PC Magazine
DOS 5
Techniques and Utilities

PC Magazine
DOS 5
Techniques and
Utilities

Jeff Prosise

Ziff-Davis Press
Emeryville, California

Development Editor	Lisa Biow
Copy Editor	Jan Jue
Technical Reviewers	Richard Ozer and Neil Rubenking
Project Coordinator	Sheila McGill
Proofreader	Jeff Barash
Cover Design	Gerard Kunkel
Book Design	Peter Tucker
Technical Illustration and Page Layout	Steph Bradshaw
Indexer	Ted Laux

This book was produced on a Macintosh IIfx, with the following applications: FrameMaker®, Microsoft® Word, MacLink*Plus*®, Adobe Illustrator®, and Collage Plus™.

Ziff-Davis Press
5903 Christie Avenue
Emeryville, CA 94608

ISBN 1-56276-007-6
10 9 8 7 6 5 4 3 2 1

For Adam, and for all my friends at
PC Magazine

■ CONTENTS AT A GLANCE

Foreword xvii

Introduction xxi

PART 1 USING DOS 5

   1. Getting Started 3

   2. Configuring Your System 39

   3. Making the Most of Memory 81

   4. Disks and Disk Management 125

   5. File and Directory Management 187

   6. Screens, Keyboards, and Printers 247

   7. A Kinder, Gentler Command Line 295

   8. Redirection and Piping 315

PART 2 PROGRAMMING DOS 5

   9. A Word on Programming 331

   10. Building the Better Batch File 375

   11. File, Directory, and Disk Utilities 459

   12. Screen, Keyboard, and Printer Utilities 531

   13. The Art and Zen of TSRs 613

PART 3 BEYOND DOS 5

   14. The Shell Game 747

   15. The QBasic Interpreter 771

APPENDICES

   Appendix A. DOS Command Reference 809

   Appendix B. Device Driver Reference 909

   Appendix C. Supplementary Utilities Reference 925

   Index 983

▆ TABLE OF CONTENTS

Foreword xvii
Introduction xxi

PART 1 USING DOS 5

1. Getting Started   **3**
In the Beginning 3
    DOS 1.x 6
    DOS 2.x 7
    DOS 3.x 9
    DOS 4.x 10
Introducing DOS 5.0 11
    Disk Handling 11
    Memory Management and Program Loading 12
    The DOS Shell, Version 2 13
    The QBasic Interpreter 14
    The DOS Editor 14
    On-Line Help 15
    Other Enhancements 16
    What's New for Programmers 17
Before You Start 18
    Hexadecimal Notation 18
    The 80x86 Family of CPUs 20
    Memory and the Bus 25
    The Basic Input/Output System 25
    The Role of the Operating System 27
    The Structure of DOS 28
    Executable and Non-Executable Files 31
    Understanding the DOS Environment 33
    DEBUG: A Special DOS Utility 35
    Preparing to Run DOS 5.0 37

2. Configuring Your System   39

The CONFIG.SYS File 40
    The 15 CONFIG.SYS Directives 41
    The BUFFERS Directive 42
    The FILES Directive 43
    The FCBS Directive 44
    The STACKS Directive 45
    The SHELL Directive 46
    The INSTALL Directive 49
    The COUNTRY Directive 50
    The LASTDRIVE Directive 52
    The DRIVPARM Directive 52
    The BREAK Directive 55
    The REM Directive 55
    The DEVICE Directive 56
    The SWITCHES Directive 58
    The DOS and DEVICEHIGH Directives 59
The AUTOEXEC.BAT File 59
    The Contents of AUTOEXEC.BAT 61
    Building a Fence Around AUTOEXEC.BAT 63
Optimizing Your System's Performance 64
    Speeding Hard-Disk Operations with SMARTDrive 64
    Speeding Disk Operations Further with FASTOPEN 68
    Speeding Disk-Intensive Applications with RAMDrive 70
    Speeding Keyboard Operations with DOSKEY and MODE 74
    Enhancing Screen and Keyboard Operations with ANSI.SYS 75
    Analyzing Memory Requirements with the MEM Command 75
    A Final Word on Device Drivers 77
Summary 80

3. Making the Most of Memory   81

Understanding Memory 82
    Conventional Memory 84
    Extended Memory 85
    The High Memory Area 86
    Expanded Memory 87
    Upper Memory 89
    Profiling Memory: The MEM Command 90
Putting Memory to Work 91
    Installing the HIMEM.SYS Driver 91

Understanding HIMEM.SYS 93

Placing DOS in High Memory 96

Placing TSRs and Device Drivers in Upper Memory 97

Using the DOS Directive 99

Using the DEVICEHIGH Directive 100

Using the LOADHIGH Command 102

Using the LOADFIX Command 105

Converting Extended Memory to Expanded 106

Converting Extended Memory to Expanded on a 286 108

Using the EMM386 Command 109

The Role of EMM386.EXE 110

More on the EMM386.EXE Driver 112

Using Alternative 386 Memory Managers 118

Windows and Other Environments 119

Summary 120

4. Disks and Disk Management   125

Working with Hard Disks 126

Low-Level Formatting 127

Hard-Disk Partitioning 129

The MS-DOS Partitioning Scheme 130

Partitioning Hard Drives with FDISK 133

SHARE.EXE and Large Partitions 137

Hard-Disk Formatting 138

Formatting a Hard Disk 141

Adding an Unsupported Hard Drive to Your System 142

Working with Floppy Disks 143

Formatting Floppy Disks 145

Adding the System Files After Formatting 148

Formatting Floppy Disks to Higher-Than-Rated Capacities 150

Copying a Disk's Contents from One Drive to Another 152

Swapping Drives with ASSIGN 152

Adding a New Floppy Drive to Your System 153

Protecting and Preserving Disk Data 154

Backing Up and Restoring Hard-Disk Data 154

Recovering Files from Defective Disks 166

Analyzing and Correcting Disk Errors with CHKDSK 167

Rebuilding Corrupted Partition Tables 175

Recovering Deleted Files 175
Recovering from an Accidental Format 178
Parking the Hard Disk's Heads 179
Third-Party Disk Maintenance Tools 181
Summary 185

5. File and Directory Management   187

Managing Disk Directories 188
Creating and Deleting Subdirectories 192
Navigating the Directory Structure 194
Displaying the Directory Structure 197
Creating Automatic Search Paths:
The PATH and APPEND Commands 199
Managing Files 205
Listing the Files in a Directory 206
Locating Files on the Hard Disk 214
Altering File Attributes 215
Comparing Files 216
Renaming Files 220
Copying Files 221
Deleting Files 228
Preventing Accidental File Erasures 230
Managing Text Files 233
Viewing Text Files with the TYPE Command 234
Editing Files with EDLIN 235
Editing Text Files with the DOS Editor 236
Summary 245

6. Screens, Keyboards, and Printers   247

Screens 247
PC Display Architecture 248
The ANSI.SYS Driver 251
Sending Commands to ANSI.SYS 252
Setting Screen Colors with ANSI.SYS 253
Setting Screen Colors Without ANSI.SYS 254
Setting Colors Without ANSI.SYS, Part II 256
Displaying More than 25 Lines of Text 257
More than 25 Lines Without ANSI.SYS 259
Customizing the Command prompt with ANSI.SYS 260

Keyboards 262
   Assigning Commands to Function Keys 265
   Using ANSI.SYS to Remap the Keyboard 268
   Setting the Keyboard's Speed 269
   Tricks for Reducing Typing Time 270
Printers 270
   Setting Print Pitch and Line Spacing 272
   Setting Print Pitch and Line Spacing on HP LaserJet Printers 273
   Using Printers Attached to Serial Ports 275
   Redirecting Output from One Parallel Port to Another 278
   Printing Text Files: The PRINT Command 280
   Quick-and-Dirty Text-File Printing 283
   Printing Graphics 284
   Why GRAPHICS? 287
Using Alternate Character Sets 287
   Displaying Alternate Character Sets 288
   Printing Alternate Character Sets 290
   Remapping the Keyboard: The KEYB Command 292
Summary 293

7. A Kinder, Gentler Command Line   295

Introducing DOSKEY 295
   Taking DOSKEY for a Test Drive 296
   Installing DOSKEY on Your System 297
   Recalling Commands from the Command Stack 298
   Editing Text on the Command Line 301
   Executing Multiple Commands 304
Command Macros 304
   Creating and Running Macros 305
   Using Replaceable Parameters in Macros 307
   Combining Macros and Redirection Operators 309
   Editing and Deleting Macros 310
   Saving Macros 311
   Putting Macros to Work on Your System 312
Summary 313

8. Redirection and Piping   315

Redirecting Output to Files and Devices 316
Using Alternate Sources of Input 319

Piping Output from One Command to Another 320
Using Filters 321
    The MORE Filter 322
    The SORT Filter 322
    The FIND Filter 324
    Building a Do-It-Yourself Phone List 325
When Redirection Will and Will Not Work 326
Summary 327

PART 2 PROGRAMMING DOS 5

9. A Word on Programming   331

A Brief Introduction to Assembly Language 332
    What Is Assembly Language 333
    Anatomy of an Assembly Language Program 334
    COM Versus EXE: What's the Difference? 341
    The Program Segment Prefix 342
The DOS Programming Environment 344
    Reading the Keyboard 345
    Displaying Characters on the Screen 354
    Transmitting Characters to the Printer 359
    Performing File Input and Output 361
    Manipulating Files 363
    Manipulating Directories 364
    Managing Memory Resources 365
    Getting and Setting the Time and Date 368
    Terminating Programs 369
    Miscellaneous DOS Functions 370
Another Sample Program 372
Summary 374

10. Building the Better Batch File   375

Batch File Basics 375
    The ECHO Command 376
    The REM Command 378
    The PAUSE Command 379
    Replaceable Parameters and the SHIFT Command 380
    The GOTO Command 382

The CALL Command 383
The FOR Command 383
The IF Command 385
Environment Variables 387
Batch File Tricks and Techniques 390
Using Subroutines in Batch Files 390
Using FOR as a Switch Statement 391
Performing String Comparisons Without Regard to Case 393
Using Redirection and Piping in Batch Files 395
Suppressing Command Output 399
Saving the Current Drive and Directory 400
Dressing Up the Screen with ANSI.SYS 403
Debugging Batch Files 407
Batch File Utilities 408
Getting Input from the User 408
Improving Screen Output 417
Getting the Time and Date 439
Determining Processor and Coprocessor Types 445
Rebooting Your PC from a Batch File 454
Compiling Batch Files for Added Speed 456
Summary 457

11. File, Directory, and Disk Utilities   459

Pruning Branches from a Directory Tree 459
Inside NUKE 461
Recursion 470
Locating Files and Subdirectories 473
Renaming Subdirectories 475
Inside RENDIR 476
Encrypting Files 482
Inside Encrypt 485
Searching for Files That Contain a Specified Text String 493
Inside FINDTEXT 496
The SEARCHDIR and SEARCHFILE Procedures 524
Changing Directories the Easy Way 527
Summary 530

12. Screen, Keyboard, and Printer Utilities   531

Setting the Screen Colors 532

Inside COLOR 538
Guarding Against Monitor Burn-In 540
Inside SAVER 554
The Installed Code 557
The DOS Multiplex Interrupt 558
Programming the Function Keys in DOS 559
Inside FKEYS 569
Toggling Caps Lock, Num Lock, and Scroll Lock 570
Inside TOGGLE 575
Capturing Printer Output to a File 577
Inside LPT2FILE 596
Transmitting Printer Control Codes 599
Running SETUP as a Memory-Resident Application 601
Changing SETUP's Hotkey with DEBUG 603
Creating PMF Files with LZSELECT 604
Printing Text Files and Saving Trees 606
Working While You Print 607
Summary 611

13. **The Art and Zen of TSRs**   **613**
An Introduction to TSR Programming 614
The Reentrancy Problem 617
Other TSR Programming Considerations 619
Logging Your Work to a File 620
Inside PC-LOG 641
Dialing Phones with Your PC 644
Using PC-DIAL 715
Customizing PC-DIAL 718
Inside PC-DIAL 720
Dialing the Phone 721
Printing PC-DIAL Data Files 724
Removing TSRs from Memory 725
Inside INSTALL and REMOVE 740
Summary 744

PART 3 BEYOND DOS 5

14. The Shell Game   **747**

Introducing the DOS Shell 747
  Working with Drives, Directories, and Files 749
  Working with Programs 754
Tips and Techniques for Using the Shell Effectively 755
  Adding Programs and Program Groups to the Program List 755
  Defining Advanced Properties for a Program Item 757
  Associating Programs and Data Files 758
  Performing Operations on Groups of Files 759
  Viewing the Contents of Files 761
  Adding Your Own Color Schemes 761
  Searching an Entire Disk for a File or Set of Files 765
  Renaming Subdirectories from Inside the Shell 766
Task Switching 767
  Some Practical Advice on Task Switching 769
Summary 770

15. The QBasic Interpreter   **771**

Getting Acquainted with the QBasic Interpreter 772
  Loading and Running Programs 774
  Converting GW-BASIC and BASICA Programs for QBasic 777
  Navigating the QBasic Help System 779
Writing Programs in the QBasic Environment 781
  Introducing *Passageways* 785
Debugging Programs in the QBasic Environment 802
  Single-Stepping Through a Program 803
  Setting and Using Breakpoints 804
  Using the Immediate Window 804
Summary 807

Appendices

Appendix A   DOS Command Reference 809
Appendix B   Device Driver Reference 909
Appendix C   Supplementary Utilities Reference 925

Index 983

# FOREWORD

JEFF PROSISE IS BEST-FRIEND MATERIAL. HE'S ONE OF THOSE STEADY, RELIABLE people who seemingly never has an unkind word to say about anyone. He's thoughtful, intelligent, and fun-loving. And, to our collective and immense good fortune, he was born with the twin gifts of caring deeply about technical topics and using words well. The results speak for themselves: an unbroken string of readable, helpful, and accurate PC Tutor columns in *PC Magazine*, a glorious history as one of *PC Magazine*'s premiere utilities authors, a scintillating column in *PC/Computing*, and this book.

MS-DOS 5.0 may be the most written-about operating system ever. Microsoft did its product development and beta testing in public, with thousands of participants. It's been poked, prodded, analyzed, and prognosticated. Any number of books have been written about it. There's extensive online help, and the manual is even pretty good. I was one of the thousands of beta testers for DOS 5.0, yet I learned a lot reading the proofs of this book. *DOS 5 Techniques and Utilities* is unique because of Prosise's extraordinary combination of talents. You can find out how to maximize memory use under DOS 5.0 from any number of sources. You can learn about the new commands. You can even read the manual. But no other source gives you Prosise's powerful utility programs, presented with a programmers's understanding of the underlying principles, an engineer's insistence on precision, and a teacher's love of accurate, concise communication.

All these books, and now there's one more. In this apparent information glut, however, ignorance abounds and misinformation is manifest. Try this pop quiz:

1. MS-DOS 5.0 gives you more usable memory even on XT-class machines. True or false?

2. You need to load ANSI.SYS to (a) use 43-line mode, (b) set screen colors, (c) print VGA screens to your printer, (d) all of the above, or (e) none of the above.

3. DOS 5.0 includes a utility to get keyboard characters and pass them to a batch file. True or False?

4. You've got a 286 and a bunch of extended memory that you'd like to use as expanded memory. You can (a) use Microsoft's EMM386 driver, or (b) go fish.

You get the idea. The answers to all these questions and far more lie in the pages ahead. The aforementioned utility programs on the enclosed disks pick up where DOS 5.0 leaves off. For instance, Microsoft could have included a 286-compatible expanded memory manager, but didn't. Prosise did. Compare the chapters in this book to the DOS 5.0 manual, and the recurring theme emerges: Microsoft didn't, but Prosise did. You'll find handy programs to make your batch files more powerful, control your screen without the overhead of ANSI.SYS, give you control over tasks by time, date—even the day of the week—all in clear, simple, fast assembly language.

Assembly language?! But, that's the hard stuff, too complicated for mere mortals, isn't it? No, on two counts. First, all these programs are on the disks, in executable form, so you don't have to understand a line of assembly to use them. Second, Prosise introduces you to assembly clearly and simply, using DOS's DEBUG program to create your own working programs, with wondrous speed, small size, and ultimate efficiency. You get all the speed and efficiency whether you elect to learn how they work or not. You also get to do things that DOS 5.0 can't do, at least not without this book. Given my long-term experience with Prosise's work, I wouldn't have expected less.

But frankly, my expectations for the chapter on QBasic were not high. After all, it's an ideal opportunity to talk about the new commands and generally fill up some pages. I should have known better. Instead of taking the easy way out, Prosise gives us an entertaining, well-conceived game, written in QBasic, using many of the new commands. He hangs out his "programmer at work" sign, and invites us to explore this exciting new implementation of BASIC with him.

Another key difference between this book and the DOS 5.0 manual is that you get what you're supposed to get from documentation: lots of what and how. This book doesn't dwell on the what, gives you a lot more of the how, and a brand new dose of the why. I've never been very good at following instructions blindly. With Prosise as your guide, you won't have to.

This book changed Jeff Prosise's life. It marks his career decision to become a full-time author, to leave behind the discipline of engineering and run a riskier road. After you've read it, you'll agree that he made the right choice.

This book won't change your life. But if you take DOS 5.0 at all seriously, it will make that part of it immeasurably better.

Bill Machrone
July, 1991

ACKNOWLEDGMENTS

No project of this magnitude could ever be completed without help from a lot of people. I'd like to thank a few key individuals who were instrumental in the development and production of this book and to say that, without them, it couldn't have happened.

My hat's off to Harry Blake, Cindy Hudson, Sheila McGill, Cheryl Holzaepfel, and the many others at Ziff-Davis Press who run the company on a day-to-day basis and somehow find time to publish books in between all the other goings-on. Thanks also to Bill Machrone and the staff of *PC Magazine* for okaying this project and putting their stamp of approval on it; to Lisa Biow and Jan Jue, for a wonderful editing job and for turning my ramblings into coherent text; to Richard Ozer, who did the technical editing for the book, and to Neil Rubenking, who did a final technical read-through; to Doug Boling, Bob Flanders, Michael Holmes, and Jay Munro, who contributed their hard work and efforts to ten of the utilities provided with the book; to my agent, Claudette Moore, who helped put everything together; to John Dickinson and Paul Somerson, who gave me my first big break as a writer; and to all the men and women at Microsoft, who put together a terrific product.

I would also like to thank the persons to whom I reported at my former employer, Martin Marietta Energy Systems, for supporting me in this endeavor. In particular, I'd like to express my gratitude to Chuck Hall, Finis Patton, and Ted Ryan.

Thanks, too, to Jack Coleman, a good friend and neighbor who was an active PC enthusiast and who provided several helpful suggestions for the programming content of this book. Jack departed this life barely weeks before the book went to press, leaving behind a devoted wife and two young daughters. He will be missed.

Most of all, thanks to my wife Lori, who put up with me during the long months I worked on the book and provided the tireless support that I needed, in the good times and the bad. She took a day or two off to deliver a bouncing baby boy during that time, too. Will wonders never cease?

≡ Introduction

ON JUNE 11, 1991, MICROSOFT ANNOUNCED AND BEGAN SHIPPING DOS 5.0. VERSION 5.0 is a far cry from the versions that preceded it. Its long list of new features includes the ability to better use memory on 286, 386, and 486 PCs; commands for undeleting files and unformatting disks; support for greater-than-32Mb hard-disk partitions, 2.88Mb floppies, and task switching; a full-screen text editor; and the new QBasic Interpreter. This is the operating system that DOS users have been waiting for. And with Microsoft's renewed commitment to making DOS, already the world's most popular operating system, an even better product, the future looks bright indeed.

This book is all about DOS 5.0: how to use it, how to configure it, and how to extend it so that you can use your PC as efficiently as possible. You'll learn the basics of using DOS 5.0 and get helpful advice on optimizing it for your system. You'll learn the tricks and techniques that DOS experts use to save keystrokes. You'll learn how to load several programs into memory at one time and switch back and forth between them. You'll learn how to use the QBasic Interpreter and its integrated debugger. You'll learn how to write more powerful batch files than ever before, and how to roll DOS commands into macros that execute instantly, just like internal DOS commands. You'll see how programmers write utilities to supplement the commands and utilities that are part of DOS, and you'll get two disks full of utilities that you can put to work giving DOS 5.0 a helping hand.

DOS 5 Techniques and Utilities is an issues-oriented book. What sets it apart from other DOS books is that when it identifies a shortcoming in the operating system, it provides you with a utility to make up the difference. For example, the REN command still won't rename a subdirectory, but the RENDIR utility that comes with this book will. Another example: DOS still doesn't do anything to help you delete subdirectories that contain files or other subdirectories. That's why you get NUKE, which removes a subdirectory just like the RD command, but does it no matter what is in that subdirectory or how extensive its network of descendant directories is. These are just two examples of the powerful utilities that are included with this book—utilities designed to help you work smarter and faster. And that, after all, is what PCs are all about.

Who Should Read This Book

Not everyone is a power user, but just about everyone would like to be. The goal of this book is to transform beginning and intermediate-level users into true power-user types—"superusers" who know their way around the operating system and know how to get from point A to point B in the shortest amount of time.

If you're already an advanced user, you'll benefit from *DOS 5 Techniques and Utilities* because it discusses not just the hows but also the whys, providing valuable insight into the ways DOS works internally. Chapter 3, for example, outlines how DOS 5.0's EMM386.EXE driver creates upper memory blocks for programs and drivers to be loaded into by switching the CPU to protected mode (that's right, protected mode!) and running DOS in a Virtual-86 mode session, where the 386's page tables are accessible. On a more practical level, it also explains how to add two statements to your CONFIG.SYS file on a 286 or 386 and gain an additional 45k of RAM.

If you're working with DOS for the first time, you'll gain from this book because it offers loads of practical advice that can only come from experience. Did you know, for example, that you can use the SHELL directive in CONFIG-.SYS to increase the size of COMMAND.COM's environment and eliminate "Out of environment space" messages when you run batch files? Or that you can double the speed of the cursor keys by adding a single command to your AUTOEXEC.BAT file? Those are the kinds of things *DOS 5 Techniques and Utilities* brings to the table—tips for better using the resources at your fingertips and for getting the most out of your system. And users at all levels will benefit from the utilities that come on the disks in the back of the book.

What this book *won't* do is teach you how to insert a floppy in drive A and hold your hand while you type FORMAT A:.It assumes that you've had some exposure to DOS before, and that you're familiar with such basic commands as CLS and DIR. It does not, however, assume that you have any prior experience with DOS 5.0. There are so many new features in DOS 5.0 that in some respects it's like starting over. We'll walk that path together to learn where both the strengths and the weaknesses lie.

How This Book Is Organized

DOS 5 Techniques and Utilities is divided into three parts. Part One, "Using DOS 5," is a guide to the operating system, its commands, its drivers, and its capabilities. Part Two, "Programming DOS 5," discusses DOS 5.0 from a utility writer's perspective and develops the source code for several useful utilities. Part Three, "Beyond DOS 5," explores the DOS Shell and the QBasic Interpreter. Three appendices document all the commands and device drivers supplied with DOS 5.0, as well as the utilities that come on the disks in the back of this book.

Part One starts off with Chapter 1 recounting the history of DOS, beginning with the development efforts that accompanied version 1.0 and continuing all the way up to version 5.0, with an emphasis on the features added to the operating system with each new release. Chapter 2 discusses configuring your system—how to choose the proper number of BUFFERS and how to use SMARTDrive to speed up disk operations, for example—and analyzes the 15 CONFIG.SYS directives that DOS 5.0 supports. Chapter 3 discusses DOS's powerful new memory-management features and offers practical advice on getting DOS set up to use the RAM in your system as efficiently as possible. Chapter 4 tackles a subject that's almost as big as DOS itself—disks and disk management—and Chapter 5 discusses the files and directories you place on those disks and the tools DOS provides for working with them. Chapter 6 talks about screens, keyboards, and printers, showing you, for example, how to display 50 lines of text on the screen and dump graphics screens to LaserJet printers. Chapter 7 discusses DOS 5.0's new DOSKEY utility, which soups up the command line with features such as command recall and editing that have been a long time in coming. To round out Part One, Chapter 8 overviews one of the most fundamentally important, yet often misunderstood, aspects of DOS—redirection and piping.

The emphasis in Part Two is on utilities. In all, *DOS 5 Techniques and Utilities* provides more than 50 one-of-a-kind utilities that will help you work more productively, and it provides them complete with source code. Chapter 9 provides a brief introduction to assembly language, to the Microsoft Macro Assembler, and to the programming resources available in DOS and in the BIOS. Chapter 10 discusses batch-file programming and provides several utilities to make batch files run smarter and faster. Chapter 11 introduces five utilities for streamlining disk operations. Chapter 12 presents nine new utilities for better utilizing your screen, keyboard, and printer. Finally, Chapter 13 takes up the subject of TSR programming and leaves you with five new utilities, including the book's crowning jewel: PC-DIAL, a pop-up phone directory and dialer.

Part Three introduces two of the most prominent new stand-alone features of DOS 5.0: the DOS Shell and the QBasic Interpreter. The Shell has been extensively reworked since DOS 4.0 and is endowed with a task-switching option that lets you load several programs at once and switch between them without losing their contexts. The QBasic Interpreter is DOS's new BASIC programming environment, modeled after Microsoft's hugely successful Quick-BASIC Compiler.

The appendices contain helpful reference material. Appendix A documents all the DOS commands, including the configuration directives that go in CONFIG.SYS. Appendix B documents the device drivers that come with DOS 5.0. Finally, Appendix C documents the supplemental utilities that are included with this book.

The Disks in the Back of the Book

The disks in the back of this book contain more than 50 utilities to help boost your productivity with DOS 5.0. Ten of them were written by *PC Magazine* programmers Doug Boling (BAT2EXEC, BCOPY, and EMS40), Bob Flanders and Michael Holmes (CDX, LASERLST, PCSPOOL, SLICE/SPLICE, and ZCOPY), and Jay Munro (LZSELECT and PCBOOK), who adapted them from versions originally published in *PC Magazine*'s "Utilities" column. All ten have been upgraded for DOS 5.0. With a few exceptions (some *PC Magazine* utilities of my own that I upgraded and enhanced for the book), the rest of the utilities appear here for the first time.

These aren't just "any" utilities; they're utilities designed to enable you get the job done faster and more efficiently. They're written specifically to exploit the features of DOS 5.0 and, where DOS 5.0 is deficient, to fill in the holes. For example, there's a FINDTEXT utility for searching out files that contain a specified text string, similar to the Norton Utilities' Text Search (TS) utility. There's also an LPT2FILE utility for capturing printer output to disk, a COLOR utility for setting the screen colors in DOS, and an FKEYS utility for assigning commands to function keys. In short, there's everything you need here to make DOS 5.0 an even better operating system than it already is. When you buy the book, you buy the utilities, too. There is no shareware here, nor are there "crippled" versions of commercial application programs. All we ask is that you read the license agreement in the back and use the software for private, noncommercial use; in other words, treat it as you would any other software package that is distributed through commercial channels.

For the programmers among you, and for those interested in learning to program, the disks in the back also contain the source code for the utilities. Most of the programs were developed in assembly language using the Microsoft Macro Assembler; a few were developed in BASIC and C. The only programs for which source code is *not* supplied are those that were developed from short DEBUG scripts. The scripts themselves are printed in the book, and thus need not be duplicated on disk.

Installing the Utilities Disks

The utilities and the accompanying source code files come in zipped format on two 360k distribution disks. To install the software, place the disk labeled "1 of 2" in drive A or B. If you inserted it in drive A, type

```
A:\ZDPRESS
```

Once the installation screen appears, press F3 to copy everything from the two disks to your hard disk. The installation program will prompt you to insert the second disk. By default, the utilities go in the \DOS5UTIL directory of drive C. If the directory doesn't exist, the installation program will create it for you. If you want to place the programs somewhere else, you can enter a new drive and path in the box labeled "Destination Drive/Path" near the top of the screen. The box immediately to its right—the one labeled "Free Space"—tells you how much room remains on the destination drive. Together, the programs and their source code require about 1.7Mb of disk space. If you don't have that much available, or if you simply want to copy a few of the programs onto floppies, press F2 twice when the installation screen comes up. You'll see a list of the files on Disk 1 with check marks by them in the window on the left. If you only want to copy a few of the files, uncheck the ones that you don't want to copy with the Enter key or the spacebar, and then press F3. Repeat this process for Disk 2. Once the software is installed, modify the PATH statement in your AUTOEXEC.BAT file to include C:\DOS5UTIL (or whatever drive and directory the utilities were installed to) so you can run the utilities no matter where you are on your hard disk.

On a More Personal Note

Friends of mine who read computer books tell me that they like to know what kind of computer a book was written on and what software was used to write it. This one was written on a stock 20 MHz IBM Model 70 with 6Mb of RAM and a 115Mb hard disk. The first several chapters were written with WordPerfect 4.2, but midway through Chapter 13 I switched to Word for Windows and never went back. To this writer at least, a WYSIWYG word processor is worth its weight in gold when it comes to crafting long documents. Throughout the process of writing the manuscript, I ran DOS 5.0 betas supplied by Microsoft. When the first beta arrived late last summer, I wasn't quite comfortable enough with it to put it on my primary machine; after all, "beta" means something in the software doesn't work, and a beta operating system could be bad news for your hard disk. So I installed and ran the very first beta on a Toshiba T3100SX laptop. It turned out that my fears were unfounded, for DOS 5.0 was surprisingly stable from the very outset. When the next beta arrived, I put it on my Model 70 and bade goodbye to DOS 3.3 forever.

I hope that you enjoy reading this book as much as I enjoyed writing it. To be sure, writing a book is a lot of work, and, as my friends and family will attest, at times you stop and wonder why you ever agreed to such a task. I won't even try to rationalize why, but I will say that since my initial involvement with microcomputers in 1983, I've been privileged to witness the birth and fulfillment of a revolution and, thanks to the fine folks at Ziff-Davis, to be a very, very small part of it. This book is my return to them, and my contribution to the furtherance of that revolution.

Finally, we've gone to great lengths to eliminate errors from *DOS 5 Techniques and Utilities*. Nonetheless, in any volume of this size, errors are bound to creep in. I take full responsibility for any inaccuracies and hope that you'll help me identify them for future editions. Should you find an error, or if you just have comments to pass on, contact me via MCI Mail (user name JPROSISE) or CompuServe Mail (user ID 72241,44). If you don't have access to either of these electronic media, write me at the following address:

Jeff Prosise
c/o Ziff-Davis Press
5903 Christie Avenue
Emeryville, CA 94608

Your comments and suggestions are greatly appreciated.

PART ONE
Using DOS 5

3
GETTING STARTED

39
CONFIGURING YOUR SYSTEM

81
MAKING THE MOST OF MEMORY

125
DISKS AND DISK MANAGEMENT

187
FILE AND DIRECTORY MANAGEMENT

247
SCREENS, KEYBOARDS, AND PRINTERS

295
A KINDER, GENTLER COMMAND LINE

315
REDIRECTION AND PIPING

1

GETTING STARTED

DOS HAS UNDERGONE NINE MAJOR REVISIONS SINCE IT WAS INTRODUCED IN April 1981. It has been transformed from a bare-bones operating system into one that supports advanced file operations, local area networks, a wide variety of peripherals ranging from disk drives to video adapters to printers, and even graphical user interfaces such as Windows.

No book on DOS would be complete without giving the reader some sense of the history of the operating system and of the PCs it was designed to run on. This history covers roughly a decade, from the time development was begun on version 1.0 in 1980 to the introduction of DOS 5.0 in 1991. During these years, it experienced some turbulent times; it even survived one short period in the late 1980s when it was widely considered to be a dying product, with OS/2 destined to take its throne. As we all know now, that didn't happen, and Microsoft recently has publicly renewed its commitment to DOS, promising there will be a version 6, a version 7, and possibly additional versions beyond that.

Version 5.0, the first tangible proof of that commitment, is a revised and reworked version of the operating system that adds many of the features users have requested over the years. DOS 5.0 is the first to take advantage of some of the powerful features of the 286, 386, and 486 microprocessors, and promises to be the first of many in a long line of releases that exploit the systems they're run on to deliver maximum benefit to the user. Following is an account of why DOS came into being and how it got to where it is today.

Before you begin, be aware that the next several sections contain numerous technical terms and references to DOS internals that may be unfamiliar to you unless you are already an advanced DOS user. Don't let yourself get too bogged down in the details; many of the basics are discussed in the final section of this chapter, and the remainder are explained in subsequent chapters. If some of the discussions mean little to you now, reread this part of the book after you've had time to work your way through some of the remaining chapters. You may be surprised at how much you've learned.

In the Beginning

To fully appreciate the impact that DOS has had on the world of microcomputers, you must understand the environment surrounding personal computing in the late 1970s and the early 1980s. At the time, there were few standards in the world of personal computers other than an 8-bit operating system called CP/M (which stood for Control Program for Microcomputers or Control Program/Monitor, depending on who you talked to), designed for Intel's 8080 microprocessor, and an emerging line of desktop computers from a company called Apple Computer that had begun in the garage of two young Silicon Valley entrepreneurs. In retrospect, the computer industry was ripe for the likes of someone such as IBM to step in and take charge. The introduction of the IBM Personal Computer in 1981 forever changed the way the world thinks about personal computing and established IBM as the dominant player in the field. IBM's success was attributable in part to an obscure operating system called DOS 1.0, marketed by a small company in the Northwest that would later become a household name in computing: Microsoft.

Legend has it that DOS 1.0 was based on the operating system 86-DOS, an operating system that strongly resembled CP/M and was written for Intel's up-and-coming microprocessor, the 8086. Legend is mostly true in this regard. In early 1980, Tim Paterson, an employee of Seattle Computer Products and later one of the primary architects of DOS at Microsoft, began development work on 86-DOS for his employer. Although Seattle Computer Products wasn't officially in the business of writing operating system software, it felt compelled to in this instance because it was also shipping a CPU board based on Intel's 16-bit 8086 microprocessor, and it needed an operating system to go with it (the 86 in 86-DOS stood for "8086"). Paterson had originally intended to rely on an 8086-specific version of CP/M called CP/M-86 from Digital Research, but Digital was late in delivering the product. So, in a pinch, the development of 86-DOS was begun.

The operating system that Paterson created borrowed heavily from CP/M because the consensus at the time was that it was important to provide a product that CP/M applications could be ported to easily. This meant many of the underlying tenets of the systems had to be the same. 86-DOS mimicked CP/M's command interface and duplicated many elements of its kernel. One important difference between the two operating systems was that rather than using CP/M's techniques for storing files on disk, 86-DOS incorporated a file system similar to one Paterson had seen demonstrated in a prototype operating system called M-DOS at the 1979 National Computer Conference by a small Bellevue, Washington-based firm named Microsoft. The 86-DOS file system was centered around a structure called a file allocation table, which divided a disk into storage units called clusters, assigned one entry in the table to each cluster, and mapped the locations where files were stored by filling in entries in the table. Four months after starting work on the new operating system, Paterson had a functioning product that was officially christened 86-DOS.

At about the same time Paterson was working on 86-DOS, officials at Microsoft were negotiating with IBM to provide a set of language products (BASIC, FORTRAN, Pascal, and COBOL development tools) for a personal computer IBM planned to introduce in early 1981. But there was one small problem: IBM still hadn't settled on an operating system. Without this key component of the system, it was difficult for Microsoft to commit to a firm date for delivering the goods. This led Microsoft to recommend that IBM talk to Digital Research about CP/M-86. The contact was made (some narratives say that Bill Gates, cofounder of Microsoft and today the company's leader and CEO, made the first contact himself on behalf of IBM), but a deal never materialized.

Exactly why a deal was never struck isn't entirely clear. Some accounts say that Digital Research wouldn't agree to IBM's strict nondisclosure agreements, put in place to keep secret from would-be competitors the fact that IBM was even endeavoring to enter the personal computer market. Other accounts say that Gary Kildall, the head of Digital Research and creator of CP/M, was away when a delegation from IBM came to Monterey, California, where Digital Research was headquartered. At any rate, the failure to come to agreement with Digital Research to obtain CP/M-86 left IBM still shopping for an operating system when the intended ship date for the IBM PC was only a few months away.

In September 1980, still searching for a realistic plan for delivering the agreed-upon language products without an operating system to develop them on, Microsoft principals Bill Gates, Paul Allen, and Kay Nishi had a brainstorm: Why not propose to IBM that Microsoft supply an operating system to go along with the other programs they were to deliver? It seemed to make sense. After all, the languages represented about 400k of code, while Microsoft estimated that an operating system could be done in about 5 percent of that, adding an almost insignificant fraction to the amount of work that had yet to be done. Plus, they were aware of Paterson's 86-DOS, and figured they could cut a deal with Seattle Computer Products to market it to IBM. Deal they did, and in short order Seattle Computer Products had agreed to license 86-DOS to Microsoft, which in turn would provide the operating system to an unspecified customer (IBM). Later, the software was sold outright to Microsoft for the sum of $50,000 plus additional perks, which included favorable language licenses and a license for Seattle Computer Products to use 86-DOS on its own machines. In October 1980, Microsoft presented a revised proposal to IBM that committed Microsoft to supplying the said language products as well as an operating system for IBM's new computer. A month later, the contract was signed and the effort to create MS-DOS version 1.0 was under way.

At Microsoft's behest, Paterson continued to work on 86-DOS, never knowing until he joined Microsoft in May 1981 that it was IBM he was doing the development for because of the tight lid on security. By February 1981, the operating system that would soon become DOS 1.0 was running on a prototype of the PC supplied to Microsoft by IBM. The IBM Personal Computer made its debut in April 1981, with DOS at its side. What many present-day users do not realize is that DOS was only one of three operating systems that IBM announced for its new computer. The other two were CP/M-86 (which finally did make its debut six months later) and SofTech Microsystem's p-System. At the time, it was far from obvious that DOS would become *the* operating system for the PC, given the relatively large installed base of CP/M applications. However, the outcome of the operating system wars is now a matter for the history books. DOS triumphed, and today it is the most widely used operating system in the world, with an installed base of around 60 million users. This figure, of course, is growing every day.

DOS 1.x

Even according to Microsoft, DOS 1.0 was no thing of beauty. However, it did what it needed to most: It ran the IBM Personal Computer and allowed PC users to run the hordes of DOS programs that soon began appearing for it. All along, Microsoft planned to upgrade it later into what would eventually become DOS 2.0. But in the haste in which version 1.0 was developed for Microsoft to meet its ship date, its designers simply ran out of time to do anything more.

Still, they did a lot. In addition to providing the basic functions that are required of an operating system—the means to read, write, and manage disk files, for example, and support for program loading and execution—DOS 1.0 sported several features that were ahead of their time for the microcomputer arena. For example, it supported two executable file formats: COM and EXE. COM files were stored on disk exactly the way they would appear in memory, similar to program files in CP/M. However, their size was restricted to 64k. EXE files allowed developers to take advantage of the new PC's full 640k address space by distributing program code, data, and stack among several segments. Once the segments were loaded into memory, DOS used information in the EXE header to dynamically alter the addresses the program made reference to. This meant that an EXE file could be loaded anywhere in memory and that segments could be loaded in any order without affecting the program's ability to run.

From the beginning, DOS was designed with device independence in mind. *Device independence* is the ability to adapt to a variety of hardware platforms without having to make dramatic changes to the core of the operating system itself. To that end, the first version of DOS communicated with peripheral devices such as the screen, keyboard, and printer through modules called *device drivers* that were loaded when the system was started. The CON device driver (CON is short for CONsole) provided the interface to the screen (for output) and the keyboard (for input), while PRN provided the interface to the parallel printer port. AUX, meanwhile, provided a link to the serial port. The idea was that if DOS were ever ported to a non-IBM PC hardware platform, these drivers would be the only components needing change. This basic operating system architecture has been retained in DOS to this day and will likely be retained in the future for compatibility with earlier versions.

DOS 1.0 featured 22 different commands for managing disks and disk files, setting the time and date, and performing other PC-related chores. Interestingly enough, there was no CLS command; that didn't appear until version 2.0. In the absence of such a command, several public domain screen-clearing utilities cropped up that may have been the meager beginnings of what is now a burgeoning market for third-party DOS utilities. DOS 1.0 did include such basic commands as COPY, DIR, and FORMAT, however, so users weren't exactly deprived of the ability to do meaningful work.

The component of the operating system that read and acted upon the users' commands, COMMAND.COM, otherwise known as the *command interpreter*, offered a unique innovation as well. When it was loaded, it split itself into two parts. The first part went near the bottom of the memory, where it necessarily occupied RAM and reduced the amount of memory available to programs that ran on top of it. The second part, however, went near the top and was permitted to be overwritten if an application program needed the space. When the lower half got control again, it went out to disk and reloaded the top half. This simple technique was a lifesaver in systems with only 64k of RAM (and believe it or not, 64k was a *lot* of RAM in those days). This modus operandi has been retained throughout all subsequent versions of DOS, including DOS 5.0, even though almost every PC now has at least 640k of RAM.

DOS 1.0 introduced the batch file interpreter, which permitted command scripts to be stored in a text file and executed as if they were being typed at the keyboard. It also dispensed with the need to *log* a disk each time a new disk was inserted in a drive, an action that was required on CP/M systems.

DOS 1.0 was only available from IBM. In 1982, version 1.1 was released, adding support for double-sided (320k) floppy disks in addition to the single-sided (160k) disks version 1.0 supported. Directory listings in DOS 1.1 included the time a file was created or last modified (version 1.0 only indicated the date). Version 1.1 also incorporated several minor bug fixes. Significantly, it was the first version of DOS to be released under the Microsoft label (Microsoft chose to call it MS-DOS 1.25), and the first to be licensed to vendors other than IBM (notably Compaq and Zenith) to package with their IBM-compatible systems.

DOS 2.x

In spring 1983 IBM introduced the PC/XT, which was a slightly souped-up version of its PC, with three additional slots, a larger power supply, and a 10Mb hard disk. At the same time, they introduced DOS 2.0, an upgraded version of DOS that was needed to interface with the XT's hard disk. Two of the most prominent changes in version 2.0 were the appearance of a new, hierarchical file system and the introduction of *installable device drivers*—software modules that could be linked into the system at runtime to provide low-level communication services to hardware devices.

The new file system was needed because the addition of a hard disk with a whopping 10Mb of storage space to the PC's arsenal presented problems for version 1.x's file system. Since a disk this size could easily hold several thousand files, it wouldn't do to have to store them all in one place. Rather, a mechanism was needed for establishing separate storage spaces on disk and keeping files apart from one another. The solution was found in the form of subdirectories. With subdirectories, files could be neatly grouped together and stowed away in different areas of the disk.

Subdirectories provided a convenient work-around for another problem, too: the fixed length of the root directory. The area of a disk where the root directory is stored is fixed in length (as we'll see in Chapter 4), permitting only a limited number of entries to be stored there, regardless of how much room remains free on the disk. On a hard disk, the root directory is limited to storing 512 files. Subdirectories, however, can hold as many entries as disk space permits, and therefore better utilize disk space.

A key component of the new file system was a set of file I/O (input/output) services that used objects called *file handles* to reference open files rather than using the traditional file control blocks. (A *file control block* is a data structure that DOS uses to hold information about open files.) The fixed length of the space set aside for file names in file control blocks precluded the use of path names, so an application program had to change to the directory a file was in before opening it. By contrast, DOS 2.0's handle-based file-open function accepted a pointer to a zero-delimited ASCII file specification that could include a path name as well as a file name, so files could be opened from anywhere on the disk. Another benefit of using the new handle-based functions was that applications that did so were ensured compatibility with future versions of DOS. As long as the data structure associated with the file was maintained by the operating system rather than by the application, changes to the internals of the file system would be transparent to application programs. Today, only a select few DOS applications—primarily holdovers from the era of DOS 1.x—use file control blocks instead of file handles for file I/O.

Before developing DOS 2.0, Microsoft realized that it needed to provide some means for third-party hardware developers to integrate support for their products into the operating system. The result was installable device drivers, which mediate between DOS and hardware elements of the system such as tape drives and CD-ROM drives. Beginning with version 2.0, new device drivers could be linked into the system with the simple addition of DEVICE= statements to CONFIG.SYS. This facility let users custom-configure DOS at runtime for the hardware attached to the system, and made DOS itself highly —and easily—extensible to third-party products.

DOS 2.0 also included the first multitasking DOS program: PRINT.COM. PRINT used the PC's internal timer and undocumented hooks in the operating system to steal occasional time slices from the CPU and print text files in the background while work continued in the foreground. Other software vendors reverse-engineered PRINT.COM and learned how to write background-processing programs, too, which led to a whole new class of utilities called *TSRs*. TSR was short for *terminate and stay resident*, the name assigned to the DOS function that programs called to remain resident in memory even after they were officially terminated. One of the most popular TSRs ever was Borland's SideKick, which integrated a text editor, calculator, calendar, appointment book, phone dialer, and ASCII chart into one program that could be popped up with a couple of keystrokes.

Version 2.0 included a host of other new features, including the ability to redirect input and output to other sources or destinations (a topic that is covered in Chapter 8 of this book), volume labels for disks, an improved batch language, the ANSI.SYS extended console driver (designed to be installed through CONFIG-.SYS and replace the default console driver, CON), support for alternate command interpreters, and support for the dynamic allocation of memory by programs. It also understood more than 20 new commands and added support for 180k and 360k disks, which contained nine sectors per track as opposed to eight on 160k and 320k disks.

Version 2.1 was introduced in March 1984, primarily to correct bugs in 2.0 and to add support for the PCjr's half-height 360k floppy drive. In most respects, it was identical to version 2.0. However, it did add support for customizing DOS for use in other countries, a move that was needed if DOS was to make the splash in the overseas markets that it had already made in this one.

DOS 3.x

In August 1984, IBM introduced its eagerly awaited IBM PC/AT, its first computer based on Intel's 80286 microprocessor and one that held the promise of someday allowing DOS users to multitask their application programs. It also introduced DOS 3.0, which added support for the AT's larger (20Mb) hard disk, high-density 1.2Mb floppy drives, and battery-powered CMOS (Complementary Metal-Oxide Semiconductor) clock-calendar.

DOS 3.0 offered a number of minor enhancements over previous versions in addition to the major ones. For example, you could now divide a hard disk into up to four partitions so that different operating systems could share the same disk (only one of those partitions could be dedicated to DOS, however). If you bought IBM-packaged DOS, you could use a new device driver, VDISK.SYS, to create a virtual disk in conventional or extended memory. And you could now run a program stored in another directory by prefixing its name with a path to where it was stored. Before, path names only applied to data files.

But the greater thrust in creating DOS 3.x was to provide support for networking, which meant rewriting many parts of the operating system from the ground up. Designing a version of DOS to run in a networked environment had hundreds of implications, some small, some large, but all of them difficult from a system developer's point of view. For example, when a call was placed to one of its file I/O services, DOS would have to determine whether the request went to a local or remote device and then handle the call accordingly. And it was clear that some sort of file-sharing module would have to be provided so that two programs wouldn't trash a file by accessing it at once. Unfortunately, the AT was ready before DOS was, and 3.0 went out the door with its networking features incomplete.

Version 3.1 followed three months later, complete with networking capabilities. One noticeable difference in 3.1 was the appearance of a pair of new commands—JOIN and SUBST—which allowed users to set up logical aliases for drives and directories. DOS 3.1 also introduced the FCBS directive to CONFIG-.SYS, which allowed the user to specify the limit on the number of files that could be open concurrently with file control blocks. By default, DOS limited this number to four to prevent programs that neglected to close their file control blocks from tying up network servers and degrading network performance as a whole.

DOS 3.2 was introduced in January 1986. Among other things, it included support for 3½-inch 720k floppy drives and added a /E switch to COMMAND.COM, allowing users to specify the size of the environment (the area of low memory where DOS stores environment strings such as PATH and COMSPEC). It also introduced the XCOPY command, an enhanced file copy command that more efficiently used the memory available to it and had the ability to copy files from multiple source directories, or even to copy entire disks.

The final upgrade to DOS in the 3.x series, version 3.3, was perhaps the most significant. Version 3.3 added support for high-density 1.44Mb floppy drives and also introduced *extended DOS partitions*, which permitted hard-disk users to devote more than 32Mb of hard-disk space to DOS by creating separate logical drives. It also introduced the FASTOPEN command for speeding up hard-disk accesses and the CALL command for calling batch files from other batch files. Several existing commands were enhanced in version 3.3. For example, the TIME and DATE commands would now set the time and date in the CMOS clock-calendar (before, that required running a separate setup utility), ATTRIB would operate throughout a range of directories rather than just one, APPEND was given additional powers to make remote directories appear to be extensions of the current one, and BACKUP and RESTORE were endowed with several new features—among them, BACKUP's ability to format a disk for you.

DOS 3.3 also made significant enhancements to DOS's *national language* support (support for languages outside the United States). It introduced a mechanism for accessing new character sets called *code page switching*, which is a fancy term for downloading new character sets to devices such as your video adapter and printer and selecting which ones to use. Code page switching is a great help if you live outside the United States, but is probably of little concern if you're a domestic user. We'll talk about it more in Chapter 6 and lay out a step-by-step procedure for putting code pages to work on your system if you so desire.

DOS 4.x

By the time DOS 4.0 rolled around in August 1988, the climate surrounding DOS had changed considerably. Microsoft had thrown many of its best operating system resources into the development effort accompanying OS/2, so it fell to programmers at IBM to do the bulk of the work on version 4.0. With an entirely new team of programmers working off Microsoft's source code for 3.3, the continuity that had benefited the development of earlier versions was gone. Too, many industry seers were predicting the imminent demise of DOS, and for a while it seemed that no one cared about DOS anymore except for the huge installed base of users. The result was the most ill-received version of DOS ever.

Ironically, DOS 4.0 offered several technological advances over previous versions. For example, it shattered the 32Mb limit on hard-disk partitions, and it introduced a useful new command called MEM, which allowed users to determine what programs were loaded in the system and where. The MODE command was given the ability to reprogram keyboards to alter typematic and delay rate timings and to program EGAs and VGAs to display 43 and 50 lines of text. The new EMM386.SYS driver shipped with the package provided expanded memory services on 386s equipped with extended memory, and selected DOS utilities such as FASTOPEN were rewritten with options for placing their buffers in expanded memory.

However, DOS 4.0 contained several well-publicized bugs that users found infuriating, and some of the subtle changes wrought to the operating system by IBM created incompatibilities with existing applications. For example, many popular utilities packages wouldn't work with large hard-disk partitions, and DOS 4.0's EMS driver wouldn't work with many non-IBM EMS boards. Worse, DOS 4.0 checked for the letters "IBM" in the OEM (Original Equipment Manufacturer) identification field of a disk's boot sector and refused to read the disk if the signature wasn't found. This meant you had to reformat your disk if it had originally been formatted by a non-IBM version of DOS. A hasty rerelease (labeled version 4.01) fixed many of the bugs that had surfaced, but not in time to quell a reputation version 4.0 had earned for being bug-ridden. Thus, users were faced with a tough decision. Should they upgrade to DOS 4.0 to take advantage of its new features, or stick to 3.3 to ensure compatibility with existing software? Most chose the latter route, preferring time-tested reliability to an operating system they weren't sure they could trust.

Introducing DOS 5.0

DOS 5.0 is the most robust, feature-filled, and user-friendly version of DOS to date, owing to an array of reworked commands, several new commands to complement the old ones, and a suite of new operating system tools that permit it to be fine-tuned for the hardware it's running on. And it should be one of the most stable major releases ever, because Microsoft (which did all the coding work for version 5.0) distributed more than 7,000 beta copies (prerelease versions of the product distributed for testing purposes) of the operating system free of charge—a remarkable number considering the time and expense involved in such an undertaking.

One of the most obvious enhancements to the operating system is an installation program (part of the DOS 5 upgrade kit) that makes it easy to upgrade from one version of DOS to another. SETUP automates the process of installing DOS 5.0 onto a hard disk or a set of floppies, and it saves the old version of DOS for you just in case something goes wrong with the installation, or your PC for some reason won't run version 5.0. To some extent, it also creates CONFIG.SYS and AUTOEXEC.BAT files that are matched to the hardware it finds in your system, or modifies existing ones to take advantage of some of the operating system's new features.

The other additions to DOS 5.0 fall into seven major categories: disk handling, memory management and program loading, the DOS Shell, the QBasic Interpreter, the DOS Editor, on-line help, and what we'll call "other" enhancements. Here's a brief introduction to what's new in DOS 5.0, and what we'll be covering in the chapters that follow.

Disk Handling

Among the most attractive of DOS 5.0's new features are those that it provides for disk management. Several substantial improvements have been made to the operating system in this area—some in the form of new commands, others simply as enhancements to existing commands and subtle refinements to the file system. It is now possible, for example, to recover an accidentally erased file without help from third-party utilities, by using DOS's new UNDELETE command. It is also possible to unformat a freshly formatted disk using DOS 5.0's UNFORMAT command and to make a backup copy of your hard disk's partition tables with the MIRROR command. These features will prove invaluable on those rare but unpleasant occasions when you discover you formatted the wrong floppy or that a wayward program has corrupted the portion of your disk that stores partitioning information.

DOS 5.0 makes the process of formatting a disk easier and more flexible than ever before, too. For those upgrading from DOS 3.3, FORMAT now supports an /F switch, which lets you specify the capacity of a floppy using easy-to-remember mnemonics rather than head, sector, and track counts. FORMAT also features a /Q option, which performs a *quick format*—one that proceeds from start to finish in seconds by skipping the redundant parts of the initialization process. If you prefer, you can perform an old-style format by running FORMAT with a /U (for "Unconditional") switch, which overwrites all the data in the files area of the disk so it can't be recovered. If you don't use either /Q or /U, the default is now a *safe format,* which stores information on the disk that can be used to unformat it later on (quick-formatted disks can be unformatted, too). And the SYS command, which transfers the DOS system files to a disk, now copies COMMAND.COM in addition to the two hidden system files and will work on any disk—not just one that is empty or that was formatted with a /B switch.

DOS 5.0 also supports a new type of floppy, the 2.88Mb extra-high density (ED) disk. These new disks, which feature barium ferrite coatings, are similar to 1.44Mb HD disks except that they pack in 36 sectors per track as opposed to just 18, enabling them to hold twice as much data.

One of the major advances in DOS 4.0 was its ability to handle logical drives that have capacities exceeding 32Mb. DOS 5.0 carries on this tradition by offering support for logical drives as large as 2Gb. If you're upgrading to DOS 5.0 from DOS 3.3, you'll be glad to know that you're no longer confined to 32Mb. If you're upgrading from DOS 4.0, you'll also be relieved that SHARE.EXE is no longer needed for large partitions. Instead, the component of SHARE.EXE that prevented certain types of programs from inadvertently destroying files in large partitions under DOS 4.0 has been moved to the DOS kernel.

DOS 5.0 is no slouch when it comes to speed, either. To increase hard-disk performance, DOS is shipped with SMARTDrive, the disk-caching driver that was originally developed for Windows. A disk cache speeds disk operations by buffering in RAM the data going to and from the disk. This data can then be obtained more quickly should it be needed again. Installing SMARTDrive will drastically increase the performance of your hard drive by reducing the number of physical disk accesses required by application programs. It will also increase the life of your hard disk by decreasing wear and tear. Furthermore, SMARTDrive will do its caching in either extended or expanded memory, so using it doesn't mean there'll be less room for your application programs to run in. RAM disks may also be placed in either extended or expanded memory under DOS 5.0, enabling you to select the most RAM-efficient way to use them in your system.

Memory Management and Program Loading

If you own a 386, you're probably already familiar with utilities such as QEMM-386 from Quarterdeck Office Systems and 386Max from Qualitas. These utilities tap features of the 386 and 486 microprocessors to make more memory available for application programs in the DOS environment. They perform other services, too, such as allowing extended memory to stand in for expanded memory, and swapping slow ROM for fast RAM so that your programs will run faster when they call on routines in the BIOS.

DOS 5.0 includes its own 386 memory manager, EMM386.EXE, which performs many of the same functions as QEMM-386 and 386Max. With EMM386.EXE installed, DOS will backfill unused regions of the *Upper Memory Area* (the term DOS uses to refer to the expanse of memory from 640k to 1Mb, which is normally reserved for adapter ROMs, video buffers, and other hardware uses) with RAM from above the 1Mb mark, creating *upper memory blocks* (UMBs) that TSRs and device drivers may be loaded into. On a typical 386 or 486 system with at least 384k of extended memory, EMM386.EXE can create from 30k to 130k of usable RAM in this area, enabling you to stuff your system full of TSRs and drivers without taking anything away from the lower 640k. In addition, EMM386.EXE will make expanded memory available to your programs the same as if you had an expanded memory board installed in your PC. And EMM386.EXE, unlike the expanded memory emulator shipped with DOS 4.0, is VCPI-compliant (VCPI, which stands for *Virtual Control Program Interface*, is a program interface that allows EMS emulators and DOS extenders to coexist on 386 and 486 PCs), which means that it won't conflict with other programs such as Lotus 1-2-3 Release 3 that use VCPI to access extended memory.

If you own a 386 or 486, you'll be glad you do when you upgrade to DOS 5.0. But you don't have to have a 386 to benefit from the new memory management features added to version 5.0. If you have a 286, 386, or 486 with at least 64k of extended memory, you can load most of DOS into the special region of memory known as the *High Memory Area*. The High Memory Area comprises the first 64k of extended memory (addresses 1024k through 1088k). The addition of a DOS=HIGH statement to CONFIG.SYS loads portions of DOS into the High Memory Area, thereby reducing its presence in conventional memory and making more room for DOS application programs. As an added bonus, the BUFFERS you allocate in CONFIG.SYS go in the High Memory Area, too. The result: On a typical AT-compatible system, there is more than 620k of RAM left free in the lower 640k after DOS is loaded, making DOS 5.0's memory requirements the lowest of any version of DOS with the exception of version 1.x.

In the area of memory use, DOS 5.0 benefits again from technology developed for Windows. For accessing upper and extended memory in a cooperative manner, DOS relies on HIMEM.SYS, Microsoft's XMS (Extended Memory Specification) memory manager originally shipped with Windows. Now that HIMEM.SYS is an integral part of DOS, it should be possible for developers to write application programs for DOS that access memory beyond 640k in a manner that's less likely to conflict with other application programs.

The DOS Shell, Version 2

For users who are more comfortable working in a highly visual environment such as Windows than a command-oriented one, DOS 5.0 offers the DOS 5.0

Shell (henceforth, simply the "Shell"). The Shell first appeared in DOS 4.0, but it has been reworked from the ground up and endowed with a slew of new features. Foremost among them is an integrated task switcher, which allows you to switch rapidly between programs by using a mouse to click on a task name in the Shell's list of currently running processes or by pressing a user-defined hotkey. With the Shell, you no longer have to end one application before running another; instead, you can simply switch to the other one, leaving the current one in memory, and leave it to DOS to handle the details associated with saving (and restoring) the current state of the system. Then, when you return to the original application, it pops back up, showing the same data that was displayed when you left it. You don't have to reload it all over again.

The Shell does other things, too. You can change directories with a click of the mouse, move or copy a file by dragging it from one directory to another, or launch a program by double-clicking on its name. The Shell also lets you do a few things that standard DOS commands won't. For example, DOS's REN command still won't rename a subdirectory, but the Rename option in the Shell's File menu will. The DOS 5.0 Shell is discussed in Chapter 14.

The QBasic Interpreter

Many programmers cut their teeth writing programs in GW-BASIC and BASICA, the BASIC interpreters that accompanied earlier versions of MS-DOS and PC-DOS, respectively. An integral part of DOS 5.0 is the new QBasic Interpreter, a BASIC development environment based on Microsoft's popular QuickBASIC compiler.

The QBasic Interpreter is a full-fledged BASIC development environment that supports structured programming, yet still will run most of the line-oriented BASIC programs written for GW-BASIC and BASICA. QBasic contains its own debugger and editor, so you don't have to supply any of the programming tools. It features built-in support for user-defined data types and EGA and VGA graphics, among other things. And Microsoft has included an assortment of sample programs to get you started and from which you can borrow routines for your own programs. Then, if you wish, you can port your programs over without change to the QuickBASIC compiler, where they can be converted into stand-alone EXE files. The QBasic environment is examined in Chapter 15.

The DOS Editor

In some ways, EDLIN—the crude, line-oriented text editor that has been a part of DOS since version 1.0—is emblematic of the problems and limitations of DOS itself. It gets the job done, but does so in an unfanciful way that makes editing a text file about as pleasurable as having a tooth pulled. It's fitting, then, that DOS 5.0 includes a new full-screen text editor called the DOS Editor to complement all the other aspects of the operating system that have been revamped for the user's benefit.

The DOS Editor is a highly interactive text editor that uses the same basic interface as DOS 5.0's QBasic Interpreter. It can be driven from the keyboard or with a mouse. It can be used to edit ASCII files that are as large as available memory (in contrast to the 64k that some editors restrict you to), and it contains an extensive on-line help facility that features hypertext-like links for navigating from one part of the help text to another. A text editor of this caliber has been a long time in coming to DOS, but it's finally here. And it's finally easy to edit files such as CONFIG.SYS and AUTOEXEC.BAT using nothing more than the tools DOS supplies. The Editor is discussed in detail in Chapter 5.

On-Line Help

Another new feature in DOS 5.0 is the on-line help facility. Now there are two ways in which you can get help with any DOS command without opening the manual: by using the new HELP command, or by running the command with a /? switch. For example, typing

```
FORMAT /?
```

produces the listing shown in Figure 1.1, which offers a 1-line description of what FORMAT does and provides a detailed list of all the command-line switches it accepts. Every DOS command has been modified in version 5.0 to accept the /? parameter, so you're never left to wonder when it can (or cannot) be used.

FIGURE 1.1

FORMAT help listing

```
Formats a disk for use with MS-DOS.

FORMAT drive: [/V[:label]] [/Q] [/U] [/F:size] [/B | /S]
FORMAT drive: [/V[:label]] [/Q] [/U] [/T:tracks /N:sectors] [/B | /S]
FORMAT drive: [/V[:label]] [/Q] [/U] [/1] [/4] [/B | /S]
FORMAT drive: [/Q] [/U] [/1] [/4] [/8] [/B | /S]

  /V[:label]  Specifies the volume label.
  /Q          Performs a quick format.
  /U          Performs an unconditional format.
  /F:size     Specifies the size of the floppy disk to format (such
              as 160, 180, 320, 360, 720, 1.2, 1.44, 2.88).
  /B          Allocates space on the formatted disk for system files.
  /S          Copies system files to the formatted disk.
  /T:tracks   Specifies the number of tracks per disk side.
  /N:sectors  Specifies the number of sectors per track.
  /1          Formats a single side of a floppy disk.
  /4          Formats a 5.25-inch 360K floppy disk in a high-density drive.
  /8          Formats eight sectors per track.
```

The HELP command does the same thing as the /? switch. In fact, all it really does is invoke the named command with a /? switch. So, typing

```
HELP FORMAT
```

also produces the listing in Figure 1.1. Using the /? switch directly is slightly faster, because it cuts out the middle man. However, the HELP command does offer one advantage: Typing HELP all by itself on the command line produces a list of all the DOS commands along with brief descriptions of each one. So, if you're stuck trying to remember the name or spelling of a command, HELP may provide the information you need to jog your memory. Also, the descriptions are obtained from the file DOSHELP.HLP stored in the DOS directory of your hard disk. If you wish, you can modify this file to add support for additional commands.

Other Enhancements

The previous sections only begin to scratch the surface of the enhancements made to DOS 5.0. Many existing DOS commands have been upgraded to provide richer functionality. For example, DIR now accepts seven different command-line switches (as opposed to two in DOS 4.0), permitting you to extend file searches into descendant directories or to sweep an entire hard disk looking for a file; sort listings by name, extension, date, or file size; list files and subdirectories separately; display files based on the attributes they possess; and more. In addition, you can now set up a DIRCMD environment variable that specifies default switches for the command.

Other commands have been enhanced, too. For example, ATTRIB now works with hidden and system file attributes as well as archive and read-only. The MEM command features a new /C switch for analyzing the contents of upper and lower memory, and the RESTORE command will now restore files backed up with any previous version of BACKUP. FDISK finally has an option for removing non-DOS partitions. And GRAPHICS now supports a long list of non-IBM printers (including the Hewlett-Packard LaserJet family) and a number of different video modes, including those that are indigenous to EGA and VGA video adapters.

Another new addition to DOS 5.0 is the SETVER command, which allows you to set the DOS version number that DOS reports when it is queried for version information by application programs. Some programs abort when they find that they're running under DOS 5.0, even though no incompatibilities exist. SETVER lets you run them anyway. Another new command, LOADFIX, offers a cure for programs that won't run properly when they're loaded into the first 64k of memory by loading and running them above the 64k mark.

One of the most exciting new commands in DOS 5.0 is DOSKEY. DOSKEY enhances the DOS command line by letting you recall commands entered earlier, edit text on the command line, enter multiple commands on a single line, and create command macros that do the work of other commands. For example, the command

```
DOSKEY WHEREIS=DIR \$1 /S /B
```

creates a command macro called WHEREIS that conducts a disk-wide search for the file whose name you specify. Typing

```
WHEREIS CHAP01.DOC
```

searches the current drive for CHAP01.DOC and lists the full path name for every copy of the file. It executes just like an internal DOS command, so it executes quickly. In fact, macros take precedence over internal DOS commands, so you could, for example, redefine CLS to execute a screen-clearing utility that sets screen colors to a combination besides white on black and accepts optional command-line parameters specifying what the colors should be. This opens up worlds of new possibilities for customizing the command-line interface and for streamlining difficult DOS commands for novices. DOSKEY and the many ways you can put it to work are discussed in Chapter 7.

What's New for Programmers

For programmers, there are several additions to the DOS 5.0 API (Application Programming Interface) that are worth noting. The information in this section leans decidedly toward the technical side, so if you're not a programmer (or simply aren't interested—yet—in what's new in DOS 5.0 for programmers) feel free to skip ahead to the next section.

For starters, there's a new function accessed through interrupt 2FH that programs can call to notify DOS that they're currently in an idle loop waiting for user input or performing some other task that is not time-critical. Programs that use it enable DOS to share CPU resources with other programs in multitasking environments such as Windows. If it's used, this function also provides a mechanism for power management software to determine when it's safe to enact energy-conservation measures.

Programs run under DOS 5.0 may also allocate blocks of upper memory for their own use, provided EMM386.EXE or a compatible 386 memory manager (e.g., 386Max or QEMM-386) has created the UMBs. However, because acquiring memory this way is injurious to some programs, UMBs can only be accessed after a program has notified DOS that memory requests can be satisfied with either upper or conventional memory. The vehicle for doing this is DOS function 58H, which now accepts a "high first" strategy that has DOS search upper memory to fulfill an allocation request before it searches low memory. Function 58H has also been retrofitted with two new subfunctions (*Get UMB Link Status* and *Set UMB Link Status*) that permit a program to determine whether or not UMBs are currently a part of the DOS memory pool and to link them in or unlink them as desired. This capability will eventually offer limited but welcome relief from the bonds of the 640k barrier on properly equipped machines once new UMB-aware applications reach the market.

One of the most significant new features of DOS 5.0 for programmers is its support for the *DOS Task Switcher API*, a comprehensive new set of API functions designed to allow DOS programs to be written in such a way that swapping them in and out of memory in a task-switching or multitasking environment will not harm them. This is important in environments such as Windows and the DOS Shell, where task-switching causes grave difficulties for some programs. Programs written according to task-switcher API guidelines should run without problems in this and future editions of DOS, as well as in future versions of real and standard mode Windows.

DOS 5.0 also features a pair of new IOCTL functions for passing information between programs and device drivers (one to get or set the volume information stored in the boot sector of a disk, the other to allow a driver to notify DOS that it supports DOS 5.0's new Query IOCTL API functions) and two new API functions for help in determining which IOCTL calls a driver supports. Finally, DOS 5.0 offers a new API function called *EnterExecState* that programs which provide their own EXEC handlers (EXEC is the DOS API function that loads and executes programs) can call on to give DOS a chance to perform certain necessary fixups before an EXEC is performed. Information about these and other API functions is contained in DOS programmers' references.

Before You Start

Before we go further, there are a few key topics that should be introduced to prepare you for some of the terms that will come up as we discuss DOS 5.0 and the way it interacts with your hardware and software. The topics include hexadecimal notation, the 80x86 family of microprocessors and the ways in which they interface to the system around them, the role that BIOS plays in the operation of the PC, and the structure of the operating system. We'll also discuss two commands that will be used frequently in this book—SET and DEBUG—and preview some of the ways in which they will be used.

Hexadecimal Notation

Many of the numbers and memory addresses presented in this book will be expressed in *hexadecimal*, or hex, form. Hex is a base 16 numbering system, similar to the base 10 numbering system we call *decimal*. It's difficult to discuss computers without discussing the hexadecimal numbering system also, because hex notation lends itself extremely well to the binary bits and bytes that computers use to represent data internally.

Let's begin by reviewing the base 10 system that we work in every day. The decimal system uses ten different symbols: the numerals 0 through 9. A decimal number is formed by stringing several numerals together with the understanding that the rightmost digit represents 1s, the next digit to the left denotes 10s, the next denotes 100s (10^2), the next 1,000s (10^3), and so on. Thus, the value of the number 356 can be calculated by evaluating three products—3 times 100, 5 times 10, and 6 times 1—and adding the results. In equation form, this can be expressed as (3*100)+(5*10)+(6*1).

There are two significant differences between decimal and hexadecimal notation. First, hexadecimal defines 16 different digits rather than ten: 0 through 9, plus A, B, C, D, E, and F. Second, the value of each successive digit as you read from right to left in a hexadecimal number increases by a factor of 16 rather than 10. The value of each place in a hex number, counting from right to left, is

1, 16, 256 (16^2), 4,096 (16^3), 65,536 (16^4), and so on. Thus, in hex, the number 356H (the "H" is a convention used to indicate that this is a hex number) reduces to (3*256)+(5*16)+(6*1), which yields 854 decimal.

Converting a hex number with numerals A through F is equally easy. The hex numerals A, B, C, D, E, and F are equivalent to decimal 10, 11, 12, 13, 14, and 15, respectively. Thus, A2CH is equivalent to (10*256)+(2*16)+(12*1), which yields 2,604 decimal. If this seems strange at first, don't worry: The familiarity that comes through use will make it easier. After you've worked with hex for a while, it will become almost as natural to you as decimal is now.

The process of converting a number from hexadecimal to decimal is illustrated graphically in Figure 1.2. The chart shows the value of each of the places in the number and how they're combined to produce the equivalent decimal number. Going from decimal to hex is slightly more difficult because it involves division rather than multiplication, but the principle is the same. The whole point is that in dealing with computers, you should think of numbers in absolute, not relative terms, and realize that once a value is arrived at, there are several different ways to express it.

FIGURE 1.2

Hexadecimal-to-decimal conversion

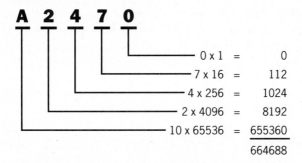

```
A 2 4 7 0
          0 x 1    =          0
          7 x 16   =        112
          4 x 256  =       1024
          2 x 4096 =       8192
         10 x 65536 =    655360
                        _____
                         664688
```

Hexadecimal is important because digital computers think in the binary, or base 2, numbering system (in this context, *digital* implies that there are only two possible states an element in the system can assume—on and off—which are ably represented by 1 and 0). Internally, a computer stores the number 193 by setting an array of eight transistors to the states on, on, off, off, off, off, off, and on. This is represented by the binary number 11000001. However, it's inconvenient to write numbers on paper in binary form. Fortunately, it turns out that since 16 is equal to 2 raised to the fourth power, binary numbers translate readily into hex numbers. The binary value 11000001 is the same as C1H, which is much easier to write down. This translation is made even more convenient by the fact that each half of an 8-digit binary number can hold a value anywhere from 0 to 15, which corresponds exactly to the storage capacity of a single hex digit. Thus, an easy way to translate 11000001 binary to hex is to observe that 1100 (the first half of the number) is equal to C hex, and that 0001 (the second half) is equal to 1 hex. Combine them and you get C1H. Similarly, you can translate the binary value 01011010, which is equivalent to 90 decimal, to 5AH because 0101 is equal to 5 hex and 1010 is equal to A hex.

The 80x86 Family of CPUs

Most everyone knows by now that CPU stands for *Central Processing Unit*, and is another name for the microprocessor chips that power our PCs. The microprocessor is often called the heart of a PC, and with good reason: It's the microprocessor that executes the instructions that make up your programs. With a few important exceptions, it's the central clearinghouse for everything that goes on inside the PC, and it's the component that's responsible for everything that happens.

It's well-known that IBM PCs and compatibles are based on Intel's 80x86 family of microprocessors, which includes no less than nine different chips ranging from the 8086 to the 486DX, with more likely to be added in the future. Table 1.1 lists the members of the 80x86 line. These chips differ from each other in several respects. For example, all the microprocessor chips that preceded the 386 were 16-bit chips, which meant they could handle units of data as large as 16 bits in one operation internally. The 386 and 486, however, are 32-bit chips. Also, three members of the family can handle larger units of data inside than they can outside. The 386SX, for example, can process 32-bit chunks of data internally, but its interface to the outside world is only 16 bits wide. As a result, when it goes to fetch a 32-bit quantity from the data bus (the channel that carries data between devices in the PC), it performs the fetch in two consecutive 16-bit operations. This slightly slows the performance of the chip, but it makes both the chip and the system around it simpler and less expensive to manufacture. Functionally, there is no difference; a 386SX can run anything a 386DX can, just as an 8088 can run anything an 8086 can. The only difference is speed.

TABLE 1.1

The Intel 80x86 Family

Microprocessor	Bits Int.	Bits Ext.	Memory (Max.)	Supported Operating Modes
8086	16	16	1Mb	Real
8088	16	8	1Mb	Real
80186*	16	16	1Mb	Real
80188*	16	8	1Mb	Real
80286	16	16	16Mb	Real, Protected
386SX	32	16	4Gb	Real, Protected, V86
386DX	32	32	4Gb	Real, Protected, V86
486SX	32	32	4Gb	Real, Protected, V86
486DX	32	32	4Gb	Real, Protected, V86

* Used primarily in intelligent controller applications

The various Intel chips also differ in how much memory they can address. Before the 286, the most memory any member of the family could use was 1Mb, which led to the 640k limit on the amount of RAM available to DOS (the remaining 384k was reserved for hardware). The 286, however, can address 16Mb of memory, while the 386 and 486 each can address a whopping 4Gb. To put that in perspective, 4Gb is the equivalent of more than 4,000Mb of RAM. That's a lot of RAM, no matter how you look at it, and it's liable to be quite some time (dare we say it?) before we see that much memory installed in one machine.

Unfortunately, how much RAM a CPU has access to depends on whether it's running in real or protected mode. *Real mode*, the mode that 8088s and 8086s run in, employs a simple addressing scheme that limits the amount of RAM the CPU can address to just 1Mb. By contrast, *protected mode*, which a 286, 386, or 486 can switch to after powering up in real mode, uses a complex memory addressing scheme that permits the CPU to access larger amounts of RAM. A 286, 386, or 486 running in real mode is limited to 1Mb, just like an 8086. In protected mode, it can use the larger address space. However, increasing the amount of RAM available to DOS is not a simple matter of switching from real to protected mode. Programs written for DOS do not run in protected mode, so DOS is relegated to running in real mode and is therefore subject to the addressing limitations that real mode imposes.

The 386 and the 486 offer a third operating mode called *Virtual-86 mode,* which enables real mode programs to run in a protected mode environment. Ostensibly, at least, Intel added Virtual-86 mode to the 386 so that real mode programs could be multitasked in separate Virtual-86 mode sessions (more than one Virtual-86 mode session can be set up and managed concurrently, and each one acts as if it were a separate PC running real mode programs). However, Virtual-86 mode tasks also enjoy a limited capacity to reach beyond the real mode limitation of 1Mb into memory that is normally accessible only in protected mode. 386 memory managers such as QEMM-386 and 386Max (and DOS 5.0's own EMM386.EXE) use this capability to make more memory available to DOS and DOS application programs run on 386 and 486 PCs.

Both the original IBM PC and the XT were based on the 8088 microprocessor, while most XT clones are now based on the 8088's 16-bit cousin, the 8086. IBM's PC/AT contained a 286, paving the way for a whole new genre of PCs based on the powerful new additions to the 80x86 line. Today, personal computers based on the AT architecture (the predominant hardware standard in the market today) are available in 286, 386, and 486 models from a wide range of manufacturers.

Each of these microprocessors is a classic example of a *stored program* or *von Neumann* processor (the latter term is in honor of mathematician John von Neumann, who devised the concept of stored program computers in the 1940s), in which instructions that tell the CPU what to do are stored in memory. At the lowest level, all a CPU does is read (fetch) an instruction from memory, decode it, execute it, and then start the cycle over again by reading another instruction from the next-higher location in memory. The 8086 understands more than 100 different instructions—the 386, more than 150. Together, the instructions make up what is called the CPU's *instruction set.* We'll discuss these instruction sets more fully when we take up the subject of assembly language and assembly language programming in Chapter 9.

Most modern microprocessors are divided internally into several operating units, with each unit assigned a role that contributes to the overall mission of the CPU. For example, the 386 contains six separate operating units. The *bus interface unit* is the CPU's gateway to the outside world, the component through which all data passes on its way to or from the microprocessor. The *instruction prefetch unit* is responsible for fetching program instructions from memory and making sure that the 386's 16-byte instruction prefetch queue is filled (or nearly filled) at all times. The *instruction decode unit* decodes the bytes coming into the prefetch queue and turns them into instructions the 386 can understand. The *execution unit* then executes the instructions. Finally, the *segmentation* and *paging* units are the two components responsible for forming actual physical memory addresses from the segmented and paged addresses the 386 uses internally (segmented memory will be explained shortly). Once a physical address is computed, a value can be read from or written to it by making the appropriate request to the bus interface unit, which deals *only* with physical addresses. One advantage to structuring a microprocessor this way is that the different units can operate in parallel so that, for example, the next instruction can be decoded while the last instruction is still executing. This increases the overall performance of the chip by overlapping the times required for such operations.

The basic units of data that 80x86s deal with are bits, bytes, words, and double words. A bit is a single transistor element that can be set to one of two states: on or off. A byte is a group of 8 bits, while a word is 16 bits (two bytes) long, and a double word is 32 bits long. 32-bit microprocessors like the 386 generally deal with double-word quantities, while 16-bit microprocessors deal with word quantities. However, any of them is capable of handling smaller units. For example, the 386 can manipulate bits, bytes, words, or double words. You'll also encounter the term *quadword* from time to time, which is a 64-bit quantity, and *paragraph*, which is the name given to a group of 16 bytes (or 128 bits).

Each of the 80x86 microprocessors contains a set of internal storage locations called *registers*. Registers are just like RAM except that they're internal to the microprocessor, not external. Figure 1.3 diagrams the registers that are common to all members of the 80x86 family. AX, BX, CX, DX, SI, DI, BP, and SP are *general registers,* which, with the exception of SP, may be used for general-purpose data storage. SP is a special case in that it is used in conjunction with the SS register to identify the current location in the microprocessor's stack. (The *stack* is a special region of memory the CPU uses to temporarily store data it knows it will need again later. Programs may also use it to store data if they so desire.) General registers are 16 bits in length. The 8-bit halves of AX, BX, CX, and DX may be referenced individually by the names AH (H for High), AL (L for Low), and so on. CS, DS, ES, and SS are *segment registers,* which identify the segments (64k regions) of memory that a program may use. In most applications, CS points to a program's code, DS and ES point to its data, and SS identifies the segment where the stack is located. Finally, the IP *(instruction pointer)* register points to the location in memory that holds the next instruction to be fetched and executed, and the FLAGS register holds an array of bit values (or *flags*) that certain microprocessor instructions rely on.

One of the fundamental concepts to understand about memory addressing on 80x86 microprocessors is that of *segmentation*. Segmentation was enacted on the 8086 as a means for permitting the CPU to address (reference) 1Mb of memory when its registers were only 16 bits wide. A 16-bit number can only hold values from 0 to 65,535, so without special provisions, a 16-bit CPU could only access 65,536 (64k) different locations in memory. To compensate, Intel declared that on the 8086, addresses have two components: a segment and an offset. The *segment address* is the base address of a region of memory 64k long that can lie anywhere in the CPU's 1Mb address space. A segment address is converted into a physical address by multiplying by 16. Thus, a segment address of A000H corresponds to the 640k mark because A000H equals 40,960 which, when multiplied by 16, yields 655,360. The *offset address* specifies the location within the segment (the offset from the base of the segment) of the targeted memory address. A typical address is specified as A000:2000, where A000 represents the segment and 2000 represents the offset from the base of the A000 segment. Both numbers are understood to be in hex. In absolute terms (if the address were specified as a single number relative to a zero base), this would correspond to A2000H.

FIGURE 1.3

The 80x86 registers

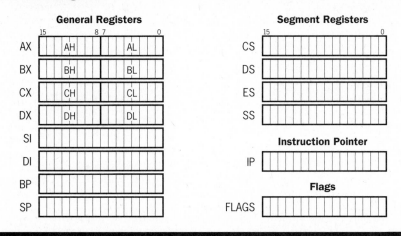

How does segmentation expand the CPU's effective addressing range to 1Mb? When a 16-bit segment register value is multiplied by 16, a 20-bit value results. In a binary numbering system, multiplying by 16 is the same as shifting a number 4 bits to the left. A 20-bit value can hold any number from 0 to 1,048,575. When that value is interpreted as a memory address, it enables the CPU to form a unique address for more than 1 million different locations in memory.

Figure 1.4 illustrates how you can convert a *segment:offset* address to an absolute address. The *segment* portion of the address is shifted one place left and a zero is substituted for the empty place on the right (in hex, you can quickly multiply a number by 16 by appending a zero to it, just as adding a zero to a decimal number multiplies it by 10). Then the *offset* is added in, and the result is an absolute (relative to zero) address. The subject of segmented memory addressing will come up several times in this book, especially in Chapter 3, which discusses DOS 5.0's powerful new memory management features.

FIGURE 1.4

Segment:offset **to absolute addressing**

Segment = A800H

Offset = 4600H

Segment	**A 8 0 0 0**
Offset	**+ 4 6 0 0**
Result	**A C 6 0 0**

It goes without saying that the CPU does not act alone in orchestrating the flow of data through a PC. It is aided by several support chips that perform critical functions apart from the CPU. In a typical PC, any or all of the following support chips may be present:

■ A math coprocessor, which performs complex math operations many times faster than the CPU (note that the 486DX has a math coprocessor, the equivalent of an 80387, built in)

■ One or more interrupt controllers, which prioritize the service requests originating from devices such as serial ports, keyboards, and disk controllers and pass them on to the CPU one at a time, in order of importance

■ One or more DMA (Direct Memory Access) controllers, which allow devices attached to the PC to transfer data to or from memory directly, without involving the CPU

■ A programmable timer chip, which provides timing for periodic RAM refresh (dynamic RAM must be reenergized every few microseconds or it will lose the data stored inside it) or which may be programmed by software for accurate event timing or speaker control

■ One or more Universal Asynchronous Receiver/Transmitter (UART) chips, which drive the serial ports

■ A clock generator chip, which provides periodic clock pulses to the CPU and to other devices in the system

This is clearly one case where the whole is greater than the sum of the parts. When separate, these chips are little more than highly specialized pieces of silicon. Together, they form a computer.

Memory and the Bus

Another important component of your PC is the bus. A *bus* is a shared circuit path that links elements on the system board to elements off the system board and allows them to pass data back and forth. In addition to data, the bus also carries timing and control signals, and addresses. When you plug a new adapter card into your PC, you're actually plugging it into the bus, where it enjoys the same access to the signals being passed around in the system that other cards installed there do.

We can get a feel for how the bus operates by examining a typical scenario in which it is used. When the CPU requests a byte of memory from the memory subsystem (the RAM installed on an add-in card or the system board, and the circuitry that accompanies it), a complicated series of events ensues. First, the CPU places the address of the RAM location it wants to read on the bus. The memory subsystem reads and decodes the address, fetches the data from the requested location, and places it back on the bus where the CPU can read it. Then it notifies the CPU that the data is available by sending a control signal along the bus. If RAM is too slow to divulge the data in the amount of time allotted by the CPU, the RAM circuitry holds off on the OK signal until the data is ready, imposing one or more *wait states* (time spent sitting idle waiting for something to happen) on the CPU. Only when the all clear is signaled does the CPU finally latch onto the data presented to it on the bus and proceed with the operation that triggered the memory access.

Data going to and from RAM isn't the only type of data that's transmitted along the bus, but it's easily the type that is transmitted the most often. There are three types of memory you can install in a PC. *Conventional memory* is the memory that makes up the first 640k. *Extended memory* is RAM that lies above 1Mb; it can only be installed on 286, 386, and 486 PCs. Finally, *expanded memory* is a special type of memory that conforms to the Lotus/Intel/Microsoft (LIM) Expanded Memory Specification (EMS). Expanded memory doesn't occupy any certain address range; rather, it's stored external to the CPU's normal memory addressing range and application programs that are EMS-aware access it by placing calls to a software module called an *expanded memory manager*.

DOS 5.0 introduces a fourth type of memory, called *upper memory*, that is defined as memory that lies between 640k and 1Mb. This region is normally reserved for hardware use. However, it's possible to load TSRs and device drivers in areas of upper memory that aren't used by the hardware on properly equipped 386 and 486 systems. This type of memory isn't physically installed in a PC like conventional, extended, or expanded memory is; it's created from extended memory by a 386 memory manager such as EMM386.EXE, one of the device drivers supplied with DOS 5.0. All four forms of memory will be examined in Chapter 3.

The Basic Input/Output System

One of the terms you'll encounter frequently in this book is *BIOS*, which stands for *Basic Input/Output System*. Most people think of the BIOS as a chip on the system board of their PCs. However, it is actually much more than that.

It contains three key components: a collection of ROM-encoded subroutines that enable programs (and operating systems) to communicate with devices attached to the system; routines for servicing hardware interrupts; and the code for the POST (*Power On Self-Test*), the series of diagnostic routines that is executed each time your PC is powered up to check for hardware errors such as malfunctioning chips or video adapters. *ROM* stands for Read-Only Memory; it's just like RAM except that it can only be read from, not written to.

The subroutines contained in the BIOS are accessed by executing *software interrupts*—CPU instructions that pass control from one code module (for example, the code that makes up a program) to another (for example, the code that makes up the BIOS). For instance, the process of sending a single character to a printer through a parallel port in assembly language involves a long and complex sequence of commands. However, the BIOS offers a set of printer I/O services accessed through interrupt 17H that allows programs to output data to the printer quickly and easily. In effect, the BIOS does all the dirty work so that all a program has to do is make a simple I/O request. Parallel printer ports aren't all the BIOS provides services for. Table 1.2 lists the categories of services that the BIOS provides and indicates what interrupts the services are accessed through.

TABLE 1.2

BIOS Services

Interrupt No.	Description
10H	Video programming services
11H	Equipment determination service
12H	Memory size determination service
13H	Disk services
14H	Serial port services
15H	Miscellaneous system services
16H	Keyboard services
17H	Parallel port services
18H	Invokes ROM BASIC
19H	Invokes the bootstrap loader
1AH	Time and date services

DOS relies on the BIOS heavily to communicate with the peripherals attached to the system. For example, when DOS's CON driver displays a character on the screen, it does so by calling one of the interrupt 10H functions in the BIOS, which takes care of the work of placing the character's ASCII code in the appropriate location in the video buffer where the video adapter's character-generating circuitry will see it. Using the BIOS in this manner rather than going out to the devices directly allows DOS to operate partially independent of the hardware it's run on, because each BIOS is adapted to a specific make and model of PC. Programs may also invoke routines in the BIOS, and most do.

Most of the large PC manufacturers such as IBM and Compaq make their own BIOS modules and only use them in machines that carry their company logos. Most clone makers, however, buy BIOS chips from third-party manufacturers such as Phoenix, Award, and AMI (American Megatrends, Inc.). Surprisingly,

IBM published the assembly language source code listings for the PC, XT, and AT BIOS modules in its technical reference manuals, so if you're curious, you can get a glimpse of what a BIOS looks like. Publishing this data undoubtedly contributed to the successful cloning of the BIOS in the early and mid-1980s, and by extension, to the widespread appearance of IBM-compatible PCs.

The Role of the Operating System

An operating system plays an important part in the grand scheme of things. Without one, a PC is a lifeless shell. You could turn it on, but it wouldn't do much for you; it wouldn't even accept your commands. In fact, there wouldn't be a command prompt for you to enter commands at. Thus, perhaps the best definition of *operating system* is that it's the software that drives a PC and also enables other software to run. DOS, of course, is one example of an operating system.

As operating systems go, DOS is one of moderate complexity. It doesn't support multitasking (the running of several programs at once) as some operating systems such as UNIX and OS/2 do, nor does it offer an integrated windowing environment as the Apple Macintosh operating system does (although you can add a windowing shell to DOS in the form of Microsoft Windows). However, it does provide a comprehensive set of core functions (collectively referred to as the *DOS kernel*) that programs may call on to read and write files, manage processes, allocate and deallocate memory, and so on. These functions greatly simplify the task of writing application programs and operating system utilities.

DOS actually performs several functions on the PC—so many, in fact, that it's difficult to draw up a complete list of exactly what it does and does not do. However, its major responsibilities include

- Reading what you type on the command line and executing your commands.

- Storing files on disk in an organized manner and ensuring that disk space is used as efficiently as possible.

- Providing a complete set of services that application programs can call on for disk and file management, memory management, program launching, device I/O, and other, similar functions.

The diagram in Figure 1.5 illustrates the relationship between DOS, application programs, the BIOS, and the hardware installed in your system. In an ideal world (or an environment such as OS/2, where the operating system controls access to all the system resources, including the hardware), application programs would go through the operating system for everything. However, in the real world, programs can and often do bypass the operating system to achieve their ends, using the BIOS or going straight to the hardware instead. As the diagram indicates, DOS programs are liable to either use services available from DOS or the BIOS, or to program the hardware directly, depending on the results they're looking for. By contrast, DOS does almost all of its interfacing with the hardware through its own device drivers, which in turn utilize services in the BIOS in order to maintain device independence.

FIGURE 1.5

The relationship between DOS and other elements of the system

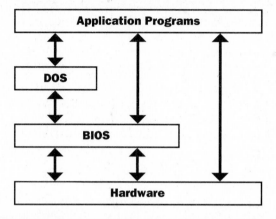

The Structure of DOS

Knowing something about the structure of DOS and the way it is loaded onto the system will help you gain a deeper understanding of what DOS is all about. Technically speaking, DOS consists of four different files or sets of files:

- The file IO.SYS, which contains the device drivers DOS loads at start-up and which performs various initialization tasks

- The file MSDOS.SYS, which contains the DOS kernel

- The file COMMAND.COM, which reads and processes your commands

- All the rest of the files that come on your DOS floppy disks, which constitute the drivers and external commands that round out the operating system

You won't see IO.SYS and MSDOS.SYS unless you type

```
DIR \ /A:HS
```

on the drive you boot from. The /A:HS switch (the /A switch is new in DOS 5.0) displays files that possess both hidden and system attributes (file attributes are discussed in Chapter 5). These attributes prevent IO.SYS and MSDOS.SYS from showing up when you type DIR without the /A modifier. In fact, you may not see them at all on some machines. In PC-DOS (the version of DOS IBM sells for its PCs), they're called IBMBIO.COM and IBM-DOS.COM. Some OEMs, the term used to refer to hardware companies such as IBM that license MS-DOS from Microsoft, adapt it to their own machines, and resell it under a different label) other than IBM have adopted IBM's conventions in an effort to be perfectly IBM-compatible. In this book, we'll refer to the system files as IO.SYS and MSDOS.SYS in keeping with the naming conventions used in plain vanilla MS-DOS.

IO.SYS is the first module loaded when DOS is started. It holds the drivers DOS uses to interface with the peripherals attached to the system, including the disk drives, screen, keyboard, and printer. It also contains an initialization module (called SYSINIT) that performs a long list of start-up operations. This task list includes initializing the device drivers and processing the CONFIG.SYS file (the file that contains your list of configuration commands). SYSINIT is discarded as soon as its work is done in order to conserve RAM.

MSDOS.SYS is the second module loaded into memory at start-up. It contains the DOS kernel, which is the name given to all the support functions DOS provides to application programs. These functions, like functions built into the BIOS, are traditionally accessed by executing software interrupts. Table 1.3 lists the interrupts that DOS uses. The most powerful one is interrupt 21H, which is the gateway to the myriad services DOS provides. Using these functions, a program can, for example, allocate a block of memory for its own use, open a file for reading or writing, get or set the current time and date, or transmit a character to the screen or printer. We'll examine these services further (especially the interrupt 21H services) and put some of them to work later on when we develop our own utility programs.

TABLE 1.3

The DOS Interrupts

Interrupt No.	Description
20H	Terminate program
21H	General programming services
22H	Terminate address
23H	Ctrl-C handler address
24H	Critical error handler address
25H	Absolute disk read
26H	Absolute disk write
27H	Terminate and stay resident
28H*	DOS idle interrupt
29H*	Fast console output
2AH*	Network support
2EH*	Execute command
2FH	DOS multiplex interrupt

* Indicates that the interrupt is undocumented

The asterisks in Table 1.3 identify interrupts that are undocumented. The interrupts that fall into this category aren't documented in Microsoft's technical reference manuals for one reason or another; usually, they're just marked "reserved," indicating that they're either used for something or are reserved for future use. Over the years, programmers have found out what most of them do anyway, thanks to some extraordinary sleuthing work on the part of several individuals and long hours spent disassembling the code that makes up DOS.

The third major component of DOS is the command processor COM-MAND.COM. COMMAND.COM is loaded after IO.SYS and MSDOS.SYS to provide DOS with an interface to the outside world—namely, the command line. It's COMMAND.COM that reads and processes what you type and that executes commands and batch files. Underneath, it relies on several of the functions in MSDOS.SYS for help. For example, it calls interrupt 21H, function 0AH to read a line of text from the command line (it's actually this code in the DOS kernel that puts characters on the screen and moves the cursor as you type a command), and it calls interrupt 21H, function 4BH to launch a program when you type the name of an executable file. It indirectly relies on drivers contained in IO.SYS to communicate with the screen, keyboard, and other external devices because the services it calls on in the kernel in turn call CON, PRN, and other DOS device drivers.

As we discussed earlier in this chapter, COMMAND.COM splits itself into two parts when it is loaded, in order to conserve memory. The transient half effectively takes no memory away from DOS and DOS programs because DOS allows it to be overwritten when an application program needs the space. When the transient half (which isn't needed while application programs are running) is destroyed, the resident half reloads it from disk, placing it back in memory where it resided before. In the course of a session, COMMAND.COM may be reloaded dozens of times without you knowing about it. Of course, that's the way it's designed to operate—transparently, with no need for you to have to be aware of what's going on in the background.

There's actually a third component of COMMAND.COM that's called on to perform various initializations when the program is first loaded. Among other things, this part is responsible for processing any command-line switches COMMAND.COM was loaded with (for example, the /E switch, which sets the environment size) and for processing AUTOEXEC.BAT. After it has run its course, the initialization module is discarded so that it won't consume precious RAM.

One of the beauties of DOS is that you don't have to use COMMAND-.COM as your command processor. Instead, you have the option of specifying an alternate command processor with a SHELL directive in CONFIG.SYS. The alternate shell might use a command-line interface like COMMAND.COM, or it might implement a richer interface that incorporates windows and objects. One of the most popular third-party command processors is J.P. Software's *4DOS,* which is a total replacement for COMMAND.COM and contains several enhancements that make working with the command line interface both easier and more productive. For example, it includes built-in command aliasing and recall features (similar to the ones DOS 5.0's DOSKEY utility provides) and an assortment of new commands. It also executes batch files from RAM rather than disk, a feature that speeds batch file processing considerably.

The fourth and final component of DOS is the collection of DOS program files such as ANSI.SYS, APPEND.EXE, and ASSIGN.COM, to name but a few. Many of the commands that DOS understands, such as CLS, DIR, TYPE, and COPY, are *internal* commands, meaning that the code for executing them is contained inside COMMAND.COM. But the code for other DOS commands, called *external* commands, resides in separate program files on disk. These include APPEND, ASSIGN, XCOPY, and others. When you type an external command, COMMAND.COM searches for a program file of the same name (with the extension .COM, .EXE, or .BAT) in the current directory, and, if it fails to find it, in the locations named in the PATH environment variable. Thus, if your system is properly configured with a PATH to the directory where the DOS files are stored on your hard disk, you don't even have to be concerned with whether a command is internal or external; you can just type it, and let DOS do the rest.

The final configuration that DOS assumes in conventional memory (memory up to 640k) once it is started and ready to go is illustrated schematically in Figure 1.6. IO.SYS's chain of system device drivers (CON, AUX, PRN, and so on) comes first, loaded at address 0700H. Next comes the DOS kernel loaded from MSDOS.SYS, and after that, the installable device drivers loaded through CONFIG.SYS and buffer spaces used internally by DOS. After that comes the resident portion of COMMAND.COM, followed by the area called the TPA, for *Transient Program Area*. It's here that DOS application programs are loaded and run. Finally, the transient portion of COMMAND.COM is loaded near the top of the TPA. You can verify most of these addresses with the listing produced when you type MEM /D at the DOS prompt.

FIGURE 1.6

DOS's configuration in memory

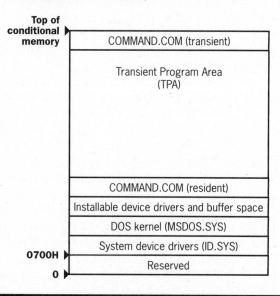

Top of conditional memory ▶	COMMAND.COM (transient)
	Transient Program Area (TPA)
	COMMAND.COM (resident)
	Installable device drivers and buffer space
	DOS kernel (MSDOS.SYS)
	System device drivers (ID.SYS)
0700H ▶	Reserved
0 ▶	

Executable and Non-Executable Files

Two more terms we'll use throughout the book are the terms *executable* and *non-executable* files. Briefly, these terms reflect the two broad categories that DOS lumps files into: those that can be executed (run like a program), and those that can't. XCOPY.EXE is an example of an executable file, while the file GRAPHICS.PRO that comes with DOS is a non-executable.

Under DOS, an executable file must have the extension .COM, .EXE, or .BAT. .BAT identifies a batch file (with this extension, DOS's batch interpreter will attempt to load and execute the file, even if it isn't a valid batch file), while .COM and .EXE identify conventional program files. The one exception to this rule is installable device drivers, which constitute a special class of executables. They can't be executed from the command line like a normal program, but they do contain code that is executed when they are installed from CONFIG.SYS. They're usually assigned the extension .SYS, but this is by convention, not necessity; they can be called anything. Similarly, non-executables may be given any 1-, 2-, or 3-letter extension you desire, or the extension may, if you wish, be omitted altogether.

There's another class of executables called *TSRs* that merit a special look. TSR stands for *terminate and stay resident*—an action that allows a program to terminate itself and pass control back to COMMAND.COM, yet remain in memory and not be written over by a subsequent program. Normally, when a program terminates, it is overwritten by the next program loaded. But not a TSR. A TSR remains in memory, temporarily inactive but with several means at its disposal for becoming active again.

For example, you've probably seen many of the *PC Magazine* utilities that pop up when a certain combination of keys is pressed. These programs are TSRs. To perform this feat, they monitor the stream of data going from the keyboard to the BIOS (which transforms raw keyboard data into intelligible ASCII codes), looking for the particular combination of codes that is their cue to pop up. When a TSR is dismissed, it allows the program it interrupted to resume executing at the same address. Thus, the program that was interrupted generally never knows it was interrupted, and the TSR slinks back into the background, waiting for you to press the magic key combination again.

Many of the utilities that come with DOS 5.0 are actually TSRs; among them are MODE, FASTOPEN, NLSFUNC, SHARE, GRAPHICS, and DOS-KEY. For example, one of MODE's jobs is to redirect printer output from an LPT port to a COM port. To do this, it becomes a TSR, and then intercepts everything sent to LPT1 and transmits it to the designated serial port. Similarly, GRAPHICS (which adds to DOS the capability to dump graphics screens to the printer when you press the Print Screen key) intercepts every occurrence of interrupt 05H, which is triggered by the keyboard BIOS when you press the Print Screen key; checks to see if your PC is currently in a graphics mode; and, if it is, transmits a screen image to the printer.

We'll give TSRs a closer look in Chapter 13 and take the time to develop a few. Until then, rest assured that the ability DOS gives a program to remain in memory after it's terminated is responsible for some of the better utility programs on the market today, including such notable examples as Borland's Side-Kick and the various command-line enhancers that are available through public domain and shareware channels.

Understanding the DOS Environment

It's inevitable that as we discuss DOS, we'll need to discuss environment strings, too. An *environment string* is a string of text, not unlike a string variable in BASIC, that DOS equates to a variable name. You can create and delete environment strings with the SET command, whose syntax is simply

```
SET [variable=[string]]
```

where *variable* is the variable name the string is to be assigned to and *string* is the text of the string. For example, the command

```
SET EXAMPLE=HELLO
```

creates an environment variable named EXAMPLE and assigns it the string "HELLO." If you type SET without any parameters after it, it will list all the currently defined environment strings. On a typical system, the list might look something like this:

```
COMSPEC=C:\COMMAND.COM
PROMPT=$p$g
PATH=C:\DOS;D:\WINDOWS;C:\WP;C:\PE;C:\UTIL;C:\MASM
EXAMPLE=HELLO
```

The COMSPEC, PROMPT, and PATH strings are placed there by default. They indicate, respectively, where on disk COMMAND.COM is located (so the resident portion of COMMAND.COM may reload the transient portion), what the DOS prompt should look like, and what the current PATH is. Each of these will be examined in subsequent chapters. The final environment string, EXAMPLE=HELLO, is there because of the command we typed earlier. COMSPEC, PROMPT, and PATH have the distinction of being the *only* environment variables that can be changed through DOS facilities other than the SET command—COMSPEC with the SHELL directive in CONFIG.SYS, PROMPT with the PROMPT command, and PATH with the PATH command. (APPEND can also be changed through means other than the SET command, but only if it has been loaded with a /E switch.)

You can delete an environment variable by retyping the SET command but omitting the *string* parameter. For example, the command

```
SET EXAMPLE=
```

deletes the variable named EXAMPLE. Similarly, you can modify an existing environment variable by assigning it a different string. The command

```
SET EXAMPLE=WORLD
```

changes the definition of EXAMPLE from "HELLO" to "WORLD."

Be careful how you enter environment strings because space characters are significant (SET is one of the few commands where space characters do make a difference). For example, the commands

```
SET EXAMPLE=HELLO
```

and

```
SET EXAMPLE= HELLO
```

and

```
SET EXAMPLE =HELLO
```

are not equivalent. The first equates a variable named "EXAMPLE" to the string "HELLO." The second sets "EXAMPLE" to " HELLO" (note the leading space). And the third creates an environment variable named "EXAMPLE," with a trailing space. To delete the last one, you'd have to type

```
SET EXAMPLE =
```

Simply typing

```
SET EXAMPLE=
```

would not do it.

What are environment strings used for? There are several ways to use them. For example, batch files can test them and make decisions based on their value. The batch command

```
IF "%CURDISK%"=="C" GOTO HARDDISK
```

tests the value of the environment variable named CURDISK and branches to the label HARDDISK if CURDISK is equal to "C." Some programs use environment variables to determine where to locate a particular set of files. For example, Windows stores temporary files in the location indicated by the TEMP environment variable and the Microsoft C Compiler looks for header files in the area spelled out by the INCLUDE environment variable. And as we'll see in Chapter 5, in DOS 5.0, you can change the defaults on the DIR command by establishing a DIRCMD variable that contains the options you'd like as the defaults. With the exception of DIRCMD and a few others, environment strings don't mean anything to DOS. DOS lets you create any environment string you want as long as there's room left in the environment to hold it.

When DOS is started, it sets aside a block of RAM in low memory to hold the environment strings you create. By default, this area is only 160 bytes long, which limits the number (and length) of the strings you can create. If a SET, PROMPT, or PATH command would exceed these limits, DOS responds with the message "Out of environment space." You can increase the size of the environment by installing COMMAND.COM with a SHELL directive in CONFIG-.SYS and passing it a /E switch, as described in Chapter 2. When a program is executed, it is given its own local copy of the environment so that any changes it makes won't affect the master environment block maintained by DOS.

DEBUG: A Special DOS Utility

One of the most powerful utilities included with DOS is DEBUG. Originally, DEBUG was intended to be used by developers to debug assembly language programs. Today, there are more sophisticated debugging tools available that provide important features DEBUG does not, such as support for source-level debugging (useful for programs written in high-level languages such as C or BASIC) and for multitasking environments such as OS/2. But DEBUG is far from being obsolete. We'll use it in this book to create short assembly language programs of our own, to modify larger programs that are created with the aid of the Microsoft Macro Assembler, and even to modify DOS itself.

DEBUG contains a built-in assembler that you can use to create stand-alone utilities. For example, starting DEBUG and typing

```
A 0100
MOV AX,0E07
INT 10
RET

N BEEP.COM
RCX
6
W
Q
```

creates a short program called BEEP.COM that, when executed from the command line or a batch file, produces a short beep on the PC's speaker. The A command tells DEBUG to begin assembling an assembly language program (assembly language is a programming language whose commands translate directly into the low-level instructions that CPUs understand) at offset address 100H—the address where all COM files begin. The three lines that follow are the actual code that makes up the program. N BEEP.COM names the program; RCX and 6 tell DEBUG what the length of the program is before it's saved to disk; W saves (Writes) the program; and Q quits DEBUG and returns to the

DOS prompt. Be sure to enter the blank line after the last assembly language instruction. It ends the assembly phase and returns DEBUG to command mode.

One way to execute this script is to start DEBUG and type the commands exactly as they are shown. A better way is to use the DOS Editor discussed in Chapter 5 or the text editor of your choice to enter the commands in a text file, and then input the commands to DEBUG using input redirection. For example, if the text file is named SCRIPT.DBG, then typing

```
DEBUG < SCRIPT.DBG
```

will execute the commands in DEBUG and produce BEEP.COM. The result is no different than if you had typed the commands at the DEBUG prompt.

Another useful way to put DEBUG to work is disassembling programs to see what makes them tick. (*Disassembling* is the process of converting the bytes that constitute a program back into the assembly language they came from.) For example, once BEEP.COM is created, type

```
DEBUG BEEP.COM
U 0100 0105
```

and DEBUG will display for you the assembly language instructions you typed in earlier. It's possible to reverse-engineer programs this way. There are also more sophisticated program debuggers available that make disassembly even easier.

You can use DEBUG to poke around inside DOS and alter the way it works. Go to the directory where COMMAND.COM is located on your hard disk and type

```
DEBUG COMMAND.COM
```

Then type

```
S 0100 C000 "AUTOEXEC"
```

and DEBUG will search COMMAND.COM for the string "AUTOEXEC" and report occurrences of it to you in the form $xxxx:yyyy$, where $xxxx$ is the segment address where the string occurred and $yyyy$ is the offset address. Type

```
D yyyy
```

and substitute the offset address DEBUG returned for $yyyy$, and DEBUG will display the portion of COMMAND.COM where the name of the batch file it looked for at start-up is stored. With one more command, you could enter the name of another batch file here and have COMMAND.COM look for something besides AUTOEXEC.BAT. In Chapter 5, we'll show you how.

That's enough for now. To quit DEBUG, type **Q** and press Enter. One thing to remember about DEBUG is that it always thinks in hex, not decimal. So when you enter numeric parameters in response to or following DEBUG commands, be sure to enter them in hex. You do not need to append an H to the values that you enter.

Preparing to Run DOS 5.0

One last detail to take care of before diving into the rest of this book is to install DOS 5.0 on your system and make sure it's ready to go. If you haven't already, read the sections in the manual about installing DOS 5.0. Thanks to the new SETUP utility included with the package, installation on most systems is a simple matter of answering a few questions, and then sitting back and letting SETUP go to work. Having DOS 5.0 running on your PC will enable you to try out the many examples in this book and do some experimenting on the side.

One of the benefits to running DOS 5.0 is that if you have a large hard disk, you can use partitions larger than 32Mb. If you install DOS on a fresh, unpartitioned hard disk, SETUP will offer to create the partitions for you (if you're unfamiliar with hard-disk partitions, the partitioning process is described in Chapter 4). However, if your hard disk is already partitioned and you'd like to repartition it to take advantage of DOS 5.0's support for greater-than-32Mb partitions, SETUP won't help. It will only use the ones that are already there. If you want to convert a hard disk that contains four 30Mb partitions into one with two 60Mb partitions, you'll have to do it the hard way by deleting the existing partitions and using FDISK to create new ones. This section explains how.

The process isn't difficult, but it is time-consuming. If you don't have a tape backup drive or some similar device, it'll take a lot of floppies, too, because repartitioning a disk destroys the files stored there. Therefore, you have to back up the data you want to save and restore it once the new partitions are created. Repartitioning your hard disk for DOS 5.0 is a seven-step process:

1. Use whatever means you have at your disposal (a tape backup drive, a commercial hard-disk backup utility such as Norton Backup, Fastback Plus, or PC Backup, or if nothing else, the DOS BACKUP command) to back up the files on your hard disk. You may also use the HDBKUP utility supplied on the installation disks, per the manual's instructions.

2. Use the SETUP /F command to install DOS 5.0 on a set of floppies so you can boot from them. If you're using 5¼-inch disks, you'll need seven of them; for 3½-inch disks, only four are required. SETUP will guide you step by step through the installation process, which will include labeling each disk with a name that SETUP provides.

3. Insert the disk you just created called "Startup" or "Startup/Support" in drive A and reboot.

4. Use the DOS 5.0 version of FDISK to remove the existing partitions and logical drives from your hard disk. Then repartition the drive as

desired. You'll find FDISK on the disk labeled "Support" or "Startup/Support." FDISK is described in Chapter 4.

5. Use FORMAT to format all the partitions and logical drives you created. FORMAT is located on the disk labeled "Startup" or "Startup /Support." FORMAT is also described in Chapter 4.

6. Restore the files to your hard disk that you backed up previously. If you used HDBKUP, use HDRSTORE to restore them.

7. Proceed with hard-disk installation as you normally would. Insert the Setup disk that came with DOS 5.0 in drive A and type **A:SETUP** to get started.

When you back up your hard disk, it's not a bad idea to back up everything, including the old DOS system files. SETUP saves the old copy of DOS on your hard disk so that you can restore the old version if something goes wrong with the installation.

If your hard disk was partitioned with a third-party disk manager such as Disk Manager from Ontrack Computer Systems or Storage Dimensions' Speedstor, there are additional steps you must take before running SETUP. See the README.TXT file on your DOS upgrade disks for details.

One last item: It's a good idea to create a set of DOS 5.0 floppies per the instructions in the manual just in case something happens to your hard disk. If your hard disk fails, for example, you'll need a DOS 5.0-formatted floppy disk to get up and running again. In most of the earlier versions of DOS, this was unnecessary because, in a pinch, you could boot off one of the DOS disks that came with the package. Not anymore. If you purchased a DOS upgrade rather than a stand-alone version, don't even have a bootable startup disk. Having a set of DOS floppies waiting in the wings as a backup will prove to be a lifesaver time and again over the life of your system.

2. CONFIGURING YOUR SYSTEM

NOW THAT DOS 5.0 IS INSTALLED ON YOUR SYSTEM, YOUR NEXT TASK IS TO SET it up to get the best return on your investment. DOS offers default configurations that will certainly run on most PCs, but there is much to be gained from customizing it for your system. If you have a 286, a 386, or a 486 with 1Mb or more of memory, for example, you can load portions of DOS into extended memory, freeing up more room in the lower 640k for programs. If you own a 386 or 486, you can load terminate-and-stay-resident (TSR) utilities and device drivers outside the lower 640k. If you have a hard disk, you can use some of that extra memory to speed up disk operations. Or, you can devote some of the memory in your system to a RAM disk to speed up application programs that are particularly disk-intensive. Even if you're running on an 8088 or 8086, you'll find that there's plenty of horsepower to spare with this operating system, and that its configuration options are as varied as they are numerous.

The key to configuring your system is a pair of special files called CONFIG.SYS and AUTOEXEC.BAT, which DOS looks for in the root directory of the drive you boot from. Both are conventional text files that you can create with the DOS Editor that comes with DOS 5.0 or with the text editor of your choice. In this chapter, we'll examine the contents of each of these files in detail and see how you can use them to tailor your system to your specific needs. Along the way, you'll learn

- What the 15 configuration directives supported in DOS 5.0 are, what they mean, and how to use them

- How to establish a list of commands that are executed every time you boot up

- How to gain the maximum possible speed from your system using DOS-supplied tools such as SMARTDrive, RAMDrive, and FASTOPEN

- How to analyze the memory requirements that result from the configuration changes you make

First we'll cover the CONFIG.SYS file and the 15 different commands, or configuration directives, that it may contain. Note that all the examples in this chapter assume that DOS files loaded at start-up with directives such as SHELL and DEVICE are located in the \DOS directory of the C drive unless otherwise noted. If these files are stored elsewhere on your PC, you'll need to modify the commands accordingly.

The CONFIG.SYS File

The commands in CONFIG.SYS are instructions that tell DOS how to configure itself at start-up. A typical CONFIG.SYS file for DOS 5.0 running on a 286 or 386 might look like this:

```
REM *******************************************************
REM
REM                       DOS 5.0
REM               System Configuration File
REM
REM *******************************************************
DEVICE=C:\DOS\HIMEM.SYS
DEVICE=C:\DOS\SMARTDRV.SYS 1024 512
DOS=HIGH
FILES=20
BUFFERS=4
SHELL=C:\COMMAND.COM C:\ /E:512 /P
```

The first several lines, all beginning with REM, are there for documentation purposes only. REM is short for REMark. Any line that begins with a REM directive is ignored during processing of CONFIG.SYS.

The DEVICE directives load two device drivers into memory: HIMEM-.SYS and SMARTDRV.SYS. HIMEM.SYS is DOS 5.0's high memory manager, a driver that arbitrates accesses to memory above 640k and provides a mechanism for other programs to use memory in this region without conflicting with each other or with DOS. SMARTDRV.SYS is DOS 5.0's equivalent of a disk-caching utility, which speeds up disk operations by buffering recently used sectors in memory where they can be accessed much more quickly than they can be straight from disk.

The third line, DOS=HIGH, tells DOS to load itself into high memory to free up room in the lower 640k on 286s, 386s, and 486s. This feature is new to version 5.0. If you have extended memory, the DOS=HIGH directive alone is enough to justify the cost of an upgrade. We'll talk more about moving DOS to high memory later in this chapter and again in Chapter 3. The FILES directive permits up to 20 files to be open in the system at any one time, while BUFFERS tells DOS how many internal disk buffers to set up. Finally, the SHELL directive installs COMMAND.COM as the command processor and has it reserve 512 bytes for environment strings rather than the default 160.

At start-up, DOS looks for CONFIG.SYS in the root directory of the boot disk and processes the commands it contains in the order in which they appear, from top to bottom. A mistake that first-time users often make is failing to reboot their PCs after modifying CONFIG.SYS. Because CONFIG.SYS is only read at start-up, changing it with a text editor doesn't do anything for the way the system is configured until the machine is restarted. If WordPerfect quits on you with a message telling you to increase the number of FILES in CONFIG.SYS, remember to press Ctrl-Alt-Del or to cycle the power on and off after you've edited the CONFIG.SYS FILES statement. Otherwise, the error message will be repeated.

Another mistake novice users make is not creating a CONFIG.SYS file at all. If your system does not have a CONFIG.SYS file, DOS will run using default configuration settings that vary from system to system, but not quite as well as it would had it been optimized for a particular system. Be smart: Learn what each of the CONFIG.SYS directives means and how it applies to your system, so you can get the most out of your PC.

The 15 CONFIG.SYS Directives

There are 15 configuration directives that you can include in a CONFIG.SYS file to customize DOS for use on your system. These directives are summarized in Table 2.1.

TABLE 2.1

The 15 CONFIG.SYS Directives

Directive	Purpose
BREAK	Enables or disables extended Ctrl-C and Ctrl-Break checking.
BUFFERS	Controls the number of internal disk buffers DOS sets aside for caching disk data.
COUNTRY	Tailors time, date, currency, and other display formats for countries other than the United States.
DEVICE	Loads an installable device driver into memory.
DEVICEHIGH	Loads an installable device driver into upper memory on 286, 386, and 486 systems.
DOS	Specifies whether the DOS kernel is to be loaded in conventional memory or in the High Memory Area just above the 1Mb mark (286-, 386-, and 486-based systems only). Also specifies whether upper memory blocks should be created.
DRIVPARM	Changes the default parameters DOS assigns to block devices such as floppy drives.
FCBS	Sets the maximum number of files that can be open in the system at any one time using file control blocks.
FILES	Sets the maximum number of files that can be open in the system at any one time using file handles.
INSTALL	Installs a RAM-resident utility.
LASTDRIVE	Specifies the highest drive letter that DOS will recognize.
REM	Causes DOS to ignore the rest of the line during CONFIG.SYS processing.
SHELL	Specifies the name of the command processor, where it is located on disk, and, optionally, what its start-up parameters are.
STACKS	Specifies the number and size of the internal stacks DOS should use to protect the system from stack overflows during the processing of hardware interrupts.
SWITCHES	Tells DOS to treat an enhanced keyboard like a conventional keyboard or that the file WINA20.386 is located somewhere other than the root directory.

For reference, a summary of the 15 CONFIG.SYS directives, their syntaxes, and notes on their use appears in Appendix A of this book. What follows here are discussions of each of these directives and tips on how best to use them.

The BUFFERS Directive

To speed up disk operations, DOS maintains an array of internal buffers in RAM, where it stores copies of the disk sectors most recently read or written (a *sector* is the basic unit of disk storage, a physical region on the disk capable of holding 512 bytes of data). Collectively, these internal buffers form an entity known as a *cache*. When a program reads a sector from disk, DOS searches the cache for the requested data and delivers it from RAM if possible, eliminating the need for a physical disk access and therefore speeding up overall drive operation. If the data does not currently reside in the cache, DOS reads the information from disk and copies as much of it to the cache as space permits in anticipation of a future read request. It also caches data written to disk, just in case the same information is requested again in a read operation.

BUFFERS lets you specify how many buffers DOS should set aside for caching. Its syntax is

```
BUFFERS=n[,m]
```

where *n* is a value from 1 to 99 designating the number of buffers and *m* specifies the size of a secondary cache. We will discuss how to determine the optimal *n* setting for your system shortly. A *secondary cache* is useful for certain types of application programs that perform sequential disk accesses as well as random disk accesses. Without the secondary cache, BUFFERS is optimized for random disk accesses. If you choose to specify a value for *m,* 4 is a good figure to use. The only sure way to tell whether a secondary cache will improve your system's performance is to try it. Even if it helps, the difference in speed may be almost imperceptible.

If no BUFFERS directive appears in your CONFIG.SYS file, *n* defaults to a number ranging from 2 to 15, depending on the amount of conventional memory and types of drives installed in your system. On a typical system, each buffer consumes approximately 532 bytes of memory—the size of one disk sector plus a few additional bytes for overhead. Thus, the more buffers you reserve room for, the less memory you'll have left over for application programs.

One way to beat the system if you have a 286, 386, or 486 with 1Mb or more of RAM is to accompany the BUFFERS directive in CONFIG.SYS with the command DOS=HIGH, which loads DOS into high memory, just beyond the 1Mb mark. With DOS loaded into high memory, disk buffers are automatically placed in high memory also. A mere 512 bytes of conventional memory is required for the buffers (total, not per buffer), saving more space for application programs. This feature is new to DOS 5.0, although DOS 4.0 did permit you to move buffers to expanded memory with the /X switch and indirectly to move them to extended memory on 386-based systems by using EMM386.SYS. The /X switch is not supported in version 5.0.

Up to a point, increasing cache space produces corresponding increases in performance—particularly if you run programs that perform frequent random accesses on a relatively small number of files. But you can quickly reach a point where it takes DOS more time to search the cache than it would for it simply to read the data from the disk. Furthermore, DOS provides a more sophisticated means of caching disk data in the form of SMARTDrive. To determine what BUFFERS setting you should use, follow these two simple rules:

- If your system is equipped with extended or expanded memory, set BUFFERS equal to 10 or less and use SMARTDrive for disk caching. You don't need both. Also, do not specify a secondary cache size in the BUFFERS command.

- If your system has neither extended nor expanded memory, forego SMARTDrive and set BUFFERS to a value that is approximately half the capacity in megabytes of your hard disk. In addition, specify a secondary cache size of 4. For example, on a 60Mb hard disk, add the statement

```
BUFFERS=30,4
```

to your CONFIG.SYS file.

It might be advantageous to omit the secondary cache size specification if you depend heavily on programs that perform frequent random disk accesses and infrequent sequential accesses. Usually, relational database managers fall into this category. In addition, disks that contain many subdirectories may benefit from higher BUFFERS settings, too. On systems that will accommodate it, it is preferable to use SMARTDrive in lieu of BUFFERS for the best all-around performance gains. SMARTDrive is discussed at length later in this chapter in the section entitled "Optimizing Your System's Performance."

The FILES Directive

Beginning with version 2.0, DOS offered application programs a new way to deal with files. Rather than using data structures borrowed from CP/M called file control blocks (FCBs), an application could open a file and obtain a *file handle*—a number that the program saves and uses in all future references to the file in the form of a parameter passed to the DOS system services. Internally, the file handle is an index into a table where DOS stores pertinent information about the file. As long as the file is open, the information that goes with it occupies one slot in the table. When the file is closed, its slot is freed up for use by another file. If the table fills up, DOS will deny further requests to open a file until one or more of the files currently open is closed.

The FILES directive controls the amount of space DOS sets aside for this internal file table, and, as a result, the limit on the number of files that can be open in the system at any one time. Its syntax is

```
FILES=n
```

where n is the maximum number of file handles DOS can support simultaneously. The default is 8; acceptable values range from 8 to 255. Many application programs require FILES to be equal to 20 or more, and some recommend adding the line FILES=99 (or higher) to your CONFIG.SYS file. Database and networking programs in particular tend to require higher FILES=*n* directives to accommodate large numbers of open files. In general, you should set FILES equal to the highest number recommended by any of the programs you run. In the absence of such advice, FILES=20 offers a reasonable compromise, allowing a respectable number of open files without consuming too much memory. Each file handle you instruct DOS to reserve room for consumes about 60 additional bytes of conventional memory. At present, DOS makes no provision for relocating the file table to high memory.

The FCBS Directive

Closely related to the FILES directive is FCBS. While FILES determines how many files may be opened using file handles, FCBS determines how many files may be opened using file control blocks, or FCBs. FCBs are carry-overs from the earliest versions of DOS, which had close ties to CP/M. An FCB is a data structure that an application sets up to hold information about an open file. Prior to DOS 2.0, file control blocks were the only means of accessing files; today, the majority of programs forsake FCBs altogether and use DOS's handle-based file I/O services instead.

The FCBS directive sets the limit on the number of FCBs that can be open at one time, causing DOS to close the file with the least recently used FCB if a program attempts to open another one after the maximum has been reached. The syntax is

```
FCBS=n
```

where *n* is the maximum number of FCBs DOS will support simultaneously. If no FCBS command is specified, DOS defaults to the equivalent of FCBS=4. The minimum value DOS will accept is 1, and the maximum is 255. If you're reusing a CONFIG.SYS file from another version of DOS, note that this syntax differs slightly from previous versions of DOS. Earlier versions of FCBS took an optional second parameter denoting the number of files to be protected against automatic closure in the event the FCBS limit was exceeded. This option has been dropped in DOS 5.0.

DOS limits the number of FCBs that can be open in the system at once because too many active FCBs can adversely affect network performance. However, some applications need to have more FCBs open than the default setting of 4 permits. The FCBS directive lets you configure your system to accommodate such programs. If an application requires it, the documentation that comes with it should tell you what to set FCBS to. In the absence of such advice, it's generally safe to assume that the default value for FCBS is sufficient or that file control blocks are not used. Note that FCBS and FILES settings are not inter-related, so values for FCBS and FILES may be determined independently.

The STACKS Directive

Although you aren't aware of them, signals from the various peripherals—keyboard, serial ports, parallel ports—and even from other chips on the system board, constantly interrupt your CPU. In technical terms, these are called *hardware interrupts: hardware* because they're generated by hardware rather than software, *interrupts* because they interrupt whatever the CPU happens to be doing at the moment and cause it to temporarily direct its attention to other matters. Typically, these interrupts are occurring at a rate of 20 or more every second. Under some circumstances, however (when you're downloading a program through a modem, for example), they can occur much faster—sometimes at the rate of several hundred per second.

Assembly language programmers are aware of what happens when a hardware interrupt occurs. The CPU stops, saves the contents of critical CPU registers on the stack, fetches the address of a routine used to service the interrupt from a table in low memory, and executes the interrupt service routine (ISR). When the ISR is complete, the CPU retrieves the register values it saved on the stack and resumes where it left off. In a well-designed system, the program that was interrupted never knows the interrupt occurred; the shift from one operating mode to another was so clean that it had little or no impact on the rest of the system.

When these interrupts occur too quickly in succession, the possibility that the stack, which is of finite length, will become overloaded is real. To guard against this, DOS attempts to preserve system integrity by maintaining a pool of internal stacks and intercepting selected hardware interrupts, directing them to use a stack from the pool rather than the current system stack. You can control the number of stacks DOS places in this pool with a STACKS directive in CONFIG.SYS.

The syntax for STACKS is

```
STACKS=n,s
```

where *n* specifies the number of stacks and *s* specifies the size of each stack in bytes. Valid values for *n* range from 8 to 64; *s* can take on any value from 32 to 512. The command

```
STACKS=8,256
```

allocates 8 stacks of 256 bytes each, requiring 2k of RAM. DOS takes this RAM from the memory used for application programs in the lower 640k; there is no provision for placing STACKS in high memory. By default, DOS uses the equivalent of STACKS=0,0 on 8086- and 8088-based PCs and STACKS=9,128 on others.

How should you set the STACKS directive on your PC? That's a highly subjective call, and one for which there's no one correct answer. Most of the time, you can disable DOS's monitoring of hardware interrupts altogether and experience no harmful effects. To do so—and to conserve about 1k of memory on most PCs—add the command

```
STACKS=0,0
```

to your CONFIG.SYS file.

If a flurry of hardware interrupts causes a system crash, DOS will display the message

```
Internal stack overflow
System halted
```

just before it goes down. At that point, your only recourse is to reboot. Once you're up and running again, tweak the STACKS directive in CONFIG.SYS (or add one if there's not already one there) to increase the number of stacks, the size of each stack, or both. It's almost impossible to tell whether a crash occurred as a result of too few stacks or not enough space in one of them, so trial-and-error is your most effective instrument to determine which number needs to be raised. Here's a tip: If a crash occurs using the defaults, a good place to start is STACKS=12,256. If that doesn't work, try incrementing the number of stacks by 3 several times before you resort to increasing the stack size.

The SHELL Directive

One of DOS's final acts during start-up is to load the command processor, COMMAND.COM. COMMAND.COM is the component of DOS that displays the command prompt, reads the command line, and acts on your commands by loading and running programs, executing batch files, and carrying out internal DOS commands such as COPY and DIR. COMMAND.COM is such an indispensable part of DOS that we usually consider it to be part of DOS itself, though technically it's no different from the numerous other program files that reside on your hard disk.

By default, DOS looks for COMMAND.COM in the root directory of the drive the PC is booted from. The SHELL directive permits you to specify an alternate command processor or an alternate location from which to load COMMAND-.COM. It also provides a means for modifying the way COMMAND.COM is loaded by passing it one or more start-up parameters. The syntax for SHELL is

```
SHELL=[d:][path]filename [parameters]
```

where *filename* is the name of the command processor to be loaded (be sure to include the 3-letter file name extension, for example, the ".COM" in COMMAND-.COM) and *parameters* is an optional set of start-up parameters specific to the command processor.

Although alternate command processors offering more features and functions than COMMAND.COM are available from third-party software houses, by far the most common uses for SHELL are

- To advise DOS that COMMAND.COM is located somewhere other than the root directory; for example in the \DOS directory with other system files

- To increase the size of the environment in low memory so that more environment strings may be entered with the SET command

If you've ever encountered the message "Out of environment space" after typing a SET command, SHELL provides a solution. When you create a new environment string, COMMAND.COM stores it in the area set aside for environment strings in low memory. By default, the size of this area is fixed at 160 bytes, restricting the combined length of all environment strings to something less than that. By loading COMMAND.COM with a SHELL directive from CONFIG.SYS with a /E switch, however, you can increase the size of this environment space to as much as 32,768 bytes—enough to satisfy even the most demanding application.

Here's what the CONFIG.SYS command to load COMMAND.COM and increase the size of the environment to 512 bytes looks like:

```
SHELL=C:\COMMAND.COM C:\ /E:512 /P
```

Note that the file name is not optional. You have to include it, even if all you want to do is increase the size of the environment. If you don't specify a drive and directory, SHELL assumes that COMMAND.COM is located in the root directory of the boot drive. To understand the subtleties of this command, you also need to know the meaning of the switches that COMMAND.COM can be passed. COMMAND.COM's full syntax is

```
COMMAND [comspec] [device] [/E:size] [/C command] [/MSG] [/P]
```

where *comspec* is the drive and directory where COMMAND.COM is located, *device* permits you to specify an alternate terminal device, *size* specifies the number of bytes to reserve for the environment, *command* is a DOS command that is to be executed when COMMAND.COM is started, /MSG tells COMMAND-.COM to store error messages in memory rather than on disk (useful for systems that do not contain hard disks), and /P makes COMMAND.COM permanently resident in memory.

Always include the /P switch when you load COMMAND.COM from CONFIG.SYS. This switch tells COMMAND.COM to ignore the EXIT command so that it will remain in memory indefinitely. It also signals COMMAND-.COM that it's the first command processor loaded and that it should read and process AUTOEXEC.BAT. Without this switch, not only will your AUTOEXEC-.BAT file be ignored, but typing EXIT will crash the system.

Believe it or not, COMMAND.COM is designed so that multiple copies may be present in memory at once. This practice is more common than you may think. Shelling out of a program (temporarily going back to the command prompt without removing the program that's running from memory) is accomplished by loading and running a second copy of COMMAND.COM. When you press Ctrl-F1 in WordPerfect, for example, to shell out to DOS, WordPerfect searches out COMMAND.COM on disk, loads it, and runs it. When you type EXIT, COMMAND.COM terminates itself and returns to WordPerfect. To see for yourself, shell out of a program and enter the command **MEM /PROGRAM** to profile the current structure and contents of memory. You should see two instances of COMMAND in the "Name" column accompanied by the designation "Program" on the right—proof that two copies of COMMAND.COM are residing in memory. (The MEM command is detailed later in this chapter under "Analyzing Memory Requirements with the MEM Command.")

The /C switch has COMMAND.COM execute a single command, and then automatically terminate itself. This may sound rather odd, too, until you realize that this was the only way in versions of DOS prior to 3.3 for one batch file to call another. The need for this was made obsolete by the advent of DOS 3.3, which introduced the CALL command to enable one batch file to call another batch file, the same way a program calls a subroutine. But there are still times when /C is useful. The BAT2EXEC utility included with this book, which compiles batch files into .EXE programs, uses this switch to invoke a secondary copy of COMMAND.COM to process internal DOS commands such as DIR, eliminating the need for the compiler to provide the code for DIR itself.

You'll probably never need COMMAND.COM's *device* parameter. It instructs COMMAND.COM to look to a device other than CON, DOS's default screen and keyboard driver, for input and output. One application for it is to direct COMMAND.COM to a remote terminal attached to a serial port, permitting you to drive the PC from the terminal. It's a neat trick, but it doesn't work nearly as nicely as it sounds, because very few programs use the CON driver for keyboard and screen I/O.

By now you can glean the meaning of the SHELL=C:\COMMAND.COM C:\ /E:512 /P directive mentioned earlier. /E:512 increases the environment size from 160 bytes to 512. It's the easiest way to make more room for environment strings. And while COMMAND.COM will accept /E values ranging from 160 to 32,768 bytes, large environment blocks are not advisable except under compelling circumstances. This is because the memory you allocate for the environment is subtracted from the room application programs have to run in. If you never see DOS's "Out of environment space" message, it's best not to bother with /E at all.

As mentioned, you must also use the SHELL directive if you plan to store COMMAND.COM somewhere other than the root directory. To load COMMAND.COM from the \DOS directory on the C drive, for example, enter the command

```
SHELL=C:\DOS\COMMAND.COM C:\DOS /P
```

in your CONFIG.SYS file. Passing the *comspec* parameter to COMMAND.COM (in this case, C:\DOS) may seem redundant, but it tells COMMAND.COM where it is, in case it needs to be reloaded from disk. You may wonder why any program would want to reload itself from disk, but with COMMAND.COM, it happens all the time. COMMAND.COM splits itself in half when it's loaded, placing one half (the resident half) near the bottom of memory and the other half (the transient half) near the top. It allows the transient half to be overwritten if an application program needs the space. If this occurs, the resident half reads a fresh copy in from disk the next time control is returned to it.

When it's started from CONFIG.SYS, COMMAND.COM transfers the *comspec* parameter to the COMSPEC environment variable. Then, when COMMAND.COM or any other program needs to know where on disk it can find COMMAND.COM, all it has to do is look to the drive and directory designated by COMSPEC.

Whether you choose to store COMMAND.COM in a subdirectory or in the root directory is a matter of personal preference. The benefit to locating it in a subdirectory is that that's one less file in your root directory. However, neither option offers any distinct advantage over the other in terms of speed, memory consumption, or convenience.

The INSTALL Directive

The INSTALL directive provides a means other than AUTOEXEC.BAT or the command line for loading RAM-resident DOS utilities such as FASTOPEN, KEYB, NLSFUNC, and SHARE into memory. You can also use it to install TSRs that are not a part of the operating system.

The syntax for INSTALL is simply

```
INSTALL=[d:][path]filename [parameters]
```

where *filename* is the name of the program you want to install and *parameters* is a set of configuration switches passed to the program being installed. The command

```
INSTALL=C:\DOS\FASTOPEN.EXE C:=60
```

loads FASTOPEN into memory from the \DOS directory on drive C and allows FASTOPEN to cache data for 60 files simultaneously. Note that you must include the 3-letter file extension with the *filename* parameter for INSTALL to work. You must also include a complete path to the file. If you omit the drive and path designators, DOS looks for the file in the root directory of the boot drive.

RAM-resident programs may also be installed from the command line, long after CONFIG.SYS has been processed. Is there any advantage to loading them from CONFIG.SYS, rather than from the command line or vice versa? Generally, no. The big difference is where they're placed in memory. If you type MEM /PROGRAM to examine memory with FASTOPEN installed two different ways—once from CONFIG.SYS, once from the command line—FASTOPEN will show up after COMMAND.COM in the latter and before it in the former. In terms of program operation, this makes no difference.

You can, however, save a small amount of memory by loading TSRs with INSTALL rather than from the command line. TSRs loaded from CONFIG-.SYS are not allocated a separate block of memory for storing environment strings, so approximately 160 bytes of memory (possibly more if you increased the size of the environment with a SHELL statement) are conserved. Some TSRs free up this block of memory anyway, in which case INSTALL doesn't save anything. Also, some TSRs may behave erratically when loaded with INSTALL because they try to do something with the environment block that isn't there or attempt to access some part of the system that is loaded *after* CONFIG.SYS is processed. If this occurs, just load the programs as you would normally: from AUTOEXEC.BAT or from the command line.

The COUNTRY Directive

One of DOS's hallmarks is its ability to adapt to the needs of users around the world. Recognizing that not everyone uses the formats for time, date, and currency that we use in the United States, DOS permits its language conventions to be modified with a COUNTRY directive placed in CONFIG.SYS.

The syntax for the COUNTRY directive is

```
COUNTRY=xxx[,yyy][,[d:][path]filename]
```

where *xxx* is a 3-digit code specifying the country whose formats you want to adopt, *yyy* is an optional 3-digit code specifying the country's default code page, and *filename* is the name of the file that contains information DOS uses in providing international support. Normally, this file is COUNTRY.SYS, which is supplied with DOS. You only need to include the *filename* parameter if you plan to use a country file other than COUNTRY.SYS or if COUNTRY.SYS is located somewhere other than the root directory of the start-up drive. If CONFIG.SYS does not contain a COUNTRY directive, DOS defaults to the settings for the United States.

Table 2.2 lists the country and language conventions DOS 5.0 supports, the corresponding 3-digit country codes, the code pages supported in each country, and examples of DOS's country-specific time and date formats. In the "Code Pages Supported" column the first number specified is the default code page for that country (the page used if the *yyy* parameter is omitted). For a given country, only the code pages listed may be entered for *yyy*. For example, the command

```
COUNTRY=045,,C:\DOS\COUNTRY.SYS
```

loaded country-specific information for Denmark on a PC where COUNTRY-.SYS resides on the C drive in the \DOS subdirectory. Since no code page is specified, 850 becomes the default. Similarly, the command

```
COUNTRY=045,865,C:\DOS\COUNTRY.SYS
```

adopts Denmark's country conventions, but makes code page 865 the default. Note that if the code page specified following COUNTRY does not coincide with your PC's *hardware code page* (the code page built into character-generating devices on your PC such as the video adapter and printer, usually code page 437), it still must be *prepared* before it can be used. The process of preparing and activating a code page is described in Chapter 6.

TABLE 2.2

Country Codes, Code Pages, and Time and Date Formats

Country/ Language	Country Code	Code Pages Supported	Time Format	Date Format
Belgium	032	850, 437	18:30:00,00	30/09/1991
Brazil	055	850, 437	18:30:00,00	30/09/1991
Canadian-French	002	863, 850	18:30:00,00	1991-09-30
Czechoslovakia	042	852, 850	18.30:00,00	1991-09-30
Denmark	045	850, 865	18.30:00,00	30-09-1991
English (Int'l)	061	437, 850	18:30:00.00	30-09-1991
Finland	358	850, 437	18.30.00,00	30.09.1991
France	033	850, 437	18:30:00,00	30/09/1991
Germany	049	850, 437	18.30:00,00	30.09.1991
Hungary	036	852, 850	18.30:00,00	1991-09-30
Italy	039	850, 437	18.30.00,00	30/09/1991
Latin America	003	850, 437	6:30:00.00p	30/09/1991
Netherlands	031	850, 437	18:30:00,00	30-09-1991
Norway	047	850, 865	18.30:00,00	30.09.1991
Poland	048	852, 850	18.30:00,00	1991-09-30
Portugal	351	850, 860	18:30:00,00	30/09/1991
Spain	034	850, 437	18:30:00,00	30/09/1991
Sweden	046	850, 437	18.30:00,00	1991-09-30
Switzerland	041	850, 437	18,30:00,00	30.09.1991
United Kingdom	044	437, 850	18:30:00.00	30-09-1991
United States	001	437, 850	6:30:00.00p	09-30-1991
Yugoslavia	038	852, 850	18.30:00,00	1991-09-30

The country conventions that you select affect DOS in three primary ways:

- They customize the way DOS displays times and dates. For example, in the United States, DOS would represent September 30, 1991, as 09-30-1991, and 6:30 p.m. as 6:30:00.00p (the digits to the right of the decimal denote hundredths of a second). In Denmark, the same date and time would be shown in the form 30-09-1991 and 18.30.00,00.

- They change the symbol used for currency. Although there are currently no DOS commands that utilize these symbols, programs may request and receive from DOS the ASCII code (or codes) for the currency symbol of any country by calling function 38H (Get or Set Country Information) from the DOS kernel. Function 38H also returns additional information that is affected by the COUNTRY setting, such as the ASCII codes for time, date, and decimal separator characters.

- They affect the sort order DOS uses when it alphabetizes listings. In effect, the COUNTRY setting determines the relative ordering of characters outside the range A to Z (for example, attached characters and punctuation symbols) in the internal collating tables DOS sets up.

COUNTRY is by no means the final word on customizing DOS for use in international settings. DOS has other commands and facilities for selecting alternate character sets and modifying the way your keyboard works, so that you don't have to have a special word processor to type accented characters or resort to typing in 3-digit codes with the Alt key and the numeric keypad. These and other aspects of customizing your PC for international use are examined in Chapter 6.

The LASTDRIVE Directive

LASTDRIVE was added to DOS 3.0 for the benefit of network users, who routinely access network resources by assigning them logical drive letters. For example, on a PC LAN running Novell NetWare, the command

```
MAP R:=VOL1:/DBASE
```

associates the drive letter R with the DBASE directory on volume VOL1. With this arrangement, all the network user has to do to access that directory on the server is type **R:**, just as if he or she were changing to another drive. DOS treats the directory as if it were a local hard disk.

The catch is that DOS puts a cap on the number of drive letters that can be assigned in the system. Trying to assign a drive letter that is not supported results in an "invalid drive specification" message from DOS. In most configurations, the highest drive letter supported is E. LASTDRIVE permits you to raise this to any letter up to and including Z. The command

```
LASTDRIVE=Z
```

legitimizes all 26 drive letters. Even if you aren't attached to a network, you may need the LASTDRIVE directive if you plan to use the SUBST command to increase effective path lengths, as described in Chapter 5.

The downside to increasing the number of logical devices DOS supports is that each additional drive letter DOS must reserve space for consumes 88 bytes of conventional memory. LASTDRIVE will work whether you're attached to a network or not, but it's wasteful to reserve room for more drive letters than you will actually use. By the same token, if the highest drive letter assigned in your system is lower than E, you can save a few bytes of memory by setting LASTDRIVE equal to the highest letter actually used.

The DRIVPARM Directive

At start-up, DOS scans your PC for devices classified as *block devices* (floppy drives, hard drives, and tape drives, which can handle blocks of data rather than just one character at a time). DOS assigns logical drive letters to each of these devices and fills in a series of internal parameter tables defining their characteristics. For a disk drive, these parameters include information such as the number of heads, number of tracks or cylinders, and the number of sectors per track or cylinder.

DRIVPARM was added in DOS 3.2 to enable DOS users to keep pace with the fast-changing world of hardware. If you add a new type of drive to your PC that for some reason DOS doesn't recognize properly, it may operate erratically or not at all. The DRIVPARM directive allows you to modify the parameters assigned to a block device, overriding DOS's defaults. The syntax is

```
DRIVPARM /D:drive [/F:form] [/H:heads] [/S:sectors]
                [/T:tracks] [/N] [/C] [/I]
```

where *drive* is a number designating the drive whose parameters are to be modified (drive A=0, drive B=1, and so on); *form* is the drive's *form factor*; *heads* is the number of heads; *sectors* is the number of sectors per track; and *tracks* is the number of tracks. A /N switch says that the drive is non-removable (for example, a hard disk is non-removable, while floppy drives and tape drives, which use removable media, are not). /C tells DOS that the drive is equipped with a change line. And the final switch, /I, designates a drive that is an electrically compatible 3½-inch drive.

A mouthful? You bet. Now let's back up and analyze some of these terms. The /D and /F switches are the only ones you'll need most of the time. The *form* parameter that follows /F is a shortcut to specifying some of the most commonly used types of devices, included so you don't have to characterize, say, a 720k drive in terms of heads, sectors, and cylinders. *Form* can be any one of the eight values shown in Table 2.3.

TABLE 2.3

DRIVPARM Form Factors

Drive Type	Form Factor
Double-density 5¼-inch (360k)	0
High-density 5¼-inch (1.2Mb)	1
Double-density 3½-inch (720k)	2
Hard disk	5
Tape drive	6
High-density 3½-inch (1.44Mb)	7
Read/write optical disk	8
Extra-high-density 3½-inch (2.88Mb)	9

Form factor 0 is also used to describe older types of 5¼-inch disks used in PCs—the 160k, 180k, and 320k models. Forerunners of today's 360k disks, these are rarely used anymore. The command

```
DRIVPARM /D:1 /F:2
```

tells DOS that drive B is a 720k drive. The numeric parameter that follows /D indicates what drive you're modifying: 0 for A, 1 for B, and so on. /F:2 says the device is a 720k drive.

You can also characterize a drive by the number of heads, sectors, and tracks. On floppy drives, *heads* is a synonym for the number of sides. Disks with capacities of 320k, 360k, 720k, 1.2Mb, or 1.44Mb have two sides; the drives that read and write them have two heads. Table 2.4 lists the head, sector, and track counts for all the floppy disk types that DOS 5.0 supports.

TABLE 2.4

Floppy Disk Characteristics

Capacity	Heads	Sectors	Tracks
160k	1	8	40
180k	1	9	40
320k	2	8	40
360k	2	9	40
720k	2	9	80
1.2Mb	2	15	80
1.44Mb	2	18	80
2.88Mb	2	36	80

Thus, an alternate way to characterize a 720k drive installed as drive B is with the directive

```
DRIVPARM /D:1 /H:2 /S:9 /T:80
```

To completely characterize the drive, you'd want to add a /C switch to the end to let DOS know that your 720k drive has change line support. Most 720k, 1.2Mb, and 1.44Mb floppy drives have change lines; 360k drives do not. A *change line* is a mechanism that alerts DOS when a drive door is opened, so it can reset the disk buffers for that drive. A bad change line will frequently manifest itself by displaying the directory of the last disk in the drive when you insert a new disk and type DIR. The reason: If the change line fails to let DOS know that the drive door was opened, DOS assumes that the old disk is still in the drive. Using this assumption, when you type DIR, DOS searches its disk buffers for the information before physically accessing the disk. If that information happens to be in the cache, DOS ignores the new disk completely.

You can use DRIVPARM to restore a drive with a faulty change line to working order. If you experience the problem described in the last paragraph—a drive that doesn't seem to know when you've removed one disk and inserted another—recharacterize the drive with a DRIVPARM directive specifying the correct number of heads, sectors, and tracks, but omit the /C switch. This will cause DOS to treat the drive as if it didn't have a change line.

The /I switch is new to DOS 5.0, and it's an important one. It is used to identify *electrically compatible* 3½-inch drives, meaning drives that are compatible with your PC at the hardware level, but that are not supported by the BIOS.

Many older machines, particularly XT clones, have equally old BIOS modules that do not support 3½-inch drives. You may have seen this if you tried to add a 720k drive to an XT clone, only to have the XT treat the new drive like a 360k model. In previous versions of DOS, DRIVPARM was no help in dealing with drives the BIOS didn't support. In DOS 5.0, it is. The command

```
DRIVPARM /D:n /F:2 /I
```

will correct this problem on most machines, even if the BIOS doesn't normally support 3½-inch drives (substitute 0 or 1 for the *n* in this command to indicate whether the drive is A or B). In Chapter 4, we'll see that DRIVER.SYS may also be used to make up for the lack of BIOS support for certain drive types. However it's preferable to use DRIVPARM when possible because DRIVER.SYS creates another logical drive in the system and forces you to refer to the modified drive using the new drive letter rather than A or B.

The BREAK Directive

Anytime DOS writes characters to the screen, reads characters from the keyboard, or accesses another character-based device such as a printer, it also checks to see if you've pressed Ctrl-Break or Ctrl-C. If it finds that you have, DOS terminates the program that's running. By adding the directive BREAK ON to your CONFIG.SYS file, you can extend break checking to the times when DOS is performing disk reads and writes, and additional operating system functions as well.

Even with BREAK set to ON, you may find that you have to press Ctrl-C or Ctrl-Break several times before DOS responds by ending the program. If a program goes for a long period without invoking one of the operating system's services, it will ignore Ctrl-C and Ctrl-Break for the duration. Fortunately, such key presses are buffered, so DOS eventually will recognize them. Break checking will also fail with the occasional program that insulates itself at the BIOS level, usually so that the program can't be crashed or otherwise compromised at a critical time.

The official syntax for BREAK is BREAK ON or BREAK OFF, with the default (if no directive is specified) being OFF. However, DOS 5.0 still recognizes BREAK using the syntax of earlier versions, where BREAK and its qualifier (ON or OFF) were separated by an equal sign.

The REM Directive

The REM directive lets you place comments in CONFIG.SYS. DOS ignores all lines that begin with REM. This can be extremely useful if you want to add comments to a CONFIG.SYS file for future reference. We've already seen a sample configuration file that used REM to create a header denoting the type of file, the version of DOS it was designed to run under, and so on. You can also use REM to comment CONFIG.SYS line by line, as shown here.

```
REM Load high memory driver
REM
```

```
DEVICE=C:\DOS\HIMEM.SYS
REM
REM Load SMARTDrive with a 1Mb
REM maximum cache size and a 512k
REM minimum cache size
REM
DEVICE=C:\DOS\SMARTDRV.SYS 1024 512
REM
REM Load DOS into high memory and set
REM FILES and BUFFERS
REM
DOS=HIGH
FILES=20
BUFFERS=4
```

While this file is no work of art, it's more readable than a CONFIG.SYS file that's devoid of comments. And there's a better chance you'll be able to understand what you did and why when you look at this file a year later than if there were no comments at all.

Another use for the REM directive is to temporarily direct DOS to ignore a line in CONFIG.SYS while you're experimenting with different configurations. (This is known as "remarking" or "commenting out" a line.) For example, if your system crashes every time you run a particular program and you suspect it's because of a conflict with a device driver, comment the line that loads the driver out of CONFIG.SYS, reboot, and try again. If the driver turns out not to be the problem, you haven't lost the line that loads it; all you have to do is remove the REM directive and you're back in business.

The DEVICE Directive

DEVICE is easily one of the most powerful of all the CONFIG.SYS directives. It permits you to load *installable device drivers,* which serve as a low-level interface between DOS and the various peripherals attached to your system. The system file IO.SYS (IBMBIO.COM in some versions) contains several device drivers DOS loads at start-up each and every time to control the console (DOS-speak for the screen and keyboard), printer, disk drives, serial ports, and real-time clock. These drivers are called *system device drivers.* DEVICE permits you to link additional drivers into the operating system at runtime to support devices such as mice, external drives, and RAM disks, which aren't part of DOS's default armament, but are a legitimate part of your system.

DOS 5.0 comes with the installable device drivers listed in Table 2.5. Divided by function, they fall into three broad categories: those that control memory (HIMEM.SYS and EMM386.SYS), those that deal with disk drives (DRIVER.SYS, RAMDRIVE.SYS, and SMARTDRV.SYS), and those that are used to enhance the operation of screens, keyboards, and printers (ANSI.SYS,

DISPLAY.SYS, EGA.SYS, and PRINTER.SYS). It also includes SETVER-.EXE, the driver used to change the version number reported to applications programs. Reference information pertaining to these drivers can be found in Appendix B. Details concerning their use appear in this and subsequent chapters.

TABLE 2.5

Installable Device Drivers

Driver	Purpose
ANSI.SYS	Replaces the default screen and keyboard device driver, CON, and adds support for extended screen and keyboard control functions. See Chapter 6 for details.
DISPLAY.SYS	Supports code page switching on the display, allowing alternate character sets to be displayed on selected video adapters. See Chapter 6 for details.
DRIVER.SYS	Sets up an additional logical drive corresponding to an existing physical drive. Optionally enables you to use drives that aren't otherwise supported by DOS or the BIOS. See Chapter 4 for details.
EGA.SYS	Allows the DOS shell to save and restore the screen when task switching is used on systems equipped with EGA video adapters. See Chapter 9 for details.
EMM386.EXE	Allows LIM 4.0 expanded memory to be emulated using extended memory on 386- and 486-based systems, and provides support for loading TSRs and device drivers high. See Chapter 3 for details.
HIMEM.SYS	Provides support for DOS and application programs that use extended memory, the High Memory Area, and upper memory. See Chapter 3 for details.
PRINTER.SYS	Supports code page switching on the printer, allowing alternate character sets to be printed on selected printers. See Chapter 6 for details.
RAMDRIVE.SYS	Creates and manages a RAM disk in conventional, extended, or expanded memory. Details later in this chapter.
SETVER.EXE	Sets the DOS version number reported to application programs.
SMARTDRV.SYS	Creates and manages a disk cache in extended or expanded memory for faster disk operations. Details later in this chapter.

The syntax for the DEVICE directive is

```
DEVICE=[d:][path]filename [parameters]
```

where *filename* is the name of the driver to be loaded and *parameters* is a list of parameters to go with it. For example, the line

```
DEVICE=C:\DOS\SMARTDRV.SYS 1024 512
```

loads SMARTDRV.SYS and specifies maximum and minimum cache sizes of 1,024 bytes and 512 bytes, respectively. If no path is specified, DOS looks for the driver in the root directory of the boot drive.

DEVICE isn't limited to installing only those device drivers that come packaged with DOS; it can load any device driver developed in accordance with the device driver specifications published by IBM and Microsoft. If you own a tape drive, chances are it came with a device driver that you had to add to your CONFIG.SYS file before you could access the drive. The manual supplied with the tape drive will probably tell you the name of the driver and what parameters to use when you install it. DOS loads it along with the others, and calls it when it needs to write data to or read data from tape.

Device drivers are normally assigned the 3-letter file extension .SYS. There are two .SYS files that come with DOS, however, that should not be loaded with the DEVICE directive: COUNTRY.SYS and KEYBOARD.SYS. Despite their names, these files are not device drivers. And because they're not device drivers, DOS will probably hang up if you attempt to load them.

Why are device drivers so important? Because they, more than any other component of the operating system, are responsible for DOS's ability to run on a variety of different hardware configurations. It's so easy to add a new device to a PC these days that we tend to take hardware-independence for granted, partly because, armed with the proper device driver, DOS can interface with almost anything.

If you still don't see the relevance of drivers, consider this: In its first and second generation PS/2s (and perhaps later ones, too), IBM left out BIOS support for 1.2Mb floppy drives. As a result, users could only attach 1.2Mb drives to their PS/2s if they had the proper device drivers to go with them. With DOS, this hardly presented a problem: Most external drives come from the manufacturer with the needed driver, and those that don't can often be run with DRIVER.SYS. But try to run the same drive under OS/2, and OS/2 won't even recognize that the drive is there. OS/2, like DOS, needs a separate driver to interface to the drive. But very few drives come with OS/2 drivers, and DOS drivers won't work under OS/2. Unless OS/2 drivers become more commonplace, PS/2 users who want to use 1.2Mb drives under OS/2 are out of luck. The moral is that DOS will handle almost any piece of hardware, but by design, not by accident. *PC Magazine* operating systems guru Ray Duncan once wrote that "Installable device drivers can only be viewed as a stroke of genius on the part of the MS-DOS designers." It's a tough point to argue.

The SWITCHES Directive

SWITCHES is a catch-all directive that will probably be expanded in future releases to accommodate needed configuration commands that don't fit neatly into one of the other categories. At present, it supports two parameters: /K and /W. The statement

```
SWITCHES=/K
```

causes DOS to treat an enhanced keyboard (one with 101 or 102 keys) as if it were a conventional (83- or 84-key) keyboard. Use it if keys that are unique to 101- and 102-key keyboards (such as F11 and F12) seem to be misinterpreted by DOS or your application programs. If you add a SWITCHES=/K statement to your CONFIG.SYS file and also load ANSI.SYS, add a /K switch to ANSI.SYS as well.

The /W switch tells DOS that you've moved the file WINA20.386, which SETUP places in the root directory during the DOS 5.0 installation process, out of the root directory and into a subdirectory. Windows uses WINA20.386 in 386 enhanced mode. The statement

```
SWITCHES=/W
```

notifies DOS that WINA20.386 is in an unspecified other location. In addition to modifying CONFIG.SYS, you'll also have to add a line to Windows's SYSTEM.INI file telling Windows where to find WINA20.386. If you move it to C:\WINDOWS, add the statement

```
DEVICE=C:\WINDOWS\WINA20.386
```

to the *386Enh* section of SYSTEM.INI. If you locate it somewhere other than C:\WINDOWS, modify the path component of this command accordingly.

The DOS and DEVICEHIGH Directives

A full discussion of the final two CONFIG.SYS directives—DOS and DEVICE-HIGH—will be deferred until the next chapter. Both directives are new to DOS 5.0 and both pertain to DOS 5.0's extensive new memory management features that allow you to put memory above 640k to work on 286-, 386-, and 486-based PCs. Chapter 3 will discuss memory management in detail and describe how best to configure your system based on processor type and the amount and type of RAM you have installed.

In a nutshell, the DOS directive lets you place portions of DOS into a special region in extended memory called the *High Memory Area* (HMA) and configures DOS for installing device drivers and TSRs into upper memory. Once configuration is complete, DEVICEHIGH loads a device driver into upper memory. DEVICEHIGH works just like DEVICE except for where it locates the drivers it loads. The benefit to using either of these directives is that they free up room in the lower 640k for running application programs. DOS 5.0's new LOADHIGH command (an actual command, not a CONFIG.SYS directive) is the third member of this trio. It permits you to load TSRs into upper memory alongside the device drivers installed with DEVICEHIGH. It, too, is examined in Chapter 3.

The AUTOEXEC.BAT File

The other file that DOS looks for in the root directory of the boot drive at startup is AUTOEXEC.BAT. As the 3-letter extension on its name implies, AUTOEXEC.BAT is a batch file—a text file containing commands that DOS executes just as if they were typed in on the command line. What sets AUTOEXEC.BAT apart from other batch files is that DOS automatically executes it each time the system is restarted.

A typical DOS 5.0 AUTOEXEC.BAT file (if there *is* such a thing as a typical AUTOEXEC.BAT file) looks something like this:

```
@ECHO OFF
REM ********************************************************
REM
REM                            DOS 5.0
REM                     System Startup File
REM
REM ********************************************************
REM
PROMPT $p$g
PATH C:\DOS;C:\WP;C:\PE;C:\UTIL;C:\MASM;C:\MSC
C:\DOS\MODE CON: RATE=32 DELAY=2
C:\MAG\PCM\UTIL\TOGGLE -N
C:\DOS\FASTOPEN C:=60
C:\DOS\DOSKEY /BUFSIZE=2048
C:\DOS\GRAPHICS LASERJETII
C:\MOUSE\MOUSE
SET TEMP=C:\DOS
```

The @ECHO OFF command prevents DOS from displaying each command as it is executed, and the @ symbol at the beginning prevents the ECHO OFF command itself from being echoed to the screen. Comment lines are prefixed with REM so that DOS will ignore them. The PROMPT command customizes the command prompt, while PATH establishes a list of directories DOS will search through for executables. The remaining lines load the TSRs FASTOPEN, DOS-KEY, GRAPHICS, and MOUSE, execute DOS commands and utilities, and establish environment variables that will later be used by programs.

If you don't create an AUTOEXEC.BAT file, DOS prompts you for the time and date each time it's started. If this suddenly begins to happen when it wasn't happening before, it's probably a clue that AUTOEXEC.BAT has been destroyed. For safety's sake, always keep a backup copy of it (and CONFIG-.SYS) in another subdirectory on your hard disk. That way, they're easily replaced if disaster strikes. Also, if DOS seems to ignore AUTOEXEC.BAT even though it's obviously present in the root directory of the boot drive, check your CONFIG.SYS file. If CONFIG.SYS contains a SHELL statement that look loads AUTOEXEC.BAT without a /P switch, then AUTOEXEC.BAT will not be executed on start-up. Adding a /P switch to the end of the statement should take care of the problem.

Note that all external commands and utilities run from the AUTOEXEC-.BAT file just shown are preceded by a complete path name, even though most of them could probably be executed by name only, since the PATH command was executed previously. Including the complete path allows AUTOEXEC.BAT to execute more quickly, because it saves DOS the trouble of searching your hard disk for the program files.

The Contents of AUTOEXEC.BAT

AUTOEXEC.BAT is a convenient mechanism for executing commands and loading terminate-and-stay-resident utilities each time you start the system, without having to type in the commands manually. You can put any DOS command in AUTOEXEC.BAT, so it's not possible to neatly capsulize the AUTOEXEC-.BAT command set the way we did the 15 CONFIG.SYS directives. However, two commands that appear in almost every AUTOEXEC.BAT file are

- A PROMPT command to customize the DOS prompt

- A PATH command to establish paths to the drives and directories where executables are stored

The PROMPT command changes the command prompt to something other than the default prompt that shows the current drive followed by a greater-than sign. For example, the command

```
PROMPT $p$g
```

changes the prompt to show the current directory as well as the current drive. (Parameters to the PROMPT command don't have to be entered in lowercase. However, when we combine PROMPT metastrings with ANSI.SYS commands in Chapter 6, case *will* be important. For consistency, we'll use lowercase characters in examples of the PROMPT command in this book except where uppercase is required.)If you're in the \DOS directory of the C drive, PROMPT pg makes the prompt read C:\DOS>, rather than simply C>. The $p metastring creates the drive and directory portion of the prompt, while $g appends the greater-than sign to the end. Appendix A lists the various metastrings you can include with the PROMPT command, including ones that add the current time and date to the prompt. Chapter 6 describes how to use these further and shows how to use ANSI.SYS to embellish the command prompt with color and to create multiline prompts.

You can create a prompt that displays the current time with the command

```
PROMPT $t$h$h$h$g
```

The three $h substrings backspace over the last three characters of the time string that DOS outputs, erasing the two digits that represent hundredths of a second. The prompt appears something like this:

```
4:17:09>
```

If you don't want to see seconds displayed, add three more $h substrings to backspace over the ":09." Note that the prompt doesn't change in real time when you use the $t parameter. Instead, it's modified to reflect the current time each time a command or program is terminated and a new prompt is displayed.

The PATH command creates a list of directories that DOS uses to search the disk for executable files. When you type DIR to list the contents of a directory, DOS doesn't need to know where executables are stored, because DIR is an internal command. Many other commonly used commands (for example, CLS, COPY, and DEL) are internal commands, too. However, when you type CHKDSK, DOS has to locate the program called CHKDSK.EXE to carry out your command. CHKDSK is an external command, not an internal one, so it's stored on disk like any other program file. If CHKDSK is not in the current directory, DOS will respond with a "Bad command or file name" message when you attempt to issue the command, unless you've set up a PATH to the directory where CHKDSK.EXE is stored. A typical PATH command looks like this:

```
PATH C:\DOS;C:\UTIL;C:\WP
```

This command places three directories on DOS's search list: \DOS, \UTIL, and \WP, all on drive C. We'll save a full discussion of the PATH command for Chapter 5, when we take on the topic of disk organization. For now, suffice it to say that if you have a hard disk, you'll need the PATH command, and AUTOEXEC.BAT is the best place to put it.

Many users like to make @ECHO OFF the first command in their AUTOEXEC.BAT file to prevent DOS from echoing batch commands as it executes them. The @ symbol prevents the command that follows it on the same line from being displayed. You can suppress the display of any single command in a batch file by preceding it with @.

AUTOEXEC.BAT is also a good place to take care of any other housekeeping chores that need to be performed each time you boot up, such as copying files to a RAM disk or executing SET commands to create environment variables. Recall from Chapter 1 that an *environment variable* is a data object to which DOS assigns a text string, not unlike string variables in BASIC. What's different about environment variables is that applications can use them to glean information about the environment they're running in. If you install the Microsoft C Compiler 6.0 on your PC, for example, you're asked to add the commands

```
SET LIB=C:\MSC\LIB
SET INCLUDE=C:\MSC\INCLUDE
SET HELPFILES=C:\MSC\HELP\*.HLP
SET INIT=C:\MSC\INIT
```

Then, at runtime, the C compiler reads these variables from the environment and uses them to determine where the files it needs to compile and link a program are located. If it requires a file with a .LIB extension, for example, it looks in C:\MSC\LIB, because that's where the LIB environment variable points. Typing SET by itself on the command line displays a list of the currently defined environment variables.

Batch files can use environment variables, too. They can create them with the SET command and test them with the IF command. We'll see examples of this in Chapter 10, when we explore the subject of batch files in depth.

Building a Fence Around AUTOEXEC.BAT

Most makers of setup and installation programs that come with application programs have gotten the idea that users don't like having their AUTOEXEC.BAT files modified for them in the process of loading a new application on their hard disk. Programs like Windows politely ask if you'd like to review the changes before they're made and even give you the option of having the setup program's proposed changes saved in a separate disk file.

But there are still a few software makers out there who believe you're not smart enough to modify AUTOEXEC.BAT by yourself and insist on doing it for you without asking permission. Fortunately, there are steps you can take to build a fence around AUTOEXEC.BAT to protect yourself from rude installation programs:

- Use the command ATTRIB +R AUTOEXEC.BAT to make AUTO-EXEC.BAT a read-only file. This will stop any installation program that doesn't examine AUTOEXEC.BAT's file attributes before it attempts to save the modified version back to disk. If they don't think you're smart enough to make your own edits to AUTOEXEC.BAT, they probably won't anticipate this move, either.

- Make AUTOEXEC.BAT a 1-line batch file that simply passes control to another batch file containing all your start-up commands. For example, copy what would normally appear in AUTOEXEC.BAT to a file called STARTUP.BAT, and then place the command STARTUP in AUTOEXEC.BAT. This way, the *real* AUTOEXEC.BAT is safely hidden, and installation programs can make all the changes they want to the file named AUTOEXEC.BAT without harming your start-up file. You may want to delete these changes later or incorporate all or part of them in STARTUP.BAT.

If you use the first of these two methods, be aware that you'll have to remove the read-only attribute with an ATTRIB –R command before some text editors (including the DOS Editor) will permit you to edit the file and save your changes to disk.

If you really want to be devious, you can patch COMMAND.COM so that it looks for a file other than AUTOEXEC.BAT when it starts up. It's easy with DEBUG. Go to the root directory of your hard disk (or to the directory where COMMAND.COM is stored) and type

```
DEBUG COMMAND.COM
```

Then, at DEBUG's hyphen prompt, type

```
S 0100 C000 "AUTOEXEC"
```

DEBUG should respond with an address in the form *xxxx:yyyy,* where *xxxx* is the segment address and *yyyy* the offset address where the string "AUTOEXEC" was found. In DOS 5.0, the *yyyy* portion of the address should be 1E70. To change the name of the start-up file to STARTUP.BAT, type

```
E yyyy "STARTUP.BAT",0
W
Q
```

Be sure to enter the offset address DEBUG returned on your system in place of *yyyy*. Furthermore, don't forget to include the comma and zero (,0) after the new file name. Zero is the delimiter that marks the end of the file name. When you're done, rename AUTOEXEC.BAT to STARTUP.BAT and reboot. DOS will now process the commands in STARTUP.BAT rather than AUTOEXEC.BAT.

If you choose to use this method, be sure to save a backup copy of the original COMMAND.COM somewhere just in case something goes wrong when you make the modifications. That way, if DOS will no longer run, you can restore your system to its original state by booting from a floppy and restoring COMMAND.COM.

Optimizing Your System's Performance

Obviously, one goal of configuring your system is to give your application programs a comfortable work environment. That means providing them with plenty of memory and adequate system resources to accomplish whatever tasks they're asked to perform. If your applications run smoothly, you'll work smoothly, too, and get the maximum benefit from your system.

A second and equally important goal is maximizing your system's speed. There are several ways you can use DOS 5.0 to make your PC run faster without spending a single dime on additional hardware or software. SMARTDRV.SYS, for example, can increase the speed of your hard disk by a factor of ten or more. So can FASTOPEN. And if you need really blinding speed from a drive, you can get it by creating a RAM disk.

The following sections describe some of the ways you can go about optimizing your PC for speed using the utilities DOS 5.0 provides and also discuss some of the inherent trade-offs between speed and memory availability.

Speeding Hard-Disk Operations with SMARTDrive

One of the easiest ways to speed up a hard disk, and one of the best ways to put extended or expanded memory to use under DOS, is to use a disk-caching utility. A *disk cache* is an area of memory where data read from the hard disk is stored so that if a program requests the same data again, it can be delivered from the cache rather than requiring another hard-disk access. Information can be retrieved from RAM several orders of magnitude faster than it can be from even the fastest hard disk. So every time hard-disk data can be retrieved from the cache, the CPU conserves valuable time. The net result is improved hard-disk performance.

Disk caches are effective because most programs tend to access the hard disk in predictable patterns. It's rare, for example, that a program reads only a single sector from disk. Usually it reads several consecutive sectors, sometimes requiring many disk accesses to do so. One of the tricks most disk-caching utilities perform is to read several sectors each time a single sector is requested. Then, if the program that made the request follows up by requesting the sector that lies after the last one requested, the data is already cached. Most caching utilities also cache data written to the hard disk, because it's not uncommon for a program to read back what it has written. By using such tried-and-true methods, it's not uncommon for a disk-caching program to achieve a *hit rate*—a percentage of disk requests delivered from the cache rather than by physically accessing the hard disk—of 90 percent or better.

Disk caches should not be (but often are) confused with *RAM caches,* which cache data going from the memory subsystem to the CPU, not data coming from the hard disk. RAM caches are commonly used on fast 386 and 486 machines, where the CPU can process data much faster than RAM can divulge it. In fact, the 486 has an 8k RAM cache built in, so every 486 uses at least an 8k RAM cache. Without a RAM cache, PC designers must resort to *wait states*—idle loops performed by the CPU while waiting for data to arrive from RAM—which penalize performance by making the CPU pause each time it accesses memory. RAM caches are normally populated with fast static RAM, which is similar to dynamic RAM (the kind of memory we normally refer to when we talk about the RAM in our systems), except that it can be accessed much faster—typically three to four times faster than even very fast dynamic RAM.

DOS performs a rudimentary form of disk caching that you can control with the BUFFERS directive in CONFIG.SYS. The number of BUFFERS you specify is the number of disk sectors that DOS caches in memory each time a disk is accessed. Each sector is 512 bytes long. BUFFERS uses a caching algorithm called *associative caching,* which is one of the simplest forms of disk caching. One characteristic of an associative cache is that a larger number of disk buffers does not necessarily improve disk-cache performance. In fact, specifying too large a number for BUFFERS can actually slow your system down, because DOS may spend more time searching the cache for a given sector than it would require to simply read the data from the hard disk. Unfortunately, there's no easy way to determine where the point of diminishing returns lies. And even if there were, it would depend on the type of applications you run and the way your hard disk is set up.

With DOS 5.0, however, comes a solution: SMARTDRV.SYS, better known as SMARTDrive. SMARTDrive is a disk-caching device driver adapted from Microsoft Windows that outperforms BUFFERS by employing larger data spaces and better, more efficient caching algorithms. Not only is SMARTDrive faster than BUFFERS, but it also allows the cache to be established in extended or expanded memory—good news for those who have lots of RAM above 640k that until now has gone largely unused under DOS. Installing SMARTDrive in your system drastically improves hard-disk performance and also prolongs the life of the drive by reducing the number of physical disk accesses.

SMARTDrive is installed with a DEVICE or DEVICEHIGH directive in CONFIG.SYS. Its syntax is

```
DEVICE=[d:][path]SMARTDRV.SYS [maxsize] [minsize] [/A]
```

where *d:* and *path* are the drive and directory where SMARTDRV.SYS is located, *maxsize* is the amount of memory in kilobytes to be set aside for caching, *minsize* specifies the minimum size the cache can be shrunk to, and /A tells SMARTDrive to use expanded memory. If /A is omitted, SMARTDrive defaults to setting up the cache in extended memory. There is no provision for loading it into conventional memory, because SMARTDrive requires at least 256k of RAM to run well and that is too much territory in the lower 640k to give up.

The *maxsize* parameter specifies the size of the cache. It can be set from 128 to 8,192 (the equivalent of 8Mb of RAM!), with 256 being the default. One feature that sets SMARTDrive apart from other disk caches is that certain programs such as Microsoft Windows can borrow memory from the cache and lend it to application programs when the need arises. That's where the *minsize* parameter comes into play: You can restrict Windows' downsizing of the cache by specifying a minimum cache size. The default is 0, meaning that if you omit the *minsize* parameter, Windows can claim all of the cache if it needs to. If you set *minsize* equal to *maxsize,* downsizing is not permitted.

Installing SMARTDrive in Extended Memory   SMARTDrive is most effective if you can allocate it at least 256k of memory. 512k or 1Mb is better, and 2Mb is better still. How much you can give it depends on how much extended or expanded memory you have in your system. If you have a 286, 386, or 486 with 1Mb of memory (640k plus 384k of extended memory), try installing SMART-Drive with a 256k cache size by adding the line

```
DEVICE=C:\DOS\SMARTDRV.SYS 256
```

assuming SMARTDRV.SYS is located in the \DOS directory of drive C. If you have 2Mb or more of memory, consider increasing the cache size to 1Mb with the command

```
DEVICE=C:\DOS SMARTDRV.SYS 1024
```

Note that if you have only 640k of RAM, SMARTDrive cannot be used.

With SMARTDrive installed, you should notice right off that your hard-disk light comes on less often, an indicator that the hard disk is being accessed less. SMARTDrive uses several techniques to minimize disk accesses, including *read buffering* and *look-ahead buffering*. The former has SMARTDrive cache sectors read from disk in RAM; the latter has it read more sectors than were actually requested when it does perform a disk read, reasoning that the program that reads a sector may soon want to read the next sector as well.

Installing SMARTDrive in Expanded Memory If you're running DOS 5.0 on an 8086 or 8088, you can't run SMARTDrive unless you have an expanded memory board. An 8088 or 8086 can't have extended memory; that's the domain of 286, 386, and 486 CPUs, which have the ability to address more than 1Mb of RAM. If you do have expanded memory, you can install SMARTDrive with a /A switch and make use of the extra RAM. The command

```
DEVICE=C:\DOS\SMARTDRV.SYS 1024 /A
```

installs SMARTDrive into expanded memory with a 1Mb cache size. Actually, saying that SMARTDrive is installed in expanded memory is slightly misleading. It's not the driver itself that goes into expanded memory, but the cache that the driver sets up and maintains. The code that makes up the driver goes into RAM below 640k, consuming something in the neighborhood of 20k of memory.

Of course, 286s, 386s, and 486s may have expanded memory, too. If your PC fits into this category, feel free to run SMARTDrive from expanded memory. There's nothing magic about the 8088 and 8086 that says they're the only ones that can place a disk cache in expanded memory. It's just that it's far more common for CPUs designated 286 and up to have extended memory rather than expanded.

As you'll see in the next chapter, it's possible to emulate expanded memory in extended memory on 386- and 486-based PCs using DOS 5.0's EMM386 driver. It's also possible to run SMARTDrive in expanded memory created by EMM386, but it's not advisable, because accessing expanded memory set up in extended memory is slightly slower than accessing extended memory directly.

Preparing to Run SMARTDrive Before you run SMARTDrive in extended memory, you must add the line

```
DEVICE=C:\DOS\HIMEM.SYS
```

to your CONFIG.SYS file (if HIMEM.SYS is located somewhere other than C:\DOS, modify the command accordingly). This command must appear before the line that loads SMARTDRV.SYS. HIMEM.SYS is the device driver DOS uses to arbitrate access to high memory so that one program doesn't overwrite sections used by another. SMARTDrive uses HIMEM.SYS to access memory without conflicting with other programs and drivers. Similarly, if you run SMARTDrive from expanded memory, you must also install an expanded memory manager in CONFIG.SYS (normally, the expanded memory manager, or EMM, comes with expanded memory hardware), and it, too, must appear before the DEVICE directive that loads SMARTDrive.

It cannot be overemphasized that SMARTDrive is one of the best ways to put memory beyond 640k to work in your system. DOS only makes limited use of extended and expanded memory to begin with, so SMARTDrive offers a rare opportunity for DOS to use the extra RAM. Other uses for RAM include setting it up as a RAM disk and, if you have extended memory, loading TSRs and device drivers into areas above 640k. Before you decide how much to allocate to SMARTDrive, you may find it advantageous to read the next section, which discusses RAM disks, and Chapter 3, which provides an overview of DOS 5.0's memory management features and ways you can use extended memory to make more memory available to application programs.

A final consideration in deciding how much RAM to devote to SMART-Drive is whether you plan to run Microsoft Windows or not. If you do, extended memory may better serve you as a resource for Windows, not as a disk cache. You won't want to do away with the disk cache altogether, but it is advisable to balance the size of the cache against Windows' own memory requirements. Assuming you have 3Mb or more of RAM to start with (which you'll want to have if you run Windows in 386 Enhanced mode), consider devoting about 512k of that to SMARTDrive, and specify a minimum cache size half that. If you have less than 3Mb and plan to run Windows, reduce SMARTDrive's allotment to 256k and reduce the minimum cache size to 0.

One last note about SMARTDrive and the way it interacts with BUFFERS: If you use SMARTDrive, set BUFFERS equal to 10 or less in your CONFIG-.SYS file. There's no need to use both of them, and setting BUFFERS to a small value minimizes its effect on the system. If, on the other hand, you have neither extended nor expanded memory or can't afford to give any of it up, skip SMARTDrive and set BUFFERS according to the directions provided earlier in this chapter. Then consider buying some additional RAM for your system so that you can use SMARTDrive. The results will be well worth the cost.

Speeding Disk Operations Further with FASTOPEN

Another DOS command that lets you speed up hard-disk accesses is FASTOPEN. Whereas SMARTDrive caches disk sectors, FASTOPEN works at the file level to provide easier access to files stored on the hard disk. It performs a different sort of caching: It caches information pertaining to where files and directories are located so that a file that is opened once may be opened quickly a second time. Hence the name FASTOPEN. With FASTOPEN installed, certain disk operations will proceed much faster than normal, and some of your application programs—especially those that use the hard disk often—will run more quickly.

Should you use SMARTDrive and FASTOPEN at the same time? The answer is a resounding "Yes!" The two are not redundant. SMARTDrive caches sectors that are read in from disk so that if the same ones are requested again, they can be delivered from fast RAM rather than from the hard disk. It works purely at the sector level; it neither understands nor cares about the concept of files, which in one sense are logical (if disjointed) groupings of sectors on the disk. FASTOPEN, on the other hand, knows nothing about sectors, but well understands how files are stored on a disk, so it can help DOS locate them.

Using both together might make your hard disk run faster than you would have believed possible.

There are two ways to install FASTOPEN: with an INSTALL directive in CONFIG.SYS, or from the command line (or, better yet, from your AUTOEXEC-.BAT file). Its syntax is

```
FASTOPEN d:[[=]n] [...] [/X]
```

where *d:* specifies the drive upon which FASTOPEN should act and *n* specifies the number of files FASTOPEN can cache data for at one time. You can specify as many as 24 drive letters (C through Z) for FASTOPEN to act on. The command

```
FASTOPEN C:=20
```

sets up a 20-entry cache for drive C, while the command

```
FASTOPEN C:=20 D:=20 E:=10
```

sets up individual caches for drives C, D, and E. FASTOPEN can only be used on hard disks. Trying to install it for a floppy drive prompts an error message from DOS.

Each FASTOPEN buffer that you reserve with the *n* parameter consumes about 48 bytes of memory. Needless to say, it pays to be judicious with memory. As a rule of thumb, allow FASTOPEN to create one buffer for every megabyte of space on the drive. For example, if your hard disk contains two logical drives—drives C and D—and drive C is 40Mb long and drive D is 20Mb, install FASTOPEN with the command

```
FASTOPEN C:=40 D:=20
```

This strikes a reasonable balance between hard-disk performance and memory consumption.

Moving FASTOPEN Out of Conventional Memory   If you omit the /X switch, FASTOPEN, like any other TSR, is installed in the region of memory known as conventional memory. This region is also used by application programs. If you have expanded memory, you can place FASTOPEN's buffers there by installing it with a /X switch. Installed this way, FASTOPEN reduces its consumption of conventional memory. The command

```
FASTOPEN.EXE C:=20 D:=20 E:=10 /X
```

installs FASTOPEN for drives C, D, and E and locates it in expanded memory.

If you don't have expanded memory, there are two other ways to move FASTOPEN out of low memory—provided that you have a 386 or 486 with extended memory. One method involves using the LOADHIGH command to move FASTOPEN to the area of memory known as upper memory. The other uses DOS 5.0's EMM386.EXE driver to make extended memory appear to be expanded memory. We'll look at both of these methods in the next chapter when we discuss the subject of DOS 5.0 memory management and the special things you can do with DOS 5.0 on a 386 or 486.

Speeding Disk-Intensive Applications with RAMDrive

Another way to increase the speed with which disk operations are performed is to use a RAM disk. A *RAM disk* is exactly what its name implies: a disk that stores information in RAM rather than on a magnetic surface. RAM disks are also called *virtual disks*. A RAM disk is accessed exactly like a real disk. You can list its contents, copy files to and from it, and even run CHKDSK on it if you like. DOS assigns it a drive letter and treats it just like all the other drives in the system. A RAM disk, however, operates much faster than a conventional disk, because the CPU can write data to and retrieve data from RAM much faster than it can to a disk.

The tool DOS provides for setting up RAM disks is RAMDRIVE.SYS, better known as RAMDrive. RAMDrive is installed with a DEVICE directive in CONFIG.SYS. The full syntax is

```
DEVICE=[d:][path]RAMDRIVE.SYS [DiskSize] [SectorSize]
       [NumEntries] [/E] [/A]
```

where *DiskSize* specifies the size of the RAM disk in kilobytes, *SectorSize* specifies the sector size in bytes, and *NumEntries* specifies the number of entries that may be stored in the RAM disk's root directory. The /E and /A switches install RAMDrive into extended and expanded memory, respectively. If you don't include either /E or /A, the RAM disk is installed in conventional memory, where it takes room away from application programs. Generally, if you don't have either extended or expanded memory, you won't want to use RAM-Drive—the size of the RAM disk you could create without affecting DOS's ability to run programs would be so small that it would be virtually useless as a disk.

The *DiskSize* parameter permits you to set the size of the virtual disk. The command

```
DEVICE=C:\DOS\RAMDRIVE.SYS 360 /E
```

sets up a 360k RAM disk in extended memory, while the command

```
DEVICE=C:\DOS\RAMDRIVE.SYS 720 /A
```

sets up a 720k disk—the equivalent of a double-density 3¹/₂-inch disk—in *expanded* memory. If you don't specify a size, RAMDrive defaults to 64k. As usual, if you install the driver into either extended or expanded memory, the line that loads the memory manager (HIMEM.SYS for extended memory or the driver that came with your expanded memory board for expanded memory) must precede the line that loads RAMDrive. And as is the case with SMART-Drive, it's counterproductive to load RAMDrive into expanded memory created in extended memory with EMM386. Instead, load RAMDrive directly into extended memory. Then you'll get the highest possible transfer speeds from your RAM disks.

You'll probably never need the *SectorSize* and *NumEntries* parameters. *SectorSize* lets you specify the size of one sector in the RAM disk. Valid values are 128, 256, and 512. DOS is set up to work with disks that use 512-byte sectors, so setting this value to anything other than 512 might cause problems. If you omit *SectorSize,* RAMDrive defaults to 512. *NumEntries* specifies the number of files that may be stored in the root directory. Valid values range from 2 to 1,024, with a default of 64. The default is good enough for most purposes. The only reason you'd want to increase the size of the root directory is if you receive a message from DOS saying it can't create another directory entry when you try to copy a file to the RAM disk or create a new file in the root directory. Even then, there may be other, better ways to work around the problem, such as creating subdirectories on the RAM disk to store files outside the root directory. As we'll see in Chapter 5, the number of files a subdirectory can hold is limited only by available disk space, while the number of entries the root directory can store is limited by additional constraints.

When you install RAMDrive, the RAM disk will assume the lowest available drive letter in the system. For example, if your PC currently has one or two floppies and a hard disk that contains logical drives C and D, the RAM disk will become drive E—provided there are no other DEVICE directives preceding it that load device drivers which create logical drives. When it is installed, RAM-Drive tells you what drive letter DOS assigned to the RAM disk in the installation message displays on the screen.

You can install multiple RAM disks in your system by loading RAMDrive more than once. For example, the following commands, entered in CONFIG-.SYS, create three 128k RAM disks:

```
DEVICE=C:\DOS\RAMDRIVE.SYS 128 /E
DEVICE=C:\DOS\RAMDRIVE.SYS 128 /E
DEVICE=C:\DOS\RAMDRIVE.SYS 128 /E
```

If D is the first drive letter available when the first command is executed, then the three drives will be addressed as D, E, and F. You can create as many RAM disks as physical memory and the range of available drive letters will allow. At most, that means you can set up 24 RAM disks, because a PC with one floppy and no hard disk has 24 available drive letters, C through Z.

When a RAM disk is created, it is initially empty, just like a freshly format-ted floppy disk. It's up to you to copy files to it. And don't forget that when a PC is powered down or recycled with Ctrl-Alt-Del, files stored on RAM disks are lost. If you want to save one or more of those files, be absolutely sure to copy them to a real disk. Once the RAM disk is destroyed, there is no way to recover the data that was on it before power was removed. If this turns out to be a per-sistent problem, you might opt to only use the RAM disk to store files that you do not intend to change. For example, you could locate executable files there, but not data files.

Now for the caveats. Unless you have a particular need for a RAM disk, it's generally better to devote the memory to a disk cache for SMARTDrive. You might choose to use a RAM disk in addition to SMARTDrive for applications that make heavy use of a small set of files stored on disk (for example, overlay files) or for applications that make extensive use of temporary files. Windows 3.0, for example, uses the TEMP environment variable to determine where to write its temporary files. Directing Windows to a RAM disk rather than to a real disk for temporary file storage can significantly improve its speed of execution.

As usual, the decision whether to use a RAM disk involves a trade-off between memory consumption and speed. Is the extra measure of speed gained worth the memory required? Could the RAM be put to better use in another capacity? That's a call only you can make, because only you know exactly how your system is set up and what kind of applications you plan to run. However, there are times when a RAM disk can help, especially if you have surplus extended or expanded memory. Following are just a few examples of how RAM disks may be put to use.

Storing Temporary Files on a RAM Disk   Some programs—Windows and the Microsoft C Compiler are two examples—use temporary disk files to store information that they need but that won't fit into RAM. Normally, these pro-grams permit you to tell them where to store the temporary files with an envi-ronment variable, usually called TMP or TEMP. Directing temporary files to a RAM disk will often increase the speed with which such applications run.

To configure your system this way, consult your programs' manuals to find out what environment variable they expect to hold the name of the drive and directory where temporary files should go. If it's TEMP, and if your RAM disk is drive D, add the command

```
SET TEMP=D:\
```

to your AUTOEXEC.BAT file. The only way to tell how much of a boost this will provide, if any, is to try it. If it helps, great. If it doesn't, then you're probably better off giving the memory to SMARTDrive for disk caching.

You may have to experiment with the size of the RAM disks you set up to hold temporary files. If a RAM disk is too small, you may encounter "out of disk space" messages, erratic program behavior, or system crashes. This is especially true if you use database programs in this manner.

Running Executables from a RAM Disk   If there are certain executable files that you run often, you can shorten the time it takes to load them by copying them to a RAM disk and modifying the PATH command in your AUTOEXEC.BAT file to address the RAM disk. For example, if you execute XCOPY.EXE, DR.COM, and WP.EXE frequently and your RAM disk is drive D, add the lines

```
COPY XCOPY.EXE D:\
COPY DR.COM D:\
COPY WP.EXE D:\
```

to your AUTOEXEC.BAT file (if they're not in the current directory, be sure to specify the paths to them), and add the designator D:\ to your PATH statement. Then, when you run one of these programs, it should load significantly faster—especially if you're not using a disk cache. Be sure to make the root directory of the RAM disk the first directory listed in your PATH statement. Otherwise, some (or all) of the added speed will go to waste.

Loading Overlay Files from a RAM Disk   Some application programs are too large to fit into memory all at once. To circumvent the limitations imposed by available memory, they divide themselves into program modules called overlays and load themselves into memory one module at a time. When a different module is needed, an overlay manager brings in the new overlay on top of the current one and passes control to it. This way, a large, voluminous program can run in a small memory space.

The only problem is that it takes time to load a new overlay, especially if it's loaded from a slow disk or, heaven forbid, a floppy. You can speed up the process of loading new overlays by copying them to a RAM disk and directing the program that uses them to the RAM disk.

For example, if you use AutoCAD Release 10, you can make AutoCAD run slightly faster by copying key overlay files to a RAM disk. The files are ACAD0.OVL, ACAD.OVL, ACAD2.OVL, ACAD3.OVL, and ACADVS.OVL. If your RAM disk is only large enough for one of these files, copy ACAD0.OVL to it. AutoCAD loads these overlay files at various times to provide the code needed to execute your AutoCAD commands and uses the PATH environment variable to find them. Thus, configuring AutoCAD to take advantage of a RAM disk is a three-step process:

1. Add a DEVICE statement to CONFIG.SYS to load RAMDrive. Make the RAM disk large enough to hold as many overlays as you plan to copy to it.

2. Add commands to AUTOEXEC.BAT to copy the .OVL files to the root directory of the RAM disk.

3. Modify the PATH command in AUTOEXEC.BAT to include the root directory of the RAM disk. For best performance, be sure to make the RAM disk the first drive named in the PATH statement.

Then reboot your PC so the configuration changes will take effect. The next time you run AutoCAD, it should run slightly (but perceptibly) faster than it did before. The increase may be small, but it may be just enough to make a difference.

Loading COMMAND.COM from a RAM Disk   Recall from the discussion of the CONFIG.SYS SHELL directive earlier in this chapter that COMMAND.COM is split in half when it is loaded into memory. When the upper half is destroyed, COMMAND.COM uses the COMSPEC environment variable to locate its own image on disk and reload itself. This causes a short pause while the disk is accessed between the time a program ends and when the command prompt reappears. To shorten this pause, you can have DOS reload COMMAND.COM from a RAM disk.

Assuming that COMMAND.COM is located in the root directory of drive C and that the RAM disk is installed as drive D, add the commands

```
COPY C:\COMMAND.COM D:\
SET COMSPEC=D:\COMMAND.COM
```

to your AUTOEXEC.BAT file. The first command physically copies COMMAND.COM to the RAM disk; the second one tells DOS where the file is now located. With these changes in place, COMMAND.COM will reload itself almost instantaneously. Be sure to make the RAM disk at least as large as COMMAND.COM itself. In DOS 5.0, this requires about 50k of space on the RAM disk. If the disk is too small, the COPY command will fail, and your system will lock up the first time COMMAND.COM is reloaded from disk.

Speeding Keyboard Operations with DOSKEY and MODE

At the risk of getting slightly ahead of ourselves, no chapter on configuration would be complete without mentioning two commands used to enhance keyboard operation: DOSKEY and MODE. DOSKEY is discussed in Chapter 7, while the form of the MODE command that controls the speed of the keyboard is discussed in Chapter 6. DOSKEY adds a variety of new features to the command line, including the ability to recall past commands, edit the text of commands, and create command macros so that, for example, the characters "LS" are equivalent to DIR /O:N /W. To install DOSKEY, add the command

```
DOSKEY
```

to your AUTOEXEC.BAT file.

The second command you might want to add to your AUTOEXEC.BAT file is

```
MODE CON: RATE=32 DELAY=2
```

This one increases the keyboard's typematic rate so that, for example, the cursor moves more quickly across the screen when you press and hold one of the arrow keys. The nice thing about it is that it doesn't take up any memory. Running it one time gives your keyboard the extra boost it needs.

Enhancing Screen and Keyboard Operations with ANSI.SYS

As we'll see in Chapter 6, DOS 5.0 permits you to do some rather fancy things with the screen and keyboard, including setting EGA and VGA displays to enhanced display modes, setting the screen colors to something other than drab white on black, and assigning DOS commands to function keys—but only if the extended console device driver ANSI.SYS is loaded. If these features sound like something you'll want to take advantage of, add the command

```
DEVICE=C:\DOS\ANSI.SYS
```

to your CONFIG.SYS file. Then typing

```
MODE CON: LINES=50
```

will set a VGA monitor to display 50 lines of text—twice as many as it normally shows. Similarly, the command

```
PROMPT $e[0;59;"MEM$_"p
```

will assign the MEM command to function key F1, so that pressing F1 automatically executes the command. The only disadvantage to using ANSI.SYS is that it consumes about 4k of RAM that could be devoted to application programs—a small price to pay for the benefits you gain.

Analyzing Memory Requirements with the MEM Command

The MEM command, first introduced in DOS 4.0, allows you to tell exactly how much memory is dedicated to the system areas DOS creates at start-up (areas whose sizes are determined by BUFFERS, FILES, FCBS, STACKS, and other CONFIG.SYS directives) and to the device drivers and TSRs you load. Type

```
MEM /PROGRAM
```

at the DOS prompt. MEM is an external command, so be sure that there's a path to the directory it's stored in or that MEM.EXE is in the current directory. You should see a listing similar to the one in Figure 2.1.

"Address" shows the address in memory where the item on the right is located. It is expressed as a hexadecimal number. "Name" tells what program or driver is loaded there. "Size" is the amount of space occupied in bytes, again in hexadecimal form. Finally, "Type" provides additional information about the

FIGURE 2.1

Listing produced by MEM /PROGRAM

```
Address     Name        Size     Type
-------     --------    ------   ------
000000                  000400   Interrupt Vector
000400                  000100   ROM Communication Area
000500                  000200   DOS Communication Area

000700      IO          000AE0   System Data

0011E0      MSDOS       001510   System Data

0026F0      IO          008510   System Data
            HIMEM       000470    DEVICE=
            SMARTDRV    0053E0    DEVICE=
            EMM386      002410    DEVICE=
                        000380    FILES=
                        000100    FCBS=
                        000200    BUFFERS=
                        0001C0    LASTDRIVE=
00AC10      MSDOS       000040   System Program

00AC60      COMMAND     000940   Program
00B5B0      MSDOS       000040   -- Free --
00B600      COMMAND     000200   Environment
00B810      MEM         000080   Environment
00B8A0      MEM         0135A0   Program
01EE50      MSDOS       081190   -- Free --
09FFF0      MSDOS       020010   System Program

0C0010      MSDOS       000070   -- Free --
0C0090      FASTOPEN    0017C0   Program
0C1860      DOSKEY      0015E0   Program
0C2E50      GRAPHICS    001680   Program
0C44E0      MOUSE       003A80   Program
0C7F70      MSDOS       018080   -- Free --


    656384 bytes total conventional memory
    655360 bytes available to MS-DOS
    608064 largest executable program size

   5505024 bytes total contiguous extended memory
         0 bytes available contiguous extended memory
   4172800 bytes available XMS memory
           MS-DOS resident in High Memory Area
```

contents of this particular memory location. Under IO, for example, "Type" tells whether the corresponding area is used by a device driver (in this case, HIMEM, SMARTDRV, or EMM386) or for FILES, FCBS, on other data structures DOS sets up. Later on in the listing, "Type" indicates whether a block of memory is free or allocated to a program. The exact format of this listing and its contents will vary depending on your system setup.

Here we learn that the device driver HIMEM.SYS occupies 1,136 bytes of memory (470 bytes, expressed in hex), SMARTDrive occupies 24,112 (53E0 in hex), and EMM386 consumes 9,232 (2,410 in hex). These figures indicate the amount of conventional memory the drivers use, but do not include any extended or expanded memory used for buffer space. We also learn that our FILES=20 statement in CONFIG.SYS resulted in a FILES area 896 bytes long (380 in hex), and that DOS has dedicated 256, 512, and 448 bytes (100, 200, and 1C0 hex) to the FCBS, BUFFERS, and LASTDRIVE data areas. As you tweak the parameters in CONFIG.SYS and restart the system, you'll see these numbers change accordingly. If you're not sure how much memory you're gaining or losing when you make configuration changes, this is one way to gauge the effects.

The bottom line is how much memory is left after your configuration changes for applications to run in. This is indicated by the "largest executable program size" line near the bottom of the listing. This, too, will change as you fine-tune CONFIG.SYS and AUTOEXEC.BAT for your system. The name of the game is to optimize for speed and efficiency without robbing the system of too much memory.

There's much more to be gleaned from the listing produced by MEM than we've touched on here. Sharp-eyed readers may have noticed that certain programs that appear in the listing—FASTOPEN, DOSKEY, and GRAPHICS, for example, all of which are TSRs—are loaded into addresses in the C0000 segment, which normally isn't available to DOS. Actually, this memory *is* available to DOS 5.0 applications when they're run on PCs built around the 386 or 486. Loading them here makes more room available for other programs in the lower 640k. That's the subject of the next chapter: using DOS 5.0 to make more memory available to applications.

A Final Word on Device Drivers

SMARTDRV.SYS and RAMDRIVE.SYS illustrate just how powerful the concept of installable device drivers is. DOS lets you link them in at runtime, and they become an integral part of the system—as if they were part of DOS itself. To a degree, this enables you to piece together a customized version of DOS that includes all the support you need for the devices attached to your system, but that doesn't waste memory and other resources on devices that *aren't* a part of your system.

One of the questions new users frequently ask is whether it's feasible to write their own device drivers. The answer is that usually it's not. Most drivers are written in assembly language, and writing them requires an intimate knowledge not only of the language, but also of the hardware characteristics of the devices the drivers are being written for. Unless you're an accomplished assembly language programmer and have experience dealing with hardware on the system level, it's best to leave writing device drivers to the experts.

In case you're curious, there are two types of device drivers:

- Character device drivers, which control devices such as serial and parallel ports that input and output data one byte, or character, at a time

- Block device drivers, which control mass-storage devices such as disk drives and tape drives that handle data in chunks rather than one character at a time

Examples of character device drivers are the ones DOS uses to send data to and read data from the serial ports, the screen, and the keyboard. By contrast, the drivers DOS uses to control your hard-disk and floppy drives are block device drivers.

We said earlier in this chapter that the system file IO.SYS contains an array of system device drivers that DOS loads automatically at start-up. Type **MEM /DEBUG** at DOS's command prompt, and the first few lines of the listing that results will look something like what's shown in Figure 2.2.

FIGURE 2.2

System device drivers

```
Address      Name        Size        Type
-------      --------     ------      ------
000000                   000400      Interrupt Vector
000400                   000100      ROM Communication Area
000500                   000200      DOS Communication Area

000700       IO          000A60      System Data
             CON                     System Device Driver
             AUX                     System Device Driver
             PRN                     System Device Driver
             CLOCK$                  System Device Driver
             A: - C:                 System Device Driver
             COM1                    System Device Driver
             LPT1                    System Device Driver
             LPT2                    System Device Driver
             LPT3                    System Device Driver
             COM2                    System Device Driver
             COM3                    System Device Driver
             COM4                    System Device Driver
```

Under IO, there are 12 system device drivers listed: CON, AUX, PRN, CLOCK$, "A: - C:," COM1, LPT1, LPT2, LPT3, COM2, COM3, and COM4. These are the internal drivers DOS loads to deal with the peripherals attached to your system. CON is DOS's default screen and keyboard driver; AUX controls the auxiliary device, normally mapped to COM1; PRN controls the printer and is normally mapped to LPT1; CLOCK$ is the interface to DOS's real-time clock; "A: - C:" is a block driver that controls drives A, B, and C (more if your hard disk has an extended DOS partition or if there is more than one hard disk installed); COM1, COM2, COM3, and COM4 are drivers for up to four serial ports installed in your system; and LPT1, LPT2, and LPT3 control up to three parallel ports. All of these drivers except the one that controls drives A through C are of the character type.

There may be more drivers listed here than you have physical devices. The block device driver for disk drives, for example, includes drive B in its list of supported devices even if you only have one floppy drive installed. DOS uses this driver to control the *logical* drive B, so that if you type **COPY A:*.* B:**, the command can be fulfilled with drive A standing in for drive B. In the absence of a physical drive B, DOS will prompt you to remove the disk from drive A and insert the disk for drive B into drive A—all thanks to the device driver, which makes it appear that you really *do* have two floppy drives.

DOS uses these drivers to communicate with all the devices attached to or resident in your system. For example, to display a character on the screen, DOS doesn't write directly to the video buffer as most application programs do; instead, it passes the character to the CON driver, and the CON driver invokes a routine in your PC's ROM BIOS to write it to video memory so that it will show up on the screen. If DOS were ported to a platform that didn't have a ROM BIOS, CON would use a different method to display the character, but would accomplish the same result. The call DOS makes to CON, however, would be identical, so by using the driver instead of interfacing directly to the hardware, DOS achieves a measure of independence from the hardware.

The DEVICE command allows additional device drivers to be installed to augment this list. If you load HIMEM.SYS and SMARTDRV.SYS from CONFIG.SYS, for example, the listing produced when you type MEM /DEBUG will contain the additional lines shown in Figure 2.3. The list of installed device drivers clearly shows that HIMEM.SYS and SMARTDRV.SYS are resident in memory, and even shows how much space they occupy.

FIGURE 2.3

Installable device drivers

```
001160    MSDOS         001460    System Data
001460
0025C0    IO            0085A0    System Data
          HIMEM         000440    DEVICE=
            XMSXXXX0               Installed Device Driver
          SMARTDRV      007170    DEVICE=
            SMARTAAR              Installed Device Driver
                        000380    FILES=
                        000100    FCBS=
                        000200    BUFFERS=
                        0001C0    LASTDRIVE=
                        000740    STACKS=
00AB70    MEM           000080    Environment
00AC00    MSDOS         000040    System Program
```

Most drivers work independently of others. Some, however, are designed to *replace* existing drivers. When you install ANSI.SYS, for example, it takes over the duties of the resident CON device driver. CON will still show up when you type MEM /DEBUG, but it's essentially taking up space doing nothing. The CON device driver is rather primitive and very limited in its capabilities. As we'll see in Chapter 6, ANSI.SYS's capabilities are a superset of CON's, and they enable us to control the screen and keyboard to a much greater degree.

You don't have to understand the inner workings of device drivers to use them in your system. In fact, you don't even have to know as much about them as we've said already. But understanding the role device drivers play is the key to appreciating the power they offer.

Summary

There. We've safely navigated our way through the mine field of using CONFIG-.SYS and AUTOEXEC.BAT to configure our PCs the way we want them. But we're not quite through with the topic of configuration. In one sense, this entire book describes how to configure DOS, because it documents in detail the commands and configuration options found in DOS 5.0. Next up is a feature that perhaps does more than any other to set DOS 5.0 apart from its predecessors: its support for extended and expanded memory. When we're done, you'll have a better idea of the many ways DOS 5.0 can exploit memory for the benefit of application programs, particularly on 286, 386, and 486 machines—and how you can take advantage of these capabilities on your system.

MAKING THE
MOST OF MEMORY

IN THE LAST CHAPTER, OUR EFFORTS TO OPTIMIZE THE CONFIGURATION OF our PCs focused primarily on speed. We saw how supplying RAM to SMART-Drive can greatly enhance hard-disk performance. We saw how RAMDrive can be used to create a RAM disk that emulates a physical disk, but operates much faster. And we saw how commands such as FASTOPEN can work in conjunction with SMARTDrive to speed file accesses even further. But we purposely avoided talking at length about one of the PC's most abundant resources: memory.

Ask 100 users what the greatest limitation of DOS is, and 99 of them will answer "the 640k barrier." Over the years, DOS has become quite famous (or infamous, to be more precise) for the 640k ceiling it imposes on usable RAM. In fact, the 640k barrier isn't wholly attributable to DOS. In certain instances, DOS is capable of using up to a megabyte of memory. However, the PC's designers made a conscious decision to reserve the upper 384k of the 1Mb address space for locating adapter ROMs and video buffers, leaving the lower 640k to be used by DOS and application programs. Had these same architects chosen to make an additional 64k or 128k available to DOS, DOS would willingly have used it. 640k seemed like a lot of memory in 1980. The designers of the PC had no way of knowing that programs and operating systems would soon require much more.

Version 5.0 does more than any other version of DOS before it to use the extended and expanded memory installed on many PCs to make more room for application programs in the lower 640k. Among other things, it permits you to

- Load most of DOS itself into extended memory on 286, 386, and 486 PCs to make more room for applications in the lower 640k

- Load TSRs and device drivers into unused regions of memory between 640k and 1Mb on 386 and 486 PCs equipped with extended memory

- Use extended memory to emulate expanded memory on 386 and 486 PCs

- Set up the buffer spaces used by BUFFERS, FASTOPEN, SMART-Drive, and RAMDrive into extended or expanded memory

DOS 5.0 contains many of the sophisticated memory-management features found in popular third-party memory managers such as QEMM-386 from Quarterdeck and 386Max from Qualitas, and then some. If you spent the extra dollars for a 386 or 486 when you bought your last PC, you finally have vindication for doing so. Many owners of non-386s now find themselves on the outside looking in, wondering how best to go about upgrading their PCs to take advantage of

DOS 5.0's 386-only features. But even if you own a 286 with 1Mb or more of memory or simply have an 8088 or 8086 with an expanded memory board, you'll be pleased to know that there are many things you can do to relieve RAM cram in the lower 640k. That's what this chapter is about: the ways in which DOS 5.0 handles memory, and how you can take advantage of these features to make more memory available to application programs.

Understanding Memory

Most of us have held a RAM chip in our hands at one time or another. RAM stands for *Random Access Memory,* and is a storage medium for electronic data. The word *random* is used because RAM allows random locations, or memory addresses, to be accessed at any time. This is in contrast to sequential storage media such as tape, whose data must be accessed in order.

A close cousin to RAM is ROM, which stands for *Read-Only Memory.* Data may be read from ROM, but it may not be written to it, hence the name *read-only.* Data contained in ROM is placed there when the ROM chip is manufactured, and it remains there permanently. ROM, unlike most RAM, does not need constant reenergizing from the PC to retain its data, a process called *memory refresh.* The BIOS of your PC is stored in ROM, and chances are that one or more of the expansion cards installed in your PC contain BIOS extensions in ROM, too. On the IBM PC, code and data in ROM are mapped into the region of memory between 640k and 1Mb, placing them firmly within the bounds of the PC's 1Mb address space.

One of the factors that drives a PC's performance is how quickly it can read from and write to memory. Two figures are normally quoted when RAM speed is at issue: *access time* and *precharge time.* Access time is the time it takes for a unit of data to be read from RAM. Precharge time is the time it takes for RAM to ready itself to be accessed again after an access has occurred. The sum of access time and precharge time is *cycle time,* which provides an indication of how frequently a cell can be accessed. Each of these quantities is measured in nanoseconds (one nanosecond is 1×10^{-9} seconds, or one one-billionth of a second). The RAM used in a typical 386 has an 80 nanosecond access time and a cycle time almost twice that. The lower these figures, the less time the CPU must spend waiting for memory accesses to be completed and the more time it can spend doing other things. Thus, up to a point (the point at which RAM speed meets or exceeds CPU and bus speed), the faster the RAM in your PC, the higher the PC's overall performance.

Over the years, many different memory architectures have evolved, all aimed at providing the quickest possible access at the lowest possible cost. Many 386s use *static RAM caches* to boost memory performance, while lesser machines use architectures such as *interleaved* and *page-mode* memory. A RAM cache operates using the same principle as a disk cache: Data going to and from RAM is cached in static RAM, which typically boasts access times of 30 nanoseconds or less. Interleaved memory weaves even and odd memory addresses together so that one bank of RAM locations can be precharging while the other one is being accessed, effectively factoring precharge times out of the equation for sequential memory accesses. Page-mode RAM divides RAM into units called pages and, with the aid of special circuitry, permits consecutive accesses within a page to occur more quickly than the chips' access times would normally allow. When the memory subsystem can't deliver data in time, the CPU is charged with *wait states*—idle time spent waiting for memory accesses to be completed—and the performance of the system as a whole is degraded.

Most of this is transparent to DOS, which views RAM simply as a series of many thousands of sequentially ordered memory locations that may be used to store data. Before we embark on a discussion of DOS 5.0 and memory usage, it's important that you understand some of the terms—specifically, what the four types of memory that DOS recognizes are and where they fall into the overall scheme of things. The four types of "DOS" memory are

- Conventional memory

- Extended memory

- Expanded memory

- Upper memory

Briefly, *conventional memory* is the memory that lies between 0 and 640k. It's this type of memory that most DOS application programs run in. *Extended memory* is the memory that lies above 1Mb and is accessible only to 286, 386, and 486 processors. Extended memory is very often confused with *expanded,* or *EMS (Expanded Memory Specification), memory.* Expanded memory is bank-switched memory (memory that is accessed by alternately mapping portions, or *banks,* of it in and out of the CPU's address space) that provides an artificial means for processors to access more than 1Mb of memory. Finally, *upper memory* is memory that lies between conventional memory and extended memory, in the range of memory addresses 640k to 1Mb. In DOS 5.0, this region is called the *upper memory area,* or UMA.

Upper memory may be new to you. Usually, when we talk about the types of memory, we talk about conventional, extended, and expanded memory. The upper memory area has always been there, but it has only recently become important. Before the 386 was introduced, this region of memory was only used as intended: to provide address space for adapter ROMs and other hardware components. But on a 386, a smart memory manager like EMM386.EXE, which is supplied with DOS 5.0, can convert extended memory into usable RAM between 640k and 1Mb and load TSRs and device drivers there.

Another term you'll become familiar with as you read this chapter is the *High Memory Area*, or HMA. Normally, a CPU can't access extended memory without switching from its default mode of operation (called *real mode*) into a special mode called *protected mode.* The HMA is a special region of extended memory that a 286, 386, or 486 can address without leaving real mode. If you have extended memory and are running DOS 5.0, you can load part of DOS into this region, freeing up more room in conventional memory for programs to run in.

Figure 3.1 shows a simplified schematic of memory on the PC and illustrates how the various types of memory are arranged. At the bottom is conventional memory, which forms all of the lower 640k on PCs equipped with 640k of RAM. Next comes upper memory, which extends upward from the top of conventional memory to the 1Mb mark. Beyond that lies extended memory, which may extend up to 16Mb on a 286 and up to 4Gb on a 386 or 486 (a gigabyte, abbreviated Gb, is equal to 1,024 megabytes). Finally, there is expanded memory, which lies outside the CPU's normal addressing range, but is mapped in and out of it in units known as *pages*. There are typically more pages than there is memory to map them to, so pages are swapped in and out of the CPU's address space a few at a time to permit all of them to be accessed in turn. Figure 3.1 also shows the location of the HMA, which extends from the 1,024k mark (1Mb) to 1,088k, comprising a total of 64k.

The following sections discuss the four forms of DOS memory in greater detail.

FIGURE 3.1

The four types of memory

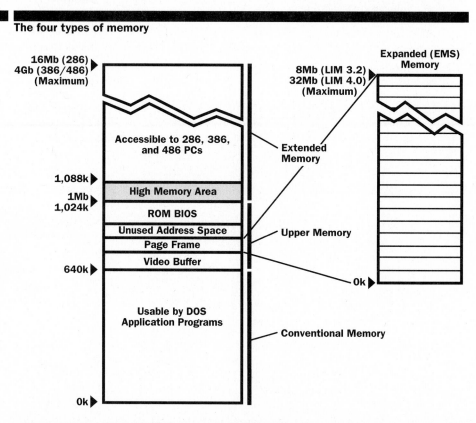

Conventional Memory

Conventional memory is the memory that most DOS programs run in. It extends from the first addressable byte of RAM in the system to 640k. Conventional memory is equally addressable by all Intel processor types.

Certain areas of conventional memory are reserved for special purposes. The first 1,024 bytes, which occupy addresses 000H through 3FFH, hold the PC's *interrupt vector table.* In the PC, an *interrupt* is a means for transferring execution from one location in memory to another. Hardware devices such as keyboards and serial ports use interrupts to signal the CPU that they need its attention; programs use interrupts to invoke subroutines contained in ROM or in the DOS kernel; and the CPU itself uses interrupts to indicate when a severe error (for example, an attempt to divide by zero) occurs.

When an interrupt is triggered, the CPU temporarily halts what it's doing, consults the interrupt vector table for the 32-bit address of an *interrupt service routine* (ISR) using the interrupt number as an index into the table, and invokes the ISR. The ISR contains the code needed to service the interrupt. Unless the CPU is a 286, 386, or 486 running in protected mode, there is no choice about where the table of interrupt vectors is located; it must go at the bottom of memory.

DOS terms the 256 bytes of memory directly above the interrupt vector table, spanning addresses 400H through 4FFH, the "ROM Communication Area." Actually, this is the region most texts refer to as the *BIOS Data Area,* where the BIOS stores critical operating parameters such as the number of rows and columns of text displayed on the screen, the I/O addresses of serial and parallel ports, and other data describing system configuration that are set dynamically each time the system is started. DOS application programs frequently use bits and bytes in this area to obtain information about the PCs they're running on.

The next 512 bytes, addresses 500H through 6FFH, form the *DOS Communication Area,* which DOS reserves for its own purposes. In past versions, this area was used to store pointers and data objects for IBM's ROM-based BASIC interpreter.

Directly above the DOS Communication Area, at address 700H, is where DOS itself is loaded. The system file IO.SYS comes first, followed by other components of the operating system such as MSDOS.SYS and DOS's internal device drivers. Beyond that is where application programs are loaded and run. The exact address where this occurs varies depending on system configuration. Typing MEM /P or MEM /D at the command prompt produces a detailed summary of how memory in this region is allocated.

Extended Memory

Extended memory begins at the 1Mb mark and is only available on 286s, 386s, and 486s. Earlier processors can't use it because they were designed to address at most 1Mb of memory. A 286 can handle as much as 16Mb of installed RAM (640k conventional, 384k upper, and 15Mb extended), while a 386 or 486 can use up to 4Gb. Even at the rapid rate that memory requirements are expanding, it seems likely that 4Gb is a sufficiently high number that it will not become a limitation on 386/486 software in the near future.

To access extended memory, the CPU has to leave real mode, in which it behaves just like an 8086, and switch into protected mode. In real mode, the same 1Mb limit on memory addressing that applies to an 8086 also applies to a 286, 386, or 486. Protected mode enables the processor to form higher-numbered addresses that in turn enable it to reach beyond 1Mb into the uppermost regions of memory.

Here's how it works. You'll recall from Chapter 1 that Intel CPUs divide each address in memory into two components: a segment and an offset. In real mode, a 20-bit address is formed by combining a 16-bit segment address with a 16-bit offset address. The segment address is shifted four bits left, effectively multiplying it by 16 and transforming it into a 20-bit quantity. Afterward, the offset address is added to the result to produce a bona fide 20-bit address. This little trick permits the 8086, whose registers are only 16 bits wide, to form the 20-bit values required to address the full range of memory between 0 and 1Mb.

In protected mode, segment and offset values are translated in a completely different way. Rather than interpreting the value you place in a segment register as the address of a physical location in memory, the CPU uses it to identify an object called a *descriptor* that is stored in a table of descriptors somewhere in memory. The descriptor, in turn, identifies a physical range of memory. The offset component of the address is added to the base address stored in the descriptor to form the address of a unique location in memory. Descriptors are 64 bits wide, so they can easily hold the 24- and 32-bit addresses used by 286 and 386 CPUs.

Alas, DOS was designed to operate in real mode regardless of CPU type, so DOS can only address 1Mb of memory. As we mentioned earlier, the IBM PC's designers reserved the upper 384k of the lower 1Mb for ROMs and video buffers. So hardware constraints limit to 640k the amount of memory DOS and DOS applications may use.

Despite this, it is possible for real mode programs to make limited use of extended memory. The AT BIOS provides functions for switching into protected mode, transferring data to or from extended memory, and switching back again to real mode. On the 286, it's also possible to use the CPU's undocumented LOADALL instruction to reach into extended memory without leaving real mode. Some DOS application programs take advantage of these facilities to use extended memory when it's available. Unfortunately, such programs are the exception rather than the rule, so the majority of DOS applications today are still subject to the 1Mb real mode cap on memory.

If opening up the realms of extended memory to DOS applications is a simple matter of running in protected mode, why does DOS stick to real mode? It turns out that real mode and protected mode are so different that existing programs would have to be completely rewritten to run in protected mode. The architects of OS/2 found this out, and it led them to develop a totally incompatible operating system that runs in protected mode but has yet to enjoy wide acceptance among the installed base of 60 million or so DOS users.

The High Memory Area

We said earlier that the CPU must shift into protected mode to access extended memory. This prevents DOS, which runs a PC in real mode, from taking wholesale advantage of the extended memory on your PC to provide more room for application programs. But as is so often the case, it turns out that there is an easier way.

A 286, 386, or 486 can access most of the first 64k of extended memory without leaving real mode. This region comprises the area of memory known as the HMA. The fact that the 8086 only has 20 address lines physically limits it to addressing 1Mb of memory. An *address line* is a physical connection between the CPU and the memory subsystem that permits the CPU to specify which of the many thousands of bytes in the system it wants to access. At any time, an address line can be in one of two states: on or off. By toggling individual address lines on and off, the CPU can form as many as 2^n unique memory addresses, where n is equal to the number of address lines in the system. For a CPU with 20 address lines, this works out to 2^{20}, or 1,048,576, different addresses, which corresponds to 1Mb of memory. The 286, 386, and 486 are endowed with additional address lines that enable them to access more than 1Mb of RAM.

The highest address that can be formed this way is FFFF:FFFFH, which translates to 10FFEFH. That's only 16 bytes short of the top of the first 64k of extended memory. Thus, by manipulating the A20 address line, a program may address all but the final 16 bytes of the first 64k of extended memory. That's exactly what DOS 5.0 does through the HIMEM.SYS driver to gain access to the HMA and allow you to place most of DOS itself there. It also lets you place disk buffers created by the BUFFERS directive there. We'll see how shortly.

Expanded Memory

Expanded memory is a special type of memory that conforms to the Lotus/Intel/Microsoft (LIM) Expanded Memory Specification. Also called *EMS memory,* it employs a bank-switching technique to permit the CPU to address more than 1Mb of RAM without switching into protected mode. Even 8088s and 8086s can take advantage of expanded memory to circumvent the 1Mb memory addressing limit imposed on them.

Expanded memory works by identifying a *page frame* (a 64k region of memory) somewhere within the first 1Mb of RAM and dividing it into four 16k units called *pages.* By making calls to an expanded memory manager, a program can map 16k chunks of EMS memory to pages in the page frame, where they can be read or written like conventional memory. Furthermore, by rotating the EMS pages in and out of the CPU's address space as needed, a program can access all of the EMS memory installed in the system. Under version 3.2 of the specification, up to 8Mb of additional memory can be managed this way. Version 4.0 increased the range to 32Mb.

This memory management scheme is illustrated in Figure 3.2. In the diagram, a 64k page frame resides in the region between 640k and 1Mb. Expanded memory is partitioned into the same 16k pages that the page frame is, and pages of EMS memory (*logical* pages) are mapped to pages in the page frame (*physical* pages) so that programs may access them. To write to EMS page 16, for example, a program could ask the expanded memory manager to map logical page 16 to physical page 0. Later, if the program needed to access logical page 8, it could map it to physical page 0, or, alternatively, to one of the other three pages in the page frame. In Figure 3.2, the logical pages 2, 3, *n*-4 (*n* is the number of logical pages there are of expanded memory), and 6 are mapped to physical pages 0, 1,

2, and 3, respectively, illustrating that memory can be set up however the application program desires, no matter how arbitrary the mapping may seem.

The Expanded Memory Specification was developed primarily as a means for easing the memory crunch that DOS programs such as Lotus 1-2-3 were experiencing in the mid-1980s. The first version of the specification, version 3.0, appeared in spring 1985. It was the product of a collaborative effort between Intel and Lotus. Microsoft, eager to solve memory woes of its own (particularly those having to do with the recently introduced Windows), joined them in time to have its name affixed to version 3.2 of the specification, which followed in the fall of that year. LIM 3.2 was quickly adapted by the software industry as a means of providing programs with access to more memory than standard addressing techniques allowed. An enhanced version of the EMS specification, version 4.0, was released in fall 1987 and also has enjoyed widespread endorsement from the industry. Today, most EMS-aware programs will run under either LIM 3.2 or 4.0. Only a subset of them requires the more advanced capabilities of version 4.0. All of the EMS-aware utilities included with DOS 5.0 will use either LIM 3.2 or LIM 4.0 EMS memory.

FIGURE 3.2

EMS memory management

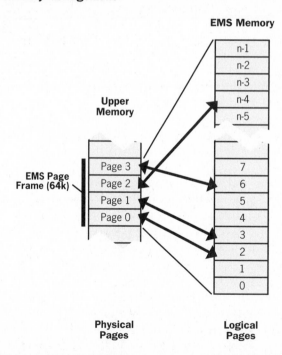

Traditionally, expanded memory is installed on an add-in memory board. The expanded memory manager that comes with it (usually a device driver loaded through CONFIG.SYS) writes data to I/O ports on the board to swap pages of

EMS memory in and out of the page frame. However, EMS memory doesn't have to be on a separate board. There are third-party utilities available that store EMS data on the hard disk rather than in physical memory. Meanwhile, 286 and 386 EMS memory managers that emulate expanded memory with extended memory are commonplace. As we'll see later, you can use the EMM386.EXE driver that comes with DOS 5.0 to convert extended memory to expanded memory if you own a 386 or 486, or one of the utilities in this book to create expanded memory on a 286.

An important point to understand is that not all programs use expanded memory. There's nothing automatic about it; to use expanded memory, a program must explicitly place calls to the expanded memory manager. This requires a substantial amount of additional programming. As a result, most software manufacturers ignore expanded memory, reasoning that only a small percentage of the PCs in the installed base have expanded memory anyway.

Upper Memory

The region of memory between 640k and 1Mb is called upper memory. In some texts, it is called *reserved memory* because it is nominally reserved for system-related purposes such as providing address space for system board and adapter ROMs. Your system's BIOS is mapped into this region, as are any additional BIOS modules installed on adapters plugged into expansion slots. The EGA, for example, contains its own BIOS, as do many hard-disk controller cards.

Upper memory is also the region where the video buffer is located. The video buffer, which we'll examine in more detail in Chapter 6, determines what appears on the screen. In text mode, bytes in the video buffer hold the ASCII codes of the characters that are displayed. They also hold attribute information that determines, among other things, what colors the characters are displayed in. In graphics mode, the video buffer defines what pixels are illuminated and what their colors are.

Expanded memory drivers usually establish their page frames in upper memory. This enables programs to use expanded memory without having to sacrifice 64k of conventional memory for the EMS page frame. It's perfectly acceptable for a driver to grab portions of upper memory for its own use as long as its needs don't conflict with the addressing needs of other devices in the system.

But what's most significant about upper memory is that on a 386, unused areas between 640k and 1Mb—holes in memory—can be backfilled with memory located above the 1Mb boundary. On most systems, not all the memory addresses in this region are occupied. Once the holes are filled with RAM, they can be used to store TSRs and device drivers so that these programs won't consume space in the lower 640k. DOS 5.0 calls these recycled chunks of memory between 640k and 1Mb *upper memory blocks,* or UMBs. Later, we'll look at how UMBs can be used to make more room for application programs in conventional memory.

Profiling Memory: The MEM Command

Chapter 2 briefly introduced a powerful tool for analyzing the makeup of memory: the MEM command. The full syntax for the command is

```
MEM [/PROGRAM] [/DEBUG] [/CLASSIFY]
```

The /PROGRAM, /DEBUG, and /CLASSIFY options may be abbreviated /P, /D, and /C. Run without a switch, MEM produces a report similar to the one shown in Figure 3.3. The exact contents of the listing will vary depending on how (or whether) you have HIMEM.SYS and EMM386.EXE installed. They will even differ if you invoke MEM from a DOS prompt window inside Windows running in 386 enhanced mode. The basic MEM listing in Figure 3.3, which was taken from a 386 with 6Mb of RAM, indicates that

- There are 655,360 bytes of memory (640k) available to DOS.

- There are 608,064 bytes remaining for application programs after DOS, TSRs, and device drivers are loaded (largest executable program size).

- The PC is equipped with 5,505,024 (5,376k) bytes of extended memory (total contiguous extended memory).

- All of the system's extended memory is controlled by HIMEM.SYS (0 bytes available contiguous extended memory), and part of this memory is already allocated for programs and drivers running in the system (MEM reports 4,172,800 bytes of available XMS memory, which is more than 1Mb less than the 5,505,024 bytes of extended memory reported). XMS is short for *Extended Memory Specification;* XMS memory is memory that is placed under the auspices of HIMEM.SYS, which is an XMS driver. Both XMS and HIMEM.SYS are discussed in detail later in this chapter.

- DOS is loaded into the HMA (MS-DOS resident in High Memory Area).

If HIMEM.SYS was not loaded, all the extended memory would have shown up as available contiguous extended memory, and there would be no readout of available XMS memory. Similarly, if EMM386.EXE is installed without a NOEMS switch, MEM lets you know how much expanded memory is present and how much of it is still available.

You saw an example of what the /P switch does in Chapter 2 when MEM was used to analyze the storage requirements of device drivers. It reveals where the DOS kernel, installable device drivers, and DOS programs are loaded. The /D switch expands on this listing by showing resident device drivers as well. We'll use the MEM command several more times throughout the remainder of this chapter to see the impact that different configurations have on the way memory is structured.

FIGURE 3.3

Output from the MEM command

```
655360 bytes total conventional memory
655360 bytes available to MS-DOS
608064 largest executable program size

5505024 bytes total contiguous extended memory
0       bytes available contiguous extended memory
4172800 bytes available XMS memory
        MS-DOS resident in High Memory Area
```

Putting Memory to Work

If you own a 286, 386, or 486 with extended memory, you're probably tired of having to let the extra memory go to waste. Chapter 2 showed how to direct SMARTDrive and RAMDrive to set up their buffers in extended memory. You may have other programs that use extended memory, too, such as a print spooler or EMS emulator, both of which are available from third-party developers.

DOS 5.0 can use some of this extra memory to make more room for application programs. You still can't use every byte of RAM in your system as one huge linear address space for programs to run in (the MEM command will never say "10340560 largest executable program size," for example), but there are several other, often equally beneficial ways to put extended memory to work in the DOS 5.0 environment. The pages that follow will discuss the various options and how they're best put in practice.

Installing the HIMEM.SYS Driver

Before DOS 5.0 can use extended memory, the installable device driver HIMEM.SYS must be loaded. If HIMEM.SYS resides in the \DOS directory of drive C, the command

```
DEVICE=C:\DOS\HIMEM.SYS
```

in CONFIG.SYS will load and install it. This command must appear *before* any other CONFIG.SYS command that uses extended memory. For example, if you load SMARTDrive into extended memory with the command

```
DEVICE=C:\DOS\SMARTDRV.SYS 1024
```

the statement that loads HIMEM.SYS must come first. To be sure, make HIMEM.SYS the first line in your CONFIG.SYS file if you plan to use it. Also note that HIMEM.SYS may not be loaded into high memory with DOS 5.0's DEVICEHIGH directive.

Like most of DOS's other installable device drivers, HIMEM.SYS accepts several optional switches when it is installed. Appendix B documents these switches. Most users won't need them, because HIMEM.SYS's default configuration is fine for most PCs. But the /MACHINE switch may be useful if HIMEM.SYS behaves erratically (or not at all) in its dealings with the High Memory Area. If you're unable to use the HMA after adding a DOS=HIGH directive to your CONFIG.SYS file, if attempting to relocate DOS to the HMA locks up your system, or if HIMEM.SYS displays the message "High Memory Area Unavailable" upon installation, it could be because the default A20 handler (the routine HIMEM.SYS uses to toggle the A20 address line on and off) is not compatible with your hardware. To compensate, you may specify a particular A20 handler with the /MACHINE switch. For example, the command

```
DEVICE=C:\DOS\HIMEM.SYS /MACHINE:5
```

or

```
DEVICE=C:\DOS\HIMEM.SYS /MACHINE:ATT6300PLUS
```

tells HIMEM.SYS to use the A20 handler for the AT&T 6300 Plus. At present, HIMEM.SYS defines 14 different A20 handlers, and more will likely be added in the future. The existing handlers are listed in Table 3.1. HIMEM.SYS attempts to install the appropriate A20 handler automatically. However, if you have one of the PCs listed in Table 3.1 with a MACHINE code of 3 or higher, you may have to use the /MACHINE switch to ensure that HIMEM.SYS operates properly.

TABLE 3.1

HIMEM.SYS MACHINE Codes

MACHINE Code	Equivalent	Type or Brand of PC Supported
1	AT	IBM PC/AT
2	PS2	IBM PS/2
3	PT1CASCADE	Phoenix Cascade BIOS
4	HPVECTRA	Hewlett-Packard Vectra (A and A+)
5	ATT6300PLUS	AT&T 6300 Plus
6	ACER1100	Acer 1100
7	TOSHIBA	Toshiba 1200XE, 1600, and 5100
8	WYSE	Wyse 12.5 MHz 286
9	TULIP	Tulip SX
10	ZENITH	Zenith ZBIOS
11	AT1	IBM PC/AT
12	AT2	IBM PC/AT (alternate delay)
	CSS	CSS Labs
13	AT3	IBM PC/AT (alternate delay)
	PHILIPS	Philips
14	FASTHP	Hewlett-Packard Vectra

So what exactly does HIMEM.SYS do? Briefly, HIMEM.SYS controls access to extended memory so that programs or device drivers that use extended memory don't step on each other's toes. Before a program stores anything in extended memory, it places a call to HIMEM.SYS to reserve a block of extended memory. If the memory is available, HIMEM.SYS passes the program a handle that may be used in future references to the block. In essence, HIMEM.SYS directs traffic: No other program may use this region of memory until the program that owns it releases it. HIMEM.SYS also controls access to the HMA and provides a device-independent means for programs to manipulate the A20 line. And finally, it controls access to upper memory, ensuring that no two programs grab the same block of RAM between 640k and 1Mb. This latter capability is extremely important when you use DOS 5.0's LOADHIGH and DEVICEHIGH commands to load TSRs and device drivers in upper memory blocks, because it permits DOS to protect these programs from other UMB-aware applications.

Depending on how deep an understanding of DOS you're looking for, this may be enough of an explanation to whet your appetite, or it may just serve to pique your curiosity. If you're eager to get on with the discussion of putting extended memory to work, then skip the next section, which offers a more detailed description of HIMEM.SYS. If, on the other hand, you're interested in a more thorough overview of the services HIMEM.SYS provides to DOS, then read on.

Understanding HIMEM.SYS

In 1984, IBM introduced its first PC based on the 286 microprocessor, the IBM PC/AT. With the 286 came the prospect of using extended memory to relieve some of the RAM cram already being experienced by DOS users. Soon, programs such as VDISK.SYS (the PC-DOS version of RAMDRIVE.SYS) began appearing that used functions in the AT BIOS and other means to reach into extended memory. However, there was a problem: DOS provided no memory management functions for extended memory, so everything beyond 1Mb was like a huge playground, with extended memory-aware programs vying for extended memory with no rules governing who could have what, and no method for a program to detect if a block of memory was already being used by another program. As a result, trying to run more than one extended memory-aware program in the system at a time was a risky proposition.

Two methods of reserving portions of extended memory for a program's private use became unofficial standards. One method involved hooking into the interrupt 15H function that reports the amount of extended memory installed in the system, and then subtracting from the amount reported the amount to be reserved. This way, a program could reserve blocks of memory from the top down and be reasonably sure that nothing else would infringe on its territory. The second method mimicked the way IBM's VDISK.SYS driver blocked off memory for itself, which involved altering the interrupt 19H vector to point to a data structure containing the address of the first free block of extended memory. With this scheme, high memory could be allocated from the bottom up. But not every program recognized these sparsely documented memory management conventions, so there was still no ironclad way to ensure that two extended memory-aware programs could run side-by-side in the same system.

In 1988, Microsoft, Intel, AST Research, and Lotus came to the rescue by proposing a method for managing memory above the 640k barrier, detailed in a document called the *Extended Memory Specification* (XMS). XMS provided what DOS didn't: a standard and agreed-upon method for programs to allocate and deallocate blocks of extended memory so they could be used cooperatively. But the specification didn't stop there. It also provided functions for allocating and deallocating blocks of upper memory, for controlling access to the HMA, for manipulating the A20 line to gain access to the HMA in real mode, and for moving data into and out of extended memory. All that was required was an XMS memory manager to sit between application programs and extended memory and provide the necessary control functions.

HIMEM.SYS is Microsoft's XMS driver. It provides 18 different functions that programs may use to access memory beyond 640k. These functions are listed in Table 3.2. With the exception of function 00H, which returns information about the driver itself, XMS services fall into four categories:

- Functions that control access to the HMA

- Functions that control the A20 address line

- Functions that control access to extended memory

- Functions that control access to upper memory

TABLE 3.2

XMS Functions

Function	Name
00H	Get XMS Version Number
HMA Functions	
01H	Request High Memory Area
02H	Release High Memory Area
A20 Address Line Functions	
03H	Global Enable A20
04H	Global Disable A20
05H	Local Enable A20
06H	Local Disable A20
07H	Query State of A20
Extended Memory Functions	
08H	Query Free Extended Memory
09H	Allocate Extended Memory Block
0AH	Free Extended Memory Block
0BH	Move Extended Memory Block
0CH	Lock Extended Memory Block
0DH	Unlock Extended Memory Block
0EH	Get Extended Memory Block Handle Information
0FH	Reallocate (Resize) Extended Memory Block
Upper Memory Functions	
10H	Request Upper Memory Block
11H	Release Upper Memory Block

A program places calls to HIMEM.SYS by executing a far call to the driver's entry point, the address of which is obtained with a call to a special interrupt known as the DOS multiplex interrupt. The XMS function that is being invoked is identified by the function code in register AH. The complete API (Application Programming Interface) for the XMS driver is documented in the XMS specification.

Functions 01H and 02H allocate and deallocate the HMA. The HMA can only be allocated as a single unit (HIMEM.SYS will not divide it up among programs), and the first program that requests it generally gets it. You can exercise some control over what program claims the HMA with HIMEM.SYS's /HMAMIN switch, which specifies the least amount of memory a program can ask for in the HMA for the request to be granted. When DOS claims the HMA, it divides it up itself and places portions of IO.SYS, MSDOS.SYS, COMMAND.COM, and other DOS internals there.

Functions 03H through 07H permit a program to toggle the A20 line on and off to gain access to the High Memory Area. The mechanics of manipulating the A20 line vary from PC to PC, so making these services a part of the XMS driver prevents a program or operating system from having to get unnecessarily close to the hardware it's running on. They're also why HIMEM.SYS offers the /MACHINE switch. With the large number of PC clones available, each with subtle differences in hardware design, no one A20 handler could hope to run on every system. The /MACHINE switch permits HIMEM.SYS to be adapted to a variety of PCs.

Functions 08H through 0FH control access to the remainder of extended memory, which starts just above the HMA at the 1,088k mark. When a program places a request for extended memory with function 09H, HIMEM.SYS carves an *Extended Memory Block* (EMB) out of available RAM and allocates it to the calling program. Once a handle to the EMB is obtained, a program can read from or write to the EMB using either of two methods. It can call on function 0BH, *Move Extended Memory Block,* to have HIMEM.SYS perform the transfer for it, or it can invoke function 0CH, *Lock Extended Memory Block,* to obtain the address of the block and perform the transfer itself. It's usually advantageous to use function 0BH, because accessing memory in this region requires either a switch to protected mode or sleight-of-hand using undocumented processor instructions. By relying on function 0BH, programs may shift the burden of protected mode memory-addressing to the XMS driver.

The final two XMS services, functions 10H and 11H, control access to upper memory—specifically, to the UMBs that are located there. The XMS driver does not create the UMBs; UMBs are only present if an external memory manager such as EMM386.EXE makes them available. HIMEM.SYS will apportion RAM in this region to make as many blocks available as space permits. UMBs may be as large as the largest block of contiguous upper memory (which by definition must be less than 384k) or as small as 16 bytes.

Placing DOS in High Memory

If you own a 286, 386, or 486 with at least 64k of extended memory, you can install most of DOS itself in the HMA—the region of memory that lies just beyond 1Mb and is accessible in real mode. Loading DOS into the HMA is the most space-efficient way to run DOS because it frees up space in conventional memory, creating more room for application programs and increasing the largest executable program size by as much as 64k .

To load DOS into the High Memory Area, add the statement

```
DOS=HIGH
```

to your CONFIG.SYS file, instructing DOS to load itself "high" rather than "low." It doesn't matter where in CONFIG.SYS it appears. You must, however, load the device driver HIMEM.SYS, otherwise DOS will respond with an error message and load itself into conventional memory. DOS uses HIMEM.SYS to reserve the HMA for itself and to manipulate the A20 address line to gain access to the HMA.

You'll know that DOS has been properly loaded into the HMA if the last line output by the MEM command contains the message "MS-DOS resident in High Memory Area." You'll also notice a significant increase in the largest executable program size that MEM reports. For example, a 386 system booted with nothing more than the statements

```
FILES=20
BUFFERS=10
```

in CONFIG.SYS reports a largest executable program size of slightly more than 595,000 bytes, the equivalent of 581k. This figure increases to nearly 623k when the statements

```
DEVICE=C:\DOS\HIMEM.SYS
DOS=HIGH
```

are added. That's a difference of more than 42k, and it costs you nothing, because only a handful of other programs are capable of using the HMA. Had the BUFFERS statement been larger (for example, BUFFERS=20 or BUFF-ERS=40), the savings would have been even greater because DOS=HIGH places BUFFERS in the HMA also.

Which brings up a question: Exactly what parts of DOS are loaded into the HMA? Portions of the system files IO.SYS and MSDOS.SYS go there; so does the resident part of COMMAND.COM. If you type MEM /P, you can see exactly how much space each of these system files occupies in conventional memory. Typically, loading DOS into the HMA will reduce the size of MSDOS.SYS in conventional memory from about 40k down to 5k and will shrink the resident half of COMMAND.COM from roughly 4k down to 2k. The transient portion of COMMAND.COM is still loaded in conventional memory, because it doesn't take anything away from the largest executable program size to begin with. Recall from the discussion of the SHELL directive in Chapter 2 that COMMAND.COM permits its transient half to be overwritten, and then reloads it on demand. The memory it occupies is never officially allocated, so it doesn't affect the amount of memory available for program loading.

BUFFERS go in the HMA if space permits. Usually, there's room for about 48 BUFFERS in the HMA after DOS is loaded. Outside the HMA, each BUFFER requires 532 bytes of conventional memory. Loaded into the HMA, however, BUFFERS requires only 512 bytes of conventional memory—total— no matter how many BUFFERS are specified. Of all the CONFIG.SYS directives that control the size of the internal buffers and data structures DOS creates at start-up, BUFFERS is the only one that places data in the HMA—and only then if the statement DOS=HIGH appears in CONFIG.SYS.

Other programs and drivers that claim the HMA may be incompatible with DOS 5.0 if DOS, too, is loaded in the HMA. Some programs that use Weitek 1167/3167/4167 math coprocessors, for example, use the HMA to communicate with the coprocessor and will crash the system if DOS is loaded there.

Placing TSRs and Device Drivers in Upper Memory

One of the most exciting aspects of running DOS 5.0 on a 386 or 486 is the ability it gives you to load TSRs and device drivers into upper memory. Normally, these programs go in conventional memory, where they subtract from the amount of RAM available to application programs. Loading programs in upper memory requires the use of four new drivers, directives, and commands. They are

- The EMM386.EXE driver, which maps extended memory into upper memory to create the UMBs (upper memory blocks) that programs are loaded into

- The DOS=UMB directive, which permits DOS to use the UMBs once they are created

- The DEVICEHIGH directive, which works just like DEVICE except that it loads a device driver into upper memory rather than conventional memory

- The LOADHIGH command, which loads a terminate-and-stay-resident program such as PRINT or FASTOPEN into upper memory rather than conventional DOS memory

You can demonstrate how easy it is to load a program or driver into upper memory by following this simple procedure. First, add the statements

```
DEVICE=C:\DOS\HIMEM.SYS
DEVICE=C:\DOS\EMM386.EXE NOEMS
DOS=HIGH,UMB
```

to your CONFIG.SYS file. If HIMEM.SYS and EMM386.EXE are located somewhere other than C:\DOS, you'll need to modify these commands accordingly. Afterwards, reboot. Once you're up and running again, enter the command

```
LOADHIGH C:\DOS\FASTOPEN C:=40
```

to load FASTOPEN into reserved memory. Then type

```
MEM /P
```

Near the end of the listing that's produced, you should see three new lines that didn't appear before:

```
0C8010      MSDOS        000050       -- Free --
0C8070      FASTOPEN     0017C0       Program
0C9840      MSDOS        0167B0       -- Free --
```

Furthermore, typing MEM /C produces a listing that includes the following lines

```
Upper Memory :


  Name              Size in Decimal         Size in Hex
- - - - - - - - -    - - - - - - - - - - -    - - - - - - -

  SYSTEM            163840     (160.0K)        28000
  FASTOPEN            6080     (  5.9K)          17C0
  FREE                 80     (  0.1K)            50
  FREE              92080     ( 89.9K)         167B0
```

The numbers may vary on your system. However, the principle is the same: There's an additional region of memory available that wasn't available before EMM386.EXE was loaded. Furthermore, the map shows unmistakably that the LOADHIGH command loaded FASTOPEN into this region of memory at address C8070H, which is well above the 640k mark. For comparison, 640k corresponds to A000H, while 1Mb is equivalent to 10000H. Better yet, loading FASTOPEN with LOADHIGH doesn't diminish the largest executable program size by a single byte. Yet FASTOPEN is resident in memory and doesn't behave any differently than it does when it is installed the normal way—in conventional memory.

FASTOPEN is safely tucked away in an upper memory block created by EMM386.EXE. Because it's still within the realm of addresses that an Intel CPU can access without switching to protected mode, FASTOPEN doesn't perceive any difference in the way it was loaded, and DOS doesn't have to do anything special to run it from there.

Not only is FASTOPEN installed outside the lower 640k, but the listing pro-deuced by MEM /C, which profiles the programs loaded in upper as well as conventional memory, indicates there is approximately 90k of RAM free in upper memory for additional programs. With this much room, you could conceivably load every TSR and device driver you normally use without subtracting anything from conventional memory. Type

```
LOADHIGH C:\DOS\DOSKEY
```

and type **MEM /C** again. This time, DOSKEY will show up in upper memory also, and the amount of free memory between 640k and 1Mb is reduced another 4k. You can continue loading programs in this area until you run out of space.

You can use DEVICEHIGH to load device drivers such as SMARTDrive and ANSI.SYS into upper memory. To try it, add the statement

```
DEVICEHIGH=C:\DOS\ANSI.SYS
```

to your CONFIG.SYS file and reboot. Type **MEM /C**. This time, ANSI.SYS will show up in upper memory also. This provides a wonderful opportunity for 386 users to economize on memory usage under DOS 5.0: Simply go through your CONFIG.SYS file and replace every occurrence of DEVICE with DEVICEHIGH.

Depending on what type of hardware you have installed, the memory EMM386.EXE makes available in the form of upper memory blocks may not be contiguous. Instead, it may be split between two or more UMBs. When DEVICEHIGH or LOADHIGH loads a program into upper memory, it loads it into the largest UMB that is available at the time and makes the remainder of the block (if any) available as a separate but smaller UMB. This means that the order in which programs are loaded can sometimes affect the number of programs you can place in upper memory. If upper memory is too small to hold all the programs you'd like to load there, experiment with different load orders, using the MEM command after each install to examine the sizes of the remaining UMBs and determine what fits best. You can use MEM /C to determine the size of the remaining UMBs at any time.

Not all TSRs and device drivers will run in upper memory. The only way to tell whether a given one will run is to try it. The sections that follow provide more detail on the commands you use to load programs and drivers in upper memory and offer tips on debugging them.

Using the DOS Directive

Twice now we've mentioned the DOS directive: once in the section on loading DOS into the HMA, and again in the section describing how to load programs in reserved memory. This directive, new to DOS 5.0, serves two purposes. It tells DOS whether to load itself into conventional memory or the High Memory Area, and it prepares the system for the issuance of DEVICEHIGH and LOADHIGH commands by establishing a link between conventional memory and upper memory. Its syntax is

```
DOS=[HIGH|LOW][,UMB|NOUMB]
```

where HIGH tells DOS to load high (in the HMA), LOW tells it to load itself low (in conventional memory), UMB tells it to claim the upper memory blocks created by EMM386.EXE so programs can be loaded into them, and NOUMB has it leave the upper memory blocks alone. In the absence of a directive telling it to do otherwise, DOS defaults to LOW and NOUMB.

The use of this directive is straightforward. If you want to conserve memory by loading DOS in the HMA, include the statement

```
DOS=HIGH
```

in your CONFIG.SYS file. It doesn't matter where in CONFIG.SYS it appears. This statement is valid only on 286-, 386-, and 486-based PCs. If you want DOS to load the old way (in conventional memory), omit the HIGH parameter or modify the statement to instead read

```
DOS=LOW
```

Similarly, if you plan to use LOADHIGH or DEVICEHIGH to load TSRs or device drivers into upper memory, you must include the statement

```
DOS=UMB
```

in CONFIG.SYS. If you want DOS loaded in the HMA *and* want to use reserved memory, combine the two operators with the statement

```
DOS=HIGH,UMB
```

This will usually be the combination you'll want on 386 and 486 systems. On the 286, the UMB option is invalid because you cannot load software into upper memory on this type of machine.

Using the DEVICEHIGH Directive

DEVICEHIGH is functionally identical to the DEVICE directive except that it loads device drivers into upper memory instead of conventional memory. Its syntax is

```
DEVICEHIGH [SIZE=size] [d:][path]filename [parameters]
```

where *filename* is the name of the driver that's being loaded (with extension) and *parameters* is a list of optional parameters passed to the driver upon installation. *Size,* meanwhile, spells out the number of bytes (in hexadecimal form) of upper memory the driver is to be allocated when it is loaded. If you do not include drive and path designators, DEVICEHIGH looks for the driver in the root directory of the boot drive.

Most of the time, you can use DEVICEHIGH the same way you use DEVICE. If your CONFIG.SYS file contains the command

```
DEVICE=C:\SYSTEM\MOUSE.SYS
```

to load a mouse driver, changing it to

```
DEVICEHIGH C:\SYSTEM\MOUSE.SYS
```

loads the driver high instead of low, conserving conventional memory. Before you can use DEVICEHIGH, you must ensure that

- HIMEM.SYS is installed

- EMM386.EXE is installed

- Your CONFIG.SYS file contains a DOS=UMB (or DOS=HIGH,UMB) directive

The lines that load HIMEM.SYS and EMM386.EXE must appear before the first DEVICEHIGH statement. However, the DOS=UMB command may appear anywhere in CONFIG.SYS.

The only thing new here is the *size* parameter, which specifies the minimum amount of upper memory that must be available for the driver to be loaded. By default, DOS uses the size of the driver to determine if there's enough upper memory remaining to hold it. This strategy is perfectly adequate for most drivers. However, some allocate additional memory for themselves after they're installed and may report errors or even lock up if memory isn't available.

That's what the SIZE switch is for. The statement

```
DEVICEHIGH SIZE=4000 C:\DOS\MOUSE.SYS
```

installs the mouse driver MOUSE.SYS if and only if there is at least 16k of upper memory remaining unallocated. This ensures that the driver won't be loaded into less than the minimum amount of space that it requires.

How do you know when to use the SIZE switch with DEVICEHIGH, and how much memory to reserve for a given driver? If changing from DEVICE to DEVICEHIGH locks your system up or causes the driver to stop working, it's possible that a SIZE switch will cure the problem. The only way to find out is to try it. To determine how much memory to set aside, install the driver in low memory with the DEVICE directive and type **MEM /P** to find out how much memory it uses. The size of the driver (in hex) appears in the "Size" column to the right of the driver's name. Use this number or one slightly larger as the *size* parameter to DEVICEHIGH. *Size* must be smaller than the amount of upper memory that remains unallocated (or, if there is more than one UMB, smaller than the *largest* remaining UMB) when the driver is installed. If there's not enough room to load a driver into upper memory, DEVICEHIGH will load it in conventional memory.

When you experiment with DEVICEHIGH, be sure to have a system-formatted floppy disk handy so you can boot from it if your system hangs up. Without the floppy, you won't be able to get up and running again to edit the offending command out of your CONFIG.SYS file.

Figure 3.4 shows what a typical CONFIG.SYS file that uses DEVICEHIGH looks like. The first two statements load HIMEM.SYS and EMM386.EXE so that extended and upper memory may be used. The next two statements load SMARTDrive and an additional driver (DASDDRVR.SYS) in upper memory with DEVICEHIGH. DOS=HIGH,UMB loads DOS into the 64k HMA and enables the use of DEVICEHIGH and LOADHIGH. The remaining statements perform other routine chores, which include installing COMMAND-.COM as the permanent command processor with an expanded environment size of 512 bytes.

Not all device drivers are compatible with upper memory. The majority, however, are. Except for HIMEM.SYS and EMM386.EXE, all of the device drivers shipped with DOS may be loaded with DEVICEHIGH. When SMARTDrive and RAMDrive are loaded into upper memory, you can still place the buffers they set up in extended or expanded memory by including the appropriate switches when they're installed. In the CONFIG.SYS file shown in Figure 3.4, SMART-Drive will go in upper memory and its buffers will go in extended memory, leaving conventional memory untouched.

Using the LOADHIGH Command

The LOADHIGH command does for TSRs what DEVICEHIGH does for device drivers: loads them in upper memory, thereby freeing room in conventional memory for other programs. The complete syntax for LOADHIGH is

```
LOADHIGH [d:][path]filename [parameters]
```

or simply

```
LH [d:][path]filename [parameters]
```

where *filename* is the name of the program to be loaded and *parameters* represents any start-up parameters you want to pass to it. You do not have to specify the file extension, although you may if you want. Also, LOADHIGH will search the currently defined PATH for the named executable if it doesn't find it in the current directory.

LOADHIGH will fail if there is not enough unused upper memory left to load the indicated program or if you neglected to add the statement DOS=UMB to your CONFIG.SYS file. If this happens, the program will be loaded in conventional memory instead. LOADHIGH doesn't tell you what happened; the only way to determine where the program was placed is by profiling memory with the MEM command.

The DOS commands APPEND, DOSKEY, DOSSHELL, GRAPHICS, KEYB, MODE, NLSFUNC, PRINT, and SHARE, which are actually terminate-and-stay-resident programs, can be loaded with LOADHIGH. So can many popular third-party TSRs such as Sidekick. The only way to tell whether a given program will run from upper memory is to try it. If it behaves strangely, if it displays error messages when it's loaded, if it locks up your PC, or if it simply doesn't work at all, then it probably does something that renders it incompatible with upper memory. Some COM programs, for example, make assumptions about the amount of memory above them because they're used to being loaded near the bottom of a 640k address space. These programs often won't work with LOADHIGH.

FIGURE 3.4

Examples of the DEVICEHIGH directive

```
REM ***********************************************************
REM
REM                          DOS 5.0
REM                  System Configuration File
REM
REM  This CONFIG.SYS file illustrates how DEVICEHIGH is
REM  used to load device drivers in upper memory. Be
REM  sure to include a UMB qualifier on the DOS directive
REM  as shown here.
REM
REM ***********************************************************
REM
DEVICE=C:\DOS\HIMEM.SYS
DEVICE=C:\DOS\EMM386.EXE NOEMS
DEVICEHIGH C:\DOS\SMARTDRV.SYS 1024 512
DEVICEHIGH C:\SYSTEM\DASDDRVR.SYS
DOS=HIGH,UMB
FILES=20
BUFFERS=4
STACKS=0,0
SHELL=C:\COMMAND.COM C:\ /E:512 /P
```

Figure 3.5 shows what a typical AUTOEXEC.BAT file that uses LOADHIGH looks like. In all, LOADHIGH is used five times: once each to load FASTOPEN, DOSKEY, and GRAPHICS, once to load Sidekick, and again to load a mouse driver. Together, these programs require about 100k of memory. The map of upper memory produced by typing MEM /P with the system set up this way is shown in Figure 3.6. On this particular system, the first program (FASTOPEN) was installed in the C000H segment at C0090H. The others followed, and nearly 30k of memory was left free at the top. It's clear that configuring the system this way saved a lot of memory that, without LOADHIGH, would have come directly out of conventional memory.

FIGURE 3.5

Examples of the LOADHIGH Command

```
@ECHO OFF
*************************************************************
REM
REM                          DOS 5.0
REM                    System Startup File
REM
REM  This AUTOEXEC.BAT file illustrates how LOADHIGH is used
REM  to load TSRs into upper memory. Before it will work,
REM  HIMEM.SYS and EMM386.EXE must be loaded from CONFIG.SYS
REM  and CONFIG.SYS must contain a DOS=UMB directive.
REM
REM *************************************************************
REM
PROMPT $P$G
PATH C:\DOS;D:\WINDOWS;C:\WP;C:\PE;C:\UTIL;C:\MASM
C:\DOS\MODE CON: RATE=32 DELAY=2
C:\MAG\PCM\UTIL\TOGGLE -N
LOADHIGH C:\DOS\FASTOPEN C:=60
LOADHIGH C:\DOS\DOSKEY /BUFSIZE=2048
LOADHIGH C:\DOS\GRAPHICS LASERJETII
LOADHIGH C:\UTIL\SIDEKICK\SK
LOADHIGH C:\MISC\MOUSE
SET TEMP=C:\DOS
```

One final note about loading TSRs and drivers high. If you can use DEVICEHIGH and LOADHIGH on 386s to indirectly load TSRs and device drivers into extended memory, you might think you could place them in expanded memory on 8086s and 286s. The unhappy truth is that DOS 5.0 makes no provision for doing so.

FIGURE 3.6

Programs loaded in upper memory

```
0C0010      MSDOS        000070      -- Free --
0C0090      FASTOPEN     0017C0      Program
0C1860      DOSKEY       001620      Program
0C2E90      GRAPHICS     0016E0      Program
0C4580      SK           000080      Environment
0C4610      SK           010A10      Program
0D5030      MOUSE        003A80      Program
0D8AC0      MSDOS        007530      -- Free --
```

Thanks to refinements made to the EMS specification between version 3.2 and 4.0, LIM 4.0 expanded memory is capable of handling code as well as data. Certain utilities on the market take advantage of this capability to let you load programs and drivers in expanded memory. One of them is Quarterdeck's QRAM (pronounced "Cram"), which is in many respects the 8086/88/286 equivalent of QEMM-386. On a system with LIM 4.0 expanded memory, QRAM can add from 30k to 130k of usable RAM to your system for storing TSRs and device drivers. As it does on a 386, this frees up additional memory in the lower 640k for application programs to run.

Using the LOADFIX Command

One problem that sometimes arises from freeing up memory in the lower 640k is that some programs can't be loaded properly in the first 64k of conventional memory. With previous versions of DOS, this generally wasn't a problem because DOS itself consumed more than 64k of RAM. With DOS installed in the HMA, however, it becomes a distinct possibility.

When a load error occurs, the program displays a "Packed file corrupt" error message and defies any further attempts to load and run it. To correct such errors, DOS 5.0 offers the LOADFIX command. Its syntax is simply

```
LOADFIX [d:][path]filename [parameters]
```

where *filename* is the program name and *parameters* is a list of parameters passed to the program. For example, if trying to run an application called FINDTEXT-.EXE with the command

```
FINDTEXT C:\ "PC Magazine" /C /I
```

results in a packed file corrupt message, starting it with the command

```
LOADFIX FINDTEXT C:\ "PC Magazine" /C /I
```

should fix the problem. What LOADFIX actually does is ensure that the program is loaded above the 64k mark. Fortunately, most programs will load fine anywhere in the lower 640k. With a little luck, you'll never have to use LOAD-FIX. But if problems do crop up, you'll know where to go.

Converting Extended Memory to Expanded

In the one example thus far showing how EMM386.EXE is installed, it was loaded with a NOEMS parameter. NOEMS means just what its name implies: that no EMS, or expanded, memory is to be supplied. If you omit the NOEMS parameter or replace it with the word RAM, as in

```
DEVICE=C:\DOS\EMM386.EXE RAM
```

EMM386.EXE provides an additional service to your programs: It makes expanded memory available to them, just as if you had a dedicated EMS memory board installed. Where does the expanded memory come from? Used in this manner, EMM386.EXE assumes the role of a LIM 4.0-compatible expanded memory manager, fielding calls from application programs and providing expanded memory services in return. Data written to expanded memory is stored in extended memory instead. The flexibility to pick and choose between extended and expanded memory offers a tremendous advantage in the DOS environment, where some programs are written to use extended memory and some to use expanded, but few are written to use both.

You can tell when and if EMM386.EXE is providing expanded memory to the system at large by typing the command EMM386. With NOEMS, the listing looks something like the one shown in Figure 3.7, which indicates that expanded memory services are not currently available.

FIGURE 3.7

EMM386 report with NOEMS option

```
MICROSOFT Expanded Memory Manager 386  Version 4.20.06X
(C) Copyright Microsoft Corporation 1986, 1990

Expanded memory services unavailable.

    Total upper memory available  . . . . . .    0 KB
    Largest Upper Memory Block available  . .    0 KB
    Upper memory starting address . . . . . .  C800 H

EMM386 Active.
```

Loaded with the RAM parameter, however, EMM386 produces a report like the one shown in Figure 3.8. This time, it reports that there is 256k of expanded memory available comprising 16 pages (at 16k per page). Another 24 pages of the total expanded memory are also available, but are already allocated for other use. Furthermore, the MEM command now reports 655,360 total bytes of EMS memory and 262,144 bytes available. If you run a program such as Lotus 1-2-3 that is capable of using EMS memory, it can make full use of those 262,144 bytes to store data.

FIGURE 3.8

EMM386 report with RAM option

```
MICROSOFT Expanded Memory Manager 386   Version 4.20.06X
(C) Copyright Microsoft Corporation 1986, 1990

    Available expanded memory . . . . . . . .    256 KB

    LIM/EMS version . . . . . . . . . . . . .    4.0
    Total expanded memory pages . . . . . . .     40
    Available expanded memory pages . . . . .     16
    Total handles . . . . . . . . . . . . . .     64
    Active handles  . . . . . . . . . . . . .      1
    Page frame segment  . . . . . . . . . . .   D000 H

    Total upper memory available  . . . . . .      0 KB
    Largest Upper Memory Block available  . .      0 KB
    Upper memory starting address . . . . . .   C800 H

EMM386 Active.
```

There is one drawback to using expanded memory this way: EMM386.EXE requires a 64k space for an EMS page frame in upper memory—the same space that TSRs and device drivers are loaded into when you use DEVICEHIGH and LOADHIGH. Thus, expanded memory created by EMM386.EXE reduces the number of programs you can load in upper memory. On systems that have 130k of reclaimable upper memory to start with, this may not be a problem. On systems with less, you may have to make a choice between using expanded memory and loading programs and device drivers high. To determine just how much upper memory is left over after your programs are loaded there, type **MEM /C**. If MEM shows less than 64k of upper memory free, you'll have to shift some of those programs to low memory in order to use expanded memory.

On the plus side, EMM386.EXE emulates LIM 4.0 expanded memory, so virtually any program written to use expanded memory—including ones that require LIM 3.2 expanded memory—should work with it.

In general, you should avoid using this form of expanded memory for DOS utilities that will use extended memory instead. For example, SMARTDrive will use extended or expanded memory; so will RAMDrive. Configuring either of them to use expanded memory created by EMM386.EXE is slower than allowing them to use extended memory directly. It works, but it is not efficient. For commands such as FASTOPEN that will use expanded memory but not extended, it's not a bad idea to use expanded memory set up by EMM386.EXE.

However, an even better idea is to load FASTOPEN into reserved memory with the LOADHIGH command, preventing it from using any conventional memory whatsoever.

Another important note is that there is a difference—a very big difference—between using the RAM parameter and using no parameter at all. Including the keyword RAM on the line where EMM386.EXE is installed provides expanded memory emulation services plus support for loading programs into reserved memory. If you specify neither RAM nor NOEMS, EMM386.EXE performs EMS emulation but does *not* allow you to load programs into UMBs.

Converting Extended Memory to Expanded on a 286

If you own a 286, you can't use EMM386.EXE to create expanded memory because EMM386.EXE only works on 386s and 486s. But you can convert extended memory to LIM 4.0 EMS memory with the help of EMS40.SYS, one of the programs included with this book. EMS40.SYS was written by *PC Magazine* contributing editor Douglas Boling, the author of a number of articles on expanded memory and expanded memory programming, and was originally published in *PC Magazine*'s "Utilities" column. Because it's so powerful, and because it fills such an obvious hole for 286 users in the otherwise comprehensive set of memory management services that DOS 5.0 offers, we've included it here.

EMS40.SYS is a device driver designed to be installed with a DEVICE directive in CONFIG.SYS. The syntax is

```
DEVICE=[d:][path]EMS40.SYS [memory]
```

where *memory* is an optional parameter that specifies the number of kilobytes of extended memory you want to set aside to serve as expanded memory, and thus the amount of expanded memory that will be made available to application programs. For example, the command

```
DEVICE=C:\UTIL\EMS40.SYS 1024
```

installs EMS40.SYS from C:\UTIL and makes 1Mb of expanded memory available to the system. Values for *memory* can range up to 15360 (which corresponds to 15Mb, the maximum the 286 will allow), but for obvious reasons cannot exceed the amount of extended memory physically installed in your system. If the *memory* parameter is omitted, EMS40.SYS defaults to 384k, which provides 24 pages of expanded memory. Note that if EMS40.SYS is used in conjunction with HIMEM.SYS, EMS40.SYS should be loaded *before* HIMEM.SYS.

Once installed, EMS40.SYS consumes approximately 69k of RAM—64k for the EMS page frame it sets up in conventional memory, and 5k for the driver itself. Though this may seem like a lot of memory to give up, the expanded memory it can provide EMS-aware application programs such as Lotus 1-2-3 will more than make up for it. And if DOS is loaded in the HMA, you'll have almost as much memory left in the lower 640k as non-286 users will with DOS installed in low memory.

EMS40.SYS will run on 386s and 486s, too, but it's not as fast as EMM386-.EXE is. EMM386.EXE has a built-in advantage in that it has access to features of the 386 that do not appear on 286s. Nor does it provide the UMB services that EMM386.EXE does. So if you own a 386 or 486, you'll still want to use EMM386-.EXE. For 286 owners who are feeling the memory crunch, this little utility may be a godsend.

Using the EMM386 Command

EMM386 serves a dual role as both a device driver and a DOS command. Once EMM386.EXE is installed through CONFIG.SYS, the EMM386 command can be executed to make certain alterations to the driver's mode of operation and to get a status report. The syntax for the command is

```
EMM386 [ON|OFF|AUTO] [W=ON|OFF]
```

where ON, OFF, and AUTO turn EMM386.EXE on and off and place it in auto mode, and W=ON and W=OFF enable and disable support for Weitek math coprocessors. If your system does not have a Weitek coprocessor, you can safely ignore this setting. If you do have a Weitek coprocessor, it probably won't work properly with EMM386.EXE installed unless Weitek support is enabled. You should enable Weitek support with the command EMM386 W=ON before running a program that uses the coprocessor, and then disable it again with EMM386 W=OFF after the program has terminated. Also note that Weitek support cannot be enabled if the High Memory Area is not available. In practical terms, this means that you can't load DOS into the HMA with the DOS=HIGH directive if you want to use a Weitek coprocessor, too.

When run with no command-line switches, EMM386 reports the status of the EMM386.EXE driver installed in memory. Figures 3.7 and 3.8 illustrate typical output from EMM386 when loaded with the NOEMS and RAM options. If the RAM option was used, EMM386 offers vital statistics on EMS memory usage such as how much remains free, where the page frame is located, and how many handles are active in the system. If NOEMS was used, EMM386 notes that expanded memory services are unavailable. The final line in the listing indicates whether the driver is currently active, inactive, or in auto mode.

You can set the operating mode with the ON, OFF, and AUTO switches. Turning it off disables expanded memory emulation, so that expanded memory will not be available to programs that request it. It also disables the use of upper memory. For this reason, EMM386 won't allow itself to be turned off if programs are using expanded or upper memory. If it did, you'd lose the data stored there because the contents of these regions of memory could be destroyed.

The differences between EMM386's ON and AUTO modes are subtle. In ON mode, EMM386.EXE reserves a fixed-length block of RAM to serve as expanded memory. This RAM is available *only* as expanded memory, and not for any other purpose. In AUTO mode, by contrast, no RAM is set aside for expanded memory ahead of time, but EMM386 will dynamically allocate RAM as expanded memory when an application program requests it. A finer, more deeply rooted difference between the two modes is that if neither upper memory nor expanded memory is being used while EMM386 is running in AUTO mode, EMM386 switches the 386 from Virtual-86 mode to real mode. With EMM386 ON, however, EMM386 runs DOS in Virtual-86 mode regardless of what services are currently in use. This isn't ordinarily a problem, but it does slow performance. Also, you'll run across occasional programs that will not run in Virtual-86 mode.

The Role of EMM386.EXE

It's obvious from reading the chapter thus far that anything DOS 5.0 does concerning reserved memory revolves around the EMM386.EXE driver. EMM386.EXE is more complicated than the examples we've shown would indicate. In fact, it can be installed with up to 17 different parameters and switches. Before you can fully appreciate them all, you need to know more about how it interacts with the CPU it's running on to customize the makeup of memory.

To create UMBs in upper memory, EMM386.EXE scans the address space from 640k to 1Mb looking for regions that are populated by neither RAM nor ROM. If your PC isn't stuffed full of adapters, you probably have at least 64k free in this area. Then it uses a mechanism known as *paging* to backfill the holes with extended memory. Technically, it doesn't really backfill the memory; it uses features of the 386 chip to redirect memory accesses from addresses in upper memory to addresses in extended memory.

To make this happen, EMM386.EXE runs in protected mode (where it can access more than 1Mb of memory) and runs DOS in Virtual-86 mode, which is similar to real mode except that it provides applications with full access to the 386's 4Gb virtual address space. Virtual-86 mode was added to the 386 for the millions of DOS users who wanted to multitask real mode DOS applications without having to rewrite them. With the 8088 and 8086, it couldn't be done; multitasking requires hardware-supported virtual memory management stratagems that can prevent two concurrent processes from conflicting with each other. The 286's protected mode has what it takes to isolate programs from one another, but while real mode programs can't run in protected mode on either the 286 or the 386, they can run without modification in Virtual-86 mode. Individual DOS programs running in separate Virtual-86 mode sessions believe that they own the machine and all of its resources (as they do in real mode under DOS). Actually, they only own the *virtual* machine they're running on—and virtual machines are physically isolated from one another by the 386 hardware.

But it's not the 386's ability to isolate tasks from one another that's important to memory managers such as EMM386.EXE; it's the fact that Virtual-86 mode programs enjoy the same access to the 386's paging capabilities that protected mode programs do. Paging is a virtual memory management technique that allows fixed-size blocks of memory 4k long, or *pages,* to be mapped to any physical address in memory. On the 386, pages are aligned on even 4k boundaries starting at the bottom of memory; page 0 is located at offset 0, page 1 starts 4k above that at offset 1000H, page 2 at 2000H, and so on.

In real mode, the contents of 16-bit segment registers are multiplied by 16 and combined with 16-bit offsets to form 20-bit physical addresses. The same thing happens in Virtual-86 mode, but there is an added level of indirection. Rather than interpreting the resulting address as a physical address, the 386 consults a *page table* if the paging-enable bit in one of its control registers is set. The page table then translates the address into a physical address that can lie anywhere in the processor's 4Gb address space. As a result, unused memory locations below 1Mb can be effectively filled with memory that actually lies outside DOS's normal 1Mb address space.

Paging is illustrated in Figure 3.9. The diagram on the left represents the 1Mb address space DOS runs in, partitioned into 256 evenly spaced pages. The one on the right depicts the 386's larger address space, which is similarly divided into pages. By setting up the page tables accordingly, EMM386.EXE can transparently reroute memory accesses from locations on the left to locations on the right. A program running in the system isn't aware that the redirection occurred, nor that the addresses it is physically accessing may actually lie above 1Mb.

By now you should see how paging is used to create the appearance that there is usable RAM in a region that is normally devoid of usable RAM. After EMM386.EXE identifies unused regions of upper memory, it simply redirects memory accesses from those addresses to addresses higher in memory that are populated with RAM. DOS's LOADHIGH and DEVICEHIGH commands then load programs and device drivers into these spaces.

The result is a flexible memory structure that can be molded to fit the requirements of the system. Figure 3.10 shows an example of how paging can be used in Virtual-86 mode to alter the layout of memory. The subject of this example is an IBM PS/2 Model 70 with an integrated VGA, a 128k ROM BIOS, and no adapter cards installed. When EMM386.EXE detects the presence of the VGA, it steers clear of segments A000H and B000H, which the VGA is likely to use for itself. It also stays away from segments E000H and F000H, where the ROM BIOS resides. That leaves 128k of RAM—segments C000H and D000H—free for UMBs. EMM386.EXE requests 128k of high memory from HIMEM.SYS, obtains the physical address of the block that is allocated, and remaps segments in upper memory to addresses in high memory. It also claims the UMB for itself (through HIMEM.SYS) to protect the programs it places there.

Had EMM386.EXE been installed with the RAM option, 64k of this memory would have been used for the EMS page frame, leaving 64k free for UMBs. To emulate expanded memory, EMM386.EXE also uses paging, but in a slightly different way. When a call is made to map a page of expanded memory into the page frame, EMM386.EXE alters the page table to map another 16k of extended memory into the CPU's address space.

The model also would have been more complicated had there been, say, an intervening adapter ROM occupying the space from D000H to D400H. Had this been the case, EMM386.EXE would have recognized the presence of the additional ROM module and created two UMBs rather than one. One UMB would have stretched from segment C000H to D000H, and the other from D400H to E000H. This way, no memory would be wasted: There would still be 112k of reserved memory in which to load programs and drivers.

FIGURE 3.9

Paging on the 386

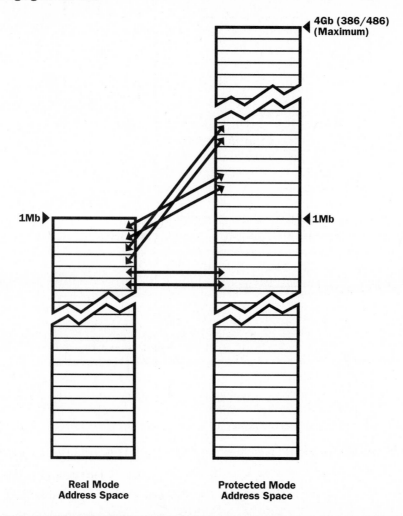

Real Mode
Address Space

Protected Mode
Address Space

More on the EMM386.EXE Driver

Before you can load TSRs and device drivers into reserved memory, DOS 5.0's
EMM386.EXE memory manager must be loaded with a DEVICE directive in
CONFIG.SYS. EMM386.EXE accepts several switches on the line that installs
it. Its full syntax is

```
EMM386.EXE [memory] [L=minXMS] [NOEMS] [RAM] [ON|OFF|AUTO]
    [I=address-address] [X=address-address] [W=ON|OFF]
    [Mx] [FRAME=address] [/Paddress] [Pn=address]
    [B=address] [A=altregs] [H=handles][D=nnn] [N=path]
```

FIGURE 3.10

Remapped memory

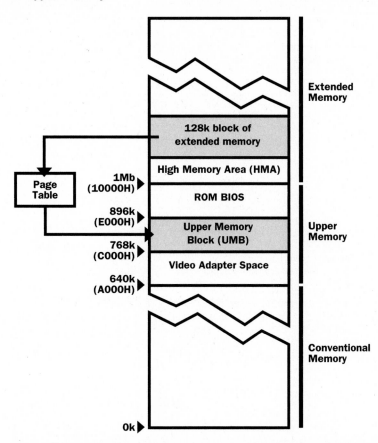

Fortunately, you won't often need any options other than NOEMS and RAM. The defaults that EMM386.EXE provides for the others are fine for most systems. These other options fall into four categories:

- Options for controlling the services EMM386.EXE provides

- Options for controlling what regions of reserved memory are used

- Options for controlling where the EMS page frame is located

- Options that control other features of EMM386.EXE

The entire range of options is listed by category and function in Table 3.3. The sections that follow explain how the options are used and when you should use them.

TABLE 3.3

EMM386.EXE Installation Options

Switch/Parameter	Description
Controlling the Services EMM386.EXE Provides	
NOEMS	Provides UMB support for LOADHIGH and DEVICEHIGH, but does not provide EMS support.
RAM	Provides UMB support for LOADHIGH and DEVICEHIGH, and EMS memory to application programs that need it.
L=*minXMS*	Specifies the minimum amount of XMS memory (in kilobytes) you want left over after EMM386.EXE is installed. The default is 0.
memory	Specifies the amount of EMS memory (in kilobytes) EMM386.EXE should make available to the system. Valid values range from 16 to 32768. If the value isn't evenly divisble by 16, EMM386.EXE rounds down to the nearest one that is. The default is 256.
Controlling the Regions of Upper Memory Used	
I=*address-address*	Specifies a range of segment addresses to be added to the ones EMM386.EXE has already determined may be used. Valid values are A000 through FFFF.
X=*address-address*	Specifies a range of segment addresses to be excluded from the ones EMM386.EXE has determined may be used. Valid values are A000 through FFFF.
Controlling Where the EMS Page Frame Is Located	
FRAME=*address*	Specifies the segment address where the EMS page frame is located. Valid values range from 8000 through 9000 and C000 through E000 in increments of 400.
M*x*	Specifies the segment address where the EMS page frame is located. Valid values for *x* are as follows:

x	Segment	*x*	Segment
1	C000H	8	DC00H
2	C400H	9	E000H
3	C800H	10	8000H
4	CC00H	11	8400H
5	D000H	12	8800H
6	D400H	13	8C00H
7	D800H	14	9000H

Switch/Parameter	Description
/P*address*	Specifies the segment address where the EMS page frame is located. Same as FRAME=*address*.
P*n*=*address*	Specifies a segment address for an EMS page. Valid values for *page* are 0 through 255. Valid values for *address* are 8000 through 9C00 and C000 through EC00, in increments of 400.
B=*address*	Specifies the lowest segment address where the EMS page frame may be located. Valid values are 1000 through 4000. The default is 4000.
Other EMM386.EXE Switches	
A=*altregs*	Specifies how many fast alternate register sets should be used. Valid values range from 0 to 254. The default is 7.
D=*nnn*	Specifies how much memory (in kilobytes) should be reserved for buffered Direct Memory Access by hardware devices.
H=*handles*	Specifies how many EMS handles may be used. Valid values range from 2 to 255. The default is 64.
W=ONIOFF	Enables or disables support for Weitek math coprocessors.
ONIOFFIAUTO	Sets EMM386.EXE's initial operating mode to ON, OFF, or AUTO.
/Y=*path*	Specifies the path to where EMM386.EXE is stored.

Controlling the Services EMM386.EXE Provides   Four switches and parameters—NOEMS, RAM, L, and *memory*—let you control how EMM386.EXE puts memory to use and how it makes it available to application programs. We've touched on the uses of RAM and NOEMS before. Briefly, NOEMS

tells EMM386.EXE to provide UMB support so that DEVICEHIGH and
LOADHIGH may be used, but without providing EMS emulation services.
RAM tells it that you want support for EMS *and* for UMBs. Omitting both param-
eters from the line where EMM386.EXE is installed enables EMS services but
not UMB support. If neither NOEMS nor RAM is specified, the commands
LOADHIGH and DEVICEHIGH may not be used.

The *memory* option specifies the number of kilobytes of EMS memory you
want EMM386.EXE to make available to the system. If you omit this parameter, EMM386.EXE defaults to 256k. The command

```
DEVICE=C:\DOS\EMM386.EXE 512 RAM
```

tells EMM386.EXE to make 512k of expanded memory available. Because the
RAM switch is used, EMM386.EXE will provide support for program loading
in upper memory in addition to support for programs that need EMS memory.
Memory is ignored if it's used on the same line as a NOEMS switch.

The L switch specifies the minimum amount of XMS memory (extended
memory managed by HIMEM.SYS) you want left over after EMM386.EXE is
installed. *MinXMS* is expressed in kilobytes. In a system with 3Mb of RAM, the
command

```
DEVICE=C:\DOS\EMM386.EXE 512 RAM L=1024
```

will make 512k of expanded memory available and leave 1,600k of XMS memory free. However, on the same system, the command

```
DEVICE=C:\DOS\EMM386.EXE 2048 RAM L=1024
```

will provide only 1,088k of expanded memory, because you instructed
EMM386.EXE to leave at least 1Mb of XMS memory free. The number following L takes precedence over a *memory* parameter appearing on the same line.

The amount of expanded memory the system provides when the L switch is
used is also affected by other drivers that are loaded if they, too, use XMS memory. For example, if SMARTDrive is loaded before EMM386.EXE, the L switch
determines the minimum amount of XMS memory left over after both SMART-
Drive and EMM386.EXE are loaded.

Controlling the Regions of Upper Memory Used EMM386.EXE allows
you to specify that certain regions of upper memory are to be included in or
excluded from the range of addresses it uses for UMBs and the EMS page
frame. These options are useful if, for example, EMM386.EXE fails to recognize
the presence of a network adapter card and erroneously tries to use the same
range of addresses the adapter is using, or if it fails to recognize that it can use a
certain region of memory that you know for a fact it *can* use without causing conflicts with other devices installed in the system.

The I switch specifies a range of segment addresses to be included. The command

```
DEVICE=C:\DOS\EMM386.EXE RAM I=C000-C7FF
```

adds every address between C0000H and C7FFFH to the addresses EMM386.EXE has already identified that it will use in upper memory. Similarly, the command

```
DEVICE=C:\DOS\EMM386.EXE RAM X=C000-C7FF
```

excludes the same region so that it will not be used, even if EMM386.EXE's initial scan of reserved memory indicated that it could be used. If you like, you can combine both I and X on the same line, and you can specify both of them more than once. For example, the command

```
DEVICE=C:\DOS\EMM386.EXE RAM I=C000-C7FF I=D000-D7FF
      X=D800-D9FF
```

tells EMM386.EXE to include segments C000H through C7FFH and D000H through D7FFH, but to leave segments D800H through D9FFH alone. If the range of addresses spelled out with the I and X switches overlap, X takes precedence.

Controlling Where the EMS Page Frame Is Located   EMM386.EXE also allows you to control where in upper memory the EMS page frame—the 64k region of memory in which physical EMS pages are located—is established. Five switches serve in this capacity: FRAME, /P, M, B, and P. FRAME and /P are two ways to express the same thing: the segment address where the page frame is to be located. The command

```
DEVICE=C:\DOS\EMM386.EXE RAM /PD000
```

locates the page frame at segment D000H, as does the command

```
DEVICE=C:\DOS\EMM386.EXE RAM FRAME=D000
```

Both switches accept address ranges from 8000 through 9000 and C000 through E000. The segment addresses specified must fall on boundaries evenly divisible by 400 (for example, C000, C400, and so on).

The M switch (which is carried over from the DOS 4.0 version of EMM386) is identical to FRAME and /P except that it takes as an argument one of several predefined codes identifying the segment address where the page is to be located. These codes are listed in Table 3.3. The command

```
DEVICE=C:\DOS\EMM386.EXE RAM M5
```

is identical to the two commands just discussed because 5 is the M code for segment D000H. Note that codes 10 through 14, which correspond to addresses between 512k and 640k, may only be used if your PC has 512k or less of conventional memory.

The B switch provides EMM386.EXE more latitude in locating the EMS page frame. By default, EMM386.EXE will never locate a page frame below segment 4000H. With the B switch, you can give it permission to establish a page frame as low as segment 1000H. The command

```
DEVICE=C:\DOS\EMM386.EXE RAM B=2000
```

designates segment 2000H as the lowest address available for locating the page frame. Valid values range from 1000 to 4000.

You may also locate a page frame with the P switch. P allows you to identify the segment address of up to 256 different EMS pages (numbered 0 through 255) individually. The command

```
DEVICE=C:\DOS\EMM386.EXE RAM P0=C000
```

locates page 0 (P0) at segment address C000H. Valid segment address values range from 8000 through 9C00 and C000 through EC00, in increments of 400. Version 3.2 of the expanded memory specification requires that pages 0 through 3 be contiguous, so if you plan to run software built for LIM 3.2 expanded memory, make sure to locate the pages accordingly. For example, don't place page 0 at D000H and page 1 at D800H. If page 0 is located at D000H, then page 1 must lie at D400H, page 2 at D800H, and page 3 at DC00H. EMM386.EXE displays a brief warning message upon installation if you set these pages up in a manner that is not compatible with LIM 3.2.

Using the Other Switches The remaining switches are rather straightforward. The A switch specifies how many *fast alternate register sets* should be allocated in the system. The default is 7. Valid values range from 0 to 254. Extra register sets permit EMM386.EXE to run slightly faster, but not without some expense: Each additional register set that you allocate requires approximately 200 bytes of memory.

The H switch specifies how many EMS handles EMM386.EXE should make available. A *handle* is a number returned by the expanded memory manager that an application program uses to identify a block of expanded memory. The default is 64. You may need more than 64 handles if you have several applications active in the system at once that use EMS memory. However, in the majority of cases, the default is more than enough to satisfy the demands of EMS-aware applications.

The ON|OFF|AUTO parameter controls the initial operating mode of the EMM386.EXE driver. The default is ON. All three modes were described earlier in this chapter. You can change the operating mode from the command line using the EMM386 command.

The D switch lets you specify how many kilobytes of memory should be set aside for buffered *Direct Memory Access* (DMA). The default is 16, which is adequate for most programs. Valid values range from 16 to 256. DMA is a mechanism for transferring data directly between block data devices (such as disk drives) and RAM, without involving the CPU. Because they don't go through the CPU, DMA memory accesses typically proceed from start to finish much faster than normal memory accesses. As a result, some application programs, notably commercial hard-disk backup utilities such as Fastback Plus and PC Backup (part of PC Tools Deluxe), use DMA to make hard-disk transfers faster. If you have difficulty running such utilities with EMM386.EXE installed, try increasing the amount of memory reserved for DMA transfers.

The /Y switch permits you to specify a path where EMM386.EXE is stored so that Windows, which attempts to locate EMM386.EXE before it starts in 386 enhanced mode by examining the DEVICE=EMM386.EXE statement in CONFIG.SYS, can track it down. If it can't find EMM386.EXE, Windows won't start. This switch is useful in networked environments where it may be desirable to locate EMM386.EXE on a remote server rather than on a local hard disk or floppy.

Finally, the W switch specifies whether Weitek coprocessor support should initially be enabled or disabled. If you don't specify a preference, EMM386.EXE defaults to the disabled state—the equivalent of W=OFF. Weitek support can be toggled on and off interactively on the command line with the EMM386 command.

Using Alternative 386 Memory Managers

The fact that DOS 5.0 includes its own memory manager doesn't preclude you from using other ones in its place. In particular, the Quarterdeck Expanded Memory Manager (QEMM-386) and 386Max from Qualitas have become quite popular over the years, and both are compatible with DOS 5.0. Both provide utilities that perform the same functions that DEVICEHIGH and LOADHIGH do, and both offer a bewildering array of installation options that enable them to run on almost any system.

They also contain features that EMM386.EXE does not. Both, for example, permit certain CONFIG.SYS-controlled data structures to be relocated to high memory, and both offer options for swapping slow ROMs for fast RAM. To do this, they perform a timing test on every byte of memory they find in the system. If it turns out that ROM, which often proves to be several times slower than RAM on 386 systems, is inhibiting performance, then these third-party memory managers copy ROM to RAM and use the 386's page tables to remap the addresses. The result: dramatically increased performance when ROM is accessed. This can really boost the performance of certain EGA and VGA video adapters, which often contain their own video ROM that is significantly slower than the RAM around it. If you wish, QEMM-386 and 386Max will also trade slow RAM below 640k for faster RAM elsewhere in memory, speeding up DOS and DOS programs that run in conventional memory.

If you include a DOS=UMB statement in CONFIG.SYS, you may use QEMM-386 or 386Max in place of EMM386.EXE and still use DOS's LOADHIGH and DEVICEHIGH commands. If you omit DOS=UMB, you must use the equivalents to LOADHIGH and DEVICEHIGH that QEMM-386 and 386Max provide.

Of course, the best thing about EMM386.EXE is that it's free. It also works, and works well, and it's compatible with Windows, while some of the older versions of QEMM-386 and 386Max were not. In the end, you decide. The bottom line is that on a 386 or 486, there's no need to let precious memory go to waste.

Windows and Other Environments

An equally viable, yet often overlooked, vehicle for putting extended or expanded memory to use is Microsoft Windows. On an 8088 or 8086, Windows 3.0 will use all the LIM 4.0 EMS memory you can give it. This enables you to have more Windows programs open simultaneously in the system without having to resort to swapping code and data in and out between RAM and the hard disk. On a 286 or 386 with at least 1Mb of memory, Windows runs in protected mode, where it can access extended memory using HIMEM.SYS.

Of course, all this extra memory is put to use running Windows applications. This means that it doesn't do you a lot of good if your primary use for Windows is to run DOS applications, unless you are using a 386 or 486 platform with at least 2Mb of memory installed. On such systems, Windows runs in *386 enhanced mode,* which enables you to run multiple DOS sessions in different windows at the same time. In this capacity, Windows not only serves as an efficient task switcher, but it also allows you to multitask DOS programs. In other words, you can have ProComm downloading a file from a bulletin board in one window while you enter text in WordPerfect in another. Windows accomplishes this by running DOS programs in separate Virtual-86 mode sessions.

An important thing to note concerning the marriage of Windows and DOS 5.0 is that while Windows is running in 386 enhanced mode, it provides EMS services to programs that request it, similar to the services provided by EMM386.EXE. Thus, you need not install EMM386.EXE for the purpose of providing EMS services if you're also running Windows in 386 enhanced mode.

There are other environments that permit extended and expanded memory to be put to work running DOS applications. DESQview 386, for example, uses the 386's Virtual-86 mode to allow several DOS programs to run simultaneously. If you look around, you'll find several alternative operating environments that work on top of DOS and put extra memory to work holding multiple application programs, especially on 386 and 486 systems.

There is also an entire class of DOS applications that use *DOS extenders* to run DOS applications in protected mode on 286, 386, and 486 PCs, where they enjoy access to extended memory. Lotus 1-2-3 Release 3 is one example of such an application; AutoCAD Release 11 is another. If you run one of these applications, it behooves you to have as much extended memory installed as possible. One of the better-known DOS extenders is Phar Lap Software's 386/DOS-Extender, which permits DOS applications run on 386s and 486s to take advantage of the extended addressing capabilities of those processors. There's a common misconception that a DOS extender is an operating environment, and that simply running a DOS application under the auspices of a DOS extender will enable it to break the 640k barrier. Unfortunately, it's not nearly that easy. An application will only use a DOS extender if it is specially written to do so.

Summary

We're ready now to paint a broad outline of what DOS 5.0 will do with extended and expanded memory. We'll start with extended memory. If you have extended memory (which also means you must have a 286, 386, or 486), you can use it to do any or all of the following:

- Store SMARTDrive's disk buffers (see Chapter 2 for instructions on installing SMARTDrive in extended memory)

- Store RAMDrive's disk buffers (see Chapter 2 for a instructions on installing RAMDrive in extended memory)

- Load DOS itself (and BUFFERS) into high memory with the DOS= HIGH directive (see "Placing DOS in High Memory" in this chapter)

- Map portions of extended memory backward into upper memory using EMM386.EXE and use DEVICEHIGH to load device drivers there (see "Using the DEVICEHIGH Directive" in this chapter)

- Load TSRs in the same upper memory using EMM386.EXE and the LOADHIGH command (see "Using the LOADHIGH Command" in this chapter)

- Emulate expanded memory with extended memory and provide EMS support for applications that are EMS-aware with EMM386.EXE (see "Converting Extended Memory to Expanded" in this chapter)

- Run any application program (or operating environment such as Windows) that is extended memory or XMS memory-aware

One of the benefits of running DOS 5.0 on a 386 or 486 is that you can create expanded memory from extended memory using the EMM386 driver. You can also install an EMS memory board to provide the same services regardless of processor type, or use the EMS40.SYS driver included with this book to convert extended memory to expanded memory on a 286. In DOS 5.0, you can use expanded memory to:

- Store SMARTDrive's disk buffers (see Chapter 2 for instructions on installing SMARTDrive in expanded memory)

- Store RAMDrive's disk buffers (see Chapter 2 for instructions on installing RAMDrive in expanded memory)

- Store FASTOPEN's buffers (see Chapter 2 for instructions on FAST-OPEN's /X switch, which installs it in expanded memory)

- Support any of the several major application programs that will use EMS memory when it is available to increase their in-memory storage capabilities

We're also ready to do now what we weren't ready to do at the end of Chapter 2: offer sample configuration files based on processor type, the amount and type of memory installed, and disk capacity. There's no way we can possibly cover every combination of CPU, memory, and hard disk you can put together, but we can choose examples that illustrate the principles involved. You can easily tailor these samples to your own system.

Listing 3.1 contains suggested configuration commands for an XT-class (8086- or 8088-based) PC with 640k of RAM, 1Mb of expanded memory, and a 30Mb hard disk. The first DEVICE directive loads the expanded memory manager that came with the EMS board (here, it's called EMM.SYS; it may go by another name on your system). The second one loads SMARTDrive with 512k of buffer space and places those buffers in expanded memory. If you have more than 1Mb of expanded memory, you may choose to increase the amount allotted to SMARTDrive. FASTOPEN is also installed and told to use expanded memory. For larger hard disks, the C:=30 parameter that follows FASTOPEN should be increased accordingly, allotting approximately one additional FASTOPEN buffer for each additional megabyte of disk space.

LISTING 3.1

```
REM  *******************************************************
REM
REM                           DOS 5.0
REM                   System Configuration File
REM
REM     For an 8086 or 8088 with 1Mb of expanded memory
REM                   and a 30Mb hard disk
REM
REM  *******************************************************
REM
DEVICE=EMM.SYS
DEVICE=C:\DOS\SMARTDRV.SYS 512 /A
INSTALL=C:\DOS\FASTOPEN C:=30 /X
FILES=20
BUFFERS=4
```

Listing 3.2 profiles a suggested configuration for a 286 with 1Mb of memory (640k of conventional memory plus 384k of extended) and a 60Mb hard disk. It's also good for a 386 with only 1Mb of RAM. HIMEM.SYS is installed so that SMARTDrive may use extended memory and DOS may be loaded into the HMA with the statement DOS=HIGH. Both actions increase the amount of memory available for program loading in the lower 640k. SMARTDrive's size is limited to 256k since there is only 384k of extended memory in the system. If your system contains more, then this size should be increased accordingly.

```
REM  *******************************************************
REM
REM                         DOS 5.0
REM                 System Configuration File
REM
REM              For a 286 with 1Mb of memory
REM          (640k conventional plus 384k extended)
REM                 and a 60Mb hard disk
REM
REM  *******************************************************
REM
DEVICE=C:\DOS\HIMEM.SYS
DEVICE=C:\DOS\SMARTDRV.SYS 256
INSTALL=C:\DOS\FASTOPEN C:=60
DOS=HIGH
FILES=20
BUFFERS=4
STACKS=0,0
SHELL=C:\COMMAND.COM C:\ /E:512 /P
```

The size of FASTOPEN is increased from 30 to 60 to accommodate the larger hard-disk size. This assumes that the entire 60Mb is devoted to one logical DOS drive—drive C. If the hard disk contains other logical drives, then the FASTOPEN statement should be adjusted accordingly. For example, if it is divided into 30Mb C and D drives, then the statement should be modified to read

```
INSTALL=C:\DOS\FASTOPEN C:=30 D:=30
```

As usual, this assumes that FASTOPEN.EXE is located in C:\DOS.

In this example, COMMAND.COM is loaded from CONFIG.SYS so the size of the environment may be increased to 512 bytes. Also, STACKS=0,0 is added to conserve memory that would otherwise be devoted to protecting the system from too many interrupts in a short time. Should you experience system crashes as a result, remove this statement from your CONFIG.SYS file.

Listing 3.3 suggests a configuration for a final system: a 386 or 486 with at least 2Mb of RAM. It is similar to the configuration file for the 286 except that it also loads EMM386.EXE and enables the use of upper memory with the addition of the UMB qualifier to the DOS=HIGH directive. The NOEMS option is used on the line where EMM386.EXE is installed so that EMS services will not be provided. You may elect to use the RAM option to configure it differently.

SMARTDrive is now loaded with a DEVICEHIGH directive instead of DEVICE, preserving a few additional kilobytes of conventional memory. Also, FASTOPEN is no longer loaded from CONFIG.SYS. It is shifted to AUTOEXEC.BAT so the LOADHIGH command can be used to place it in reserved memory. From CONFIG.SYS, the only option is to load it with INSTALL, which locates it in conventional memory. Loading it that way is a waste of resources when reserved memory is available for program loading.

LISTING 3.3

```
REM ************************************************************
REM
REM                           DOS 5.0
REM                   System Configuration File
REM
REM       For a 386 or 486 with 2Mb or more of memory
REM
REM ************************************************************
REM
DEVICE=C:\DOS\HIMEM.SYS
DEVICE=C:\DOS\EMM386.EXE NOEMS
DEVICEHIGH C:\DOS\SMARTDRV.SYS 1024
REM *** Install FASTOPEN with LOADHIGH in AUTOEXEC.BAT ***
DOS=HIGH,UMB
FILES=20
BUFFERS=4
STACKS=0,0
SHELL=C:\COMMAND.COM C:\ /E:512 /P
```

It's possible that you may find the sheer number of memory management options available under DOS 5.0 and their dependency on CPU type somewhat bewildering. To help, Table 3.4 provides a checklist of DOS 5.0 memory usage options versus processor type. Not only does it provide a concise summary of what DOS 5.0 will do with extended and expanded memory, but it also indicates what CPU types the features are supported on. One glance tells you that your options are limited unless you own at least a 286, and that a 386 or 486 is required to squeeze the most from the operating system.

TABLE 3.4

DOS 5.0 Memory Usage Options versus CPU Type

Action	8086/88	286	386/486
Use expanded memory for FASTOPEN	x	x	x
Use expanded memory for SMARTDrive	x	x	x
Use expanded memory for RAMDrive	x	x	x
Use extended memory for SMARTDrive		x	x
Use extended memory for RAMDrive		x	x
Load DOS into the High Memory Area		x	x
Use DEVICEHIGH to load device drivers in upper memory			x
Use LOADHIGH to load TSRs in upper memory			x
Use extended memory to emulate expanded memory			x

DISKS AND DISK MANAGEMENT

IF YOU'RE NEW TO COMPUTING, YOU MAY FIND IT HARD TO IMAGINE PCS WITH-out hard disks—or for that matter, PCs with cassette decks attached to them. Yet one of the options on the first IBM PC was a cassette deck that could be used in place of floppy drives for mass data storage. Disks fit so seamlessly into our systems today that we tend to take them for granted. And why not? It wasn't long ago that a 10Mb hard disk was more than most people could afford. Now a hard disk with several times that capacity can be had for less than what a single floppy drive cost on the original IBM PC.

DOS provides an arsenal of commands and utilities for dealing with hard disks and floppy disks that every user should be familiar with. Some of these commands are new to DOS 5.0, adding features to the operating system that before were available only as third-party utilities. Others are not new, but have been revamped for greater utility and ease of use. And still others appear in DOS 5.0 intact from earlier versions, unchanged but also undiminished in importance. We'll look at several of these commands in this chapter, including:

- FDISK, used to partition hard disks

- FORMAT, used to format disks

- SYS, used to place the DOS system files on a disk after formatting

- ASSIGN, used to redirect disk accesses from one floppy drive to another

- BACKUP and RESTORE, used to back up and restore hard-disk files

- RECOVER, used to extract files from damaged disks

- CHKDSK, used to detect and repair logical errors on disks

- MIRROR, UNDELETE, and UNFORMAT, used to repair damaged hard-disk partition tables and recover from accidental formats and erasures

We'll also look at some of the commands DOS left out—commands for defragmenting hard-disk files and performing low-level formats, for example—and discuss where you can get them. In the end, you'll have a better understanding of how DOS interacts with hard disks and floppies, how you can protect your files from harm and salvage them when trouble strikes, and how you can work your knowledge of DOS's file system to your advantage.

Working with Hard Disks

A typical hard disk today actually contains many disks, called *drive platters*, on which information is stored magnetically. Platters are coated with a thin magnetic medium containing small metal or oxide particles that can be aligned in one of two orientations by passing a magnetic field over them. The surface of each platter is divided into concentric rings (usually several hundred of them) called *cylinders*. Cylinders, in turn, are divided into several smaller storage units called *sectors*. On most PCs, one sector holds 512 bytes of data.

In discussions of hard-disk technology, you'll also hear the term *heads*, which refers to the number of surfaces on which data may be stored. Strictly speaking, this term refers to the number of heads on the drive itself. But since there is a one-to-one relationship between drive heads and recording surfaces, "heads" is used to describe both. On most drives, the number of heads is either two times the number of drive platters or two times the number of platters, minus one. On floppies, the term *sides* is normally used in place of heads and *tracks* in place of cylinders. Floppies, which never contain more than one drive platter, are always either single- or double-sided.

Figure 4.1 shows the physical makeup of a typical hard-disk drive containing 7 heads, 855 cylinders, and 17 sectors per cylinder. Having 7 heads requires at least four drive platters; here, three are double-sided and one is single-sided. When a drive has an odd number of sides, the extra side is usually used to record special signals that the controller uses to locate cylinders on the disk. The 855 cylinders form a series of thin rings emanating outward from the center of the disk. The sectors are the short, arc-shaped segments in each cylinder. You can calculate a drive's capacity by multiplying the number of heads by the number of cylinders, multiplying the result by the number of sectors per cylinder, and, finally, multiplying that result by 512 to determine the total number of bytes represented. For this example, the calculation yields 52,093,440 bytes, which is equivalent to approximately 50Mb.

Before a hard disk is ready to be used by DOS, three conditions must be met. First, it must be low-level formatted. *Low-level formatting* defines where the sectors and cylinders lie on the disk. Second, it must be partitioned. *Partitioning* divides a hard disk up into one or more *logical drives*, which DOS assigns separate drive letters to and treats as if they were separate physical disks. Third, it must be formatted. *Formatting* (sometimes called high-level formatting to distinguish this formatting process from low-level formatting) creates the data structures DOS uses to record the locations of files on the disk. In the next several sections, we'll look at these three processes in more detail and at what they do to the disk. We'll also examine the tools you use to perform them.

FIGURE 4.1

Structure of a hard disk

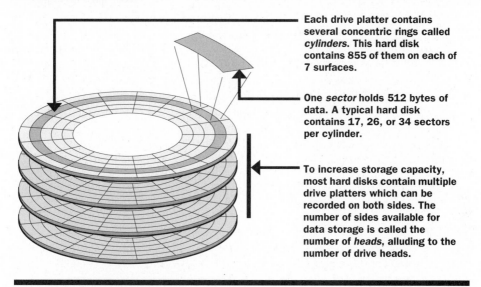

Each drive platter contains several concentric rings called *cylinders*. This hard disk contains 855 of them on each of 7 surfaces.

One *sector* holds 512 bytes of data. A typical hard disk contains 17, 26, or 34 sectors per cylinder.

To increase storage capacity, most hard disks contain multiple drive platters which can be recorded on both sides. The number of sides available for data storage is called the number of *heads*, alluding to the number of drive heads.

Low-Level Formatting

Before being used for the first time, a hard disk must be low-level formatted. Low-level formatting creates the sectors and cylinders on the disk by writing sector ID information to its surface that defines where individual sectors are located and how they're numbered.

The ID information is stored in units called *sector ID headers* that precede each sector on the disk. An ID header typically contains a head, sector, and cylinder number; an address mark defining where the ID header begins; and CRC (Cyclical Redundancy Check) data for detecting errors in the header. When it is told to final a particular sector on the disk, the hard-disk controller uses this information to locate its target.

Sector numbering takes into account several factors that later have an impact on the performance of the hard disk. The most important of these is *sector interleave*, which matches the disk's rate of rotation (3,600 rpm for most hard disks) to the rate at which the controller can physically process data passing underneath the drive head. Interleave separates consecutively numbered sectors on the disk so that, for example, sector 2 and sector 3 might actually lie anywhere from two to six sectors apart. Sectors are arranged this way because not all PCs are capable of reading a sector, writing the information to RAM, and getting ready to read another in the short time it takes the next sector to spin around to the drive head. If the controller has to wait an entire revolution for the sector to come around again, time is wasted. By properly spacing out the sectors on the disk, however, you can arrange to have the next sector arrive beneath the drive head at about the same time the controller is ready for it, and thus obtain the highest possible data-transfer rates.

Low-level formatting also marks bad sectors on the disk so that they won't be used to store data. Generally, the disk is tested before it leaves the factory and bad sectors are either marked on the spot or, if the drive is being supplied to an OEM who will do the low-level formatting after the drive is received, recorded in a *defect list*. ESDI (Enhanced Small Device Interface) drives, which are popular on 386 PCs for their speed, store defect lists right on the disk. Don't be alarmed if DOS reports that a drive contains several hundred thousand bytes in bad sectors. Because of the huge storage capacities of today's hard disks, almost all of them contain at least a few bad sectors. You don't need to worry about them unless there are so many that they take away a significant fraction of the total disk space.

Under normal circumstances, a hard disk only needs a low-level format once in its lifetime. Once the sectors and cylinders are mapped out, they needn't be remapped unless the magnetic contents of the disk are damaged, lost, or destroyed. However, the following other factors might lead you to low-level format a hard disk more often:

- If bad sectors develop on a hard disk as a result of normal use, a new low-level format will repair the disk by flagging the defective sectors so they won't be used to store data.

- Over time, stresses induced by normal wear and tear may cause the drive heads to creep out of alignment with the cylinders on the disk. When this happens, a new low-level format is the most effective and economical way to restore alignment.

- If a hard disk isn't low-level formatted with the optimum sector interleave value, you pay a price in performance. Reformatting with the proper interleave value will ensure that you're getting the fastest possible performance from your system.

Some drives, particularly the IDE (Intelligent Drive Electronics) disks that have become so popular on 286 and 386 systems, can only be low-level formatted at the factory. Others may be reformatted at will provided you have the right software to do it. We'll examine more closely the reasons for low-level formatting a drive later in this chapter in the section entitled "Protecting and Preserving Hard-Disk Data."

If you do want to low-level format a hard disk, you'll have to provide your own utility for doing it. DOS doesn't provide one. Fortunately, most hard disks come from the manufacturer or dealer already low-level formatted. Some hard disks come with low-level formatters, and some hard-disk controllers contain low-level formatting logic that may be invoked with DEBUG. All of these, however, destroy data that's already on the disk. Later in this chapter, we'll also look at third-party low-level formatters that not only perform their work non-destructively, but also offer value-added features such as the ability to test for and apply optimum interleave values during formatting.

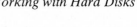

Hard-Disk Partitioning

To make large hard disks more manageable, DOS permits them to be subdivided into units called *partitions*. Partitions are treated like separate physical drives and are even assigned separate drive letters like physical drives. Having a 40Mb hard disk divided into two 20Mb partitions is just like having two 20Mb hard disks.

There are three types of hard-disk partitions: primary DOS partitions, extended DOS partitions, and non-DOS partitions. A *primary DOS partition* is the first DOS partition you place on a hard disk and is the only type of partition from which you can boot DOS. A primary DOS partition may take up all of the hard disk or only a part of it. If it only encompasses a part of the disk, the remainder of the disk can be allocated to an extended DOS partition, one or more non-DOS partitions, or a combination of the two. The maximum number of partitions that DOS supports on any hard disk is four.

Prior to version 3.3, only the first 32Mb of a hard disk could be used by DOS because primary DOS partitions were limited to 32Mb each and because hard disks were limited to a single DOS partition.

Versions of DOS from 3.3 onward support *extended DOS partitions*, which permit you to divide large hard disks into several additional logical drives. A primary DOS partition is assigned a single drive letter, but an extended DOS partition may be divided into as many logical drives as hard-disk space and the range of available drive letters permit. On a typical system with one or two floppy drives (A and B) and a hard disk with a primary DOS partition (drive C), an extended DOS partition may contain as many as 23 logical drives (D through Z).

Non-DOS partitions are for other operating systems that you want DOS to share space with on your hard disk. In general, DOS doesn't do anything with these partitions except steer clear of them. Two examples of non-DOS partitions are ones set up for OS/2's High-Performance File System (HPFS) and for the UNIX file system.

As recently as version 3.3, the largest logical drive DOS supported was 32Mb. DOS 4.0 and 5.0 permit logical drives to be up to 2Gb in length. Even with this increased capacity, you can still break up a large disk into as many as 24 logical drives to make it more manageable. In general, it's a good idea to set up one logical drive for each major program grouping. For example, the PC this book was written on contains two logical drives: one for DOS and DOS application programs, and another for Windows and Windows applications. It also contains a non-DOS partition that holds OS/2. At one time, it contained a third logical drive that was used to store programs that were waiting to be reviewed. Maintaining these systems in separate areas of the hard disk reinforces the notion that they are three separate entities on the disk and also builds a fence around them that clearly stakes out how much of the disk each one may use. Creating too many logical drives, on the other hand, can cause trouble down the road with programs that need lots of disk space. As a rule of thumb, you should keep the number of logical drives on your hard disk to the minimum you judge is required to get the job done.

The MS-DOS Partitioning Scheme

When it partitions a disk, DOS sets up a data structure called a *master partition table* at offset 1BEH (the 447th byte from the beginning of the sector) in the disk's first sector. Figure 4.2 shows the format of this table. It contains four 16-byte entries. Each entry is divided into ten fields of varying lengths containing all the information necessary to describe one partition on the hard disk, including

- The head, sector, and cylinder where the partition starts

- The head, sector, and cylinder where the partition ends

- The length of the partition in sectors

- How many sectors precede the partition

- How the partition is formatted or what operating system is installed on it

- Whether the partition is the active partition—that is, the one that is booted at start-up

With starting and ending partition addresses stored as they are, partitions don't have to be of fixed length or occupy a certain amount of space on the hard disk; they can be as small as a few sectors long or as large as an entire disk.

The bytes in the sector and cylinder number slots (offsets 02H, 03H, 06H, and 07H) aren't interpreted strictly as 8-bit values. The lower 6 bits of the sector field indicate the actual sector number, while the upper 2 bits are joined with the 8-bit value in the cylinder field to form a 10-bit cylinder number, in keeping with the conventions used by BIOS disk functions. This way, DOS may use hard disks with as many as 64 sectors per cylinder and 1,024 cylinders—64 sectors because a 6-bit value may hold any number from 0 to 63, and 1,024 cylinders because a 10-bit value can represent any value from 0 to 1,023. Disks that exceed these limits must be accompanied by special device drivers or be equipped with controllers that can mask the physical characteristics of the drive and make it appear that the sector and cylinder counts fall within the maximums.

The system indicator byte (offset 04H) reveals what operating system is installed on the partition and, for DOS partitions, what *type* of partition it is. Primary DOS partitions are marked with 01H, 04H, or 06H, depending on the length of the partition. In general, partitions less than approximately 16Mb long are labeled type 01H; partitions between 16 and 32Mb, type 04H; and partitions larger than 32Mb, type 06H. A value of 05H identifies an extended DOS partition. Any other positive value identifies a non-DOS partition. A 00H in this slot means that the partition hasn't been defined.

The active partition contains the value 80H in its boot indicator field. Only one partition may bear this mark. When your PC is started from the hard disk, a short routine in ROM reads the sector that contains the master partition table and executes a short program located at the base of the sector. This program scans the partition table for an entry with the value 80H in the boot indicator field. The first sector of the corresponding partition is subsequently read into memory and called on to execute a routine that loads DOS (or whatever operating system owns the partition) from disk.

FIGURE 4.2

Format of the MS-DOS partition table

Offset within the Partition Table Entry

	00H	01H	02H	03H	04H	05H	06H	07H	08-0BH	0C-0FH
01BEH	BI	H	S	C	SI	H	S	C	SP	N
01CEH	BI	H	S	C	SI	H	S	C	SP	N
01DEH	BI	H	S	C	SI	H	S	C	SP	N
01EEH	BI	H	S	C	SI	H	S	C	SP	N

Offset from the Beginning of the Sector (left label)

Starting head, sector, and cylinder — Ending head, sector, and cylinder — Length of partition in sectors

Offset	Size	Symbol	Description
00H	Byte	BI	Boot indicator
			00H = Not active
			80H = Active partition
01H	Byte	H	Starting head number
02H	Byte	S	Starting sector number
03H	Byte	C	Starting cylinder number
04H	Byte	SI	System indicator
			00H = Unused
			01H = DOS (0 to 16Mb)
			04H = DOS (16 to 32Mb)
			05H = Extended DOS partition
			06H = DOS (more than 32Mb)
			07H = OS/2 High-Performance File System
05H	Byte	H	Ending head number
06H	Byte	S	Ending sector number
07H	Byte	C	Ending cylinder number
08H	DWord	SP	Number of sectors preceding this partition
0CH	DWord	N	Number of sectors in this partition

Figure 4.3 shows a hex dump of the partition table on a 40Mb hard disk set up by DOS 5.0 as one large 40Mb partition. The boot indicator is set to 80H to mark this (the only one on the hard disk) as the active partition. The system indicator byte is 06H, identifying this as a DOS partition larger than 32Mb. The partition starts at head 1, sector 1, cylinder 0, and is 142B0H, or 82,608, sectors long. That checks out with what we know the length of partition to be, for one sector is 512 bytes long. The remaining partition table entries are zeroed out, indicating no additional partitions are defined.

FIGURE 4.3

Sample partition table

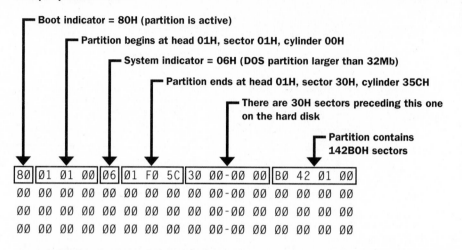

Extended DOS Partitions If you want a hard disk to contain more than one logical drive, you must set up an extended DOS partition. The difference between a primary DOS partition and an extended DOS partition is that the extended DOS partition may be divided up into several logical drives, while the primary one may not. Rather than identifying the location of a physical partition, the starting head, sector, and cylinder numbers for an extended DOS partition identify the location of another partition table that describes a logical volume. If there are additional logical drives defined in the extended DOS partition, the second entry in this pseudo-partition table contains the address of yet another partition table holding information about the next logical drive. Partition tables may be chained together as many levels deep as is required to fully describe all the logical drives defined in an extended DOS partition.

The hex dump in Figure 4.4 shows the chain of partition table entries on a 40Mb hard disk that contains a 20Mb primary DOS partition and a 20Mb extended DOS partition. The extended DOS partition is subdivided into two 10Mb logical drives.

The master partition table contains entries for one type 04H partition (the primary DOS partition) and one extended (type 05H) partition. Reading the sector whose address is head 00H, sector 41H, cylinder ABH (the numbers spelled out for the starting head, sector, and cylinder in the entry for the extended DOS partition) reveals partition table number 2, which contains two entries: one for a type 01H partition and one for a type 05H partition. The type 01H partition is the first logical drive in the extended DOS partition. Reading the starting sector for the type 05H partition reveals yet another partition table, this one containing a single entry for a type 01H partition. This type 01H partition is the second of the two logical drives.

FIGURE 4.4

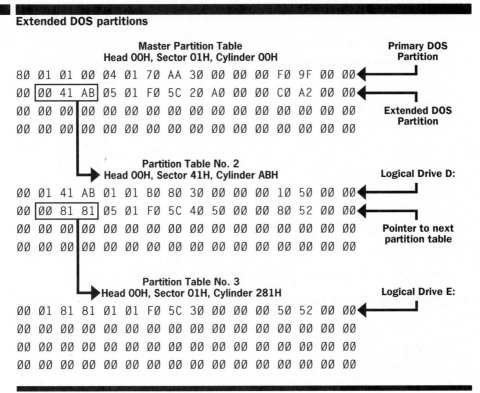

Extended DOS partitions

In DOS 5.0, you can get a glimpse of the partition tables on your hard disk by typing

```
UNFORMAT /PARTN /L
```

UNFORMAT will respond with one or more tables summarizing the contents of each of the partition tables it finds. The entry for each partition will tell you what type of partition it is and how large it is, the beginning and ending head, sector, and cylinder, and how many sectors precede this partition on the hard disk.

Partitioning Hard Drives with FDISK

The tool DOS provides for setting up and deleting hard-disk partitions is FDISK. There's nothing inherently difficult about running FDISK. It's menu driven, and it displays plain-English error messages when you attempt to do something illegal, such as create a primary DOS partition on a drive where a primary DOS partition already exists. In general, FDISK is used to

■ Create primary DOS partitions

- Create extended DOS partitions
- Create logical drives in extended DOS partitions
- Delete partitions and logical drives
- Set the active partition
- View partition information

Before you partition a new hard disk, you should decide how many logical drives you want set up for DOS and what size they should be. Then use the guidelines in the following sections to set up your hard disk accordingly. If you're upgrading to DOS 5.0 directly from version 3.3, you may want to repartition your hard disk to take advantage of DOS 5.0's support for greater-than-32Mb logical drives.

Creating a Primary DOS Partition   The first partition you'll create on a new hard disk is the primary DOS partition. Your hard disk must have a primary DOS partition if you plan to use DOS with it. To create a primary DOS partition, start FDISK. You'll see the menu shown in Figure 4.5.

FIGURE 4.5

The FDISK Options menu

```
                      FDISK Options


Current fixed disk drive: 1

Choose one of the following:

1. Create DOS Partition or Logical DOS Drive
2. Set active partition
3. Delete DOS Partition or Logical DOS Drive
4. Display partition information


Enter choice: [1]
```

The cursor will be positioned inside the square brackets after "Enter choice," waiting for you to type **1**, **2**, **3**, or **4** and press Enter. Select **1**. FDISK will then display the menu shown in Figure 4.6.

Select **1** and press Enter. FDISK will ask you if you wish to use all available space for the partition. If you want the entire disk set up as one logical drive, answer yes. If you want to create additional logical drives later or reserve room for a non-DOS operating system, answer no, and then tell FDISK how much space to allocate to the primary partition. This number may be expressed either as a number of megabytes or, by ending it with a percent sign, as a percentage of available disk space. Enter a number and FDISK will write the entry defining the primary DOS partition to the disk's master partition table. Then press Esc until you reach the FDISK Options menu shown in Figure 4.5.

FIGURE 4.6

The FDISK "Create DOS Partition or Logical DOS Drive" menu

```
                    Create DOS Partition or Logical DOS Drive

Current fixed disk drive: 1

Choose one of the following:

1. Create Primary DOS Partition
2. Create Extended DOS Partition
3. Create Logical DOS Drive(s) in the Extended DOS Partition


Enter choice: [1]
```

Setting the Active Partition   If the primary DOS partition you set up doesn't take up the entire disk, you'll need to make it the active partition (if it's the *only* partition on the hard disk, FDISK makes it the active partition by default). To do so, choose option **2** from FDISK's FDISK Options menu and enter **1** for the primary DOS partition.

It's not hard to guess what FDISK is doing here: It's writing the value 80H to the partition's boot indicator byte in the partition table. Once the partition is formatted, this will enable you to boot DOS from the hard disk.

Creating an Extended DOS Partition   If you didn't dedicate all available disk space to the primary DOS partition, you may use option 2 from FDISK's "Create DOS Partition or Logical DOS Drive" menu to create an extended DOS partition. You can't create an extended DOS partition unless a primary DOS partition already exists (the one exception occurs when you have more than one hard disk; only the first disk must have a primary DOS partition). If you try, FDISK will warn you that no primary DOS partition exists.

Setting up an extended DOS partition is similar to creating a primary DOS partition. FDISK asks you how much of the remaining disk space should be allocated to the extended DOS partition. If you don't plan to install other operating systems, accept the default, which allocates it all. In response, FDISK will write an entry for an extended DOS partition to the next available slot in the master partition table. But one step remains: Before you can address the extended DOS partition, you must use FDISK to establish logical drives inside it.

Creating Logical Drives in the Extended DOS Partition   Option number 3 under FDISK's "Create DOS Partition or Logical DOS Drive menu" permits you to assign one or more drive letters to the extended DOS partition. Since the primary partition is assigned the letter C, letters D through Z are available if there are no other hard disks in your system. You may use the entire extended DOS partition as one drive or break it up into as many as 23 logical drives.

FDISK will ask you how much space you want allocated to the first logical drive. If you want all available space allocated to it, press Enter to accept the default. If you don't, tell FDISK how much to allocate it. FDISK will continue prompting you for drive sizes (each time displaying the amount of space remaining on the disk as the default) until the entire extended DOS partition is allocated—or until you press Esc to end the process.

Deleting DOS Partitions   You may also use FDISK to delete partitions and remove logical drive assignments from extended DOS partitions. Pressing 3 on the FDISK Options menu displays the menu shown in Figure 4.7.

FIGURE 4.7

The FDISK "Delete DOS Partition or Logical DOS Drive" menu

```
            Delete DOS Partition or Logical DOS Drive

Current fixed disk drive: 1

Choose one of the following:

1.   Delete Primary DOS Partition
2.   Delete Extended DOS Partition
3.   Delete Logical DOS Drive(s) in the Extended DOS Partition
4.   Delete Non-DOS Partition


Enter choice: [ ]
```

If you choose to delete a primary DOS partition, FDISK will ask you for the partition number. If you elect to delete a logical drive instead, DOS will ask you for the drive letter to delete. Be very careful. *All* the files stored in the deleted areas will be lost. As a precaution, FDISK asks for the drive's label and will not delete the drive unless the label is entered correctly. If you want to preserve the information, back up the files first.

Older versions of DOS assumed that a partition that belonged to another operating system should only be deleted by that operating system, using its equivalent of FDISK. As a result, the DOS version of FDISK would not delete non-DOS partitions. The DOS 5.0 FDISK, however, provides an option for removing non-DOS partitions.

Why would you want to delete a partition or logical drive in the first place? Because if you want to change the way your hard disk is partitioned, you'll have to delete the old partitions first. If you decide to do this, be sure to back up everything in it before it's deleted. You can restore the backed-up files once the disk is repartitioned.

Viewing Partition Information   The final option under FDISK's "FDISK Options" menu—option number 4—lets you see how your hard disk is set up. For each partition that is defined, FDISK tells you whether the partition is the active one, what type of partition (primary DOS, extended DOS, or non-DOS) it is, what the partition's volume label is (if it's a primary DOS partition), how large the partition is (in megabytes), what type of file system it is set up with, and what percentage of the total disk space the partition consumes. If the disk contains an extended DOS partition, FDISK will display similar information for each of the logical drives defined.

SHARE.EXE and Large Partitions

DOS 4.0, the first version of DOS to support logical drives larger than 32Mb, recommended that SHARE.EXE be loaded on systems with large partitions. SHARE.EXE contained a module that prevented the inadvertent destruction of files stored in large partitions by programs that used file control blocks (FCBs) to read and write disk files.

In many cases, SHARE.EXE was loaded without users knowing it, consuming precious memory that could otherwise have been used for application programs. When DOS 4.0 booted up on a system whose hard disk contained large partitions and detected that SHARE.EXE had not been loaded, it automatically looked for SHARE.EXE in the root directory of the boot drive and in the location addressed by the SHELL directive in CONFIG.SYS. Failing that, it displayed the warning

```
WARNING! SHARE should be loaded for large media
```

warning you (somewhat ambiguously) to proceed at your own risk.

DOS 5.0 does not require that SHARE.EXE be installed on systems with large partitions. Instead, the component of SHARE.EXE that provided FCB fixups has been made part of the operating system kernel. That's good news to non-network users, who need protection from programs that use FCB file services, but don't need the excess baggage of SHARE.EXE's network file sharing services.

Hard-Disk Formatting

Before a logical drive created by FDISK may be used, it must be formatted with the FORMAT command. Formatting divides the drive into two areas: the *system area*, where system information is stored, and the *files area*, where files are stored. It also initializes the system area by writing information to the first sector in the logical volume (the *boot sector*), setting up two copies of the file allocation table (FAT), and creating the root directory.

Figure 4.8 shows the arrangement of these components. The boot sector is 512 bytes long and is always the first sector in the logical drive. It is followed by the FAT, whose length varies with the size of the logical drive. Two copies are maintained in case one of them is corrupted. The root directory is next; on hard disks, its length is always 16k, which provides enough room for 512 file and subdirectory entries to be recorded in the root directory.

FIGURE 4.8

Structure of a logical drive

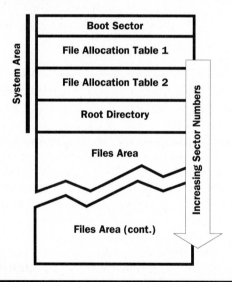

The Boot Sector   The boot sector contains a short program called the *bootstrap loader* that loads the DOS kernel into memory at start-up or displays the message

```
Non-System disk or disk error
Replace and press any key when ready
```

if the system files IO.SYS and MSDOS.SYS are nowhere to be found. It also contains a table known as the BIOS Parameter Block (BPB), which holds information about the logical structure of the disk (number of sectors in the disk, number of sectors per cluster, the size of the FAT and root directory, and more). Additional fields before and after the BPB contain data about the physical makeup of the disk and the signature of the brand and version of DOS that formatted the disk.

DOS uses the information in the BPB to determine what type of disk it's dealing with when a drive is accessed. For a hard disk, DOS only has to consult the BPB one time, because a hard disk can't be removed. But floppies may be inserted and removed at will, leaving it up to DOS to determine each time drive A is accessed, for example, whether the drive now holds a low-density 360k or perhaps a high-density 1.2 Mb disk. When it detects that a new disk has been inserted, DOS must rebuild the internal data structures it uses to access that disk. To do so, it rereads the boot sector and calls on functions in its own kernel to build the data structures based on information obtained from the BPB.

The File Allocation Table DOS views the area of a disk where files are stored as a collection of storage units called *clusters*. A cluster is a group of one or more sectors. On hard disks, clusters are typically four or eight sectors long, yielding, respectively, a 2k or 4k cluster size. When DOS writes a file to a disk, it copies the contents of the file to unused clusters in the files area. To keep track of which clusters are used and which ones remain available for file storage, DOS uses a structure called a *file allocation table*, or FAT. Think of the FAT as a roadmap to the files area. Each entry in the FAT corresponds to one cluster in the data area. If a FAT entry is 0, then the corresponding cluster is unused. If it's not 0, then the cluster is currently in use.

There are two types of FATs: FATs that use 12-bit entries and FATs that use 16-bit entries. A 16-bit FAT can handle a greater number of clusters than a 12-bit FAT, because a 16-bit number can form a value 16 times higher than the highest 12-bit number. When a logical drive is formatted, DOS decides what type of FAT to use based on the drive's size. In general, drives less than approximately 16Mb long are formatted with 12-bit FATs, while larger ones are formatted with 16-bit FATs.

To some extent, this method of divvying up space in the logical drive's files area is wasteful, because no file may be allocated less than a full cluster. A one-byte file will consume 4,096 bytes of disk space if the cluster size is 4k. But such allocation inefficiencies are offset by other factors, including shorter FATs and the ability to address more sectors than a one-to-one mapping of sectors to clusters would permit.

Every file stored on a disk is marked by a 32-byte directory entry that records the file's name, size, and other information. To map the location of a file on disk, DOS records the file's starting cluster number in a reserved field in the file's directory entry. Then it records the number of each cluster allocated to the file in the FAT entry for the previous cluster, establishing a chain of entries that, if traced from beginning to end, maps out (in sequence) every cluster that contains a piece of the file. The last cluster in every chain is marked with a special value that DOS recognizes as an end-of-chain token.

Let's say that DOS is asked to create a file on the disk that will require three clusters for storage, and that clusters 10H, 2AH, and 40H are the first three found to be free. DOS will create a new directory entry for the file and place the value 10H in the field reserved for the starting cluster number. Next, DOS will place a 2AH in FAT entry number 10H and a 40H in FAT entry number 2AH. Finally, it will terminate the chain of allocation entries by writing the value FFFFH (for 16-bit FATs) or FFFH (for 12-bit FATs) to FAT entry number 40H.

The beauty of the FAT system of file tracking is that files do not have to be stored in contiguous locations on disk. Instead, they can be fragmented as needed to make the most efficient use of disk space. Also, to erase a file from disk, DOS doesn't have to modify anything in the files area. It can simply zero out the entries in the FAT so that the space will be reused (and overwritten) by subsequent files.

Certain non-zero FAT entries have special meanings. Table 4.1 shows what they are. The hexadecimal digits in parentheses to the left of the entries appear in 16-bit FAT entries only. (F)FF7H marks bad clusters (clusters that contain bad sectors and shouldn't be used), while (F)FF0 through FFF6H mark clusters DOS chooses to reserve for any other purpose. (F)FF8 through FFFH indicates that this cluster is the last one in the chain. Any other non-zero entry is interpreted as the number of the next cluster in an allocation chain.

TABLE 4.1

File Allocation Table Entries

FAT Entry	Meaning
00H	Available cluster
(F)FF0 - FF6H	Reserved cluster
(F)FF7H	Bad cluster
(F)FF8 - FFFH	Last cluster in allocation chain
Any other non-zero value	Cluster in use by a file

The Root Directory   The root directory is the section of the disk where DOS stores the 32-byte entries that describe files and subdirectories in the root directory. Each entry stores the name of the associated file or subdirectory, its attributes (hidden, read-only, and so on), the time and date it was created or last updated, its size, and its starting cluster number.

Because the size of this area is set when the disk is formatted, all disks are limited to storing as many files in the disk's root directory as the size of this fixed-length area permits. On hard disks, the limit is 512 files. That's one reason it's wise not to clutter a hard disk's root directory with files, but to store files in subdirectories instead.

Formatting a Hard Disk

To format a primary DOS partition so that you can boot DOS from it, use the command

```
FORMAT d: /S [/V:label]
```

where *d:* is the partition's drive letter. The /S switch copies the system files IO.SYS, MSDOS.SYS, and COMMAND.COM to the partition so you can boot from it. Use the /V switch if you want to specify a volume label. If you don't specify a label, DOS will prompt you for one after formatting is complete. You can add a label at a later date (or change the current volume label) with DOS's LABEL command. The command

```
FORMAT C: /S /V:DOS-DISK-1
```

formats drive C, places the system files on it, and gives it the name DOS-DISK-1.

To format a logical drive in an extended DOS partition (or a primary partition on a second hard disk), use the same command, but leave off the /S switch. The command

```
FORMAT D: /V:DOS-DISK-2
```

formats logical volume D and gives it the name DOS-DISK-2. Omitting the system files from extended DOS partitions (which can't be booted from anyway) and from primary DOS partitions on secondary drives saves more than 100k of disk space.

As DOS formats a hard disk, it also checks for defective sectors that cannot reliably hold data. Those it finds it marks off by placing the code for a bad cluster (FF7H or FFF7H) in the FAT. Don't be alarmed if FORMAT reports several thousand bad bytes when it formats a hard disk. That's normal; hard disks are so voluminous, it's virtually impossible to manufacture a perfect one. Fortunately, the bad bytes won't affect any of the data you store on your hard disk, because DOS will keep your files safe.

Once the formatting process is complete, your hard disk is ready to be used by DOS. You should never have to format it again unless you repartition it (after a disk is repartitioned, the new partitions must be formatted) or unless the system area of the disk is damaged so badly that CHKDSK (DOS's disk diagnosis and repair utility) can't repair it. As a precaution, you should run CHKDSK on each logical volume periodically to ensure the volume's integrity and to catch problems before they become more severe. Later in this chapter, we'll look more closely at CHKDSK and at how you can use it to keep your hard disk running smoothly and reliably.

Adding an Unsupported Hard Drive to Your System

You can't add just any hard disk to any PC. A PC has to know certain things about the drive—how many heads, sectors, and cylinders there are; where the landing zone (the area the drive heads retract to when they're parked to avoid coming in contact with surfaces that contain data) is; and where write precompensation (the strengthening of the magnetic field written to the innermost cylinders of a disk to compensate for the higher data density near the center) begins. Usually this information is derived from the drive's *type number*.

If your PC is one of those that stores configuration information in CMOS RAM, its setup program will ask you for the drive type number. (CMOS RAM is battery-powered RAM used to store configuration data in most 286s and 386s.) The PC uses this number as an index into a table stored in ROM that defines the physical characteristics of several different types of drives. If a hard disk is characterized in ROM, adding it to the system is as easy as plugging it in and rerunning the setup procedure to notify the PC of the drive type.

Table 4.2 shows the drive types defined in IBM ROMs. The AT supports types 1 through 15; the XT/286, types 1 through 24; and the PS/2s, types 1 through 32. Drive types are specific to the BIOS, so a drive that's a type 20 on one PC may be a type 24 on another. Most clone-makers define drive types 1 through 15 the same way IBM does, for compatibility. One exception is Compaq, which defined its own drive tables to match Compaq-brand drives.

The manufacturer of your PC's BIOS can supply you with a list of supported drive types and thus, of the drives you may add to your PC. If you want to add a drive that is not supported, you have four options:

- Upgrade the ROM to a version that does support the drive.

- Use a third-party disk utility that adds support for drives that are not supported in ROM.

- Use a supported drive type number that matches the physical parameters of the new drive as closely as possible.

- Purchase one of the newer drives that uses sector translation to adapt itself to one of the other drive types.

A ROM upgrade is the most direct solution, provided a newer version is available that supports the drive in question. As an alternative, there are third-party programs available such as Ontrack Computer Systems' Disk Manager and Storage Dimensions' SpeedStor that enable you to use a drive even if it's not supported in ROM. These work well unless you run software that gets very close to the hardware (such as Windows) or run non-DOS operating systems (such as OS/2, UNIX, or NetWare).

The third alternative is to use a drive type that doesn't match the drive exactly, but comes close. If your drive has 1,024 cylinders, 5 heads, and 17 sectors per cylinder, for example, you could use IBM drive type 17 (977 cylinders, 5 heads, 17 sectors per cylinder). The drive would work—the first 977 cylinders, anyway. You'd lose the last 47 cylinders, amounting to about 2Mb of disk space.

But at least you'd be able to use the drive. It's important to pick a drive type with fewer cylinders than your drive actually has to ensure that the heads don't try to seek too far and that DOS isn't fooled into thinking the disk is larger than it really is.

TABLE 4.2

IBM Drive Types

Type	Heads	Sectors	Cylinders	Write Precomp	Landing Zone	Cap. (Mb)
1	4	17	306	128	305	10
2	4	17	615	300	615	21
3	6	17	615	300	615	31
4	8	17	940	512	940	64
5	6	17	940	512	940	48
6	4	17	615	None	615	21
7	8	17	462	256	511	31
8	5	17	733	None	733	31
9	15	17	900	None	901	115
10	3	17	820	None	820	21
11	5	17	855	None	855	36
12	7	17	855	None	855	51
13	8	17	306	128	319	21
14	7	17	733	None	733	44
15*	—	—	—	—	—	—
16	4	17	612	0	663	21
17	5	17	977	300	977	41
18	7	17	977	None	977	58
19	7	17	1,024	512	1,023	61
20	5	17	733	300	732	31
21	7	17	733	300	732	44
22	5	17	733	300	733	31
23	4	17	306	None	336	10
24	4	17	612	305	663	21
25	4	17	306	None	340	10
26	4	17	612	None	670	21
27	7	17	698	300	732	41
28	5	17	976	488	977	41
29	4	17	306	0	340	10
30	4	17	611	306	663	21
31	7	17	732	300	732	43

*Drive type 15 is reserved for unsupported drives

A fourth and final alternative is to purchase a drive that can make itself appear to have the same number of heads, sectors, and cylinders as one of the supported drive types using a process known as *sector translation*, in which logical sector numbers requested by the hard-disk BIOS are converted to physical sector numbers by the hard-disk controller. Many IDE drives offer this capability. If you install one of these drives as a type 9, the drive will automatically configure itself so that it appears to have 15 heads, 17 sectors per cylinder, and 900 cylinders.

Working with Floppy Disks

Its support for mass storage devices of various types, including a wide variety of floppy-disk formats, has long been one of DOS's strongest suits. Ignoring the now obsolete single-sided 160k and 180k floppy disks and double-sided 320k disks (all of which are still supported by DOS for compatibility reasons but none of which you're likely to see used on present-day systems), DOS 5.0 supports five different types of floppy disks:

- Double-density 5¼-inch disks (360k formatted capacity)

- Double-density 3½-inch disks (720k formatted capacity)

- High-density 5¼-inch disks (1.2Mb formatted capacity)

- High-density 3½-inch disks (1.44Mb formatted capacity)

- Extra-high-density 3½-inch disks (2.88Mb formatted capacity)

Future versions of DOS will undoubtedly add support for additional floppy-disk types, including the much talked-about 20Mb floppy that is just now emerging from the research labs.

On the surface, all floppy disks of a given size may appear the same. Hold a 720k 3½-inch disk in one hand and a 1.44Mb 3½-inch disk in the other, and the only difference you'll see is an extra hole in the casing of the latter identifying it as a high-density disk.

Inside, they're much different. High-density disks have higher-quality coatings than double-density disks, enabling flux transitions to be packed closer together on the surface of the disk. There is also a difference in the way DOS formats high-density and low-density disks. A 1.44Mb floppy is formatted with 18 sectors per track, while 720k floppies are only formatted with 9 sectors per track. For comparison purposes, Table 4.3 lists the numbers of tracks, sectors per track, and bytes per sector for all the double-sided disk formats DOS 5.0 supports.

TABLE 4.3

Physical Characteristics of Double-Sided Floppy Disks

Capacity	Tracks	Sectors Per Track	Bytes Per Sector
320k	40	8	512
360k	40	9	512
720k	80	9	512
1.2Mb	80	15	512
1.44Mb	80	18	512
2.88Mb	80	36	512

Knowing how many tracks, sectors per track, bytes per sector, and sides there are on a disk, you can calculate its capacity (in kilobytes) using this formula:

$$K = \frac{\text{Tracks} * (\text{Sectors/Track}) * (\text{Bytes/Sector}) * (\text{No. of Sides})}{1,024}$$

For double-sided disks with 512 bytes per sector like those listed in Table 4.3, this reduces to

```
K = Tracks * Sectors
```

Checking this calculation for a 1.44Mb disk yields 80 * 18, or 1,440k, which is equivalent to 1.44Mb.

In most respects, DOS treats a floppy just like a logical drive on a hard disk. A floppy contains a boot sector, two FATs, a root directory, and a files area. Except for the boot sector, the length of these areas is downsized to accommodate the lower capacity of the disk. Floppies do not contain partition tables, and therefore may not be partitioned. Also, you never need to low-level format a floppy because the drive controller performs the equivalent of a low-level format when you format the disk with the FORMAT command.

Formatting Floppy Disks

Like a hard disk, a floppy must be formatted before it can be used. The DOS 5.0 FORMAT command's handling of floppy disks is greatly improved over previous versions. You can now

- Specify the capacity the disk should be formatted to by using easy mnemonics rather than the old /N and /T switches. (Remember typing **FORMAT A: /T:80 /N:9** to format a 720k disk in a 1.44Mb drive?)

- Perform a quick format to reformat a disk that has been formatted before. This saves time by bypassing the surface scan performed when a new disk is initialized.

- Perform a safe format, which allows the disk to be unformatted should the need arise.

- Perform an unconditional format, which obliterates everything on the disk so that it cannot be unformatted.

The sections that follow describe how to use these formatting procedures and when they should be applied.

Formatting a Fresh, Never-Before-Formatted Disk To format a fresh, never-before-formatted disk, use a command of the form

```
FORMAT d: [/F:size] [/V:label] [/S]
```

where *d:* is a drive designator such as A or B; *size* specifies the capacity the disk is to be formatted to; *label* is the volume label you want attached to the disk; and /S copies the system files to the disk so it can be used to boot the PC. Including a /V switch and a volume label with the FORMAT command prevents FORMAT from asking you for a volume label when formatting is complete.

The *size* parameter enables you to format a disk to something other than the default capacity of the drive without knowing anything about the structure of the disk in terms of tracks and sectors. Valid values are shown in Table 4.4.

TABLE 4.4	

Valid Disk Sizes for the FORMAT Command

Disk Size	Parameter Following /F Switch
160k	160, 160K, or 160KB
180k	180, 180K, or 180KB
320k	320, 320K, or 320KB
360k	360, 360K, or 360KB
720k	720, 720K, or 720KB
1.2Mb	1200, 1200K, 1200KB, 1.2, 1.2M, or 1.2MB
1.44Mb	1440, 1440K, 1440KB, 1.44, 1.44M, or 1.44MB
2.88Mb	2880, 2880K, 2880KB, 2.88, 2.88M, or 2.88MB

Thus the command

```
FORMAT A: /F:1.44
```

formats the disk in drive A to 1.44Mb. This is only valid if the drive itself supports 1.44Mb media.

If you don't include an /F switch, DOS defaults to the highest capacity supported by the drive on most systems. The command

```
FORMAT A:
```

is sufficient to format, say, a 1.44Mb disk in a high-density 3½-inch drive, or a 1.2Mb disk in a high-density 5¼-inch drive. If you want to format a 720k disk in a 1.44Mb drive A, use the command

```
FORMAT A: /F:720
```

Internally, DOS will respond by formatting the disk with 9 sectors per track rather than the 18 it would use on a 1.44Mb disk.

Reformatting a Disk That Has Been Formatted Before   To reformat a disk in drive A that has been formatted before, use the command

```
FORMAT A: [/F:size] [/V:label] [/S]
```

Once again, you must use the /F switch to specify the capacity the disk should be formatted to if it's less than the capacity of the drive. Otherwise, DOS will attempt to format the disk to a higher-than-rated capacity.

When a disk is formatted for the second time, FORMAT applies a bit of intelligence to the formatting process. Rather than reinitialize the entire disk, it erases the record of the files from the FAT and root directory and leaves the files area of the disk largely intact. It also scans the disk for bad sectors and marks off any it finds. This is somewhat faster than the type of format performed on a new disk, because there's less writing to be done. It's also safer, because you can later recover the contents of the disk with the UNFORMAT command if you discover you formatted the wrong floppy. For this reason, DOS calls this a *safe format*.

Quick Formatting   To quickly reformat the disk in drive A, type

```
FORMAT /Q [/V:label] [/S]
```

The /Q parameter tells DOS to perform a *quick format*. This time, there's no need for an /F switch because DOS formats the disk to the same capacity it was formatted to the first time. Quick formatting works just like a safe format, except that it skips the surface scan so it can proceed from start to finish in seconds. If you want to erase a disk that contains subdirectories, FORMAT /Q is considerably faster than DEL ERASE. The UNFORMAT command can also be used to unformat a quick-formatted disk. You can speed the formatting process even more by combining the /Q and /U switches. However, a disk formatted this way cannot be unformatted reliably.

Unconditional Formatting   When it formats a disk for the first time, FORMAT performs what DOS calls an *unconditional format*. FORMAT fills in the disk's boot sector, writes 0's to the FAT and root directory (except for the reserved bytes at the beginning of the FAT), and writes F6's to the files area. It also scans the files area of the disk for bad sectors.

When it reformats a disk, FORMAT defaults to a safe format. But you can force a full, unconditional format on a preformatted disk by including a /U switch with the FORMAT command. The command:

```
FORMAT A: /U
```

unconditionally reformats the disk in drive A, completely destroying all the data on it. Be careful: An unconditionally formatted disk can't be reconstructed with the UNFORMAT command. The /U switch is useful when you want to dispose of a floppy and make sure no one else can recover the files on it.

The hex dumps in Figures 4.9 through 4.11 illustrate the difference between safe and unconditional formats. Each listing shows the first 64 bytes in the boot sector, FAT, root directory, and files area of a 1.44Mb disk. Figure 4.9 shows what these areas look like with several files stored on the disk.

Figure 4.10 shows what the disk looks like after being unconditionally formatted, which is exactly how it would appear had it just been formatted for the first time. Entries in the FAT and root directory are zeroed, while everything in the data area of the disk is overwritten with F6's. The listing in Figure 4.11 shows the same areas of the disk after a safe format. The FAT and root directory entries are gone, but the data area appears exactly as it did before the format. This, combined with information FORMAT stored elsewhere on the disk, allows UNFORMAT to restore the floppy to the condition it was in before the format occurred.

FIGURE 4.9

System area and files area before reformatting

```
                    Boot Sector

EB 3C 90 4D 53 44 4F 53-35 2E 30 00 02 01 01 00    .<.MSDOS5.0.....
02 E0 00 40 0B F0 09 00-12 00 02 00 00 00 00 00    ...@............
00 00 00 00 00 00 29 CC-11 14 15 4E 4F 20 4E 41    ......)....NO NA
4D 45 20 20 20 20 46 41-54 31 32 20 20 20 FA 33    ME    FAT12   .3


                 File Allocation Table

F0 FF FF 03 40 00 05 60-00 07 80 00 09 A0 00 0B    ....@..`........
C0 00 0D E0 00 0F 00 01-11 20 01 13 40 01 15 60    ......... ..@..`
01 17 80 01 19 A0 01 1B-C0 01 1D E0 01 1F 00 02    ................
21 20 02 23 40 02 25 60-02 27 80 02 29 A0 02 2B    ! .#@.%`.'..)..+


                   Root Directory

46 4F 52 4D 41 54 20 20-43 4F 4D 20 00 00 00 00    FORMAT  COM ....
00 00 00 00 00 00 A0 28-68 16 02 00 B1 80 00 00    .......(h.......
4B 45 59 42 20 20 20 20-43 4F 4D 20 00 00 00 00    KEYB    COM ....
00 00 00 00 00 00 A0 28-68 16 43 00 8A 3A 00 00    .......(h.C..:..


                    Files Area

E9 3B 80 43 6F 6E 76 65-72 74 65 64 00 00 00 00    .;.Converted....
4D 5A 26 00 41 00 00 00-20 00 F9 00 FF FF D4 08    MZ&.A... .......
80 00 00 00 10 00 C6 07-1E 00 00 00 01 00 00 00    ................
00 00 00 00 00 00 00 00-00 00 00 00 00 00 00 00    ................
```

Adding the System Files After Formatting

If you want to add the DOS system files to a hard disk or floppy that wasn't formatted with an /S switch, you can do so with the SYS command. To copy the system files from drive C to drive A and make the disk in drive A bootable, type

```
SYS C: A:
```

or, if C is already the default drive, simply type

```
SYS A:
```

which tells DOS to copy the system files from drive C to the disk in drive A. SYS copies the three system files IO.SYS, MSDOS.SYS, and COMMAND.COM to the indicated disk (this is an improvement on previous versions of DOS, which only copied IO.SYS and MSDOS.SYS and left it to you to copy COMMAND-.COM). In DOS 5.0, this works on any disk with enough free space to hold the system files, even if the first two slots in the root directory (the only location that IO.SYS and MSDOS.SYS can go) are already occupied. If SYS informs you that it couldn't transfer COMMAND.COM onto the target disk, make sure that the COMSPEC environment variable is pointing to a directory that contains a valid copy of COMMAND.COM and that there is sufficient free space on the disk to store that file.

FIGURE 4.10 ▬▬▬▬▬▬▬▬▬▬▬▬▬▬▬▬▬▬▬▬▬▬▬▬▬▬▬▬

System area and files area after unconditional formatting

```
                        Boot Sector
EB 3C 90 4D 53 44 4F 53-35 2E 30 00 02 01 01 00    .<.MSDOS5.0.....
02 E0 00 40 0B F0 09 00-12 00 02 00 00 00 00 00    ...@...........
00 00 00 00 00 00 29 CC-11 14 15 4E 4F 20 4E 41    ......)....NO NA
4D 45 20 20 20 20 46 41-54 31 32 20 20 20 FA 33    ME    FAT12   .3

                    File Allocation Table
F0 FF FF 00 00 00 00 00-00 00 00 00 00 00 00 00    ...............
00 00 00 00 00 00 00 00-00 00 00 00 00 00 00 00    ...............
00 00 00 00 00 00 00 00-00 00 00 00 00 00 00 00    ...............
00 00 00 00 00 00 00 00-00 00 00 00 00 00 00 00    ...............

                       Root Directory
00 00 00 00 00 00 00 00-00 00 00 00 00 00 00 00    ...............
00 00 00 00 00 00 00 00-00 00 00 00 00 00 00 00    ...............
00 00 00 00 00 00 00 00-00 00 00 00 00 00 00 00    ...............
00 00 00 00 00 00 00 00-00 00 00 00 00 00 00 00    ...............

                         Files Area
F6 F6 F6 F6 F6 F6 F6 F6-F6 F6 F6 F6 F6 F6 F6 F6    ...............
F6 F6 F6 F6 F6 F6 F6 F6-F6 F6 F6 F6 F6 F6 F6 F6    ...............
F6 F6 F6 F6 F6 F6 F6 F6-F6 F6 F6 F6 F6 F6 F6 F6    ...............
F6 F6 F6 F6 F6 F6 F6 F6-F6 F6 F6 F6 F6 F6 F6 F6    ...............
```

FIGURE 4.11

System area and files area after safe formatting

```
                      Boot Sector
EB 3C 90 4D 53 44 4F 53-35 2E 30 00 02 01 01 00    .<.MSDOS5.0.....
02 E0 00 40 0B F0 09 00-12 00 02 00 00 00 00 00    ...@...........
00 00 00 00 00 00 29 CD-11 14 26 4E 4F 20 4E 41    ......)...&NO NA
4D 45 20 20 20 20 46 41-54 31 32 20 20 20 FA 33    ME    FAT12   .3

                 File Allocation Table
00 FF FF 00 00 00 00 00-00 00 00 00 00 00 00 00    ................
00 00 00 00 00 00 00 00-00 00 00 00 00 00 00 00    ................
00 00 00 00 00 00 00 00-00 00 00 00 00 00 00 00    ................
00 00 00 00 00 00 00 00-00 00 00 00 00 00 00 00    ................

                   Root Directory
00 00 00 00 00 00 00 00-00 00 00 00 00 00 00 00    ................
00 00 00 00 00 00 00 00-00 00 00 00 00 00 00 00    ................
00 00 00 00 00 00 00 00-00 00 00 00 00 00 00 00    ................
00 00 00 00 00 00 00 00-00 00 00 00 00 00 00 00    ................

                    Files Area
E9 F3 80 43 6F 6E 76 65-72 74 65 64 00 00 00 00    .;.Converted....
4D 5A 26 00 41 00 00 00-20 00 F9 00 FF FF D4 08    MZ&.A... .......
80 00 00 00 10 00 C6 07-1E 00 00 00 01 00 00 00    ................
00 00 00 00 00 00 00 00-00 00 00 00 00 00 00 00    ................
```

Formatting Floppy Disks to Higher-Than-Rated Capacities

Most high-density 3½-inch drives will format 720k disks to 1.44Mb, usually without error. Having discovered this, many users routinely substitute 720k disks for 1.44Mb disks, rather than pay the premium price manufacturers demand for high-density disks.

There are physical differences in 720k and 1.44Mb disks that could cause trouble, however. High-density disks have higher-quality, finer-grained coatings that permit the flux transitions representing binary 1's and 0's on the surface of the disk to be packed closer together. The closer these flux transitions can be placed, the more data the disk can hold. 720k disks have slightly inferior coatings that were not designed for high-density bit spacing.

One measurement of coating quality is *surface coercivity*. In physics, coercivity is defined as the magnitude of the opposing magnetic force required to remove the residual magnetism from a saturated magnetic material. In magnetic media, coercivity is a measure of the magnetic field required to force a flux transition (or the resistivity that flux transition displays to being changed once it's written to the disk).

The coercivity of a typical 1.44Mb disk measures 700 oersted (an *oersted* is a unit of magnetic intensity, named after 19th-century physicist Hans Christian Oersted). The coercivity of a typical 720k disk is about 100 oersted less. As a result, the flux transitions on the surface of a 720k disk formatted to 1.44Mb may not be able to withstand the force enacted on them by neighboring flux transitions, and may, over time, begin to cancel each other out. This is called self-erasure, because data on the disk will mysteriously disappear for no apparent reason.

Another problem with using double-density disks in place of high-density disks is the result of the tight tolerances placed on bit timings. As a disk spins inside a drive, flux transitions in the disk's magnetic coating cause electromagnetic pulses in the drive head, which are interpreted by the drive as bits of data with the value 1. The absence of a pulse is interpreted as a bit with the value 0. Timing (and the precise placement of flux transitions on the disk) is critical, because the drive must know when it's time for the next pulse to appear to distinguish 1's from 0's. Pulses, or the lack thereof, must occur within the narrow windows of time when the drive electronics are looking for them. The higher head current used to write to high-density disks sometimes saturates double-density coatings, blurring pulses to the point that the drive can't pick them up within the window of time allotted. Bits that miss this window are lost. Conversely, pulses may also occur when none are expected. Either way, the result is data error.

Despite such risks, IBM PS/2s willingly format 720k disks to 1.44Mb unless you use an /F switch with the FORMAT command. IBM elected not to build into the PS/2 family the inexpensive optical sensors needed to differentiate between high-density and double-density media. In 3½-inch disks these optical sensors detect the *high-density indicator hole* (opposite the hole that houses the write-protect tab) that distinguishes high-density from double-density disks.

Some users resort to drilling holes in 720k disks to fool their drives into thinking they're genuine 1.44Mb disks. This is dangerous. At best, these disks are subject to the same physical limitations that all other 720k disks are. At worst, particles of plastic could fall into the disk's housing and damage the magnetic coating, leading to surface defects and eventual data loss.

The new 2.88Mb extra-high-density disks supported in DOS 5.0 combine a fundamentally different type of coating with a new recording technology to achieve data densities twice that of conventional HD 3½-inch disks. On DD and HD 3½-inch disks, bits are recorded when needle-shaped particles lying in the plane of the disk are polarized from end to end. ED coatings, however, contain barium ferrite particles, which are polarized from top to bottom—perpendicular to the plane of the disk. Toshiba, the developer of the barium ferrite disk, calls this *perpendicular recording technology*. Because the barium ferrite particles are hexagon-shaped, they can be packed closer together than the long, slender particles in conventional coatings. This tighter packing is responsible for the higher data capacities.

Copying a Disk's Contents from One Drive to Another

You can copy the contents of one floppy to another floppy of the same type with the DISKCOPY command. The command

```
DISKCOPY A: B:
```

performs a sector-by-sector copy of the disk in drive A, faithfully duplicating it in drive B. Adding a /V switch to the command turns verify on, which has DISKCOPY read back what it writes to the target disk to make sure it was written correctly. It also slows the copying process down and is therefore rarely used.

You cannot use DISKCOPY to copy data between unlike disk types. It will not, for example, copy a 360k disk to a 720k disk. Nor can you use it on hard disks. You can always fall back to the COPY command to copy everything from one disk to another, but it becomes unwieldy if the source disk contains subdirectories as well as files. COPY leaves it to you to create the subdirectories on the destination disk and to copy the files one subdirectory at a time.

You can copy everything from one disk to another, regardless of disk types, with DOS's XCOPY command (XCOPY is examined in detail in Chapter 5). To copy all the files from A to B, type

```
XCOPY A:\ B: /S /E
```

The /S switch tells XCOPY to reproduce subdirectories and their contents on the destination disk; /E tells it to do so even if those subdirectories are empty. Since the starting point on drive A is the root directory, the /S switch will encompass everything on the disk. When you use this method of transferring files from one disk to another, note that XCOPY, unlike DISKCOPY, does not copy hidden or system files.

Swapping Drives with ASSIGN

Despite the general increase in the sophistication of software packages we've seen over the past few years, there are still a few dinosaurs out there—primarily game programs and installation utilities—that insist on running from or retrieving data from drive A or B. The problem is that it's not always possible to accommodate such requirements. How do you run an installation program provided on a 5¼-inch disk, for example, if it won't run from anywhere but drive A, and the A drive on your PC is a 3½-inch drive?

The ASSIGN command provides an easy solution. The command

```
ASSIGN A=B
```

reroutes every disk access intended for drive A to drive B. This is a quick fix for programs that want to run from drive A but can only run from drive B on your system. Conversely, the command

```
ASSIGN B=A
```

lets a program that thinks it's running in drive B be run from drive A instead. To unassign all drives, type **ASSIGN** by itself on the command line. All redirection will be canceled. To get a list of current ASSIGNed drives, type **ASSIGN /STATUS**.

ASSIGN is a risky command to use. Running BACKUP, RESTORE, LABEL, JOIN, or SUBST on ASSIGNed drives can be disastrous. Microsoft recommends that you use SUBST instead of ASSIGN, because SUBST is guaranteed to be compatible with future versions of DOS, while ASSIGN is not. (SUBST is examined in detail in Chapter 5.) The command

```
SUBST A: B:\
```

is equivalent to ASSIGN A=B, serving to redirect accesses from drive A to drive B. The only limitation in using SUBST this way is that the first drive letter following the SUBST command cannot be the current drive.

Neither ASSIGN nor SUBST will be of any help when it comes to running self-booting game programs from drive B rather than drive A. For these commands to be effective, DOS has to be booted and running. But self-booting programs boot themselves rather than DOS. There are commercial programs available that permit PCs to boot off drive B specifically for this purpose. An equally workable but far more awkward solution is to swap drive connectors internally so that drive A becomes drive B and vice versa. PCs that store configuration information in CMOS RAM would need to be notified of the change through their setup programs.

Adding a New Floppy Drive to Your System

If you add a floppy drive to your system that is not supported by the BIOS, you'll need to install DRIVER.SYS with a DEVICE or DEVICEHIGH command in CONFIG.SYS to let DOS know what type of drive it is. The full syntax for DRIVER.SYS is documented in Appendix B. The command

```
DEVICE=C:\DOS\DRIVER.SYS /D:2 /F:7
```

adds a third drive (a 1.44Mb drive) to a system that already contains two floppy drives. /D:2 tells DOS that the drive is the third physical drive (0=first, 1=second, 2=third, and so on), and /F:7 identifies it as a 1.44Mb drive. Similarly, the command

```
DEVICE=C:\DOS\DRIVER.SYS /D:2 /F:1
```

adds a 1.2Mb drive to the system. The new drive assumes the lowest available drive letter. If your hard disk contains a primary DOS partition (drive C) and an extended DOS partition with two logical drives (drives D and E), and there are no RAM disks or other block devices loaded before DRIVER.SYS, then the drive installed with DRIVER.SYS will become drive F:. Many add-on drives come with their own device drivers that may be used in lieu of DRIVER.SYS if desired.

Another use for DRIVER.SYS is to assign a second drive letter to an existing drive so that files can be copied from one disk to another in the same drive. Let's say, for example, that you have two floppy-disk drives in your system—A and B—and that drive A is a 1.44Mb drive and drive B is a 1.2Mb drive. To set up your system so you could copy files from one 1.44Mb disk to another, add the statement

```
DEVICE=C:\DOS\DRIVER.SYS /D:0 /F:7
```

to CONFIG.SYS. Then, assuming the new logical drive created by DRIVER.SYS was assigned drive letter F, you could copy files to and from disks in drive A by entering

```
COPY A:*.* F:
```

DOS will prompt to insert disks for drives A and F as required. Note that if your system is only equipped with one floppy drive, DOS automatically creates a logical drive B that is equivalent to drive A. Under such circumstances, DRIVER.SYS is not required.

Protecting and Preserving Disk Data

DOS provides an assortment of tools for protecting files stored on disks and for recovering them if something goes wrong. BACKUP and RESTORE let you back up hard-disk data to floppies; RECOVER lifts files from damaged disks; and CHKDSK scans a disk for logical errors (errors in the disk's FAT or directory entries) and helps repair trouble spots when they do occur. In addition, the new UNDELETE, UNFORMAT, and MIRROR utilities supplied with DOS 5.0 are capable of restoring most erased files, reversing accidental formats, and restoring corrupted hard-disk partition tables. If you know how to use these utilities, you'll be able to work your way through 90 percent of the trouble you'll ever encounter—or, if you're willing to make regular backups of your data, potentially *all* the trouble you'll ever encounter.

Backing Up and Restoring Hard-Disk Data

When hard-disk trouble strikes, the best defense is a backup of your files. Make no mistake about it: Every hard disk will fail. It may be a matter of months or it may be years. But eventually something inside will wear out—maybe the head mechanism, maybe the drive electronics, maybe the magnetic coating on the platters. If you're not prepared, you'll lose everything stored there.

DOS 5.0 provides two utilities for backing up and restoring hard-disk data: BACKUP and RESTORE. They're not as flashy as third-party backup programs, nor are they as fast, but they do get the job done. Used properly, these programs provide the best and most effective insurance there is against data loss.

Backing Up Hard-Disk Data   The BACKUP command lets you back up hard-disk data to floppies. If you wish, you may also back files up to another hard disk or even back up one floppy to another. The full syntax for the DOS 5.0 version of BACKUP is

```
BACKUP source destination [/S] [/M] [/A] [/F[:size]]
     [/D:date [/T:time]] [/L[:log]]
```

where *source* is the name and location of the files to be backed up (for example, C:*.* or C:\DATA*.WK1) and *destination* is the drive the files are to be copied to (for example, A:). All command-line switches are optional. These switches and their meanings are summarized in Table 4.5.

TABLE 4.5

BACKUP Command-Line Switches

Switch	Description
/S	Back up the source directory and all subdirectories stemming from it.
/M	Back up only those files that have been modified since the last backup (only those files whose archive bits are set).
/A	Add backed-up files to the destination disks without destroying the backups already there.
/F[:size]	Format the destination disks. If the disks need to be formatted to a capacity lower than the maximum capacity the drive supports, include a *size* switch specifying the desired formatted capacity. Valid values for *size* are

Capacity	Parameter Following /F Switch
160k	160, 160K, or 160KB
180k	180, 180K, or 180KB
320k	320, 320K, or 320KB
360k	360, 360K, or 360KB
720k	720, 720K, or 720KB
1.2Mb	1200, 1200K, 1200KB, 1.2, 1.2M, or 1.2MB
1.44Mb	1440, 1440K, 1440KB, 1.44, 1.44M, or 1.44MB
2.88Mb	2880, 2880K, 2880KB, 2.88, 2.88M, or 2.88MB

Switch	Description
/D:date	Back up only those files that were modified on or after the specified date.
/T:time	Back up only those files that were modified at or after the specified time.
/L[:log]	Write a log file summarizing the latest backup operation. If this switch appears on the command line but *log* (the name and location of the log file) isn't specified, the log is created in the root directory of the source drive with the name BACKUP.LOG.

As BACKUP runs, it keeps you posted on its progress by showing what file is being backed up. If there is information on the destination drive that will be destroyed by the backup, BACKUP warns you and gives you a chance to abort the procedure. The transcript of a typical session appears in Figure 4.12. In this example, the /L switch is used to create a log file called BACKUP.LOG in the

\MISC directory of the C drive. The contents of this file are shown in Figure 4.13. The log tells you that the backup was performed at 12:07 P.M. on October 19, 1990. It also lists all the files backed up to disk number 01.

FIGURE 4.12

A typical BACKUP session

```
C:>BACKUP C:\UTIL\*.* A: /L:C:\MISC\BACKUP.LOG

Insert backup diskette 01 in drive A:

WARNING! Files in the target drive
A:\ root directory will be erased
Press any key to continue . . .

*** Backing up files to drive A: ***
Diskette number: 01

Logging to file C:\MISC\BACKUP.LOG

\UTIL\PRN2FILE.COM
\UTIL\BROWSE.COM
\UTIL\DR.COM
\UTIL\MSCOPE.EXE
\UTIL\TOGGLE.COM
\UTIL\LL.COM
\UTIL\SYSCTRL.COM
\UTIL\PICEM.EXE
\UTIL\EXECBOOK.COM
```

If more than one disk is required for the backup, BACKUP will prompt you to insert new ones as needed. It's important that you write the BACKUP disk number on each disk's label, so you can keep the disks in sequence. RESTORE—the counterpart to BACKUP that copies the files back to the hard disk—requires that the disks be reinserted in numeric order.

If you list the directory of the first floppy that you use for a backup, you will see two files listed: BACKUP.001 and CONTROL.001. BACKUP.001 contains the backed-up files, compressed into a single file to conserve disk space. CONTROL.001 contains information about the backup that will be used when the files are RESTOREd. The three-digit file extension—.001—indicates that this is disk number 1. If the disks get shuffled or if you forget to label them, you can use this file extension to determine the disk number.

FIGURE 4.13

A BACKUP log file

```
10-19-1990 12:07:08
001 \UTIL\PRN2FILE.COM
001 \UTIL\BROWSE.COM
001 \UTIL\DR.COM
001 \UTIL\MSCOPE.EXE
001 \UTIL\TOGGLE.COM
001 \UTIL\LL.COM
001 \UTIL\SYSCTRL.COM
001 \UTIL\PICEM.EXE
001 \UTIL\EXECBOOK.COM
```

Should you later decide to use a floppy that contains these backup files for something other than restoring data to the hard disk, you're in for a surprise if you try to delete BACKUP.001 or CONTROL.001. DOS will respond to the DEL command with the error message "Access denied." The reason? BACKUP makes the files read-only, which prevents DEL from erasing them. To work around this, first type

```
ATTRIB -R A:*.*
```

to convert them to normal files (this assumes the floppy is in drive A). Then the DEL command will work.

In general, BACKUP will copy any type of file, including hidden files. It will not, however, make backup copies of the three system files IO.SYS, MSDOS.SYS, and COMMAND.COM. This is to prevent it from inadvertently overwriting the system files on a disk that has undergone a DOS upgrade since the last backup.

Making Full Backups of Hard-Disk Data   You can have BACKUP copy everything on drive C to floppies in drive A with the command

```
BACKUP C:\*.* A: /S
```

The C:*.* tells BACKUP to start with all the files in the root directory; /S tells it to back up the subdirectories stemming from the root directory (and all the files in them) as well.

If the floppies are not already formatted, BACKUP will format them for you as it goes. If you need them formatted to something less than the full capacity of the drive, add an /F switch specifying the size, as in:

```
BACKUP C:\*.* A: /S /F:1.44
```

BACKUP may also be used to back up individual files and subdirectories. To copy every file in the \WP\WPFILES directory of drive C, type

```
BACKUP C:\WP\WPFILES\*.* A:
```

If there are subdirectories stemming from \WP\WPFILES (for example, \WP\WPFILES\LETTERS and \WP\WPFILES\BUDGETS), you may want them backed up as well. Rather than issue one BACKUP for every area you want backed up, use the /S switch, which tells BACKUP to back up the specified directory and all subdirectories underneath it. The command

```
BACKUP C:\WP\WPFILES\*.* A: /S
```

copies everything from \WP\WPFILES on down.

Normally, BACKUP erases all files stored in the root directory of the destination disk before starting the backup, including files placed there by a previous backup operation. If you want to add the backup files to backup files already on the disk, use the /A switch. For example, if you want to back up the directories C:\WP\WPFILES, C:\123\DATA, and C:\DBASE\DATA onto one 2.88Mb floppy, use the commands

```
BACKUP C:\WP\WPFILES\*.* A:
BACKUP C:\123\DATA\*.* A: /A
BACKUP C:\DBASE\DATA\*.* A: /A
```

The first BACKUP command erases any old files on the disk in drive A before it starts. The second two, however, append data to the existing backup files by virtue of the /A switch.

When you use the /A switch, BACKUP prompts you to insert a disk in the destination drive with the message

```
Insert last backup diskette in drive A:
Press any key to continue . . .
```

Many users find this prompt confusing. What BACKUP is telling you is that you should place the highest-numbered backup disk in the drive. For example, if you have five backup disks labeled 01 through 05, disk number 05 should be inserted. If disk 05 is already in the drive, all you need to do is press Enter. What it's *not* telling you to do is remove the disk currently in the drive and insert disk number 04—the last disk if you interpret "last" to mean previous, not highest-numbered.

Making Incremental Backups of Hard-Disk Data   If you back up your hard disk regularly, you can save time by performing a full backup at specified intervals and incremental backups in between. An *incremental backup* backs up only those files that have changed since the last backup. By employing this strategy, you eliminate the redundant backing up of files that do not change often, or don't change at all.

The /M switch tells BACKUP to copy only files that have been modified since the disk was last backed up. The command

```
BACKUP C:\WP\WPFILES\*.* A: /S /M
```

backs up all the files on drive C that have changed since the last backup. The /M switch can be used in conjunction with all the other command-line switches. If /M is omitted, BACKUP backs up every file it finds, rather than just those that were modified.

How can BACKUP tell which files were modified and which ones weren't? Along with the name of each file that it stores on disk, DOS also stores a series of attribute bits that contain information about the file. One of these bits, the *archive bit*, is automatically set when a file is created or written to. When it's invoked with an /M switch, BACKUP inspects the archive bit of every file it encounters and backs up only those whose archive bits are set. Then it clears the archive bits so the same files won't be backed up again.

You can perform a similar type of backup—a *dated* backup—by leaving off the /M switch and specifying a date with the /D switch. This causes BACKUP to copy only files that are stamped with a date equal to or more recent than the one specified. In the United States, dates are entered in *mm-dd-yy* format. The commands

```
BACKUP C:\*.* /S A: /D:06-01-91
BACKUP C:\*.* /S A: /D:06-01-1991
BACKUP C:\*.* /S A: /D:06/01/1991
BACKUP C:\*.* /S A: /D:06/01/91
```

are all valid. If your CONFIG.SYS file contains a COUNTRY directive to configure your PC for use in another country, this format may vary (the COUNTRY directive and the time and date formats used outside the United States are summarized in Chapter 2). For example, if CONFIG.SYS contains the line

```
COUNTRY=049
```

to configure your PC for use in Germany, dates should be entered in *dd.mm.yy* format. There, the BACKUP command equivalent to the ones just listed would be

```
BACKUP C:\*.* /S A: /D:01.06.1991
```

or simply

```
BACKUP C:\*.* /S A: /D:01.06.91
```

For even more precise control over dated backups, BACKUP also permits you to specify a time with a /T switch. Only files stamped with a time equal to or later than the time specified are backed up. The format that time is entered in following the /T switch also depends on the COUNTRY setting of your PC. For sample time and date formats, refer to your DOS manual or to Table 2.2 in this book.

One way in which BACKUP differs from the COPY and XCOPY commands is that it will split files among floppies to make use of all available storage space. It will even copy files larger than the floppies the files are being written to. If you ever need to transport a file from one PC to another via floppy, but the file is too large to fit on the highest-capacity floppy you have at your disposal, use BACKUP to split it among two or more floppies. Then, at the destination, use RESTORE to splice the pieces back together on the hard disk.

Restoring Files from Backups When the time comes to restore your backed-up files to your hard disk, you can't simply copy them back to the disk with the COPY command as you would normal files. BACKUP stores them in a special format designed to make the most efficient use of disk space, requiring a special utility to restore the files to their original formats. This "special utility" is DOS's RESTORE command. Its syntax is

```
RESTORE source destination [/S] [/P] [/M] [/N]
    [/B:date] [/A:date] [/E:time] [/L:time] [/D]
```

This time, *source* is the drive where the backup files will be read from, and *destination* is both the drive to which the files should be restored and the names and locations of the files to be restored. The functions of all of RESTORE's command-line switches are summarized in Table 4.6.

RESTORE's /S switch works like the /S switch on BACKUP to recursively restore the indicated files in the specified directory and all the directories beneath it. To restore an entire hard disk, use the command

```
RESTORE A: C:\*.* /S
```

This assumes that you'll be inserting the backup disks in drive A and that the destination disk is drive C. Note that the file specification is entered *after* the drive specifier, just the opposite of where it is entered for the BACKUP command. This way, you can selectively restore a portion of the files on a backup disk without restoring all of them. Once it is started, RESTORE will prompt you to insert backup disk 01, then 02, and so on, until the restoration is completed. If you want to see a list of the files that will be restored without actually restoring them, run RESTORE with a /D switch.

TABLE 4.6

RESTORE Command-Line Switches

Switch	Description
/S	Restore specified directory and all the subdirectories stemming from it.
/P	Prompt for confirmation before restoring files marked with read-only attributes. Also ask for confirmation before restoring files that have been modified since they were last backed up.
/M	Restore only those files modified since the last backup.
/N	Restore only those files that do not exist on the destination disk.
/B:*date*	Restore only those files that were modified on or before the specified date.
/A:*date*	Restore only those files that were modified on or after the specified date.
/E:*time*	Restore only those files that were modified at or earlier than the specified time.
/L:*time*	Restore only those files that were modified at or later than the specified time.
/D	Display a list of the files that will be restored.

You don't have to restore every file that was backed up. If you have a stack of ten backup disks and want to restore only the files that were backed up out of the \WP\WPFILES directory of drive C you could use the command

```
RESTORE A: C:\WP\WPFILES\*.*
```

To restore one particular file named LETTER.DOC rather than all the files in \WP\WPFILES, use the command

```
RESTORE A: C:\WP\WPFILES\LETTER.DOC
```

If you're not sure which of the ten disks the files reside on, refer to the log file created when BACKUP was run (provided you started it with an /L switch). Also note that the subdirectory names you provide to the RESTORE command must be the same subdirectory names the files were stored under before they were backed up.

If you encounter a defective disk while restoring files to a drive, RESTORE will choke and probably cause you to abort the restoration process. You can recover the files on subsequent disks by restarting RESTORE and inserting the disk after the one that's defective. RESTORE will respond with the message:

```
WARNING! Diskette is out of sequence
Replace diskette or continue if OK
```

Verify that you know the disk is out of sequence by pressing any key. RESTORE will resume file restoration with that disk and proceed with file restoration.

If you mix full and incremental backups, you must restore data in the proper sequence. First restore the data from the last full backup. Then, in separate operations, restore data from incremental backups performed since then, in the order that they were performed. For example, if you had created two incremental backups dated 6/1 and 6/15 since the last full one, restoring the hard disk would be a three-step process:

1. Restore the files from the full backup

2. Restore the files from the incremental backup dated 6/1

3. Restore the files from the incremental backup dated 6/15

Then—and only then—would the hard disk be restored to the state it was in on 6/15.

One way to avoid having to perform multiple restores is to use BACKUP's /A switch to append each incremental file backup to the backup files already created rather than start from scratch with a new set of disks. In other words, the first time you do an incremental backup, include the /A switch. Then, when BACKUP prompts you to insert the last disk in the series, insert the highest-numbered disk created by the last full backup. The next time you do an incremental backup, repeat the procedure but insert the highest-numbered disk from the last incremental backup, and so on. In the end, you'll have a single set of disks that contains everything you need to restore the hard disk to the state it was in on the date of the last incremental backup.

Devising and Implementing a Backup Strategy   How often you back up should be determined by how mission-critical your files are and how frequently they're updated. If they're extremely important (for example, if losing them would be disastrous for your company) and updated daily, consider performing a full backup once a week and an incremental backup once a day. At the other extreme, you may elect to perform a full backup once every month and an incremental at the close of each week.

It's prudent to use two complete sets of disks for backups rather than just one. Each time you perform a backup, alternate between sets of disks, always using the older set for the current backup and leaving the more recent set intact. When you perform a restore operation, use the set that contains the most recent backup. This way, if something goes wrong with the most recent set of disks, you've got a second set to fall back on with data that's only slightly less recent than the first.

The following batch files will help you meet these goals by making backups as painless as possible. You may need to modify them to suit particular needs. Nonetheless, the versions shown here provide a starting point to illustrate the principles and actions involved. With luck, you'll never need to use these backups to restore lost data. But if disaster does strike, you'll be prepared.

The first one, FBACKUP.BAT, performs a full backup of all the files on drives C and D. It assumes that the floppies used for the backup are preformatted and that you want log files placed in the root directories of the drives backed up. When the backup is complete, FBACKUP.BAT either prints the message "Backup successfully completed" or, if BACKUP returned an ERRORLEVEL code indicating an error occurred, a message reflecting the nature of the error.

LISTING 4.1

```
@ECHO OFF
REM ********************************************************
REM
REM FBACKUP.BAT backs up all the files on drives C and D
REM to floppies in drive A.  It writes log files to the
REM root directories of the backed-up drives.
REM
REM ********************************************************
ECHO Starting backup of drive C:...
BACKUP C:\*.* A: /S /L:C:\FBACKUP.LOG
IF ERRORLEVEL 4 GOTO ERROR4
IF ERRORLEVEL 3 GOTO ERROR3
IF ERRORLEVEL 2 GOTO ERROR2
IF ERRORLEVEL 1 GOTO ERROR1
ECHO Starting backup of drive D:...
BACKUP D:\*.* A: /S /L:D:\FBACKUP.LOG
IF ERRORLEVEL 4 GOTO ERROR4
IF ERRORLEVEL 3 GOTO ERROR3
IF ERRORLEVEL 2 GOTO ERROR2
IF ERRORLEVEL 1 GOTO ERROR1
GOTO DONE
:ERROR1
ECHO **** WARNING! ****
ECHO The drive contained no files to back up
GOTO END
:ERROR2
ECHO **** WARNING! ****
ECHO Some files were not backed up because of sharing conflicts
GOTO END
:ERROR3
ECHO **** WARNING! ****
ECHO BACKUP was terminated by a press of Ctrl-C
GOTO END
:ERROR4
ECHO **** ERROR! ****
ECHO BACKUP failed due to an unknown error
GOTO END
:DONE
```

```
ECHO **** Backup successfully completed ****
:END
```

The next batch file, IBACKUP.BAT, performs an incremental backup of all the files on drives C and D. Only files that have been modified since the last backup are backed up. Because the BACKUP commands include /A switches, you may use the same set of disks to store full and incremental backups and restore both the C and D drives with a single restore operation.

LISTING 4.2

```
@ECHO OFF
REM *********************************************************
REM
REM IBACKUP.BAT performs an incremental backup on all the
REM files on drives C and D to floppies in drive A.  Log
REM files are written to the root directories of the backed-
REM up drives.
REM
REM *********************************************************
ECHO Starting backup of drive C:...
BACKUP C:\*.* A: /S /M /A /L:C:\IBACKUP.LOG
IF ERRORLEVEL 4 GOTO ERROR4
IF ERRORLEVEL 3 GOTO ERROR3
IF ERRORLEVEL 2 GOTO ERROR2
IF ERRORLEVEL 1 GOTO ERROR1
ECHO Starting backup of drive D:...
BACKUP D:\*.* A: /S /M /A /L:D:\IBACKUP.LOG
IF ERRORLEVEL 4 GOTO ERROR4
IF ERRORLEVEL 3 GOTO ERROR3
IF ERRORLEVEL 2 GOTO ERROR2
IF ERRORLEVEL 1 GOTO ERROR1
GOTO DONE
:ERROR1
ECHO **** WARNING! ****
ECHO The drive contained no files to back up
GOTO END
:ERROR2
ECHO **** WARNING! ****
ECHO Some files were not backed up because of sharing conflicts
GOTO END
:ERROR3
ECHO **** WARNING! ****
ECHO BACKUP was terminated by a press of Ctrl-C
```

```
GOTO END
:ERROR4
ECHO **** ERROR! ****
ECHO BACKUP failed due to an unknown error
GOTO END
:DONE
ECHO **** Backup successfully completed ****
:END
```

Should you ever need to restore the backed-up files, use the next batch file, called RECALL.BAT. RECALL mirrors the procedure carried out in FBACKUP and IBACKUP with the RESTORE command to restore all the files on drives C and D from the most recent backup or backups.

LISTING 4.3

```
@ECHO OFF
REM ************************************************************
REM
REM RECALL.BAT restores all the files backed up from drives
REM C and D by FBACKUP.BAT or IBACKUP.BAT.
REM
REM ************************************************************
ECHO Starting restoration of drive C:...
RESTORE A: C:\*.* /S
IF ERRORLEVEL 4 GOTO ERROR4
IF ERRORLEVEL 3 GOTO ERROR3
IF ERRORLEVEL 1 GOTO ERROR1
ECHO Starting restoration of drive D:...
RESTORE A: D:\*.* /S
IF ERRORLEVEL 4 GOTO ERROR4
IF ERRORLEVEL 3 GOTO ERROR3
IF ERRORLEVEL 1 GOTO ERROR1
GOTO DONE
:ERROR1
ECHO **** WARNING! ****
ECHO RESTORE found no files to restore
GOTO END
:ERROR3
ECHO **** WARNING! ****
ECHO RESTORE was terminated by a press of Ctrl-C
GOTO END
:ERROR4
ECHO **** ERROR! ****
```

```
ECHO RESTORE failed due to an unknown error
GOTO END
:DONE
ECHO **** Restore successfully completed ****
:END
```

Recovering Files from Defective Disks

Unfortunately, disks can—and sometimes do—develop bad sectors through normal use. When DOS tries to read a file that contains a bad sector, it quits when it encounters the bad sector and displays a "Data error" or "Sector not found" message indicating that it was unable to read the file as directed. The kicker is that 99 percent of the file may be stored in undamaged sectors, but DOS refuses to read any part of it because of the one sector that's defective.

That's why DOS offers the RECOVER command. Run with a file name as its argument, RECOVER works its way through the file a cluster at a time, patching the disk's file allocation table as needed to work around the defective areas. When it's done, RECOVER leaves behind a modified version of the damaged file that is readable.

If, for example, you tried to copy the file BUDGET.WK1 from your hard disk to a floppy and DOS responded with a message indicating a read error had occurred, the command

```
RECOVER BUDGET.WK1
```

would allow you to recover all parts of the file that it is possible to recover. How much of it is successfully recovered depends on the length of the file and the number of bad sectors in the chain of clusters where the file is stored. A 200-byte file would be irretrievable, because the entire file is contained in one sector. A 20,000-byte file, however, might be recoverable except for one or two thousand bytes. To help you assess the damage, RECOVER reports how many bytes were in the original file and how many were recovered.

Although the recovered file is readable, it may not necessarily be usable by the application program that created it. It may be missing critical header information, or the program that created it may store data in a linked-list format that requires all parts of the file to be intact. If the file was a plain text file, you can probably reuse most or all of the data that was recovered. If it was an AutoCAD or Lotus 1-2-3 file, you may be out of luck.

The damage is more severe if a surface defect develops in the disk's root directory. If this happens, several files may be affected rather than just one. If subdirectories stored in the root directory are affected too, all or a large portion of the files on the disk may be lost. When disaster of this magnitude strikes, you can put RECOVER to work disk-wide, salvaging as many files as it can, by passing it a drive letter (rather than a file name) as an argument, like this:

```
RECOVER C:
```

This command recovers all recoverable data from the disk in drive C, but at a cost: The entire disk will be wiped out. RECOVER erases all files from the disk and recreates them in the root directory with the names FILE0001.REC, FILE0002.REC, and so on. The fact that the root directory of a hard disk is limited to 512 entries means that the maximum number of files RECOVER can recover using this method is 512. Should you have more files to recover, you can copy the 512 files to another disk or subdirectory, delete them from the root directory, and run RECOVER again, repeating the process as many times as needed to recover all the files on the disk.

It's up to you to browse through the files with DEBUG, a text editor, or whatever tools are at your disposal and determine what REC file is what—no easy task unless you're dealing with generic text files. Even files that didn't contain bad sectors may not be the same length they were before. Needless to say, RECOVER should only be used this way as a last resort. The last thing you'd ever want to do is type **RECOVER C:** by accident. Your entire C drive would be obliterated.

The bottom line: RECOVER is a helpful tool for recovering individual files from hard disks and from floppies inflicted with bad sectors. But don't attempt to RECOVER files from a disk with a damaged directory until you've exhausted all other means of file retrieval first. RECOVER warns you that the entire drive will be reconstructed and directories destroyed and asks if you're sure before it proceeds. Don't say yes unless you're prepared to deal with the consequences.

Analyzing and Correcting Disk Errors with CHKDSK

For diagnosing and repairing errors in a disk's file structures—errors in directory entries and file allocation tables—DOS provides the CHKDSK (pronounced "Check Disk") command. The most common use for CHKDSK is simply to check the disk for errors (in the pre–DOS 4.0 days, before there was a MEM command, CHKDSK was also used to get a reading on free memory). But CHKDSK is also capable of fixing most errors when they're found, albeit sometimes at the expense of some of the files stored on the disk.

Typing **CHKDSK C:** produces a report like the one in Figure 4.14. The report provides high-level disk statistics such as the amount of disk space, how much of it is available, how much of it is used and by how many files, and the number of bytes per cluster (CHKDSK calls clusters "allocation units"). And yes, it still reports the amount of conventional memory available and free.

But CHKDSK does more than this simple report implies. As it runs, CHKDSK looks for errors in the logical structure of the disk. It traces through the allocation chain for every file and subdirectory and makes sure that everything is intact. It checks for clusters that are referenced more than once and for clusters that are marked in the FAT but aren't referenced by a file. It checks for bad sectors in the FAT. It verifies that the dot and double-dot entries (representing the current subdirectory and its parent directory, respectively) are intact for every subdirectory. In short, it looks for nearly every error imaginable in the FAT and directory entries, and reports the errors it finds. What many users do not realize is that it does not check the files area of the disk where files are stored. A bad sector in that part of the disk will go undetected by CHKDSK unless there happens to be a file or subdirectory entry stored there.

FIGURE 4.14

The CHKDSK display

```
Volume DOS 5 DISK created 10-22-1990 4:18p
Volume Serial Number is 2875-17D8

42194944 bytes total disk space
   69632 bytes in 2 hidden files
  120832 bytes in 55 directories
25513984 bytes in 739 user files
16490496 bytes available on disk

    2048 bytes in each allocation unit
   20603 total allocation units on disk
    8052 available allocation units on disk

  655360 total bytes memory
  557856 bytes free
```

Run without an /F switch, CHKDSK runs in *diagnostic mode*. Errors are checked for but not corrected. In effect, a report like the one shown earlier, which doesn't contain error messages, is a clean bill of health for your disk. If CHKDSK does detect an error, you'll be notified of it with the message

```
Errors found, F parameter not specified
Corrections will not be written to disk
```

It will then display additional information pinpointing the nature of the error. If lost clusters are found, for example, CHKDSK will say something like:

```
56 lost allocation units found in 8 chains
Convert lost chains to files (Y/N)?
```

(The terms "lost allocation units" and "lost chains" will be explained shortly.) If it wasn't started with an /F switch, CHKDSK will not write corrections to disk— even if you answer yes to the on-screen query. To correct the errors, rerun CHKDSK, this time with an /F switch. The command

```
CHKDSK C: /F
```

runs CHKDSK on drive C in *fixup mode*. If CHKDSK reports lost clusters and you answer yes to its query, the lost clusters will be converted to files in the root directory.

CHKDSK can be run on hard disks and floppies. It will not run on non-DOS partitions, nor would it make any sense to do so, because other operating systems aren't likely to use the same file structure DOS does. Occasionally CHKDSK will display the message

```
Probable non-DOS disk
Continue (Y/N)?
```

In fact, it probably *is* a DOS disk, else DOS wouldn't have recognized it to begin with. This is usually symptomatic of a hard disk that wasn't formatted before it was used (yes, that can happen) or a disk whose FAT has been badly damaged.

How often should you run CHKDSK? As a general rule, the more the better. It runs so quickly that giving your disk a quick once-over is relatively painless. Some users install it in AUTOEXEC.BAT so it's run every time their PC is started. One thing's for sure: When there are errors in your disk's system areas, you can't correct them too soon. Sometimes errors can beget other errors. Periodic checkups can head off severe trouble at the pass.

CHKDSK is an extremely powerful tool for correcting disk errors. But to use it effectively, you need to understand what's going on when CHKDSK reports errors—know how to speak its language, as it were. Here are the most common errors you'll encounter and what to do about them.

Repairing Lost Clusters By far the most common error CHKDSK will report is lost allocation units, or clusters. When it tracks through the chain of allocated clusters for every file on the disk, CHKDSK makes a list of every cluster that was referenced. Then, when it's done, it compares that list to the list of allocated clusters in the FAT. If there are clusters marked in the FAT that are not part of any file, CHKDSK reports them as lost clusters. By examining the FAT entries for the lost clusters, CHKDSK can also determine how many different chains are represented. Thus the message

```
56 lost allocation units found in 8 chains
Convert lost chains to files (Y/N)?
```

means 56 orphaned clusters were found that formerly belonged to eight different files.

If you answer yes to the question "Convert lost chains to files?" (and if you started it with an /F switch), CHKDSK will convert the lost chains to files in the disk's root directory, assigning them the names FILE0000.CHK, FILE0001.CHK, and so on. There will be one .CHK file for every lost chain. By converting the lost chains to files, CHKDSK effectively corrects the errors in the FAT, because after

CHKDSK is finished, the lost clusters belong to files. To verify this, run CHKDSK a second time. You should receive a clean report.

As CHKDSK creates these files in the root directory, it's still subject to the limit on the number of files that can be placed there. If the root directory fills up, CHKDSK will halt and display the message

```
Insufficient room in root directory
Erase files in root and repeat CHKDSK
```

To recover, just do as the warning says: Erase the files from the root directory (copy them to another disk or subdirectory first if you want to save them). Then run CHKDSK again. It will pick up where it left off.

Determining what to do with all the .CHK files CHKDSK places in the root directory is another matter. If the lost clusters in a .CHK file once belonged to an ASCII text file, you may be able to reuse the file in its present form. As a test, TYPE it to the screen and see if the listing is intelligible. If you recognize the information there as something that originated in a text file, rename the .CHK file, call it up with your word processor or text editor, and reconstruct the missing data. If a large portion of a text file is missing, it's possible that some of the missing data is stored inside another .CHK file. Don't delete anything until you've TYPEd each .CHK file to the screen. In the next chapter, we'll look at how you can append one text file to another using the COPY command.

If the listing contains unrecognizable characters but you recognize text that was once part of a word processing document, try calling the .CHK file up in your word processor. If it was indeed once a word processing document, a large part of the data may be intact. If you find other parts of the document in other .CHK files, call them up in your word processor, too, and merge them with the parts you've already reconstructed. With effort (and a little bit of luck), you may be able to recover 90 percent or more of the document.

If listing a .CHK file to the screen produces unintelligible garbage, the lost clusters that comprise it probably belonged to some sort of binary file—perhaps an executable file with a .COM or .EXE extension, or a file created by an application program. There's usually nothing you can do with these files except delete them to free up room on your hard disk. If you think you recognize a file and can identify the application that created it, try calling it up inside that application. If you're successful, patch the file up and save it under a new name.

This whole process is complicated by the fact that there may be hundreds of .CHK files to deal with. If you're less concerned about data recovery than you are about getting back to business quickly, delete the .CHK files from the root directory and proceed. The data may be gone, but at least your hard disk is repaired.

Repairing Cross-Linked Files Another common error you'll encounter is cross-linked files. When two separate allocation chains (each representing a file) converge on the same cluster, the files are said to be *cross-linked*. Normally, each allocated cluster on the disk belongs to one—and only one—file. Cross-linked files share a cluster. The dangers are many. If one of the files is deleted, the other file will be affected, too, because deleting a file zeroes out the corresponding entries in the FAT. CHKDSK will later report finding *invalid clusters.* Similarly, if one file's data is updated, the other file may change, too. Any way you look at them, cross-linked files are a sure recipe for disaster.

CHKDSK will notify you of cross-linked files with a message similar to this one:

```
C:\WP\DOC\LETTERS.DOC
Is cross linked on allocation unit 32
C:\123\BUDGET.WK1
Is cross linked on allocation unit 32
```

indicating LETTERS.DOC and BUDGET.WK1 are cross-linked at cluster number 32.

To correct the problem, make a copy of both files using new file names. Then delete the originals. If you want, rename the copies to restore the old file names. Then call up both files from the applications that created them. Generally, when cross-linking occurs, one of the files will be intact in its original form and the other will be corrupted. Calling them up this way will tell you which one is good and which one is bad. The farther into the allocation chain the cross-link occurred, the greater the amount of data that will be intact in the corrupted file.

Recovering from Invalid Clusters If, as CHKDSK traces through a file's allocation chain, it comes upon a FAT entry that contains zero or a cluster number that is higher than the highest-numbered cluster on the disk, it will report having found an invalid allocation unit. "Invalid allocation unit" simply means that the value found in the FAT can't possibly be correct. It also means that the part of the file that follows the invalid cluster entry is lost.

The error report looks something like this:

```
C:\WP\DOC\LETTERS.DOC
Has invalid allocation unit, file truncated
```

If CHKDSK was started with an /F switch, it mends the error by replacing the invalid entry with an end-of-chain marker (effectively truncating the file) and truncating the file length value stored in the file's directory entry. CHKDSK apprises you of this with the message

```
First allocation unit is invalid
Entry truncated
```

If the invalid cluster happens to be the starting cluster number recorded in the file's directory entry, the length is truncated to zero.

Once CHKDSK has truncated the entry, the remainder of the file may still be on the disk in the form of lost clusters. If so, CHKDSK will offer to convert them to files in the root directory. Answer yes, then inspect the .CHK files CHKDSK created. There's a good chance that one of them will contain the truncated part of the file.

Recovering from Allocation Errors   A similar but slightly more benign error is one CHKDSK calls an *allocation error*. It warns you with the message

```
C:\WP\DOC\LETTERS.DOC
Allocation error, size adjusted
```

An allocation error is reported when the number of clusters mapped out for a file in the FAT doesn't agree with the file size stored in the file's directory entry. If the file size is, say, 4,000 bytes, and the cluster size is 2,048 bytes, CHKDSK will expect to see two clusters reserved for the file. If there are more or less, and if CHKDSK was run in fixup mode, CHKDSK will adjust the file size field inside the directory entry to match what's recorded in the FAT.

Several things may happen as a result. If the directory entry's file size value was wrong to begin with, then the file is restored 100 percent. If the FAT entries were wrong and the file size was right, then the file will either be wrongfully truncated (if the FAT showed fewer clusters than it should have) or data from another file will be wrongfully appended (if the FAT showed too many clusters).

Fixing Bad Sectors in the FAT   When a bad sector develops in the portion of the disk where the FAT is stored and CHKDSK is unable to read the FAT as a result, CHKDSK responds with the error message

```
Disk error reading FAT x
```

where x is 1 or 2, depending on which FAT CHKDSK found to be damaged. Your response should be to make a backup copy of all the files on the affected disk. DOS will cooperate by using the undamaged copy of the FAT to read the files. That's why it placed two copies of the FAT on the disk in the first place.

If the FAT error occurred on a floppy, just discard the disk after the files are copied off of it and replace it with another one. If the damaged FAT is on a hard disk, try giving the hard disk a new low-level format with a utility that does a surface analysis as it formats. If that fails, the error may not be correctable, and you may have to replace the hard disk.

Fixing Invalid Subdirectory Entries   Unlike root directory entries, subdirectory entries are not stored in a fixed area on the disk. Rather, they're stored like files and marked with a special attribute that tells DOS they're to be treated differently. But they, like files, may be corrupted. CHKDSK checks subdirectory entries for errors as it scans the logical structure of the disk and reports any inconsistencies it finds. A typical error report looks like this:

```
Invalid sub-directory entry
Convert lost directory to file (Y/N)?
```

If you answer yes to the offer to convert the damaged directory to a file, CHKDSK will create a new file bearing the name of the former subdirectory. Before you answer yes, terminate CHKDSK and copy everything out of the directory and its descendant directories that DOS permits you to copy. Then rerun CHKDSK and allow it to convert the lost directory to a file. The problem with losing a subdirectory is that you lose all the files in it, too. That's why it's worthwhile to recover as much information from it as possible.

When CHKDSK converts a subdirectory to a file, all the files that formerly were stored inside the subdirectory become lost chains. Answer yes when CHKDSK asks you if you want to convert them to files. Then you can recreate the subdirectory with a MKDIR command and copy all the .CHK files you can identify into the new subdirectory after restoring any files that DOS allowed you to copy out of the damaged directory.

A Case Study   Figure 4.15 illustrates schematically what happens when a FAT entry is accidentally zeroed and CHKDSK is called upon to fix it. The diagram on the left shows the file in its uncorrupted state. The starting cluster field in the file's directory entry points to cluster number A0H. FAT entry A0H points to cluster A1H; FAT entry A1H points to A2H; FAT entry A2H, to A3H; and so on, until the end-of-file marker FFFFH is reached in FAT entry CDH.

The middle diagram shows what the allocation chain looks like after a way-ward program inadvertently overwrites the value in FAT entry number A6H with a 0. The allocation chain is now broken, because the pointer to the last four clusters of the file no longer exists. CHKDSK will report finding an invalid cluster when it encounters the 0, and, if it's run in fixup mode, replace it with the value FFFFH (effectively truncating the file) and adjust the file size value in the directory entry accordingly.

CHKDSK will then display the error message

```
4 lost allocation units found in 1 chain
Convert lost chains to files (Y/N)?
```

The four lost clusters are those that were orphaned when CHKDSK truncated the file. The rightmost diagram in Figure 4.15 shows how CHKDSK recovers the lost clusters by converting them to files. First, it creates a directory entry in the root directory with the name FILE0000.CHK. Then it patches the starting cluster field in the directory entry with the value of the first cluster in the lost chain, turning the chain into a stand-alone file. If you can identify the file, you can append it to the old one and come very close to recovering the original intact.

FIGURE 4.15

Converting lost chains to files

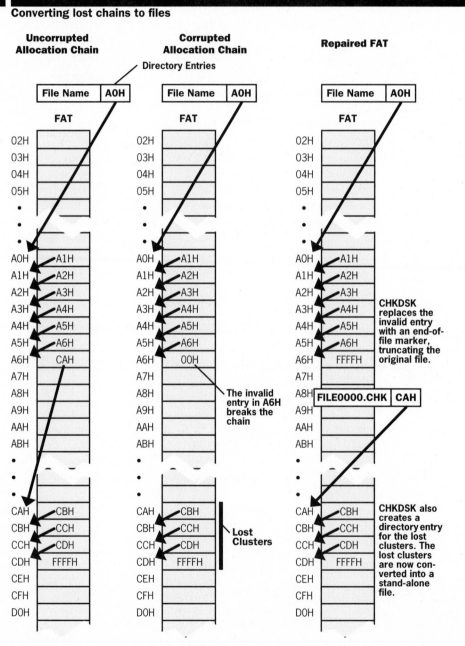

Rebuilding Corrupted Partition Tables

One of the most serious hard-disk-related problems occurs when a partition table is corrupted. When this happens, DOS generally won't recognize one or more of the logical drives defined on the hard disk, and you'll be reduced to booting off a system-formatted DOS floppy.

The MIRROR command (new in DOS 5.0) allows you to recover from such disasters, but only if you'll take a few minutes up front to run it. MIRROR makes a backup copy of the partition information stored on your hard disk. To use it, type

```
MIRROR /PARTN
```

MIRROR will ask you which drive you want the information copied to. Answer **A:** or **B:** (copying it to the hard disk won't do any good because if the partition table is corrupted, you won't be able to retrieve the backup copy). MIRROR will create a file called PARTNSAV.FIL on the specified drive containing all the information necessary to recreate the structure of your hard disk.

If you suspect your partition table is corrupted because DOS suddenly responds with "Invalid drive specification" when you attempt to access your hard disk, pull out the floppy that contains PARTNSAV.FIL and type

```
UNFORMAT /PARTN
```

At the prompt, enter a drive letter to direct the UNFORMAT utility to the floppy with the backup information and the disk will be restored. Then reboot, and with a little luck (if the partition table was the only thing damaged) the drive will be as good as new.

Recovering Deleted Files

DOS users have waited for a long time to recover deleted files without having to rely on third-party utilities. With DOS 5.0, that capability is finally here. If you delete a file only to realize that you needed it or that you deleted the wrong one, help is just one short command away.

The syntax for the new UNDELETE command is

```
UNDELETE [[d:][path]filename] [/LIST|/ALL] [/DOS|/DT]
```

where *filename* specifies what file or files you want to recover; /LIST lists all the files that may be recovered without actually recovering them; /ALL recovers the specified files automatically, without prompting you to supply the first letter of the file name for each one; /DOS recovers files without help from a file called a *delete-tracking* file created by MIRROR; and /DT recovers erased files using the delete-tracking file.

That may seem like a lot of command-line options, but in reality, UNDE-LETE isn't all that difficult to use. Most of the time, using UNDELETE immediately after DEL will recover a file. For example, if you type

```
DEL LETTERS.DOC
```

and then type

```
UNDELETE LETTERS.DOC
```

DOS will display the file name with a question mark in place of the first character and ask you if you want to undelete it. If you answer yes, DOS will prompt you to enter the first character of the file name, then proceed to undelete the file. Similarly, you can recover a whole directory full of files deleted with DEL *.* by typing

```
UNDELETE *.*
```

or simply

```
UNDELETE
```

and supplying the missing first letter for each file name as DOS lists the names of the deleted files to the screen. If you want to see a list of the files that are recoverable without actually recovering any of them, run UNDELETE with a /LIST switch.

To have DOS supply the first letter in a file name for you, use UNDE-LETE's /ALL switch. /ALL restores each file matching the file specification you supply and replaces the first character in each file name with a # symbol. If a file with that name already exists, /ALL substitutes other characters (numerals, symbols, and letters of the alphabet) until it finds one that it can use. The /ALL switch is particularly useful when you're undeleting a large number of files. You can always restore the original file names later with the REN command.

File recovery such as this is possible because when DOS deletes a file, it doesn't physically remove it from the disk. All it does is replace the first character in the file name with a byte of value E5H, marking the file as deleted, and zero out the file's entries in the FAT. The file itself is left intact, able to be recovered by a disk utility with the smarts to replace the missing character in the file's directory entry and reconstruct the chain of FAT entries. It's important to note that the space a deleted file resides in may be overwritten when another file is written to the disk, eliminating the possibility that the deleted file can be recovered. The sooner you run UNDELETE after erasing a file, the better. Occasionally even running other DOS commands can permanently wipe out an erased file.

You can acquire an extra measure of protection against accidental file deletions by using the MIRROR command to create a delete-tracking file, which holds information about deleted files that makes recovering them easier. The syntax is

```
MIRROR /Td[-nnn] ...
```

where *d* is the letter of the drive delete-tracking is to be performed on (without the usual colon), and *nnn* specifies the number of entries in the delete-tracking file (one entry corresponds to one deleted file). The default, which varies depending on the size of the drive, ranges from 25 for a 360k floppy to 303 for a drive larger than 32Mb. You can set it anywhere from 1 to 999. The command

```
MIRROR /TC /TD-500
```

establishes a delete-tracking file for drives C and D, accepting the default number of entries for drive C and reserving room for information about 500 files on drive D. In addition to creating the delete-tracking file, MIRROR also installs a memory-resident program that monitors file deletions and updates the tracking file each time a file is deleted. If the limit is reached, new entries replace old ones so that information about the *nnn* most recent files will always be on hand.

The delete-tracking file enables you to undelete some files that conventional methods alone could not. It also prevents you from having to supply the first character in the file name. But even it cannot undelete a file whose space has been reclaimed and reused by another file. Once again, the sooner you get around to undeleting a file after it's deleted, the greater the chance that you'll be able to recover it.

When UNDELETE is called on to restore a file, it checks for a delete-tracking file and uses it if it finds it. If no delete-tracking file exists for the specified drive, UNDELETE resorts to its usual methods. You can tell it explicitly which technique to use with the /DOS and /DT switches. /DOS causes UNDELETE to use the conventional method of undeleting a file, ignoring a delete-tracking file if it exists, while /DT has it undelete only those files listed in the tracking file, even if it might be possible to delete additional files using the other method. For a list of the files currently recorded in the delete-tracking file, type UNDELETE /LIST /DT.

There are two things you should keep in mind when you use these commands.

■ You should never use delete-tracking on a drive for which a JOIN or SUBST command is in effect. You can use it with ASSIGN, but only after the ASSIGN command has been issued, not before.

■ UNDELETE can't restore files in subdirectories that no longer exist. Sometimes recreating a subdirectory with the MD command will enable you to recover some of the files formerly stored there. However, your

best bet for recovering lost files *and* subdirectories is a utility such as
The Norton Utilities' UD (Unremove Directory) command.

Recovering from an Accidental Format

Another new DOS 5.0 command that will be useful in a clutch is UNFORMAT.
UNFORMAT makes it possible to restore disks that were formatted without a
/U switch with DOS 5.0's FORMAT command, or that contain a mirror file (a
special file that contains a copy of the disk's FAT and root directory) created by
the MIRROR command. The complete syntax for UNFORMAT is

```
UNFORMAT [/PARTN] [/L]
UNFORMAT d: [/TEST] [/L] [/P] [/U]
UNFORMAT d: [/J]
```

where *d:* specifies the drive to be unformatted; /PARTN restores hard-disk partition tables; [/L] lists partition information if it's used with the /PARTN switch
or lists file and subdirectory names as the disk is unformatted if it's used without
it; /TEST previews the restoration process for unformats performed without a
mirror file; /P sends output from the UNFORMAT command to the printer; /U
unformats a disk without using a mirror file; and /J verifies that a mirror file
exists and that its contents are consistent with other information on the disk.

The first form of the UNFORMAT command restores hard-disk partition
tables. Its use was discussed in the section entitiled "Rebuilding Corrupted Partition Tables." Also, you can list the partition information for a drive by typing
UNFORMAT /PARTN /L. The /P switch doesn't work if the /PARTN switch is
specified too, but you can get a hard copy of the output from this form of the
UNFORMAT command by typing

```
UNFORMAT /PARTN /L > LPT1
```

If the printer you want to print the listing on is other than LPT1, substitute the
name of the port it's connected to—LPT2, LPT3, COM1, COM2, COM3, or
COM4—for LPT1.

The second form of the UNFORMAT command unformats a disk. If the
disk you want to restore was not formatted with FORMAT's /U switch, you can
unformat it very easily. The command

```
UNFORMAT A:
```

unformats the disk in drive A. When used without a /U switch on a preformatted
disk, the FORMAT command creates a mirror file on the disk containing a copy
of the disk's FAT and root directory. UNFORMAT restores the FAT and root
directory from this file and by so doing restores the drive to approximately the
same state it was in before the format. If you run UNFORMAT immediately
after formatting the disk, the disk will be restored 100 percent. The longer you

wait, the more data you'll lose. Note that UNFORMAT works equally well on hard disks and floppies.

You can also unformat a disk that doesn't contain a mirror file as long as it wasn't unconditionally formatted. If UNFORMAT can't find a mirror file on the disk, it will do what it can with the information currently in the FAT and root directory. Undoing a format this way is slower and less reliable, but it's probably better than losing everything on the disk. If a mirror file does exist, you can tell UNFORMAT to ignore it by starting it with a /U switch, as in

```
UNFORMAT C: /U
```

Before you run UNFORMAT without benefit of a mirror file, run it with /TEST and /L to see how well the unformatting process would work. The command

```
UNFORMAT C: /TEST /L
```

has it analyze the disk and list every file and subdirectory that an unformat would recover, but without actually recovering them. If the results aren't to your liking, you'll know not to proceed with the real thing. If it's not clear whether the disk contains a mirror file, type

```
UNFORMAT C: /J
```

UNFORMAT will tell you if there is a mirror file and validate it against information in the system area of the disk if there is.

UNFORMAT is the kind of utility you're glad to have but hope you never have to use. If you avoid using FORMAT /U and stick to the FORMAT command supplied with DOS rather than relying on other formatting utilities, UNFORMAT is as effective in protecting hard-disk data from accidental formats as doing a daily backup of your files, and far less time-consuming. For floppy disks, it's even better, because you probably don't worry too much about backing up your floppies. But remember: If all else fails, particularly when a hard disk is concerned, there's no substitute for a good backup of your data.

Parking the Hard Disk's Heads

When a hard disk is powered down, the drive heads, which are separated from the magnetic surface of the disk by a thin cushion of air while the disk is spinning, are lowered to their resting position in contact with the surface. Unfortunately, since the intervening layer of air is created by the high-speed motion of the disk, the heads normally make contact before the disk has stopped spinning. Over time, this mechanical wear and tear can cause damage to the magnetic coating where flux transitions representing bits and bytes are recorded. For this reason, some hard drives move their heads to an area known as the *landing zone* (an area of the disk where no data is stored) when power is removed, to preserve the coating in areas where data is stored. This is called *parking the heads*.

But not all drives automatically park their heads at power-down. For the most part, drives that actuate (move) the heads with voice coils do, while drives that use stepper motors do not. If you have one of the latter types of drives, taking time to park the heads each day before you shut your machine off can help preserve your data and extend the life of the drive.

DOS doesn't provide a head-parking utility for hard disks, but you can create one with this short DEBUG script:

LISTING 4.4

```
A 0100
JMP      013F
DB       "Park failed",0D,0A,"$"
DB       "Heads parked",0D,0A
DB       "Your PC must now be restarted",0D,0A,"$"
DB       80
MOV      AH,08                  ;Get drive data from
MOV      DL,[013E]              ;   the BIOS
INT      13
JNB      0151                   ;Continue if it worked
MOV      AH,09                  ;Display error message
MOV      DX,0102                ;   and exit
INT      21
RET
MOV      AH,0C                  ;Seek to the highest-
MOV      DL,[013E]              ;   numbered cylinder
INT      13                     ;   on the disk
JB       0149                   ;Display "heads parked"
MOV      AH,09                  ;   message
MOV      DX,0110
INT      21
CLI                             ;Disable interrupts
HLT                             ;Halt the CPU

N PARK.COM
RCX
64
W
Q
```

PARK parks the heads on your hard disk. On some hard drives, you'll actually hear the drive heads moving toward the center of the disk and may hear a clunking sound as they reach their destination. If you have two hard drives, you can create a separate utility to park drive number two's heads by changing the line "DB 80" to read "DB 81" and changing the name of the program to something like PARK2.COM.

If you park the drive heads and then decide you want to continue computing, just proceed as normal. The first time the hard disk is accessed, the heads will seek to the proper track, and you'll be back in business.

PARK takes a simple approach to deciding where to park the drive heads. Since it's difficult to determine where a drive's landing zone is (the value is usually encoded in ROM-based drive parameter tables that the BIOS references with a drive type number), PARK calls on BIOS interrupt 13H, function 08H (Read Drive Parameters) to determine what the highest-numbered cylinder on the disk is. Then it calls interrupt 13H, function 0CH (Seek) to seek to that cylinder. The landing zone doesn't always coincide with the highest-numbered cylinder, but it's invariably close. And since DOS writes to a disk from the outside in (starting on the outermost, or lowest-numbered, cylinders and working toward the center), in most instances this will prove effective in keeping the heads away from data.

Third-Party Disk Maintenance Tools

The relative lack of sophistication of the tools DOS provides for protecting hard-disk data and performing routine disk maintenance has spawned an entire industry of third-party programs seeking to bridge the gap. These packages fall into three broad categories:

- Hard-disk backup utilities that outclass BACKUP and RESTORE in terms of speed, ease of use, and error recovery

- Data-recovery utilities that help you recover data lost to accidental erasures, inadvertent formats, and programs that corrupt system areas of the disk such as the partition table

- Preventative-maintenance/performance-enhancement utilities that let you defragment hard-disk files, perform low-level formats, and check disks for developing surface defects

The need for many of these utilities is gone now that DOS 5.0 includes commands and utilities for recovering deleted files, unformatting formatted disks, and rebuilding corrupted partition tables. But packages such as The Norton Utilities and PC Tools Deluxe are far from obsolete. There are still many tools DOS does not provide, among them utilities for editing disks at the sector level, defragmenting disk files, and performing low-level formats non-destructively. All these capabilities and more are available from outside sources. Here's a brief survey of what you can find in third-party disk utilities.

Hard-Disk Backup Utilities   The one thing BACKUP and RESTORE have going for them is that they're free. Any other way you look at them, they're inferior to many of the backup utilities available commercially.

High-performance backup programs such as Fastback Plus from Fifth Generation Systems and PC Backup from Central Point Software do everything possible to make backups fast and painless. Typically, these programs employ a fast format routine that can format an unformatted floppy in seconds (even one that has never been formatted before). Most use data-compression algorithms to squeeze more data (up to two times as much) on the backup disks and use advanced error correction to recover data even from damaged backups. And they program DMA (Direct Memory Access) channels in the PC to carry data directly from drive to drive without tying up the CPU. Data transfer rates of 2.5Mb per minute are not uncommon.

This is in stark contrast to DOS's BACKUP utility, which is slow, uses no form of data compression, and chokes on the most menial of errors. Run it one time on an 80Mb hard disk, and you'll see why a commercial backup program is worthwhile.

Hard-Disk File Defragmenting Utilities One of the benefits DOS gains from mapping files on disk using the FAT is that files can be stored in non-contiguous locations. The downside to this system for file allocation and tracking is that files can become so badly fragmented that they slow down the system as a whole each time they're accessed. The reason: If a file is scattered out in several different places on the disk, the drive mechanism has to perform more movements to reach all parts of it. The resultant decrease in performance can be severe.

The solution to the problem of file fragmentation is a file-defragmenting utility. Both The Norton Utilities and PC Tools Deluxe contain one, and there are several shareware defragmenters available. Defragmenters rearrange clusters on the disk so that all files are stored in contiguous locations. The process isn't easy, nor is it quick: Some defragmenters can take hours to run. But the result is well worth it. Files will load as quickly as they did when the disk was brand new. If the disk was badly fragmented before, you'll be amazed at the difference in performance.

Low-Level Formatting Utilities Giving your hard disk a new low-level format from time to time can be effective in combating two common causes of hard-disk data errors: misalignment between the drive heads and cylinders on the disk, and defective sectors that have cropped up since the disk was last formatted. Here's why—and what you can do to ease the tedious chore of performing a low-level format.

The part of a sector where data is stored is refreshed every time the sector is rewritten. If the drive head mechanism creeps over time due to mechanical stresses, the sectors on the disk will creep with it. But the sector ID headers— the blocks of information that allow DOS to locate sectors on the disk— remain where they were positioned when the disk was last low-level formatted. If head misalignment becomes severe enough, the drive heads may end up so far out of line with the ID headers that they can't locate them, and thus can't locate sectors on the disk. When this happens, DOS will bomb with a "Sector not found" message.

This misalignment problem is illustrated in Figure 4.16. The sector ID headers remain where they were when the disk was last low-level formatted, but the portions of the sectors where file data is stored have moved outward, away from the center of the disk. A new low-level format will realign the sectors with the drive heads.

FIGURE 4.16

Misalignment between heads and cylinders

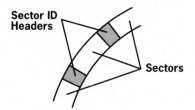

Sector ID Headers

Sectors

A low-level format refreshes sectors and sector ID headers, ensuring that they line up with each other.

Over time, the drive heads may creep and cause sectors (which are refreshed every time they're written) to drift out of alignment with the sector ID headers. If the misalignment becomes severe enough, DOS will no longer be able to locate sectors on the disk.

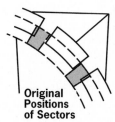

Misaligned Sectors and New Path of Drive Heads

Original Positions of Sectors

Fortunately, modern hard-disk designs minimize misalignment by employing measures to permit the drive heads to adjust to the position of cylinders on the disk on the fly. One technique that drive makers often rely on uses special signals called *servos* to guide the controller to a specific location on the disk with a high degree of precision. Until recently, servos were usually stored on a dedicated platter. Many drive makers now place the servos right alongside the sectors and cylinders of the hard disk, giving rise to a technology called *embedded servos*. Drives that use embedded servos usually cannot be low-level formatted outside the factory because conventional controllers lack the electronics necessary to avoid overwriting the servos and to create new ones. That's the primary reason why many IDE drives can't be low-level formatted.

Another reason to give your hard disk a new low-level format periodically is to repair surface defects that have developed since the last time it was formatted. A good low-level formatter will repair some defects and mark off those it can't repair so they won't be used.

Disk maintenance utilities such as SpinRite II from Gibson Research make low-level formatting almost a pleasure. While conventional low-level formatting utilities destroy files on the hard disk, SpinRite II preserves them so you don't have to do a time-consuming backup-and-restore before and after the format. It also moves files around as needed to move them away from bad sectors. Recent versions of SpinRite will even repair defective sectors on drives that can't be low-lovel formatted. Applying it or a utility like it regularly is one of the best preventative measures you can take to guard against data loss due to the adverse effects of normal—and unavoidable—wear and tear.

Choosing the Right Interleave   Some low-level formatters will also test your disk for the optimum sector interleave and apply it during the format. Doing so ensures that you get the maximum possible performance from your hard drive by performance-matching its rate of rotation to the rate at which the rest of your system can process data coming from and going to it.

FIGURE 4.17

Sector interleave

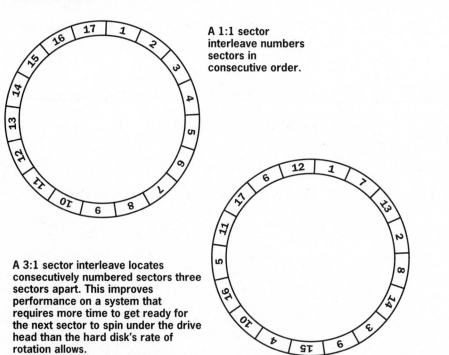

A 1:1 sector interleave numbers sectors in consecutive order.

A 3:1 sector interleave locates consecutively numbered sectors three sectors apart. This improves performance on a system that requires more time to get ready for the next sector to spin under the drive head than the hard disk's rate of rotation allows.

Sector interleave is illustrated in Figure 4.17. On a hard disk with a 3:1 interleave ratio, consecutively numbered sectors are placed three physical sectors apart. This is ideal for a system where the controller can't be ready for the next sector until two additional sectors pass beneath the drive head. Rather than have the drive head wait a full revolution for the sector to come back around, the proper interleave will bring the sector around at about the same time the controller is ready for it. Most 386-based PCs can handle a 1:1 interleave, but slower PCs usually benefit from higher values. What's best for your PC can only be determined by experimentation. That's why it's best to leave the dirty work to a low-level formatting utility such as SpinRite II or The Norton Utilities' CALIBRATE that can determine what that optimum value is for you.

Summary

If, after reading this chapter, you feel overwhelmed with everything you need to know to set up and maintain a hard disk, don't be dismayed. With luck, nothing will ever go wrong with any of your disks and you'll never need to run UNFOR-MAT or employ any of the data recovery methods outlined here. But if disaster does strike, you'll be prepared. You'll also know that most of the time, you can recover all or at least part of the data lost in a disk failure if you know the right place to start.

In the next chapter, we'll look at how to organize a hard disk once it's partitioned and formatted. There are good ways and bad ways to store files on a hard disk, and ways that can get you in real trouble if you're not aware of them up front. We'll also look more closely at subdirectories and at the different types of files you can store on a disk. At the end, your education in using hard disks and floppies for everyday storage needs will be complete.

5 FILE AND DIRECTORY MANAGEMENT

EVERY NOW AND THEN A NEW IDEA COMES ALONG THAT FUNDAMENTALLY changes the way we work with computers. The GUI, or graphical user interface, was one such idea; but new concepts can be more subtle than that and still have far-reaching effects. One of the best examples to illustrate this point is that of *tree-structured directories*, which were introduced in DOS 2.0 to permit hard-disk users to organize the hundreds or perhaps thousands of files that could now be stored on a single disk. Imagine, if you will, what a hard disk would be like without tree-structured directories. A 100Mb disk might have 25,000 files in the root directory. Just listing all the files stored there might take several minutes. And locating a particular file could take even longer.

That's why tree-structured directories are important. They permit you to divide a volume into smaller, more easily managed units called *subdirectories*. If you picture your hard disk as a filing cabinet and the partitions on it as the different drawers, the subdirectories are the folders inside the drawers. Properly set up, subdirectories can greatly increase the ease with which your hard disk is accessed and the efficiency with which it is used.

Figure 5.1 illustrates the directory structure of a typical hard disk. Every disk contains a top-level directory called the *root directory,* which is denoted by a backslash character. The root directory of the disk in this example contains eight subdirectories, some of which contain subdirectories themselves. The overall structure of the disk resembles an upside-down tree, starting at a single point and branching out to encompass a much wider area. If you prefer, think of this directory structure as the root system of a tree, which gets larger as it gets deeper.

The idea behind using subdirectories is a simple one. Each subdirectory serves as a local repository on the hard disk where files may be stored apart from other files. The directory you're currently in (whether it's the root directory or a subdirectory) is called the *current directory*. There is always a current directory, just as there is always a current drive—A, B, C, D, and so on. When you execute a DOS file command, it acts on the files in the current directory unless you specify otherwise. In this way the groups of files stored on the disk are insulated from each other, and rather than having to deal with up to several thousand files in one storage unit, you can deal with several smaller storage units containing as many or as few files as you please. Note that the terms "directory" and "subdirectory" are often used interchangeably.

This chapter introduces the concepts you'll need to know to effectively organize the directory structure on your hard disk. It also offers an overview of the tools DOS provides for managing files and subdirectories on a day-by-day basis. Lastly, it introduces commands for displaying, creating, and editing text files, including EDIT, which invokes DOS 5.0's new full-screen text editor.

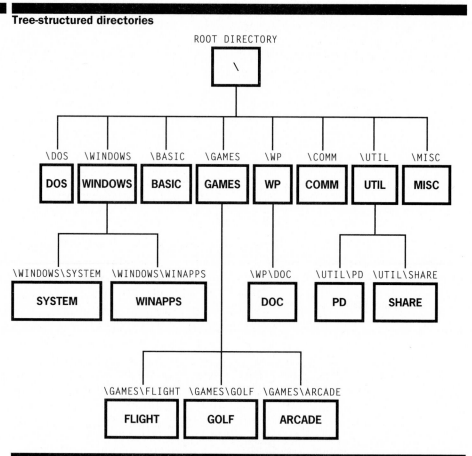

FIGURE 5.1

Tree-structured directories

Managing Disk Directories

There are few rules governing what the directory structure of a hard disk must look like. Within the latitude that provides you, you can organize a hard disk just about any way you want to. However, there is one axiom that you should keep in mind when you set up a new hard disk: That the root directory should contain at most three files—CONFIG.SYS, AUTOEXEC.BAT, and COMMAND-.COM. Everything else should be stored in subdirectories.

The reason is partly a matter of necessity. Because the area of the disk where root directory entries are stored is fixed in size (recall the discussion of the root directory area in the last chapter), the root directory is limited to a finite number of file or subdirectory entries, no matter how large the disk is or how much room is left on it. On a hard disk, the limit is 512 entries. Subdirectories, however, suffer no such limitations. If there is sufficient room, a subdirectory may contain thousands of files. Thus, subdirectories provide a convenient mechanism for surpassing the 512-file limit DOS places on a hard disk's root directory.

Restricting the number of files in the root directory is also good, sound organization. The more you can compartmentalize files, the easier it will be to find them when you need them. Other than the system files IO.SYS and MSDOS.SYS, the only two files that *must* reside in the root directory are CONFIG.SYS and AUTOEXEC.BAT. Most users place COMMAND.COM there, too, but it is possible to move COMMAND.COM into a subdirectory using the SHELL directive as shown in Chapter 2. DOS's installation program may have placed a file called WINA20.386 in the root directory of your hard disk, which Windows uses in 386 enhanced mode when it's run with DOS 5.0. This file, too, can be located somewhere other than the root directory by making the appropriate modifications to CONFIG.SYS and SYSTEM.INI. These modifications were also described in Chapter 2.

It's a common practice to store DOS files (ANSI.SYS, APPEND.EXE, ASSIGN.COM, and so on) in the root directory. The better way, because it avoids clutter in the root, is to set up a separate subdirectory (call it DOS or SYSTEM or something with a similar connotation) to store the system files. Then, by using a PATH command to point DOS to the DOS directory, you can execute any DOS command from anywhere on the hard disk. This also makes it easier to upgrade DOS versions, because it stores DOS files apart from other files.

Most users also find it convenient to store applications in separate subdirectories. This helps isolate programs from each other to prevent them (and their data files) from being mixed up. You might, for example, create a subdirectory called WP for word processing and another called EXCEL for Microsoft Excel. Many users go one step further and create additional subdirectories within the application directories for the purpose of storing data files. This reduces the number of files you have to search through to find a particular file and lets DOS load it slightly faster. Storing data files and program files in separate subdirectories has another benefit, too: It makes backing up easier. You can skip the program directories after you back them up once, because the files stored there aren't modified nearly as often as the files stored in data directories.

Using tree-structured directories requires that you modify the way you think about the locations of files on a disk. Normally, when you reference a file by passing its name to a program or DOS command, you implicitly assume that the file is located in the current directory. For example, the command

```
TYPE TEXTFILE.TXT
```

works if TEXTFILE.TXT resides in the current directory, but not if it's located elsewhere on the disk. Without outside help from DOS commands such as APPEND, there are two ways to remedy this: by changing to the directory where the file is stored before executing the command, or by modifying the command to spell out the path to TEXTFILE.TXT. The command

```
TYPE C:\DATA\TEXT\TEXTFILE.TXT
```

will work from any drive or directory, because it specifies both the drive (C) and the directory (\DATA\TEXT) where the text file whose name is passed to the TYPE command is located. This type of file specifier is called a *fully qualified file name,* because it fully and unambiguously spells out the name of the file as well as its location on disk.

The general syntax for a fully qualified file name is

```
[d:][path][filename]
```

where *d:* is the drive where the file is stored, *path* is the path to the file (the directory where it is stored), and *filename* is the file's name and extension. Here, the brackets don't indicate that any part of the string is optional; they're simply used to separate the components of the string. You'll never get in trouble providing fully qualified file names. DOS will use them anytime and anywhere to correctly locate a file on disk.

In DOS 4.0 and 5.0, you can use the undocumented TRUENAME command to generate a fully qualified file name. To test it out, type TRUENAME followed by the file name that you want converted. If you're in the \WP\WPFILES directory of drive C, typing

```
TRUENAME ANYFILE.DOC
```

will elicit the response

```
C:\WP\WPFILES\ANYFILE.DOC
```

from DOS. Note that TRUENAME does not check to make sure the file exists. Interestingly enough, TRUENAME will see through aliases created with the SUBST, JOIN, and ASSIGN commands. It also works with network drives. If you had formerly typed the command

```
SUBST W: C:\WP\WPFILES
```

then TRUENAME W:ANYFILE.DOC would also return

```
C:\WP\WPFILES\ANYFILE.DOC.
```

It's not always convenient to spell out the entire path to a file. What if the file is nested four directory levels deep and you're already in that directory? It's far easier to type

```
TYPE TEXTFILE.TXT
```

than it is to type

```
TYPE C:\FILES\DATA\TEXT\ASCII\TEXTFILE.TXT
```

You can leave off the parts of the fully qualified file name that coincide with the current drive and directory. If you leave off the *d:* component that specifies the drive, DOS assumes that the file is located on the current drive. Similarly, if you leave off the *path* component, DOS assumes the file is located in the current directory.

Choosing whether to include the *path* portion of the file name isn't an all-or-nothing proposition; the path to the file may be broken down even further. DOS provides two ways to specify the path to a file: relative to the root directory or relative to the current directory. If the path name begins with a backslash character, the path is assumed to stem from the *root directory*. Without the leading backslash, DOS assumes that the specified path is relative to the *current directory*.

If the current directory is \FILES\DATA, for example, the path to TEXT-FILE.TXT could be specified either as

```
\FILES\DATA\TEXT\ASCII\TEXTFILE.TXT
```

or simply as

```
TEXT\ASCII\TEXTFILE.TXT
```

because the latter path name lacks a leading backslash; DOS appends it to the name of the current directory, \FILES\DATA, yielding the path name \FILES\-DATA\TEXT\ASCII\TEXTFILE.TXT. If the current directory were \WP rather than \FILES\DATA, the path name

```
TEXT\ASCII\TEXTFILE.TXT
```

would be interpreted instead as

```
\WP\TEXT\ASCII\TEXTFILE.TXT
```

DOS remembers the current directory for each drive in the system. Thus, if you're working in the \WP directory of drive D and type **C:** to switch to drive C, the file name

```
D:TEXTFILE.TXT
```

evaluates to D:\WP\TEXTFILE.TXT. Alternately, the file name could have been entered as

```
D:\WP\TEXTFILE.TXT
```

But the \WP portion of the name is redundant, so leaving it off saves a few keystrokes. These conventions for spelling out the location of a file don't apply just to data files; they also apply to executables. For example, if you want to execute the program INSTALL.COM in the \UTIL directory, but you're currently in the \FILES directory, you could type

```
\UTIL\INSTALL
```

DOS would look for the executable named INSTALL in the \UTIL directory of the current drive.

Before you begin creating and using subdirectories on your hard disk, you'll need to know what commands DOS provides for doing so. The next several sections will examine seven such commands, including

- The MD command, for creating subdirectories

- The RD command, for deleting subdirectories

- The CD command, for changing the current directory

- The TREE command, for graphing the directory structure

- The SUBST command, for assigning logical drive letters to subdirectories

- The PATH command, for establishing automatic search paths for executables

- The APPEND command, for establishing automatic search paths for non-executables

Creating and Deleting Subdirectories

DOS provides two commands for creating and deleting subdirectories. They are

- The MKDIR command (abbreviated MD), short for *MaKe DIRectory,* which creates a subdirectory

- The RMDIR command (abbreviated RM), short for *ReMove DIRectory,* which deletes a subdirectory

The syntax for the commands is simply

```
MD [d:]path
RD [d:]path
```

where *d:* is an optional drive specifier and *path* is the name of the directory to be created or deleted. Just as you can specify whether the path to a file starts from the root directory or from the current directory with the inclusion or omission of a leading backslash, you can locate a subdirectory relative to the current directory or to the root directory when using MD and RD. For example, the command

```
MD NEWDIR
```

creates a new subdirectory called NEWDIR as a descendant of the current directory. The command

```
MD \NEWDIR
```

attaches NEWDIR to the root directory. If the root directory is the current directory, these two commands are equivalent.

The only limitation in the number of levels of subdirectories that you can create is that the total length of the path name string, including backslashes, cannot exceed 63 characters. Using shorter names for subdirectories permits you to create more of them stemming from a particular directory. In practice, you'll find that directory structures that are more than three or four levels deep are usually more trouble than they're worth. One reason is that they simply create a lot of typing. Another is that long path names affect other DOS commands, too. For example, a PATH statement can only be 127 characters long. The shorter your subdirectory names are, the more of them you can include in a PATH command.

The RD command removes a subdirectory from disk. To prevent you from accidentally losing all the files in a subdirectory that's not empty, DOS won't let you remove subdirectories that contain files or other subdirectories. If a valid RD command results in the message

```
Invalid path, not directory,
or directory not empty
```

then one of three things is true:

- The subdirectory you specified does not exist, or it does exist, but the path you supplied to it is invalid.

- The name following the RD command was the name of a file, not a subdirectory.

- The subdirectory is not empty; it contains files, other subdirectories, or both.

If you determine that the subdirectory isn't empty, delete the files and subdirectories inside it and try again. RD should work the next time around. Note that the root directory may never be deleted.

Sometimes you'll have to start several subdirectories deep, deleting files and removing subdirectories to remove a higher-level subdirectory. At present, there's no easy way to do this from the DOS command line except by brute force. In Chapter 11, we'll develop a utility called NUKE that removes subdirectories, cleaning out lower-level files and subdirectories automatically if needed.

Deleting Stubborn Subdirectories　If there appear to be no files in a particular directory but repeated RD commands produce an error message indicating that the directory is not empty, then there are probably hidden or system files still stored in the directory. Files marked with hidden or system attributes do not show up when you type DIR. But they're there, and they prevent the DEL command from working just the same as if they *did* show up in directory listings. To verify this, go to the subdirectory and type

```
DIR /A
```

In DOS 5.0, this form of the DIR command lists *everything* stored in the current directory, even files marked with hidden or system attributes. If such files do show up, you can turn them into normal files by typing

```
ATTRIB -H -S -R *.*
```

Then delete the files and you should be able to remove the subdirectory. The ATTRIB command, which will be examined later in this chapter, allows you to change the attributes attached to a file. In addition to stripping hidden and system attributes, the ATTRIB command used here also removes read-only attributes, which, if left intact, could prevent a file from being deleted even after the other attributes were removed.

Navigating the Directory Structure

The CHDIR (*CHange DIRectory*) command, which may be abbreviated CD, changes the current directory. For example, you could use the command

```
CD \
```

to switch to the root directory, or

```
CD \UTIL
```

to change to the \UTIL directory. As usual, path names are interpreted as being relative to the root directory if they are preceded by a backslash or relative to the current directory if they are not. Thus, typing

```
CD UTIL
```

is equivalent to typing

```
CD \UTIL
```

if the root directory is the current directory.

If you include a drive specifier in front of the path name in a CD command, DOS will make the indicated directory the current one on the specified drive, but will not automatically switch to that drive. The next time you switch to that drive, you'll be dropped into its current directory.

If you type CD by itself, DOS will display the current drive and directory. A better way to keep track of where you are on the disk at all times is to customize the DOS prompt to display the current directory with the command

```
PROMPT $p$g
```

Then, instead of reading C> when you're on the C drive, the prompt will read C:\> to indicate you're in the root directory, C:\WP\WPFILES> to indicate you're in the WPFILES subdirectory of the \WP subdirectory, and so on. For convenience, add this PROMPT command to your AUTOEXEC.BAT file so that it will be automatically executed every time you boot up. Chapters 2 and 6 contain more detailed discussions of the PROMPT command and of the various options you may use with it.

The Dot and Double-Dot Entries   DOS provides two special entries for directory navigation: the dot and double-dot entries. When you type DIR to display a list of files in a subdirectory, DOS displays the dot and double-dot entries at the top of the listing, as shown in Figure 5.2.

FIGURE 5.2

The Dot and Double-Dot entries

```
Volume in drive C is DOS 5 DISK
Volume Serial Number is 2875-17D8
Directory of C:\MISC

.                 <DIR>      10-22-90    4:39p
..                <DIR>      10-22-90    4:39p
INTERRUP LST      429461 10-14-90    3:59p
PCXSPEC  DOC       23266 11-11-90   11:48a
SKY      GIF      112896 08-10-90   11:46p
TRAIN    GIF       59776 08-15-90    8:02p
GIFSPEC  DOC       85478 07-31-90    9:47p
NODITHER GIF       54144 08-17-90    9:01p
TIFFSPEC TXT      128541 08-16-90    5:28a
TIFFSPEC DOC      127213 08-16-90    5:32a
DITHER   GIF       86528 08-17-90    9:19p
PHONES   TXT        1547 11-10-90   12:01a
CONFIG   SYS         382 09-01-90    9:02p
INTERRUP 1ST       13906 04-30-89    8:28a
COMDEX   TXT         953 11-11-90   11:34a
        15 file(s)     1124091 bytes
                      16414720 bytes free
```

The double-dot is shorthand for the current directory's *parent directory* (the directory one level up in the directory structure). Thus, typing

```
CD ..
```

moves you up one directory level. If you're currently in the \WP\WPFILES directory, for example, typing **CD ..** moves you up to the \WP directory. Typing **CD ..** a second time lands you in the root directory. Similarly, the command

```
CD..\..
```

combines both actions into one to move you up two directory levels with a single command.

The single-dot entry is shorthand for the current directory. You won't need it often, but it is useful at times. If a program prompts you for a directory name, for example, and you want to point it to the current directory, you don't have to type the entire name of the directory; instead, you can answer with a period. To DOS, that's the same as typing the current directory's name.

You can also use the single-dot entry to run programs or batch files that have the unfortunate distinction of having the same name as internal DOS commands. For example, if you create a batch file called DIR.BAT and type

```
DIR
```

DOS will execute the DIR command (not the batch file DIR.BAT), because internal commands take precedence over program files of the same name. However, if you type

```
.\DIR
```

DIR.BAT will be executed because the .\ that preceded the command tells DOS that you want to execute an external command or program located in the current directory. This is a convenient way to ensure that only you can execute a particular program on your hard disk. Just rename it with the name of an internal DOS command, and it'll be impossible to execute without knowing the .\ trick. Of course, you must be in the directory the program is in for this to work. If you're someplace else on the hard disk, just substitute the appropriate path name for .\, and the file will execute just the same.

You can use the dot and double-dot directory entries in path names passed to any DOS command. For example, if you're in the \MSC\SRC directory and you want to see what's in the \MSC\INCLUDE directory, you can type

```
DIR ..\INCLUDE
```

The double-dot component of the path tells DIR to go up one directory (to \MSC); the \INCLUDE component tells it to look in the INCLUDE directory of \MSC. The alternative is to type

```
DIR \MSC\INCLUDE
```

which works equally well but requires more typing.

Displaying the Directory Structure

Since a typical hard disk contains several subdirectories and subdirectory levels, it's not difficult to lose track of the big picture and forget exactly how the disk is structured. To help, DOS offers the TREE command, which displays a graphical listing of all the subdirectories on a drive stemming from the specified directory. If you start from the root directory, TREE depicts the directory structure of the entire drive.

The syntax for the TREE command is

```
TREE [d:][path] [/F] [/A]
```

where *path* is the name of the directory where TREE should start, /F displays file names along with directory names, and /A substitutes conventional ASCII characters for the graphics characters normally used to draw lines in the directory tree.

Typing **TREE C:** displays the directory structure of drive C. Figure 5.3 shows the results of running TREE on a typical hard disk. Each level of indentation reflects one additional level of subdirectories. *Child directories* (the subdirectories of a particular directory) are joined by lines to their parent directories.

The /A switch is important if you output the directory tree to a printer whose character set isn't completely compatible with the IBM character set. For example, if you type

```
TREE C:\ >PRN
```

to print the output from the TREE command on an early-model Epson printer, the line-draw characters that you see on the screen will show up as italics on the printer, because the upper-order Epson and IBM character sets that are used to produce these characters do not match. But by modifying the command to read

```
TREE C:\ /A >PRN
```

you direct DOS to substitute conventional characters—hyphens, plus signs, backslashes, and vertical bars—which are present in nearly every printer's character set.

FIGURE 5.3

Output from the TREE Command

```
Directory PATH listing for Volume DOS 5 DISK
Volume Serial Number is 2875-17D8
```

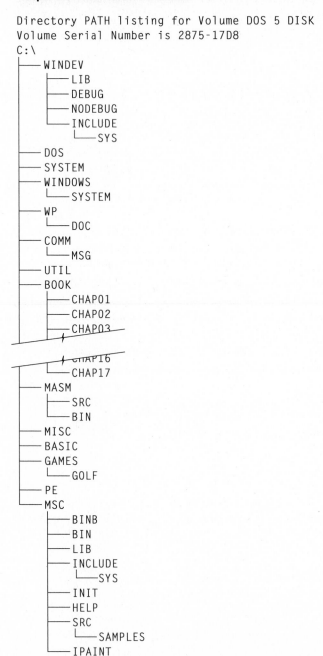

If your hard disk contains more than a handful of subdirectories, the output from TREE won't fit onto one screen. To prevent the information from scrolling by too quickly, use the MORE command. The command

```
TREE | MORE
```

captures the output from TREE and displays it one screenful at a time, pausing at the bottom of each screen for a keystroke.

Creating Automatic Search Paths: The PATH and APPEND Commands

As we've seen, you can reference any file stored on disk—whether it's an executable file or a data file—by spelling out the path to it. But most of the time it's not convenient to type in a full path name. Imagine having to type \DOS\CHKDSK every time you wanted to run CHKDSK and weren't in the directory where CHKDSK.EXE is stored. Pretty soon you'd grow tired of the extra typing and avoid using CHKDSK altogether.

That's why DOS provides the PATH and APPEND commands. PATH establishes a list of subdirectories that DOS checks when it searches for executable files. APPEND does the same for non-executable files. It creates a list of directories that are treated as logical extensions of the current directory, so that data files (for example, document files created by WordPerfect or spreadsheet files created by Lotus 1-2-3) can be accessed without a path name.

One of the benefits of using these commands is that you can separate data files from program files, but can access either of them without typing in long path names. For example, if you keep WordPerfect in a subdirectory called \WP and WordPerfect document files in \WP\DOC, you can set up a PATH to \WP and CD to \WP\DOC before starting WordPerfect. Then, all your document files are stored in the current directory where they're easy to get to, and, thanks to the PATH command, WordPerfect will run as if it were stored there, too. Conversely, you could direct DOS to the \WP\DOC subdirectory with an APPEND command, and then CD to \WP and execute WordPerfect from there. However, it turns out that APPEND can be dangerous if it's not used carefully, so it's preferable to use the PATH command instead. We'll see why in a moment.

The PATH Command   The syntax for PATH is

```
PATH [[d:]path[;[d:]path][;...]]
```

where *path* is the path to a directory and *d:* is the drive where it is located. Multiple *path* entries on a single line must be separated by semicolons. The command

```
PATH C:\DOS;C:\WP;C:\UTIL
```

instructs DOS to look for executables in the C:\DOS, C:\WP, and C:\UTIL directories, in that order.

When you enter a command, DOS tries three different ways to process it. First, it compares it against its list of internal commands such as DIR and COPY. If it's an internal command, it is executed from inside COMMAND.COM. If not, DOS checks for a file with the same name and the extension .COM, .EXE, or .BAT (in that order) in the current directory. Failing that, it turns to the list of directories specified with the PATH command. Entering the PATH command in the previous paragraph ensures that programs located in C:\DOS, C:\WP, or C:\UTIL can be executed without entering path names. If CHKDSK-.EXE is stored in the C:\DOS directory, it can now be executed simply by typing CHKDSK.

Executing PATH without any command-line parameters displays the current PATH. Typing PATH after entering the PATH command just shown would produce

```
PATH=C:\DOS;C:\WP;C:\UTIL
```

You may also inspect the PATH by typing SET. SET displays a list of all the currently defined environment strings. DOS stores the PATH string in an environment variable named PATH. Typing SET produces a display similar to this one:

```
COMSPEC=C:\COMMAND.COM
PROMPT=$p$g
PATH=C:\DOS;C:\WP;C:\UTIL
```

It's a good idea to include a drive specifier with every subdirectory named in the PATH command. Why? Because without the drive specifier, DOS assumes that the subdirectory is located on the current drive, which isn't always the case. For example, let's assume that the PATH command in your AUTOEXEC.BAT file reads simply

```
PATH \DOS;\WP;\UTIL
```

and that \DOS, \WP, and \UTIL are all meant to reference subdirectories on drive C. As long as drive C is the current drive, this works just fine. But switch to drive D and DOS will no longer be able to find CHKDSK.EXE. The problem is, with D as the current drive, DOS looks for CHKDSK in D:\DOS, not C:\DOS. Not every hard-disk user has a drive D, but the same problem occurs if you switch to drive A or B. By being explicit with your intentions and specifying a drive as well as a subdirectory, you can ensure that DOS will search the proper locations no matter where you are on your system.

Overcoming PATH Limitations　One problem users frequently encounter with the PATH command is that DOS limits the number of characters that can be entered in one command to 127, which in turn limits the number of subdirectories you can specify in a PATH statement. For example, if you wanted to add the following list of subdirectories to the PATH:

```
C:\USER\PEOPLE\SMITH\DOS
C:\USER\PEOPLE\SMITH\MSC\BIN
C:\USER\PEOPLE\SMITH\SYSTEM
C:\USER\PEOPLE\SMITH\UTIL
C:\USER\PEOPLE\SMITH\WP
```

On the surface, at least, it would seem that the command

```
PATH C:\USER\PEOPLE\SMITH\DOS;C:\USER\PEOPLE\SMITH\MSC\BIN;
C:\USER\PEOPLE\SMITH\SYSTEM;C:\USER\PEOPLE\SMITH\UTIL;C:\US
ER\PEOPLE\SMITH\WP
```

would do it. But look more closely. This command contains 136 characters, so you can't enter them all in the command line. Even if the command is executed from a batch file, DOS will ignore the last nine characters. In effect, the directory C:\USER\PEOPLE\SMITH\WP is omitted from the PATH statement because, upon execution, it is truncated to simply C:\USER\PEOPLE\.

The SUBST command provides a convenient work-around. SUBST allows logical drive letters to be equated to other drives and directories. For example, after entering the command

```
SUBST Z: \USER\PEOPLE\SMITH\UTIL
```

typing DIR Z: is the same as typing DIR \USER\PEOPLE\SMITH\UTIL. You can take advantage of this abbreviated means of referencing a subdirectory to expand the number of subdirectories that may be named in a PATH statement. Rather than enter the PATH statement listed earlier, enter the following series of commands:

```
SUBST V: C:\USER\PEOPLE\SMITH\DOS
SUBST W: C:\USER\PEOPLE\SMITH\MSC\BIN
SUBST X: C:\USER\PEOPLE\SMITH\SYSTEM
SUBST Y: C:\USER\PEOPLE\SMITH\UTIL
SUBST Z: C:\USER\PEOPLE\SMITH\WP
PATH V:;W:;X:;Y:;Z:
```

Using this method, you can direct DOS to as many locations for executables as there are available drive letters in your system. If you use this method, don't forget that you'll also need to add a LASTDRIVE command to your CONFIG.SYS file for DOS to recognize drive letters above E. If Z is the highest drive designator you plan to use, add the line

```
LASTDRIVE = Z
```

to CONFIG.SYS. You can conserve a few kilobytes of memory by using the lowest drive letters possible. If your system has A through D drives, for example, you might opt to use E through I, rather than V through Z.

SUBST was introduced in DOS 3.1 to help users overcome problems with older programs that would only accept drive letters—not subdirectory names— as file locations. Today, such programs are rare. But if you come across one of them, you can use SUBST to make it subdirectory aware.

If you frequently find yourself adding directories to your PATH command on the fly, you're probably frustrated by the fact that you have to retype the whole directory list just to add a new one to the end. You can remedy this with a simple batch file called APATH.BAT (APATH for *Add PATH*). APATH should contain a single line:

```
PATH=%PATH%;%1
```

Then, to add C:\MASM to the PATH, type

```
APATH C:\MASM
```

When the batch file executes, %PATH% is replaced by the current PATH string, and %1 is replaced by what you type on the command line—in this case, C:\MASM. Both these forms of substitution work only in batch files; they will not work on the command line. We'll learn more about batch files and the tricks you can do with them in Chapter 10.

The APPEND Command   The APPEND command is similar to PATH except that it works for non-executable files, not executables. In other words, it works with the data files that programs create rather than with the programs themselves.

The APPEND command makes a specified list of directories a logical extension of the current directory so that when a program or DOS command goes to look for a file, it may find it in any of those other directories. To help understand what the APPEND command really does, try this experiment. First, assuming you have an AUTOEXEC.BAT file stored in the root directory of your hard disk, enter the command

```
APPEND C:\
```

to make the root directory of drive C a logical extension of whatever directory you happen to be in later. Then go to any directory on the disk other than the root directory and type

```
EDIT AUTOEXEC.BAT
```

and up will pop the DOS Editor showing the contents of your AUTOEXEC.BAT file (to exit, press Alt-F, and then press X). Because of the APPEND command, EDIT was able to find AUTOEXEC.BAT, even though it wasn't located in the current directory.

The complete syntax for APPEND is

```
APPEND [[d:]path[;[d:]path][;...] [/PATH:ON|OFF] [/X:ON|OFF] [/E]
```

Again, *path* is the path to a directory on the disk. Each *path* parameter may be accompanied by a *d:* parameter designating what drive the directory is located on.

The /E switch causes the list of APPENDed directories to be stored as an environment string. To prove it, type **APPEND /E**, and then, at the command line, type **SET**. APPEND will show up in the list of environment variables. One implication of this is that the APPEND list may be modified using the SET command. Is there ever a time when this will come in handy? You bet. Recall the APATH.BAT batch file we concocted in the last section. You could create a similar batch file to add directory names to the APPEND list, but only if you install APPEND with a /E switch so that it appears as an environment variable. On the downside, storing APPEND in the environment requires more environment space. If you add the /E switch and suddenly start getting "Out of environment space" messages when you boot up, you'll need to increase the size of the environment with the SHELL command. The /E switch may only be used the first time APPEND is executed. Also, if you use /E, you can't include any *path* parameters in the same command. They must be entered in separate—and subsequent—commands.

The /X:ON switch gives APPEND more far-reaching power to make APPENDed directories appear to be extensions of the current one. Normally, APPEND only intervenes when a program attempts to open a file or obtain a file's size. With /X:ON, however, APPEND extends its services to additional DOS kernel functions that a program is likely to use before it attempts to open a file. The practical implication of this is that if a particular application you run seems not to recognize APPENDed directories, /X:ON may help. This capability may be toggled on and off by rerunning APPEND with /X:ON and /X:OFF switches.

The /PATH:ON and /PATH:OFF options also affect the extent to which APPENDed directories are used. If a program attempts to open a file for which you have not specified a complete path, then DOS will search for it in APPENDed directories. With /PATH:ON (the default), it will also search the list of APPENDed directories if the file name includes a path name. With /PATH:OFF, it won't. DOS will interpret your inclusion of a path name as an indication that you want only that particular directory searched. Like /X, /PATH can be toggled on and off by rerunning APPEND with a /PATH:ON or /PATH:OFF switch.

An example may help clarify the effect the /PATH switch has on APPEND. Let's say you want to edit the file AUTOEXEC.BAT and that it's stored in the root directory of drive C. If you've formerly entered the command

```
APPEND C:\
```

then the command

```
EDIT AUTOEXEC.BAT
```

will bring up AUTOEXEC.BAT for editing, no matter what directory you're currently in. But what happens if you type

```
EDIT \BACKUP\AUTOEXEC.BAT
```

and there is no file named AUTOEXEC.BAT in the directory named \BACKUP? DOS could interpret this in either of two ways: as a signal that you want to create a new file named AUTOEXEC.BAT in \BACKUP, or as an indication that you'd like the APPEND command to automatically take you to where AUTOEXEC.BAT really is—in the root directory. The /PATH switch determines which action is taken. With /PATH:ON, DOS will open the copy of AUTOEXEC.BAT in the root directory. With /PATH:OFF, DOS will ignore the list of APPENDed directories because the file specification you typed contained a path name as well as a file name. As a result, EDIT will create a new file named AUTOEXEC.BAT in the current directory.

You can cancel APPEND with the command

```
APPEND;
```

APPEND still remains in memory, but its directory list is nullified. You can renew the directory list with subsequent APPEND commands. If APPEND was installed with a /E switch, you may also remove the directory list with the command

```
SET APPEND=
```

Now for the caveats. You should never, ever use APPEND except as a last resort. That may seem a strange thing to say after going to the trouble of explaining how it's used, but consider these reasons:

- The APPEND command can get you in trouble. For example, if you open a word processing file from a remote location on the hard disk, modify it, and then save it back to disk, the file will be written to the *current directory*—not the directory where the original file was located. If you're unaware of this, you may go back to the original directory later and wonder why the changes you made to the file weren't saved.

- APPEND can cause no end of difficulties on networks, especially those based on IBM's PC LAN Program. Why IBM chose to name one of the programs included with the PC LAN package APPEND we'll never know, but woe to the hapless user who confuses the two.

The bottom line is that there is nothing APPEND can do for you that sound organization will not. Instead of using APPEND, set up a PATH to the directories where executables are stored and then CD to the directory in which your data files are stored before starting an application program. Then you're sure of where the file is and where modified versions will be placed when they're saved.

If you do decide to use APPEND, be sure to include drive names with the path names. Otherwise you might run into the same sort of trouble you do when you omit drive names in the PATH command: Without a drive specifier, DOS assumes that a directory named in a PATH or APPEND statement is located on the current drive. On other drives, APPEND will not work as intended unless you specify drives as well as directories.

Managing Files

One of the questions new users frequently ask is "What is a file?" That's a legitimate question, but one for which there's no easy answer. Technically, a file is nothing more than a collection of bytes grouped together as one logical unit. The operating system assigns a name to it and keeps track of where it is stored on disk. It also provides commands for us to deal with it and kernel functions to enable programs to read and write it.

Subjectively, we know that a file is much more than that. A file is only a collection of bytes in the sense that a book is merely a collection of words. Perhaps a better way to say it is that a file is an object that stores data. Since the object is owned by the operating system, a program may manipulate that object—read data from it or write data to it—without knowing much about it other than the name under which it was stored.

When you save a document inside a word processing program, the document is saved to disk in the form of a file, utilizing file services built into the DOS kernel. In other words, the word processing program lets DOS do the dirty work of picking out empty sectors on the disk, copying the document to those empty sectors in 512-byte chunks, and keeping a record of what sectors were used for retrieval purposes. When it is later recalled, the file is reloaded from disk, again utilizing DOS file services.

DOS places a few simple restrictions on file names. A file may be given a name up to eight characters long and an extension up to three characters long. The names may include letters of the alphabet, numbers, underscores (_), carets (^), dollar signs ($), tildes (~), exclamation points (!), pound signs (#), percent signs (%), ampersands (&), hyphens (-), braces ({}), and parentheses, among others. A file name may not contain spaces, periods, or symbols that DOS uses for other purposes—greater-than and less-than signs, for example. Finally, certain names are reserved for the operating system and may not be used for files: CLOCK$, CON, AUX, COM*x*, LPT*x*, PRN, and NUL.

In general, there are two types of files that DOS recognizes: executable and non-executable. Executable files are files that contain code. When you type a command on the command line, DOS looks for a file of the same name with the extension .BAT (batch files), .COM, or .EXE (unless it's an internal command, in which case the command is executed from within COMMAND.COM). If it finds a file matching that criterion, DOS loads it and runs it. Thus, you should never assign a data file the extension .BAT, .COM, or .EXE. If you do, DOS will think it's an executable and may try to run it.

You can use this knowledge to your advantage when someone hands you a floppy and tells you to take a look at the program on it without telling you the program's name. It doesn't matter that the floppy may contain hundreds of files; program files must have the extension .COM,.EXE, or .BAT. You can tell which one or ones are programs simply by looking at their file extensions.

Although there are few hard-and-fast guidelines about assigning file name extensions to non-executable files, certain extensions have become widely recognized in the DOS world. Table 5.1 lists just a few of them. A complete and comprehensive list would take up several pages in this book. But this gives you an idea of what commonly encountered extensions are, and helps you identify a file's source and intended purpose even if you don't know anything about it besides its name.

DOS provides several commands for dealing with files, including tools for copying, comparing, deleting, and renaming them. In the next several sections, we'll examine several of these commands, including

- The DIR command, for listing the files in a directory

- The ATTRIB command, for changing file attributes

- The COMP and FC commands, for comparing files

- The RENAME command, for changing file names

- The COPY and XCOPY commands, for copying files

- The DEL and ERASE commands, for deleting files

We'll also look at some of the common pitfalls in using them and creative ways you can put them to work on your system.

Listing the Files in a Directory

Unless this is the first time you've ever used DOS, you know about the DIR command. It lists all the files in a directory. It's probably the most commonly used DOS command. But you may not already know that the DOS 5.0 DIR command is greatly enhanced, offering a plethora of new and long-awaited options for formatting directory listings and for controlling what's shown.

The complete syntax for the command is

```
DIR [d:][path][filename] [/A:attr] [/O:order]
    [/B] [/L] [/P] [/S] [/W]
```

So that you'll have a concise summary of what all the command-line switches do, Table 5.2 lists them in alphabetical order.

When run without command-line parameters, DIR displays a list of the files and subdirectories in the current directory as shown in Figure 5.4. The lines at the top of the listing spell out the disk's volume label (the name assigned to a disk during formatting or with the LABEL command) and serial number, and the directory whose contents are displayed. The two lines at the bottom inform you how many files and subdirectories were counted, how many bytes are used by them, and how many bytes remain free on the disk. The count of bytes used reflects the storage space consumed by files only; subdirectories are assumed to have zero length. In the middle lies the list of files and subdirectories, complete with numbers specifying file lengths (or "<DIR>" identifying subdirectories) and time and date stamps.

TABLE 5.1

Commonly Used File Extensions

Extension	File Type
Executable Files	
BAT	Batch files
COM	Program files (COM format)
EXE	Program files (EXE format)
SYS	DOS device drivers
Non-Executable Files	
ASM	Assembly language source code files
BAS	BASIC source code files
BMP	BMP-format graphics files
C	C source code files
CGM	CGM-format graphics files
DBF	dBASE data files
DEF	Module definition files
DLL	Windows dynamic link libraries
DOC	Word processing document files
DRV	Printer and other device drivers
DWG	AutoCAD drawing files
DXF	DXF-format graphics files
EPS	Encapsulated PostScript graphics files
FON	Font files
FOR	FORTRAN source code files
GIF	GIF-format graphics files
H	C header files
ICO	Windows icon files
IGS	IGES-format graphics files
LIB	Compiler library files
OBJ	Object files (created by LINK)
OVL	Overlay files
PAS	Pascal source code files
PCX	PCX-format graphics files
PIF	Windows program information files
RC	Windows resource compiler files
RES	Windows resource files
TIF	TIFF-format graphics files
TXT	ASCII text files
WKS	Lotus 1-2-3 spreadsheet files (version 1.x)
WK1	Lotus 1-2-3 spreadsheet files (versions 2 and higher)
WPG	WordPerfect graphics files
XLS	Excel spreadsheet files

You can omit the file size and date information with the /B and /W switches. /B lists files and subdirectories minus everything that normally appears to their right. /W (for *Wide*) compresses the directory display by displaying five file or subdirectory names per line. If you prefer lowercase (rather than the uppercase characters DOS displays almost everything in), include a /L (for *Lowercase*) switch with the DIR command.

TABLE 5.2

DIR Command-Line Switches

Switch	Description
/A:*attr*	Displays only those files or subdirectories with the attributes you specify. Valid values for *attr* are

	Nothing	Display everything
	A	Display files whose archive bits are set
	-A	Display files whose archive bits are not set
	D	Display subdirectories only
	-D	Display files only
	H	Display hidden files
	-H	Display files that are not hidden
	R	Display read-only files
	-R	Display files that are not read-only
	S	Display system files
	-S	Display non-system files

Switch	Description
/B	Lists file and subdirectory names only, omitting file sizes and time and date stamps
/L	Displays all file and subdirectory names in lowercase
/O:*order*	Sorts the file name listing before displaying it. Valid values for *order* are

	Nothing	Display subdirectories first, files second, sorted by name
	D	Sort by date and time from oldest to newest
	-D	Sort by date and time from newest to oldest
	E	Sort by extension in alphabetical order
	-E	Sort by extension in reverse alphabetical order
	G	Display directories before files (no sort)
	-G	Display files before directories (no sort)
	N	Sort by name in alphabetical order
	-N	Sort by name in reverse alphabetical order
	S	Sort by file size from smallest to largest
	-S	Sort by file size from largest to smallest

Switch	Description
/P	Pauses for a keystroke between each screenful of information so the listing doesn't scroll off the screen
/S	Searches the specified directory and all its descendant directories
/W	Displays a wide directory listing (five file or subdirectory names per line, omitting file sizes and time and date stamps)

The /P (for *Pause*) switch is convenient to use when the directory listing is more than one screen long. Including this switch causes DIR to pause for a keystroke at the bottom of each screen, ensuring that information doesn't scroll off the screen until you're ready. The DIR command is sensitive to screens displaying more than 25 lines of text, so if you're using a VGA and have 50 lines showing, the /P switch will halt every 50th line rather than every 25th. In Chapter 6, we'll look at how you can use ANSI.SYS in conjunction with the MODE command to achieve 43- and 50-line displays.

Listing by File Attribute   In DOS 5.0, that's only the start of what you can do with directory listings. The /A switch (for *Attribute*) allows you to select entries to include in the listing by attribute. There are five attributes a directory entry may have: archive, hidden, read-only, system, and directory. A *directory attribute* means simply that an entry corresponds to a subdirectory, not a file. The *archive* *attribute* is used by commands such as BACKUP and XCOPY to determine whether a file has been modified since the last time it was backed up, and to selectively copy only those files that were modified. *Read-only* files can be read from but not written to. *System files* are files such as IO.SYS and MSDOS.SYS that are part of the operating system. Finally, *hidden files* are files that do not normally show up in directory listings, hence the name "hidden." System files are normally suppressed in directory listings, too. It's not uncommon for files to be marked with more than one attribute. IO.SYS and MSDOS.SYS, for example, are hidden, read-only, system files, and their archive attributes are set. If a file doesn't contain a read-only, hidden, or system attribute, it's said to be a *normal* file.

FIGURE 5.4

Output from the DIR command

```
Volume in drive C is DOS 5 DISK
Volume Serial Number is 2875-17D8
Directory of C:\

COMMAND  COM      41765 08-15-90    3:33a
WINDEV       <DIR>       11-22-90   11:01a
DOS          <DIR>       10-22-90    4:20p
SYSTEM       <DIR>       10-22-90    4:23p
WINDOWS      <DIR>       10-22-90    4:23p
WP           <DIR>       10-22-90    4:34p
COMM         <DIR>       10-22-90    4:36p
UTIL         <DIR>       10-22-90    4:37p
BOOK         <DIR>       10-22-90    4:38p
MASM         <DIR>       10-22-90    4:38p
MISC         <DIR>       10-22-90    4:39p
BASIC        <DIR>       10-22-90    4:40p
GAMES        <DIR>       10-22-90    4:40p
PE           <DIR>       11-02-90    3:20p
MSC          <DIR>       11-22-90   10:10a
CONFIG   SYS        480 12-05-90    1:09p
AUTOEXEC BAT        656 12-04-90    7:20p
       17 file(s)        42901 bytes
                      16418816 bytes free
```

Briefly put, the /A switch lets you include or exclude certain files and subdirectories from the listing based on the attributes they possess. For example, the command

```
DIR /A
```

displays everything in a directory, including hidden and system files, which are normally suppressed in directory listings. The command

```
DIR /A:H
```

displays *only* hidden files and subdirectories, while the command

```
DIR /A:-H
```

displays only those that are *not* hidden. You include files with a given attribute by including an attribute identifier after the /A switch, and exclude files with a given attribute by preceding the attribute identifier with a minus sign.

In previous versions of DOS, the command

```
DIR *.
```

was often used to obtain a listing of subdirectories in the current directory. (As explained under "Listing the Contents of Other Drives and Directories," the asterisk is a wildcard character that can be used to represent any sequence of characters.) This technique worked as long as all the files had extensions and none of the subdirectories did. In DOS 5.0, you can list the subdirectories by using an /A:D switch, as in

```
DIR /A:D
```

The switch tells DIR to exclude file names from its output. Similarly, you can display files only (no subdirectories) with the command

```
DIR /A:-D
```

You can combine attribute identifiers to further narrow the list of files displayed. The command

```
DIR /A:HSR
```

displays files whose hidden, system, and read-only attributes are set. A file must possess all three attributes to be included in the listing. This command will *not* display the name of a file that is marked hidden and system but not read-only.

Sorting the Listing   The DIR command's /O switch (O for *Order*) allows you to sort the directory listing using one of several sort criteria. Note that this sorts the *listing only*. It does not sort the actual order in which the files appear in the directory.

Table 5.2 provides a summary of the options that may follow /O on the command line. Using the /O switch with no modifiers displays the contents of the directory with subdirectory names first, file names second, in alphabetical order. Had the directory listing in Figure 5.4 been obtained with the command

```
DIR /O
```

it would have appeared as shown in Figure 5.5. Note that the information that precedes and follows the listing remains the same; only the order of the file and subdirectory names is changed.

FIGURE 5.5

Sorted DIR output

```
Volume in drive C is DOS 5 DISK
Volume Serial Number is 2875-17D8
Directory of C:\

BASIC        <DIR>       10-22-90    4:40p
BOOK         <DIR>       10-22-90    4:38p
COMM         <DIR>       10-22-90    4:36p
DOS          <DIR>       10-22-90    4:20p
GAMES        <DIR>       10-22-90    4:40p
MASM         <DIR>       10-22-90    4:38p
MISC         <DIR>       10-22-90    4:39p
MSC          <DIR>       11-22-90   10:10a
PE           <DIR>       11-02-90    3:20p
SYSTEM       <DIR>       10-22-90    4:23p
UTIL         <DIR>       10-22-90    4:37p
WINDEV       <DIR>       11-22-90   11:01a
WINDOWS      <DIR>       10-22-90    4:23p
WP           <DIR>       10-22-90    4:34p
AUTOEXEC BAT        656  12-04-90    7:20p
COMMAND  COM      41765  08-15-90    3:33a
CONFIG   SYS        480  12-05-90    1:09p
         17 file(s)       42901 bytes
                   16416768 bytes free
```

You can list files first and subdirectories second with the command

```
DIR /O:-G
```

In effect, using the /O switch with no modifiers is equivalent to using /O:G, which groups files and subdirectories separately, subdirectories first.

The N, E, S, and D modifiers let you sort the listing by name, extension, size, and date, respectively. Normally, /O:N and /O:E list entries in alphabetical order (the first by name, the second by extension), /O:S lists them from smallest to largest, and /O:D from oldest to newest. Preceding any of these modifiers with a minus sign reverses the order of the sort. To list files from largest to smallest, for example, enter the command

```
DIR /O:-S
```

You can sort on two criteria by including two modifiers after an /O switch. For example, **DIR /O:NE** sorts first by name, then by extension. **DIR /O:GNE** does the same, but displays directory names before file names.

Listing the Contents of Other Drives and Directories   All the examples we've given thus far display in some form the contents of the current directory. You can list the contents of a directory other than the current one by including a path specifier and, optionally, a drive specifier, after the DIR command. The command

```
DIR C:\UTIL
```

displays the contents of the \UTIL directory on the C drive. If you want to list a particular set of files—for example, those with the extension .COM—you can append a file specifier to the end, as in

```
DIR C:\UTIL\*.COM
```

The asterisk appearing in the file name is a wildcard character; it stands for any sequence of characters. To list the .COM files in the \UTIL directory in alphabetical order, type

```
DIR C:\UTIL\*.COM /O:N
```

DOS's other wildcard character is the question mark; it stands for any one character in a file name. For example, the command

```
DIR C:\UTIL\CHAP??.DOC /O:N
```

lists, in alphabetical order, every file in the C drive's \UTIL directory that begins with CHAP, has exactly four, five, or six characters in its name, and has the extension .DOC. This would include CHAP.DOC, CHAP6.DOC, and CHAP06.DOC, as well as any other files that match the description. Almost every other DOS command that deals with files accepts wildcards, too. As we go along, we'll point out those that do not.

Note that DOS commands aren't always consistent in the way they interpret wildcard file specifications. For example, the command

```
DIR A*
```

will list all the files in the current directory that begin with the letter "A," but the command

```
DEL A*
```

will only delete files that begin with A and have no extension. However, the command

```
DEL A*.*
```

will successfully delete everything that begins with A. Most of them were probably oversights in early versions of DOS. However, over time, users come to rely on small quirks in DOS commands to elicit certain behavior from programs and batch files. As a result, the architects of DOS are compelled to replicate these quirks in subsequent versions, lest they render future releases of the operating system incompatible with earlier ones.

Presetting the Default Switches You can change DIR's default behavior by defining an environment variable named DIRCMD and setting it equal to the switches you want included on the DIR command. For example, if you want DIR to always behave as if it had been entered with a /O:N switch, type

```
SET DIRCMD=/O:N
```

to define DIRCMD and equate it to /O:N. Then type **DIR**. The resulting listing will be sorted alphabetically by name, just as if you had typed DIR /O:N.

Any combination of switches that is valid following the DIR command is also valid for DIRCMD. You can even use DIRCMD to specify a default file specification. If you want DIR to list only the files with extension .DOC, enter the command

```
SET DIRCMD=*.DOC
```

If a switch or file specification entered on the command line conflicts with DIRCMD, the command line always takes precedence. If DIRCMD is set to /O:N, for example, and you execute DIR with a /O:-N or /O:E switch, the /O:N will be ignored. Similarly, the command

```
DIR *.COM
```

will display the files with the extension .COM, regardless of how DIRCMD is defined.

You can determine what the defaults are at any time by looking at the value of DIRCMD. To do so, type **SET** at the DOS prompt. DOS will list every environment variable that's defined, including DIRCMD if it exists. To permanently remove any default options defined with DIRCMD, enter the command

```
SET DIRCMD=
```

This removes the DIRCMD definition from memory and erases the accompanying switch settings as a result.

Locating Files on the Hard Disk

The only DIR command-line switch we haven't discussed so far is /S, which lists not only the files and subdirectories in the current or specified directory, but also the files and subdirectories in all its descendant subdirectories.

The reason we saved this switch for last is that it's probably far from obvious why you'd ever want to use it. Consider this: Old DOS hands know a trick with the CHKDSK command that lets them search a hard disk for a particular file. The command

```
CHKDSK C: /V | FIND "CHAP05.DOC"
```

searches drive C for a file named CHAP05.DOC. But this is a highly inefficient way to search for a file. First of all, it doesn't just search for the file; it takes the time to check the entire logical structure of the disk, too. Second, this command actually runs two programs—CHKDSK and FIND—rather than just one, doubling the amount of overhead incurred. And third, you can't include wildcards in the file name, because the FIND command interprets everything inside quotation marks—including asterisks and question marks—literally.

The /S switch, new in DOS 5.0, provides a much more elegant way to perform disk-wide file searches. The command

```
DIR C:\CHAP05.DOC /S
```

searches drive C for CHAP05.DOC, but without carrying any unnecessary baggage along. CHAP05.DOC doesn't have to be in the root directory. Because you included the /S switch, it can be located in any descendant of the root directory, which by definition means any subdirectory on the disk. DIR will list any and all occurrences of the file you specified, along with the names of the directories they're located in. If no matching file is found, DIR will answer "No files found." You can suppress this message by including a /B switch on the command line. /B also omits the file size, time, and date information usually displayed on the right so that the listing is more succinct.

Another advantage to using DIR instead of CHKDSK is that it accepts wildcards. You could search for all files named CHAP05, regardless of extension, with the command

```
DIR C:\CHAP05.* /S
```

Similarly, you could restrict the search to the \DOC directory and all its descendants with the command

```
DIR C:\DOC\CHAP05.* /S
```

In Chapter 7, we'll convert this command (whose length makes it somewhat unwieldy) into a DOS command macro so you can search for a file simply by typing LOCATE followed by the file name.

Altering File Attributes

In the last chapter, we briefly touched on the subject of the directory entries DOS uses to store information about files on the disk. Each entry is 32 bytes long and contains the name of the file, its length, its starting cluster number, and the date and time it was created or last modified. It also contains a record of the file's attributes—properties that files may be assigned that distinguish them from normal, unattributed files. Each attribute is assigned one bit in the directory entry. If an attribute bit is set, then the file possesses that attribute. Thus, you'll sometimes hear it said that a file's read-only bit is set. That's another way of saying that the file possesses a read-only attribute, or simply that it is a read-only file.

The subject of attributes came up again in the discussion of the DIR command, where the /A switch allows us to list files by attribute. We said then that there are five possible attributes an entry may possess. Technically, if the directory bit is set, it's no longer a file, but a subdirectory. There's actually one other attribute that may be assigned: the volume label attribute. DOS uses it to mark volume labels, which are stored in the root directory in the same format as the directory entries for files and subdirectories.

Table 5.3 lists the four attributes that a *file* may possess and that may be altered by the ATTRIB command. The syntax for ATTRIB is

```
ATTRIB [+A|-A] [+H|-H] [+R|-R] [+S|-S] [d:][path]filename [/S]
```

where A stands for archive, H for hidden, R for read-only, and S for system. You can set or clear an attribute by including its identifier in the command and preceding it with a plus sign (to set the attribute) or a minus sign (to clear it). For example, the command

```
ATTRIB +H CHAPØ5.DOC
```

makes CHAP05.DOC a hidden file. Conversely, the command

```
ATTRIB -H CHAPØ5.DOC
```

strips the hidden attribute so that CHAP05.DOC is no longer a hidden file. You can use wildcards in file names passed to the ATTRIB command and combine attribute identifiers to set or clear several attributes in one fell swoop. The command

```
ATTRIB -H -R -S *.DOC
```

makes sure every file with the extension .DOC in the current directory is a normal file by removing any hidden, read-only, and system attributes it encounters. If you run ATTRIB without command-line switches, it displays the attributes of the file whose name you specified.

TABLE 5.3

File Attributes

Attribute	ATTRIB Code	Meaning
Archive	A	The file has been created or modified since the last time it was backed up.
Hidden	H	The file will not show up in directory listings.
Read-only	R	The file may be read but not written. If a program attempts to open the file with read/write privileges, DOS will fail the attempt.
System	S	The file is an operating system file. System files, like hidden files, are suppressed in directory listings.

The /S switch has ATTRIB sweep through all the directories below the current or specified one. For example, the command

```
ATTRIB +R \WP\DOC\*.* /S
```

converts every file in the subdirectory \WP\DOC and all its descendant subdirectories to read-only. Similarly, the command

```
ATTRIB -H C:\*.* /S
```

"unhides" every hidden file on drive C.

There are several reasons you might want to manipulate file attributes. For example, a hidden, read-only, or system file cannot be deleted. But strip its attributes with ATTRIB, and then it can be deleted. Another example: When you perform an incremental backup on your hard disk, BACKUP copies every file whose archive attribute is set. If you wanted to conserve space on the backup floppies, you could go through the hard disk clearing the archive attributes on files you didn't want to back up.

Comparing Files

DOS provides two commands for comparing two files: COMP and FC. Historically, FC has been available only to users of MS-DOS. For reasons known only to IBM, it is omitted from PC-DOS.

COMP is the more Spartan of the two. Its syntax is

```
COMP [[d:][path]filename1] [[d:][path]filename2]
     [/A] [/C] [/D] [/L] [/N:lines]
```

where *filename1* and *filename2* are the names of the two files being compared. The filenames are optional because COMP will prompt you for them if you omit one or both of them. In addition, if you specify a drive or path name only for the second parameter, COMP will automatically look for a file with the same name as *filename1*, but at the indicated location.

COMP reads the two files you specify and compares them byte for byte. The /A and /D switches control how the differences are displayed. /A displays bytes that differ as *characters*, while /D, the default, displays them as *character codes* in hexadecimal format. Use /A if you're comparing two text files, /D if you're comparing binary files. The /L and /C switches are also useful for comparing text files. Rather than display the location where the difference occurred as a byte offset from the beginning of the file, /L displays it as a line number. And /C performs the comparison without regard to case, so that "A," for example, is equivalent to "a." The final switch, /N, is also reserved for text files only. It restricts the comparison to the number of lines specified with the *lines* parameter.

To compare the contents of two binary files, use the COMP command without any command-line switches. A typical command looks like this:

```
COMP TRAIN.PCX BOXCAR.PCX
```

And, if the two files don't match, the typical output for a single mismatched byte looks like this:

```
Compare error at OFFSET 7F00
file1 = A8
file2 = E4
```

indicating the bytes at offsets 7F00H within the files contain different values. COMP will continue comparing bytes until it encounters 10 errors. At that point, it quits. At the end, it asks you if you want to compare more files. If you answer yes, you can enter the new file names right there rather than having to reissue the COMP command.

To compare the contents of two text files, use the /A and /L switches and, if you want to ignore case, the /C switch as well. A typical command line might be

```
COMP \AUTOEXEC.BAT \BACKUP\AUTOEXEC.BAT /A /L
```

while a typical error report might look like this:

```
Compare error at LINE 14
file1 = C
file2 = P
```

This output is slightly more intelligible, because the location where the mismatch occurred is given as a line number, not an offset into the file (/L), and the mismatched bytes themselves are displayed as characters, rather than character codes (/A).

One of the chief limitations of this command is that if the two files aren't the same length, COMP won't compare them. Instead, it displays the message "Files are different sizes," assumes the files can't be the same, and asks if you want to compare more files. It's true that two files of different lengths can't be identical, but it doesn't mean you don't want to compare them anyway. You might, for example, want to compare them up to a point to see if one is a subset of the other. Unfortunately, COMP won't help you there.

But the FC (for *File Compare*) command will. FC is COMP's more sophisticated cousin. Its syntax is

```
FC [d:][path]filename1 [d:][path]filename2
   [/A] [/B] [/L] [/C] [/LBn] [/N] [/T] [/W] [/lines]
```

where *filename1* and *filename2* are the names of the two files being compared; /A abbreviates output by displaying only the first and last lines in a set of differences; /B performs a comparison between two binary files; /L performs a comparison between two text files; /C performs the comparison without regard to case; /LB*n* sets FC's internal line buffer to *n* lines; /N displays line numbers on text comparisons; /T prevents FC from expanding tabs to spaces in text comparisons; and /W causes FC to treat several consecutive spaces or tabs (white space) as a single entity in text files, effectively ignoring the length of the white space. The */lines* switch specifies the number of consecutive lines that must match for FC to resynchronize after encountering a mismatch during a text file comparison.

Whew! That's a mouthful. Let's back up and make some sense out of these switches. First, FC runs in two modes: binary and text. Use binary mode to compare binary files and text mode to compare text files. The difference lies in how FC reports discrepancies between the files.

To perform a binary comparison, use FC's /B switch. /B isn't necessary if one or both of the files have .EXE, .COM, .SYS, .OBJ, .LIB, or .BIN extensions; FC defaults to a binary comparison for these files. The command

```
FC TRAIN.PCX BOXCAR.PCX /B
```

performs a binary comparison between TRAIN.PCX and BOXCAR.PCX. A typical discrepancy is reported as follows:

```
00007F00: A8 E4
```

indicating that the byte at offset 7F00H is A8H in TRAIN.PCX and E4H in BOXCAR.PCX. Had there been more differences, they would have been listed, too. FC doesn't stop until it reaches the end of the shorter of the two files.

All the remaining switches apply to comparisons between text files only. FC really shines when it comes to comparing text files. Whereas COMP simply blunders through the file byte by byte reporting differences, FC attempts to be more helpful by showing you the lines that differ. For example, the command

```
FC \AUTOEXEC.BAT \BACKUP\AUTOEXEC.BAT /L
```

produced the following error report on one system:

```
***** \AUTOEXEC.BAT
set temp = c:\windows\temp
For Microsoft C Compiler 6.0 and Windows SDK
set path=%path%;c:\msc\binb;c:\msc\bin;c:\windev
***** \BACKUP\AUTOEXEC.BAT
set temp = c:\windows\temp
REM For Microsoft C Compiler 6.0 and Windows SDK
set path=%path%;c:\msc\binb;c:\msc\bin;c:\windev
```

A quick glance shows that the second line in the first file lacks the REM statement that the same line in the second file contains. FC not only shows you the entire text of the line, but also the lines on either side of it to help you locate it. Actually, there's a little more to it than that. The third line in each listing is the line where resynchronization occurred after the mismatch. Once a difference is detected, FC attempts to pick up again at the point the two files converge. If the attempt fails, FC displays the message "Resynch failed" and terminates. This effort to preserve synchronicity between files is important when one of the files you're comparing contains lines the other does not, and is one way in which FC is superior to COMP.

If there are several mismatched lines in a row, you can abbreviate the listing by including a /A switch. Rather than displaying every mismatched line, FC will substitute ellipses (...) for all but the first and last in each set.

The /L switch was our signal to FC telling it to perform a text comparison, not a binary one. In truth, it wasn't necessary to include it in this example, because FC would have defaulted to text mode after examining the files' extensions. But spelling these things out explicitly is a good practice—especially since DOS commands and their defaults tend to change from version to version.

Executing the same command with a /N switch produces this report:

```
***** \AUTOEXEC.BAT
    13:  set temp = c:\windows\temp
    14:  For Microsoft C Compiler 6.0 and Windows SDK
    15:  set path=%path%;c:\msc\binb;c:\msc\bin;c:\windev
***** \BACKUP\AUTOEXEC.BAT
    13:  set temp = c:\windows\temp
```

```
14:   REM For Microsoft C Compiler 6.0 and Windows SDK
15:   set path=%path%;c:\msc\binb;c:\msc\bin;c:\windev
```

This time the line numbers are displayed so there's no doubt about exactly where the discrepancy occurred.

The /T and /W switches help you control how FC treats *white space*—computerese for tabs and spaces—in text files. In many cases, you're not concerned about whether a word on a line is preceded by six spaces or seven spaces; you're concerned about the word itself. The /W switch compresses tabs and spaces so that, for example, six consecutive spaces in one file and seven consecutive spaces in the other are treated as if they were alike. This is a particularly useful feature for comparing program files, because most language compilers ignore white space. The /T switch is slightly different. By default, FC expands tabs to spaces with stops at every eighth character. To prevent FC from performing this expansion, start it with a /T.

You won't often need to use the /LB and */lines* switches. The number following /LB specifies the size of FC's *line buffer*—the buffer where it stores text while it makes a comparison. The default value is 100. When FC attempts to regain synchronization after a discrepancy is encountered, it can survive a discrepancy as large as there are lines in the line buffer. With the default value of 100, any difference greater than 100 lines terminates the comparison. You can increase (or decrease) this number with /LB. The */lines* switch plays a similar role. It specifies the number of lines that must match after synchronization is lost for FC to conclude that the files have reconverged. The default is 2 in DOS 5.0. Many users prefer to set *lines* to 1. The command

```
FC \AUTOEXEC.BAT \BACKUP\AUTOEXEC.BAT /L /LB200 /1
```

sets the size of the line buffer to 200 and the number of lines that must match after a difference is detected to 1.

Renaming Files

You can rename a file with DOS's RENAME command, which may be abbreviated REN. The syntax for REN is

```
REN [d:][path]filename1 filename2
```

where *filename1* is the name of the file being renamed and *filename2* is the new name you want to give it. A drive and directory are not accepted with *filename2* because REN does not have the power to move a file from one drive and directory to another. The command

```
REN CHAP05.DOC CHAP05.BAK
```

renames CHAP05.DOC to CHAP05.BAK. The REN command does accept wildcard characters. Therefore, the command

```
REN *.DOC *.WPD
```

changes the extension of every file in the current directory with the extension .DOC from .DOC to .WPD.

Logic would tell you that the RENAME command would also rename subdirectories. But that's not the case. Attempting to do so results in the error message "Invalid path or file name."

DOS provides two methods for changing the name of a subdirectory:

■ Create a new directory of the desired name, copy the contents of the original directory to the new directory, delete the contents of the original directory, and remove the original directory with an RD command.

■ Use the DOS 5.0 shell's Rename command.

The first one is awkward. There's a lot of work involved, especially if the subdirectory you're renaming contains other subdirectories (which may contain further subdirectories). The XCOPY command's /S switch, which copies files and subdirectories recursively, will help for small jobs. But there must be enough disk space to store a duplicate copy of the files. A batch file isn't the answer either, because that would require commands for deleting files and subdirectories recursively. In DOS 5.0, there are no such commands. Clearly there has to be a better way.

That better way is the DOS shell. Even if you choose not to run the shell full time, it's worth the time to fire it up to rename subdirectories. To do so, type **DOSSHELL**. Then highlight the subdirectory you want to change in the Directory Tree window and pull down the File menu. Select Rename, and then enter the new name for the subdirectory. To exit, press Alt-F4. The DOS shell will be explored in depth in Chapter 9.

Ironically, the RENAME function that programs may call on in the DOS kernel possesses the capability to rename subdirectories as well as files. In Chapter 11, we'll take advantage of this fact to develop a command-line utility for renaming subdirectories.

Copying Files

DOS provides two commands for copying files: COPY and XCOPY. COPY is an internal command and has been around since version 1.0. XCOPY is an external command and only appeared in version 3.2. Many of their functions overlap, but each offers some functions that the other doesn't. So although either of them may be used in typical situations, there's usually a good reason to use one rather than the other. We'll discuss those reasons as we examine each of the command's capabilities.

The COPY Command   The COPY command is actually two commands in one. It has two uses: copying files and concatenating (joining) two or more files into one. Used the first way, its syntax is

```
COPY source [/A|/B]
     destination [/A|/B] [/V]
```

where *source* identifies the file or files to be copied and (optionally) their location, while *destination* specifies the location they're to be copied to, the names they're to be given, or both. If you specify a drive or directory for *destination* but no file name, COPY gives the files the same names at the other location. The command

```
COPY CHAPØ5.DOC A:
```

copies CHAP05.DOC to drive A's current directory, while the command

```
COPY CHAPØ5.DOC \BACKUP\DOC
```

copies it to the directory \BACKUP\DOC on the current drive. Similarly, the command

```
COPY CHAPØ5.DOC \BACKUP\DOC\CHAPØ5.BAK
```

copies the file, but changes the name to CHAP05.BAK at the destination. This saves you the extra step of having to rename it at the other end.

You must be careful if you specify a directory name but not a file name for *destination*. If you execute the command COPY CHAP05.DOC \BACKUP\ DOC and there is no DOC directory in \BACKUP, then COPY will interpret DOC as a file name and copy CHAP05.DOC to the \BACKUP directory with the name DOC. It won't give you any warning that it has done this, so it may appear that the copied file simply disappeared. This is one instance when using XCOPY rather than COPY will help. XCOPY (used with exactly the same syntax) will pause and ask you to clarify whether DOC is a directory name or a file name. If the former, XCOPY will create the directory for you if it doesn't already exist. You should also keep in mind that if a file with the specified name already exists at the destination, the new file is written over the old—and DOS neither warns you nor asks for confirmation.

You can use wildcard characters to copy several files at once. The command

```
COPY *.DOC A:
```

copies every file with the extension .DOC in the current directory to drive A. You may also copy an entire directory to another directory by specifying path names rather than file names. For example, the command

```
COPY \COMM \TERMINAL
```

copies everything from the \COMM directory to \TERMINAL. This is equivalent to typing

```
COPY \COMM\*.* \TERMINAL
```

Again, it's your responsibility to ensure that the \TERMINAL directory exists. If it doesn't, the COPY command will appear to have succeeded, when in fact each file in the \COMM directory was copied to the root directory and given the file name TERMINAL. Each file that is copied this way is appended to the destination file, so in the end the root directory will contain a file named TERMINAL that is an aggregate of all the files in \COMM.

The /V switch turns copy verification on. To verify that a file was copied correctly to its destination, COPY rereads what it has written to the destination disk and compares it to what was actually written. Contrary to popular belief, the /V switch does *not* do a physical comparison of the source and destination files. Its primary intent is to ensure that what was written was written correctly. You can make /V the default by executing a VERIFY ON command from the command line.

The /A and /B switches tell COPY that it's copying text and binary files, respectively. These switches are shown twice in the syntax statement because they may be used twice on the same command line—once for *source* and once for *destination.* If no switches are specified, COPY defaults to /B when it is simply copying files and not concatenating them. A switch affects only the file name immediately preceding it. However, if there is a switch after the first but not after the second, the switch is applied to both.

The /A and /B switches determine how COPY treats Ctrl-Z characters, which normally mark the end of text files. If *source* is a text file, COPY copies only up to the first Ctrl-Z in the file. If it's a binary file, COPY copies the entire file from beginning to end, regardless of its contents. If *destination* is a text file, COPY appends a Ctrl-Z to the end of it. If *destination* is a binary file, COPY does not append a Ctrl-Z to the end.

Most of the time you don't have to worry about the distinction between text and binary files. A binary copy (the default) will copy text files just fine. COPY offers these options primarily because of its CP/M heritage.

The second form of the COPY command concatenates files. The syntax is

```
COPY [d:][path]filename1 [/A|/B]
    +[d:][path]filename2 [/A|/B] [+...]
    [destination] [/A|/B] [/V]
```

where *filename1, filename2,* and so on are the names of the files to be joined, and destination is the name and optimally the location of the resultant file. If destination is omitted, the other files are simply appended to *filename1.* The first file named in this command will be overwritten with the concatenated version if you leave off the final parameter.

The command

```
COPY CHAP05A.DOC+CHAP05B.DOC+CHAP05C.DOC CHAP05.DOC
```

combines three files—CHAP05A.DOC, CHAP05B.DOC, and CHAP05C-.DOC—into one named CHAP05.DOC. The only limit on the number of files that can be joined with one command is the 127-character limit DOS places on commands. If you need to concatenate more, divide the operation into several stages. Join a few files at a time, each time using the file created by the previous command as the *filename1* parameter.

The meanings of the /A, /B, and /V are identical to the meanings used with the other form of the COPY command. The one additional point that bears mentioning is that when an /A or /B switch is used, it affects not only the file name that precedes it, but all subsequent file names until another switch is encountered. For example, in the command

```
COPY CHAP05A.DOC /A +
CHAP05B.DOC+CHAP05C.DOC CHAP05.DOC /B
```

CHAP05A.DOC, CHAP05B.DOC, and CHAP05C.DOC are all treated as text files, while CHAP05.DOC is treated as a binary file. When a subsequent switch is encountered, it takes effect with the file name preceding it, not following it.

When files are concatenated, COPY defaults to /A rather than /B, treating the files as if they were text files. If you know that the files are binary, be sure to include a /B switch, as in

```
COPY FILE1.BIN /B +FILE2.BIN BIGFILE.BIN
```

In fact, if you don't know for sure what kind of files you're concatenating, you'll rarely go wrong doing it this way. On the other hand, things can go terribly wrong if you copy binary files as text files. Any file that contains a binary 26 will be only partially copied and the destination will be corrupted when COPY appends a binary 26 to the end of it.

There are occasions when you'll have to use the /B switch. Some users store printer control strings in binary files that can be copied to LPT1 to set the printer to print in compressed mode, for example, or to change from one font to another. Sometimes it's expedient to send two or more control strings with the same COPY command, as in

```
COPY SETCOMP.PRN+CHGFONT.PRN LPT1
```

Here, SETCOMP.PRN contains the instructions to enable compressed print, and CHGFONT.PRN contains the instructions to change printer fonts. LPT1 is the name of the device that the data is being copied to (we'll look more closely at device names in the next chapter). However, there's a problem. These printer control strings, which are binary, will be treated as if they were text strings. Thus, this COPY command may not get the job done. The solution is to modify it to read

```
COPY SETCOMP.PRN /B +CHGFONT.PRN LPT1
```

to treat the files—properly—as binary files.

Here's a short trick for updating the time and date stamp on a file to the current time and date. It requires the /B switch also. The command

```
COPY ANYFILE.DOC /B +,,
```

updates the time and date on ANYFILE.DOC. If you omit the /B, the updated file will come out one byte longer than it originally was if it's a binary file because DOS will append a Ctrl-Z character to the end of it. Similarly, the two commas at the end of the command serve as placeholders, indicating that no additional data should be appended to the end of the file.

The XCOPY Command   The XCOPY command is one of DOS's best-kept secrets. It is similar to COPY in many respects, except that it cannot be used to concatenate files. It will do anything else COPY will, however, and then some.

The syntax for XCOPY is

```
XCOPY source [destination]
      [/A] [/D:date] [/E] [/M] [/P] [/S] [/V] [/W]
```

The command

```
XCOPY CHAPØ5.DOC A:
```

copies CHAP05.DOC to drive A, and the command

```
XCOPY CHAPØ5.DOC \BACKUP\DOC
```

copies CHAP05.DOC to the directory BACKUP\DOC. As we've already noted, XCOPY stops and asks you whether DOC refers to a directory or to a file name, and, if you answer D for directory, creates the directory if it doesn't already exist.

XCOPY is faster than the COPY command in two situations:

- When the file or files you are copying are more than 64k long

- When you're copying more than one file with a single command

This speed advantage stems from two major differences in the way XCOPY and COPY operate. First, to copy files larger than about 64k, COPY divides them into 64k blocks and copies them one block at a time. For a large file, this slows the process down, because more disk accesses are required. XCOPY, by contrast, uses all available memory below 640k to perform the copy. If there is 500k or more free in the system, XCOPY will copy a 500k file in only two disk accesses—one to read the file, the second to write it out to the destination.

XCOPY also cuts down the number of disk accesses when more than one file is being copied. It reads as many files as it can into RAM, writes the information to the destination disk, and then repeats the procedure until all the source files are copied. COPY, on the other hand, copies one file at a time. You'll see a big difference if you use both COPY and XCOPY to transfer a large number of relatively small files. XCOPY will finish much sooner.

This latter technique XCOPY uses to speed up disk transfers offers another advantage, too. Many users today only have one floppy drive on their systems, and the one drive serves as both drives A and B. If you use the command

```
COPY A:*.* B:
```

to copy everything on drive A to drive B on a one-drive system and there are 50 files on the disk, COPY will require you to swap disks in and out of drive A no less than 99 times. If all the files will fit in available RAM, XCOPY will only force you to swap disks once. Even if all the files are large, XCOPY will require less disk handling than COPY and will proceed much faster.

The *source* parameter following XCOPY does not have to contain a file name; it may include a drive or path name only. For example, the command

```
XCOPY A:\*.* B:\
```

copies everything from the root directory of drive A to B. The command

```
XCOPY A:\ B:\
```

does the same thing. There's no need to include the wildcard file specification; the A: is enough for XCOPY to infer that you want to copy everything from the root directory of drive A. However, you may include the *.* if you wish.

XCOPY accepts a number of command-line switches. The /A switch copies only files whose archive bits are set. /D copies only files modified on or after the specified date. Like /A, /M copies only files whose archive bits are set, but it also clears the archive bits afterward. /P has XCOPY prompt you for confirmation before each file is copied. /V enables copy verification, just like it does for the COPY command. And /W has XCOPY wait before it starts copying, providing you the opportunity to swap disks if needed.

The two XCOPY switches we didn't mention in the preceding paragraph— /S and /E—are among the most important. They also serve a related purpose. /S tells XCOPY to copy the files in the current or specified directory, plus *all those in its descendant directories.* In other words, it allows you to perform a recursive copy. In the last chapter, we saw how you can use this capability to copy entire disks. The command

```
XCOPY A:\ B: /S /E
```

copies everything from drive A to drive B, even if A contains subdirectories. The /E switch tells XCOPY to create empty subdirectories on the destination disk. Without this switch, XCOPY passes over empty directories on the source disk.

These switches, combined with the /A, /D, and /M switches, allow XCOPY to serve in a backup capacity similar to the BACKUP command. The command

```
XCOPY C:\ D:\ /S /E
```

duplicates drive C on drive D (the equivalent of a full backup), while the command

```
XCOPY C:\ D:\ /S /E /M
```

copies all the files from drive C that have been modified since the last backup (the equivalent of an incremental backup). One drawback to using XCOPY as a replacement for BACKUP is that XCOPY will not split, say, a 700k file into three pieces to fit onto 360k disks. BACKUP will. In addition, if you're backing up to floppies, BACKUP will make far more efficient use of disk space by bridging parts of files from one disk to another. On the other hand, XCOPY's copies are readable as is; you don't have to run RESTORE before you can use them again.

XCOPY's /M switch, combined with DOS's ATTRIB command, offers an easy solution to the problem of copying a large group of files from a hard disk to floppies when the files won't fit onto a single floppy. First, go to the directory where the source files are stored and type

```
ATTRIB +A *.*
```

Then insert the first floppy in drive A and type

```
XCOPY *.* A: /M
```

When XCOPY indicates that the first disk is full, insert a fresh floppy in drive A and repeat the last command. Continue doing so until all the files are copied.

What's magic about this is that XCOPY knows what files it has already copied onto the previous floppies, so it doesn't duplicate them on later ones. How? Through the archive bit. The ATTRIB command sets the archive bit on every file in the directory. The /M switch on XCOPY copies only those files with archive bits set and clears each one after it's copied. Thus, when you run the XCOPY command anew, it skips over the files that have already been copied.

You can extend this to entire disks or parts of disks, subdirectories included, by adding /S switches to ATTRIB and XCOPY to make the operations extend downward to all the descendant directories.

So when should you choose COPY and when should you choose XCOPY? Use these few simple rules to help you decide between the two on a case-by-case basis:

- To concatenate files, use COPY. XCOPY won't do file concatenation.

- To copy a single file less than approximately 64k long, use COPY. Since it's an internal command, it starts faster. And for small files, there's virtually no speed difference between the two once the copy begins.

- To copy a file larger than 64k, use XCOPY. By requiring fewer disk accesses, XCOPY saves time.

- To copy more than one file, use XCOPY. Again, its increased efficiency in dealing with disks saves time—lots of it if there are many small files. XCOPY is especially helpful when the group of files being copied is too large for one disk.

Follow these guidelines and you can be assured that you're performing the copy in the fastest manner DOS provides for.

Deleting Files

DOS provides two commands for deleting files from hard disks and floppies: DEL and ERASE. Both are internal commands, and both act identically. They also accept the same command-line switches. In fact, COMMAND.COM uses the same internal routine to process both commands, so the two may be used interchangeably. However, since most users prefer DEL for its compactness, we'll use DEL in our examples here.

The syntax for DEL is simply

```
DEL [d:][path]filename [/P]
```

where *filename* is the name of the file or files to be deleted, *d:* and *path* are optional drive and directory specifiers, and /P is an optional switch that has DEL prompt you for confirmation before deleting each file.

The command

```
DEL CHAP05.DOC
```

deletes the copy of the CHAP05.DOC in the current directory, while

```
DEL \WP\DOC\CHAP05.DOC
```

deletes CHAP05.DOC from the \WP\DOC directory. DEL does not accept multiple file names on the command line, but you can use wildcard characters

to delete groups of files that share common characteristics. For example, the command

```
DEL *.DOC
```

erases all files with the extension .DOC from the current directory, while

```
DEL CHAP??.DOC
```

deletes all files that match the specification CHAP??.DOC in one fell swoop.

When you type DEL *.* to delete everything in the current directory, DEL pauses and displays the warning

```
All files in directory will be deleted!
Are you sure (Y/N)?
```

On the chance that you entered DEL *.* by mistake, this warning gives you one last chance to avert disaster. But it's often not effective, because it doesn't list the names of the files you're about to delete. If you're in the wrong directory, you're liable to go right ahead and answer yes, only to discover later on that you should have answered no.

That's why the /P switch was added. Run with a /P switch, DEL displays the name of each file before it deletes it and asks you the question "Delete (Y/N)?" For example, if you're currently in the \WP\DOC directory and type

```
DEL CHAPØ5.DOC /P
```

DOS answers back with

```
C:\WP\DOC\CHAPØ5.DOC,    Delete (Y/N)?
```

Only files that you answer yes to are deleted. This method makes it painfully clear what files are about to be deleted and offers a safeguard against common mistakes such as typing DEL *.* in the wrong directory.

Deleting Stubborn Files   DOS will refuse to delete a file whose read-only attribute is set. We'll use that to our advantage in the next section, which pre-scribes methods for preventing files from being erased. DOS will respond to an attempt to delete a read-only file with the message "Access denied." To work around this, remove the file's read-only attribute by running ATTRIB with a -R switch. For example, to remove the read-only attribute from a file called CHAP05.DOC, type

```
ATTRIB -R CHAPØ5.DOC
```

The ATTRIB command can also be used to remove hidden and system attributes, which will also prevent a file from being deleted.

You may occasionally encounter files with invalid characters in their names, such as spaces. If you attempt to delete a file named MAN MACH.DOC, for example, with the command

```
DEL MAN MACH.DOC
```

DOS will think you're trying to delete a file named MAN (no extension) and interpret MACH.DOC as a separate—and invalid—parameter. The file will not be deleted. If there happens to be a file named MAN in the current directory, it *will* be deleted, even though you didn't intend for it to. Although spaces are technically invalid characters in file names, there are several ways to create such files, usually inside programs that don't fully respect DOS's file-naming conventions.

The solution is to replace the invalid character in the file name with a question mark. The command

```
DEL MAN MACH.DOC
```

isn't valid, but

```
DEL MAN?MACH.DOC
```

is. If there are other files in the directory that match this file specification (unlikely, but possible), you'll need to rename them first so that they won't be deleted also.

Preventing Accidental File Erasures

There are several measures you can use to guard against accidental file erasures. These might be particularly handy if you're a departmental PC manager who finds yourself devoting time and resources to recovering files inadvertently erased by others. Of course, the best news is that DOS 5.0 contains an UNDELETE command for recovering deleted files. But UNDELETE doesn't work under all circumstances, so the best defense is to prevent important files from being erased in the first place.

The simplest of these safeguards is to use the ATTRIB command to make files that you want preserved read-only. Both DEL and ERASE are ineffective against read-only files. For example, to render the file WP.EXE impervious to DEL, go to the directory it's stored in and type

```
ATTRIB +R WP.EXE
```

If someone attempts to delete this file, DOS will answer with "Access denied." This is a great way to build a fence around executable files, but it may have undesirable side effects on data files. If the file is modified, the program that modified it may not be able to write it back to disk. Worse, it may not be able to retrieve it in the first place. As a result, you should normally remove the read-only attribute before you actually use the file.

DOS 5.0's new DOSKEY command, which is discussed in detail in Chapter 7, provides a second way to prevent accidental file erasures. Install the following two commands in your AUTOEXEC.BAT file:

```
DOSKEY DEL=DEL $1 /P
DOSKEY ERASE=ERASE $1 /P
```

These commands create command macros that replace the default definitions of DEL and ERASE with ones that include /P. (The effect is similar to what you get by defining a DIRCMD environment variable for the DIR command.) Then, when you use DEL or ERASE, the /P switch is appended automatically, resulting in a file-by-file list that makes it clear exactly what's about to be deleted.

A more radical but equally effective way to prevent files from being inadvertently deleted is to disable these commands altogether. (This is an especially attractive option if you have an alternative to DEL and ERASE in the form of a third-party file management utility.) One way to achieve this is to change the two commands shown in the last paragraph to

```
DOSKEY DEL=XYZ
DOSKEY ERASE=XYZ
```

Then, provided there is no executable named XYZ.BAT, XYZ.COM, or XYZ.EXE in the current directory or PATH, DEL and ERASE will be rendered ineffective because DOS will try to execute the non-existent XYZ command when DEL or ERASE is typed.

A more permanent way to effect the same change is to patch the portion of COMMAND.COM where the names of internal commands such as DEL and ERASE are stored, a task that's accomplished easily enough with DEBUG. To disable DEL and ERASE in DOS 5.0, go to the directory where COMMAND.COM is stored and, after making a backup copy just in case something goes wrong, type

```
DEBUG COMMAND.COM
E A914 "XYZXY"
E A91F "XYZ"
W
Q
```

This series of commands overwrites the text strings "DEL" and "ERASE" in the table of command names, replacing them with the fictitious names "XYZ" and "XYZXY." Once you reboot, DEL and ERASE will no longer work. If you must delete a file, use the XYZ command (which, after the patch, is a valid command) in place of DEL.

To patch other versions of COMMAND.COM, you'll have to determine the offset addresses of the locations to patch. To do so, start DEBUG with the command DEBUG COMMAND.COM, and type

```
S 0100 C000 "ERASE"
S 0100 C000 "DEL"
```

To each command, DEBUG will respond with one or more hexadecimal addresses in the form *xxxx:yyyy*. If only one address is offered after each command, then you're done. Write the offset addresses down, and then execute the last four lines of the DEBUG script in the previous paragraph, substituting the *yyyy* components of the addresses DEBUG returned for A914 and A91F.

If one or both of the S commands produce two or more addresses, however, you've one step left. Use DEBUG's D command to dump the contents of memory at that address and look for something on the right side of the screen similar to what's shown in Figure 5.6 for DOS 5.0—DOS's table of internal command names. Use the addresses that DEL and ERASE appear at in this listing as the patch points for invalidating the commands.

FIGURE 5.6

COMMAND.COM's table of internal command names

```
0C11:A900  45 4E 41 4D 45 03 DF 1A-0E 85 03 52 45 4E 03 DF    ENAME......REN..
0C11:A910  1A 0E 85 05 45 52 41 53-45 03 57 1A CA 84 03 44    ....ERASE.W....D
0C11:A920  45 4C 03 57 1A CA 84 04-54 59 50 45 03 8D 1B 24    EL.W....TYPE...$
0C11:A930  85 03 52 45 4D 06 04 01-3A 85 04 43 4F 50 59 03    ..REM...:..COPY.
0C11:A940  C3 38 B4 84 05 50 41 55-53 45 06 4A 1A 3E 85 04    .8...PAUSE.J.>..
0C11:A950  44 41 54 45 02 C4 2F C4-84 04 54 49 4D 45 02 2D    DATE../...TIME.-
0C11:A960  30 1E 85 03 56 45 52 02-B7 1D 28 85 03 56 4F 4C    0...VER...(..VOL
0C11:A970  03 BB 1C 30 85 02 43 44-03 77 25 A8 84 05 43 48    ...0..CD.w%...CH

0C11:A980  44 49 52 03 77 25 A8 84-02 4D 44 03 E2 25 EA 84    DIR.w%...MD..%..
0C11:A990  05 4D 4B 44 49 52 03 E2-25 EA 84 02 52 44 03 56    .MKDIR..%...RD.V
0C11:A9A0  26 0A 85 05 52 4D 44 49-52 03 56 26 0A 85 05 42    &...RMDIR.V&...B
0C11:A9B0  52 45 41 4B 02 BC 37 9E-84 06 56 45 52 49 46 59    REAK..7...VERIFY
0C11:A9C0  02 FF 37 2C 85 03 53 45-54 06 D7 22 16 85 06 50    ..7,..SET..”...P
0C11:A9D0  52 4F 4D 50 54 06 BD 22-F6 84 04 50 41 54 48 02    ROMPT..”...PATH.
0C11:A9E0  1F 1F EE 84 04 45 58 49-54 00 19 22 E6 84 04 43    .....EXIT..”...C
0C11:A9F0  54 54 59 03 6B 20 C0 84-04 45 43 48 4F 06 82 37    TTY.k ...ECHO..7
```

A slightly unusual but no less inventive way to prevent a particular file from being deleted is to embed an upper-order ASCII character (one with an ASCII value greater than 127) in its name. The character whose ASCII code is 255 is a popular one for this purpose because it shows up as a space on the screen. To try this out, pick a file you want to protect. Say its name is CHAP05.DOC. Enter the command

```
REN CHAP05.DOC CHAPx05.DOC
```

but rather than type the lowercase x in the second file name, hold down the Alt key and type 255 on the numeric keypad. This will embed an ASCII 255 in the file name. When you list the files in the directory, this particular one will show up as

```
CHAP Ø5.DOC
```

but will defy your attempts to delete it unless you also enter ASCII 255 when you enter the file's name after the DEL command. Actually, you could delete this file the same way you would a file with a space in its name: by substituting a question mark for the space (or, in this case, for the ASCII 255 character). But how many of your colleagues are going to know that?

Managing Text Files

Many of the files you encounter every day as a DOS user are text files—files composed primarily of printable letters, numerals, and punctuation symbols. Earlier, you saw that the COPY command treats text files and binary files differently. So do certain other of the DOS commands, including PRINT, which works with text files only. Before we discuss the three commands that DOS provides for viewing and editing text—TYPE, EDLIN, and EDIt—it's important that you understand what a text file is and what it is that differentiates it from a binary file.

The character set on the IBM PC contains 256 printable characters. The first 128 are modeled after those defined in the American National Standard Institute's specification for the ASCII character set (ANSI Standard X3.4-1977). ASCII stands for *American Standard Code for Information Interchange*. It is a table of 128 characters and control codes assigned numbers from 0 to 127. With the exception of ASCII code 127, which is the code to delete a character, ASCII codes numbered 32 and higher are printable characters (letters, numerals, and other symbols), while codes numbered 31 and lower (the *control codes*) are reserved for special purposes such as marking the end of a line or a page break. The other 128 members of the IBM PC's character set—those with ASCII codes 128 through 255—were devised especially for the IBM PC. This half of the set includes letters accented with diacritics, line-draw symbols for constructing simple boxes, mathematical tokens, and other symbols. Most computers in the world today, with the exception of IBM mainframes (which use a similar but incompatible code called EBCDIC), use some form of the ASCII character set for the representation of data.

The terms *ASCII file* and *text file* are often used interchangeably. By definition, a text file is a file that contains printable text (ASCII codes 32 and higher) organized into lines, with each line delimited by a carriage return (ASCII 13), line feed (ASCII 10), or both. Many text files also contain form feed characters (ASCII 12) marking page breaks in long documents, and tab characters (ASCII 9) denoting tabs. And some text files have end-of-file characters (ASCII 26) marking the points at which they terminate. Other than these, characters with ASCII codes less than 32 are used only sparingly in text files.

Unfortunately, this definition still doesn't go far enough to separate text files from binary files. A binary file can contain any character from 0 to 255, so it's possible to create a binary file that meets the criteria described in the previous paragraph that still isn't what we would normally think of as a text file. As a result, we generally apply a second, more subjective rule when we distinguish between binary files and text files: A text file must be *readable* in the sense that text normally is. In other words, when you TYPE a text file to the screen, it should contain recognizable words and phrases. When you TYPE a binary file, you typically get a lot of strange-looking graphics characters and letters from foreign alphabets, in no particular order. To see for yourself, go to the directory where COMMAND.COM is stored and type

```
TYPE COMMAND.COM
```

The odd assortment of characters that results may be many things, but it's certainly not text. Thus, we don't take too much of a risk when we apply a bit of subjective reasoning to the process of determining the text or binary nature of a file.

Many of the files you use every day are text files. CONFIG.SYS is a text file; so is AUTOEXEC.BAT. Other common text files include batch files, BASIC source code files from DOS 5.0's QBasic Interpreter, DEBUG script files like the ones in this book, and any file created with a program editor or text editor. Text files offer a concise, human-readable means of storing character-based data. It's difficult to look at a binary spreadsheet file and tell what's in it unless you can call it up inside the application that created it or have access to a sophisticated file viewer such as Lotus Magellan. But one glance at a text file with a standard ASCII text editor or file browser is usually enough to reveal exactly what lies within.

Because text files are so important in the DOS environment, it's important that you know how to deal with them. The next several sections show you how.

Viewing Text Files with the TYPE Command

The TYPE command is the most rudimentary of the commands DOS offers for viewing text files. It reads a text file from disk and writes it to the screen a line at a time, continuing to write until the entire file is displayed. There are no command-line switches supported. The command

```
TYPE TEXTFILE.TXT
```

displays the contents of the file named TEXTFILE.TXT. TYPE is one of the few file-handling commands that does not accept wildcards.

For lines that are longer than the width of the screen, TYPE wraps around to the next line, and the next, and to as many as are required to display the line in question. If the listing is more than one screen long, TYPE scrolls the screen with each new line once the screen is filled. You may pause the listing as it scrolls past by pressing the Pause key (or Ctrl-Num Lock on 83- and 84-key keyboards) or by pressing Ctrl-S. A listing temporarily halted may be resumed by pressing any character key. A listing may be interrupted altogether by pressing Ctrl-Break or Ctrl-C. TYPE makes no provisions for scrolling backward in a file.

You can also list files to the screen a screenful at a time without having to hover over the Pause key by piping output from TYPE to the MORE filter (piping and filters will be discussed in Chapter 8). For example, the command

```
TYPE TEXTFILE.TXT | MORE
```

displays TEXTFILE.TXT one screen at a time. At the bottom of each screen, MORE pauses for a keystroke before proceeding to the next one. To use this command, make sure the directory where MORE.COM is stored (normally the directory where other DOS files reside) is in the current PATH. If your system is equipped with an EGA or VGA display adapter, switching into 43- or 50-line mode will enable you to pack more information onto each screen.

The TYPE command is particularly useful when you're trying to locate a file whose contents you remember but whose file name escapes you. TYPEing the file to the screen lets you get a quick peek at the file. You can even use it to take a cursory look at most word processing documents, because even word processors such as WordPerfect and Wordstar that use proprietary formats store most of their text in plain ASCII format. Special codes embedded in the documents (binary codes for boldfacing and underlining, for example) may show up as upper-order ASCII characters, but most of the file's contents will be recognizable.

Editing Files with EDLIN

Every version of DOS has included the simple line-oriented text editor called EDLIN. Legend has it that EDLIN was originally developed by Tim Paterson for his own use in developing tools for the operating system he called 86-DOS. 86-DOS, of course, was the operating system that was eventually transformed into DOS 1.0. In this regard, it was the progenitor of the DOS that we're familiar with today.

By today's standards, EDLIN is crude compared with the many screen-oriented text editors that are available commercially, as shareware, and in the public domain. Line-oriented editors such as EDLIN generally work in command mode rather than interactive mode. For example, to delete a line in EDLIN, you first have to determine its line number, then type

```
10D
```

if it's, say, the tenth line in the file. By contrast, a screen-oriented editor lets you scroll through the file until the cursor reaches the desired line, and then use a key combination such as Alt-D or Ctrl-Y to delete the line. The difference in ease-of-use is striking and becomes more pronounced as text files grow longer.

We won't discuss EDLIN any further here because DOS 5.0 comes with a screen-oriented text editor called the *DOS Editor* that renders EDLIN nearly obsolete. If you aren't familiar with EDLIN already but feel compelled to learn it, refer to the DOS manual for an overview of EDLIN commands and operation.

Then feel free to forget what you've learned; with a little luck, you'll never have to use EDLIN again.

Editing Text Files with the DOS Editor

If EDLIN is a workhorse, then DOS 5.0's new DOS Editor—actually an interactive, full-screen text editing utility based on the program editors used in Microsoft's Quick language series—is a sleek Ferrari. Menu-driven rather than command-driven, the DOS Editor (henceforth, simply the "Editor") presents the entire file to you in an on-screen window and allows you to navigate to different parts of the file with conventional cursor movement keys—PgUp, PgDn, the arrow keys, Ctrl-Home, and Ctrl-End, to name a few—or, if you prefer, with the mouse. It also provides comprehensive on-line help, so you're never stuck wondering what this key does or what menu options to use to carry out a basic operation.

The best way to get acquainted with the Editor is to jump in and take it for a test drive. To start it, type **EDIT** followed by the name of the file you want to edit. When it comes up, you'll see a screen similar to the one shown in Figure 5.7. At the top of the window are the menus that contain the Editor commands and the name of the file being edited (in this case, AUTOEXEC.BAT). To the right of and below the edit windows are scroll bars, which enable you to scroll through the file with the mouse. And in the lower-right corner of the screen the text "00001:001" appears, indicating that the cursor is currently in row 1, column 1.

FIGURE 5.7

The DOS Editor

```
   File  Edit  Search  Options                                 Help
                          AUTOEXEC.BAT
 @ECHO OFF
 REM *********************************************************************
 REM
 REM                              DOS 5.0
 REM                         System Startup File
 REM
 REM *********************************************************************
 REM
 PROMPT $p$g
 PATH C:\DOS;d:\windows;c:\wp;c:\pe;c:\util;c:\masm
 C:\DOS\mode con: rate=32 delay=2
 c:\mag\pcm\util\toggle -n
 loadhigh c:\dos\fastopen c:=60
 loadhigh c:\dos\doskey /bufsize=2048
 loadhigh c:\dos\graphics LASERJETII
 loadhigh c:\util\lpt2file lpt3:=c:\misc\p.txt
 loadhigh c:\util\saver
 loadhigh c:\misc\mouse
 SET TEMP=C:\DOS

 MS-DOS Editor  <F1=Help> Press ALT to activate menus       00001:001
```

The Editor's overhead menus, which you may pull down with the mouse or by pressing the Alt key and the first letter of the menu's name, contain the commands you'll use to create and edit text, manage files, and obtain on-line help. Table 5.4 lists what these commands are.

TABLE 5.4		

DOS Editor Commands

Group	Command	Description
File	New	Begin a new text file
	Open...	Open an existing text file
	Save	Save the current file
	Save As...	Save the current file under a different name or to a different location
	Print...	Print the current file
	Exit	Exit to DOS
Edit	Cut	Delete the selected text and copy it to the clipboard
	Copy	Copy the selected text to the clipboard, leaving the original text intact
	Paste	Insert text from the clipboard at the current cursor position
	Clear	Delete the selected text without copying it to the clipboard
Search	Find...	Search for a specified string
	Repeat last find	Search again for the specified string
	Change...	Search and replace
Options	Display...	Specify screen preferences
	Help Path...	Specify the path to the help file
Help	Getting Started	Invoke general help
	Keyboard	Get help on keystrokes
	About...	Display information about the DOS Editor

An ellipsis (three periods) following a menu option indicates that the command calls up a dialog box for further input. For example, when you select Open from the File menu, the Editor pops up the dialog box shown in Figure 5.8, from which you may select the file you want to open from any drive or directory simply by pointing and shooting. Or, if you prefer, you may enter the file name in the box labeled File Name. Either way, you're asked to make some kind of input. Like a Windows program, the Editor has you do this inside dialog boxes rather than in the main edit window.

The Editor allows you to edit files that are as large as available memory. On a typical 640k PC, that amounts to files as large as approximately 300k. A final note regarding the use of the DOS Editor is that it will not run unless QBASIC.EXE is in the current directory, the PATH, or the directory where EDIT.COM is stored. Why? Because the code for the DOS Editor is actually contained inside QBASIC.EXE, the QBasic program file, not EDIT.COM. All EDIT does when it's executed is invoke QBASIC.EXE with a /EDCOM switch. Therefore, you can't delete QBASIC.EXE to save space on your hard disk if you plan to run the DOS Editor, too. The sections that follow describe some of the Editor's basic features and provide examples of its use.

Basic Text Editing　Creating text with the Editor is not unlike creating it in your word processor. One difference is that lines do not automatically wrap around at the end (lines may be up to 256 characters long, however). Another is that the files created inside the Editor are saved in pure ASCII format, devoid of any formatting information. Other than that, the ways in which they operate are probably very similar.

FIGURE 5.8

The Open dialog box

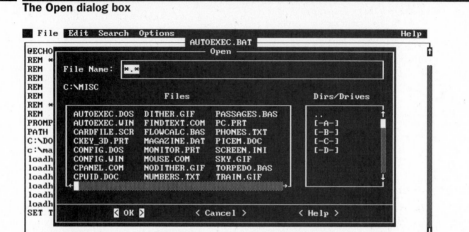

If you're using a mouse, you may position the cursor in the document by clicking on the desired location with the mouse pointer. Similarly, you can scroll through the document using the scroll bar on the right, or scroll sideways with the scroll bar at the bottom of the edit window. You may move the cursor through the document under keyboard control using the keys and key combinations listed in Table 5.5. Some of these key combinations—and other key combinations employed by the Editor—will be familiar to Wordstar users.

The purpose of most of these keys and key combinations is self-explanatory. One exception may be the Ctrl-K and Ctrl-Q series of keystrokes, which permit you to place "bookmarks" in the document—up to four of them—and return to them instantly. For example, if you want to mark a location in the text, press Ctrl-K-0. Then, when you want to return, press Ctrl-Q-0. The Editor will move the cursor back to the spot it was in when the bookmark was placed.

The Ins key toggles insert mode on and off. At startup, the Editor defaults to insert mode. When you switch to overstrike mode, the cursor takes on a block shape as a visual reminder that the text you type will replace existing text.

You can delete characters with the Del and Backspace keys. The key combination Ctrl-Y deletes the current line, while Ctrl-T deletes the rest of the word that the cursor is resting on. Shift-Tab deletes leading spaces from the current line. Finally, Ctrl-Q-Y deletes the text from the cursor to the end of the line. The next section describes how to delete a block of text and, if desired, paste it back in at other locations.

You can save your work at any time by pulling down the File menu and selecting Save. If you want to save the file under a name other than the one shown at the top of the edit window (or in a different location on disk), select

Save As. You'll be prompted with a dialog box where you may enter a new file name, a new location for the file, or both. The first time you save a file, the Save dialog box will come up by default so that you may assign the file a name.

TABLE 5.5

DOS Editor Cursor-Movement Keys

Key(s)	Description
Up Arrow	Move up one line
Down Arrow	Move down one line
Left Arrow	Move left one character
Right Arrow	Move right one character
Ctrl-Left Arrow	Move one word to the left
Ctrl-Right Arrow	Move one word to the right
Home	Move to the beginning of the line
End	Move to the end of the line
Ctrl-Enter	Move to the beginning of the next line
Ctrl-Home	Move to the top of the document
Ctrl-End	Move to the end of the document
Ctrl-Up Arrow	Scroll screen down one line
Ctrl-Down Arrow	Scroll screen up one line
Ctrl-PgUp	Scroll screen one screen-width left
Ctrl-PgDn	Scroll screen one screen-width right
PgUp	Scroll screen up one page
PgDn	Scroll screen down one page
Ctrl-K-0	Place bookmark number 1
Ctrl-K-1	Place bookmark number 2
Ctrl-K-2	Place bookmark number 3
Ctrl-K-3	Place bookmark number 4
Ctrl-Q-0	Go to bookmark number 1
Ctrl-Q-1	Go to bookmark number 2
Ctrl-Q-2	Go to bookmark number 3
Ctrl-Q-3	Go to bookmark number 4

To erase all the current text and start a new file, select New from the File menu. To load an existing file from disk, select Open from the File menu. If the current file hasn't been saved, the Editor asks you if you want to save it before overwriting it with the file about to be loaded. When you're ready to end the editing session, select Exit from the File menu. Once again, if you haven't saved your work, you'll get one last chance to do so.

Cutting and Pasting The Edit menu contains four options for cutting and pasting text: Cut, Copy, Paste, and Clear. *Cut* deletes the selected block of text and copies it to the clipboard. *Copy* copies the selected text to the clipboard. *Paste* inserts text cut or copied to the clipboard back into the file being edited. And *Clear* deletes the selected text without copying it to the clipboard.

Two terms need to be defined here. The *clipboard* is an unseen buffer where the Editor temporarily stores any text that is deleted. Text buffered in the clipboard may be *pasted* to, or inserted at, another location. Second, *selected text* means text that has been highlighted (*selected*) with the mouse or keyboard. You must select text before using the Editor's Cut, Copy, or Clear options. The easy way to select text is with the mouse. To select a block of text with the mouse, move the mouse pointer to one corner of the text, press and hold the left mouse button, drag the pointer to the opposite corner of the block, and release the button. The selected text is highlighted in reverse video. Selecting a block of text using the keyboard involves a similar operation. Move the cursor to the beginning of the block, press and hold one of the Shift keys, and use the cursor movement keys to move to the end of the block. Again, the block is highlighted in reverse video so that it's obvious what the selection encompasses.

Initially, all four options in the Edit menu are grayed out, indicating that they can't be invoked. However, once a block of text is selected, the Cut, Copy, and Clear options turn to black. There are three basic actions that these menu options, in conjunction with Paste (which becomes active once text is copied to the clipboard), permit you to perform:

- To move the selected text from one location to another, cut it by selecting Cut from the Edit menu, move the cursor to the new insertion point, and select Paste. The text will be moved from the first location to the second.

- To duplicate the selected text elsewhere in the document, choose Copy from the Edit menu. Then place the cursor where the text should be copied to, and select Paste.

- To simply delete the selected text, select Clear. Cut does the same thing, but also copies the selected text to the clipboard. Using Cut lets you change your mind if you decide after doing it that you didn't want to delete the text after all. If the clipboard contains text you don't want to overwrite by using Cut, however, Clear is the way to go.

Once a block of text is copied to the clipboard, it remains there until a subsequent Cut or Copy operation replaces it. Thus, you may paste the text back into the document as many times and in as many locations as you want after a Cut or Copy is performed.

Cut and Copy aren't the only two operations that copy text to the clipboard. So does Ctrl-Y, which deletes a line. The line is copied to the clipboard so that you can undo a deleted line by selecting Paste from the Edit menu. In fact, this provides a quick method for cutting and pasting a single line. Rather than take the time to select the line as if a Cut or Copy was about to be performed, delete the line with Ctrl-Y, move the cursor to the new insertion point, and select Paste (or press Shift-Ins). The deleted line will appear at the new location with a minimum of keystrokes required.

Shift-Ins, which is the equivalent of Paste, is one of several *accelerator keys* the Editor offers for quickly performing commonly used operations. These key combinations are especially useful if you don't have a mouse. Rather than press Alt-E to pull down the Edit menu and press C to select Cut, for example, you can press Shift-Del instead. Similarly, Ctrl-Ins is the equivalent of Copy, and Del is the same as Clear. For reference, accelerator keys are listed to the right of menu selections in the pull-down menus.

You may also use the clipboard to cut and paste text between documents. To copy a block of text from one file to another, cut (or copy) the text to the clipboard from the first document, open the second document, move the cursor to the desired insertion point, and select Paste. This works because the contents of the clipboard are retained across documents; they are only discarded when you exit the Editor.

There is no method for determining what is in the clipboard other than actually performing a paste operation. However, you can tell whether there's anything in the clipboard. If Paste is not grayed out in the Edit menu, then the clipboard contains text; if Paste *is* grayed out, then the clipboard is currently empty.

Searching and Replacing   The Search menu contains three menu options: Find, Repeat last find, and Change. *Find* lets you search the current document for a specified text string. *Repeat last find* repeats the search using the same search criteria. And *Change* lets you perform search-and-replace operations.

When you select Find, the MS-DOS Editor pops up the dialog box shown in Figure 5.9. Enter the text you're looking for in the Find What box. By default, the search is not case sensitive. If you want it to be sensitive to case (so that "DEVICE" is not the same as "device," for example), check the "Match Upper/ Lowercase" box located below Find What. Similarly, if you want only whole words matched (so that a search for "OK" does not stop at "INVOKE," for example), check the "Whole Word" box. When you're ready for the search to begin, press Enter or click the OK button at the bottom of the dialog box. The dialog box will disappear, and the cursor will be positioned at the first occurrence of the string. The string will also be highlighted so that you may perform a Cut, Copy, or Clear on it if desired.

FIGURE 5.9

The Find dialog box

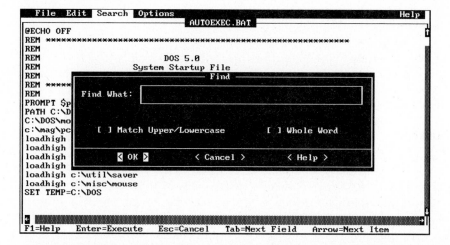

There may be more than one instance of the string you specified. If so, you can continue the search by pressing F3 (or selecting "Repeat last find" from the Search menu). Each successive search stops at the next occurrence of the string. If the string is not found, the Editor will display a "Match not found" message.

The Change menu option permits you to perform automatic search-and-replace operations. The Change dialog box is identical to the Find dialog box, except that it contains an additional text entry box labeled "Change To" and two additional options at the bottom: "Find and Verify" and "Change All." Enter the text you want to replace the original text with in the "Change To" box. Then, if you want the Editor to prompt you before each change is made, click on "Find and Verify." Otherwise, click on "Change All." If you opt for the latter, all occurrences of the target string will be replaced with the new text automatically.

As you can in any of the Editor's dialog boxes, you may elect not to go through with an operation by selecting "Cancel" to dismiss the dialog box.

Printing Your Work   You can print files—or parts of files—from inside the Editor. Selecting Print from the File menu pops up a dialog box with two options: "Selected Text Only" and "Complete Document." As the names imply, these options permit you to print only the selected text or the entire file. If you want to print only a portion of a file, select the text you want to print as if you were about to perform a Cut, Copy, or Clear operation. Then select Print, click "Selected Text Only," and press OK. The selected text will be output to your printer.

One caveat applies to printing text files: the Editor outputs text to the printer using DOS's PRN device driver. One consequence of this is that the Editor assumes that your printer is connected to LPT1. If you use a serial printer connected to a COM port, you'll need to use a MODE command as described in Chapter 6 to redirect printer output from LPT1 to the appropriate serial port before starting the Editor. Similarly, if your printer is connected to LPT2 or LPT3, you'll need to use Chapter 6's LPT2LPT utility to reroute output from LPT1 to the desired LPT port—or print the file outside the Editor, using any of the several means that are discussed in Chapter 6.

Getting On-line-Help   The Editor has an on-line help facility to get you out of trouble spots without having to reach for the manual. This is especially handy when you're on the road with a laptop and don't have access to a printed manual. In most cases, the Editor can offer enough information about the subject at hand to get you up and running again.

Help comes in several varieties. First, notice that when you pull down a menu and drag the highlight bar through the various menu options, the bottom line of the screen displays a one-line description of the command. For further help, press F1. The Editor will pop up a help window with a detailed description of the command and tips on using it. No matter what menu is pulled down or what option is highlighted, F1 will always bring context-sensitive help.

F1, the Editor's designated Help key, brings context-sensitive help at other times, too. For example, pressing F1 with the Editor's Open dialog box displayed (invoked by selecting Open from the File menu) displays the screen shown in Figure 5.10 diagramming the parts of the dialog box and offering advice on what goes where. This type of help is available for all the dialog boxes featured in the MS-DOS Editor with the exception of the About box. Help may also be invoked by pressing the Help button on the last line of the dialog box.

FIGURE 5.10

The File dialog box Help screen

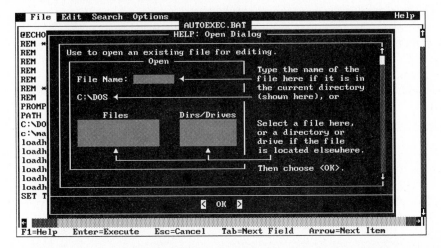

Pressing F1 with no menu or dialog box showing invokes the Editor's general help facility, which divides on-line help into two categories: Getting Started and Keyboard. *Getting Started* includes help on using the help facility itself, using menus and commands, using dialog boxes, options for starting the Editor, and copyright and trademark information. *Keyboard* outlines all the keys that may be used inside the Editor for such actions as selecting text, cutting and pasting, and moving the cursor. Either of these help categories may be invoked directly by going through the Help menu in the upper-right corner of the screen. In addition, the Getting Started window may be displayed at any time by pressing Shift-F1.

When you invoke on-line help, the help appears in a separate window (the help window) resting on top of the edit window, which is downsized so that both windows may share the screen. This is illustrated in Figure 5.11. If you like, you can leave the help window up and continue editing in the edit window. To move the cursor to the edit window, press F6. To move it back to the help window, press F6 again. If you're using a mouse, you can simply move the mouse pointer into the window you want to become active and click once. You may also resize the windows so that each one occupies proportionally more or less room on the screen. From the keyboard, pressing Alt-Plus or Alt-Minus (the gray plus and minus keys on the numeric keypad) makes the active window (the one whose name is highlighted) larger or smaller, respectively. With the mouse, you can resize the windows by dragging the line that divides them up or down. Position the mouse pointer over the line, hold down the left mouse button, and drag. When the windows are sized the way you want them, release the mouse button.

You can even print help if you wish. To do so, use the help menus to display the help topic of interest, and then select Print from the File menu. Rather than say "Selected Text Only" and "Complete Document" as it normally does, the Print dialog box will now offer the choices "Selected Text Only" and "Current Window." If the help window is the active one, selecting the second option— "Current Window"—will print the contents of the help window. If you want to print only part of the help text, use the mouse or keyboard to select the text to be printed the same way you would select text in the edit window; then select the "Selected Text Only" option from the dialog box.

FIGURE 5.11

Help and edit windows displayed simultaneously

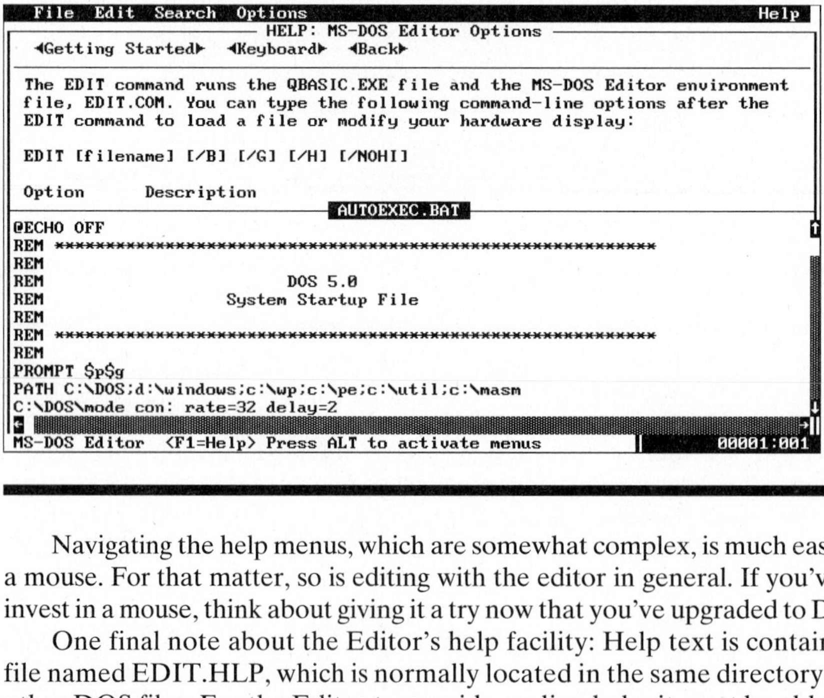

```
   File  Edit  Search  Options                                    Help
┌───────────────────── HELP: MS-DOS Editor Options ─────────────────────┐
│  ◄Getting Started►  ◄Keyboard►  ◄Back►                                 │
│                                                                        │
│  The EDIT command runs the QBASIC.EXE file and the MS-DOS Editor environment │
│  file, EDIT.COM. You can type the following command-line options after the   │
│  EDIT command to load a file or modify your hardware display:          │
│                                                                        │
│  EDIT [filename] [/B] [/G] [/H] [/NOHI]                                │
│                                                                        │
│  Option      Description                                               │
│              ┌────────────── AUTOEXEC.BAT ──────────────┐              │
│ @ECHO OFF                                                              ↑
│ REM ******************************************************************  │
│ REM                                                                     │
│ REM                       DOS 5.0                                       │
│ REM                  System Startup File                                │
│ REM                                                                     │
│ REM ******************************************************************  │
│ PROMPT $p$g                                                             │
│ PATH C:\DOS;d:\windows;c:\wp;c:\pe;c:\util;c:\masm                     │
│ C:\DOS\mode con: rate=32 delay=2                                      ↓│
├─◄──────────────────────────────────────────────────────────────────►──┤
│  MS-DOS Editor  <F1=Help> Press ALT to activate menus      00001:001  │
└────────────────────────────────────────────────────────────────────────┘
```

Navigating the help menus, which are somewhat complex, is much easier with a mouse. For that matter, so is editing with the editor in general. If you've yet to invest in a mouse, think about giving it a try now that you've upgraded to DOS 5.0.

One final note about the Editor's help facility: Help text is contained in a file named EDIT.HLP, which is normally located in the same directory as your other DOS files. For the Editor to provide on-line help, it must be able to find EDIT.HLP. It looks in two places: the current directory and every directory in the current PATH. If EDIT.HLP is located in neither location, use the Help Path option under the Options menu to specify the drive and directory where it is located.

Customizing the Editor   The Display option under the Options menu allows you to set the foreground and background colors in the edit window, display or hide the scroll bars at the edges of the edit window, and specify how many spaces separate tab stops. In most cases, the defaults are adequate. However, you may prefer a different selection of text colors; if so, you can change them here. If you don't use a mouse, you may elect to hide the scroll bars so they don't occupy valuable real estate on the screen. The Editor saves the changes you make in a file called QBASIC.INI so your preferences will be preserved from one editing session to the next.

The switches that follow EDIT on the command line provide further opportunities for customization. The full syntax for the command is

```
EDIT [[d:][path]filename] [/B] [/G] [/H] [/NOHI]
```

The *filename* parameter is the name of the file that is loaded when the Editor is started. /B runs the Editor in monochrome for the benefit of users who pair monochrome monitors with color video adapters. /G enables fast screen updates on CGA video adapters. By default, if the Editor detects that it is running on a CGA, it uses a method for writing to the screen that prevents a snow-like interference (the result of the CPU and the CGA video refresh circuitry contending for access to video RAM at the same time) from appearing, but also inhibits display performance. /G speeds up the display; it also produces snow on true CGA clones. /G is the default on non-CGA video adapters. The /H switch has the Editor alter the video mode to display the maximum number of lines possible on your video adapter. For a VGA, this is 50 lines; for an EGA, it's 43. Either way, this switch enables you to pack almost twice as much information onto the screen as a conventional 25-line display. Finally, /NOHI is for the small subset of monitors that do not support high-intensity (bold) characters.

The /B and /NOHI switches are useful on laptops. If you're running EDIT on an LCD screen that doesn't do a very good job of translating color levels to shades of gray, try one or both of these switches. If that doesn't work to your satisfaction, try adjusting the screen colors with the Display command.

Summary

DOS 5.0 provides the most sophisticated set of file and directory management tools that any version has offered to date. There isn't much you can't do when you apply these tools resourcefully. However, it's equally important to know how and when they'll get you into trouble. It is hoped that you'll come away from this chapter with a better feel for how these commands work and for how to overcome common problems, such as files that refuse to be deleted or directions that resist your attempts to remove them.

The next chapter goes beyond drive, directory, and file management and introduces the subject of how DOS interacts with some of the other devices attached to your system—namely, the screen, keyboard, and printer. Earlier, we mentioned that it's possible to display more than 25 rows of text on the screen with EGA and VGA video adapters. It's also possible to program the keyboard to assign commands to function keys, speed up the cursor, and more. No matter how you use your system, you should find something there to help make using it just a little bit easier.

6 SCREENS, KEYBOARDS, AND PRINTERS

FEW WOULD ARGUE THAT DOS'S SUPPORT FOR HARD DISKS AND FLOPPY DISKS of all types is anything less than robust. But there are other devices attached to your system that are just as important and that DOS has traditionally been found lacking in its support for: namely, your screen, keyboard, and printer.

While it's certainly no panacea, DOS 5.0 does a lot to atone for the sins of versions past. For example, it's now possible to use ANSI.SYS to set the screen colors to something besides white-on-black without experiencing the problems this caused in earlier versions. If you have an EGA or VGA video adapter, DOS 5.0 will display more than 25 lines of text. Through ANSI.SYS, it is also possible to remap keys on the keyboard and assign them macro-like character strings so that pressing one key has the same effect as pressing many. To make typing faster, you now have the option of specifying typematic rates and delay intervals on AT and enhanced keyboards. And DOS 5.0 provides better support for printers than any version before it, thanks to an updated GRAPHICS command that supports EGA and VGA display adapters as well as LaserJet printers.

In the course of this chapter, you'll learn how to use all these features of DOS 5.0 and more. You'll also learn how video adapters, keyboards, and printers work on the IBM PC and how DOS interacts with them. Where DOS falls short in its handling of these devices, we'll introduce short DEBUG utilities to take up the slack. Finally, at the end of the chapter we'll take up the subject of code page switching, which permits users in countries other than the United States to adapt the character sets used on their PCs for international settings.

Screens

In the early days, video options for the IBM PC were limited. When the IBM PC was introduced in 1981, IBM only offered two display adapters to go with it: a monochrome card called the *Monochrome Display Adapter (MDA)*, and a color card called the *Color/Graphics Adapter (CGA)*. The MDA offered crisp, readable text with each character displayed in a 9-by-14-dot-character matrix, but lacked the ability to display graphics. The CGA offered graphics resolutions up to 640 by 200 and as many 16 colors in selected video modes, but at a cost: Characters on a CGA, which were rendered in a fuzzy 4-by-8-dot-character matrix, appeared indistinct when compared to characters displayed on an MDA. Thus, buyers were faced with a tough choice: Choose text clarity and give up the ability to display graphics images and color, or pick color and graphics and live with lower text resolutions.

Other manufacturers rushed to fill the void left by IBM. The Hercules Graphics Card, a monochrome card that was compatible with IBM's MDA in text mode but that could also be programmed for graphics, became a popular alternative to the MDA and CGA. The *Enhanced Graphics Adapter (EGA),* introduced in 1984, was IBM's solution to the functionality gap between the two adapters. The designers of the EGA combined desirable qualities from both the CGA and the MDA and threw in a few twists of their own to produce a graphics adapter with high text legibility. The *Video Graphics Array (VGA)* followed in 1987. The VGA did the EGA one better in terms of color, resolution, and text legibility, and quickly became a standard in the IBM world, partly because it was a system board component on IBM's Micro Channel-based PS/2 machines and partly because video manufacturers successfully cloned it, making low-cost VGAs available to owners of non-Micro Channel PCs.

Regardless of the type of video adapter installed in a system, DOS interacts with it through the CON device driver, which is automatically loaded into memory each time DOS is booted. CON provides simple character-oriented services to the operating system that permit DOS to write characters to the screen by calling the CON driver via a software interrupt. CON, in turn, relies on functions built into the video BIOS to drive the video hardware. By doing so, it effectively insulates DOS from the nuances of dealing with video adapters at the hardware level and renders the operating system somewhat independent of the video platform it is run on.

DOS comes with an extended console driver called ANSI.SYS that may be installed with a DEVICE directive in CONFIG.SYS. When it is loaded, ANSI.SYS replaces CON as the default console driver and provides a set of services that is a superset of those offered by CON. The advantage to using it is that while CON is a plain vanilla driver unable to accommodate color or to reprogram a video adapter to unlock its hidden capabilities, ANSI.SYS is far more sensitive to the hardware it's running on and willing to exploit it for your gain. In subsequent sections, we'll explore the capabilites of ANSI.SYS more fully and show how you can use it to select screen colors, display more than 25 lines of text, and personalize the DOS prompt.

Before we embark on a discussion of ANSI.SYS, however, it would be beneficial for you to have a basic understanding of how video works on the IBM PC—how characters are displayed on the screen, what determines the colors they're displayed in, and so on. If you're not familiar with these tenets already, the next section provides a brief introduction to PC display architecture that will help bring you up to speed.

PC Display Architecture

On the IBM PC, characters are displayed on the screen by entering their ASCII values into a portion of memory known as the *video buffer*. In color text modes, the video buffer starts at absolute address B8000H (the 736k mark); in monochrome text modes, it begins at address B0000H (704k). Character-generating circuitry in the video adapter translates ASCII values stored in memory to pixel patterns on the screen so that the value 41H, for example (the ASCII code for

"A"), produces the letter "A." Hence, we say that video on the IBM PC is memory-mapped, because what's stored in the video buffer is mapped directly to the screen by the display system hardware.

Figure 6.1 shows the structure of the video buffer in 80-column-by-25-line (or row) text mode. For each character cell on the screen, there are two corresponding bytes in the video buffer. One byte holds the ASCII code of the character displayed in that cell (empty cells are assigned the value 20H, the ASCII code for the space character); the other holds the character's *attribute*. On color systems, the attribute byte determines the character's foreground and background color, whether it is displayed with bold or normal intensity, and whether it is blinking or non-blinking. In monochrome modes, where color has no meaning, the attribute byte determines the character's intensity, whether it is underlined, whether it blinks, and whether it's displayed in normal or reverse video.

FIGURE 6.1

The text-mode video buffer

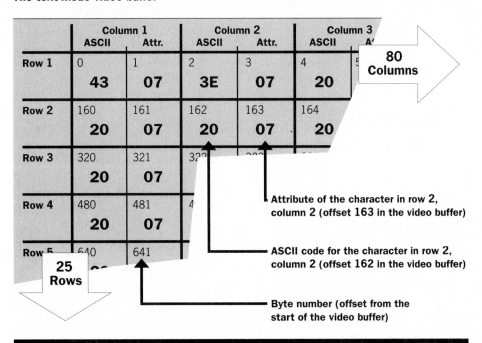

On color systems, the foreground and background colors a character is displayed in are determined by the settings of the bits in the attribute byte. There are three color bits available for specifying foreground colors and three for background, corresponding to the three color guns on a color RGB monitor: red, green, and blue. Setting the red bit for foreground and the blue bit for background, for example, produces a red character on a blue background. Colors other than red, green, and blue can be obtained by combining colors. White, for example, is produced by setting all three color bits. Cyan comes from combining blue and green but leaving red off. Since there are eight different combinations that can be formed from three bits, foreground and background colors on an IBM PC can be selected from any of eight colors. These colors, and the RGB values used to generate them, are listed in Figure 6.2. Note that each foreground color may be displayed in bold or normal intensity, increasing the effective number of foreground colors available from 8 to 16.

FIGURE 6.2

Mapping of the color attribute byte

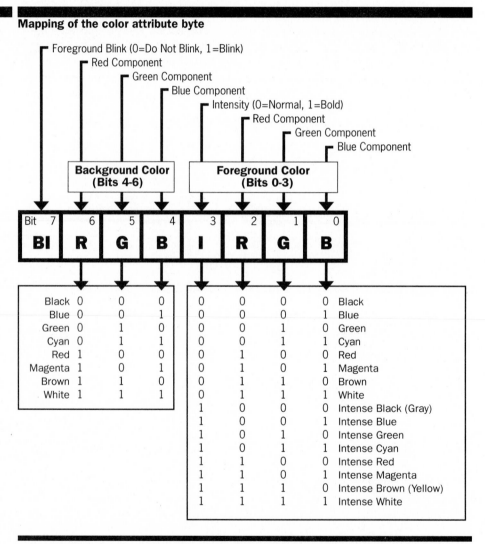

Character bytes and attribute bytes are interleaved such that the first byte in the video buffer determines what character is displayed in the upper-left corner of the screen, the second byte determines how it is displayed, the third byte determines what character is displayed one cell to the right of the one in the upper-left corner, and so on. Another way to look at it is that even-numbered bytes (starting at offset 0) hold character codes, while odd-numbered bytes hold character attributes. Character cells on the screen are numbered from left to right, top to bottom, in sequential order. Bytes 978 and 979 in the video buffer correspond to the 490th character on the screen, which is the tenth character from the left on the seventh line of an 80-column display.

Knowing this, you can better understand the nature of DOS's interactions with the video hardware. First, DOS uses the CON device driver as a go-between for nearly all its interactions with the screen. DOS doesn't understand color because CON doesn't understand color. CON (using routines in the BIOS) writes text to the screen by poking ASCII codes into even-numbered bytes, leaving the attribute bytes in between alone. Furthermore, when you clear the screen with CLS, DOS writes the value 07H to all the attribute bytes so that everything is set to white on black. ANSI.SYS, however, writes attribute bytes as well as character bytes to video memory. That's why, with ANSI.SYS installed, you can select color schemes other than DOS's default white-on-black by passing the appropriate commands to the ANSI.SYS console driver—commands that we'll examine in detail in subsequent parts of this chapter.

The ANSI.SYS Driver

ANSI.SYS is an extended screen and keyboard control device driver that permits PCs to emulate terminals using a subset of the terminal control functions defined in ANSI standard 3.64-1979. Before the days of memory-mapped video and one-user, one-CPU computing architectures, it was customary for programs run on mainframes to send escape sequences (character strings preceded by an escape character, ASCII 27) to terminals to perform such display-related functions as moving the cursor and changing text colors. With ANSI.SYS installed, a PC becomes the equivalent of one of these terminals. If they wish, DOS application programs may send commands to ANSI.SYS to manipulate the display.

Not many programs rely on ANSI.SYS for screen control, for two reasons. First, the PC's video BIOS contains screen control functions that are faster, more versatile, and more far-reaching than ANSI.SYS. For example, to move the cursor to a certain row and column, it's more expedient to call function 02H in the video BIOS (which sets the cursor position) than it is to output a long escape sequence to ANSI.SYS, which ultimately calls function 02H anyway. Second, using ANSI.SYS screen services requires ANSI.SYS to be installed. In many earlier versions of DOS, this presented a problem because ANSI.SYS had inherent flaws that sometimes caused conflicts with other programs. If that weren't enough, it also consumed valuable memory that many users weren't willing to take away from their already RAM-starved application programs.

Many of these flaws were corrected in DOS 5.0. For example, ANSI.SYS is now compatible with 43- and 50-line screens and may now be installed in high memory on compatible systems with DOS 5.0's new DEVICEHIGH directive. But because these features have come so late, few applications currently (or ever will) use it. Although ANSI.SYS may be of limited use to application programs, it is still extremely useful for enhancing the DOS command line. And as we'll see later, it's also useful for enhancing keyboard operations.

Before you can use the examples in this section, ANSI.SYS must be installed with a DEVICE or DEVICEHIGH directive in CONFIG.SYS. Its complete syntax is

```
DEVICE=ANSI.SYS [/K] [/X]
```

The /K switch directs ANSI.SYS to ignore certain keys on 101- and 102-key keyboards, including function keys F11 and F12. With this switch, an enhanced keyboard acts very much like an XT- or AT-style keyboard. If you install ANSI.SYS with a /K switch, you should also add a SWITCHES=/K statement to your CONFIG.SYS file. The /X switch tells ANSI.SYS that duplicate keys on 101- and 102-key keyboards are to be mapped separately. This means that if you redefine the Home key, only the Home key on the numeric keypad will be affected; the Home key to the left of the keypad will still act as Home. Without /X, both Home keys are remapped.

Sending Commands to ANSI.SYS

Before you can use ANSI.SYS to spruce up the display, you have to find a way to pass commands to it. Your mechanism for doing so is any DOS command that writes to *standard output*—the predefined I/O channel that DOS provides as a means for programs to transmit data to the CON device driver. By default, standard output goes to the screen, but users may redirect it to a file or to another physical device (a printer attached to COM1 or LPT1, for example) by using a redirection or piping operator on the command line. ANSI.SYS examines the stream of characters written to standard output and interprets any that are preceded by escape characters as commands for the keyboard or screen.

There are three DOS commands that write to standard output: PROMPT, TYPE, and ECHO. For our purposes, the most utilitarian of these is PROMPT, which lets you represent escape characters, line terminators, and piping and redirection operators with special metastrings that are easily entered at the keyboard. For example, the command

```
PROMPT $e[2J
```

clears the screen just like CLS does. The $e is the PROMPT equivalent of the escape character; when PROMPT sees it, it outputs an ASCII 27 in its place. ESC[2J is the ANSI.SYS command to clear the screen. Issuing the same command using TYPE or ECHO would require that you enter it in a text file and embed an actual escape character by typing **027** on the numeric keypad with the Alt key held down or by some similar method.

One annoying side effect of using PROMPT to output ANSI.SYS escape sequences is that the DOS prompt is destroyed. If your AUTOEXEC.BAT file contains a command such as PROMPT pg to set the system prompt, you'll have to enter PROMPT pg again to restore it. You can restore the default DOS prompt C> by entering PROMPT without any parameters.

Setting Screen Colors with ANSI.SYS

Setting screen colors in DOS has always been a problem. Were Henry Ford alive today, he might quip that DOS comes in any color you like—as long as what you like is white on black. The color attribute 07H (0, or black, for the background, and 7, or white, for the foreground) hardcoded into COMMAND.COM ensures that typing CLS will clear the screen to white on black. But with ANSI.SYS installed, you can override the default screen attributes and specify the color scheme of your choice.

You tell ANSI.SYS what colors to use with a command of the form

```
PROMPT $e[code;code; ...m
```

where *code* is a foreground color, background color, or attribute value code taken from Table 6.1.

TABLE 6.1

ANSI.SYS Attributes and Color Codes

Code	Attribute	Code	Foreground Color	Code	Background Color
0	All attributes off	30	Black	40	Black
1	Bold (intensify foreground color)	31	Red	41	Red
4	Underline (monochrome displays only)	32	Green	42	Green
5	Blink	33	Yellow	43	Yellow
7	Reverse video	34	Blue	44	Blue
8	Concealed	35	Magenta	45	Magenta
		36	Cyan	46	Cyan
		37	White	47	White

Foreground colors are specified with the values 30 through 37; background colors with the values 40 through 47; and other text attributes with the values 0, 1, 4, 5, 7, and 8. The command

```
PROMPT $e[37;44m
```

sets the screen colors to white on blue. All text that DOS writes to the screen will use this color combination, and typing CLS will clear the screen to these colors. A "1" in the escape sequence turns on the bold attribute. The command

```
PROMPT $e[1;37;44m
```

sets the screen colors to bright white against a blue background, while the command

```
PROMPT $e[0;37;44m
```

turns bold off, restoring the screen to unintensified white on blue. The bold attribute affects only the foreground color, not the background. ANSI.SYS lets you choose from any combination of 16 foreground colors (eight different colors in bold or normal intensity) and eight different background colors. The *concealed* option (code 8) places ASCII character codes in memory, but sets the foreground color equal to the background color to render characters invisible.

Setting Screen Colors Without ANSI.SYS

There are several ways to produce other color combinations on the command line without ANSI.SYS, but few of them are as simple—or as effective—as patching COMMAND.COM to clear the screen to something other than white on black.

COMMAND.COM is an assembly language program that is similar to application programs in many respects. It even uses DOS and BIOS services like application programs do. In fact, when you type CLS, COMMAND.COM calls on function 06H in the video BIOS (accessed through interrupt 10H) to clear the screen. With DEBUG, it's easy enough for assembly language programmers to find the code sequence that does this and patch it to write an attribute value other than 07H (black on white) to the video buffer.

Here's how. First, make a backup copy of COMMAND.COM just in case something goes wrong when you modify the original. Also, make sure you have a system-formatted floppy (one you can boot from) handy so that if COMMAND.COM is damaged beyond repair, you can boot from the floppy and restore COMMAND.COM from the backup.

Once that's done, go to the directory where COMMAND.COM is stored and type

```
DEBUG COMMAND.COM
```

Then, at DEBUG's hyphen prompt, type

```
S 0100 8000 CD 10
```

In DOS 5.0, DEBUG will respond with the following listing:

```
1BCC:432B
1BCC:4337
1BCC:435F
1BCC:436C
1BCC:4370
1BCC:4376
```

These are the addresses in memory where the code sequence CD 10 (machine code for INT 10H) is located. The four digits to the left of the colon—1BCC in this listing—will probably differ on your machine. The S command (for Search)

you typed told DEBUG to search the current code segment from offsets 0100 through 8000 for every occurrence of CD followed by 10. DEBUG responded with a list of addresses in segment:offset form.

Now that you've identified the general range of addresses that the instructions occur at with the S command, use DEBUG's U (Unassemble) command to disassemble the code in and around these addresses. In DOS 5.0, you'll find on a code sequence beginning at offset 4362 that looks like this:

```
XOR     AX,AX
MOV     CX,AX
MOV     AH,06
MOV     BH,07
XOR     BL,BL
INT     10
```

This is the code that clears the screen when you type CLS. It calls on interrupt 10H, function 06H in the BIOS to perform the deed. Before the call is placed, the video attribute to be used on the screen is loaded into register BH. Note that in this code sequence, the value 07H, which corresponds to white on black, is used. If you trace further on through the code, you'll also see that COMMAND-.COM returns the cursor to the upper-left corner of the screen after clearing it.

All you need do to produce your own color combination is change the 07 in the instruction MOV BH,07, which resides at offset 4369 in the DOS 5.0 version of COMMAND.COM. First, form a 2-digit attribute byte from the foreground and background values shown in Table 6.2. The background value should be the left digit, the foreground value, the right. Then use DEBUG's E command to patch the value into COMMAND.COM.

TABLE 6.2

IBM PC Foreground and Background Color Codes

Color	Background	Foreground
Black	0	0
Blue	1	1
Green	2	2
Cyan	3	3
Red	4	4
Magenta	5	5
Brown	6	6
White	7	7
Gray	—	8
Intense Blue	—	9
Intense Green	—	A
Intense Cyan	—	B
Intense Red	—	C
Intense Magenta	—	D
Yellow	—	E
Intense White	—	F

To have CLS clear the screen to intense white on blue rather than white on black, for example, change 07 to 1F. Or for green on black, use 02. To patch the value into COMMAND.COM, use the following series of DEBUG commands:

```
DEBUG COMMAND.COM
E 4369 xx
W
Q
```

Substitute the attribute value you selected for *xx*. The E command (short for Enter) replaces the byte at offset 4369 with the value you supply. The W command (Write) saves the modified version of COMMAND.COM to disk, and Q quits DEBUG. After you've made the change, remember to restart your PC. The modifications won't take effect until COMMAND.COM is reloaded. Also make sure that ANSI.SYS is not loaded; if it is, it will override the changes you made to COMMAND.COM.

One more tip: The offset address of COMMAND.COM's color attribute and the code that clears the screen change from release to release. This method works with any existing version of DOS (and conceivably with future versions as well) provided you know enough about assembly language to search out the code that clears the screen and determine the exact address of the attribute byte loaded into BH before making changes with DEBUG. Remember that the addresses listed here are valid for DOS 5.0 only. If you're not familiar with assembly language and are working with a version of DOS other than 5.0, you may be interested in the procedure for setting screen colors outlined in the next section.

Setting Colors Without ANSI.SYS, Part II

There's an even easier way to get the screen colors you want from DOS, one that doesn't require patching COMMAND.COM or installing ANSI.SYS. To try it, make sure that ANSI.SYS is not installed and type in the following DEBUG listing to create a short utility called CLEAR.COM:

```
A 0100
MOV     AH,12           ;Test for EGA/VGA
MOV     BL,10
INT     10
MOV     AX,0040         ;Point DS to BIOS data area
MOV     DS,AX
MOV     AX,0600         ;Clear the screen using BIOS
MOV     BH,1F           ;  interrupt 10H, function
SUB     CX,CX           ;  06H
MOV     DH,18
CMP     BL,10
JZ      011D
```

```
MOV     DH,[0084]
MOV     DL,[004A]
DEC     DL
INT     10
MOV     AH,02                    ;Home the cursor
MOV     BH,[0062]
SUB     DX,DX
INT     10
RET

N CLEAR.COM
RCX
30
W
Q
```

Place CLEAR.COM in a directory in your DOS PATH. Then, to clear the screen to white on blue, type **CLEAR** rather than CLS. Or, for a different color combination, change the 1F in the line MOV BH,1F (the line that loads the color attribute the BIOS function uses to clear the screen) to the color attribute you want.

As we'll see in Chapter 7, DOS 5.0 lets you create command macros that take precedence over internal commands such as CLS. You can use this feature of version 5.0 to create a macro that runs CLEAR.COM every time you enter CLS, in effect coercing CLS into clearing the screen using the colors of your choice. To demonstrate, make sure CLEAR.COM is in the current PATH and type

```
DOSKEY CLS=CLEAR
```

Thereafter, when you type CLS, the screen will be cleared to white-on-blue (or to whatever color you selected in CLEAR.COM). To delete the macro and restore CLS's default mode of operation, type DOSKEY CLS= at the DOS prompt.

Displaying More than 25 Lines of Text

On selected video adapters, it's possible to display more than 25 lines of text on the screen by reprogramming the adapter to alter its timing parameters and loading a smaller screen font from ROM to reduce the character height. One of the most popular articles ever published in *PC Magazine* was a two-part series in which Charles Petzold examined the EGA in-depth and offered a short utility for changing the display density from 25 lines to 43.

One feature you'll love about DOS 5.0 is that if you have an EGA or VGA video adapter, you can use DOS to switch to alternate text modes that display more than 25 lines of text. This form of the MODE command first appeared in DOS 4.0, but it's still one of DOS's best-kept secrets. The syntax is

```
MODE CON: LINES=rows
```

where *rows* is the number of rows of text you want displayed. The *rows* parameter can be set to 43 on EGAs and 43 or 50 on VGAs. If you're a VGA user, the command

```
MODE CON: LINES=50
```

compresses text vertically so that there are 50 lines displayed. Similarly, the command

```
MODE CON: LINES=25
```

restores the default 25-line display. You can use this same command to switch between 40 and 80 columns by substituting a COLS parameter for LINES. The command

```
MODE CON: COLS=40
```

displays 40 columns rather than 80. The old ways of switching between 40 and 80 columns—MODE 40 and MODE 80—still work, too. You can also combine LINES and COLS on one line to switch to, say, a 50-line by 40-column video mode. For example, the command

```
MODE CON: LINES=50 COLS=40
```

displays 50 lines and 40 columns. To switch back to 25-line by 80-column mode, type

```
MODE CON: LINES=25 COLS=80
```

DOS's ANSI.SYS console driver must be installed for the MODE command to work with the LINES parameter. Otherwise, MODE will respond with the message "ANSI.SYS must be installed to perform requested function."

Earlier versions of ANSI.SYS only used the top 25 lines of the display, no matter how many more were displayed. The DOS 5.0 version of ANSI.SYS, however, has been updated to be compatible with different display densities. Likewise, DOS 5.0 utilities such as EDIT (the full-screen text editor) have been designed to work with any number of screen rows. If you haven't tried it, you may be surprised to find how much easier it is to edit or browse a long text file with 43 or 50 lines displayed than with only 25.

More than 25 Lines Without ANSI.SYS

Using the MODE command to display more than 25 lines of text requires that the ANSI.SYS extended console driver be installed. In DOS 5.0, this usually isn't a problem, because ANSI.SYS has been upgraded for EGA and VGA users and the DEVICEHIGH command permits ANSI.SYS to be loaded into upper memory on 386 systems. But if you're really pressed for memory, ANSI.SYS may be the first to go from your CONFIG.SYS file. Here's how to switch to 43 lines or 50 lines without it.

This DEBUG script creates 50.COM, which switches a VGA to 50-line mode (yes, program names *can* begin with numerics):

```
A 0100
MOV     AX,0500             ;Switch to page 0
INT     10
MOV     AX,1112             ;Load 8 by 8 font from ROM and
SUB     BL,BL               ;  let the BIOS reprogram the
INT     10                  ;  video adapter
MOV     AH,12               ;Select alternate print screen
MOV     BL,20               ;  routine from the video BIOS
INT     10
RET                         ;Exit

N 50.COM
RCX
13
W
Q
```

50.COM does no checking to make sure that you're in fact running it on a VGA, so be careful. Running it on other adapters could produce strange—and potentially harmful—results.

Listing 6.1 creates 43.COM, which switches an EGA to 43-line mode:

LISTING 6.1

```
A 0100
MOV     AX,0500             ;Switch to page 0
INT     10
MOV     AX,1112             ;Load 8 by 8 font from ROM and
SUB     BL,BL               ;  let the BIOS reprogram the
INT     10                  ;  video adapter
MOV     AH,12               ;Select alternate print screen
MOV     BL,20               ;  routine from the video BIOS
INT     10
MOV     AX,0040             ;Point DS to BIOS data area
MOV     DS,AX
```

```
MOV     DL,[0087]               ;Save EGA info byte
OR      BYTE PTR [0087],01      ;Toggle low bit on
MOV     AH,01                   ;Reset the cursor mode
MOV     CX,0600
INT     10
MOV     [0087],DL               ;Restore EGA info byte
MOV     DX,03B4                 ;Fix EGA underline bug
MOV     AX,0714
OUT     DX,AX
RET                             ;Exit


N 43.COM
RCX
33
W
Q
```

To get back to 25-line mode, type **MODE 80** (or **MODE 40** if you prefer 40-column displays to 80). Both these utilities rely on a function built into the video BIOS (interrupt 10H, function 11H) to program the video adapter for denser displays and to select an alternate print-screen routine in the video BIOS that makes the Print Screen key work with more than 25 lines. The EGA utility includes some additional code to compensate for flaws in the EGA BIOS.

Customizing the Command Prompt with ANSI.SYS

You've probably used DOS's PROMPT command before. Most users include the command

```
PROMPT $p$g
```

or one similar to it in their AUTOEXEC.BAT file so the command prompt will show the current drive and directory. With ANSI.SYS installed, you can further customize the DOS prompt by embedding ANSI.SYS escape sequences inside PROMPT commands to control the color and appearance of the prompt.

First, Table 6.3 shows the metastrings you may include in a PROMPT command, with or without ANSI.SYS. The pg in PROMPT pg means show the current drive and directory in the DOS prompt followed by a greater-than character. Other metastrings let you include the time, date, and DOS version number in the prompt, for example, and embed characters in prompt strings that require special treatment—carriage returns and backspaces, for instance.

Table 6.4 lists some of the ANSI.SYS escape sequences that you might find useful in PROMPT commands in addition to those for setting screen colors. They're divided into two categories: those that control the cursor position and those that erase text from the screen.

TABLE 6.3

PROMPT Metastrings

Substring	Output
$b	I character
$d	Current date
$e	Escape character
$g	> character
$h	Backspace (delete last character)
$l	< character
$n	Current drive
$p	Current drive and directory
$q	= character
$t	Current time
$v	DOS version number
$$	$ character
$_	Carriage return/line-feed pair (new line)

TABLE 6.4

ANSI.SYS Cursor Control and Screen Control Commands

Cursor Control

Escape Sequence	Description
$e[s	Save the current cursor position
$e[u	Restore the last cursor position saved with $e[s
$e[xxA	Move the cursor up xx rows
$e[xxB	Move the cursor down xx rows
$e[xxC	Move the cursor right xx columns
$e[xxD	Move the cursor left xx columns
$e[xx;yyH	Move the cursor to row xx, column yy
$e[H	Move the cursor to the upper left corner of the screen

Screen Control

Escape Sequence	Description
$e[2J	Clear the screen
$e[K	Erase everything from the current cursor position to the end of the line

With a little imagination, you can use these escape sequences to come up with some really inventive command prompts. For kicks, make sure ANSI.SYS is loaded, and then try out this PROMPT command:

```
PROMPT $e[s$e[;5ØH$d   $t$h$h$h$h$h$h$e[u$p$g
```

Can you predict what it's going to do? This one's a little sneaky: It saves the current cursor position (using the ANSI.SYS escape sequence $e[s), moves the cursor to the upper-right corner of the screen ($e[;50H), displays the time and date ($d $t), backspaces six times to erase the seconds and hundredths of seconds displays from the time (hhhhhh), and then returns the cursor to its original position ($e[u) and displays a pg-type prompt—one that shows the current drive and directory.

You may also include ANSI.SYS escape sequences that change text colors or text attributes in PROMPT commands. *PC Magazine* programmer Michael Mefford concocted this little goody, which also requires ANSI.SYS:

```
PROMPT $p=$g $e[8m $e[Øm$e[D
```

This one is trickier still. It hides the flashing cursor until you type the first character of a command (remember the concealed attribute code in Table 6.1?). To add a little more flair to your prompt, try this command:

```
PROMPT $e[1;37;41mPC Magazine$g$e[Ø;37;40m
```

Substitute the name of your company for the substring "PC Magazine" to customize the prompt even further. This command displays the text sandwiched between "$e[1;37;41m" and "$g" in bright white on red so that it stands out from everything else on the screen. The codes for changing text colors and attributes were presented in Table 6.1.

You can use PROMPT's $_ metastring, which moves the cursor to the start of the next line, to create multiline prompts, as in

```
PROMPT $e[Ø;36;40mDate: $d$_Time: $t$h$h$h$_$e[37m$p$g
```

This one uses ANSI.SYS to change the color of the prompt to cyan, display the date and time on separate lines, and switch back to the default white-on-black before the cursor is displayed.

Keyboards

Keyboards for the IBM PC and PC clones come in several varieties. The original IBM PC keyboard featured 83 keys, ten of which were function keys arranged in two columns on the left side of the keyboard, and a layout similar to that of an IBM Selectric typewriter. The 84-key keyboard introduced with the AT in 1984 rearranged the keys slightly (to the consternation of those whose fingers had grown accustomed to the 83-key layout) and added an extra key, labeled SysReq, which was ostensibly to be used in a future version of DOS.

When IBM introduced its PS/2 line of computers in 1987, it brought forth yet another new keyboard, this time one with 101 keys (102 in systems sold outside the United States). The 101-key keyboard, or *enhanced* keyboard as it came to be called, departed radically from the conventions of the past. Primary features included a row of 12 function keys spaced along the top of the keyboard, a separate cursor keypad located between the numeric keypad and character keys, dual Ctrl and Alt keys, and a dedicated Pause key. This keyboard layout was and continues to be widely duplicated by clonemakers and is presently featured on the majority of the keyboards shipped with IBM-compatible PCs.

Despite the changes in style and appearance, the inner workings of the keyboard have remained relatively constant over the years. Each time a key is pressed or released, a microprocessor inside the keyboard sends a one-byte *scan code* that identifies which key was pressed or released to the keyboard controller on the system board. (On 101- and 102-key keyboards, there are some scan codes that are longer than one byte, but those are the exception rather than the rule.) The keyboard controller, in turn, notifies the CPU that a keyboard event has occurred by generating a hardware interrupt that the interrupt controller passes on to the CPU. In response, the CPU stops what it's doing (provided it's not servicing a higher-priority interrupt at the time) and transfers control to an interrupt-handling routine in the ROM BIOS. The interrupt handler reads the scan code from the keyboard and takes action based on which key was activated and whether it was pressed or released.

When a character key is pressed, the BIOS converts the scan code to an ASCII character code and inserts both the original scan code and the ASCII code into a region of memory known as the *keyboard buffer*. By default, the keyboard buffer can store up to 16 two-byte key codes, enough to keep a fast typist from outracing even an old 4.77MHz PC.

When a Ctrl, Alt, or Shift key is pressed, the BIOS doesn't insert a key code into the keyboard buffer. Instead, it sets a bit that corresponds to the key that was pressed in a reserved portion of low memory to 1 so that it can tell which, if any, of these keys was pressed when it processes a subsequent character key. When the key is released, the BIOS sets the bit back to 0, indicating that the key is no longer held down.

The BIOS also provides a set of routines that programs (and operating systems) may call on to read key codes from the keyboard buffer. A typical code sequence (in the native machine code that all programs, regardless of the language they were written in, are eventually reduced to) looks like this:

```
MOV         AH,Ø
INT         16H
```

The zero placed in register AH is a function code designating which of the several services available through interrupt 16H is being invoked. The instruction INT 16H generates a software interrupt that invokes the BIOS keyboard service routines. This function reads a key code from the keyboard buffer and returns the key's scan code in AH and ASCII code in AL. Certain keys—function keys and cursor-movement keys, for example—do not have corresponding ASCII codes and return 0 in AL. These keys are identified by the scan code in AH.

Figure 6.3 illustrates the circuitous route a key code must travel before it can be read by an application program. The key code originates in the keyboard itself in the form of a scan code, and is passed through the keyboard cable to the keyboard controller. The keyboard BIOS reads the scan code from the keyboard controller, converts it into a two-byte key code, and deposits it in the next available slot in the keyboard buffer. The application program ultimately reads the key code from the buffer by placing a call to the BIOS. If the buffer is empty at the time the call is made, the BIOS waits for a key code to come available before returning to the caller.

FIGURE 6.3

IBM PC keyboard processing

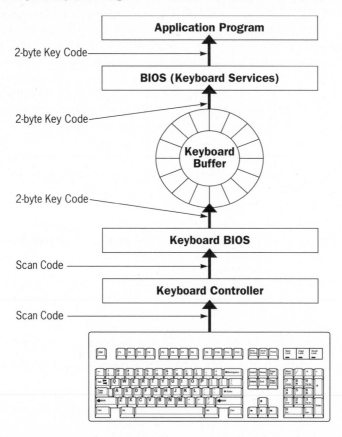

To insulate itself from the hardware, DOS places an additional layer of software between itself and the keyboard buffer: the CON device driver. To read a key code, DOS places a call to CON, which in turn calls on interrupt 16H to retrieve the next key code waiting in the queue. When ANSI.SYS is installed in place of CON, it provides keyboard services of its own that also rely on the interrupt 16H services built into the BIOS. This added level of indirection is employed to enable DOS to be ported to other hardware platforms. The idea is that an identical call to CON will return a key code on any system; all that has to be changed is the CON driver itself.

Application programs may also call on the CON device driver to perform keyboard I/O. But because it is slow by comparison to a direct call to interrupt 16H, and because the driver lacks the additional keyboard processing functions interrupt 16H provides (functions for detecting when non-character keys such as Ctrl, Alt, and Shift are pressed, for example), most programs bypass DOS and go straight to the BIOS instead.

Complicated? At first, yes—but the complexity is outweighed by the sheer elegance of this scheme for deciphering and buffering key presses. You don't have to understand the mechanics of keyboard processing to type DOS commands, or even to write keyboard utilities that run under DOS. But knowing it will give you a better feel for what DOS is doing while it awaits your keyboard input on the command line—and a better appreciation for the special things that it does.

The same ANSI.SYS that enables you to customize the screen also lets you customize operation of the keyboard. You'll learn how to use this feature of ANSI.SYS to assign commands to function keys on the DOS command line, remap the keyboard, reduce typing time, and obtain on-line help for any DOS command. Finally, you'll learn how DOS 5.0 lets you specify the typematic rates and delays for 84-, 101-, and 102-key keyboards. This trick will make keyboard-intensive applications such as word processors and spreadsheets easier to use.

Assigning Commands to Function Keys

The ANSI.SYS extended screen and keyboard driver in DOS 5.0 lets you assign text strings to keys such that pressing a key has the same effect as typing an entire command. The general syntax for redefining a key (in the form of an ANSI escape sequence transmitted with the PROMPT command) is

```
PROMPT $e[code;"string"p
```

where *code* is either a single character enclosed in quotation marks (the character produced by the key you want to redefine) or one of the numeric identifiers shown in Table 6.5, and *string* is the character string to be assigned to the key, enclosed in quotation marks.

To see how this works, make sure ANSI.SYS is installed in your CONFIG-.SYS file and type

```
PROMPT $e[0;59;"MEM"p
```

followed by

```
PROMPT $p$g
```

to restore the system prompt. Then press function key F1. The command "MEM" will appear to the right of the DOS prompt, ready to be executed when you press Enter. Go ahead and press Enter and then type

```
PROMPT $e[0;59;"MEM$_"p
```

Press F1 again and this time MEM will be typed *and* executed. The reason: The "$_" at the end of the MEM command represents a carriage return, which signifies to the command interpreter that the command is to be executed as soon as F1 is pressed.

TABLE 6.5

ANSI Keyboard Codes

Key	By Itself	With Shift	With Ctrl	With Alt	Key	By Itself	With Shift	With Ctrl	With Alt
F1	0;59	0;84	0;94	0;104	K	107	75	11	0;37
F2	0;60	0;85	0;95	0;105	L	108	76	12	0;38
F3	0;61	0;86	0;96	0;106	M	109	77	13	0;50
F4	0;62	0;87	0;97	0;107	N	110	78	14	0;49
F5	0;63	0;88	0;98	0;108	O	111	79	15	0;24
F6	0;64	0;89	0;99	0;109	P	112	80	16	0;25
F7	0;65	0;90	0;100	0;110	Q	113	81	17	0;16
F8	0;66	0;91	0;101	0;111	R	114	82	18	0;19
F9	0;67	0;92	0;102	0;112	S	115	83	19	0;31
F10	0;68	0;93	0;103	0;113	T	116	84	20	0;20
F11	0;133	0;135	0;137	0;139	U	117	85	21	0;22
F12	0;134	0;136	0;138	0;140	V	118	86	22	0;47
					W	119	87	23	0;17
Home	0;71	55	0;119	—	X	120	88	24	0;45
Up Arrow	0;72	56	(0;141)	—	Y	121	89	25	0;21
PgUp	0;73	57	0;132	—	Z	122	90	26	0;44
Left Arrow	0;75	52	0;115	—					
Right Arrow	0;77	54	0;116	—	1	49	33	—	0;120
End	0;79	49	0;117	—	2	50	64	—	0;121
Down Arrow	0;80	50	(0;145)	—	3	51	35	—	0;122
PgDn	0;81	51	0;118	—	4	52	36	—	0;123
Ins	0;82	48	(0;146)	—	5	53	37	—	0;124
Del	0;83	46	(0;147)	—	6	54	94	—	0;125
Print Screen	—	—	0;114	—	7	55	38	—	0;126
					8	56	42	—	0;127
Home	(224;71)	(224;71)	(224;119)	(224;151)	9	57	40	—	0;128
Up Arrow	(224;72)	(224;72)	(224;141)	(224;152)	0	58	41	—	0;129
Page Up	(224;73)	(224;73)	(224;132)	(224;153)					
Left Arrow	(224;75)	(224;75)	(224;115)	(224;155)	–	45	95	31	0;130
Right Arrow	(224;77)	(224;77)	(224;116)	(224;157)	=	61	43	—	0;131
End	(224;79)	(224;79)	(224;117)	(224;159)	[	91	123	27	0;26
Down Arrow	(224;80)	(224;80)	(224;145)	(224;160)	]	93	125	29	0;27
Page Down	(224;81)	(224;81)	(224;118)	(224;161)	\	92	124	28	0;43
Insert	(224;82)	(224;82)	(224;146)	(224;162)	;	59	58	—	0;39
Delete	(224;83)	(224;83)	(224;147)	(224;163)	'	39	34	—	0;40
					,	44	60	—	0;51
A	97	65	1	0;30	.	46	62	—	0;52
B	98	66	2	0;48	/	47	63	—	0;53
C	99	67	3	0;46	`	96	126	—	(0;41)
D	100	68	4	0;32					
E	101	69	5	0;18	Tab	9	0;15	(0;148)	(0;165)
F	102	70	6	0;33	Null	0;3	—	—	—
G	103	71	7	0;34	Backspace	8	8	127	—
H	104	72	8	0;35	Enter	13	13	10	(0;28)
I	105	73	9	0;23	Esc	27	27	27	(0;1)
J	106	74	10	0;36	Space	32	32	32	32

Keycodes shaded in gray correspond to the gray keys on enhanced keyboards.
Keycodes enclosed in parentheses are not available on all keyboards.

In like manner, DOS 5.0 permits you to assign commands to any of the 48 different combinations of function keys F1 through F12 (F1 through F10 if you have an 83- or 84-key keyboard) and the Ctrl, Alt, and Shift keys. In fact, you're not limited to function keys only; virtually any key on the keyboard, with a few exceptions, can be assigned macro-like character strings.

   In Table 6.5, each key that ANSI.SYS allows to be redefined is identified by a 1- or 2-number code. The code differs depending on whether the key is pressed by itself or shifted by Ctrl, Alt, or Shift. Because the ANSI code for Alt-F10 is 0;113, the command

```
PROMPT $e[Ø;113;"DIR$_"p
```

assigns the DIR command to Alt-F10, and, by virtue of the $_ metastring inside the quotation marks, automatically executes it when Alt-F10 is pressed. Similarly, the command

```
PROMPT $e[Ø;134;"EDIT "p
```

assigns EDIT to function key F12, but pauses so you can enter a file name before pressing Enter to execute the command. Any command that can be entered on the command line, including ones that use redirection and piping operators, can be assigned to a key using ANSI.SYS.

   The one type of command you have to be careful with is a PROMPT command that assigns another PROMPT command to a key. Let's say, for instance, that you wanted to write a PROMPT command to change the color scheme from white on black to green on black when you press F1. On the surface, it would appear that the command

```
PROMPT $e[Ø;59;"PROMPT $e[32;4Øm$_"p
```

should do it. But look more closely: The $e inside the quotation marks will be interpreted as an escape character not only by the PROMPT command inside the marks, but also by the one on the outside. For our purposes, the $e inside the quotation marks needs to be interpreted literally rather than symbolically. Here's how to do it:

```
PROMPT $e[Ø;59;"PROMPT $$e[32;4Øm$_"p
```

This command programs function key F1 to change the screen colors to green on black. The $e inside the quotation marks was changed to $$e so that the outside PROMPT command would leave it untouched (PROMPT interprets "$$" as "$", so "$$e" becomes "$e"). If this sounds a little confusing, don't worry. Just remember to double up on all the dollar signs inside the quotation marks except for the one on the line terminator $_ whenever you nest two PROMPT commands together like this. Although it has always been possible to do this, some versions of ANSI.SYS (including the one in DOS 3.3) contained bugs that sometimes prevented nested PROMPT commands from working correctly. The DOS 5.0 ANSI-.SYS, however, is sound in this regard.

Reversing a Key Assignment Once a key has been assigned a text string, you can "unassign" it—restore it to its default mode of operation—by defining the key as itself. For example, if F1 had been redefined with the command

```
PROMPT $e[0;59;"MEM$_"p
```

you could restore it by typing

```
PROMPT $e[0;59;0;59p
```

The code 0;59 is the one that identifies function key F1. In effect, this command tells ANSI.SYS that pressing F1 is to produce the key code for F1, restoring the key's default operation.

On-line Help for DOS Commands If you press a key that has been assigned a text string after entering text on the command line, the text assigned to the key is appended to the existing text rather than used to replace it. You can take advantage of this to build a simple but effective on-line help facility for DOS commands. Enter this command:

```
PROMPT $e[0;59;" /?$_"p
```

Then type any DOS command and, instead of pressing Enter, press F1. The result: DOS displays a summary of the command and the command syntax. All DOS 5.0 commands respond with help messages when they're executed with /?. This assignment simply appends a /? switch to what was already typed and executes the resultant command.

Using ANSI.SYS to Remap the Keyboard

You can also use ANSI.SYS's key redefinition capability to swap one key for another. For example, the command

```
PROMPT $e["\";"/"p$e["/";"\"p
```

swaps the forward slash and backslash keys, something that might be useful if you chronically reverse the two. This command takes advantage of the fact that you can string as many ANSI escape sequences together on one line as the command line will hold (127 characters). Just be sure to precede each individual escape sequence with the escape character $e.

You cannot, unfortunately, use ANSI.SYS to remap any of the shift keys (Ctrl, Alt, Shift), the toggle keys (Scroll Lock, Caps Lock, Num Lock), or the Pause key. You're limited to the keys either that are listed in Table 6.5 or that can be identified by the printable character they produce.

One last note: Be careful about the function keys you remap. As we'll see in the next chapter, DOS 5.0 offers extensive command recall and editing features not found in previous versions of DOS, features which rely rather heavily on the function keys, particularly F7 through F10, Alt-F7, and Alt-F10. You may want to leave these keys as is so that you can easily access those editing capabilities.

Setting the Keyboard's Speed

Another of DOS 5.0's little-known features is the ability to set the keyboard's typematic rate and delay interval using the MODE command. *Typematic rate* is the rate at which characters are repeated when a key is held down; *delay interval* is the length of the pause between the time the key is pressed and typematic repeat begins. ANSI.SYS is not required for this feature. The syntax for this form of the MODE command is

```
MODE CON: RATE=rate DELAY=delay
```

where *rate* is a value from 1 to 32 that determines the typematic rate. The value specified for *rate* translates roughly to characters per second. The higher the value, the faster the characters are repeated. The *delay* value, from 1 to 4, specifies whether the delay between the first and second character should be $1/4$ of a second, $1/2$ second, $3/4$ second, or a full second. In most configurations, the default delay is $1/2$ second. The "CON:" in the command refers to the CON device driver, which, in this context, means the keyboard. The command

```
MODE CON: RATE=32 DELAY=2
```

sets the typematic rate to its highest setting, leaving a $1/2$-second pause between the time a key is pressed and repeat begins. Type this command, and then press and hold down the "A" key. The cursor will scamper across the screen much more quickly than before. Among other things, this makes it much easier to scroll through long word processing documents by pressing and holding the Up-Arrow or Down-Arrow key. Conversely, the command

```
MODE CON: RATE=16 DELAY=2
```

resets the typematic rate to approximately what it was when the system was started. And

```
MODE CON: RATE=1 DELAY=2
```

slows it to a crawl. If the maximum typematic rate of 32 isn't fast enough for you, lower *delay* to 1 to cut the delay time down to $1/4$ of a second and gain an extra measure of speed. Once you've found the most comfortable setting, add the appropriate MODE command to your AUTOEXEC.BAT file to have it execute each time you boot up.

Unfortunately, you cannot use the MODE command in this way to control 83-key keyboards. On IBM PCs and XTs, where the 83-key layout was standardized, the keyboard's typematic rate and delay interval were hardcoded in silicon. The delay interval was fixed at $\frac{1}{2}$ second, the typematic rate at approximately 10 characters per second. With the AT, IBM introduced the 84-key keyboard, which was programmable and therefore capable of accepting user-input values. This feature, which the MODE command relies on to alter the keyboard's default mode of operation, is also present in 101- and 102-key keyboards.

Tricks for Reducing Typing Time

To soup up your system and cut down on the time you spend typing commands, add the following lines to your AUTOEXEC.BAT file:

```
MODE CON: RATE=32 DELAY=2
PROMPT $e[0;59;" /?$_"p
PROMPT $e[0;60;"CLS$_"p
PROMPT $e[0;61;"DIR /O$_"p
PROMPT $e[0;62;"MEM$_"p
PROMPT $e[0;63;"CD ..$_"p
PROMPT $e[0;64;"EDIT "p
PROMPT $e[0;94;"PROMPT $$e[0;37;40m$$p$$g$_"p$p$g
PROMPT $e[0;95;"PROMPT $$e[1;37;44m$$p$$g$_"p$p$g
PROMPT $p$g
```

Thereafter, function key F1 will invoke context-sensitive help (type the command you want help on, and then press F1); F2 will clear the screen; F3 will list the contents of the current directory; F4 will execute the MEM command; F5 will move you up one directory level; and F6 will type EDIT on the command line and wait for you to enter a file name. Ctrl-F1 and Ctrl-F2 will toggle back and forth between DOS's default black-on-white color scheme and a more pleasing one that displays text in brilliant white-on-blue. And all keys will repeat at about twice their normal rate when held down.

Make sure that ANSI.SYS is loaded from CONFIG.SYS before you boot your computer with this enhanced AUTOEXEC.BAT file. And keep in mind that DOS 5.0 lets you assign commands to all 48 combinations of the function keys and the Ctrl, Alt, and Shift keys, including those that use F11 and F12. Keep a list of the DOS commands you use most often. Then add them to this list, so you won't have to type them in repeatedly.

Printers

DOS's interaction with printers is handled by the device drivers PRN, LPT1, LPT2, and LPT3. LPT1, LPT2, and LPT3 refer to the parallel ports of the same name. PRN is the logical name assigned to the system print device, which by default DOS maps to parallel port LPT1.

When one of these device drivers outputs a character to the printer, it does so using the interrupt 17H printer I/O functions built into the system BIOS. Function 00H transmits a character to the printer attached to the indicated parallel port; function 01H initializes the port; and function 02H returns the status of the indicated port in register AH. The strength of these BIOS functions lies in the fact that they take care of the rather complicated process of sending a character out a parallel port and acknowledging that the transmission succeeded (or detecting that an error occurred if the transmission didn't succeed). Ironically, the one function DOS provides to application programs for printer I/O—interrupt 21H, function 05H—is so limited that it is rarely used. One fault is that it makes no provision for directing output to any port but LPT1. It also provides no means for polling the status of the printer before outputting a character and no error information when a transmission fails.

Data sent to a printer usually consists of a mixture of ASCII codes (the ASCII codes of the characters being printed) and control codes that instruct the printer to perform a control function such as switching from normal print to bold or from an upright font to italics. On an HP LaserJet II, for example, the escape sequence

```
ESC(s16.66H
```

changes the print pitch to 16.66 characters per inch. On most IBM and Epson printers, a single byte of value 0FH (15 decimal) does the same thing. There is no standard that governs what printer control languages should look like, so manufacturers create their own. Some languages have become so popular that they are now being emulated by other vendors. For instance, Hewlett-Packard's PCL (Printer Control Language), standard on all its LaserJet printers, is so widely supported by software makers that even IBM laser printers now offer HP PCL emulation modes.

Of course, when you think about printers, you think about PostScript, too. PostScript is an advanced printer control language (the term "page description language" is more frequently used and perhaps more appropriate) from Adobe Systems that turns a printer into a computer in and of itself. In essence, PostScript is a programming language that permits you to define how ink is applied to a page. Once a page is defined through a series of PostScript commands, a PostScript interpreter (usually housed in ROM inside the printer) performs the scan conversions necessary to transform the image into a dot-by-dot bit map that can be output to the printed page.

All this goes way beyond DOS, whose interactions with the printer are comparatively simple. But DOS 5.0 does provide several commands for manipulating printers and obtaining hard-copy output. In this section, you'll learn how to use these commands to

■ Set the print pitch and line spacing on IBM, Epson, and LaserJet printers

- Configure DOS and DOS applications to output to a printer attached to a serial port rather than to a parallel port and troubleshoot the DOS-to-serial-port interface

- Redirect printer output from one LPT port to another

- Print text files

- Get screen dumps of CGA, EGA, and VGA screens on a wide range of printers

The latter capability is perhaps the most important of all, since DOS 5.0 is the first to support graphics-mode screen dumps on EGA and VGA video adapters *and* to support non-IBM printers. Who says you can't teach an old dog new tricks?

Setting Print Pitch and Line Spacing

If your printer's command set is compatible with that of IBM's original Graphics Printer (most Epson dot-matrix printers are, but HP LaserJets are not), you can set the print pitch (normal or compressed) and number of lines per inch (6 or 8) using the MODE command. The command

```
MODE LPT1: COLS=132 LINES=8
```

sets the printer attached to LPT1 to print in compressed mode (132 columns on an 8½-inch-wide page) at 8 lines per inch. What this command actually does is output the hexadecimal control code sequence

```
0F 1B 30
```

to the PRN device, parallel port LPT1. To an IBM or Epson printer, 0FH is the signal to switch to compressed print and 1B 30 is the escape code for ⅛-inch line spacing. Similarly, the command

```
MODE LPT1: COLS=80 LINES=6
```

restores normal printing: 80-character-wide pages and ⅙-inch line spacing. Valid values for COLS are 80 and 132; for LINES, 6 and 8. If you'd like, you may drop the COLS= and LINES= keywords from the command and simply type

```
MODE LPT1:132,8
```

to set the printer for 132 characters per line and 8 lines per inch. To direct the command to a printer other than LPT1, simply substitute the appropriate device name (LPT2 or LPT3) for LPT1.

Setting Print Pitch and Line Spacing on HP LaserJet Printers

The MODE command is fine for setting print parameters if you happen to have an IBM or Epson dot-matrix printer or one that emulates the IBM/Epson command set. But what if you're an HP LaserJet user?

The following DEBUG script creates CPI.COM, a short utility that sets an HP LaserJet printer to print 10, 12, or 16.66 characters per inch:

```
A 0100
JMP       0106                    ;Start program
DB        1B,28,73,48
CLD                               ;Clear direction flag
MOV       SI,0081                 ;Advance to first non-space
LODSB
CMP       AL,20
JZ        010A
CMP       AL,0D
JZ        0131
DEC       SI                      ;Point SI to first non-space
MOV       DI,SI                   ;Save string address in DI
MOV       SI,0102                 ;Send escape sequence to printer
MOV       DX,0000                 ;0=LPT1, 1=LPT2, 2=LPT3
MOV       CX,0003
CALL      0132
MOV       SI,DI                   ;Retrieve string address
MOV       CX,0002                 ;Output the string to the printer
CALL      0132
SUB       AH,AH                   ;Send final code in sequence
MOV       AL,[0105]
INT       17
RET                               ;Exit
SUB       AH,AH                   ;Subroutine to send a string to
LODSB                             ;  the printer (string length
INT       17                      ;  in CX)
LOOP      0132
RET

N CPI.COM
RCX
3A
W
Q
```

To use it, type **CPI 10**, **CPI 12**, or **CPI 16** at the DOS prompt. CPI 10 is equivalent to typing MODE LPT1:80 for IBM and Epson printers, while CPI 16 is the same as MODE LPT1:132. To send printer commands to a port other than LPT1, change the line that reads MOV DX,0000 in the DEBUG script to MOV DX,0001 for LPT2 or MOV DX,0002 for LPT3.

This DEBUG script creates another utility, LPI.COM, that sets the number of lines per inch to 4, 6, or 8 on HP LaserJet printers:

```
A 0100
JMP     0107                    ;Start program
DB      1B,26,6C,3F,44
CLD                             ;Clear direction flag
MOV     SI,0081                 ;Advance to first non-space
LODSB
CMP     AL,20
JZ      010B
CMP     AL,0D
JZ      0127
MOV     [0105],AL               ;Insert character entered on the
MOV     SI,0102                 ;  command line into the escape
MOV     DX,0000                 ;  sequence and output the
MOV     CX,0005                 ;  string
SUB     AH,AH
LODSB
INT     17
LOOP    0120
RET                             ;Exit


N LPI.COM
RCX
28
W
Q
```

Thus, the command

```
LPI 8
```

configures an HP LaserJet to print 8 lines per inch. To use LPI with other than the default of LPT1, change the line MOV DX,0000 to MOV DX,0001 or MOV DX,0002 for LPT2 or LPT3, respectively.

Using Printers Attached to Serial Ports

Most application programs have configuration options that permit you to specify what port your printer is attached to. But not DOS. By default, DOS assumes that the PRN device is attached to LPT1. If this is the case, you don't need to do anything else to have DOS send output to your printer. If, however, your printer is attached to a serial port (as is the case if you have an Apple LaserWriter attached to your PC, for example), you need to redirect DOS output from LPT1 to the appropriate COM port. Your mechanism for doing so is the MODE command, used as follows:

```
MODE LPT1:=COMx:
```

where COMx is COM1, COM2, COM3, or COM4. For example, the command

```
MODE LPT1:=COM2:
```

reroutes printer output from LPT1 to the printer attached to COM2. The command

```
MODE LPT1:
```

cancels output redirection, restoring LPT1 output to LPT1. Contrary to popular belief, the MODE command cannot be used to redirect printer output to a file, or even to another LPT port. It only works going from an LPT port to a COM port.

How does MODE work? MODE is a small TSR (terminate-and-stay-resident program) that intercepts interrupt 17H, the software interrupt that DOS and almost all application programs use to output data to the printer. When a program invokes interrupt 17H to output a character, MODE executes a call to interrupt 14H instead, the entry point to the BIOS serial port services. Because MODE intercepts *all* LPT output (not just LPT output from DOS commands), it can be used as a general cure for application programs that otherwise wouldn't recognize a printer attached to a serial port. Just use MODE to redirect output to the COM port your printer is attached to, tell your application programs to print to the redirected LPT port, and in all but a few cases (the exceptions: programs that write to the parallel port hardware directly rather than through interrupt 17H), output will go there.

Let's say your system has two printers: a laser printer attached to LPT1 and a dot-matrix printer attached to COM1. Furthermore, let's assume you have an application program that recognizes LPT ports only, but that you'd like to be able to use it with your serial printer. Before you run the application, type

```
MODE LPT2:=COM1:
```

Then, to use the laser printer, print to LPT1. To use the dot-matrix printer, print to LPT2. By virtue of the MODE command executed earlier, LPT2 output is transparently rerouted to COM1. It doesn't matter that there *is* no LPT2 port. DOS intercepts what's sent there, and the application program is blissfully unaware that it's really printing to a serial printer.

Initializing the Serial Port   If you redirect printer output from an LPT port to a COM port, you'll also need to issue a MODE command to initialize that particular serial port. The command

```
MODE COM1: BAUD=96 PARITY=N DATA=8 STOP=1
```

initializes serial port COM1 to 9,600 bits per second, no parity, 8 data bits, and 1 stop bit. Valid values for bit rate, parity, data bits, and stop bits are shown in Table 6.6. You may omit the BAUD, PARITY, DATA, and STOP keywords if you wish, so the command

```
MODE COM1:96,N,8,1
```

is equivalent to the one above.

TABLE 6.6

MODE Communications Parameters

Parameter	Meaning
Bit Rate	
11	110 bits per second
15	150 bits per second
30	300 bits per second
60	600 bits per second
12	1,200 bits per second
24	2,400 bits per second
48	4,800 bits per second
96	9,600 bits per second
19	19,200 bits per second
Parity	
N	No parity
E	Even parity
O	Odd parity
M	Mark parity (always 1)
S	Space parity (always 0)
Data Bits	
5	5 data bits per frame
6	6 data bits per frame
7	7 data bits per frame
8	8 data bits per frame
Stop Bits	
1	1 stop bit per frame
1.5	1.5 stop bits per frame
2	2 stop bits per frame

Different printers operate with different data rates and communications settings. Common settings are 9,600 bps (bits per second), no parity, 8 data bits, and 1 stop bit (MODE 96 N,8,1), and 9,600 bps, even parity, 7 data bits, and 1 stop bit (MODE 96, E,7,1). Consult your printer manual to determine the correct setting for your system.

Why does the serial port have to be initialized before DOS will use it? There's a tiny chip that drives the serial port called a UART, short for Universal Asynchronous Receiver/Transmitter. Initializing the port really means initializing the UART, which involves writing a series of values to UART registers (a task DOS calls on the BIOS to perform). The UART *must* be initialized before it will work.

Fine. But why do you have to initialize the serial port with a MODE command before using it with DOS, but not with applications such as ProComm that use the serial ports themselves? Because ProComm initializes the serial port internally and DOS does not. DOS relies on you to enter a MODE command to perform the initialization.

If you don't specify values for parity, data bits, and stop bits, MODE defaults to even parity, 7 data bits, and 1 stop bit. Thus, the command

```
MODE COM2:12
```

initializes COM2 to 1,200 bps, even parity, 7 data bits, and 1 stop bit, the same as the command MODE COM2:12,E,7,1.

Troubleshooting Serial Printers   Unfortunately, DOS won't work with just any serial printer. Serial communications between devices are fraught with potential pitfalls, the result of there being so many ways for two serial devices to talk to each other, with no standard governing how they *should* communicate. Here's what DOS expects of a serial printer, and what you can do to coerce a stubborn printer into working.

All serial ports used on PCs have at least nine pins: TD (Transmit Data) and RD (Receive Data), used to transmit and receive bits of data; DTR (Data Terminal Ready), RTS (Request To Send), CTS (Clear To Send), and DSR (Data Set Ready), used for handshaking between the sender and receiver; DCD (Data Carrier Detect), used to indicate the presence of a carrier in modem communications; RI (Ring Indicator), asserted when an incoming call is detected; and ground. Of these, four pins are critically important to whether DOS will work with a given printer: DTR, RTS, CTS, and DSR.

When DOS outputs a character to a serial port, it uses a BIOS routine that transmits the character through the UART only after asserting DTR and RTS and waiting for CTS and DSR to be asserted in return. Using this form of handshaking, the BIOS ensures that it will only send characters when the printer is ready for them. The problem is that not all printers are set up to use this type of handshaking. If the printer, for example, fails to assert CTS after the BIOS asserts RTS, DOS will steadfastly refuse to print. Most application programs are more forgiving because they program the serial port directly rather than going through the BIOS, and thus exercise better control over the port. As a result, application programs will work when DOS won't.

There are two ways to correct the problem. One is to check your printer for DIP switch or jumper settings that cause it to employ RTS/CTS and DTR/DSR handshaking. If your printer has an option for doing so, you're home free.

Solution number two is to rig up a serial printer cable that fools the BIOS into *thinking* handshaking is being performed. If the printer asserts CTS but not DSR, for example, a special cable with DTR looped into DSR on the PC end would ensure that DSR were asserted, too. Also watch for printers that won't accept characters unless DCD is asserted. The solution is to use a cable that ties the PC's DTR or RTS output into DCD. If you know what control logic is being exercised on both ends of the cable, you can usually devise a solution that's compatible with the device on either end.

An indispensable tool for troubleshootiung serial PC-to-printer connections is a small device called an *RS-232 breakout box* or *quick cabler*. The device is installed in the line between the PC and the printer where it can monitor (or modify) the signals passed back and forth between the two. About the size of a mouse, a typical breakout box features LEDs that indicate which pins are being asserted by the devices on either of the line and jumpers or switches for altering the connections. It's a simple matter, for example, to channel the PC's DTR output to the printer's DCD input for testing purposes. A quick cabler is a simplified breakout box that allows you to select from several predefined line combinations with the flip of a few switches. Once you've determined what handshaking protocols are being employed, you can wire a special cable to match.

Redirecting Output from One Parallel Port to Another

The command MODE LPT1:=COM1: redirects printer output from LPT1 to COM1 so that DOS (and application programs that do not support serial printers) may drive printers connected to COM ports. But how about redirecting output from one parallel port to another, say LPT1 to LPT2? If you issue the command MODE LPT1:=LPT2:, DOS will respond with the error message "Invalid parameter – =LPT2:." Instead, to redirect printer output from one LPT port to another, you'll need a custom utility. To create one, start DEBUG and enter the following script:

```
A 0100
JMP        015D
DB         "Syntax: MODELPT LPTx[:]=LPTx[:]",0D,0A,"$"
DB         "Must be LPT1, LPT2, or LPT3",0D,0A,"$"
DB         0,0,0,0,0,0,0,0
PUSHF                          ;Interrupt handler to intercept
CS:                           ;  interrupt 17H and alter the
CMP        DX,[0146]          ;  printer number in DX for
JNZ        0157               ;  redirected printers
CS:
MOV        DX,[0148]
```

```
POPF
CS:
JMP     FAR [0142]
CLD                             ;Parse the command line for
MOV     SI,0081                 ;  input
CALL    0194
JNB     016F
MOV     AH,09                   ;Exit on syntax error
INT     21
MOV     AX,4C01
INT     21
MOV     [0146],AX
CALL    0194
JB      0166
MOV     [0148],AX
MOV     AX,3517                 ;Get current interrupt 17H vector
INT     21
MOV     [0142],BX               ;Save it
MOV     [0144],ES
MOV     AX,2517                 ;Point interrupt 17H to our own
MOV     DX,014A                 ;  interrupt handler
INT     21
MOV     DX,015D                 ;Become memory-resident
INT     27
LODSB                           ;Subroutine called to parse
CMP     AL,0D                   ;  the command line
JZ      01AB
CMP     AL,30                   ;Less than"0"?
JB      0194                    ;Yes, then loop
CMP     AL,39                   ;Greater than "9"?
JA      0194                    ;Yes, then loop
SUB     AL,31                   ;ASCII => binary
CMP     AL,02                   ;Syntax error if
JA      01B0                    ;  greater than 2
SUB     AH,AH
CLC
RET                             ;Return
MOV     DX,0102
STC
RET
MOV     DX,0124
```

```
STC
RET

N MODELPT.COM
RCX
B5
W
Q
```

Once MODELPT.COM is created, type

```
MODELPT LPT1:=LPT2:
```

to redirect output from LPT1 to LPT2. Any combination of LPT ports 1, 2, and 3 is valid. The only limitation is that once LPT output is redirected, you'll have to reboot to cancel redirection—or use utilities such as INSTALL and REMOVE (Chapter 14) to remove MODELPT from memory.

Printing Text Files: The PRINT Command

For printing text files, DOS provides the PRINT command. PRINT does more than just read a file and dump it to the printer; it spools printer output so that printing can proceed in the background while you run other programs in the foreground. It's the closest that DOS, an inherently single-tasking operating system, comes to multitasking.

PRINT accepts an assortment of switches and command-line parameters. Its full syntax is

```
PRINT [/D:device] [/B:size] [/U:ticks1] [/M:ticks2]
      [/S:ticks3] [/Q:qfiles] [/T] [[d:][path]filename] [...]
      [/C] [/P]
```

Each of these command-line switches is detailed in Appendix A. Of them, you're only likely to need three: *filename*, /P, and /C. *Filename* is the name of the file to be printed. Typing

```
PRINT TEXTFILE.DOC
```

queues TEXTFILE.DOC for printing. If it's the first file in the queue PRINT sets up, printing will begin immediately; otherwise, it will be printed after the files that precede it in the queue. You can queue up several files for printing at once by entering their names following a single PRINT command. The command

```
PRINT JAN92.DOC FEB92.DOC MAR92.DOC
```

adds three files to the print queue: JAN92.DOC, FEB92.DOC, and MAR92-
.DOC. They're printed in the order in which they appear on the command line.
You can delete a file from the queue with the /C (for "Cancel") switch. The
command

```
PRINT MAR92.DOC /C
```

removes MAR92.DOC from the print queue. The command has to be issued
before PRINT begins to print the file, else it will have no effect. You can even
add files to the print queue and remove others in the same command. A /C or
/P switch applies to the file name that precedes it and to all subsequent file
names until another /P or /C switch is encountered. The command

```
PRINT MAR92.DOC /C APR92.DOC /P MAY92.DOC
```

deletes MAR92.DOC from the print queue but adds APR92.DOC and
MAY92.DOC. Running PRINT with no command-line switches displays the
current list of files in the print queue.

Using PRINT with Ports Other than LPT1   The first time PRINT is run, it asks
you for the name of the "list" device. The default is PRN, which corresponds to
LPT1. You may specify an alternate output device—LPT2, LPT3, COM1, COM2,
COM3, or COM4—by entering its name here or by including a /D switch on the
command line when PRINT is installed. For example, the command

```
PRINT /D:LPT2
```

installs the resident portion of PRINT in memory and tells it to print to LPT2.
If you install PRINT from a batch file, include a /D switch (even if the destination is PRN) to prevent PRINT from pausing and prompting you for the name
of the list device. Another note: If your printer is attached to a COM port, but
you've redirected output from LPT to COM with a MODE command, you can
give PRINT the name of *either* port. But for good form, refer it to the LPT port.

Changing Print Parameters   The /B, /S, and /Q switches allow you to customize the way PRINT works by controlling the size of the print buffer (the region
of memory where data output to the printer is stored when it's read in from
disk), the number of timeslices PRINT gets as a background task, and the maximum number of files that may be queued at any time. The default values are
adequate for most users. But you may have special needs that call for values
other than the defaults.

   The default print buffer is 512 bytes long—meager by any standard. You can
speed up printing and reduce disk accesses by installing PRINT with a more spa-
cious print buffer. The command

```
PRINT /B:16384
```

installs PRINT with a 16k buffer size (the maximum PRINT allows), at the expense of 16k of RAM that would otherwise be available to application programs. Unfortunately, PRINT does not permit its buffer to be placed in extended or expanded memory unless you have a 386 and install PRINT.COM in upper memory with a LOADHIGH command.

Your PC contains an internal clock that, on average, ticks approximately 18.2 times every second. PRINT uses this clock tick to grab control of the PC every so often and output one or more characters from its print buffer. You can adjust the priority of this background process with the /S switch, which accepts a value from 1 to 255 that specifies how many clock ticks, or timeslices, PRINT is allocated. The *ticks3* value you specify only has meaning in relative, not absolute, terms. The higher the value, the more time PRINT steals from the process that is running in the foreground, and the faster printing is performed.

The default *ticks3* value is 8. If printing is too slow for you, reinstall PRINT (yes, you have to reinstall it; the /S, /Q, and /B switches only work when PRINT is first installed) with a higher *ticks3* value. Reinstalling it requires either a reboot or a utility that will remove TSRs from memory. For example, the command

```
PRINT /S:16
```

will speed printing up slightly. The command

```
PRINT /S:128
```

will speed printing up a lot. Why not just default to the highest value permitted? Two reasons. One, because the more timeslices PRINT is allotted, the slower foreground processes will run. Installing PRINT with too high a /S value may slow a word processor or spreadsheet to a crawl. Two, PRINT is limited by the speed of your printer. At some point, further adjustments to *ticks3* will have no incremental effect on printing speed because the printer is already being driven at the maximum possible speed. Once the break-even point is reached, devoting additional timeslices to PRINT is a waste of system resources.

The number of files that may be queued at any one time (default: 10) is independent of the print buffer size. If you need to print more than ten files at a time, install PRINT with a /Q switch denoting the maximum number of files that may be queued. The minimum is 4, the maximum, 32. The command

```
PRINT /Q:20
```

doubles the size of the print queue from its default of 10 to allow up to 20 files to be in the queue at once.

Some Practical Advice   If you plan to use the PRINT command, it's wise to load it from your AUTOEXEC.BAT file or with an INSTALL directive from

CONFIG.SYS. The reason: PRINT leaves behind a RAM-resident wedge that, if installed after other TSRs, may prevent them from being uninstalled. Loading it from AUTOEXEC.BAT allows you to control where and when it's loaded. The first time PRINT is run, it's installed in memory. As a general rule, make PRINT among the first TSRs loaded in your system unless another one explicitly states that it is to be loaded first.

If you have a 386, consider installing PRINT with a LOADHIGH command and a larger buffer size to increase printing efficiency. LOADHIGH puts it in upper memory, out of the way of programs that reside in the lower 640k that need all the conventional memory they can get.

As a suggested configuration, install PRINT with the following parameters, which assume you plan to use PRINT on LPT1 and don't anticipate the need to queue up more than eight files at once:

```
PRINT /D:LPT1 /B:4096 /Q:8
```

The 4,096-byte print buffer and maximum queue size of eight files strike a reasonable compromise between performance and memory consumption.

Keep in mind that PRINT was designed to print text files only. If you use it to print a file that contains binary printer control codes, the output may be garbled. This is because PRINT, assuming it will only be used for text files, expands characters with the value 09H (the ASCII code for a tab character) into the number of spaces (ASCII code 20H) needed to reach the next tab stop. It also interprets any character with the value 1AH (the ASCII code for the character that marks the end of a text file) as end of the file and stops printing, even if data remains. This type of error often occurs when PRINT is used to print files that were printed to disk from application programs that send setup strings or formatting codes to the printer.

Quick-and-Dirty Text-File Printing

You don't have to use the PRINT command to print text files from DOS. If all you need is a quick hard copy of a short text file, try the command

```
COPY filename PRN
```

or

```
COPY filename LPTx
```

instead, where *filename* is the name of the file you want to print and LPT*x* is LPT1, LPT2, or LPT3. These commands copy the file directly to the indicated device. You can also type

```
TYPE filename > PRN
```

This method uses the output redirection operator to funnel output from the TYPE command to PRN. These commands have the added advantage that they do not leave a resident program behind in memory which may, under certain circumstances, prevent other TSRs from being uninstalled. Type **ECHO^L** to eject the final page from the printer.

We noted in the last section that the PRINT command should not be used to print binary files. The TYPE command warrants a similar caveat because it, like PRINT, stops at the first occurrence of a character with the value 1AH. The COPY command, however, works with binary files as well as text files. So if you want to print a file that was captured to disk from an application program and that you know contains binary printer setup strings, use the COPY command to output it to the printer.

Printing Graphics

Prior to DOS 4.0, the GRAPHICS command, which permits you to dump graphics screens to the printer by pressing the Print Screen key, only worked with CGA screens and printers that understood the IBM command set. GRAPHICS was upgraded for newer EGA and VGA screens in DOS 4.0, but printer support remained a glaring weakness. The DOS 5.0 GRAPHICS command has finally been upgraded to accommodate a wider range of printers, including the HP LaserJets that have become ubiquitous on the desktops of corporate America.

Before you can use the Print Screen key to print graphics screens, you must install GRAPHICS. Its syntax is

```
GRAPHICS [printer] [[d:][path]filename] [/R] [/B] [/LCD]
    [/PB:id]
```

where *printer* identifies the type of printer attached to your system, selected from the list in Table 6.7; *filename* is the name of the data file that contains printer information; /R reverses white and black in the printed image; /B prints the background in color on color printers; /LCD adjusts the aspect ratio of the printed image to match the LCD screen on the IBM PC Convertible; and *id* provides an alternate way to control the aspect ratio (what the DOS manual calls the "print box size") of the printed image. At present, the *id* parameter can be set to either STD or LCD. Specifying /PB:LCD is the same as using the /LCD switch.

If you don't specify a printer type when GRAPHICS is installed, DOS defaults to HPDEFAULT, which works with any PCL-type printer. PCL is the control language built into HP printers.

There are subtle differences in the ways that HPDEFAULT, LASERJET, and LASERJETII handle LaserJet printers. For example, LASERJET prints everything in the LaserJet's 75 dpi mode, while LASERJETII uses 100- and 150-dpi printer modes for added clarity. If you own an HP LaserJet of any type, you might want to try all three and see which one gives you the best results. The highest resolution that GRAPHICS uses on any LaserJet printer is 150 dpi, so the half megabyte of RAM that comes standard on most LaserJets is adequate for screen dumps in any video mode.

TABLE 6.7

MODE Command Printer Parameters

Parameter	Printer Type
COLOR1	IBM Color Printer with monochrome ribbon
COLOR4	IBM Color Printer with four-color RGB (red, green, blue, and black) ribbon
COLOR8	IBM Color Printer with four-color CMY (cyan, magenta, yellow, and black) ribbon
DESKJET	Hewlett-Packard DeskJet
GRAPHICS	IBM Graphics Printer, IBM Proprinter, or IBM Quietwriter (also most Epson dot-matrix printers)
GRAPHICSWIDE	Wide-carriage IBM Graphics Printer
HPDEFAULT	Hewlett-Packard PCL printer
LASERJET	Hewlett-Packard LaserJet
LASERJETII	Hewlett-Packard LaserJet II (also Laser Jet III)
PAINTJET	Hewlett-Packard PaintJet
QUIETJET	Hewlett-Packard QuietJet
QUIETJETPLUS	Hewlett-Packard QuietJet Plus
RUGGEDWRITER	Hewlett-Packard Rugged Writer
RUGGEDWRITERWIDE	Wide-carriage Hewlett-Packard Rugged Writer
THERMAL	IBM PC Convertible thermal printer
THINKJET	Hewlett-Packard ThinkJet

You can adapt the GRAPHICS command to most Epson dot-matrix printers (and printers that emulate the Epson command set) using the GRAPHICS printer type. This causes GRAPHICS to output commands to the printer using the command set found on IBM's original Graphics Printer, which functions identically to Epson's MX-series printers. Epson's RX-series and FX-series printers, as well as several others, feature compatible command sets. For wide-carriage IBM or Epson printers, specify GRAPHICSWIDE as the *printer*.

By default, GRAPHICS obtains its printer information from a file called GRAPHICS.PRO, which resides in the same directory as your other DOS system files. GRAPHICS.PRO is a text file that defines everything DOS needs to know to duplicate a screen image on the printer—the video modes that are supported, the control codes used to initialize the printer to print graphics and to reset it once it's done, the relationship between printer pixels and screen pixels, and more.

You can snoop around inside GRAPHICS.PRO with a text editor to see how the GRAPHICS command handles printers. In particular, you'll see several PRINTER statements that define what printers the information that follows applies to. You'll see DISPLAYMODE statements followed by numbers that define the supported video modes. Following each DISPLAYMODE statement, you'll see SETUP, GRAPHICS, and RESTORE statements that list the control codes DOS issues to the printer when the printing process starts, at the beginning of each line, and when printing is finished. Finally, you'll see PRINTBOX statements that define how many printer pixels correspond to each screen pixel and whether the image should be printed sideways or upright on the page for each supported /PB switch.

If GRAPHICS is executed from a directory other than the one that contains GRAPHICS.PRO and GRAPHICS.PRO isn't in the same directory that GRAPHICS.COM is in, you'll need to specify a path to GRAPHICS.PRO when GRAPHICS is installed. For example, the command

```
GRAPHICS DESKJET C:\DOS\GRAPHICS.PRO
```

tells DOS that GRAPHICS.PRO can be found in the \DOS directory of the C drive and that GRAPHICS is being installed to work with an HP DeskJet. Alternatively, if you use a printer information file other than GRAPHICS.PRO, you must enter its name here.

The optional /R and /B switches tell DOS to print reverse-field and color images, respectively. The /B switch is only valid if the printer type is COLOR4 or COLOR8. If you don't include a /B switch when using GRAPHICS with a color printer, the background color may be printed as white due to the way the BIOS handles colors in graphics mode. The /R switch simply reverses the field so that what's normally printed in black comes out white, and vice versa.

If GRAPHICS.PRO is stored in the \DOS directory of your hard disk along with GRAPHICS.COM, the command

```
GRAPHICS LASERJETII
```

sets your PC up to dump graphics screens to HP LaserJet-series printers. If GRAPHICS.PRO is located elsewhere (and if it's not in the current directory), modify this to read

```
GRAPHICS LASERJETII C:\SYSTEM\GRAPHICS.PRO
```

assuming GRAPHICS.PRO is located in the \SYSTEM subdirectory of the C drive. Similarly, the command

```
GRAPHICS GRAPHICS
```

configures a PC to print graphics screens on IBM, IBM-compatible, and most Epson dot-matrix printers. Finally, the command

```
GRAPHICS COLOR4
```

installs GRAPHICS for IBM color printers equipped with RGB ribbons.

Once you have installed GRAPHICS, press the Print Screen key whenever you're ready for a screen dump. (On some keyboards, you'll have to press Shift as well; on 101-key models, there is a dedicated Print Screen key.) After a brief pause, the image will come rolling out of your printer. A common misconception among new users is that the GRAPHICS command itself prints the screen. GRAPHICS must be installed before DOS will print a graphics mode screen, but you must press the Print Screen key to actually initiate a screen dump.

Exactly how the screen dump will appear depends on what type of printer you have and what the current graphics mode is. On black-and-white printers, some images are printed in monochrome, while others are printed using up to four shades of gray. In general, you'll find that the fewer colors there are on the screen, the better the hard-copy rendition DOS will produce.

Why GRAPHICS?

You might wonder why a GRAPHICS command is necessary for your PC to dump graphics screens to the printer. After all, the key is labeled "Print Screen," and it works fine in text mode, with or without GRAPHICS installed. So why GRAPHICS?

The answer lies in the BIOS. When the Print Screen key is pressed, the BIOS keyboard handler generates an interrupt 05H, which immediately passes control to a special routine elsewhere in the BIOS that dumps the screen to the printer. That's fine in text mode, but not in graphics mode: The BIOS routine is written to handle text-mode screens only. It reads the video mode before starting, and, if the screen is currently in a graphics mode, kicks out without printing a single pixel.

That's where GRAPHICS comes in. GRAPHICS is a TSR that intercepts occurrences of interrupt 05H and prints graphics screens itself. In text mode, GRAPHICS defers execution on to the BIOS. But in graphics mode, it reads the contents of the video buffer pixel by pixel, converts what it sees there to equivalent printer commands, and reproduces the pixels on the printer. That's not an easy task given the plethora of video modes and printers available, because all of them have to be treated differently. But GRAPHICS does a pretty fair job of accommodating all of them.

One limitation you should be aware of in using the GRAPHICS command is that it only supports video modes that are supported by the video BIOS. You cannot, for example, dump an 800 by 600 SuperVGA graphics screen to the printer or print a screen from an application that reprograms the VGA to a video mode not normally supported by the BIOS. One example of such a mode is the VGA's 256-color 360 by 480 graphics mode. Some programs use it, but the BIOS does not support it.

Using Alternate Character Sets

So that it may be adapted for use in other countries, DOS supports the use of alternate character sets on your screen, keyboard, and printer through a process known as *code page switching*. A *code page* is simply the set of 256 characters your printer or video adapter uses to determine what characters correspond to what ASCII codes and how they should appear. In code page 437, for example (the hardware code page built into most IBM-compatible equipment), the character whose ASCII code is 244 appears as the upper half of an integral sign

(∫). In code page 850, the same character appears as a paragraph marker (¶). You can take advantage of the code page switching facilities built into DOS to select the character set that is most appropriate for the country you are working in and substitute it for the one your PC defaults to. DOS provides two device drivers for this purpose: DISPLAY.SYS for screens and PRINTER.SYS for printers. In addition, it provides an assortment of commands for preparing and switching among the various code pages once the requisite drivers are loaded.

Displaying Alternate Character Sets

Part of DOS 5.0's support for use in international settings is its ability to download alternate character sets (code pages) to EGA and VGA video adapters. By default, both the EGA and VGA contain fonts in ROM that the DOS documentation calls *hardware code pages*—a fancy term for the character bit maps that determine what character corresponds to what ASCII code. But they also accept downloaded character sets, the same way laser printers accept downloaded fonts. DOS comes packaged with six EGA/VGA-compatible code pages that may be downloaded to the video hardware so characters not commonly used in the United States (letters of the alphabet accented with diacritics, for example) may be displayed.

The six code pages, their 3-digit ID codes, and the languages they support are listed in Table 6.8. Your DOS manual shows what each code page looks like. Code page 437 is identical to the default character set stored in ROM on EGAs and VGAs. So for all intents and purposes, DOS adds five new character sets to the arsenals of EGA and VGA users.

TABLE 6.8

Code Pages and Code Page IDs

Code	Code Page	Languages Supported
437	United States	English and most European languages
850	Multilingual	English and most other languages
852	Slavic	Slavic languages
860	Portuguese	English and Portuguese
863	Canadian-French	English and Canadian-French
865	Nordic	English, Norwegian, and Danish

Until you tell it otherwise, DOS uses code page 437, the one built into your video adapter. You can verify this by typing CHCP (the CHange Code Page command) without any parameters or switches following it. DOS will display the message

```
Active code page: 437
```

Selecting one of the alternate code pages for use is a four-step process:

1. Load the DISPLAY.SYS device driver.

2. Execute an NLSFUNC command to add national language support functions to DOS itself.

3. Load the code page into RAM ("prepare" the code page in DOS-speak) from disk with the MODE command.

4. Use the CHCP or MODE command to download the code page to the video hardware ("select" the code page).

The effect of selecting an alternate code page is to change the way characters are displayed. With code page 437 selected, a value of 189 in a character cell in the video buffer is displayed as a box corner; with code page 850 selected, it is displayed as a cent sign. The ASCII code for the character doesn't change; rather, the way the video hardware treats the ASCII code changes.

The first step in setting your PC up to use alternate code pages is to load the display driver DISPLAY.SYS. The statement

```
DEVICE=C:\DOS\DISPLAY.SYS CON=(EGA,437,1)
```

in CONFIG.SYS installs DISPLAY.SYS from the \DOS directory of drive C, tells it that it will be used on an EGA or VGA and that the display adapter's default code page is 437, and reserves room for one additional code page to be defined later on. If your PC is set up to load device drivers into upper memory, DISPLAY.SYS may also be installed with a DEVICEHIGH directive.

After the DEVICE directive that loads DISPLAY.SYS should come an INSTALL directive that loads NLSFUNC (short for National Language Support FUNCtions). NLSFUNC is a TSR that DOS uses to load and switch between code pages and to read information from COUNTRY.SYS, the DOS file where country-specific information is stored. The command

```
INSTALL=C:\DOS\NLSFUNC.EXE C:\DOS\COUNTRY.SYS
```

in CONFIG.SYS loads NLSFUNC from C:\DOS and tells DOS that COUNTRY-.SYS is also located in C:\DOS. If COUNTRY.SYS is located in the root directory of the boot drive, you can leave off the C:\DOS\COUNTRY.SYS. Otherwise, you need to spell out the path to where it is on your hard disk. NLSFUNC may also be installed from AUTOEXEC.BAT, where it runs and installs itself the way a normal TSR does.

The MODE command allows you to load a code page into RAM in the space reserved for code pages when DISPLAY.SYS was loaded. The command

```
MODE CON CP PREPARE=((850)C:\DOS\EGA.CPI)
```

reads code page 850 into RAM ("prepares" the code page) from the file C:\DOS-\EGA.CPI, one of the five code page information files that comes with DOS.Then, the command

```
MODE CON CP SELECT=850
```

activates it. A code page must be prepared before it can be used with a MODE CON CP SELECT command. Otherwise, DOS will respond with the message "Code page not prepared."

After code page 850 is selected, typing

```
MODE CON CODEPAGE /STATUS
```

displays the message

```
Active code page for device CON is 850
Hardware code pages: code page 437
Prepared code pages: code page 850
```

And typing

```
MODE CON CODEPAGE SELECT=437
```

directs DOS to revert to your PC's default code page.

To see the effect of code page switching, clear the screen, switch to code page 437, and, on the command line, type the character whose ASCII code is 189 by holding down the Alt key and entering 189 on the numeric keypad. Press Enter and ignore the "Bad command or file name" message. Then switch to code page 850. You'll immediately see the character you typed on the last line switch to a cent sign. Switch back to code page 437, and the character will switch back, too.

MODE CON CODEPAGE SELECT isn't the only way to switch from one code page to another. DOS also provides the simpler, more concise CHCP command. The command

```
CHCP 850
```

switches to code page 850 just like MODE CON CODEPAGE SELECT=850. The difference is that CHCP makes the code page active for all devices, not just the display device CON. As explained in the next section, code pages must be prepared for the printer the same as they must be for displays. If code page switching has been enabled for both the screen and the printer, the command CHCP 850 activates that code page for both devices.

Printing Alternate Character Sets

Code page switching isn't unique to the display device. So that you can print what you see on the screen, DOS permits code pages to be prepared and selected for printers also—provided your printer is one of the following: an IBM Proprinter 4201, 4202, 4207, or 4208, or an IBM Quietwriter III Model 5202. Code page switching is not supported on other printers, so this capability will be of limited worth to most users.

Why do code pages have to be loaded for the printer if it's to print what appears on the screen? Remember that in text mode, your PC thinks in terms of ASCII codes, not character bit maps. To a video adapter, the value 41H represents a capital "A." Your printer thinks the same way. You send it an ASCII code, and it looks up the bit map for the code in an internal character table. If the printer's character table doesn't match the video adapter's character table, what's printed won't be the same as what's shown on the screen. Configuring both devices to use identical code pages ensures that the internal character tables match.

Preparing a printer for code page switching is exactly analogous to preparing a display, except that the device driver PRINTER.SYS is used in place of DISPLAY.SYS. Adding the commands

```
DEVICE=C:\DOS\PRINTER.SYS LPT1=(4201,437,1)
INSTALL=C:\DOS\NLSFUNC.EXE C:\DOS\COUNTRY.SYS
```

to CONFIG.SYS configures DOS for code page switching on the printer attached to LPT1. The component on the PRINTER.SYS command that specifies what type of printer code page switching is being installed for (4201 in the preceding example) can be any of the codes shown in Table 6.9. As they do in DRIVER.SYS, the other two numeric parameters in parentheses specify the printer's hardware code page (again, 437) and the number of additional code pages DOS should reserve room for in memory.

TABLE 6.9

PRINTER.SYS Code Page Information Files

Code	Code Page Information File	Printer
4201	4201.CPI	IBM Proprinter 4201 or 4202
4208	4208.CPI	IBM Proprinter 4207 or 4208
5202	5202.CPI	IBM Quietwriter III Model 5202

Once PRINTER.SYS and NLSFUNC are installed, the command

```
MODE LPT1 CODEPAGE PREPARE=((850)C:\DOS\4201.CPI)
```

prepares code page 850 for use by loading it from the code page information file 4201.CPI, which is supplied with DOS. The names of the code page information files that correspond to the printers that support code page switching are also shown in Table 6.9.

Finally, the command

```
MODE LPT1 CODEPAGE SELECT=850
```

activates the code page so the printer uses the character set imported from 4201.CPI rather than its ROM-based character set. You can also use the command CHCP 850 to activate that code set for both the printer and the screen.

You can use DISPLAY.SYS without PRINTER.SYS if you have an EGA or VGA video card but don't have one of the IBM printers just listed. The only problem is that printed copies may not reflect what you see on the screen. If that's a problem, you may choose to forego code page switching altogether—or to be careful what characters you use when code page switching is enabled.

Remapping the Keyboard: The KEYB Command

Having alternative character sets at your disposal for the screen and printer is one thing, but typing them is another. One way to enter a character that doesn't appear on the keyboard is to enter its three-digit ASCII code on the numeric keypad while the Alt key is held down. For example, depress Alt and type 160 on the keypad, and when you let go of the Alt key, a lowercase "a" accented with an acute diacritic (á) appears. That's the character whose ASCII code is 160, as shown in your DOS manual's code page tables for all code pages but 863.

If you live and work in a foreign country, this method of entering characters is more hindrance than help. That's why DOS includes the KEYB command. KEYB permits you to alter the layout of the keyboard to accommodate foreign languages. The command

```
KEYB BE,,C:\DOS\KEYBOARD.SYS
```

remaps your keyboard to the Belgian layout. This layout and others are diagrammed in your DOS manual. Table 6.10 lists the keyboard country codes that DOS 5.0 accepts. KEYBOARD.SYS is the file from which DOS extracts the information it uses to remap the keyboard. You must spell out the path to KEYBOARD.SYS unless it is located in the current directory or the current path. Also note that KEYB may be installed in CONFIG.SYS with the INSTALL command.

TABLE 6.10

KEYB Codes

Country	Code	Country	Code
Australia	US	Netherlands	NL
Belgium	BE	Norway	NO
Brazil	BR	Poland	PL
Canadian-French	CF	Portugal	PO
Czechoslovakia (Czech)	CZ	Spain	SP
Czechoslovakia (Slovak)	SL	Sweden	SV
Denmark	DK	Swiss-French	SF
Finland	SU	Swiss-German	SG
France	FR	United Kingdom	UK
Germany	GR	United States	US
Hungary	HU		
Italy	IT		
Latin America	LA		

KEYB works by installing a memory-resident keyboard handler that supplants the one in the BIOS. KEYB affects the keyboard in two ways. First, it alters the way the keyboard is laid out, in most cases adding characters to it that weren't there before. In some layouts, a single key can produce as many as four different characters, depending on what other keys are pressed at the same time. Second, KEYB lets you enter characters with diacritics by typing the diacritic followed the character it's to be used with. For example, typing apostrophe-a (the apostrophe key followed by the "a" key) produces "á"; quotation mark-a produces "ä"; a tilde followed by "n" produces "ñ"; and apostrophe-c produces "ç." For characters to be displayed properly, they must be supported in the active code page. Your DOS manual contains diagrams of the keyboard layouts for the various countries supported.

Once KEYB is installed, you can switch back to the default layout by pressing Ctrl-Alt-F1. To revert to the alternate layout, press Ctrl-Alt-F2.

Summary

This chapter is by no means the last word on screens, keyboards, and printers. Despite the improvements, DOS still lacks many of the sophisticated tools you'd like to have at your disposal for interfacing with these devices. In Chapter 12, we'll take up the subject of screens, keyboards, and printers again, this time with the goal of developing some of the utilities that DOS left out—for example, utilities to blank the screen after a predetermined amount of time has elapsed with no keyboard or mouse activity and to capture output from the printer to a file.

So what's next? The enhancements that ANSI.SYS and KEYB add to the keyboard aren't all DOS does to make your life as a typist easier. In the next chapter, we'll look at one of version 5.0's most surprising new features—the DOSKEY command—which lets you recall past commands, edit text typed on the command line, and build command macros. After you've read it, you'll probably agree that DOS users have never had it so good.

7 A KINDER, GENTLER COMMAND LINE

IT WOULDN'T SEEM THAT THE ACT OF TYPING COMMANDS ON THE COMMAND line would be all that arduous a task. And it's not—at least not on the surface. Nor would you think that something as small and seemingly unimportant as a command line would evoke strong emotions from DOS users. Yet it does. DOS's command line interface is something of a paradox. Some users love it, some users hate it, and some users endure a tempestuous love-hate relationship with it that leads them at times to seek refuge in DOS shells and menu systems that hide the command line altogether. But despite the diversity of opinions, the one thing nearly all DOS users would agree on is that the command line is long overdue for a few minor but very needed improvements.

Throughout all versions of DOS up to and including DOS 4.0, the part of COMMAND.COM that reads and interprets your commands remained relatively unchanged. The kernel function it calls upon to read text from the command line (the same kernel function, by the way, that other DOS utilities such as DEBUG and EDLIN call to read a line of input) offered only limited provisions for editing text, lacking even the capability to move the cursor back to previously typed characters without erasing intervening characters as it went. Nor did it make provisions for recalling any command other than the last one entered, or for any of the myriad command-line enhancements available from third-party utilities.

DOS 5.0 changes all that with a better, more flexible command line than ever. In this chapter, you'll learn how to edit text on the command line, recall old commands, enter multiple commands and create command macros. All these features are new to DOS 5.0. They're all part of a grander scheme to make working on the command line easier than ever—and to let you work faster and smarter as a result.

Introducing DOSKEY

At the heart of DOS 5.0's improved command line is the new DOSKEY command. DOSKEY is actually a small terminate-and-stay-resident utility program that attaches itself to the operating system and enhances the command line by giving you the ability to

- Recall past commands
- Search the list of past commands for ones that begin with a specified text string
- Execute two or more commands from the same command line

- Edit commands

- Create command macros, where typing **LS**, for instance, executes the command DIR /O:N, just as if LS were a native DOS command

DOSKEY resembles third-party command-line utilities such as Chris Dunford's CED and *PC Magazine*'s own DOSKEY (no relation to the DOS command of the same name, though they bear similar features), which added similar capabilities to earlier versions of DOS.

Taking DOSKEY for a Test Drive

Before we delve into the details, let's take a quick look at DOSKEY's talents. In future sections, we will explore each of those capabilities in depth. If you haven't already, install DOSKEY by entering its name on the command line (as always, make sure there's a path to the \DOS directory on your hard disk—or to whatever directory DOS 5.0's external command files are stored in). Then execute a few DOS commands.

Afterward, press the Up Arrow key a few times and watch the commands you typed cycle back across the screen. If you want to execute one of them, just strike the Enter key when the command is displayed—just as if you had entered it manually. Up Arrow cycles backward through the command stack, and Down Arrow cycles forward. DOSKEY records every command you type, so you can play it back later and edit it if you like, to modify it before it's reused.

When you're finished cycling through the command stack, press Esc to clear the command line. Notice that with DOSKEY installed, pressing Esc actually clears the command line rather than just moving the cursor to the next line. Then type

```
DOSKEY /HISTORY
```

DOSKEY will list all the commands you've typed, in the order in which they were entered.

Next, enter the command

```
TYPE README.DOC | MORE
```

but don't press the Enter key. Instead, press Home and watch what happens. The cursor jumps back to the beginning of the line, ready for you to edit the command just as if you were working with a line of text inside your word processor. The full range of cursor-movement and editing keys that you can use will be discussed shortly under "Editing Text on the Command Line." For now, just try pressing the Left Arrow and Right Arrow keys to move the cursor backward and forward through the text.

Then position the cursor under the "T" in TYPE and press Del to delete the character at the cursor and pull the remaining text in to fill the void. Now press the Ins key to activate insert mode and type **T**, reinserting that character into the existing text.

DOSKEY also lets you piece together command macros that incorporate other DOS commands. Press Esc again to clear the command line and type

```
DOSKEY WHEREIS=DIR \$1 /S
```

Then type

```
WHEREIS *.DOC
```

DOS responds with a list of files on the current drive with the extension .DOC. DOSKEY assigns the command DIR \$1 /S (which tells DOS to look for all occurrences of a given file in the root directory and all the subdirectories below it, which by definition encompass the entire disk) to the command WHEREIS and substitutes the file specification you type after WHEREIS for $1. When you type **WHEREIS *.DOC**, DOS actually executes the command DIR *.DOC /S, although you can't see it because all the processing goes on behind the scenes. In effect, you've created a new command, one that DOS didn't recognize before and that you can use to locate files on your hard disk.

Installing DOSKEY on Your System

If your system is configured for loading TSRs high, install DOSKEY with the LOADHIGH command. Otherwise, install it as you would any other TSR. The syntax for the DOSKEY command is

```
DOSKEY [/REINSTALL] [/BUFSIZE=size] [/MACROS] [/HISTORY]
   [/INSERT | /OVERSTRIKE] [macro=[command]]
```

The /MACROS and /HISTORY parameters tell DOSKEY to display all the macros currently defined and a command history, respectively. A command history is a list of all the commands that are currently buffered in the command stack and that can be recalled using the Up Arrow, Down Arrow, and other command-recall keys.

The *size* parameter following BUFSIZE specifies how many bytes of memory DOSKEY should reserve internally to store commands and command macros. The default is 512 bytes, enough to store roughly five hundred characters of command and macro text. DOSKEY won't run out of room for stacking old commands because it pushes older ones off the stack when it needs room for more. But it can run out of space for storing macros. If you try to create a command macro and DOSKEY responds with the message "Macro storage depleted," increase its internal buffer size with the BUFSIZE switch.

There are two ways to increase the buffer size. You can reboot your computer and install DOSKEY from scratch with the correct *size* parameter. (If DOSKEY is installed from AUTOEXEC.BAT, be sure to edit the appropriate line in that file.) Alternatively, you can reinstall DOSKEY by issuing a DOSKEY command with a REINSTALL switch, and using an increased *size* parameter. For example, you can reinstall DOSKEY with a buffer size of 2,048 bytes, with the command

```
DOSKEY /REINSTALL /BUFSIZE=2048
```

The /REINSTALL switch tells DOSKEY that it has already been installed once and that it's about to be installed a second time (without this command-line switch, DOSKEY will not reinstall itself, so that you won't reinstall it by accident). The advantage to using /REINSTALL is that you don't have to take time out to reboot. The disadvantage is that it wastes memory because the old copy of the program is left behind, occupying space to no use. You can see this by typing **MEM /C** after a second copy of DOSKEY is installed. DOSKEY will show up twice in the program listing.

You can use the /INSERT and /OVERSTRIKE switches to determine DOSKEY's default editing mode. When it's first installed, DOSKEY's command-line editor defaults to character overstrike mode unless you specify otherwise with the /INSERT switch. These text-entry modes are exactly analogous to insert and overstrike modes in most word processors. It's easy to tell which mode is currently in effect: DOSKEY increases the size of the cursor in insert mode as a visual reminder that as you type, characters to the right of the cursor will be pushed farther to the right. In overstrike mode, what you type replaces the text that's already there. You can always press the Ins key to switch back and forth between the two editing modes. However, as soon as you press Enter to execute a command, DOSKEY reverts to the default text-insertion mode—the one that was set when the program was installed. DOSKEY always remembers what mode it was originally set to, even if you press Ins during a command-line edit.

The final command-line switch, *macro=command*, lets you create command macros that DOSKEY will recognize on the command line. Command macros are similar to batch files except that they are run from RAM rather than from disk and can be used to replace internal DOS commands such as DIR and DEL. We'll take a closer look at macros later. But first, let's examine one of DOS-KEY's foremost means of cutting down on the number of keystrokes: the ability it gives you to recall past commands.

Recalling Commands from the Command Stack

DOSKEY automatically records every command you type on the command line in an internal storage buffer known as the *command stack* and lets you recall them. You can display a complete list of commands currently recorded with the command

```
DOSKEY /HISTORY
```

You can also get a list of commands, complete with line numbers, by pressing F7. A summary of the keys DOSKEY provides for accessing and managing the command stack is shown in Table 7.1.

TABLE 7.1

DOSKEY's Command-Recall Keys

Key	Action
Up Arrow	Cycles backward through the command stack, displaying one command at a time
Down Arrow	Cycles forward through the command stack, displaying one command at a time
PgUp	Recalls the oldest command in the command stack
PgDn	Recalls the most recent command in the command stack
F7	Displays a numbered list of all the commands currently recorded in the command stack
F8	Cycles through the command stack recalling only those commands that begin with the text entered on the command line
F9	Recalls a command by number (a numbered list is displayed when you press F7)
Alt-F7	Clears the command stack of all commands
Alt-F10	Clears all macros

The Up Arrow and Down Arrow keys move backward and forward through the command stack, displaying one command at a time. Once a command is displayed, you can edit it, execute it, or press Up Arrow or Down Arrow again to proceed to the next command. If you know that the command you want is only a few commands back, Up Arrow is the easiest way to get there. Press Up Arrow repeatedly until the command you want is displayed, and then edit it as needed or press Enter to execute it. If you overshoot a command, press Down Arrow to work your way back down the command stack.

If, as you peruse the stack with the Arrow keys, you lose track of where you are in the command stack, press F7 for a list of commands. The current command will be marked with a greater-than symbol, as shown here:

```
1: CD \WP\DOC
2: COPY CHAP07.DOC A:
3: CLS
4:>MEM /PROGRAM
5: DOSKEY /MACROS
   .
   .
   .
16: EMM386
17: DOSKEY /HISTORY
```

The next press of Up Arrow will display the command above the one that is marked, while pressing Down Arrow will display the command that is currently marked. When a command is executed, DOSKEY automatically resets the pointer so that the next press of Up Arrow will display the last command entered.

To quickly get to the top of the stack, press PgUp. The oldest command in the stack will be displayed. To get to the bottom, press PgDn. These keys work no matter where you are in the stack when you press them. They're useful when you know that the command you're looking for is somewhere near the top or bottom of the stack, but you don't want to press Up Arrow or Down Arrow 50 times to get there.

As the stack grows, finding a specific command for recall becomes more difficult. To help, DOSKEY provides two special keys:

■ Function key F8, which works like Up Arrow, except that it recalls only those commands that begin with the text you enter on the command line

■ Function key F9, which recalls a command from anywhere in the command stack by number

One way to quickly recall a certain command is to press F7 for a list of commands, followed by F9 and the number of the command you want. The command history displayed by function key F7 is numbered so that you can identify the one you want. If the list looked like this:

```
 1: CD \WP\DOC
 2: COPY CHAP07.DOC A:
 3: CLS
 4: MEM /PROGRAM
 5: DOSKEY /MACROS

     .

     .

     .

16: EMM386
17: DOSKEY /HISTORY
```

you could recall the command COPY CHAP07.DOC A: by pressing F9, and then, at the "Line number:" prompt, typing **2** and pressing Enter. DOSKEY does not provide a way for you to delete individual commands from the stack, nor does it permit you to edit them. You can, however, edit a command once it's recalled or delete *every* command from the stack by pressing Alt-F7.

Function key F8 invokes DOSKEY's smart recall feature. Let's say that somewhere back you typed the command

```
LINK PMCARD, /ALIGN:16, NUL, OS2, PMCARD.DEF
```

and you want to use it again, but you know that it's buried deep in the command stack—perhaps dozens of commands deep. You can recall it quickly by typing **LINK** and pressing function key F8. F8 reads the text currently entered on the command line and searches the command stack, recalling only those commands that begin with the same characters. If there's more than one command matching the specified pattern, repeated presses of F8 cycle you through all of them in the reverse order in which they were entered.

Naturally, the more text you enter before pressing F8, the more selective DOSKEY will be in its search. If you had executed several LINK commands and wanted to zero in on a particular one, you could do so by typing enough of the command to separate it from the rest. Typing

```
LINK PM
```

followed by pressing F8 is sufficient to separate

```
LINK PMCARD, /ALIGN:16, NUL, OS2, PMCARD.DEF
```

from

```
LINK MODULE1+MODULE2
```

With a little practice, you can retrieve any command from the stack without a second thought. And once you grow accustomed to the new way of doing things, you'll rarely, if ever, type the same command twice in one session.

Editing Text on the Command Line

Next to command stacking, one of the greatest pleasures you'll find in using DOSKEY is the flexibility it gives you in editing text on the command line. Whereas previous versions of DOS offered a relatively crude set of character-at-a-time editing tools based on function keys F1 through F5, DOS 5.0, with the help of DOSKEY, offers much more. The old features are still there, should you choose to use them, but the new ones are so powerful and so robust that most users will find it just as convenient to forget about the old way of doing things and embrace the new with vigor.

Table 7.2 lists the keys DOSKEY provides for editing commands. Function keys F1 through F5 work basically the same as they did in previous versions of DOS, copying characters between an unseen command template and the current command line or, in the case of function key F4, simply moving the cursor forward in the command template. If, for example, you entered the command

```
EDLIN AUTOEXEC.BAT
```

the string "EDLIN AUTOEXEC.BAT" would become the command template. Then, pressing F1 would reproduce the command one character at a time, each press copying one character from the template to the command line. Pressing F2 immediately followed by a character key would copy everything from the template to the command line up to the character specified. Pressing F2 followed by the period key, for example, would produce the string

```
EDLIN AUTOEXEC
```

Pressing F3 would copy the remainder of the template to the command line, or, if the command line were empty, simply repeat the last command. Pressing F4 followed by a character key would move the pointer identifying the current location in the command template forward to the specific character. For example, to type

```
EDLIN DO.BAT
```

you could press F2 followed by **A** (to produce EDLIN and a space), type **DO**, press F4 followed by the period key (to move the pointer forward to the period after AUTOEXEC), and finish up by pressing F3 to copy BAT to the command line. The F5 key works slightly differently: Pressing it copies the current text of the command line to the command template, essentially duplicating the action of the F3 key.

TABLE 7.2

DOSKEY's Command-Line Editing Keys

Key	Action
F1	Copies one character from the command template to the current command line
F2	Copies text from the command template to the command line up to the character pressed immediately after F2
F3	Copies the remainder of the command template to the current command line; if pressed with the cursor at the beginning of the line, F3 repeats the entire command
F4	Moves the pointer that identifies the current location in the command template forward to the character pressed immediately after F4
F5	Copies the current text of the command line to the command template and clears the command line
Left Arrow	Moves the cursor one character to the left
Right Arrow	Moves the cursor one character to the right
Ctrl-Left	Moves the cursor one word to the left
Ctrl-Right	Moves the cursor one word to the right
Home	Moves the cursor to the beginning of the line
End	Moves the cursor to the end of the line
Ctrl-Home	Deletes text from the character immediately left of the cursor to the beginning of the line
Ctrl-End	Deletes text from the cursor position to the end of the line
Del	Deletes the character at the cursor
Backspace	Deletes the character left of the cursor in insert mode and functions like Left Arrow in overstrike mode, unless you begin backspacing from the end of the line, in which case Backspace deletes the character left of the cursor regardless of the text insertion mode
Esc	Clears the command line
Ins	Toggles between insert and overstrike modes

The only difference in DOSKEY's handling of these function keys is that the command template doesn't necessarily reflect the last command entered. If a command is recalled from the command stack, the template is automatically updated to reflect the last *recalled* command. In addition, you no longer need to use function keys to edit commands. They're retained primarily for compatibility with older versions of DOS. Instead, you can use the additional keys listed in Table 7.2, which fall into three categories:

- Keys that move the cursor around the command line: Left Arrow and Right Arrow, Ctrl-Left and Ctrl-Right, Home, and End

- Keys that delete text: Backspace, Del, Ctrl-Home, Ctrl-End, and Esc

- The key that toggles between insert and overstrike modes: Ins

The six cursor movement keys move the cursor nondestructively on the command line. Left Arrow and Right Arrow move it one character at a time; Ctrl-Left and Ctrl-Right move it a word at a time (words are separated by spaces or tabs); and Home and End move the cursor to the beginning and end of the command line, respectively. Once the cursor is positioned, you can add, delete, or change text as needed to modify the command.

The Ins key toggles insert mode on and off. DOSKEY increases the size of the cursor in insert mode to remind you that text will be inserted rather than overwritten. It also returns to the default mode when the Enter key is struck. If, for example, overstrike mode is the default, and you temporarily switch to insert mode and edit and execute a command, DOSKEY will revert to overstrike mode as soon as a new command prompt is displayed. If DOSKEY was installed with an /INSERT switch, then insert mode is the default, and DOSKEY will automatically revert to insert mode with each new command prompt. There is no provision for causing the most recently selected text insertion mode to become the default.

Five keys and key combinations delete text from the command line. Del deletes the character at the cursor, drawing everything to the right of it one cell to the left. Backspace deletes the character left of the cursor, Ctrl-End deletes everything from the cursor to the end of the line, and Ctrl-Home deletes everything from the character immediately left of the cursor to the beginning of the line. Esc clears all text from the command line.

DOSKEY also permits you to edit commands that are longer than the width of the screen. In previous versions, the cursor would not wrap back around to the top line once it reached the second line of a two-line command. With DOSKEY installed, it will.

The best way to get comfortable with these editing keys is simply to use them. Take time to play around with them, experimenting with different ways to position the cursor and to add, delete, and modify text. If you've used word processors or full-screen text editors before, these functions will feel comfortable to you.

Executing Multiple Commands

Another feature that DOSKEY brings to the command line is the ability to execute more than one command per command line. All you have to do is separate each command by pressing Ctrl-T, which shows up on the screen as a paragraph marker symbol (¶). The following command combines two other commands—an MD and a CD command—to create a subdirectory and then change to it:

```
MD \TMPDIR ¶ CD \TMPDIR
```

Similarly, the next command moves a file from one directory to another by first copying it to the destination, then deleting it from the current directory:

```
COPY CHAP07.DOC \BACKUP ¶ DEL CHAP07.DOC
```

You can combine as many commands on one command line as the 127-character limit permits; and commands may include special symbols, such as redirection and piping operators.

Command Macros

The ability to record and manipulate a stack of commands is only part of what DOSKEY has to offer. DOSKEY also lets you create command macros to increase efficiency, minimize mistakes, or simplify DOS operations for novice users. A macro is a command you enter on the command line that executes another command or series of commands. In many respects, macros are similar to batch files, with the following exceptions:

- Macros are stored in RAM where DOS can get to them quickly. Batch files require from one to several disk accesses each time they're run.

- Macros can be executed anywhere, anytime. Batch files must be located in the current directory or somewhere in the current PATH so DOS can find them.

- Macros are limited to 127 characters of text (the maximum amount of text that can be entered on one command line), while the length of batch files is virtually unlimited.

- Macros cannot perform conditional branching based on the outcome of other commands like batch files can by using IF and GOTO commands.

- You can run a batch file from within another batch file. You cannot, however, invoke a macro from inside another macro. DOSKEY also does not allow macros to be run from batch files; macros can only be executed on the command line.

- You can use macros to replace DOS commands (both internal and external) such as DEL and FORMAT. You can't replace an internal command with a batch file.

You can demonstrate DOSKEY's macro feature by typing these two commands:

```
DOSKEY LS=DIR /O:N
LS
```

The first command creates a macro called LS (LS is the UNIX command to display a directory listing, similar to DIR in DOS). The second one runs it. When you type **LS**, DOS displays the same sorted directory listing that DIR /O:N does. But by assigning the command to a macro, you've cut the number of keystrokes required by more than half and simplified the syntax of the command. Once a macro is created, you can save it to disk for later use, as described in the section "Saving Macros."

The importance of the fact that macros are stored in RAM rather than as files on disk cannot be overstated. First, your hard disk, even if it's a fast one with a sub-20-millisecond access time, is one of the slowest components of your system. Macros are executed instantaneously, but DOS must pause to load batch files each time they're run. Second, many users have dozens of short batch files, perhaps one or two lines long, sitting on their hard disk occupying much more space than needed. A 20-byte batch file on a hard disk with a 4k cluster size consumes more than 4,000 bytes of disk space. Consolidating these short batch files into macros that are RAM-based rather than disk-based not only speeds up operation, but also conserves precious disk space.

Another significant difference between macros and batch files is that environment variable substitution works in batch files, but not in macros. For example, the statement

```
PATH=%PATH%;%1
```

in a batch file adds a string entered on the command line (represented by %1) to the current PATH environment variable because DOS's batch file interpreter substitutes the PATH text string for %PATH% in the batch file. In a macro, no substitution is performed. The equivalent command executed as a macro would destroy the PATH environment variable, because DOSKEY would interpret the %PATH% component of the command literally.

There are two reasons to create macros: to save typing and to minimize errors. Any frequently used command that is more than a few characters long is a candidate for a macro. It is far easier to type **FMT**, for example, than it is to type **FORMAT A: /F:720**. Similarly, if a command that you use every day includes a long list of parameters, why bother memorizing them, or risk entering them incorrectly, when you can have the computer do it for you?

Creating and Running Macros

The syntax for the command to create a macro is

```
DOSKEY macro=command
```

where *macro* is the macro name and *command* is the command or series of commands to be executed when *macro* is typed on the command line. For example, the command

```
DOSKEY DDIR=DIR /W
```

creates the command macro DDIR and assigns it the command DIR /W. Once the macro is defined, typing **DDIR** is the same as typing **DIR /W**. DOS doesn't know the difference, because DOSKEY reads what you type on the command line and substitutes DIR /W for DDIR before COMMAND.COM even gets a look at it. In effect, you've created a new command—DDIR—that wasn't previously in DOS's vocabulary, and you've taught DOS how to interpret it.

What happens if you give a macro the same name as a DOS command? The macro takes precedence. This macro equates DIR to DIR /W, with the result that entering DIR produces the same listing as DIR /W:

```
DOSKEY DIR=DIR /W
```

It doesn't matter whether the command that's replaced is internal (stored inside COMMAND.COM) or external (stored as a program file on disk). DOS always gives macros higher priority.

You can take advantage of this order of priority to neutralize DOS commands that are dangerous if misused. If you manage a group of PC users and are often called to recover files that were accidentally deleted, try adding this macro to your users' machines:

```
DOSKEY DEL=DEL $1 /P
```

This DEL command will prompt users for verification before it deletes a file and display the name of the file as well. Better yet, the person sitting at the PC won't even have to remember to type **DEL /P** rather than **DEL**—DOSKEY will do it automatically. This should all but eliminate the loss of entire directories full of files that results when someone types **DEL *.*** in the wrong location on the hard disk.

When invoking a macro, avoid inserting any spaces before the macro name. Why? Because DOSKEY starts at the beginning of the line and compares what you type there character-for-character with its list of macros. A leading space causes the lookup routine to fail. If you've redefined a DOS command, you can use this to your advantage if you want to execute the real command rather than the macro. If DEL were redefined as just shown, typing

```
C:\>DEL *.DOC
```

would invoke the macro. But typing

```
C:\> DEL *.DOC
```

would run the real DEL command instead.

You can have a macro execute more than one command by separating individual commands on the right side of the equal sign with the character string "$T". The syntax is

```
DOSKEY macro=command [$T command] [$T command] [...]
```

You can string together as many commands in one macro as the command line will hold (up to 127 characters). For example, the command

```
DOSKEY CP=MD TMP $T COPY *.DOC TMP
```

creates a macro called CP that creates the subdirectory TMP in the current directory and copies to it all the files with the extension .TMP. Likewise, the command

```
DOSKEY MV=MD TMP $T COPY *.TMP TMP $T DEL *.TMP
```

creates a macro called MV that is identical to CP except that it deletes all the .TMP files from the current directory when it's done.

Unlike batch files, macros with multiple commands can't use the outcome of one command to affect the execution of other commands in the sequence; the GOTO command doesn't work for macros. Once a macro is started, it blindly proceeds from left to right, executing each command in turn. Also, macros cannot call other macros. You can interrupt macro processing by pressing Ctrl-C or Ctrl-Break, but for macros with multiple commands, you'll have to press it at least once for each command contained in the macro. Be prepared to sit on the Break key if you need to halt a long macro once it's started.

You can list all of the macros currently defined by typing

```
DOSKEY /MACROS
```

We'll combine this feature with output redirection later in this chapter to devise a method for storing macros to disk so they can be recreated later on.

Using Replaceable Parameters in Macros

In batch files, you can use replaceable parameters (represented by the symbols %1 through %9) to reference parameters entered on the command line. Macros can also have replaceable parameters, represented by the symbols $1 through $9. The first parameter entered on the command line when the macro is invoked is substituted for $1, the second parameter for $2, and so on. For example, the command

```
DOSKEY TY=TYPE $1
```

sets up a macro named TY that is equivalent to the TYPE command. When you type **TY FILE.TXT**, DOS interprets it as TYPE FILE.TXT, because the text string FILE.TXT is substituted for the symbol $1 when the macro is executed. Another example is

```
DOSKEY LIST=FOR %F IN ($1) DO TYPE %F
```

This macro, LIST, creates a super TYPE command which, unlike DOS's TYPE command, will accept wildcard characters in file names. DOS won't accept the command

```
TYPE *.TXT
```

because TYPE won't take wildcards. But it will accept

```
LIST *.TXT
```

You can reference up to nine different command-line parameters with the symbols $1 through $9. Most commands only require one or two, but should you ever need more, the capability is there. There is no macro equivalent of the SHIFT command used to access more than ten parameters in batch files. Nor is there an equivalent to %0, which, in a batch file, assumes the name of the batch file itself.

The $* Parameter: A Special Case There will occasionally be times when you'd like to assign all the text that follows the command that invokes a macro to a single parameter. That's what $* is for. The command

```
DOSKEY D=DIR $*
```

passes anything and everything entered after D to DIR. If you type

```
D /A:D /O:N
```

the $* parameter assumes the value /A:D /O:N, so this command has the same effect as typing

```
DIR /A:D /O:N
```

If, on the other hand, the macro had simply been defined as

```
DOSKEY D=DIR
```

you wouldn't be able to pass command modifiers to the D command, because with no replaceable parameters designated when the macro was defined, no substitution would occur. And if it had been defined with the command

```
DOSKEY D=DIR $1
```

only the first parameter—/A:D—would be passed. Using $* ensures that everything entered on the command line is passed to the macro.

Combining Macros and Redirection Operators

There's another problem associated with macro definitions that results from DOS's interpretation of the symbols <, >, and | on the command line to mean you want input or output redirected. (If you're not familiar with redirection and piping, they're discussed in detail in the next chapter.) To illustrate the problem, type

```
DOSKEY D=DIR /O:N | MORE
```

At first glance, it would appear that this command creates a macro that displays a sorted directory listing one screenful at a time by piping output from the DIR command to MORE. But enter it and type DOSKEY /MACRO to display a list of the currently defined macros, and it will show up as

```
D=DIR /O:N
```

What happened to the end of the macro? Simple: DOS thought you wanted to pipe output from the DOSKEY command to MORE. It didn't realize you wanted | MORE to be part of the macro. To compensate, DOSKEY reserves the special symbol $B to insert in place of the | operator in the macro definition. The command

```
DOSKEY D=DIR /O:N $B MORE
```

does what we intended to do in the first place: It creates a macro that executes the DIR command with a /O:N switch and pipes the output to the MORE filter. You can incorporate the < and > redirection operators the same way with the symbols $L and $G, respectively. For example, the command

```
DOSKEY PRINTDIR=DIR /O:N $G PRN
```

creates a macro named PRINTDIR that issues the command

```
DIR /O:N > PRN
```

which outputs a listing of the contents of the current directory to your printer. Similarly, the command

```
DOSKEY DELALL=DEL *.* $L YES.TXT
```

creates a macro that executes the command DEL *.* and looks to a text file called YES.TXT (which presumably contains a response to the DEL command's query "Are you sure (Y/N)?") for input. Table 7.3 summarizes all the special symbols DOSKEY accepts in macro definitions.

TABLE 7.3

Reserved Symbols in Macro Definitions

Symbol	Meaning
$*	Assumes the value of all text entered on the command line following a macro name when the macro is invoked. In the command MAC FILE1 FILE2, $* becomes FILE1 FILE2.
$1 through $9	Assume the values of individual parameters entered on the command line following a macro name when the macro is invoked. DOSKEY substitutes the first parameter following the macro for $1, the second for $2, and so on.
$B	Represents the piping operator I in macro definitions. Causes output to be piped from one command to another.
$G	Represents the output redirection operator > in macro definitions. Redirects output to a destination other than the screen.
$L	Represents the input redirection operator < in macro definitions. Redirects input to a source other than the keyboard.
$T	Separates individual commands in a macro that contains multiple commands.
$$	Represents the dollar sign $ in macro definitions.

If you want to include a dollar sign in a macro definition, designate it with the $$ symbol. If you enter just a single dollar sign, DOSKEY will interpret it as a replaceable parameter if it's followed by a number, or as a piping operator, redirection operator, or command separator if it is followed by the letter "B," "G," "L," or "T." With $$, there's no mistaking your intentions.

Editing and Deleting Macros

There are two ways to delete macros once they're defined: individually or all at once. To erase a single macro, type

```
DOSKEY macro=
```

where *macro* is the name of the macro to be deleted. If you had created the following macro:

```
DOSKEY WHEREIS=DIR \$1 /S
```

The command

```
DOSKEY WHEREIS=
```

would delete it. Type **DOSKEY /MACROS** to list all the macros currently defined, and WHEREIS will no longer show up. You can delete all the macros currently defined by pressing Alt–F10.

Unfortunately, there's no way to edit a macro once it's been entered. If you reenter it, however, the new definition supersedes the old. The ability to recall old commands could help here. If you entered the macro on the keyboard rather than from a batch file, and if the command stack is deep enough, just recall the command you used to enter the macro, edit it as needed, and reexecute the command to replace the old macro with the new.

Saving Macros

It would be convenient if DOSKEY were to provide you with an easy way to write macros out to a file so that you could call them up later, like some third-party keyboard enhancers do. Unfortunately, DOSKEY makes you go about saving macros the hard way: by saving all currently defined macros to a file and using a text editor to convert the macro definitions to batch commands.

To save the macros to a file, enter the command

```
DOSKEY /MACROS > filename
```

where *filename* is the name (and optionally, the location) of the file you want created to hold the macro definitions. Let's say the file that is generated looks like this:

```
WHEREIS=DIR \$1 /S
MOVE=COPY $1 $2 $T DEL $1
D=DIR /O:N $B MORE
LIST=FOR %F IN ($1) DO TYPE %F
```

Give the file the extension .BAT. Then, use EDIT to add the word DOSKEY to the beginning of each line as shown here:

```
DOSKEY WHEREIS=DIR \$1 /S
DOSKEY MOVE=COPY $1 $2 $T DEL $1
DOSKEY D=DIR /O:N $B MORE
DOSKEY LIST=FOR %F IN ($1) DO TYPE %F
```

The result: a batch file that, when run, will recreate the entire list of macros. The only difference between the list DOSKEY outputs and the commands needed to create the macros is the "DOSKEY" at the beginning of each line. You're taking advantage of that fact to concoct a means for saving macros.

Putting Macros to Work on Your System

So what can you do with macros now that you know how to use them? Plenty. No discussion of DOSKEY's powerful macro capabilities would be complete without a list of suggested macros to get you started. Type in the following listing and save it as MACRO.BAT:

```
DOSKEY D=DIR $1 /O:N /P
DOSKEY LOCATE=DIR $2\$1 /S /B
DOSKEY MOVE=COPY $1 $2 $T DEL $1
DOSKEY LIST=FOR %F IN ($1) DO TYPE %F
DOSKEY MDEL=FOR %F IN ($*) DO DEL %F
DOSKEY DCOPY=XCOPY $1 $2 /S /E
```

Then add the statement

```
CALL \BATCH\MACRO
```

to your AUTOEXEC.BAT file. This example assumes that the file MACRO-.BAT is stored in the \BATCH directory; if you stored the file elsewhere, substitute the appropriate directory name.

MACRO.BAT adds the following macro commands to your system:

Command: D
Example: D *.DOC
Purpose: Displays a sorted directory listing and automatically pauses between screens if there is more than one screenful of information.

Command: LOCATE
Example: LOCATE PICFILE.PCX
LOCATE PICFILE.PCX D:
Purpose: Searches an entire drive for a specified file and lists all occurrences of it. If the drive parameter is omitted, the current drive is searched by default.

Command: MOVE
Example: MOVE \GRAPHICS\PICFILE.PCX D:\PCXFILES
Purpose: Moves a file from one location (drive, directory, or both) to another. The file is deleted from the old directory. If there is not enough space for the file at the destination, the file will be lost and must be recovered with the UNDELETE command.

Command: LIST
Example: LIST *.TXT

Purpose: Lists the specified file or files to the screen (or to a file or device if output is redirected). Similar to TYPE except that it accepts wildcard characters.

Command: MDEL
Example: MDEL XXX.DAT YYY.DAT ZZZ.DAT
Purpose: Deletes one or more files. Similar to DEL except that it accepts multiple file names.

Command: DCOPY
Example: DCOPY A: B:
Purpose: Copies the entire contents of one disk to another, duplicating directory structures in the process. Similar to DISKCOPY except that it can work with floppy drives of dissimilar types.

As you think of new commands, add them to MACRO.BAT so that over time you'll accumulate a macro collection of your own. The possibilities are endless.

Summary

Some third-party command-line enhancers add more features to the command line than DOS 5.0 does, but don't let that detract from your enjoyment of it. Two years ago pundits were predicting the demise of DOS as the world prepared for the onslaught of OS/2. Two years later DOS is going strong and growing stronger, thanks to Microsoft's renewed commitment to making DOS the best it can be. The inclusion of DOSKEY in version 5.0 is but one indication that this commitment is genuine.

The next chapter introduces another topic important to your mastery of the command line: redirection and piping. Input and output redirection are mechanisms for pointing DOS to sources other than the keyboard for input (a disk file, for example) and for routing output from DOS commands to destinations other than the screen (to a disk file or printer, for example). Piping combines aspects of both input and output redirection to funnel the output from one command to the input of another. If you've ever been stymied trying to figure out how to get a hard copy of a disk directory or prevent a long list from scrolling off the screen, the next chapter's for you.

8 REDIRECTION AND PIPING

YOU'VE SEEN THEM BEFORE: LONG COMMANDS THAT COMBINE OTHER DOS commands with greater-than and less-than signs and vertical bars and produce all sorts of strange output. Commands like

```
DIR \ /S /B | FIND "DOC" | SORT > DOCFILES.LST
```

which searches the current drive for files whose names contain the letters "DOC," sorts them alphabetically, and writes the list to a file named DOCFILES-.LST. At first, this example would seem to be ammunition for those who claim that a command-oriented user interface is too difficult to learn and that graphical interfaces are far easier to work with. Yet when you break it down into its component parts as shown in Figure 8.1, it turns out that it's not that complex a command after all.

FIGURE 8.1

Anatomy of a redirection command

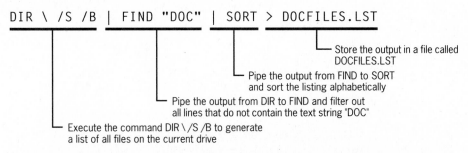

The first part of the command—DIR \ /S /B—generates a list of all the files on the current drive. The output from DIR is piped to the FIND command, which filters out all file names that do not contain the string "DOC" and pipes the ones that do to the SORT command. SORT rearranges the file names so that they appear in alphabetical order. Finally, the output from SORT is directed to a file called DOCFILES.LST.

This one command line contains no less than four separate DOS commands, yet they act as one command. The capability DOS gives you to string commands together like this, with each one acting on the output of the last, provides a flexibility in formatting output that can only be had in a command-driven environment.

This rerouting of input and output to another source or destination is called *redirection*. Output redirection sends output that would normally go to the screen to a file or device instead. Input redirection causes DOS to look to a file or device other than the keyboard for input. And a special form of redirection called *piping* directs the output of one DOS command to the input of another.

Redirection works because DOS commands use a pair of predefined I/O channels called *standard input* and *standard output* to perform most of their screen and keyboard I/O. Normally, data written to standard output goes to the screen, while data that is read from standard input comes from the keyboard. Internally, DOS maintains a table of file handles (numbers that programs use to reference open files and devices) that map standard input and standard output to the CON device driver. However, when it sees an output redirection operator on the command line, DOS closes the handle that corresponds to standard output and opens the named file or device, which assumes the file handle that was formerly assigned to standard output. Then, when the program on the left side of the > symbol writes to the file handle normally associated with standard output, it unknowingly sends its output to the file or device that is the target of the redirection rather than to CON.

DOS provides three special command-line operators for redirecting input and output:

- The > operator, which redirects command output from the screen to the file or device of your choice

- The < operator, which redirects command input from the keyboard to the file or device of your choice

- The | operator, which pipes the output of one command to the input of another

Anytime DOS sees these symbols on the command line, it assumes that you intended for redirection to occur. As a result, you can't use them in file names or for any other purpose on the command line besides redirecting input and output.

Redirecting Output to Files and Devices

You can redirect the text that a DOS command writes to the screen by using the following command format:

```
command > destination
```

where *command* is the DOS command whose output you want to redirect and *destination* is the name of the file or device where you want the output to go. The command

```
DIR /O:N > FILES.TXT
```

outputs a sorted directory listing (DIR /O:N) to a disk file named FILES.TXT. If FILES.TXT doesn't exist, DOS will create it for you. If it does exist, the old contents of the file will be replaced by the output from the DIR command. If the file exists and you want its original contents preserved, type

```
DIR /O:N >> FILES.TXT
```

The >> operator tells DOS to append the output from DIR /O:N to the current contents of the file rather than to overwrite it.

The *destination* parameter may also specify any character device that is supported by a character device driver. By default, DOS supplies the logical device names listed in Table 8.1.

TABLE 8.1

Character Devices Available for Redirected Input and Output

Driver	Input Device	Output Device
NUL	None	None
CON	Keyboard	Screen
AUX	Auxiliary (COM1)	Auxiliary (COM1)
PRN	—	System Printer (LPT1)
LPT1	—	Parallel Port LPT1
LPT2	—	Parallel Port LPT2
LPT3	—	Parallel Port LPT3
COM1	Serial port COM1	Serial Port COM1
COM2	Serial port COM2	Serial Port COM2
COM3	Serial port COM3	Serial Port COM3
COM4	Serial port COM4	Serial Port COM4

"—" indicates the corresponding device is used as a destination for output only, not as a source of input.
Device names in parentheses indicate what physical device the driver corresponds to.

All but one of these, NUL, appears in the listing generated by the command MEM /DEBUG. The NUL device driver is a special one that you can use when you want to suppress output from a command. For example, the command

```
DIR /O:N
```

normally displays a directory listing on the screen. But type

```
DIR /O:N > NUL
```

and nothing happens. The reason? The NUL device driver simply discards any text sent to it, earning it the name "NUL," short for "null," or "nothing." It's like a black hole for command output: Anything you send there simply disappears.

There are occasions, believe it or not, when it's convenient to suppress command output. For example, if your AUTOEXEC.BAT file contains several COPY commands to copy files to a RAM disk at start-up, the message "*xx* file(s) copied" is shown on the screen for each COPY command executed, even if ECHO OFF was the first statement in the batch file. But by redirecting COPY's screen output to the NUL device, you can prevent COPY from littering the screen with messages. Changing the command

```
COPY \DOS\*.* F:\
```

to

```
COPY \DOS\*.* F:\ > NUL
```

copies all the files in the current directory just the same, but sends the "files copied" message to never-never land, where it won't be seen again.

Another way to suppress output from DOS commands is to use the CTTY command, which directs DOS to use a device besides CON for input and output. To use it, place the command

```
CTTY NUL
```

immediately before the command or commands you want output redirected from, and the command

```
CTTY CON
```

immediately after. Anything written to standard output will be swallowed up, just as if you had redirected output from each one of the commands individually. What's more, error messages, which DOS normally writes to a separate predefined I/O channel called *standard error,* will also be redirected, something you can't accomplish with the > operator. Be careful, however. If one of the intervening commands requires input from you or if something goes wrong with it, your PC may lock up and will probably require a reboot.

A far more common use of DOS's willingness to send output to a device other than the screen is to send it to the system printer. To get a hard-copy listing of the files in the current directory, you could type

```
DIR /O:N > PRN
```

PRN is the logical name for the system printer, which DOS assumes by default is attached to parallel port LPT1. If your printer is attached to a port other than LPT1, you can access it by specifying the name of the port explicitly—COM1, COM2, or COM3 for serial ports; LPT1, LPT2, LPT3, or LPT4 for parallel ports. The command

```
DIR /O:N > LPT2
```

redirects output to LPT2. A quick-and-dirty way to print text files (and avoid having PRINT become resident in memory) is to redirect output from the TYPE command to the printer. The command

```
TYPE TEXTFILE.DOC > PRN
```

sends TEXTFILE.DOC to port LPT1. If there's a printer attached, it will print the listing. Note that DOS does not automatically output a form feed at the end as many word processors do, so if you're using a laser printer, you may have to type ECHO^L >PRN to eject the final page (enter ^L by pressing L with the Ctrl Key held down).

There's a common misconception among new users that redirection can somehow be used to capture printer output to a file. Third-party utilities (like the ones we'll develop in Chapter 12) can, but DOS can't. One form of the MODE command does permit printer output to be rerouted from an LPT to a COM port as described in Chapter 6, but that's another type of redirection that is unique to MODE. Remember, output redirection allows you to redirect screen output to a file or device. Its capabilities begin and end there.

Using Alternate Sources of Input

By default, DOS commands look to the keyboard for typed input. You can change the default by entering commands in the form

```
command < source
```

where *command* is the DOS command that will *receive* the input and *source* is the file or device that will *supply* the input.

By far the most common use for input redirection is to automate execution of a command by supplying input from a text file. For example, FORMAT prompts you to press Enter before it begins formatting. When it's done, it prompts you for a volume label and asks if you want to format another disk before it returns to the command line. In all, a minimum of four keystrokes is required. To automate this process, use EDIT to create a text file containing two blank lines followed by an N and a carriage return , and then run FORMAT with redirected input by supplying a statement of the form

```
FORMAT A: < filename
```

where *filename* is the name of the file you just created. Each time it pauses for input, FORMAT will read the text file instead of the keyboard, get its answer from there, and go on.

Even full-blown DOS utilities such as DEBUG can be driven totally from a text file. For example, the following series of commands, executed in DEBUG, will create a short program named BEEP.COM that emits a short beep when you run it:

```
A 0100
MOV      AX,0E07
INT      10
RET

N BEEP.COM
RCX
6
W
Q
```

If you type this in, be sure to include a blank line between RET and N BEEP-
.COM. You can automate the execution of these commands by entering them in
a text file (call it BEEP.SCR) and typing

```
DEBUG < BEEP.SCR
```

DEBUG won't even know the difference. It'll think you typed everything in at
its hyphen prompt, when in reality the commands were read from the text file
and passed through as if they had been entered at the keyboard.

The other common application for input redirection is to pass streams of
data to the DOS commands MORE, SORT, and FIND. The command

```
SORT < NAMES.TXT
```

sorts the lines in a text file named NAMES.TXT and outputs them to the
screen. To capture the sorted output to a file, you could modify the command
to read

```
SORT < NAMES.TXT > SORTED.TXT
```

See what's happening? This command tells SORT to get its input from
NAMES.TXT and to send its output to a file named SORTED.TXT. You've
combined input and output redirection on a single line to customize a command
to work the way you want it to, not the way DOS has it operate by default.

Piping Output from One Command to Another

The piping operator | redirects the output of one command to the input of
another. For example, if you wanted to view the entire listing produced by MEM
/DEBUG but didn't want to hover over the Pause key to keep it from scrolling
off the screen, you could use the command

```
MEM /DEBUG | MORE
```

to display it one screenful at a time. The piping operator makes the output of MEM the input to MORE. You could do the same thing without the piping operator by using these two commands, which store the output from MEM in an intermediate file and input the file to MORE:

```
MEM /DEBUG > TMPFILE.TXT
MORE < TMPFILE.TXT
```

But why do in two steps what you could do in one? Piping combines input and output redirection so that two related operations can be performed with a single command.

In principle, piping is no different from input and output redirection. From the user's perspective, the difference between redirection and piping is that the text to the right of a piping operator will always be a command or program name (for example, SORT), while the text to the right of a > symbol will always be a device name or file name. In response to a piping request, DOS loads and runs the program on the left side of the | symbol and pipes the output from it to the program on the right. In a true multitasking environment, these two processes would be run concurrently; in DOS's single-tasking environment they're run sequentially, but the output from the first is captured before the second is started, so that it can *appear* that both programs are running simultaneously.

Using Filters

The most frequent beneficiaries of piped input/output are the three filters DOS provides for searching, sorting, and displaying lines of text. Filters are unique in that they have no capacity to read or write data files themselves; instead, they rely on input redirection or piping for data input and write their output to the screen unless directed to do otherwise with an output redirection operator.

The filters supplied with DOS 5.0 are

- MORE, which displays text one screenful at a time, pausing for a keypress between screens

- SORT, which sorts a text file based on criteria specified at runtime

- FIND, which searches a text file for occurrences of a specified string

Experienced users will be interested to know that these filters have changed little since previous versions of DOS, with the exception of an optional /I switch added to FIND for performing searches without regard to case. C and assembly language programmers can easily write additional filters to perform tasks such as stripping the high bits off 8-bit characters and encrypting and decrypting text files.

The MORE Filter

The MORE filter buffers text sent to it and displays it one screen at a time, pausing for a keystroke between each screen. Its syntax is

```
MORE < source
```

where *source* is the name of the file or device from which input will be taken. Output from MORE is automatically sent to the screen. Alternatively, input can be piped to MORE using the following command syntax:

```
command | MORE
```

where *command* is a command such as MEM or TYPE. MORE, like any other external DOS program file, must be in the current directory or in a PATH directory for DOS to find it. If DOS responds with "Bad command or file name" when you use a MORE filter, make sure MORE.COM is in the current PATH.

Use MORE anytime you want to view a text file without having it scroll off the screen, as in

```
MORE < TEXTFILE.DOC
```

or

```
TYPE TEXTFILE.DOC | MORE
```

Of course, a browse utility or DOS 5.0's full-screen editor is an even better way to peruse long text files. But that's cheating if you're a DOS purist. Besides, you may not always have access to a file browser or editor. What happens if you're sitting in front of someone else's PC trying to analyze a long text file? Now you can handle it using nothing other than the tools DOS provides.

Experienced users will be glad to know that the DOS 5.0 version of MORE works with screens displaying more than 25 lines of text, with or without ANSI-.SYS loaded. In previous versions, MORE assumed there were always 25 lines displayed and only used part of the screen when there were more.

The SORT Filter

The SORT filter reads lines of ASCII text and outputs them in alphabetical order. The syntax is

```
SORT [/R] [/+nn] < source [> destination]
```

or

```
command | SORT [/R] [/+nn] [> destination]
```

where /R tells SORT to sort text in reverse alphabetical order (from Z to A rather than A to Z), *nn* is the column number on which the sort should be based, *source* is the name of the input file or device, and *destination* is the name of an output file or device. If *destination* is omitted, sorted output goes to the screen. If the /+ switch is omitted, sorting begins with the first character in each line.

A classic use for SORT in versions of DOS prior to 5.0 was to obtain a sorted directory listing. The command

```
DIR | SORT
```

generates a directory listing sorted by file name. The command

```
DIR | SORT > DIRLIST.TXT
```

writes the listing to a text file. To sort the directory listing by file size, you could use the /+ switch as follows:

```
DIR | SORT /+13
```

This tells SORT to ignore the first 12 characters in each line and to begin sorting with the 13th. And it just so happens that column 13 is where DOS places the number that indicates file size when you type **DIR**. Of course, DOS 5.0 provides a better way to get sorted directory listings: the DIR command's /O switch. In earlier versions, running output through SORT was the *only* way to sort a directory listing.

Text passed to the SORT filter doesn't have to come from a DOS command. SORT may also be used to sort text files. If you have a list of names and phone numbers stored in last-name-first format in a file called PHONES.DAT, for example, you could sort the list by last name with the command

```
SORT <PHONES.DAT >PHONES.SRT
```

With a little preplanning, you could also arrange to store the names in first-name-first format, yet still manage to sort the listing by last name. To do so, begin each person's last name in the same column, even though some names will have more than one space between the first and the last. If last names begin in column 20, the command

```
SORT /+20 <PHONES.DAT >PHONES.SRT
```

will sort the list by last name. Later, we'll carry this idea one step further and combine it with the other DOS filters to learn how to set up and manage small databases.

The FIND Filter

The FIND filter searches text files for occurrences of specified text strings. The syntax is

```
FIND [/C] [/I] [/N] [/V] "string" < source [>destination]
```

or

```
command | FIND [/C] [/I] [/N] [/V] "string" [> destination]
```

where *source* and *destination* specify file or device names for input and output and *"string"* specifies the text string to search for. Run without any modifiers, FIND outputs each line it finds that contains the text string to the screen. /C suppresses this output and has FIND output only a count of the number of lines containing the string, while /V displays the lines that *don't* contain the string. If both /V and /C are used, FIND counts the number of lines that do not contain the string. /N adds line numbers indicating each line's position in the text file, and /I specifies that the search is not case sensitive. If /I is omitted, the search is sensitive to case.

A classic use for FIND is as an aid in searching your hard disk for files with certain characters in their name. The command

```
DIR \ /S /B | FIND "PCM"
```

locates any and all files with "PCM" embedded in their file names, regardless of where they are on the disk. If you simply wanted a count of how many files matching this criterion there are, you could type

```
DIR \ /S /B | FIND /C "PCM"
```

Remember that FIND's searches are case sensitive without a /I switch. Since DIR lists file names in all caps, this command wouldn't work with "pcm" rather than "PCM," unless it were also accompanied by /I.

FIND is the only one of the three DOS filters that doesn't have to rely on piping or redirection to read data files; it can also be run as a stand-alone DOS command. An alternate way to run it uses the syntax

```
FIND [/C] [/I] [/N] [/V] "string" [d;][path]filename
```

where *filename* is the name of the file to be examined. FIND does not accept wildcard characters in the file specification, so searches must be performed one file at a time.

Although FIND was designed to work with pure ASCII text files, it can be used to a limited extent on word processing documents stored in proprietary formats. Most word processors store text as ASCII characters and formatting instructions as binary codes or code sequences. As a result, text lookups will still work. For example, if you're trying to find the WordPerfect file that contains a greeting to Ed Smith, the command

```
FIND /C "Ed Smith" LETTERØ7.DOC
```

will tell you if LETTER07.DOC is the one—even though WordPerfect doesn't store documents in strict ASCII format.

Building a Do-It-Yourself Phone List

Would you believe that you can set up and maintain small databases using DOS 5.0? EDIT, MORE, SORT, and FIND are powerful tools for dealing with text files. Used correctly, they can do most of what some flat-file database managers can—and then some.

To build a phone list for names and phone numbers, use EDIT to set up a text file with the names and phone numbers of friends or business associates. Place one name (last name first) and one phone number on each line, like this:

```
Rubenking, Neil     555-7220
Hummel, Robert      555-2066
Davis, Fred         555-1667
Winer, Ethan        555-5892
Shaw, Richard       555-5876
```

Let's assume that the file is named PHONES.DAT and that it's stored in the \DATA directory of the C drive.

To sort and display the phone list, type

```
SORT < C:\DATA\PHONES.DAT
```

or, if the file is more than one screen long:

```
SORT < C:\DATA\PHONES.DAT | MORE
```

To quickly find Richard Shaw's number, type

```
FIND /I "SHAW" < C:\DATA\PHONES.DAT
```

It's even easier if you roll these commands into macros. To do so, add these commands to your AUTOEXEC.BAT file:

```
DOSKEY SHOW=SORT $L C:\DATA\PHONES.DAT $B MORE
DOSKEY SRCH=FIND /I "$1" $L C:\DATA\PHONES.DAT
DOSKEY PRNT=SORT $L C:\DATA\PHONES.DAT $G PRN
```

With these macros in effect, type **SHOW** to list all names and phones. To look up Richard Shaw's phone number, type **SRCH SHAW**. Or, to send a sorted listing of all the names and numbers to the printer, type **PRNT**. If your database needs are sufficiently modest, you may never fire up your old database manager again.

When Redirection Will and Will Not Work

Will input and output redirection and piping work with programs other than DOS commands? Yes, but only with programs that use DOS's internal programming functions—as opposed to BIOS services—to read the keyboard and write to the screen. To see what the difference is, start DEBUG and type in the following script (or better yet, save the script as a text file and use input redirection to enter it!):

```
A 0100
JMP    010F
DB     "Hello, world$"
MOV    AH,9
MOV    DX,0102
INT    21
RET

N HELLO1.COM
RCX
17
W
Q
```

This series of commands creates a short program called HELLO1.COM in the current directory. When you run HELLO1, it writes "Hello, world" to the screen. And if you type

```
HELLO1 > TESTFILE.TXT
```

the message is redirected and captured in the text file TESTFILE.TXT.

Now start DEBUG again and enter this command script:

```
A 0100
JMP    010F
DB     "Hello, world$"
CLD
MOV    SI,0102
LODSB
CMP    AL,24
```

```
JZ    011E
MOV   AH,0E
INT   10
JMP   0113
RET

N HELLO2.COM
RCX
1F
W
Q
```

This one creates HELLO2.COM, another program that displays "Hello, world" on the screen. Now type

```
HELLO2 > TEXTFILE.TXT
```

and what happens? "Hello, world" is displayed anyway! Moreover, the text file that is created has a length of zero bytes. It's almost as if DOS didn't see the output redirection operator entered on the command line. What went wrong?

Actually, DOS *did* see the > symbol on the command line. HELLO1 uses a DOS output routine (interrupt 21H, function 09H) to write to the screen. HELLO2 uses a BIOS output routine (interrupt 10H, function 0EH) instead. DOS can only intercept input or output if it is performed using DOS routines because only DOS routines use standard input and standard output. Unfortunately, most programs use BIOS services instead (or program the hardware directly) because the screen and keyboard services DOS offers are notoriously slow and feature-limited. That's why you can't capture output from WordPerfect or Lotus 1-2-3 to a text file. But all DOS commands use DOS I/O services, so you can count on piping and redirection working—always—with DOS commands.

If you program in C, you can guarantee that your programs will work with redirection by using keyboard and screen I/O functions that read from standard input and write to standard output. Your C runtime reference will tell you which functions fall into this category. Functions such as *printf*, *scanf*, *puts*, and *getche* do, but *_outtext* does not.

Summary

Redirection and piping enable you to do things with DOS that would otherwise require third-party utilities. Without output redirection, for example, an act as simple as printing the directory listing of a disk would require a special program. But by redirecting output from the DIR command to PRN, it's a snap. FIND, SORT, and MORE add to these capabilities even further, enabling you to perform common operations such as sorts and searches on text files without bringing in additional tools to do so.

The next chapter introduces the DOS 5.0 shell, which places an additional layer of operating system software—the graphical user interface—between you and the DOS kernel. This shell is greatly enhanced over the one included with DOS 4.0, to the point that its quality rivals (and in some cases exceeds) that of many of the third-party shells available. One can't help but note the irony in the fact that the first version of DOS to be packaged with a usable shell also introduced the best command line ever, for the shell was designed to insulate us from the very features that were added.

PART TWO

Programming DOS 5

331
A WORD ON PROGRAMMING

375
BUILDING THE BETTER BATCH FILE

459
FILE, DIRECTORY, AND DISK UTILITIES

531
SCREEN, KEYBOARD, AND PRINTER UTILITIES

613
THE ART AND ZEN OF TSRS

9 A Word on Programming

TO THE PROGRAMMER, THE PC IS A WORLD OF POSSIBILITIES WAITING TO happen. Non-programmers are restricted to working within the bounds that the operating system defines for them. Programmers, on the other hand, are free to create programs of their own that go above and beyond what the operating system has to offer. You saw this illustrated several times in Part 1, when DEBUG was used to create small but useful utilities.

Chapters 9 through 13 will develop even more DOS utilities and explain how they were developed so that you can write utilities of your own. If you read *PC Magazine*, you know that one of the most popular columns in the magazine is the "Utilities" column, where in each issue the magazine's writers present one or more utilities to help make life with DOS a bit easier. Think of Part 2 of this book as one big "Utilities" column, where we'll tackle several of the problems that confront DOS users daily and develop solutions to them in the form of custom programs.

It can't be emphasized enough that you don't have to be a programmer to benefit from the next few chapters of this book. Even if you skip the program listings altogether, you'll still gain several new utilities designed to fill the holes left by DOS. As powerful and feature-filled as it is, DOS 5.0 still leaves something to be desired in a few areas. Without special utilities to help, for example, you still can't capture printer output to a file or delete a subdirectory that contains other files and subdirectories. We will address these and other important needs in the chapters to come.

Every utility that we develop here is included on the disks at the back of the book, in both source code and executable form. The disks also include a sampling of utilities from other *PC Magazine* authors who have contributed their time and talent to making this book a complete resource for getting the most out of your PC. Individual programs are discussed at appropriate times throughout the book, and the syntaxes for all of them are documented in Appendix C.

Before we start writing programs, a brief introduction to programming in general is in order. It's not possible in a single chapter to acquaint you with everything you have to know to write a DOS program, but it is possible to provide a quick overview of the programming language we'll be using and of the DOS programming environment. This chapter discusses some of the basic elements of assembly language programming and introduces some of the resources that these programs routinely use to do their work.

A Brief Introduction to Assembly Language

All of the programs presented here were written in assembly language using the Microsoft Macro Assembler (MASM) version 5.1. You don't have to own the Macro Assembler to use these utilities; you only need it if you plan to modify the source code for them. Even without an assembler, these examples will be a big help in familiarizing you with the language and getting you acquainted with some basic assembly language programming techniques.

An assembler is a program that converts source code files that contain assembly language instructions into program files (executables) that you can store on your hard disk and run when you need them. The assembler produces a file called an *object file* that is later converted into a program file having an .EXE extension using a separate utility called a *linker*. Some EXE files are then converted into COM files with a third utility called a *binary converter*. Both the linker and the converter are normally included in the same package as the assembler. MASM is the assembler written and marketed by Microsoft Corporation, the same company that created DOS. Microsoft calls their linker LINK and their converter EXE2BIN. Other companies market compatible language tools that may be used in the place of MASM, LINK, and EXE2BIN. This book refers to them by their Microsoft names.

Why assembly language? Today, it's possible to write utilities in almost any contemporary language, including Pascal, C, and BASIC. These are examples of high-level languages—languages that offer their own commands such as PRINT and printf that are later translated into instructions the CPU understands. Programs written in assembly language are smaller, more concise, and faster-running than programs written in high-level languages. That's why the majority of the utilities published in *PC Magazine* are written in assembly language. That's also why we'll rely on assembly language in this book.

To be sure, there is a downside to working in assembler. It's more cryptic than other languages, because there are no English-like commands such as PRINT. There is usually more work involved in writing a program in assembly language because you're working at a much lower level. Writing "Hello, world" to the screen in C, for example, requires just one line of code. In assembly, it would take pages of code if it weren't for the fact that DOS and BIOS contain built-in functions that assembly language programs may call on to output text to the screen. As such, programming in assembler requires an intimate knowledge of what's available from DOS and the BIOS. Later in this chapter, we'll highlight some of the most important DOS and BIOS functions to prepare you for them later on when they show up in code listings.

It isn't the goal of this book to teach you assembly language from the ground up. That's a book in itself. However, it will give you a taste of what it's like. Assembler has a reputation for being difficult. In reality, it's probably one of the easier languages to master. However, it doesn't necessarily follow that writing assembly language programs is easy. It's quite possible to know the language inside out and still not be able to write a functioning program on the IBM PC. That's because to program the IBM PC in assembly language, you must understand the environment you're working in as well as the language you're using.

The source code listings in this book will provide numerous examples and a working education in the way professional and non-professional programmers alike get their programs to do the things they do.

What Is Assembly Language?

The heart of your PC is a small chip called the microprocessor, or CPU. The first IBM PC used an Intel 8088 chip, which was a slightly modified version of the 8086. The AT used the 80286. Subsequent PCs from a variety of manufacturers use other CPU chips, including the Intel 80386 and the 80486. Before long, we'll see PCs based on the 80586, which at this writing was a mere design on a drawing board.

Built into the microprocessor is a set of commands that cause it to perform tasks such as reading data from a memory location, loading a register with a value, comparing the contents of two registers, and so on. Collectively, these commands are known as the microprocessor's *instruction set*. A program is merely a set of instructions that tell the CPU what to do, when to do it, and how to go about it. When you write a program in a high-level language such as BASIC, the compiler (or interpreter) translates each BASIC command you enter into the tens or perhaps hundreds of CPU instructions that are required to execute that one command.

Assembly language is the middle ground between high-level languages and the instructions that CPUs understand. What's unique about assembly language is that each statement corresponds to one CPU instruction. There is no PRINT command in assembly language; only more primitive commands that, for example, move data from one location in memory to another, or read an I/O port. In assembly language, the equivalent of BASIC's PRINT "Hello, world" might look like this:

```
msg     db   "Hello, world$"

        mov  ah,09h
        mov  dx,offset msg
        int  21h
```

In assembler, every CPU instruction is assigned a short mnemonic such as CALL or MOV. The mnemonic is carefully chosen to provide a clue as to the instruction's purpose. CALL, for example, calls a subroutine. MOV moves data from one location to another. The fact that instructions in an assembly language program translate directly to CPU instructions makes assembly language the most direct route to programming the PC.

The 8086 instruction set contains approximately 110 different instructions, some of them simple, some of them quite complex. Most of the instructions have several different forms. The MOV instruction, for example, comes in nine forms; which form is used in a given situation depends on the type of data being transferred and where it is stored (in memory, in a general register, in a segment register, and so on). If you were to count the different forms as different instructions, you could argue that the 8086 actually understands several hundred different instructions. That's one reason to use an assembler rather than to assemble machine code programs by hand: The assembler takes care of many of the details for you. Simply include the MOV instruction in a program, for example, and the assembler decides which of the several forms of MOV should be used.

Table 9.1 lists all the instructions that appear in the 8086 instruction set. Programs that restrict themselves to this basic subset of the full 80x86 instruction set can be run without modification on all Intel processor types. The 286 and 386 offer additional instructions not shown here.

Don't let the size of this list intimidate you. Just to put things into perspective, if you program in QuickBASIC, you're working in an environment that supports more than 200 functions and statements. Meanwhile, the Microsoft C 6.0 runtime library contains more than 500 different functions and macros. Compared with these, assembly language isn't that difficult a language to master.

Anatomy of an Assembly Language Program

At this point, it's appropriate to take a look at a living, breathing assembly language program to see what makes it tick. The program we'll examine is HELLO1.ASM, which prints the message "Hello, world" on the screen. The source code is shown in Listing 9.1.

LISTING 9.1 HELLO1.ASM

```
                page    66,132
;******************************************************************************
; HELLO1 writes "Hello, world" to the screen.
;******************************************************************************


code            segment
                assume  cs:code,ds:code
                org     100h
begin:          jmp     short main

msg             db      13,10,"Hello, world",13,10,"$"


;******************************************************************************
; Procedure MAIN
;******************************************************************************


main            proc    near
                mov     ah,09h                  ;Display message with DOS
                mov     dx,offset msg           ;  function 09H
                int     21h

exit:           mov     ax,4C00h                ;Call function 4CH to exit
                int     21h
main            endp

code            ends
                end     begin
```

TABLE 9.1

The 8086 Instruction Set

Mnemonic	Meaning	Mnemonic	Meaning
AAA	ASCII Adjust for Add	JP	Jump on Parity
AAD	ASCII Adjust for Divide	JPE	Jump on Parity Even
AAM	ASCII Adjust for Multiply	JPO	Jump on Parity Odd
AAS	ASCII Adjust for Subtract	JS	Jump on Sign
ADC	Add with Carry	JZ	Jump on Zero
ADD	Add	LAHF	Load AH with Flags
AND	Logical AND	LDS	Load Data Segment register
CALL	Call	LEA	Load Effective Address
CBW	Convert Byte to Word	LES	Load Extra Segment register
CLC	Clear Carry flag	LOCK	Lock
CLD	Clear Direction flag	LODS	Load String
CLI	Clear Interrupt flag	LOOP	Loop
CMC	Complement Carry flag	LOOPE	Loop while Equal
CMP	Compare	LOOPNE	Loop while Not Equal
CMPS	Compare String	LOOPNZ	Loop while Not Zero
CWD	Convert Word to Double word	LOOPZ	Loop while Zero
DAA	Decimal Adjust for Add	MOV	Move
DAS	Decimal Adjust for Subtract	MOVS	Move String
DEC	Decrement	MUL	Multiply (unsigned)
DIV	Integer Divide (unsigned)	NEG	Negate
ESC	Escape	NOP	No Operation
HLT	Halt	NOT	Logical NOT
IDIV	Divide (signed)	OR	Logical OR
IMUL	Integer Multiply (signed)	OUT	Output
IN	Input	POP	Pop
INC	Increment	POPF	Pop Flags
INT	Interrupt	PUSH	Push
INTO	Interrupt on Overflow	PUSHF	Push Flags
IRET	Interrupt Return	RCL	Rotate through Carry Left
JA	Jump on Above (unsigned)	RCR	Rotate through Carry Right
JAE	Jump on Above or Equal (unsigned)	REP	Repeat
JB	Jump on Below (unsigned)	REPE	Repeat while Equal
JBE	Jump on Below or Equal (unsigned)	REPNE	Repeat while Not Equal
JC	Jump on Carry set	REPNZ	Repeat while Not Zero
JCXZ	Jump on CX Zero	REPZ	Repeat while Zero
JE	Jump on Equal	RET	Return
JG	Jump on Greater than (signed)	ROL	Rotate Left
JGE	Jump on Greater than or Equal (signed)	ROR	Rotate Right
JL	Jump on Less than (signed)	SAHF	Store AH into Flags
JLE	Jump on Less than or Equal (signed)	SAL	Shift Arithmetic Left
JMP	Jump	SAR	Shift Arithmetic Right
JNA	Jump on Not Above (unsigned)	SBB	Subtract with Borrow
JNAE	Jump on Not Above or Equal (unsigned)	SCAS	Scan String
JNB	Jump on Not Below (unsigned)	SHL	Shift Left
JNBE	Jump on Not Below or Equal (unsigned)	SHR	Shift Right
JNC	Jump on No Carry	STC	Set Carry flag
JNE	Jump on Not Equal	STD	Set Direction flag
JNG	Jump on Not Greater than (signed)	STI	Set Interrupt flag
JNGE	Jump on Not Greater than or Equal (signed)	STOS	Store String
JNL	Jump on Not Less than (signed)	SUB	Subtract
JNLE	Jump on Not Less than or Equal (signed)	TEST	Test
JNO	Jump on No Overflow	WAIT	Wait
JNP	Jump on No Parity	XCHG	Exchange
JNS	Jump on No Sign	XLAT	Translate
JNZ	Jump on Not Zero	XOR	Logical XOR (Exclusive OR)
JO	Jump on Overflow		

The first line sets the page length to 66 lines and the page width to 132 columns. This isn't absolutely necessary, but it is helpful in formatting listings output by the assembler. The PAGE directive is particularly useful if you ask the assembler to produce a LST file (which we will in just a moment). Without it, the LST file may contain a lot of unwanted 80-column line wraps.

The next three lines begin with semicolons, indicating that they are comment lines. In assembly language, anything that follows a semicolon is ignored by the assembler. Scanning ahead shows that several lines in the body of the program contain semicolons, too, followed by comments explaining what's going on in that section of code. This is a common technique for documenting assembly language programs.

The next four lines (ignoring the blank line following the comment lines at the top of the listing) form a standard header that we'll use for most of the utilities in this book. The line

```
code    segment
```

defines the segment where our code will be stored (recall from Chapter 1 that a *segment* is a 64k region of memory pointed to by one of the CPU's segment registers). The segment is given the name "code." The name could have been anything, but "code" is an obvious name to give a segment that holds program code. The next line,

```
assume  cs:code,ds:code
```

is there for the benefit of the assembler. It tells MASM that both the CS and DS segment registers will point to (contain the segment address of) the segment named "code" unless otherwise notified. Recall that addresses on the PC are expressed in *segment:offset* form, and that a segment register is involved in every memory access. It follows that if MASM is to generate the code to access a location in memory, it must know what regions of memory the segment registers point to each time an access is made. It has no way of determining this except by your ASSUME statements. ASSUME CS:CODE,DS:CODE tells MASM that it can resolve references to any variable in the "code" segment with either the CS or DS register. If DS is later loaded with another value, the programmer should include a second ASSUME statement to let MASM know that DS has changed. ASSUME remains in effect until a subsequent ASSUME statement supersedes it.

The line

```
org     100h
```

tells the assembler that the address of this location in the program is 100h bytes from the beginning of the code segment. All subsequent addresses will be relative to this one. For example, the offset address of the JMP that appears next will be exactly 100h bytes from the base of the segment. This is a requirement for COM files, because DOS always begins executing a COM-formatted program at offset 100h.

All the lines thus far have merely been for the benefit of the assembler. The next one is the first actual assembly language instruction. JMP is the command to jump from one point in the program to another, similar to a GOTO in BASIC. In this case, execution goes to the line labeled MAIN. The SHORT that appears between JMP and MAIN isn't necessary, but including it makes the program one byte shorter and thus saves one byte of memory. This little trick only works if there are fewer than 128 bytes of code or data between where the JMP instruction appears and the location that is the target of the jump.

Assembly language programs, like programs written in high-level languages, usually contain data as well as code. The line

```
msg     db      13,10,"Hello, world",13,10,"$"
```

defines the string that will be output to the screen. MSG is the name of the memory location where the string starts. DB is short for *define byte,* an assembler directive that defines one or more bytes of data. After DB comes the string itself. Everything between quotation marks is interpreted literally; MASM converts the characters to ASCII codes and stores them in consecutive memory locations starting at the offset that corresponds to MSG. The numbers at the beginning and end of the string that aren't enclosed in quotation marks—13 and 10—are the ASCII codes for a carriage-return/line-feed pair, which sends the cursor to the next line. The dollar sign delimits the string. HELLO1 uses DOS function 09H to output the string, and function 09H requires that the final character in the string be a dollar sign. This way, when the string is being output, DOS knows where to stop. The dollar sign is not output with the rest of the string.

Next comes the heart of the program. The line

```
main    proc    near
```

defines a near procedure named MAIN. This is the point that the JMP instruction vectored program execution to at start-up. In assembly language, subroutines are called *procedures.* A NEAR procedure is one that is only called by other procedures within the same segment. The opposite of a NEAR procedure is a FAR one, which may be called from any segment. All the procedures in our programs (with one or two exceptions) will be of the NEAR variety, for the simple reason that COM files may, in contrast to EXE files, only contain one segment.

The line

```
main    endp
```

near the end of the listing marks the end of the procedure. For every line that contains a PROC directive, there must be a line with an ENDP (END Procedure) directive to balance it. PROC and ENDP are like BEGIN and END in Pascal or { and } in C; they mark the beginning and end of every procedure that's defined in the program.

The three lines

```
mov    ah,09h
mov    dx,offset msg
int    21h
```

invoke DOS function 09H (one of the many functions contained in the DOS kernel that programs may call on) to display the string "Hello, world." MOV AH,09H moves the function code (09H) into the AH register. MOV DX,OFF-SET MSG moves the offset address of the string MSG into the DX register. In this example, MSG begins at offset 0102H, so the assembler substitutes the value 0102H for OFFSET MSG. MASM resolves address references this way to prevent you from having to know the exact location of every data object in your programs. The instruction INT 21H triggers a software interrupt and invokes the DOS function. Executing a software interrupt is analogous to calling a subroutine. The code that is executed lies inside the DOS kernel. Almost all DOS functions are invoked with interrupt 21H.

The final two instructions,

```
mov    ax,4C00h
int    21h
```

invoke DOS function 4CH, which terminates the program and returns to DOS. Because of the 00H placed in register AL prior to the call, the program returns an *exit code* of 0. If HELLO1 is run from a batch file, this exit code can be tested with an IF ERRORLEVEL statement. In this case, the value has no significance. But at times the capability to pass an exit code back to DOS can be very useful, particularly if an error occurred as the program executed.

The final two lines in the listing,

```
code    ends
        end    begin
```

tell the assembler that the code segment ends here and that the program ends here also. In assembly language, ENDS is short for END Segment. The BEGIN that follows the END directive tells DOS where to begin executing the program when it is run—in this case, at the line labeled BEGIN at the beginning of the program. For COM programs, the point where execution begins must be the line that follows the ORG 100H directive.

Once the source code is saved to disk, the following sequence of commands assembles it, links it, and converts the binary EXE file into a COM file:

```
MASM HELLO1;
LINK HELLO1;
EXE2BIN HELLO1 HELLO1.COM
```

The command MASM HELLO1; creates an object file (a file that contains the machine code generated from the assembly language instructions in the source code file) with the extension .OBJ. LINK HELLO1; converts the OBJ file into an EXE file. And EXE2BIN HELLO1 HELLO1.COM converts the program to its final form, a COM file that can be loaded and run by DOS. If you wish, you may delete the OBJ and EXE files that are left over.

Veteran assembly language programmers often roll these commands into the following batch file:

```
@ECHO OFF
MASM %1;
IF ERRORLEVEL 1 GOTO END
LINK %1;
EXE2BIN %1 %1.COM
DEL %1.EXE
DEL %1.OBJ
:END
```

If you name the batch file ASM.BAT, then the command

```
ASM HELLO1
```

will create HELLO1.COM for you. ASM.BAT automatically deletes the left-over OBJ and EXE files. It also checks the exit code returned by MASM and skips the LINK and EXE2BIN commands if the assembly process failed.

If you execute the command

```
MASM HELLO1,,HELLO1;
```

MASM will generate a special file called a list file named HELLO1.LST that shows exactly what the assembler did with the source code. This file is shown in Listing 9.2. On the right three-fourths of each page you see the source code as you entered it. On the left, you see the binary machine code generated from the source code and the offset addresses of all the lines in the program. Notice that the first instruction in the program, JMP, appears at offset 0100 because the instruction ORG 100H set the current address to 0100 immediately before it. The EB 11 that follows the line offset is the machine code MASM generated for the JMP instruction. The instruction is two bytes long, so the next line lies at offset 0102. You can trace through the entire program this way, examining the binary code generated from your instructions and incrementing offsets by the length of the last instruction to arrive at the next offset. The last instruction, INT 21H, lies at offset 011D and translates to CD 21. The "R" following the machine code at offset 0115 indicates that MASM had to resolve an address reference. In this case, it had to resolve the reference "OFFSET MSG" to 0102.

LISTING 9.2

```
                              page    66,132


                       ;**********************************************************
                       ; HELLO1 writes "Hello, world" to the screen.
                       ;
                       ; Copyright (c) 1991 Jeff Prosise
                       ;**********************************************************

0000                   code    segment
                               assume  cs:code,ds:code
0100                           org     100h
0100  EB 11            begin:  jmp     short main

0102  0D 0A 48 65 6C 6C  msg   db      13,10,"Hello, world",13,10,"$"
      6F 2C 20 77 6F 72
      6C 64 0D 0A 24


                       ;**********************************************************
                       ; Procedure MAIN
                       ;**********************************************************

0113                   main    proc    near
0113  B4 09                    mov     ah,09h          ;Display message with DOS
0115  BA 0102 R                mov     dx,offset msg   ;  function 09H
0118  CD 21                    int     21h

011A  B8 4C00          exit:   mov     ax,4C00h        ;Call function 4CH to exit
011D  CD 21                    int     21h
011F                   main    endp

011F                   code    ends
                               end     begin
```

The final page of the LST file (shown in Listing 9.3) contains summary information regarding segments and symbols. For example, it lists every line that has a label associated with it (BEGIN, MSG, MAIN, and so on) and the offset address that corresponds to it. It also reveals that HELLO1 contained 30 lines of source code and that the assembly process was completed with no errors or warnings. For large assembly language programs, this list can grow quite long.

LISTING 9.3

```
Segments and Groups:

                Name                   Length   Align   Combine Class

CODE . . . . . . . . . . . .           011F     PARA    NONE

Symbols:

                Name                   Type     Value   Attr

BEGIN . . . . . . . . . . .            L NEAR   0100    CODE
```

```
EXIT . . . . . . . . . . . . . .       L NEAR   011A     CODE

MAIN . . . . . . . . . . . . . .       N PROC   0113     CODE     Length = 000C
MSG  . . . . . . . . . . . . . .       L BYTE   0102     CODE

@CPU . . . . . . . . . . . . . .       TEXT   0101h
@FILENAME  . . . . . . . . . . .       TEXT   hello1
@VERSION . . . . . . . . . . . .       TEXT   510


      30 Source  Lines
      30 Total   Lines
      10 Symbols

   47362 Bytes symbol space free

       0 Warning Errors
       0 Severe  Errors
```

COM Versus EXE: What's the Difference?

DOS supports two different binary executable file types: COM and EXE. The three-letter extension on the file name reveals which category a program falls into. COM programs are the simpler of the two, and therefore the simpler to write. All the programs in this book are of the COM variety. An inspection of the directory of your hard disk where DOS files are stored reveals that many of the programs that make up DOS itself are also COM files.

COM files are simpler because they're subject to more restrictions than EXE files are. For example, COM files are limited to one segment for code and data. EXE files, on the other hand, may contain multiple code and data segments, and separate segments for the stack. COM files also cannot be more than 64k long. All the program's code and data must fit into that space. EXE files, by contrast, may be virtually any length. Also, COM files cannot contain symbolic debugging information required by source-level debuggers such as CodeView. They must, therefore, be debugged without benefit of many of the sophisticated tools available for debugging EXE files.

However, it turns out that these restrictions aren't that severe for the majority of utilities. A 64k utility is a large utility, indeed, when it's written in assembly language. Most of the ones we'll develop here will be 2k or less in length. Also, a program that is only 2k long is much easier to debug than one written in a high-level language, which is likely to be several thousand or tens of thousands of bytes long.

One characteristic that distinguishes COM files from EXE files is that COM-formatted programs are stored on disk exactly as they appear in memory. DOS loads COM files very quickly because it doesn't have to do anything besides read them in from disk and jump to the instruction at offset 100H. By contrast, EXE-formatted programs contain header information that DOS uses to, among other things, resolve references to segments within the program at runtime (EXE files can be loaded anywhere in memory, so some memory references can only be resolved after the program is loaded). The process required to load an EXE file into memory is time-consuming, so it is advantageous to use the COM format for short utilities. An added benefit is that COM programs, which do not contain headers, consume less disk space than EXE files.

One peculiarity of COM files that results from this lack of header information is that COM-formatted programs, when loaded into memory, are allocated all available memory by DOS. If there is 500k of RAM free in the system when a 2k COM file is loaded, all 500k is allocated to the program. If the program calls DOS functions that require memory of their own or wants to cooperate with TSR processes that require memory, it must use DOS function 4AH (which will be described later in this chapter) to shrink its memory allocation. By contrast, EXE files are only allocated the amount of memory they need when they're started because the EXE header contains information about memory requirements.

All MASM programs are of the EXE variety when they are first linked. That's why, when you're creating a COM program, you have to run EXE2BIN after you run LINK. EXE2BIN converts the EXE file produced by LINK into a COM file. Before it does so, it verifies that certain criteria for COM files are met.

One final note: When you run EXE2BIN to convert an EXE file to the COM format, it will probably display an error message saying that the program contains no stack segment. Ignore the warning. COM files use the code segment for the stack, so there's no need to declare a stack segment separately. In fact, if you try, you'll violate the rule that COM files may only contain a single segment, and EXE2BIN will inform you that the "File cannot be converted," and quit without creating the COM file.

The Program Segment Prefix

Before it loads any program into memory, DOS creates a 256-byte structure called a *program segment prefix,* or PSP. The program itself is loaded immediately after the PSP. That's why the first instruction in a COM file is always at offset 100H: The first 256 (100H) bytes are set aside for the program segment prefix.

The PSP contains a wealth of information that is useful to programs and to DOS itself. Figure 9.1 shows the fields that the PSP is divided into. The field at 00H contains an INT 20H instruction, which programs may use to terminate if they wish. (This method of terminating a program has since been replaced by DOS function 4CH, which we'll examine later in this chapter.) The word at offset 02H contains the segment address of the top of the program's allocated memory block, enabling programs to determine how much memory they were allocated initially. Offset 05H holds the CPU instructions for an intersegment CALL to DOS's function request handler. This field was originally included for compatibility with CP/M and is no longer used. The double words at offsets 0AH, 0EH, and 12H hold the contents of the interrupt 22H, 23H, and 24H vectors as they appeared when the program was started. DOS uses the information in these fields to restore the interrupt vectors when the program terminates.

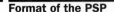

FIGURE 9.1

Format of the PSP

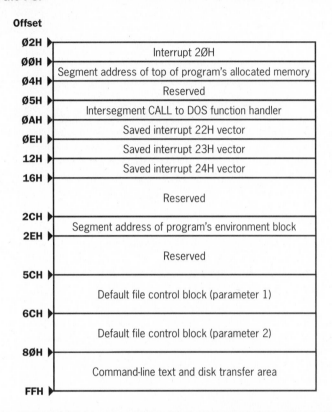

The word at offset 2CH within the PSP contains the segment address of the environment block DOS allocated to the program. The environment block contains a local copy of the environment strings present in the master environment block DOS maintains in low memory. If a program needs information from these strings, it can go to the PSP to obtain the segment address of its own environment block, and then read the strings from there.

When you start a program by typing its name on the command line, DOS parses the first two parameters it finds following the file name and, if they qualify as file names themselves, sets up two default file control blocks at offsets 5CH and 6CH in the PSP containing them. Now that file control blocks are rarely used, having been superseded by DOS's easier to use and more versatile handle-based file functions, these PSP fields aren't tremendously important any more. However, the field at offset 80H is, because in it, DOS places everything that appeared on the command line following the program name. Many of the utilities in this book will go to the PSP and parse the command line for switches, so you'll see plenty of examples of how to read and interpret the parameters entered there.

The area from 80H to FFH within the PSP also serves as the default disk transfer area, used by DOS to return information from several DOS functions. (The disk transfer area is discussed later in this chapter and again in Chapter 11.) If you use any of these functions, you should read the command line first because anything that DOS placed there when the program was started will be destroyed. As an alternative, you may relocate the transfer area by placing a call to function 1AH. Then, the information in this part of the PSP will be preserved.

The DOS Programming Environment

If it fell to the programmer to manage all the resources in the system and to interface directly with all the devices that can be attached to a PC (for example, screens, keyboards, and printers), life as an assembly language programmer would be very difficult. Fortunately, assembly language programming is made much easier by the myriad functions provided by DOS and by the BIOS. You saw an example of one such function in action in the program listing for HELLO1, where DOS function 09H was called upon to output a string of text to the screen. A knowledge and understanding of such resources is vital to writing assembly language programs, because without them it would take mounds of code to write even the most primitive utility.

Through interrupt 21H, DOS provides a set of approximately 100 different functions programmers may call on to perform basic tasks such as reading or writing a disk file, sending data to a printer, or allocating a block of memory. In general, these functions can be grouped into seven different categories:

- Functions for performing input and output to the character devices (screens, keyboards, printers, and serial ports)

- Functions for performing input and output to files

- Functions for managing files, directories, and disks

- Functions for managing system resources such as memory

- Functions for getting and setting the time and date

- Functions for controlling network resources

- Miscellaneous functions

A function is invoked by placing a function code in AH (a number that uniquely identifies the function) and executing an INT 21H instruction. Many of the functions take other parameters in other registers as well, and some of them are many functions in one. When this is the case, a subfunction code passed in AL indicates what service is being invoked. With a few exceptions, the contents of registers that do not return values are preserved across function calls.

Many of the interrupt 21H functions (particularly those added in DOS 2.0 or later) indicate success or failure by the state of the carry flag on return. (The *carry flag* is one of the bit-sized flags in the CPU's FLAGS register.) Carry clear means the request was met, while carry set indicates it was not. This convention makes it easy for assembly language programmers to test for errors with a single JC (Jump on Carry) or JNC (Jump on No Carry) instruction after each function call and to branch when errors occur. When an error does occur, AX is loaded with an error code that offers more precise information about the nature of the error. In DOS 3.0 and later, additional information can be obtained by calling function 59H (Get Extended Error Information) before another function call is placed.

So that programs and operating systems may run somewhat independently of the hardware they're executed on, the IBM PC contains a module called the Basic Input/Output System (BIOS) that offers a variety of low-level I/O services that software may call on to interact with the hardware components of the system. The BIOS is contained in ROM and is part of every IBM PC-compatible microcomputer. DOS relies on it extensively for device I/O, as do many of the popular application programs and utilities that run in the DOS environment. For example, to output a character to the screen, DOS's CON device driver calls on one of the BIOS video services, interrupt 10H, function 0AH, which inserts the character's ASCII code into the address in the video buffer that corresponds to the current position of the cursor. Applications, too, may use this service, or any of the others that the BIOS provides to the system.

BIOS services, like DOS services, are accessed through software interrupts. As with DOS interrupts, function codes are placed in AH prior to the call, and registers that do not return values are preserved. The three interrupts that will be the most useful to us are interrupts 10H, 16H, and 17H, which provide interfaces to the screen, keyboard, and printer, respectively. Other devices the BIOS interfaces with include disk drives, serial ports, and the system timer.

At this point, it may be helpful to refer back to Figure 1.6 in Chapter 1, which illustrates the relationship between application programs, DOS, the BIOS, and the devices in the system. The BIOS sits just above the hardware but just below DOS and programs that run on top of DOS. In most cases, a program can choose among three methods for performing I/O with a device: through DOS, through the BIOS, or by going directly to the device itself, bypassing DOS and the BIOS. Which method is best depends on the device being accessed and the circumstances requiring the access.

The remainder of this chapter is devoted to a discussion of such basic programming tasks as reading the keyboard and writing characters to the screen, and to the DOS and BIOS functions that are instrumental in accomplishing them. It's more a quick tour than an exhaustive overview, but don't worry; you'll see plenty of examples of these and other functions at work in the chapters that follow.

Reading the Keyboard

There are two widely accepted methods for reading the keyboard under DOS. The first is to use the BIOS keyboard services that are available through interrupt 16H. The second is to use DOS services that read from standard input, whose name is synonymous with the keyboard unless input has been redirected on the command line. The primary distinction between the two sets of services is that BIOS keyboard services are more versatile than their counterparts in the DOS kernel. Also, BIOS keyboard input routines are less susceptible to external events such as presses of Ctrl-C and input redirection. In most cases, the proper choice of keyboard input services depends on the type of utility that is being written. For command-line utilities such as NUKE (which we'll develop in Chapter 11), DOS input functions should be used. For programs such as Lotus 1-2-3 and WordPerfect, which take over the screen, and especially for TSRs, it makes much more sense to use BIOS keyboard functions.

BIOS Keyboard Functions The BIOS keyboard I/O functions accessed through interrupt 16H provide an easy and device-independent means for programs to read the keyboard. With them, you can extract codes from the keyboard buffer (the area where key codes processed by the BIOS are stored while they wait to be read), find out if there are any key codes awaiting processing in the keyboard buffer, and read the status of non-character keys such as Shift, Ctrl, and Alt. On 84- and 101-key keyboards, you may also use the BIOS keyboard functions to set the keyboard's typematic and delay rates. The interrupt 16H functions supported by the BIOS are listed in Table 9.2.

TABLE 9.2

BIOS Keyboard Functions

Function	Name/Description
00H	Read keyboard
01H	Get keyboard buffer status
02H	Get shift status
03H	Set typematic and delay rates
05H	Write character to keyboard buffer
10H	Read keyboard (extended)
11H	Get keyboard buffer status (extended)
12H	Get shift status (extended)

Not all keyboard functions are available on all machines. Whether a given function is supported depends upon the type of keyboard you have and how recent the BIOS is. At the very least, however, you can count on the presence of functions 00H, 01H, and 02H. These were included in the very first IBM BIOS and today form the foundation of the BIOS keyboard services.

Function 00H reads a key code from the keyboard buffer. Key codes on the IBM PC are two bytes long. For most keys, one byte is the scan code that was transmitted from the keyboard, and the other is the ASCII code that corresponds to the key. If there is a key code available at the time the call is made, the function returns immediately with the ASCII code in AL and the scan code in AH. If the keyboard buffer is empty, function 00H doesn't return until a key is pressed.

For reference, Table 9.3 lists the ASCII codes returned by function 00H and the keys that correspond to them. Note that certain codes can be produced two ways (for example, pressing Enter or Ctrl-M will produce an ASCII 13). Also note that no single key produces any of the ASCII codes numbered 28 through 31. However, you may enter these and any other ASCII codes directly by holding down the Alt key and typing the ASCII code number on the PC's numeric keypad.

TABLE 9.3

ASCII Key Codes

Code Key(s)	Code	Key	Code	Key	Code	Key
1 Ctrl-A	33	!	65	A	97	a
2 Ctrl-B	34	"	66	B	98	b
3 Ctrl-C	35	#	67	C	99	c
4 Ctrl-D	36	$	68	D	100	d
5 Ctrl-E	37	%	69	E	101	e
6 Ctrl-F	38	&	70	F	102	f
7 Ctrl-G	39	'	71	G	103	g
8 Ctrl-H (Backspace)	40	(	72	H	104	h
9 Ctrl-I (Tab)	41	)	73	I	105	i
10 Ctrl-J	42	*	74	J	106	j
11 Ctrl-K	43	+	75	K	107	k
12 Ctrl-L	44	,	76	L	108	l
13 Ctrl-M (Enter)	45	–	77	M	109	m
14 Ctrl-N	46	.	78	N	110	n
15 Ctrl-O	47	/	79	O	111	o
16 Ctrl-P	48	0	80	P	112	p
17 Ctrl-Q	49	1	81	Q	113	q
18 Ctrl-R	50	2	82	R	114	r
19 Ctrl-S	51	3	83	S	115	s
20 Ctrl-T	52	4	84	T	116	t
21 Ctrl-U	53	5	85	U	117	u
22 Ctrl-V	54	6	86	V	118	v
23 Ctrl-W	55	7	87	W	119	w
24 Ctrl-X	56	8	88	X	120	x
25 Ctrl-Y	57	9	89	Y	121	y
26 Ctrl-Z	58	:	90	Z	122	z
27 Esc	59	;	91	[	123	{
28 (None)	60	<	92	\	124	l
29 (None)	61	=	93	]	125	}
30 (None)	62	>	94	^	126	~
31 (None)	63	?	95	_		
32 Spacebar	64	@	96	`		

You may have noticed that Table 9.3 does not include codes for keys such as the function keys and the cursor movement keys. That's because these keys do not have corresponding ASCII codes. To uniquely identify them, the BIOS returns an *extended key code* in register AH. To indicate that AH contains an extended key code, it places a 0 in AL. To differentiate between ASCII key codes and extended key codes, most programs examine AL first and, if it contains 0, branch to a routine that processes the key based upon the extended key code found in AH. This logic is illustrated by the following code fragment:

```
mov   ah,00h
int   16h
cmp   al,0
je    extended_key_code
      .
      .
      .
```

```
(Process ASCII code in AL)
    .
    .
    .

extended_key_code:
    .
    .
    .

(Process extended key code in AH)
    .
    .
    .
```

The instruction MOV AH,00H places the function code 00H in the AH register, while INT 16H executes the function. CMP AL,0 compares the value returned in the AL register to 0. If the comparison is positive, the instruction JE EXTENDED_KEY_CODE jumps to the line labeled EXTENDED_KEY_-CODE, which begins the routine that handles extended key codes. If AL is not 0, execution falls through to the instruction immediately following the JE instruction, where begins the routine that processes conventional ASCII key codes.

Table 9.4 lists the extended key codes supported by function 00H. Extended key codes cover the function keys F1 through F10 (alone and in combination with Shift, Ctrl, and Alt), the cursor movement keys, various keys shifted with Ctrl or Alt, the Insert and Delete keys, and Shift-Tab (the key combination used for backward tabs).

Again, however, there are certain keys and key combinations conspicuously missing from Table 9.4 including function keys F11 and F12. The original IBM PC keyboard only had ten function keys, so the BIOS did not define key codes for F11 and F12. Nor did IBM see fit to add support for F11 and F12 to function 00H when it introduced the 101-key keyboard in 1987. What IBM did instead was define a new keyboard function, function 10H, which is identical to function 00H except that it supports an array of new extended key codes, including codes for function keys F11 and F12. These new codes are listed in Table 9.5. It is important to note that the codes listed there are *only* returned by function 10H. Pressing any of these keys or key combinations in response to a function 00H has the same effect as pressing no key at all. Thus, utilities that recognize F11 and F12 must use function 10H rather than function 00H to retrieve key codes.

Another important note regarding Table 9.5 is that extended codes 151 through 163 can only be produced using the dedicated keys that appear between the main part of the keyboard and the numeric keypad on 101-key keyboards. When you press a numeric key on the keypad with Alt held down, the BIOS assumes you're trying to enter a 3-digit ASCII character code.

TABLE 9.4

Extended Key Codes Returned by Function 00H

Code(s)	Key(s)
15	Shift-Tab
16-25	Alt-Q, W, E, R, T, Y, U, I, O, P
30-38	Alt-A, S, D, F, G, H, J, K, L
44-50	Alt-Z, X, C, V, B, N, M
59-68	F1, F2, F3, F4, F5, F6, F7, F8, F9, F10
71	Home
72	Up Arrow
73	PgUp
75	Left Arrow
77	Right Arrow
79	End
80	Down Arrow
81	PgDn
82	Ins
83	Del
84-93	Shift-F1, F2, F3, F4, F5, F6, F7, F8, F9, F10
94-103	Ctrl-F1, F2, F3, F4, F5, F6, F7, F8, F9, F10
104-113	Alt-F1, F2, F3, F4, F5, F6, F7, F8, F9, F10
114	Ctrl-PrtSc
115	Ctrl-Left Arrow
116	Ctrl-Right Arrow
117	Ctrl-End
118	Ctrl-PgDn
119	Ctrl-Home
120-129	Alt-0, 1, 2, 3, 4, 5, 6, 7, 8, 9
130	Alt- (Alt-Hyphen)
131	Alt-= (Alt-Equal)
132	Ctrl-PgUp

There's one other thing that's different about function 10H: It sometimes returns an E0H rather than 0 in AL to indicate that AH holds an extended key code. If you press one of the ten gray keys that lie just to the left of the numeric keypad on 101-key keyboards—Ins, Del, Home, End, PgUp, PgDn, and the arrow keys—AL is set to E0H. This enables programs that need to differentiate between, say, the dedicated PgDn key and the PgDn key on the numeric keypad to tell one from the other. It also means that the keyboard processing logic that we outlined a few paragraphs back must be modified to account for this possibility. Fortunately, the modification is only slight. A keyboard processing routine that employs function 10H might look like this:

```
mov   ah,00h
int   16h
cmp   al,0
je    extended_key_code
cmp   al,E0h
```

```
        je   extended_key_code
             .
             .
             .

        (Process ASCII code in AL)
             .
             .
             .

extended_key_code:
             .
             .
             .

        (Process extended key code in AH)
             .
             .
             .
```

TABLE 9.5

Extended Key Codes Returned by Function 10H

Code	Key(s)	Code	Key(s)
1	Alt-Esc	142	Ctrl-Keypad –
14	Alt-Backspace	143	Ctrl-Keypad 5
26	Alt-[	144	Ctrl-Keypad +
27	Alt-]	145	Ctrl-Down Arrow
28	Alt-Enter	146	Ctrl-Ins
39	Alt-;	147	Ctrl-Del
40	Alt-'	148	Ctrl-Tab
41	Alt-`	149	Ctrl-Keypad /
43	Alt-\	150	Ctrl-Keypad *
51	Alt-,	151	Alt-Home
52	Alt-.	152	Alt-Up Arrow
53	Alt-/	153	Alt-PgUp
55	Alt-Keypad *	155	Alt-Left Arrow
133	F11	157	Alt-Right Arrow
134	F12	159	Alt-End
135	Shift-F11	160	Alt-Down Arrow
136	Shift-F12	161	Alt-PgDn
137	Ctrl-F11	162	Alt-Ins
138	Ctrl-F12	163	Alt-Del
139	Alt-F11	164	Alt-Keypad /
140	Alt-F12	165	Alt-Tab
141	Ctrl-Up Arrow	166	Alt-Keypad Enter

Not every key on the keyboard produces a buffered key code. The states of the Ctrl, Alt, and Shift keys are determined by placing a call to function 02H, which returns in AL the shift status byte diagrammed in Figure 9.2. Each bit corresponds to a key or to a locked shift state; if the bit is set, the key is pressed or the corresponding shift state is active. Function 12H is identical to function 02H except that it returns the extended shift status byte (also diagrammed in Figure 9.2) in AH as well as the shift status byte in AL.

FIGURE 9.2

Shift status and extended shift status bytes

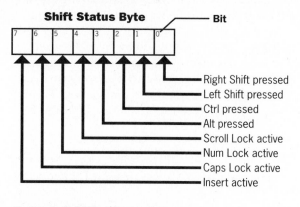

Shift Status Byte

- Right Shift pressed
- Left Shift pressed
- Ctrl pressed
- Alt pressed
- Scroll Lock active
- Num Lock active
- Caps Lock active
- Insert active

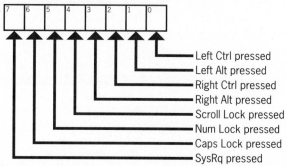

Extended Shift Status Byte

- Left Ctrl pressed
- Left Alt pressed
- Right Ctrl pressed
- Right Alt pressed
- Scroll Lock pressed
- Num Lock pressed
- Caps Lock pressed
- SysRq pressed

Other keys that do not produce a buffered key code include PrtSc and Pause. These receive special treatment from the BIOS. When PrtSc is pressed, the BIOS automatically invokes an internal routine that dumps the screen to LPT1. If Pause is pressed, the BIOS enters a do-nothing loop that continues until another key is pressed. Trapping presses of either key requires forsaking the BIOS and intercepting the scan codes emanating from the keyboard. Fortunately, such drastic measures are seldom needed, because most of the time it's perfectly acceptable to let these keys function as they were intended.

Functions 01H and 11H allow a program to check the keyboard buffer for buffered keystrokes. By verifying that there is an entry in the keyboard buffer before calling function 00H or 10H, a program can ensure that the BIOS doesn't wait until one becomes available. On return, the CPU's zero flag is set if the buffer is empty and clear if it's not. Also, if the buffer is not empty, AH and AL are set to the values they'll assume when function 00H or 10H is next called. The only difference between functions 01H and 11H is that function 01H ignores the additional extended key codes supported by function 11H.

The final two BIOS keyboard functions, 03H and 05H, are found in most (but not all) BIOS modules manufactured since 1986. Function 03H alters the keyboard's typematic and delay rates. To use it, set AH to 03H (the function code), AL to 05H, BL to a value from 0 to 31 representing the desired key repeat rate (the higher the input value, the slower the rate; 0 corresponds to 30 characters per second, 31 to 2 characters per second), and BH to a value between 0 and 3 representing the delay interval (0 corresponds to 0.25 second, 1 to 0.50 second, 2 to 0.75 second, and 1 to 1.0 second). This function is not supported on most systems with XT (83-key) keyboards. Function 05H permits programs to insert key codes into the keyboard buffer, simulating typing action. This is useful for keyboard macro programs and other utilities that must fool applications into thinking characters were typed.

DOS Keyboard Functions   DOS provides six input functions for reading characters and character strings from the keyboard. These functions are listed in Table 9.6. All are accessed through interrupt 21H, and all benefit (or suffer, depending upon your point of view) from the fact that if input is redirected on the command line, they will look to the indicated file or device for input rather than the keyboard. Thus, these DOS services must be used with a healthy dose of caution. They're entirely appropriate for command-line utilities, but not for programs that work in full-screen mode.

TABLE 9.6

DOS Keyboard Functions

Function	Name/Description
01H	Character input with echo
07H	Unfiltered character input without echo
08H	Filtered character input without echo
0AH	Buffered input
0BH	Get input status
0CH	Reset input buffer, then input

Function 01H is similar to interrupt 16H, function 10H. It waits for a key to be pressed and returns an ASCII code in AL. It also displays the character on the screen and advances the cursor one cell to the right in anticipation of further input. However, its handling of extended key codes is a little clumsy. If AL returns 0, function 01H must be called a second time to obtain the second half of the 2-byte extended key code. In general, DOS 5.0 responds to any key code that the BIOS's interrupt 16H, function 10H input function responds to. An important distinction is that the DOS input function never returns E0H in AL for the first half of an extended key code as the BIOS function does for certain keys; AL will always return 0 to signify the start of a 2-byte key code.

Functions 07H and 08H are similar to function 01H except that they don't echo input to the screen. Like function 01H, they return an ASCII code in AL. And like function 01H, they must be called twice to process extended key codes.

The only difference between them is that function 07H does not respond to Ctrl-C, while function 08H does.

Function 0AH allows a program to input an entire string of characters rather than just one character. You pass it the address of an input buffer in DS:DX that will receive string input. Input ends when the Enter key is pressed. Before this service is invoked, the caller must place a value indicating the maximum number of characters that will be accepted (including the carriage return at the end) in the first byte of the input buffer so the buffer won't be overrun. On return, DOS places the actual number of characters entered (excluding the terminating carriage return) in the second byte. The characters that were typed start in the third byte. Sound familiar? It should. Function 0AH is the one DOS calls to read your input on the command line.

Function 0BH is the DOS equivalent of interrupt 16H, functions 01H and 11H in the BIOS. AL returns 0 if the keyboard buffer is empty and 255 if it is not. Unlike its counterparts in the BIOS, however, function 0BH can be interrupted by pressing Ctrl-C.

Function 0CH clears the keyboard buffer and then invokes the DOS input function whose function code is passed in AL. For example, calling function 0CH with AL set to 0AH and DS:DX pointing to an input buffer clears the keyboard buffer, and then reads a character string. Unfortunately, this is the only function either DOS or the BIOS provides for clearing the keyboard buffer, and to use it, you must call another input function, too. Should you ever need to clear the keyboard buffer under program control, you can do so with the following code fragment:

```
push    ds
mov     ax,40h
mov     ds,ax
cli
mov     ax,[1Ah]
mov     [1Ch],ax
sti
pop     ds
```

This method works by setting equal to each other the two pointers the BIOS maintains indicating where the next key codes will be read from and written to. These pointers are stored in a region of memory called the BIOS Data Area, which will be discussed later in this chapter. The instructions PUSH DS and POP DS save and restore the value of the DS register (PUSH and POP place data on and remove data from the stack, respectively). CLI (for Clear Interrupt) temporarily disables interrupts so that the BIOS will not process any keystrokes while this routine is active (recall from Chapter 6 that the keyboard gets the CPU's attention when a key is pressed by generating a hardware interrupt), and STI reenables interrupts so that the keyboard will not permanently remain dysfunctional. The instructions

```
mov     ax,40h
mov     ds,ax
mov     ax,[1Ah]
mov     [1Ch],ax
```

actually do the work of clearing the buffer. The first two initialize segment register DS to point to the BIOS Data Area at segment 40H. The third one places the value at absolute address 0040:001AH into AX, and the fourth one places that value back in the memory location at 0040:001CH. (The brackets indicate that the number inside represents an offset address, not an actual value; the 0040 portion of the address is derived from the value of the DS register, which bracketed addresses are assumed to be relative to unless otherwise specified.) Why couldn't we have used the instruction

```
mov     [1Ch],[1Ah]
```

and eliminated one instruction? Because the 80x86 does not support the direct transfer of data from one memory location to another. Attempting to code a memory-to-memory instruction like this one would result in an error message from the assembler. Similarly, the AX register had to be used as an intermediary to place the value 40H in the DS register because the 80x86 does not permit immediate values (values hard-coded into the program, not stored in a memory location or a register) to be loaded into segment registers.

Displaying Characters on the Screen

DOS programmers can choose from three resources for writing characters to the screen: BIOS video functions, DOS video functions, and direct writes to the video buffer. The BIOS video functions are accessed through interrupt 10H, DOS video functions through interrupt 21H. As usual, which method is best depends on the type of program you're writing. DOS output functions should be used for command-line utilities where speed is not a concern and where the user should be able to redirect output to another file or device if desired. BIOS output functions should be used for programs that operate in full-screen mode and for any program that needs to establish a more intimate contact with the display environment than DOS functions allow. Direct video writes are a replacement for the video BIOS's character output functions and should be used when raw speed is of utmost importance.

BIOS Video Functions   One of the most useful elements of the BIOS is the set of services it provides for manipulating video. Through the BIOS, you can set the video mode, display characters on the screen, set the appearance of the cursor, scroll text up and down, clear the screen, and more. These functions are faster and more versatile than DOS's display I/O functions, which simply don't provide the degree of control over the video environment that the BIOS does. Furthermore, all the BIOS functions are available without loading additional drivers. For DOS to support the use of color in what you write to screen, ANSI.-SYS must be loaded. Table 9.7 lists the 20 video functions that are common to most machines and the function codes assigned to them. Note that functions 10H and higher are only available on systems equipped with EGA and VGA video adapters.

TABLE 9.7

BIOS Video Functions

Function	Name/Description
00H	Set video mode
01H	Set cursor type
02H	Set cursor position
03H	Read cursor position
04H	Read light pen position
05H	Select active video page
06H	Scroll active video page up
07H	Scroll active video page down
08H	Read character and attribute
09H	Write character and attribute
0AH	Write character only
0BH	Select color palette
0CH	Write dot (pixel)
0DH	Read dot (pixel)
0EH	Write teletype
0FH	Get video information
10H	Set palette registers
11H	Program character generator
12H	Alternate select
13H	Write string

The three functions that will be the most useful to us are functions 02H, 06H, and 09H. Function 02H moves the cursor to the row-and-column address passed in DH (row) and DL (column). Row and column numbers are zero-based, so the address of the character cell in the upper-left corner of the screen is 0,0. Function 02H also requires that a page number be passed in BH, because the BIOS maintains separate cursor addresses for up to eight different video pages. If you're not sure what the active video page is, you can get that information by calling function 0FH, which returns the number of the active (displayed) video page in BH, the number of columns displayed in AH, and the current video mode in AL.

Function 06H allows you to block out a rectangular region on the screen and then either clear it or scroll the text in it upward. Function 07H is identical except that it scrolls text down rather than up. You saw an example of function 06H at work in Chapter 6, where we examined the code in COMMAND.COM that clears the screen when you type CLS. Both functions take as parameters the row and column address of the upper-left corner of the region to be acted upon (CH and CL), the row-and-column address of the lower-right corner (DH and DL), the attribute to be used on lines that are left blank after scrolling is completed (BH), and the number of lines to be scrolled (AL). If AL is set to 0, the entire region is blanked out using the attribute in BH. Both functions default to the active video page.

Function 09H writes a character and its attribute to the screen. You can illustrate its use by starting DEBUG and typing the following script. Don't type the comments to the right of the code; they're there for instructional purposes only. Also, be sure to include the blank line after RET to signal DEBUG to exit program entry mode.

```
A 0100
MOV  AH,0F     ;Get active video page in BH
INT  10
MOV  AH,2      ;Set cursor to row 0, column 0
MOV  DX,0
INT  10
MOV  AH,09     ;Display heart (ASCII 03H)
MOV  AL,03
MOV  BL,4F
MOV  CX,1
INT  10
RET

G
```

When you type G to run the program you just entered, you should see a small heart appear in the upper-left corner of the screen. Three BIOS video routines were used here: one to get the number of the active video page (function 0FH), one to position the cursor (function 02H), and one to display the character (function 09H). Afterward, the cursor will remain in the upper-left corner. That's no problem. Just type **Q** and press Enter, and you'll be back at the DOS command prompt.

Function 09H accepts three parameters other than the function code in AH: the ASCII code of the character to display (AL), the attribute to be used (BL), and the number of the characters you want to output (CX). Setting CX to 1 produces just one character. However, setting it to a higher value replicates the character as many times as desired, and does so very quickly. Function 0AH also accepts the same parameters, except that it does not take an attribute value in BL. Instead, it uses the existing attribute for the character cell where the cursor currently resides.

The preceding example should give you a good idea of how commercial DOS application programs craft beautiful, colored screens. It's a matter of painting every cell on the screen with a character and an attribute. In assembly language, the easiest way to do this is through the BIOS.

If you simply want to write text to the screen without regard to color or location, function 0EH offers a convenient means for doing it. All it requires is an ASCII code in AL. Function 0EH displays the character at the current cursor position (using the color that's already there) and advances the cursor one cell to the right. At the end of a line, the cursor wraps around to the beginning of the next one. When the cursor reaches the bottom of the screen, the BIOS automatically scrolls everything up a line so text won't run off the bottom. With function 0EH, the three lines

```
mov     ah,0Eh
mov     al,"a"
int     10h
```

are all it takes to display an "A" on the screen. For sheer simplicity, it can't be beat.

DOS Video Functions   That's not to say that the BIOS is the only way to do it, however. DOS offers two screen-output functions of its own, which come with the usual caveat related to redirection: If the user redirects output on the command line, DOS will send the text to the indicated file or device rather than to the screen. Function 02H outputs a character. You pass it the ASCII character code in DL, and it displays the character at the current cursor position. Any similarity you may have perceived between it and function 0EH in the video BIOS is not coincidental; DOS function 02H calls BIOS function 0EH to output the character.

The other DOS screen-output function is function 09H. We'll use it a lot, particularly to output messages from command-line-type utilities. All it requires is the address of an ASCII string in DS:DX. The string must be delimited by a dollar sign. The following code snippet prints "Syntax error" using function 09H:

```
msg     db      "Syntax error$"

        mov     ah,09h
        mov     dx,offset msg
        int     21h
```

That's all there is to it. One assumption made in this example is that DS is already pointing to the segment where the string is stored. If this is not the case, then DS must be loaded accordingly before the call to function 09H is made.

You may have noticed that DOS functions do not allow you to control output color or to set the cursor position. And therein lie two of the greatest deficiencies of DOS functions: To set color or to set cursor position, you have to load the ANSI.SYS extended console driver and pass cryptic color and cursor-positioning escape codes to it through the standard output device. It's slow, it's clumsy, and it offers no advantage over using BIOS interrupt 10H video functions, which provide much more control over the video environment. That's why DOS's character output functions are only useful for programs that make limited use of the screen.

Direct Video Writes

There's a third way to write to the screen that involves neither DOS nor the BIOS. Instead, it involves writing data (ASCII character codes and character attributes) directly to the video buffer. Recall from Chapter 6 that the IBM PC uses memory-mapped video, and that, in text mode, each character cell on the screen has two bytes that correspond to it that hold the ASCII code and attribute for the character displayed there. The attribute byte determines what color the character is displayed in, whether it's blinking or non-blinking, bold or normal, and so on. The region of memory where these characters and attributes are held is called the *video buffer*. Inserting data into the buffer is the fastest way to get information on the screen, but also the most fraught with peril. There are many complicating factors: the fact that there may be multiple pages in the video buffer, that the video buffer is located at different addresses on different machines, that certain adapters such as the IBM CGA don't react very well to direct video writes unless some special precautions are taken, and more. However, a lot of popular programs interact with the display this way for reasons that can be summed up with three simple words: speed, speed, and speed.

Writing to the screen through the BIOS incurs a lot of overhead. For example, the BIOS has to find out what video mode the display adapter is currently in, how many columns of text are displayed, and other, similar, information. Then when it finally does insert a character code or attribute into the display buffer, it may time the writes to the buffer so that they only occur when the raster beam that illuminates the display is disabled as it travels from one side of the screen to the other to start a new horizontal stroke. Sometimes there are good reasons for doing that, but it imposes a severe penalty on performance.

When it comes to overhead, DOS is even worse. First it does some checking of its own (for example, to see if Ctrl-C has been pressed or output has been redirected), and then it travels a very roundabout way to a point where it finally calls a BIOS video output routine! The result: It crawls. DOS may take a hundred or more times longer than direct video writes to fill a screen with characters.

You'll see an example of direct writes to the video buffer when we develop the utility called FINDTEXT in Chapter 11 and again when we develop PC-DIAL in Chapter 13. There are several factors you must take into account when you write data directly to the video buffer. For example, you can no longer locate simply by a row-and-column address the position on the screen where a write will occur. Instead, you must determine what offset in the video buffer corresponds to the desired row and column. Just to give you an idea of how much additional responsibility this incurs, the list that follows describes the four-step process involved in translating a row-and-column address into a physical memory address:

1. Determine where the start of the video buffer lies. On monochrome systems, it lies at segment B000H in text mode; on color systems, it starts at B800H. Call this address *BufferAddress*.

2. Determine the offset from the beginning of the video buffer where the active *page* lies. Call it *PageAddress*. Add this offset to *BufferAddress* to determine the address of the byte that corresponds to row 0, column 0.

3. Determine how many columns of text are currently displayed. Call this value *NumberOfColumns*.

4. To determine the address in the video buffer that corresponds to a given row and column, use the following formula:

ByteAddress = *BufferAddress* + *PageAddress*

+ (2 * ((*RowNumber* * *NumberOfColumns*)

+ *ColumnNumber*))

The resulting address is the address of the byte in memory that determines what character is displayed at row *RowNumber,* column *ColumnNumber.* Add 1 to it and you have the address of the byte that determines the character's attribute.

As you can see, it *is* more complicated to do it this way. But in the right situations, the extra trouble is well worth it.

If you want to see just how fast direct writes are (and if you have a color system), try this experiment. Start DEBUG and type the following script:

```
A 0100
CLD
MOV        AX,B800
MOV        ES,AX
MOV        DI,0
MOV        AX,4F03
MOV        CX,7D0
REP        STOSW
RET

G
```

When you press Enter after the G, your screen should be covered instantaneously with small white hearts displayed against a red background. The instruction REP STOSW transferred 2,000 instances of the ASCII code for the heart symbol and the attribute for white on red into the video buffer. Doing the same thing with the video BIOS is fast, but not nearly as fast as what you just saw demonstrated.

Transmitting Characters to the Printer

To merely say that DOS is weak when it comes to communicating with printers is being charitable. The sole output function DOS provides for printers—interrupt 21H, function 05H—offers no means for communicating with printer ports other than LPT1 nor for polling the status of the port before transmitting characters to it. That's why most application programs use functions in the BIOS to drive printers attached to the system's parallel ports. BIOS printer I/O functions are accessed through interrupt 17H. The three that are common to all PCs are listed in Table 9.8.

TABLE 9.8

BIOS Printer Functions

Function	Name/Description
00H	Print character
01H	Initialize parallel port
02H	Get parallel port status

Function 00H outputs a character to the printer. The ASCII character code is passed in AL, and the value in DX (0, 1, or 2) indicates what port the output will go to—LPT1, LPT2, or LPT3. On return, AH indicates the success or failure of the operation. If bit 3 is set, the call failed. Conversely, if bit 3 is clear, then the character was successfully transmitted. If the printer is unable to accept data when the function call is made, the BIOS will retry the operation several times before giving up. It will only return after a short time-out (which may vary from a fraction of a second to several seconds).

The simplicity of this function belies the complex two-way exchange of information that takes place between the BIOS and the parallel port in the background. After sending the character to the port, the BIOS is responsible for enabling and disabling the printer's strobe line, which indicates to the printer's internal decoding circuits that the data lines hold a valid value. Then, after toggling the strobe line, the BIOS latches a status value from the port to return in AH. Without the BIOS to intercede for them, programs would have to perform these functions themselves. Needless to say, it would be much more difficult to write a utility that used the printer if this was the case.

To avoid long delays caused by printers that are not ready to accept data, you can use function 02H to obtain the status of the parallel port before attempting to transmit a character. It returns a status value in AH using the bit assignments shown in Figure 9.3. On most systems, AH returns with bit 3 set if the printer is powered off or is off line or if no printer is attached to the port. If bit 3 and bit 5 (which is set when the printer is out of paper) are clear, then it's safe to go. Do not wait for a zero return; bit 7 will be set anytime the printer is capable of accepting characters.

Interrupt 17H, function 01H initializes the parallel port by toggling the INIT line on the parallel port interface (one of the lines that connects the parallel port to the printer) off and on, and by asserting the SLCT IN line that "selects" the printer. In most instances, it's not necessary to initialize a parallel port on an IBM PC before using it. Also note that with most printers this function does not, as is often supposed, reset the printer to its power-up condition. To do that, you must transmit a reset command to the printer using function 00H. For a Laser-Jet, that command is an escape character (1BH) followed by the ASCII code for the letter E (45H).

FIGURE 9.3

Printer status bits

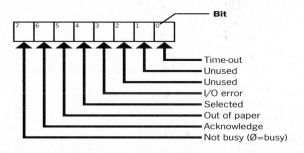

Performing File Input and Output

DOS provides the functions listed in Table 9.9 to enable programs to perform input and output to disk files. In general, these functions take their input in one of two forms: either as an ASCIIZ file specification (a file name and, optionally, a path name and drive name to go with it), or as a file handle returned from one of DOS's file open or file create functions. A *file handle* is an operating system object that insulates application programs from many of the nuances of file I/O. Once DOS assigns a file handle to a file, it may be used in all future references to that file until the file (and the handle) is formally closed by calling function 3EH.

TABLE 9.9

File I/O Functions

Function	Name/Description	Input
3CH	Create file	ASCIIZ
3DH	Open file	ASCIIZ
3EH	Close file	Handle
3FH	Read file	Handle
40H	Write file	Handle
42H	Move file pointer	Handle
5AH	Create temporary file	ASCIIZ
5BH	Create file	ASCIIZ

Functions 3CH and 5BH permit a program to create a file. The caller passes the address of an ASCIIZ file specifier in DS:DX and a series of bits defining the attributes the file is to be assigned in CX. On return, the carry flag reveals whether the function call succeeded. If carry is clear, AX holds the file handle. The only difference between functions 3CH and 5BH is what happens if a file of the specified name already exists. Function 3CH truncates the file to zero length, destroying its contents. Function 5BH will fail if a file of the same name exists, preventing existing file data from being inadvertently destroyed.

Existing files can be opened for reading and writing with function 3DH. The caller passes a code in AL that indicates what type of access is requested (read, write, or read/write) and what file sharing mode is desired, and the address of an ASCIIZ file specifier in DS:DX. On return, AX contains a file handle if carry is clear.

Once a file handle is obtained, the file can be read and written with functions 3FH and 40H. Both functions accept a file handle in BX, the number of bytes to be read or written in CX, and the address of a buffer in DS:DX. Function 3FH (Read File) copies the file data to this buffer, while function 40H (Write File) copies data from it. On return, the carry flag indicates success or failure, and AX contains the number of bytes read or written if the call succeeded. If function 40H writes fewer bytes than requested, then the disk is probably full.

For every file handle that an application opens, DOS maintains a record of where the next byte in the corresponding file will be read from or written to in the form of an imaginary object called a *file pointer*, which is actually nothing more than a byte offset from the beginning of the file. Read and write operations advance the file pointer the number of bytes indicated in the CX register when function 3FH or 40H is called. Alternatively, programs may manipulate the file pointer directly by calling function 42H, which accepts a file handle in BX, a 32-bit offset in CX:DX, and a value in AL that specifies how the 32-bit offset should be interpreted. You'll see an example of this in Chapter 11 when we develop the code for FINDTEXT.

Function 42H also provides a convenient means for programs to determine the size of a file. The procedure involves opening the file, and then moving the file pointer to the end of the file by calling function 42H with CX and DX set to 0, and AL set to 2. On return, DX:AX holds a value that is equal to the length of the file in bytes.

When access to an open file is no longer required, the file should be closed with a call to function 3EH, which accepts a file handle in BX. The function will only fail if the handle is invalid or does not correspond to an open file. When a program terminates, DOS automatically closes any files that the program has open.

Function 5AH is useful when a program needs to create a temporary file and doesn't want to conjure up a unique name for it that's guaranteed not to conflict with existing programs. With function 5AH, DOS picks the file's name. The caller passes an attribute code for the new file in CX and the address of an ASCIIZ path name in DS:DX. On return, AX contains a file handle and, just in case it's needed, the address of the file's ASCIIZ file specification in DS:DX.

This set of file I/O functions is collectively known as DOS's *handle-based file functions*. There is another set of file I/O functions that uses file control blocks (FCBs) to access files, and that offers similar, often overlapping services. Function 0FH, for instance, also opens a file, but rather than accepting an ASCIIZ file specifier, it expects the address of a partially filled-in FCB to be passed to it in DS:DX. This set of functions is known as DOS's *FCB-based file functions*. FCBs date back to DOS 1.0 and are no longer the preferred means for dealing with files of any type. With few exceptions, new programs use handle-based functions almost exclusively because the functions themselves are more versatile and because it is easier to open, read, write, and close files with handles than it is with FCBs. We'll exclusively use handle-based functions here when we deal with files.

Manipulating Files

To complement the file I/O functions outlined in the preceding section, DOS also offers a set of six functions for manipulating files. A list appears in Table 9.10. All the functions but one—function 57H—accept an ASCIIZ file specifier as input. Function 57H accepts a handle to a previously opened file, so the file must be opened with function 3DH first.

TABLE 9.10

File Management Functions

Function	Name/Description	Input
41H	Delete file	ASCIIZ
43H	Get or set file attributes	ASCIIZ
4EH	Search for first match	ASCIIZ
4FH	Search for next match	ASCIIZ
56H	Rename file or subdirectory	ASCIIZ
57H	Get or set file date and time	Handle

Function 41H deletes the file specified by the string in DS:DX. Function 56H renames a file given the address of a file specifier in DS:DX and a pointer to the new name in ES:DI. It will also, if asked, rename a subdirectory. There are two similar FCB-based functions for deleting and renaming files which offer one advantage their counterparts do not: the FCB versions will accept wildcard characters in file names, while functions 41H and 56H will not.

Function 43H permits a program to get or set a file's attributes. Four attributes are recognized: hidden, system, read-only, and archive. The caller passes a subfunction code in AL (00H to get file attributes, 01H to set them) and the address of an ASCIIZ string in DS:DX. Subfunction 01H also takes an attribute value in CX. This value is a bit-wise combination of the following codes:

Archive	20H
System	04H
Hidden	02H
Read-only	01H

Thus, passing a 22H in CX sets the file's archive and hidden attributes, but leaves the system and read-only attributes turned off. Subfunction 00H returns the specified file's attributes in CX using the same data format.

Function 57H is similar, except that it gets or sets the date and time a file is stamped with. The subfunction code passed in AL indicates whether the date and time are being set or retrieved; 00H invokes a get operation, while 01H indicates a set. Both subfunctions require a file handle to be passed in BX. On entry into subfunction 01H, the time and date are passed in registers CX and DX in the following format:

- Bits 11 through 15 of CX indicate the hour (0 through 23).

- Bits 5 through 10 indicate minutes (0 through 59).

- Bits 0 through 4 indicate seconds (0 through 59).

■ Bits 9 through 15 of DX indicate the year (since 1980).

■ Bits 5 through 8 indicate the month (1 through 12).

■ Bits 0 through 4 indicate the day (0 through 31).

Subfunction 00H returns the date and time in the same registers and in the same format.

Functions 4EH and 4FH are two of the most powerful file control functions DOS offers. Programs use them to search for a file of a specified name. Because wildcards may be included in the file specification, these functions can be used to build an entire list of files matching the indicated pattern. Function 4EH locates the first file that matches the search criteria, while function 4FH locates the second, third, and so on. When either function returns, the current disk transfer area is filled out as shown in Table 9.11. Carry set indicates that no match was made. You'll see several examples of how these functions are used in Chapter 11.

TABLE 9.11

Format of the Information Returned by DOS Functions 4EH and 4FH

Offset	Size	Description
0	21 Bytes	Reserved for use by DOS
21	Byte	Attribute of file
22	Word	Time stamp
24	Word	Date stamp
26	Word	File size (least significant word)
28	Word	File size (most significant word)
30	13 Bytes	ASCIIZ file name and extension

Manipulating Directories

DOS also provides four directory control functions that give programs the ability to create and delete subdirectories, change directories, and determine what the current directory is. These functions are listed in Table 9.12. Functions 39H, 3AH, and 3BH accept in DS:DX the *segment:offset* address of an ASCIIZ path name that identifies the directory. Function 47H accepts a drive code in DL and the address of a buffer in DS:SI that will hold an ASCIIZ string identifying the current directory on return.

TABLE 9.12

Directory Management Functions

Function	Name/Description
39H	Create subdirectory
3AH	Remove subdirectory
3BH	Set current directory
47H	Get current directory

A program can create a subdirectory by calling function 39H with DS:DX pointing to an ASCIIZ path name string designating the name of (and, optionally, the path to) the subdirectory to be created. On return, the state of the carry flag indicates whether the call succeeded. Carry clear means the operation was carried out; carry set means an error occurred and that AX holds an error code revealing the exact nature of the error. The code fragment

```
dirname    db    "\MSC",0


           mov   ah,39h
           mov   dx,offset dirname
           int   21h
           jc    error
```

creates the subdirectory \MSC on the current drive and checks for an error return from DOS. In general, the function will fail if the path name was invalid or the subdirectory already exists. It will also fail if it's asked to create a subdirectory in the root directory and the root directory is full.

Function 3AH is similar to function 39H except that it deletes rather than creates a subdirectory. The calling parameters are the same: a function code in AH and a pointer to an ASCIIZ path name string in DS:DX. On return, the carry flag again indicates the success or failure of the operation. The request will fail if the path name string is invalid, if the subdirectory does not exist, if it is not empty (it contains other subdirectories or files), or if the subdirectory is also the current directory.

Function 3BH sets the current directory. This is equivalent to using the CD (or CHDIR) command on the command line. Once again, DS:DX points to an ASCIIZ path name string, and on exit the carry flag indicates whether the function succeeded. Function 3BH will fail if the path name is invalid or the indicated directory does not exist.

Function 47H accepts a drive code in DL (0=default, 1=A, 2=B, and so on) and the address of a 64-byte buffer in DS:SI. On return, the buffer contains an ASCIIZ string that identifies the current directory. The path to it is specified all the way from the root directory, but the name placed in the buffer does not contain a leading backslash.

Managing Memory Resources

One of the challenges that confronts any operating system is managing the memory resources available to it as effectively and efficiently as possible. The system DOS uses to manage memory is a simple one. Memory is divided into variable-length blocks that are chained together as a linked list. Each block is preceded by a 16-byte header called a *memory control block* (MCB) that specifies how large it is, what program it is allocated to (which program "owns" it), and whether there are more blocks succeeding it in memory.

When a program requests a block of memory, DOS searches the chain for an unused block whose size is equal to or larger than the one requested. If the one it finds is larger, DOS carves from it a block of the requested size and creates a new block from the amount left over. The new block may then be allocated to other programs. When the owner of the block releases it, DOS returns it to the free memory pool. If there is free memory directly above or below the block that is being released, DOS consolidates it into one contiguous block so that it may be used to satisfy further requests for memory.

Until DOS 5.0, this memory management scheme only applied to conventional memory, which limited DOS to 640k. However, DOS 5.0, if requested to, will also create a chain of memory control blocks linking the upper memory blocks created by EMM386.EXE and make the resultant memory available to application programs. As a result, it is possible to have as much as 130k or so of extra RAM available when DOS 5.0 is run on 386 and 486 systems.

DOS provides four memory management functions that programs may use to request and release blocks of memory, and to control how that memory is allocated. Function 48H requests memory; function 49H releases it; function 4AH resizes a block that was previously allocated; and function 58H controls the strategy DOS uses in the search for free memory and also determines whether upper memory blocks may be used to satisfy requests for memory. These functions are summarized in Table 9.13.

TABLE 9.13

Memory Management Functions

Function	Name/Description
48H	Allocate memory
49H	Release memory
4AH	Resize allocated memory block
58H	Get or set memory allocation strategy/get or set upper memory block link status

Function 48H places a request for a block of memory. The only parameter it expects other than the function code in AH is the size of the requested block in paragraphs (16-byte units) in BX. On return, carry clear indicates the request was granted, while carry set indicates there was not enough free memory to satisfy the request. If the call was successful, AX returns holding the segment address of the block. If it was not, BX holds the size of the largest available block in paragraphs. As a result, the program knows immediately how much it *can* request and can judge whether that's enough memory for it to proceed.

To determine the size of the largest available memory block at any time, all a program has to do is call function 48H with BX set equal to FFFFH. Since there can't possibly be a megabyte of memory free (not in current versions of DOS, anyway), the call will fail and the size of the largest available block will be returned in BX.

Function 49H releases a block of memory that was previously obtained with function 48H. The block is returned to the free memory pool so that subsequent programs may use it. The caller passes the segment address of the block in ES. The address must correspond exactly to the segment address returned in AX by function 48H, else the call will fail. The state of the carry flag on return indicates whether the operation succeeded or failed.

Function 4AH permits programs to shrink or expand memory blocks that they have been allocated. On entry, BX holds the requested size in paragraphs of the resized block, and ES holds the block's segment address. Again, this segment address must be the one that was returned earlier by function 48H. On return, carry clear means the block was successfully resized; carry set indicates it was not. In general, this function will rarely fail if the size of the block is being reduced. However, it will succeed in expanding a block of memory only if there is enough free memory directly above it so that the combined length of the two blocks is enough to satisfy the request.

The most common use for function 4AH is for COM programs to shrink the amount of memory they're allocated at start-up. By default, DOS gives them all available memory because COM files, unlike EXE files, do not contain headers that specify how much memory they require. However, certain DOS functions will fail unless there is some minimum amount of memory available. Thus, the first action many COM programs take is to shrink the amount of memory they were initially allocated down to some reasonable amount (usually 64k) with function 4AH. The code to do so looks like this:

```
MOV     AH,4AH
MOV     BX,1000H
INT     21H
JC      ERROR
```

These lines call function 4AH with BX set to 1000H, requesting that the memory block whose segment address is passed in ES be shrunk from its present size down to 64k (1000H paragraphs). The statement JC ERROR traps errors when they occur and jumps to the line labeled ERROR.

The final memory management function, function 58H, is actually four functions in one. Subfunctions 00H and 01H let programs set or get the current memory allocation strategy, which governs how DOS conducts a search for free memory to satisfy a function 48H request. DOS 5.0 supports three allocation strategies: first fit, last fit, and best fit. In *first fit,* DOS searches the chain of memory blocks from the bottom of memory up and uses the first one it finds that is sufficient to meet the request. *Last fit* does the same, but searches from the top of memory down. *Best fit* has DOS examine all the memory blocks available in the system and use the one that most closely matches the requested block size. In addition, if there are UMBs that are controlled by DOS, programs may specify whether the search begins in conventional memory or in upper memory. This is called *low first* or *high first* strategy.

Subfunction 00H returns a code in AX that reveals what the current allocation strategy is. The lowest three bits indicate the general strategy: 0 means first fit, 1 means best fit, and 2 means last fit. The highest bit indicates what region of memory is searched first: 0 means low, 1 means high. The default in DOS 5.0 is first fit, low first. Subfunction 01H allows a program to *set* the allocation strategy. The strategy code, whose format is identical to that of the code returned in AX by subfunction 00H, is passed in BX.

Subfunction 02H lets a program determine whether UMBs created by EMM386.EXE will be included when DOS searches for memory to fulfill an allocation request. If AL returns 0, UMBs are excluded from the search; if AL returns set to 1, then UMBs are included. DOS calls this the *link status*. If the UMBs are free to be allocated just like the rest of memory, then they're said to be *linked*; if they're separate from the rest of memory and are not available to application programs, then they're not linked. Subfunction 03H allows a program to set the link status. Passing a 0 to this subfunction in BX unlinks UMBs, while passing a 1 links them. Subfunctions 02H and 03H are only valid if DOS was started with the statement DOS=UMB in CONFIG.SYS and if UMBs do exist. Carry set on return from either subfunction means the call failed.

Getting and Setting the Time and Date

DOS offers four functions for getting and setting the system's current record of the time and date. These functions are listed in Table 9.14. In DOS 3.3 and later versions, including version 5.0, setting the date or time with these functions also sets the date or time in the system's battery-operated clock-calendar so that the new settings will be retained even after power is shut off. In prior versions, changing the permanent record of the time and date required direct communication with the clock-calendar hardware through the I/O ports assigned to it.

TABLE 9.14

Time and Date Functions

Function	Name/Description
2AH	Get date
2BH	Set date
2CH	Get time
2DH	Set time

Functions 2AH and 2CH take no input parameters other than the function codes passed as usual in AH. Function 2AH returns the year in CX (1980 through 2099), the month in DH (1 through 12), and the day in DL (1 through 31). It also returns a value in AL that indicates the current day of the week, with 0 corresponding to Sunday, 1 to Monday, and so on. Function 2CH returns hours in CH (0 through 23), minutes in CL (0 through 59), seconds in DH (0 through 59), and hundredths of a second in DL (0 through 99).

Although it reports time in increments of hundredths of a second, function 2CH cannot be used to time the passage of events on the PC with a great deal of accuracy because most PC system clocks do not possess hundredths-of-a-second resolution. In addition, the overhead incurred in making the call is often sufficient to skew the results. Thus, the value returned in DL by function 2CH is usually ignored.

The values passed to functions 2BH and 2DH exactly mirror the values returned by functions 2AH and 2CH and the registers in which they are returned. To set the system date, a program invokes function 2BH with the year in CX, the month in DH, and the day in DL. On return, a 0 in AL indicates that the call was carried out successfully. To set the system time, a program calls function 2DH with hours in CH, minutes in CL, seconds in DH, and hundredths of a second in DL. Again, a value of 0 in AL on return indicates successful completion. A non-zero return from either of these functions usually indicates that one or more of the values passed to it was out of range.

Terminating Programs

There are several ways to terminate a program under DOS. The preferred method is to call DOS function 4CH, which closes any file handles the program left open, returns the memory allocated to it to the free memory pool, and returns control to the program that launched it (usually COMMAND.COM). Function 4CH also allows the terminating program to return an exit code from 0 to 255 that the parent program (the program that started it) can retrieve with a call to function 4DH or that batch files may test with an IF ERRORLEVEL statement. The return code is placed in AL prior to the call to function 4CH.

The following code sequence ends a program and returns an ERROR-LEVEL value of 1:

```
MOV    AX,4C01H
INT    21H
```

The instruction MOV AX,4C01H places a 4CH (the function code) in AH and 01H (the return code) in AL. Upon return, the line

```
IF ERRORLEVEL 1 GOTO END
```

in a batch file would transfer execution to the batch statement labeled END. Function 4CH has the added advantage in that it works equally well for COM and EXE program types.

In Chapter 13, you'll be introduced to terminate-and-stay-resident programs, which remain in memory even after they're officially terminated. TSRs have to terminate in a special way so that DOS will not return the memory they occupy to the pool of available memory. Since the memory a TSR occupies stays reserved, the program remains in memory by virtue of the fact that programs loaded after it are placed elsewhere in memory. There are two operating system services that allow a program to terminate but remain resident in memory: function 31H and interrupt 27H. The former is the preferred method, and the one that we'll use for all the TSRs we develop in this book. We'll discuss it fully in Chapter 13.

Miscellaneous DOS Functions

There are several other DOS functions that may be useful to programmers but that don't fall neatly into any one category. Table 9.15 contains a partial list of these functions. Some of the functions listed here were never documented in the official technical references published by Microsoft and IBM. Functions that are undocumented are indicated with an asterisk following the function number.

TABLE 9.15

Miscellaneous DOS Functions

Function	Name/Description
1AH	Set disk transfer area address
2FH	Get disk transfer area address
25H	Set interrupt vector
35H	Get interrupt vector
30H	Get DOS version number
33H	Get or set break check status
34H*	Get InDOS flag address
4BH	Execute program (EXEC)
4DH	Get return code
50H*	Set active program segment prefix address
51H*	Get active program segment prefix address
59H	Get extended error information
5DH*	Get critical error flag address/set extended error information
60H*	Return fully qualified file name
62H	Get active program segment prefix address
69H*	Get or set disk serial number and volume label

* Indicates the function is undocumented in official texts

When any of DOS's FCB-based functions are used to read, write, or search a disk directory for files, or when functions 4EH and 4FH are used to search for files, DOS uses a 128-byte buffer called the *disk transfer area* (DTA) to hold the file data that is read or written. Programs can obtain the address of the current DTA with a call to function 2FH or change its address with function 1AH. Function 1AH reads the address of the new DTA from DS:DX. Function 2FH returns the address of the DTA in ES:BX. TSRs that use any of the functions that use the DTA should save the current address, change it to something else, and then restore the original DTA address before relinquishing control. This action ensures that other programs that use the DTA will not be disturbed.

Functions 25H and 35H provide mechanisms for programs to alter and inspect interrupt vectors. The PC supports 256 different interrupts, numbered 0 to 255, and the interrupt vector for each one is stored in a table of interrupt vectors at the bottom of memory. All the TSRs we'll develop later on in this book will use these functions to hook interrupts and, when applicable, save the current interrupt vector before changing it. Function 25H, which sets an interrupt vector, takes an interrupt number in AL and the address of a new interrupt service routine in DS:DX. Its counterpart, function 35H, accepts an interrupt number in AL and returns the address of the associated interrupt service routine in ES:BX.

Function 30H returns a code in AX that reveals what version of DOS is running. AL returns holding the major version number (for example, the 5 in DOS 5.0), AH the minor version number (the 0 in DOS 5.0). This seems straightforward, and it is. However, bear in mind that the SETVER command, added in DOS 5.0, may lead DOS to report a false version number to selected programs.

Function 33H permits programs to get or set the state of a flag that determines how often DOS pauses and looks to see if Ctrl-C or Ctrl-Break has been pressed. Rather than enter into a lengthy discussion of exactly what break-checking entails, let it suffice to say that enabling or disabling break-checking is equivalent to typing BREAK ON or BREAK OFF on the command line or entering the same statements in CONFIG.SYS. You'll see function 33H in action in Chapter 11.

At once one of the most powerful and one of the most complex interrupt 21H functions, function 4BH, also called EXEC, loads and executes a program. It may also be used to load programs or overlays without executing them. DOS uses it; so do DOS shells and most debuggers. We won't use it directly in any of the utilities in this book, but we will intercept calls to EXEC in Chapter 13 to create a log of all the programs that are run on your PC.

Function 4DH allows a program that spawned a child process with DOS's EXEC function to retrieve the 1-byte return code returned via function 4CH. On return, AL holds the return code.

Function 60H is among the most useful of the undocumented functions. Given a file name, it returns a fully qualified version of that file name—one that includes a drive letter and a complete path to the file. Using fully qualified file names is particularly important to TSRs that perform file I/O, because the current directory is likely to be changed by the user between each invocation of the TSR. A side benefit of using this function is that it sees through drive and directory aliases set up by SUBST, ASSIGN, JOIN, and network redirectors. On entry, DS:SI points to the ASCIIZ file name to be converted and ES:DI points to a 128-byte buffer where the fully qualified file name will be placed. On return, carry clear indicates that the buffer contains a valid and fully qualified file name.

Function 69H, which was added in DOS 4.0, is an interesting one. With it, you can obtain a disk's serial number and volume label, or you can set the serial number and volume label. On entry, AL holds the subfunction number (0 to get the information, 1 to set it), BL contains a drive code (0=default, 1=A, 2=B, and so on), and DS:DX contains the address of a buffer that will receive the serial number and volume label when subfunction 00H is invoked, or set the serial number and volume label for subfunction 01H. The first word of the block contains 0. The next four bytes hold the encoded serial number. And the next 11 bytes hold the ASCII text of the volume label. Without this function, getting or setting this information (particularly the volume label) requires some rather complicated machinations.

Functions 34H, 50H, 51H, 59H, 5DH, and 62H are primarily of interest to TSRs. You'll see each of them used in Chapter 13. For now, it's enough to say that these functions permit programs to control the environment they're running in without disturbing other programs. Without these functions, it would be virtually impossible to write a well-behaved TSR, and we wouldn't have some of the famous application programs DOS users have become enamored of over the years, such as Borland's SideKick. It's unfortunate that many of these functions are only sparsely documented if they are documented at all, because this lack of information has led to some fairly well-regarded programs that in fact are downright dangerous to run on your system. Chapter 13 will clear up some of the mysteries surrounding these functions and provide real-life examples of how they're used.

Another Sample Program

At this point, we're ready to embellish the HELLO1 program presented earlier in the chapter with features that demonstrate the use of DOS and BIOS functions. HELLO2, shown in Listing 9.4, prompts the user to enter "S" or "P" to send output—the message "Hello, world"—to the screen or printer. As before, DOS function 09H is used to display the message on the screen. But if the user elects to send it to the printer instead, BIOS interrupt 17H, function 00H is used to send it to LPT1. CX is loaded with the length of the string, and the LOOP instruction loops the indicated number of times to output the text.

LISTING 9.4

```
;****************************************************************************
; HELLO2 demonstrates the use of DOS and BIOS functions in sending the
; message "Hello, world" to the screen or printer.
;****************************************************************************

code            segment
                assume  cs:code,ds:code
                org     100h
begin:          jmp     short main

msg1            db      13,10,"Screen or printer (S/P)? $"
msg2            db      13,10,"Hello, world",13,10,"$"


;****************************************************************************
; Procedure MAIN
;****************************************************************************

main            proc    near
                mov     ah,09h                  ;Prompt user for "S" or "P"
                mov     dx,offset msg1
                int     21h

getkey:         mov     ah,01h                  ;Wait for a key to be
                int     21h                     ;  pressed

                and     al,0DFh                 ;Capitalize the letter
                cmp     al,"S"                  ;  by clearing bit 5 of
                je      screen                  ;  the ASCII code returned
                cmp     al,"P"
                jne     main
```

```
                call    out2prn              ;Output to printer
                jmp     short exit

screen:         mov     ah,09h               ;Output to screen
                mov     dx,offset msg2
                int     21h

exit:           mov     ax,4C00h             ;Exit
                int     21h
main            endp

;*************************************************************************
; Procedure OUT2PRN outputs "Hello, world" to LPT1
;*************************************************************************

out2prn         proc    near
                cld                          ;Clear direction flag
                mov     cx,14                ;CX = Number of characters
                mov     dx,0                 ;DX = Printer number
                mov     si,offset msg2       ;DS:SI => String address

outloop:        lodsb                        ;Get a character
                mov     ah,00h               ;Print it
                int     17h
                loop    outloop              ;Loop until done
                ret                          ;Return to caller
out2prn         endp

code            ends
                end     begin
```

HELLO2 also illustrates how one procedure may call another in assembly language. The CALL instruction calls another procedure like a subroutine. When the CALLed procedure ends by executing a RET instruction, execution resumes at the instruction immediately following the CALL statement.

HELLO2 uses DOS function 01H to solicit input from the user. Function 01H waits for a key press and echoes it to the screen. If the character entered is neither "S" nor "P," HELLO2 repeats the prompt and tries again. Because a DOS function is used, you may automate the execution of this program by passing an "S" or "P" response to it from the command line using a redirection operator. For example, if you set up a text file called RESPONSE.TXT that contains the letter "P," the command

```
HELLO2  < RESPONSE.TXT
```

will run HELLO2 and send output to the printer. Similarly, if RESPONSE.TXT contains an "S" instead of a "P," the command

```
HELLO2  < RESPONSE.TXT
```

will send output to the screen. In neither case will the program wait for you to press a key in response to its prompt.

The instruction AND AL,0DFH is an old assembly language trick for reducing the number of comparisons. Performed on an ASCII code for a letter of the alphabet, this instruction capitalizes it. So, if "p" was entered, the AND instruction converts it to "P," but if "P" was entered, it remains the same. This way, the program only has to check for two return values: capital "S" and capital "P."

Summary

If you haven't programmed in assembly language before, this may seem like a lot of information to digest in one sitting. You'll see examples of nearly all the DOS and BIOS functions discussed here in the next four chapters. Unlike higher-level languages such as C and BASIC, assembler doesn't have built-in functions and commands for reading the keyboard, reading a line of text from a file stored on disk, and so on. Programming in assembly language invariably involves relying on functions in DOS and the BIOS and on other resources such as the information DOS stores in a program's PSP. Once you become familiar with these resources, you'll find that assembly language is no more difficult an environment to work in than many of the more contemporary languages in use today.

With introductions aside, it's time now to start writing utilities. We'll start by developing several that you can use to enhance batch file operations in Chapter 10. While we're at it, we'll also review batch file programming and present some of the batch file tricks and techniques that experienced DOS users rely on. Chapter 11 will introduce utilities aimed at making disk operations easier, and Chapter 12 will follow through with a sampling of utilities designed to provide better control over screens, keyboards, and printers. Finally, Chapter 13 will present a thorough overview of TSRs complete with lots of sample code demonstrating how they're written. It will also introduce the most prolific of all the utilities developed in this book—a pop-up phone list that you can use to store the names and phone numbers of friends or business associates and even to dial the phone if you own a Hayes or Hayes-compatible modem.

Building the Better Batch File

YOU COULD BE A PROGRAMMER AND NOT KNOW IT. IF YOU'VE EVER CREATED A batch file to automate a task such as backing up a hard disk or switching to another drive and subdirectory to launch an application program, then you are a programmer. Batch files are programs in every sense of the word. The only difference between batch files and the programs you run every day is that commands in batch files are DOS commands stored as ASCII text, while the COM and EXE files on your hard disk are binary files that contain compiled machine code.

Writing batch files is one of the surest and quickest ways to increase your productivity. They're guaranteed timesavers: Any task that you perform day in and day out and that requires you to type more than one or two DOS commands is a candidate for a batch file. Batch files eliminate careless typing mistakes and cut down on the amount of typing you have to do by allowing you to enter commands just once. They also give you access to facilities in DOS that you can't get to from the command line. For example, you can write a batch file that appends an additional directory name onto the end of the current PATH environment variable. But try the same thing from the command line, and all you'll succeed in doing is destroying PATH altogether.

This chapter will introduce you to the basics of batch file programming, discuss some tricks and techniques that make batch files easier to write and more convenient to use, and develop an assortment of utilities for enhancing your batch programs. Even veteran DOS users may be surprised at some of the things they can do with the tools introduced here.

Batch File Basics

A batch file is a collection of DOS commands stored in an ASCII text file. Anything you can do on the command line, you can do in a batch file, and in some cases you can do more. A simple batch file that switches to the \WINDOWS directory of your hard disk and starts Windows looks like this:

```
CD \WINDOWS
WIN
```

Like commands typed on the command line, lines inside a batch file are limited to 127 characters. DOS ignores anything beyond that. When you type a command at the DOS prompt, DOS searches the current directory and the directories named in the PATH environment variable for a file that has that name and has an extension of .COM, .EXE, or .BAT (provided the command is not an internal DOS command). If it does locate a BAT file with the specified name, DOS opens it and attempts to execute the commands inside. A batch file may be given any legal DOS file name as long as it has the extension .BAT. The name AUTOEXEC.BAT is reserved for a special purpose: DOS looks for an AUTOEXEC.BAT file in the root directory at start-up and, if it finds one, automatically executes it.

There are several ways to create batch files. The easiest way to create a batch file is with a text editor such as the DOS Editor or, if you prefer, EDLIN. You may also use a word processor if it has an ASCII save option so you can store the file as an ASCII text file rather than as a word processing file. You can also create a text file with the command

```
COPY CON filename
```

which copies everything you enter at the keyboard (the "CON" device) to a file named *filename*. When you're through entering text, press Ctrl-Z. DOS will save the file to disk for you.

Batch files may contain any combination of internal or external DOS commands, the names of other batch files or programs, or the eight special batch commands DOS provides. The batch commands supported in DOS 5.0 are

- REM, which precedes remarks in a batch file

- ECHO, which outputs text to the screen

- PAUSE, which pauses for a key press

- GOTO, which transfers control from one point in a batch program to another

- CALL, which executes another batch file

- IF, which conditionally executes a command after testing an exit code returned by a program, the value of a string, or for the existence of a file

- FOR, which repeats a command once for each member of a set

- SHIFT, which allows batch files to access more than ten command-line parameters

Before you begin to write batch files, it is essential that you understand these commands. As such, they are the subject of the next several sections.

The ECHO Command

The ECHO command serves two purposes. One, it lets you output messages to the screen from a batch file. For example, the command

```
ECHO Hello, world
```

displays "Hello, world." Two, it lets you turn command echoing on and off. When ECHO is enabled (which it is by default), DOS displays or *echoes* each command on the screen before executing it. This may be helpful if you're debugging a batch file, but most of the time it just clutters up the screen needlessly. You can disable command echoing by including the command

```
ECHO OFF
```

in your batch file. Should you need to reenable it, enter the command

```
ECHO ON
```

at the point where you want echoing to resume.

You can suppress echoing of any command in a batch file by preceding it with a @ symbol. This feature has been available in batch files since DOS 3.3. For example, the command

```
@CLS
```

clears the screen, but prevents CLS from being displayed if ECHO is on. If ECHO is off, the @ modifier has no effect because the command isn't echoed anyway. One useful application for @ is to suppress even ECHO OFF from being displayed. The first line in many batch files is

```
ECHO OFF
```

which turns command echoing off but is itself displayed because commands are echoed *before* they are executed. However, modifying the command to read

```
@ECHO OFF
```

prevents even this one command from being displayed.

You can also use ECHO to display a blank line, but only by using version-specific tricks. If you simply place the command

```
ECHO
```

all by itself on a line, DOS responds with the message "ECHO is off" or "ECHO is on." In most previous versions of DOS, you had to fool DOS into displaying a blank line by entering a space and an ASCII 255 character after ECHO. (ASCII 255 is a non-displaying character that you can enter on most keyboards by depressing the Alt key and typing 255 on the numeric keypad.) In DOS 5.0, there's an easier way: Simply place a period after ECHO. The lines

```
ECHO Hello, world
ECHO.
ECHO.
ECHO.
ECHO And a good evening to you
```

will display two messages separated by three blank lines.

Because ECHO sends its output to standard output, the text it transmits can be directed to a file or to an alternate device. One use for this capability is to create short text files from the command line (yes, batch commands can be executed from the command line) or to append text to existing files by redirecting output. For example, to create an AUTOEXEC.BAT file containing the commands PROMPT pg and PATH C:\DOS, you could type

```
ECHO PROMPT $p$g > AUTOEXEC.BAT
ECHO PATH C:\DOS;C:\UTIL >> AUTOEXEC.BAT
```

Be careful, though. The first of these two commands will wipe out an existing AUTOEXEC.BAT file. In addition, this technique may not be used to save lines that contain redirection or piping operators because the operator will be interpreted as a command to redirect or to pipe input or output on the command line itself.

The REM Command

REM allows you to place comments in batch files. It's just like the REM directive in CONFIG.SYS files: Anything that comes after it is ignored by DOS. One helpful use for it is to comment batch programs so you can understand what they're doing and why they're doing it months or even years down the road. It's not a bad idea to place a header at the top of every batch file documenting its purpose and its calling conventions. Such a header might look like this:

```
@ECHO OFF
REM *********************************************
REM
REM APATH.BAT appends a new directory name to the
REM existing PATH.  Its syntax is
REM
REM          APATH dirname;dirname...
REM
REM where "dirname" is a new directory name.  If
REM running APATH results in the message "Out of
REM environment space" from DOS, then the size of
REM the environment should be increased with a
```

```
REM SHELL directive in CONFIG.SYS.
REM
REM ********************************************
```

Because of the @ECHO OFF command that precedes the first REM statement, these remarks will not be echoed to the screen.

Another use for REM is to temporarily "comment out" statements so that they will be ignored while you DEBUG or fine-tune a batch file. When you want to add them back in, all you have to do is remove the REM from in front of them. That's substantially easier than deleting and later retyping each command, especially if the commands are long, complicated, and possibly difficult to duplicate.

The PAUSE Command

The PAUSE command suspends the execution of a batch file and displays the message "Press any key to continue...." When the user presses a key, execution resumes. Ironically, "any key" doesn't really mean any key; certain keys, including Ctrl, Alt, and Shift, will not restart execution.

If Ctrl-C or Ctrl-Break is pressed while a batch file executes, DOS stops and displays the message "Terminate batch job (Y/N)?", providing you the opportunity to abort the program. If you want to give the user the option of stopping a batch file at a certain point, insert a PAUSE command there, as shown in the following example:

```
ECHO Press Ctrl-C or Ctrl-Break to exit ...
PAUSE
```

When used this way, it's usually helpful to precede the PAUSE statement with an ECHO command as a reminder that Ctrl-C or Ctrl-Break will terminate the program.

If you want to have a little fun with your friends, substitute the following program for PAUSE in your (or their) batch files. The program, called NEW-PAUSE.COM, is created with this DEBUG script:

```
A 0100
JMP  0141
DB   "Press any key to continue . . .",0D,0A,"$"
DB   "Any key but that one . . .",0D,0A,"$"
MOV  AH,09
MOV  DX,0102
INT  21
CALL 015A
MOV  AH,09
MOV  DX,0124
```

```
INT   21
CALL  015A
MOV   AX,4C00
INT   21
MOV   AH,08
INT   21
CMP   AL,0
JNZ   0166
MOV   AH,08
INT   21
RET

N NEWPAUSE.COM
RCX
67
W
Q
```

When run, NEWPAUSE displays the same message PAUSE does, but in response to the first key pressed, it answers back with "Any key but that one...." Only after a second key press will it finally terminate itself and allow the batch program to continue.

Unfortunately, PAUSE is the only batch command DOS provides that permits any type of keyboard input. Later in this chapter, we'll develop a utility you can use to solicit keyboard input in batch files. This utility returns a code that batch files can test to determine what key was pressed.

Replaceable Parameters and the SHIFT Command

Many application programs accept command-line parameters that tell them what to do or what to do it on. (A *parameter* is any word, number, or text string that follows a command or program name.) For example, if you're a WordPerfect user, you might type

```
WP BUDGET.DOC
```

to start WordPerfect and have it load the document BUDGET.DOC. Here, BUDGET.DOC is an example of a command-line parameter.

Batch files, too, may be passed parameters from the command line. You can use this fact to build generic batch programs that accept input from the command line. DOS makes such parameters available to batch files in the form of variables numbered %0 through %9. To illustrate, create a short batch file called TEST.BAT that contains these lines:

```
@ECHO OFF
ECHO Program: %0
ECHO Parameter 1: %1
ECHO Parameter 2: %2
ECHO Parameter 3: %3
```

Save it, and then type

```
TEST ONE TWO THREE
```

TEST will display the following lines on the screen:

```
Program: TEST
Parameter 1: ONE
Parameter 2: TWO
Parameter 3: THREE
```

You can see what happened. The parameters ONE, TWO, and THREE on the command line became %1, %2, and %3 in the batch file. %0 assumed the name of the batch file itself. With this convention, batch files can access as many as nine different command-line parameters—ten command-line parameters if you include the program name.

These variables are called *replaceable parameters*. You can reference them as many times as you wish in a batch file. For example, a batch file that contains the lines

```
COPY %1 %2
DEL %1
```

will move a file to another drive or directory. If the batch file is named MOVE.BAT, then the command

```
MOVE FILE1.TXT C:\TEXT
```

will copy FILE1.TXT to C:\TEXT, and then delete it from the current directory.

On some occasions, nine replaceable batch file parameters will not be enough. To compensate, DOS offers the SHIFT command, which moves everything entered on the command line one position to the left, enabling a batch file to access as many parameters as you can cram into one command. After a SHIFT, what was %1 is now %0, what was %2 is now %1, and so on. More importantly, the tenth parameter following the batch file name on the command line, which was once inaccessible, is now %9. You can execute SHIFT as many times as needed to access all the parameters that were entered.

You can also use SHIFT to enable batch files to operate on an unknown number of parameters. For example, you can create a DEL command that accepts multiple entries with the batch file:

```
@ECHO OFF
:BEGIN
IF "%1"=="" GOTO END
DEL %1
SHIFT
GOTO BEGIN
:END
```

Call it MDEL.BAT and place it in a directory in the PATH. Then, the command

```
DEL FILE1.TXT FILE2.TXT FILE3.TXT
```

will delete all three files named on the command line. Each time a file is deleted, the SHIFT command makes the next parameter the new %1. When all the parameters have been processed, "%1" will be equal to "" and the batch file will end.

The GOTO Command

The GOTO command jumps from one location in a batch file to another. It is similar in function to the GOTO command in BASIC. The destination of a GOTO must be a line that consists of a colon followed by a name. The syntax is illustrated by the following batch file excerpt:

```
GOTO END
   .
   .
   .
:END
```

Note that the colon is omitted from the line label in the GOTO command itself. It is required, however, on the line that GOTO branches to. Otherwise, the line label will be interpreted as a command, and DOS will attempt to execute it.

You can use to your advantage the fact that DOS considers any line that begins with a colon to be a destination for GOTO. If you want to temporarily comment a command out of a batch file, enter a colon at the beginning of the line. This requires a couple fewer keystrokes than typing REM. Later, when you're ready to reinsert the line, just remove the colon. Also, many programmers use a line with nothing but a colon on it to separate sections of a batch program. This prevents blank lines, which DOS interprets as null commands, from slowing batch execution.

At the risk of getting slightly ahead of ourselves, it should be said that the GOTO command is frequently used in conjunction with the IF command to branch to another location in the program based on the results of a test. We'll see plenty of examples of this later when we examine the IF command in all its forms.

The CALL Command

When one batch file starts another, the first batch file is terminated and the second one started. When the second batch file has terminated, DOS does not go back and finish executing the first one. However, at times it is useful to call one batch file from another (like a subroutine) and have control return to the first one when the second one has finished. In versions of DOS before 3.3, the only way to accomplish this was with the command

```
COMMAND /C filename
```

where *filename* was the name of the second batch file. However, DOS 3.3 introduced the CALL command, which allows one batch file to call another and resume executing when the second one has run its course. The command

```
CALL BACKUP
```

calls the batch file BACKUP.BAT. If you wish, parameters may also be passed to the batch program being CALLed. For example, the command

```
CALL BACKUP C: D:
```

passes the parameters "C:" and "D:" to BACKUP as %1 and %2.

CALL statements may be nested, so there is no restriction that says a CALLed program can't CALL another. A batch file can even call itself. Be aware, however, that a batch file that calls itself must make some provision for exit (for example, a statement that says "Continue (Y/N)?") so that it won't get stuck in an endless loop.

The FOR Command

The FOR command allows a batch file to execute one command repeatedly for each member in a set of parameters you specify. Its syntax is

```
FOR %%variable IN (set) DO command
```

where *variable* is a letter of the alphabet (A to Z) and *set* is the set of parameters the command is to act upon. FOR executes *command* once for each member of the set. Each time through, the next set member is substituted for %%*variable*. For example, the command

```
FOR %%P IN (One Two Three Four Five) DO ECHO %%P
```

displays

```
One
Two
Three
Four
Five
```

on the screen. You can repeat a single command several times in a batch file by including dummy parameters in *set*. For example, the command

```
FOR %%P IN (1 2 3 4 5 6 7 8 9 10) DIR
```

executes DIR ten times.

One peculiarity of the FOR command is that when a member of *set* contains a wildcard, FOR automatically expands the wildcard and executes one time for each singular parameter that is generated. You can take advantage of this fact to coerce DOS commands that normally don't accept wildcard characters to accept them anyway. For example, the command

```
TYPE *.BAT
```

returns the error message "Invalid filename or file not found" from DOS. However, set up a batch file called TY.BAT with the line

```
FOR %%F IN (%1) DO TYPE %%F
```

and type

```
TY *.BAT
```

and DOS will TYPE all files with the extension .BAT to the screen.

One of the restrictions DOS places on the FOR command is that FOR loops can't be nested. However, there's a way around this should the need arise. You can execute a FOR command within a FOR command by invoking the second one from an auxiliary copy of COMMAND.COM. This is illustrated by the command

```
FOR %%A IN (1 2 3) DO COMMAND /C FOR %%B IN (1 2 3) ECHO command
```

which executes *command* nine times. It doesn't happen fast; this batch file loads, executes, and terminates COMMAND.COM nine times. But it gets the job done, and in clutch situations it's better than not having the capability at all.

The IF Command

The IF command is the sole mechanism DOS provides to batch programs for executing commands conditionally. It is used in three distinctly different ways. The first, which has the syntax

```
IF [NOT] ERRORLEVEL exitcode command
```

permits a program to test the exit code (ERRORLEVEL number) returned by a program and execute a command based on that value. Any COM or EXE program may return an exit code from 0 to 255 when it terminates through DOS function 4CH. The command

```
IF ERRORLEVEL 4 GOTO END
```

tests the exit code returned by the program just executed and jumps to the line labeled END if the code is 4 or higher. Note that *command* is executed if the exit code is *equal to or greater than* the value specified after the IF command, not just if they are equal. By contrast, the statement

```
IF NOT ERRORLEVEL 4 GOTO END
```

reverses the test and branches if the exit code is 3 or less.

Batch file programmers employ two methods for testing for a specific ERRORLEVEL value. The first one is the longer of the two. The lines

```
IF ERRORLEVEL 40  GOTO CONTINUE
IF ERRORLEVEL 39 GOTO ELSEWHERE
:CONTINUE
```

branch to the line labeled ELSEWHERE if and only if ERRORLEVEL is equal to 39. However, why do in three lines what you could do in one? The statement

```
IF ERRORLEVEL 39 IF NOT ERRORLEVEL 40 GOTO ELSEWHERE
```

also jumps to ELSEWHERE if and only if ERRORLEVEL is equal to 39. This technique takes advantage of the fact that DOS permits IF statements to be compounded. The only real restriction is that the 127-character limit on individual lines in a batch file must not be exceeded. It also illustrates that the *command* parameter following an IF statement does not have to be a GOTO. It can be any other DOS command, batch command, or program name.

Only a few DOS commands return ERRORLEVEL values. Your DOS manual tells which ones they are and what the various exit codes mean. The term ERRORLEVEL itself is something of a misnomer. It doesn't necessarily indicate that an error occurred. For example, the GETKEY utility we'll develop in this chapter uses ERRORLEVEL to return the ASCII code of the key that was pressed.

The second form of the IF command allows a batch program to compare two strings. Its syntax is

```
IF [NOT] string1==string2 command
```

where *string1* and *string2* are text strings and *command*, again, is the command to be executed if the test proves true. Strings can be either literal strings or batch variables. For example, the command

```
IF "%1"=="123" GOTO LOTUS
```

branches to the line labeled LOTUS if the first parameter entered on the command line following the name of the batch file was 123. It's a good idea to always enclose strings in quotes, even though it's not strictly a requirement. To test for a null parameter, use the command

```
IF "%1"=="" command
```

This works because if %1 is a null string, "%1" reduces to simply "".

String comparisons performed with the IF command are case sensitive. If the user starts the batch file START.BAT by typing

```
START Word
```

and START.BAT contains the line

```
IF "%1"=="WORD" GOTO WP
```

the comparison will fail because DOS will not equate "WORD" to "Word." One way to defeat this is to perform several comparisons based on all the combinations that the batch program is likely to see. For example, the lines

```
IF "%1"=="WORD" GOTO WP
IF "%1"=="Word" GOTO WP
IF "%1"=="word" GOTO WP
```

will catch most of the variations a user is likely to enter. You can roll this into one line with the FOR command, as in

```
FOR %%P IN (WORD Word word) DO IF "%1"=="%%P" GOTO WP
```

However, this technique, useful as it is, still won't catch odd combinations such as "WOrd" and "wORD." Later on, we'll examine a technique for performing string comparisons without regard to case that you can use to make batch programs less sensitive to input variations.

The third and final form of the IF command allows a decision to be made based on the existence or non-existence of a particular file. The syntax for this form is

```
IF [NOT] EXIST filename command
```

where *filename* is the name of the file the test is based on. The command

```
IF EXIST WIN.COM GOTO WINDOWS
```

branches to WINDOWS if and only if WIN.COM exists in the current directory. The NOT modifier causes *command* to be executed if the file does *not* exist. The command

```
IF NOT EXIST C:\WINDOWS\WIN.COM ECHO File not found!
```

displays the message "File not found!" if WIN.COM is not to be found in C:\WINDOWS.

Environment Variables

Almost every programming language provides some mechanism for storing and accessing information in the form of variables. The batch language uses *environment variables*—text strings stored in an area of RAM known as the DOS environment. Batch files can create, modify, or delete environment variables with DOS's SET command. For example, the command

```
SET GREETING=Hello, world
```

creates a variable called GREETING and assigns it the string "Hello, world." Afterward, the command

```
SET GREETING=Goodbye
```

redefines GREETING to "Goodbye" and

```
SET GREETING=
```

deletes it altogether. Similarly, you can create environment variables from the values passed to your batch program from the command line. The command

```
SET GREETING=%1
```

creates an environment variable out of the first parameter following the batch file name, while

```
SET GREETING=%1%2
```

joins the first and second parameters together and assigns the result to GREETING. Without additional software, this is about as involved as string handling in batch files gets. DOS allows you to join strings and add other text to them if you wish, but it does not provide any string functions to extract a substring from a string or perform similar operations that are standard fare in other languages.

One consequence of storing variables as environment variables is that every string you define takes up room in the environment. If your batch programs make extensive use of environment variables, you may run out of room to store them in. By default, DOS sets aside 160 bytes of RAM for environment variables, which is just enough to store the PATH, PROMPT, and COMSPEC strings on some systems. You can increase the size of the environment by adding a SHELL directive to CONFIG.SYS. One example of such a directive is

```
SHELL=C:\COMMAND.COM C:\ /E:512 /P
```

The key is the /E switch, which specifies the desired size for the environment in bytes. If 512 bytes isn't enough, increase this value to 1,024 or to whatever is necessary to store all the strings your batch files will create. Also remember to delete environment variables when they're no longer needed; doing so will free up room for other ones to be defined. Accordingly, it's wise to keep environment variable names short.

Batch programs can reference environment variables by sandwiching them between percent signs. For example, the command

```
ECHO %PATH%
```

displays the contents of the PATH string. If PATH had been defined as C:\DOS;C:\UTIL;C:\WP, then the above command would display

```
C:\DOS;C:\UTIL;C:\WP
```

on the screen. It is important to note that this only works from inside a batch file. On the command line, entries such as %PATH% are interpreted literally.

You can use this means of accessing environment variables to your advantage. For example, you could create a batch file to append additional directory names onto the current PATH using the line

```
PATH=%PATH%;%1
```

The semicolon is included because directory names in PATH lists must be separated by semicolons. If the batch file were named APATH.BAT, then typing

```
APATH C:\MISC
```

would add C:\MISC to the list of directories in the PATH. You can use percent signs on the left side of the equal sign, too. Try to predict what the following lines will do:

```
SET VARNAME=GREETING
SET VARVALUE=Hello, world
SET %VARNAME%=%VARVALUE%
```

If you guessed that they would create an environment variable named GREETING and equate it to "Hello, world," then you guessed correctly. This is not all that different from using pointers in C and Pascal, where one variable contains the address of another. In this case, DOS substitutes GREETING for %VARNAME% and "Hello, world" for %VARVALUE% in the SET command on the last line.

One thing you should note about environment variables is that they can be passed to any batch command this way, not just to SET. They can even be the object of a GOTO command, a fact that we'll use later to develop a technique for implementing batch file subroutines. Another item worth noting is that everything on the left side of the equal sign in a SET command is capitalized before it is actually placed in the environment. Thus,

```
SET GREETING=Hello, world
```

is the same as

```
SET Greeting=Hello, world
```

Both create an environment variable named GREETING and assign it "Hello, world." However, case is preserved on the right side of the equal sign. Thus, the statement

```
SET GREETING=HELLO, WORLD
```

is not equivalent to either of the preceding lines. You can prove this by creating and running the following batch file:

```
@ECHO OFF
SET TEST1=Hello, world
SET TEST2=HELLO, WORLD
IF %TEST1%==%TEST2% GOTO EQUAL
ECHO Not Equal!
GOTO END
:EQUAL
Equal!
:END
```

When run, the program will display the message "Not equal!" because the string comparison performed with the IF command will fail, and execution will fall through to the line below.

Batch File Tricks and Techniques

Knowing the basics gives you the tools you need to write some pretty sophisticated batch files. But there's something to be said for going beyond the basics, too. There are several tricks and techniques batch file programmers often rely on to make batch programs easier to use, more compact, and more resistant to input error. For example, there's a simple trick that lets you perform IF string comparisons without regard to case so that batch files won't be sensitive to mixed upper- and lowercase characters when parameters are passed to them. The next few sections describe some of these methods and provide examples of their use.

Using Subroutines in Batch Files

Encapsulating segments of code that are used more than once into subroutines is one technique programmers use to keep code length to a minimum. A *subroutine* is a section of code that is set apart from the rest and that may be called by other parts of the program when its services are needed. Unfortunately, the batch language doesn't support the use of subroutines unless those subroutines are stored in the form of separate batch files so that they may be invoked with the CALL command. But there is a way to incorporate subroutines into your batch file. The following batch program illustrates how.

```
@ECHO OFF
SET RETURN=LABEL1
GOTO HELLO
:LABEL1
SET RETURN=LABEL2
GOTO HELLO
```

```
:LABEL2
SET RETURN=LABEL3
GOTO HELLO
:LABEL3
GOTO END
:HELLO
ECHO Hello, world
GOTO %RETURN%
:END
```

Here, the subroutine HELLO, which consists of the two lines

```
ECHO Hello, world
GOTO %RETURN%
```

is called three times to display the message "Hello, world" on the screen. Before HELLO is invoked, the batch program sets an environment variable named RETURN to the name of the label following the line that invokes it. Then, when the subroutine is finished, it executes a GOTO %RETURN% to return to the point in the program where it left off. The key to making this work is realizing that GOTO doesn't mind if it's not given the name of a label directly; it's perfectly happy to accept an environment variable that *holds* the name of the label. Programmers call this using *indirection*, because it permits objects to be referenced indirectly.

This procedure is like the one high-level language compilers use to call a subroutine and return to the statement following the one that made the call. Typically, a subroutine call causes the address of the next statement in the program to be saved on the stack. When the subroutine returns, the address saved on the stack is where execution is resumed. The only real difference is that in DOS's batch language, the return address must be saved manually, and it's stored in the environment, not on the stack. But the results are the same, and this technique can significantly reduce the length of some batch programs by eliminating redundant code.

Using FOR as a Switch Statement

C programmers are familiar with the *switch* statement, which tests a variable or expression against a series of constant values and branches accordingly. For example, the statement

```
switch (var) {
    case 0:
        CaseOne ();
        break;
    case 1:
```

```
        CaseTwo ();
        break;
    case 2:
        CaseThree ();
        break;
}
```

calls the function *CaseOne*, *CaseTwo*, or *CaseThree*, depending on the value of *var*. This is very similar to the CASE statement in Pascal and SELECT CASE in BASIC.

The batch language doesn't provide an equivalent construct, but you can create one using the FOR command. Let's say your batch file should be designed to accept three different parameters on the command line—WP for word processing, SS for spreadsheet, and DB for database—and that you want to branch based on the parameter that is input. Indirection will help you accomplish this, as shown here:

```
FOR %%P IN (WP wp SS ss DB db) DO IF "%1"=="%%P" GOTO %1
ECHO Invalid parameter or parameter missing
GOTO END
:WP
ECHO Word Processing
GOTO END
:SS
ECHO Spreadsheet
GOTO END
:DB
Echo Database
:END
```

If one of the three supported parameters is entered (in either upper- or lower-case), execution will branch to the appropriate label—WP, SS, or DB. If an invalid parameter is entered, or if no parameter is entered at all, the batch program will display an error message indicating as much. One of the keys here is that the GOTO command is not sensitive to case, so you don't have to enter labels in both upper- and lowercase.

A variation on this theme uses the result returned in ERRORLEVEL as the basis for the test. This is particularly useful when you use a program such as the one we'll develop later in this chapter to solicit input from the keyboard. Let's say you want to branch based on which ERRORLEVEL value is returned: 0, 1, 2, or 3. This is easily done with the following logic.

```
FOR %%E IN (Ø 1 2 3) DO IF ERRORLEVEL %%E GOTO CASE%%E
ECHO Unsupported value
GOTO END
:CASEØ
ECHO ERRORLEVEL=Ø
GOTO END
:CASE1
ECHO ERRORLEVEL=1
GOTO END
:CASE2
ECHO ERRORLEVEL=2
GOTO END
:CASE3
ECHO ERRORLEVEL=3
:END
```

If the ERRORLEVEL values you're testing aren't contiguous, you'll need to add code to test for unsupported values. Let's say that ERRORLEVEL is set to the ASCII code of the last key pressed, and that you want to test for the values 13 (Enter), 27 (Esc), 78 (the "N" key), and 89 (the "Y" key). First, modify the FOR statement to read

```
FOR %%E IN (13 14 27 28 78 79 89 9Ø) DO IF ERRORLEVEL %%E
        GOTO CASE%%E
```

and substitute CASE13, CASE27, CASE78, and CASE89 for CASE0, CASE1, CASE2, and CASE3 in the body of the program. Next, add four lines containing the statements :CASE14, :CASE28, :CASE79, and :CASE90 just after the FOR statement. With this arrangement, the batch file will say "Unsupported value" if ERRORLEVEL is set to any value other than the four you're looking for. Note that values must appear in the FOR statement in ascending order for this technique to work.

Performing String Comparisons Without Regard to Case

A well-written batch file should recognize parameters passed to it from the command line regardless of case. Earlier, we looked at one method for trapping the different ways a user might enter command-line parameters by anticipating the various permutations and including a test for each. For example, the lines

```
IF "%1"=="SMARTDRIVE" GOTO SD
IF "%1"=="SMARTDrive" GOTO SD
IF "%1"=="SmartDrive" GOTO SD
IF "%1"=="Smartdrive" GOTO SD
IF "%1"=="smartdrive" GOTO SD
```

would catch the five most common variations of "SMARTDrive." However, an odd variation such as "SMARTdrive" would slip right through. Clearly, there needs to be some way for a batch file to trap any and all the combinations of upper- and lowercase a user might enter so that it can recognize an entry no matter how it's typed.

Fortunately, there is. You can take advantage of the fact that DOS capitalizes the names of environment variables created with the SET command to perform string comparisons that are not case sensitive. The following batch file illustrates how.

```
@ECHO OFF
SET %1=$$
IF "%SMARTDRIVE%"=="$$" GOTO SAYYES
ECHO No!
GOTO END
:SAYYES
ECHO Yes!
:END
SET %1=
```

This program recognizes SMARTDRIVE as a command-line parameter no matter how it's entered—even if you spell it "SmArTdRiVe." To verify as much, it writes "Yes!" to the screen when it recognizes the parameter as SMARTDRIVE, "No!" when you enter anything else.

The program works by creating an environment variable with the same name as the command-line parameter. Assuming the command-line parameter is SMARTDRIVE, entered in any combination of upper- and lowercase, the line

```
SET %1=$$
```

creates an environment variable named SMARTDRIVE and sets it equal to a dummy string containing two dollar signs. Next, the program tests whether there is an environment variable named SMARTDRIVE that's equal to $$ with the command

```
IF "%SMARTDRIVE%"=="$$" GOTO SAYYES
```

The test could be fooled if there were already an environment variable named SMARTDRIVE, but only if it happened to be set to $$. It's highly unlikely that this would occur, especially if the dummy variable were chosen wisely. That's also why it's important to delete the environment variable at the end of the program. Otherwise, subsequent comparisons would return true even if a parameter other than SMARTDRIVE were entered.

One thing you should do when you use this technique is insert a separate test for a null parameter before the SET %1=$$ command. Otherwise, if no %1 parameter is entered on the command line, you'll get a "Syntax error" message when SET is executed. You can fix this in the previous batch file by modifying it to read:

```
@ECHO OFF
IF "%1=="" GOTO SAYNO
SET %1==$$
IF "%SMARTDRIVE%"== "$$" GOTO SAYYES
:SAYNO
ECHO No!
GOTO END
:SAYYES
ECHO Yes!
:END
SET %1=
```

The line

```
IF "%1"=="" GOTO SAYNO
```

averts the error message by recognizing when there is no command-line parameter entered and branching directly to SAYNO.

Using Redirection and Piping in Batch Files

DOS doesn't support redirection or piping on lines that invoke batch files. But it does support redirection and piping *inside* batch files. There are lots of different ways you can put this to use. The one-line batch file

```
ECHO ^L > PRN
```

is a well-known way to send a form feed to your printer (^L is entered by pressing Ctrl-L). Ctrl-L produces an ASCII 12, which most printers recognize as the code to eject a page. The command works equally well from a batch file or from the command line. However, storing it in a batch file called FF.BAT permits you to eject a page simply by typing FF.

The following batch file, TY.BAT, uses piping to create a smart TYPE command. It works just like TYPE, but it automatically appends a piping operator and the MORE command to prevent long listings from scrolling off the screen. It also checks to see that a file name was entered and displays a message if one was not.

```
@ECHO OFF
IF "%1"=="" GOTO ERROR
```

```
TYPE %1 | MORE
GOTO END
:ERROR
ECHO Syntax: TY filename
:END
```

You might also want to use piping to greet the user with today's time and date by adding these two lines to the batch file:

```
ECHO | MORE | DATE | FIND "Current"
ECHO | MORE | TIME | FIND "Current"
```

The output will look something like this:

```
Current date is Fri 03-15-1991
Current time is 12:21:44.14p
```

How does it work? ECHO | MORE outputs a carriage return followed by some meaningless text. This output is piped to DATE and TIME, which interpret the carriage return as a press of the Enter key and therefore terminate with the date and time unchanged. The output from DATE and TIME is then piped to FIND, which only displays lines that contain the text string "Current." You could use this little eye-opener to add some pizzazz to an otherwise dull AUTOEXEC.BAT file. Better yet, if you wanted to keep a record of when you get into the office every day and turn your PC on (or to tell when and if your PC is being turned on in your absence), you could add these lines to AUTOEXEC.BAT:

```
ECHO | MORE | DATE | FIND "Current" >> USAGE.TXT
ECHO | MORE | TIME | FIND "Current" >> USAGE.TXT
ECHO. >> USAGE.TXT
```

The first statement outputs today's date to a file named USAGE.TXT; the second statement outputs the current time; and the third one outputs a blank line so that consecutive entries in the file will be separated by white space. In this way, a log is built up that contains a record of the time and date for every time AUTOEXEC.BAT is executed. Note that the >> operator in the first command will create USAGE.TXT if it doesn't already exist. If the file does exist, then new output will be appended to the old. As shown, USAGE.TXT will be created in the current directory. If you want to store it somewhere else, add a drive name, path name, or both to the file name in all three lines. Also, since both FIND and MORE are external commands, make sure these statements appear after the PATH statement in your AUTOEXEC.BAT file. Otherwise, you'll have to include path names indicating where the files are stored.

You can get a lot more sophisticated than this if you wish. Consider, for example, the batch program in Listing 10.1, which creates a file called SYSINFO.TXT that records important system parameters such as currently defined environment variables, the contents of CONFIG.SYS and AUTOEXEC.BAT, the amount and types of memory installed, and the time and date the listing was created. This type of listing can be very valuable if a system crash wipes out your start-up files and you have to rebuild them from scratch, or if you need a list of pertinent system parameters for when you talk to a technical support person.

LISTING 10.1   SYSINFO.BAT

```
@ECHO OFF
REM **********************************************
REM
REM SYSINFO.BAT writes a summary of important
REM system parameters to the file SYSINFO.TXT.
REM
REM **********************************************
:
ECHO | MORE | DATE | FIND "Current" >SYSINFO.TXT
ECHO | MORE | TIME | FIND "Current" >>SYSINFO.TXT
ECHO. >>SYSINFO.TXT
:
ECHO :::::::::: DOS VERSION :::::::::::>>SYSINFO.TXT
ECHO. >>SYSINFO.TXT
VER >>SYSINFO.TXT
ECHO. >>SYSINFO.TXT
:
ECHO :::::::::: CONFIG.SYS :::::::::::>>SYSINFO.TXT
ECHO. >>SYSINFO.TXT
TYPE C:\CONFIG.SYS >>SYSINFO.TXT
ECHO. >>SYSINFO.TXT
:
ECHO ::::::::: AUTOEXEC.BAT :::::::::::>>SYSINFO.TXT
ECHO. >>SYSINFO.TXT
TYPE C:\AUTOEXEC.BAT >>SYSINFO.TXT
ECHO. >>SYSINFO.TXT
:
ECHO ::::::::::::: MEMORY :::::::::::::>>SYSINFO.TXT
ECHO. >>SYSINFO.TXT
MEM >>SYSINFO.TXT
ECHO. >>SYSINFO.TXT
```

```
:
ECHO ::::::::::: ENVIRONMENT :::::::::::>>SYSINFO.TXT
ECHO. >>SYSINFO.TXT
SET >>SYSINFO.TXT
ECHO. >>SYSINFO.TXT
:
ECHO ::::::::::: HARD DISK ::::::::::::>>SYSINFO.TXT
ECHO. >>SYSINFO.TXT
CHKDSK C:>>SYSINFO.TXT
ECHO. >>SYSINFO.TXT
:
ECHO :::::: DIRECTORY STRUCTURE :::::>>SYSINFO.TXT
ECHO. >>SYSINFO.TXT
TREE C:\>>SYSINFO.TXT
ECHO. >>SYSINFO.TXT
```

To get a hard copy of the listing produced by SYSINFO.BAT, run the program, and then type

```
COPY SYSINFO.TXT PRN
```

to print the file on LPT1. If your printer is connected to a port other than LPT1, you can substitute LPT2, LPT3, COM1, COM2, COM3, or COM4 for PRN in this statement. Make a new copy of this listing anytime you make a major configuration change to your PC, and file it away somewhere. You never know when it might prove useful.

You can also use redirection to enable a batch file to dial the phone for you if you have a modem connected to your PC. Assuming the modem is connected to COM1 and is Hayes-compatible (understands the AT command set), this short batch program will dial numbers entered on the command line:

```
@ECHO OFF
MODE COM1:1200 >NUL
IF "%1"=="" GOTO ERROR
ECHO ATDT%1; >COM1
PAUSE
ECHO ATH0 >COM1
GOTO END
:ERROR
ECHO Syntax: DIAL number
:END
```

If the batch file is named DIAL.BAT, then typing

```
DIAL 1-800-555-1212
```

will dial 800-number information for you. You may include spaces and hyphens in the number if you wish; Hayes and Hayes-compatible modems simply ignore them. Also, you can force the modem to pause by placing one or more commas where you want the pause to occur. Each comma produces a delay approximately 2 seconds in duration. If you have to dial a one-digit access code to get an outside line, you may have to insert a comma or two between the access code and the number to allow the modem time to get the dial tone.

DIAL.BAT initializes the COM port to 1,200 bps using the MODE command, and then ECHOes ATDT (the Hayes command to dial the phone) followed by the phone number and a semicolon, which returns the modem to command state. Finally, it pauses for a keystroke and outputs an ATH0 command to disconnect the modem from the line. Don't press a key until after the number is dialed and you've picked up the handset; otherwise, the connection will be terminated and you'll have to dial again.

You can make the modem dial faster by substituting the command

```
ECHO ATS11=55DT%1; >COM1
```

for the command

```
ECHO ATDT%1;>COM1
```

This outputs an additional command to the modem—ATS11=55—which shortens the pause between tones transmitted by the modem to 55 milliseconds. Also, if your phone uses pulse rather than tone dialing, you'll need to change ATDT to ATDP. You can make DIAL.BAT work with serial port COM2 by replacing every instance of COM1 with COM2. It will work with COM3 and COM4 also if the ports are configured with the I/O addresses that DOS's COM3 and COM4 device drivers expect.

Suppressing Command Output

Redirection can also be useful for suppressing unwanted output from DOS commands. Let's say you installed the command

```
COPY C:\DOS\*.* F:
```

in your AUTOEXEC.BAT file to copy everything from your DOS directory to a RAM disk at start-up. When the command executes, it writes to the screen the name of every file copied to drive F followed by the message "*xx* files(s) copied." If you don't want the screen cluttered with text, you can modify this command to read

```
COPY C:\DOS\*.* F: >NUL
```

to route screen output from COPY to the NUL device.

But even this little trick isn't foolproof. If the source files do not exist, it will display an error message on the screen, despite the fact that output was redirected to the NUL device. The problem? DOS commands output error messages to another predefined I/O channel called *standard error* rather than standard output, and the > operator only affects messages written to standard output. DOS does this because if you don't receive the error message, you may be unaware that the error occurred.

You can hide all output from DOS commands by redirecting it to the NUL device with the CTTY command, which specifies what device DOS should use for console input and output. To do so, place the command

```
CTTY NUL
```

immediately before the COPY command, and

```
CTTY CON
```

right after it. The one danger in using this method is that it effectively disconnects DOS from the screen and keyboard. So if an error occurs while CTTY NUL is in effect that requires input from you, your system will lock up and you'll have to reboot. Also note that even the CTTY command can't suppress output from utilities that write directly to the video buffer or use video functions in the BIOS for screen output.

Saving the Current Drive and Directory

Batch files are frequently used to switch to another drive and directory before loading an application program. It's easy for a batch program to get to another drive and directory, but it's not so easy for it to return to where it started. DOS doesn't provide any overt means for batch programs to return to the drive and directory that were current when they were started. What's needed is a way for batch programs to record the current defaults and restore them on exit.

With hard work and a healthy dose of imagination, it's possible to save and restore the default drive and directory using nothing more than DOS commands. The following batch file shows how.

```
@ECHO OFF
SET OLD_PROMPT=%PROMPT%
ECHO PROMPT CD $P >C:\MISC\SETRETN.BAT
```

```
PROMPT $N: @
COMMAND /C C:\MISC\SETRETN.BAT >C:\MISC\RETURN.BAT
SET PROMPT=%OLD_PROMPT%
REM
REM Change drive and directory
REM
CALL C:\MISC\RETURN
```

The return is set up by the lines

```
ECHO PROMPT CD $P >C:\MISC\SETRETN.BAT
PROMPT $N: @
COMMAND /C C:\MISC\SETRETN.BAT >C:\MISC\RETURN.BAT
```

which create a batch file called RETURN.BAT that contains the necessary commands to restore the default drive and directory. It's probably far from obvious from looking at these statements what's going on. The first statement creates a batch file named SETRETN.BAT in the \MISC directory of the C drive containing the command PROMPT CD $P ($P is the PROMPT metastring for the current directory). It's important to specify an absolute path name here because after the drive and directory are changed, the batch file must have a fixed point of reference. The next statement changes the prompt to the letter of the default drive (as a result of the $N) followed by a colon, a space, and a @ symbol (the latter is a placeholder to make sure there's at least one space after the colon). The third statement loads and runs a secondary copy of COMMAND.COM, which in turn executes SETRETN.BAT and changes the DOS prompt a second time. The trick is that while the second COMMAND.COM is running, every prompt it displays is captured to a file named RETURN.BAT. If you started out in C:\WP\DOC, RETURN.BAT would contain these lines:

```
C: @PROMPT CD $P
CD C:\WP\DOC
```

When this batch file is executed, it will restore the drive and directory to C:\WP\DOC. Everything on the first line from the @ symbol on is ignored by DOS; in other words, typing

```
C: @PROMPT CD $P
```

is equivalent to typing simply C:. The two SET commands preserve and later restore the PROMPT environment variable and therefore the prompt itself. If you'd like, you may also include DEL commands to delete the two batch files that are created.

If traveling such a circuitous path to a destination makes you uneasy, you can use the following pair of utilities to set up a return to a remote drive and directory. The first, ECHODRV.COM, writes to standard output the command to return to the current drive. You can create it by typing these DEBUG commands:

```
A 0100
MOV   AH,19
INT   21
ADD   AL,41
MOV   [0111],AL
MOV   AH,9
MOV   DX,0111
INT   21
RET
DB    "x:",0D,0A,"$"

N ECHODRV.COM
RCX
16
W
Q
```

ECHODRV obtains the current drive by calling DOS function 19H, which returns a code in AL that identifies the default drive, where 0=A, 1=B, and so on. It then converts the drive code into a drive letter by adding 41H (so that 0, for example, becomes 41H, the ASCII code for the letter "A"). Finally, it transmits the drive letter, a colon, and a carriage-return/line-feed pair to standard output using DOS function 09H.

The second utility, ECHOCD.COM, sends to standard output the characters "CD" followed by a space. It is created with this DEBUG script:

```
A 0100
MOV   AH,09
MOV   DX,0108
INT   21
RET
DB    "CD $"

N ECHOCD.COM
RCX
0C
W
Q
```

This one simply uses the DOS function 09H to output the letters "CD" and a space. Once you have these utilities, you can use them to build a batch file that returns to the default drive and directory. In a batch program, use these commands to set up the return:

```
ECHODRV >C:\MISC\RETURN.BAT
ECHOCD >>C:\MISC\RETURN.BAT
CD >>C:\MISC\RETURN.BAT
```

Then, when you're ready to return, execute the command

```
CALL C:\MISC\RETURN
```

There are no tricks here. The first command creates the batch file RETURN.BAT and writes to it the command that returns to the default drive. The second command writes a CD command to the file (note the >> operator so that data is *appended* to the file, not written over it), and the third command adds the name of the current directory to the line that contains CD. When RETURN.BAT is executed, the current drive and directory are restored. Once again, you may want to delete RETURN.BAT from the disk so as not to leave any stray files behind.

Dressing Up the Screen with ANSI.SYS

If ANSI.SYS is installed, it's possible for batch files to take greater control of the screen and use the display as more than a simple teletype device. We saw examples of how ANSI.SYS can be used to control text color and cursor position in Chapter 6 when we embedded escape sequences in PROMPT commands to customize the appearance of the DOS prompt. You can use similar techniques to add spice to your batch files. The batch program in Listing 10.2 shows how.

LISTING 10.2 ANSIDEMO.BAT

```
@ECHO OFF
REM ********************************************
REM
REM ANSIDEMO.BAT demonstrates the use of ANSI.SYS
REM escape sequences to create custom batch file
REM screens
REM
REM ********************************************
:
ANSIOUT [1;37;44m
CLS
```

```
:
ANSIOUT [1;37;41m
ANSIOUT [8;33H
ECHO    Main Menu
:
ANSIOUT [1;33;44m
ANSIOUT [1Ø;33H
ECHO 1.
ANSIOUT [11;33H
ECHO 2.
ANSIOUT [12;33H
ECHO 3.
ANSIOUT [13;33H
ECHO 4.
:
ANSIOUT [1;37;44m
ANSIOUT [1Ø;36H
ECHO WordPerfect
ANSIOUT [11;36H
ECHO Lotus 1-2-3
ANSIOUT [12;36H
ECHO dBASE
ANSIOUT [13;36H
ECHO Exit to DOS
```

In this example, commands are sent to ANSI.SYS by outputting escape sequences (streams of characters preceded by a binary 27, the ASCII code for an escape character) to standard output via a utility called ANSIOUT.COM, which will be discussed momentarily. For a list of the cursor movement commands ANSI.SYS supports, refer back to Table 6.4. For a list of the color and attribute codes you can use to change text attributes, see Table 6.1. This information also appears in the documentation for ANSI.SYS in Appendix B. ANSIDEMO.BAT uses two escape sequences repeatedly: one to position the cursor, one to set the text color. The escape sequence [8;33H positions the cursor at row 8, column 33, while [1;33;44m sets the text output color to yellow (33) on blue (44). The "1" in the command means the foreground color (yellow) should be high-intensity.

As mentioned, ANSIDEMO.BAT uses a small utility called ANSIOUT-.COM to send escape sequences to ANSI.SYS. This utility is needed because the DOS Editor does not allow you to enter escape characters directly (not even by tapping out 027 on the numeric keypad while holding down the Alt key). Also, you can't write to standard output from a batch file using the PROMPT command because PROMPT doesn't send anything out until the command prompt is displayed, and with ECHO off, the prompt isn't displayed

again until the batch program has terminated. You can create your own copy
of ANSIOUT.COM with the following DEBUG script:

```
A 0100
MOV  SI,0081
MOV  CL,[SI-01]
CMP  CL,02
JB   011A
CLD
SUB  CH,CH
MOV  BYTE PTR [SI],1B
LODSB
MOV  DL,AL
MOV  AH,02
INT  21
LOOP 0111
RET

N ANSIOUT.COM
RCX
1B
W
Q
```

The syntax for ANSIOUT.COM is simply

```
ANSIOUT string
```

where *string* is the escape sequence, minus the leading escape character. When
run, ANSIOUT.COM uses DOS function 02H to output an escape character followed by the text you entered on the command line to standard output. If ANSI-
.SYS is installed, it will see the escape sequences and act on them accordingly.
We can dissect ANSIDEMO.BAT line for line to see how it works. The lines

```
ANSIOUT [1;37;44m
CLS
```

set the screen colors to intense white on a blue background and clear the screen
to effect the new color combination. Next, the lines

```
ANSIOUT [1;37;41m
ANSIOUT [8;33H
ECHO   Main Menu
```

set the current text color to white on red, position the cursor at row 8, column 33, and write "Main Menu." Afterward, the lines

```
ANSIOUT [1;33;44m
ANSIOUT [10;33H
ECHO 1.
ANSIOUT [11;33H
ECHO 2.
ANSIOUT [12;33H
ECHO 3.
ANSIOUT [13;33H
ECHO 4.
```

display the menu numbers 1 through 4 in yellow on blue, and the lines

```
ANSIOUT [1;37;44m
ANSIOUT [10;36H
ECHO WordPerfect
ANSIOUT [11;36H
ECHO Lotus 1-2-3
ANSIOUT [12;36H
ECHO dBASE
ANSIOUT [13;36H
ECHO Exit to DOS
```

display the text accompanying those numbers in white on blue. Notice that each ECHO command is preceded by an escape sequence that positions the cursor at the location where text will appear.

If you rely on ANSI.SYS to soup up your batch programs and plan to distribute them to other people, your programs should verify that ANSI.SYS is installed before outputting commands to it. To do so, they need a special utility. You can create one with the following DEBUG script:

```
A 0100
MOV  AX,1A00
INT  2F
INC  AL
JZ   010B
MOV  AL,1
MOV  AH,4C
INT  21
```

```
N CHKANSI.COM
RCX
ØF
W
Q
```

The utility is called CHKANSI.COM, and it works for versions of DOS from 4.0 on. It returns an ERRORLEVEL value of 0 if ANSI.SYS is installed, 1 if it's not. This is demonstrated in the following batch file excerpt:

```
CHKANSI
IF ERRORLEVEL 1 GOTO ERROR
ECHO ANSI.SYS installed!
GOTO END
:ERROR
ECHO ANSI.SYS not installed!
:END
```

Fortunately, there are better ways to dress up the screen than placing calls to ANSI.SYS, but these require utilities that DOS doesn't provide. Later in this chapter, we'll develop four such utilities that are faster, more flexible, and easier to use than ANSI.SYS.

Debugging Batch Files

The longer a batch program is, the greater the chance that it will contain bugs. It's difficult to debug batch programs because DOS places a limited number of tools for doing so at your disposal. However, applying a few simple techniques will help keep the errors in your programs to a minimum and make it easier to swat bugs when they do occur.

The first line of defense is to comment your programs thoroughly. You know exactly why you included a certain line today, but your memory may not be so good a year from now when a seemingly minor modification to the code causes it to start behaving erratically. A few well-placed REM statements are just the ticket. Too many of them will slow a program down, but one or two here and there won't make that great a difference in speed.

When bugs do occur, you can usually track them down by turning ECHO on so that DOS will echo every command it executes to the screen. That's similar to the trace facility offered by many debuggers, which lets you see exactly where a program is going and what branches it's taking. If the first line of your batch program is @ECHO OFF, just comment it out with a REM statement for the time being. When the bug is corrected, remove the REM and you're back in business. And remember that as a batch file executes, you can freeze it by pressing Ctrl-S or Pause.

For very long and complicated batch files, it may be beneficial to make strategically placed debugging commands a permanent part of the program. For example, at the start of a critical section of code, you could insert an ECHO command describing what's about to take place, or when the value of an environment variable is of concern, you could echo it to the screen. Furthermore, you could set it up so that these commands are only executed when an environment variable named DEBUG is set to "YES," as demonstrated by the line

```
IF "%DEBUG%"=="YES" ECHO ENVVAR=%ENVVAR%
```

Prior to starting the batch file, typing

```
SET DEBUG=YES
```

would enable the debugging statements. You could even key the ECHO OFF command to DEBUG by making

```
@IF NOT "%DEBUG%"=="YES" ECHO OFF
```

the first statement in the program. Then, setting DEBUG to YES before executing the batch file would automatically turn command echoing on.

Batch File Utilities

DOS's batch language may seem powerful until you realize that the only command it offers for performing keyboard I/O (the PAUSE command) doesn't provide any feedback to let you know what key was pressed. The batch language suffers many shortcomings, many of which can be corrected with stand-alone utilities. For instance, it's easy to concoct a keyboard input utility for use in batch files. It's also possible to incorporate color without ANSI.SYS, write batch files that execute at a certain time of day or on a particular day of the week or month, and much, much more, provided you have a few well-fitted utilities at your disposal.

In the next few sections we'll develop several such utilities. Among other things, you'll learn to write batch files that read the keyboard, that build professional-looking screens with pop-up windows and screen borders, that use information about the time and date to execute conditionally, that identify the processor and coprocessor type, and that reboot your PC. And so that you can use these batch file utilities as a first step toward creating your own, they're presented here complete with source code.

Getting Input from the User

One capability that the batch language doesn't provide is a means for batch programs to receive input from the keyboard. This is a severe limitation if you want to write interactive batch files that respond to user input. Fortunately, it's possible to read the keyboard from batch files much the same way application programs do by writing a utility to return key codes that can be tested with IF ERRORLEVEL.

We can use DEBUG to whip up a quick-and-dirty program for getting an ASCII key code from the keyboard. The program, GETKEY.COM, is created with this short DEBUG script:

```
A 0100
MOV  AH,08
INT  21
CMP  AL,00
JNZ  010E
MOV  AH,08
INT  21
MOV  AL,00
MOV  AH,4C
INT  21

N GETKEY.COM
RCX
12
W
Q
```

GETKEY uses DOS function 08H to read a keystroke and returns in ERROR-LEVEL the ASCII code of the first key pressed. If the key that is pressed is one of those that produces an extended key code as described in Chapter 9, the ASCII code will be zero. Thus, the one limitation imposed on GETKEY is that it can't be used to differentiate between keys such as F1 and F2 that return extended key codes.

The following batch file illustrates how GETKEY could be used to get a yes or no response from the user:

```
@ECHO OFF
:READ
ECHO Answer Yes or No (Y/N)
GETKEY
IF ERRORLEVEL 89 IF NOT ERRORLEVEL 90 GOTO YES
IF ERRORLEVEL 121 IF NOT ERRORLEVEL 122 GOTO YES
IF ERRORLEVEL 78 IF NOT ERRORLEVEL 79 GOTO NO
IF ERRORLEVEL 110 IF NOT ERRORLEVEL 111 GOTO NO
GOTO READ
:YES
ECHO You answered yes
GOTO END
```

```
:NO
ECHO You answered no
:END
```

GETKEY is called to get the key code, and four IF ERRORLEVEL statements test for the ASCII codes for Y, y, N, and n, respectively. If the ASCII code returned by GETKEY is not one of these, the batch file loops back to the beginning, redisplays the prompt, and calls GETKEY again. The loop continues until a valid key code is entered (or until you press Ctrl-C). You can test for any valid ASCII code, so you can also use GETKEY to check for the numbers 0 through 9 and for keys such as Enter and Esc. All you have to do is add logic to test for the corresponding ASCII codes.

GETKEY is fine for some applications, but it doesn't help if you want to trap extended key codes as well as plain ASCII codes. To that end, the source code for a more sophisticated input utility, BATCHKEY, is provided in Listing 10.3. Like GETKEY, BATCHKEY returns a code in ERRORLEVEL that indicates what key was pressed. But it also supports extended key codes and makes it easier to be selective about the keys that are accepted.

LISTING 10.3 BATCHKEY.ASM

```
;****************************************************************************
; BATCHKEY allows batch files to get keyboard input.  Its syntax is:
;
;       BATCHKEY [keylist]
;
; where keylist is an optional list of accepted values.  If no list is
; supplied, BATCHKEY returns the ASCII code of any key that is pressed in
; ERRORLEVEL (extended key codes return Ø).  If a list is supplied,
; BATCHKEY returns an ERRORLEVEL value that reflects the key's position in
; the list.  An ERRORLEVEL value of 255 means the key code entered was not
; one of those in the list.
;
; Keylist values can be entered in three forms:
;
;       Literal         "Y"     Y key
;       ASCII code      13      Enter key
;       Extended code   (59)    Function key F1
;
; Literal values are not case-sensitive.  Thus, the command
;
;       BATCHKEY "YN" 27 13 (59)
;
; would return 1 if "Y" or "y" was pressed, 2 if "N" or "n" was pressed,
; 3 if Esc (ASCII 27) was pressed, 4 if Enter (ASCII 13) was pressed, 5
; if function key F1 was pressed, or 255 if any other key was pressed.
;****************************************************************************

code            segment
                assume  cs:code,ds:code
                org     100h
```

```
begin:          jmp     main

msg             db      13,10,"Invalid parameter",13,10,"$"
buffer          db      64 dup (?)
keyflags        db      64 dup (0)
keycount        dw      ?


;*************************************************************************
; Procedure MAIN
;*************************************************************************

main            proc    near
                cld                             ;Clear direction flag
                sub     cx,cx                   ;Initialize count in CX
                mov     di,offset buffer        ;Initialize SI and DI
                mov     si,81h
                call    findchar                ;Advance to first character
                jnc     main2
;
; No key list was entered.  Return the ASCII code of the first key pressed.
;
main0:          mov     ah,08h                  ;Read the keyboard
                int     21h
                or      al,al                   ;Exit if AL is not 0
                jnz     main1
                mov     bl,al                   ;Save key code
                mov     ah,08h                  ;Read extended key code
                int     21h
                mov     al,bl                   ;Retrieve original code
main1:          mov     ah,4Ch                  ;Exit with key code in AL
                int     21h
;
; Parse the command line and build the key list.
;
main2:          lodsb                           ;Get a character
                cmp     al,28h                  ;Branch if "("
                je      extended
                cmp     al,22h                  ;Branch if quotation mark
                jne     ascii
;
; Process a string of literal key codes
;
literal:        lodsb                           ;Get a character
                cmp     al,22h                  ;Exit when closing quotation
                je      nextchar                ;  mark is encountered
                cmp     al,0Dh                  ;Error if EOL
                je      error
                call    lc2cap                  ;Capitalize the character
                stosb                           ;Store it in the key list
                inc     cx                      ;Increment count
                jmp     literal                 ;Loop back for more
;
; Process an extended key code entry
```

```
;
extended:       call    asc2bin                 ;ASCII => binary
                jnc     error                   ;Exit on error
                cmp     bl,29h                  ;Error if ")" not found
                jne     error
                stosb                           ;Store the key code
                inc     si                      ;Advance SI beyond ")"
                inc     cx                      ;Increment count
                push    di                      ;Set flag indicating this
                dec     di                      ;  is an extended key
                sub     di,offset buffer        ;  code
                add     di,offset keyflags
                mov     byte ptr [di],1
                pop     di
                jmp     short nextchar          ;Continue
;
; Process an ASCII key code entry
;
ascii:          dec     si                      ;Decrement SI
                call    asc2bin                 ;ASCII => binary
                jc      error                   ;Exit on error
                call    lc2cap                  ;Capitalize the character
                stosb                           ;Store it in the key list
                inc     cx                      ;Increment count
;
; Advance to the next character
;
nextchar:       call    findchar                ;Advance to next character
                jnc     main2                   ;Loop back if found
;
; Read a key code and check for extended key codes.
;
                jcxz    main0                   ;Exit if no codes entered
                mov     keycount,cx             ;Save count
                mov     si,offset buffer        ;Initialize SI and DI
                mov     di,offset keyflags
                mov     ah,08h                  ;Read the keyboard
                int     21h
                or      al,al                   ;Branch if extended key
                jz      exonly                  ;  code
;
; Search the list for conventional key codes.
;
                call    lc2cap                  ;Capitalize the character
                mov     bl,al                   ;Save it in BL
search1:        mov     al,[di]                 ;Get flag for next code
                inc     di
                or      al,al                   ;Branch if extended code
                jnz     next1
                mov     al,[si]                 ;Test key code against list
                cmp     al,bl
                je      match                   ;Exit on match
next1:          inc     si                      ;Otherwise loop back for more
```

```
                loop    search1

                jmp     short nomatch           ;No match if search exhausted

;
; Search the list for extended key codes.
;
exonly:         mov     ah,08h                  ;Read extended code
                int     21h
                mov     bl,al                   ;Save it in BL
search2:        mov     al,[di]                 ;Get flag for next code
                inc     di
                or      al,al                   ;Branch if not extended code
                jz      next2
                mov     al,[si]                 ;Test key code against list
                cmp     al,bl
                je      match                   ;Exit on match
next2:          inc     si                      ;Otherwise loop back for more
                loop    search2
;
; No match was found.
;
nomatch:        mov     ax,4C00h                ;Exit with ERRORLEVEL=0
                int     21h
;
;An error was encountered while parsing the command line.
;
error:          mov     ah,09h                  ;Display error message
                mov     dx,offset msg
                int     21h
                jmp     nomatch                 ;Exit with ERRORLEVEL=255
;
; A match was found.
;
match:          mov     ax,keycount             ;Set ERRORLEVEL and exit
                sub     ax,cx
                inc     al
                mov     ah,4Ch
                int     21h
main            endp

;**********************************************************************
; FINDCHAR advances SI to the next non-space or non-comma character.
; On return, carry set indicates EOL was encountered.
;**********************************************************************

findchar        proc    near
                lodsb                           ;Get the next character
                cmp     al,20h                  ;Loop if space
                je      findchar
                cmp     al,2Ch                  ;Loop if comma
                je      findchar
                dec     si                      ;Point SI to the character
```

```
                cmp     al,0Dh                  ;Exit with carry set if end
                je      eol                     ;  of line is reached

                clc                             ;Clear carry and exit
                ret

eol:            stc                             ;Set carry and exit
                ret
findchar        endp


;**************************************************************************
; ASC2BIN converts a decimal number entered in ASCII form into a binary
; value in AL.  Carry set on return indicates that an error occurred in
; the conversion.
;**************************************************************************

asc2bin         proc    near
                sub     ax,ax                   ;Initialize registers
                sub     bh,bh
                mov     dl,10

a2b_loop:       mov     bl,[si]                 ;Get a character
                inc     si
                cmp     bl,20h                  ;Exit if space
                je      a2b_exit
                cmp     bl,2Ch                  ;Exit if comma
                je      a2b_exit
                cmp     bl,0Dh                  ;Exit if carriage return
                je      a2b_exit

                cmp     bl,"0"                  ;Error if character is not
                jb      a2b_error               ;  a number
                cmp     bl,"9"
                ja      a2b_error

                mul     dl                      ;Multiply the value in AL by
                jc      a2b_error               ;  10 and exit on overflow
                sub     bl,30h                  ;ASCII => binary
                add     ax,bx                   ;Add latest value to AX
                cmp     ax,255                  ;Error if sum > 255
                jna     a2b_loop                ;Loop back for more

a2b_error:      dec     si                      ;Set carry and exit
                stc
                ret

a2b_exit:       dec     si                      ;Clear carry and exit
                clc
                ret
asc2bin         endp


;**************************************************************************
; LC2CAP capitalizes the ASCII code in AL
;**************************************************************************
```

```
lc2cap          proc    near
                cmp     al,"a"                  ;Exit if less than "a"
                jb      l2c_exit
                cmp     al,"z"                  ;Exit if greater than "z"
                ja      l2c_exit
                and     al,0DFh                 ;Capitalize
l2c_exit:       ret
lc2cap          endp

code            ends
                end     begin
```

The syntax for **BATCHKEY** is

```
BATCHKEY [keylist]
```

where *keylist* is a list of characters and key codes. If *keylist* is not supplied, BATCHKEY behaves just like GETKEY: It returns an ASCII key code to ERRORLEVEL. If you include *keylist*, however, BATCHKEY returns to ERRORLEVEL a code that reflects the position that the key code appeared at in *keylist*. For example, the command

```
BATCHKEY "YN"
```

returns 1 if "Y" or "y" is pressed (BATCHKEY is not case sensitive) and 2 if "N" or "n" is pressed. If any other key is pressed, BATCHKEY returns zero, providing the batch file a chance to notify the user that the input was not accepted. A batch file equivalent to the one above that solicits a yes or no response to a question could be built with these lines:

```
@ECHO OFF
:READ
ECHO Answer Yes or No (Y/N)
BATCHKEY "YN"
IF ERRORLEVEL 2 GOTO NO
IF ERRORLEVEL 1 GOTO YES
GOTO READ
:YES
ECHO You answered yes
GOTO END
:NO
ECHO You answered no
:END
```

If a key other than Y or N is pressed, ERRORLEVEL is set to 0 and execution loops back to the line labeled :READ to redisplay the prompt and read the keyboard again.

With BATCHKEY, you can represent key codes three different ways: as literal strings enclosed in quotation marks, as numeric ASCII codes, or as extended codes. The following example illustrates how:

```
BATCHKEY "ABCDE" 13 27 (59) (60) (61)
```

This command tests for ten different keys: "A" through "E," Enter and Esc (ASCII codes 13 and 27), and function keys F1 through F3 (extended codes 59, 60, and 61). If "A," "B," "C," "D," or "E" is pressed, BATCHKEY returns 1, 2, 3, 4, or 5. If Enter or Esc is pressed, it returns 6 or 7. And in response to F1, F2, or F3, it returns 8, 9, or 10. BATCHKEY recognizes extended codes by the parentheses surrounding them. A list of the extended codes supported by the PC is provided in Tables 9.4 and 9.5. Among the more useful ones are function keys F1 through F10 (59 through 68), Shift-F1 through F10 (84 through 93), Ctrl-F1 through F10 (94 through 103), Alt-F1 through F10 (104 through 113), and F11 and F12 (133 and 134).

There are two procedures in BATCHKEY that you may find useful in your own programs and that we'll use often in this book. The first is FINDCHAR. On entry, DS:SI points to a location on the command line. FINDCHAR advances SI to the next character that is neither a comma nor a space. If carry is clear on exit from FINDCHAR, then SI points to the first character in the next command-line parameter. If carry is set, then there are no more parameters; FINDCHAR reached the end of the line. Using FINDCHAR to locate entries on the command line will prevent your programs from being sensitive to extraneous separator characters. After all, occasionally a finger will slip and there will be two spaces between the program name and the first parameter. Your programs should recognize this common error and adjust to it rather than fail.

The second procedure to examine is ASC2BIN, which converts a string of ASCII digits representing a number between 0 and 255 to a binary value in AL. On entry, SI holds the offset address of the string relative to segment register DS. On return, carry is set if an error occurred in the conversion (for example, if the string contained an invalid character) or clear if the conversion proceeded without error. Thus, the caller can test for an error with a simple JC instruction and use it to branch to an error handler when errors do occur.

One other item to note is just how the command line is parsed. When DOS starts a program, it copies the contents of the command line to the area beginning at offset 81h in the program's program segment prefix (PSP). The byte at offset 80h contains a count of the number of characters present, not including the carriage return at the end. Thus, all a program has to do to examine the command line is to look inside its own PSP. Like many programs, BATCHKEY sets the SI register to 81H when it starts and uses the 80x86 LODS (Load String) instruction to fetch one byte at a time from the PSP, examine it, and decide what to do with it. Segment register DS does not have to be set before parsing begins because DOS loads all four segment registers with the segment address of the PSP when a COM program is started.

Improving Screen Output

Earlier, we saw how batch files can escape the black-and-white doldrums and create color screens by sending escape sequences to ANSI.SYS. There are two reasons why it's preferable not to have to rely on ANSI.SYS. One, not all users load it in their systems. It takes up RAM, and it has a bad reputation from years past that keeps many veteran users from adding it to their CONFIG.SYS files. Two, it's slow. It takes time to output long escape sequences and for ANSI.SYS to decipher them. Batch files are so slow already that additional delays should be avoided whenever possible. Fortunately, a few simple screen utilities can do anything ANSI.SYS can, and then some.

We'll develop four such utilities in this section: one to display text in your choice of colors, one to position the cursor so that text can be displayed anywhere you want, one to clear the screen (or a part of the screen) to the desired color, and one to draw boxes on the screen. The source code for the first, TEXTOUT, is shown in Listing 10.4. Its syntax is

```
TEXTOUT attr "string"
```

where *attr* is a hexadecimal code specifying the foreground and background colors the text is to be displayed in, and *string* is the text itself, enclosed in quotation marks. Why quotation marks? Because this way, you can include leading or trailing spaces in your strings. With ECHO, which doesn't use quotation marks, it's hard to tell where a string with extra spaces begins and ends.

LISTING 10.4 TEXTOUT.ASM

```
;*****************************************************************************
; TEXTOUT echoes a string to the screen using the attribute specified.
; Its syntax is:
;
;       TEXTOUT attr "string"
;
; where "attr" is a hex number indicating what color attribute is to
; be used, and "string" is the text to be output.  For example, the
; command
;
;       TEXTOUT 1E "Hello, world"
;
; displays "Hello, world" in yellow on blue at the current cursor position.
; The cursor can be positioned with the separate SETPOS utility.
;*****************************************************************************

code            segment
                assume  cs:code,ds:code
                org     100h
begin:          jmp     short main
```

```
msg1            db      13,10,"Syntax: TEXTOUT nn ",34,"string",34,13,10,"$"
msg2            db      13,10,"Invalid parameter",13,10,"$"
start           dw      ?
attr            db      ?


;****************************************************************************
; Procedure MAIN
;****************************************************************************

main            proc    near
                cld                             ;Clear direction flag
                mov     si,81h                  ;Point SI to command line
                call    findchar                ;Advance to first character
                jnc     getattr                 ;Branch if found

error1:         mov     dx,offset msg1          ;Display error message
error2:         mov     ah,09h
                int     21h
                mov     ax,4C01h                ;Exit with ERRORLEVEL=1
                int     21h
;
; Parse the strings entered on the command line.
;
getattr:        call    hex2bin                 ;Convert the attribute
                mov     dx,offset msg2          ;   value to binary and
                jc      error2                  ;   store it for later
                mov     attr,bl

                call    findchar                ;Advance to next character
                jc      error1                  ;Error if EOL encountered
                cmp     al,22h                  ;Error if character is not
                jne     error1                  ;   a quotation mark
                inc     si                      ;Advance SI to string
                mov     start,si                ;Save string address

mloop:          lodsb                           ;Get a character
                cmp     al,0Dh                  ;Error if EOL encountered
                je      error1
                cmp     al,22h                  ;Loop back if it's not a
                jne     mloop                   ;   quotation mark

                mov     byte ptr [si-1],0       ;Mark end of string
;
; Output the string using BIOS interrupt 10H video I/O functions.
;
                mov     ah,0Fh                  ;Get active page number
                int     10h                     ;   in BH
                mov     ah,03h                  ;Get current cursor position
                int     10h                     ;   in DH and DL
                mov     bl,attr                 ;Get attribute in BL
                mov     si,start                ;Point SI to string

outloop:        lodsb                           ;Get a character
```

```
                or      al,al                   ;Exit if zero
                jz      exit
                mov     ah,09h                  ;Output the character
                mov     cx,1
                int     10h
                mov     ah,02h                  ;Advance the cursor for
                inc     dl                      ;  next write
                int     10h
                jmp     outloop                 ;Loop back for more

exit:           mov     ax,4C00h                ;Exit with ERRORLEVEL=0
                int     21h
main            endp

;************************************************************************
; FINDCHAR advances SI to the next non-space or non-comma character.
; On return, carry set indicates EOL was encountered.
;************************************************************************

findchar        proc    near
                lodsb                           ;Get the next character
                cmp     al,20h                  ;Loop if space
                je      findchar
                cmp     al,2Ch                  ;Loop if comma
                je      findchar
                dec     si                      ;Point SI to the character
                cmp     al,0Dh                  ;Exit with carry set if end
                je      eol                     ;  of line is reached

                clc                             ;Clear carry and exit
                ret

eol:            stc                             ;Set carry and exit
                ret
findchar        endp

;************************************************************************
; HEX2BIN converts a hex number entered in ASCII form into a binary
; value in BL.  Carry set on return indicates that an error occurred in
; the conversion.
;************************************************************************

hex2bin         proc    near
                sub     ah,ah                   ;Initialize registers
                sub     bx,bx

h2b_loop:       lodsb                           ;Get a character
                cmp     al,20h                  ;Exit if space
                je      h2b_exit
                cmp     al,2Ch                  ;Exit if comma
                je      h2b_exit
                cmp     al,0Dh                  ;Exit if carriage return
                je      h2b_exit
```

```
                cmp     al,"0"                  ;Check for digits "0"
                jb      h2b_error               ;  through "9"
                cmp     al,"9"
                ja      h2b2

                sub     al,30h                  ;ASCII => binary
h2b1:           mov     cl,4                    ;Multiply BX by 16 and
                shl     bx,cl                   ;  add the latest
                add     bx,ax                   ;  digit
                cmp     bx,255                  ;Error if sum > 255
                ja      h2b_error
                jmp     h2b_loop                ;Loop back for more

h2b2:           and     al,0DFh                 ;Capitalize the letter
                cmp     al,"A"                  ;Check range and exit if
                jb      h2b_error               ;  not "A" through "F"
                cmp     al,"F"
                ja      h2b_error
                sub     al,37h                  ;ASCII => binary
                jmp     h2b1                    ;Finish and loop back

h2b_error:      dec     si                      ;Set carry and exit
                stc
                ret

h2b_exit:       dec     si                      ;Clear carry and exit
                clc
                ret
hex2bin         endp


;*********************************************************************
; ASC2BIN converts a decimal number entered in ASCII form into a binary
; value in AL.  Carry set on return indicates that an error occurred in
; the conversion.
;*********************************************************************
;

asc2bin         proc    near
                sub     ax,ax                   ;Initialize registers
                sub     bh,bh
                mov     dl,10

a2b_loop:       mov     bl,[si]                 ;Get a character
                inc     si
                cmp     bl,20h                  ;Exit if space
                je      a2b_exit
                cmp     bl,2Ch                  ;Exit if comma
                je      a2b_exit
                cmp     bl,0Dh                  ;Exit if carriage return
                je      a2b_exit

                cmp     bl,"0"                  ;Error if character is not
                jb      a2b_error               ;  a number
```

```
               cmp     bl,"9"
               ja      a2b_error

               mul     dl                      ;Multiply the value in AL by
               jc      a2b_error               ;  10 and exit on overflow
               sub     bl,30h                  ;ASCII => binary
               add     ax,bx                   ;Add latest value to AX
               cmp     ax,255                  ;Error if sum > 255
               jna     a2b_loop                ;Loop back for more

a2b_error:     dec     si                      ;Set carry and exit
               stc
               ret

a2b_exit:      dec     si                      ;Clear carry and exit
               clc
               ret
asc2bin        endp

code           ends
               end     begin
```

The hexadecimal attribute code is formulated by pairing one digit designating the background color with another one designating the foreground color. The color codes supported by the IBM PC were summarized in Table 6.2. The command

```
TEXTOUT 1E "Hello, world"
```

prints "Hello, world" in yellow on blue because 1 corresponds to blue and E, to yellow. The first digit determines the background color, the second, the foreground color. You could print the same message in white on red by changing 1E to 4F, or dark blue on light blue (cyan) by changing it to 31.

Text output by TEXTOUT is displayed at the current cursor position. The second utility in this set, SETPOS, shown in Listing 10.5, lets you reposition the cursor to a particular row and column. Its syntax is

```
SETPOS row col
```

Row and column numbers are zero-based, so the upper-left corner of the screen is row 0, column 0. By the same token, the lower-right corner of an 80 by 25 screen is row 24, column 79.

LISTING 10.5 SETPOS.ASM

```
;*****************************************************************************
; SETPOS sets the cursor position to the row and column specified.  Its
; syntax is:
;
;       SETPOS row col
;
```

```
; where "row" is the row where the cursor should be placed and "col" is
; the column.  Row and column numbers are zero-based, so the upper left
; corner of the screen is 0,0.
;***************************************************************************

code            segment
                assume  cs:code,ds:code
                org     100h
begin:          jmp     short main

msg1            db      13,10,"Syntax: SETPOS row col",13,10,"$"
msg2            db      13,10,"Invalid parameter",13,10,"$"
row             db      ?


;***************************************************************************
; Procedure MAIN
;***************************************************************************

main            proc    near
                cld                             ;Clear direction flag
                mov     si,81h                  ;Point SI to command line
                call    findchar                ;Advance to first character
                jnc     parse                   ;Branch if found

error1:         mov     dx,offset msg1          ;Display error message
error2:         mov     ah,09h
                int     21h
                mov     ax,4C01h                ;Exit with ERRORLEVEL=1
                int     21h
;
; Parse the command line entries.
;
parse:          call    asc2bin                 ;Get the row number
                mov     dx,offset msg2
                jc      error2
                mov     row,al

                call    findchar                ;Advance to next character
                jc      error1

                call    asc2bin                 ;Get the column number
                mov     dx,offset msg2
                jc      error2
                mov     dl,al                   ;Place row and column in
                mov     dh,row                  ;   DH and DL
;
; Set the cursor position and exit.
;
                mov     ah,0Fh                  ;Get active page number
                int     10h                     ;   in BH
                mov     ah,02h                  ;Set cursor position
                int     10h
                mov     ax,4C00h                ;Exit with ERRORLEVEL=0
```

```
                int     21h
main            endp

;***********************************************************************
; FINDCHAR advances SI to the next non-space or non-comma character.
; On return, carry set indicates EOL was encountered.
;***********************************************************************

findchar        proc    near
                lodsb                           ;Get the next character
                cmp     al,20h                  ;Loop if space
                je      findchar
                cmp     al,2Ch                  ;Loop if comma
                je      findchar
                dec     si                      ;Point SI to the character
                cmp     al,0Dh                  ;Exit with carry set if end
                je      eol                     ;  of line is reached

                clc                             ;Clear carry and exit
                ret

eol:            stc                             ;Set carry and exit
                ret
findchar        endp

;***********************************************************************
; ASC2BIN converts a decimal number entered in ASCII form into a binary
; value in AL.  Carry set on return indicates that an error occurred in
; the conversion.
;***********************************************************************

asc2bin         proc    near
                sub     ax,ax                   ;Initialize registers
                sub     bh,bh
                mov     dl,10

a2b_loop:       mov     bl,[si]                 ;Get a character
                inc     si
                cmp     bl,20h                  ;Exit if space
                je      a2b_exit
                cmp     bl,2Ch                  ;Exit if comma
                je      a2b_exit
                cmp     bl,0Dh                  ;Exit if carriage return
                je      a2b_exit

                cmp     bl,"0"                  ;Error if character is not
                jb      a2b_error               ;  a number
                cmp     bl,"9"
                ja      a2b_error

                mul     dl                      ;Multiply the value in AL by
                jc      a2b_error               ;  10 and exit on overflow
                sub     bl,30h                  ;ASCII => binary
```

```
                    add     ax,bx              ;Add latest value to AX
                    cmp     ax,255             ;Error if sum > 255
                    jna     a2b_loop           ;Loop back for more

a2b_error:          dec     si                 ;Set carry and exit
                    stc
                    ret

a2b_exit:           dec     si                 ;Clear carry and exit
                    clc
                    ret
asc2bin             endp

code                ends
                    end     begin
```

Normally, you'll use SETPOS and TEXTOUT in combination to print what you want where you want. For example, the following lines print "PC Magazine" in the center of an 80-column screen:

```
SETPOS 12 33
TEXTOUT 4F " PC Magazine "
```

Sometimes in a batch file it's distracting to have a flashing cursor sitting somewhere on the screen when it's not being used. You can make the cursor disappear with SETPOS. All you have to do is set it to a row address that is higher than the number of rows currently displayed. For example, on an 80 by 25 screen, the command

```
SETPOS 25 Ø
```

temporarily hides the cursor. It will reappear when you use another SETPOS command to move it back onto the visible area of the screen.

The utility shown in Listing 10.6, CLRSCR, clears all or part of the screen and does so using a color you supply. Its syntax is

```
CLRSCR attr [row1 col1 row2 col2]
```

where *attr* is a hexadecimal color code identical to the one passed to TEXTOUT, *row1* and *col1* designate the row and column address of the upper-left corner of the region to be cleared, and *row2* and *col2* designate the row and column address of the lower-right corner. If row and column addresses are not specified, CLRSCR defaults to clearing the entire screen. If they *are* specified, however, CLRSCR only clears the rectangle you identified and leaves the rest of the screen untouched.

LISTING 10.6 CLRSCR.ASM

```
;**************************************************************************
; CLRSCR clears the screen or a specified region of the screen using the
; attribute specified.  Its syntax is:
;
;       CLRSCR attr [row1 col1 row2 col2]
;
; where "attr" is the attribute to be used, "row1" and "column1" are
; the row and column numbers of the upper left corner of the region to
; be cleared, and "row2" and "col2" are the row and column numbers of the
; lower right corner.  Row and column numbers are zero-based, so the upper
; left corner of the screen is 0,0.  If row and column numbers are omitted,
; the entire screen is cleared.
;**************************************************************************

code            segment
                assume  cs:code,ds:code
                org     100h
begin:          jmp     short main

msg1            db      13,10,"Syntax: CLRSCR attr [row1 col1 "
                db      "row2 col2",13,10,"$"
msg2            db      13,10,"Invalid parameter",13,10,"$"
attr            db      ?
row1            db      0
col1            db      0
row2            db      24
col2            db      ?


;**************************************************************************
; Procedure MAIN
;**************************************************************************

main            proc    near
                cld                             ;Clear direction flag
                mov     si,81h                  ;Point SI to command line
                call    findchar                ;Advance to first character
                jnc     parse                   ;Branch if found

error1:         mov     dx,offset msg1          ;Display error message
error2:         mov     ah,09h
                int     21h
                mov   · ax,4C01h                 ;Exit with ERRORLEVEL=1
                int     21h
;
; Parse the command line for attribute and row and column entries.
;
parse:          call    hex2bin                 ;Get attribute value and
                mov     dx,offset msg2          ; save it
                jc      error2
                mov     attr,bl

                call    findchar                ;Advance to next character
```

```
                jnc       readcoords            ;Branch if found
;
; Determine the coordinates for the lower left corner of the screen.
;
                mov       ah,0Fh                ;Get the number of columns
                int       10h                   ; displayed (minus 1)
                dec       ah
                mov       col2,ah

                mov       ah,12h                ;Check for an EGA with
                mov       bl,10h                ; video function 12H
                int       10h
                cmp       bl,10h                ;Branch if no EGA detected
                je        clrscr
                mov       ax,40h                ;Get number of rows from
                mov       es,ax                 ; the BIOS Data Area
                mov       al,es:[84h]
                mov       row2,al
                jmp       short clrscr
;
; Read row and column coordinates from the command line
;
readcoords:     call      asc2bin               ;Read "row1" parameter
                mov       dx,offset msg2
                jc        error2
                mov       row1,al
                call      findchar
                jc        error1

                call      asc2bin               ;Read "col1" parameter
                mov       dx,offset msg2
                jc        error2
                mov       col1,al
                call      findchar
                jc        error1

                call      asc2bin               ;Read "row2" parameter
                mov       dx,offset msg2
                jc        error2
                mov       row2,al
                call      findchar
                jc        error1

                call      asc2bin               ;Read "col2" parameter
                mov       dx,offset msg2
                jc        error2
                mov       col2,al
;
; Clear the region.
;
clrscr:         mov       ax,0600h              ;Use DOS function 06H
                mov       bh,attr               ;BH = attribute
                mov       ch,row1               ;CH = upper left row
```

```
                mov       cl,col1              ;CL = upper left column
                mov       dh,row2              ;DH = lower right row
                mov       dl,col2              ;DL = lower right column
                int       10h                  ;Do it

                mov       ax,4C00h             ;Exit with ERRORLEVEL=0
                int       21h
main            endp

;****************************************************************************
; FINDCHAR advances SI to the next non-space or non-comma character.
; On return, carry set indicates EOL was encountered.
;****************************************************************************

findchar        proc      near
                lodsb                          ;Get the next character
                cmp       al,20h               ;Loop if space
                je        findchar
                cmp       al,2Ch               ;Loop if comma
                je        findchar
                dec       si                   ;Point SI to the character
                cmp       al,0Dh               ;Exit with carry set if end
                je        eol                  ;  of line is reached

                clc                            ;Clear carry and exit
                ret

eol:            stc                            ;Set carry and exit
                ret
findchar        endp

;****************************************************************************
; HEX2BIN converts a hex number entered in ASCII form into a binary
; value in BL.  Carry set on return indicates that an error occurred in
; the conversion.
;****************************************************************************

hex2bin         proc      near
                sub       ah,ah                ;Initialize registers
                sub       bx,bx

h2b_loop:       lodsb                          ;Get a character
                cmp       al,20h               ;Exit if space
                je        h2b_exit
                cmp       al,2Ch               ;Exit if comma
                je        h2b_exit
                cmp       al,0Dh               ;Exit if carriage return
                je        h2b_exit

                cmp       al,"0"               ;Check for digits "0"
                jb        h2b_error            ;  through "9"
                cmp       al,"9"
                ja        h2b2
```

```
                 sub      al,30h              ;ASCII => binary
h2b1:            mov      cl,4                ;Multiply BX by 16 and
                 shl      bx,cl               ;  add the latest
                 add      bx,ax               ;  digit
                 cmp      bx,255              ;Error if sum > 255
                 ja       h2b_error
                 jmp      h2b_loop            ;Loop back for more

h2b2:            and      al,0DFh             ;Capitalize the letter
                 cmp      al,"A"              ;Check range and exit if
                 jb       h2b_error           ;  not "A" through "F"
                 cmp      al,"F"
                 ja       h2b_error
                 sub      al,37h              ;ASCII => binary
                 jmp      h2b1                ;Finish and loop back

h2b_error:       dec      si                  ;Set carry and exit
                 stc
                 ret

h2b_exit:        dec      si                  ;Clear carry and exit
                 clc
                 ret
hex2bin          endp
```

```
;****************************************************************************
; ASC2BIN converts a decimal number entered in ASCII form into a binary
; value in AL.  Carry set on return indicates that an error occurred in
; the conversion.
;****************************************************************************
```

```
asc2bin          proc     near
                 sub      ax,ax               ;Initialize registers
                 sub      bh,bh
                 mov      dl,10

a2b_loop:        mov      bl,[si]             ;Get a character
                 inc      si
                 cmp      bl,20h              ;Exit if space
                 je       a2b_exit
                 cmp      bl,2Ch              ;Exit if comma
                 je       a2b_exit
                 cmp      bl,0Dh              ;Exit if carriage return
                 je       a2b_exit

                 cmp      bl,"0"              ;Error if character is not
                 jb       a2b_error           ;  a number
                 cmp      bl,"9"
                 ja       a2b_error

                 mul      dl                  ;Multiply the value in AL by
                 jc       a2b_error           ;  10 and exit on overflow
```

```
                sub      bl,30h                  ;ASCII => binary
                add      ax,bx                   ;Add latest value to AX
                cmp      ax,255                  ;Error if sum > 255
                jna      a2b_loop                ;Loop back for more

a2b_error:      dec      si                      ;Set carry and exit
                stc
                ret

a2b_exit:       dec      si                      ;Clear carry and exit
                clc
                ret
asc2bin         endp

code            ends
                end      begin
```

The final utility in this set, DRAWBOX, is shown in Listing 10.7. DRAW-BOX.ASM draws a box on the screen whose upper-left corner lies at the current cursor position and of the width and height specified on the command line. Its syntax is

```
DRAWBOX attr width height [style]
```

where *attr* is the usual hexadecimal color code, *width* is the width of the box in screen columns, *height* is the box height in screen rows, and *style* is an optional parameter that determines whether single- or double-line graphics characters will be used to draw the box. A "1" selects single lines, while "2" selects double lines. If no *style* parameter is supplied, DRAWBOX defaults to drawing single-line boxes. The height and width parameters include the borders of the box. Thus, the smallest box you can create has a height and width of 2. Specifying 0 or 1 for *width* or *height* results in an "Invalid parameter" message from DRAWBOX.

LISTING 10.7   DRAWBOX.ASM

```
;*************************************************************************
; DRAWBOX draws a box on the screen.  Its syntax is:
;
;       DRAWBOX attr width height [style]
;
; where "attr" specifies the attribute to be used, "width" specifies the
; box width in columns, "height" specifies the height of the box in rows,
; and "style" is an optional parameter that specifies whether a single or
; double-line box is to be drawn (1=single, 2=double).  If "style" is
; omitted, DRAWBOX defaults to a single-line box.  The upper left corner
; of the box is drawn at the current cursor position.  The cursor can be
; positioned with the separate SETPOS utility.
;*************************************************************************

code            segment
                assume   cs:code,ds:code
                org      100h
```

```
begin:          jmp     short main

msg1            db      13,10,"Syntax: DRAWBOX attr width height "
                db      "[style]",13,10,"$"
msg2            db      13,10,"Invalid parameter",13,10,"$"

attr            db      ?
boxwidth        db      ?,0
boxheight       db      ?,0

row1            db      ?
col1            db      ?
row2            db      ?
col2            db      ?

upleft          db      218
upright         db      191
loleft          db      192
loright         db      217
horizontal      db      196
vertical        db      179

altchars        db      201,187,200,188,205,186


;*****************************************************************************
; Procedure MAIN
;*****************************************************************************

main            proc    near
                cld                             ;Clear direction flag
                mov     si,81h                  ;Point SI to command line
                call    findchar                ;Advance to first character
                jnc     parse                   ;Branch if found

error1:         mov     dx,offset msg1          ;Display error message
error2:         mov     ah,09h
                int     21h
                mov     ax,4C01h                ;Exit with ERRORLEVEL=1
                int     21h
;
; Parse the command line.
;
parse:          call    hex2bin                 ;Read "attr"
                mov     dx,offset msg2
                jc      error2
                mov     attr,bl
                call    findchar                ;Advance to next character
                jc      error1

                call    asc2bin                 ;Read "width"
                mov     dx,offset msg2
                jc      error2
                sub     al,2                    ;Normalize "width"
```

```
                jc      error2              ;Error if less than 2
                mov     boxwidth,al
                call    findchar            ;Advance to next character
                jc      error1

                call    asc2bin             ;Read "height"
                mov     dx,offset msg2
                jc      error2
                sub     al,2                ;Normalize "height"
                jc      error2              ;Error if less than 2
                mov     boxheight,al
                call    findchar            ;Advance to next character
                jc      drawbox             ;Branch if there is none

                call    asc2bin             ;Read "style"
                mov     dx,offset msg2
                jc      error2
                cmp     al,1                ;Error if greater than 2
                jb      error2              ;  or less than 1
                cmp     al,2
                ja      error2
                dec     al                  ;Branch if "style"=1
                jz      drawbox

                mov     si,offset altchars  ;Copy alternate graphics
                mov     di,offset upleft    ;  characters to table
                mov     cx,6
                rep     movsb
;
; Draw the box.
;
drawbox:        mov     ah,0Fh              ;Get active page number
                int     10h                 ;  in BH
                mov     ah,03h              ;Get current cursor position
                int     10h                 ;  in DH and DL

                mov     row1,dh             ;Compute corner coordinates
                mov     col1,dl             ;  of box and store them
                add     dh,boxheight        ;  away
                inc     dh
                mov     row2,dh
                add     dl,boxwidth
                inc     dl
                mov     col2,dl

                mov     ah,09h              ;Draw upper left corner
                mov     al,upleft
                mov     bl,attr
                mov     cx,1
                int     10h

                mov     dh,row1             ;Draw upper horizontal
                mov     dl,col1
                inc     dl
```

```
                mov     cx,word ptr boxwidth
                call    drawhorizontal

                mov     ah,02h                  ;Draw upper right corner
                mov     dl,col2
                int     10h
                mov     ah,09h
                mov     al,upright
                mov     cx,1
                int     10h

                inc     dh                      ;Draw right vertical
                mov     cx,word ptr boxheight
                call    drawvertical

                mov     ah,02h                  ;Draw lower right corner
                mov     dh,row2
                int     10h
                mov     ah,09h
                mov     al,loright
                mov     cx,1
                int     10h

                mov     dl,col1                 ;Draw lower horizontal
                inc     dl
                mov     cx,word ptr boxwidth
                call    drawhorizontal

                mov     ah,02h                  ;Draw lower left corner
                dec     dl
                int     10h
                mov     ah,09h
                mov     al,loleft
                mov     cx,1
                int     10h

                mov     dh,row1                 ;Draw left vertical
                inc     dh
                mov     cx,word ptr boxheight
                call    drawvertical

                mov     ah,02h                  ;Home the cursor
                dec     dh
                int     10h

                mov     ax,4C00h                ;Exit with ERRORLEVEL=0
                int     21h
main            endp

;**************************************************************************
; DRAWHORIZONTAL draws a horizontal line at the cursor position passed in
; DH and DL.  Length is specified in CX, attribute in BL, and page number in
; BH.  The line is drawn left to right.
;**************************************************************************
```

```
drawhorizontal  proc    near
                jcxz    dh_exit             ;Exit if length=0
                mov     ah,02h              ;Position the cursor
                int     10h
                mov     ah,09h              ;Draw horizontal
                mov     al,horizontal
                int     10h
dh_exit:        ret
drawhorizontal  endp


;*********************************************************************
; DRAWVERTICAL draws a vertical line at the cursor position passed in
; DH and DL.  Length is specified in CX, attribute in BL, and page number
; in BH.  The line is drawn top to bottom.
;*********************************************************************

drawvertical    proc    near
                jcxz    dv_exit             ;Exit if length=0
dv_loop:        mov     ah,02h              ;Position the cursor
                int     10h
                push    cx                  ;Save CX
                mov     ah,09h              ;Draw one character
                mov     al,vertical
                mov     cx,1
                int     10h
                inc     dh
                pop     cx                  ;Retrieve CX
                loop    dv_loop             ;Loop until done
dv_exit:        ret
drawvertical    endp


;*********************************************************************
; FINDCHAR advances SI to the next non-space or non-comma character.
; On return, carry set indicates EOL was encountered.
;*********************************************************************

findchar        proc    near
                lodsb                       ;Get the next character
                cmp     al,20h              ;Loop if space
                je      findchar
                cmp     al,2Ch              ;Loop if comma
                je      findchar
                dec     si                  ;Point SI to the character
                cmp     al,0Dh              ;Exit with carry set if end
                je      eol                 ; of line is reached

                clc                         ;Clear carry and exit
                ret

eol:            stc                         ;Set carry and exit
                ret
findchar        endp
```

```
;***********************************************************************
; HEX2BIN converts a hex number entered in ASCII form into a binary
; value in BL.  Carry set on return indicates that an error occurred in
; the conversion.
;***********************************************************************

hex2bin         proc    near
                sub     ah,ah                   ;Initialize registers
                sub     bx,bx

h2b_loop:       lodsb                           ;Get a character
                cmp     al,20h                  ;Exit if space
                je      h2b_exit
                cmp     al,2Ch                  ;Exit if comma
                je      h2b_exit
                cmp     al,0Dh                  ;Exit if carriage return
                je      h2b_exit

                cmp     al,"0"                  ;Check for digits "0"
                jb      h2b_error               ;  through "9"
                cmp     al,"9"
                ja      h2b2

                sub     al,30h                  ;ASCII => binary
h2b1:           mov     cl,4                    ;Multiply BX by 16 and
                shl     bx,cl                   ;  add the latest
                add     bx,ax                   ;  digit
                cmp     bx,255                  ;Error if sum > 255
                ja      h2b_error
                jmp     h2b_loop                ;Loop back for more

h2b2:           and     al,0DFh                 ;Capitalize the letter
                cmp     al,"A"                  ;Check range and exit if
                jb      h2b_error               ;  not "A" through "F"
                cmp     al,"F"
                ja      h2b_error
                sub     al,37h                  ;ASCII => binary
                jmp     h2b1                    ;Finish and loop back

h2b_error:      dec     si                      ;Set carry and exit
                stc
                ret

h2b_exit:       dec     si                      ;Clear carry and exit
                clc
                ret
hex2bin         endp

;***********************************************************************
; ASC2BIN converts a decimal number entered in ASCII form into a binary
; value in AL.  Carry set on return indicates that an error occurred in
; the conversion.
;***********************************************************************
```

```
asc2bin        proc    near
               sub     ax,ax                   ;Initialize registers
               sub     bh,bh
               mov     dl,10

a2b_loop:      mov     bl,[si]                 ;Get a character
               inc     si
               cmp     bl,20h                  ;Exit if space
               je      a2b_exit
               cmp     bl,2Ch                  ;Exit if comma
               je      a2b_exit
               cmp     bl,0Dh                  ;Exit if carriage return
               je      a2b_exit

               cmp     bl,"0"                  ;Error if character is not
               jb      a2b_error               ;  a number
               cmp     bl,"9"
               ja      a2b_error

               mul     dl                      ;Multiply the value in AL by
               jc      a2b_error               ;  10 and exit on overflow
               sub     bl,30h                  ;ASCII => binary
               add     ax,bx                   ;Add latest value to AX
               cmp     ax,255                  ;Error if sum > 255
               jna     a2b_loop                ;Loop back for more

a2b_error:     dec     si                      ;Set carry and exit
               stc
               ret

a2b_exit:      dec     si                      ;Clear carry and exit
               clc
               ret
asc2bin        endp

code           ends
               end     begin
```

The command

```
DRAWBOX 2F 20 10 1
```

draws a single-line white-on-green box 20 characters wide and 10 characters high at the current cursor position, while the command

```
DRAWBOX 2F 20 10 2
```

draws a double-line box to the same specification. Normally, you'll call SET-POS before you call DRAWBOX to position the cursor where you want the upper-left corner of the box to be. You can draw a filled box in the center of the screen with the message "Hello, world" with these commands:

```
CLRSCR 6E 9 20 15 59
SETPOS 9 20
DRAWBOX 6E 40 7 1
SETPOS 12 34
TEXTOUT 6E "Hello, world"
```

In fact, there's almost no limit to the number of ways you can come up with to dress up batch file screens with these commands. To illustrate, the batch program in Listing 10.8 combines SETPOS, TEXTOUT, CLRSCR, and DRAW-BOX to build an interactive batch program that pops windows up and down on the screen in response to key presses. Except for the fact that it runs slower than a real application program (an unavoidable consequence of the fact that batch programs are *interpreted*—translated into machine code on the fly—rather than *compiled*, as programs written in languages such as C usually are), DEMO.BAT is virtually indistinguishable from application programs written in professional programming languages that permit programs to take full control of the screen.

LISTING 10.8   DEMO.BAT

```
@ECHO OFF
REM *********************************************
REM
REM DEMO.BAT demonstrates how the keyboard and
REM screen utilities in this chapter may be used
REM to create visual, interactive batch programs.
REM
REM *********************************************
:
CLRSCR 07
:
:DRAWMAIN
CLRSCR 1F 8 30 15 49
SETPOS 8 30
DRAWBOX 1F 20 8
SETPOS 8 34
TEXTOUT 1F " MAIN MENU "
SETPOS 10 32
TEXTOUT 1F "1. Submenu One"
SETPOS 11 32
TEXTOUT 1F "2. Submenu Two"
```

```
SETPOS 12 32
TEXTOUT 1F "3. Submenu Three"
SETPOS 13 32
TEXTOUT 1F "4. Exit to DOS"
SETPOS 26 Ø
:
:GETKEY
BATCHKEY "1" (59) "2" (6Ø) "3" (61) "4" (62)
IF ERRORLEVEL 7 GOTO END
IF ERRORLEVEL 5 GOTO DRAW3
IF ERRORLEVEL 3 GOTO DRAW2
IF ERRORLEVEL 1 GOTO DRAW1
GOTO GETKEY
:
:DRAW1
CLRSCR 4F 2Ø Ø 24 79
SETPOS 2Ø Ø
DRAWBOX 4F 8Ø 5
SETPOS 2Ø 32
TEXTOUT 4F " SUBMENU NO. 1 "
SETPOS 22 31
TEXTOUT 4F "Press Esc to exit"
SETPOS 26 Ø
:DRAW1A
BATCHKEY 27
IF NOT ERRORLEVEL 1 GOTO DRAW1A
CLRSCR Ø7 2Ø Ø 24 79
GOTO GETKEY
:
:DRAW2
CLRSCR 2F Ø Ø 1Ø 79
SETPOS Ø Ø
DRAWBOX 2F 8Ø 11
SETPOS Ø 32
TEXTOUT 2F " SUBMENU NO. 2 "
SETPOS 5 31
TEXTOUT 2F "Press Esc to exit"
SETPOS 26 Ø
:DRAW2A
BATCHKEY 27
IF NOT ERRORLEVEL 1 GOTO DRAW2A
```

```
CLRSCR 07 0 0 10 79
GOTO DRAWMAIN
:
:DRAW3
CLRSCR 6E 10 10 20 69
SETPOS 10 10
DRAWBOX 6E 60 11
SETPOS 10 32
TEXTOUT 6E " SUBMENU NO. 3 "
SETPOS 15 31
TEXTOUT 6E "Press Esc to exit"
SETPOS 26 0
:DRAW3A
BATCHKEY 27
IF NOT ERRORLEVEL 1 GOTO DRAW3A
CLRSCR 07 10 10 20 69
GOTO DRAWMAIN
:
:END
CLRSCR 07
CLRSCR 4F 0 0 0 79
SETPOS 0 1
TEXTOUT 4F "DEMO Finished"
SETPOS 1 0
```

Something you'll notice as you look over the source code for these utilities is that a significant part of the code—often 50 percent or more—is devoted to parsing text entered on the command line. FINDCHAR and ASC2BIN, the two parsing procedures used in BATCHKEY, are used again, and a new procedure called HEX2BIN is introduced to parse hexadecimal strings. The calling and return conventions for HEX2BIN are almost identical to those of ASC2BIN except that the result is returned in BL rather than AL.

A great deal of code is also devoted to error checking. For example, if these utilities find that they're missing a command-line parameter, they'll output a message outlining their syntax. If they encounter an invalid character while converting an ASCII string to its binary equivalent, they'll warn you that an "invalid parameter" was entered. In short, they try to flag errors so the user will know how and why they occurred. It's a good idea to incorporate this type of logic in any utility you write so that new users won't be left wondering why they keep receiving error messages.

These utilities also rely rather heavily on the video BIOS functions accessed through interrupt 10H. SETPOS, for example, sets the cursor position with function 02H; TEXTOUT and DRAWBOX output characters with function

09H; and CLRSCR clears the screen with function 06H. Without these BIOS functions, the code would have had to be considerably more complex, because it would have been forced to interact directly with the display hardware. As we stated in Chapter 9, it's normally advantageous to use BIOS video functions for this reason. These utilities are the first we've come across that illustrate how powerful the BIOS video routines are and how convenient they are to use.

Getting the Time and Date

It's fairly easy to write a batch program that executes one or more commands on a certain day of the month or a particular day of the week. All you need are programs to tap into the system's real-time clock/calendar and tell you what today's date is or what day of the week it is. You can create two such utilities with DEBUG. The first one, WHATDATE.COM, returns an ERRORLEVEL value that reveals the current day of the month (for example, 16 for June 16th). Build it with the following DEBUG script:

```
A 0100
MOV  AH,2A
INT  21
MOV  AH,4C
MOV  AL,DL
INT  21

N WHATDATE.COM
RCX
0A
W
Q
```

The second, WHATDAY.COM, is similar to WHATDATE except that it returns a value from 0 to 6 indicating what day of the week it is, where 0 represents Sunday, 1 represents Monday, and so on. It is created with this DEBUG script:

```
A 0100
MOV  AH,2A
INT  21
MOV  AH,4C
INT  21

N WHATDAY.COM
RCX
08
```

```
W
Q
```

You can place WHATDATE in your AUTOEXEC.BAT file to execute a command on a certain date every month. For example, you might choose to run CHKDSK the first of every month to make sure hard-disk problems don't slip by unnoticed. You could do so with the following addition to AUTOEXEC.BAT:

```
WHATDATE
IF NOT ERRORLEVEL 2 CHKDSK
```

Better yet, you could use WHATDAY to execute CHKDSK every Monday by modifying these statements to read:

```
WHATDAY
IF ERRORLEVEL 1 IF NOT ERRORLEVEL 2 CHKDSK
```

Both utilities rely on DOS function 2AH to get the current date. Function 2AH returns the year in CX, the month (1 through 12) in DH, the day of the month (1 through 31) in DL, and the day of the week (0 through 6) in AL. Thus, you could just as easily write a utility to return the year or month to ERROR-LEVEL. The one catch is that ERRORLEVEL cannot be greater than 255, so the year would have to be adjusted to fit this constraint. You could, for example, return the number of years elapsed since 1980 by subtracting 1,980 from the value function 2AH returns in CX.

It's equally easy to build short DEBUG utilities to return the time in hours and minutes so you can create batch programs that wait until a certain time to act. The following utility, GETHOUR.COM, returns the current hour, 0 through 23:

```
A 0100
MOV  AH,2C
INT  21
MOV  AH,4C
MOV  AL,CH
INT  21

N GETHOUR.COM
RCX
0A
W
Q
```

GETHOUR gets its information from DOS function 2CH, which returns the hour in CH, minutes (0 through 59) in CL, seconds (0 through 59) in DH, and hundredths of a second (0 through 99) in DL. Thus, you could construct a utility to return the current minute with this DEBUG script:

```
A 0100
MOV   AH,2C
INT   21
MOV   AH,4C
MOV   AL,CL
INT   21

N GETMIN.COM
RCX
0A
W
Q
```

The only difference between the two is a single instruction—the one that transfers the value to be returned into AL. Armed with these two utilities, you could build a batch file that waits until a certain time of day to execute a sequence of commands, as follows:

```
:LOOP1
GETHOUR
IF NOT ERRORLEVEL 21 GOTO LOOP1
IF ERRORLEVEL 22 GOTO LOOP1
:LOOP2
GETMIN
IF NOT ERRORLEVEL 30 GOTO LOOP2
CHKDSK
```

This batch file waits until 9:30 p.m. to execute CHKDSK because it waits for GETHOUR to return 21 and GETMIN to return 30 before allowing execution to fall through to the line that calls CHKDSK. Of course, you probably wouldn't need to run CHKDSK this way, but this could be quite useful for running a hard-disk backup program while everyone is away from the office. If your PC is equipped with a tape drive, chances are backups can be performed unattended.

There's an even better way to have batch files wait until an appointed time to launch an operation. Listing 10.9 contains the code for WAITTIL, a small utility that delays until the time entered on the command line arrives. Its syntax is

```
WAITTIL hh:mm[:ss]
```

where *hh* represents hours, *mm* represents minutes, and *ss* represents seconds. Hours should be entered in military time (0 to 23) and seconds are optional. If seconds are omitted, WAITTIL defaults to the equivalent of 00. A batch file equivalent to the one above could be built using WAITTIL with the two simple lines

```
WAITTIL 21:30
CHKDSK
```

Like GETHOUR and GETMIN, WAITTIL uses DOS function 2CH to get the current time from the system's real-time clock. It also checks the keyboard buffer periodically with DOS function 0BH and removes any pending keystrokes with DOS function 08H, so that the loop may be interrupted with a press of Ctrl-C or Ctrl-Break.

LISTING 10.9 WAITTIL.ASM

```
;************************************************************************
; WAITTIL delays until a specified hour, minute, and, optionally, second
; is reached.  Its syntax is:
;
;       WAITTIL hh:mm[:ss]
;
; where "hh" represents hours (miltary format), "mm" minutes, and "ss"
; seconds.  Example:
;
;       WAITTIL 18:30:00
;
; causes a batch file to pause until 6:30 p.m.  The delay loop can be
; interrupted with Ctrl-C or Ctrl-Break.
;************************************************************************

code            segment
                assume  cs:code,ds:code
                org     100h
begin:          jmp     short main

msg1            db      13,10,"Syntax: WAITTIL hh:mm[:ss]",13,10,"$"
msg2            db      13,10,"Invalid parameter",13,10,"$"
hours           db      ?
minutes         db      ?
seconds         db      0


;************************************************************************
; Procedure MAIN
;************************************************************************

main            proc    near
                cld                     ;Clear direction flag
                mov     si,81h          ;Point SI to command line
                call    findchar        ;Advance to first character
                jnc     parse           ;Branch if found
```

```
error1:         mov     dx,offset msg1          ;Error if no command line
error2:         mov     ah,09h                  ;   parameters entered
                int     21h
                mov     ax,4C01h                ;Exit with ERRORLEVEL=1
                int     21h
;
; Parse the command line and determine the specified time.
;
parse:          call    asc2bin                 ;Get hours
                jc      error1
                mov     hours,al
                cmp     bl,3Ah                  ;Syntax error if no colon
                jne     error1
                mov     dx,offset msg2          ;Error if greater than 23
                cmp     al,23
                ja      error2

                call    asc2bin                 ;Get minutes
                jc      error1
                mov     minutes,al
                mov     dx,offset msg2          ;Error if greater than 59
                cmp     al,59
                ja      error2
                cmp     bl,3Ah                  ;Done if no colon
                jne     delay

                call    asc2bin                 ;Get seconds
                jc      error1
                mov     seconds,al
                mov     dx,offset msg2          ;Error if greater than 59
                cmp     al,59
                ja      error2
;
; Wait until the specified time arrives, then terminate.
;
delay:          mov     ah,0Bh                  ;Check the keyboard buffer
                int     21h
                or      al,al                   ;Branch if no key codes are
                jz      gettime                 ;   awaiting processing

                mov     ah,08H                  ;Read character
                int     21h
                or      al,al                   ;Branch if not an extended
                jz      gettime                 ;   key code
                mov     ah,08h                  ;Read extended key code
                int     21h

gettime:        mov     ah,2Ch                  ;Get current time
                int     21h                     ;   from DOS
                cmp     ch,hours                ;Compare hours
                jne     delay
                cmp     cl,minutes              ;Compare minutes
                jb      delay
```

```
                cmp     dh,seconds              ;Compare seconds
                jb      delay
                mov     ax,4C00h                ;Exit with ERRORLEVEL=0
                int     21h
main            endp


;**************************************************************************
; FINDCHAR advances SI to the next non-space character.  On return,
; carry set indicates EOL was encountered.
;**************************************************************************

findchar        proc    near
                lodsb                           ;Get the next character
                cmp     al,20h                  ;Loop if space
                je      findchar
                dec     si                      ;Point SI to the character
                cmp     al,0Dh                  ;Exit with carry set if end
                je      eol                     ;  of line is reached

                clc                             ;Clear carry and exit
                ret

eol:            stc                             ;Set carry and exit
                ret
findchar        endp


;**************************************************************************
; ASC2BIN converts a decimal number entered in ASCII form into a binary
; value in AL.  Carry set on return indicates that an error occurred in
; the conversion.
;**************************************************************************

asc2bin         proc    near
                sub     ax,ax                   ;Initialize registers
                sub     bh,bh
                mov     dl,10

a2b_loop:       mov     bl,[si]                 ;Get a character
                inc     si
                cmp     bl,20h                  ;Exit if space
                je      a2b_exit
                cmp     bl,3Ah                  ;Exit if colon
                je      a2b_exit
                cmp     bl,0Dh                  ;Exit if carriage return
                je      a2b_exit

                cmp     bl,"0"                  ;Error if character is not
                jb      a2b_error               ;  a number
                cmp     bl,"9"
                ja      a2b_error

                mul     dl                      ;Multiply the value in AL by
                jc      a2b_error               ;  10 and exit on overflow
```

```
              sub     bl,30h                ;ASCII => binary
              add     ax,bx                 ;Add latest value to AX
              cmp     ax,255                ;Error if sum > 255
              jna     a2b_loop              ;Loop back for more

a2b_error:    stc                           ;Set carry and exit
              ret

a2b_exit:     clc                           ;Clear carry and exit
              ret
asc2bin       endp

code          ends
              end     begin
```

You can also use WAITTIL to turn your PC into a simple alarm clock. First, type in the following DEBUG script to create a short COM file to beep your PC's speaker:

```
A 0100
MOV  AX,0E07
INT  10
RET

N BEEP.COM
RCX
06
W
Q
```

Then, use EDIT or your favorite text editor to create the following batch file, called ALARM.BAT:

```
WAITTIL %1
:LOOP
BEEP
GOTO LOOP
```

When you want to start the clock ticking, type **ALARM** followed by the time you want the alarm to sound. When the time comes, your PC will start beeping. It won't stop until you press Ctrl-C or Ctrl-Break to terminate the batch file.

Determining Processor and Coprocessor Types

There are occasions when it's useful to know what type of CPU your batch programs are running on. For example, you could check the CPU before running 386-specific applications and abort if the PC contained anything but a 386 or a

486. The same goes for math coprocessors. With a test to determine if a math coprocessor was installed, batch programs could choose to run or avoid running programs that require a floating-point chip.

It's possible to write a utility that returns an ERRORLEVEL code identifying the type of CPU by relying on documented differences between the various Intel CPUs. For example, you can distinguish a 386 from a 486 by toggling a special bit in the EFLAGS register called the *Alignment Check bit* and verifying that EFLAGS changed. On a 386, the Alignment Check bit can't be changed, but on a 486, it can. CPUTYPE, the program whose listing appears in Listing 10.10, demonstrates this and other techniques for identifying Intel CPU chips.

LISTING 10.10 CPUTYPE

```
;******************************************************************************
; CPUTYPE identifies the type of CPU installed in a PC.  On return,
; ERRORLEVEL is set as follows:
;
;       0          8086 or 8088
;       1          80286
;       2          80386
;       3          80486
;
; A CPU identified as a 386 could be either a 386DX or 386SX.
;******************************************************************************

code            segment
                assume  cs:code,ds:code
                org     100h
begin:          jmp     short main

text            db      13,10,"CPU is an 80$"
cpu_8086        db      "86 or 8088$"
cpu_286         db      "286$"
cpu_386         db      "386$"
cpu_486         db      "486$"
crlf            db      13,10,"$"
errorlevel      db      0


;******************************************************************************
; Procedure MAIN
;******************************************************************************

main            proc    near
                mov     ah,09h                      ;Print opening message
                mov     dx,offset text
                int     21h
;
; Test for an 8086/8088 by determing whether SP is decremented before
; or after a PUSH.
;
                mov     dx,offset cpu_8086
                push    sp
                pop     ax
```

```
                cmp     sp,ax
                jne     exit
;
; Test for a 286 by attempting to set the Nested Task (NT) bit in the
; FLAGS register.
;
                mov     dx,offset cpu_286
                inc     errorlevel
                pushf                       ;Push FLAGS
                pop     ax                  ;AX = FLAGS
                or      ax,4000h            ;Set NT bit (bit 14)
                push    ax                  ;Push new value
                popf                        ;Pop it into FLAGS
                pushf                       ;Push FLAGS
                pop     ax                  ;Pop FLAGS into AX
                test    ax,4000h            ;Test bit 14 and exit
                jz      exit                ;  if it's not set

                and     ax,not 4000h        ;Clear the NT bit before
                push    ax                  ;  proceeding
                popf
;
; Separate 386s from 486s by attempting to toggle the Alignment Check (AC)
; bit in the EFLAGS register.
;
                .386
not_286:        mov     dx,offset cpu_386
                inc     errorlevel
                mov     ebx,esp             ;Zero lower 2 bits of ESP
                and     esp,0FFFFFFFCh      ;  to avoid AC fault on 486
                pushfd                      ;Push EFLAGS register
                pop     eax                 ;EAX = EFLAGS
                mov     ecx,eax             ;ECX = EFLAGS
                xor     eax,40000h          ;Toggle AC bit (bit 18) in
                                            ;  EFLAGS register
                push    eax                 ;Push new value
                popfd                       ;Put it in EFLAGS
                pushfd                      ;Push EFLAGS
                pop     eax                 ;EAX = EFLAGS
                and     eax,40000h          ;Isolate bit 18 in EAX
                and     ecx,40000h          ;Isolate bit 18 in ECX
                cmp     eax,ecx             ;Are EAX and ECX equal?
                je      is_386              ;Yes, then it's a 386

                mov     dx,offset cpu_486   ;No, then it's a 486
                inc     errorlevel
                push    ecx                 ;Restore EFLAGS
                popfd

is_386:         mov     esp,ebx             ;Restore ESP
;
; Display CPU type, set return code, and exit.
;
```

```
exit:           mov     ah,09h                  ;Display CPU type
                int     21h
                mov     ah,09h
                mov     dx,offset crlf
                int     21h
                mov     ah,4Ch                  ;Exit with ERRORLEVEL set
                mov     al,errorlevel           ;  indicating CPU type
                int     21h
main            endp

code            ends
                end     begin
```

CPUTYPE returns a value to ERRORLEVEL that identifies the type of CPU installed. A 0 identifies an 8086 or 8088; 1, a 286; 2, a 386 (DX or SX); and 3, a 486. It also sends a message to the screen identifying the CPU that, if desired, can be directed to another file or device (the NUL device if you want output suppressed) using an output redirection operator.

CPUTYPE steps through a decision tree to determine whether a CPU is an 8086/8088, 286, 386, or 486. First, it separates 8086s and 8088s from the rest by seeing if the stack pointer register SP is decremented before or after a PUSH. The 8086 and 8088 decrement SP *before* a value is pushed onto the stack, while all other Intel CPUs decrement it *after* the PUSH occurs. The code sequence

```
push    sp
pop     ax
cmp     sp,ax
jne     exit
```

weeds 8086s and 8088s out of the pack. If a branch occurs, as it will if SP is equal to AX after the PUSH/POP, then the CPU is an 8086 or 8088.

The next test separates 286s from 386s and 486s and involves attempting to set bit 14 (the Nested Task, or NT, bit) of the CPU's FLAGS register. A 286 will not allow this bit to be set, but a 386 or 486 will. If the test

```
pushf
pop     ax
or      ax,4000h
push    ax
popf
pushf
pop     ax
test    ax,4000h
jz      exit
```

branches on the final instruction, then the CPU must be a 286 because the bit remained 0 even though it was set to 1 with the instruction OR AX,4000H. Why all the pushes and pops? The FLAGS register can't be manipulated directly, so CPUTYPE has to get to it in a roundabout way. The instructions

```
pushf
pop      ax
```

retrieve the current value of the FLAGS register into AX. After AX is modified, the statements

```
push     ax
popf
```

copy the value in AX to FLAGS. Using these techniques, an assembly language program can get or set the value of the FLAGS register at will.

Distinguishing a 386 from a 486 requires one more step. The 486 EFLAGS register (EFLAGS is the 32-bit version of FLAGS) contains a bit that is not implemented on the 386: bit 18, better known as the Alignment Check bit. This bit can't be changed on a 386, but it can on a 486. CPUTYPE tests the bit with the following code fragment:

```
pushfd
pop      eax
mov      ecx,eax
xor      eax,40000h
push     eax
popfd
pushfd
pop      eax
and      eax,40000h
and      ecx,40000h
cmp      eax,ecx
je       is_386
```

If this looks remarkably like the code used to test for a 286, that's because it is. The same technique is used to get at the EFLAGS register, the only difference being that the 386 test uses 32-bit registers and instructions. If, at the end, registers EAX and ECX are equal, then the Alignment Check bit was not changed and the CPU must therefore be a 386. Note the .386 directive in the source code, which tells MASM to permit 386 instructions to be included.

Listing 10.11 contains the source code for a companion program, NDPTYPE, which reveals whether or not an NDP (the official name for math coprocessors, which stands for *numeric data processor*) is installed and, if it is, whether it is an 8087, an 80287, or an 80387. The type of NDP installed doesn't necessarily follow from the CPU installed, because in some cases 80287s are paired with 386 CPUs. NDPTYPE returns 0 to ERRORLEVEL if there is no NDP installed; 1, for an 8087; 2, for an 80287; and 3, for an 80387. Note that 486DXs have the equivalent of an 80387 built in, so if you run NDPTYPE on a 486DX, it will report finding an 80387 math coprocessor.

LISTING 10.11 NDPTYPE.ASM

```
;****************************************************************************
; NDPTYPE determines whether or not a math coprocessor is installed and
; identifies it as an 8087, 80287, or 80387.  On return, ERRORLEVEL is
; set as follows:
;
;       0       No coprocessor installed
;       1       8087
;       2       80287
;       3       80387
;
; 486-based PCs will report that an 80387 is installed because the 486
; has the equivalent of an 80387 built in.
;****************************************************************************

                .8087

code            segment
                assume  cs:code,ds:code
                org     100h
begin:          jmp     short main

no_ndp          db      13,10,"No coprocessor installed",13,10,"$"
ndp_is          db      13,10,"Coprocessor is an 80$"
ndp_8087        db      "87$"
ndp_80287       db      "287$"
ndp_80387       db      "387$"
crlf            db      13,10,"$"
cword           dw      0
errorlevel      db      1


;****************************************************************************
; Procedure MAIN
;****************************************************************************

main            proc    near
                fninit                          ;Check for coprocessor
                fnstcw  cword                   ;  by initializing it
                cmp     byte ptr [cword+1],3    ;  and checking to see
                je      ndp_installed           ;  if FNINIT works
                mov     ah,09h                  ;Print "No coprocessor
                mov     dx,offset no_ndp        ;  installed" message
                int     21h
                mov     ax,4C00h                ;Set ERRORLEVEL and exit
                int     21h
```

```
;
; Test for an 8087 by seeing if the FDISI instruction sets the IEM bit
; in the coprocessor control word.
;
ndp_installed:  mov     ah,09h                      ;Print opening message
                mov     dx,offset ndp_is
                int     21h

                mov     dx,offset ndp_8087
                and     cword,0FF7Fh
                fldcw   cword                       ;Load control word
                fdisi                               ;Disable NDP interrupts
                fstcw   cword                       ;Store control word
                test    cword,0080h                 ;Test bit 7
                jnz     exit                        ;Exit if set
;
; Separate 287s from 387s by seeing whether the coprocessor defaults to
; affine (387) or projective closure (287)
;
                mov     dx,offset ndp_80287
                inc     errorlevel
                finit                               ;Initialize the coprocessor
                fld1                                ;Push 1.0 onto the stack
                fldz                                ;Push 0.0 onto the stack
                fdiv                                ;Divide 1.0 by 0.0
                fld     st                          ;Duplicate infinity
                fchs                                ;Change the sign of one
                fcompp                              ;Compare the two infinities
                fstsw   cword                       ;Get status word from compare
                fwait
                mov     ax,cword                    ;Transfer it to FLAGS
                sahf
                jz      exit                        ;287 if infinities equal

                mov     dx,offset ndp_80387         ;It's a 387!
                inc     errorlevel
;
; Display NDP type, set return code, and exit.
;
exit:           mov     ah,09h                      ;Display NDP type
                int     21h
                mov     ah,09h
                mov     dx,offset crlf
                int     21h
                mov     ah,4Ch                      ;Exit with ERRORLEVEL set
                mov     al,errorlevel               ;  indicating NDP type
                int     21h
main            endp

code            ends
                end     begin
```

NDPTYPE also relies on documented differences to distinguish among members of Intel's family of NDPs. The first test checks to see if a math coprocessor is even installed. The code

```
fninit
fnstcw      cword
cmp                 byte ptr [cword+1],3
je                  ndp_installed
```

initializes the NDP (if present) with an FNINIT instruction, transfers the coprocessor control word to CWORD, and then checks to see if the lower half of CWORD is equal to 3. If no coprocessor is installed, CWORD will still be 0— the value it was set to when the program was started. If the compare operation returns true, then NDPTYPE concludes that there must be some type of coprocessor installed in the PC.

The next test separates 8087s from 287s and 387s. On the 8087, an FDISI instruction disables coprocessor interrupts by setting the Interrupt Enable Mask (IEM) bit in the coprocessor control word to 1. The 287 and the 387 ignore FDISI. NDPTYPE manually clears the IEM bit with the statement

```
and         cword,0ff7fh
```

Then it executes the code

```
fldcw       cword
fdisi
fstcw       cword
test        cword,0080h
jnz         exit
```

A branch occurs if FDISI succeeded in setting the IEM bit, indicating that the NDP is of the 8087 variety.

The final test separates 287s from 387s. The basis for the test is that the 287 supports two different forms of infinity control (affine and projective), while the 386 supports only one (affine). *Affine closure* allows infinity to be positive or negative, while *projective closure* uses a single representation for positive and negative infinity. NDPTYPE tests this by initializing the NDP, dividing 1.0 by 0.0 to generate infinity, copying the result and changing the sign, and finally comparing the two infinities. If they are not equal, then closure is affine and the NDP is a 387. If they *are* equal, then projective closure is evidenced and the NDP must, by inference, be a 287. This procedure is embodied in the following fragment of code:

```
finit
fld1
fldz
fdiv
fld       st
fchs
fcompp
fstsw     cword
fwait
mov       ax,cword
sahf
jz        exit
```

If the branch occurs as a result of the JZ instruction, then the coprocessor is a 287. By process of elimination, anything else must be a 387—or the 486 equivalent of a 387.

In a batch file, NDPTYPE might be used like this:

```
NDPTYPE >NUL
IF ERRORLEVEL 1 GOTO RUN
ECHO Math coprocessor required
GOTO END
:RUN
```

An ERRORLEVEL value of 0 indicates that there is no coprocessor installed and gives the batch program a chance to stop before a program requiring a math coprocessor is executed.

With CPUTYPE and NDPTYPE in hand, you can jazz up SYSINFO.BAT (the batch program introduced earlier in this chapter) by adding the following lines to it:

```
ECHO ::::::::::: PROCESSORS ::::::::::::>>SYSINFO.TXT
ECHO. >>SYSINFO.TXT
CPUTYPE >>SYSINFO.TXT
NDPTYPE >>SYSINFO.TXT
ECHO. >>SYSINFO.TXT
```

With this addition, the output file will contain information about the processor and coprocessor types along with everything else. Not bad for a batch file, right?

CPUTYPE and NDPTYPE are useful for more than just making batch files smarter. They're also useful if you're a system manager faced with the task of supporting dozens or perhaps hundreds of PCs. With these utilities, you can quickly determine what CPU a PC is based on and whether it contains a math coprocessor simply by popping in a disk. The alternative is to take the cover off and look inside, which sometimes requires that you remove boards or other hardware components such as disk drives to get a look at the chips on the system board. Most users would agree that the software method is easier.

Rebooting Your PC from a Batch File

In these days of multiple operating systems and operating environments, 386 memory managers, expanded memory simulators, and DOS-extended applications, it's not unusual for PC users to have to maintain multiple CONFIG.SYS and AUTOEXEC.BAT files and to switch between them. For example, many DOS 5.0 users who also run Windows 3 keep two different sets of system configuration files—one for DOS, one for Windows—and boot from the set that starts the operating environment that is most appropriate to the task at hand. If you do this, you probably rename files and press Ctrl-Alt-Del often. A batch file and a small utility you can create with DEBUG can make the chore of maintaining multiple system files much easier.

The batch file in Listing 10.12 shows how. Let's say you keep one set of configuration files for DOS and one set for Windows. With DOS running, you'd like to be able to switch to Windows by typing BOOT WINDOWS. Similarly, with Windows running, typing BOOT DOS should restart the system without Windows. That's what BOOT.BAT does. To start DOS, BOOT renames the DOS configuration files CONFIG.DOS and AUTOEXEC.DOS as CONFIG.SYS and AUTOEXEC.BAT. To boot Windows, it renames CONFIG.WIN and AUTOEXEC.WIN the same way. It both cases, it renames the existing system files using the extension .WIN or .DOS so that they will be preserved. BOOT can easily be modified to accommodate even more configuration options.

LISTING 10.12

```
BOOT.BAT
@ECHO OFF
REM **********************************************
REM
REM            BOOT.BAT boots DOS or Windows
REM
REM **********************************************
:
IF "%1"=="" GOTO SYNTAX
SET %1=$$
IF "%DOS%"=="$$" GOTO DOS
IF "%WINDOWS%"=="$$" GOTO WINDOWS
:SYNTAX
ECHO Syntax: BOOT DOS or WINDOWS
GOTO END
:
:DOS
```

```
REN C:\CONFIG.SYS CONFIG.WIN
REN C:\CONFIG.DOS CONFIG.SYS
REN C:\AUTOEXEC.BAT AUTOEXEC.WIN
REN C:\AUTOEXEC.DOS AUTOEXEC.BAT
REBOOT
:
:WINDOWS
REN C:\CONFIG.SYS CONFIG.DOS
REN C:\CONFIG.WIN CONFIG.SYS
REN C:\AUTOEXEC.BAT AUTOEXEC.DOS
REN C:\AUTOEXEC.WIN AUTOEXEC.BAT
REBOOT
:
:END
```

To reboot your PC, BOOT uses REBOOT.COM, which you can create with this DEBUG script:

```
A 0100
MOV   AX,40
MOV   ES,AX
ES:
MOV   WORD PTR [72],1234
JMP   FFFF:0000

N REBOOT.COM
RCX
11
W
Q
```

REBOOT.COM performs a warm restart by jumping to the same point in the ROM BIOS that the CPU jumps to when your PC is powered on. When an Intel CPU is started up, its first act is to execute the instruction at FFFF:0000. In the IBM PC, that address contains a JMP instruction that jumps to another location in ROM and starts the POST (Power On Self-Test) sequence. REBOOT simulates this by jumping to FFFF:0000 with a JMP instruction of its own, but only after placing a 1234H in the word at 0040:0072. During start-up, the BIOS looks at this word value to determine whether to perform a warm reset (the kind you get when you press Ctrl-Alt-Del) or a cold reset (the kind you get when you flip the power switch off and on); a 1234H forces a warm reset. Thus, running REBOOT has the same effect as pressing Ctrl-Alt-Del.

Compiling Batch Files for Added Speed

One of the drawbacks to running batch files is that they're slow compared to binary executable files with .COM or .EXE extensions. That's because batch files are *interpreted*, meaning they're read one line at a time and each line is translated into machine code as the program is executed. Compiled programs, by contrast, are translated into machine code ahead of time and stored on disk as series of binary CPU instructions, allowing them to execute more quickly. One example that illustrates the difference between interpreted and compiled programming environments compares DOS 5.0's QBasic interpreter with Microsoft's QuickBASIC compiler. Both run the same BASIC-language programs, but programs compiled with QuickBASIC run slightly faster than those run in the QBasic environment.

This book comes with a utility called BAT2EXEC, which compiles batch programs the same way QuickBASIC compiles BASIC programs. It produces fast-running, stand-alone COM files that perform the same functions as the BAT files they were generated from. BAT2EXEC was written by *PC Magazine* programmer Doug Boling and was originally published in *PC Magazine*'s "Utilities" column. Its syntax is simply

```
BAT2EXEC [d:][path]filename
```

where *filename* is the name of the batch file you want to compile, complete with .BAT extension. When run, BAT2EXEC produces a file with the same name and the extension .COM. You can run it as you can any other .COM file: by typing its name or by invoking it by name from another batch file.

COM files produced by BAT2EXEC will run several times faster than the equivalent BAT files, and the longer the batch file, the greater the difference in speed. If, while compiling a program, BAT2EXEC encounters a command it doesn't understand, it will apprise you with an error message. In general, it's a good idea to write and debug a batch file in BAT form, and then to convert it to COM form once everything is working. Note that if you make changes to a BAT file after compiling it with BAT2EXEC, you'll have to recompile it to incorporate those changes in the COM version. Also be aware that if the program references any external commands, program names, or other batch files, the corresponding files must be available on disk. For example, if the program contains the command CHKDSK, then CHKDSK.EXE must be in the current directory or in the PATH. CHKDSK.EXE does *not* become part of the compiled batch program.

There are some batch files that should not be compiled. For example, DOS will not recognize AUTOEXEC.BAT if it is compiled to COM form. Also, you should not compile batch programs that load TSR-type utilities, because once the TSR is installed, DOS cannot reclaim the memory that belonged to the COM file that loaded the TSR. Other than that, you can use BAT2EXEC to compile just about any batch program you want.

There are a few other differences between compiled and interpreted batch files, aside from speed. First, batch programs compiled with BAT2EXEC do not echo commands to the screen, even if ECHO was not turned off. Also, pressing Ctrl-C or Ctrl-Break as a compiled batch program runs does not produce the message "Terminate batch job (Y/N)?"; instead, it terminates the program altogether. Finally, running another batch file without a CALL command does not terminate the current program.

Summary

With the techniques and utilities presented in this chapter, you now have the ability to

- Call subroutines from batch files

- Perform batch string comparisons ignoring case

- Use a batch file to create a complete system summary

- Dial your phone from a batch file

- Have a batch file return to the drive and directory it started from

- Dress up batch file screens with color and pop-up windows

- Get input from the keyboard to a batch file

- Execute a batch routine at a certain time, on a certain date, or on a certain day of the week

- Have a batch file determine what type of CPU and math coprocessor your PC contains

- Reboot your PC from a batch file

- Compile batch files for added speed

You can probably think of several more utilities that would be useful to batch file programmers. It wouldn't hurt to have utilities to produce tones on the PC's speaker and to perform string operations on environment variables so that, for example, you could extract one string from the middle of another one and do a comparison on the result. Some useful batch file utilities are trivial to write given the multitude of DOS and BIOS functions available. ECHODRV.COM and ECHOCD.COM are two very good examples. ECHODRV.COM only required two DOS functions; ECHOCD.COM, just one. If nothing else, it is hoped that this chapter will help you when it comes to writing your own batch file utilities, not only by providing working examples, but also by providing useful assembly language routines that you can reuse in your own programs.

FILE, DIRECTORY, AND DISK UTILITIES

IT ALMOST GOES WITHOUT SAYING THAT DOS IS A VERY FILE- AND DISK-ORIENTED operating system, as any operating system must be. As such, it offers a wide variety of tools for managing files and the disks those files are stored on. Be that as it may, it's not too difficult to come up with a list of useful disk and file management commands that are *not* included with DOS—commands for renaming subdirectories, for example, and for removing subdirectories that contain subdirectories of their own.

The five utilities introduced in this chapter will help remedy some of DOS's shortcomings in these areas. In the order in which they are presented, they are

- NUKE, which deletes a subdirectory and everything in it, including files and other subdirectories

- RENDIR, which renames subdirectories just like REN renames files

- ENCRYPT, which password-encrypts files to secure them against unauthorized access

- FINDTEXT, which searches a disk (or part of a disk) for files that contain a specified text string

- CDX, which changes directories based on partial path or directory names, or based on the files contained inside a directory

These utilities illustrate how easy it is to create full-fledged utilities to run in the DOS environment. With the exception of FINDTEXT (and CDX, which was written in C and whose source code is not presented here), they are relatively compact—a tribute both to the power of assembly language and to the programming support that DOS provides.

Pruning Branches from a Directory Tree

How often have you found yourself needing to remove a subdirectory from your hard disk, only to discover that it contains other subdirectories, and that those subdirectories contain even more subdirectories? Suddenly, what appeared to be a quick and easy job has become a long and arduous one. Without a special utility to help, your only recourse is to manually walk the directory tree from the bottom up, deleting subdirectories and files as you go. If this particular branch of the directory tree contains many subtrees, getting rid of it in its entirety could take a long time.

Now you have a utility, NUKE, that does this work for you. NUKE works its way recursively through all the branches of a directory tree until it has removed them all. It's simple, it's fast, and it's easy to use. And at less than 1k long, it will scarcely dent the free space on your hard disk.

The syntax for NUKE is

```
NUKE [d:]path
```

where *d:* is the drive where the action is to be performed and *path* is the name of the directory to be removed. The command

```
NUKE C:\ACAD
```

nukes everything from the ACAD directory of the C drive on down. When NUKE is done, ACAD will no longer exist on the drive—nor will any of the files or subdirectories that were previously in it. If drive C is the default drive, the command

```
NUKE \ACAD
```

will do the same thing. NUKE deletes *everything* from the specified directory and its descendants, including hidden, system, and read-only files. It will even delete hidden subdirectories. The *d:* parameter to NUKE is optional, but the *path* parameter is not, for the simple reason that NUKE could be a very dangerous utility if misused. By forcing you to specify a path name, NUKE makes you think about what you're doing and attempts to avert the kind of disaster that might be brought on if you could type NUKE all by itself on the command line and have NUKE delete everything from the current directory on down.

To get help with NUKE, type

```
NUKE /?
```

You know by now that DOS 5.0 has standardized the /? switch as a means for getting help with command-line utilities. Run any DOS command with a /? switch and you'll get anywhere from one or two lines to a whole screenful of information describing what it does and how it's used. For consistency, NUKE (and the other programs presented in this chapter) also recognizes this convention.

You can erase an entire disk by having NUKE start at the root directory, which by definition must be the highest directory on the disk. For example, the command

```
NUKE A:\
```

deletes all the files and subdirectories from the disk in drive A. Be very careful when using NUKE, especially when you use it this way. Once you prune a branch from the directory tree, most of the files that were stored there will be unrecoverable. You may be able to recover the files stored in the topmost directory with the UNDELETE command, but you won't be able to recover the other ones without restoring the deleted subdirectories, too. And restoring subdirectories is something UNDELETE doesn't do.

Inside NUKE

For budding utilities writers, there's much to be learned from the source code listing for NUKE, shown in Listing 11.1. Even though the listing is fairly short, its length still prohibits dissecting it line by line here. However, for this and the other programs in this chapter, areas of interest in the code will be highlighted. Also, how the program works will be discussed, so later on you can apply some of its procedures and methods to programs of your own.

LISTING 11.1 NUKE.ASM

```
;**************************************************************************
; NUKE deletes an entire directory full of files and all the files
; and subdirectories in it.  Its syntax is:
;
;        NUKE [d:]path
;
; where "path" is the name of the top-level subdirectory to be removed.
; NUKE will delete files and subdirectories with hidden, read-only, and
; system attributes, but it cannot delete the root directory.  Careful:
; Starting NUKE at the root directory level will erase an entire disk.
;**************************************************************************

code            segment
                assume  cs:code,ds:code
                org     100h
begin:          jmp     main

helpmsg         db      "Deletes a subdirectory and everything in it.",13,10
                db      13,10
                db      "NUKE [d:]path",13,10,"$"

errmsg1         db      "Syntax: NUKE [d:]path",13,10,"$"
errmsg2         db      "Invalid drive specification",13,10,"$"
errmsg3         db      "Invalid path specification",13,10,"$"
errmsg4         db      "Unable to remove attribute(s) from $"
errmsg5         db      "Unable to delete $"
errmsg6         db      "Unable to remove $"
errmsg7         db      "Not enough memory",13,10,"$"
msg1            db      "Removed $"

drive           db      ?                       ;Home drive
updir           db      "..",0                  ;Command to move up a level
filespec        db      "*.*",0                 ;File spec for searches
homedir db      "\",64 dup (?)                  ;Name of home directory
currdir db      "x:\",64 dup (?)                ;Name of current directory
```

```
;**************************************************************************
; Procedure MAIN
;**************************************************************************

main            proc    near
                cld                             ;Clear direction flag
                mov     si,81h                  ;Point SI to command line
                call    scanhelp                ;Scan for "/?" switch
                jnc     checkmem                ;Branch if not found
                mov     ah,09h                  ;Display help text and exit
                mov     dx,offset helpmsg       ;   with ERRORLEVEL=0
                int     21h
                mov     ax,4C00h
                int     21h

checkmem:       mov     dx,offset errmsg7       ;Make sure there's enough
                cmp     sp,4000h                ;   memory to run the
                ja      parse                   ;   program

error:          mov     ah,09h                  ;Display error message and
                int     21h                     ;   exit with ERRORLEVEL=1
                mov     ax,4C01h
                int     21h
;
; Parse the command line.
;
parse:          call    findchar                ;Find first parameter
                jnc     charfound               ;Branch if found
error1:         mov     dx,offset errmsg1       ;Error if not
                jmp     error
;
; Save the current drive and directory.
;
charfound:      push    si                      ;Save address
                mov     ah,19h                  ;Get default drive and
                int     21h                     ;   save it in DRIVE
                mov     drive,al
                mov     ah,47h                  ;Get current directory and
                sub     dl,dl                   ;   save it in HOMEDIR
                mov     si,offset homedir+1
                int     21h
                pop     si
;
; Go to the drive and directory entered on the command line.
;
                push    si
                call    finddelim               ;Find end of entry
                mov     byte ptr [si],0         ;Convert to ASCIIZ
                pop     si                      ;Retrieve starting address
                cmp     byte ptr [si+1],":"     ;Branch if path does not
                jne     nodrive                 ;   contain a drive code

                mov     al,byte ptr [si+2]      ;Make sure a directory name
                cmp     al,20h                  ;   appears after the drive
                je      error1                  ;   code
```

```
                cmp     al,2Ch
                je      error1
                cmp     al,0
                je      error1

                lodsb                           ;Get drive code
                and     al,0DFh                 ;Capitalize it
                sub     al,41h                  ;Normalize it (0=A, 1=B...)
                mov     ah,0Eh                  ;Set default drive
                mov     dl,al
                int     21h
                mov     ah,19h                  ;See if it worked by seeing
                int     21h                     ;  what is now the default
                cmp     al,dl                   ;Error if AL != DL
                mov     dx,offset errmsg2
                jne     error
                inc     si                      ;Point SI to directory name

nodrive:        mov     ah,19h                  ;Get default drive and add
                int     21h                     ;  it to CURRDIR for
                add     al,41h                  ;  status messages
                mov     currdir,al
                mov     ah,3Bh                  ;Change directories
                mov     dx,si
                int     21h
                jnc     nukem                   ;Branch if the call succeeded
                mov     ah,0Eh                  ;Restore the default drive
                mov     dl,drive                ;  and exit if it did not
                int     21h
                mov     dx,offset errmsg3
                jmp     error
;
; Nuke everything from the current directory down.
;
nukem:          call    nuke                    ;Nuke everything

                mov     ah,47h                  ;Get current directory
                sub     dl,dl
                mov     si,offset currdir+3
                int     21h
                mov     ah,3Bh                  ;Go up one level
                mov     dx,offset updir
                int     21h
                jc      root                    ;Branch if root directory

                mov     ah,3Ah                  ;Remove the final
                mov     dx,offset currdir       ;  subdirectory
                int     21h
                jnc     showdir                 ;Branch if call succeeded
                mov     dx,offset errmsg6       ;Error if subdirectory could
                jmp     fatal_exit              ;  not be removed

showdir:        call    status                  ;Display directory name

root:           mov     ah,0Eh                  ;Restore default drive
                mov     dl,drive
```

```
                int     21h
                mov     ah,3Bh                  ;Restore current directory
                mov     dx,offset homedir
                int     21h

main_exit:      mov     ax,4C00h                ;Exit with ERRORLEVEL=0
                int     21h
main            endp


;***************************************************************************
; FINDCHAR advances SI to the next non-space or non-comma character.
; On return, carry set indicates EOL was encountered.
;***************************************************************************

findchar        proc    near
                lodsb                           ;Get the next character
                cmp     al,20h                  ;Loop if space
                je      findchar
                cmp     al,2Ch                  ;Loop if comma
                je      findchar
                dec     si                      ;Point SI to the character
                cmp     al,0Dh                  ;Exit with carry set if end
                je      eol                     ;  of line is reached

                clc                             ;Clear carry and exit
                ret

eol:            stc                             ;Set carry and exit
                ret
findchar        endp


;***************************************************************************
; FINDDELIM advances SI to the next space or comma character.  On return,
; carry set indicates EOL was encountered.
;***************************************************************************

finddelim       proc    near
                lodsb                           ;Get the next character
                cmp     al,20h                  ;Exit if space
                je      fd_exit
                cmp     al,2Ch                  ;Exit if comma
                je      fd_exit
                cmp     al,0Dh                  ;Loop back for more if end
                jne     finddelim               ;  of line isn't reached

                dec     si                      ;Set carry and exit
                stc
                ret

fd_exit:        dec     si                      ;Clear carry and exit
                clc
                ret
finddelim       endp
```

```
;*************************************************************************
; SCANHELP scans the command line for a /? switch.  If found, carry returns
; set and SI contains its offset.  If not found, carry returns clear.
;*************************************************************************

scanhelp        proc    near
                push    si                      ;Save SI
scanloop:       lodsb                           ;Get a character
                cmp     al,0Dh                  ;Exit if end of line
                je      scan_exit
                cmp     al,"?"                  ;Loop if not "?"
                jne     scanloop
                cmp     byte ptr [si-2],"/"     ;Loop if not "/"
                jne     scanloop

                add     sp,2                    ;Clear the stack
                sub     si,2                    ;Adjust SI
                stc                             ;Set carry and exit
                ret

scan_exit:      pop     si                      ;Restore SI
                clc                             ;Clear carry and exit
                ret
scanhelp        endp


;*************************************************************************
; NUKE clears out files and subdirectories.  It sets up a DTA on the stack
; and calls itself recursively to get the job done.  The directory that is
; current when NUKE is called is the one that is cleared out.
;*************************************************************************

nuke            proc    near
                push    bp                      ;Save BP
                mov     ah,2Fh                  ;Get current DTA address
                int     21h
                push    bx                      ;Save it
                push    es
                sub     sp,2Bh                  ;Make room on the stack
                mov     bp,sp                   ;Establish addressability
                mov     ah,1Ah                  ;Set DTA address to a
                mov     dx,bp                   ;  location in the
                int     21h                     ;  stack
;
; Find the first file or subdirectory name.
;
                mov     ah,4Eh                  ;Call function 4Eh (DOS
                mov     cx,17h                  ;  Find First)
                mov     dx,offset filespec
                int     21h
                jnc     testname                ;Proceed if call succeeded
;
; Restore BP, the DTA, and the stack, then exit.
;
nuke_exit:      add     sp,2Bh                  ;Adjust the stack pointer
                mov     ah,1Ah                  ;Restore the DTA to where
                mov     bx,ds                   ;  it was on entry
```

```
                pop     ds
                pop     dx
                int     21h
                mov     ds,bx
                pop     bp                  ;Restore BP
                ret                         ;Return to caller
;
; Find another entry and decide what to do with it.
;
findnext:       mov     ah,4Fh              ;Call function 4Fh (DOS
                int     21h                 ;  Find Next)
                jc      nuke_exit           ;Exit if nothing found

testname:       cmp     byte ptr [bp+30],2Eh   ;Skip . and .. entries
                je      findnext
                test    byte ptr [bp+21],10h   ;Branch if name returned is
                jnz     rmdir               ;  a subdirectory name
;
; Delete the file whose name was just returned.
;
                mov     ax,4301h            ;Remove any existing file
                sub     cx,cx               ;  attributes with a call
                mov     dx,bp               ;  to DOS function 43h
                add     dx,30
                int     21h
                mov     dx,offset errmsg4
                jc      fatal_exit          ;Exit if call failed

                mov     ah,41h              ;Delete the file
                mov     dx,bp
                add     dx,30
                int     21h
                mov     dx,offset errmsg5
                jc      fatal_exit          ;Exit if call failed
                jmp     findnext            ;Loop back for more
;
; Clear out and remove the subdirectory whose name was just returned.
;
rmdir:          mov     ah,3Bh              ;Change to the subdirectory
                mov     dx,bp
                add     dx,30
                int     21h

                call    nuke                ;Clear it out

                mov     ah,47h              ;Get current directory
                sub     dl,dl
                mov     si,offset currdir+3
                int     21h
                mov     ah,3Bh              ;Go up a directory level
                mov     dx,offset updir
                int     21h
                mov     ah,3Ah              ;Remove the subdirectory
                mov     dx,bp
                add     dx,30
                int     21h
```

```
                mov     dx,offset errmsg6       ;Exit on error
                jc      fatal_exit

                call    status                  ;Show directory name
                jmp     findnext                ;Loop back for more
;
; A fatal error occurred.  Say what it was and terminate.
;
fatal_exit:     mov     bx,dx                   ;Save DX in BX
                mov     ah,09h                  ;Display error message
                int     21h
                cmp     bx,offset errmsg6       ;Branch if file delete
                jne     showfile                ;  error

                call    status2                 ;Display directory name
                jmp     short fatal2            ;  and exit

showfile:       mov     si,offset currdir       ;Display directory name
                call    textout
                cmp     byte ptr [si-2],"\"     ;Append a backslash if
                je      noslash                 ;  it's not the root
                mov     ah,02h                  ;  directory
                mov     dl,"\"
                int     21h
noslash:        mov     si,bp                   ;Display file name too
                add     si,30
                call    textout

fatal2:         mov     ah,0Eh                  ;Restore default drive
                mov     dl,drive
                int     21h
                mov     ah,3Bh                  ;Restore current directory
                mov     dx,offset homedir
                int     21h
                mov     ax,4C01h                ;Exit with ERRORLEVEL=1
                int     21h
nuke            endp


;***********************************************************************
; STATUS displays the name of the subdirectory that was just removed.
;***********************************************************************

status          proc    near
                mov     ah,09h                  ;Print "Removed"
                mov     dx,offset msg1
                int     21h
status2:        mov     si,offset currdir       ;Display directory name
                call    textout
                mov     ah,09h                  ;Move cursor to next line
                mov     dx,offset errmsg1+21
                int     21h
                ret
status          endp
```

```
;*********************************************************************
; TEXTOUT displays the ASCIIZ text string pointed to by DS:SI.
;*********************************************************************

textout         proc    near
                lodsb                           ;Get a character
                or      al,al                   ;Exit if zero
                jz      to_exit
                mov     ah,02h                  ;Display it using DOS
                mov     dl,al                   ;  function 02H
                int     21h
                jmp     textout                 ;Loop back for more
to_exit:        ret
textout         endp

code            ends
                end     begin
```

The first thing NUKE does when it is started is prepare to parse the command line by clearing the direction flag (the flag that determines whether string instructions such as LODSB work in forward or reverse), pointing SI to the text of the command line in the PSP, and scanning for a /? switch with the code

```
cld
mov     si,81h
call    scanhelp
```

The procedure SCANHELP appears midway through the listing. All it does is scan the command line for "/" characters and, when it finds one, checks to see if it is followed by a question mark. If SCANHELP returns with the carry flag clear, then no /? switch was found. If, however, carry returns set, then SCAN-HELP *did* find a /? switch, and NUKE executes the lines

```
mov     ah,09h
mov     dx,offset helpmsg
int     21h
mov     ax,4C00h
int     21h
```

to display the help message HELPMSG (using DOS function 09H) and exit with a return code of 0 (using DOS function 4CH). Since the command line is scanned for /? switches from beginning to end and all other parameters are ignored during the scan, NUKE will stop and display a help message if it's started with a /?, no matter what else appears on the command line.

NUKE's next act is to verify that there's enough memory for it to run in. When a COM file is loaded into memory, DOS picks a 64k segment for it to reside in and initializes all four segment registers—CS, DS, ES, and SS—to the address of the segment. The PSP occupies the first 100H bytes of the segment, code and data come next (at offset 100H), and the stack goes at the top, where it grows downward in memory. NUKE's code and data together take less than 1k of RAM, and while the size of the stack is both variable and dynamic, a stack will rarely ever exceed about 1k in length. 64k is plenty of space for NUKE to work in because the stack would have to grow to approximately 63k before it would threaten to overwrite code and data.

The problem is that there's no guarantee that the program will be assigned a 64k data space. If there is less than 64k of RAM available when NUKE is executed, DOS will load it anyway and leave it to NUKE to adjust to the lesser amount of RAM or decide to terminate itself if it judges that the memory it was allocated is not sufficient. 64k may not seem like much memory, but if you shell out to DOS from a large application program on a 640k PC, it's quite likely that there will be less than half that amount of RAM available—possibly even less than 64k.

NUKE verifies that it has enough memory by checking the value of the SP register, which points to the bottom of the stack and is therefore a pretty good indicator of the size of the segment the program was loaded into. The code that performs the check looks like this:

```
MOV     DX,OFFSET ERRMSG7
CMP     SP,4000H
JA      PARSE
```

Normally, when a COM program is allocated a full 64k segment, SP is set to FFFEH on entry. If SP is less than 4000H, indicating that the segment in which the program was loaded is smaller than 16k, NUKE aborts with an error message saying there isn't enough memory. NUKE could probably work with less memory than that, but it's important to leave a comfortable margin of error here to avoid a system crash, which is exactly what will happen if the stack grows downward until it collides with code or data. As you'll see in a moment, NUKE is unusually stack-intensive for a program of its size, so that's even more reason to provide the stack plenty of room to grow in.

NUKE calls the procedure FINDCHAR to locate the first character beyond the command name on the command line, which should correspond to the name of the directory (and possibly the drive) where NUKE will begin working. If no parameter is found (if the end of the line is encountered before a character is), NUKE aborts and displays a message that reminds the user of its syntax. How does it detect the end of the line? The end of the command line is marked by a carriage return character, ASCII code 13. As it scans the command line for characters, FINDCHAR also looks for carriage returns. If it encounters a carriage return before it encounters text, FINDCHAR sets the carry flag before returning so that the caller may take appropriate action.

Provided FINDCHAR returns with carry clear, NUKE's next act is to save the current drive and directory so that it may return to them later. The instructions

```
mov     ah,19h
int     21h
mov     drive,al
```

save the code for the current drive in the byte-sized memory location named DRIVE, while the instructions

```
mov     ah,47h
sub     dl,dl
mov     si,offset homedir+1
int     21h
```

save the name of the current directory. The current drive is obtained through DOS function 19H, which returns a value in AL that indicates what drive is the default (0=A, 1=B, 2=C, and so on). The current directory is obtained by placing a call to DOS function 47H, which accepts a drive code in DL (0=default drive, 1=A, 2=B, and so on) and the address of a 64-byte text buffer in DS:SI. On return, the buffer holds an ASCII string denoting the current directory, minus a leading backslash. Because the directory name returned by function 47H must include a backslash, NUKE initializes the first character in the buffer to "\" and passes DOS the address of the character *after* the backslash. Later, it can return to the same directory by calling DOS function 3BH with DS:DX pointing to the beginning of the buffer.

The next several lines of code parse the path name entered on the command and change to the indicated drive and directory. First, NUKE has to determine whether the parameter even contains a drive code. If the second character is a colon, NUKE assumes that the first character is a drive letter and attempts to change to that drive using DOS function 0EH. Unlike most DOS functions, function 0EH does not indicate success or failure by the state of the carry flag. To make sure the call succeeded, NUKE asks DOS for the default drive and compares it to the one just set. If the two drive codes are not equal, it terminates and prints an "Invalid drive specification" error message.

After the drive issue is settled, NUKE changes to the directory named on the command line by placing a call to DOS function 3BH. If carry returns set, NUKE terminates with the error message "Invalid path specification." If, however, carry returns clear, then NUKE is at the drive and directory location specified on the command line and is finally ready to start to work.

Recursion

At this point, NUKE is ready to start deleting files and removing subdirectories, acts that are accomplished easily enough with DOS functions 41H (Delete File) and 3AH (Remove Subdirectory). These functions are the kernel equivalents of the DEL and RD commands. However, there's a problem: If the current directory contains subdirectories of its own, NUKE must remove those subdirectories before it can remove the current one. And if those contain still more subdirectories, it needs to regress yet another level deeper into the directory structure before it begins its work.

To accomplish this, NUKE places a call to the procedure named NUKE. When the procedure call returns, all the files and subdirectories from the current directory down are gone. How does it work? NUKE (the procedure) employs a technique called *recursion*. By definition, recursion occurs when a procedure calls itself. A recursive procedure may call itself many times if necessary, each time repeating the instructions that determine if another call is required. When NUKE is called, it searches for subdirectories in the current directory. If it finds a subdirectory, it makes it the current one, then it calls itself to check *that* subdirectory for even more subdirectories, and so on, until it has worked its way to the very bottom of the directory tree.

Once it reaches a directory that contains no subdirectories of its own, NUKE deletes all the files in it, and then returns to the procedure that called it by executing a RET instruction. The procedure that called it, of course, is probably another instance of NUKE. On return, this latter instance of NUKE calls DOS function 3BH with DS:DX pointing to the string ".." to move up a directory level and DOS function 3AH to erase the subdirectory it just came from. Then it searches what is now the current directory for yet another subdirectory and descends into it. Only when all the subdirectories have been removed does NUKE finally erase the files in this directory and execute a RET instruction to return to the procedure that called it.

Eventually, NUKE will work its way back to the directory it started from. Then it clears out that final directory, removes it, and its job is finished. At that point, the procedure MAIN takes over again, restores the default drive and directory, and terminates. If it can't return to the default directory because that directory was removed, NUKE moves to the parent directory of the branch of the tree that was pruned.

Figure 11.1 depicts this process pictorially for a branch of the directory tree that comprises a total of five subdirectories. In step 1, NUKE descends to the subdirectory \WP\DOC, sees that there is a subdirectory named BUSINESS, and, in step 2, descends to \WP\DOC\BUSINESS. In step 3, NUKE removes all the files from the \WP\DOC\BUSINESS subdirectory, and, in step 4, ascends back to \WP\DOC and removes \WP\DOC\BUSINESS. In steps 5 through 7, it repeats this procedure for \WP\DOC\PERSONAL. In steps 8 and 9, with all the subdirectories now deleted from \WP\DOC, NUKE erases all the files there, goes back to the WP directory, and removes \WP\DOC. In steps 10 through 12, NUKE descends to \WP\TMP, erases all the files there, returns to \WP, and removes \WP\TMP. Finally, in step 13, it deletes all the files from \WP—the directory in which it started.

One complication that recursion brings with it is that before a procedure calls itself, it must save everything it's going to need later on. NUKE uses a

FIGURE 11.1

Traversing the directory tree

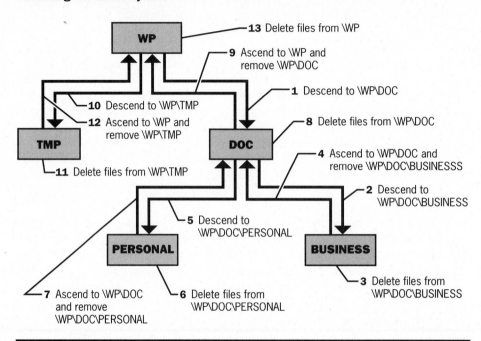

technique that high-level languages such as C and Pascal use: It saves data on the stack. The first thing NUKE does when it is called is execute the instructions

```
push    bp
mov     ah,2Fh
int     21h
push    bx
push    es
sub     sp,2Bh
```

which saves the current value of the BP register, saves the address of the current Disk Transfer Area, or DTA, and makes room on the stack for more data by subtracting 2BH (37 decimal) from SP. Remember that the stack grows downward in memory, so decrementing SP increases the size of the stack. These 37 bytes become the new DTA when the instructions

```
mov     bp,sp
mov     ah,1Ah
mov     dx,bp
int     21h
```

are executed (each instance of NUKE that is executed needs a unique area for its DTA that will not be overwritten by other instances of the same procedure). Conversely, the last thing NUKE does before it returns to the procedure that called it is execute the instructions

```
add    sp,2Bh
mov    ah,1Ah
mov    bx,ds
pop    ds
pop    dx
int    21h
mov    ds,bx
pop    bp
```

which undoes everything that was done on entry. It shrinks the size of the stack by 37 bytes, restores the address of the DTA, and restores the value of BP. When execution returns to the caller, the system is restored to the exact state it was in when the call was placed.

Earlier, it was stated that NUKE was unusually stack-intensive. Now you understand why. For every level it descends into the directory structure, it requires another 43 bytes of stack space (37 bytes for the DTA, plus two each to store BP, BX, and ES, which it PUSHes onto the stack) for temporary storage. This may sound like a lot, and it is, compared with the modest needs of most programs. But in reality it's not all that unreasonable because the directory structure can never be more than 32 levels deep. DOS places a 64-character limit on the length of path names, and each directory name in the path must be separated by a backslash character. Thus, the longest directory name you could create would be 32 levels deep if each subdirectory name were but 1 character long. As a result, the maximum amount of temporary storage space that NUKE could ever require on the stack would be 32 times 37, or 1,184 bytes. Compared with the minimum of 16k it ensures it has available when it is started, that is a small amount of memory indeed.

Devising and putting in place a recursive algorithm such as this isn't nearly as difficult as it sounds. You can modify this technique for traversing the directory tree and adapt it to just about *any* program to work in descendants of a given directory as well as in the directory itself. In fact, we'll use a modified version of it later when we develop the utility called FINDTEXT. DOS itself uses a routine that is no doubt similar to this when you execute a DIR or ATTRIB command with a /S switch.

Locating Files and Subdirectories

To identify files and subdirectories in the current directory, NUKE relies on DOS functions 4EH and 4FH. To locate the first file or subdirectory, a program calls function 4EH (Find First) with the attributes of the files or subdirectories it is looking for in CX and DS:DX pointing to an ASCIIZ file specification. So that it may identify *all* files and subdirectories, NUKE uses the file specification *.*. It also sets CX to 17H, which locates any file or subdirectory, regardless of the attributes (hidden, read-only, or system) it is assigned. The true purpose of the DTA when it's used in this context is to serve as a repository for data returned by function 4EH. On return, the DTA contains several interesting items of information about the file or subdirectory located, including its name (at offset 1EH), its attributes (at offset 15H), and the file size (in the two words starting at offset 1AH). If no such file or subdirectory exists, function 4EH returns with the carry flag set.

Once the first file or subdirectory is located, others are found by calling function 4FH repeatedly until it, too, returns with the carry flag set. Function 4FH takes no input values; instead, it uses the information placed in the DTA by function 4EH. You can see this demonstrated in the procedure NUKE, which searches for files and subdirectories until one or both of these functions returns with carry set.

Once a file or subdirectory is located, NUKE determines what its name is by looking inside the DTA. How does it know where the DTA is? It sets it when it is first called by placing a call to DOS function 1AH, which accepts the *segment:offset* address of the DTA in DS:DX (recall from the last section that NUKE reserves room for the DTA on the system stack). To distinguish files from subdirectories, NUKE inspects bit 4 of the attribute byte located at offset 15H in the DTA. If the bit is set, it's a subdirectory; if it's clear, then it's a file. When NUKE finds a subdirectory, it uses the name returned in the DTA to change to that subdirectory. And once all subdirectories are removed from the current directory, NUKE uses file names returned in the DTA to delete files.

The process of identifying a file and then deleting it is illustrated by the following code sequence, which was extracted from the procedure NUKE:

```
mov     ah,4Fh
int     21h
jc      nuke_exit
   .
   .
   .
test    byte ptr [bp+21],10h
jnz     rmdir
   .
   .
   .
mov     ah,41h
mov     dx,bp
add     dx,30
int     21h
```

The first three lines retrieve the name of the next file or subdirectory and exit if carry returns set indicating that there are no more to be found. The next two lines verify that the name returned is that of a file by testing bit 4 of the attribute byte in the DTA. And the final four lines delete the file by calling DOS function 41H after loading the address of the file name into register DX. In this example, BP points to the base of the DTA, so the address passed in DX is formulated by adding 30 to it—the offset at which the file name appears in the DTA.

Before it deletes a file, NUKE places a call to DOS function 43H to remove attributes from the file that could prevent it from being deleted. Hidden, system, and read-only files cannot be deleted. The code sequence

```
mov     ax,4301h
sub     cx,cx
mov     dx,bp
add     dx,30
int     21h
```

does the trick. The 01H placed in AL is a subfunction code telling DOS to change the file's attributes (subfunction 00H returns the file's attributes in CX). The zero in CX resulting from the instruction SUB CX,CX becomes the file's new attribute byte, effectively deleting any existing file attributes. DS:DX points to the name of the file. Once again, the address of the file name is returned by adding an offset to BP, which contains the address of the DTA itself.

Renaming Subdirectories

One of the shortcomings of DOS's REN command is that it will rename files, but not subdirectories. You can use the Rename function under the File menu in the DOS Shell to rename a subdirectory. But unless you're already in the Shell, starting it up to rename a subdirectory is probably too much trouble, unless there's simply no alternative.

We can create an alternative in the form of RENDIR.COM, which allows you to rename subdirectories from the command line. Its syntax, which is modeled after that of the REN command, is

```
RENDIR [d:][path]dirname1 dirname2
```

where *dirname1* is the name of the subdirectory to be renamed, and *dirname2* is the new name it's to be given. The command

```
RENDIR \WP\DOC WPFILES
```

renames the DOC subdirectory in \WP to WPFILES. Similarly, the command

```
RENDIR TEMP TMP
```

renames the subdirectory TEMP in the current directory to TMP. Note that you cannot specify a drive or path with *dirname2*; the drive and path specified for *dirname1* is assumed for both.

RENDIR will fail if any of the following conditions is true:

- It is run under a version of DOS earlier than 3.0.

- The subdirectory *dirname1* does not exist.

- *Dirname1* names a file, not a subdirectory.

- *Dirname2* includes a drive or path specifier.

- A file or subdirectory named *dirname2* already exists.

RENDIR incorporates descriptive error messages that alert you to the cause of the problem when errors do occur. Note that RENDIR requires DOS 3.0 or later because the Kernel function that it uses to rename subdirectories renames files only in version 2.x.

RENDIR will also fail if you try to rename the root directory, because the root directory cannot be renamed. In some versions of DOS (including DOS 5.0), RENDIR also will fail if you try to rename the *current* directory. As a rule, you should avoid renaming the current directory even if the version of DOS you're running will permit you to, because doing so can confuse DOS and cause it to temporarily lose track of its location on the disk. You can demonstrate this by renaming a subdirectory that is a parent of the current directory. Try to ascend to the parent directory with the command **CD ..** and DOS will respond that it's an invalid directory. To get DOS back on track, you must CD to the directory that was renamed by spelling out the path to it in full, or CD to one *above* the one that was renamed. For this reason, it's also prudent not to rename a subdirectory that lies between the current directory and the root directory in the directory chain. If the subdirectory you want to rename fits this description, CD to a different directory chain, and *then* use RENDIR.

Inside RENDIR

The program listing for RENDIR is shown in Listing 11.2. Compared with NUKE, RENDIR is a very simple program, requiring even less code. At the start, it calls SCANHELP to scan the command line for a /? switch and then, provided it doesn't find one, calls FINDCHAR to locate the first parameter entered on the command line. Next RENDIR parses the command line, searching for two entries: the current directory name and the new directory name. When it finds them, it saves the addresses and places a zero at the end of each one to convert it to the ASCIIZ format that DOS understands. If it doesn't find both of them, it terminates with a syntax error.

LISTING 11.2 RENDIR.ASM

```
;******************************************************************************
; RENDIR renames subdirectories.  Its syntax is:
;
;        RENDIR [d:][path]dirname1 dirname2
```

```
;
; where "dirname1" is the current name of the subdirectory and "dirname2"
; is the new name it's to be given.  RENDIR requires DOS 3.0 or later.
;************************************************************************

code            segment
                assume  cs:code,ds:code
                org     100h
begin:          jmp     main

helpmsg         db      "Renames a subdirectory.",13,10,13,10
                db      "RENDIR [d:][path]dirname1 dirname2",13,10,13,10
                db      "  dirname1    Current subdirectory name."
                db      13,10
                db      "  dirname2    New subdirectory name.",13,10,"$"

errmsg1         db      "DOS 3.0 or later required",13,10,"$"
errmsg2         db      "Syntax: RENDIR [d:][path]dirname1 dirname2",13,10,"$"
errmsg3         db      "Subdirectory not found or path invalid",13,10,"$"
errmsg4         db      "Not a subdirectory",13,10,"$"
errmsg5         db      "A file or subdirectory of that name already "
                db      "exists",13,10,"$"
errmsg6         db      "Cannot rename the current directory",13,10,"$"
errmsg7         db      "Subdirectory could not be renamed",13,10,"$"

param1          dw      ?                       ;Address of first parameter
endparam1       dw      ?                       ;Ending address of parameter
param2          dw      ?                       ;Address of second parameter

;************************************************************************
; Procedure MAIN
;************************************************************************

main            proc    near
                cld                             ;Clear direction flag
                mov     si,81h                  ;Point SI to command line
                call    scanhelp                ;Scan for "/?" switch
                jnc     checkver                ;Branch if not found
                mov     ah,09h                  ;Display help text and exit
                mov     dx,offset helpmsg       ;  with ERRORLEVEL=0
                int     21h
                mov     ax,4C00h
                int     21h
;
; Check DOS version and exit if less than 3.0.
;
checkver:       mov     ah,30h                  ;Get DOS version
                int     21h
                cmp     al,3                    ;Continue of 3.0 or
                jae     parse                   ;  later

                mov     dx,offset errmsg1       ;Display error message and
error:          mov     ah,09h                  ;  exit with ERRORLEVEL=1
                int     21h
                mov     ax,4C01h
                int     21h
```

```
;
; Parse the command line for parameters.
;
parse:          mov     dx,offset errmsg2       ;Initialize error pointer
                call    findchar                ;Find first entry
                jc      error                   ;Error if not found
                mov     param1,si               ;Save address
                call    finddelim               ;Find end of entry
                jc      error                   ;Exit if end of line
                mov     byte ptr [si],0         ;Convert to ASCIIZ
                mov     endparam1,si            ;Save address

                inc     si                      ;Advance SI past 0
                call    findchar                ;Find second entry
                jc      error                   ;Error if not found
                mov     param2,si               ;Save address
                cmp     byte ptr [si+1],":"     ;Error if "dirname2" has a
                jc      error                   ;  drive specifier attached
                call    finddelim               ;Find end of entry
                mov     byte ptr [si],0         ;Convert to ASCIIZ

                mov     cx,si                   ;Get length of "dirname2"
                sub     cx,param2               ;  in CX
                inc     cx
                mov     di,param2               ;Point DI to "dirname2"
                mov     al,"\"                  ;Scan "dirname2" for "\"
                repne   scasb                   ;  characters
                je      error                   ;Error if found
;
; Make sure the subdirectory exists and that it's not a file.
;
                mov     ax,4300h                ;Get attributes
                mov     dx,param1
                int     21h
                mov     dx,offset errmsg3       ;Error if entry does not
                jc      error                   ;  exist
                mov     dx,offset errmsg4       ;Error if entry is a file,
                test    cx,10h                  ;  not a subdirectory
                jz      error
;
; Build the specification for the new subdirectory name.
;
                mov     cx,endparam1            ;Get length of "dirname1"
                sub     cx,param1               ;  in CX
                mov     di,endparam1            ;Point DI to the end of
                dec     di                      ;  "dirname1"
                mov     al,"\"
                std
                repne   scasb                   ;Scan for "\" character
                cld
                mov     di,offset newname
                jne     copyname                ;Branch if none found

                mov     si,param1               ;Copy everything up to and
                inc     cx                      ;  including the final "\"
                rep     movsb                   ;  to NEWNAME
```

```
copyname:       mov     si,param2               ;Append "dirname2" to the
copy2:          movsb                           ; end of the string
                cmp     byte ptr [si-1],0
                jne     copy2
;
; Make sure a file or directory with the new name doesn't already exist.
;
                mov     ax,4300h                ;Get attributes
                mov     dx,offset newname
                int     21h
                mov     dx,offset errmsg5       ;Error if entry already
                jnc     goto_error              ; exists
;
; Rename the subdirectory and exit.
;
                mov     ah,56h                  ;Rename it with DOS
                mov     dx,param1               ; function 56H
                mov     di,offset newname
                int     21h
                jnc     exit                    ;Exit if call succeeded

                mov     dx,offset errmsg6       ;Error if user tried to
                cmp     ax,10h                  ; rename current directory
                je      goto_error
                mov     dx,offset errmsg7       ;All other errors
goto_error:     jmp     error

exit:           mov     ax,4C00h                ;Exit with ERRORLEVEL=0
                int     21h
main            endp


;****************************************************************************
; FINDCHAR advances SI to the next non-space or non-comma character.
; On return, carry set indicates EOL was encountered.
;****************************************************************************

findchar        proc    near
                lodsb                           ;Get the next character
                cmp     al,20h                  ;Loop if space
                je      findchar
                cmp     al,2Ch                  ;Loop if comma
                je      findchar
                dec     si                      ;Point SI to the character
                cmp     al,0Dh                  ;Exit with carry set if end
                je      eol                     ; of line is reached

                clc                             ;Clear carry and exit
                ret

eol:            stc                             ;Set carry and exit
                ret
findchar        endp


;****************************************************************************
; FINDDELIM advances SI to the next space or comma character.  On return,
```

```
; carry set indicates EOL was encountered.
;****************************************************************************

finddelim       proc    near
                lodsb                           ;Get the next character
                cmp     al,20h                  ;Exit if space
                je      fd_exit
                cmp     al,2Ch                  ;Exit if comma
                je      fd_exit
                cmp     al,0Dh                  ;Loop back for more if end
                jne     finddelim               ;  of line isn't reached

                dec     si                      ;Set carry and exit
                stc
                ret

fd_exit:        dec     si                      ;Clear carry and exit
                clc
                ret
finddelim       endp


;****************************************************************************
; SCANHELP scans the command line for a /? switch.  If found, carry returns
; set and SI contains its offset.  If not found, carry returns clear.
;****************************************************************************

scanhelp        proc    near
                push    si                      ;Save SI
scanloop:       lodsb                           ;Get a character
                cmp     al,0Dh                  ;Exit if end of line
                je      scan_exit
                cmp     al,"?"                  ;Loop if not "?"
                jne     scanloop
                cmp     byte ptr [si-2],"/"     ;Loop if not "/"
                jne     scanloop

                add     sp,2                    ;Clear the stack
                sub     si,2                    ;Adjust SI
                stc                             ;Set carry and exit
                ret

scan_exit:      pop     si                      ;Restore SI
                clc                             ;Clear carry and exit
                ret
scanhelp        endp

newname         =       $                       ;New subdirectory name

code            ends
                end     begin
```

The heart of the program is the code sequence

```
mov     ah,56h
mov     dx,param1
mov     di,offset newname
int     21h
```

which places the offset address of the subdirectory's current name in DX and the offset address of the new name in DI, and then calls DOS function 56H to rename the subdirectory. If carry is set on return, then the subdirectory could not be renamed and an error message is displayed. The real reason function 56H exists is to rename files. However, in version 3.0 it gained the ability to rename subdirectories, too. RENDIR places a call to DOS function 30H to make sure it's running with DOS 3.0 or later. Function 30H returns the major version number of the version of DOS running on the system (for example, the 3 in 3.0) in AL and the minor version number (the 0 in 3.0) in AH.

Most of the code prior to the segment that actually renames the subdirectory is there for the purpose of building a full path name to the directory based on the first parameter the user input on the command line. Let's say, for example, that you had typed

```
RENDIR \WP\DOC WPFILES
```

to invoke RENDIR. Simply passing function 56H the addresses of \WP\DOC and WPFILES wouldn't work. Function 56H requires that the second parameter passed to it include the same path name that the first one does. In this case, RENDIR must pass function 56H the address of the strings \WP\DOC and \WP\WPFILES. As a result, RENDIR is forced to go to the trouble of determining what part of the first parameter is a path (\WP) and what portion of it is an actual directory name. Then it combines the path component with the second string input on the command line.

To do so, RENDIR scans the first parameter for backslash characters. Everything up to and including the final backslash, which marks the end of the path portion of the string, is copied to the location named NEWTEXT. If there is no backslash, then no copy is performed. Afterward, RENDIR appends the directory name entered for *dirname2* to NEWNAME. Then it passes the address of NEWNAME to function 56H and the directory is renamed.

RENDIR demonstrates yet again that when you program in assembly language, a significant part of the programming you do is directed toward parsing the command line. We could have taken the easy way out and required the user to enter a path name along with *dirname2*. But doing so would unfairly handicap the program with an awkward syntax and therefore make it difficult to use. The way it's written, RENDIR shoulders the burden of the work itself. And that, after all, is what using computers is all about.

Encrypting Files

Every day it seems that information flows a little more freely, thanks to inexpensive PCs, CD-ROMs and CD-ROM drives, local area networks, and on-line services such as CompuServe and GEnie, which can be accessed by anyone with a modem and a credit card. As information becomes easier to obtain, data security becomes harder to maintain. What's to prevent someone from taking the helm of your PC while you're away and browsing through business-sensitive word processing or spreadsheet files? And how secure can you feel storing sensitive data files on the hard disk of a network server when anyone with a privileged account can access your area of the network and read anything you can?

Enter ENCRYPT, which allows you to password-encrypt sensitive data files so that no one but you can read them. A file encrypted with ENCRYPT is transformed into a meaningless jumble of characters that can only be restored to its original form with the same password that it was encrypted with. The syntax for running ENCRYPT is

```
ENCRYPT [d:][path]filename "password"
```

where *filename* is the name of the file that's to be encrypted and *password* is the password to encrypt it with. The password can be any length you like (with a minimum of 1 character), and it may contain any character (including spaces) except for redirection and piping symbols. The password must also be enclosed in quotation marks. For example, the command

```
ENCRYPT BUDGET.DOC "King Arthur"
```

encrypts BUDGET.DOC using the password (or, more accurately, the pass *phrase*) "King Arthur."

To restore a file to its original form, run it through ENCRYPT again with the same password. This time, ENCRYPT will unencrypt the data rather than encrypt it. The command

```
ENCRYPT BUDGET.DOC "King Arthur"
```

restores a file encrypted with the password "King Arthur" to its original form. Be very careful when using this utility. Once a file is encrypted, it cannot be restored without the password. Also, passwords are case sensitive, so "King Arthur" is not the same as "king arthur" or "KING ARTHUR." Note that if you enter the wrong password when unencrypting a file, you'll have to undo the effects of *that* password before you can rerun it to undo the effects of the original one.

If you're extremely security-minded, you can use to your advantage the fact that multiple passwords operate independently, and you can double-encrypt files that are especially sensitive. If a file is encrypted with the commands

```
ENCRYPT BUDGET.DOC "Arthur"
```

```
ENCRYPT BUDGET.DOC "King of all he surveys"
```

it can only be unencrypted with the commands

```
ENCRYPT BUDGET.DOC "King of all he surveys"
ENCRYPT BUDGET.DOC "Arthur"
```

in that order. Again, if you forget the password or passwords, there is no way to restore the file short of manually breaking the code. If you encrypt an important file, it's not a bad idea to keep a backup copy of it in unencrypted form, just in case your memory fails you. Be sure to store the backup in a safe place so someone snooping on your hard disk won't find it.

If an attempt to encrypt or unencrypt a file produces the error message "File could not be opened for writing," then the file is probably marked read-only. You can verify this by typing

```
ATTRIB filename
```

where *filename* is the name of the file you're trying to access. DOS will display an "R" next to the file name if the file's read-only attribute is set. In this case, use the command

```
ATTRIB -R filename
```

to remove the read-only attribute. ENCRYPT should then work.

If the problem isn't a read-only attribute, or if you get the message "File could not be opened for reading," the problem may be a lack of available file handles. To correct the error, increase the number following the FILES= statement in your PC's CONFIG.SYS file and reboot.

ENCRYPT uses an encryption technique called a *Vernam cipher*, named after Gilbert Vernam, who is credited with inventing it in 1917, while working for AT&T. The Vernam cipher is one of the simplest, yet most effective, encryption methods that there is, and it lends itself extremely well to implementations on digital computers. It's also called the *exclusive-or* cipher.

All the Vernam cipher does is perform an exclusive-or between each character in the password and each character in the file. Exclusive-or, abbreviated XOR, is a logical operation that compares two bits, and sets a resultant bit to 0 if the two bits were both 1 or both 0, or sets it to 1 if one was 0 and one was 1. This is illustrated by the following four lines:

```
0 XOR 0 = 0
0 XOR 1 = 1
1 XOR 0 = 1
1 XOR 1 = 0
```

In other words, the result is 1 *if and only if* there was one—and only one—1 in the two bits that were compared. To XOR two values other than 1 or 0 together, a computer breaks them down to their binary equivalents and XORs each bit individually. XORing 151 and 49 produces 166, as demonstrated in this diagram:

```
        1 Ø Ø 1 Ø 1 1 1 = 151
XOR     Ø Ø 1 1 Ø Ø Ø 1 = 49
        - - - - - - - - - - - - - -
        1 Ø 1 Ø Ø 1 1 Ø = 166
```

To the right of each 8-bit binary number is shown its decimal equivalent. Eight different XOR operations are performed, one on each of the eight columns of digits shown. Reading from left to right, 1 XOR 0 equals 1, 0 XOR 0 equals 0, 0 XOR 1 equals 1, and so on. The result is a binary number whose decimal equivalent is 166.

To encrypt an entire file, ENCRYPT XORs the first character of the password with the first character of the file, the second character of the password with the second character of the file, and so on, until it reaches the end of the password. Then it loops back to the beginning of the password and starts again. For a simple file containing the line "King of all he surveys" matched up with the password "PCMag," the pairings would look like this:

```
K i n g   o f   a l l   h e   s u r v e y s
P C M a g P C M a g P C M a g P C M a g P C
```

The result is a seemingly random mix of values between 0 and 255 that are no longer recognizable as text when they're TYPEd to the screen.

What's remarkable about the Vernam cipher is that XORing an encrypted file with the same password again restores the file to its original form. Why? Because if XORing A with B produces C, then XORing C with B produces A. Recall the previous example, where we showed that XORing 151 with 49 produces 166. When you XOR 166 with 49, you get 151, as shown here:

```
        1 Ø 1 Ø Ø 1 1 Ø = 166
XOR     Ø Ø 1 1 Ø Ø Ø 1 = 49
        - - - - - - - - - - - - - -
        1 Ø Ø 1 Ø 1 1 1 = 151
```

As a result, ENCRYPT doesn't require a separate utility for unencrypting encrypted files. You can just run it a second time with the same password, and the file will be restored to its original state.

The Vernam cipher was used by the Germans in World War II for their famous Lorenz cipher machines. Given a random password that is as long as the file is long, a Vernam cipher is virtually unbreakable. If the password is shorter, a trained cryptographer who knows the length of the password can sometimes break a Vernam cipher given enough time to do so. Fortunately, unless you work at CIA headquarters in Langley, Virginia, chances are that not many of your coworkers are trained cryptographers. That means most of us can rest assured that ENCRYPT provides a safe and reliable means for securing our data files from prying eyes.

Inside ENCRYPT

The source code for ENCRYPT is shown in Listing 11.3. Like NUKE and RENDIR, ENCRYPT's first action at start-up is to scan the command line for a /? switch invoking help. Then, like NUKE, it checks to make sure it has enough memory to run in. ENCRYPT doesn't use recursion like NUKE does; it checks available memory for a different reason. Recall our discussion of the 64K segment that a COM program is loaded into. ENCRYPT uses some of this 64k (32k of it) as buffer space for reading and writing file data. The buffer, named BUFFER in the source code listing, is located at the end of the program. ENCRYPT requires about 700 bytes for code and data (the length of the COM file itself), 32k for file I/O buffering, and additional space for the stack. When it starts, ENCRYPT checks the value in the SP register to ensure that there is at least 40k of RAM available to it, which should be enough to ensure that there is never a collision between the stack and file data.

LISTING 11.3 ENCRYPT.ASM

```
;**************************************************************************
; ENCRYPT.ASM encrypts a data file using a variation on the Vernam cipher
; technique, which XORs each character of a message with each character
; of a password.  Its syntax is:
;
;       ENCRYPT [d:][path]filename "password"
;
; where "file1" is the name of the file to be encrypted and "password" is
; the password used to encrypt the file.  The password must be enclosed in
; quotation marks and may be as long as the command line permits.
;
; Files are unencrypted by passing them through ENCRYPT.ASM again with the
; same password.  If a password is forgotten, there is no way to recover
; the original file short of manually breaking the code.
;**************************************************************************

code            segment
                assume  cs:code,ds:code
                org     100h
begin:          jmp     main

helpmsg         db      "Encrypts a file for data security.",13,10,13,10
                db      "ENCRYPT [d:][path]filename ",22h,"password",22h
                db      13,10,13,10
                db      "  filename  Name of the file to be encrypted",13,10
                db      "  password  Password used for encryption",13,10
                db      13,10
                db      "To unencrypt a file, run it through ENCRYPT again "
                db      "with the same password.",13,10,"$"
```

```
errmsg1         db      "Syntax: ENCRYPT [d:][path]filename "
                db      22h,"password",22h,13,10,"$"
errmsg2         db      "File not found or path invalid",13,10,"$"
errmsg3         db      "File could not be opened for reading",13,10,"$"
errmsg4         db      "File could not be opened for writing",13,10,"$"
errmsg5         db      "File read error",13,10,"$"
errmsg6         db      "File write error",13,10,"$"
errmsg7         db      "Disk full error",13,10,"$"
errmsg8         db      "Not enough memory",13,10,"$"

filename        dw      ?                       ;Address of file name
r_handle        dw      ?                       ;File handle for reading
w_handle        dw      ?                       ;File handle for writing
password        dw      ?                       ;Password address
count           dw      ?                       ;Password length
blocksize       dw      ?                       ;Block size for file I/O
bytesread       dw      ?                       ;Bytes read from input file


;****************************************************************************
; Procedure MAIN
;****************************************************************************

main            proc    near
                cld                             ;Clear direction flag
                mov     si,81h                  ;Point SI to command line
                call    scanhelp                ;Scan for "/?" switch
                jnc     checkmem                ;Branch if not found
                mov     ah,09h                  ;Display help text and exit
                mov     dx,offset helpmsg       ;  with ERRORLEVEL=0
                int     21h
                mov     ax,4C00h
                int     21h

checkmem:       mov     dx,offset errmsg8       ;Make sure there's enough
                cmp     sp,0A000h               ;  memory to run the
                ja      parse                   ;  program

error:          mov     ah,09h                  ;Display error message and
                int     21h                     ;  exit with ERRORLEVEL=1
                mov     ax,4C01h
                int     21h
;
; Parse the command line.
;
parse:          call    findchar                ;Find first parameter
                jnc     parse2                  ;Branch if found
error1:         mov     dx,offset errmsg1       ;Error if not
                jmp     error

parse2:         cmp     byte ptr [si],22h       ;Error if quotation mark
                je      error1
                mov     filename,si             ;Save address
                call    finddelim               ;Find end of string
                jc      error1                  ;Error if end of line
                mov     byte ptr [si],0         ;Convert to ASCIIZ
```

```
                inc     si                      ;Advance SI

                call    findchar                ;Find next parameter
                jc      error1                  ;Error if end of line
                cmp     byte ptr [si],22h       ;Error if NOT quotation
                jne     error1                  ;  mark this time
                inc     si                      ;Skip quotation mark
                mov     password,si             ;Save address
                sub     cx,cx                   ;Initialize counter
readnext:       lodsb                           ;Find the closing quotation
                cmp     al,0Dh                  ;  mark and exit on error
                je      error1                  ;  if end of line is
                cmp     al,22h                  ;  encountered first
                je      quotefound
                inc     cx
                jmp     readnext
quotefound:     jcxz    error1                  ;Error if length is 0
                mov     count,cx                ;Save password length
;
; Open the file with separate handles for reading and writing.
;
                mov     ax,3D00h                ;Open the file for reading
                mov     dx,filename             ;  using DOS function 3DH
                int     21h
                mov     r_handle,ax             ;Save file handle
                jnc     open                    ;Continue if no error

                mov     dx,offset errmsg3       ;Determine what the error
                cmp     ax,2                    ;  was and point DX to the
                jb      goto_error              ;  appropriate error
                cmp     ax,3                    ;  message
                ja      goto_error
                mov     dx,offset errmsg2
goto_error:     jmp     error                   ;Exit on error

open:           mov     ax,3D01h                ;Open the file for writing
                mov     dx,filename             ;  using DOS function 3Dh
                int     21h
                mov     w_handle,ax             ;Save file handle
                mov     dx,offset errmsg4       ;Branch on error
                jc      error
;
; Read the file, encrypt it, and write it back out to disk.
;
                mov     ax,8000h                ;Compute block size for
                sub     dx,dx                   ;  file I/O
                div     count                   ;Quotient in AX
                mul     count                   ;Product in AX (<8000H)
                mov     blocksize,ax            ;Save block size

readblock:      mov     ah,3Fh                  ;Read one block using
                mov     bx,r_handle             ;  DOS function 3FH
                mov     cx,blocksize
                mov     dx,offset buffer
                int     21h
                mov     dx,offset errmsg5
```

```
                jc        goto_error              ;Error if call failed
                jcxz      exit                    ;Done if zero bytes read
                mov       bytesread,ax            ;Save bytes read count

                call      encrypt                 ;Encrypt the block

                mov       ah,40h                  ;Write one block using
                mov       bx,w_handle             ;  DOS function 40H
                mov       cx,bytesread
                mov       dx,offset buffer
                int       21h
                mov       dx,offset errmsg6
                jc        goto_error              ;Error if call failed
                cmp       ax,bytesread            ;Proceed if bytes written
                je        check                   ;  equals bytes read
                mov       dx,offset errmsg7       ;Queue up "Disk full"
                jmp       error                   ;  message and exit

check:          mov       ax,bytesread            ;Loop back for more if
                cmp       ax,blocksize            ;  bytes read is less
                jnb       readblock               ;  than bytes requested
;
; Close file handles and exit.
;
exit:           mov       ah,3Eh                  ;Close the read handle
                mov       bx,r_handle
                int       21h
                mov       ah,3Eh                  ;Close the write handle
                mov       bx,w_handle
                int       21h
                mov       ax,4C00h                ;Exit with ERRORLEVEL=0
                int       21
main            endp


;***************************************************************************
; FINDCHAR advances SI to the next non-space or non-comma character.
; On return, carry set indicates EOL was encountered.
;***************************************************************************

findchar        proc      near
                lodsb                             ;Get the next character
                cmp       al,20h                  ;Loop if space
                je        findchar
                cmp       al,2Ch                  ;Loop if comma
                je        findchar
                dec       si                      ;Point SI to the character
                cmp       al,0Dh                  ;Exit with carry set if end
                je        eol                     ;  of line is reached

                clc                               ;Clear carry and exit
                ret

eol:            stc                               ;Set carry and exit
                ret
findchar        endp
```

```
;***********************************************************************
; FINDDELIM advances SI to the next space or comma character.  On return,
; carry set indicates EOL was encountered.
;***********************************************************************

finddelim       proc    near
                lodsb                           ;Get the next character
                cmp     al,20h                  ;Exit if space
                je      fd_exit
                cmp     al,2Ch                  ;Exit if comma
                je      fd_exit
                cmp     al,0Dh                  ;Loop back for more if end
                jne     finddelim               ;  of line isn't reached

                dec     si                      ;Set carry and exit
                stc
                ret

fd_exit:        dec     si                      ;Clear carry and exit
                clc
                ret
finddelim       endp


;***********************************************************************
; SCANHELP scans the command line for a /? switch.  If found, carry returns
; set and SI contains its offset.  If not found, carry returns clear.
;***********************************************************************

scanhelp        proc    near
                push    si                      ;Save SI
scanloop:       lodsb                           ;Get a character
                cmp     al,0Dh                  ;Exit if end of line
                je      scan_exit
                cmp     al,"?"                  ;Loop if not "?"
                jne     scanloop
                cmp     byte ptr [si-2],"/"     ;Loop if not "/"
                jne     scanloop

                add     sp,2                    ;Clear the stack
                sub     si,2                    ;Adjust SI
                stc                             ;Set carry and exit
                ret

scan_exit:      pop     si                      ;Restore SI
                clc                             ;Clear carry and exit
                ret
scanhelp        endp


;***********************************************************************
; ENCRYPT encrypts a block of data using an XOR algorithm.
;***********************************************************************

encrypt         proc    near
                mov     di,offset buffer        ;Point DI to buffer
                mov     si,password             ;Point SI to password
                mov     cx,bytesread            ;Initialize CX with count
```

```
enloop:         lodsb                           ;Get password character
                cmp     al,22h                  ;Branch if not a quotation
                jne     notquote                ;  mark
                mov     si,password             ;Reset BX to start of
                lodsb                           ;  password
notquote:       xor     [di],al                 ;Encrypt the character
                inc     di                      ;Advance buffer pointer
                loop    enloop                  ;Loop until done
                ret
encrypt         endp

buffer          =       $                       ;File I/O buffer

code            ends
                end     begin
```

Next ENCRYPT parses the command line for a file name and a password. It converts the file name to ASCIIZ format by placing a zero at the end of it and saves its address. Then it computes the length of the password and saves its address. If either of these parameters is not found, ENCRYPT displays a syntax error message and terminates.

In Chapter 9, we talked briefly about DOS function 3DH, which opens a file for reading or writing. Function 3DH returns a number called a *file handle* to the caller, which is used in all subsequent references to the file. Once the handle is obtained, a program can read from or write to the file using DOS functions 3FH and 40H. You can see these functions in action in procedure MAIN. ENCRYPT calls function 3DH twice—once to get a handle for reading the file, a second time to get a handle for writing to the file—and saves the handles in R_HANDLE and W_HANDLE, respectively. The instructions

```
mov     ax,3D00h
mov     dx,filename
int     21h
mov     r_handle,ax
```

open the file for reading and save the read handle, while the instructions

```
mov     ax,3D01h
mov     dx,filename
int     21h
mov     w_handle,ax
```

open it for writing and save the write handle. Function 3DH takes as input an *access code* in AL and the address of the file name in DS:DX. The access code tells DOS what type of access to the file (read, write, or read/write) is being requested. A 00H requests permission to read the file, 01H requests permission to write to it, and 02H says the program wants to read *and* write it. If the request succeeds, carry returns clear and the file handle is returned in AX.

Once ENCRYPT has the handles it needs, it alternately reads a block of data, encrypts it, and writes the encrypted block back to disk. If the file is smaller than approximately 32k, the entire file is read into memory at once, and one pass through the encryption cycle encrypts the whole thing. If, however, the file is too large to fit into ENCRYPT's internal 32k buffer space, the program processes one block at a time until the entire file has been encrypted.

To read a block of data from the file, ENCRYPT uses the following code:

```
mov     ah,3Fh
mov     bx,r_handle
mov     cx,blocksize
mov     dx,offset buffer
int     21h
```

Function 3FH accepts three parameters: a file handle in BX, the number of bytes requested from the file in CX, and the address of file I/O buffer (the area where the data read from the file will be placed) in DS:DX. ENCRYPT starts with a block size of exactly 32k and rounds down to the nearest even multiple of the password length. Then it requests that number of bytes each time it reads the file. Function 3FH returns the actual number of bytes read in AX. ENCRYPT checks this return value each time and knows it has reached the end of the file when the number of bytes read is less than the number of bytes requested.

To encrypt the block of data, ENCRYPT calls the procedure ENCRYPT, which consists of the lines

```
            mov     di,offset buffer
            mov     si,password
            mov     cx,bytesread

enloop:     lodsb
            cmp     al,22h
            jne     notquote
            mov     si,password
            lodsb
notquote:   xor     [di],al
            inc     di
            loop    enloop
            ret
```

In effect, this procedure loads SI with the address of the password, DI with the address of the file data (BUFFER), and CX with the length of the block of data read from the file. Then it works its way through the buffer a byte at a time, XORing one character in the password with one character from the file. Each time a character from the password is read, the procedure checks to see if it has reached the end of the password by seeing if AL (which holds the ASCII code for the password character) is equal to 22H—the ASCII code for a quotation mark. When the end of the password is reached, SI is reset to the first character in the password.

When the entire block is encrypted, ENCRYPT writes the data back out to the file with the instructions

```
mov     ah,40h
mov     bx,w_handle
mov     cx,bytesread
mov     dx,offset buffer
int     21h
```

Function 40H is similar to function 3FH except that it writes, not reads, file data. In fact, the input parameters are exactly the same as those for function 3FH. It accepts a handle in BX, the count of bytes to write in CX, and a buffer address in DS:DX. On return, AX contains the number of bytes actually written. If this number is less than what was specified, that's an indication that the disk is full and cannot hold more data. In the unlikely event that this occurs, ENCRYPT will terminate with a "Disk full error" message.

Before it ends, ENCRYPT closes both file handles by placing two separate calls to DOS function 3EH, which accepts as its sole parameter a file handle in BX. DOS only permits a limited number of files to be open in the system at once, so closing these file handles allows other programs to open files later on. If you neglect to close a handle, DOS will do it for you anyway when it terminates the program. If ENCRYPT encounters an error condition that merits termination, it relies on DOS to close any open file handles for it. This keeps the error-handling code simple by not forcing it to determine what, if any, handles are open before it ends the program.

At this point, you may be wondering why ENCRYPT requests two handles for the file when it could do with only one, provided that handle was opened with read *and* write access privileges. The reason is that ultimately, it keeps the code simpler. Consider this. ENCRYPT reads a block of data with the read handle, encrypts the block, and writes it out with the write handle. As such, it never has to tinker with the *file pointer*—the invisible pointer DOS uses to remember where the next byte to be read from the file will come from or the next byte written to the file will go. Had it opened the file with a single handle for reading and writing, ENCRYPT would have to read a block, reset the file pointer with DOS function 42H before writing data back out to the file and then reset it again before reading the next block. With two handles, no call to function 42H is required because DOS maintains a separate file pointer for each and every file handle. This method is slightly faster than using a single handle when large files are involved, because it eliminates function calls that would otherwise be required.

Searching for Files That Contain a Specified Text String

The fourth utility in this chapter may turn out to be the most useful one of all. If you've used The Norton Utilities before, you may be familiar with the utility called TS (for Text Search). TS performs disk-wide searches for files containing a specified text string. FINDTEXT, the utility presented here, is similar to TS. It lets you search for files based on their contents rather than their names. FINDTEXT is a life saver when you need to locate a file stored on your hard disk and all you remember about it is that it contained a certain word or phrase.

The syntax for FINDTEXT is

```
FINDTEXT [d:][path][filename] "text" [/S] [/C] [/I]
        [/A] [/M] [/7]
```

where *filename* is an optional parameter that denotes what files to search for (omitting *filename* is the same as typing *.*) and *text* is the text to search for, enclosed in quotation marks. The /S switch tells FINDTEXT to search the specified directory and all the directories below it (if you omit *path*, FINDTEXT begins in the current directory by default); /C tells it to perform the search with regard to case (so that "TEXT," for example, is not equivalent to "Text"); /I runs the program in full-screen interactive mode, which will be described shortly; /A searches all files that are encountered, regardless of their attributes (without the /A switch, FINDTEXT ignores files marked with hidden and system attributes); /M runs the program in monochrome mode on color monitors, which is useful on laptops that pair color adapters with black-and-white LCD or gas plasma screens; and /7 tells FINDTEXT to ignore the eighth bit in comparisons, which is useful when searching files created by programs such as Wordstar that use the eighth bit for special, non-text-related purposes.

A few examples will help. Let's say you need to locate a word processing file somewhere on drive C that you know contains the string "PC Magazine," but you have no idea what you named the file or what directory you stored it in. The command

```
FINDTEXT C:\ "PC Magazine" /S
```

searches every directory in drive C for files that contain "PC Magazine." If you're sure the string was entered with this exact mix of uppercase and lowercase characters, you can speed the search up somewhat by typing

```
FINDTEXT C:\ "PC Magazine" /S /C
```

to make it case sensitive. If you want FINDTEXT to search hidden and system files, too, include the /A switch to search *all* files, regardless of their attributes, as in

```
FINDTEXT C:\ "PC Magazine" /S /C /A
```

Finally, if the file was created in Wordstar or some other word processor that uses 7-bit representations for characters and reserves the eighth bit for other purposes, type

```
FINDTEXT C:\ "PC Magazine" /S /C /A /7
```

to instruct FINDTEXT to ignore the uppermost bit in each character. If you don't know how the application that created the file uses the eighth bit, it usually doesn't hurt to include the /7 switch as a precaution. Also note that switches can be entered in any order that you like.

Let's modify this example a bit and say that you know the file is located in C:\WP\WPFILES and think it has the extension .DOC. Furthermore, assume drive C is currently the default drive. You can narrow the search by typing

```
FINDTEXT \WP\WPFILES\*.DOC "PC Magazine"
```

This will eliminate the recursive directory search so that *only* the directory \WP\WPFILES will be searched. If \WP\WPFILES happens to be the current directory, you can simplify the command even further by typing

```
FINDTEXT *.DOC "PC Magazine"
```

or, to search files with any extension in the current directory,

```
FINDTEXT "PC Magazine"
```

FINDTEXT will report the name of every file it finds that contains the specified text and its location on disk. At the end of the search, a search summary is displayed indicating how many directories were searched, how many files were searched, and how many files containing the text string were found. A typical response looks something like this:

```
C:\WP\WPFILES\PCM1990.DOC
C:\WP\WPFILES\PCM1991.DOC
C:\WP\WPFILES\PRINTERS.DOC

55 file(s) searched in 1 directory; 3 file(s) found
    containing "PC Magazine"
```

This indicates that PCM1990.DOC, PCM1991.DOC, and PRINTERS.DOC all contain the specified text string. You can capture this list of files to a file or send it to your printer by adding an output redirection operator to the command. For example, the command

```
FINDTEXT "PC Magazine" > FILELIST.TXT
```

routes the output from FINDTEXT to the text file FILELIST.TXT, while the command

```
FINDTEXT "PC Magazine" > LPT1
```

outputs it to the printer attached to LPT1.

A disk-wide search for files could take awhile, particularly if your hard disk contains many hundreds or perhaps thousands of files.. You can terminate a search at any time by pressing Ctrl-C or Ctrl-Break.

All the examples we've seen thus far run FINDTEXT in non-interactive mode, in which it simply reports the names of the files that meet the search criterion you specified. For a real kick, try running it in interactive mode with the /I switch. In interactive mode, FINDTEXT displays a colorful screen that shows what files and directories are being searched, *and* it displays the contents of any file (with the search text highlighted) it finds that contains the text you're looking for.

Figure 11.2 shows what a typical interactive-mode screen looks like. At the center of the screen is a status window that tells you what string FINDTEXT is looking for ("Searching for"), the drive and directory that is being searched ("Location"), and the name of the file that is currently being examined ("File"). The line at the bottom of the screen lists the number of files and directories that have been searched and the number of files that have been found containing the specified text. As the search goes on, these on-screen indicators are updated to keep you informed on the progress of the search.

FIGURE 11.2

The FINDTEXT status window

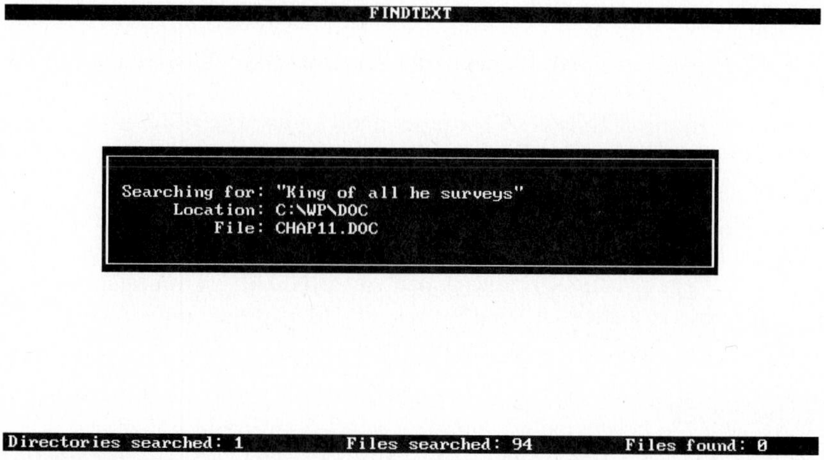

```
FINDTEXT
```

```
Searching for: "King of all he surveys"
     Location: C:\WP\DOC
         File: CHAP11.DOC
```

```
Directories searched: 1     Files searched: 94     Files found: 0
```

When FINDTEXT locates the searched-for text string in interactive mode, it pops the status window down and displays a screen similar to the one in Figure 11.3, which shows the string you're searching for and the text that surrounds it. The text is unformatted, but in most cases it will be more than enough to let you know whether this is the file you're looking for. Graphics characters, control characters, and other non-text characters show up as periods. The search string itself is highlighted in red (reverse video on monochrome displays), and the file name is displayed at the top of the screen. You can press Esc to terminate the search and go back to the command line, Enter to continue searching the file that is displayed, or the spacebar to skip to the next file and continue the search. These options are spelled out for you on the last line of the screen. When all the files have been searched, FINDTEXT displays the message "No more files" in the status window. Pressing any key takes you back to the command line.

FIGURE 11.3

The FINDTEXT display

```
                        C:\UP\DOC\CHAP11.DOC
th the same password.  This time, ENCRYPT will.unencrypt the data rather than en
crypt it.  The command...ENCRYPT BUDGET.DOC "King Arthur"..restores a file encry
pted with the password "King Arthur" to its.original form.  Be very careful when
using this utility.  Once a._........file is encrypted, it cannot be restored w
ithout the password. .Also, passwords are case.sensitive, so "King Arthur" is no
t the.same as "king arthur" or "KING ARTHUR."  And note that if you.enter the wr
ong password when unencrypting a file, you'll have to.undo the effects of .that.
 password before you can rerun it to undo.the effects of the original one...If y
ou're extremely security.minded, you can use the fact.that multiple passwords op
erate indpendently to your advantage to.doubly.encrypt files that are especially
 sensitive.  If a file is.encrypted with the commands......ENCRYPT BUDGET.DOC "
Arthur"..ENCRYPT BUDGET.DOC "King of all he surveys".....it can only be unencry
pted with the commands......ENCRYPT BUDGET.DOC "King of all he surveys"..ENCRYP
T BUDGET.DOC "Arthur".....in that order.  Again, if you forget the password or
password,.there is no way to restore the file short of manually breaking.^......
..the code.  If you encrypt an important file, it's not a bad idea.to keep a bac
kup copy of it in unencrypted form just in case your.memory fails you...If attem
pting to encrypt or unencrypt a file produces the.error message "File could not
be opened for writing," then the.file is probably marked read.only.  You can ver
ify this by typing...ATTRIB .filename...where .filename. is the name of the file
 you're trying to access. .DOS should display an "R" next to the file name, indi
cating that.the file's read.only attribute is set.  If this happens, use the.com
mand...ATTRIB .R .filename...to remove the read.only attribute.  ENCRYPT should
       Press Enter to continue, Esc to stop, or Space to go to next file
```

In interactive mode, FINDTEXT adapts itself to use the full extent of the screen if there are more than 25 lines of text displayed. It also determines whether it's being run on a color or monochrome video adapter and adjusts its output accordingly. However, many laptops have "color" video adapters that use gray-scale summing to simulate a color display with shades of gray on black-and-white LCD or gas plasma screens. If you run FINDTEXT on a laptop and find that the display is difficult to read, try restarting it with a /M switch. On many systems, this will increase the contrast significantly.

Inside FINDTEXT

The program listing for FINDTEXT is shown in Listing 11.4. FINDTEXT is far and away the longest of the utilities presented in this chapter, primarily because it takes more code to write a full-screen utility than it does to write a conventional command-line utility. FINDTEXT is really two utilities in one, because it will run in either full-screen or command-line mode. To the extent possible, code is shared among the procedures that enact the two output modes so that there is as little redundancy as possible.

LISTING 11.4 FINDTEXT.ASM

```
;***************************************************************************
; FINDTEXT searches the files in a directory (and optionally its descendant
; directories) for a specified text string.  Its syntax is:
;
;       FINDTEXT [d:][path][filename] "text" [/S] [/C] [/I] [/A] [/M] [/7]
;
; where
;
;       filename   Specifies the file or files to search
;       "text"     Specifies the text to search for
;       /S         Search descendant directories
;       /C         Make the search case-sensitive
;       /I         Run in full-screen interactive mode
;       /A         Search hidden and system files as well as normal files
;       /M         Use monochrome video attributes on color adapters
;       /7         Do 7-bit comparisons (ignore 8th bit)
;
; If no path name is specified, the search begins in the current directory.
; Similarly, if no file name is specified, all files are searched.  If the
; /I switch is not specified, FINDTEXT lists the names of all the files that
; contain the specified text.  /I causes FINDTEXT to run in interactive mode,
; displaying the contents of the files as well as their names.  The /7 switch
; is useful for searching word processing files that use the high bit of each
; character for non-text purposes.  By default, FINDTEXT only searches files
; whose hidden and system attribute bits aren't set.  /A has it search those
; files, too.  Finally, /M has FINDTEXT use monochrome attributes in inter-
; active mode, useful for laptops that pair color adapters with black-and-
; white LCD or gas plasma screens.
;***************************************************************************


code            segment
                assume  cs:code,ds:code
                org     100h
begin:          jmp     main

helpmsg         db      "Searches for files that contain a specified "
                db      "text string.",13,10,13,10
                db      "FINDTEXT [d:][path][filename] ",22h,"text",22h
                db      " [/S] [/C] [/I] [/A] [/M] [/7]",13,10,13,10
                db      "  filename  Specifies the file or files to "
                db      "search.",13,10
                db      "  text      Specifies the text to search for."
                db      13,10
                db      "  /S        Search descendant directories."
                db      13,10
                db      "  /C        Make the search case-sensitive."
                db      13,10
                db      "  /I        Run in full-screen interactive mode."
                db      13,10
```

```
                  db      "    /A          Search hidden and system files also."
                  db      13,10
                  db      "    /M          Use monochrome video attributes "
                  db      "(interactive mode only).",13,10
                  db      "    /7          Do 7-bit comparisons (ignore 8th bit)."
crlf              db      13,10,"$"

errmsg1           db      "Syntax: FINDTEXT [d:][path][filename] ",22h,"text"
                  db      22h," [/S] [/C] [/I] [/A] [/M] [/7]",13,10,"$"
errmsg2           db      "Invalid drive specification",13,10,"$"
errmsg3           db      "Invalid path specification",13,10,"$"
errmsg4           db      "Error opening $"
errmsg5           db      "Error reading $"
errmsg6           db      "Not enough memory",13,10,"$"

msg1              db      " file(s) searched in $"
msg2a             db      " directory; $"
msg2b             db      " directories; $"
msg3              db      " file(s) found containing ",22h,"$"
msg4              db      22h,13,10,"$"

defspec           db      "*.*",0                  ;Default file spec
filespec          dw      offset defspec          ;Address of file spec
srchtext          dw      0                       ;Address of search text
textsize          dw      ?                       ;Length of search text
endspec           dw      ?                       ;Address of end of file spec
rootdir           db      "\",0                   ;Command to go to root
updir             db      "..",0                  ;Command to go up one level

descflag          db      0                       ;1=Search descendants
caseflag          db      0                       ;1=Case sensitive
scrnflag          db      0                       ;1=Full-screen mode
bitflag           db      0                       ;1=7-bit comparisons
fileattr          dw      1                       ;File attributes

drive             db      ?                       ;Default drive
directory         db      "\",64 dup (?)          ;Current directory
pathstring        db      "x:\",64 dup (?)        ;Current drive and directory
bytesbefore       dw      ?                       ;Offset to search text
filessearched     dw      0                       ;Files searched
dirssearched      dw      0                       ;Directories searched
filesfound        dw      0                       ;Files found
foundflag         db      ?                       ;1=Match found in this file
bytesread         dw      ?                       ;Bytes read from file
breakflag         db      ?                       ;Ctrl-Break flag
handle            dw      ?                       ;File handle

rows              db      24                      ;Rows displayed (minus 1)
cursor            dw      ?                       ;Cursor mode
pageno            db      ?                       ;Active display page
videoseg          dw      0B800h                  ;Video segment address
videobuf          dw      ?                       ;Video buffer offset

window_color1     db      1Fh                     ;Primary window color
window_color2     db      1Ah                     ;Secondary window color
hilite_color      db      4Fh                     ;Highlighted text color
```

```
text_color      db      07h                     ;Normal text color
scrn_color      db      ?                       ;Screen color on entry

scrntxt1        db      "FINDTEXT",0
scrntxt2        db      "Directories searched:",12 dup (20h)
                db      "Files searched:",12 dup (20h)
                db      "Files found:",0
scrntxt3        db      6 dup (20h),"Press xxxxx to continue, "
                db      "xxx to stop, or xxxxx to go to next file"
                db      7 dup (20h),0
scrntxt4        db      "Searching for:",0
scrntxt5        db      "Location:",0
scrntxt6        db      "File:",0
scrntxt7        db      22h,0
scrntxt8        db      "No more files",0
scrntxt9        db      "Enter",0
scrntxt10       db      "Esc",0
scrntxt11       db      "Space",0

row1            db      ?                       ;Starting row for DRAWBOX
col1            db      ?                       ;Starting column for DRAWBOX
row2            db      ?                       ;Ending row for DRAWBOX
col2            db      ?                       ;Ending column for DRAWBOX
boxwidth        db      ?,0                     ;Box width for DRAWBOX
boxheight       db      ?,0                     ;Box height for DRAWBOX

;****************************************************************************
; Procedure MAIN
;****************************************************************************

main            proc    near
                cld                             ;Clear direction flag
                mov     si,81h                  ;Point SI to command line
                call    scanhelp                ;Scan for "/?" switch
                jnc     checkmem                ;Branch if not found
                mov     ah,09h                  ;Display help text and exit
                mov     dx,offset helpmsg       ;  with ERRORLEVEL=0
                int     21h
                mov     ax,4C00h
                int     21h

checkmem:       mov     dx,offset errmsg6       ;Make sure there's enough
                cmp     sp,0F000h               ;  memory to run the
                ja      parse                   ;  program

error:          mov     ah,09h                  ;Display error message and
                int     21h                     ;  exit with ERRORLEVEL=1
                mov     ax,4C01h
                int     21h
error1:         mov     dx,offset errmsg1
                jmp     error
;
; Parse the command line.
;
parse:          call    findchar                ;Find next parameter
                jnc     parse2                  ;Continue if found
```

```
                jmp     check                   ;Branch if not

parse2:         lodsb                           ;Get next character
                cmp     al,"/"                  ;Branch if it's a "/"
                je      switch
                cmp     al,22h                  ;Branch if it's a
                je      readtext                ;  quotation mark

                cmp     filespec,offset defspec ;Error if this parameter has
                jne     error1                  ;  already been entered
                dec     si                      ;Move back one character
                mov     filespec,si             ;Save address
                call    finddelim               ;Find the end of it
                mov     byte ptr [si],0         ;Convert it to ASCIIZ
                mov     endspec,si              ;Save ending address
                jc      check                   ;Branch if end of line
                inc     si                      ;Advance to next character
                jmp     parse                   ;Return to parsing loop

readtext:       cmp     srchtext,0              ;Error if this parameter has
                jne     error1                  ;  already been entered
                mov     srchtext,si             ;Save address
                sub     cx,cx                   ;Initialize count
readloop:       lodsb                           ;Get next character
                cmp     al,22h                  ;Done if quotation mark
                je      readdone
                cmp     al,0Dh                  ;Error if end of line
                je      error1
                inc     cx                      ;Increment count
                jmp     readloop                ;Go back for more
readdone:       jcxz    error1                  ;Error if count is 0
                mov     textsize,cx             ;Save count
                mov     byte ptr [si-1],0       ;Convert to ASCIIZ string
                jmp     parse                   ;Go back for more

switch:         lodsb                           ;Get character after switch
                cmp     al,"7"                  ;Set bitflag if it's /7
                jne     switch1
                mov     bitflag,1
                jmp     parse

switch1:        and     al,0DFh                 ;Capitalize the character
                cmp     al,"C"                  ;Set CASEFLAG if it's /C
                jne     switch2
                mov     caseflag,1
                jmp     parse

switch2:        cmp     al,"I"                  ;Set SCRNFLAG if it's /I
                jne     switch3
                mov     scrnflag,1
                jmp     parse

switch3:        cmp     al,"S"                  ;Set DESCFLAG if it's /S
                jne     switch4
                mov     descflag,1
                jmp     parse
```

```
switch4:        cmp     al,"A"                  ;Set FILEATTR if it's /A
                jne     switch5
                mov     fileattr,07h
                jmp     parse

switch5:        cmp     al,"M"                  ;Replace color attributes
                je      switch6                 ;  with monochrome if /M
goto_error:     jmp     error1                  ;  was entered
switch6:        call    setmono
                jmp     parse

check:          cmp     srchtext,0              ;Make sure text string was
                je      goto_error              ;  entered before going on
;
; If a path name was entered, go to the drive and directory named.
;
                mov     ah,19h                  ;Save the default drive
                int     21h
                mov     drive,al
                mov     ah,47h                  ;Save the current directory
                sub     dl,dl
                mov     si,offset directory+1
                int     21h

                cmp     filespec,offset defspec ;Branch if no path string
                je      gotosrch                ;  was entered

                mov     si,filespec             ;Point SI to path
                cmp     byte ptr [si+1],":"     ;Branch if path did not
                jne     nodrive                 ;  contain a drive code
                mov     ah,0Eh                  ;Otherwise set the default
                mov     dl,[si]                 ;  drive to the one
                and     dl,0DFh                 ;  specified
                sub     dl,41h
                int     21h
                mov     ah,19h                  ;See if it worked by seeing
                int     21h                     ;  what is now the default
                cmp     al,dl                   ;Error if AL != DL
                mov     dx,offset errmsg2
                je      checkpath

error3:         jmp     error

checkpath:      add     filespec,2              ;Advance past drive code
                cmp     byte ptr [si+2],0       ;If there's no path string
                jne     nodrive                 ;  after the drive code,
                mov     filespec,offset defspec ;  begin search now
gotosrch:       jmp     short beginsrch

nodrive:        mov     ah,3Bh                  ;Try to set the current
                mov     dx,filespec             ;  directory using the
                int     21h                     ;  path string entered
                jc      checkend                ;  on the command line
                mov     filespec,offset defspec ;If it worked, set FILESPEC
                jmp     short beginsrch         ;  equal to *.* and branch
```

```
checkend:      mov     di,endspec            ;If it failed, make sure the
               cmp     byte ptr [di-1],"\"   ;  path didn't end in "\"
               je      badpath

               mov     cx,di                 ;Get length in CX
               sub     cx,filespec
               dec     di
               mov     al,"\"                ;Initialize AL
               std                           ;Set direction flag
               repne   scasb                 ;Search for "\"
               cld                           ;Clear direction flag
               jne     beginsrch             ;Begin search if no "\"

               mov     dx,filespec           ;Point DX to path
               mov     filespec,di           ;Point FILESPEC to new
               add     filespec,2            ;  file spec string
               mov     byte ptr [di+1],0     ;Convert path to ASCIIZ
               mov     ah,3Bh                ;Try to set the current
               mov     si,dx                 ;  directory again
               cmp     byte ptr [si],0       ;Reset DX if path pointed
               jne     chdir                 ;  to the root directory
               mov     dx,offset rootdir
chdir:         int     21h
               jnc     beginsrch             ;Continue if it worked

badpath:       mov     ah,0Eh                ;Restore default drive
               mov     dl,drive              ;  and exit if it
               int     21h                   ;  failed
               mov     dx,offset errmsg3
               jmp     error
;
; Perform initializations and do the search.
;
beginsrch:     mov     ah,19h                ;Initialize path string with
               int     21h                   ;  the letter of the current
               add     al,41h                ;  drive
               mov     pathstring,al

               mov     si,srchtext           ;Copy the search string to
               mov     di,offset text        ;  buffer at end of program
               mov     cx,textsize
               rep     movsb

               cmp     caseflag,0            ;Convert search string to
               jne     docase                ;  uppercase if /C was not
               mov     si,offset text        ;  entered
               mov     cx,textsize
               call    stripcase

docase:        cmp     bitflag,0             ;Strip high bits from the
               je      do8bits               ;  search string if /7 was
               mov     si,offset text        ;  entered
               mov     cx,textsize
               call    striphigh

do8bits:       mov     ax,3300h              ;Get the state of Ctrl-
```

```
                int     21h                     ;  Break checking
                mov     dl,breakflag
                mov     ax,3301h                ;Turn Ctrl-Break checking
                mov     dl,1                    ;  on
                int     21h
                mov     ax,2523h                ;Point interrupt 23H to
                mov     dx,offset exit          ;  internal Ctrl-Break
                cmp     scrnflag,0              ;  handler
                je      exit_ok
                mov     dx,offset abort
exit_ok:        int     21h

                cmp     scrnflag,0              ;Initialize video if full-
                je      dosearch                ;  screen mode
                call    init_video

dosearch:       call    searchdir               ;Do the search

                cmp     scrnflag,0              ;Branch if not full-screen
                je      show_results
                mov     ax,0600h                ;Blank the window
                mov     cx,090Bh
                mov     dx,0D44h
                mov     bh,window_color1
                int     10h
                mov     si,offset scrntxt8      ;Display "No more files"
                mov     dx,0B21h
                mov     bl,window_color1
                call    bios_outtext
                mov     ah,0                    ;Wait for a keypress
                int     16h
abort:          call    restore_video           ;Clear the screen and exit
                jmp     short exit
;
; Summarize the results of the search.
;
show_results:   mov     ah,09h                  ;Advance cursor to next line
                mov     dx,offset crlf
                int     21h
                mov     ax,filessearched        ;Echo number of files
                call    dos_outnum              ;  searched
                mov     ah,09h
                mov     dx,offset msg1
                int     21h
                mov     ax,dirssearched         ;Echo number of directories
                call    dos_outnum              ;  searched
                mov     ah,09h
                mov     dx,offset msg2a
                cmp     dirssearched,1
                je      singular
                mov     dx,offset msg2b
singular:       int     21h
                mov     ax,filesfound           ;Echo number of files
                call    dos_outnum              ;  found containing
                mov     ah,09h                  ;  the text string
                mov     dx,offset msg3
```

```
                int     21h
                mov     si,srchtext             ;Echo the text string
                call    dos_out
                mov     ah,09h
                mov     dx,offset msg4
                int     21h
;
; Restore the default drive and directory and exit.
;
exit:           mov     ax,3301h                ;Restore the state of Ctrl-
                mov     dl,breakflag            ;  Break checking
                int     21h
                mov     ah,0Eh                  ;Restore default drive
                mov     dl,drive
                int     21h
                mov     ah,3Bh                  ;Restore current directory
                mov     dx,offset directory
                int     21h
                mov     ax,4C00h                ;Exit with ERRORLEVEL=0
                int     21h
main            endp

;************************************************************************
; FINDCHAR advances SI to the next non-space or non-comma character.
; On return, carry set indicates EOL was encountered.
;************************************************************************

findchar        proc    near
                lodsb                           ;Get the next character
                cmp     al,20h                  ;Loop if space
                je      findchar
                cmp     al,2Ch                  ;Loop if comma
                je      findchar
                dec     si                      ;Point SI to the character
                cmp     al,0Dh                  ;Exit with carry set if end
                je      eol                     ;  of line is reached

                clc                             ;Clear carry and exit
                ret

eol:            stc                             ;Set carry and exit
                ret
findchar        endp

;************************************************************************
; FINDDELIM advances SI to the next space or comma character.  On return,
; carry set indicates EOL was encountered.
;************************************************************************

finddelim       proc    near
                lodsb                           ;Get the next character
                cmp     al,20h                  ;Exit if space
                je      fd_exit
                cmp     al,2Ch                  ;Exit if comma
                je      fd_exit
                cmp     al,0Dh                  ;Loop back for more if end
```

```
                 jne     finddelim           ;  of line isn't reached

                 dec     si                  ;Set carry and exit
                 stc
                 ret

fd_exit:         dec     si                  ;Clear carry and exit
                 clc
                 ret
finddelim        endp


;***********************************************************************
; SCANHELP scans the command line for a /? switch.  If found, carry returns
; set and SI contains its offset.  If not found, carry returns clear.
;***********************************************************************

scanhelp         proc    near
                 push    si                  ;Save SI
scanloop:        lodsb                       ;Get a character
                 cmp     al,0Dh              ;Exit if end of line
                 je      scan_exit
                 cmp     al,22h              ;Branch if it's a quotation
                 je      skip                ;  mark
                 cmp     al,"?"              ;Loop if not "?"
                 jne     scanloop
                 cmp     byte ptr [si-2],"/" ;Loop if not "/"
                 jne     scanloop

                 add     sp,2                ;Clear the stack
                 sub     si,2                ;Adjust SI
                 stc                         ;Set carry and exit
                 ret

scan_exit:       pop     si                  ;Restore SI
                 clc                         ;Clear carry and exit
                 ret

skip:            lodsb                       ;Get a character
                 cmp     al,0Dh              ;Exit if end of line
                 je      scan exit
                 cmp     al,22h              ;Reenter the loop if it's
                 je      scanloop            ;  a quotation mark
                 jmp     skip                ;Continue scanning
scanhelp         endp


;***********************************************************************
; SEARCHDIR searches files in the current directory for a text string.  If
; FINDTEXT was started with a /S switch, SEARCHDIR calls itself recursively
; to search the current directory and all its descendants.
;***********************************************************************

searchdir        proc    near
                 push    bp                  ;Save BP
                 mov     ah,2Fh              ;Get current DTA address
                 int     21h
                 push    bx                  ;Save it
```

```
                push    es
                sub     sp,2Bh                  ;Make room on the stack
                mov     bp,sp                   ;Establish addressability
                mov     ah,1Ah                  ;Set DTA address to a
                mov     dx,bp                   ;  location in the
                int     21h                     ;  stack

                inc     dirssearched            ;Increment directory count
                mov     ah,47h                  ;Add the current directory
                sub     dl,dl                   ;  to the path string for
                mov     si,offset pathstring+3  ;  output
                int     21h

                cmp     scrnflag,0              ;Branch if not full-screen
                je      findfirstfile
                call    win_showdir             ;Display directory name
                mov     dh,rows                 ;Blank the directory count
                mov     dl,23                   ;  currently displayed
                mov     cx,5
                mov     bl,window_color1
                call    blankcells
                mov     ax,dirssearched         ;Display the new number of
                mov     dl,23                   ;  directories searched
                call    bios_outnum
;
; Search all the files in the current directory.
;
findfirstfile:  mov     ah,4Eh                  ;Find first file matching
                mov     cx,fileattr             ;  the search criteria
                mov     dx,filespec
                int     21h
                jc      findfirstdir            ;Branch if no files found

search_another: call    searchfile              ;Search the file

                mov     ah,4Fh                  ;Find next file matching
                int     21h                     ;  the search criteria
                jnc     search_another
;
; Search for a subdirectory to go to if /S was specified.
;
findfirstdir:   cmp     descflag,0              ;Exit if /S was not entered
                je      sd_exit
                mov     ah,4Eh                  ;Find first file or
                mov     cx,17h                  ;  subdirectory
                mov     dx,offset defspec
                int     21h
                jc      sd_exit                 ;Exit if nothing found

testdir:        cmp     byte ptr [bp+30],2Eh    ;Skip . and .. entries
                je      findnextdir
                test    byte ptr [bp+21],10h    ;Branch if name returned
                jz      findnextdir             ;  is not a subdirectory

                mov     ah,3Bh                  ;Change to the subdirectory
                mov     dx,bp                   ;  whose name was just
```

```
                        add     dx,30                   ;  returned
                        int     21h

                        call    searchdir               ;Search it too

                        mov     ah,3Bh                  ;Go up a directory level
                        mov     dx,offset updir
                        int     21h

findnextdir:            mov     ah,4Fh                  ;Find next subdirectory
                        int     21h
                        jnc     testdir                 ;Loop back if found
;
; Restore BP, the DTA, and the stack, then exit.
;
sd_exit:                add     sp,2Bh                  ;Adjust the stack pointer
                        mov     ah,1Ah                  ;Restore the DTA to where
                        mov     bx,ds                   ;  it was on entry
                        pop     ds
                        pop     dx
                        int     21h
                        mov     ds,bx
                        pop     bp                      ;Restore BP
                        ret                             ;Return to caller
searchdir               endp


;**************************************************************************
; SEARCHFILE searches the file whose name is at [BP+30] for a text string.
;**************************************************************************

searchfile      proc    near
                        mov     foundflag,0             ;Initialize flag
                        inc     filessearched           ;Increment search count
                        cmp     scrnflag,0              ;Branch if not full-screen
                        je      openfile
                        call    win_showfile            ;Display file name
                        mov     dh,rows                 ;Blank the file count
                        mov     dl,50                   ;  currently displayed
                        mov     cx,5
                        mov     bl,window_color1
                        call    blankcells
                        mov     ax,filessearched        ;Display the new number of
                        mov     dl,50                   ;  files searched
                        call    bios_outnum
;
; Open the file.
;
openfile:               mov     ax,3D00h                ;Open the file for
                        mov     dx,bp                   ;  reading
                        add     dx,30
                        int     21h
                        jnc     savehandle              ;Branch if no error
                        mov     dx,offset errmsg4       ;Exit on error
search_error:   cmp     scrnflag,0              ;Branch if not full-screen
                        je      serror1
                        push    dx                      ;Save DX
```

```
                      call    restore_video           ;Restore video before exit
                      pop     dx                      ;Restore DX
          serror1:    mov     ah,09h                  ;Output the error message
                      int     21h
                      call    dos_outname             ;Followed by the file name
                      mov     ah,09h                  ;Advance cursor to next
                      mov     dx,offset crlf          ;  line before exit
                      int     21h
                      jmp     exit                    ;Terminate the program
          savehandle: mov     handle,ax               ;Save file handle
          ;
          ; Read a block of data and search it.
          ;
          readblock:  mov     ah,3Fh                  ;Read one 24K block of data
                      mov     bx,handle               ;  from the file
                      mov     cx,6000h
                      mov     dx,offset buffer1
                      int     21h
                      mov     dx,offset errmsg5       ;Exit on error
                      jc      search_error
                      cmp     ax,textsize             ;Done if bytes read is less
                      jae     search1                 ;  than search text length
                      jmp     search_done

          search1:    mov     bytesread,ax            ;Save bytes read count
                      cmp     bitflag,0               ;Strip the high bits off
                      je      search2                 ;  characters in the buffer
                      mov     si,offset buffer1       ;  if /7 was entered
                      mov     cx,bytesread
                      call    striphigh

          search2:    cmp     caseflag,0              ;Branch if /C was not entered
                      jne     search3
                      cmp     scrnflag,0              ;Also branch if /I was not
                      je      nocopy                  ;  entered
                      mov     si,offset buffer1       ;Copy everything in BUFFER1
                      mov     di,offset buffer2       ;  to BUFFER2
                      mov     cx,bytesread
                      rep     movsb
          nocopy:     mov     si,offset buffer1       ;Capitalize everything in
                      mov     cx,bytesread            ;  BUFFER1
                      call    stripcase

          search3:    mov     cx,bytesread            ;Compute number of string
                      sub     cx,textsize             ;  comparisons to be
                      inc     cx                      ;  performed
                      mov     si,offset buffer1       ;Point SI to buffer

          search4:    push    cx                      ;Save CX and SI
                      push    si
                      mov     di,offset text          ;Point DI to search string
                      mov     cx,textsize             ;Initialize CX with length
                      repe    cmpsb                   ;Compare the strings
                      je      match                   ;Branch if match found
          continue:   pop     si                      ;Restore SI and CX
                      pop     cx
```

```
                inc     si                      ;Increment SI
                loop    search4                 ;Loop back for more

                cmp     bytesread,6000h         ;Search done if end of
                jb      search_done             ;   file reached

                mov     ax,textsize             ;Set the file pointer
                neg     ax                      ;   back to make sure
                cwd                             ;   text strings that
                mov     cx,dx                   ;   straddle buffer
                mov     dx,ax                   ;   boundaries are
                mov     bx,handle               ;   not missed
                mov     ax,4201h
                int     21h
                jmp     readblock               ;Process another block
;
; Process a match.
;
match:          cmp     scrnflag,0              ;Branch if not full-screen
                je      match2
                cmp     foundflag,0             ;Increment files found count
                jne     alreadyfound            ;   if this is the first match
                mov     foundflag,1             ;   in this file
                inc     filesfound
                push    si                      ;Save SI
                mov     dh,rows                 ;Blank the found count
                mov     dl,74                   ;   currently displayed
                mov     cx,5
                mov     bl,window_color1
                call    blankcells
                mov     ax,filesfound           ;Display the new number of
                mov     dl,74                   ;   files found
                call    bios_outnum
                pop     si                      ;Restore SI

alreadyfound:   call    showfile                ;Show the file
                or      ah,ah                   ;Reenter the search loop
                je      continue                ;   if Enter was pressed
                add     sp,4                    ;Clean off the stack
                cmp     ah,2                    ;Search complete if spacebar
                je      search_done             ;   was pressed
                call    restore_video           ;Restore video and terminate
                jmp     exit                    ;   if Esc was pressed

match2:         add     sp,4                    ;Clean off the stack
                call    dos_outname             ;Display the file name
                inc     filesfound              ;Increment files found count
;
; Close the file and exit.
;
search_done:    mov     ah,3Eh                  ;Close file with DOS
                mov     bx,handle               ;   function 3EH
                int     21h
                ret
searchfile      endp
```

```
;**************************************************************************
; SHOWFILE displays the contents of a file surrounding the point where
; a match was found in the search for matching text.  On entry, SI points
; to the address just after the text string in BUFFER1 and [BP+30] points
; to the name of the file.  On exit, AH=0 if Enter was pressed, AH=1 if
; Esc was pressed, or AH=2 if the spacebar was pressed.
;**************************************************************************

showfile        proc    near
                push    si                      ;Save SI
                mov     dx,0020h                ;Blank "FINDTEXT" at the
                mov     cx,8                    ;  top of the screen
                mov     bl,window_color1
                call    blankcells
;
; Display the file name at the top of the screen and instructions at bottom.
;
                mov     di,offset pathstring    ;Compute length of path
                call    strlen                  ;  name string
                mov     bx,cx                   ;Save it in BX
                mov     di,bp                   ;Compute length of file
                add     di,30                   ;  name string
                call    strlen
                add     bx,cx                   ;Add it to BX
                mov     dx,79                   ;Calculate where to write
                sub     dx,bx                   ;  string such that it is
                shr     dx,1                    ;  centered
                sub     dh,dh
                mov     bl,window_color1
                mov     si,offset pathstring    ;Output path string
                call    bios_outtext
                cmp     byte ptr [bp+3],0       ;Branch if this is the
                je      show1                   ;  root directory
                mov     si,offset rootdir       ;Output a "\" to separate
                call    bios_outtext            ;  the path and file names
show1:          mov     si,bp                   ;Output file name
                add     si,30
                call    bios_outtext

                mov     dh,rows                 ;Display instructions at the
                mov     dl,1                    ;  bottom of the screen
                mov     bl,window_color2
                mov     si,offset scrntxt3
                call    bios_outtext
                mov     bl,window_color1
                mov     dl,13
                mov     si,offset scrntxt9
                call    bios_outtext
                mov     dl,32
                mov     si,offset scrntxt10
                call    bios_outtext
                mov     dl,48
                mov     si,offset scrntxt11
                call    bios_outtext

                mov     ax,0600h                ;Clear the screen
```

```
                mov     cx,0100h
                mov     dh,rows
                dec     dh
                mov     dl,79
                mov     bh,text_color
                call    exec10h
;
; Calculate starting and ending buffer offsets and show the file.
;
                pop     si                      ;Retrieve buffer pointer
                sub     si,textsize             ;Point SI to start of text
                mov     dx,si                   ;Save it in DX
                mov     al,80                   ;Compute the maximum number
                mov     bl,rows                 ;  of characters that can be
                dec     bl                      ;  displayed
                mul     bl
                push    ax                      ;Save it
                mov     al,80                   ;Redo the calculation, this
                mov     bl,rows                 ;  time making sure that the
                shr     bl,1                    ;  number of rows is an even
                shl     bl,1                    ;  number
                dec     bl
                mul     bl
                sub     ax,textsize             ;Now compute the buffer
                shr     ax,1                    ;  offset where display
                sub     si,ax                   ;  should begin
                cmp     si,offset buffer1
                jnb     start_ok
                mov     si,offset buffer1
start_ok:       pop     cx                      ;Retrieve count
                sub     dx,si                   ;Calculate offset to text
                push    si                      ;Save starting offset
                add     si,cx                   ;Compute ending offset
                mov     di,offset buffer1       ;Compute maximum offset
                add     di,bytesread
                cmp     si,di                   ;Compare the offsets
                jbe     end_ok                  ;CX okay if end < maximum
                sub     si,di                   ;Otherwise subtract the
                sub     cx,si                   ;  difference from CX
end_ok:         pop     si                      ;Retrieve starting offset
                cmp     caseflag,0
                jne     blast_it
                add     si,6000h                ;Adjust if case-sensitive
blast_it:       push    es                      ;Save ES
                mov     es,videoseg             ;Point ES:DI to video buffer
                mov     di,videobuf
                add     di,160
out_loop1:      lodsb                           ;Get a character
                cmp     al,32                   ;Substitute a period if
                jb      period                  ;  it's non-displayable
                cmp     al,126
                jbe     copy_it
period:         mov     al,"."
copy_it:        stosb                           ;Copy it to the video buffer
                inc     di                      ;Advance to next character
                loop    out_loop1               ;Loop until done
```

```
;
; Highlight the search text.
;
                mov     di,videobuf             ;Point DI to the byte that
                add     di,160                  ;  corresponds to the first
                shl     dx,1                    ;  attribute of the search
                add     di,dx                   ;  text
                inc     di
                mov     al,hilite_color         ;Load attribute in AL
                mov     cx,textsize             ;Load string length in CX
out_loop2:      stosb                           ;Highlight the search text
                inc     di
                loop    out_loop2
                pop     es                      ;Restore ES
;
; Get a keyboard response from the user.
;
getkey:         mov     ah,0                    ;Read keyboard
                int     16h
                sub     ah,ah                   ;Set AH to 0
                cmp     al,0Dh                  ;Exit if Enter was pressed
                je      show_exit
                inc     ah                      ;Set AH to 1
                cmp     al,1Bh                  ;Exit if Esc was pressed
                je      show_abort
                mov     ah,2
                cmp     al,20h                  ;Exit if spacebar was pressed
                jne     getkey                  ;Otherwise loop back for more
;
; Redraw the title bar, status bar, and search window, then exit.
;
show_exit:      push    ax                      ;Save return code
                mov     ax,0600h                ;Clear the screen
                mov     cx,0100h
                mov     dh,rows
                dec     dh
                mov     dl,79
                mov     bh,text_color
                call    exec10h
                call    drawtitle               ;Redraw the title bar
                call    drawstatus              ;Redraw the status bar
                call    drawwindow              ;Redraw the window
                call    win_showdir             ;Display directory name
                call    win_showfile            ;Display file name
                pop     ax                      ;Retrieve return code
show_abort:     ret
showfile        endp


;****************************************************************************
; DOS_OUTNUM converts the number in AX to ASCII and displays it.
;****************************************************************************


dos_outnum      proc    near
                mov     bx,10                   ;Initialize BX with divisor
                sub     cx,cx                   ;Initialize digit counter
divide:         inc     cx                      ;Increment counter
```

```
                        sub     dx,dx               ;Zero high word of DX:AX
                        div     bx                  ;Divide AX by 10
                        push    dx                  ;Save remainder on stack
                        or      ax,ax               ;Loop if AX != 0
                        jnz     divide
        output:         mov     ah,02h              ;Use DOS function 02H
                        pop     dx                  ;Retrieve digit from stack
                        add     dl,30h              ;Convert to ASCII
                        int     21h                 ;Output it
                        loop    output              ;Loop until done
                        ret
        dos_outnum      endp

;****************************************************************************
; DOS_OUTNAME displays the ASCIIZ file name addressed by [BP+30] prefixed
; by the ASCIIZ string PATHSTRING.
;****************************************************************************

        dos_outname     proc    near
                        mov     si,offset pathstring    ;Output path string
                        call    dos_out
                        mov     ah,02h
                        mov     si,offset pathstring    ;Output "\" if this is
                        cmp     byte ptr [si+3],0       ;  not the root directory
                        je      notroot
                        mov     ah,02h
                        mov     dl,"\"
                        int     21h
        notroot:        mov     si,bp                   ;Output file name
                        add     si,30
                        call    dos_out
                        mov     ah,09h                  ;Move cursor to next line
                        mov     dx,offset crlf
                        int     21h
                        ret
        dos_outname     endp

;****************************************************************************
; WIN_SHOWDIR displays the name of the directory being searched in
; the search window.
;****************************************************************************

        win_showdir     proc    near
                        mov     dx,0B1Bh                ;Blank the directory name
                        mov     cx,42                   ;  currently displayed
                        mov     bl,window_color1
                        call    blankcells
                        mov     si,offset pathstring    ;Point SI to PATHSTRING
                        mov     dx,0B1Bh                ;Starting row and column
                        mov     di,si                   ;Get length of PATHSTRING
                        call    strlen
                        cmp     cx,41                   ;Branch if it's greater
                        ja      wsd1                    ;  than 41
                        call    bios_outtext            ;Output PATHSTRING
                        ret                             ;Return to caller
        wsd1:           mov     cx,41                   ;Output first 41 characters
```

```
                        call    bios_out                ;  of PATHSTRING
                        ret                             ;Return to caller
        win_showdir     endp

        ;************************************************************************
        ; WIN_SHOWFILE displays the name of the file being searched in the
        ; search window.  On entry, [BP+30] points to the file name.
        ;************************************************************************

        win_showfile    proc    near
                        mov     dx,0C1Bh                ;Blank the file name
                        mov     cx,42                   ;  currently displayed
                        mov     bl,window_color1
                        call    blankcells
                        mov     si,bp
                        add     si,30
                        mov     dx,0C1Bh                ;Display the file name
                        call    bios_outtext
                        ret
        win_showfile    endp

        ;************************************************************************
        ; STRIPCASE converts lowercase characters to uppercase in the buffer
        ; pointed to by DS:SI.  On entry, CX the buffer length.
        ;************************************************************************

        stripcase       proc    near
                        cmp     byte ptr [si],"a"       ;Skip if less than "a"
                        jb      notlower
                        cmp     byte ptr [si],"z"       ;Skip if greater than "z"
                        ja      notlower
                        and     byte ptr [si],0DFh      ;Capitalize the character
        notlower:       inc     si                      ;Advance SI
                        loop    stripcase               ;Loop until done
                        ret
        stripcase       endp

        ;************************************************************************
        ; STRIPHIGH strips the high bits off the characters in the buffer pointed
        ; to by DS:SI.  On entry, CX holds the buffer length.
        ;************************************************************************

        striphigh       proc    near
                        and     byte ptr [si],7Fh       ;Zero the high bit
                        inc     si                      ;Advance SI
                        loop    striphigh               ;Loop until done
                        ret
        striphigh       endp

        ;************************************************************************
        ; DOS_OUT displays the ASCIIZ text string pointed to by DS:SI using DOS
        ; function 02H.  Text is displayed at the current cursor position.
        ;************************************************************************

        dos_out         proc    near
                        lodsb                           ;Get a character
```

```
                or      al,al                   ;Exit if zero
                jz      dos_exit
                mov     ah,02h                  ;Display it using DOS
                mov     dl,al                   ;  function 02H
                int     21h
                jmp     dos_out                 ;Loop back for more
dos_exit:       ret
dos_out         endp


;**************************************************************************
; INIT_VIDEO sets the video environment for full-screen mode.
;**************************************************************************

init_video      proc    near
                push    es                      ;Point ES to the BIOS
                mov     ax,40h                  ;  Data Area
                mov     es,ax
                mov     al,es:[49h]             ;Get display mode in AL
                cmp     al,7                    ;Continue if mode 2, 3,
                je      mode_ok                 ;  or 7
                cmp     al,2
                je      mode_ok
                cmp     al,3
                je      mode_ok
                mov     ax,0003h                ;Reset video mode
                test    byte ptr es:[63h],40h
                jnz     reset
                mov     ax,0007h
reset:          int     10h
mode_ok:        test    byte ptr es:[63h],40h   ;Determine whether video is
                jnz     is_color                ;  color or monochrome
                call    setmono                 ;Switch to monochrome video
                mov     videoseg,0B000h
is_color:       mov     ax,es:[4Eh]             ;Get starting page address
                mov     videobuf,ax
                mov     al,es:[62h]             ;Get active page number
                mov     pageno,al
                mov     ax,es:[60h]             ;Get cursor type
                mov     cursor,ax
                mov     ah,12h                  ;Find out if there's an
                mov     bl,10h                  ;  EGA, VGA, or XGA
                int     10h                     ;  installed
                cmp     bl,10h
                je      noega
                mov     al,es:[84h]             ;Determine number of rows
                mov     rows,al                 ;  displayed if there is
noega:          pop     es                      ;Restore ES
                mov     ah,08h                  ;Get the color of the
                mov     bh,pageno               ;  character at the
                int     10h                     ;  cursor
                mov     scrn_color,ah
;
; Paint the screen.
;
                mov     ah,01h                  ;Hide the cursor
                mov     ch,20h
```

```
                        int     10h
                        mov     ax,0600h                ;Clear the screen
                        sub     cx,cx
                        mov     dh,rows
                        mov     dl,79
                        mov     bh,text_color
                        int     10h
                        call    drawtitle               ;Display the title bar
                        call    drawstatus              ;Display the status bar
                        call    drawwindow              ;Display the status window
                        ret
        init_video      endp


;**************************************************************************
; RESTORE_VIDEO cleans up the screen before the program terminates.
;**************************************************************************

        restore_video   proc    near
                        mov     ax,0600h                ;Clear the screen
                        sub     cx,cx
                        mov     dh,rows
                        mov     dl,79
                        mov     bh,scrn_color
                        int     10h
                        mov     ah,02h                  ;Home the cursor
                        mov     bh,pageno
                        sub     dx,dx
                        int     10h
                        mov     ah,01h                  ;Redisplay the cursor
                        mov     cx,cursor
                        int     10h
                        ret
        restore_video   endp


;**************************************************************************
; SETMONO replaces color video attributes with monochrome attributes.
;**************************************************************************

        setmono proc    near
                        mov     window_color1,70h
                        mov     window_color2,70h
                        mov     hilite_color,70h
                        mov     text_color,07h
                        ret
        setmono endp


;**************************************************************************
; DRAWTITLE displays the screen title at the top of the screen.
;**************************************************************************

        drawtitle       proc    near
                        sub     dx,dx                   ;Blank the line
                        mov     cx,80
                        mov     bl,window_color1
                        call    blankcells
                        mov     dx,0024h                ;Display title
```

```
                        mov     si,offset scrntxt1
                        call    bios_outtext
                        ret
        drawtitle       endp


;************************************************************************
; DRAWSTATUS displays the status bar at the bottom of the screen.
;************************************************************************

        drawstatus      proc    near
                        mov     dh,rows                 ;Blank the line
                        sub     dl,dl
                        mov     cx,80
                        mov     bl,window_color1
                        call    blankcells
                        mov     dl,1                    ;Display status bar text
                        mov     si,offset scrntxt2
                        mov     bl,window_color2
                        call    bios_outtext

                        mov     ax,dirssearched         ;Display number of
                        mov     bl,window_color1        ;  directories searched
                        mov     dl,23
                        call    bios_outnum

                        mov     ax,filessearched        ;Display number of files
                        mov     dl,50                   ;  searched
                        call    bios_outnum

                        mov     ax,filesfound           ;Display number of files
                        mov     dl,74                   ;  found containing the
                        call    bios_outnum             ;  search string
                        ret
        drawstatus      endp


;************************************************************************
; DRAWWINDOW displays the search window on the screen.
;************************************************************************

        drawwindow      proc    near
                        mov     ax,0600h                ;Blank the area where the
                        mov     cx,080Ah                ;  window will lie
                        mov     dx,0E45h
                        mov     bh,window_color1
                        call    exec10h

                        mov     cx,080Ah                ;Draw a border around the
                        mov     dx,0E45h                ;  window
                        mov     bh,pageno
                        mov     bl,window_color1
                        call    drawbox

                        mov     dx,0A0Ch                ;Display "Searching for:"
                        mov     si,offset scrntxt4
                        mov     bl,window_color2
                        call    bios_outtext
```

```
                mov     dx,ØB11h                ;Display "Location:"
                mov     si,offset scrntxt5
                call    bios_outtext
                mov     dx,ØC15h                ;Display "File:"
                mov     si,offset scrntxt6
                call    bios_outtext

                mov     dx,ØA1Bh                ;Display opening quotation
                mov     bl,window_color1        ;  mark
                mov     si,offset scrntxt7
                call    bios_outtext

                mov     si,srchtext             ;Display search text
                mov     di,si
                call    strlen
                cmp     cx,39
                ja      dw1
                call    bios_outtext
                jmp     short dw2
dw1:            mov     cx,39
                call    bios_out

dw2:            mov     si,offset scrntxt7      ;Display closing quotation
                call    bios_outtext            ;  mark
                ret
drawwindow      endp

;*************************************************************************
; EXEC1ØH executes an INT 1ØH and preserves BP across the call.
;*************************************************************************

exec1Øh         proc    near
                push    bp                      ;Save BP
                int     1Øh                     ;Do the interrupt
                pop     bp                      ;Restore BP
                ret
exec1Øh         endp

;*************************************************************************
; STRLEN returns the length of the ASCIIZ string pointed to by ES:DI in CX.
;*************************************************************************

strlen          proc    near
                mov     cx,ØFFFFh               ;Initialize count
                sub     al,al                   ;Intialize AL
                repne   scasb                   ;Search for zero
                inc     cx                      ;Calculate number of
                mov     ax,ØFFFFh               ;  bytes that were
                xchg    ax,cx                   ;  examined
                sub     cx,ax
                ret
strlen          endp
```

```
;**********************************************************************
; BIOS_OUT displays an ASCII string.  On entry, DS:SI points to the string,
; DH and DL hold the starting row and column, BL holds the attribute to be
; used, and CX holds the character count.
;**********************************************************************

bios_out        proc    near
                mov     ah,02h                  ;Set the cursor position
                mov     bh,pageno
                call    exec10h
                push    cx                      ;Save count
                lodsb                           ;Get a character
                mov     ah,09h                  ;Display it
                mov     cx,1
                call    exec10h
                inc     dl                      ;Advance column number
                pop     cx                      ;Retrieve count
                loop    bios_out                ;Loop until done
                ret
bios_out        endp


;**********************************************************************
; BIOS_OUTTEXT displays the ASCIIZ text string pointed to by DS:SI using
; BIOS text output functions.  On entry, DH and DL hold the row and column
; where output should begin and BL holds the attribute to be used.
;**********************************************************************

bios_outtext    proc    near
                mov     ah,02h                  ;Set the cursor position
                mov     bh,pageno
                call    exec10h
                lodsb                           ;Get a character
                or      al,al                   ;Exit if zero
                jz      bios_exit
                mov     ah,09h                  ;Display it
                mov     cx,1
                call    exec10h
                inc     dl                      ;Advance column number
                jmp     bios_outtext            ;Loop back for more
bios_exit:      ret
bios_outtext    endp


;**********************************************************************
; BIOS_OUTNUM converts the number in AX to ASCII form and displays it using
; BIOS output functions.  On entry, AX holds the number, DH and DL hold the
; row and column address, and BL holds the attribute to be used.
;**********************************************************************

bios_outnum     proc    near
                mov     si,bx                   ;Save BX and DX
                mov     di,dx
                mov     bx,10                   ;Initialize BX with divisor
                sub     cx,cx                   ;Initialize digit counter
bnum1:          inc     cx                      ;Increment counter
                sub     dx,dx                   ;Zero high word of DX:AX
                div     bx                      ;Divide AX by 10
```

```
                push    dx                          ;Save remainder on stack
                or      ax,ax                       ;Loop if AX != 0
                jnz     bnum1

                mov     bx,si                       ;Retrieve BX and DX
                mov     dx,di
                mov     bh,pageno                   ;Place page number in BH

bnum2:          mov     ah,02h                      ;Position the cursor
                call    exec10h
                pop     ax                          ;Retrieve digit from stack
                add     al,30h                      ;Convert to ASCII
                mov     ah,09h                      ;Output it using BIOS
                push    cx                          ;  function 09H
                mov     cx,1
                call    exec10h
                pop     cx
                inc     dl                          ;Advance the cursor
                loop    bnum2                       ;Loop until done
                ret
bios_outnum     endp


;**************************************************************************
; BLANKCELLS blanks a line or part of a line.  On entry, DH and DL hold the
; starting row and column, CX holds the number of cells to blank, and BL
; holds the attribute to be used.
;**************************************************************************

blankcells      proc    near
                mov     ah,02h                      ;Position the cursor
                mov     bh,pageno
                call    exec10h
                mov     ax,0920h                    ;Blank the cells
                call    exec10h
                ret
blankcells      endp


;**************************************************************************
; DRAWBOX draws a single line box.  On entry, CH and CL hold the row and
; column address of the upper left corner of the box, DH and DL the address
; of the lower right corner, BH the page number, and BL the attribute to be
; used.
;**************************************************************************

drawbox         proc    near
                mov     row1,ch                     ;Save box coordinates and
                mov     col1,cl                     ;  compute the box height
                mov     row2,dh                     ;  and box width
                mov     col2,dl
                push    cx
                sub     dh,ch
                dec     dh
                mov     boxheight,dh
                sub     dl,cl
                dec     dl
```

```
        mov     boxwidth,dl

        mov     ah,02h                  ;Position the cursor at the
        pop     dx                      ;   upper left corner
        call    exec10h

        mov     ah,09h                  ;Draw upper left corner
        mov     al,218
        mov     cx,1
        call    exec10h

        mov     dh,row1                 ;Draw upper horizontal
        mov     dl,col1
        inc     dl
        mov     cx,word ptr boxwidth
        call    drawhorizontal

        mov     ah,02h                  ;Draw upper right corner
        mov     dl,col2
        call    exec10h
        mov     ah,09h
        mov     al,191
        mov     cx,1
        call    exec10h

        inc     dh                      ;Draw right vertical
        mov     cx,word ptr boxheight
        call    drawvertical

        mov     ah,02h                  ;Draw lower right corner
        mov     dh,row2
        call    exec10h
        mov     ah,09h
        mov     al,217
        mov     cx,1
        call    exec10h

        mov     dl,col1                 ;Draw lower horizontal
        inc     dl
        mov     cx,word ptr boxwidth
        call    drawhorizontal

        mov     ah,02h                  ;Draw lower left corner
        dec     dl
        call    exec10h
        mov     ah,09h
        mov     al,192
        mov     cx,1
        call    exec10h

        mov     dh,row1                 ;Draw left vertical
        inc     dh
        mov     cx,word ptr boxheight
        call    drawvertical
```

```
                        ret
drawbox         endp


;*************************************************************************
; DRAWHORIZONTAL draws a horizontal line at the cursor position passed in
; DH and DL.  Length is specified in CX, attribute in BL, and page number in
; BH.  The line is drawn left to right.
;*************************************************************************

drawhorizontal  proc    near
                mov     ah,02h                  ;Position the cursor
                call    exec10h
                mov     ah,09h                  ;Draw horizontal
                mov     al,196
                call    exec10h
dh_exit:        ret
drawhorizontal  endp


;*************************************************************************
; DRAWVERTICAL draws a vertical line at the cursor position passed in
; DH and DL.  Length is specified in CX, attribute in BL, and page number
; in BH.  The line is drawn top to bottom.
;*************************************************************************

drawvertical    proc    near
                mov     ah,02h                  ;Position the cursor
                call    exec10h
                push    cx                      ;Save CX
                mov     ah,09h                  ;Draw one character
                mov     al,179
                mov     cx,1
                call    exec10h
                inc     dh
                pop     cx                      ;Retrieve CX
                loop    drawvertical            ;Loop until done
dv_exit:        ret
drawvertical    endp

text            =       $                       ;Text being searched for
buffer1         =       $+80h                   ;File I/O buffer 1 (24K)
buffer2         =       $+6080h                 ;File I/O buffer 2 (24K)

code            ends
                end     begin
```

FINDTEXT's first act at start-up, as usual, is to scan the command line for a /? switch and display a help screen if a /? was entered. If help is not requested, FINDTEXT checks to make sure it has at least 60k of memory available to it by checking the value of the SP register. In addition to the 3.5k it needs for the code itself, FINDTEXT also requires 48k of buffer space between the end of the code and bottom of the stack for file I/O, plus room for the stack itself. If you start FINDTEXT with a /S switch, it operates recursively in a manner similar to NUKE, so additional stack space may be required. If there is less than 60k of

RAM available to it when it is started, FINDTEXT aborts with a "Not enough memory" message.

If a path name was entered on the command line, FINDTEXT saves the current drive and directory and switches to the drive and directory specified. It also checks to see if the path name contained a file name, and, if it did, stores it to use as a file specification string later on when it begins reading files. To determine whether a file specification was included, FINDTEXT attempts to set the current directory using the path name entered on the command line. If the call fails, FINDTEXT assumes everything following the final backslash in the path name must be a file specification. To test this theory, it saves the address of the possible file specification, and then replaces the terminating backslash in the path name with a zero, effectively converting it to an ASCIIZ path name. Next it tries to change directories with the converted path name. If it works, then the assumption about the file specification was good and FINDTEXT is all set to go in the directory that was specified. If the call fails, however, FINDTEXT displays the message "Invalid path specification" and terminates.

FINDTEXT takes care of a final few chores before beginning the search. First, provided it wasn't started with a /C switch, it converts the characters in the string to uppercase so that case will not be a factor in comparisons. Later, it will also convert the text of the files it reads to uppercase. If a /7 switch was entered, FINDTEXT strips the eighth bit from each character in the text string, and will do likewise for text read from disk. If it was started with a /I switch, FINDTEXT calls the procedure INIT_VIDEO to prepare itself to run in full-screen mode. Among other things, INIT_VIDEO changes to an 80-column text mode if fewer than 80 columns are displayed, selects the video attributes that will be used based on whether it finds itself running on a monochrome or color video adapter, hides the cursor so it won't be distracting, and paints the screen as shown in Figure 11.2.

FINDTEXT also saves the current status of *break-checking* (which determines how often DOS checks for presses of Ctrl-C and Ctrl-Break) and then enables break-checking. When break-checking is disabled, DOS only checks for presses of Ctrl-C and Ctrl-Break at the infrequent times when certain DOS functions are called. By enabling break-checking, FINDTEXT ensures that you can get its attention at almost any time by pressing Ctrl-C or Ctrl-Break. DOS function 33H is the vehicle both for determining the current status of break-checking and for setting it. FINDTEXT saves the current state with the instructions

```
mov     ax,3300h
int     21h
mov     dl,breakflag
```

and enables break-checking with

```
mov     ah,3301h
```

```
mov     dl,1
int     21h
```

Had DL been set to 0 in this last code sequence, break-checking would have been disabled. Before it terminates, FINDTEXT restores break-checking to the state it was in when it was started so that other programs won't be affected by its actions. FINDTEXT also alters the interrupt 23H vector, which holds the address of the routine that DOS executes when Ctrl-C or Ctrl-Break is pressed, to point to a location in the code that aborts the program.

The SEARCHDIR and SEARCHFILE Procedures

The heart of FINDTEXT is the procedure SEARCHDIR, which searches each file in the current directory for the text specified on the command line. If the program was started with a /S switch, SEARCHDIR calls itself recursively to search all the files in the descendants of the current directory, too. The logic employed is similar to that used in NUKE, except that SEARCHDIR traverses the directory tree from top to bottom rather than from bottom to top.

For each file it finds in the current directory, SEARCHDIR calls another procedure called SEARCHFILE to perform the actual search for the text string. SEARCHFILE reads the file into a 24k buffer at the end of the program. If the program is running in interactive mode and was not started with a /C switch, SEARCHFILE copies the contents of the buffer to a second buffer and converts all the characters in the first one to uppercase. All the string comparisons are performed in the first buffer. If FINDTEXT finds a match in interactive mode, it uses the second buffer to display the file in its original, unaltered form.

To search the buffered file data for instances of the text string entered on the command line, SEARCHFILE uses a classic string comparison algorithm. If there are *m* bytes in the buffer and the search text is *n* bytes long, then a total of *m-n*+1 string comparisons is performed. It works like this. Let's say the buffer contains 11 characters—the string "PC Magazine"—and that we're searching for the string "Mag." The first time through the search loop, the strings are compared like this:

```
P C   M a g a z i n e
- - -
M a g
```

The characters "PC" are compared to the characters "Mag," so no match is made. The second time through the loop, the comparison begins one byte further into "PC Magazine," as in

```
P C   M a g a z i n e
  - - -
  M a g
```

This time, "C M" is compared with "Mag," and again no match is made. However, the fourth time through the loop, the search is set up like this:

```
P C   M a g a z i n e
      - - -
      M a g
```

Now the search will turn up a match, and SEARCHFILE will either display the name of the file the text is contained in if it's running in non-interactive mode, or display the contents of the file around the letters "Mag" if instead it's running in interactive mode. Afterward, the search proceeds, and on the ninth and final pass through the text buffer, the characters "ine" will be compared to "Mag" and nothing will turn up. The beauty of this algorithm is that it works no matter how large the buffer is or how small the search string is. A large differential between the two just means that more comparisons must be performed.

If a file is larger than 24k, SEARCHFILE reads it in separate 24k blocks. There is one precaution it is forced to take as a result. To make sure it won't miss strings that happen to fall on the boundary between two 24k blocks, SEARCHFILE calls DOS function 42H to move the file pointer back a number of bytes equal to the length of the search string before each new block is read. The code looks like this:

```
mov     ax,textsize
neg     ax
cwd
mov     cx,dx
mov     dx,ax
mov     bx,handle
mov     ax,4201h
int     21h
```

Function 42H accepts a *method code* in AL, a file handle in BX, and a 32-bit value in CX:DX. The method code determines how the value in CX:DX is interpreted. A 0 means it specifies the new position for the file pointer as an offset from the beginning of the file; a 1 means it specifies an offset relative to the current position in the file; and a 2 means it's interpreted as a byte offset from the end of the file. SEARCHFILE employs method number 1 and passes a negative integer in CX:DX to set the file pointer back the specified number of bytes. In assembly language, you can convert a positive integer smaller than 32,768 in AX into a negative integer in DX:AX with the two instructions

```
neg     ax
cwd
```

NEG AX negates the value in AX, while CWD converts the word in AX to a double word in DX:AX. If the length of the search text is, say, 16 bytes, then the call to function 42H ultimately sets the file pointer back 16 bytes.

When SEARCHFILE locates an occurrence of the searched-for text string in interactive mode, it calls a third procedure named SHOWFILE to display the contents of the file surrounding the string. To keep things simple, SHOWFILE doesn't attempt to format the text like a word processor would; instead, it simply fills the screen with text, ignoring formatting characters such as tabs and carriage returns. To make the display fast, SHOWFILE writes the text directly to video memory rather than use the text output routines in the video BIOS. As a result, the text appears to literally pop up on the screen, even on an 8086. Had SHOW-FILE used the BIOS instead, the display rate would appear sluggish by comparison—even on fast 386 PCs.

To write directly to the video buffer, SHOWFILE uses two of the values stashed away by INIT_VIDEO. In text mode, the segment address of the video buffer is always B000H for monochrome modes and B800H for color modes. INIT_VIDEO places the appropriate segment value in the memory location labeled VIDEOSEG. It also retrieves the word from offset 4EH in the BIOS Data Area that marks the location in the video buffer where the active page begins and stores it in VIDEOBUF. (In text modes, the video buffer is divided into units called *pages*, and programs can choose which page to display; if a program chooses to write directly to video memory, it's up to the program to determine what the active page is and to compute its address.) With these values in hand, SHOWFILE uses the 80x86 LODSB and STOSB instructions to transfer data from BUFFER1 into the video buffer. As it does, it replaces characters with ASCII codes lower than 32 or higher than 126 with the ASCII code for a period to keep from cluttering the display with non-text.

When it's run in interactive mode, FINDTEXT uses video output routines in the BIOS, accessed through interrupt 10H, for all other screen I/O. You can see examples of these functions by examining procedures such as DRAWWINDOW, DRAWBOX, and BIOS_OUT, to name a few. In non-interactive mode, FINDTEXT uses DOS text output functions for all its screen I/O.

One final procedure in FINDTEXT that may interest you is EXEC10H, which consists of just three lines:

```
push    bp
int     10h
pop     bp
```

This routine is included because of a bug in some of the early IBM video BIOS modules that destroys the value of BP when an interrupt 10H is executed. Because FINDTEXT uses BP as a pointer to the name of the file that is currently being searched (it has to—the file name is saved on the stack, and only BP and SP can specify offsets relative to the SS register), it is essential that this value be preserved. Therefore, rather than sandwich every INT 10H instruction between a PUSH BP and a POP BP, FINDTEXT calls on EXEC10H to perform most calls to interrupt 10H. This slows the program down slightly, but it keeps the code length down and ensures that FINDTEXT will run on old as well as new PCs.

Changing Directories the Easy Way

Long path names are a bore. They also create a lot of work because DOS's CD command demands that the path to the directory you want to change be spelled out in full unless it happens to be a descendant of the current directory. To cut down on the typing required to navigate directory trees, the disks included with this book contain a utility by Michael Holmes and Bob Flanders called CDX that supplements the DOS CD command and applies a bit of intelligence to the process of switching from one directory to another.

The syntax for CDX is

```
CDX [/B] [/+] [/F filename] [drivelist]p1 p2 ... pn
```

where /B has CDX stop at the first directory it finds that matches the criteria you specified elsewhere on the command line without prompting for a yes or no response; /+ includes floppies as well as hard disks and other logical drives in the search; /F switches to the directory that contains a file named *filename*; *drivelist* identifies one or more drives; and *p1, p2,* and so on are parameters that identify, in whole or in part, the names of one or more directories.

Basically, CDX lets you do three things that CD doesn't. First, it lets you specify just part of the name of the directory you want to change to, and it doesn't require you to enter a path name. Second, it lets you change to a directory that contains a file of a certain name without requiring you to know the name of the directory itself. Third, it lets you change drives as well as directories if needed, and search more than one drive for a directory specification.

Let's say that you're somewhere on drive C and that you want to switch to \WP\DOC\LETTERS. With CDX, rather than type

```
CD \WP\DOC\LETTERS
```

you can type

```
CDX LET
```

CDX will search the current drive for all directories that begin with the letters LET. Then it will display the name of each one followed by a question mark, your prompt to type **Y** to change to that directory or **N** to continue the search. If there is not a directory whose name begins with "LET," or if you press **N** and no more are found, CDX notifies you that the requested path/file was not found. You can eliminate the yes/no prompt by including a /B switch. The command

```
CDX /B LET
```

changes to the first directory beginning with "LET" that CDX locates on the current drive.

You can narrow the directories that CDX will search by supplying additional components of the path name. For example, you could also change to \WP\DOC\LETTERS by typing

```
CDX W D LET
```

or simply

```
CDX WP L
```

This capability is especially useful if you use the /B switch to ensure that only one directory can possibly match the search criteria. For example, the command

```
CDX /B LET
```

will switch to \123\LETTERS if such a directory exists and CDX finds it before it finds \WP\DOC\LETTERS. However, the command

```
CDX /B W LET
```

will skip \123\LETTERS and go directly to \WP\DOC\LETTERS, because no directory in the path to \123\LETTERS has a name that begins with W.

CDX also permits you to switch to a directory based on the name of a file contained in that directory. If \WP\DOC\LETTERS contains a file named MINUTES.DOC, then the command

```
CDX /F MINUTES.DOC
```

will change to it. You can use wildcards in the file name if you wish. The command

```
CDX /F MIN*.*
```

is equivalent to the previous command but requires less typing. As usual, CDX will display the name of each directory containing a file of the specified name and prompt you to answer yes or no to switch to the indicated directory. You can go to the first directory that contains a file of the specified name by combining the /B and /F switches, as in

```
CDX /B /F MIN*.*
```

CDX will search other drives in addition to the default drive if you ask it to, and it will switch drives for you if it finds a directory on a remote drive fitting the search criteria. The command

```
CDX D:WIN
```

will switch to a directory on drive D that begins with the letters WIN. CDX will also accept multiple drive identifiers. The command

```
CDX CDE:WIN
```

searches drives C, D, and E for directories beginning with "WIN," while the command

```
CDX *:WIN
```

searches all drives except A and B. You can include A and B also with the /+ switch. The command

```
CDX /+ *:WIN
```

searches all drives, including drives A and B.

In like manner, you can exclude one or more drives from the search by preceding the list of drive identifiers with a minus sign. In this case, CDX searches all the drives you didn't specify, except drives A and B. For example, the command

```
CDX -EF:WIN
```

searches all drives but A, B, E, and F for the specified directory, while the command

```
CDX /+ -EF
```

searches all but E and F. You can even combine the list of drive identifiers with the /F switch to search for directories on remote drives that contain a particular file. The command

```
CDX /F *.DOC ACD:
```

displays only the names of directories that contain a file with the extension .DOC and that are located on drive A, C, or D.

CDX isn't a total replacement for CD. You'll still want to use the CD command if you know the name of the directory you want to go to and the path to it isn't prohibitively long. Also, the CD command will tell you what the current directory is on another drive (for example, CD D:), while CDX will only echo the name of the current directory on the default drive. Used in the right situations, however, CDX will save you a lot of time and trouble.

Summary

In addition to having five useful new utilities to add to your collection, you've now been exposed to some of the basic techniques that DOS application programs use to operate on files and disks. Among other things, the assembly language listings presented in this chapter provide graphic examples of how to

- Search a directory for files and subdirectories

- Design a recursive directory search algorithm to perform an operation throughout a range of subdirectories

- Perform basic file I/O operations such as opening, reading, writing, and closing files, and moving the file pointer

- Delete files, rename files and subdirectories, remove subdirectories, and change from one directory to another

- Parse the command line and break a string that contains a drive name, a path name, and a file specification into three separate components

- Scan the command line for switches and display a help screen when /? is entered

- Use BIOS video output routines to take over the display and generate interactive color screens

The utilities in this chapter probably bring to mind other utilities that would also be useful. It wouldn't be too hard to convert the part of FINDTEXT that performs recursive directory searches into the beginnings of a WHEREIS utility that searches an entire disk for files. The need for such a utility isn't as urgent now that DIR will operate recursively with the /S option, but there are plenty of other uses for such an algorithm. If you've been reading *PC Magazine* for a few years, for example, you might remember Charles Petzold's SWEEP utility, which used a form of recursion to execute a DOS command in every directory of a hard disk.

If you're just now learning assembly language, you might try modifying the code for some of these utilities to add features to them. For example, you could add a /D switch to NUKE (for Delete-only) to have it delete all the files from the directories it visits, but leave the directories themselves intact. Or if you don't like the encryption algorithm that ENCRYPT uses, you could replace the procedure named ENCRYPT with one that performs a more sophisticated form of encryption and completely transform the way the program works. Finally, you could substantially improve the utility of FINDTEXT by replacing the SHOWFILE procedure with one that shows text in *formatted* form, where a carriage return breaks a line and a tab moves to the next 8-space boundary. The possibilities are endless.

12 SCREEN, KEYBOARD, AND PRINTER UTILITIES

IN THIS CHAPTER, WE'LL DEVELOP UTILITIES TO HELP YOU BETTER UTILIZE your screen, keyboard, and printer. Although DOS 5.0 is richer in commands for dealing with these devices than any previous version of DOS, it still leaves room for improvement.

Some of the utilities introduced here have appeared in *PC Magazine*'s "Utilities" column in past years, and have been upgraded by their original authors for this book. LASERLST, for example, the classic utility developed by Michael Holmes and Bob Flanders for printing text files on laser printers, has been revised so that it now works with all members of the HP LaserJet family. Others, such as LPT2FILE and SAVER, appear here for the first time. Those come complete with source code so that you can see how they work and perhaps use them as a model for developing utilities of your own.

In all, this chapter will introduce nine new utilities designed to interface to screens, keyboards, and printers. They are

- COLOR, which sets the screen colors in DOS

- SAVER, which automatically blanks the screen after a specified time-out period has elapsed without mouse or keyboard activity

- FKEYS, which lets you assign DOS commands to function keys

- TOGGLE, which lets you toggle Caps Lock, Num Lock, and Scroll Lock from the command line or from within a batch file

- LPT2FILE, which captures printer output to disk

- SETUP and LZSELECT, which let you send escape codes and setup strings to printers from the command line, from inside a pop-up control window, or from inside a menu-driven shell tailored especially for LaserJet printers

- LASERLST, which prints text files on LaserJet and LaserJet-compatible printers, fitting two pages of information onto each 8½-by-11-inch page

- PCSPOOL, which spools printer output so that you can keep working while your documents print

No matter how you use your PC, or what you use it for, you should find something in here that will help you work more productively.

Setting the Screen Colors

In Chapter 6, you learned to use the ANSI.SYS driver to set the DOS screen colors to the combination of foreground and background colors you want. Selecting colors involved using the PROMPT command to send a series of cryptic codes preceded by an escape character, as in

```
PROMPT $e[1;37;44m
```

which causes DOS to display text in bright white against a blue background. Useful as it may be, this method leaves something to be desired when it comes to ease of use. Unless you carry a list of ANSI.SYS escape codes around in your head, you need a reference on hand to determine what parameters correspond to what colors. It shouldn't take so much effort to do something as simple as select the colors you want to work in.

The utility shown in Listing 12.1, COLOR, takes the tedium out of setting the screen colors. It accepts English words such as RED and MAGENTA, translates them into the equivalent ANSI.SYS commands, and transmits them to the ANSI.SYS driver. The syntax for using it is

```
COLOR foreground background
```

where *foreground* specifies the foreground color and *background* specifies the background color. The command

```
COLOR WHITE BLUE
```

tells DOS to display text in white on blue. Valid color identifiers are BLACK, BLUE, GREEN, CYAN, RED, MAGENTA, YELLOW, and WHITE. If you wish, you may substitute BROWN or ORANGE for YELLOW (depending on what type of video adapter and monitor you have, this color is liable to show up in any of the three hues). In addition, you may select bold foreground colors by preceding the color identifier with an underscore character. The command

```
COLOR _WHITE BLUE
```

selects bright white on blue. COLOR makes it easy to experiment with the myriad color combinations. Once you settle on a color scheme, add a COLOR command to your AUTOEXEC.BAT file to activate it every time you boot up.

LISTING 12.1

```
;****************************************************************************
; COLOR sets the screen to the specified combination of colors.  Its
; syntax is
;
;         COLOR foreground background
;
; where "foreground" specifies the foreground color and "background"
; specifies the background color.  Valid values for these parameters are:
;
;         BLACK          RED
;         BLUE           MAGENTA
;         GREEN          YELLOW, ORANGE, or BROWN
;         CYAN           WHITE
;
; Preceding a color identifier with an underscore selects the intense
; version of that color (foreground colors only).  The ANSI.SYS driver
; must be installed.
;****************************************************************************

code            segment
                assume  cs:code,ds:code
                org     100h
begin:          jmp     main

helpmsg         db      "Sets the screen to the specified combination of "
                db      "colors.",13,10,13,10
                db      "COLOR foreground background",13,10,13,10
                db      "  foreground  Foreground color.",13,10
                db      "  background  Background color.",13,10,13,10
                db      "Valid colors are BLACK, BLUE, GREEN, CYAN, RED, "
                db      "MAGENTA, YELLOW, and WHITE.",13,10
                db      "ORANGE or BROWN may be substituted for YELLOW.  "
                db      "Preceding a color identifier",13,10
                db      "with an underscore highlights the color "
                db      "(foreground colors only).",13,10,"$"

errmsg1         db      "Syntax: COLOR foreground background",13,10,"$"
errmsg2         db      "DOS 4.0 or higher required",13,10,"$"
errmsg3         db      "ANSI.SYS not installed",13,10,"$"
errmsg4         db      "Invalid color identifier",13,10,"$"

color_ids       db      "BROWN",0               ;Color ID table
                db      "ORANGE",0
                db      "WHITE",0
                db      "CYAN",0
                db      "MAGENTA",0
                db      "BLUE",0
                db      "YELLOW",0
                db      "GREEN",0
                db      "RED",0
                db      "BLACK",0

command         db      27,"[0;3x;4xm$"         ;ANSI command string
```

```
;****************************************************************************
; Procedure MAIN
;****************************************************************************

main            proc    near
                cld                             ;Clear direction flag
                mov     si,81h                  ;Point SI to command line
                call    scanhelp                ;Scan for "/?" switch
                jnc     checkver                ;Branch if not found
                mov     ah,09h                  ;Display help text and exit
                mov     dx,offset helpmsg       ;   with ERRORLEVEL=0
                int     21h
                mov     ax,4C01h
                int     21h
;
; Make sure this is DOS 4.0 or higher and that ANSI.SYS is installed
; before proceeding.
;
checkver:       mov     dx,offset errmsg2       ;Exit if DOS version
                mov     ah,30h                  ;   is less than 4.0
                int     21h
                cmp     al,4
                jae     checkansi

error:          mov     ah,09h                  ;Display error message and
                int     21h                     ;   exit with ERRORLEVEL=1
                mov     ax,4C01h
                int     21h

checkansi:      mov     ax,1A00h                ;Check for ANSI.SYS using
                int     2Fh                     ;   the DOS multiplex
                mov     dx,offset errmsg3       ;   interrupt
                cmp     al,0FFh
                jne     error                   ;Error if not installed
;
; Capitalize everything on the command line.
;
                mov     si,81h                  ;Point SI to start
                mov     cl,[si-1]               ;Get character count in CX
                sub     ch,ch
                jcxz    parse                   ;Branch if nothing entered
capsloop:       lodsb                           ;Get a character
                cmp     al,"a"                  ;Branch if lower than "a"
                jb      skipchar
                cmp     al,"z"                  ;Branch if higher than "z"
                ja      skipchar
                and     byte ptr [si-1],0DFh    ;Capitalize the character
skipchar:       loop    capsloop                ;Loop until done
;
; Parse the command line for identifiers and build the command string.
;
parse:          mov     si,81h                  ;Reset SI again
                call    findchar                ;Find first parameter
                mov     dx,offset errmsg1       ;Error if no parameter
                jc      error                   ;   found
                cmp     byte ptr [si],5Fh       ;Test for an underscore
```

```
                jne     not_uscore              ;Branch if found
                inc     si                      ;Advance SI past underscore
                inc     byte ptr command[2]     ;Select intense foreground
not_uscore:     call    convert_color           ;Convert to a color code
                mov     dx,offset errmsg4       ;Exit if error occurred in
                jc      error                   ;  the conversion
                add     cl,30h                  ;Convert binary to ASCII
                mov     command[5],cl           ;Store in command string

                call    finddelim               ;Find end of parameter
                mov     dx,offset errmsg1       ;Exit if parameter ended
                jc      error                   ;  with a carriage return

                call    findchar                ;Find second parameter
                mov     dx,offset errmsg1       ;Error if no parameter
                jc      error                   ;  found
                call    convert_color           ;Convert to color code
                mov     dx,offset errmsg4       ;Exit if error occurred in
                jc      error                   ;  the conversion
                add     cl,30h                  ;Convert binary to ASCII
                mov     command[8],cl           ;Store in command string
;
; Output the command string to ANSI.SYS and terminate.
;
                mov     ah,09h                  ;Output the string with
                mov     dx,offset command       ;  DOS function 09H
                int     21h
                mov     ax,4C00h                ;Exit with ERRORLEVEL=0
                int     21h
main            endp


;****************************************************************************
; FINDCHAR advances SI to the next non-space or non-comma character.
; On return, carry set indicates EOL was encountered.
;****************************************************************************

findchar        proc    near
                lodsb                           ;Get the next character
                cmp     al,20h                  ;Loop if space
                je      findchar
                cmp     al,2Ch                  ;Loop if comma
                je      findchar
                dec     si                      ;Point SI to the character
                cmp     al,0Dh                  ;Exit with carry set if end
                je      eol                     ;  of line is reached

                clc                             ;Clear carry and exit
                ret

eol:            stc                             ;Set carry and exit
                ret
findchar        endp
```

```
;*************************************************************************
; FINDDELIM advances SI to the next space or comma character.  On return,
; carry set indicates EOL was encountered.
;*************************************************************************

finddelim       proc    near
                lodsb                           ;Get the next character
                cmp     al,20h                  ;Exit if space
                je      fd_exit
                cmp     al,2Ch                  ;Exit if comma
                je      fd_exit
                cmp     al,0Dh                  ;Loop back for more if end
                jne     finddelim               ;  of line isn't reached

                dec     si                      ;Set carry and exit
                stc
                ret

fd_exit:        dec     si                      ;Clear carry and exit
                clc
                ret
finddelim       endp


;*************************************************************************
; SCANHELP scans the command line for a /? switch.  If found, carry returns
; set and SI contains its offset.  If not found, carry returns clear.
;*************************************************************************

scanhelp        proc    near
                push    si                      ;Save SI
scanloop:       lodsb                           ;Get a character
                cmp     al,0Dh                  ;Exit if end of line
                je      scan_exit
                cmp     al,"?"                  ;Loop if not "?"
                jne     scanloop
                cmp     byte ptr [si-2],"/"     ;Loop if not "/"
                jne     scanloop

                add     sp,2                    ;Clear the stack
                sub     si,2                    ;Adjust SI
                stc                             ;Set carry and exit
                ret

scan_exit:      pop     si                      ;Restore SI
                clc                             ;Clear carry and exit
                ret
scanhelp        endp


;*************************************************************************
; CONVERT_COLOR compares the string pointed to by DS:SI against a list
; of ASCIIZ strings and returns carry clear if there's a match, carry set
; if there's not.  If carry is clear, CX holds the number of the string
; that was matched.
;*************************************************************************

convert_color   proc    near
```

```
                push    si                      ;Save SI on stack
                mov     bx,si                   ;Also save it in BX
;
; Compare the parameter to the list of color identifiers.
;
                mov     si,offset color_ids     ;Point SI to table
                mov     cx,9                    ;Initialize CX
cc1:            mov     di,bx                   ;Point DI to parameter
cc2:            lodsb                           ;Get a character
                or      al,al                   ;Is it zero?
                je      match                   ;Match if it is
                scasb                           ;Compare the characters
                je      cc2                     ;Loop if they're equal
                jcxz    nomatch                 ;Finished if CX is 0
                dec     cx                      ;Decrement count
cc3:            lodsb                           ;Skip to the first character
                or      al,al                   ;  beyond the next zero and
                jnz     cc3                     ;  compare the next string
                jmp     cc1                     ;  in the list
;
; Set the carry flag to 1 or 0, then exit.
;
nomatch:        pop     si                      ;Restore SI
                stc                             ;Set carry and exit
                ret

match:          cmp     cx,8                    ;Set CX to 3 if it's
                jb      match1                  ;  greater than 8
                mov     cx,3
match1:         pop     si                      ;Restore SI
                clc                             ;Clear carry and exit
                ret
convert_color   endp

code            ends
                end     begin
```

COLOR works by transmitting commands to the ANSI.SYS driver. If ANSI.SYS is not installed, COLOR will output the error message "ANSI.SYS not installed." You can install ANSI.SYS by adding the command

```
DEVICE=C:\DOS\ANSI.SYS
```

to your CONFIG.SYS file (assuming ANSI.SYS is stored in the \DOS directory of the C drive) and rebooting. If your PC is set up to load drivers in upper memory, you can also load ANSI.SYS with the command

```
DEVICEHIGH=C:\DOS\ANSI.SYS
```

instead. This places ANSI.SYS in RAM above the 640k mark, leaving more room for applications in the first 640k.

Inside COLOR

COLOR's first act at start-up after scanning the command line for a /? switch is to verify that ANSI.SYS is installed. It does so by executing the lines

```
mov     ax,1A00h
int     2Fh
mov     dx,offset errmsg3
cmp     al,0FFh
jne     error
```

which call interrupt 2FH (also known as the *DOS multiplex interrupt*) with AH set to 1AH and AL set to 00H, and test the value returned in AL. If ANSI.SYS is installed, AL will return FFH; if it's not, then AL will return unchanged, still set to 0. COLOR compares the value in AL to FFH with a CMP instruction and branches to error handling code if AL is *not* FFH. This method of testing for ANSI.SYS is only valid if the DOS version is 4.0 or later. COLOR calls DOS function 30H to check the version number and aborts if it's an earlier version.

Recall from Chapter 6 that a command string of the form ESC[*x*;*yy*;*zz*m transmitted to ANSI.SYS sets the screen colors. *yy* is a 2-digit code identifying the foreground color, and *zz* is a 2-digit code that identifies the background color. The *x* is a 1-digit code that specifies the intensity to be used; a 1 selects bold foreground colors, while a 0 selects normal ones. Values for *yy* lie between 30 and 37, while values for *zz* lie between 40 and 47.

COLOR's ultimate objective is to formulate a command string suitable for outputting to ANSI.SYS. It starts off with a string defined with MASM's DB (Define Byte) directive like this:

```
command         db      27,"[0;3x;4xm$"
```

The dollar sign serves as the string delimiter. COLOR's first task is to replace the 0 just after the square bracket in the command string with a 1 if the foreground color identifier begins with an underscore. To do so, it executes the following sequence of instructions:

```
            call    findchar
              .
              .
              .

            cmp     byte ptr [si],5Fh
            jne     not_uscore
            inc     si
            inc     byte ptr command[2]
not_uscore:     .
```

.

.

The call to FINDCHAR advances SI to the first character on the command line beyond the command name itself, which should be the first character of the foreground color. If the character is not an underscore (ASCII 5CH), COLOR branches and leaves the 0 in the command string untouched. If, on the other hand, it *is* 5CH, then COLOR uses an INC (INCrement) instruction to change the 0 to a 1. INC works because the ASCII code for 0 is 30H and the ASCII code for 1 is 31H.

Next COLOR capitalizes everything entered on the command line and calls the procedure CONVERT_COLOR to convert the string identifying the foreground color into a binary value that it can use. CONVERT_COLOR performs a byte-by-byte comparison of what it finds on the command line to a table of ASCII color names labeled COLOR_IDS in Listing 12.1. If it finds a match, CONVERT_COLOR returns with carry clear and CX holding a value from 0 to 9 that indicates which of the ten strings in the table matches the string entered on the command line. If there was no match, then CONVERT_COLOR returns with carry set, and COLOR terminates with a syntax error.

If the value in CX is 8 or 9, corresponding to BROWN or ORANGE in the table of color names, COLOR converts the code to 3, which corresponds to YELLOW. This way, YELLOW, BROWN, and ORANGE are equivalent. Then it converts the number in CX to an ASCII numeral by adding 30H and writes it to the command string just after the "3" to finalize the part of the string that specifies the foreground color. At this point, if the foreground color that was entered was, say, _RED, the command string would look like this:

```
27,"[1;31;4xm$"
```

COLOR finishes parsing the command line by calling FINDCHAR to advance SI to the background color identifier and again calling CONVERT_COLOR to read the command line and return a binary color code. Once the code is obtained, it, too, is converted to ASCII format and written to the command string, this time after the "4" near the end of the string. If the specified background color was BLACK, the command string would end up looking like this:

```
27,"[1;31;40m$"
```

COLOR's final act before terminating is to transmit the command with the instructions

```
mov     ah,09h
mov     dx,offset command
int     21h
```

Normally, DOS function 09H transmits a string to standard output. However, ANSI.SYS monitors everything written to standard output and extracts anything that begins with an escape character. As a result, function 09H is a convenient means for sending escape codes to ANSI.SYS from inside a program.

Guarding Against Monitor Burn-In

In the early days of the IBM PC, monochrome monitors were popular because they were less expensive than color monitors and because IBM's Monochrome Display Adapter (MDA) produced a higher-quality text than did the only color adapter available at the time, the Color Graphics Adapter (CGA). However, because it used high-persistence phosphors to display images on the screen, IBM's Monochrome Display was especially susceptible to a phenomenon known as *burn-in*, where an image that is displayed for too long is permanently imprinted in the display. You may have seen images ghosted on the glass of some old monitors. This led to a whole new genre of utilities called *screen savers*, which blanked the screen automatically after a specified period had elapsed without any keyboard activity. Newer monitors are generally less vulnerable to burn-in, but it's still a good idea to turn your monitor off if you're going to leave it for any significant length of time or to use a screen saver to have it blanked automatically.

SAVER, the program in Listing 12.2, is a screen saver with a twist. Not only does it monitor the keyboard to detect when the PC has been left unattended, but it also monitors the mouse so that the display won't suddenly blank out if you use the mouse rather than the keyboard. Unlike many screen savers from years past, SAVER works with virtually any type of video adapter, from the lowly MDA and CGA all the way up to the EGA, MCGA, VGA, and XGA.

The syntax for using the program is

```
SAVER [mm]
```

where *mm* is the number of minutes the mouse and keyboard must be inactive before the screen is blanked. For example, the command

```
SAVER 3
```

sets the countdown timer (the internal clock that determines when the screen will be blanked) to 3 minutes. Acceptable values for *mm* are 0 to 60. The command

```
SAVER Ø
```

disables the countdown timer for the time being (so that the screen will not be blanked). If you don't specify a number of minutes, SAVER defaults to 5. Typing SAVER all by itself on the command line tells you the countdown timer setting. You can change it by rerunning SAVER with a different *mm* value.

LISTING 12.2

```
;***************************************************************************
; SAVER blanks the screen after a specified amount of time has elapsed
; with no mouse or keyboard activity.  Its syntax is
;
;        SAVER [mm]
;
; where "mm" is the length of time that must pass before the screen is
; blanked (in minutes).  Valid values range from 1 to 60.  Typing SAVER 0
; disables SAVER until a non-zero value is entered.  You may also blank the
; screen on demand by pressing both Shift keys.
;
; SAVER must be installed after the mouse driver if it's to monitor
; the actions of the mouse.  Once the screen is blanked, pressing any key,
; moving the mouse, or pressing a mouse button will restore video output.
;***************************************************************************

code            segment
                assume  cs:code
                org     100h
begin:          jmp     init

signature       db      0,1,2,"SAVER",2,1,0     ;Program signature
mouseflag       db      0                       ;0=No mouse installed
scancode        db      ?                       ;Keyboard scan code
blanked         db      0                       ;1=Screen blanked
prog_id         db      ?                       ;Multiplex ID number
adapter         db      ?                       ;Video adapter ID
ac_addr         dw      ?                       ;Attribute controller address
mcount          dw      0                       ;Nested INT 33h calls
time            dw      5460                    ;Countdown timer reset value
count           dw      5460                    ;Countdown timer
mset            db      2Ch,28h,2Dh,29h         ;CGA/MDA mode select values
                db      2Ah,2Eh,1Eh,29h

int08h          dd      ?                       ;Interrupt 08H vector
int09h          dd      ?                       ;Interrupt 09H vector
int2Fh          dd      ?                       ;Interrupt 2FH vector
int33h          dd      ?                       ;Interrupt 33H vector

buttons         dw      ?                       ;Mouse button status
vertical        dw      ?                       ;Mouse horizontal position
horizontal      dw      ?                       ;Mouse vertical position

;***************************************************************************
; TIMER_INT handles interrupt 08H.
;***************************************************************************

timer_int       proc    far
                pushf                           ;Push FLAGS register
                call    cs:[int08h]             ;Call previous handler
                sti                             ;Enable interrupts
                cmp     cs:[time],0             ;Exit if countdown timer is
                je      timer_exit              ;  disabled
                cmp     cs:[blanked],1          ;Branch if the screen is
                je      timer3                  ;  already blanked
;
```

```
; Reset the countdown timer if mouse has moved, decrement it if it has not.
;
                cmp     cs:[mouseflag],0        ;Branch if no mouse installed
                je      timer2
                call    check_mouse             ;See if the mouse has moved
                jc      timer4                  ;Branch if it has

timer2:         dec     cs:[count]              ;Decrement countdown timer
                cmp     cs:[count],0            ;Has the countdown reached 0?
                jne     timer_exit              ;Branch if not
                call    disable_video           ;Blank the screen
                iret                            ;Return from interrupt
;
; Unblank the screen if the mouse has moved.
;
timer3:         cmp     cs:[mouseflag],0        ;Exit if no mouse installed
                je      timer_exit
                call    check_mouse             ;See if the mouse has moved
                jnc     timer_exit              ;Unblank the screen if it
                call    enable_video            ;  has
timer4:         push    cs:[time]               ;Reset countdown timer
                pop     cs:[count]
timer_exit:     iret                            ;Return from interrupt
timer_int       endp


;****************************************************************************
; KB_INT handles interrupt 09H.
;****************************************************************************

kb_int          proc    far
                pushf                           ;Save FLAGS
                push    ax                      ;Save AX
                in      al,60h                  ;Read the scan code
                mov     cs:[scancode],al        ;Save it
                pop     ax                      ;Restore AX
                popf                            ;Restore FLAGS
                pushf                           ;Push FLAGS
                call    cs:[int09h]             ;Call previous handler
                sti                             ;Enable interrupts

                test    cs:[scancode],80h       ;Exit if high bit of scan
                jnz     kb_exit                 ;  code is set

                push    ax                      ;Save AX and ES
                push    es
                mov     ax,40h                  ;Point ES to the BIOS
                mov     es,ax                   ;  Data Area
                mov     al,es:[17h]             ;Get keyboard flags
                and     al,03h                  ;Zero the upper 6 bits
                cmp     al,03h                  ;Are the Shift keys pressed?
                pop     es                      ;Restore AX and ES
                pop     ax
                jne     kb2                     ;Branch if they're not
                call    disable_video           ;Blank the screen
                iret                            ;Return from interrupt
```

```
kb2:            push    cs:[time]           ;Reset countdown timer
                pop     cs:[count]
                cmp     cs:[blanked],0      ;Is the screen blanked?
                je      kb_exit             ;If not, then exit
                call    enable_video        ;Unblank the screen
kb_exit:        iret                        ;Return from interrupt
kb_int          endp


;***********************************************************************
; MPLEX_INT handles interrupt 2FH.  If, on entry, AH is set to SAVER's
; multiplex ID number, MPLEX_INT uses the value in AL as a function code.
; The functions supported are:
;
;    00H    Returns FFH in AL to indicate the program is installed
;           and returns the address of its signature in ES:DI.
;
;    01H    Sets the countdown timer to the value passed in BX.
;           A value of 0 temporarily disables the timer.
;
;    02H    Returns the timer reset value in AX.
;***********************************************************************

mplex_int       proc    far
                pushf                       ;Save FLAGS register
                cmp     ah,cs:[prog_id]     ;Branch if AH holds the
                je      mplex2              ;  multiplex ID
                popf                        ;Restore FLAGS
                jmp     cs:[int2Fh]         ;Pass the interrupt on
;
; Function 00H verifies that the program is installed.
;
mplex2:         popf                        ;Restore FLAGS
                or      al,al               ;Branch if function code
                jnz     mplex3              ;  is other than 00H
                mov     al,0FFh             ;Set AL to FFH
                push    cs                  ;Point ES:DI to the program
                pop     es                  ;  signature
                mov     di,offset signature
                iret                        ;Return from interrupt
;
; Function 01H sets the countdown timer.
;
mplex3:         cmp     al,01h              ;Branch if function code
                jne     mplex4              ;  is other than 01H
                mov     cs:[time],bx        ;Load new timer value
                mov     cs:[count],bx
                iret                        ;Return from interrupt
;
; Function 02H returns the timer reset value.
;
mplex4:         mov     ax,cs:[time]        ;Get value in AX
                iret                        ;Return from interrupt
mplex_int       endp
```

```
;*************************************************************************
; MOUSE_INT handles interrupt 33H.
;*************************************************************************

mouse_int       proc    far
                pushf                           ;Save FLAGS
                inc     cs:[mcount]             ;Increment count
                popf                            ;Restore FLAGS
                pushf                           ;Push FLAGS
                call    cs:[int33h]             ;Call mouse driver
                pushf                           ;Save FLAGS
                dec     cs:[mcount]             ;Decrement count
                popf                            ;Restore FLAGS
                ret     2                       ;Return from interrupt
mouse_int       endp


;*************************************************************************
; DISABLE_VIDEO disables the video output signal.
;*************************************************************************

disable_video   proc    near
                push    ax                      ;Save registers
                push    bx
                push    dx
                push    es
                cli                             ;Disable interrupts
                cmp     cs:[adapter],2          ;Branch if EGA or VGA
                jae     dv2
;
; Blank a CGA or MDA screen.
;
                mov     ax,40h                  ;Point ES to the BIOS
                mov     es,ax                   ;  Data Area
                mov     al,es:[49h]             ;Get mode number in AL
                sub     ah,ah                   ;Convert it to a word and
                mov     bx,ax                   ;  transfer to BX
                mov     al,cs:[bx+offset mset]  ;Get mode select value
                and     al,0F7h                 ;Clear bit 3
                mov     dx,es:[63h]             ;Get CRTC base address
                add     dx,4                    ;Compute mode select address
                out     dx,al                   ;OUT the value
                jmp     short dv_exit           ;Exit
;
; Blank an EGA or VGA screen.
;
dv2:            mov     dx,cs:[ac_addr]         ;Get register address
                in      al,dx                   ;Reset addr/data flip-flop
                sub     al,al                   ;Clear bit 5 of the address
                mov     dx,3C0h                 ;  register
                out     dx,al
                mov     dx,cs:[ac_addr]         ;Reset the flip-flop again
                in      al,dx

dv_exit:        mov     cs:[blanked],1          ;Set screen flag
                sti                             ;Enable interrupts
                pop     es                      ;Restore registers and exit
```

```
                pop     dx
                pop     bx
                pop     ax
                ret
disable_video   endp

;***************************************************************************
; ENABLE_VIDEO enables the video output signal.
;***************************************************************************

enable_video    proc    near
                push    ax                      ;Save registers
                push    bx
                push    dx
                push    es
                cli                             ;Disable interrupts
                cmp     cs:[adapter],2          ;Branch if EGA or VGA
                jae     ev2
;
; Unblank a CGA or MDA screen.
;
                mov     ax,40h                  ;Point ES to the BIOS
                mov     es,ax                   ;  Data Area
                mov     al,es:[49h]             ;Get mode number in AL
                sub     ah,ah                   ;Convert it to a word and
                mov     bx,ax                   ;  transfer to BX
                mov     al,cs:[bx+offset mset]  ;Get mode select value
                mov     dx,es:[63h]             ;Get CRTC base address
                add     dx,4                    ;Compute mode select address
                out     dx,al                   ;OUT the value
                jmp     short ev_exit           ;Exit
;
; Unblank an EGA or VGA screen.
;
ev2:            mov     dx,cs:[ac_addr]         ;Get register address
                in      al,dx                   ;Reset addr/data flip-flop
                mov     al,20h                  ;Set bit 5 of the address
                mov     dx,3C0h                 ;  register
                out     dx,al
                mov     dx,cs:[ac_addr]         ;Reset the flip-flop again
                in      al,dx

ev_exit:        mov     cs:[blanked],0          ;Clear screen flag
                sti                             ;Enable interrupts
                pop     es                      ;Restore registers and exit
                pop     dx
                pop     bx
                pop     ax
                ret
enable_video    endp

;***************************************************************************
; CHECK_MOUSE returns with the carry flag clear if the mouse status has not
; changed since the last call, set if it has.
;***************************************************************************
```

```
check_mouse     proc    near
                cmp     cs:[mcount],Ø             ;Exit now if another INT
                je      cmØ                      ;   33H is in progress
                clc
                ret

cmØ:            push    ax                       ;Save registers
                push    bx
                push    cx
                push    dx

                mov     ax,Ø3h                   ;Get information with
                int     33h                      ;   mouse function Ø3H
                cmp     bx,cs:[buttons]          ;Branch and set the carry
                jne     cm2                      ;   flag if anything has
                cmp     cx,cs:[horizontal]       ;   changed since the
                jne     cm2                      ;   last call
                cmp     dx,cs:[vertical]
                jne     cm2

cm1:            clc                              ;Clear the carry flag
                jmp     short cm3                ;Jump to exit

cm2:            mov     cs:[buttons],bx          ;Save return values
                mov     cs:[horizontal],cx
                mov     cs:[vertical],dx
                stc                              ;Set the carry flag
cm3:            pop     dx                       ;Restore registers and
                pop     cx                       ;   exit
                pop     bx
                pop     ax
                ret
check_mouse     endp

;*****************************************************************************
; Data that will be discarded when the program becomes memory-resident.
;*****************************************************************************

helpmsg         db      "Blanks the screen after a period of mouse or "
                db      "keyboard inactivity.",13,1Ø,13,1Ø
                db      "SAVER [mm]",13,1Ø,13,1Ø
                db      "  mm  Number of minutes before blanking occurs "
                db      "(1 to 6Ø, default=5).",13,1Ø,13,1Ø
                db      "Typing SAVER Ø disables SAVER until a non-zero "
                db      "value is entered.",13,1Ø,"$"

errmsg1         db      "Syntax: SAVER [mm]",13,1Ø,"$"
errmsg2         db      "Requires DOS 3.Ø or higher",13,1Ø,"$"
errmsg3         db      "Minutes must be 6Ø or less",13,1Ø,"$"
errmsg4         db      "Program could not be installed",13,1Ø,"$"

msg1            db      "SAVER 1.Ø installed",13,1Ø,"$"
msg2            db      "Countdown timer set to $"
msg3            db      " minute(s)",13,1Ø,"$"
msg4            db      "Countdown timer disabled",13,1Ø,"$"
```

```
parmflag        db      Ø                       ;Ø=No command line parameter
minutes         db      5                       ;Minutes in countdown timer

;**************************************************************************
; INIT makes the program resident in memory.
;**************************************************************************

                assume  cs:code,ds:code

init            proc    near
                cld                             ;Clear direction flag
                mov     si,81h                  ;Point SI to command line
                call    scanhelp                ;Scan for "/?" switch
                jnc     checkver                ;Branch if not found
                mov     ah,Ø9h                  ;Display help text and exit
                mov     dx,offset helpmsg       ;  with ERRORLEVEL=Ø
                int     21h
                mov     ax,4CØØh
                int     21h
;
; Check the DOS version and parse the command line.
;
checkver:       mov     dx,offset errmsg2       ;Exit if DOS version
                mov     ah,3Øh                  ;  is less than 3.Ø
                int     21h
                cmp     al,3
                jae     parse

error:          mov     ah,Ø9h                  ;Display error message and
                int     21h                     ;  exit with ERRORLEVEL=1
                mov     ax,4CØ1h
                int     21h

parse:          call    findchar                ;Find parameter (if any)
                jc      checkprog               ;Branch if none found
                mov     parmflag,1              ;Set PARMFLAG to 1
                call    asc2bin                 ;Convert ASCII to binary
                mov     dx,offset errmsg3       ;Exit on error
                jc      error
                cmp     al,60                   ;Error if value entered is
                ja      error                   ;  greater than 6Ø

                mov     minutes,al              ;Save number of minutes
                sub     ah,ah                   ;Multiply value entered by
                mov     bx,1092                 ;  1,Ø92 and save it away
                mul     bx
                mov     time,ax
                mov     count,ax

checkprog:      call    check_install           ;See if program is installed
                jnc     install                 ;Branch if it's not
;
; Communicate with an installed copy of the code.
;
                cmp     parmflag,Ø              ;Branch if no time was
                jne     cp2                     ;  entered
```

```
              mov      al,02h                   ;Get counter reset value
              int      2Fh                      ;  from installed code
              sub      dx,dx                    ;Divide it by 1,092
              mov      bx,1092
              div      bx
              mov      minutes,al               ;Save it
              jmp      short cp3                ;Branch and display it

cp2:          mov      al,01h                   ;AL = Function code
              mov      bx,time                  ;BX = Reset value
              int      2Fh                      ;Set the value

cp3:          call     showtime                 ;Display minutes
              mov      ax,4C00h                 ;Exit with ERRORLEVEL=0
              int      21h
;
; Install the program.
;
install:      call     mplex_id                 ;Find a multiplex ID number
              mov      dx,offset errmsg4        ;Error if none available
              jc       error
              mov      prog_id,ah               ;Save the ID number

              call     video_id                 ;ID the video adapter
              mov      adapter,al               ;Save ID value
              mov      ax,40h                   ;Get and save the address of
              mov      es,ax                    ;  the attribute controller
              mov      ax,es:[63h]              ;  for EGAs and VGAs
              add      ax,6
              mov      ac_addr,ax

              mov      ah,00h                   ;Check for mouse driver
              int      33h
              or       ax,ax                    ;Branch if no mouse
              jz       nomouse1
              mov      mouseflag,1              ;Set flag for mouse

nomouse1:     mov      ax,3508h                 ;Hook interrupt 08H
              int      21h
              mov      word ptr int08h,bx
              mov      word ptr int08h[2],es
              mov      ax,2508h
              mov      dx,offset timer_int
              int      21h

              mov      ax,3509h                 ;Hook interrupt 09H
              int      21h
              mov      word ptr int09h,bx
              mov      word ptr int09h[2],es
              mov      ax,2509h
              mov      dx,offset kb_int
              int      21h

              mov      ax,352Fh                 ;Hook interrupt 2FH
              int      21h
              mov      word ptr int2Fh,bx
```

```
                mov     word ptr int2Fh[2],es
                mov     ax,252Fh
                mov     dx,offset mplex_int
                int     21h

                cmp     mouseflag,0             ;Branch if no mouse
                je      nomouse2                ;  installed
                mov     ax,3533h                ;Hook interrupt 33H
                int     21h
                mov     word ptr int33h,bx
                mov     word ptr int33h[2],es
                mov     ax,2533h
                mov     dx,offset mouse_int
                int     21h

nomouse2:       mov     ah,49h                  ;Get the segment address of
                mov     es,ds:[2Ch]             ;  the environment block
                int     21h                     ;  and free the segment

                mov     ah,09h                  ;Display message verifying
                mov     dx,offset msg1          ;  the installation
                int     21h
                call    showtime                ;Display minutes

                mov     ax,3100h                ;Terminate with function 31H
                mov     dx,(offset helpmsg - offset code + 15) shr 4
                int     21h
init            endp

;*************************************************************************
; FINDCHAR advances SI to the next non-space or non-comma character.
; On return, carry set indicates EOL was encountered.
;*************************************************************************

findchar        proc    near
                lodsb                           ;Get the next character
                cmp     al,20h                  ;Loop if space
                je      findchar
                cmp     al,2Ch                  ;Loop if comma
                je      findchar
                dec     si                      ;Point SI to the character
                cmp     al,0Dh                  ;Exit with carry set if end
                je      eol                     ;  of line is reached

                clc                             ;Clear carry and exit
                ret

eol:            stc                             ;Set carry and exit
                ret
findchar        endp

;*************************************************************************
; SCANHELP scans the command line for a /? switch.  If found, carry returns
; set and SI contains its offset.  If not found, carry returns clear.
;*************************************************************************
```

```
scanhelp        proc    near
                push    si                      ;Save SI
scanloop:       lodsb                           ;Get a character
                cmp     al,0Dh                  ;Exit if end of line
                je      scan_exit
                cmp     al,"?"                  ;Loop if not "?"
                jne     scanloop
                cmp     byte ptr [si-2],"/"     ;Loop if not "/"
                jne     scanloop

                add     sp,2                    ;Clear the stack
                sub     si,2                    ;Adjust SI
                stc                             ;Set carry and exit
                ret

scan_exit:      pop     si                      ;Restore SI
                clc                             ;Clear carry and exit
                ret
scanhelp        endp

;****************************************************************************
; CHECK_INSTALL returns carry set if the program is already installed,
; carry clear if it's not.  If carry returns set, AH holds the program's
; multiplex ID number.
;****************************************************************************

check_install   proc    near
                mov     ax,8000h                ;Initialize AH and AL
                mov     cx,80h                  ;Initialize count

chinst1:        push    ax                      ;Save AX and CX
                push    cx
                sub     di,di                   ;Set ES and DI to 0
                mov     es,di
                int     2Fh                     ;Interrupt 2Fh
                cmp     al,0FFh                 ;Nothing here if AL isn't
                jne     chinst2                 ;  equal to FFH

                mov     si,offset signature     ;See if program signature
                mov     cx,11                   ;  appears at the address
                repe    cmpsb                   ;  returned in ES:DI
                jne     chinst2                 ;Branch if it does not

                pop     cx                      ;Clear the stack and exit
                pop     ax                      ;  with carry set
                stc
                ret

chinst2:        pop     cx                      ;Retrieve AX and CX
                pop     ax
                inc     ah                      ;Next multiplex ID
                loop    chinst1                 ;Loop until done

                clc                             ;Exit with carry clear
                ret
check_install   endp
```

```
;**************************************************************************
; MPLEX_ID searches for an unused multiplex ID number.  If one is found,
; it is returned in AH with carry clear.  Carry set means no multiplex
; ID numbers are currently available.
;**************************************************************************

mplex_id        proc    near
                mov     ax,8000h                ;Initialize AH and AL
                mov     cx,80h                  ;Initialize count

mxid1:          push    ax                      ;Save AX and CX
                push    cx
                int     2Fh                     ;Interrupt 2Fh
                or      al,al                   ;Branch if AL=0
                jz      mxid2
                pop     cx                      ;Retrieve AX and CX
                pop     ax
                inc     ah                      ;Increment ID number
                loop    mxid1                   ;Loop until done

                stc                             ;Exit with carry set
                ret

mxid2:          pop     cx                      ;Clear the stack and exit
                pop     ax                      ;  with carry clear
                clc
                ret
mplex_id        endp

;**************************************************************************
; VIDEO_ID returns 2 in AL if the video adapter is an EGA or VGA, 1 if it's
; a CGA, or 0 if it's an MDA or other monochrome adapter.
;**************************************************************************

video_id        proc    near
                mov     ah,12h                  ;Test for EGA/VGA
                mov     bl,10h
                int     10h
                mov     al,2                    ;Initialize AL
                cmp     bl,10h                  ;EGA/VGA installed if BL
                jne     video_exit              ;  returned changed
                dec     al                      ;Set AL to 1
                mov     bx,40h                  ;Point ES to BIOS Data Area
                mov     es,bx
                test    byte ptr es:[63h],40h   ;Test 6845 address word
                jnz     video_exit              ;CGA installed if bit 6 set
                dec     al                      ;Set AL to 0 and exit
video_exit:     ret
video_id        endp

;**************************************************************************
; SHOWTIME displays the length of the countdown in minutes.
;**************************************************************************

showtime        proc    near
```

```
                  cmp     minutes,0              ;Branch if minutes is
                  jne     st2                    ;  not 0
                  mov     ah,09h                 ;Display "Countdown timer
                  mov     dx,offset msg4         ;  disabled" message
                  int     21h
                  ret

st2:              mov     ah,09h                 ;Display "Countdown timer"
                  mov     dx,offset msg2         ;  part of message
                  int     21h
                  mov     al,minutes             ;Display the number of
                  sub     ah,ah                  ;  minutes
                  call    bin2asc
                  mov     ah,09h                 ;Display "minute(s)"
                  mov     dx,offset msg3
                  int     21h
                  ret
showtime          endp

;*************************************************************************
; ASC2BIN converts a decimal number entered in ASCII form into a binary
; value in AL.  Carry set on return indicates that an error occurred in
; the conversion.
;*************************************************************************

asc2bin           proc    near
                  sub     ax,ax                  ;Initialize registers
                  sub     bh,bh
                  mov     dl,10

a2b_loop:         mov     bl,[si]                ;Get a character
                  inc     si
                  cmp     bl,20h                 ;Exit if space
                  je      a2b_exit
                  cmp     bl,2Ch                 ;Exit if comma
                  je      a2b_exit
                  cmp     bl,0Dh                 ;Exit if carriage return
                  je      a2b_exit

                  cmp     bl,"0"                 ;Error if character is not
                  jb      a2b_error              ;  a number
                  cmp     bl,"9"
                  ja      a2b_error

                  mul     dl                     ;Multiply the value in AL by
                  jc      a2b_error              ;  10 and exit on overflow
                  sub     bl,30h                 ;ASCII => binary
                  add     ax,bx                  ;Add latest value to AX
                  cmp     ax,255                 ;Error if sum > 255
                  jna     a2b_loop               ;Loop back for more

a2b_error:        dec     si                     ;Set carry and exit
                  stc
                  ret

a2b_exit:         dec     si                     ;Clear carry and exit
```

```
                clc
                ret
asc2bin         endp

;************************************************************************
; BIN2ASC converts a binary value in AX to ASCII form and displays it.
;************************************************************************

bin2asc         proc    near
                mov     bx,10                   ;Initialize divisor word and
                xor     cx,cx                   ;  digit counter
b2a1:           inc     cx                      ;Increment digit count
                xor     dx,dx                   ;Divide by 10
                div     bx
                push    dx                      ;Save remainder on stack
                or      ax,ax                   ;Loop until quotient is zero
                jnz     b2a1
b2a2:           pop     dx                      ;Retrieve a digit from stack
                add     dl,30h                  ;Convert it to ASCII
                mov     ah,2                    ;Display it
                int     21h
                loop    b2a2                    ;Loop until done
                ret
bin2asc         endp

code            ends
                end     begin
```

Every time a key is pressed, the mouse is moved, or a mouse button is pressed, the countdown timer is reset to the value you specified when you installed or last ran SAVER. As long as you keep typing or using the mouse, the screen will remain on. But if the specified amount of time passes with no perceivable activity, SAVER disables video output, forcing the screen to go black. You can reactivate video output by pressing a key, moving the mouse, or clicking a mouse button. If you don't want to disturb the program that's running, press a key that doesn't mean anything to it. The left and right Shift keys normally fit this criterion. Once output is reactivated, the countdown starts over, and the screen will be blanked again if the keyboard and mouse become idle.

With SAVER installed you can blank the screen yourself by pressing both Shift keys. This is useful for hiding the information displayed on the screen when someone walks into your office, or for blanking the screen before you leave the room without waiting for the countdown timer to expire. As usual, pressing any key or moving the mouse will restore the video signal.

SAVER only monitors mouse activity if, when it's installed, it finds that a mouse driver is loaded. Therefore, if you load SAVER from your AUTOEXEC-.BAT file and want it to watch the mouse as well as the keyboard, be sure to place the line that loads the screen saver *after* the line that loads the mouse driver. Loading the mouse driver from CONFIG.SYS enforces this order of loading by default, because DOS reads and processes CONFIG.SYS before it processes AUTOEXEC.BAT.

There are certain programs you should not use with SAVER. Microsoft Windows is one of them. Windows processes scan codes transmitted from the keyboard itself rather than relying on the keyboard BIOS, and it uses an internal driver to communicate with the mouse. With Windows running, SAVER can't reliably monitor either the keyboard or the mouse, leading the screen to blank out within minutes of starting Windows—despite the fact that you may have been busily pounding keys or clicking mouse buttons. Furthermore, because SAVER can't tell when a key is pressed, you may be unable to restore the screen after SAVER blanks it out.

If you must run programs such as Windows with SAVER loaded, disable SAVER's screen blanking feature with the command

```
SAVER Ø
```

before you start. Then, when you exit the application, rerun SAVER to restore screen blanking.

Installed, SAVER consumes about 750 bytes of memory. If you have a 386 or 486 with extended memory, you can place it in upper memory with the LOADHIGH command, where it won't take memory away from application programs. The command

```
LOADHIGH SAVER 1Ø
```

loads SAVER in upper memory and sets the timer to 10 minutes. If, after using LOADHIGH the first time SAVER is run, you then run SAVER again to alter or check the time interval, you needn't use LOADHIGH again. Simply typing

```
SAVER 5
```

will set the countdown timer to 5 minutes, regardless of whether SAVER is installed in upper or lower memory.

Inside SAVER

SAVER is the first example of a TSR we've seen thus far. TSR stands for *terminate and stay resident*, and is the term used to describe a whole class of utilities that, when terminated, remain in memory waiting to be run again. In most instances, you don't reactivate them by typing a command. A TSR typically latches onto one or more interrupts by inserting the address of one of its own routines in the interrupt vector table in low memory. When an interrupt occurs, the TSR takes control, does its job, and then relinquishes control back to DOS or the program that was temporarily interrupted. Many times you're not even aware that the TSR is working.

To become memory-resident, SAVER doesn't terminate in the conventional way by calling DOS function 4CH. Instead, it calls DOS function 31H. The code looks like this:

```
mov     ax,3100h
mov     dx,(offset helpmsg - offset code + 15) shr 4
int     21h
```

Function 31H accepts an exit code in AL (the same exit code placed in AL before function 4CH is called) and the number of paragraphs of memory the TSR wants to reserve for itself in DX. The first instruction, MOV AX,3100H, loads the function code in AH (31H) and the exit code in AL (00H). The next one calculates the amount of memory to reserve. The expression (OFFSET HELPMSG - OFFSET CODE + 15) evaluates to 15 more than the offset of the label HELPMSG; SHR 4 shifts the result four bits to the right, effectively dividing it by 16 and converting a byte value to a paragraph value. With this call, everything beyond HELPMSG is discarded once the program becomes resident; only the code that counts timer ticks, blanks and unblanks the screen, and so on, is retained.

Before it terminates, SAVER takes several actions that enable it to work once it has become memory-resident. Starting at the line labeled INIT, it verifies that it's running under DOS 3.0 or later, parses the command line to determine the number of minutes you want the countdown timer set to, and checks to see if a copy of SAVER is currently resident in memory. If SAVER has already been installed once, the newly launched copy either passes a new countdown timer value to the installed copy or, if you didn't specify a command-line parameter, requests the current value of the countdown timer from the installed copy so that it can display it.

If SAVER is already installed, it terminates the conventional way—through DOS function 4CH—so that two copies won't reside in memory at once. Allowing a second copy of SAVER to be installed would consume memory needlessly. If a copy is not already installed, however, SAVER calls the procedure VIDEO_ID to tell it what type of video adapter—CGA, MDA, EGA, VGA, or perhaps MCGA or XGA—is installed in the system, information that it will need later on when it tries to blank or unblank the screen. Then it checks to see if a mouse driver is installed with the code

```
mov     ah,00h
int     33h
```

If, on return, AX is 0, then no mouse driver is installed and SAVER leaves a flag called MOUSEFLAG set to 0, in effect making a note to itself that mice need not be considered. If AX returns non-zero indicating that there is a mouse driver installed, MOUSEFLAG is set to 1. Once it's resident, SAVER will examine this flag to decide whether to check for mouse movements and button presses.

SAVER then modifies the table of interrupt vectors in low memory so that it will be activated when one of several events occurs. In order, it alters the vectors for interrupts 08H (the timer interrupt, generated slightly more than 18 times per second by the PC's hardware timer chip), interrupt 09H (the keyboard interrupt, generated anytime a key is pressed or released), interrupt 2FH (the DOS multiplex interrupt, frequently used by memory-resident programs to enable a program running in DOS's transient program area to communicate with a TSR), and interrupt 33H (the mouse interrupt, used by application programs to place calls to the mouse driver, the same way interrupt 21H is used to place calls to DOS). The code to set an interrupt vector looks like this:

```
mov     ax,2508h
mov     dx,offset timer_int
int     21h
```

Function 25H patches the *segment:offset* address in registers DS and DX into the interrupt table for the interrupt whose number is contained in AL. In this example, interrupt 08H is altered to point to the procedure named TIMER_INT.

Before SAVER changes these interrupt vectors, it saves the old ones so that it can call the original interrupt service routines when necessary. SAVER uses the following snippet of code to grab the interrupt 08H vector before changing it:

```
mov     ax,3508h
int     21h
mov     word ptr int08h,bx
mov     word ptr int08h[2],es
```

This routine uses DOS function 35H, which accepts an interrupt number in AL, to retrieve the interrupt vector 08H. On return, ES:BX holds the interrupt vector. SAVER stores the vector away in the variable named INT08H.

Its final act before calling function 31H to terminate is to deallocate its own environment block with the three instructions:

```
mov     ah,49h
mov     es,ds:[2Ch]
int     21h
```

DOS function 49H releases the block of memory whose segment address is passed in ES, returning it to the free memory pool for use by other programs. Here, the segment address passed is that of the program's environment block, whose address is stored at offset 2CH in the PSP and retrieved with the instruction MOV ES,DS:[2CH] (at the time this code is executed, segment register DS points to the PSP). When DOS loads a program—any program—into memory, it initially allocates it two blocks of memory: one to hold the program itself, and another to hold a local copy of the environment strings defined with the SET command. SAVER doesn't use any information in the environment block, so by returning the memory it occupies to DOS, it can reduce the amount of memory it will consume once it's memory-resident by approximately 160 bytes—more if the size of the environment was expanded with a SHELL statement in CONFIG-.SYS and the environment is nearly full.

The Installed Code

What happens next may be a little more difficult to grasp conceptually. After SAVER terminates, it sits idle waiting for something to happen. When one of the interrupts that it tapped into is generated, the procedure whose address SAVER patched into the interrupt vector table is activated. For example, every time the system timer ticks, the procedure TIMER_INT receives control; and when a key is pressed or released on the keyboard, KB_INT is activated. Each time, the procedure that gains control does its work, and then ends the interrupt by executing an IRET instruction. So that SAVER can cohabitate with other elements of the system, the procedures TIMER_INT and KB_INT also call the original ISRs (interrupt service routines) whose addresses were found in the vector table when SAVER was installed.

It's important to note that when a routine such as TIMER_INT or KB_INT receives control, there's no telling where the segment registers besides CS are pointing (CS will point to SAVER's code segment). Therefore, when these ISRs reference a named memory location such as MOUSEFLAG, they use a segment override (an instruction that tells the CPU to use a segment register other than the default) to make the reference relative to the CS register as opposed to the DS register, which is normally the default. In addition, they take care to save any registers they will be modifying on the stack and to restore them before they exit. If register values are not preserved across interrupts, especially hardware interrupts such as these, the system will crash.

It's TIMER_INT that does the bulk of the work. Each time it's called—again, it's called on average about 18.2 times per second at regular intervals, or about every 55 milliseconds—it decrements a timer value that was initialized to 1,092 times the number of minutes you specified for the blanking interval (18.2 ticks per second equals 1,092 ticks per minute). When the count reaches 0, TIMER_INT calls the procedure DISABLE_VIDEO to blank the screen. Each time a keyboard interrupt is generated, the counter is reset so that the countdown will begin anew. Similarly, each time the mouse is moved or a button is pressed, the countdown timer is reset. This way, video will not be disabled unless the specified number of ticks go by without a mouse or keyboard event. Once the screen is blanked, KB_INT calls ENABLE_VIDEO to reenable the video output signal if a key is pressed, or TIMER_INT calls it if the mouse is used. To detect mouse events, TIMER_INT calls the procedure CHECK_MOUSE, which in turn invokes interrupt 33H, function 03H to determine whether the mouse has moved or one of its buttons has been pressed.

KB_INT serves another purpose, too. Every time a key is pressed, it checks to see if both Shift keys are held down by checking bits 0 and 1 of the shift status byte diagrammed in Figure 9.2. If they are, KB_INT calls DISABLE_VIDEO to blank the screen. Once again, the screen is unblanked when a key is pressed, the mouse is moved, or a mouse button is pressed.

The routines DISABLE_VIDEO and ENABLE_VIDEO use one procedure for blanking and unblanking CGA and MDA screens and another for handling EGA, MCGA, VGA, and XGA screens. The video output signal is disabled on a CGA or MDA by zeroing bit 3 of the adapter's *mode select register*, which is located at I/O address 3B8H on an MDA, 3D8H on a CGA. Conversely, output is reenabled by setting bit 3 back to 1. Because it is important not to alter the bits that surround bit 3, and because mode select is a write-only register, SAVER has to employ some special logic to set or clear bit 3 without affecting the rest of the register. To accomplish this feat, it writes the same value to the register that the BIOS writes to it when interrupt 10H, function 00H is called to switch to another video mode, with bit 3 altered as needed. SAVER stores a table of register values in its own data space and, based on the current video mode (determined by inspecting the byte at absolute address 0040:0049H), decides which one to send.

On adapters with EGA-like architectures (which include the VGA, MCGA, and XGA in addition to the EGA itself), SAVER uses a different strategy for blanking and unblanking the screen. To disable video output, it zeros bit 5 of the adapter's *attribute address register*, which is accessed through I/O port 3C0H. To enable video, it sets bit 5 to 1. Before it can access the attribute address register, it must perform an IN on the port at 3DAH on color systems and 3BAH on monochrome systems to reset an internal address flip-flop. This is necessary because port 3C0H does double duty, serving as the channel both for accessing the attribute address register and the attribute data register. The IN resets the flip-flop so that the next value OUTed to 3C0H will go to the address register, not to the data register.

SAVER's installed code is fairly typical of TSR code, which uses hardware and software interrupts in the PC to gain control of the machine, if only for a moment. If you're interested, the best way to get a feel for what's happening is to go through the code listing line by line and see what happens and when. The next chapter will examine the subject of TSR programming more fully.

The DOS Multiplex Interrupt

SAVER makes unique use of the DOS multiplex interrupt, interrupt 2FH. Before it is installed, SAVER calls the procedure MPLEX_ID to find an unused multiplex ID number between 128 and 255. Certain DOS drivers and TSRs such as ANSI.SYS and PRINT also use the multiplex interrupt, and use preassigned ID numbers, usually between 0 and 127. SAVER calls interrupt 2FH repeatedly with an ID number in AH and a 0 in AL until AL returns still set to 0, indicating that the ID number in AH is unused by DOS or by other TSRs. Then it saves away the number in AH as its own ID number.

In addition, SAVER supplies its own interrupt handler for interrupt 2FH. This interrupt handler accepts a function code in AL. When SAVER is run from the command line, it can find out whether a copy of SAVER is already installed in memory by testing every possible ID code between 128 and 255 for one that returns FFH in AL *and* returns with ES:DI pointing to an 11-byte header that uniquely identifies SAVER. If a copy of SAVER is resident in memory, it receives the interrupt and sets AL and ES:DI appropriately. If, on the other hand, every call to interrupt 2FH returns 0 in AL, then SAVER knows that a copy of itself is not already installed.

The term "multiplex interrupt" may be a bit misleading. It's not a different type of interrupt; it's simply the name DOS technical manuals assign to interrupt 2FH. "Multiplex" means the interrupt is shared among several programs. Interrupt 2FH is the interrupt that TSRs run from the command line use to tell whether they have already been installed and if so, to exchange information with the installed copy. Fortunately, a TSR that *we* write can use this interrupt, too, provided it can ensure that the multiplex ID number it assumes is not one of those reserved for use by DOS. That's why SAVER goes to the trouble of finding an unused ID number, and why, once it does, it can use the multiplex interrupt the way DOS does without fear of crashing the system.

SAVER's interrupt 2FH handler (called MPLEX_INT in Listing 12.2) accepts two other function codes, too: 01H and 02H. When function 01H is called, the installed copy of SAVER saves the value passed to it in BX to use when a key press or mouse action resets the countdown timer. This is the mechanism SAVER uses to pass a new timer value to the installed copy when you run it a second time. The third function, function 02H, allows a copy of SAVER run from the command line to determine from an installed copy of the code what the countdown value is. The current timer value is returned in AX. Note that when MPLEX_INT receives control, it examines the ID code in AH and passes the interrupt on to the original interrupt 2FH if the code is not that of SAVER's.

Again, this is pretty sophisticated material, and if you want to understand it at the nuts and bolts level, the only way to do so is to examine the source code. Most of the logic is embodied in the procedures MPLEX_INT, MPLEX_ID, and CHECK_INSTALL. You'll see these routines again in the LPT2FILE utility developed later in this chapter, and again in the next chapter when we develop more TSRs.

There are other methods that a TSR can use to detect whether it is already installed, but none is as reliable as this one. Plus, the multiplex interrupt method works even if the TSR is installed in upper memory. Some methods only work if the TSR is loaded in the lower 640k. With DOS 5.0, which permits TSRs to be loaded high with the LOADHIGH command, such methods are not acceptable.

Programming the Function Keys in DOS

In addition to showing how to set the screen colors, Chapter 6 also demonstrated how to program the function keys to produce DOS commands. Once more, this involved sending escape sequences to the ANSI.SYS driver and required a considerable knowledge both of the keyboard and of the codes the individual keys are assigned.

The utility shown in Listing 12.3 fixes that. FKEYS lets you program the function keys using English-like commands rather than cryptic and hard-to-remember escape sequences. Its syntax is

```
FKEYS [shift-]key ["command"[*]]
```

where *shift* identifies a shift key (Ctrl, Alt, or Shift), *key* identifies a function key, and *command*, enclosed in quotation marks, is the command to assign to the function key. The command

```
FKEYS F1 "MEM /C"
```

assigns the command MEM /C to function key F1 so that pressing F1 spells out "MEM /C" on the command line. The command will not be executed until you press Enter. If you want the command executed as soon as you press the function key, include an asterisk after the closing quotation mark. The command

```
FKEYS F1 "MEM /C"*
```

assigns MEM /C to F1 and automatically executes it when F1 is pressed. You can delete a function key assignment by running FKEYS with the function key name but without a *command* parameter. Typing

```
FKEYS F1
```

removes F1's new key assignment and restores it to its normal mode of operation.

LISTING 12.3

```
;*********************************************************************
; FKEYS programs the function keys to produce DOS commands.  Its syntax is
;
;        FKEYS [shift-]key ["command"[*]]
;
; where "shift" designates a shift state (CTRL, ALT, or SHIFT), "key"
; designates the function key to be programmed (F1 through F12), "command"
; is the command to assign to the function key, and "*" indicates that the
; command should be executed when the function key is pressed.  Omitting
; "command" cancels a function key assignment.  The following metastrings
; may be used in the "command" parameter to specify special symbols:
;
;        $B        Piping operator (|)
;        $G        Output redirection operator (>)
;        $L        Input redirection operator (<)
;        $T        Ctrl-T (command separator)
;        $$        Dollar sign
;
; FKEYS requires DOS 4.0 or higher and requires that ANSI.SYS be installed.
;*********************************************************************

code            segment
```

```
                assume  cs:code,ds:code
                org     100h
begin:          jmp     main

helpmsg         db      "Programs the function keys to produce DOS commands."
                db      13,10,13,10
                db      "FKEYS [shift-]key [",22h,"command",22h,"[*]]"
                db      13,10,13,10
                db      "  shift      Identifies a shift key (Ctrl, Alt, or "
                db      "Shift).",13,10
                db      "  key        Identifies a function key (F1 through "
                db      "F12).",13,10
                db      "  command  Command to be assigned to the function "
                db      "key.",13,10
                db      "  *            Indicates the command should be auto-"
                db      "executed.",13,10,13,10
                db      "Running FKEYS without a ",22h,"command",22h
                db      " parameter cancels a function key assignment."
                db      13,10,"$"

errmsg1         db      "Syntax: FKEYS [shift-]key [",22h,"command",22h
                db      "[*]]",13,10,"$"
errmsg2         db      "DOS 4.0 or higher required",13,10,"$"
errmsg3         db      "ANSI.SYS not installed",13,10,"$"

altkey          db      "ALT"
ctrlkey         db      "CTRL"
shiftkey        db      "SHIFT"
adder1          db      58
adder2          db      122

command         db      27,"[0;",128 dup (?)


;***************************************************************************
; Procedure MAIN
;***************************************************************************

main            proc    near
                cld                             ;Clear direction flag
                mov     si,81h                  ;Point SI to command line
                call    scanhelp                ;Scan for "/?" switch
                jnc     checkver                ;Branch if not found
                mov     ah,09h                  ;Display help text and exit
                mov     dx,offset helpmsg       ;  with ERRORLEVEL=0
                int     21h
                mov     ax,4C01h
                int     21h
;
; Make sure this is DOS 4.0 or higher and that ANSI.SYS is installed
; before proceeding.
;
checkver:       mov     dx,offset errmsg2       ;Exit if DOS version
                mov     ah,30h                  ;  is less than 4.0
                int     21h
                cmp     al,4
                jae     checkansi
```

```
error:          mov     ah,09h                  ;Display error message and
                int     21h                     ;  exit with ERRORLEVEL=1
                mov     ax,4C01h
                int     21h

checkansi:      mov     ax,1A00h                ;Check for ANSI.SYS using
                int     2Fh                     ;  the DOS multiplex
                mov     dx,offset errmsg3       ;  interrupt
                cmp     al,0FFh
                jne     error                   ;Error if not installed
;
; Capitalize everything that's not between quotation marks.
;
                mov     si,81h                  ;Point SI to command line
tocaps1:        lodsb                           ;Get a character
                cmp     al,0Dh                  ;Branch if end of line
                je      parse
                cmp     al,22h                  ;Branch if not quotation
                jne     tocaps3                 ;  mark

tocaps2:        lodsb                           ;Get a character
                cmp     al,0Dh                  ;Branch if end of line
                je      parse
                cmp     al,22h                  ;Is it a quotation mark?
                je      tocaps1                 ;Branch if it is
                jmp     tocaps2                 ;Loop if it's not

tocaps3:        cmp     al,"a"                  ;Leave it if less than "a"
                jb      tocaps1
                cmp     al,"z"                  ;Leave it if greater than "z"
                ja      tocaps1
                and     byte ptr [si-1],0DFh    ;Capitalize it
                jmp     tocaps1                 ;Loop until done
;
; Parse the command line for a function key identifier.
;
parse:          mov     dx,offset errmsg1       ;Initialize error pointer
                mov     si,81h                  ;Reset SI
                call    findchar                ;Find first parameter
                jc      error                   ;Error if nothing found

                cmp     byte ptr [si],"A"       ;Is the character an "A?"
                jne     not_alt                 ;No, then branch
                mov     cx,3                    ;Set CX to string length
                mov     di,offset altkey        ;Point DI to "ALT"
                add     adder1,45               ;Update adders
                add     adder2,6
                repe    cmpsb                   ;Compare the strings
                jne     error                   ;Error if they don't match
                jmp     short checkdash

not_alt:        cmp     byte ptr [si],"C"       ;Is the character a "C?"
                jne     not_ctrl                ;No, then branch
                mov     cx,4                    ;Set CX to string length
                mov     di,offset ctrlkey       ;Point DI to "CTRL"
```

```
                add     adder1,35           ;Update adders
                add     adder2,4
                repe    cmpsb               ;Compare the strings
                jne     error               ;Error if they don't match
                jmp     short checkdash

not_ctrl:       cmp     byte ptr [si],"S"   ;Is the character an "S?"
                jne     fkey                ;No, then branch
                mov     cx,5                ;Set CX to string length
                mov     di,offset shiftkey  ;Point DI to "SHIFT"
                add     adder1,25           ;Update adders
                add     adder2,2
                repe    cmpsb               ;Compare the strings
                jne     error1              ;Error if they don't match

checkdash:      lodsb                       ;Get the next character
                cmp     al,"-"              ;Should be a hyphen
                jne     error1              ;Error if it's not

fkey:           lodsb                       ;Get next character
                cmp     al,"F"              ;Is it "F?"
                je      fkey1               ;Branch if it is
error1:         jmp     error               ;Error if it's not
fkey1:          call    asc2bin             ;Convert to binary
                mov     dx,offset errmsg1   ;Initialize error pointer
                jc      error1              ;Exit on error
                cmp     al,1                ;Error if number is less
                jb      error1              ;  than 1
                cmp     al,12               ;Error if number is greater
                ja      error1              ;  than 12
                cmp     al,10               ;Is it F1 through F10?
                jbe     fkey2               ;Branch if it is
                add     al,adder2           ;Convert to ANSI.SYS code
                jmp     short fkey3         ;Branch around the next line
fkey2:          add     al,adder1           ;Convert to ANSI.SYS code
fkey3:          mov     di,offset command+4 ;Point DI to end of command
                call    bin2asc             ;Convert binary to ASCII
                mov     al,";"              ;Append a semicolon
                stosb
;
; Parse the command line for a command string.
;
                call    findchar            ;Find next parameter
                jnc     fkey4               ;Branch if one found

                mov     si,offset command+2 ;Point SI to key code
                mov     cx,di               ;Compute length of string
                sub     cx,offset command+3 ;  entered thus far
                rep     movsb               ;Copy the key code
                jmp     short exit          ;Output and exit

fkey4:          movsb                       ;Copy the next character
                mov     dx,offset errmsg1   ;Initialize error pointer
                cmp     byte ptr [si-1],22h ;Error if it was not a
                jne     error1              ;  quotation mark
```

```
fkey5:          lodsb                           ;Read another character
                cmp     al,0Dh                  ;Error if it's a carriage
                je      error1                  ;  return
                cmp     al,22h                  ;Branch if it's a quotation
                je      fkey7                   ;  mark

                cmp     al,"$"                  ;Branch if character is not
                jne     fkey6                   ;  a dollar sign
                call    convert_mstring         ;Convert metastring if it is
fkey6:          stosb                           ;Write it to the string
                jmp     fkey5                   ;Loop back for more

fkey7:          cmp     byte ptr [si],"*"       ;Is next character a "*"?
                jne     fkey8                   ;Branch if it's not
                mov     byte ptr [di],0Dh       ;Append a carriage return
                inc     di
fkey8:          stosb                           ;Add closing quotation mark
;
; Output the command string to ANSI.SYS and terminate.
;
exit:           mov     ax,0070h                ;Append a "p" and binary
                stosw                           ;  zero to the command
                mov     si,offset command       ;Transmit the string to
                call    dos_out                 ;  ANSI.SYS
                mov     ax,4C00h                ;Exit with ERRORLEVEL=0
                int     21h
main            endp


;***************************************************************************
; FINDCHAR advances SI to the next non-space or non-comma character.
; On return, carry set indicates EOL was encountered.
;***************************************************************************
;

findchar        proc    near
                lodsb                           ;Get the next character
                cmp     al,20h                  ;Loop if space
                je      findchar
                cmp     al,2Ch                  ;Loop if comma
                je      findchar
                dec     si                      ;Point SI to the character
                cmp     al,0Dh                  ;Exit with carry set if end
                je      eol                     ;  of line is reached

                clc                             ;Clear carry and exit
                ret

eol:            stc                             ;Set carry and exit
                ret
findchar        endp


;***************************************************************************
; FINDDELIM advances SI to the next space or comma character.  On return,
; carry set indicates EOL was encountered.
;***************************************************************************
;

finddelim       proc    near
```

```
                lodsb                           ;Get the next character
                cmp     al,20h                  ;Exit if space
                je      fd_exit
                cmp     al,2Ch                  ;Exit if comma
                je      fd_exit
                cmp     al,0Dh                  ;Loop back for more if end
                jne     finddelim               ;  of line isn't reached

                dec     si                      ;Set carry and exit
                stc
                ret

fd_exit:        dec     si                      ;Clear carry and exit
                clc
                ret
finddelim       endp


;*************************************************************************
; SCANHELP scans the command line for a /? switch.  If found, carry returns
; set and SI contains its offset.  If not found, carry returns clear.
;*************************************************************************

scanhelp        proc    near
                push    si                      ;Save SI
scanloop:       lodsb                           ;Get a character
                cmp     al,0Dh                  ;Exit if end of line
                je      scan_exit
                cmp     al,22h                  ;Branch if it's a quotation
                je      skip                    ;  mark
                cmp     al,"?"                  ;Loop if not "?"
                jne     scanloop
                cmp     byte ptr [si-2],"/"     ;Loop if not "/"
                jne     scanloop

                add     sp,2                    ;Clear the stack
                sub     si,2                    ;Adjust SI
                stc                             ;Set carry and exit
                ret

scan_exit:      pop     si                      ;Restore SI
                clc                             ;Clear carry and exit
                ret

skip:           lodsb                           ;Get a character
                cmp     al,0Dh                  ;Exit if end of line
                je      scan_exit
                cmp     al,22h                  ;Reenter the loop if it's
                je      scanloop                ;  a quotation mark
                jmp     skip                    ;Continue scanning
scanhelp        endp


;*************************************************************************
; CONVERT_MSTRING converts a $B, $G, $L, $T, or $$ into a single character.
; On entry, AL holds the ASCII code for the dollar sign that prompted the
; call.  On exit, AL holds the character to be used in the command.
;*************************************************************************
```

```
convert_mstring proc    near
                mov     ah,7Ch                  ;Substitute "|" for $B
                cmp     byte ptr [si],"b"
                je      cm_convert
                cmp     byte ptr [si],"B"
                je      cm_convert

                mov     ah,3Eh                  ;Substitute ">" for $G
                cmp     byte ptr [si],"g"
                je      cm_convert
                cmp     byte ptr [si],"G"
                je      cm_convert

                mov     ah,3Ch                  ;Substitute "<" for $L
                cmp     byte ptr [si],"l"
                je      cm_convert
                cmp     byte ptr [si],"L"
                je      cm_convert

                mov     ah,14h                  ;Substitute Ctrl-T for $T
                cmp     byte ptr [si],"t"
                je      cm_convert
                cmp     byte ptr [si],"T"
                je      cm_convert

                mov     ah,24h                  ;Substitute "$" for $$
                cmp     byte ptr [si],"$"
                je      cm_convert
                cmp     byte ptr [si],"$"
                jne     cm_exit

cm_convert:     mov     al,ah                   ;Store code in AL
                inc     si                      ;Skip next character

cm_exit:        ret                             ;Exit to caller
convert_mstring endp

;****************************************************************************
; ASC2BIN converts a decimal number entered in ASCII form into a binary
; value in AL.  Carry set on return indicates that an error occurred in
; the conversion.
;****************************************************************************

asc2bin         proc    near
                sub     ax,ax                   ;Initialize registers
                sub     bh,bh
                mov     dl,10

a2b_loop:       mov     bl,[si]                 ;Get a character
                inc     si
                cmp     bl,20h                  ;Exit if space
                je      a2b_exit
                cmp     bl,2Ch                  ;Exit if comma
                je      a2b_exit
                cmp     bl,0Dh                  ;Exit if carriage return
```

```
                je      a2b_exit

                cmp     bl,"0"                  ;Error if character is not
                jb      a2b_error               ;  a number
                cmp     bl,"9"
                ja      a2b_error

                mul     dl                      ;Multiply the value in AL by
                jc      a2b_error               ;  10 and exit on overflow
                sub     bl,30h                  ;ASCII => binary
                add     ax,bx                   ;Add latest value to AX
                cmp     ax,255                  ;Error if sum > 255
                jna     a2b_loop                ;Loop back for more

a2b_error:      dec     si                      ;Set carry and exit
                stc
                ret

a2b_exit:       dec     si                      ;Clear carry and exit
                clc
                ret
asc2bin         endp
```

```
;****************************************************************************
; BIN2ASC converts a binary value in AX to ASCII form.  On entry, ES:DI
; holds the address the string will be written to.
;****************************************************************************
```

```
bin2asc         proc    near
                mov     bx,10                   ;Initialize divisor word and
                xor     cx,cx                   ;  digit counter
b2a1:           inc     cx                      ;Increment digit count
                xor     dx,dx                   ;Divide by 10
                div     bx
                push    dx                      ;Save remainder on stack
                or      ax,ax                   ;Loop until quotient is zero
                jnz     b2a1
b2a2:           pop     ax                      ;Retrieve a digit from stack
                add     al,30h                  ;Convert it to ASCII
                stosb                           ;Store it
                loop    b2a2                    ;Loop until done
                ret
bin2asc         endp
```

```
;****************************************************************************
; DOS_OUT outputs the ASCIIZ string pointed to by DS:SI.
;****************************************************************************
```

```
dos_out         proc    near
                lodsb                           ;Get a character
                or      al,al                   ;Exit if it's zero
                jz      dos_exit
                mov     ah,02h                  ;Output it using DOS
                mov     dl,al                   ;  function 02H
                int     21h
                jmp     dos_out                 ;Loop until done
```

```
dos_exit:      ret
dos_out        endp

code           ends
               end     begin
```

You can use FKEYS to program any of the function keys F1 through F12. You can also use it to program any function key modified with a Ctrl, Alt, or Shift key. For example, the command

```
FKEY CTRL-F1Ø "DIR /O:D"*
```

programs Ctrl-F10 to list the contents of the current directory sorted by date, from oldest to newest. Similarly, the command

```
FKEY ALT-F3 "CLS"*
```

programs Alt-F3 to clear the screen, and

```
FKEY SHIFT-F12 "MEM"*
```

programs F12 in combination with the left or right Shift key to show how much memory is installed and available.

If you want to include redirection or piping operators or Ctrl-T command separators in a command you assign to a function key, you can use one of the five special metastrings employed by FKEYS in lieu of the actual operators to represent these characters. The metastrings are

- ▪ $B, which represents a piping operator (|)
- ▪ $G, which represents an output redirection operator (>)
- ▪ $L, which represents an input redirection operator (<)
- ▪ $T, which represents a Ctrl-T command separator (¶)
- ▪ $$, which represents a dollar sign ($)

Use these metastrings with FKEYS anytime you assign a command to a function key that contains a piping or redirection operator, a Ctrl-T command separator, or a dollar sign. For example, the command

```
FKEYS SHIFT-F1 "MEM /C $B MORE"
```

assigns the command MEM | MORE to Shift-F1. This is equivalent to entering

```
FKEYS SHIFT-F1 "MEM /C | MORE"
```

but using metacharacters is more consistent with the way other DOS commands, such as PROMPT and DOSKEY, work. Plus, it enables FKEYS to recognize that a syntax error occurred if you omit the opening or closing quotation mark (if you omit one of them, DOS will act on the redirection or piping operator or the command separator itself and effectively truncate the command, lopping off everything to the right of the operator). Similarly, the command

```
FKEYS ALT-F12 "DIR /A:-D $G PRN"*
```

programs Alt-F12 to send a listing of the files in the current directory to the printer. The $G between DIR and PRN becomes an output redirection operator that routes the output from DIR to the printer rather than to the screen. The $L metastring works the same way, except that it evaluates to an input redirection symbol (<) rather than a greater-than sign.

Recall from Chapter 7 that DOSKEY permits multiple commands to be entered on the command line if they're separated by a Ctrl-T character (¶). If you want a function key programmed by FKEYS to be assigned more than one command, separate them with a $T. For example, the command

```
FKEYS F6 "CLS $T MEM"*
```

programs F6 to clear the screen, and then execute a MEM command. If you want to include a dollar sign in a command assignment, enter it as $$ to ensure that FKEYS will not interpret the character that comes after it as the second character of a metastring.

It's important to note that function keys programmed with FKEYS will work *only* while you're on the command line, not while you're inside application programs. The only exceptions are applications that read strings from standard input using DOS function OAH, such as EDLIN and DEBUG. Like COLOR, FKEYS will only run if ANSI.SYS is installed. If you're not sure how to install ANSI.SYS, go back and read the discussion of the COLOR command earlier in this chapter.

Inside FKEYS

From a programming perspective, there's not much in FKEYS that you haven't seen before. Like most of the utilities in this book it begins by scanning the command line for a /? switch. However, the SCANHELP routine that FKEYS calls to do the scanning is slightly different from the one used in the other programs. This one does not return carry set indicating that a /? was found if it appears inside quotation marks. If not for this simple modification, FKEYS wouldn't accept the command

```
FKEYS F1 " /?"*
```

which turns F1 into a help key for DOS commands (type a command, press F1, and DOS will offer help for the command). Instead, it would see the /? and execute its help routine.

Most of the logic in FKEYS is devoted to parsing the command line and turning what you type into an ANSI.SYS command. You saw in Chapter 6 that a command of the form ESC[*code*;"*string*"p sent to ANSI.SYS programs a key that corresponds to *code* to produce a command ("*string*"). So ESC[0;59;"MEM"p assigns MEM to function key F1. FKEYS turns the *shift-key* parameter you enter on the command line into a 2-number key code (for example, the code for F1 is 0;59) and places after it everything you entered between quotation marks. Then it transmits the command to ANSI.SYS. After that, it's ANSI.SYS that takes care of outputting a command when a function key is pressed.

If FKEYS encounters a dollar sign as it parses text you placed between quotation marks, it calls CONVERT_MSTRING to convert what could be a metastring into a special symbol such as a redirection or piping operator. On entry, AL holds the ASCII code for the dollar sign that was just read. On return, it still holds the code for a dollar sign if the character following the dollar sign was not B, G, L, T, or $. Otherwise, it holds the ASCII code for the symbol that the metastring represents. For example, if the command contains a $T, CONVERT_MSTRING returns a 14H in AL—the ASCII code for Ctrl-T. FKEYS then writes that value to the command string, effectively substituting for the metastring the symbol that it represents.

Toggling Caps Lock, Num Lock, and Scroll Lock

One of the little problems that nags users day in and day out is the fact that most PCs' configuration utilities do not allow them to designate the state of Caps Lock, Num Lock, and Scroll Lock at start-up. Most people thought nothing of it until IBM introduced the PS/2, which broke tradition by booting up with Num Lock on. Suddenly everyone wanted a means for manipulating these keyboard states from the command line so they could set them from AUTOEXEC.BAT.

Fortunately, it's not that difficult to write a utility to turn Caps Lock, Num Lock, and Scroll Lock on and off, as TOGGLE, the utility shown in Listing 12.4, demonstrates. The syntax for running TOGGLE is

```
TOGGLE [+C|-C] [+N|-N] [+S|-S] [/L]
```

where + enables a keyboard state and - disables it. The C, N, and S parameters stand for Caps Lock, Num Lock, and Scroll Lock, respectively. The command

```
TOGGLE +C
```

turns Caps Lock on, while the command

```
TOGGLE -N
```

turns Num Lock off. You can combine these operators in any way you like to toggle two or even three keyboard states at once. For example, the command

```
TOGGLE +C -N -S
```

turns Caps Lock on, Num Lock off, and Scroll Lock off, all in one operation.

LISTING 12.4

```
;**********************************************************************
; TOGGLE turns Caps Lock, Num Lock, and Scroll Lock on or off.  Its syntax
; is
;
;         TOGGLE [+C|-C] [+N|-N] [+S|-S] [/L]
;
; where +C or -C turns Caps Lock on or off, +N or -N turns Num Lock on or
; off, and +S or -S turns Scroll Lock on or off.  /L turns the keyboard
; indicator lights on or off also (on most PCs, the lights will toggle
; without the /L switch).  Running TOGGLE with no switches displays the
; current settings of Caps Lock, Num Lock, and Scroll Lock.
;**********************************************************************


code            segment
                assume  cs:code,ds:code
                org     100h
begin:          jmp     main

helpmsg         db      "Turns Caps Lock, Num Lock, and Scroll Lock on "
                db      "or off.",13,10,13,10
                db      "TOGGLE [+C|-C] [+N|-N] [+S|-S] [/L]",13,10,13,10
                db      "  +C  Turns Caps Lock on.",13,10
                db      "  -C  Turns Caps Lock off.",13,10
                db      "  +N  Turns Num Lock on.",13,10
                db      "  -N  Turns Num Lock off.",13,10
                db      "  +S  Turns Scroll Lock on.",13,10
                db      "  -S  Turns Scroll Lock off.",13,10
                db      "  /L  Toggles keyboard indicator lights.",13,10
                db      13,10
                db      "On most PCs, the keyboard indicator lights will "
                db      "toggle without the /L switch.",13,10
                db      "/L is included for those that do not.",13,10,"$"

errmsg1         db      "Syntax: Toggle [+C|-C] [+N|-N] [+S|-S] [/L]"
                db      13,10,"$"

msg1            db      13,10,"   Caps Lock   : $"
msg2            db      "   Num Lock    : $"
msg3            db      "   Scroll Lock : $"
msg4            db      "Off",13,10,"$"
msg5            db      "On",13,10,"$"

syncflag        db      0                       ;0=No /L switch


;**********************************************************************
; Procedure MAIN
;**********************************************************************
```

```
main            proc    near
                cld                             ;Clear direction flag
                mov     si,81h                  ;Point SI to command line
                call    scanhelp                ;Scan for "/?" switch
                jnc     parse                   ;Branch if not found
                mov     ah,09h                  ;Display help text and exit
                mov     dx,offset helpmsg       ;  with ERRORLEVEL=0
                int     21h
                mov     ax,4C01h
                int     21h
;
; Parse the command line and toggle keyboard states.
;
parse:          mov     ax,40h                  ;Point ES to the BIOS
                mov     es,ax                   ;  Data Area
nextparm:       call    findchar                ;Advance SI to next entry
                jc      checklites              ;Branch if end of line
                lodsb                           ;Get the character
                cmp     al,"+"                  ;Branch if "+"
                je      toggle
                cmp     al,"-"                  ;Branch if "-"
                je      toggle
                cmp     al,"/"                  ;Branch if "/"
                je      slash

error:          mov     ah,09h                  ;Display error message and
                mov     dx,offset errmsg1       ;  exit with ERRORLEVEL=1
                int     21h
                mov     ax,4C01h
                int     21h

slash:          lodsb                           ;Get next character
                and     al,0DFh                 ;Capitalize it
                cmp     al,"L"                  ;Error if not equal to "L"
                jne     error
                mov     syncflag,1              ;Set SYNCFLAG
                jmp     nextparm                ;Loop back for more

toggle:         lodsb                           ;Get next character
                and     al,0DFh                 ;Capitalize it
                mov     ah,40h                  ;Set AH for Caps Lock
                cmp     al,"C"                  ;Branch if "C" was entered
                je      on_off
                shr     ah,1                    ;Set AH for Num Lock
                cmp     al,"N"                  ;Branch if "N" was entered
                je      on_off
                shr     ah,1                    ;Set AH for Scroll Lock
                cmp     al,"S"                  ;Branch if "S" was entered
                jne     error

on_off:         cmp     byte ptr [si-2],"-"    ;Branch if leader was a "-"
                je      off
                or      byte ptr es:[17h],ah    ;Toggle a state bit on
                jmp     nextparm                ;Loop back for more
off:            not     ah                      ;Reverse all the bits
```

```
            and      byte ptr es:[17h],ah    ;Toggle a state bit off
            jmp      nextparm                ;Loop back for more
    ;
    ; Make sure the BIOS and the indicator lights are in sync if /L was entered.
    ;
    checklites:  cmp    syncflag,0           ;Exit now if SYNCFLAG
            je       echo                    ;  isn't set
            mov      bl,es:[17h]             ;Get keyboard flags
            and      bl,70h                  ;Zero unused bits
            mov      cl,4                    ;Shift four bits right
            shr      bl,cl
            cli                              ;Disable interrupts
            mov      al,0EDh                 ;Output command to keyboard
            out      60h,al                  ;  to set the indicator
            jmp      short $+2               ;  lights
            mov      al,bl                   ;Then output the new status
            out      60h,al                  ;  byte
            sti                              ;Enable interrupts
    ;
    ; Display the current keyboard status before exiting.
    ;
    echo:       mov      ah,09h              ;Echo state of Caps Lock
            mov      dx,offset msg1
            int      21h
            mov      ah,09h
            mov      dx,offset msg4
            test     byte ptr es:[17h],40h
            jz       nocaps
            mov      dx,offset msg5
    nocaps:     int      21h

            mov      ah,09h                  ;Echo state of Num Lock
            mov      dx,offset msg2
            int      21h
            mov      ah,09h
            mov      dx,offset msg4
            test     byte ptr es:[17h],20h
            jz       nonum
            mov      dx,offset msg5
    nonum:      int      21h

            mov      ah,09h                  ;Echo state of Scroll Lock
            mov      dx,offset msg3
            int      21h
            mov      ah,09h
            mov      dx,offset msg4
            test     byte ptr es:[17h],10h
            jz       noscroll
            mov      dx,offset msg5
    noscroll:   int      21h

            mov      ax,4C00h                ;Exit with ERRORLEVEL=0
            int      21h
    main        endp
```

```
;*************************************************************************
; FINDCHAR advances SI to the next non-space or non-comma character.
; On return, carry set indicates EOL was encountered.
;*************************************************************************

findchar        proc    near
                lodsb                           ;Get the next character
                cmp     al,20h                  ;Loop if space
                je      findchar
                cmp     al,2Ch                  ;Loop if comma
                je      findchar
                dec     si                      ;Point SI to the character
                cmp     al,0Dh                  ;Exit with carry set if end
                je      eol                     ;  of line is reached

                clc                             ;Clear carry and exit
                ret

eol:            stc                             ;Set carry and exit
                ret
findchar        endp


;*************************************************************************
; SCANHELP scans the command line for a /? switch.  If found, carry returns
; set and SI contains its offset.  If not found, carry returns clear.
;*************************************************************************

scanhelp        proc    near
                push    si                      ;Save SI
scanloop:       lodsb                           ;Get a character
                cmp     al,0Dh                  ;Exit if end of line
                je      scan_exit
                cmp     al,"?"                  ;Loop if not "?"
                jne     scanloop
                cmp     byte ptr [si-2],"/"     ;Loop if not "/"
                jne     scanloop

                add     sp,2                    ;Clear the stack
                sub     si,2                    ;Adjust SI
                stc                             ;Set carry and exit
                ret

scan_exit:      pop     si                      ;Restore SI
                clc                             ;Clear carry and exit
                ret
scanhelp        endp

code            ends
                end     begin
```

On most PCs, TOGGLE will also toggle the keyboard indicator lights. If the lights do not change when you run TOGGLE, try running it with a /L switch. /L (L for Lights) outputs the command to the keyboard to turn the LEDs (Light Emitting Diodes) on or off to match the current state of Num Lock, Caps Lock, and Scroll Lock. Normally, the keyboard BIOS takes care of this for you.

However, the BIOS on some older PCs does not. If you've retrofitted an older PC with a third-party keyboard or added a keyboard that was not specifically designed to work with your PC, the lights may have to be toggled without help from the BIOS. The /L switch takes care of this problem on most systems.

If there's any doubt as to the current state of Caps Lock, Num Lock, and Scroll Lock, run TOGGLE without any command line switches. It will display the current settings of all three. A typical display will look like this:

```
Caps Lock   : On
Num Lock    : Off
Scroll Lock : Off
```

If the keyboard LEDs are out of sync with the states indicated here, run TOGGLE with a /L switch and nothing else, as in

```
TOGGLE /L
```

If your keyboard is 100 percent IBM-compatible, TOGGLE will turn the LEDs on or off as needed to match them up with the keyboard states recorded in the BIOS.

Inside TOGGLE

The settings of Caps Lock, Num Lock, and Scroll Lock are determined by the settings of three bits in the BIOS Data Area. In the byte at address 0040:0017H, also known as the *shift status byte*, bit 6 controls Caps Lock, bit 5 controls Num Lock, and bit 4 controls Scroll Lock. Setting one of these bits to 1 enables the corresponding keyboard state, and setting it to 0 disables it. You can demonstrate this with the following DEBUG script:

```
A 0100
MOV     AX,40
MOV     DS,AX
OR      BYTE PTR [17],20
RET

G=0100
```

Start DEBUG, and then type the commands exactly as shown. When you execute the script with the G command, Num Lock will be enabled. Provided your keyboard has indicator lights and the keyboard and BIOS are compatible with each other, the Num Lock light will come on. If it doesn't, you can still verify that Num Lock is enabled by typing a few numbers on the numeric keypad.

This DEBUG script works because the component of the BIOS that processes scan codes emanating from the keyboard checks the status of Caps Lock and Num Lock before it decides what to do with the scan code for a character key. For example, if "A" is pressed, the BIOS checks to see if one of the Shift keys is pressed *and* checks to see if Caps Lock is active before deciding whether to place the ASCII code for an upper- or lowercase "A" in the keyboard buffer. Similarly, if the "7" key on the numeric keypad is pressed, the BIOS checks the Num Lock bit in the shift status byte and the Shift keys before deciding whether to place a "7" in the buffer or to place the code for the Home key. As you would suspect, when Caps Lock, Num Lock, or Scroll Lock is pressed, the BIOS toggles the corresponding bit in the BIOS Data Area.

The shift status byte was diagrammed in Chapter 9 in Figure 9.2. In addition to recording the state of Caps Lock, Num Lock, and Scroll Lock, this byte also tells us whether Ctrl, Alt, and the Shift keys are pressed (if a key is currently pressed, the bit that corresponds to it is set to 1), and whether Insert is currently active. The BIOS treats the Insert key as a toggle key just like it does the three Lock keys. However, because it produces a buffered key code like most of the other keys on the keyboard, the Insert key is easy enough to track without relying on the BIOS. As a result, most programs ignore bit 7 of the byte at 0040:0017H and process presses of the Insert key themselves.

The only real work TOGGLE has to do is translate the pluses and minuses you type on the command line (and the letters that follow them) into bit assignments. Once it decides that, say, an "N" means turn Num Lock on or off, it either sets or clears bit 5 of the shift status byte, depending on whether the "N" was preceded by a plus or a minus. In toggling the bit, TOGGLE has to be careful to leave the other bits unchanged, thereby avoiding unwanted side effects. To set the bit to 1, TOGGLE executes the instruction

```
OR      BYTE PTR ES:[17H],AH
```

where AH holds the value 20H if it's bit 5 that's being set (20H is the value you get if you zero all the bits in a byte but bit 5) and ES holds 40H—the segment address of the BIOS Data Area. The OR operation toggles bit 5 on while leaving the bits that surround it unchanged. Conversely, if the bit is being cleared rather than set, TOGGLE reverses the settings of all bits in AH (turning 1s to 0s and 0s to 1s) with the instruction

```
NOT AH
```

and then clears bit 5 with the instruction

```
AND     BYTE PTR ES:[17H],AH
```

The AND instruction performs a logical AND between the bits in the destination byte (in this case, the byte at ES:[17H]) and the bits in the source byte (AH). Thus, if all the bits in AH but bit 5 are set to 1, an AND instruction will set bit 5 to 0 and leave the others unaffected.

To display the current settings of Caps Lock, Num Lock, and Scroll Lock before it terminates, TOGGLE rereads bits 4, 5, and 6 from the shift status byte and indicates the corresponding lock state is "Off" if the bit is 0 or "On" if it's set to 1. Its work done, TOGGLE then calls DOS function 4CH to terminate.

Capturing Printer Output to a File

Many of today's application programs offer an option for printing to a file, which sends output that would normally go to a printer to disk instead. This feature can be quite useful. For example, if you want to print from an application program but don't have a printer attached to your machine, you can print to a file, and then carry a disk with the file to a PC that does have a printer attached and print it there. Yet not all programs offer such a feature. And when it comes to redirecting printer output to a file, DOS is of no help.

LPT2FILE, the utility whose program listing is shown in Listing 12.5, allows you to generically capture printer output from a program and direct it to a file on disk. Its syntax is

```
LPT2FILE [LPTn[:]=[[d:][path]filename]] [/B=size] [/C]
```

where *n* is the number of the printer to be redirected (LPT1, LPT2, or LPT3), *filename* specifies the name of the file that data is to be captured to, *size* specifies the number of kilobytes to be allocated to LPT2FILE's data buffer, and /C cancels redirection. The valid values for *size* range from 2 to 64. If you don't specify a buffer size, LPT2FILE defaults to 4k. The larger the buffer, the less often LPT2FILE will pause to access the disk, but the more memory it will consume. Installed with the default buffer size of 4k, LPT2FILE consumes about 5k of RAM. Installed with a different buffer size, it consumes proportionally more or less.

LISTING 12.5

```
;****************************************************************************
; LPT2FILE captures printer output to a file.  Its syntax is
;
;       LPT2FILE [LPTn[:]=[[d:][path]filename] [/B=size] [/C]
;
; where LPTn specifies the printer output is to be rerouted from (LPT1,
; LPT2, or LPT3), "filename" specifies the name of the file, and "size"
; specifies the size of LPT2FILE's internal data buffer (in kilobytes).
; "Size" defaults to 4k; acceptable values range from 2k to 64k.  Run
; without command line parameters, LPT2FILE displays which (if any)
; printer is redirected.  Running it with /C cancels redirection.
;****************************************************************************

code            segment
                assume  cs:code
                org     100h
begin:          jmp     init

signature       db      0,1,2,"LPT2FILE",2,1,0   ;Program signature
prog_id         db      ?                        ;Multiplex ID number
```

```
int08h          dd      ?                       ;Interrupt 08H vector
int13h          dd      ?                       ;Interrupt 13H vector
int17h          dd      ?                       ;Interrupt 17H vector
int21h          dd      ?                       ;Interrupt 21H vector
int25h          dd      ?                       ;Interrupt 25H vector
int26h          dd      ?                       ;Interrupt 26H vector
int28h          dd      ?                       ;Interrupt 28H vector
int2Fh          dd      ?                       ;Interrupt 2FH vector

errorflag       dd      ?                       ;Critical error flag address
intflags        db      0                       ;Disk interrupt flags
indos           dd      ?                       ;InDOS flag address
bufsize         dw      4096                    ;Internal buffer size
bufhalf         dw      2048                    ;Half buffer size
bufptr          dw      0                       ;Buffer pointer
bufseg          dw      ?                       ;Buffer segment
bytecount       dw      ?                       ;Number of bytes in buffer
counter         db      91                      ;Countdown timer
lptport         db      0FEh,0                  ;Redirected LPT port
filename        db      128 dup (?)             ;File specification


;******************************************************************************
; TIMER_INT handles interrupt 08H.
;******************************************************************************

timer_int       proc    far
                pushf                           ;Push FLAGS
                call    cs:[int08h]             ;Call previous handler
                cli                             ;Disable interrupts

                cmp     cs:[counter],0          ;Branch if timer has
                je      timer1                  ;  already expired
                dec     cs:[counter]            ;Decrement counter
                jnz     timer_exit              ;Exit if not zero
                cmp     cs:[bufptr],0           ;Branch if there is data
                jne     timer1                  ;  in the buffer
                mov     cs:[counter],91         ;Reset the counter and exit
                jmp     short timer_exit        ;  if there's not

timer1:         push    di                      ;Save ES and DI
                push    es
                cmp     cs:[intflags],0         ;Branch if a disk interrupt
                jne     timer2                  ;  flag is set
                les     di,cs:[indos]           ;Branch if the InDOS flag
                cmp     byte ptr es:[di],0      ;  is set
                jne     timer2
                les     di,cs:[errorflag]       ;Branch if the critical error
                cmp     byte ptr es:[di],0      ;  flag is set
                jne     timer2
                call    flush                   ;Flush the output buffer
timer2:         pop     es                      ;Restore ES and DI
                pop     di
timer_exit:     iret
timer_int       endp
```

```
;*************************************************************************
; PRINTER_INT handles interrupt 17H.
;*************************************************************************

printer_int     proc    far
                cmp     cs:[lptport],ØFFh       ;Branch if redirection is
                jne     prn_check               ;  enabled
prn_bios:       jmp     cs:[int17h]             ;Jump to BIOS handler

prn_check:      cmp     dx,word ptr cs:[lptport];Exit if this LPT port is not
                jne     prn_bios                ;  currently redirected
                cmp     ah,Ø2h                  ;Exit if function code is
                ja      prn_bios                ;  greater than Ø2h

                push    di                      ;Save ES and DI
                push    es
;
; Process interrupt 17H, function ØØH (transmit character to printer).
;
                or      ah,ah                   ;Branch if AH is not Ø
                jnz     prn1
                mov     cs:[counter],91         ;Reset timer
                mov     di,cs:[bufptr]          ;Point DI to buffer
                cmp     di,cs:[bufsize]         ;Error if the buffer is
                je      prn_error               ;  full
                mov     es,cs:[bufseg]          ;Point ES to buffer segment
                mov     es:[di],al              ;Buffer the character
                inc     di                      ;Increment the buffer pointer
                mov     cs:[bufptr],di          ;Store the new pointer
                cmp     di,cs:[bufhalf]         ;Exit if the buffer is less
                jb      prn_exit                ;  than half full

prn_clear:      cmp     cs:[intflags],Ø         ;Branch if a disk interrupt
                jne     prn_exit                ;  flag is set
                les     di,cs:[indos]           ;Branch if the InDOS flag
                cmp     byte ptr es:[di],Ø      ;  is set
                jne     prn_exit
                les     di,cs:[errorflag]       ;Branch if the critical error
                cmp     byte ptr es:[di],Ø      ;  flag is set
                jne     prn_exit
                call    flush                   ;Flush the output buffer
                jmp     short prn_exit          ;Then exit
;
; Process interrupt 17H, function Ø1H (initialize printer).
;
prn1:           cmp     ah,Ø1h                  ;Branch if AH is not 1
                jne     prn2
                cmp     cs:[bufptr],Ø           ;Exit if the buffer
                je      prn_exit                ;  is empty
                jmp     prn_clear               ;Flush it if it's not
;
; Process interrupt 17H, function Ø2H (get printer status).
;
prn2:           mov     di,cs:[bufptr]          ;Get buffer pointer
                cmp     di,cs:[bufsize]         ;Is the buffer full?
                je      prn_error               ;Error if it is
```

```
prn_exit:       mov     ah,90h              ;Return OK signal in AH
                pop     es                  ;Restore ES and DI
                pop     di
                iret                        ;Return from interrupt

prn_error:      mov     ah,08h              ;Return I/O error in AH
                pop     es                  ;Restore ES and DI
                pop     di
                iret                        ;Return from interrupt
printer_int     endp

;*************************************************************************
; DOS_INT handles interrupt 21H.
;*************************************************************************

dos_int         proc    near
                pushf                       ;Save FLAGS
                cmp     cs:[bufptr],0       ;Exit if the buffer is
                je      dos_exit            ;  empty

                push    di
                push    es
                cmp     cs:[intflags],0     ;Branch if a disk interrupt
                jne     dos_busy            ;  flag is set
                les     di,cs:[indos]       ;Branch if the InDOS flag
                cmp     byte ptr es:[di],0  ;  is set
                jne     dos_busy
                les     di,cs:[errorflag]   ;Branch if the critical error
                cmp     byte ptr es:[di],0  ;  flag is set
                jne     dos_busy
                call    flush               ;Flush the buffer
dos_busy:       pop     es                  ;Restore registers
                pop     di

dos_exit:       popf                        ;Restore FLAGS
                jmp     cs:[int21h]         ;Exit to original handler
dos_int         endp


;*************************************************************************
; DOSIDLE_INT handles interrupt 28H.
;*************************************************************************

dosidle_int     proc    far
                pushf                       ;Push FLAGS
                call    cs:[int28h]         ;Call previous handler
                cli                         ;Disable interrupts

                cmp     cs:[bufptr],0       ;Exit if the buffer
                je      dosidle_exit        ;  is empty

                cmp     cs:[intflags],0     ;Branch if a disk interrupt
                jne     dosidle_exit        ;  flag is set
                push    di                  ;Save ES and DI
                push    es
                les     di,cs:[errorflag]   ;Check the state of the
                cmp     byte ptr es:[di],0  ;  critical error flag
```

```
                        pop     es                  ;Restore ES and DI
                        pop     di
                        jne     dosidle_exit        ;Exit if the flag is set
                        call    flush               ;Yes, then flush it
        dosidle_exit:   iret                        ;Return from interrupt
        dosidle_int     endp


;*************************************************************************
; DISK_INT handles interrupt 13H.
;*************************************************************************

        disk_int        proc    far
                        pushf                       ;Save FLAGS
                        or      cs:[intflags],02h   ;Set disk flag
                        popf                        ;Retrieve FLAGS
                        pushf                       ;Push FLAGS
                        call    cs:[int13h]         ;Call previous handler
                        pushf                       ;Save FLAGS
                        and     cs:[intflags],0FDh  ;Clear disk flag
                        popf                        ;Retrieve FLAGS
                        ret     2                   ;Return with FLAGS intact
        disk_int        endp


;*************************************************************************
; ABS_READ_INT handles interrupt 25H.
;*************************************************************************

        abs_read_int    proc    far
                        pushf                       ;Save FLAGS
                        or      cs:[intflags],04h   ;Set disk flag
                        popf                        ;Retrieve FLAGS
                        call    cs:[int25h]         ;Call previous handler
                        pushf                       ;Save FLAGS
                        and     cs:[intflags],0FBh  ;Clear disk flag
                        popf                        ;Retrieve FLAGS
                        ret                         ;Return with FLAGS on stack
        abs_read_int    endp


;*************************************************************************
; ABS_WRITE_INT handles interrupt 26H.
;*************************************************************************

        abs_write_int   proc    far
                        pushf                       ;Save FLAGS
                        or      cs:[intflags],08h   ;Set disk flag
                        popf                        ;Retrieve FLAGS
                        call    cs:[int26h]         ;Call previous handler
                        pushf                       ;Save FLAGS
                        and     cs:[intflags],0F7h  ;Clear disk flag
                        popf                        ;Retrieve FLAGS
                        ret                         ;Return with FLAGS on stack
        abs_write_int   endp
```

```
;************************************************************************
; MPLEX_INT handles interrupt 2FH.  If, on entry, AH is set to LPT2FILE's
; multiplex ID number, MPLEX_INT uses the value in AL as a function code.
; The functions supported are:
;
;    00H    Returns FFH in AL to indicate the program is installed
;           and returns the address of its signature in ES:DI.
;
;    01H    Returns the number of the printer currently redirected
;           (0, 1, or 2) in AL, or FFH if none are redirected.  If AL
;           contains 0, 1, or 2, then ES:DI holds the address of the
;           name of the file output is redirected to.
;
;    02H    Accepts the number of the printer to be redirected (0, 1,
;           or 2) in BL and the address of a file name in DS:SI.  FFH
;           cancels redirection.  This function causes the output
;           buffer to be flushed.
;************************************************************************

mplex_int       proc    far
                pushf                           ;Save FLAGS register
                cmp     ah,cs:[prog_id]         ;Branch if AH holds the
                je      mplex2                  ;  multiplex ID
                popf                            ;Restore FLAGS
                jmp     cs:[int2Fh]             ;Pass the interrupt on
;
; Function 00H verifies that the program is installed.
;
mplex2:         popf                            ;Restore FLAGS
                or      al,al                   ;Branch if function code
                jnz     mplex3                  ;  is other than 00H
                mov     al,0FFh                 ;Set AL to FFH
                push    cs                      ;Point ES:DI to the program
                pop     es                      ;  signature
                mov     di,offset signature
                iret                            ;Return from interrupt
;
; Function 01H reports the status of redirection.
;
mplex3:         cmp     al,01h                  ;Branch if function code
                jne     mplex4                  ;  is other than 01H
                mov     al,cs:[lptport]         ;Put printer number in AL
                push    cs                      ;Point ES to this segment
                pop     es
                mov     di,offset filename      ;Point DI to file name
                iret                            ;Return from interrupt
;
; Function 02H designates a new printer and file name for redirection.
;
mplex4:         cmp     cs:[bufptr],0           ;Branch if the output
                je      mplex5                  ;  buffer is empty
                call    flush                   ;Flush the buffer
mplex5:         mov     cs:[lptport],bl         ;Store printer number
                cmp     bl,0FFh                 ;Branch if redirection
                je      mplex_exit              ;  cancelled
                push    es                      ;Save ES
```

```
                push    cs                      ;Point ES to this segment
                pop     es
                mov     di,offset filename      ;Point DI to file name
                cld                             ;Clear direction flag
mplex6:         movsb                           ;Copy one character
                cmp     byte ptr [si-1],0       ;Was it a zero?
                jne     mplex6                  ;No, then loop back
                pop     es                      ;Restore ES
mplex_exit:     iret                            ;Return from interrupt
mplex_int       endp


;**************************************************************************
; FLUSH flushes the output buffer.
;**************************************************************************

flush           proc    near
                push    ax                      ;Save registers
                push    bx
                push    cx
                push    dx
                push    ds

                mov     ax,cs                   ;Point DS to the code
                mov     ds,ax                   ;  segment
                assume  ds:code

                mov     counter,91              ;Reset the counter
                mov     ax,bufptr               ;Retrieve buffer pointer
                mov     bytecount,ax            ;Save it for later
                mov     bufptr,0                ;Reset the pointer
                sti                             ;Enable interrupts

                call    openfile                ;Attempt to open the file
                jc      flush_exit              ;Branch if it failed

                mov     bx,ax                   ;Transfer file handle to BX

                mov     ax,4202h                ;Move the file pointer to
                sub     cx,cx                   ;  the end of the file
                mov     dx,cx
                int     21h

                mov     ah,40h                  ;Copy the output buffer
                mov     cx,bytecount            ;  to disk
                sub     dx,dx
                mov     ds,bufseg
                assume  ds:nothing
                int     21h

                mov     ah,3Eh                  ;Close the file
                int     21h

flush_exit:     pop     ds                      ;Restore registers and exit
                pop     dx
                pop     cx
                pop     bx
```

```
                pop     ax
                ret
flush           endp

;**********************************************************************
; OPENFILE attempts to open or create the file output is redirected to.
; On return, carry is clear if the attempt was successful and the file
; handle is in AX.  Carry set means the attempt failed.  On entry, DS
; must point to the code segment.
;**********************************************************************

openfile        proc    near
                mov     ax,3D01h                ;Attempt to open the file
                mov     dx,offset filename      ;  for writing
                int     21h
                jnc     opened                  ;Branch if it worked

                mov     ax,4301h                ;Attempt to strip all the
                sub     cx,cx                   ;  attributes off the file
                mov     dx,offset filename
                int     21h

                mov     ax,3D01h                ;Then attempt to open it
                mov     dx,offset filename      ;  for writing again
                int     21h
                jnc     opened                  ;Branch if it worked

                mov     ah,3Ch                  ;Attempt to create the
                sub     cx,cx                   ;  file from scratch
                mov     dx,offset filename
                int     21h
                jnc     opened                  ;Branch if it worked

                stc                             ;Set the carry flag and
                ret                             ;  exit

opened:         clc                             ;Clear the carry flag and
                ret                             ;  exit
openfile        endp

;**********************************************************************
; Data that will be discarded when the program becomes memory-resident.
;**********************************************************************

helpmsg         db      "Captures printer output to a file.",13,10,13,10
                db      "LPT2FILE [LPTn[:]=[[d:][path]filename]] [/B=size] "
                db      "[/C]",13,10,13,10
                db      " LPTn      Specifies the LPT port number.",13,10
                db      " /B=size   Specifies the internal buffer size in "
                db      "kilobytes (default=4k).",13,10
                db      " /C        Cancels redirection.",13,10,13,10
                db      "Running LPT2FILE with no parameters displays the "
                db      "status of redirection.",13,10,"$"

errmsg1         db      "Syntax: LPT2FILE [LPTn[:]=[[d:][path]filename]] "
                db      "[/B=size] [/C]",13,10,"$"
```

```
errmsg2         db          "Requires DOS 3.0 or higher",13,10,"$"
errmsg3         db          "Buffer size is fixed once the program is installed"
crlf            db          13,10,"$"
errmsg4         db          "Invalid buffer size (minimum=2, maximum=64)"
                db          13,10,"$"
errmsg5         db          "Invalid port number (must be LPT1, LPT2, or LPT3)"
                db          13,10,"$"
errmsg6         db          "File could not be opened",13,10,"$"
errmsg7         db          "Program could not be installed",13,10,"$"
errmsg8         db          "Not enough memory",13,10,"$"

msg1            db          "LPT2FILE 1.0 installed",13,10,"$"
msg2            db          "No printers are currently redirected",13,10,"$"
msg3            db          "LPTn: is currently redirected to $"


installed       db          0                       ;0=Not installed
eoladdr         dw          0                       ;End of line address


;****************************************************************************
; INIT makes the program resident in memory.
;****************************************************************************


                assume   cs:code,ds:code

init            proc     near
                cld                                 ;Clear direction flag
                mov      si,81h                     ;Point SI to command line
                call     scanhelp                   ;Scan for "/?" switch
                jnc      checkver                   ;Branch if not found
                mov      ah,09h                     ;Display help text and exit
                mov      dx,offset helpmsg          ;  with ERRORLEVEL=0
                int      21h
                mov      ax,4C00h
                int      21h
;
; Check the DOS version and see if the program is already installed.
;
checkver:       mov      dx,offset errmsg2          ;Exit if DOS version
                mov      ah,30h                     ;  is less than 3.0
                int      21h
                cmp      al,3
                jae      checkprog

error:          mov      ah,09h                     ;Display error message and
                int      21h                        ;  exit with ERRORLEVEL=1
                mov      ax,4C01h
                int      21h

checkprog:      push     es                         ;Save ES
                call     check_install              ;See if a copy is installed
                jnc      reset                      ;Branch if not
                mov      installed,1                ;Set flag if it is
                mov      prog_id,ah                 ;Also store the ID number
reset:          pop      es                         ;Restore ES
;
; First capitalize everything on the command line.
```

```
;
parse:          mov     si,81h                  ;Point SI to command line
                mov     cl,[si-1]               ;CL = Number of characters
                sub     ch,ch                   ;Convert byte to word in CX
                jcxz    parse3                  ;Done if CX=0
parse1:         cmp     byte ptr [si],"a"       ;Leave it if less than "a"
                jb      parse2
                cmp     byte ptr [si],"z"       ;Leave it if greater than "z"
                ja      parse2
                and     byte ptr [si],0DFh      ;Capitalize it
parse2:         inc     si                      ;Advance SI
                loop    parse1                  ;Loop until done
parse2a:        mov     si,81h                  ;Reset SI
;
; Parse the command line for entries.
;
parse3:         call    findchar                ;Find parameter
                jnc     parse3a                 ;Branch if not end of line
                jmp     done                    ;Exit the parsing loop
parse3a:        cmp     byte ptr [si],"/"       ;Branch if the character
                jne     getportinfo             ;  is not a forward slash
;
; Process a /B switch.
;
                inc     si                      ;Advance SI
                lodsb                           ;Get character
                cmp     al,"B"                  ;Branch if it's not a "B"
                jne     slashc
                cmp     installed,0             ;Error if /B entered with the
                mov     dx,offset errmsg3       ;  program already installed
                jne     error
                lodsb                           ;Get the next character
                cmp     al,"="                  ;Error if not a "="
                mov     dx,offset errmsg1
                jne     error
                call    asc2bin                 ;Get the number after the "="
                mov     dx,offset errmsg4       ;Exit if error occurred in
                jc      error                   ;  the conversion
                cmp     al,2                    ;Error if less than 2
                jb      error
                cmp     al,64                   ;Error if greater than 64
                ja      error
                sub     ah,ah                   ;Compute the buffer size
                mov     cl,10                   ;  in bytes by shifting
                shl     ax,cl                   ;  AX left 10 bits
                or      ax,ax                   ;Branch if not equal to 0
                jnz     not_zero
                dec     ax                      ;Set AX to FFFFH
not_zero:       mov     bufsize,ax              ;Record the buffer size
                shr     ax,1                    ;Divide buffer size by 2
                mov     bufhalf,ax              ;Record it
                jmp     parse3                  ;Return to parsing loop
;
; Process a /C switch.
;
slashc:         mov     dx,offset errmsg1       ;Initialize error pointer
```

```
              cmp     al,"C"                  ;Error if it's not a "C"
              jne     error1
              mov     lptport,0FFh            ;Cancel redirection
              jmp     parse3                  ;Return to input loop
;
; Process an LPT port number.
;
getportinfo:  mov     dx,offset errmsg1       ;Initialize error pointer
              mov     di,offset errmsg1+8     ;Point DI to "LPT"
              mov     cx,3                    ;Load CX with count
              repe    cmpsb                   ;Compare the strings
              jne     error1                  ;Error if not equal

              mov     dx,offset errmsg5       ;Initialize error pointer
              lodsb                           ;Get port number
              cmp     al,"1"                  ;Error if less than "1"
              jb      error1
              cmp     al,"3"                  ;Error if greater than "3"
              ja      error1
              sub     al,31h                  ;Convert to port number
              mov     lptport,al              ;Save it

              mov     dx,offset errmsg1       ;Initialize error pointer
              cmp     byte ptr [si],":"       ;Is next character a colon?
              jne     gpi3                    ;No, then branch
              cmp     byte ptr [si],0Dh       ;Error if end of line
              je      error1
              inc     si                      ;Skip colon

gpi3:         lodsb                           ;Get next character
              cmp     al,"="                  ;Error if it's not "="
              jne     error1
;
; Process the file name that goes with the port number.
;
              push    si                      ;Save string address
              call    finddelim               ;Find end of file name
              jc      gpi4                    ;Branch if end of line
              mov     eoladdr,si              ;Save end of line address
gpi4:         mov     byte ptr [si],0         ;Convert to ASCIIZ string
              pop     si                      ;Retrieve string address
              mov     di,offset filename      ;Point DI to file name buffer
              mov     ah,60h                  ;Turn it into a fully
              int     21h                     ;  qualified file name
              jnc     gpi5                    ;Branch if no error

error2:       mov     dx,offset errmsg6       ;Exit on error
error1:       jmp     error

gpi5:         call    openfile                ;Attempt to open the file
              jc      error2

              mov     bx,ax                   ;Close the file
              mov     ah,3Eh
              int     21h
```

```
                cmp     eoladdr,0               ;Reached end of line?
                je      done                    ;Yes, then quit parsing
                mov     si,eoladdr              ;Point SI to end of file name
                inc     si                      ;Advance past the zero byte
                jmp     parse3                  ;Loop back for more
;
; Come here when parsing is done.
;
done:           cmp     installed,0             ;Branch if the program is
                jne     done1                   ;  already installed
                cmp     lptport,0FEh            ;Port number equal to FEH?
                jne     install                 ;No, then go install
                inc     lptport                 ;Set port number to FFH
                jmp     short install           ;Go install

done1:          cmp     lptport,0FEh            ;Port number equal to FEH?
                je      done2                   ;Yes, then we're done
                mov     ah,prog_id              ;Send new printer number
                mov     al,02h                  ;  and file name to an
                mov     bl,lptport              ;  installed copy of
                mov     si,offset filename      ;  the program
                int     2Fh

done2:          call    showstatus              ;Show redirection status
                mov     ax,4C00h                ;Exit with ERRORLEVEL=0
                int     21h
;
; Install the program.
;
install:        call    mplex_id                ;Find a multiplex ID number
                mov     dx,offset errmsg7       ;Error if none available
                jc      error1
                mov     prog_id,ah              ;Save the ID number

                mov     ah,34h                  ;Get and save the address of
                int     21h                     ;  the InDOS flag
                mov     word ptr indos,bx
                mov     word ptr indos[2],es

                push    ds                      ;Save DS
                mov     ax,5D06h                ;Get and save the address of
                int     21h                     ;  the critical error flag
                mov     word ptr cs:[errorflag],si
                mov     word ptr cs:[errorflag+2],ds
                pop     ds                      ;Restore DS
                mov     dx,offset errmsg7       ;Error if function returned
                jc      error1                  ;  with carry set

                mov     ax,3508h                ;Hook interrupt 08H
                int     21h
                mov     word ptr int08h,bx
                mov     word ptr int08h[2],es
                mov     ax,2508h
                mov     dx,offset timer_int
                int     21h
```

```
        mov     ax,3513h                ;Hook interrupt 13H
        int     21h
        mov     word ptr int13h,bx
        mov     word ptr int13h[2],es
        mov     ax,2513h
        mov     dx,offset disk_int
        int     21h


        mov     ax,3517h                ;Hook interrupt 17H
        int     21h
        mov     word ptr int17h,bx
        mov     word ptr int17h[2],es
        mov     ax,2517h
        mov     dx,offset printer_int
        int     21h


        mov     ax,3521h                ;Hook interrupt 21H
        int     21h
        mov     word ptr int21h,bx
        mov     word ptr int21h[2],es
        mov     ax,2521h
        mov     dx,offset dos_int
        int     21h


        mov     ax,3525h                ;Hook interrupt 25H
        int     21h
        mov     word ptr int25h,bx
        mov     word ptr int25h[2],es
        mov     ax,2525h
        mov     dx,offset abs_read_int
        int     21h


        mov     ax,3526h                ;Hook interrupt 26H
        int     21h
        mov     word ptr int26h,bx
        mov     word ptr int26h[2],es
        mov     ax,2526h
        mov     dx,offset abs_write_int
        int     21h


        mov     ax,3528h                ;Hook interrupt 28H
        int     21h
        mov     word ptr int28h,bx
        mov     word ptr int28h[2],es
        mov     ax,2528h
        mov     dx,offset dosidle_int
        int     21h


        mov     ax,352Fh                ;Hook interrupt 2FH
        int     21h
        mov     word ptr int2Fh,bx
        mov     word ptr int2Fh[2],es
        mov     ax,252Fh
        mov     dx,offset mplex_int
        int     21h
```

```
                mov     ah,49h                  ;Get the segment address of
                mov     es,ds:[2Ch]             ;  the environment block
                int     21h                     ;  and free the segment

                mov     ah,4Ah                  ;Shrink the memory block
                mov     bx,(offset helpmsg - offset code + 15) shr 4
                mov     cx,cs                   ;  the program is
                mov     es,cx                   ;  loaded in
                int     21h

                mov     ah,48h                  ;Request a new block of
                mov     bx,bufsize              ;  memory for the data
                mov     cl,4                    ;  buffer
                shr     bx,cl
                inc     bx
                int     21h
                mov     dx,offset errmsg8       ;Error if there's not
                jnc     no_error                ;  enough memory
                jmp     error
no_error:       mov     bufseg,ax               ;Save the segment address

                mov     ah,09h                  ;Display message verifying
                mov     dx,offset msg1          ;  the installation
                int     21h
                call    showstatus              ;Show redirection status

                mov     ax,3100h                ;Terminate with function 31H
                mov     dx,(offset helpmsg - offset code + 15)
                int     21h
init            endp

;****************************************************************************
; FINDCHAR advances SI to the next non-space or non-comma character.
; On return, carry set indicates EOL was encountered.
;****************************************************************************

findchar        proc    near
                lodsb                           ;Get the next character
                cmp     al,20h                  ;Loop if space
                je      findchar
                cmp     al,2Ch                  ;Loop if comma
                je      findchar
                dec     si                      ;Point SI to the character
                cmp     al,0Dh                  ;Exit with carry set if end
                je      eol                     ;  of line is reached

                clc                             ;Clear carry and exit
                ret

eol:            stc                             ;Set carry and exit
                ret
findchar        endp
```

```
;*******************************************************************************
; FINDDELIM advances SI to the next space or comma character.  On return,
; carry set indicates EOL was encountered.
;*******************************************************************************

finddelim       proc    near
                lodsb                           ;Get the next character
                cmp     al,20h                  ;Exit if space
                je      fd_exit
                cmp     al,2Ch                  ;Exit if comma
                je      fd_exit
                cmp     al,0Dh                  ;Loop back for more if end
                jne     finddelim               ;  of line isn't reached

                dec     si                      ;Set carry and exit
                stc
                ret

fd_exit:        dec     si                      ;Clear carry and exit
                clc
                ret
finddelim       endp


;*******************************************************************************
; SCANHELP scans the command line for a /? switch.  If found, carry returns
; set and SI contains its offset.  If not found, carry returns clear.
;*******************************************************************************

scanhelp        proc    near
                push    si                      ;Save SI
scanloop:       lodsb                           ;Get a character
                cmp     al,0Dh                  ;Exit if end of line
                je      scan_exit
                cmp     al,"?"                  ;Loop if not "?"
                jne     scanloop
                cmp     byte ptr [si-2],"/"     ;Loop if not "/"
                jne     scanloop

                add     sp,2                    ;Clear the stack
                sub     si,2                    ;Adjust SI
                stc                             ;Set carry and exit
                ret

scan_exit:      pop     si                      ;Restore SI
                clc                             ;Clear carry and exit
                ret
scanhelp        endp


;*******************************************************************************
; CHECK_INSTALL returns carry set if the program is already installed,
; carry clear if it's not.  If carry returns set, AH holds the program's
; multiplex ID number.
;*******************************************************************************

check_install   proc    near
                mov     ax,8000h                ;Initialize AH and AL
```

```
                      mov      cx,80h                    ;Initialize count

chinst1:              push     ax                        ;Save AX and CX
                      push     cx
                      sub      di,di                     ;Set ES and DI to 0
                      mov      es,di
                      int      2Fh                       ;Interrupt 2Fh
                      cmp      al,0FFh                   ;Nothing here if AL isn't
                      jne      chinst2                  ;  equal to FFH

                      mov      si,offset signature       ;See if program signature
                      mov      cx,14                     ;  appears at the address
                      repe     cmpsb                     ;  returned in ES:DI
                      jne      chinst2                  ;Branch if it does not

                      pop      cx                        ;Clear the stack and exit
                      pop      ax                        ;  with carry set
                      stc
                      ret

chinst2:              pop      cx                        ;Retrieve AX and CX
                      pop      ax
                      inc      ah                        ;Next multiplex ID
                      loop     chinst1                   ;Loop until done

                      clc                                ;Exit with carry clear
                      ret
check_install         endp

;**************************************************************************
; MPLEX_ID searches for an unused multiplex ID number.  If one is found,
; it is returned in AH with carry clear.  Carry set means no multiplex
; ID numbers are currently available.
;**************************************************************************
;

mplex_id              proc     near
                      mov      ax,8000h                  ;Initialize AH and AL
                      mov      cx,80h                    ;Initialize count

mxid1:                push     ax                        ;Save AX and CX
                      push     cx
                      int      2Fh                       ;Interrupt 2Fh
                      or       al,al                     ;Branch if AL=0
                      jz       mxid2
                      pop      cx                        ;Retrieve AX and CX
                      pop      ax
                      inc      ah                        ;Increment ID number
                      loop     mxid1                     ;Loop until done

                      stc                                ;Exit with carry set
                      ret

mxid2:                pop      cx                        ;Clear the stack and exit
                      pop      ax                        ;  with carry clear
                      clc
                      ret
```

```
mplex_id        endp

;*********************************************************************
; ASC2BIN converts a decimal number entered in ASCII form into a binary
; value in AL.  Carry set on return indicates that an error occurred in
; the conversion.
;*********************************************************************

asc2bin         proc    near
                sub     ax,ax                   ;Initialize registers
                sub     bh,bh
                mov     dl,10

a2b_loop:       mov     bl,[si]                 ;Get a character
                inc     si
                cmp     bl,20h                  ;Exit if space
                je      a2b_exit
                cmp     bl,2Ch                  ;Exit if comma
                je      a2b_exit
                cmp     bl,0Dh                  ;Exit if carriage return
                je      a2b_exit

                cmp     bl,"0"                  ;Error if character is not
                jb      a2b_error               ;  a number
                cmp     bl,"9"
                ja      a2b_error

                mul     dl                      ;Multiply the value in AL by
                jc      a2b_error               ;  10 and exit on overflow
                sub     bl,30h                  ;ASCII => binary
                add     ax,bx                   ;Add latest value to AX
                cmp     ax,255                  ;Error if sum > 255
                jna     a2b_loop                ;Loop back for more

a2b_error:      dec     si                      ;Set carry and exit
                stc
                ret

a2b_exit:       dec     si                      ;Clear carry and exit
                clc
                ret
asc2bin         endp


;*********************************************************************
; SHOWSTATUS displays the current status of printer redirection.
;*********************************************************************

showstatus      proc    near
                cmp     installed,0             ;See if program is installed
                je      show1                   ;Branch if not

                mov     ah,prog_id              ;Use the multiplex interrupt
                mov     al,01h                  ;  (function 01H) to find out
                int     2Fh                     ;  what printer (if any) is
                jmp     short show2             ;  redirected
```

```
show1:          mov     al,lptport              ;Get printer number
                mov     bx,cs                   ;Point to ES to this segment
                mov     es,bx
                mov     di,offset filename      ;Point DI to file name

show2:          cmp     al,0FFh                 ;Branch if a printer is
                jne     show3                   ;  currently redirected
                mov     ah,09h                  ;Display "No printers
                mov     dx,offset msg2          ;  redirected" message
                int     21h                     ;  and exit
                ret

show3:          add     al,31h                  ;Convert printer number to
                mov     msg3[3],al              ;  ASCII and store it
                mov     dx,offset msg3          ;Display printer name
                mov     ah,09h
                int     21h
                call    dos_out                 ;Display file name too
                mov     ah,09h                  ;End the line
                mov     dx,offset crlf
                int     21h
                ret
showstatus      endp


;****************************************************************************
; DOS_OUT displays the ASCIIZ string pointed to by ES:DI.
;****************************************************************************

dos_out         proc    near
                mov     dl,es:[di]              ;Get a character
                or      dl,dl                   ;Exit if it's zero
                jz      out_exit
                mov     ah,02h                  ;Output it using DOS
                int     21h                     ;  function 02H
                inc     di                      ;Advance DI to next one
                jmp     dos_out                 ;Loop until done
out_exit:       ret
dos_out         endp

code            ends
                end     begin
```

LPT2FILE is a TSR. The first time it is run, it installs itself in memory where it can monitor data going to the printer. The command

```
LPT2FILE LPT1:=C:\TEXT\PRINTER.TXT /B=16
```

installs LPT2FILE with a buffer size of 16k and creates a file called PRINTER-.TXT in the \TEXT directory of drive C to hold data sent to LPT1. A buffer size can only be specified on a line that *installs* LPT2FILE; once it's installed, the buffer size is fixed. If the path name or the file name you supply is invalid, LPT2-FILE will display the message "File could not be opened" and terminate without installing itself. If the file whose name you specified doesn't exist, LPT2FILE will create it for you. If the file does exist, LPT2FILE will append output to the end of it to preserve the existing data.

You can change the printer that is redirected by running LPT2FILE with a new LPT port number. The command

```
LPT2FILE LPT2:=OUTPUT.TXT
```

redirects LPT2 to OUTPUT.TXT in the current directory. You can cancel redirection altogether by typing

```
LPT2FILE /C
```

LPT2FILE will redirect output to any LPT port, even if that port is not physically installed in the PC. You can use this feature to choose whether to capture printer output from a program without leaving the application. Let's say you're running a word processor and want to selectively redirect printer output to disk and that you have a printer connected to LPT1. Before starting the word processor, type

```
LPT2FILE LPT3:=PRINTER.TXT
```

Then, when you want to print to a file, direct the output of the word processor to LPT3. Conversely, to bypass LPT2FILE and send data directly to the printer, direct output to LPT1. Output to LPT3 will continue to be captured in the file PRINTER.TXT until you cancel redirection with another LPT2FILE command, tell LPT2FILE to switch to another printer, or change the filename.

You can determine the status of redirection at any time by running LPT2-FILE with no command-line parameters. If a printer is redirected, LPT2FILE will tell you which one and the name of the file it is redirected to. If redirection is disabled at the moment, LPT2FILE will advise you that "No printers are currently redirected."

For most applications, LPT2FILE's default buffer size of 4k will suffice. However, if you notice that certain programs don't seem to work very well with LPT2FILE—if you experience persistent printer I/O errors, for example, or if data is missing from the files that are captured from them—try increasing the size of the buffer. Programs that transmit data to the printer using DOS function 40H (Write to File or Device) will overwhelm LPT2FILE if they output blocks of data larger than the length of the internal buffer. You can see an example of this by COPYing a file that is larger than LPT2FILE's output buffer to a redirected printer using the form

```
COPY filename LPT1
```

If the file is less than 64k long, COPY will transmit the file in its entirety to LPT1 with a single call to DOS function 40H; if it's more than 64k long, it will be sent

64k at a time. Either way, if the length of the file exceeds the buffer size, an error will result. LPT2FILE will accept characters until its internal buffer fills up. Then, unable to dump the buffer to disk because the call to DOS function 40H is still in progress, it will signal DOS that it can't accept any more. DOS will respond with an "Abort, Retry, Ignore, Fail" message and stop transmitting data. The only way to circumvent this problem is to increase the buffer size to a value sufficient to meet function 40H's demands. Since the maximum number of bytes that can be transmitted with a single call to function 40H is 65,535, installing LPT2FILE with a buffer size of 64k will enable it to handle just about anything DOS can throw at it. Fortunately, programs that write to the printer using DOS function 40H are relatively rare, so there's a very good chance you'll never run into this problem and can keep LPT2FILE's memory requirements to modest levels.

LPT2FILE is compatible with DOS 5.0's LOADHIGH command. If you have room for it in upper memory, consider installing it with LOADHIGH to free up room in the lower 640k.

Inside LPT2FILE

The premise behind LPT2FILE is simple. It works by intercepting interrupt 17H—the BIOS printer I/O interrupt—and capturing characters that are transmitted to the printer through interrupt 17H in its own internal buffer. At the earliest available opportunity, it copies the contents of the buffer to disk, zeros the pointer to the location in the buffer that the next character will be written to, and resumes capturing printer output. Because interrupt 17H is used almost universally to transmit data to printers, LPT2FILE will work with most application programs in use today.

The tricky part of coding a utility like LPT2FILE is ensuring that the buffer is flushed often enough to prevent buffer overruns, but to do this without encroaching upon other parts of the system. If DOS were a multitasking operating system, writing a utility like LPT2FILE would be almost trivial. Every time the buffer accumulated a given number of characters, LPT2FILE could just use the operating system's file I/O services to copy the buffer to disk, and then proceed with business. But with DOS, it doesn't work that way. The routine inside the DOS kernel that handles interrupt 21H is *non-reentrant*, meaning once it's called, it can't be called again until it has finished processing the first call. If a second call is made before the first one is completed, the system will probably crash. To tell if it's safe to place a call to DOS, a program can check two flags internal to DOS itself: the *InDOS flag*, which is non-zero if an interrupt 21H call is currently in progress, and the *critical error flag*, which is non-zero if DOS is currently attempting to rectify a critical error (for example, if you tried to access a floppy disk with the drive door open and haven't answered DOS's "Abort, Retry, Fail" message). If both of these flags are zero, then it's safe to use interrupt 21H. If either flag is not, then, except under special circumstances, placing a call to interrupt 21H invites disaster.

Both the InDOS flag and the critical error flag figure prominently in TSR programming. We'll see them again in the next chapter when we develop a utility to store names and phone numbers and to dial the phone. LPT2FILE obtains the address of the InDOS flag during its initialization procedure by placing a call to interrupt 21H with the instructions

```
mov     ah,34h
int     21h
mov     word ptr indos,bx
mov     word ptr indos[2],es
```

DOS function 34H, which was officially undocumented until the *MS-DOS Encyclopedia* was published in 1988, returns the address of the InDOS flag in ES:BX. With the address safely tucked away, the resident portion of LPT2FILE can check the flag at any time to see if it's safe to call DOS. Similarly, the address of the critical error flag is obtained with the instructions

```
push    ds
mov     ax,5D06h
int     21h
mov     word ptr cs:[errorflag],si
mov     word ptr cs:[errorflag+2],ds
pop     ds
```

This routine relies on undocumented DOS function 5DH, subfunction 06H, to obtain the flag's address. This function, which has only been available since DOS 3.0, returns the address of the critical error flag in DS:SI. Because the DS register is used to return a value, LPT2FILE saves the current value of DS on the stack before calling the function and restores it when the function ends. It's also necessary to access the memory location named ERRORFLAG with a CS segment override, because DS does not point to the code segment when function 5DH returns.

LPT2FILE also maintains a flag that is non-zero if any type of disk access is currently in progress and checks it before performing disk accesses of its own. This flag, called INTFLAGS in the source code listing, is initially set to 0. LPT2FILE sets up interrupt handlers for interrupts 13H, 25H, and 26H, and sets a bit in INTFLAGS when any of these interrupts is generated. When the interrupt is complete, LPT2FILE zeros the corresponding bit in INTFLAGS as a signal to itself that it's safe to perform a disk access provided InDOS and the critical error flag are clear. This strategy works because nearly all disk accesses on the IBM PC are performed through one of these three interrupts (interrupt 13H is the BIOS disk interrupt, while interrupts 25H and 26H are the DOS interrupts for reading and writing a disk, respectively). By taking this precaution, LPT2FILE ensures that it will not try to perform a disk write of its own while another disk operation is in progress. If it did, the result would probably be lost data.

Once it becomes resident, and with the addresses of all these flags in hand, LPT2FILE employs a four-pronged strategy to try to copy its output buffer to disk before the buffer fills up:

1. Each time a program transmits a character with interrupt 17H, function 00H, LPT2FILE buffers the character, and then checks to see if the buffer is more than half full. If it is, then LPT2FILE immediately flushes the buffer provided InDOS, the critical error flag, and INTFLAGS are not set.

2. Each time interrupt 21H is called, LPT2FILE checks InDOS, the critical error flag, and INTFLAGS and attempts to flush the buffer if there are any characters in it waiting to be copied to disk.

3. Each time interrupt 28H is called (this interrupt is normally triggered when a program terminates and the DOS prompt is redisplayed), LPT2-FILE again checks the critical error flag and INTFLAGS and attempts to flush the buffer if it contains any characters. InDOS does not have to be checked because it's safe to call DOS functions numbered 0DH and higher from inside an interrupt 28H handler, even if InDOS is set.

4. As a last resort, LPT2FILE taps into the PC's timer interrupt and attempts to flush the buffer if more than 5 seconds have passed since the last character was received and there is data waiting to be written. The buffer is not flushed if InDOS, the critical error flag, or INTFLAGS is set.

With this strategy, seldom will LPT2FILE *not* be able to find an opportunity to flush the output buffer, especially if the buffer size is sufficiently large. Knowing this, you can now understand why programs that output characters to the printer with DOS function 40H give LPT2FILE such a fit. If the buffer size is 4k and function 40H is called to output a block of data, say, 8k long, the buffer will fill up when only half the block has been output. From the time the buffer is half full until it fills up, LPT2FILE tries every means at its disposal to flush the buffer; it never gets the opportunity because the InDOS flag is set the whole time (InDOS is set because the call to function 40H is in progress). When the buffer reaches capacity, LPT2FILE returns an I/O error to DOS saying it can't accept more characters.

Another challenge that confronts LPT2FILE is to look like a printer to the programs from which it captures output. To accomplish this, LPT2FILE takes over interrupt 17H and provides its own routines to handle interrupt 17H, functions 00H, 01H, and 02H. Function 00H prints a character and returns an 8-bit status code in AH (the meanings of the individual bits in the status code were diagrammed back in Figure 9.3). If the character was buffered, LPT2FILE returns the value 90H in AH, indicating that the printer is not busy and that it is currently selected. If, however, the buffer is full, LPT2FILE returns a status code of 08H, indicating an I/O error occurred. These are exactly the same values the BIOS returns in AH after outputting a character to a real printer.

Function 01H initializes a printer. When it processes this function, LPT2-FILE flushes the buffer if there is any data in it and returns a 90H in AH. For function 02H, which programs call to determine the status of the printer, LPT2-FILE returns 90H if the buffer is not full, 08H if it is. In this way, it lets any program that cares to check know whether it is capable of accepting more characters. When the buffer fills up, LPT2FILE effectively is telling an application program trying to output data that the printer is unable to accept data because it is powered off, off-line, or otherwise unable to accept characters.

Transmitting Printer Control Codes

In the back of most printer manuals you'll find a list of control codes and commands that can be sent to the printer to control its modes of operation. For example, outputting the value 15 to most IBM and Epson dot-matrix printers turns on compressed print mode, permitting you to fit 132 columns of text on an 8^1/$_2$-by-11-inch page. Similarly, outputting the string "(s16.66H" preceded by an escape character (binary 27) does the same thing for a LaserJet printer. It turns out that most printers are far more intelligent than we give them credit for. By transmitting the proper control codes, you can achieve all sorts of interesting effects, from changing the print pitch or selecting a font, to drawing lines across the page on some printers. Some printers even understand the language called PostScript, which enables them to respond to and act upon high-level graphics commands sent from the PC in much the same way that QBasic responds when you type a command to draw a line or a circle at its input prompt.

All that's lacking is a convenient means for sending these commands to the printer from the command line or from inside an application program. Several years ago, *PC Magazine* published a utility called SETUP for transmitting control codes to a printer. The disks that came with this book contain SETUP 3.0, an enhanced version of the original SETUP (and its successor, SETUP 2.0) that makes communicating commands to your printer easier than ever. SETUP's syntax is

```
SETUP [[d:][path]filename] [/C codes] [/Pn]
```

where *filename* is the name of a printer menu file; *codes* is one or more output codes entered in hex, decimal, or ASCII form; and /P*n* designates to what printer the output will go. Valid values for *n* are 1, 2, and 3, corresponding to LPT1, LPT2, and LPT3, respectively. If the /P switch is omitted from the command line, SETUP defaults to LPT1.

The /C switch allows you to transmit printer control codes from the command line. The command

```
SETUP /C 12
```

transmits a single byte—a binary 12, the code for a form feed—to LPT1. What follows a /C switch may be any mixture of ASCII text (enclosed in quotation marks) and binary values expressed in decimal or hexadecimal form. For example, the command

```
SETUP /C 27,"(s16.66H"
```

outputs the command to switch a LaserJet to compressed print to LPT1. Anything that appears between quotation marks—in this case, "(s16.66H"—is interpreted literally. Everything else is interpreted as a control code. SETUP recognizes any number that begins with the character **0x** as a hexadecimal number, borrowing from the convention set forth by the C programming language. For example, the command SETUP /C 27,"(s16.66H" could be entered as

```
SETUP /C 0x1B,"(s16.66H"
```

or as a series of binary values with the command

```
SETUP /C 0x1B 40 115 49 54 46 54 54 72
```

If you'll look closely, you'll notice that 40 is the ASCII code for **(**, 115 is the ASCII code for **s**, and so on. Entries may be separated by spaces or commas, whichever you prefer.

With SETUP, it's easy to create short batch files to send often-used commands to your printer. For example, the command

```
SETUP /C 12
```

outputs the ASCII code for a form feed to eject a page from the printer. For convenience, you could enter the command in a batch file called EJECT.BAT and type

```
EJECT
```

to eject a page. Similarly, you could create a batch file to perform a software reset on a LaserJet printer attached to LPT2 with the command

```
SETUP /C 27 69 /P2
```

If the batch file is named RESET.BAT, then typing RESET will restore the printer to its default conditions at power-up, just as if the power had been cycled off and back on. And just to illustrate that control codes can be as complex as they can be simple, the command

```
SETUP /C 27,"&l1o2e5.647c66F",27,"@k2S"
```

prepares a LaserJet printer to output compressed print in landscape mode with the space between lines reduced to fit more information on the page—perfect for printing spreadsheets that you used to print on wide-carriage printers. Better yet, incorporate these commands in command macros with DOSKEY so they won't take up disproportionate amounts of disk space as short batch files do.

Running SETUP as a Memory-Resident Application

If you run it without a /C switch, SETUP becomes RAM-resident, waiting for you to call it up by pressing a hotkey. Installed, it requires slightly more than 4k of memory, plus the memory it uses to store the menus you load for it. The larger the menus, the more RAM is consumed. When you press Ctrl in combination with the right Shift key, SETUP pops up a window that offers a menu of printer control options. Menu options can be selected in two ways: by pressing the corresponding function key (a function key name is listed to the left of each menu item), or by pressing Enter with the desired menu option highlighted. You can move the menu bar that highlights menu options with the Up Arrow and Down Arrow keys. And if there is more than one page of menu items, you can flip through them with the PgUp and PgDn keys. Pressing the Escape key closes the window and allows DOS to resume running whatever was interrupted when Ctrl-Shift was pressed.

The text of the menus and the control codes that correspond to the menu items come from a special file called a *printer menu file*, or PMF file for short, whose name you pass to SETUP when it is installed. Because there is such a wide variety of printers in use today, SETUP leaves it to you to generate the PMF files for specific makes and models of printers. The rules for creating PMF files are simple:

- PMF files are composed of plain ASCII text. Thus, you can use any text editor or word processor that features an ASCII save option, including the DOS Editor discussed in Chapter 5.

- The first line of a PMF file specifies the title to appear at the top of the window. Normally, this line will contain the name of the printer the PMF was created for, such as "Epson RX-80" or "HP LaserJet III." The title may contain as many as 26 characters; anything more than that is ignored.

- Succeeding lines in the PMF file identify the items in the menu and the binary control codes that correspond to them. A sample line is

```
Reset Printer;      27 69
```

Here, "Reset Printer" will be what's shown in the menu, and 27 and 69 are the control codes that will be sent when this item is selected from the menu. Menu text and control codes must be separated by a semicolon, and menu text may be up to 20 characters long. Each menu item may be assigned as many as 255 control codes.

- Any line with a # character in column 1 is interpreted as a comment line. Blank lines are ignored.

Figure 12.1 shows a sample PMF file for an IBM or Epson dot-matrix printer or for any printer that emulates the IBM/Epson command set. If the file is named EPSON.PMF, then typing

```
SETUP EPSON.PMF
```

will install SETUP with the menus contained in EPSON.PMF. Control codes are entered in the PMF file exactly as they are on the command line. They can contain any mixture of ASCII text and decimal or hexadecimal values that you wish. If, as SETUP parses the PMF file, it encounters an error, it outputs an error message and tells you what line the error is on. An error will result if a numeric entry contains an invalid character or if you omit the semicolon separating menu text from the control codes on a line.

FIGURE 12.1

Sample PMF file

```
#**************************************************
#              Printer Menu File
#    For IBM and Epson Dot-Matrix Printers
#**************************************************

   IBM and Epson Printers


Compressed Mode On;          15
Compressed Mode Off;         18
Expanded Mode On;            27,"W1"
Expanded Mode Off;           27,"W0"
Emphasized Mode On;          27,"E"
Emphasized Mode Off;         27,"F"
Double-Strike On;            27,"G"
Double-Strike Off;           27,"H"
Miniature Mode On;           15,27,83,0,27,65,6
Miniature Mode Off;          18,27,84,27,50


Elite Mode On;               27,"M"
Elite Mode Off;              27,"P"
Skip Perforation On;         27,78,8
Skip Perforation Off;        27,79
1/8" Line Spacing;           27,"0"
7/72" Line Spacing;          27,"1"
1/6" Line Spacing;           27,"2"
Line Feed;                   10
Form Feed;                   12
Reset Printer;               27,"@"
```

When SETUP is installed with the PMF file in Figure 12.1, there will be two full pages of menus available in the pop-up window. You can switch between them with the PgUp and PgDn keys. The "Page of" indicator in the lower-left corner of the window tells you what page you're on at all times and how many pages there are.

With the printer control window showing, you can toggle between LPT ports with the * key. Initially, the text in the lower-right corner of the window will say "Port: LPT1," or whatever port you designated as the default with a /P switch when the program was installed. Pressing the * key once changes it to read LPT2; a second time, to LPT3; and the third time, to LPT1. If you have two printers attached to your PC, you can build separate menus for each one and use SETUP to control them both. If your printer is off-line or powered off when you transmit a control code, SETUP will beep and display the message "Printer not ready" at the bottom of the window. The next key you press will clear the message.

You can also type in control codes directly from the pop-up window if you need to output a sequence of codes that you did not assign to a menu item. To do so, press the forward slash key. A cursor will appear in the gray bar near the bottom of the window. Type in any text or control codes you want to send to the printer, in the same format you enter them in following a /C switch on the command line. When you press Enter, the string will be transmitted to the LPT port shown in the lower-right corner.

Changing SETUP's Hotkey with DEBUG

SETUP's default hotkey combination of Ctrl and the right Shift key may conflict with other memory-resident programs that you use. If so, you can change the hotkey with DEBUG using this simple procedure.

First, determine what combination of Ctrl, Alt, left Shift, and right Shift you want to use to pop up the window. Then formulate a *shift mask value* (a number that specifies which of the four keys should be monitored) by adding up the values in the following table that correspond to the keys you selected:

Alt	8
Ctrl	4
Left Shift	2
Right Shift	1

For example, the value that corresponds to Ctrl-Alt is 12, and the value that corresponds to the combination of Alt and the left Shift key is 10. You could even assign SETUP a 3-key combination by adding values for three of the keys. For example, a 13 would change the hotkey to Ctrl, Alt, and right Shift.

Second, use DEBUG to insert the shift mask value into SETUP.COM at offset address 0160H. If the value you want to enter is 3 (which will change SETUP to pop up when both Shift keys are pressed), then go to the directory where SETUP.COM is stored and type

```
DEBUG SETUP.COM
E 0160 03
W
Q
```

It's important that you enter the code for the hotkey in hexadecimal form, because DEBUG always thinks in hex. Had the value you selected been 12, for example, you would have entered

```
E 0160 0C
```

in place of E 0160 03. Also, for caution's sake, make a backup copy of SETUP-.COM before you patch it. Then, if something goes wrong, you can delete the modified copy and restore the original. Once the changes are made, reinstall SETUP and the new hotkey combination will be ready to use.

Creating PMF Files with LZSELECT

The downside to creating your own PMF files is that you have to be pretty familiar with all of your printer's capabilities and have a reference manual that lists the commands it understands. For a typical 1980s-vintage dot-matrix printer, that may not be so bad; but for a printer as complex as a LaserJet, it can be downright intimidating.

LZSELECT, developed by *PC Magazine* programmer Jay Munro, greatly simplifies the process of creating PMF files for LaserJet printers. Its syntax is

```
LZSELECT [/2] [/B] [/F [d:][path]filename]
```

where /B runs the program in black-and-white on color monitors (useful on LCD and gas plasma laptop screens); /2 sends output to LPT2, which is meaningful only if you're outputting commands directly from LZSELECT; and *filename* specifies the name of the PMF file you're creating. If you don't specify a file name on the command line, LZSELECT will prompt you for one before you save the file.

Creating a PMF file in LZSELECT is a multistep process. First you define the text for a menu item at LZSELECT's opening prompt, and then you select commands from its main menu to associate with the menu item. Initially, the main menu displays a list of command categories. You add a command to the current menu item by highlighting the desired category, pressing Enter, and then going through the same motions to select a printer command. Each time a command is selected, it is added to the list in the window on the right side of the screen, and the actual codes that correspond to it are appended to the list at the bottom. Continue selecting commands until you've defined all the ones you want to define for the current menu item, then press F2 to move on to a new one, and repeat the process until all menu items are defined. When you're done, pressing F10 saves the commands to disk in the form of a PMF file, and pressing Alt-Q exits the program.

You can assign up to 100 commands to a single menu item provided the aggregate length of the control codes that comprise those commands does not exceed 255 bytes. You can take advantage of this feature to create complex commands that are carried out with a single keystroke. For example, you could create a command to reset the printer, switch to landscape mode, and set the pitch to 16.66 characters per inch by combining the "Printer Reset" and "Landscape" commands from the Job Control category with the "16.66 Pitch" command from the main menu's Font Selection category. At the bottom of the screen, the sequence of escape codes produced would look like this:

```
27,"E",27,"&l1O",27,"(s16.66H"
```

27,"E" resets the printer; 27,"&l1O" switches to landscape mode; and 27,"(s16.66H" sets the pitch. In addition to supporting 100 commands per menu item, LZSELECT permits up to 100 different menu items to be defined, corresponding to ten pages of menus in SETUP.

If, as you select the commands to go with a menu item, you make a mistake, you can delete a command by pressing F7. Pressing F8 lets you insert a command. In addition, Alt-F7 deletes all the commands assigned to the current menu item, while Ctrl-F7 deletes everything, menu items included.

Once a PMF file is saved to disk, you can edit it with a text editor, but you cannot call it back up and edit it inside LZSELECT. You can also save the string of escape codes shown at the bottom of the screen to disk as a set of printer-ready codes by pressing F9. The file that is created can be output directly to the printer with the COPY command. If you only need to output a single command from a batch file, this provides an alternative to using SETUP's /C switch.

Other function keys perform other duties. You can get help with LZSELECT at any time by pressing F1. You can also send the list of codes displayed in the window at the bottom of the screen to the printer by pressing F3. You can download soft fonts to a printer with F4 and Alt-F4. F4 downloads a *permanent* soft font—one that will remain after a software reset is performed, while Alt-F4 downloads a *temporary* font, which is destroyed if a reset command is issued. F5 toggles what's displayed in the window on the right side of the LZSELECT screen, alternately showing menu item text and the commands assigned to a menu item. Finally, F6 toggles back and forth between the two methods of storing printer commands: individually or combined. In combined mode, LZSELECT will combine escape codes, when possible, to shorten the resultant command; in individual mode, commands are stored separately. For example, if LZSELECT is running in individual mode (indicated by "F6 Mode > I" at the bottom of the screen), the commands

```
27,"&a10L"
```

and

```
27,"&a75M"
```

will be stored as

```
27,"&a10L",27,"&a75M"
```

However, in combined mode, they will be combined to form the single command

```
27,"&a10175M"
```

On a LaserJet, two or more commands that begin with the same first two characters can be combined by dropping the leading characters from all but the first command and entering the terminating character for all but the final command in lowercase rather than uppercase. Combining them this way reduces the number of bytes that must be transmitted to the printer and helps LZSELECT stay under the 255-byte limit SETUP places on the length of the codes that can be assigned to a single menu item.

Printing Text Files and Saving Trees

One of the handiest and most popular printer utilities ever to appear in *PC Magazine*'s "Utilities" column was Michael Holmes and Bob Flanders's LASER-LST. The short way to describe LASERLST is to say that it prints text files. But that hardly does this gem of a program justice. On LaserJet printers, LASER-LST turns the page on its side and uses the LaserJet's 16.66 character-per-inch line printer font to fit two pages of text on each 8½-by-11-inch sheet. Not only does it save trees (real trees, the kind that grow in a forest, not hard-disk directory trees) by cutting paper consumption in half, it also allows you to fit more information on a page—a real help if you're dissecting a long program listing or complex text files.

The syntax for LASERLST is

```
LASERLST [d:][path]filename [[d:][path]outfile] [/Tn]
```

where *filename* is the name of the file to be printed and /T*n* specifies the number of columns between tab stops (default=8). The command

```
LASERLST PROGLIST.ASM
```

prints PROGLIST.ASM, while

```
LASERLST PROGLIST.ASM /T4
```

prints it with tab stops set every fourth column rather than every eighth. The highest value LASERLST will accept for tabs is 16.

If you wish, you can print to a file rather than to a printer by including an *outfile* parameter. This capability is useful if, for example, you don't have a LaserJet connected to your PC but know someone who does. With *outfile*, you can direct the output from LASERLST to a file, copy the file to a floppy, and then print the file on some other PC with the command

```
COPY outfile PRN
```

You can also use this feature to send the listing to a printer other than LPT1 by first printing to *outfile*, and then using the COPY command as shown in the previous example, but substituting a device name such as LPT1 or COM1 for PRN.

LASERLST works with all members of the LaserJet family, and with printers that are LaserJet-compatible. As a rule, it works best if none of the lines in the text file is more than 81 characters long—the most it can fit on half of an 8½-by-11-inch page in landscape mode. Lines that are longer wrap around to the next line. Also, LASERLST expects the files it prints to be pure ASCII text files. If you want to use it to print a document file from your word processor, you must save it in ASCII format first.

Working While You Print

It's absurd when you think about it. Pair a fast 386 or 486 PC with a 4-page-per-minute laser printer, and your PC will be tied up for 25 minutes while you print a 100-page document. It's not that the PC isn't capable of transmitting characters faster than that; it's that characters will be lost if the PC sends them any faster than the printer can print them. Add it up and over time you might amass enough hours of down time to justify the cost of a printer upgrade—or the cost of a second computer so you can continue working while your printer churns out paper.

A more practical way to free up your PC while documents print is to use a print spooler. A *print spooler* is a utility that intercepts data going to the printer, buffers it in RAM, and then transmits it to the printer in the background while you work in the foreground. To the application program that transmits the printer data, printing seems to proceed in less time because the spooler can accept data much faster than a real printer can. The net result: You get back to work sooner, because you no longer have to wait for printing to finish before you regain control of your PC.

This book comes with a print spooler called PCSPOOL, written by *PC Magazine* programmers Michael Holmes and Bob Flanders. PCSPOOL loads as a TSR, intercepts interrupt 17H to buffer data en route to the printer, and uses the periodic timer interrupt to transmit data on to the printer. Installed, PCSPOOL consumes about 23k of RAM unless you change its default buffer size with the /C switch. The syntax for installing it is

```
PCSPOOL /I [/1] [/2] [/3] [/Cnn | /D[d:][path]]
```

where /I tells it to install itself in memory; /1, /2, and /3 identify the printers to be spooled (/1, /2, and /3 correspond to LPT1, LPT2, and LPT3, respectively); /C specifies the size of PCSPOOL's print queue (in kilobytes); and /D locates the print queue on disk rather than in RAM. The command

```
PCSPOOL /I /1 /2 /C32
```

tells PCSPOOL to spool output to LPT1 and LPT2 and to set the size of the print queue to 32k. If you don't use the /C switch, the queue size defaults to 16k. Similarly, the command

```
PCSPOOL /I /1 /DE:\SPOOL
```

tells it to spool LPT1 only and to place the print queue in the \SPOOL directory of drive E. If you do not specify a drive and path name following a /D switch, PCSPOOL places the queue in the root directory of drive C. The /D option is best utilized to make use of extended or expanded memory by placing the print queue on a RAM disk.

You can uninstall PCSPOOL with the command

```
PCSPOOL /U
```

When it is uninstalled, PCSPOOL releases the memory it formerly owned so that other programs can use it and restores the interrupt vectors it patched into. If an attempt to uninstall it produces the error message "Can't uninstall at this time," then it can't uninstall itself because another TSR was installed after it. In most cases, it's only safe to uninstall TSRs in the reverse order in which they were loaded.

Once PCSPOOL is installed, pressing Ctrl-Alt-P pops up a window that displays information about the queue and about the printers that are being served. On the left side of the window is a series of five status indicators. "Gauge" tells you what percentage of the queue is in use by a particular printer; "CPS" is the rate characters are being printed at; "CP" is a count of characters printed; "CIQ" tells you how many characters still reside in the queue; and "Time" shows the current time.

On the right is a list of the commands you can issue through the pop-up window. D (for Disable) disables spooling until the G (Go) command is issued; P (Pause) pauses printing until G is pressed; F (FormFeed) sends a form-feed character to the printer; C (Cancel) flushes the remaining data from the queue so that it will not be printed; R (Reset) resets the printer to its power-up conditions; and J (JobSkip) skips to the next print job. Which of the three possible printers is affected by these command keys is determined by what keys you press. An unshifted command key affects LPT1 only; a command key shifted with Ctrl affects LPT2; and a command key pressed in conjunction with Alt affects LPT3. Pressing Alt-P, for example, pauses printing on LPT3, Ctrl-F sends a form feed to LPT2, and D disables spooling on LPT1. When you're done, pressing Esc closes the pop-up window.

You can issue some of these commands from the command line. For example, the command

```
PCSPOOL /P /2
```

pauses the printer attached to LPT2. Actually, it doesn't pause the printer immediately as does pressing P with the window displayed. Instead, it inserts a *pause record* in the print queue. When the pause record comes up, PCS-POOL pauses the printer until you pop up the window and press G. If you wish, you may attach a comment to the command to insert a message that will show up in the pop-up window. Let's say, for example, that you're sending three jobs to the printer with COPY commands, and that the third job will require legal-size paper rather than letter-size. You could arrange the commands as follows:

```
COPY FILE1.TXT LPT1
COPY FILE2.TXT LPT1
PCSPOOL /P /1 *** Insert legal tray ***
COPY FILE3.TXT LPT1
```

Before FILE3.TXT is printed, LPT1 will pause for you to replace the paper tray. And if you pop up the control window, you'll see the message "*** Insert legal tray ***" displayed next to LPT1. Pause records come into play at one other time, too: when you issue a JobSkip command from the window. JobSkip skips forward to the next pause record waiting in the queue. If there are no pause records, pressing JobSkip has the same effect as pressing Cancel.

You can also issue a form-feed command from the command line, which is useful for separating documents that do not contain their own form-feed characters to eject the last page from the printer. For example, the commands

```
COPY FILE1.TXT LPT1
PCSPOOL /F /1
COPY FILE2.TXT LPT1
PCSPOOL /F /1
```

queue up FILE1.TXT and FILE2.TXT for printing and eject a page after each one. You could output a blank page between documents by inserting *two* PCS-POOL /F commands. Note that you do not have to use the COPY command to send files to PCSPOOL. PCSPOOL intercepts output from any application, whether it's the DOS COPY command or a word processing program. COPY is just the command we chose for our examples here. Also, be aware that some applications such as WordPerfect have their own print spoolers built in.

If PCSPOOL's default hotkey combination of Ctrl-Alt-P conflicts with other RAM-resident programs you have loaded, you can change it with DEBUG. First, derive a shift mask value the same way you did earlier in this chapter for SETUP. Call it *xx.* Then, from the list of scan codes in Table 12.1, select the code for the key you want to use in place of P. Call it *yy.* Then go to the directory where PCSPOOL is stored and, after making a backup copy of the PCSPOOL.COM, type

```
DEBUG PCSPOOL.COM
E 025C xx
E 025D yy
W
Q
```

For example, changing the byte at 025C to 04 and the byte at offset 025D to 01 would change the hotkey to Alt-Esc. Or using values of 03 and 19 would change it to Shift-Shift-P. Once the modifications are made, reinstall PCSPOOL so that the changes will take effect.

TABLE 12.1

Keyboard Scan Codes

Key	Scan Code	Key	Scan Code
A	1E	0	0B
B	30	1	02
C	2E	2	03
D	20	3	04
E	12	4	05
F	21	5	06
G	22	6	07
H	23	7	08
I	17	8	09
J	24	9	0A
K	25		
L	26	F1	3B
M	32	F2	3C
N	31	F3	3D
O	18	F4	3E
P	19	F5	3F
Q	10	F6	40
R	13	F7	41
S	1F	F8	42
T	14	F9	43
U	16	F10	44
V	2F	F11	57
W	11	F12	58
X	2D		
Y	15	Enter	1C
Z	2C	Spacebar	39
		Esc	01
		Tab	0F

Summary

Let's quickly summarize what you gained from this chapter. With the utilities presented here, you now possess the capability to

- Set screen colors and assign commands to function keys through the ANSI.SYS driver without having to remember arcane escape sequences

- Protect your monitor from burn-in by having it automatically blanked after a specified number of minutes passes with no keyboard or mouse activity

- Toggle Caps Lock, Num Lock, and Scroll Lock on and off from AUTOEXEC.BAT, from another batch file, or from the command line

- Send setup codes to printers from the command line, from inside a pop-up window, or from inside a menu-driven shell; capture printer output to a file; print text files on laser printers in a two-pages-per-sheet format; and spool printer output so you can work while files print in the background

Once again, these utilities serve to illustrate that armed with a copy of MASM and a little know-how, it is possible to create many of the commands that DOS forgot.

13 THE ART AND ZEN OF TSRs

IF YOU WANT TO START A FIGHT AMONG A GROUP OF DOS USERS, SAY SOME-thing like "Gee, aren't TSRs great?" and find an exit. The subject of TSRs tends to evoke strong emotions from DOS users. On the one hand, there's the crowd that couldn't imagine what life would be like without them. These are the folks who stuff their systems with every TSR imaginable. Step up to one of their PCs and type in a few oddball key combinations and you're likely to see colorful win-dows popping up all over the screen. On the other hand, there's the crowd that doesn't trust TSRs, the past victims of inexplicable system crashes and other TSR-induced mishaps who wouldn't load a TSR on their system if you paid them to.

TSR stands for *terminate and stay resident*. TSRs are a special type of DOS utility that doesn't terminate the way normal application programs (called *tran-sient* application programs) do. They remain in memory after they've termi-nated, waiting to be run again. And run they do, usually triggered by an external stimulus such as the press of a key or a tick from the PC's internal hardware timer chip. They evoke strong feelings because they enable DOS to do wonder-ful things that it's not possible to do with transient applications alone, yet they can compromise the integrity of the system around them. DOS was designed to be a single-tasking operating system, where only one program is active in the system at a time. With TSRs, however, it's possible to have many programs active at once. A TSR must perform a delicate balancing act to keep from inter-fering with other parts of the system. Considering that DOS isn't much help in propping it up, and that many of the facilities DOS does provide to support TSRs have never been officially documented by IBM and Microsoft, it's a won-der that TSRs can be made to work at all.

The previous chapter introduced several TSRs. Two of them, SAVER and LPT2FILE, were presented along with source code. The chapter also outlined how TSRs become memory-resident in the first place, how they patch them-selves into the PC's interrupt vector table, and how they gain control asynchro-nously when an interrupt occurs. This chapter plumbs the subject of TSR programming a level deeper and introduces four new utilities that illustrate the art and zen of TSR programming. They are

- PC-LOG, which maintains a log of all the programs you run on your PC in an ASCII text file, complete with times and dates

■ PC-DIAL, a pop-up phone directory and dialer that lessens the chore of keeping up with all your telephone contacts

■ INSTALL and REMOVE, two TSR managers that work together to allow TSRs installed on your system to be uninstalled on command

These utilities are more than just examples of TSRs; as usual, they're useful programs that you can put to work on your system. Before you begin, however, a short introduction to the topic of TSR programming is in order. The next few sections provide a brief overview of TSR programming and of the DOS functions, documented and undocumented, that make it possible for DOS programmers to write full-functioning, well-behaved TSRs.

An Introduction to TSR Programming

Perhaps the best place to begin a discussion of TSR programming is to write a simple TSR, something akin to writing the classic "Hello, world" program the first time you sit down with a new programming language. TSRs don't have to be complex; in fact, they can be quite simple. As evidence of this assertion, consider the short TSR named BEEP, whose source code is shown in Listing 13.1.

LISTING 13.1 BEEP.COM

```
;*****************************************************************************
; BEEP is a small TSR that beeps the PC's speaker once a minute.
;*****************************************************************************


code            segment
                assume  cs:code
                org     100h
begin:          jmp     short init

int08h          dd      ?                       ;Interrupt 08H vector
counter         dw      1092                    ;Countdown timer


;*****************************************************************************
; TIMER_INT handles interrupt 08H.
;*****************************************************************************


timer_int       proc    far
                pushf                           ;Push FLAGS register
                call    cs:[int08h]             ;Call previous handler
                sti                             ;Enable interrupts

                dec     cs:[counter]            ;Decrement countdown timer
                jnz     timer_exit              ;Branch if it's not zero

                mov     cs:[counter],1092       ;Reset the countdown timer
                push    ax                      ;Save AX and BP on the
                push    bp                      ;  stack
                mov     ax,0E07h                ;Sound the speaker
                int     10h
                pop     bp                      ;Restore AX and BP from
                pop     ax                      ;  the stack
timer_exit:     iret                            ;Return from interrupt
```

```
timer_int       endp

;*****************************************************************************
; INIT makes the program resident in memory.
;*****************************************************************************

                assume  cs:code,ds:code

init            proc    near
                mov     ax,3508h                ;Get the interrupt 08H
                int     21h                     ; vector in ES:BX
                mov     word ptr int08h,bx      ;Save BX
                mov     word ptr int08h[2],es   ;Save ES
                mov     ax,2508h                ;Set the interrupt 08H
                mov     dx,offset timer_int     ; vector to point to
                int     21h                     ; our own timer ISR

                mov     ax,3100h                ;Terminate with function 31H
                mov     dx,(offset init - offset code + 15) shr 4
                int     21h
init            endp

code            ends
                end     begin
```

BEEP's mission in life is simple. Once installed, it sits quietly in the background counting timer ticks until 1 minute has gone by. Then it produces an audible beep on the PC's internal speaker, resets the countdown timer, and starts counting again. As long as it remains in memory, it continues to beep at 1-minute intervals, reminding you that it's still there and still working.

Here's how it works. When BEEP is started, it executes the procedure named INIT. INIT uses DOS function 35H to retrieve the interrupt 08H vector. Interrupt 08H is the PC's timer interrupt, executed every 55 milliseconds in response to a pulse output from a timer chip inside the PC. After grabbing the interrupt vector, INIT saves it in the double-word variable called INT08H so that later on it can call the BIOS routine that services the interrupt. The code to obtain and then save the interrupt vector looks like this:

```
mov     ax,3508h
int     21h
mov     word ptr int08h,bx
mov     word ptr int08h[2],es
```

Then, BEEP uses DOS function 25H to patch the address of its own TIMER_INT procedure into the interrupt vector table so that every time an interrupt 08H is executed, TIMER_INT will receive control. This is accomplished with the following code sequence:

```
mov     ax,2508h
mov     dx,offset timer_int
int     21h
```

Finally, BEEP calls DOS function 31H to terminate and stay resident, as shown here:

```
mov     ax,3100h
mov     dx,(offset init - offset code + 15) shr 4
int     21h
```

When function 31H is called, AL holds the exit code that will be returned to the parent program and DX holds the number of paragraphs of memory to reserve. BEEP reserves just enough memory to ensure that TIMER_INT will remain behind intact and unchanged. The memory allocated for INIT, by contrast, is discarded, because INIT is never called again once BEEP resides in memory.

At this point, BEEP is resident in memory, where it lies dormant until an interrupt 08H comes along to activate it. The first time an interrupt is generated by the timer, and each time thereafter, the procedure TIMER_INT is executed. Its first act upon coming to life is to use the interrupt vector it saved away earlier to call the original interrupt 08H service routine. It does so with the instructions

```
pushf
call    cs:[int08h]
```

The reason for doing this is to give the BIOS, which provides the default handler for interrupt 08H, a chance to perform the up-to-the-minute housekeeping chores it is responsible for, chores that will not be performed if it is deprived of the timer tick. There are also certain actions that must be performed anytime a hardware interrupt is generated, and if TIMER_INT didn't share the interrupt with the BIOS, it would have to accept responsibility for those actions itself. Moreover, passing the interrupt on in this manner gives any other TSRs that may have tapped into the timer interrupt the chance to execute their own timer tick service routines. The PUSHF instruction before the CALL is necessary because we're trying to simulate a real interrupt here, and a real interrupt places the FLAGS register on the stack before performing the equivalent of a far CALL to the associated interrupt handler. Why doesn't BEEP just use the INT instruction? Because if it did, execution would go back to TIMER_INT (the routine that the interrupt 08H vector points to), and INT would be executed again, and again, and again, locking the CPU in an endless loop and therefore locking up the PC.

Next, TIMER_INT enables interrupts with an STI instruction. This is necessary because interrupts are initially disabled when an interrupt handler is called, preventing any further interrupts from occurring until interrupts are explicitly enabled again. Then it decrements its internal countdown timer (the variable named COUNTER) and branches to the end of the interrupt routine if the countdown timer has not reached zero with the instructions

```
dec     cs:[counter]
jnz     timer_exit
```

The CS override is used because there's no telling where the DS register, which the CPU normally uses to reference COUNTER, is pointing when TIMER_INT receives control. If the counter *has* reached zero, TIMER_INT sounds a beep by passing the ASCII code for a bell tone (ASCII 07H) to function 0EH in the video BIOS (the BIOS's teletype-style output routine) with the instructions

```
push    ax
push    bp
mov     ax,0E07h
int     10h
pop     bp
pop     ax
```

Note that AX and BP are saved prior to the call and restored afterward so that they will have the same values coming out of the interrupt routine that they did going in (technically, you shouldn't have to change BP because TIMER_INT doesn't modify it; however, a bug in some IBM PC video BIOS modules alters the value of BP when certain interrupt 10H functions are called, so BEEP preserves the value of BP as a precaution). It's important to preserve register values going into and coming out of an interrupt handler like this, because otherwise asynchronous hardware interrupts will randomly change the register values set by application programs, resulting in system crashes. At the conclusion, TIMER_INT executes the instruction

```
iret
```

to end the interrupt and terminate itself until the next interrupt 08H comes along to reactivate it. When another timer tick occurs, the process starts all over again. This scenario is repeated as long as TIMER_INT remains active in memory.

The Reentrancy Problem

That's one end of the TSR spectrum. You can expand on this simple shell to construct more elaborate TSRs, adding interrupt service routines as needed to accomplish whatever you want. SAVER, the mouse- and keyboard-sensitive screen saver introduced in Chapter 12, wasn't much more complicated than this. In addition to tapping into the timer interrupt, it also hooked the keyboard interrupt (interrupt 09H) so it could tell when a key was pressed in case it needed to unblank the screen. It also tapped into interrupt 33H, the interrupt used by the mouse driver, and interrupt 2FH, which it used as a mechanism for determining whether it was already installed and, if it was, to pass information between the resident copy and the copy executing in DOS's transient program area.

At the other end of the spectrum are TSRs that use DOS functions for file I/O and other operations. As you saw in the last chapter, TSRs that call interrupt 21H must take special precautions before doing so to make sure that calls to interrupt 21H do not overlap each other. The first line of defense involves checking the InDOS flag (the internal flag DOS maintains that indicates when a call to DOS is in progress) and avoid placing calls to DOS when InDOS is non-zero. The danger in nesting calls to interrupt 21H arises from the fact that, when it is activated, DOS's interrupt 21H service routine switches to one of three internal stacks. If two calls to interrupt 21H overlap each other, DOS may switch to the same stack twice, destroying the information that was placed there by the first call. The lost data will eventually cause the system to crash. Because calls to DOS functions can't be nested, we say that the interrupt 21H service routine is a *non-reentrant* ISR. Therefore, TSRs must avoid reentering DOS if they're to preserve the integrity of the system.

Another mechanism that plays a role in circumventing the non-reentrant limitations of DOS is interrupt 28H, also called the *DOS Idle* interrupt. DOS calls interrupt 28H repeatedly while it awaits your input on the command line. The important thing to know is that it's safe to call DOS functions numbered 0DH and higher from an interrupt 28H handler, even if InDOS is set. Therefore, a TSR can set up its own interrupt 28H ISR and use it as a safety valve to gain control of the PC, ignoring the state of InDOS. This is particularly important because InDOS is set the whole time the command prompt is displayed. COMMAND.COM calls DOS function 0AH to read what you type on the command line, so technically you're "in DOS" the whole time. If it weren't for interrupt 28H, TSRs that won't act while InDOS is set would be handcuffed as long as the user were on the command line.

A second flag that figures prominently into TSR programming is the critical error flag, which DOS sets when a critical error has occurred. In general, avoid calling DOS for any reason whatsoever while a critical error (the type of error that results in an "Abort, retry, ignore, fail?" message from DOS) is being processed. In DOS 3.0 and later, you can obtain the address of the critical error flag by calling DOS function 5DH with AL set to 06H. On return, DS:SI holds the flag's address.

Armed with this knowledge, a TSR can safely place calls to the DOS kernel without fear of crashing the system if it takes a few necessary precautions. If InDOS and the critical error flag are both clear (equal to zero) when the TSR takes control, it's safe to call interrupt 21H. If the critical error flag is clear and InDOS is not, but control was gained through an interrupt 28H handler, then it's also safe to call interrupt 21H as long as you restrict yourself to DOS functions numbered 0DH and higher. It's never safe to call interrupt 21H when the critical error flag is set, because DOS enters an unstable state when a critical error occurs. Even a single function call could push it over the edge and trigger a system crash.

If a TSR plans to use DOS services that result in disk accesses, there's an additional precaution it should take: It should intercept the three interrupts that applications use to read and write sectors on a disk—interrupts 13H, 25H, and 26H—and defer calling any DOS function that also accesses the disk if any of these interrupts is in progress. LPT2FILE demonstrated how this is done by selectively setting bits in a flag in its own code segment when one of these interrupts is called. You'll see this technique demonstrated again in this chapter when we develop the source code for PC-DIAL. This strategy virtually ensures that one disk access won't overlap with another.

Other TSR Programming Considerations

Unfortunately, there's more to writing a well-behaved TSR than simply avoiding nested interrupt 21H calls. A cardinal rule of TSR programming is that a TSR has to keep from disturbing other active processes or writing data to regions of memory it doesn't own. In keeping with this rule, there are several additional precautions it must take.

Precaution No. 1: If a TSR uses any DOS function that writes to the DTA, it must first relocate the DTA to a location in its own data space. Otherwise, data placed in the DTA by another program will be destroyed. DOS's FCB-based Find First and Find Next functions, functions 11H and 12H, modify the DTA; so do their handle-based counterparts, functions 4EH and 4FH. A TSR that uses these functions should first call DOS function 2FH to get the current DTA address, then call DOS function 1AH to relocate it. Then, on exit, it must restore the entry-level DTA address by placing a final call to function 1AH.

Precaution No. 2: A TSR run under DOS 3.10 or later should preserve the extended error information that DOS makes available through function 59H. One of the new features introduced in DOS 3.0 is the ability for a program to request additional information—extended error information, in DOS parlance—about an interrupt 21H call that failed. The information is only available for the most recent call; when another DOS function is invoked, the information that was previously available is destroyed. The key here is that DOS function 5D06H, which is officially undocumented, can be called upon to *set* the extended error information available from DOS. Before calling any DOS function, the TSR should retrieve the information that is currently available with function 59H. Then, before it exits, it should restore that information with function 5D06H.

Precaution No.3: If a TSR will be opening any files or allocating any memory after it becomes resident, it should use undocumented DOS function 50H, which accepts a segment address in BX, to activate itself. DOS keeps a record of which process is the active one at all times, and uses that information when files are opened and closed and memory is allocated. Processes are identified by the segment address of their PSPs. On entry, a TSR should call upon another undocumented DOS function, function 51H, to save the PSP address of the process that is currently active before activating itself. Then, on exit, it should reactivate the process that was active before.

To illustrate the perils of TSR programming, consider that in DOS 2.x, calling function 50H or 51H from inside an interrupt 28H handler will crash the system if the critical error flag isn't set. That's because DOS 2.x uses the same stack to process calls to functions 50H and 51H that it used for functions that generate interrupt 28H. However, the DOS 2.x interrupt 21H handler examines the critical error flag before performing the stack switch and switches to an alternate if the flag is set. Thus, a TSR can avert a stack conflict by setting the critical error flag before calling functions 50H and 51H, forcing DOS to switch to a safe stack. This anomaly was fixed by the time version 3.0 rolled around, so TSRs running under any version of DOS from 3.0 on can call functions 50H and 51H without first ensuring that the critical error flag is set.

Another point to consider is that a TSR that uses the stack in any capacity should switch to an internal stack just in case the caller's stack is almost full. Furthermore, the internal stack should be large enough to handle several nested function calls to the BIOS in case the TSR is interrupted by another TSR that doesn't switch to an internal stack. The bottom line is that a well-behaved TSR must take whatever steps are necessary to make sure it doesn't disturb other parts of the system and that it has adequate resources for itself. That's one reason protected mode operating systems such as OS/2 are technologically attractive: There, processes are physically isolated in memory, so it doesn't take Herculean programming efforts to write programs that will run safely alongside each other. DOS, however, is a far cry from OS/2. As such, it's important to follow the rules of the game to ensure that TSRs operate in an orderly, cooperative manner.

Logging Your Work to a File

Listing 13.2 contains the program listing for PC-LOG, a TSR that records the name of every program you run on your PC, the time it was started and ended, and the command-line parameters it was started with. The information is written to a text file so that you can print it or edit it with conventional text handling tools such as the DOS Editor. Installed, PC-LOG takes up slightly less than 2k of RAM. The syntax for installing it is

```
PC-LOG [[d:][path]filename]
```

where *filename* is the name of the log file you want information logged to. If a file by that name doesn't exist, PC-LOG creates it for you; if it does exist, PC-LOG will append data to the end so that the information written to it previously won't be destroyed. If you omit the *filename* parameter, PC-LOG defaults to a file named USAGE.LOG in the root directory of the current drive. Log files can grow quite large, so you shouldn't try to maintain them on floppies. Hard disks serve the purpose much better.

LISTING 13.2 PC-LOG.ASM

```
;****************************************************************************
; PC-LOG maintains a log of all the programs run on your PC in an ASCII
; text file.  Its syntax is
;
;         PC-LOG [[d:][path]filename]
;
; where "filename" is the name of the ASCII file programs will be logged
; to.  If "filename" is not specified, the program creates a file called
; USAGE.LOG in the root directory of the current drive.
;****************************************************************************

code            segment
                assume  cs:code
                org     100h
begin:          jmp     init

signature       db      0,1,2,"PC-LOG",2,1,0         ;Program signature
prog_id         db      ?                           ;Multiplex ID number

int21h          dd      ?                           ;Interrupt 21H vector
int2Fh          dd      ?                           ;Interrupt 2FH vector

dosversion      dw      ?                           ;DOS version number
handle          dw      ?                           ;File handle for log file
level           dw      0                           ;EXEC level number (0 thru 9)
execflag        db      0                           ;0=Entering EXEC function

xerror_ax       dw      ?                           ;Storage array for DOS
xerror_bx       dw      ?                           ;  extended error
xerror_cx       dw      ?                           ;  information
xerror_dx       dw      ?
xerror_si       dw      ?
xerror_di       dw      ?
xerror_ds       dw      ?
xerror_es       dw      ?
                dw      3 dup (0)

months          db      "JanFebMarAprMayJunJulAugSepOctNovDec"

header          db      "Log file created by PC-LOG version 1.0",13,10
                db      "Copyright (c) 1991 ",254," Jeff Prosise ",254
                db      " Ziff-Davis Press",13,10

titles          db      "START",5 DUP (32),"END",5 DUP (32)
                db      "ELAPSED",4 DUP (32),"LEVEL",4 DUP (32)
                db      "PROGRAM",10 DUP (32),"PARAMETERS",13,10

logfile         db      "x:\USAGE.LOG", 116 dup (0)

;****************************************************************************
; DOS_INT handles interrupt 21H.
;****************************************************************************

dos_int         proc    far
                pushf                               ;Save FLAGS
```

```
                cmp     ax,4B00h                ;Exit immediately if this
                jne     exec0                   ;  isn't a call to EXEC
                cmp     cs:[level],9            ;Exit if we've exceeded
                jb      exec1                   ;  reentrancy limits
exec0:          popf                            ;Restore FLAGS
                jmp     cs:[int21h]             ;Exit to DOS EXEC handler
;
; Save registers passed to EXEC.
;
exec1:          sti                             ;Interrupts on
                push    ax                      ;Save registers
                push    bx
                push    cx
                push    dx
                push    si
                push    di
                push    bp
                push    ds
                push    es
;
; Record the program start/end time and write an entry to the log file.
;
                push    bx                      ;Save registers set for
                push    dx                      ;  EXEC call
                push    ds
                push    es
                push    cs                      ;Point DS to the code
                pop     ds                      ;  segment
                assume  ds:code

                inc     level                   ;Increment reentrancy count
                call    record_time             ;Record the current time
                cmp     level,1
                je      skipwrite1
                call    open_file               ;Open the log file
                mov     si,level                ;Point SI to start time and
                dec     si                      ;  DI to end time
                shl     si,1
                shl     si,1
                add     si,offset times
                mov     di,si
                add     di,4
                mov     al,byte ptr level       ;Store previous level number
                dec     al                      ;  in AL
                call    write_entry             ;Write log entry
                call    close_file              ;Close the log file
skipwrite1:     mov     execflag,1              ;Set EXEC flag

                assume  ds:nothing
                pop     es                      ;Restore EXEC registers
                pop     ds
                pop     dx
                pop     bx
;
; Record the name of the program just EXECed.
;
```

```
                push    es                          ;Save ES and BX
                push    bx
                push    ds                          ;Set ES equal to DS
                pop     es
                mov     di,dx                       ;Scan for terminating zero
                sub     al,al                       ;   in ASCIIZ file name
                mov     cx,128
                cld                                 ;Clear the direction flag
                repne   scasb
                mov     bx,127                      ;Transfer string length
                sub     bx,cx                       ;   to CX
                mov     cx,bx
                mov     si,di                       ;Get ending address in SI
                sub     si,2                        ;Point SI to last character
                std                                 ;Set the direction flag
exec2:          lodsb                               ;Scan backward for first
                cmp     al,"\"                      ;   character in file name
                je      exec3
                cmp     al,":"
                je      exec3
                loop    exec2
                dec     si
exec3:          add     si,2                        ;Point SI to first character
                sub     bx,cx                       ;Compute length of file name
                mov     cx,bx                       ;Transfer length to CX
                cld                                 ;Clear direction flag again
                push    cs                          ;Point ES to code segment
                pop     es
                mov     al,13                       ;Compute offset into table
                mov     dl,byte ptr cs:[level]      ;   of program names
                mul     dl
                mov     di,ax
                add     di,offset names
                mov     al,cl                       ;Write file name character
                stosb                               ;   count into table
exec5:          lodsb                               ;Convert lowercase characters
                cmp     al,"a"                      ;   to upper and copy file
                jb      exec6                       ;   name into table
                cmp     al,"z"
                ja      exec6
                and     al,0DFh
exec6:          stosb
                loop    exec5
                pop     bx                          ;Restore ES and BX
                pop     es
;
; Record the command line passed to the program just EXECed.
;
                lds     si,es:[bx+2]                ;Load string address
                mov     cl,[si]                     ;Get string length in CX
                sub     ch,ch
                inc     cx
                push    cs                          ;Point ES:DI to command line
                pop     es                          ;   buffer in code segment
                mov     di,offset cmdline
                rep     movsb                       ;Copy the command line
```

```
;
; Restore the register values passed to EXEC.
;
                pop     es
                pop     ds
                pop     bp
                pop     di
                pop     si
                pop     dx
                pop     cx
                pop     bx
                pop     ax
                popf
;
; Save registers again since the EXEC function destroys them.
;
                push    bx
                push    cx
                push    dx
                push    si
                push    di
                push    bp
                push    ds
                push    es
;
; Save the values of SS and SP, call EXEC, and restore the stack.
;
                pushf                           ;Save FLAGS
                mov     cs:[handle],bx          ;Save BX temporarily
                mov     bx,cs:[level]           ;Compute an index into the
                dec     bx                      ;  STACKSEG and STACKPTR
                shl     bx,1                    ;  tables
                popf                            ;Restore FLAGS
                mov     word ptr cs:[stackseg+bx],ss    ;Save the SS and SP
                mov     word ptr cs:[stackptr+bx],sp    ;  registers
                mov     bx,cs:[handle]          ;Restore BX

                pushf                           ;Push FLAGS
                cli                             ;Disable interrupts
                call    int21h                  ;Call the DOS EXEC function

                mov     cs:[handle],ax          ;Save the return code
                lahf                            ;Store FLAGS in AH for now
                mov     bx,cs:[level]           ;Recompute the table index
                dec     bx
                shl     bx,1
                cli                             ;Disable interrupts
                mov     ss,word ptr cs:[stackseg+bx]    ;Restore SS and SP
                mov     sp,word ptr cs:[stackptr+bx]
                sti                             ;Enable interrupts
                sahf                            ;Restore the FLAGS register
                mov     ax,cs:[handle]          ;Restore return code in AX
;
; Restore the registers to their conditions before EXEC was called.
;
                pop     es
```

```
                pop     ds
                pop     bp
                pop     di
                pop     si
                pop     dx
                pop     cx
                pop     bx
;
; Save registers again while post-processing is performed.
;
                pushf
                push    ax
                push    bx
                push    cx
                push    dx
                push    si
                push    di
                push    bp
                push    ds
                push    es
;
; Save extended error information if DOS version is 3.10 or later.
;
                push    cs                      ;Point DS to code segment
                pop     ds
                assume  ds:code
                cmp     dosversion,030Ah        ;Skip if not 3.10 or later
                jb      exec7
                push    ds                      ;Save DS
                mov     ah,59h                  ;Get extended error
                sub     bx,bx                   ;  information
                int     21h
                mov     cs:[xerror_ds],ds       ;Save return value of DS
                pop     ds                      ;Set DS to code segment again
                mov     xerror_ax,ax            ;Save return values in
                mov     xerror_bx,bx            ;  XERROR array
                mov     xerror_cx,cx
                mov     xerror_dx,dx
                mov     xerror_si,si
                mov     xerror_di,di
                mov     xerror_es,es
;
; Record the program start/end time and write an entry to the log file.
;
exec7:          dec     level                   ;Decrement reentrancy count
                call    record_time             ;Record the current time
                call    open_file               ;Open the log file
                mov     si,level                ;Point SI to start time and
                inc     si                      ;  DI to end time
                shl     si,1
                shl     si,1
                add     si,offset times
                mov     di,si
                sub     di,4
                mov     al,byte ptr level       ;Store previous level number
                inc     al                      ;  in AL
```

```
                call    write_entry                 ;Write log entry
                call    close_file                  ;Close the log file
                mov     execflag,0                  ;Clear EXEC flag
;
; Restore extended error information if DOS version is 3.10 or later.
;
                cmp     dosversion,030Ah            ;Skip if not 3.10 or later
                jb      exec8
                mov     ax,5D0Ah                    ;Restore information with
                mov     dx,offset xerror_ax         ;  DOS function 5Dh
                int     21h
;
; Restore registers a final time and exit to the parent program.
;
                assume  ds:nothing
exec8:          pop     es
                pop     ds
                pop     bp
                pop     di
                pop     si
                pop     dx
                pop     cx
                pop     bx
                pop     ax
                popf
                ret     2                           ;Return with FLAGS intact
dos_int         endp

;***************************************************************************
; MPLEX_INT handles interrupt 2FH.  If, on entry, AH is set to PC-LOG's
; multiplex ID number, MPLEX_INT uses the value in AL as a function code.
; The functions supported are:
;
;     00H     Returns FFH in AL to indicate the program is installed
;             and returns the address of its signature in ES:DI.
;***************************************************************************

mplex_int       proc    far
                pushf                               ;Save FLAGS register
                cmp     ah,cs:[prog_id]             ;Branch if AH holds the
                je      mplex2                      ;  multiplex ID
                popf                                ;Restore FLAGS
                jmp     cs:[int2Fh]                 ;Pass the interrupt on
;
; Function 00H verifies that the program is installed.
;
mplex2:         popf                                ;Restore FLAGS
                or      al,al                       ;Branch if function code
                jnz     mplex3                      ;  is other than 00H
                mov     al,0FFh                     ;Set AL to FFH
                push    cs                          ;Point ES:DI to the program
                pop     es                          ;  signature
                mov     di,offset signature
mplex3:         iret                                ;Return from interrupt
mplex_int       endp
```

```
;************************************************************************
; OPEN_FILE attempts to open or create the file output is redirected to.
; On return, carry is clear if the attempt was successful and the file
; handle is in AX.  Carry set means the attempt failed.  On entry, DS
; must point to the code segment.
;************************************************************************

callflag        db      0

open_file       proc    near
                assume  ds:code
                mov     ax,3D01h                ;Attempt to open the file
                mov     dx,offset logfile       ;  for writing
                int     21h
                jnc     opened                  ;Branch if it worked

                mov     ax,4301h                ;Attempt to strip all the
                sub     cx,cx                   ;  attributes off the file
                mov     dx,offset logfile
                int     21h

                mov     ax,3D01h                ;Then attempt to open it
                mov     dx,offset logfile       ;  for writing again
                int     21h
                jc      create_file             ;Branch if it failed

opened:         mov     handle,ax               ;Store the file handle
                mov     bx,ax                   ;Move the file pointer
                mov     ax,4202h                ;  to the end of the
                sub     cx,cx                   ;  file
                mov     dx,cx
                int     21h
                cmp     callflag,0              ;Branch if this routine has
                jne     open_exit               ;  been called before
set_flag:       mov     callflag,1              ;Set flag indicating it has
                call    write_date              ;Write date to the log file
                call    Write_header            ;Write header to the log file
open_exit:      clc                             ;Clear the carry flag and
                ret                             ;  exit

create_file:    mov     ah,3Ch                  ;Attempt to create the
                sub     cx,cx                   ;  file from scratch
                mov     dx,offset logfile
                int     21h
                jc      not_created             ;Branch if it failed

                mov     handle,ax               ;Store the file handle
                mov     bx,ax                   ;Transfer handle to BX
                mov     ah,40h                  ;Write the header to the
                mov     cx,94                   ;  file
                mov     dx,offset header
                int     21h
                jmp     set_flag                ;Exit

not_created:    stc                             ;Set the carry flag and
                ret                             ;  exit
```

```
open_file       endp

;****************************************************************************
; CLOSE_FILE closes the log file.
;****************************************************************************

close_file      proc    near
                assume  ds:code
                mov     ah,3Eh
                mov     bx,handle
                int     21h
                ret
close_file      endp


;****************************************************************************
; WRITE_ENTRY writes a 1-line entry to the log file.  On entry, DS:SI
; points to the start time, DS:DI points to the end time, and AL holds the
; latest reentrancy level.
;****************************************************************************

lastlevel       db      ?

write_entry     proc    near
                assume  ds:code
                mov     lastlevel,al            ;Store last level number
                call    write_time              ;Write out the starting
                mov     cx,4                    ;  time
                call    write_spaces            ;Pad it with spaces

                push    si                      ;Save starting time
                mov     si,di                   ;Write out the ending
                call    write_time              ;  time
                mov     cx,3
                call    write_spaces            ;Pad it with spaces
                pop     si                      ;Retrieve start time

                call    write_diff              ;Write elapsed time
                mov     cx,5
                call    write_spaces            ;Pad it with spaces

                mov     al,lastlevel            ;Write out the reentrancy
                mov     bl,1                    ;  level
                call    write_num
                mov     cx,6
                call    write_spaces            ;Pad it with spaces

                mov     al,13                   ;Compute offset into table
                mul     lastlevel               ;  of program names
                mov     dx,ax
                add     dx,offset names
                mov     ah,40h                  ;Write the program name to
                mov     bx,dx                   ;  the log file
                mov     cl,[bx]
                sub     ch,ch
                push    cx
                mov     bx,handle
```

```
                inc     dx
                int     21h
                pop     bx

                cmp     execflag,Ø              ;Exit now if this is called
                je      write_exit              ; on entry to EXEC

                mov     cx,12                   ;Compute number of spaces
                sub     cx,bx                   ; to skip
                add     cx,5
                call    write_spaces            ;Output spaces
                mov     bx,offset cmdline       ;Write command line to the
                mov     cl,[bx]                 ; log file
                sub     ch,ch
                jcxz    write_exit
                mov     ah,4Øh
                mov     bx,handle
                mov     dx,offset cmdline+1
                int     21h

write_exit:     call    write_crlf              ;End line with CR/LF
                ret
write_entry     endp


;****************************************************************************
; WRITE_TIME writes the time to the log file.  On entry, DS:SI points to
; the time.  The byte at [SI] holds the number of minutes, while the byte
; at [SI+1] holds the number of hours.
;****************************************************************************

colon           db      ":"

write_time      proc    near
                assume  ds:code
                mov     al,[si+1]               ;Write hours to log file
                mov     bl,1
                call    write_num
                mov     ah,4Øh                  ;Write ":" to separate
                mov     bx,handle               ; hours and minutes
                mov     cx,1
                mov     dx,offset colon
                int     21h
                mov     al,[si]                 ;Write minutes to log file
                sub     bl,bl
                call    write_num
                ret
write_time      endp


;****************************************************************************
; WRITE_DIFF writes the elapsed time to the log file.  On entry, DS:SI
; points to the start time and DS:SI points to the end time.
;****************************************************************************

delta           db      3 dup (?)

write_diff      proc    near
```

```
                assume  ds:code
                mov     al,[di]                 ;Retrieve starting and ending
                mov     bl,[si]                 ;  seconds, minutes, and
                mov     cl,[di+1]               ;  hours
                mov     dl,[si+1]
                mov     ah,[di+2]
                mov     bh,[si+2]
;
; Prepare to compute differences between hours, minutes, and seconds.
;
                cmp     ah,bh                   ;If ending seconds is less
                jae     wrdiff1                 ;  than starting, add 60 to
                add     ah,60                   ;  ending seconds and
                dec     al                      ;  decrement ending minutes

wrdiff1:        cmp     al,bl                   ;If ending minutes is less
                jge     wrdiff2                 ;  than starting, add 60 to
                add     al,60                   ;  ending minutes and
                dec     cl                      ;  decrement ending hours

wrdiff2:        cmp     cl,dl                   ;If ending hours is less
                jge     wrdiff3                 ;  than starting, add 24
                add     cl,24                   ;  to ending hours
;
; Compute the difference and write it to the log file.
;
wrdiff3:        sub     ah,bh                   ;Calculate seconds difference
                mov     delta+2,ah              ;Store it
                sub     al,bl                   ;Calculate minutes difference
                mov     delta,al                ;Store it
                sub     cl,dl                   ;Calculate hours difference
                mov     delta+1,cl              ;Store it

                mov     si,offset delta         ;Write hours and minutes to
                call    write_time              ;  the log file
                mov     ah,40h                  ;Write ":" to log file
                mov     bx,handle
                mov     cx,1
                mov     dx,offset colon
                int     21h
                mov     al,[si+2]               ;Write seconds to log file
                sub     bl,bl
                call    write_num
                ret
write_diff      endp


;****************************************************************************
; WRITE_NUM converts a binary byte value in AL to ASCII and writes it to
; the log file.  Value must be between 0 and 99, inclusive.  On entry, BL=0
; means include leading zeroes; BL=1 means don't include leading zeroes.
;****************************************************************************

fileword        dw      ?

write_num       proc    near
                assume  ds:code
```

```
                aam                         ;Convert to BCD in AX
                add     ax,3030h            ;Convert to ASCII
                or      bl,bl               ;Convert leading zero to
                jz      wrnum1              ;  space if BL=1
                cmp     ah,30h
                jne     wrnum1
                mov     ah,20h
wrnum1:         xchg    ah,al               ;Swap bytes
                mov     fileword,ax         ;Store them
                mov     ah,40h              ;Then write them to the
                mov     bx,handle           ;  log file
                mov     cx,2
                mov     dx,offset fileword
                int     21h
                ret
write_num       endp


;****************************************************************************
; WRITE_CRLF writes a carriage return/line feed to the log file.
;****************************************************************************

crlf            db      13,10

write_crlf      proc    near
                assume  ds:code
                mov     ah,40h
                mov     bx,handle
                mov     cx,2
                mov     dx,offset crlf
                int     21h
                ret
write_crlf      endp


;****************************************************************************
; WRITE_SPACES writes the designated number of spaces to the log file.  On
; entry, CX holds the number of spaces to write.
;****************************************************************************

space           db      32

write_spaces    proc    near
                assume  ds:code
                push    cx                  ;Save count
                mov     ah,40h              ;Write one space
                mov     bx,handle
                mov     cx,1
                mov     dx,offset space
                int     21h
                pop     cx                  ;Retrieve count
                loop    write_spaces        ;Loop until done
                ret
write_spaces    endp


;****************************************************************************
; RECORD_TIME records the current time in the slot designated by LEVEL.
;****************************************************************************
```

```
record_time     proc    near
                assume  ds:code
                mov     ah,2Ch                  ;Get the current time
                int     21h                     ;  from DOS
                mov     bx,level                ;Compute offset into table
                shl     bx,1                    ;  of start/end times
                shl     bx,1
                mov     word ptr times[bx],cx   ;Store current time
                mov     byte ptr times[bx+2],dh
                ret
record_time     endp

;***************************************************************************
; WRITE_DATE writes the current date to the log file.
;***************************************************************************

century         db      "19"

write_date      proc    near
                assume  ds:code
                call    write_crlf              ;Skip one line
                mov     ah,2Ah                  ;Get today's date from DOS
                int     21h
                push    cx                      ;Save it
                push    dx

                mov     al,dl                   ;Write day of the month to
                sub     bl,bl                   ;  the log file
                call    write_num
                mov     cx,1                    ;Skip a space
                call    write_spaces

                pop     dx                      ;Retrieve month from stack
                dec     dh                      ;Compute offset into month
                mov     cl,dh                   ;  table of the name of
                sub     ch,ch                   ;  the current month
                mov     dx,offset months
                jcxz    wrdate2
wrdate1:        add     dx,3
                loop    wrdate1
wrdate2:        mov     ah,40h                  ;Write month name to the
                mov     bx,handle               ;  log file
                mov     cx,3
                int     21h
                mov     cx,1                    ;Skip a space
                call    write_spaces

                mov     ah,40h                  ;Write "19" portion of year
                mov     cx,2
                mov     dx,offset century
                int     21h
                pop     cx                      ;Retrieve year from stack
                sub     cx,1900                 ;Subtract century portion
                mov     al,cl                   ;Write year to the log file
                sub     bl,bl
```

```
                call    write_num
                call    write_crlf              ;Finish with CR/LF pairs
                call    write_crlf
                ret
write_date      endp


;*********************************************************************
; WRITE_HEADER writes the column titles to the log file.
;*********************************************************************

equalsign       db      "="

write_header    ·proc   near
                assume  ds:code
                mov     ah,40h                  ;Write column titles
                mov     bx,handle
                mov     cx,67
                mov     dx,offset titles
                int     21h

                mov     cx,79                   ;Write row of "=" symbols
wrhead1:        push    cx
                mov     ah,40h
                mov     cx,1
                mov     dx,offset equalsign
                int     21h
                pop     cx
                loop    wrhead1

                call    write_crlf              ;End it with a CR/LF pair
                ret
write_header    endp


;*********************************************************************
; Buffer areas to be used after installation.
;*********************************************************************

names           =       $                       ;Program names
times           =       $ + 130                 ;Start and end times
stackseg        =       $ + 170                 ;Saved values of SS register
stackptr        =       $ + 190                 ;Saved values of SP register
cmdline         =       $ + 210                 ;Command line buffer
lastbyte        =       $ + 338                 ;Last byte


;*********************************************************************
; Data that will be discarded when the program becomes memory-resident.
;*********************************************************************

helpmsg         db      "Maintains a log of the programs run on your PC."
                db      13,10,13,10
                db      "PC-LOG [[d:][path]filename]",13,10,13,10
                db      "  filename  Name of the ASCII log file.",13,10,13,10
                db      "If no file name is specified, the program creates a "
                db      "log file named USAGE.LOG",13,10
                db      "in the root directory of the current drive."
                db      13,10,"$"
```

```
errmsg1         db      "Syntax: PC-LOG [[d:][path]filename]",13,10,"$"
errmsg2         db      "Requires DOS 3.0 or higher",13,10,"$"
errmsg3         db      "Program is already installed",13,10,"$"
errmsg4         db      "Invalid time value (max=59:59)",13,10,"$"
errmsg5         db      "Invalid file specification",13,10,"$"
errmsg6         db      "Invalid file specification or file could not be "
                db      "opened",13,10,"$"
errmsg7         db      "Program could not be installed",13,10,"$"

msg1            db      "PC-LOG 1.0 installed",13,10
                db      "Entries will be written to $"


;****************************************************************************
; INIT makes the program resident in memory.
;****************************************************************************

                assume  cs:code,ds:code

init            proc    near
                cld                             ;Clear direction flag
                mov     si,81h                  ;Point SI to command line
                call    scanhelp                ;Scan for "/?" switch
                jnc     checkver                ;Branch if not found
                mov     ah,09h                  ;Display help text and exit
                mov     dx,offset helpmsg       ;  with ERRORLEVEL=0
                int     21h
                mov     ax,4C00h
                int     21h
;
; Check the DOS version and see if the program is already installed.
;
checkver:       mov     dx,offset errmsg2       ;Get the DOS version number
                mov     ah,30h
                int     21h
                mov     byte ptr dosversion,ah  ;Save it
                mov     byte ptr dosversion[1],al
                cmp     al,3                    ;Exit if the version number
                jae     checkins                ;  is less than 3.0

error:          mov     ah,09h                  ;Display error message and
                int     21h                     ;  exit with ERRORLEVEL=1
                mov     ax,4C01h
                int     21h

checkins:       call    check_install           ;Error if the program is
                mov     dx,offset errmsg3       ;  already installed
                jc      error

                mov     ah,19h                  ;Get default drive code with
                int     21h                     ;  DOS function 19H
                add     al,41h                  ;Convert it to ASCII
                mov     logfile,al              ;Store it
;
; Parse the command line.
;
```

```
            mov     si,81h                  ;Reset SI
            call    findchar                ;Find first parameter
            jc      checkfile               ;Branch if none found

            mov     bx,si                   ;Save starting address
            call    finddelim               ;Find the end of the string
            mov     byte ptr [si],0         ;Convert string to ASCIIZ
            mov     ah,60h                  ;Call DOS function 60H to
            mov     si,bx                   ;  convert the string to a
            mov     di,offset logfile       ;  full qualified file
            mov     bx,cs                   ;  name
            mov     es,bx
            int     21h
            mov     dx,offset errmsg5       ;Error if carry returns set
            jc      error

checkfile:  call    open_file               ;Make sure the log file can
            mov     dx,offset errmsg6       ;  be opened
            jc      error                   ;Error if it can't
            call    close_file              ;Close the file
            call    record_time             ;Record the time
;
; Install the program.
;
            call    mplex_id                ;Find a multipex ID number
            mov     dx,offset errmsg7       ;Error if none available
            jc      error
            mov     prog_id,ah              ;Save the ID number

            mov     ax,3521h                ;Hook interrupt 21H
            int     21h
            mov     word ptr int21h,bx
            mov     word ptr int21h[2],es
            mov     ax,2521h
            mov     dx,offset dos_int
            int     21h

            mov     ax,352Fh                ;Hook interrupt 2FH
            int     21h
            mov     word ptr int2Fh,bx
            mov     word ptr int2Fh[2],es
            mov     ax,252Fh
            mov     dx,offset mplex_int
            int     21h

            mov     ah,49h                  ;Get the segment address of
            mov     es,ds:[2Ch]             ;  the environment block
            int     21h                     ;  and free the segment

            mov     ah,09                   ;Display message verifying
            mov     dx,offset msg1          ;  the installation
            int     21h
            mov     si,offset logfile       ;Display the name of the
            call    dos_out                 ;  log file

            mov     ax,3100h                ;Terminate with function 31H
```

```
                mov     dx,(offset lastbyte - offset code + 15) shr 4
                int     21h
init            endp


;*************************************************************************
; FINDCHAR advances SI to the next non-space or non-comma character.
; On return, carry set indicates EOL was encountered.
;*************************************************************************

findchar        proc    near
                lodsb                           ;Get the next character
                cmp     al,20h                  ;Loop if space
                je      findchar
                cmp     al,2Ch                  ;Loop if comma
                je      findchar
                dec     si                      ;Point SI to the character
                cmp     al,0Dh                  ;Exit with carry set if end
                je      eol                     ;  of line is reached

                clc                             ;Clear carry and exit
                ret

eol:            stc                             ;Set carry and exit
                ret
findchar        endp


;*************************************************************************
; FINDDELIM advances SI to the next space or comma character.  On return,
; carry set indicates EOL was encountered.
;*************************************************************************

finddelim       proc    near
                lodsb                           ;Get the next character
                cmp     al,20h                  ;Exit if space
                je      fd_exit
                cmp     al,2Ch                  ;Exit if comma
                je      fd_exit
                cmp     al,0Dh                  ;Loop back for more if end
                jne     finddelim               ;  of line isn't reached

                dec     si                      ;Set carry and exit
                stc
                ret

fd_exit:        dec     si                      ;Clear carry and exit
                clc
                ret
finddelim       endp


;*************************************************************************
; SCANHELP scans the command line for a /? switch.  If found, carry returns
; set and SI contains its offset.  If not found, carry returns clear.
;*************************************************************************

scanhelp        proc    near
                push    si                      ;Save SI
```

```
scanloop:       lodsb                           ;Get a character
                cmp     al,0Dh                  ;Exit if end of line
                je      scan_exit
                cmp     al,"?"                  ;Loop if not "?"
                jne     scanloop
                cmp     byte ptr [si-2],"/"     ;Loop if not "/"
                jne     scanloop

                add     sp,2                    ;Clear the stack
                sub     si,2                    ;Adjust SI
                stc                             ;Set carry and exit
                ret

scan_exit:      pop     si                      ;Restore SI
                clc                             ;Clear carry and exit
                ret
scanhelp        endp


;****************************************************************************
; CHECK_INSTALL returns carry set if the program is already installed,
; carry clear if it's not.  If carry returns set, AH holds the program's
; multiplex ID number.
;****************************************************************************

check_install   proc    near
                mov     ax,8000h                ;Initialize AH and AL
                mov     cx,80h                  ;Initialize count

chinst1:        push    ax                      ;Save AX and CX
                push    cx
                sub     di,di                   ;Set ES and DI to 0
                mov     es,di
                int     2Fh                     ;Interrupt 2Fh
                cmp     al,0FFh                 ;Nothing here if AL isn't
                jne     chinst2                 ;   equal to FFH

                mov     si,offset signature     ;See if program signature
                mov     cx,12                   ;   appears at the address
                repe    cmpsb                   ;   returned in ES:DI
                jne     chinst2                 ;Branch if it does not

                pop     cx                      ;Clear the stack and exit
                pop     ax                      ;   with carry set
                stc
                ret

chinst2:        pop     cx                      ;Retrieve AX and CX
                pop     ax
                inc     ah                      ;Next multiplex ID
                loop    chinst1                 ;Loop until done

                clc                             ;Exit with carry clear
                ret
check_install   endp


;****************************************************************************
```

```
; MPLEX_ID searches for an unused multiplex ID number.  If one is found,
; it is returned in AH with carry clear.  Carry set means no multiplex
; ID numbers are currently available.
;****************************************************************************

mplex_id        proc    near
                mov     ax,8000h                ;Initialize AH and AL
                mov     cx,80h                  ;Initialize count

mxid1:          push    ax                      ;Save AX and CX
                push    cx
                int     2Fh                     ;Interrupt 2Fh
                or      al,al                   ;Branch if AL=0
                jz      mxid2
                pop     cx                      ;Retrieve AX and CX
                pop     ax
                inc     ah                      ;Increment ID number
                loop    mxid1                   ;Loop until done

                stc                             ;Exit with carry set
                ret

mxid2:          pop     cx                      ;Clear the stack and exit
                pop     ax                      ; with carry clear
                clc
                ret
mplex_id        endp


;****************************************************************************
; ASC2BIN converts a decimal number entered in ASCII form into a binary
; value in AL.  Carry set on return indicates that an error occurred in
; the conversion.
;****************************************************************************

asc2bin         proc    near
                sub     ax,ax                   ;Initialize registers
                sub     bh,bh
                mov     dl,10

a2b_loop:       mov     bl,[si]                 ;Get a character
                inc     si
                cmp     bl,20h                  ;Exit if space
                je      a2b_exit
                cmp     bl,3Ah                  ;Exit if colon
                je      a2b_exit
                cmp     bl,0Dh                  ;Exit if carriage return
                je      a2b_exit

                cmp     bl,"0"                  ;Error if character is not
                jb      a2b_error               ; a number
                cmp     bl,"9"
                ja      a2b_error

                mul     dl                      ;Multiply the value in AL by
                jc      a2b_error               ; 10 and exit on overflow
                sub     bl,30h                  ;ASCII => binary
```

```
                add     ax,bx                   ;Add latest value to AX
                cmp     ax,255                  ;Error if sum > 255
                jna     a2b_loop                ;Loop back for more

a2b_error:      dec     si                      ;Set carry and exit
                stc
                ret

a2b_exit:       dec     si                      ;Clear carry and exit
                clc
                ret
asc2bin         endp

;****************************************************************************
; DOS_OUT displays the ASCIIZ string pointed to by DS:SI.
;****************************************************************************

dos_out         proc    near
                lodsb                           ;Get a character
                or      al,al                   ;Exit if it's zero
                jz      out_exit
                mov     ah,02h                  ;Output it using DOS
                mov     dl,al                   ;  function 02H
                int     21h
                jmp     dos_out                 ;Loop until done
out_exit:       ret
dos_out         endp

code            ends
                end     begin
```

Once PC-LOG is installed, it automatically keeps track of all the programs you run and writes an entry for each one to the log file. Figure 13.1 shows a typical log file. START and END tell you what time a program was started and what time it ended; ELAPSED reveals the elapsed time; LEVEL indicates what level the program ran at (more on this in a moment); PROGRAM is the name of the program that was run; and PARAMETERS lists the parameters and switches the program was started with. In this example, WordPerfect (WP.EXE) was active from 11:19 to 11:34 A.M. (all times are reported in military format), from 11:36 to 11:44, and also from 11:45 to 12:27. In between invocations of WordPerfect, other programs and external DOS commands were given turns.

The only column in the log file whose purpose may not be obvious is the one labeled LEVEL. Under DOS, programs can (and often do) load and execute other programs. LEVEL tells you how many levels deep a program was run relative to the primary command processor, which by definition runs at level 0. Most programs run at level 1, which means they were started from the command line. However, if you use a DOS shell, the shell itself is run at level 1 and other programs you start from it execute at level 2 or higher. Similarly, if you "Go to DOS" from WordPerfect or otherwise shell out of an application program, you'll see an entry for a secondary copy of COMMAND.COM run one level higher than the program that launched it.

FIGURE 13.1

PC-LOG log file

START	END	ELAPSED	LEVEL	PROGRAM	PARAMETERS
11:19	11:19	0:00:00	1	MEM.EXE	
11:19	11:34	0:14:15	1	WP.EXE	chap13.doc
11:34	11:34	0:00:06	1	CHKDSK.EXE	
11:34	11:34	0:00:00	1	EDIT.COM	\config.sys
11:34	11:35	0:00:48	2	QBASIC.EXE	/EDCOM \config.sys
11:35	11:35	0:00:00	1	EDIT.COM	
11:36	11:44	0:08:11	1	WP.EXE	chap13.doc
11:44	11:44	0:00:06	2	COMMAND.COM	
11:44	11:44	0:00:01	3	UNDELETE.EXE	/?
11:44	11:44	0:00:14	2	COMMAND.COM	
11:44	11:44	0:00:02	3	UNDELETE.EXE	/list
11:44	11:44	0:00:11	2	COMMAND.COM	
11:44	11:45	0:00:14	3	UNDELETE.EXE	
11:45	11:45	0:00:02	2	COMMAND.COM	
11:45	12:27	0:42:04	1	WP.EXE	
12:27	12:27	0:00:00	1	PC-DIAL.COM	\masm\book\zd.dat
12:30	12:30	0:00:00	1	REMOVE.COM	/1
12:30	12:30	0:00:04	1	MEM.EXE	/c

As a result, programs may be nested several levels deep. You can see this in the log file in Figure 13.1 in the entry for EDIT.COM (the DOS Editor) and again in the entry for WP.EXE that starts at 11:36 A.M. When you use the EDIT command, it actually invokes QBASIC.EXE (The QBasic interpreter) with a /EDCOM switch. It's actually the QBasic editor you're using when you run the DOS Editor (it's no coincidence that the two bear strong resemblances to each other). PC-LOG reports that EDIT.COM was run at level 1, and that QBASIC-.EXE, which was loaded and run by EDIT.COM, was run at level 2. This isn't at all unusual. In fact, if you use PC-LOG regularly, you'll find that many DOS applications call on other programs to do their work for them. Run the Microsoft C Compiler with PC-LOG loaded, for example, and there'll be dozens of entries written to the log file each time the compiler is invoked.

The 11:36 entry for WordPerfect shows what happens when you shell out to DOS from an application program. The log file contains a level 1 entry for WP.EXE, a level 2 entry for COMMAND.COM, and a level 3 entry for UNDELETE.EXE. By definition, programs shell out to DOS by loading and running another copy of COMMAND.COM. The primary copy of COMMAND-.COM is still in memory; it doesn't go away. WordPerfect is still there, too. The second copy of COMMAND.COM is loaded at a higher memory address, where it won't overwrite the other COMMAND.COM or the copy of WordPerfect that is interposed between instances of COMMAND.COM. Programs run from the secondary command prompt run at level 3, as the entry for UNDELETE.EXE illustrates. When you type EXIT to go back to WordPerfect, PC-LOG writes another entry to the file for WP.EXE, just as if it had been started all over again. In truth, you were in WordPerfect all the time. But WordPerfect wasn't always the active application. PC-LOG will report programs run as many as 10 levels deep—far deeper than you're likely ever to go because of the practical constraints imposed by available memory.

PC-LOG keeps a record of every program that is run on your PC, including external DOS commands such as MEM and CHKDSK. If you use PC-LOG for billing purposes (to keep track of the time spent on a client's job, for instance) and want to omit some of these entries from the log file, use the DOS Editor to edit the unwanted entries out of the log file. You can add text as well as delete it. For example, you might add a note to certain entries indicating who the time is being billed to, or add a numerical job code to some of the entries for bookkeeping purposes.

Each time PC-LOG is started, it writes a record of the current date to the log file. It does not check the date at any other time. If you start an application running at 8:00 A.M. on Friday and leave it until 5:00 P.M. on Monday, PC-LOG will report that the program was active for nine hours. The best way to use PC-LOG is to add it to your AUTOEXEC.BAT file and then get in the habit of turning your PC on in the morning and off again before you leave for the night. That's good medicine for your PC also; it prevents both the stress caused by turning the machine on and off too often and the needless wear to mechanical components of the system, particularly the hard drive.

Inside PC-LOG

When DOS loads and executes a program, it does so by placing a call to DOS function 4BH, *Execute Program*, also called the DOS EXEC function. When PC-LOG becomes memory-resident, it patches itself into interrupt 21H and watches for calls to function 4BH. When a call occurs, PC-LOG inspects the register values passed to the function to determine what program is being EXECed and what parameters are being passed to it. Then it buffers the information in memory along with the time the program was started. When the program terminates, PC-LOG writes an entry for it to the log file.

The calling conventions for function 4BH are as follows. On entry, register AH holds the function number (4BH), while AL holds a 00H if the program is to be loaded and executed, or a 03H if an overlay is being loaded (in the old days, when PCs with 64k of memory were common, large executables were frequently divided into multiple modules called *overlays;* overlays were loaded from disk as needed, so the entire program would not have to reside in memory at once). There's a third value that may be passed in AL—01H—which tells DOS to load a program file but not to execute it. This option, undocumented in official texts, is used by programs such as DEBUG to load programs into memory for debugging. PC-LOG only reports on programs loaded with AL equal to 00H so that log files won't contain the names of overlays or programs loaded for debugging purposes.

When function 4BH is called, DS:DX points to an ASCIIZ file specification that holds the name and location of the program being EXECed, and ES:BX points to a data structure that contains, in order, the segment address of the environment block the program will receive (every program that is EXECed receives its own local copy of the environment), the *segment:offset* address of the command tail (the text passed to the program from the command line), and the *segment:offset* addresses of a pair of file control blocks. What does EXEC do with this information? The address of the environment block is placed in the program's PSP at offset 2CH; the command tail is copied to the PSP beginning at offset 80H; and the file control blocks are copied to the PSP at offsets 5CH and 6CH, respectively.

PC-LOG inspects the string pointed to by DS:DX to determine the name of the program being loaded and the information pointed to by ES:BX to find out what switches and parameters it is being started with. The following code copies the text of the command tail passed to the program to a local buffer named CMDLINE:

```
lds     si,es:[bx+2]
mov     cl,[si]
sub     ch,ch
inc     cx
push    cs
pop     es
mov     di,offset cmdline
rep     movsb
```

The instruction

```
lds     si,es:[bx+2]
```

loads the *segment:offset* address of the command tail, which is located 2 higher than the base of the list pointed to by ES:BX, into DS:SI. The first byte of the command tail contains a count of the number of characters, not including the carriage return at the end, so the instructions

```
mov     cl,[si]
sub     ch,ch
inc     cx
```

place the count (plus 1, to include the carriage return) in CX. Next, the instructions

```
push    cs
pop     es
mov     di,offset cmdline
```

point ES:DI to the local buffer named CMDLINE, and the instruction

```
rep     movsb
```

copies the number of bytes in CX from DS:SI to ES:DI. Later, when PC-LOG writes an entry to the log file, the text that was buffered in CMDLINE goes into the PARAMETERS column.

The strategy that PC-LOG employs in logging EXEC calls to a file goes something like this. Each time EXEC is called, PC-LOG increments the level number, which is initially zero, and records the time that the function call was placed. If the level number is greater than 1, PC-LOG writes an entry to the log file for the program that performed the EXEC, which, by definition, just ended. Next, it records the name of the program being EXECed by examining the ASCIIZ string pointed to by DS:DX. So the log file won't be cluttered with path names, PC-LOG ignores drive and path names and only buffers the file name itself. Then it records the command tail passed to the program and saves all the registers on the stack.

This last step—saving the registers passed to EXEC—is necessary because in some versions of DOS, EXEC destroys all registers but CS and IP, including SS and SP. SS and SP require special attention because they can't be saved and restored like other registers can. Just before it puts the call through to EXEC, PC-LOG saves SS and SP in two special buffer areas called STACKSEG and STACKPTR, using the current level number as an index. Since EXEC calls may be nested several levels deep, it's important that successive SS and SP values be stored apart from each other so that consecutive calls to EXEC will not destroy values written there earlier.

Finally, the call to EXEC is made. When the call returns, PC-LOG regains control, restores SS and SP so that the stack is once more addressable, and restores the register values that were saved before the function was called. Then it checks the version of DOS that is running and, if it's 3.10 or later, uses DOS function 59H to save the extended error information that DOS made available as a result of the EXEC call. This is important because if the EXEC call failed, the program that called it may request additional information about the error from DOS through function 59H. But PC-LOG is about to make a few interrupt 21H calls of its own, and if one of them fails, the extended error information for it will replace the extended error information that pertains to EXEC. Later, before it returns to the program that placed the call to EXEC, PC-LOG will use undocumented DOS function 5D0AH to restore the extended error information.

Before returning from interrupt, PC-LOG decrements the level number and records the current time. Then it writes an entry to the log file for the program that just terminated (by definition, when a call to EXEC returns, a program has just ended). Finally, it executes a RET 2 instruction to end the call to interrupt 21H. Why RET 2, and not IRET, the instruction normally used to return from interrupt? Because interrupt 21H returns information in the FLAGS register (remember that the carry flag is generally used to indicate whether a function call succeeded or failed), and IRET restores the FLAGS register to the value it held when the call to the interrupt was placed. RET 2 returns from interrupt leaving the values of FLAGS intact. This is a simple but effective technique for returning from interrupt without affecting what's in the FLAGS register.

You can see all this in action by tracing through the program listing for PC-LOG, particularly for the procedure named DOS_INT, which is the interrupt handler that intercepts calls to EXEC. A final point that remains to be made about PC-LOG is that it doesn't bother to check InDOS or the critical error flag before calling interrupt 21H itself. Why? Because it intercepts calls to interrupt 21H and places its own calls to interrupt 21H from inside the interrupt handler *before* the original call to interrupt is patched through. Therefore, no stack switch has occurred, and it's safe to call interrupt 21H. It also makes interrupt 21H calls after EXEC has returned, but the same logic applies under those circumstances, too. The original call to interrupt 21H has returned, so we're no longer "in DOS." If it wanted to, PC-LOG could verify this by checking the state of the InDOS flag. However, there's nothing to be gained from doing so, so to save time and to operate as unobtrusively as possible, it doesn't indulge in unnecessary actions.

Dialing Phones with Your PC

This next utility could be one of the most useful ones you've ever owned. On the surface, it's a pop-up phone directory with lots of bells and whistles. But it does more than store names and phone numbers. If you own a modem, it will dial the phone for you, too. And because it's implemented as a TSR, you can pop it up just about anytime you need it—even if you're currently in the middle of another application program.

The name of the program is PC-DIAL. Its source code listing appears in Listing 13.3. Installed, it consumes anywhere from 13k to 60k of RAM, depending on the size of the buffer you allocate for it. Like the other TSRs in this book, PC-DIAL may be loaded in upper memory with the LOADHIGH command on properly configured systems. The syntax for installing it is

```
PC-DIAL [[d:][path]filename] [/B=size] [/M]
```

where *filename* is the name of a data file to load at start-up, *size* is the number of kilobytes of memory to allocate for data storage, and /M tells PC-DIAL to run in monochrome, even if the video adapter it's run on reports itself as a color adapter. Like the /M switch on the FINDTEXT command in Chapter 11, this switch is included so that laptop users can obtain the highest degree of contrast possible on black-and-white displays that simulate color with shades of gray.

LISTING 13.3 PC-DIAL.ASM

```
; PC-DIAL is a popup phone directory and dialer that lets you store names,
; company names, and phone numbers and dial the phone with the touch of a
; key provided you have a modem.  Its syntax is
;
;       PC-DIAL [[d:][path]filename] [/B=size] [/M]
;
; where "filename" is the name of the data file to load at start-up,
; "size" is the size of the data buffer (in kilobytes), and /M runs the
; program in monochrome mode on color video adapaters -- useful for lap-
; tops with color adapters but LCD or gas plasma screens.  Once PC-DIAL
```

```
; is installed, pressing Alt-Rt Shift pops it up.
;************************************************************************

defaultsize     equ     16384                   ;Default buffer size

border_color    equ     [bx]                    ;Color table equates
window_color_1  equ     [bx+1]
window_color_2  equ     [bx+2]
hilite_color_1  equ     [bx+3]
hilite_color_2  equ     [bx+4]
shadow_color    equ     [bx+5]
menu_color1     equ     [bx+6]
menu_color2     equ     [bx+7]
title_color     equ     [bx+8]
error_color     equ     [bx+9]


;************************************************************************
; Program code and data.
;************************************************************************

code            segment
                assume  cs:code
                org     100h
begin:          jmp     init

signature       db      0,1,2,"PC-DIAL",2,1,0   ;Program signature
prog_id         db      ?                       ;Multiplex ID number

int08h          dd      ?                       ;Interrupt 08H vector
int09h          dd      ?                       ;Interrupt 09H vector
int10h          dd      ?                       ;Interrupt 10H vector
int13h          dd      ?                       ;Interrupt 13H vector
int1Bh          dd      ?                       ;Interrupt 1Bh vector
int23h          dd      ?                       ;Interrupt 23H vector
int24h          dd      ?                       ;Interrupt 24H vector
int25h          dd      ?                       ;Interrupt 25H vector
int26h          dd      ?                       ;Interrupt 26H vector
int28h          dd      ?                       ;Interrupt 28H vector
int2Fh          dd      ?                       ;Interrupt 2FH vector

dosversion      dw      ?                       ;DOS version number
bufferptr       dw      offset databuffer       ;Address of current record
buffertop       dw      offset databuffer       ;Address of top of data
bufferlimit     dw      offset databuffer+defaultsize
buffersize      dw      defaultsize             ;Buffer size (in bytes)
filename        db      128 dup (0)             ;Data file name
inbuffer        db      128 dup (0)             ;String input buffer
progfile        db      128 dup (0)             ;Program file name
egaflag         db      1                       ;1=EGA/VGA/XGA installed
popupflag       db      0                       ;Non-zero if window is up
requestflag     db      0                       ;Non-zero if hotkey pressed
errorflag       dd      ?                       ;Critical error flag address
indos           dd      ?                       ;InDOS flag address
intflags        db      0                       ;User interrupt flags
oldpsp          dw      ?                       ;Active process ID
records         dw      0                       ;Number of records
```

```
recordno        dw      0                       ;Current record number
recordlength    dw      0                       ;Length of deleted record
del_record      db      74 dup (0)              ;Last record deleted
searchtext      db      27 dup (0)              ;Text to search for
counter         db      0                       ;Internal countdown timer
ss_register     dw      ?                       ;Contents of SS register
sp_register     dw      ?                       ;Contents of SP register

color_table     db      1Bh,3Fh,1Fh,1Eh         ;Color video attributes
                db      4Fh,07h,7Fh,70h
                db      1Fh,4Fh

mono_table      db      70h,07h,70h,70h         ;Monochrome video attributes
                db      07h,07h,0Fh,0Fh
                db      70h,70h

key_table       db      "QWERTYUIOP",0,0,0,0    ;Alt key character codes
                db      "ASDFGHJKL",0,0,0,0,0
                db      "ZXCVBNM"

menu_cols       db      1,11,22,31,42,53,63,72

color_ptr       dw      offset color_table      ;Pointer to color table
video_segment   dw      0B800h                  ;Video buffer segment
video_offset    dw      ?                       ;Video buffer offset
small_cursor    dw      0607h                   ;Small cursor shape
big_cursor      dw      0407h                   ;Bug cursor shape
line_length     dw      ?                       ;Bytes per video line
cursor_mode     dw      ?                       ;Cursor mode
cursor_pos      dw      ?                       ;Cursor position
video_page      db      ?                       ;Video page number
window_start    db      ?                       ;Starting row of window
columns         dw      0                       ;Number of columns in window
rows            dw      0                       ;Number of rows in window

menutext        db      " F1-Setup  F2-Search  F3-Next  F4-Insert "
                db      " F5-Delete  F6-Paste  F7-Save  F8-Open ",0

title1          db      " Name ",0
title2          db      " Company ",0
title3          db      " Phone ",0

search_prompt   db      "Search For:",0
save_prompt     db      "Save As:",0
open_prompt     db      "File Name:",0
keep_prompt     db      "Save changes to disk (Y/N)?",0
setup_prompt    db      "Save To:",0

errtxt1         db      "No matching records were found",0
errtxt2         db      "There's not enough room for another record",0
errtxt3         db      "You must delete a record before you can paste it",0
errtxt4         db      "There's not enough room to paste the record",0
errtxt5         db      "There are no records to save",0
errtxt6         db      "Invalid path or file name.  File was not saved.",0
errtxt7         db      "An error occurred while the file was being saved",0
errtxt8         db      "Disk full error.  File was only partially saved.",0
```

```
errtxt9        db      "Invalid path or file name",0
errtxt10       db      "The file was not found or could not be opened",0
errtxt11       db      "The file is too large to fit in the data buffer",0
errtxt12       db      "The file was not created by PC-DIAL",0
errtxt13       db      "An error occurred while the file was being read",0
errtxt14       db      "There's not enough room to edit this record",0
errtxt15       db      "Either your modem is off or there is no modem "
               db      "attached to COMx",0
errtxt16       db      "The address must be a valid hex number",0
errtxt17       db      "The file was not found or could not be opened for "
               db      "writing",0
errtxt18       db      "An error occurred as the setup information was "
               db      "being written",0
errtxt19       db      "There is no COM port at ",4 dup (0)

msg1a          db      "Wait until the phone begins to ring.  Then pick",0
msg1b          db      "up the handset and press any key to disconnect the",0
msg1c          db      "modem from the line.",0

config1        db      "COM Port",0
config2        db      "COM Port Address",0
config3        db      "Communications Setting",0
config4        db      "Initialization Command",0
config5        db      "Dial Command",0
config6        db      "Dial Command Suffix",0
config7        db      "Disconnect Command",0
config8        db      "Dialing Prefix",0

divisor_data   dw      384,384,96,96,48,48      ;Baud rate data values used
               dw      24,24,12,12              ;  to initialize the UART

format_data    db      03h,1Ch,03h,1Ch,03h     ;Data format values used
               db      1Ch,03h,1Ch,03h,1Ch     ;  to initialize the UART

comm_table     db      "300-N81 ",0
               db      "300-E71 ",0
               db      "1200-N81",0
               db      "1200-E71",0
               db      "2400-N81",0
               db      "2400-E71",0
               db      "4800-N81",0
               db      "4800-E71",0
               db      "9600-N81",0
               db      "9600-E71",0

addr_table     db      "3F8",0                  ;COM port addresses
               db      "2F8",0
               db      "3E8",0
               db      "2E8",0

initcmd        db      "ATS11=55M1",7 dup (0)   ;Modem init command
dialcmd        db      "ATDT",13 dup (0)        ;Dial command
suffix         db      ";",16 dup (0)           ;Dial command suffix
hangcmd        db      "ATH0",13 dup (0)        ;Disconnext command
prefix         db      17 dup (0)               ;Dial prefix
comport        db      0                        ;COM port number
```

```
commptr         db      2                       ;Pointer into COMM_TABLE
setup_index     db      0                       ;Setup window index
comstring       db      "COM",0
endcmd          db      13,0

text_table      dw      offset initcmd
                dw      offset dialcmd
                dw      offset suffix
                dw      offset hangcmd
                dw      offset prefix

xerror_ax       dw      ?                       ;Storage array for
xerror_bx       dw      ?                       ;  extended error
xerror_cx       dw      ?                       ;  information
xerror_dx       dw      ?
xerror_si       dw      ?
xerror_di       dw      ?
xerror_ds       dw      ?
xerror_es       dw      ?
                dw      3 dup (0)


;****************************************************************************
; TIMER_INT handles interrupt 08H.
;****************************************************************************

timer_int       proc    far
                pushf                           ;Push FLAGS
                call    cs:[int08h]             ;Call previous handler

                cmp     cs:[counter],0          ;Decrement internal counter
                je      timer0                  ;  if it's not 0 (used by
                dec     cs:[counter]            ;  the DIAL procedure)

timer0:         cmp     cs:[requestflag],0      ;Exit if REQUESTFLAG is
                je      timer_exit              ;  not set

                push    di                      ;Save DI and ES
                push    es
                cmp     cs:[intflags],0         ;Exit if a user interrupt
                jne     timer1                  ;  flag is set
                les     di,cs:[indos]           ;Exit if the InDOS flag
                cmp     byte ptr es:[di],0      ;  is non-zero
                jne     timer1
                les     di,cs:[errorflag]       ;Exit if the critical error
                cmp     byte ptr es:[di],0      ;  flag is non-zero
                jne     timer1
                mov     cs:[requestflag],0      ;Clear REQUESTFLAG
                mov     cs:[popupflag],1        ;Set POPUPFLAG
                call    popup                   ;Pop up the window
                mov     cs:[popupflag],0        ;Clear POPUPFLAG
                jmp     short timer2            ;Exit

timer1:         dec     cs:[requestflag]        ;Decrement counter
timer2:         pop     es                      ;Restore DI and ES
                pop     di
timer_exit:     iret                            ;Return from interrupt
```

```
timer_int       endp

;****************************************************************************
; KB_INT handles interrupt Ø9H.
;****************************************************************************

kb_int          proc    far
                pushf                           ;Push FLAGS
                call    cs:[intØ9h]             ;Call previous handler

                cmp     cs:[popupflag],1        ;Exit now if POPUPFLAG
                je      kb_exit                 ;  is already set

                push    ax                      ;Save AX and ES
                push    es
                mov     ax,4Øh                  ;Point ES to the BIOS
                mov     es,ax                   ;  Data Area
                mov     al,es:[17h]             ;Get keyboard flags
                and     al,ØFh                  ;Zero the upper 4 bits
                cmp     al,Ø9h                  ;Is Alt-Rt Shift pressed?
                pop     es                      ;Restore AX and ES
                pop     ax
                jne     kb_exit                 ;No, then branch

                push    di                      ;Save DI and ES
                push    es
                cmp     cs:[intflags],Ø         ;Exit if a user interrupt
                jne     kb1                     ;  flag is set
                les     di,cs:[indos]           ;Exit if the InDOS flag
                cmp     byte ptr es:[di],Ø      ;  is non-zero
                jne     kb1
                les     di,cs:[errorflag]       ;Exit if the critical error
                cmp     byte ptr es:[di],Ø      ;  flag is non-zero
                jne     kb1
                mov     cs:[requestflag],Ø      ;Clear REQUESTFLAG
                mov     cs:[popupflag],1        ;Set POPUPFLAG
                call    popup                   ;Pop up the window
                mov     cs:[popupflag],Ø        ;Clear POPUPFLAG
                jmp     short kb2               ;Exit

kb1:            mov     requestflag,18          ;Set request flag
kb2:            pop     es                      ;Restore DI and ES
                pop     di
kb_exit:        iret                            ;Return from interrupt
kb_int          endp


;****************************************************************************
; VIDEO_INT handles interrupt 1ØH.
;****************************************************************************

video_int       proc    far
                pushf                           ;Save FLAGS
                or      cs:[intflags],Ø1h       ;Set video interrupt flag
                popf                            ;Retrieve FLAGS
                pushf                           ;Push FLAGS
                call    cs:[int1Øh]             ;Call previous handler
```

```
                pushf                           ;Save FLAGS
                and     cs:[intflags],ØFEh      ;Clear video interrupt flag
                popf                            ;Retrieve FLAGS
                ret     2                       ;Return with FLAGS intact
video_int       endp

;**************************************************************************
; DISK_INT handles interrupt 13H.
;**************************************************************************

disk_int        proc    far
                pushf                           ;Save FLAGS
                or      cs:[intflags],Ø2h       ;Set disk flag
                popf                            ;Retrieve FLAGS
                pushf                           ;Push FLAGS
                call    cs:[int13h]             ;Call previous handler
                pushf                           ;Save FLAGS
                and     cs:[intflags],ØFDh      ;Clear disk flag
                popf                            ;Retrieve FLAGS
                ret     2                       ;Return with FLAGS intact
disk_int        endp

;**************************************************************************
; ERROR_INT handles interrupt 24H (and 1BH and 23H).
;**************************************************************************

error_int       proc    far
                mov     al,Ø3h                  ;Fail the call
error_exit:     iret                            ;Return from interrupt
error_int       endp

;**************************************************************************
; ABS_READ_INT handles interrupt 25H.
;**************************************************************************

abs_read_int    proc    far
                pushf                           ;Save FLAGS
                or      cs:[intflags],Ø4h       ;Set disk flag
                popf                            ;Retrieve FLAGS
                call    cs:[int25h]             ;Call previous handler
                pushf                           ;Save FLAGS
                and     cs:[intflags],ØFBh      ;Clear disk flag
                popf                            ;Retrieve FLAGS
                ret                             ;Return with FLAGS on stack
abs_read_int    endp

;**************************************************************************
; ABS_WRITE_INT handles interrupt 26H.
;**************************************************************************

abs_write_int   proc    far
                pushf                           ;Save FLAGS
                or      cs:[intflags],Ø8h       ;Set disk flag
                popf                            ;Retrieve FLAGS
                call    cs:[int26h]             ;Call previous handler
                pushf                           ;Save FLAGS
```

```
                and     cs:[intflags],ØF7h        ;Clear disk flag
                popf                              ;Retrieve FLAGS
                ret                               ;Return with FLAGS on stack
abs_write_int   endp


;****************************************************************************
; DOSIDLE_INT handles interrupt 28H.
;****************************************************************************

dosidle_int     proc    far
                pushf                             ;Push FLAGS
                call    cs:[int28h]               ;Call previous handler

                cmp     cs:[requestflag],Ø        ;Exit if REQUESTFLAG is
                je      dosidle_exit              ;  not set

                push    di                        ;Save DI and ES
                push    es
                cmp     cs:[intflags],Ø           ;Exit if a user interrupt
                jne     dosidle2                  ;  flag is set
                les     di,cs:[errorflag]         ;Exit if the critical error
                cmp     byte ptr es:[di],Ø        ;  flag is non-zero
                jne     dosidle2
                mov     cs:[requestflag],Ø        ;Clear REQUESTFLAG
                mov     cs:[popupflag],1          ;Set POPUPFLAG
                call    popup                     ;Pop up the window
                mov     cs:[popupflag],Ø          ;Clear POPUPFLAG
dosidle2:       pop     es                        ;Restore DI and ES
                pop     di
dosidle_exit:   iret                              ;Return from interrupt
dosidle_int     endp


;****************************************************************************
; MPLEX_INT handles interrupt 2FH.  If, on entry, AH is set to PC-DIAL's
; multiplex ID number, MPLEX_INT uses the value in AL as a function code.
; The functions supported are:
;
;    ØØH    Returns FFH in AL to indicate the program is installed
;           and returns the address of its signature in ES:DI.
;****************************************************************************

mplex_int       proc    far
                pushf                             ;Save FLAGS register
                cmp     ah,cs:[prog_id]           ;Branch if AH holds the
                je      mplex2                    ;  multiplex ID
                popf                              ;Restore FLAGS
                jmp     cs:[int2Fh]               ;Pass the interrupt on
;
; Function ØØH verifies that the program is installed.
;
mplex2:         popf                              ;Restore FLAGS
                or      al,al                     ;Branch if function code
                jnz     mplex3                    ;  is other than ØØH
                mov     al,ØFFh                   ;Set AL to FFH
                push    cs                        ;Point ES:DI to the program
                pop     es                        ;  signature
```

```
                mov     di,offset signature
mplex3:         iret                            ;Return from interrupt
mplex_int       endp


;****************************************************************************
; POPUP pops up the PC-DIAL window.
;****************************************************************************

popup           proc    near
                cli                             ;Disable interrupts
                mov     cs:[ss_register],ss     ;Save the SS register
                mov     cs:[sp_register],sp     ;Save the SP register
                push    cs                      ;Switch to the internal
                pop     ss                      ;   stack
                mov     sp,offset mystack
                sti                             ;Enable interrupts
                cld                             ;Clear direction flag
                push    ax                      ;Save registers
                push    bx
                push    cx
                push    dx
                push    si
                push    bp
                push    ds
                mov     ax,cs                   ;Point DS to the code
                mov     ds,ax                   ;   segment
                assume  ds:code
;
; Save extended error information available from DOS.
;
                cmp     dosversion,030Ah        ;Skip if not 3.10 or later
                jb      save_psp
                push    ds                      ;Save DS
                mov     ah,59h                  ;Get extended error
                sub     bx,bx                   ;   information
                int     21h
                mov     cs:[xerror_ds],ds       ;Save return value of DS
                pop     ds                      ;Set DS to code segment again
                mov     xerror_ax,ax            ;Save return values in
                mov     xerror_bx,bx            ;   XERROR array
                mov     xerror_cx,cx
                mov     xerror_dx,dx
                mov     xerror_si,si
                mov     xerror_di,di
                mov     xerror_es,es
;
; Save the ID for the active process and make this the active one.
;
save_psp:       mov     ah,51h                  ;Get the PSP address of
                int     21h                     ;   the current process
                mov     oldpsp,bx               ;Save it
                mov     ah,50h                  ;Make this the active
                mov     bx,cs                   ;   process by calling
                int     21h                     ;   DOS function 50H
;
; Vector interrupts 1BH, 23H, and 24H to internal routines.
```

```
;
                mov     ax,351Bh                ;Hook interrupt 1BH
                int     21h
                mov     word ptr int1Bh,bx
                mov     word ptr int1Bh[2],es
                mov     ax,251Bh
                mov     dx,offset error_exit
                int     21h


                mov     ax,3523h                ;Hook interrupt 23H
                int     21h
                mov     word ptr int23h,bx
                mov     word ptr int23h[2],es
                mov     ax,2523h
                mov     dx,offset error_exit
                int     21h


                mov     ax,3524h                ;Hook interrupt 24H
                int     21h
                mov     word ptr int24h,bx
                mov     word ptr int24h[2],es
                mov     ax,2524h
                mov     dx,offset error_int
                int     21h
;
; Get information about the video environment.
;
                mov     ax,40h                  ;Point ES to the BIOS Data
                mov     es,ax                   ;  Area
                mov     al,es:[49h]             ;Get video mode number in AL
                cmp     al,2                    ;Continue if mode number is
                je      popup1                  ;  2, 3, or 7
                cmp     al,3
                je      popup1
                cmp     al,7
                je      popup1
popup_exit:     jmp     end_popup               ;Exit if it's not

popup1:         mov     ax,es:[4Ah]             ;Get number of columns in AX
                cmp     ax,80                   ;Exit if less than 80 are
                jb      popup_exit              ;  displayed
                shl     ax,1                    ;Compute bytes per video line
                mov     line_length,ax          ;Store it in LINE_LENGTH

                mov     ax,es:[4Eh]             ;Get offset address of the
                mov     video_offset,ax         ;  video buffer
                test    byte ptr es:[63h],40h   ;Branch if this is a color
                jnz     popup2                  ;  video mode
                mov     color_ptr,offset mono_table     ;Prepare for mono-
                mov     video_segment,0B000h            ;  chrome if not
                mov     small_cursor,0B0Ch
                mov     big_cursor,080Ch

popup2:         mov     window_start,24         ;Initialize WINDOW_START
                cmp     egaflag,0               ;Branch if this is a CGA
                je      popup3                  ;  or MDA
```

```
                mov     al,es:[84h]             ;Get number of rows displayed
                mov     window_start,al         ;Store it in WINDOW_START
popup3:         sub     window_start,11         ;Compute window location

                mov     ax,es:[60h]             ;Get the cursor mode
                mov     cursor_mode,ax          ;Store it
                mov     dx,es:[63h]             ;Place CRTC address in DX
                mov     bl,es:[62h]             ;Get the active page
                sub     bh,bh                   ;  number in BX
                mov     video_page,bl           ;Save it
                shl     bx,1                    ;Multiply it by 2
                mov     ax,es:[bx+50h]          ;Get the cursor address
                mov     cursor_pos,ax           ;Store it
;
; Save the screen and display the popup window.
;
                mov     ch,window_start         ;Load CX with the address of
                sub     cl,cl                   ;  the upper left corner
                mov     dh,ch                   ;Load DX with the address of
                add     dh,11                   ;  the lower right corner
                mov     dl,79
                push    cx                      ;Save CX and DX
                push    dx
                mov     ax,cs                   ;Point ES:DI to the primary
                mov     es,ax                   ;  screen buffer
                mov     di,offset screenbuffer1
                call    saveregion              ;Save the screen
                pop     dx                      ;Restore CX and DX
                pop     cx

                push    cx                      ;Save CX and DX again
                push    dx
                dec     dh
                mov     bx,color_ptr            ;Load AH with the border's
                mov     ah,border_color         ;  color attribute
                call    drawbox                 ;Draw the window border
                pop     dx                      ;Restore CX and DX
                pop     cx

                push    cx                      ;Save CX and DX yet again
                push    dx
                add     cx,0101h                ;Blank the interior of
                sub     dx,0201h                ;  the window using
                mov     bh,window_color_1       ;  interrupt 10H,
                mov     ax,0600h                ;  function 06H in
                int     10h                     ;  the video BIOS

                mov     dh,window_start         ;Draw the highlight bar
                add     dh,5                    ;  across the center of
                mov     dl,1                    ;  the window
                mov     bx,color_ptr
                mov     al,hilite_color_1
                mov     cx,78
                call    write_attr

                mov     ah,border_color         ;Draw the top of the left
```

```
        mov     al,0C2h              ;   inside vertical bar
        mov     dh,window_start
        mov     dl,29
        call    write_char

        mov     dh,window_start      ;Draw the top of the right
        mov     dl,58                ;   inside vertical bar
        call    write_char

        mov     al,0C1h              ;Draw the bottom of the
        mov     dh,window_start      ;   left inside vertical
        add     dh,10                ;   bar
        mov     dl,29
        call    write_char

        mov     dh,window_start      ;Draw the bottom of the
        add     dh,10                ;   right inside vertical
        mov     dl,58                ;   bar
        call    write_char

        push    ax                   ;Draw the left inside
        mov     dh,window_start      ;   vertical bar
        inc     dh
        mov     dl,29
        call    compute_address
        mov     di,ax
        mov     es,video_segment
        pop     ax
        mov     cx,9
        call    drawvertical

        push    ax                   ;Draw the right inside
        mov     dh,window_start      ;   vertical bar
        inc     dh
        mov     dl,58
        call    compute_address
        mov     di,ax
        pop     ax
        mov     cx,9
        call    drawvertical

        mov     ah,title_color       ;Display "Name" title
        mov     dh,window_start
        mov     dl,12
        mov     si,offset title1
        call    write_string

        mov     dh,window_start      ;Display "Company" title
        mov     dl,39
        mov     si,offset title2
        call    write_string

        mov     dh,window_start      ;Display "Phone" title
        mov     dl,65
        mov     si,offset title3
        call    write_string
```

```
                mov     dh,window_start         ;Display the menu at the
                add     dh,11                   ;  bottom of the window
                sub     dl,dl
                push    dx
                mov     bx,color_ptr
                mov     ah,menu_color2
                mov     si,offset menutext
                call    write_string
                pop     dx
                mov     al,menu_color1
                mov     si,offset menu_cols
                mov     cx,8
popup4:         push    cx
                push    dx
                mov     dl,[si]
                inc     si
                mov     cx,3
                call    write_attr
                pop     dx
                pop     cx
                loop    popup4

                mov     si,bufferptr            ;Point SI to data
                call    showpage                ;Display the data

                mov     ah,01h                  ;Hide the cursor
                mov     cx,2000h
                int     10h
;
; Process keystrokes with the window displayed.
;
getkey:         call    readkey                 ;Read a keystroke
                or      al,al                   ;Branch if it's an extended
                jz      extended                ;  code

                cmp     al,13                   ;Process the Enter key
                jne     escape
                call    dial
                jmp     getkey

escape:         cmp     al,27                   ;Process the Esc key
                jne     tab
                jmp     close

tab:            cmp     al,9                    ;Process the Tab key
                jne     getkey
                call    edit
                cmp     ax,4800h                ;Branch if Up-Arrow was
                je      up                      ;  pressed
                cmp     ax,5000h                ;Branch if Down-Arrow was
                je      down                    ;  pressed
                jmp     getkey
;
; Process extended keycodes.
;
```

```
extended:      cmp     ah,59              ;Process F1 (Setup)
               jne     f2
               call    setup
               jmp     getkey

f2:            cmp     ah,60              ;Process F2 (Search)
               jne     f3
               call    search
               jmp     getkey

f3:            cmp     ah,61              ;Process F3 (Next)
               jne     f4
               call    next
               jmp     getkey

f4:            cmp     ah,62              ;Process F4 (Insert)
               jne     f5
               call    insert
               jmp     getkey

f5:            cmp     ah,63              ;Process F5 (Delete)
               jne     f6
               call    delete
               jmp     getkey

f6:            cmp     ah,64              ;Process F6 (Paste)
               jne     f7
               call    paste
               jmp     getkey

f7:            cmp     ah,65              ;Process F7 (Save)
               jne     f8
               call    save
               jmp     getkey

f8:            cmp     ah,66              ;Process F8 (Open)
               jne     up
               call    open
               jmp     getkey

up:            cmp     ah,72              ;Process the Up-Arrow key
               jne     down
               cmp     recordno,0         ;Ignore if we're already
               je      up1                ;  at the top
               dec     recordno           ;Decrement the record number
               mov     al,1               ;Compute the address of the
               mov     di,bufferptr       ;  record previous to this
               call    findlast           ;  one
               mov     bufferptr,di       ;Save it in BUFFERPTR
               mov     si,di              ;Transfer it to SI
               call    showpage           ;Display the page
up1:           jmp     getkey             ;Return to the input loop

down:          cmp     ah,80              ;Process the Down-Arrow key
               jne     pgup
               mov     ax,recordno        ;Ignore if we're already
```

```
                cmp     ax,records              ;  at the bottom
                je      down1
                inc     recordno                ;Increment the record number
                mov     al,1                    ;Compute the address of the
                mov     di,bufferptr            ;  record following this
                call    findnext                ;  one
                mov     bufferptr,di            ;Save it in BUFFERPTR
                mov     si,di                   ;Transfer it so SI
                call    showpage                ;Display the page
down1:          jmp     getkey                  ;Return to the input loop

pgup:           cmp     ah,73                   ;Process the PgUp key
                jne     pgdn
                cmp     recordno,0              ;Ignore if we're already at
                je      pgup2                   ;  the top
                mov     cx,recordno             ;Compute the new record
                sub     cx,9                    ;  number by subtracting
                cmp     cx,0                    ;  9 and adjusting to 0
                jge     pgup1                   ;  if necessary
                mov     cx,0
pgup1:          mov     ax,recordno             ;Compute the relative
                sub     ax,cx                   ;  displacement
                mov     recordno,cx             ;Store the new record number
                mov     di,bufferptr            ;Retrieve the buffer pointer
                call    findlast                ;Find the address of the new
                mov     bufferptr,di            ;  record and save it
                mov     si,di                   ;Transfer address to SI
                call    showpage                ;Display the page
pgup2:          jmp     getkey                  ;Return to the input loop

pgdn:           cmp     ah,81                   ;Process the PgDn key
                jne     homekey
                mov     ax,recordno             ;Ignore it if we're already
                cmp     ax,records              ;  at the bottom
                je      pgdn2
                add     ax,9                    ;Compute the new record
                cmp     ax,records              ;  number by adding 9 and
                jbe     pgdn1                   ;  adjusting to the highest
                mov     ax,records              ;  number if necessary
pgdn1:          mov     cx,recordno             ;Compute the relative
                mov     recordno,ax             ;  displacement
                sub     ax,cx
                mov     di,bufferptr            ;Retrieve the buffer pointer
                call    findnext                ;Find the address of the new
                mov     bufferptr,di            ;  record and save it
                mov     si,di                   ;Transfer address to SI
                call    showpage                ;Display the page
pgdn2:          jmp     getkey                  ;Return to the input loop

homekey:        cmp     ah,71                   ;Process the Home key
                jne     endkey
                cmp     recordno,0              ;Ignore it if we're already
                je      homekey1                ;  at the top
                mov     recordno,0              ;Set record number to 0
                mov     si,offset databuffer    ;Reset SI and BUFFERPTR
                mov     bufferptr,si
```

```
                call    showpage                ;Display the page
homekey1:       jmp     getkey                  ;Return to the input loop

endkey:         cmp     ah,79                   ;Process the End key
                jne     altchar
                mov     ax,records              ;Ignore it if we're already
                cmp     ax,recordno             ;  at the bottom
                je      endkey1
                mov     recordno,ax             ;Determine the address of
                call    findrec                 ;  the final record
                mov     bufferptr,di            ;Save it in BUFFERPTR
                mov     si,di                   ;Transfer address to SI
                call    showpage                ;Display the page
endkey1:        jmp     getkey                  ;Return to the input loop

altchar:        cmp     ah,16                   ;Branch if scan code is less
                jb      altchar1                ;  than 16 (Alt-Q)
                cmp     ah,50                   ;Also branch if it's greater
                ja      altchar1                ;  than 50 (Alt-M)
                mov     al,ah                   ;Transfer key code to AL
                sub     al,16                   ;Subtract 16 from it
                mov     bx,offset key_table     ;Point BX to table of codes
                xlat                            ;Get the ALth byte from it
                or      al,al                   ;Exit if AL holds 0
                jz      altchar1
                call    qsearch                 ;Do a quick search
altchar1:       jmp     getkey                  ;Return to the input loop
;
; Close the window.
;
close:          pop     dx                      ;Retrieve window coordinates
                pop     cx
                mov     si,offset screenbuffer1 ;Point SI to saved video data
                call    restregion              ;Restore the screen
                mov     ah,02h                  ;Restore the cursor position
                mov     bh,video_page
                mov     dx,cursor_pos
                int     10h
                mov     ah,01h                  ;Restore the cursor mode
                mov     cx,cursor_mode
                int     10h
;
; Reactivate the old PSP, restore interrupt vectors, and restore extended
; error information before exiting.
;
                mov     ah,50h                  ;Reactivate the PSP that was
                mov     bx,oldpsp               ;  current when this process
                int     21h                     ;  took over

                assume  ds:nothing
                mov     ax,251Bh                ;Restore interrupt 1BH
                lds     dx,cs:[int1Bh]          ;  vector
                int     21h
                mov     ax,2523h                ;Restore interrupt 23H
                lds     dx,cs:[int23h]          ;  vector
                int     21h
```

```
                mov     ax,2524h            ;Restore interrupt 24H
                lds     dx,cs:[int24h]      ;  vector
                int     21h

                cmp     cs:[dosversion],030Ah   ;Skip if not 3.10 or later
                jb      end_popup
                mov     ax,cs               ;Make sure DS points to
                mov     ds,ax               ;  this segment
                mov     ax,5D0Ah            ;Restore information with
                mov     dx,offset xerror_ax ;  DOS function 5Dh
                int     21h
;
; Restore register values, restore the stack, and exit.
;
end_popup:      pop     ds
                pop     bp
                pop     si
                pop     dx
                pop     cx
                pop     bx
                pop     ax
                cli
                mov     ss,cs:[ss_register]
                mov     sp,cs:[sp_register]
                sti
                ret
popup           endp

;****************************************************************************
; READKEY reads a keycode from the keyboard buffer.  While it waits for
; a key to be pressed, READKEY generates interrupt 28H over and over to
; give other TSRs a chance to pop up.
;****************************************************************************

readkey         proc    near
                assume  ds:code
                mov     ah,01h              ;Check keyboard buffer and
                int     16h                 ;  branch if it contains
                jnz     rkey1               ;  a keycode
                int     28h                 ;Execute an INT 28H and
                jmp     readkey             ;  loop back
rkey1:          mov     ah,00h              ;Read the keycode and exit
                int     16h
                ret
readkey         endp

;****************************************************************************
; SAVEREGION saves a region of video memory to a user-specified buffer.
; On entry, CX holds the row and column address of the region's upper left
; corner, DX holds the row and column address of the lower right corner,
; and ES:DI points to the buffer where data will be stored.
;****************************************************************************

saveregion      proc    near
                sub     dh,ch               ;Compute the number of rows
                inc     dh                  ;  that will be read and
```

```
                mov     byte ptr rows,dh         ;  buffered
                sub     dl,cl                    ;Then compute the number of
                inc     dl                       ;  columns
                mov     byte ptr columns,dl


                mov     dx,cx                    ;Place starting address in DX
                call    compute_address          ;Compute the memory address
                mov     si,ax                    ;Transfer result to SI
                push    ds                       ;Save DS
                mov     ds,video_segment         ;Point DS to the video buffer
                assume  ds:nothing


                mov     cx,rows                  ;Load CX with row count
sr_loop:        push    cx                       ;Save count
                push    si                       ;Save starting address
                mov     cx,columns               ;Load CX with column count
                rep     movsw                    ;Buffer one row of text
                pop     si                       ;Retrieve SI
                add     si,line_length           ;Point it to the next row
                pop     cx                       ;Rerieve count
                loop    sr_loop                  ;Loop until all rows are done


                pop     ds                       ;Restore DS and exit
                assume  ds:code
                ret
saveregion      endp
```

```
;****************************************************************************
; RESTREGION restores a region of video memory from a user-specified buffer.
; On entry, CX holds the row and column address of the region's upper left
; corner, DX holds the row and column address of the lower right corner,
; and DS:SI points to the buffer the data will be retrieved from.
;****************************************************************************


restregion      proc    near
                sub     dh,ch                    ;Compute the number of rows
                inc     dh                       ;  that will be written
                mov     byte ptr rows,dh         ;
                sub     dl,cl                    ;Then compute the number of
                inc     dl                       ;  columns
                mov     byte ptr columns,dl


                mov     dx,cx                    ;Place starting address in DX
                call    compute_address          ;Compute the memory address
                mov     di,ax                    ;Transfer result to DI
                mov     es,video_segment         ;Point ES to the video buffer


                mov     cx,rows                  ;Load CX with row count
rr_loop:        push    cx                       ;Save count
                push    di                       ;Save starting address
                mov     cx,columns               ;Load CX with column count
                rep     movsw                    ;Buffer one row of text
                pop     di                       ;Retrieve DI
                add     di,line_length           ;Point it to the next row
                pop     cx                       ;Rerieve count
                loop    rr_loop                  ;Loop until all rows are done
```

```
                ret
restregion      endp

;*************************************************************************
; DRAWBOX draws a box in text mode using single-line graphics characters.
; On entry, CX holds the row and column address of the upper left corner,
; and DX holds the row and column address of the lower right corner.  AH
; holds the video attribute used to draw the box.
;*************************************************************************

drawbox         proc    near
                sub     dh,ch                   ;Compute the number of rows
                dec     dh                      ;  inside the box
                mov     byte ptr rows,dh
                sub     dl,cl                   ;Then compute the number of
                dec     dl                      ;  columns
                mov     byte ptr columns,dl

                push    ax                      ;Save video attribute
                mov     dx,cx                   ;Place starting address in DX
                call    compute_address         ;Compute the memory address
                mov     di,ax                   ;Transfer result to DI
                mov     es,video_segment        ;Point ES to the video buffer
                pop     ax                      ;Retrieve video attribute
                push    di                      ;Save video buffer address

                mov     al,0DAh                 ;Draw the upper left corner
                stosw                           ;  of the box
                mov     al,0C4h                 ;Draw the upper horizontal
                mov     cx,columns
                rep     stosw
                mov     al,0BFh                 ;Draw the upper right corner
                stosw                           ;  of the box

                sub     di,2                    ;Point DI to the end of the
                add     di,line_length          ;  second row of the box
                mov     cx,rows                 ;Draw right vertical
                call    drawvertical
                mov     al,0D9h                 ;Draw the lower right corner
                stosw                           ;  of the box

                pop     di                      ;Retrieve address
                add     di,line_length          ;Point DI to the second row
                mov     cx,rows                 ;Draw left vertical
                call    drawvertical
                mov     al,0C0h                 ;Draw the lower left corner
                stosw                           ;  of the box

                mov     al,0C4h                 ;Draw the lower horizontal
                mov     cx,columns
                rep     stosw
                ret
drawbox         endp

;*************************************************************************
; DRAWVERTICAL draws a vertical line.  On entry, ES:DI points to the
```

```
; location in the video buffer, AH holds the video attribute, and CX
; holds the length of the line in rows.
;***********************************************************************

drawvertical    proc    near
                mov     al,0B3h                 ;Load AL with ASCII code
dv_loop:        stosw                           ;Write one character
                sub     di,2                    ;Point DI to the character
                add     di,line_length          ;  cell on the next row
                loop    dv_loop                 ;Loop until done
                ret
drawvertical    endp


;***********************************************************************
; WRITE_STRING writes an ASCIIZ string at the row and column address
; specified in DH and DL.  On entry, AH contains the video attribute and
; DS:SI points to the string.
;***********************************************************************

write_string    proc    near
                push    ax                      ;Save video attribute
                call    compute_address         ;Compute the memory address
                mov     di,ax                   ;Transfer result to DI
                mov     es,video_segment        ;Point ES to the video buffer
                pop     ax                      ;Retrieve video attribute

ws_loop:        lodsb                           ;Get a character
                or      al,al                   ;Exit if it's zero
                jz      ws_exit
                stosw                           ;Display it
                jmp     ws_loop                 ;Loop back for more
ws_exit:        ret
write_string    endp


;***********************************************************************
; WRITE_CHAR writes a character and attribute at the row and column
; address specified in DH and DL.  On entry, AH holds the video attribute
; and AL holds the character's ASCII code.
;***********************************************************************

write_char      proc    near
                push    ax                      ;Save video attribute
                call    compute_address         ;Compute the memory address
                mov     di,ax                   ;Transfer result to DI
                mov     es,video_segment        ;Point ES to the video buffer
                pop     ax                      ;Retrieve video attribute
                stosw                           ;Write the character and
                ret                             ;  attribute and exit
write_char      endp


;***********************************************************************
; SHOW_STRING writes an ASCIIZ string at the row and column address
; specified in DH and DL.  On entry, DS:SI points to the string.  Video
; attributes are preserved.
;***********************************************************************
```

```
show_string      proc    near
                 call    compute_address        ;Compute the memory address
                 mov     di,ax                  ;Transfer result to DI
                 mov     es,video_segment       ;Point ES to the video buffer
ss_loop:         lodsb                          ;Get a character
                 or      al,al                  ;Exit if it's zero
                 jz      ss_exit
                 stosb                          ;Display it
                 inc     di                     ;Skip attribute byte
                 jmp     ss_loop                ;Loop back for more
ss_exit:         ret
show_string      endp

;********************************************************************************
; SHOW_CHAR writes a character only (no attribute) at the row and column
; address specified in DH and DL.  On entry, the character is in AL.
;********************************************************************************

show_char        proc    near
                 push    ax                     ;Save the character
                 call    compute_address        ;Compute the memory address
                 mov     di,ax                  ;Transfer it to DI
                 pop     ax                     ;Retrieve the character
                 mov     es,video_segment       ;Point ES to the video buffer
                 stosb                          ;Display the character
                 ret
show_char        endp


;********************************************************************************
; WRITE_ATTR writes the attribute in AL to the row and column address
; passed in DH and DL.  On entry, CX holds the number of consecutive
; attribute bytes to write.
;********************************************************************************

write_attr       proc    near
                 push    ax                     ;Save video attribute
                 push    cx                     ;Save count
                 call    compute_address        ;Compute the memory address
                 mov     di,ax                  ;Transfer result to DI
                 inc     di                     ;Point DI to attribute bytes
                 mov     es,video_segment       ;Point ES to the video buffer
                 pop     cx                     ;Retrieve count
                 pop     ax                     ;Retrieve video attribute
wa_loop:         stosb                          ;Write one attribute
                 inc     di                     ;Advance DI to next one
                 loop    wa_loop                ;Loop until done
wa_exit:         ret
write_attr       endp


;********************************************************************************
; COMPUTE_ADDRESS returns in AX the video buffer address that corresponds
; to the row and column number passed in DH and DL.  Before this procedure
; is called, LINE_LENGTH must contain the number of bytes per video line
; and VIDEO_OFFSET must contain the offset within the video buffer of the
; current video page.
;********************************************************************************
```

```
compute_address proc    near
                mov     cl,dl                   ;Save DL in CL
                mov     al,dh                   ;Get starting row in AL
                cbw                             ;Convert byte to word in AX
                mul     line_length             ;Multiply by bytes per row
                mov     dl,cl                   ;Load DL with column number
                shl     dx,1                    ;Multiply starting column by 2
                add     ax,dx                   ;Add it to AX
                add     ax,video_offset         ;Add video buffer offset
                ret
compute_address endp

;**********************************************************************
; STRLEN returns the length of the ASCIIZ string pointed to by DS:SI in CX.
;**********************************************************************

strlen          proc    near
                push    si                      ;Save SI
                sub     cx,cx                   ;Initialize count
strlen1:        lodsb                           ;Get a character
                or      al,al                   ;Exit if it's zero
                jz      strlen_exit
                inc     cx                      ;Otherwise increment the
                jmp     strlen1                 ;  count and loop back
strlen_exit:    pop     si                      ;Restore SI and exit
                ret
strlen          endp


;**********************************************************************
; STRCAT appends the ASCIIZ string pointed to by ES:DI to the one at DS:SI.
;**********************************************************************

strcat          proc    near
                call    strlen                  ;Compute the string length
                add     si,cx                   ;Add the result to SI
                xchg    si,di                   ;Exchange SI and DI
                call    copyz                   ;Append the string
                ret
strcat          endp


;**********************************************************************
; EDIT_STRING permits a string to be edited.  On entry, DS:SI points to
; the string, DH and DL identify the row and column where the string is
; displayed, and CX holds the maximum number of characters that will be
; accepted.  If AL is 0 when the routine is called, the cursor is
; positioned at the beginning of the string; if it's 1, the cursor is
; positioned at the end.  If BH is 0 when the routine is called, Tab and
; Shift-Tab are ignored; if BH is 1, Tab and Shift-Tab will terminate input
; If BL is 0 when the routine is called, Up- and Down-Arrow are ignored;  if
; BL is 1, Up- and Down-Arrow will terminate input.
;
; On return, CX holds the length of the string, not including the string
; delimiter at the end, and AX holds the key code for the key that was
; pressed to terminate input.
;
```

```
                ; NOTE: The values of DX (the current row and column numbers) and SI (the
                ; pointer to the current location in the string) are maintained throughout.
                ;*************************************************************************

chars           dw      ?                       ;Character count
maxchars        dw      ?                       ;Maximum number of characters
stringstart     dw      ?                       ;String starting address
stringend       dw      ?                       ;String ending address
insflag         db      ?                       ;0=Insert off, 1=Insert on
tabflag         db      ?                       ;0=Ignore Tab and Shift-Tab
updnflag        db      ?                       ;0=Ignore Up- and Down-Arrow

edit_string     proc    near
                mov     maxchars,cx             ;Initialize pointers and
                mov     stringstart,si          ;  variables
                mov     tabflag,bh
                mov     updnflag,bl
                mov     insflag,0
                push    ax
                call    strlen
                pop     ax
                mov     chars,cx
                mov     stringend,cx
                add     stringend,si
                or      al,al
                jz      edstr1
                add     dl,cl
                add     si,cx
edstr1:         mov     ah,02h                  ;Position the cursor at
                mov     bh,video_page           ;  the beginning or end
                int     10h                     ;  of the string
                mov     ah,01h                  ;Display the cursor
                mov     cx,small_cursor
                int     10h
;
; Wait for a keypress and process conventional key codes.
;
editkey:        call    readkey                 ;Get a key code
                or      al,al                   ;Branch if it's not an
                jnz     ekey1                   ;  extended code
                jmp     ekey10                  ;Jump if it is

ekey1:          cmp     al,8                    ;Process the Backspace key
                jne     ekey2
                cmp     si,stringstart
                je      editkey
                mov     ah,02h
                mov     bh,video_page
                dec     dl
                int     10h
                dec     si
                jmp     ekey16a

ekey2:          cmp     al,9                    ;Process the Tab key
                jne     ekey3
                cmp     tabflag,0
```

```
                je      editkey
ekey2a:         jmp     edstr_exit


ekey3:          cmp     al,13                   ;Process the Enter key
                je      ekey2a


ekey4:          cmp     al,27                   ;Process the Esc key
                je      ekey2a


ekey5:          cmp     insflag,Ø               ;Process a character key
                jne     ekey6                   ;Branch if the character
                cmp     si,stringend            ;  will be inserted
                je      ekey6
                mov     [si],al
                push    dx
                call    show_char
                pop     dx
ekey5a:         inc     dl
                mov     ah,Ø2h
                mov     bh,video_page
                int     1Øh
                inc     si
                jmp     editkey


ekey6:          mov     cx,chars                ;Insert a character at the
                cmp     cx,maxchars             ;  current cursor location
                je      editkey
                mov     cx,stringend
                sub     cx,si
                inc     cx
                push    ax
                push    si
                mov     si,stringend
                mov     di,si
                inc     di
                mov     bx,cs
                mov     es,bx
                std
                rep     movsb
                cld
                pop     si
                pop     ax
                mov     [si],al
                inc     stringend
                inc     chars
                push    dx
                push    si
                call    show_string
                pop     si
                pop     dx
                jmp     ekey5a
;
; Process extended key codes.
;
ekey1Ø:         cmp     ah,15                   ;Process Shift-Tab
                jne     ekey11
```

```
                cmp     tabflag,0
                je      ekey11a
                jmp     edstr_exit

ekey11:         cmp     ah,71                   ;Process the Home key
                jne     ekey12
                mov     cx,si
                sub     cx,stringstart
                mov     ah,02h
                mov     bh,video_page
                sub     dl,cl
                int     10h
                mov     si,stringstart
ekey11a:        jmp     editkey

ekey12:         cmp     ah,75                   ;Process the Left-Arrow key
                jne     ekey13
                cmp     si,stringstart
                je      ekey12a
                mov     ah,02h
                mov     bh,video_page
                dec     dl
                int     10h
                dec     si
ekey12a:        jmp     editkey

ekey13:         cmp     ah,77                   ;Process the Right-Arrow key
                jne     ekey14
                cmp     si,stringend
                je      ekey13a
                mov     ah,02h
                mov     bh,video_page
                inc     dl
                int     10h
                inc     si
ekey13a:        jmp     editkey

ekey14:         cmp     ah,79                   ;Process the End key
                jne     ekey15
                mov     cx,stringend
                sub     cx,si
                mov     ah,02h
                mov     bh,video_page
                add     dl,cl
                int     10h
                mov     si,stringend
                jmp     editkey

ekey15:         cmp     ah,82                   ;Process the Ins key
                jne     ekey16
                xor     insflag,1
                mov     cx,small_cursor
                cmp     insflag,0
                je      ekey15a
                mov     cx,big_cursor
ekey15a:        mov     ah,01h
```

```
                int    10h
                jmp    editkey

ekey16:         cmp    ah,83                  ;Process the Del key
                jne    ekey17
ekey16a:        mov    cx,stringend
                sub    cx,si
                jcxz   ekey16b
                mov    di,si
                mov    bx,cs
                mov    es,bx
                push   si
                inc    si
                rep    movsb
                pop    si
                push   dx
                push   si
                call   show_string
                mov    byte ptr es:[di],32
                pop    si
                pop    dx
                dec    chars
                dec    stringend
ekey16b:        jmp    editkey

ekey17:         cmp    updnflag,0             ;Loop back if Arrow keys
                je     ekey16b               ;  are ignored
                cmp    ah,72                 ;Terminate input if Up-
                je     edstr_exit            ;  Arrow was pressed
                cmp    ah,80                 ;Terminate input if Down-
                jne    ekey16b               ;  Arrow was pressed
;
; Hide the cursor, place the string length in CX, and exit.
;
edstr_exit:     push   ax                    ;Save exit character
                mov    ah,01h                ;Hide the cursor
                mov    ch,20h
                int    10h
                mov    si,stringstart        ;Compute the length of
                call   strlen                ;  the string
                pop    ax                    ;Retrieve exit character
                ret
edit_string     endp


;*********************************************************************
; COPYZ copies an ASCIIZ string from one location to another.  On entry,
; DS:SI points to the string and ES:DI points to its new location.
;*********************************************************************

copyz           proc   near
                lodsb                        ;Get a character
                stosb                        ;Copy it to the destination
                or     al,al                 ;Loop back for more if it
                jnz    copyz                 ;  wasn't a zero
                ret
copyz           endp
```

```
;****************************************************************************
; INSTRING returns carry clear if the string pointed to by DS:SI is a
; subset of the string pointed to by DS:DI, carry set if it's not.  The
; string comparisons are performed without regard to case.
;****************************************************************************

strlength       dw      ?

instring        proc    near
                push    si                      ;Save substring address
                mov     si,di                   ;Compute the length of the
                call    strlen                  ;  primary string
                mov     dx,cx                   ;Save it in DX
                pop     si                      ;Compute the length of the
                call    strlen                  ;  substring
                mov     strlength,cx            ;Save it
                sub     dx,cx                   ;Subtract it from DX
                inc     dx                      ;Increment DX
                mov     cx,dx                   ;Transfer result to CX
                cmp     cx,1                    ;No match if the result is
                jl      instr6                  ;  less than 1 (signed)

instr1:         push    cx
                push    si
                push    di
                mov     cx,strlength

instr2:         lodsb                           ;Get character from string 1
                cmp     al,"a"                  ;Capitalize it if necessary
                jb      instr3
                cmp     al,"z"
                ja      instr3
                and     al,0DFh
instr3:         mov     ah,[di]                 ;Get character from string 2
                inc     di                      ;Advance DI to next character
                cmp     ah,"a"                  ;Capitalize it if necessary
                jb      instr4
                cmp     ah,"z"
                ja      instr4
                and     ah,0DFh
instr4:         cmp     ah,al
                jne     instr5
                loop    instr2
                jmp     instr7

instr5:         pop     di
                inc     di
                pop     si
                pop     cx
                loop    instr1

instr6:         stc                             ;Set carry and exit
                ret

instr7:         add     sp,6                    ;Clean off the stack
```

```
                        clc                             ;Clear carry and exit
                        ret
        instring        endp


        ;*************************************************************************
        ; SHOWPAGE displays a page of data with record number RECORDNO in the
        ; center of the window.  On entry, DS:SI must point to the address of
        ; record number RECORDNO.
        ;*************************************************************************

        nullrec         db      0,0,0
        blanklines      dw      ?
        linesback       db      ?
        lines           dw      ?

        showpage        proc    near
                        mov     dh,window_start         ;Set DH to the starting
                        inc     dh                      ;  row number
                        mov     blanklines,0            ;Initialize variables
                        mov     linesback,4
                        mov     lines,9
                        cmp     records,0               ;Exit if there are no
                        je      sp_exit                 ;  records to display

                        mov     cx,4                    ;Compute the number of blank
                        sub     cx,recordno             ;  lines at the top of the
                        cmp     cx,0                    ;  window
                        jle     sp2                     ;Branch if it's less than 0

                        sub     linesback,cl            ;Adjust LINESBACK
                        sub     lines,cx                ;Adjust LINES
                        push    si                      ;Save address in SI
        sp1:            push    cx                      ;Save CX and DX
                        push    dx
                        mov     si,offset nullrec       ;Point SI to null record
                        call    showline                ;Blank one line
                        pop     dx                      ;Retrieve DX
                        inc     dh                      ;Increment line number
                        pop     cx                      ;Retrieve count in CX
                        loop    sp1                     ;Loop until done
                        pop     di                      ;Restore SI into DI

        sp2:            mov     al,linesback            ;Compute the address of the
                        mov     di,bufferptr            ;  first record to be
                        call    findlast                ;  displayed
                        mov     si,di

                        mov     cx,recordno             ;Compute the number of blank
                        add     cx,5                    ;  lines at the bottom of
                        sub     cx,records              ;  the window
                        cmp     cx,0                    ;Branch if the result is
                        jle     sp3                     ;  less than 0
                        mov     blanklines,cx           ;Save it
                        sub     lines,cx                ;Adjust LINES

        sp3:            mov     cx,lines                ;Place line count in CX
```

```
sp4:            push    cx                      ;Save CX and DX
                push    dx
                call    showline                ;Display one line
                pop     dx                      ;Retrieve DX
                inc     dh                      ;Increment line number
                pop     cx                      ;Retrieve count in CX
                loop    sp4                     ;Loop until done

                mov     cx,blanklines           ;Retrieve blank line count
                jcxz    sp_exit                 ;Exit if zero
sp5:            push    cx                      ;Save CX and DX
                push    dx
                mov     si,offset nullrec       ;Point SI to null record
                call    showline                ;Display one blank line
                pop     dx                      ;Retrieve DX
                inc     dh                      ;Increment line number
                pop     cx                      ;Retrieve count in CX
                loop    sp5                     ;Loop until done
sp_exit:        ret
showpage        endp


;***************************************************************************
; SHOWLINE displays a line of data.  On entry, DS:SI points to the record
; and DH identifies the line on which it will be displayed.
;***************************************************************************

showline        proc    near
                mov     dl,2                    ;Place column number in DL
                call    compute_address         ;Compute the address
                mov     di,ax                   ;Transfer it to DI
                mov     es,video_segment        ;Point ES to video
                mov     cx,26                   ;Display the name field
                call    showfield
                add     di,6                    ;Advance DI
                mov     cx,26                   ;Display the company field
                call    showfield
                add     di,6                    ;Advance DI
                mov     cx,18                   ;Display the phone field
                call    showfield
                ret
showline        endp


;***************************************************************************
; SHOWFIELD displays one zero-delimited field.  On entry, ES:DI points
; to the address in the video buffer, DS:SI points to the data, and CX
; holds the length of the field.  If the length of the text string is
; less than the length of the field, the extra character cells are
; filled with spaces.  On exit, SI points to the start of the next field.
;***************************************************************************

showfield       proc    near
                lodsb                           ;Get a character
                or      al,al                   ;Exit if it's zero
                jz      sf2
                stosb                           ;Display it
                inc     di                      ;Skip attribute byte
```

```
               loop      showfield               ;Loop if CX isn't zero
sf1:           lodsb                              ;Get a character
               or        al,al                    ;Loop back it's not zero
               jnz       sf1
sf2:           jcxz      sf_exit                  ;Exit if CX is zero
               mov       al,20h                   ;Place space in AL
sf3:           stosb                              ;Write one space
               inc       di                       ;Skip attribute byte
               loop      sf3                      ;Loop until done
sf_exit:       ret
showfield      endp


;***************************************************************************
; FINDREC returns in DI the address of the record whose number is passed
; in AX.
;***************************************************************************

three          db        3,0

findrec        proc      near
               mov       di,offset databuffer     ;Point DI to the data
               mov       bx,cs                    ;Point ES to the segment
               mov       es,bx                    ;  where the data is stored
               mul       word ptr three           ;Multiply AX by 3
               mov       cx,ax                    ;Transfer result to CX
               sub       al,al                    ;Zero AL
fr1:           push      cx                       ;Save count
               mov       cx,255                   ;Initialize CX
               repne     scasb                    ;Search for the next 0
               pop       cx                       ;Retrieve count
               loop      fr1                      ;Loop until done
               ret
findrec        endp


;***************************************************************************
; FINDLAST computes the address of a record relative to a specified record
; whose address is passed in DI.  On entry, the value of AL specifies the
; relative position of the desired record.  On exit, DI holds its address.
;***************************************************************************

findlast       proc      near
               mul       three                    ;Multiply AL by 3
               mov       cx,ax                    ;Transfer result to CX
               inc       cx                       ;Increment it
               mov       ax,cs                    ;Point ES to this segment
               mov       es,ax
               dec       di                       ;Decrement DI
               sub       al,al                    ;Zero AL
               std                                ;Set direction flag
fl1:           push      cx                       ;Save counter
               mov       cx,255                   ;Reset CX
               repne     scasb                    ;Search for a 0
               pop       cx                       ;Retrieve counter
               loop      fl1                      ;Loop until done
               add       di,2                     ;Add 2 for record address
               cld                                ;Clear direction flag
```

```
                    ret                             ;Return to caller
        findlast    endp


;****************************************************************************
; FINDNEXT computes the address of a record relative to a specified record
; whose address is passed in DI.  On entry, the value of AL specifies the
; relative position of the desired record.  On exit, DI holds its address.
;****************************************************************************

        findnext    proc    near
                    mul     three               ;Multiply AL by 3
                    mov     cx,ax               ;Transfer result to CX
                    mov     ax,cs               ;Point ES to this segment
                    mov     es,ax
                    sub     al,al               ;Zero AL
        fn1:        push    cx                  ;Save counter
                    mov     cx,255              ;Reset CX
                    repne   scasb               ;Search for a 0
                    pop     cx                  ;Retrieve counter
                    loop    fn1                 ;Loop until done
                    ret                         ;Return to caller
        findnext    endp


;****************************************************************************
; QSEARCH displays the next record that starts with the ASCII code in AL.
;****************************************************************************

        qsearch     proc    near
                    mov     ah,al               ;Transfer code to AH
                    or      ah,20h              ;Convert it to lowercase
                    mov     bx,recordno         ;Initialize BX and DI for
                    mov     di,bufferptr        ;  the search
                    mov     cx,cs               ;Points ES to the segment
                    mov     es,cx               ;  where data is stored

        qs1:        push    ax                  ;Save ASCII codes
                    call    nextrec             ;Advance to the next record
                    pop     ax                  ;Retrieve ASCII codes
                    cmp     bx,recordno         ;Exit if we've reached the
                    je      qsearch_exit        ;  current record
                    cmp     [di],al             ;Branch if the name field
                    je      qs2                 ;  starts with the code in
                    cmp     [di],ah             ;  AH or AL
                    je      qs2
                    jmp     qs1                 ;Loop back if it doesn't

        qs2:        mov     recordno,bx         ;Store the record number
                    mov     bufferptr,di        ;Store the address also
                    mov     si,di               ;Transfer address to SI
                    call    showpage            ;Display the record
        qsearch_exit: ret
        qsearch     endp


;****************************************************************************
; NEXTREC accepts a record number in BX and the corresponding record
; address in DI, then returns the next record number and its address in
```

```
; the same registers.  On entry, ES must point to the segment where data
; is stored.
;***********************************************************************

nextrec         proc    near
                inc     bx                      ;Increment record number
                cmp     bx,records              ;Branch if it's equal to
                jae     reset                   ;   the number of records

                sub     al,al                   ;Zero AL
                mov     cx,255                  ;Initialize CX
                repne   scasb                   ;Advance to the next zero...
                repne   scasb                   ;And the next...
                repne   scasb                   ;And the next
                ret                             ;Return to caller

reset:          sub     bx,bx                   ;Set record number to 0
                mov     di,offset databuffer    ;Point DI to the base
                ret                             ;Return to caller
nextrec         endp


;***********************************************************************
; SETUP lets the program be configured interactively.
;***********************************************************************

nine            db      9
changed         db      ?
exitcode        dw      ?
spaces          db      27 dup (32),0

setup           proc    near
                mov     changed,0               ;Initialize changed flag
                mov     bx,color_ptr            ;Place attributes in AH,
                mov     ah,border_color         ;   AL, and BH
                mov     al,window_color_2
                mov     bh,shadow_color
                mov     ch,window_start         ;Load CX with the window's
                sub     ch,4                    ;   starting coordinates
                mov     cl,17
                mov     dh,ch                   ;Load DX with the window's
                add     dh,9                    ;   ending coordinates
                mov     dl,62
                push    cx                      ;Save window coordinates
                push    dx
                push    cs                      ;Point ES:DI to the buffer
                pop     es                      ;   for screen data
                mov     di,offset screenbuffer2
                call    openwindow              ;Display the window

                mov     dh,window_start         ;Compute row and column
                sub     dh,3                    ;   address to begin
                mov     dl,19                   ;   writes
                push    dx                      ;Save row and column
                mov     si,offset config1       ;Point DS:SI to the text
                call    show_string             ;Display "COM Port" string
                pop     dx                      ;Retrieve row and column
```

```
        inc     dh                      ;Display "COM Port Address"
        push    dx
        mov     si,offset config2
        call    show_string
        pop     dx

        inc     dh                      ;Display "Communications
        push    dx                      ;  Setting"
        mov     si,offset config3
        call    show_string
        pop     dx

        inc     dh                      ;Display "Initialization
        push    dx                      ;  Command"
        mov     si,offset config4
        call    show_string
        pop     dx

        inc     dh                      ;Display "Dial Command"
        push    dx
        mov     si,offset config5
        call    show_string
        pop     dx

        inc     dh                      ;Display "Dial Command
        push    dx                      ;  Suffix"
        mov     si,offset config6
        call    show_string
        pop     dx

        inc     dh                      ;Display "Disconnect Command"
        push    dx
        mov     si,offset config7
        call    show_string
        pop     dx

        inc     dh                      ;Display "Dialing Prefix"
        mov     si,offset config8
        call    show_string

        mov     dh,window_start         ;Display the COM port
        sub     dh,3                    ;  number
        mov     dl,45
        push    dx
        mov     si,offset comstring
        call    show_string
        mov     al,comport
        add     al,31h
        stosb
        pop     dx

        inc     dh                      ;Display COM port address
        push    dx
        mov     al,comport
        cbw
```

```
            shl     ax,1
            shl     ax,1
            add     ax,offset addr_table
            mov     si,ax
            call    show_string
            pop     dx

            inc     dh                      ;Display communications
            push    dx                      ;  setting
            mov     al,commptr
            mul     nine
            add     ax,offset comm_table
            mov     si,ax
            call    show_string
            pop     dx

            inc     dh                      ;Display initialization
            push    dx                      ;  command
            mov     si,offset initcmd
            call    show_string
            pop     dx

            inc     dh                      ;Display dial command
            push    dx
            mov     si,offset dialcmd
            call    show_string
            pop     dx

            inc     dh                      ;Display dial command
            push    dx                      ;  suffix
            mov     si,offset suffix
            call    show_string
            pop     dx

            inc     dh                      ;Display disconnect
            push    dx                      ;  command
            mov     si,offset hangcmd
            call    show_string
            pop     dx

            inc     dh                      ;Display dialing prefix
            push    dx
            mov     si,offset prefix
            call    show_string
            pop     dx
;
; Take input from the keyboard.
;
setup1:     mov     bx,color_ptr            ;Draw the selection bar at
            mov     al,hilite_color_2       ;  the location addressed
            mov     cx,44                   ;  by SETUP_INDEX
            mov     dh,window_start
            add     dh,setup_index
            sub     dh,3
            mov     dl,18
            call    write_attr
```

```
setup2:         call    readkey                 ;Get a keystroke
                or      al,al                   ;Branch if it's an extended
                jnz     setup2z                 ;   key code
                jmp     setup3
setup2z:        cmp     al,27                   ;Exit if Esc was pressed
                jne     setup2a
                jmp     setup_exit
setup2a:        cmp     al,9                    ;Branch if Tab, Enter, or
                je      setup2b                 ;   spacebar was pressed
                cmp     al,13
                je      setup2b
                cmp     al,32
                jne     setup2                  ;Ignore anything else

setup2b:        cmp     setup_index,0           ;Branch if SETUP_INDEX is
                je      setup2c                 ;   either 0 or 2
                cmp     setup_index,2
                jne     setup2d
setup2c:        jmp     setup6a

setup2d:        cmp     setup_index,1           ;Branch if SETUP_INDEX is
                je      get_address             ;   other than 1
                jmp     get_string
;
; Input a COM port address.
;
get_address:    mov     al,comport              ;Compute the address of the
                cbw                             ;   string that denotes the
                shl     ax,1                    ;   COM port address
                shl     ax,1
                add     ax,offset addr_table
                push    ax                      ;Save it
                mov     si,ax                   ;Transfer it to AX
                mov     di,offset inbuffer      ;Point DI to input buffer
                mov     bx,cs                   ;Point ES to this segment
                mov     es,bx
                call    copyz                   ;Copy string to input buffer

getaddr1:       mov     al,01h                  ;Prepare for call to
                mov     bx,01h                  ;   EDIT_STRING
                mov     cx,3
                mov     dh,window_start
                sub     dh,2
                mov     dl,45
                mov     si,offset inbuffer
                call    edit_string             ;Let the string be edited
                mov     exitcode,ax             ;Save the exit code

                cmp     al,27                   ;Branch if ESC was not
                jne     getaddr2                ;   pressed
                mov     dh,window_start         ;Redisplay the old COM
                sub     dh,2                    ;   port address and exit
                mov     dl,45
                push    dx
                mov     si,offset spaces+24
```

```
                        call    show_string
                        pop     dx
                        pop     si
                        call    show_string
                        jmp     setup2

getaddr2:               mov     changed,1               ;Set CHANGED flag
                        mov     si,offset inbuffer       ;Convert the address just
                        call    hex2bin                 ;  entered to binary
                        jnc     getaddr3                ;Branch if call succeeded

                        mov     ah,01h                  ;Turn off the cursor
                        mov     ch,20h
                        int     10h
                        mov     si,offset errtxt16      ;Point SI to error message
                        mov     di,offset screenbuffer3 ;Point DI to buffer area
                        call    strlen                  ;Get message length in CX
                        add     cx,3                    ;Add 3 to it
                        call    msg_window              ;Display the error message
                        jmp     getaddr1                ;Reenter the input loop

getaddr3:               pop     di                      ;Retrieve string address
                        push    di                      ;Save it on the stack again
                        mov     bx,cs                   ;Point ES to this segment
                        mov     es,bx
                        call    bin2hex                 ;Convert binary to ASCIIZ
                        mov     dh,window_start         ;Blank the string currently
                        sub     dh,2                    ;  displayed
                        mov     dl,45
                        push    dx
                        mov     si,offset spaces+24
                        call    show_string
                        pop     dx                      ;Then redisplay the ASCII
                        pop     si                      ;  equivalent of the number
                        call    show_string             ;  just entered and exit
                        cmp     exitcode,4800h
                        je      getstr2
                        cmp     exitcode,5000h
                        je      getstr3
                        jmp     setup2
;
; Input a modem command string.
;
get_string:             mov     bl,setup_index          ;Compute offset address of
                        sub     bl,3                    ;  the string to be edited
                        sub     bh,bh
                        shl     bx,1
                        mov     si,[bx+offset text_table]
                        push    si                      ;Save it
                        mov     di,offset inbuffer      ;Point DI to input buffer
                        mov     bx,cs                   ;Point ES to this segment
                        mov     es,bx
                        call    copyz                   ;Copy string to input buffer

                        mov     al,01h                  ;Prepare for call to
                        mov     bx,01h                  ;  EDIT_STRING
```

```
                mov     cx,16
                mov     dh,window_start
                sub     dh,3
                add     dh,setup_index
                mov     dl,45
                mov     si,offset inbuffer
                call    edit_string                 ;Let the string be edited

                pop     di                          ;Retrieve its address in DI
                cmp     al,27                       ;Branch if the Esc key was
                jne     getstr1                     ;  not pressed
                mov     dh,window_start            ;Otherwise redisplay the
                sub     dh,3                        ;  original string and
                add     dh,setup_index             ;  return to the input
                mov     dl,45                       ;  loop
                push    dx
                push    di
                mov     si,offset spaces+11
                call    show_string
                pop     si
                pop     dx
                call    show_string
                jmp     setup2

getstr1:        mov     changed,1                  ;Set CHANGED flag
                mov     bx,ax                      ;Save exit code in BX
                mov     si,offset inbuffer         ;Copy the new string to the
                mov     ax,cs                      ;  original string address
                mov     es,ax
                call    copyz
                cmp     bx,4800h                   ;Branch if input was termin-
getstr2:        je      setup3a                    ;  ated with Up-Arrow
                cmp     bx,5000h                   ;Also branch if it was term-
getstr3:        je      setup4a                    ;  inated with Down-Arrow
                jmp     setup2                     ;Return to input loop
;
; Process the Up- and Down-Arrow keys.
;
setup3:         cmp     ah,72                      ;Process the Up-Arrow key
                jne     setup4
setup3a:        mov     bx,color_ptr               ;Erase the selection bar
                mov     al,window_color_2
                mov     cx,44
                mov     dh,window_start
                add     dh,setup_index
                sub     dh,3
                mov     dl,18
                call    write_attr
                dec     setup_index                ;Decrement index
                cmp     setup_index,0FFFFh
                jne     setup3b
                mov     setup_index,7
setup3b:        jmp     setup1

setup4:         cmp     ah,80                      ;Process the Down-Arrow key
                jne     setup5
```

```
setup4a:        mov     bx,color_ptr                ;Erase the selection bar
                mov     al,window_color_2
                mov     cx,44
                mov     dh,window_start
                add     dh,setup_index
                sub     dh,3
                mov     dl,18
                call    write_attr
                inc     setup_index                 ;Increment index
                cmp     setup_index,8
                jne     setup4b
                mov     setup_index,0
setup4b:        jmp     setup1
;
; Process the Left- and Right-Arrow keys.
;
setup5:         cmp     ah,75                       ;Process the Left-Arrow key
                jne     setup6
                mov     dh,window_start             ;Initialize DX with row and
                sub     dh,3                        ;  column number
                mov     dl,45
                cmp     setup_index,0               ;Branch if SETUP_INDEX is
                jne     setup5a                     ;  other than 0
                mov     changed,1                   ;Set CHANGED flag
                dec     comport                     ;Decrement COM port number
                cmp     comport,0FFFFh
                jne     setup6b
                mov     comport,3
                jmp     short setup6b               ;Go display the setting

setup5a:        cmp     setup_index,2               ;Branch if SETUP_INDEX is
                jne     setup6c                     ;  other than 2
                mov     changed,1                   ;Set CHANGED flag
                dec     commptr                     ;Decrement the pointer to
                cmp     commptr,0FFh                ;  communications settings
                jne     setup6e
                mov     commptr,9
                jmp     short setup6e               ;Go display the new setting

setup6:         cmp     ah,77                       ;Process the Right-Arrow key
                jne     setup6c
setup6a:        mov     dh,window_start             ;Initialize DX with row and
                sub     dh,3                        ;  column number
                mov     dl,45
                cmp     setup_index,0               ;Branch if SETUP_INDEX is
                jne     setup6d                     ;  other than 0
                mov     changed,1                   ;Set CHANGED flag
                inc     comport                     ;Increment the COM port
                cmp     comport,4                   ;  number
                jne     setup6b
                mov     comport,0
setup6b:        push    dx                          ;Display the COM port number
                add     dl,3
                mov     al,comport
                add     al,31h
                call    show_char
```

```
                    pop     dx
                    inc     dh                      ;Display COM port address
                    push    dx
                    mov     si,offset spaces+24
                    call    show_string
                    pop     dx
                    mov     al,comport
                    cbw
                    shl     ax,1
                    shl     ax,1
                    add     ax,offset addr_table
                    mov     si,ax
                    call    show_string
setup6c:            jmp     setup2                  ;Return to input loop

setup6d:            cmp     setup_index,2           ;Branch if SETUP_INDEX is
                    jne     setup6f                 ;  other than 2
                    mov     changed,1               ;Set CHANGED flag
                    inc     commptr                 ;Increment the pointer to
                    cmp     commptr,10              ;  communications settings
                    jne     setup6e
                    mov     commptr,0
setup6e:            mov     al,commptr              ;Display the new settings
                    mul     nine
                    add     ax,offset comm_table
                    mov     si,ax
                    add     dh,2
                    call    show_string
setup6f:            jmp     setup2                  ;Return to input loop
;
; Save the changes, close the window, and exit.
;
setup_exit:         cmp     changed,0               ;Exit now if there were
                    jne     setup9                  ;  no changes
                    jmp     setup_close

setup9:             mov     bx,color_ptr            ;Place attributes in AH,
                    mov     ah,border_color         ;  AL, and BH
                    mov     al,window_color_2
                    mov     bh,shadow_color
                    mov     ch,window_start         ;Load CX with the window's
                    add     ch,4                    ;  starting coordinates
                    mov     cl,5
                    mov     dh,ch                   ;Load DX with the window's
                    add     dh,2                    ;  ending coordinates
                    mov     dl,74
                    push    cx                      ;Save window coordinates
                    push    dx
                    push    cs                      ;Point ES:DI to the buffer
                    pop     es                      ;  for screen data
                    mov     di,offset screenbuffer3
                    call    openwindow              ;Display the window

                    mov     dh,window_start         ;Compute row and column
                    add     dh,5                    ;  address for message
                    mov     dl,26
```

```
                mov     si,offset keep_prompt      ;Prompt "Save changes to
                call    show_string                ;   disk (Y/N)?"

setup10:        call    readkey                    ;Get an answer to the
                or      al,al                      ;   question
                jz      setup10                    ;Loop back on extended key
                cmp     al,27                      ;Branch if the Esc key was
                jne     setup10a                   ;   not pressed
                pop     dx                         ;Close the prompt window
                pop     cx                         ;   by restoring what was
                add     dx,0101h                   ;   under it
                mov     si,offset screenbuffer3
                call    restregion
                jmp     setup2                     ;Return to setup window
setup10a:       and     al,0DFh                    ;Capitalize the response
                cmp     al,"Y"                     ;Continue if it's "Y"
                je      setup11
                cmp     al,"N"                     ;Exit if it's "N" or loop
                jne     setup10                    ;   back if it's not
                jmp     setup17

setup11:        mov     dh,window_start            ;Compute row and column
                add     dh,5                       ;   address
                mov     dl,26
                mov     si,offset spaces           ;Erase the prompt from the
                call    show_string                ;   window
                mov     dh,window_start
                add     dh,5
                mov     dl,7
                push    dx
                mov     si,offset setup_prompt     ;Display "Save To:" prompt
                call    show_string

                mov     si,offset progfile         ;Point SI to the file name
                call    strlen                     ;Compute the string length
                cmp     cx,57                      ;Branch if it's <= 57
                jna     setup12
                mov     progfile,0                 ;Erase it if it's not
setup12:        mov     di,offset inbuffer         ;Point DI to input buffer
                mov     ax,cs                      ;Point ES to this segment
                mov     es,ax
                call    copyz                      ;Copy file name to buffer

                pop     dx                         ;Display the file name
                add     dl,9                       ;   used the last time
                push    dx                         ;   changes were saved
                mov     si,offset progfile
                call    show_string
                pop     dx                         ;Prepare for call to
                mov     al,01h                     ;   EDIT_STRING
                mov     bx,00h
                mov     cx,57
                mov     si,offset inbuffer
                call    edit_string                ;Input the file name
                mov     exitcode,ax                ;Save the exit code
                pop     dx                         ;Close the prompt window
```

```
                pop     cx                      ;  by restoring what was
                add     dx,0101h                ;  under it
                mov     si,offset screenbuffer3
                call    restregion
                cmp     byte ptr exitcode,27    ;Loop back if input was
                je      setup_return            ;  ended with the Esc key

                mov     si,offset inbuffer      ;Convert the file name
                mov     di,offset progfile      ;  into a fully qualified
                mov     ax,cs                   ;  file name
                mov     es,ax
                mov     ah,60h
                int     21h
                mov     si,offset errtxt9       ;Branch if an error
                jc      setup_err               ;  occurred

                call    savesetup               ;Save the configuration
                jnc     setup_close             ;  changes

                mov     si,offset errtxt17      ;Point SI to error message
                cmp     al,01H
                je      setup_err
                mov     si,offset errtxt18
setup_err:      mov     di,offset screenbuffer3 ;Point DI to buffer area
                call    strlen                  ;Get message length in CX
                add     cx,3                    ;Add 3 to it
                call    msg_window              ;Display the error message
setup_return:   jmp     setup2                  ;Go back for more

setup_close:    pop     dx                      ;Close the window by
                pop     cx                      ;  restoring what was
                add     dx,0101h                ;  under it
                mov     si,offset screenbuffer2
                call    restregion
setup_end:      ret

setup17:        pop     dx                      ;Close the prompt window
                pop     cx                      ;  by restoring what was
                add     dx,0101h                ;  under it
                mov     si,offset screenbuffer3
                call    restregion
                jmp     setup_close
setup           endp

;****************************************************************************
; SEARCH searches for the first record containing a specified string.
;****************************************************************************

recaddress      dw      ?
searchcount     dw      ?

search          proc    near
                mov     si,offset searchtext    ;Point SI to search string
                mov     di,offset inbuffer      ;Point DI to input buffer
                mov     ax,cs                   ;Point ES to this segment
                mov     es,ax
```

```
            call    copyz                   ;Copy the search string

            mov     ch,26                   ;Prepare for call to
            mov     cl,41                   ;  PROMPT_WINDOW
            mov     si,offset search_prompt
            mov     di,offset inbuffer
            call    prompt_window           ;Input the search string

            cmp     al,13                   ;Exit if input wasn't ended
            jne     setup_end               ;  with the Enter key
            mov     si,offset inbuffer      ;Point SI to input buffer
            mov     di,offset searchtext    ;Point DI to search string
            mov     ax,cs                   ;Point ES to this segment
            mov     es,ax
            call    copyz                   ;Copy the search string

            mov     si,offset searchtext    ;Point SI to search string
            call    strlen                  ;Compute its length in CX
            or      cx,cx                   ;Exit if there is no
            jz      search_exit             ;  search string
            cmp     records,0               ;Exit if there are no
            je      search_exit             ;  records to search

search1:    mov     bx,recordno             ;Initialize BX and DI
            mov     di,bufferptr
            mov     cx,records              ;Initialize counter
            mov     searchcount,cx

search2:    call    nextrec                 ;Advance to the next record
            mov     recaddress,di           ;Save the record address
            mov     si,offset searchtext    ;Point SI to search string
            push    di
            call    instring                ;Compare the search string to
            pop     di                      ;  the Name field and branch
            jnc     search3                 ;  if there's a match
            sub     al,al                   ;Find the beginning of the
            mov     cx,255                  ;  Company field
            repne   scasb
            mov     si,offset searchtext    ;Point SI to search string
            push    di
            call    instring                ;Search the field
            pop     di
            jnc     search3                 ;Branch if there's a match
            sub     al,al                   ;Find the beginning of the
            mov     cx,255                  ;  Phone field
            repne   scasb
            mov     si,offset searchtext    ;Point SI to search string
            push    di
            call    instring                ;Search the field
            pop     di
            jnc     search3                 ;Branch if there's a match

            dec     searchcount             ;Decrement counter
            jz      search4                 ;Exit if it has reached zero
            mov     di,recaddress           ;Retrieve record address
            jmp     search2                 ;Continue the search
```

```
search3:        mov     recordno,bx             ;Store the record number
                mov     di,recaddress           ;Retrieve the record address
                mov     bufferptr,di            ;Store the address also
                mov     si,di                   ;Transfer address to SI
                call    showpage                ;Display the record
                ret

search4:        mov     si,offset errtxt1       ;Point SI to error message
                mov     di,offset screenbuffer2 ;Point DI to buffer area
                call    strlen                  ;Get message length in CX
                add     cx,3                    ;Add 3 to it
                call    msg_window              ;Display the error message
search_exit:    ret
search          endp


;**************************************************************************
; NEXT searches for the next record containing a specified string.
;**************************************************************************

next            proc    near
                cmp     records,0               ;Exit if there are no
                je      next_exit               ;  records to search
                mov     ax,cs                   ;Point ES to this segment
                mov     es,ax
                cmp     searchtext,0            ;Branch if the search string
                je      next1                   ;  isn't null
                jmp     search1
next1:          mov     bx,recordno             ;Place record number if BX
                mov     di,bufferptr            ;Place record address in DI
                call    nextrec                 ;Find the next record
                mov     bufferptr,di            ;Save its address
                mov     recordno,bx             ;Save its number
                mov     si,di                   ;Transfer address to SI
                call    showpage                ;Display the next record
next_exit:      ret
next            endp


;**************************************************************************
; INSERT inserts a new (blank) record at the current position.
;**************************************************************************

insert          proc    near
                mov     ax,recordno             ;Exit if we're just past
                cmp     ax,records              ;  the final record
                je      ins_exit

                mov     ax,bufferlimit          ;Compute the number of bytes
                sub     ax,buffertop            ;  left in the buffer
                cmp     ax,3                    ;Branch if it's more than 3
                ja      insert1
                mov     si,offset errtxt2       ;Point SI to error message
                mov     di,offset screenbuffer2 ;Point DI to buffer area
                call    strlen                  ;Get message length in CX
                add     cx,3                    ;Add 3 to it
                call    msg_window              ;Display the error message
```

```
                ret                          ;  and exit

insert1:        mov     si,buffertop         ;Point SI to data to move
                dec     si
                mov     di,si                ;Point DI to destination
                add     di,3                 ;  (three bytes higher)
                mov     ax,cs                ;Point ES to this segment
                mov     es,ax
                mov     cx,buffertop         ;Compute number of bytes
                sub     cx,bufferptr         ;  to move in CX
                std                          ;Set direction flag
                rep     movsb                ;Perform the move
                cld                          ;Clear direction flag
                add     buffertop,3          ;Adjust BUFFERTOP
                inc     records              ;Increment record count
                mov     si,bufferptr         ;Load SI with BUFFERPTR
                mov     byte ptr [si],0      ;Insert three zeroes
                mov     byte ptr [si+1],0
                mov     byte ptr [si+2],0
                call    showpage             ;Display the page
ins_exit:       ret
insert          endp


;****************************************************************************
; PASTE inserts the most recently deleted record.
;****************************************************************************

paste           proc    near
                cmp     recordlength,0       ;Branch if there is a
                jne     paste1               ;  record to paste
                mov     si,offset errtxt3    ;Point SI to error message
                mov     di,offset screenbuffer2 ;Point DI to buffer area
                call    strlen               ;Get message length in CX
                add     cx,3                 ;Add 3 to it
                call    msg_window           ;Display the error message
                ret                          ;  and exit

paste1:         mov     cx,bufferlimit       ;Compute the number of bytes
                sub     cx,buffertop         ;  left in the buffer
                cmp     cx,recordlength      ;Branch if it's more than the
                ja      paste2               ;  length of the paste record
                mov     si,offset errtxt4    ;Point SI to error message
                mov     di,offset screenbuffer2 ;Point DI to buffer area
                call    strlen               ;Get message length in CX
                add     cx,3                 ;Add 3 to it
                call    msg_window           ;Display the error message
                ret                          ;  and exit

paste2:         mov     si,buffertop         ;Point SI to data to move
                dec     si
                mov     di,si                ;Point DI to destination
                add     di,recordlength
                mov     ax,cs                ;Point ES to this segment
                mov     es,ax
                mov     cx,buffertop         ;Compute number of bytes
                sub     cx,bufferptr         ;  to move in CX
```

```
                    std                             ;Set direction flag
                    rep     movsb                   ;Perform the move
                    cld                             ;Clear direction flag
                    mov     ax,recordlength         ;Get record length in AX
                    add     buffertop,ax            ;Adjust BUFFERTOP
                    inc     records                 ;Increment record count
                    mov     si,offset del_record    ;Point SI to deleted record
                    mov     di,bufferptr            ;Point DI to current record
                    mov     cx,recordlength         ;Load CX with record length
                    rep     movsb                   ;Insert the deleted record
                    mov     si,bufferptr            ;Point SI to current record
                    call    showpage                ;Display the page
paste_exit:         ret
paste               endp


;************************************************************************
; DELETE deletes the current record.
;************************************************************************

delete              proc    near
                    cmp     records,0               ;Exit if there are no
                    je      del_exit                ;  records
                    mov     ax,recordno             ;Exit if we're just past
                    cmp     ax,records              ;  the final record
                    je      del_exit

                    mov     di,bufferptr            ;Point DI to current record
                    mov     ax,cs                   ;Point ES to this segment
                    mov     es,ax
                    sub     al,al                   ;Zero AL
                    mov     cx,255                  ;Initialize CX
                    repne   scasb                   ;Skip past the next
                    repne   scasb                   ;  three zeroes
                    repne   scasb
                    push    di                      ;Save next record address
                    mov     si,bufferptr            ;Point SI to current record
                    mov     cx,di                   ;Compute length of record to
                    sub     cx,si                   ;  delete in CX
                    mov     recordlength,cx         ;Save the result
                    mov     di,offset del_record    ;Point DI to record buffer
                    rep     movsb                   ;Save the deleted record
                    pop     si                      ;Retrieve next record address
                    mov     di,bufferptr            ;Point DI to current record
                    mov     cx,buffertop            ;Compute number of bytes to
                    sub     cx,si                   ;  move in CX
                    rep     movsb                   ;Delete the current record
                    mov     cx,recordlength         ;Subtract record length
                    sub     buffertop,cx            ;  from BUFFERTOP
                    dec     records                 ;Decrement record count
                    jz      delete1                 ;Branch if RECORDS is 0
                    mov     si,bufferptr            ;Point SI to current record
                    call    showpage                ;Display the page
                    ret

delete1:            mov     dh,window_start         ;Load row number in DH
                    add     dh,5
```

```
                mov     si,offset nullrec       ;Point SI to null record
                call    showline                ;Delete the current line
del_exit:       ret
delete          endp


;*************************************************************************
; SAVE saves the current data to disk.
;*************************************************************************

save            proc    near
                cmp     records,Ø               ;Branch if RECORDS is not
                jne     save1                   ;  equal to Ø
                mov     si,offset errtxt5       ;Point SI to error message
                mov     di,offset screenbuffer2 ;Point DI to buffer area
                call    strlen                  ;Get message length in CX
                add     cx,3                    ;Add 3 to it
                call    msg_window              ;Display the error message
                ret                             ;  and exit

save1:          mov     si,offset filename      ;Point SI to file name
                call    strlen                  ;Compute the string length
                cmp     cx,57                   ;Branch if it's less than or
                jna     save2                   ;  equal to 57
                mov     filename,Ø              ;Erase it if it's longer
save2:          mov     di,offset inbuffer      ;Point DI to input buffer
                mov     ax,cs                   ;Point ES to this segment
                mov     es,ax
                call    copyz                   ;Copy the file name

                mov     ch,57                   ;Prepare for call to
                mov     cl,69                   ;  PROMPT_WINDOW
                mov     si,offset save_prompt
                mov     di,offset inbuffer
                call    prompt_window           ;Input the file name

                cmp     al,13                   ;Exit if input wasn't ended
                jne     save_exit               ;  with the Enter key
                mov     ah,60h
                mov     si,offset inbuffer      ;Point SI to input buffer
                mov     di,offset filename      ;Point DI to file name
                mov     bx,cs                   ;Point ES to this segment
                mov     es,bx
                int     21h                     ;Make fully qualified name
                mov     si,offset errtxt6       ;Error if the call failed
                jc      save4

                call    savefile                ;Save the data
                jnc     save_exit               ;Branch if call succeeded

                mov     si,offset errtxt6       ;Point SI to error message
                cmp     al,Ø1H
                je      save4
                mov     si,offset errtxt7
                cmp     al,Ø2H
                je      save4
                mov     si,offset errtxt8
```

```
save4:          mov     di,offset screenbuffer2 ;Point DI to buffer area
                call    strlen                  ;Get message length in CX
                add     cx,3                    ;Add 3 to it
                call    msg_window              ;Display the error message
save_exit:      ret
save            endp


;****************************************************************************
; OPEN opens a new data file.
;****************************************************************************

open            proc    near
                mov     si,offset filename      ;Point SI to file name
                call    strlen                  ;Compute the string length
                cmp     cx,57                   ;Branch if it's less than or
                jna     open1                   ;  equal to 57
                mov     filename,0              ;Erase it if it's longer
open1:          mov     di,offset inbuffer      ;Point DI to input buffer
                mov     ax,cs                   ;Point ES to this segment
                mov     es,ax
                call    copyz                   ;Copy the file name

                mov     ch,57                   ;Prepare for call to
                mov     cl,69                   ;  PROMPT_WINDOW
                mov     si,offset open_prompt
                mov     di,offset inbuffer
                call    prompt_window           ;Input the file name

                cmp     al,13                   ;Exit if input wasn't ended
                jne     open_exit               ;  with the Enter key
                mov     ah,60h
                mov     si,offset inbuffer      ;Point SI to input buffer
                mov     di,offset filename      ;Point DI to file name
                mov     bx,cs                   ;Point ES to this segment
                mov     es,bx
                int     21h                     ;Make fully qualified name
                mov     si,offset errtxt9       ;Error if the call failed
                jc      open3

                call    readfile                ;Save the data
                jc      open2                   ;Branch if call succeeded

                mov     recordno,0             ;Display the new file
                mov     si,offset databuffer
                mov     bufferptr,si
                call    showpage
open_exit:      ret

open2:          mov     si,offset errtxt10      ;Point SI to error message
                cmp     al,01H
                je      open3
                mov     si,offset errtxt11
                cmp     al,02H
                je      open3
                mov     si,offset errtxt12
                cmp     al,03h
```

```
                je      open3
                mov     si,offset errtxt13
open3:          mov     di,offset screenbuffer2 ;Point DI to buffer area
                call    strlen                  ;Get message length in CX
                add     cx,3                    ;Add 3 to it
                call    msg_window              ;Display the error message
                ret
open            endp


;****************************************************************************
; EDIT allows the current record to be edited.  On return, AX holds the
; key code for the key that terminated input.
;****************************************************************************

field_addr      dw      offset inbuffer         ;Field addresses
                dw      offset inbuffer+32
                dw      offset inbuffer+64
field_col       dw      2,31,60                 ;Field column numbers
field_len       dw      26,26,18                ;Field lengths
field_num       dw      ?                       ;Field number
rec_length      dw      ?                       ;Record length
next_record     dw      ?                       ;Address of next record

edit            proc    near
                mov     field_num,0             ;Initialize field number
                mov     ax,recordno             ;Branch if the pointer is
                cmp     ax,records              ;  highlighting a record
                jne     edit2

                mov     ax,bufferlimit          ;Compute the number of bytes
                sub     ax,buffertop            ;  left in the buffer in AX
                cmp     ax,73                   ;Error if there's not enough
                ja      edit1                   ;  room to edit the record

edit_error:     mov     si,offset errtxt14      ;Point SI to error message
                mov     di,offset screenbuffer2 ;Point DI to buffer area
                call    strlen                  ;Get message length in CX
                add     cx,3                    ;Add 3 to it
                call    msg_window              ;Display the error message
                sub     ax,ax                   ;Zero the return code
                ret
;
; Prepare the input buffer to receive input.
;
edit1:          mov     byte ptr inbuffer,0     ;Zero the three bytes where
                mov     byte ptr inbuffer[32],0 ;  editing will begin and
                mov     byte ptr inbuffer[64],0 ;  branch ahead
                jmp     short edit3

edit2:          mov     si,bufferptr            ;Point SI to current record
                mov     ax,cs                   ;Point ES to this segment
                mov     es,ax
                call    strlen                  ;Compute the length of the
                mov     rec_length,cx           ;  string in the Name field
                mov     di,offset inbuffer      ;Copy the string to the
                call    copyz                   ;  input buffer
```

```
                call    strlen                  ;Compute the length of the
                add     rec_length,cx           ;  string in the next field
                mov     di,offset inbuffer+32   ;Copy the string to the
                call    copyz                   ;  input buffer
                call    strlen                  ;Compute the length of the
                add     rec_length,cx           ;  string in the Phone field
                add     rec_length,3            ;Add 3 to account for zeroes
                mov     di,offset inbuffer+64   ;Copy the string to the
                call    copyz                   ;  input buffer
                mov     next_record,si          ;Save the next record address
                mov     cx,73                   ;Subtract the record size
                sub     cx,rec_length           ;  from 73 in CX
                mov     ax,bufferlimit          ;Compute the number of bytes
                sub     ax,buffertop            ;  left in the buffer in AX
                cmp     ax,cx                   ;Error if there's not enough
                jb      edit_error              ;  room to edit the record
;
; Let the record be edited.
;
edit3:          mov     bx,field_num            ;Get the field number in BX
                mov     si,offset field_len     ;Get the length of the field
                mov     cx,[si+bx]              ;  in CX
                mov     dh,window_start         ;Get the starting row number
                add     dh,5                    ;  in DH
                mov     si,offset field_col     ;Get the starting column
                mov     dl,[si+bx]              ;  number in DL
                mov     si,offset field_addr    ;Get the field address in SI
                mov     si,[si+bx]
                mov     al,00h
                mov     bx,0101h
                call    edit_string             ;Edit the field

                mov     bp,ax                   ;Save the exit code
                cmp     al,13                   ;Exit if Enter was pressed
                je      edit5
                cmp     al,27                   ;Exit if Esc was pressed
                je      edit5a
                cmp     ax,4800h                ;Exit if Up-Arrow was
                je      edit5                   ;  pressed
                cmp     ax,5000h                ;Exit if Down-Arrow was
                je      edit5                   ;  pressed

                cmp     al,9                    ;Branch if Tab was not
                jne     edit4                   ;  pressed
                add     field_num,2             ;Move the cursor to the
                cmp     field_num,6             ;  next field if input was
                jne     edit3                   ;  terminated with the Tab
                mov     field_num,0             ;  key
                jmp     edit3
edit4:          sub     field_num,2             ;Move the cursor to the
                cmp     field_num,0             ;  previous field if input
                jnl     edit3                   ;  was terminated with
                mov     field_num,4             ;  Shift-Tab
                jmp     edit3
;
; Move the records above the new one up or down in memory.
```

```
;
edit5:          mov     ax,cs                   ;Point ES to this segment
                mov     es,ax
                mov     si,offset inbuffer      ;Point SI to first field
                call    strlen                  ;Compute the string length
                mov     bx,cx                   ;Transfer it to BX
                mov     si,offset inbuffer+32   ;Point SI to second field
                call    strlen                  ;Compute the string length
                add     bx,cx                   ;Add it to BX
                mov     si,offset inbuffer+64   ;Point SI to third field
                call    strlen                  ;Compute the string length
                add     bx,cx                   ;Add it to BX
                add     bx,3                    ;Add 3 for record length
                mov     cx,bx                   ;Transfer the result to CX
                mov     ax,recordno             ;Branch if this record will
                cmp     ax,records              ;  not be appended to the end
                jne     edit6

                cmp     cx,3                    ;Exit if the input buffer
                ja      edit5b                  ;  is empty
edit5a:         jmp     short edit_exit
edit5b:         inc     records                 ;Increment record count
                add     buffertop,cx            ;Adjust BUFFERTOP
                jmp     short edit8             ;Go add the new record

edit6:          cmp     cx,rec_length           ;Branch if the new record is
                jae     edit7                   ;  longer than the old one
                mov     ax,rec_length           ;Compute length difference in
                sub     ax,cx                   ;  AX
                mov     si,next_record          ;Point SI to the data to move
                mov     di,si                   ;Point DI to the new
                sub     di,ax                   ;  location below it
                mov     cx,buffertop            ;Compute the number of bytes
                sub     cx,next_record          ;  to move
                rep     movsb                   ;Move the data
                sub     buffertop,ax            ;Adjust BUFFERPTR
                jmp     short edit8             ;Go add the new record

edit7:          sub     cx,rec_length           ;Compute length difference
                jcxz    edit8                   ;Branch if difference is 0
                mov     si,buffertop            ;Point SI to the top of the
                dec     si                      ;  data in the buffer
                mov     di,si                   ;Point DI to the new
                add     di,cx                   ;  location above it
                mov     ax,cx                   ;Transfer difference to AX
                mov     cx,buffertop            ;Compute the number of bytes
                sub     cx,next_record          ;  to move
                std                             ;Set direction flag
                rep     movsb                   ;Move the data
                cld                             ;Clear direction flag
                add     buffertop,ax            ;Adjust BUFFERTOP
;
; Copy the new record to the data buffer and exit.
;
edit8:          mov     si,offset inbuffer      ;Point SI to first field
                mov     di,bufferptr            ;Point DI to data buffer
```

```
                    call    copyz                       ;Copy the first field
                    mov     si,offset inbuffer+32       ;Point SI to second field
                    call    copyz                       ;Copy it
                    mov     si,offset inbuffer+64       ;Point SI to third field
                    call    copyz                       ;Copy it
edit_exit:          mov     si,bufferptr                ;Point SI to current record
                    call    showpage                    ;Display the page
                    mov     ax,bp                       ;Retrieve the return code
                    ret
edit                endp

;************************************************************************
; DIAL dials the phone number currently displayed.
;************************************************************************

uart_addr           dw      ?

dial                proc    near
                    cmp     records,0                   ;Exit if there are no
                    jne     dial1                       ;  records
dial_abort:         ret
dial1:              mov     ax,records                  ;Also exit if the pointer
                    cmp     ax,recordno                 ;  is at the end of the
                    je      dial_abort                  ;  data

                    mov     al,comport                  ;Get the UART's base
                    cbw                                 ;  address
                    shl     ax,1
                    shl     ax,1
                    add     ax,offset addr_table
                    mov     si,ax
                    call    hex2bin
                    mov     uart_addr,ax                ;Save it
                    mov     dx,ax                       ;Transfer it to DX
;
; Initialize the serial port.
;
                    add     dx,3                        ;Point DX to line control
                    mov     bl,commptr                  ;Retrieve format byte from
                    sub     bh,bh                       ;  table
                    mov     al,[bx+offset format_data]
                    push    ax                          ;Save it
                    or      al,80h                      ;Set bit 7 (DLAB)
                    out     dx,al                       ;Write it to the UART
                    sub     dx,3                        ;Point DX to LSB divisor
                    shl     bx,1                        ;Double the table pointer
                    mov     al,[bx+offset divisor_data]     ;Output the divisor
                    out     dx,al                       ;  LSB to the UART
                    inc     dx                          ;Point DX to MSB divisor
                    mov     al,[bx+offset divisor_data+1]   ;Output the divisor
                    out     dx,al                       ;  MSB to the UART
                    pop     ax                          ;Retrieve format byte
                    add     dx,2                        ;Point DX to line control
                    out     dx,al                       ;Output data to the UART
;
; Make sure there's a serial port at this address.
```

```
;
                mov     bl,al                   ;Copy format byte to BL
                mul     bl                      ;Dummy opcode for I/O delay
                in      al,dx                   ;Read line control register
                cmp     al,bl                   ;Are the values the same?
                je      dial2                   ;Yes, then continue
                mov     al,comport              ;Compute address of COM port
                cbw                             ;  address
                shl     ax,1
                shl     ax,1
                add     ax,offset addr_table
                mov     si,ax                   ;Transfer it to SI
                mov     di,offset errtxt19+24   ;Point DI to error message
                mov     ax,cs                   ;Point ES to this segment
                mov     es,ax
                call    copyz                   ;Append the COM port address
                mov     si,offset errtxt19      ;Point SI to error message
                mov     di,offset screenbuffer2 ;Point DI to buffer area
                call    strlen                  ;Get message length in CX
                add     cx,3                    ;Add 3 to it
                call    msg_window              ;Display the error message
                ret
;
; Make sure there's a modem attached and ready.
;
dial2:          add     dx,3                    ;Point DX to modem status
                in      al,dx                   ;Read modem status
                test    al,10h                  ;See if CTS is asserted
                jnz     dial3                   ;Branch if it is
                mov     si,offset errtxt15      ;Point SI to error message
                mov     di,offset screenbuffer2 ;Point DI to buffer area
                call    strlen                  ;Get message length in CX
                add     cx,3                    ;Add 3 to it
                mov     al,comport              ;Get COM port number in AL
                add     al,31h                  ;Convert binary to ASCII
                mov     errtxt15[61],al         ;Write it to ERRTXT15
                call    msg_window              ;Display the error message
                ret                             ;  and exit
;
; Initialize the modem.
;
dial3:          mov     si,offset initcmd       ;Copy the command to
                mov     di,offset inbuffer      ;  initialize the modem
                mov     ax,cs
                mov     es,ax
                call    copyz
                mov     si,offset inbuffer      ;Append a carriage return
                mov     di,offset endcmd        ;  to the end of it
                call    strcat
                mov     dx,uart_addr            ;Load DX with UART address
                mov     si,offset inbuffer      ;Transmit the command
                call    transmit_string

                mov     counter,18              ;Initialize counter
dial4:          cmp     counter,0               ;Pause for about 1 second
                jne     dial4                   ;  before proceeding
```

```
;
; Dial the phone number.
;
                mov     si,offset dialcmd       ;Build the command to dial
                mov     di,offset inbuffer      ;  the phone, starting with
                call    copyz                   ;  the "ATDT" string
                mov     si,offset inbuffer      ;Append the dialing prefix
                mov     di,offset prefix
                call    strcat
                mov     si,offset inbuffer      ;Append the number itself
                mov     di,bufferptr
                mov     cx,255
                sub     al,al
                repne   scasb
                repne   scasb
                call    strcat
                mov     si,offset inbuffer      ;Append the dial command
                mov     di,offset suffix        ;  suffix
                call    strcat
                mov     si,offset inbuffer      ;Append a carriage return to
                mov     di,offset endcmd        ;  terminate the command
                call    strcat

                mov     dx,uart_addr            ;Load DX with UART address
                mov     si,offset inbuffer      ;Transmit the command
                call    transmit_string
;
; Display the message window saying what to do next.
;
                mov     bx,color_ptr            ;Place attributes in AH,
                mov     ah,border_color         ;  AL, and BH
                mov     al,window_color_2
                mov     bh,shadow_color
                mov     ch,window_start         ;Load CX with the window's
                add     ch,3                    ;  starting coordinates
                mov     cl,13
                mov     dh,ch                   ;Load DX with the window's
                add     dh,4                    ;  ending coordinates
                mov     dl,66
                push    cx                      ;Save window coordinates
                push    dx
                push    cs                      ;Point ES:DI to the buffer
                pop     es                      ;  for screen data
                mov     di,offset screenbuffer2
                call    openwindow              ;Display the window

                mov     dh,window_start         ;Display the message itself
                add     dh,4
                mov     dl,15
                push    dx
                mov     si,offset msg1a
                call    show_string
                pop     dx
                inc     dh
                push    dx
                mov     si,offset msg1b
```

```
                call    show_string
                pop     dx
                inc     dh
                mov     si,offset msg1c
                call    show_string

                call    readkey                 ;Wait for a keypress

                pop     dx                      ;Close the message window
                pop     cx                      ;  by restoring what was
                add     dx,0101h                ;  under it
                mov     si,offset screenbuffer2
                call    restregion
;
; Disconnect the modem from the line and exit.
;
                mov     si,offset hangcmd       ;Build the command to
                mov     di,offset inbuffer      ;  disconnect the modem
                mov     ax,cs                   ;  from the line
                mov     es,ax
                call    copyz
                mov     si,offset inbuffer
                mov     di,offset endcmd
                call    strcat
                mov     dx,uart_addr            ;Load DX withe UART address
                mov     si,offset inbuffer      ;Transmit the command
                call    transmit_string
dial_exit:      ret
dial            endp


;**************************************************************************
; TRANSMIT_STRING transmits an ASCIIZ string to a COM port.  On entry,
; DS:SI points to the string and DX contains the COM port's I/O address.
;**************************************************************************

transmit_string proc    near
                lodsb                           ;Get a character
                or      al,al                   ;Exit if it's zero
                jz      trans_exit
                call    transmit_char           ;Transmit it to the COM port
                jmp     transmit_string         ;Loop back for more
trans_exit:     ret
transmit_string endp


;**************************************************************************
; TRANSMIT_CHAR transmits a character to a COM port.  On entry, AL holds
; the character and DX contains the COM port's I/O address.
;**************************************************************************

transmit_char   proc    near
                push    ax                      ;Save the character
                add     dx,5                    ;Point DX to line status
trans_loop:     in      al,dx                   ;Read line status from UART
                test    al,20h                  ;Loop until transmit holding
                jz      trans_loop              ;  register comes empty
                pop     ax                      ;Retrieve the character
```

```
              sub      dx,5                  ;Point DX to output port
              out      dx,al                 ;Transmit the character
              ret
transmit_char endp


;******************************************************************************
; OPENWINDOW opens a window for input.  On entry CH and CL hold the
; coordinates of the window's upper left corner; DH and DL hold the
; coordinates of the lower right corner; AH holds the window's border
; color; AL holds the color of its interior; BH holds the drop shadow
; color; and ES:DI points to the buffer where video data will be stored.
;******************************************************************************

ul_col        db       ?                     ;Upper left column
ul_row        db       ?                     ;Upper left row
lr_col        db       ?                     ;Lower right column
lr_row        db       ?                     ;Lower right row
border_attr   db       ?                     ;Border attribute
window_attr   db       ?                     ;Window attribute
shadow_attr   db       ?                     ;Shadow attribute

openwindow    proc     near
              mov      word ptr ul_col,cx    ;Save window coordinates
              mov      word ptr lr_col,dx
              mov      border_attr,ah        ;Store video attributes
              mov      window_attr,al
              mov      shadow_attr,bh

              add      dx,0101h              ;Include drop shadow
              call     saveregion            ;Save the screen

              mov      ah,border_attr        ;Retrieve attribute
              mov      cx,word ptr ul_col    ;Retrieve window coordinates
              mov      dx,word ptr lr_col
              call     drawbox               ;Draw the window border

              mov      bh,window_attr        ;Retrieve attribute
              mov      cx,word ptr ul_col    ;Retrieve window coordinates
              add      cx,0101h
              mov      dx,word ptr lr_col
              sub      dx,0101h
              mov      ax,0600h              ;Blank the interior of the
              int      10h                   ;  window

              mov      al,shadow_attr        ;Retrieve attribute
              mov      cl,lr_col             ;Compute length of the
              sub      cl,ul_col             ;  horizontal portion
              inc      cl                    ;  of the drop shadow
              sub      ch,ch                 ;Byte to word in CX
              mov      dh,lr_row             ;Load DX with the starting
              mov      dl,ul_col             ;  row and column address
              add      dx,0101h
              call     write_attr            ;Write the attribute

              mov      cl,lr_row             ;Compute length of the
              sub      cl,ul_row             ;  vertical portion of
```

```
                  inc      cl                      ;  the drop shadow
                  sub      ch,ch                   ;Byte to word in CX
                  push     cx                      ;Save it
                  mov      dh,ul_row               ;Load DX with the starting
                  mov      dl,lr_col               ;  row and column address
                  add      dx,0101h
                  call     compute_address         ;Compute the address
                  mov      di,ax                   ;Transfer offset to DI
                  inc      di                      ;Point DI to attribute
                  mov      es,video_segment        ;Point ES to video segment
                  pop      cx                      ;Retrieve length
                  mov      al,shadow_attr          ;Retrieve attribute
open_loop:        stosb                            ;Write one attribute
                  add      di,line_length          ;Point DI to next attribute
                  dec      di                      ;  byte
                  loop     open_loop               ;Loop until done
                  ret
openwindow        endp

;*****************************************************************************
; PROMPT_WINDOW opens a window for string input.  On entry, CL holds the
; length of the window horizontally, CH holds the maximum number of char-
; acters that will be accepted, DS:SI points to the prompt string, and DS:DI
; points to the default input string.  On exit, AX holds the return code
; from EDIT_STRING.
;*****************************************************************************

straddr1          dw       ?                       ;String address 1
straddr2          dw       ?                       ;String address 2
charlimit         db       ?                       ;Maximum character count

prompt_window     proc     near
                  mov      straddr1,si             ;Save string addresses
                  mov      straddr2,di
                  mov      charlimit,ch            ;Save maximum character count
                  mov      al,cl                   ;Copy window length to AL
                  mov      ah,cl                   ;Copy window length to AH
                  inc      al                      ;Increment length by 1
                  shr      al,1                    ;Then divide it by 2

                  mov      ch,window_start         ;Load CX and DX with the
                  add      ch,4                    ;  window coordinates
                  mov      cl,40
                  sub      cl,al
                  mov      dh,ch
                  add      dh,2
                  mov      dl,cl
                  add      dl,ah
                  mov      bx,color_ptr            ;Place video attributes in
                  mov      ah,border_color         ;  AH, AL, and BH
                  mov      al,window_color_2
                  mov      bh,shadow_color
                  push     cs                      ;Point ES:DI to the buffer
                  pop      es                      ;  where screen data will
                  mov      di,offset screenbuffer2 ;  be saved
                  push     cx                      ;Save window coordinates
```

```
                push    dx
                call    openwindow              ;Display the prompt window
                pop     dx                      ;Retrieve window coordinates
                pop     cx

                push    cx                      ;Save the window coordinates
                push    dx                      ;  again
                mov     dx,cx                   ;Compute location to display
                add     dx,0102h                ;  prompt
                mov     si,straddr1             ;Point SI to the prompt
                call    show_string             ;Display the prompt
                pop     dx                      ;Retrieve window coordinates
                pop     cx

                push    cx                      ;Save the window coordinates
                push    dx                      ;  again
                mov     dx,cx                   ;Compute location to display
                add     dx,0103h                ;  the input string
                push    cx
                mov     si,straddr1
                call    strlen
                add     dl,cl
                pop     cx
                push    dx
                mov     si,straddr2             ;Point SI to the input string
                call    show_string             ;Display the input string
                pop     dx

                mov     al,01h                  ;Prepare registers for call
                mov     bx,00h                  ;  to EDIT_STRING
                mov     cl,charlimit
                sub     ch,ch
                mov     si,straddr2
                call    edit_string             ;Input a new string

                pop     dx                      ;Retrieve window coordinates
                pop     cx
                add     dx,0101h
                push    ax                      ;Save the return code
                mov     si,offset screenbuffer2 ;Close the window
                call    restregion
                pop     ax                      ;Retrieve return code and
                ret                             ;  return to caller
prompt_window   endp

;****************************************************************************
; MSG_WINDOW opens a window and displays a message.  On entry, CL holds
; the length of the window horizontally, DS:SI points to the ASCIIZ message
; string, and DS:DI points to the buffer where video data will be stored.
;****************************************************************************

msg_window      proc    near
                push    di                      ;Save buffer address
                push    si                      ;Save string address
                mov     al,cl                   ;Copy window length to AL
                mov     ah,cl                   ;Copy window length to AH
```

```
                inc     al              ;Increment length by 1
                shr     al,1            ;Then divide it by 2

                mov     bx,ds           ;Point ES to this segment
                mov     es,bx
                mov     ch,window_start ;Load CX and DX with the
                add     ch,4            ;  window coordinates
                mov     cl,40
                sub     cl,al
                mov     dh,ch
                add     dh,2
                mov     dl,cl
                add     dl,ah
                mov     bx,color_ptr    ;Place video attributes in
                mov     ah,error_color  ;  AH, AL, and BH
                mov     al,ah
                mov     bh,shadow_color
                push    cx              ;Save window coordinates
                push    dx
                call    openwindow      ;Display the error window
                pop     dx              ;Retrieve window coordinates
                pop     cx

                pop     si              ;Retrieve message address
                push    cx              ;Save the window coordinates
                push    dx              ;  again
                mov     dx,cx           ;Compute the row and column
                add     dh,1            ;  to display the error
                call    strlen          ;  message
                shr     cl,1
                mov     dl,40
                sub     dl,cl
                call    show_string     ;Display the error message

                call    readkey         ;Wait until a key is pressed

                pop     dx              ;Retrieve window coordinates
                pop     cx              ;  and close the window
                add     dx,0101h
                pop     si
                call    restregion
                ret
msg_window      endp


;******************************************************************************
; READFILE loads a data file.  Carry set on return means an error occurred.
; If carry is set, AL holds one of the following error codes:
;
;       01H     File was not found or could not be opened
;       02H     File is too large to fit in the internal buffer
;       03H     File was not created by PC-DIAL (header is not valid)
;       04H     An error occurred while reading the file
;
; On entry, both DS and ES must point to the segment that holds the file
; specification and the data buffer.
;******************************************************************************
```

```
bytestoread      dw      ?

readfile         proc    near
                 mov     ax,3D02h                ;Open the file with read/
                 mov     dx,offset filename      ;  write access privilege
                 int     21h
                 jc      read_error1             ;Error if call failed

                 mov     bx,ax                   ;Transfer file handle to BX
                 mov     ax,4202h                ;Determine the file's size
                 sub     cx,cx                   ;  by positioning the file
                 mov     dx,cx                   ;  pointer at the end of
                 int     21h                     ;  the file
                 or      dx,dx                   ;Error if file is larger
                 jnz     read_error2             ;  than 64k
                 cmp     ax,15                   ;Error if the file is less
                 jb      read_error3             ;  than 15 bytes long
                 sub     ax,15                   ;Adjust file size
                 mov     bytestoread,ax          ;Save the result
                 cmp     ax,buffersize           ;Error if file is larger
                 ja      read_error2             ;  than the buffer size

                 push    ax                      ;Save the file size
                 mov     ax,4200h                ;Reset the file pointer to
                 sub     cx,cx                   ;  the beginning of the
                 mov     dx,cx                   ;  file
                 int     21h

                 mov     ah,3Fh                  ;Read the 13-byte header
                 mov     cx,13                   ;  from the file
                 mov     dx,offset databuffer
                 int     21h
                 jc      read_error4             ;Branch on error
                 mov     si,offset signature     ;Compare strings to see if
                 mov     di,offset databuffer    ;  this is a valid PC-DIAL
                 mov     cx,13                   ;  data file
                 repe    cmpsb
                 pop     cx                      ;Retrieve file size
                 jne     read_error3             ;Error if strings don't match

                 mov     ah,3Fh                  ;Read the number of records
                 mov     cx,2                    ;  from the data file
                 mov     dx,offset records
                 int     21h
                 jc      read_error4             ;Branch on error

                 mov     ah,3Fh                  ;Read the file into the
                 mov     cx,bytestoread          ;  data buffer
                 mov     dx,offset databuffer
                 int     21h
                 jc      read_error4             ;Branch on error

                 mov     ah,3Eh                  ;Close the file
                 int     21h
                 mov     bufferptr,offset databuffer     ;Reset pointers
```

```
                    mov     ax,offset databuffer
                    add     ax,bytestoread
                    mov     buffertop,ax
                    clc                             ;Clear carry and exit
                    ret

read_error1:        mov     al,01h                  ;Set AL to 01H and exit
                    jmp     short read_error
read_error2:        mov     ah,3Eh                  ;Close the file, set AL to
                    int     21h                     ;  02H, and exit
                    mov     al,02h
                    jmp     short read_error
read_error3:        mov     ah,3Eh                  ;Close the file, set AL to
                    int     21h                     ;  03H, and exit
                    mov     al,03h
                    jmp     short read_error
read_error4:        mov     ah,3Eh                  ;Close the file, set AL to
                    int     21h                     ;  04H, and exit
                    mov     al,04h
read_error:         stc
                    ret
readfile            endp


;**************************************************************************
; SAVEFILE writes the contents of the data buffer to disk.  Carry set on
; return means an error occurred.  If carry is set, AL holds one of the
; following error codes:
;
;       01H     The file could not be created
;       02H     An error occurred during a write
;       03H     The destination disk is full
;**************************************************************************

bytestowrite        dw      ?

savefile            proc    near
                    mov     ah,3Ch                  ;Create the file or truncate
                    sub     cx,cx                   ;  it to zero length if it
                    mov     dx,offset filename      ;  already exists
                    int     21h
                    jc      save_error1             ;Exit if the call failed

                    mov     bx,ax                   ;Transfer file handle to BX
                    mov     ah,40h                  ;Write the 13-byte header to
                    mov     cx,13                   ;  the file to identify it
                    mov     dx,offset signature     ;  as a PC-DIAL file
                    int     21h
                    jc      save_error2             ;Exit if the call failed
                    cmp     ax,13                   ;Also exit if the disk is
                    jb      save_error3             ;  full

                    mov     ah,40h                  ;Write the record count to
                    mov     cx,2                    ;  the file
                    mov     dx,offset records
                    int     21h
                    jc      save_error2             ;Exit if the call failed
```

```
                        cmp     ax,2                    ;Also exit if the disk is
                        jb      save_error3             ;  full

                        mov     ah,40h                  ;Write the contents of the
                        mov     cx,buffertop            ;  data buffer to the file
                        sub     cx,offset databuffer
                        mov     dx,offset databuffer
                        mov     bytestowrite,cx
                        int     21h
                        jc      save_error2             ;Exit if the call failed
                        cmp     ax,bytestowrite         ;Also exit if the disk is
                        jb      save_error3             ;  full

                        mov     ah,3Eh                  ;Close the file and exit
                        int     21h                     ;  with carry clear
                        clc
                        ret

save_error1:            mov     al,01h                  ;Set AL to 01H and exit
                        jmp     short save_error
save_error2:            mov     ah,3Eh                  ;Close the file, set AL to
                        int     21h                     ;  02H, and exit
                        mov     al,02h
                        jmp     short save_error        ;Close the file, set AL to
save_error3:            mov     ah,3Eh                  ;  03H, and exit
                        int     21h
                        mov     al,03h
save_error:             stc
                        ret
savefile                endp

;*****************************************************************************
; SAVESETUP writes setup information to disk.  Carry set on return means an
; error occurred.  If carry is set, AL holds one of the following error
; codes:
;
;       01H     PC-DIAL.COM was not found or could not be opened
;       02H     An unknown error occurred during the write operation
;*****************************************************************************

savesetup               proc    near
                        mov     ax,3D01h                ;Open the program file for
                        mov     dx,offset progfile      ;  writing
                        int     21h
                        jc      setup_error1            ;Branch if call failed

                        mov     bx,ax                   ;Transfer file handle to BX
                        mov     ax,4200h                ;Move the file pointer to the
                        sub     cx,cx                   ;  beginning of the setup
                        mov     dx,offset addr_table    ;  information
                        sub     dx,0100h
                        int     21h

                        mov     ah,40h                  ;Write the setup information
                        mov     cx,offset commptr+1     ;  to disk
                        sub     cx,offset addr_table
```

```
                mov     dx,offset addr_table
                int     21h
                jc      setup_error2

                mov     ah,3Eh                  ;Close the file and exit
                int     21h                     ;  with carry clear
                clc
                ret

setup_error1:   mov     al,01h                  ;Set AL to 01H and exit
                jmp     short setup_error
setup_error2:   mov     ah,3Eh                  ;Close the file, set AL to
                int     21h                     ;  01H, and exit
                mov     al,02h
setup_error:    stc
                ret
savesetup       endp

;***************************************************************************
; HEX2BIN converts a hex number entered in ASCIIZ form into a binary
; value in AX.  On entry, DS:SI points to the string.  Carry set on return
; indicates that an error occurred in the conversion.
;***************************************************************************

sixteen         dw      16

hex2bin         proc    near
                sub     ax,ax                   ;Initialize registers
                sub     bh,bh

h2b_loop:       mov     bl,[si]                 ;Get a character
                inc     si
                or      bl,bl                   ;Exit if it's 0
                jz      h2b_exit

                cmp     bl,"0"                  ;Error if character is less
                jb      h2b_error               ;  than "0"
                cmp     bl,"9"                  ;Branch if it's between "0"
                jbe     h2b_shift               ;  and "9"
                and     bl,0DFh                 ;Capitalize the character
                cmp     bl,"A"                  ;Error if it's less than "A"
                jb      h2b_error
                cmp     bl,"F"                  ;Error if it's greater than
                ja      h2b_error               ;  "B"
                sub     bl,7                    ;Convert hex digit to number

h2b_shift:      mul     sixteen                 ;Multiply the value in AX by
                jc      h2b_error               ;  16 and exit on overflow
                sub     bl,30h                  ;ASCII => binary
                add     ax,bx                   ;Add latest value to AX and
                adc     dx,0                    ;  DX
                or      dx,dx                   ;Error if DX is not 0
                jz      h2b_loop                ;Loop back for more

h2b_error:      dec     si                      ;Set carry and exit
                stc
```

```
                        ret

h2b_exit:       dec     si                      ;Clear carry and exit
                clc
                ret
hex2bin         endp

;***********************************************************************
; BIN2HEX converts a binary value in AX to an ASCIIZ number in hex format.
; On entry, ES:DI points to the location where the string will be written.
;***********************************************************************

bin2hex         proc    near
                mov     bx,16                   ;Initialize divisor word and
                xor     cx,cx                   ;  digit counter
b2h1:           inc     cx                      ;Increment digit count
                sub     dx,dx                   ;Divide by 16
                div     bx
                push    dx                      ;Save remainder on stack
                or      ax,ax                   ;Loop until quotient is zero
                jnz     b2h1
b2h2:           pop     ax                      ;Retrieve last digit
                cmp     al,10                   ;Branch if it's less than 10
                jb      b2h3
                add     al,7                    ;Otherwise add 7
b2h3:           add     al,30h                  ;binary => ASCII
                stosb
                loop    b2h2                    ;Loop until done
                sub     al,al                   ;Append the terminating
                stosb                           ;  zero to the string
                ret
bin2hex         endp

;***********************************************************************
; Buffer areas to be used after installation.
;***********************************************************************

screenbuffer1   =       $                       ;Screen buffer (1920 bytes)
screenbuffer2   =       $ + 1920                ;Screen buffer (1034 bytes)
screenbuffer3   =       $ + 2954                ;Screen buffer (568 bytes)
mystack         =       $ + 4034                ;Internal stack (512 bytes)
databuffer      =       $ + 4038                ;Data buffer

;***********************************************************************
; Data that will be discarded when the program becomes memory-resident.
;***********************************************************************

helpmsg         db      "Installs a popup phone directory and dialer."
                db      13,10,13,10
                db      "PC-DIAL [[d:][path]filename] [/B=size] [/M]"
                db      13,10,13,10
                db      "  filename  Data file to load at start-up."
                db      13,10
                db      "  /B=size   Buffer size in kilobytes (default=16)."
                db      13,10
                db      "  /M        Use monochrome video attributes."
```

```
                db      13,10,13,10
                db      "Once PC-DIAL is installed, pressing Alt and the "
                db      "right Shift key pops ",13,10
                db      "up the phone directory window.",13,10,"$"

errmsg1         db      "Syntax: PC-DIAL [[d:][path]filename] [/B=size] "
                db      " [/M]",13,10,"$"
errmsg2         db      "Requires DOS 3.0 or higher",13,10,"$"
errmsg3         db      "Program could not be installed",13,10,"$"
errmsg4         db      "Program is already installed",13,10,"$"
errmsg5         db      "Invalid buffer size (minimum=1, maximum=48)"
                db      13,10,"$"
errmsg6         db      "Invalid path or file name",13,10,"$"
errmsg7         db      "File not found or could not be opened",13,10,"$"
errmsg8         db      "File is too large for the data buffer",13,10,"$"
errmsg9         db      "File was not created by PC-DIAL",13,10,"$"

msg1            db      "PC-DIAL 1.0 installed",13,10
                db      "Hotkey is Alt-Right Shift",13,10,"$"

eol_flag        db      0                       ;1=End of line reached


;****************************************************************************
; INIT makes the program resident in memory.
;****************************************************************************

                assume  cs:code,ds:code

init            proc    near
                cld                             ;Clear direction flag
                mov     si,81h                  ;Point SI to command line
                call    scanhelp                ;Scan for "/?" switch
                jnc     checkver                ;Branch if not found
                mov     ah,09h                  ;Display help text and exit
                mov     dx,offset helpmsg       ;  with ERRORLEVEL=0
                int     21h
                mov     ax,4C00h
                int     21h
;
; Check the DOS version and terminate if the program is already installed.
;
checkver:       mov     dx,offset errmsg2       ;Get the DOS version number
                mov     ah,30h
                int     21h
                mov     byte ptr dosversion,ah  ;Save it
                mov     byte ptr dosversion[1],al
                cmp     al,3                    ;Exit if version number is
                jae     checkins                ;  less than 3.0

error:          mov     ah,09h                  ;Display error message and
                int     21h                     ;  exit with ERRORLEVEL=1
                mov     ax,4C01h
                int     21h

checkins:       push    es                      ;Save ES
                call    check_install           ;Get installed status
```

```
              pop     es                      ;Restore ES
              mov     dx,offset errmsg4       ;Error if the program is
              jc      error                   ;  already installed
              mov     si,81h                  ;Reset SI
;
; Parse the command line.
;

parse:        call    findchar                ;Find first parameter
              jc      endparse                ;Branch if none found
              cmp     byte ptr [si],"/"       ;Branch if it's a "/"
              je      slashb                  ;  character

              mov     bx,si                   ;Save SI temporarily
              call    finddelim               ;Find the end of the name
              jnc     parse1                  ;Branch if not end of line
              mov     eol_flag,1              ;Set EOL flag to 1
parse1:       mov     byte ptr [si],0         ;Convert string to ASCIIZ
              inc     si                      ;Advance SI past the zero
              push    si                      ;Save SI
              mov     ah,60h                  ;Convert the file name into
              mov     si,bx                   ;  a fully qualified file
              mov     di,offset filename      ;  name
              int     21h
              pop     si                      ;Retrieve SI
              mov     dx,offset errmsg6       ;Initialize error pointer
              jc      error                   ;Error if call failed
              cmp     eol_flag,0              ;Branch if end of line was
              jne     endparse                ;  reached
              jmp     parse                   ;Otherwise loop back
;
; Process a /B switch.
;
slashb:       mov     dx,offset errmsg1       ;Initialize error pointer
              inc     si                      ;Skip the "/" character
              lodsb                           ;Get a character
              and     al,0DFh                 ;Capitalize it
              cmp     al,"B"                  ;Branch if it's not a "B"
              jne     slashm

              lodsb                           ;Get the next character
              cmp     al,"="                  ;Error if it's not a "="
              jne     error
              cmp     byte ptr [si],"0"       ;Error if the next character
              jb      error                   ;  is not a number
              cmp     byte ptr [si],"9"
              ja      error
              call    asc2bin                 ;Convert the number to binary
              mov     dx,offset errmsg5       ;Error if it's less than 1 or
              cmp     al,1                    ;  greater than 48
              jb      error
              cmp     al,48
              ja      error

              cbw                             ;Convert kilobytes to bytes
              mov     cl,10                   ;  by shifting left 10
              shl     ax,cl                   ;  places
```

```
                mov     buffersize,ax           ;Store the result
                sub     bufferlimit,defaultsize ;Adjust address of top of
                add     bufferlimit,ax          ;  data buffer
                jmp     parse                   ;Reenter the parse loop
;
; Process a /M switch.
;
slashm:         cmp     al,"M"                  ;Error if the character is
                jne     error1                  ;  not an "M"
                push    si                      ;Save SI
                mov     si,offset mono_table    ;Point SI to mono attributes
                mov     di,offset color_table   ;Point DI to color attributes
                mov     cx,10                   ;Initalize counter
                rep     movsb                   ;Copy mono to color
                pop     si                      ;Restore SI
                jmp     parse                   ;Reenter the parsing loop
;
; Read the data file if a name was specified.
;
endparse:       cmp     filename,0              ;Go install if no file name
                je      install                 ;  was entered
                call    readfile                ;Read the data file
                jnc     install                 ;Go install if no error
                mov     dx,offset errmsg7       ;Initialize DX with address
                cmp     al,1                    ;  of error message and exit
                je      error1
                mov     dx,offset errmsg8
                cmp     al,2
                je      error1
                mov     dx,offset errmsg9
error1:         jmp     error
;
; Install the program.
;
install:        call    mplex_id                ;Find a multiplex ID number
                mov     dx,offset errmsg3       ;Error if none available
                jc      error1
                mov     prog_id,ah              ;Save the ID number

                mov     ah,34h                  ;Get and save the address of
                int     21h                     ;  the InDOS flag
                mov     word ptr indos,bx
                mov     word ptr indos[2],es

                push    ds                      ;Save DS
                mov     ax,5D06h                ;Get and save the address of
                int     21h                     ;  the critical error flag
                mov     word ptr cs:[errorflag],si
                mov     word ptr cs:[errorflag+2],ds
                pop     ds                      ;Restore DS
                mov     dx,offset errmsg3       ;Error if function returned
                jc      error1                  ;  with carry set

                mov     si,offset databuffer-1  ;Zero the byte just before
                mov     byte ptr [si],0         ;  the data buffer
```

```
              mov     ah,12h                  ;Test for EGA/VGA
              mov     bl,10h
              int     10h
              cmp     bl,10h                  ;EGA/VGA installed if BL
              jne     set_vectors             ;  returned changed
              mov     egaflag,0               ;Zero video adapter flag

set_vectors:  mov     ax,3508h                ;Hook interrupt 08H
              int     21h
              mov     word ptr int08h,bx
              mov     word ptr int08h[2],es
              mov     ax,2508h
              mov     dx,offset timer_int
              int     21h

              mov     ax,3509h                ;Hook interrupt 09H
              int     21h
              mov     word ptr int09h,bx
              mov     word ptr int09h[2],es
              mov     ax,2509h
              mov     dx,offset kb_int
              int     21h

              mov     ax,3510h                ;Hook interrupt 10H
              int     21h
              mov     word ptr int10h,bx
              mov     word ptr int10h[2],es
              mov     ax,2510h
              mov     dx,offset video_int
              int     21h

              mov     ax,3513h                ;Hook interrupt 13H
              int     21h
              mov     word ptr int13h,bx
              mov     word ptr int13h[2],es
              mov     ax,2513h
              mov     dx,offset disk_int
              int     21h

              mov     ax,3525h                ;Hook interrupt 25H
              int     21h
              mov     word ptr int25h,bx
              mov     word ptr int25h[2],es
              mov     ax,2525h
              mov     dx,offset abs_read_int
              int     21h

              mov     ax,3526h                ;Hook interrupt 26H
              int     21h
              mov     word ptr int26h,bx
              mov     word ptr int26h[2],es
              mov     ax,2526h
              mov     dx,offset abs_write_int
              int     21h

              mov     ax,3528h                ;Hook interrupt 28H
```

```
              int     21h
              mov     word ptr int28h,bx
              mov     word ptr int28h[2],es
              mov     ax,2528h
              mov     dx,offset dosidle_int
              int     21h

              mov     ax,352Fh                    ;Hook interrupt 2FH
              int     21h
              mov     word ptr int2Fh,bx
              mov     word ptr int2Fh[2],es
              mov     ax,252Fh
              mov     dx,offset mplex_int
              int     21h

              mov     ah,49h                      ;Get the segment address of
              mov     es,ds:[2Ch]                 ;  the environment block
              int     21h                         ;  and free the segment

              mov     ah,09h                      ;Display message verifying
              mov     dx,offset msg1              ;  the installation
              int     21h

              mov     ax,3100h                    ;Terminate with function 31H
              mov     dx,offset databuffer+15 ;Compute amount of memory to
              add     dx,buffersize               ;  reserve in DX first
              mov     cl,4
              shr     dx,cl
              int     21h
init          endp


;***************************************************************************
; FINDCHAR advances SI to the next non-space or non-comma character.
; On return, carry set indicates EOL was encountered.
;***************************************************************************

findchar      proc    near
              lodsb                               ;Get the next character
              cmp     al,20h                      ;Loop if space
              je      findchar
              cmp     al,2Ch                      ;Loop if comma
              je      findchar
              dec     si                          ;Point SI to the character
              cmp     al,0Dh                      ;Exit with carry set if end
              je      eol                         ;  of line is reached

              clc                                 ;Clear carry and exit
              ret

eol:          stc                                 ;Set carry and exit
              ret
findchar      endp


;***************************************************************************
; FINDDELIM advances SI to the next space or comma character.  On return,
; carry set indicates EOL was encountered.
```

```
;************************************************************************

finddelim       proc    near
                lodsb                           ;Get the next character
                cmp     al,20h                  ;Exit if space
                je      fd_exit
                cmp     al,2Ch                  ;Exit if comma
                je      fd_exit
                cmp     al,0Dh                  ;Loop back for more if end
                jne     finddelim               ;  of line isn't reached

                dec     si                      ;Set carry and exit
                stc
                ret

fd_exit:        dec     si                      ;Clear carry and exit
                clc
                ret
finddelim       endp


;************************************************************************
; SCANHELP scans the command line for a /? switch.  If found, carry returns
; set and SI contains its offset.  If not found, carry returns clear.
;************************************************************************

scanhelp        proc    near
                push    si                      ;Save SI
scanloop:       lodsb                           ;Get a character
                cmp     al,0Dh                  ;Exit if end of line
                je      scan_exit
                cmp     al,"?"                  ;Loop if not "?"
                jne     scanloop
                cmp     byte ptr [si-2],"/"     ;Loop if not "/"
                jne     scanloop

                add     sp,2                    ;Clear the stack
                sub     si,2                    ;Adjust SI
                stc                             ;Set carry and exit
                ret

scan_exit:      pop     si                      ;Restore SI
                clc                             ;Clear carry and exit
                ret
scanhelp        endp


;************************************************************************
; CHECK_INSTALL returns carry set if the program is already installed,
; carry clear if it's not.  If carry returns set, AH holds the program's
; multiplex ID number.
;************************************************************************

check_install   proc    near
                mov     ax,8000h                ;Initialize AH and AL
                mov     cx,80h                  ;Initialize count

chinst1:        push    ax                      ;Save AX and CX
```

```
                push    cx
                sub     di,di                   ;Set ES and DI to 0
                mov     es,di
                int     2Fh                     ;Interrupt 2Fh
                cmp     al,0FFh                 ;Nothing here if AL isn't
                jne     chinst2                 ;  equal to FFH

                mov     si,offset signature     ;See if program signature
                mov     cx,13                   ;  appears at the address
                repe    cmpsb                   ;  returned in ES:DI
                jne     chinst2                 ;Branch if it does not

                pop     cx                      ;Clear the stack and exit
                pop     ax                      ;  with carry set
                stc
                ret

chinst2:        pop     cx                      ;Retrieve AX and CX
                pop     ax
                inc     ah                      ;Next multiplex ID
                loop    chinst1                 ;Loop until done

                clc                             ;Exit with carry clear
                ret
check_install   endp

;*****************************************************************************
; MPLEX_ID searches for an unused multiplex ID number.  If one is found,
; it is returned in AH with carry clear.  Carry set means no multiplex
; ID numbers are currently available.
;*****************************************************************************

mplex_id        proc    near
                mov     ax,8000h                ;Initialize AH and AL
                mov     cx,80h                  ;Initialize count

mxid1:          push    ax                      ;Save AX and CX
                push    cx
                int     2Fh                     ;Interrupt 2Fh
                or      al,al                   ;Branch if AL=0
                jz      mxid2
                pop     cx                      ;Retrieve AX and CX
                pop     ax
                inc     ah                      ;Increment ID number
                loop    mxid1                   ;Loop until done

                stc                             ;Exit with carry set
                ret

mxid2:          pop     cx                      ;Clear the stack and exit
                pop     ax                      ;  with carry clear
                clc
                ret
mplex_id        endp


;*****************************************************************************
```

```
; ASC2BIN converts a decimal number entered in ASCII form into a binary
; value in AL.  Carry set on return indicates that an error occurred in
; the conversion.
;****************************************************************************

asc2bin         proc    near
                sub     ax,ax                   ;Initialize registers
                sub     bh,bh
                mov     dl,10

a2b_loop:       mov     bl,[si]                 ;Get a character
                inc     si
                cmp     bl,20h                  ;Exit if space
                je      a2b_exit
                cmp     bl,2Ch                  ;Exit if comma
                je      a2b_exit
                cmp     bl,0Dh                  ;Exit if carriage return
                je      a2b_exit

                cmp     bl,"0"                  ;Error if character is not
                jb      a2b_error               ;   a number
                cmp     bl,"9"
                ja      a2b_error

                mul     dl                      ;Multiply the value in AL by
                jc      a2b_error               ;   10 and exit on overflow
                sub     bl,30h                  ;ASCII => binary
                add     ax,bx                   ;Add latest value to AX
                cmp     ax,255                  ;Error if sum > 255
                jna     a2b_loop                ;Loop back for more

a2b_error:      dec     si                      ;Set carry and exit
                stc
                ret

a2b_exit:       dec     si                      ;Clear carry and exit
                clc
                ret
asc2bin         endp

code            ends
                end     begin
```

The larger the buffer size you specify, the greater the number of entries you can store. The minimum buffer size that PC-DIAL will accept with the /B switch is 1, corresponding to 1k, and the maximum it will accept is 48, for 48k. If you don't specify a buffer size, it defaults to 16k. Combined with the approximately 12k of RAM needed for code, data, stack, and other purposes, PC-DIAL requires approximately 28k of memory to run using the default configuration. The exact number of entries you can fit into the allotted buffer space depends on the length of the entries that you make. Each entry in the PC-DIAL database is divided into three fields—Name, Company, and Phone—and each field may hold up to 26, 26, and 18 characters, respectively. Assuming the *average* length of a record is 50 characters, a 16k buffer has room for more than 300 names and phone numbers. The maximum buffer size of 48k provides space for about 1,000 entries of comparable length. Note that the buffer size may only be specified when PC- DIAL is installed; once the program is resident in memory, the buffer size is fixed.

If 1,000 records still isn't enough, or if you don't want to give up that much memory to one TSR, you can break your database of names and phone numbers into several data files and load them as needed. In its minimum configuration, PC-DIAL consumes only 13k of usable memory and has room for about 20 entries of 50 characters each. You can load a data file when PC-DIAL is installed by specifying the file name on the command line. After the program is installed, you can load data files by pressing the F8 key with the PC-DIAL window displayed on the screen.

Using PC-DIAL

The hotkey combination for PC-DIAL is Alt and the right Shift key. Pressing these keys pops up the window shown in Figure 13.2. The database that PC-DIAL maintains is structured as a series of records, each divided into three fields: one for names, one for company names, and one for phone numbers. The record highlighted by the bar in the center of the window is what we'll call the *current record*. All you have to do to dial a phone number is highlight the record that contains the number you want to dial and then press Enter. It's that easy.

FIGURE 13.2

The PC-DIAL window

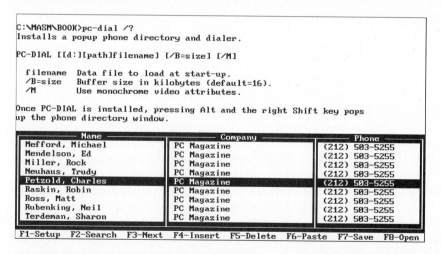

The function keys are your shortcut to many of the features of PC-DIAL. The menu line at the bottom of the screen lists what these function key assignments are. F1 calls up PC-DIAL's Setup window, which lets you customize PC-DIAL for use with your system by specifying the COM port your modem is attached to, the COM port address, and other configuration parameters. The finer points of customizing PC-DIAL are discussed in the next section. F2 pops up the Search window, where you define search strings, and F3 moves you to the next record that contains the current search string. F4 inserts a blank record above the current record. F5 deletes the current record, and F6 pastes the last record you deleted back into the database at the current record position. F7 saves the current database to disk so that you can recall it later, and F8 loads a new data file into memory.

The first thing you'll want to do when you use PC-DIAL is to enter some names and phone numbers. To create the first record, press the Tab key. A cursor will appear in the Name field. Type a name and press Tab to proceed to the Company field; then type a company name and press Tab again to move the cursor to the Phone field. You can move the cursor to the next field whenever you like by pressing Tab. Likewise, you can move it to the previous field by pressing Shift-Tab. When you're done typing the record, press Enter. The information you just typed will be entered into the database and the cursor will go away.

As you enter text, you can use the Left Arrow and Right Arrow keys to move the cursor, the Home and End keys to move to the beginning and end of the field, and Del and Backspace to delete. The Insert key toggles between insert and overstrike mode. In insert mode, the cursor increases in size to remind you that the text you type will be inserted, pushing text to the right of the cursor further to the right, toward the end of the field.

To enter the second record, either cursor to the blank line following the record you just entered by pressing the Down Arrow key, or press F4 to insert a new record above the current one. Then press Tab to enter the data, and Enter when you're done. Continue entering records this way until you've entered everything you want to enter. When you're ready to save, press function key F7, enter a file name at the "Save As" prompt, and press Enter. The data will be written to disk under the name you specified.

To scroll through the database, you can move up or down one line at a time with the Up Arrow and Down Arrow keys, a page at a time with the PgUp and PgDn keys, or move directly to the top or bottom of the list with the Home and End keys. To edit an entry, highlight the one you want to edit, press Tab to make the cursor visible, and make the desired changes to the record, again using Tab and Shift-Tab to move between fields. When you're finished, press Enter (or Up Arrow or Down Arrow) to register the changes. If, as you edit a record, you have second thoughts about what you've done, press the Escape key and the changes will be undone. If you're severely short on buffer space when you press the Tab key to begin editing a record, PC-DIAL will respond with an error message saying there's not enough space left in the buffer to edit the record. If this happens, you must free up some space by deleting other records before you can edit the current one—or reinstall PC-DIAL with a larger buffer size.

You can make space in the database for a new entry in two ways. If you want to add a new record to the end of the list, simply cursor to the blank line following the final record and press Tab to enter new text. If you want to insert a new record in the middle of the file, highlight the entry at the location where you want the new record to go and press F4. PC-DIAL will insert a blank line for you, which you can add text to by pressing the Tab key to obtain a cursor.

To delete a record, highlight it and press F5. If you discover you deleted the wrong one, press F6 to paste it back in. PC-DIAL's paste feature is more than a tool for fixing mistakes; you can also use it to reorder the records in the database. To move a record, cut it from its current position with F5, move to the new location you want it to appear in, and press F6. Repeat this operation as often as necessary to completely reorder the database.

After you enter or modify a group of records, press F7 to save them. PC-DIAL will ask you to enter the name of the file the data will be saved under. If you've saved the data before, PC-DIAL will provide the file name you used last as the default. If you haven't saved your data but have loaded a data file either from the command line when the program was installed or with the F8 key, PC-DIAL will use the name of that file as the default. If you want to save it under a name other than the default, all you have to do is enter the new name for the file at the "Save As" prompt. Conversely, to load a new data file, press F8 and enter a file name at the "File Name" prompt. Since PC-DIAL is a TSR and any directory is likely to be the current directory when it is popped up, you may have to specify a path to the file in addition to the file name for PC-DIAL to find it.

To dial a number, highlight the one you want to dial and press the Enter key. By default, PC-DIAL is configured to work with a Hayes or Hayes-compatible modem that supports data rates of at least 1,200 bits per second (bps) and is connected to COM1. If this description doesn't fit your system, you can change the configuration through the setup window invoked with function F1. After it transmits the command to the modem to dial the phone, PC-DIAL pops up a message window that tells you to wait until the phone at the receiving end begins to ring, and then to pick up the handset and press any key to disconnect the modem from the line. It's important that you pick up the telephone handset *before* you press a key; if you don't, the connection will be lost and you'll have to redial the number.

PC-DIAL provides two means for searching the database. The first involves defining a search string with the F2 key. Pressing F2 pops up a window in which you may enter a string of text to serve as the basis for the search. Once you enter a string and press Enter, PC-DIAL will proceed to the *next* record that contains that string. The search string can be any word or phrase, whole or in part, that appears in any of the three fields. For example, to search for "Smith," you could enter "Smith" or simply "Sm." Once the search string is defined, pressing F3 proceeds to the next record that contains the search string. The quick way to locate an individual who works for IBM, for example, is to press F2, type the letters "IBM," press Enter, and press F3 repeatedly until you find the record you're looking for.

The second means for searching out a particular record requires even less effort. Pressing the Alt key with any letter of the alphabet displays the next record whose Name field begins with that letter. To locate a name that begins with the letter M, for example, press Alt-M. To locate the next one, press Alt-M again. What's great about this feature is that it doesn't matter whether names are stored in last-name-first or first-name-first format, and it even works if the names aren't alphabetized. Best of all, it only takes one keystroke. To do better than that, the program would have to read your mind.

Customizing PC-DIAL

If your modem isn't Hayes-compatible, you'll need to make a few configuration changes before PC-DIAL can dial the phone for you. Even if it is Hayes-compatible, you may need to alter PC-DIAL's default configuration parameters for other reasons: for example, if your modem is connected to COM2 rather than COM1, or if you want to change the command that initializes the modem to something other than the default.

Function key F1 pops up the window depicted in Figure 13.3. From this central command console, you can change eight important setup parameters. You indicate which of the parameters you want to modify by using the Up Arrow and Down Arrow keys to move the red highlighting bar. With "COM Port" highlighted, pressing Enter, the spacebar, or the Tab key toggles between COM1, COM2, COM3, and COM4. With "Communications Setting" highlighted, the same keys allow you to choose from five different data rates (ranging from 300 bps to 9,600 bps) and two different data formats: no parity, 8 data bits, and 1 stop bit (abbreviated N81); and even parity, 7 data bits, and 1 stop bit (abbreviated E71). Note that the data format you select has no impact on the way the phone is dialed. This setting is provided for convenience, in case you want the serial port initialized to a particular setting after PC-DIAL is used. However, you must make sure that the data rate you select is one that your modem supports. You can't send commands at 2,400 bps to a modem that only supports 1,200 bps. Also note that in addition to using the Enter, spacebar, and Tab keys, you can move backward or forward through these selection sets with the Left Arrow and Right Arrow keys.

FIGURE 13.3

The PC-DIAL configuration window

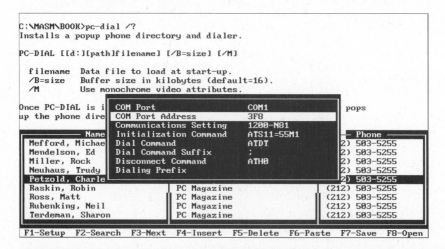

Pressing Enter, Tab, or the spacebar with any other configuration option highlighted displays a cursor so that you can enter text. Under "COM Port Address," you can enter a new I/O address for the COM port displayed on the line above. The address is understood to be in hexadecimal format. For COM1 and COM2, you'll probably never need to change it. By convention, COM1 is always assigned 3F8H and COM2 is assigned 2F8H. The addresses for COM3 and COM4 vary from system to system, however. If you want to use PC-DIAL with COM3 or COM4 and they're configured to use addresses other than 3E8H and 2E8H, you'll need to advise PC-DIAL what the actual addresses are. For help, turn to the manual that came with the serial ports, or, if they came installed in your PC, the PC documentation. The manuals should tell you what the I/O addresses are. Note that some PCs permit the I/O addresses to be changed with jumper or DIP switch settings; if this is the case, you may have to examine the board the serial ports are installed on to determine what they're mapped to.

If there are any digits you want PC-DIAL to dial before dialing a phone number, enter them in the field labeled "Dialing Prefix" at the bottom of the window. Some phone systems require you to dial 9 to get an outside line. If yours is one of those, enter "9" as the dialing prefix, and PC-DIAL will automatically prefix every number it dials with a 9 to request an outside line. On some phone systems, you may have to include one or two commas after the 9 to induce a short pause after the 9 is dialed (a comma signals a Hayes modem to pause, usually for about 2 seconds). By the same token, if every number you dial is long distance, this is an excellent way to avoid having to enter a 1 in front of every number in your database. Just enter a 1 for the dialing prefix and you'll be set.

The remaining four entries in the configuration window define commands that are sent to the modem when the phone is dialed. Each entry may be up to 16 characters long. "Initialization Command" is the command sent to the modem before the number is dialed. The default is ATS11=55M1, which sets the interval between touch tones to 55 milliseconds for fast dialing and turns the modem's speaker on until a carrier is detected. "Dial Command" is the command sent to dial the phone. The default is ATDT. If your phone requires pulse dialing rather than tone dialing, change this to ATDP. "Dial Command Suffix" is the string of text that is sent to the modem immediately following the phone number. By default, this is a semicolon, which returns a Hayes modem to command state after the current command is processed. Finally, "Disconnect Command" is the command that is sent to disconnect the modem once dialing is complete. By default, it is ATH0. You can use these configuration parameters to customize PC-DIAL to work with non-Hayes modems if you substitute the commands that your modem uses to dial and hang up the phone. As you make changes, be aware that most Hayes modems will accept a maximum of 40 characters as part of any one command, including the digits that make up the phone number. Therefore, if you set *all* of these fields to the maximum of 16 characters, you may not get the results you expect.

When all your configuration changes are made, press Esc to exit setup. PC-DIAL will ask you if you want to save the changes to disk. If you answer no, your changes will remain for the duration of this session, but will revert to the defaults the next time PC-DIAL is installed. If you answer yes, you'll be prompted to enter the name of the file to save the changes to. Enter the name *and location* of PC-DIAL.COM. For example, if PC-DIAL.COM is stored in the \UTIL directory of the C drive, answer C:\UTIL\PC-DIAL.COM to the query. PC-DIAL will copy the new parameters to its image on disk so that the next time it's loaded, the changes you made will automatically take effect.

Inside PC-DIAL

As TSRs go, PC-DIAL is about as sophisticated as they get. Because it uses DOS file I/O functions to read and write data files, it's careful to check the InDOS flag and critical error flag before it pops up to ensure that calls to interrupt 21H will not be nested. It also maintains a flag of its own called INTFLAGS (similar to the flag of the same name used by LPT2FILE in Chapter 12) that is non-zero when a call to interrupt 13H, 25H, or 26H is currently in progress. By not allowing itself to pop up when any of these interrupts is being processed, PC-DIAL provides all the insurance it can that it will not interfere with an ongoing disk operation.

PC-DIAL is only the second example we've seen of a utility that writes directly to video memory (the first one was FINDTEXT, presented in Chapter 10). Notice that when you press the hotkey, the PC-DIAL window literally pops up onto the screen. Contrast this to SETUP, which was introduced in Chapter 12. SETUP draws its window onto the screen slowly; so slowly, in fact, that even on a fast 386 PC you can see the window go up and down. PC-DIAL is fast because it places character codes and attributes directly into the video buffer, while SETUP uses video output functions in the BIOS. Run side by side, these two programs vividly illustrate the difference between programming the official way (going through DOS and the BIOS) and programming the other way (bypassing DOS and the BIOS and programming the hardware). A downside to writing directly to the video buffer is that PC-DIAL will not pop up if you're currently running in any sort of graphics mode. (The architectures of text and graphics modes are entirely different and video routines that work in text mode must be rewritten if they're to work in graphics mode, too.) That means if you use PC-DIAL with the DOS 5.0 Shell, you'll either need to run the Shell in text mode or wait until you're running a character-based application to pop up PC-DIAL.

PC-DIAL is also the first TSR we've examined that displays a window on the screen. It accomplishes this via two procedures called SAVEREGION and RESTREGION. SAVEREGION accepts the row and column address of the upper-left corner of a rectangular region of the screen in CX and the row and column address of the lower-right corner of the region in DX. It also accepts the address of a buffer in ES:DI. Then it copies all the character and attribute data in the specified area of the screen to the buffer. RESTREGION (short for *RESTore REGION*) does just the opposite: You pass it the coordinates of a rectangle in CX and DX and the address of the buffer the data was written to earlier in DS:SI, and it restores that part of the screen. That's how you erase a window displayed by a TSR; you simply restore the image that was on the screen before the window was drawn.

When the hotkey combination is pressed, PC-DIAL calls the procedure POPUP, which, among other things, determines how many lines are showing on the screen and calls SAVEREGION to save the last 12 lines displayed. Then it paints the window onto the screen by inserting character and attribute data into the video buffer. Later, when you press Esc to close the window, PC-DIAL calls RESTREGION to restore the part of the screen that was overwritten by the pop-up window. You can use similar methods for writing TSRs with pop-up windows of your own. In fact, you can borrow SAVEREGION and RESTREGION right from the source code for PC-DIAL. Just make sure that before you call either of them, the variables named VIDEO_SEGMENT and LINE_LENGTH are initialized. VIDEO_SEGMENT holds the segment address of the video buffer (B000H in monochrome video modes, B800H in color). LINE_LENGTH is the number of bytes in the video buffer it takes to represent one line on the screen, which is exactly two times the number of columns displayed. In PC-DIAL, these variables are set by POPUP before SAVEREGION and RESTREGION are called.

If you run PC-DIAL on an old IBM Color Graphics Adapter, you'll see an unsightly, snow-like interference on the screen when the window goes up and down and as you scroll through the database. That's because the CGA lacks the circuitry required to coordinate accesses to the video buffer when the CPU and the video adapter's on-board character generator try to read or write video memory at the same time. In the past, many programs employed software work-arounds that eliminated the errant video signals but adversely affected performance. PC-DIAL doesn't. With VGAs available for less than $100, there's no good reason to run a CGA anymore—and no reason to cripple otherwise good software to compensate for flawed hardware that is long out of date.

Dialing the Phone

Writing a program to dial the phone for you isn't nearly as difficult as it may sound. In reality, the modem does most of the work; all the program has to do is transmit the proper commands to the modem to tell it to dial the phone. Hayes and Hayes-compatible modems understand a modem language called the *AT command set*. AT doesn't mean AT as in IBM PC/AT; instead, it represents the ASCII codes for the letters A and T. "AT" is the string a Hayes modem recognizes as the beginning of a command, similar to an escape character transmitted to ANSI.SYS. For example, the ASCII string

```
ATDT5551212
```

followed by a carriage return commands a Hayes modem to dial the number 555-1212. AT (short for "ATtention") tells the modem that a command is forthcoming; D is the command to dial the phone; and T tells it to tone dial, the same way a touch-tone phone dials a number. Similarly, the command

```
ATH0
```

tells the modem to go "on hook"—in effect, to hang up the phone. When the modem is on-line, it is said to be "off hook." In all, the AT command set comprises approximately 50 different commands enabling the modem to do everything from dialing the phone to adjusting its own speaker volume. If a modem doesn't understand the AT command set, then it's not truly Hayes-compatible.

Pressing the Enter key with a phone number displayed in PC-DIAL initiates a series of events that culminates in the dialing of the phone. First, PC-DIAL transmits the command to initialize the modem. By default, this command is ATS11=55M1. S11=55 sets the spacing between touch tones to 55 milliseconds. This speeds up dialing considerably. On most modems, any value from 50 to 255 is acceptable. M1 turns the modem's speaker on. Once the modem detects the presence of a carrier, the speaker is automatically turned off.

After it initializes the modem, PC-DIAL sends the command to dial the phone, followed by the phone number and a command suffix, which by default is a semicolon. If you dialed 555-1212, the string of characters sent to the modem would look like this:

```
ATDT555-1212;<CR>
```

The <CR> at the end represents a carriage return (ASCII 13), which Hayes modems recognize as a command terminator. Why the semicolon at the end of the phone number? When a dial command ends in a semicolon, the modem immediately returns to command state, ready to accept more commands. This is important because as soon as the number is dialed, PC-DIAL displays a message box telling you to wait until you hear the phone begin to ring, and then to pick up the handset and press a key. When you press a key, PC-DIAL sends an ATH0 command to the modem to disconnect it from the line. If the modem isn't in command state, the command will be ignored unless it's preceded by a special escape code. This way, the escape code isn't needed, because the modem is in command state already.

The only tricky part about dialing the phone is sending the modem commands out the serial port. The BIOS offers a convenient set of serial port I/O services through interrupt 14H that programs can use to transmit serial data, but there's a problem: Most BIOS modules won't send data to the serial port unless the device on the receiving end (the modem) asserts the CTS and DSR lines on the RS-232 interface (the physical connections between two serial devices). CTS stands for Clear to Send, DSR for Data Set Ready. In classical RS-232 communications, these are signals used by the receiving device to tell the sender it's okay to send data. However, modems don't always assert DSR. Setting DIP switch 6 to the up position on a Hayes Smartmodem 1200, for example, disables DSR except when there is a connection established. And if DSR is not asserted, the BIOS won't transmit data. To compensate, PC-DIAL does what commercial communications programs do: It supplies its own serial port output routines that ignore the settings of pins on the RS-232 interface. TRANSMIT_STRING sends an ASCIIZ string to the serial port whose I/O address is passed in DX, and TRANSMIT_CHAR does the same for a single character.

You can see from the source code how these routines work. TRANSMIT_-CHAR polls the serial port's Line Status register until bit 5 is set, indicating that the Transmit Holding register (the register that data is sent to for output) is ready to accept another byte of data. Then the data is written to the Transmit Holding register with an OUT instruction. In code, it looks like this:

```
                   push    ax
                   add     dx,5
trans_loop:        in      al,dx
                   test    al,20h
                   jz      trans_loop
                   pop     ax
                   sub     dx,5
                   out     dx,al
```

On entry, AL holds the character to be transmitted and DX holds the base address of the serial port, which also happens to be the address of the Transmit Holding register. The instructions

```
push    ax
add     dx,5
```

save the byte to be transmitted on the stack and point DX to the Line Status register, whose address is equal to the base address of the serial port plus 5. Then, the code sequence

```
trans_loop:        in      al,dx
                   test    al,20h
                   jz      trans_loop
```

delays until bit 5 of the Line Status register comes clear, and the instructions

```
pop     ax
sub     dx,5
out     dx,al
```

retrieve the output value, point DX back to the Transmit Holding register, and output the byte of data. Once the character is received by the Transmit Holding register, the serial port UART breaks it down into individual bits and places them on the line, effectively transmitting the character to the receiver on the other end. (UART, which stands for Universal Asynchronous Receiver/Transmitter, is the chip that drives the serial port.)

As usual, you can pull these serial port output routines straight out of PC-DIAL and use them in your own programs if you wish. They'll come in handy anytime you want to send data out a serial port, provided there's no possibility that the sender can transmit data faster than the receiver can process it. (If that's a possibility, you'll need additional logic to implement a handshaking scheme using the pins on the RS-232 interface.) Otherwise, all you need to know is the address where the serial port is based. The rest is automatic.

Printing PC-DIAL Data Files

PC-DIAL saves the data you enter in a special format that is similar but not identical to plain ASCII text files. That's fine as long as you don't have to use the files outside PC-DIAL, but it's a stumbling block if you want to print them or export them to a separate database package such as dBASE or Paradox. What you need is a tool to convert a PC-DIAL data file to an ASCII text file. To that end, this book comes with a companion program to PC-DIAL called PC-LIST that lists the contents of PC-DIAL data files to the standard output device (the screen) in plain ASCII format suitable for capturing to a file or sending to a printer.

The syntax for running PC-LIST is

```
PC-LIST [d:][path]filename
```

where filename is the name of the data file you want listed. To print the contents of a file, use an output redirection operator to direct output to a printer instead of the screen. You could, for example, print a PC-DIAL file named BUSINESS.DAT with the following command:

```
PC-LIST BUSINESS.DAT > PRN
```

Similarly, you could print the output on LPT2 with the command

```
PC-LIST BUSINESS.DAT > LPT2
```

If all you want to do is convert a PC-DIAL data file into an ASCII file, you can use an output redirection operator to capture the output from PC-LIST to a file. The command

```
PC-LIST BUSINESS.DAT > BUSINESS.TXT
```

creates an ASCII file called BUSINESS.TXT that contains the same information BUSINESS.TXT does, but in standard ASCII format. If you're curious to know how PC-LIST works, the source code for it (PC-LIST.ASM) is included on the disks. We won't print it here because it includes nothing that you haven't seen before.

Removing TSRs from Memory

Now that you have a few TSRs to use on your system (in addition to the ones that come with DOS—GRAPHICS, FASTOPEN, and others), you need a way to remove them from memory once they're installed. Installing them is easy; uninstalling them is not. While DOS provides an easy mechanism for programs to terminate and remain resident in memory, it does not provide a built-in means for removing them. Once a TSR is installed, it's generally there until you reboot.

You can fix that with INSTALL and REMOVE, the pair of utilities shown in Listings 13.4 and 13.5. These programs are TSR managers that use a book-mark metaphor to let you mark TSRs and unload them on demand. With INSTALL, you insert a bookmark in memory and give the bookmark a name if you wish. Later, you can use REMOVE to uninstall all the TSRs installed after that bookmark. You can create as many bookmarks as you like, and you can remove the bookmarks one at a time or several at once. Each bookmark that you create requires about 1,400 bytes of memory.

The syntax for INSTALL is

```
INSTALL [bookmark]
```

where *bookmark* is the name you want to assign to the bookmark. The name is optional; if you don't specify one, INSTALL installs a bookmark anyway and assigns it the name "(No Name)." Normally, *bookmark* will be the name of the TSR or TSRs you're going to install after INSTALL. Names can be up to 32 characters long; anything more than that is ignored.

LISTING 13.4 INSTALL.ASM

```
;*************************************************************************
; INSTALL inserts a bookmark in memory that allows TSRs installed above it
; to be uninstalled.  Its syntax is
;
;       INSTALL [bookmark]
;
; where "bookmark" is the name of the bookmark.  This parameter can be
; passed to REMOVE when a TSR is uninstalled.  Only the first 32 characters
; of the bookmark name are used.
;*************************************************************************

code            segment
                assume  cs:code
                org     100h
begin:          jmp     init

nextblock       dw      0FFFFh                  ;Pointer to next block
bookmark        db      "(No Name)",24 dup (0Dh);Bookmark name
signature       db      0,1,2,"INSTALL",2,1,0   ;Program signature
vectors         dw      512 dup (?)             ;Interrupt vectors
prog_id         db      ?                       ;Multiplex ID number
int2Fh          dd      ?                       ;Interrupt 2FH vector


;*************************************************************************
```

```
; MPLEX_INT handles interrupt 2FH.  If, on entry, AH is set to INSTALL's
; multiplex ID number, MPLEX_INT uses the value in AL as a function code.
; The functions supported are:
;
;    00H    Returns FFH in AL to indicate the program is installed
;           and returns the address of its signature in ES:DI.
;****************************************************************************

mplex_int       proc    far
                pushf                           ;Save FLAGS register
                cmp     ah,cs:[prog_id]         ;Branch if AH holds the
                je      mplex2                  ;   multiplex ID
                popf                            ;Restore FLAGS
                jmp     cs:[int2Fh]             ;Pass the interrupt on
;
; Function 00H verifies that the program is installed.
;
mplex2:         popf                            ;Restore FLAGS
                or      al,al                   ;Branch if function code
                jnz     mplex3                  ;   is other than 00H
                mov     al,0FFh                 ;Set AL to FFH
                push    cs                      ;Point ES:DI to the program
                pop     es                      ;   signature
                mov     di,offset signature
mplex3:         iret                            ;Return from interrupt
mplex_int       endp


;****************************************************************************
; Data that will be discarded when the program becomes memory-resident.
;****************************************************************************

helpmsg         db      "Places a bookmark in memory that allows TSRs to "
                db      "be uninstalled.",13,10,13,10
                db      "INSTALL [bookmark]",13,10,13,10
                db      "  bookmark   Name of the bookmark being installed."
                db      13,10,13,10
                db      "Once a bookmark is placed, TSRs installed above "
                db      "it in memory can be",13,10
                db      "uninstalled with INSTALL's companion program, "
                db      "REMOVE.",13,10,"$"

errmsg1         db      "Requires DOS 3.0 or higher",13,10,"$"
errmsg2         db      "INSTALL cannot be loaded high",13,10,"$"
errmsg3         db      "Program could not be installed",13,10,"$"

msg1            db      "Bookmark created.  Use REMOVE to remove it."
                db      13,10,"$"


;****************************************************************************
; INIT makes the program resident in memory.
;****************************************************************************

                assume  cs:code,ds:code

init            proc    near
                cld                             ;Clear direction flag
```

```
                mov     si,81h              ;Point SI to command line
                call    scanhelp            ;Scan for "/?" switch
                jnc     checkver            ;Branch if not found
                mov     ah,09h              ;Display help text and exit
                mov     dx,offset helpmsg   ;  with ERRORLEVEL=0
                int     21h
                mov     ax,4C00h
                int     21h
;
; Check the DOS version and make sure the program isn't loaded high.
;
checkver:       mov     dx,offset errmsg1   ;Exit if DOS version
                mov     ah,30h              ;  is less than 3.0
                int     21h
                cmp     al,3
                jae     checkaddr

error:          mov     ah,09h              ;Display error message and
                int     21h                 ;  exit with ERRORLEVEL=1
                mov     ax,4C01h
                int     21h

checkaddr:      mov     dx,offset errmsg2   ;Exit if program is loaded
                mov     ax,cs               ;  at segment A000H or
                cmp     ax,0A000h           ;  higher
                jae     error
;
; Parse the command line.
;
                call    findchar            ;Advance to first character
                jc      copy                ;Branch if no parameters
                mov     di,offset bookmark  ;Point DI to buffer
                mov     cx,32               ;Initialize counter
parse1:         lodsb                       ;Get a character
                cmp     al,"a"              ;Capitalize it if it's
                jb      parse2              ;  between "a" and "z"
                cmp     al,"z"
                ja      parse2
                and     al,0DFh
parse2:         stosb                       ;Store it
                cmp     al,0Dh              ;Branch if was a carriage
                je      copy                ;  return
                loop    parse1              ;Loop back for more
;
; Copy the interrupt vector table from low memory.
;
copy:           push    ds                  ;Save DS
                sub     si,si               ;Point DS:SI to 0000:0000
                mov     ds,si
                assume  ds:nothing
                mov     di,offset vectors   ;Point DI to storage area
                mov     cx,512              ;Initialize counter
                cli                         ;Disable interrupts
                rep     movsw               ;Copy the vector table
                sti                         ;Enable interrupts
                pop     ds                  ;Restore DS
```

```
                assume  ds:code
;
; Install the program.
;
                call    check_install           ;Branch if a copy of INSTALL
                jnc     install_full            ;  is not already installed

                mov     di,offset nextblock     ;Point DI to NEXTBLOCK
install1:       cmp     word ptr es:[di],0FFFFh ;Branch if this is not the
                jne     install2                ;  last block in the chain
                mov     word ptr es:[di],cs     ;Record the address of this
                jmp     short install_part      ;  block if it is
install2:       mov     es,es:[di]              ;Point ES to next block in
                jmp     install1                ;  the chain and loop back

install_full:   call    mplex_id                ;Find a multiplex ID number
                mov     dx,offset errmsg3       ;Error if none available
                jc      error
                mov     prog_id,ah              ;Save the ID number

                mov     ax,352Fh                ;Hook interrupt 2FH
                int     21h
                mov     word ptr int2Fh,bx
                mov     word ptr int2Fh[2],es
                mov     ax,252Fh
                mov     dx,offset mplex_int
                int     21h

install_part:   mov     ah,49h                  ;Get the segment address of
                mov     es,ds:[2Ch]             ;  the environment block
                int     21h                     ;  and free the segment

                mov     ah,09h                  ;Display message verifying
                mov     dx,offset msg1          ;  the installation
                int     21h

                mov     ax,3100h                ;Terminate with function 31H
                mov     dx,(offset helpmsg - offset code + 15) shr 4
                int     21h
init            endp

;**************************************************************************
; FINDCHAR advances SI to the next non-space or non-comma character.
; On return, carry set indicates EOL was encountered.
;**************************************************************************

findchar        proc    near
                lodsb                           ;Get the next character
                cmp     al,20h                  ;Loop if space
                je      findchar
                cmp     al,2Ch                  ;Loop if comma
                je      findchar
                dec     si                      ;Point SI to the character
                cmp     al,0Dh                  ;Exit with carry set if end
                je      eol                     ;  of line is reached
```

```
                clc                             ;Clear carry and exit
                ret

eol:            stc                             ;Set carry and exit
                ret
findchar        endp


;***********************************************************************
; SCANHELP scans the command line for a /? switch.  If found, carry returns
; set and SI contains its offset.  If not found, carry returns clear.
;***********************************************************************

scanhelp        proc    near
                push    si                      ;Save SI
scanloop:       lodsb                           ;Get a character
                cmp     al,0Dh                  ;Exit if end of line
                je      scan_exit
                cmp     al,"?"                  ;Loop if not "?"
                jne     scanloop
                cmp     byte ptr [si-2],"/"     ;Loop if not "/"
                jne     scanloop

                add     sp,2                    ;Clear the stack
                sub     si,2                    ;Adjust SI
                stc                             ;Set carry and exit
                ret

scan_exit:      pop     si                      ;Restore SI
                clc                             ;Clear carry and exit
                ret
scanhelp        endp


;***********************************************************************
; CHECK_INSTALL returns carry set if the program is already installed,
; carry clear if it's not.  If carry returns set, AH holds the program's
; multiplex ID number.
;***********************************************************************

check_install   proc    near
                mov     ax,8000h                ;Initialize AH and AL
                mov     cx,80h                  ;Initialize count

chinst1:        push    ax                      ;Save AX and CX
                push    cx
                sub     di,di                   ;Set ES and DI to 0
                mov     es,di
                int     2Fh                     ;Interrupt 2Fh
                cmp     al,0FFh                 ;Nothing here if AL isn't
                jne     chinst2                 ;  equal to FFH

                mov     si,offset signature     ;See if program signature
                mov     cx,13                   ;  appears at the address
                repe    cmpsb                   ;  returned in ES:DI
                jne     chinst2                 ;Branch if it does not

                pop     cx                      ;Clear the stack and exit
```

```
                        pop     ax                      ;  with carry set
                        stc
                        ret

chinst2:                pop     cx                      ;Retrieve AX and CX
                        pop     ax
                        inc     ah                      ;Next multiplex ID
                        loop    chinst1                 ;Loop until done

                        clc                             ;Exit with carry clear
                        ret
check_install           endp

;**************************************************************************
; MPLEX_ID searches for an unused multiplex ID number.  If one is found,
; it is returned in AH with carry clear.  Carry set means no multiplex
; ID numbers are currently available.
;**************************************************************************

mplex_id                proc    near
                        mov     ax,8000h                ;Initialize AH and AL
                        mov     cx,80h                  ;Initialize count

mxid1:                  push    ax                      ;Save AX and CX
                        push    cx
                        int     2Fh                     ;Interrupt 2Fh
                        or      al,al                   ;Branch if AL=0
                        jz      mxid2
                        pop     cx                      ;Retrieve AX and CX
                        pop     ax
                        inc     ah                      ;Increment ID number
                        loop    mxid1                   ;Loop until done

                        stc                             ;Exit with carry set
                        ret

mxid2:                  pop     cx                      ;Clear the stack and exit
                        pop     ax                      ;  with carry clear
                        clc
                        ret
mplex_id                endp

code                    ends
                        end     begin
```

Once a bookmark is installed, you can remove it with REMOVE. The syntax for REMOVE is

```
REMOVE [bookmark] [/L]
```

where bookmark is the name of the bookmark you want to remove. The /L switch lists all the bookmarks that REMOVE finds when it scans through memory, but without actually uninstalling any of them. If you run it without specifying the name of a bookmark, it simply removes the last bookmark you created. If you run REMOVE with the name of a bookmark, it removes that bookmark and any bookmarks installed after it. In other words, if you create bookmarks 1, 2, and 3, in that order, and then remove bookmark 2, bookmark 3 is automatically removed also.

The important thing to grasp here is that when you remove a bookmark, you also remove any TSRs installed after it. Let's say you created a bookmark called DOS 5 UTILS and then loaded PC-DIAL and LPT2FILE. When you remove the bookmark, PC-DIAL and LPT2FILE go away, too. By locating bookmarks in strategic places, you can remove any TSRs you want to, one at a time or in groups.

LISTING 13.5　REMOVE.ASM

```
;**************************************************************************
; REMOVE removes TSRs installed with INSTALL.  Its syntax is
;
;        REMOVE [bookmark] [/L]
;
; where "bookmark" is the name of the bookmark (assigned with INSTALL)
; to be removed from memory, and /L lists the bookmarks that are currently
; resident in memory.  When a bookmark is removed, all the TSRs installed
; above it are removed also.  Run with no command line parameters, REMOVE
; removes the highest bookmark in memory.
;**************************************************************************

nextblock       equ     0103h                   ;Offset of NEXTBLOCK field
bm_addr         equ     0105h                   ;Offset of bookmark field
vectors         equ     0133h                   ;Offset of vector field

code            segment
                assume  cs:code,ds:code
                org     100h
begin:          jmp     main

helpmsg         db      "Removes TSRs installed with INSTALL.",13,10,13,10
                db      "REMOVE [bookmark] [/L]",13,10,13,10
                db      "  bookmark  Name of the bookmark to remove.",13,10
                db      "  /L        List the bookmarks currently "
                db      "installed.",13,10,13,10
                db      "Run with no parameters, REMOVE removes the "
                db      "highest bookmark in memory ",13,10
                db      "and everything above it.",13,10,"$"

errmsg1         db      "Syntax: REMOVE [bookmark] [/L]",13,10,"$"
errmsg2         db      "Requires DOS 3.0 or higher",13,10,"$"
errmsg3         db      "No bookmarks are installed",13,10,"$"
errmsg4         db      "No bookmark of that name is installed",13,10,"$"
errmsg5         db      "Memory deallocation failed",13,10,"$"

msg1            db      "Bookmark $"
msg2            db      " removed"
crlf            db      13,10,"$"

lastblock       dw      ?                       ;Segment of last block
bookmark        db      33 dup (0Dh)            ;Bookmark name
```

```
signature       db      0,1,2,"INSTALL",2,1,0   ;INSTALL signature

;****************************************************************************
; Procedure MAIN
;****************************************************************************

main            proc    near
                cld                             ;Clear direction flag
                mov     si,81h                  ;Point SI to command line
                call    scanhelp                ;Scan for "/?" switch
                jnc     checkver                ;Branch if not found
                mov     ah,09h                  ;Display help text and exit
                mov     dx,offset helpmsg       ;   with ERRORLEVEL=0
                int     21h
                mov     ax,4C00h
                int     21h
;
; Check the DOS version.
;
checkver:       mov     dx,offset errmsg2       ;Exit if DOS version
                mov     ah,30h                  ;   is less than 3.0
                int     21h
                cmp     al,3
                jae     checkins

error:          mov     ah,09h                  ;Display error message and
                int     21h                     ;   exit with ERRORLEVEL=1
                mov     ax,4C01h
                int     21h

checkins:       call    check_install           ;See if INSTALL is installed
                mov     dx,offset errmsg3
                jnc     error                   ;Exit if it's not
;
; Parse the command line.
;
                mov     lastblock,cs            ;Initialize LASTBLOCK
                mov     si,81h                  ;Reset SI
                call    findchar                ;Find the first parameter
                jc      search1                 ;Branch if there are none
                cmp     byte ptr [si],"/"       ;Branch if the character
                jne     parse                   ;   is not a "/"
;
; Process a /L switch.
;
list:           inc     si                      ;Skip the "/" character
                lodsb                           ;Get the next character
                and     al,0DFh                 ;Capitalize it
                mov     dx,offset errmsg1       ;Initialize error pointer
                cmp     al,"L"                  ;Error if the character is
                jne     error                   ;   not an "L"

nextname:       mov     di,bm_addr              ;Point DI to bookmark name
                call    dos_out                 ;Display bookmark name
                mov     ah,09h                  ;Move the cursor to the
                mov     dx,offset crlf          ;   next line
```

```
                int     21h
                cmp     word ptr es:[nextblock],0FFFFh  ;Exit if this is the
                je      list_exit               ;   last block
                mov     es,es:[nextblock]       ;Get segment of next block
                jmp     nextname                ;Go back and output its name

list_exit:      mov     ax,4C00h                ;Exit with ERRORLEVEL=0
                int     21h
;
; Read the bookmark name from the command line.
;
parse:          mov     di,offset bookmark      ;Point DI to buffer
                mov     cx,32                   ;Initialize counter
parse1:         lodsb                           ;Get a character
                cmp     al,"a"                  ;Capitalize it if it's
                jb      parse2                  ;   between "a" and "z"
                cmp     al,"z"
                ja      parse2
                and     al,0DFh
parse2:         mov     [di],al                 ;Store it
                inc     di                      ;Increment DI
                cmp     al,0Dh                  ;Branch if it was a carriage
                je      search                  ;   return
                loop    parse1                  ;Loop back for more
;
; Search out a bookmark.
;
search:         mov     si,offset bookmark      ;Point SI to local name
                mov     di,bm_addr              ;Point DI to remote name
                call    compare_names           ;Compare the two
                je      endchain                ;Branch if they're equal
                mov     dx,offset errmsg4
                cmp     word ptr es:[nextblock],0FFFFh
                je      error                   ;Error if last block
                mov     lastblock,es            ;Save last block address
                mov     es,es:[nextblock]       ;Get address of next block
                jmp     search                  ;Return to search loop

search1:        cmp     word ptr es:[nextblock],0FFFFh
                je      endchain                ;Branch if last block
                mov     lastblock,es            ;Save last block address
                mov     es,es:[nextblock]       ;Get address of next block
                jmp     search1                 ;Continue the search
;
; Terminate the chain of INSTALLed blocks and restore interrupt vectors.
;
endchain:       push    es                      ;Save ES
                mov     es,lastblock            ;Retrieve last block address
                mov     word ptr es:[nextblock],0FFFFh  ;Terminate the chain
                pop     es                      ;Restore ES
                mov     lastblock,es            ;Save ES in LASTBLOCK

                push    ds                      ;Save DS and ES
                push    es
                mov     ax,es                   ;Point DS:SI to copy of
                mov     ds,ax                   ;   interrupt vectors in
```

```
                assume  ds:nothing             ;  INSTALLed block
                mov     si,vectors
                sub     di,di                  ;Point ES:DI to 0000:0000
                mov     es,di
                mov     cx,512                 ;Initialize counter
                cli                            ;Disable interrupts
                rep     movsw                  ;Restore interrupt vectors
                sti                            ;Enable interrupts
                pop     es                     ;Restore DS and ES
                pop     ds
                assume  ds:code
;
; Search out every PSP block above INSTALL and deallocate the memory that
; belongs to it.
;
                mov     bx,es                  ;Transfer ES to BX
                mov     ah,49h                 ;Deallocate the memory used
                int     21h                    ;   by INSTALL
                mov     dx,offset errmsg5      ;Initialize error pointer
                jc      error1                 ;Error if call failed

remove:         dec     bx                     ;Point BX to MCB
                mov     es,bx                  ;Transfer BX to ES
                add     bx,es:[03h]            ;Compute next MCB address
                inc     bx
                mov     es,bx                  ;Transfer segment to ES
                inc     bx                     ;Point BX to segment beyond
                cmp     bx,es:[01h]            ;Does the segment own itself?
                jne     remove                 ;No, then continue searching
                mov     ax,cs                  ;Record current segment in AX
                cmp     bx,ax                  ;Have we reached our own PSP?
                je      done                   ;Yes, then we're done

                push    bx                     ;Save PSP segment address
                call    freemem                ;Free all memory it owns
                pop     bx                     ;Retrieve the address
                mov     dx,offset errmsg5      ;Loop back if no error
                jnc     remove                 ;   occurred

error1:         jmp     error                  ;Exit on error
;
; Announce that REMOVE succeeded and terminate.
;
done:           mov     ah,09h                 ;Display message verifying
                mov     dx,offset msg1         ;   that the bookmark was
                int     21h                    ;   removed
                mov     es,lastblock
                mov     di,bm_addr
                call    dos_out
                mov     ah,09h
                mov     dx,offset msg2
                int     21h

                mov     ax,4C00h               ;Exit with ERRORLEVEL=0
                int     21h
main            endp
```

```
;**************************************************************************
; FINDCHAR advances SI to the next non-space or non-comma character.
; On return, carry set indicates EOL was encountered.
;**************************************************************************

findchar        proc    near
                lodsb                           ;Get the next character
                cmp     al,20h                  ;Loop if space
                je      findchar
                cmp     al,2Ch                  ;Loop if comma
                je      findchar
                dec     si                      ;Point SI to the character
                cmp     al,0Dh                  ;Exit with carry set if end
                je      eol                     ;  of line is reached

                clc                             ;Clear carry and exit
                ret

eol:            stc                             ;Set carry and exit
                ret
findchar        endp


;**************************************************************************
; SCANHELP scans the command line for a /? switch.  If found, carry returns
; set and SI contains its offset.  If not found, carry returns clear.
;**************************************************************************

scanhelp        proc    near
                push    si                      ;Save SI
scanloop:       lodsb                           ;Get a character
                cmp     al,0Dh                  ;Exit if end of line
                je      scan_exit
                cmp     al,"?"                  ;Loop if not "?"
                jne     scanloop
                cmp     byte ptr [si-2],"/"     ;Loop if not "/"
                jne     scanloop

                add     sp,2                    ;Clear the stack
                sub     si,2                    ;Adjust SI
                stc                             ;Set carry and exit
                ret

scan_exit:      pop     si                      ;Restore SI
                clc                             ;Clear carry and exit
                ret
scanhelp        endp


;**************************************************************************
; CHECK_INSTALL returns carry set if a copy of INSTALL is installed,
; carry clear if it's not.  If carry returns set, AH holds INSTALL's
; multiplex ID number and ES holds its segment address.
;**************************************************************************

check_install   proc    near
                mov     ax,8000h                ;Initialize AH and AL
```

```
                    mov     cx,80h                  ;Initialize count

chinst1:            push    ax                      ;Save AX and CX
                    push    cx
                    sub     di,di                   ;Set ES and DI to 0
                    mov     es,di
                    int     2Fh                     ;Interrupt 2Fh
                    cmp     al,0FFh                 ;Nothing here if AL isn't
                    jne     chinst2                 ;   equal to FFH

                    mov     si,offset signature     ;See if program signature
                    mov     cx,13                   ;   appears at the address
                    repe    cmpsb                   ;   returned in ES:DI
                    jne     chinst2                 ;Branch if it does not

                    pop     cx                      ;Clear the stack and exit
                    pop     ax                      ;   with carry set
                    stc
                    ret

chinst2:            pop     cx                      ;Retrieve AX and CX
                    pop     ax
                    inc     ah                      ;Next multiplex ID
                    loop    chinst1                 ;Loop until done

                    clc                             ;Exit with carry clear
                    ret
check_install       endp

;***************************************************************************
; FREEMEM frees all the memory blocks owned by the process whose PSP
; address is passed in BX.  Carry is set on return if a call to release
; a block of memory failed.
;***************************************************************************

freemem             proc    near
                    push    bx                      ;Save BX
                    mov     ah,52h                  ;Get address of the first
                    int     21h                     ;   MCB with DOS function 52H
                    mov     dx,es:[bx-2]            ;Copy the address to DX
                    mov     es,dx                   ;Also copy it to ES
                    pop     bx                      ;Restore BX

free1:              cmp     bx,es:[01h]            ;Branch if the ownership
                    jne     free2                   ;   word does not match

                    inc     dx                      ;Increment DX
                    mov     es,dx                   ;Point ES to segment
                    mov     ah,49h                  ;Deallocate the segment
                    int     21h
                    jc      free_exit               ;Exit if called failed
                    dec     dx                      ;Decrement DX
                    mov     es,dx                   ;Point ES back to the MCB

free2:              add     dx,es:[03h]            ;Compute the address of the
                    inc     dx                      ;   next MCB
```

```
                mov     es,dx                   ;Transfer address to ES
                cmp     byte ptr es:[00h],"Z"   ;End of the MCB chain?
                jne     free1                   ;No, then continue the search
                clc                             ;Clear carry and exit
free_exit:      ret
freemem         endp


;****************************************************************************
; COMPARE_NAMES compares the two ASCII strings addressed by DS:SI and ES:DI.
; On return, the Z flag indicates whether or not the two are equal.
;****************************************************************************

compare_names   proc    near
                lodsb                           ;Get a character
                cmp     al,0Dh                  ;Exit if it's a carriage
                je      compare_exit            ;  return
                scasb                           ;Compare it ES:[DI]
                je      compare_names           ;Loop back if they're equal
compare_exit:   ret                             ;Return to caller
compare_names   endp


;****************************************************************************
; DOS_OUT displays the ASCII string pointed to by ES:DI.
;****************************************************************************

dos_out         proc    near
                mov     dl,es:[di]              ;Get a character
                cmp     dl,0Dh                  ;Exit if it's a carriage
                je      dos_exit                ;  return
                mov     ah,02h                  ;Output it using DOS
                int     21h                     ;  function 02H
                inc     di                      ;Advance DI to next one
                jmp     dos_out                 ;Loop until done
dos_exit:       ret
dos_out         endp

code            ends
                end     begin
```

A few examples will help clarify how INSTALL and REMOVE are used. For starters, let's say that you want to load PC-DIAL into memory and uninstall it later on, before you start a program that needs the memory. The commands

```
INSTALL PC-DIAL
PC-DIAL
```

set this up. The first command creates a bookmark called PC-DIAL, while the second actually installs PC-DIAL. To uninstall PC-DIAL, all you have to do is type

```
REMOVE PC-DIAL
```

and REMOVE will remove it. You could save a few keystrokes by simply typing

```
REMOVE
```

This works when the bookmark you want removed is the last one that was created.

You can have more than one TSR assigned to a bookmark if you wish. If you want to install PC-DIAL, LPT2FILE, and SAVER and be able to unload them with one stroke, load them with the commands

```
INSTALL ALL
LPT2FILE
SAVER
PC-DIAL
```

(You could also enter the word INSTALL by itself or INSTALL LPT2FILE in place of INSTALL ALL.) Then, typing

```
REMOVE ALL
```

will unload them all. By the same token, if you want to be able to unload them one at a time, place a bookmark in front of each one, as illustrated by the commands

```
INSTALL LPT2FILE
LPT2FILE
INSTALL SAVER
SAVER
INSTALL PC-DIAL
PC-DIAL
```

Then you can unload them individually. But remember that when you remove one bookmark, you remove all the ones installed after it, too. That means that if you type

```
REMOVE SAVER
```

both SAVER and PC-DIAL will be removed from memory. By contrast, the command

```
REMOVE PC-DIAL
```

will remove PC-DIAL only, leaving LPT2FILE and SAVER intact.

If you've forgotten what bookmarks are installed, you can get a list of them by running REMOVE with a /L (for List) switch. /L lists all the currently installed bookmarks without actually removing any of them. If you entered the following commands:

```
INSTALL LPT2FILE
LPT2FILE
INSTALL SAVER
SAVER
INSTALL PC-DIAL
PC-DIAL
```

and then typed

```
REMOVE /L
```

REMOVE would respond with the following list of names:

```
LPT2FILE
SAVER
PC-DIAL
```

Note that you don't *have* to install any TSRs after INSTALL. If you wanted to, you could execute these three commands in sequence:

```
INSTALL LPT2FILE
INSTALL SAVER
INSTALL PC-DIAL
```

The command

```
REMOVE LPT2FILE
```

would still remove all three bookmarks—even though there are no TSRs separating them.

As a rule, INSTALL and REMOVE work with the majority of TSRs. However, there are certain types of TSRs that they cannot uninstall completely. If a TSR uses expanded memory, for example, REMOVE will not deallocate the expanded memory that is allocated to the TSR. The expanded memory manager will think that the memory is still being used and will not let other programs have access to it. Try INSTALL and REMOVE out on the TSRs you want them to work with and note any strange behavior after a TSR is removed. If everything seems fine, then it probably is. If, however, the system behaves erratically after a particular TSR is removed, you should avoid using INSTALL and REMOVE with that TSR.

A final caveat about INSTALL and REMOVE concerns programs loaded high with the LOADHIGH command. INSTALL and REMOVE cannot be used to uninstall programs loaded in upper memory. The reason why leans a bit toward the technical side (we'll discuss this issue further in the next section). For now, suffice it to say that when DOS places a program in upper memory, it uses a different set of rules to determine where to place it relative to programs loaded earlier than it does when it loads a program into conventional memory. This difference, though subtle, is enough to prevent INSTALL and REMOVE from working effectively. If you try to place a bookmark in upper memory by loading INSTALL with the LOADHIGH command, INSTALL will respond with an error message saying it can't be loaded high. If you go the other route and load INSTALL low and the TSR high, REMOVE will remove the bookmark without removing the TSR.

Inside INSTALL and REMOVE

The principle that permits INSTALL and REMOVE to work is simple. What distinguishes a TSR from a transient application program is that the memory allocated to it remains allocated even after it terminates. In addition, most TSRs patch themselves into the PC's interrupt vector table that's located at the very bottom of memory. What INSTALL does is place a RAM-resident wedge in memory that contains a copy of the interrupt vector table as it appeared when INSTALL was run. REMOVE locates the wedge (the bookmark) in memory, restores the interrupt vector table, and releases the memory allocated to everything that was installed after INSTALL. The result: TSRs installed after the bookmark are effectively removed from memory.

The key to this strategy is the fact that when DOS loads a program, TSR or not, it loads it at the lowest available memory address. When INSTALL becomes memory-resident itself, it knows that any TSRs loaded after it will be located higher in memory. REMOVE uses this knowledge to identify the memory blocks that belong to a TSR and to deallocate them.

DOS divides conventional memory into a series of blocks. Each block is preceded by a 16-byte header called a *memory control block*, or MCB, that contains information about the size of the ensuing block, who (what program) owns it, and whether there are more blocks following this one. The blocks are linked together in linked list fashion (that is, each control block contains the address of the next block in the chain). If you can determine the address of the lowest MCB in memory, you can walk the chain, so to speak, and examine the entire chain of control blocks that determine the logical makeup of memory.

The format of the MCB is diagrammed in Figure 13.4. The first byte contains the value 4DH if this isn't the final block in the chain, 5AH if it is. Not coincidentally, these values are the ASCII values for the letters "M" and "Z," which happen to be the initials of Mark Zbikowski, one of the principal architects of DOS. The next two bytes form a word value that is the Program Segment Prefix address of the program that owns the ensuing block of memory. For unallocated blocks (free memory), this value is 0. The next two bytes in the MCB form another word value, this time one that reveals the length (in paragraphs) of the ensuing block of memory. You can determine the address of the next higher MCB by adding the value in this field to the segment address of the current MCB. Finally, the eight bytes from offset 08H to 0FH in the MCB contain the name of the program that owns the block of memory, in ASCII format. This field was only added in DOS 4.0; prior to that, it was unused.

FIGURE 13.4

Format of the Memory Control Block

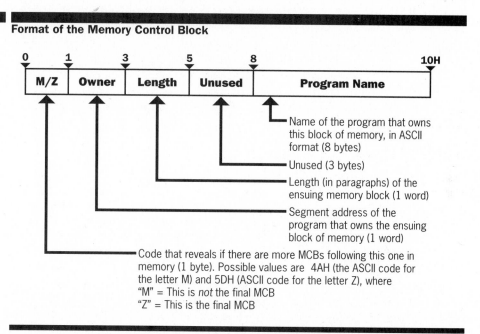

To uninstall one or more TSRs, REMOVE follows this simple procedure. First, it locates the first copy of INSTALL installed in memory by placing a call to CHECK_INSTALL, which returns a segment address in ES. Using this address as a base, it then works its way upward in memory, locating other copies of INSTALL by inspecting the double-word value at offset 0103H (called NEXTFIELD in the program listing) within each INSTALL wedge, which contains the address of the *next* copy of INSTALL. Each new instance of INSTALL that is loaded into memory writes its segment address to this field in the previous copy, with the result that all the INSTALL wedges that are present in memory at once are joined together in linked list format. REMOVE continues searching the chain of installed wedges until it finds the one that contains the name of the bookmark you specified on the command line, or until it reaches the wedge that is uppermost in memory. In the final copy of INSTALL, NEXTBLOCK is set to FFFFH to mark the end of the chain.

Once it has located the searched-for INSTALL wedge, REMOVE writes the value FFFFH to NEXTBLOCK to terminate the linked list of INSTALL wedges. Then it copies the interrupt vectors from the wedge to the interrupt vector table in low memory. The following lines show the code to accomplish this.

```
mov       ax,es
mov       ds,ax
assume    ds:nothing
mov       si,vectors
sub       di,di
mov       es,di
mov       cx,512
cli
rep       movsw
sti
```

The instructions

```
mov       ds,ax
assume    ds:nothing
mov       si,vectors
```

point DS:SI to the copy of the interrupt vector table inside INSTALL (VEC-TORS is the offset within the wedge where the interrupt vectors are stored), while the instructions

```
sub       di,di
mov       es,di
```

point ES:DI to 0000:0000, the address of the interrupt vector table in low memory. The vectors are copied with a REP MOVSW instruction, which moves the number of words in CX (in this case, 512) from the address specified by DS:SI to the one specified by ES:DI. Interrupts are disabled before the operation begins so that none will occur while the interrupt vector table is being modified. If an interrupt *did* occur during this time, all havoc would result if it occurred at the same time that its own vector was being modified. Conceivably, the segment portion of the interrupt vector could be pointing to one destination and the off-set portion to another, causing the interrupt to fire off to some unknown (and unintended) location in memory, ultimately crashing the system.

REMOVE's next task is to deallocate the memory that belongs to TSRs loaded after INSTALL. The key here is that TSRs loaded after INSTALL *must be loaded at a higher address*. Fortunately, this is the case for TSRs loaded in conventional memory, but it is *not* always true of TSRs loaded in upper memory (more on this in a moment). REMOVE scans the chain of memory control blocks from the specified INSTALL wedge forward. As it does, it identifies blocks of memory that have programs loaded in them by checking for blocks that "own" themselves. Only a block that contains a program may own other blocks of memory, and such blocks are identifiable because the owner field in the MCB preceding them contains the block's own segment address. Each time

REMOVE finds a block that contains a program, it calls DOS function 49H to deallocate it, and then scans the entire chain of MCBs from the very first one forward looking for other memory blocks that are owned by the program whose memory was just deallocated. When it finds them, it deallocates them, too. In the end, REMOVE removes every memory block owned by any TSR that was installed after the bookmark.

Once the interrupt vector table is restored and the memory blocks are released, the system is restored to the state it was in the last time INSTALL was run. More importantly, any TSRs loaded after INSTALL are removed because they no longer own any memory and the interrupt vectors they patched into in order to function are now restored to the state they were in before the TSR was installed.

One item that's worthy of note is the technique REMOVE uses to locate the first MCB. Since MCBs are stored in a linked list, you can locate all of them if you can locate the first one, but first you must find the first one. REMOVE gets the segment address of the first MCB by placing a call to DOS function 52H as follows:

```
mov     ah,52h
int     21h
mov     dx,es:[bx-2]
```

Function 52H, also called "Get List of Lists," is officially undocumented. It returns a pointer in ES:BX to a list of other pointers and control structures that DOS maintains internally. The word at ES:[BX-2] holds the segment address of the first MCB. Although using this function carries with it the same risk that using any undocumented DOS function does—the risk that it will not be implemented in some future version of DOS—function 52H has become so well known in the programming community that it is likely to be retained in all foreseeable future releases.

Now that you have an idea how INSTALL and REMOVE work, you can also understand why they won't work in upper memory. REMOVE relies on the assumption that the order in which programs appear in memory reflects the order in which they were loaded. When a program is loaded into conventional memory, this assumption is valid. However, LOADHIGH loads a TSR into the largest UMB that is available at the time. If upper memory is fragmented into two or more UMBs, the order in which TSRs loaded high are placed is likely to be staggered. Therefore, the key assumption that permits REMOVE to work is no longer valid. INSTALL guards against being placed in upper memory by checking its own segment address when it is loaded. If that segment address is greater than A000H (the beginning of the upper memory area), INSTALL displays the message "INSTALL cannot be loaded high" and terminates without becoming memory-resident. This logic is embodied in the following code fragment.

```
mov     ax,cs
cmp     ax,0A000h
jae     error
```

If the value of the CS register is greater than or equal to A000H, execution branches to the line labeled ERROR. If any of the programs you write should not be loaded high, you can use this same technique to terminate them gracefully rather than to allow a system crash.

Summary

This concludes the discussion of creating utilities for DOS 5.0. In this chapter, you learned what differentiates TSRs from normal application programs and also learned how they're written. As you've seen, there's more to writing a TSR than there is to an application that will not become memory-resident, especially if your program will use DOS services. But in the end, the results are worth the effort. Programs such as PC-DIAL are more useful because they are TSRs, and because you can pop them up over other application programs with the flick of a key.

Learning to program the IBM PC is the key to unlocking its power. Nonprogrammers are forced to work within the bounds laid down for them by utilities and application programs that others have written. Programmers, by contrast, can create utilities and application programs of their own. There's nothing quite like the feeling you get when a program that you've been working on for days or perhaps weeks or months runs for the first time. Even if you're not interested in programming, perhaps the code and discussions presented in these last few chapters will give you a greater appreciation for the inner workings and complexities of DOS, for the work that goes into creating an application program, and, most important of all, for the programmers that create them.

PART THREE

Beyond DOS 5

747
THE SHELL GAME

771
THE QBASIC INTERPRETER

14. THE SHELL GAME

NEXT TO TSRS, THE SUBJECT THAT'S MOST LIKELY TO STIR DEBATE AMONG experienced DOS users is the use of DOS shells. Some swear by them, claiming they can get more work done in less time. Others claim that once you grow accustomed to the command-line interface, graphical user interfaces seem like toys by comparison. The sentiments and general indignation of the latter camp was perhaps summed up best by fellow *PC Magazine* columnist John Dvorak, who once wrote that DOS Shells are for people who can't memorize tough commands like CLS. In the end, the decision whether to use a DOS Shell is one that only you can make. To help you make a more informed decision, this chapter discusses the general merits and capabilities of the Shell that comes with DOS 5.0 (henceforth, the *DOS Shell*, or simply, the *Shell*).

What this chapter *won't* do is rehash the DOS manual and show you how to type text into dialog boxes, pull down menus with the mouse, or use command-line switches when starting the Shell. We'll assume that you're comfortable with the basic tenets of working in a graphical environment and that you already know, for example, how to double-click on an object with the mouse to initiate an action. We'll also assume, in most of the examples, that you are indeed using a mouse. In truth, anything that can be done inside the Shell with a mouse can also be done with the keyboard. But operating the Shell solely from the keyboard frequently involves entering arcane series of keystrokes that aren't intuitive to anyone except perhaps the programmers that wrote them. With that in mind, here's the lowdown on the DOS 5.0 Shell—what you can do with it, and how you can use it to best advantage.

Introducing the DOS Shell

If you haven't started it already, you can boot up the DOS Shell and put it through its paces by typing

```
DOSSHELL
```

at the DOS command prompt. Ideally, the directory where DOSSHELL.COM and other DOS files are located should be named in your PATH statement so that DOS can find DOSSHELL.COM and the other files (DOSSHELL.EXE, DOSSHELL.HLP, and so on) that it uses. However, if there is no PATH to the directory where the files that constitute the DOS Shell are stored, you can CD to the directory where DOSSHELL.COM is located and start it from there.

When the Shell is started for the first time, you'll see a screen similar to the one shown in Figure 14.1. (Using the Display option under the Options menu or command-line switches, you can select from several different display modes; all the examples shown in this chapter were shot in 25-line graphics mode.) Near the top of the screen, just below the menu bar, is a set of drive icons you can click on to change the current drive. Below that, the screen is divided into three areas: the directory tree area, the file list area, and the program list area. The *directory tree area* shows a graphical depiction of the directory structure for the current drive, similar to the type of output you get when you type **TREE ** at the command prompt. The *file list area* lists the files in the drive and directory currently selected in the drive and directory tree areas. Finally, the *program list area* lists the programs and program groups that you can currently access with a couple of clicks of the mouse. You indicate which area you want to work in by clicking anywhere inside the area with the mouse, or, if you aren't using a mouse, pressing Tab or Shift-Tab until the title bar above the area you want to work in is highlighted. In general, you work in one area at a time, and switch between them as needed to accomplish your task.

FIGURE 14.1

The DOS Shell's main screen

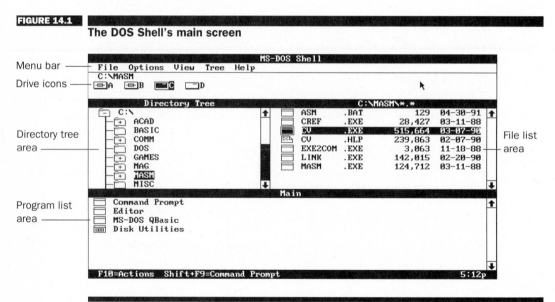

At the top of the screen is a menu bar through which you access many of the Shell's features. Initially, there are five options displayed: File, Options, View, Tree, and Help. The File menu contains all the commands you'll need to perform basic file operations such as copying, deleting, and renaming files, viewing file contents, and associating data files with the applications that created them. The Options menu contains several user-selectable options that affect the way the Shell looks and operates. The View menu determines what working areas are displayed. The Tree menu lets you control the format of the information displayed in the directory tree area. The Help menu is the entry point to the many levels of on-line help that the Shell puts at your fingertips.

In general, you can display a drop-down menu from any of the options in the menu bar by clicking on the menu option with the mouse and dragging the pointer down to the option you want to select (when you let go of the mouse button, the option is automatically selected; alternatively, you can click on the menu option, let go of the mouse button, and then click again on the option you want to select). If you're not using a mouse, you can pull down a menu by pressing the Alt key or function key F10, moving the highlight that appears in the menu bar with the Left Arrow and Right Arrow keys, and pressing Enter or Up Arrow or Down Arrow to display the menu. For reference, a complete list of all the menu options available in each of the five categories is shown in Table 14.1.

Not all menu options are available at all times. The Shell enables and disables menu options on the fly so that commands can't be selected out of context. In addition, when the program list area is the active area, the Tree menu goes away and the commands in the File menu are replaced by an entirely different set of commands. Some of the menu options are followed by three periods, otherwise known as an ellipsis. The ellipsis indicates that the command will not be carried out immediately, but will pop up a dialog box prompting you for confirmation or additional information before proceeding. Menu options that are *not* followed by an ellipsis are executed immediately.

You can alter the appearance of the Shell by selecting a different view from the View menu. There are five views available: Single File List, Dual File Lists, All Files, Program/File Lists, and Program List. The default view is Program/File Lists, which shows the directory tree area, the file list area, and the program list area. Selecting Single File List removes the program list area from the screen, leaving only the directory tree area and the file list area, while Dual File Lists displays two directory tree and file list areas. All Files lists every file on the current drive in one long list. Finally, the Program List option removes the directory tree and file list areas from the screen and displays only the program list area.

If you haven't already, select each of the options in the View menu one at a time to see what effect they have on the screen. Note that if you enable task switching by selecting the Enable Task Swapper option in the Options menu, the program list area shrinks to half its normal size and a fourth area labeled "Active Task List" appears to the right of it. With task switching enabled, the active task list shows all the programs that are active in the system. Task switching will be discussed in detail later in this chapter, in the section entitled "Task Switching."

Working with Drives, Directories, and Files

The greatest difference between working in the Shell and working on the command line is that you no longer have to type commands to get things done. Instead, you work in a visually oriented point-and-shoot environment where you point at something with the mouse and click the mouse button to initiate an action. For example, all you have to do to change the default drive is click on one of the drive icons near the top of the screen. The Shell will make that drive the

TABLE 14.1

Summary of DOS Shell Menu Options

Menu Option	Shortcut Key	Description
File Menu		
Open		Starts the program selected in the file list area or, if a data file is selected, starts the application associated with that file and automatically loads the data file
Run...		Displays a dialog box from which you can launch a program by entering its name
Print		Prints the file selected in the file list area (only valid if PRINT.COM is installed)
Associate...		Associates one or more file name extensions with an application program
Search...		Searches the current drive for a file or group of files
View File Contents	F9	Displays the contents of the file selected in the file list area
Move...	F7	Moves the file or files selected in the file list area to another drive or directory
Copy...	F8	Copies the file or files selected in the file list area to another drive or directory
Delete...	Del	Deletes the subdirectory or subdirectories selected in the directory tree area or the file or files selected in the file list area
Rename...		Renames the file selected in the file list area or the subdirectory selected in the directory tree area
Change Attributes...		Displays the attributes of the file selected in the file list area and lets you change them
Create Directory...		Creates a subdirectory on the current drive
Select All		Selects all the files in the current directory
Deselect All		Cancels selections made with Select All
Exit	Alt-F4	Exits the DOS Shell and returns to the DOS command line
Options Menu		
Confirmation...		Sets confirmation options for file operations
File Display Options...		Sets the criterion used for displaying files in the file list area, controls whether files are listed in descending or ascending order, and controls the display of hidden and system files
Select Across Directories		Enables and disables the ability to select files in multiple directories
Show Information...		Displays information about the file or files selected in the file list area, the current directory, and the current drive
Enable Task Swapper		Enables and disables task switching
Display...		Sets the screen mode used by the Shell and lets you specify how many lines to display
Colors...		Sets the screen colors used by the Shell
View Menu		
Single File List		Displays the directory tree area and the file list area
Dual File Lists		Displays two side-by-side directory tree areas and file list areas
All Files		Displays every file on the current drive and information about the files and directories on it
Program/File Lists		Displays the directory tree area, the file list area, and the program list area
Program List		Displays the program list area
Repaint Screen	Shift-F5	Redraws the screen
Refresh	F5	Rereads the current drive and updates file and directory information for it

TABLE 14.1

(Continued)

Menu Option	Shortcut Key	Description
Tree Menu		
Expand One Level	+	Displays an additional level of subdirectories for the directory selected in the directory tree area
Expand Branch	*	Displays all subdirectories that are descendants of the subdirectory selected in the directory tree area
Expand All	Ctrl-*	Displays all subdirectories on the current drive in the directory tree area
Collapse Branch	-	Hides all subdirectories that are descendants of the subdirectory selected in the directory tree area
Help Menu		
Index		Opens the Help window and displays the help index
Keyboard		Opens the Help window and displays a list of shortcut keys that the Shell supports
Shell Basics		Opens the Help window and displays a list of basic skills you can get help with
Commands		Opens the Help window and displays a list of Shell commands
Procedures		Opens the Help window and displays a list of Shell procedures
Using Help		Opens the Help window and displays a list of topics for help on Help
About Shell		Displays information about the Shell

current one and update the information in the directory tree and file list areas to reflect the change.

Changing directories is equally simple. With the directory tree area selected, scroll up or down in that window until the directory you want to change to is displayed, and then click on it with the mouse. The Shell will make that directory current, and then update the file list to list the files in the current directory.

The options in the Tree menu let you control the display of information in the directory tree window. Selecting Expand One Level or pressing the + key displays one additional level of subdirectories for the directory that is currently highlighted in the directory tree window. Selecting Collapse Branch or pressing the - key collapses it again. Directories that are candidates for either operation are marked with a plus or minus in the directory tree list. You can also expand or collapse directories by clicking on the plus or minus in the folder icon. If a directory contains subdirectories that are not currently displayed, the Shell displays a plus sign in the icon for that directory. Similarly, if the subdirectories for the directory are already shown, the Shell displays a minus sign in the directory's icon indicating that you can press the - key to collapse that directory. If an icon contains neither a plus nor a minus sign, then the associated directory doesn't contain any subdirectories.

You can also expand more than one level of a directory tree simultaneously. Selecting Expand Branch or pressing the * key when a directory containing a plus sign is highlighted displays all the subdirectories that are descendants of that directory, no matter how many levels that comprises. Also, selecting Expand All or pressing Ctrl-* displays *every* subdirectory on the current drive.

As a rule, you can display as much or as little information about the structure of the drive as you like.

As an example, let's say you want to show one level of subdirectories for the current drive, but don't want to show any subdirectories lower than that. To do it, click once on the icon for the root directory (the first directory listed in the directory tree window), and then press the - key. The tree will collapse so that only the root directory is shown. Then press the + key. The tree will expand to show the first level of subdirectories. If you had pressed * instead, *every* subdirectory would have been displayed. Pressing * at the root directory level is equivalent to pressing Ctrl-*, because every subdirectory on the drive is by definition a descendant of the root directory. If you press + or * with any directory other than the root directory highlighted, the tree is only expanded to show the descendants of the current directory.

The drive icons and directory list are merely tools for displaying the right information in the file list area. Once the file list contains the name of the file you want to perform an operation on, you're ready to go to work. In general, the idea is to select the file you want to work with by clicking on it once with the mouse. Then, you select the operation you want to perform from the File menu. Let's say, for example, that you want to delete a file called BUDGET.DOC in the \WP\WPFILES directory of the C drive. Here's how you'd go about it. First, if drive C isn't already the current drive, click on the drive C icon at the top of the screen. Next, select the \WP directory in the directory list and, if the \WP branch isn't already expanded, press + or * to display the subdirectories stemming from \WP. Then select WPFILES. At this point, the file list will contain the names of all the files in \WP\WPFILES. Go to the file list window and scroll until you see BUDGET.DOC. (If the file is way down in the list, you can press B to automatically scroll down to the first file name that begins with the letter B.) Select BUDGET.DOC. Next, either press the Del key or pull the File menu down from the top of the screen and select Delete. Then press Enter or click the Yes button when the Shell displays a dialog box asking for confirmation before deleting the file. The file will be removed from the disk.

You can perform two of the most common types of file operations—moving and copying—without involving menus. Suppose you want to move a file from one directory to another. First, scroll the information in the directory tree area up or down until the directory that you want to move the file to is showing in the window. Then, in the file list area, position the mouse pointer over the file you want to move, and, without letting up on the mouse button, drag the file over and place it on top of the directory you want it to go into. Then release the mouse button. The Shell will ask you to confirm the move in a dialog box, and then it will move the file for you. You can copy a file the same way. The only difference in the procedure is that you press and hold the Ctrl key the whole time.

There are lots of other operations you can perform on a file, including renaming it, displaying its contents, printing it, changing its file attributes, and more. From the Options menu, you can also invoke the Show Information option to display information about the file such as its size and the total number of bytes in the directory it's stored in.

From the Options menu, you can control the settings of two parameters that determine (1) when the Shell prompts you for confirmation before proceeding with an operation, and (2) what files are displayed in the file list and how they're ordered. The Confirmation menu item pops up a dialog box with three check boxes: Confirm on Delete, Confirm on Replace, and Confirm on Mouse Operation. Initially, all three are checked. Confirm on Delete causes the Shell to prompt you for confirmation before deleting a file (as you saw in the example earlier); Confirm on Replace has it prompt you for confirmation when a file is being moved or copied to another location and a file of the same name already exists at the destination; and Confirm on Mouse Operation prompts you for confirmation when a file is being moved or copied with the mouse. If you find the confirmation prompts annoying, unclick the check boxes and the prompts will go away. Be careful, though: It's easy to delete a file accidentally by pressing the Del key when Confirm on Delete is disabled.

The File Display Options menu item lets you control what is displayed in the file list and how. The File Display Options dialog box contains four fields: Name, Display hidden/system files, Descending order, and Sort by. The Name field contains the file specification used to filter the files in the file list. The default is *.*. If you only wanted to display, say, files that end in .BAK, you could enter *.BAK in this field. By default, hidden and system files are not included in the file list. However, you can add them in by checking the Display hidden/system files check box. Similarly, files are listed in ascending order by default, but you can reverse the order by checking the Descending order check box. Lastly, you can control whether files are sorted by name, extension, date, size, or the natural order in which they appear on the disk by clicking on the corresponding button in the Sort by field.

One of the beauties of working in the Shell environment is that you don't have to work on just one file at a time; instead, you can work on several at once, extending the operations that you perform to entire groups of files. The techniques and procedures for doing this will be discussed later in this chapter, in the section entitled "Performing Operations on Groups of Files."

You can also use options in the File menu to manipulate subdirectories. Create Directory creates a subdirectory (equivalent to MD on the command line); Delete removes a subdirectory (the same as RD); and Rename renames a subdirectory (no command-line equivalent). Should you ever need to get to the command line, you can do so by pressing Shift-F9. The Shell will run a secondary copy of COMMAND.COM and present you with a DOS command prompt. Note that if you make changes to the structure of the disk while you're on the command line (for example, if you remove or create a subdirectory or delete a file), you'll need to notify the Shell of the changes when you return. To do so, press F5 or select Refresh from the View menu. The Shell will reread the contents of the disk and reinitialize the directory tree and file list displays. Also note that when you're at a command prompt started from the Shell, you should type **EXIT** to get back to the Shell. One mistake that novice users often make is attempting to get back to the Shell by typing DOSSHELL a second time. Doing so will start a second, separate instance of the Shell running and will accomplish nothing except to decrease the amount of memory available.

Working with Programs

The DOS Shell also provides convenient mechanisms for launching application programs. There are five ways to start a program running:

- Switch to the directory that contains the program and activate the file list. Then double-click on the name of the program, or highlight the program name and select Open from the File menu.

- From the program list, double-click on a program icon, or highlight the icon and select Open from the File menu.

- From the File menu, select Run and enter the name of the program. Use the full path name if the directory that contains the program is neither currently selected nor included in your PATH statement.

- Press Shift-F9 to go to the command prompt, and then type the command to start the program.

- Double-click on the name of a data file that is associated with a program, or highlight the data file name and select Open from the File menu.

The first two methods involve nothing more than mouse-selecting an object in a list. The third and fourth are the most manual of the five, requiring you to actually type in the program name. In both of these cases, you can include any parameters that you would normally include on the command line. When loading WordPerfect, for example, you can include the name of a data file to be loaded as soon as the program starts. We'll put off a more comprehensive discussion of the fifth method, double-clicking on a data file name associated with a program, until the section entitled "Associating Programs and Data Files."

There are two basic actions you can perform in the program list. One is clicking on a program icon to start a program. (If you're running the Shell in text mode, you'll only see the *name* of the program in the program list; there will be no icon for it.) You'll learn to create program icons of your own and add them to the file list in the next section. The other is opening a program *group* to display the program icons contained in the group. The Shell permits you to organize program icons stored in the program list into groups of programs that share common traits or functions. By default, the Shell provides two program groups: Main and Disk Utilities. Main is displayed when you first bring up the Shell; it contains icons for three programs (what the DOS manual calls *program items*) and an icon for the Disk Utilities Group. Double-clicking on the Disk Utilities icon or highlighting it and selecting Open from the File menu displays the contents of the group. Initially, it contains icons labeled Disk Copy, Backup Fixed Disk, Restore Fixed Disk, Quick Format, Format, and Undelete, which launch the DISKCOPY, BACKUP, RESTORE, FORMAT /Q, FORMAT, and UNDELETE commands, respectively. You can run any of these commands by double-clicking on the icon. In addition, you can go back to the Main group by double-clicking on its icon, which by default appears at the top of the program list when the contents of Disk Utilities is displayed. As described in the next section, the Shell also gives you the power to alter the program list as needed, adding or deleting program groups, and adding or deleting program items to go in them.

Tips and Techniques for Using the Shell Effectively

The DOS manual tells you all you need to know about the mechanics of using the Shell—how to launch programs by double-clicking on program names or program icons, how to enter text in dialog boxes, and so forth. But it doesn't always make it clear how to use the myriad commands and options available in the Shell most productively. The sections that follow describe tips and techniques that will transform you from a Shell novice to a Shell power user, and provide practical advice on customizing the Shell to suit your own particular needs and tastes.

Adding Programs and Program Groups to the Program List

The first time you start the Shell, the program list at the bottom of the screen shows the contents of the Main program group, which includes three programs (Command Prompt, Editor, and QBasic) and one program group (Disk Utilities). You can modify this selection to add groups of your own or to add new programs to the existing groups. In general, you should create icons for all your frequently used programs so you can start them without having to navigate through directory trees and file lists.

The first step in adding a new program group is to activate the program list window by clicking anywhere inside it with a mouse or tabbing down to it with the Tab or Shift-Tab keys. Then, pull down the File menu. Right off, you'll notice that many of the menu items that are normally part of the File menu are no longer there, having been replaced by six new ones: New, Open, Copy, Delete, Properties, and Reorder. New allows you to define a new program group or program item; Open runs the program or displays the contents of the program group selected in the program list; Copy copies a program item from one program group to another; Delete deletes a program item or program group; Properties allows you to define the properties (group name, program title, and so on) associated with a program item or program group; and Reorder lets you change the order in which program items and program groups appear in the program list. For your convenience, the Shell equates the Enter key and the Del key to the Open and Delete menu items, respectively, when the program list window is the active area.

To create a new program group, select New from the File menu. The Shell will display a dialog box asking you to specify via a pair of buttons whether the object you want to add is a program group or a program item. Select Program Group and click the dialog box's OK button. The Shell will then display a second dialog box prompting you for the title of the new program group (the text that will appear alongside its icon in the program list) and, optionally, for any help text you want associated with it and a password for restricting access to it. Fill in the entry fields and press OK, and the new program group icon will appear in the program list. Later, if you want to change any of the properties you defined for the program group—for example, if you want to add or change a password or modify the group title—select the group icon in the program list and then select Properties from the File menu. You'll be presented with the same dialog box again for editing the group's properties.

Removing a program group is even easier. Select the program group's icon in the program list and press Del, and the Shell will pop up a dialog box asking for confirmation before proceeding. If you press Enter or press the OK button, the program group will be erased, along with any program items and other program groups that it contains. Note that deleting a program group that contains program items does *not* affect the program files themselves, so you don't have to worry about accidentally deleting files, too, when you remove a program group.

Restricting access to a program group by assigning it a password is a reasonably effective way to keep novices from running the programs in the group. However, the Shell's password security scheme is easily circumvented by starting the program using any of the various other methods at your fingertips for starting a program from the Shell—for example, by starting the program from the command prompt or with the Run command from the File menu. So don't count too much on the password feature's ability to prevent certain operations from taking place.

To add a new program item to a program group, change to the group you want it added to and select New from the File menu. Make sure the Program Item button in the dialog box is selected and press OK. Then fill in the fields in the dialog box that appears. Program Title is the name that will appear beside the program's icon in the program list; Commands is the command or commands that will start the program; Startup Directory is the directory the Shell will CD to before starting the program; Application Shortcut Key is the key combination that will switch to the program when the program is running with task switching enabled (we'll talk more about defining shortcut keys when we discuss task switching near the end of the chapter); and Password is a password that must be entered before the program can be started. You can also specify whether the Shell will pause and display a "Press any key to return to the Shell" message when the program is terminated by selecting or deselecting the check box labeled "Pause after exit."

When you enter the command to start the program into the Command field, there are a couple of things to keep in mind. First, if there's not a PATH to the directory where the program is stored, you should enter a complete path name along with the file name. In fact, by specifying the path to the file here rather than relying on PATH, you can cut down on the amount of time it takes the Shell to launch the program. Second, by including replaceable parameters in the command (similar to replaceable parameters in batch files), you can have the Shell automatically prompt you for additional information when the program is started. Let's say you're filling out the dialog box for WordPerfect, and you want it to prompt you for a file name each time it's started. Furthermore, assume that WordPerfect is located in the \WP directory of drive C and that you want the

Shell to change to the \WP\WPFILES directory before launching WordPerfect. You could put all of this in place by filling in the first three fields of the dialog box with the following information:

```
Program Title:          WordPerfect
Commands:               C:\WP\WP %1
Startup Directory:C:\WP\DOC
```

After you OK the entries, another dialog box appears. The information you enter in this one determines what the dialog box that the Shell pops up to get your input for %1 will look like. Here, you can define the dialog box title, information you want to appear in the top of the window, the prompt message that will be displayed, and default parameters. You can define prompts for up to nine replaceable parameters this way, represented in the Commands field by the identifiers %1 through %9.

A third point to remember about the Commands field is that it may contain more than one command, as long as the commands are separated by a semicolon. Say, for example, that you want to add the MEM command to the program list so that you can get a reading on the amount of memory available by clicking on an icon. You might also want to clear the screen before MEM is executed, for a cleaner, neater-looking display. You could accomplish this by entering

```
CLS; MEM
```

for Commands in the dialog box. You'd also want to make sure that the "Pause before exit" check box was selected so that the Shell wouldn't be redisplayed before you had a chance to read the output from the MEM command.

The procedure for deleting a program item is exactly the same as the one for deleting a program group. Select the program item to be deleted and press Del or select the Delete option from the File menu. The program item will go away. Once again, deleting a program item does not delete the program file that corresponds to it; it only deletes the program name and icon from the program list.

Defining Advanced Properties for a Program Item

As you defined properties for a program item in the Program Item Properties dialog box, you may have noticed that there's a button in the lower-left corner of the window labeled "Advanced." Clicking on this button permits you to define additional properties for the program item that provide more intimate control over the environment. With the exception of the Help Text field, these options pertain only to programs that will be run with the Shell's task switching feature enabled.

The good news is that most of the time you can get away without entering anything in the Advanced dialog box. Should you choose to do so anyway, or should a particular program require it, here's how the individual fields in the dialog box are used. You use the Help Text field to enter text to be displayed if the user presses F1 with the program item highlighted in the program list (pressing F1 at any time while you're in the Shell invokes context-sensitive help). Entries may be up to 255 characters long. You can embed carriage returns (line breaks) in the help text by typing a caret (^) followed by an M (^M stands for Ctrl-M, the equivalent of a carriage return character). The next two fields—Conventional Memory KB Required and XMS Memory KB Required—let you specify the minimum amount of conventional and extended memory the program will require, in kilobytes. The defaults are 128 and 0, respectively. These values are only meaningful when task switching is enabled, so that the Shell will know how much memory at a minimum to allocate the program. The XMS Memory KB Limit field specifies the *maximum* amount of extended memory that will be allocated to the program with task switching enabled. The default is 384 or the amount of extended memory available in the system, whichever is less. The Video Mode buttons tell the Shell whether the program will run in text or graphics mode. This option need only be specified if the program is being run on a system equipped with a CGA video adapter and if task switching is enabled. The Prevent Program Switch check box, if checked, prevents the user from switching from this program to another one with task switching enabled. Finally, the Reserve Shortcut Keys check boxes let you disable certain key combinations used by the switcher if the program uses those key combinations itself.

The decision about when to define advanced properties for a program item must be made on a case-by-case basis. Choosing to define a help message (or *not* to define a help message) for a program item is a personal choice. If your PC has a CGA video adapter and you plan to use task switching, you should use the Advanced dialog box to inform the Shell whether the program runs in text or graphics mode. This information helps the Shell determine how much memory to reserve for the program's video buffer when a task switch occurs. Use the Reserve Shortcut Keys check boxes if the program uses Alt-Tab, Alt-Esc, or Ctrl-Esc. Fortunately, programs that use these rather esoteric key combinations are generally the exception rather than the rule. Finally, exercise control over the memory allocation options the Advanced dialog box provides if the program in question crashes or otherwise behaves erratically because there isn't enough memory available to it or if the program itself reports that there isn't enough memory available. If, for example, you can determine, either from guidance provided by the program manual or through experimentation, that the program will run fine if there's at least 512k of conventional memory available to it, then enter 512 in the Conventional Memory KB Required field. If the Shell can't free up at least that much room for the program, it will inform you that there's not enough memory when you attempt to start it. Similarly, if an application requires more than 384k of extended memory to run, increase the maximum amount the Shell will make available to it by adjusting XMS Memory KB Limit.

Associating Programs and Data Files

One of the DOS Shell's most useful features is that it lets you associate data files with the applications that created them so that clicking on a data file name in the file list area automatically launches the application *and* loads the data file. To make this connection, you associate an application program with a certain file name extension (for example, the .DOC in BUDGET.DOC). Then, if you click on any file with that extension, the program is automatically loaded, too.

To illustrate, suppose you want WordPerfect loaded anytime you click on a file in the file list that has the extension .DOC. Go to the file list area and select WP.EXE, the WordPerfect program file. Then pull down the File menu and select Associate. The Shell will display a dialog box in which you can enter the extension to be associated with WP.EXE. Enter **DOC** in the Extensions field and press OK. Alternately, highlight any .DOC file in the file list area and select Associate. The Shell will prompt you for the name of the application to associate with that file name extension. Thereafter, anytime you click on a file that ends in .DOC, the Shell will launch WordPerfect for you and load the document file for editing. You can associate more than one extension with a program name by entering all the extensions in the Extensions field, separated by spaces. Should you ever want to delete an association, all you have to do is go back to the Associate File dialog box and delete the extension name or names.

When you start it, the Shell provides two default file associations for you. Files that end in .TXT are automatically associated with the DOS Editor, and files that end in .BAS are associated with the QBasic Interpreter. Therefore, you can load and edit a BASIC program into QBasic or load a text file with the extension .TXT for editing in the DOS Editor simply by clicking on the name of the file.

Performing Operations on Groups of Files

You've already seen how a file selected in the file list area can be the subject of commands invoked from the File menu. But what may be less obvious unless you've read the section in the manual on the DOS Shell thoroughly is that File commands can be applied to entire *groups* of files. With this capability, you can make sweeping changes to the files on your hard disk in a single operation, and with only a little more effort than it would have taken to perform the action on just a single file.

The first step toward performing a group operation is to select the files that will make up the group. This is called making an *extended selection*. There are several ways to go about it. If the files you want to select are listed in contiguous order (if, say, you want to select lines 1 through 10 in the file list), then click on the first file name in the group, move down to the last file name in the set, press Shift, and click again. All the files between the two points you selected will be highlighted. All that remains then is to go to the File menu and select a command. The command will be applied to every member of the extended selection set.

There's a shortcut you can use if you want to select every file displayed in the file list. Pull down the File menu and choose Select All. All the files in the file list area of the screen will automatically be highlighted. If you change your mind about the selection, the Deselect All menu option, also in the File menu, will undo the effects of Select All. If you're using the keyboard rather than a mouse, the key combination Ctrl-/ is equivalent to Select All. Make sure the file list window is the active window before you press Ctrl-/; otherwise, the operation will not be carried out.

If the files you want to add to the group are not in contiguous, uninterrupted order, you can form an extended selection set anyway by holding down the Ctrl key as you select the file names in the file list window. Each new file that you select will be added to the group, and the ones selected previously will remain highlighted. You can use a variation of this basic strategy to combine contiguous *groups* of files into one consolidated group. Let's say that you want to combine files 4 through 10, file number 12, and files 20 through 29 into one group to perform a group delete. First, click on file number 4 in the file list, then click on file number 10 with the Shift key held down. Next, click on file number 12 with the Ctrl key depressed. Finally, click on file number 20 with the Ctrl key still depressed, and click on file number 29 with both Ctrl and Shift held down. All the indicated files will become members of the extended selection set. If you don't have a mouse, you can do the same thing using only the keyboard. It's not the best way to go about it, but if you *must* do it that way, your DOS manual describes how.

The files that you designate to go into an extended selection set don't all have to be in the same directory, or even on the same drive, for that matter. If you go into the Options menu and select Select Across Directories, a small bullet will appear next to the menu item indicating that the Shell's Select Across Directory feature is now enabled (choosing this menu item when it is already enabled *disables* it). With this feature enabled, the same basic keystrokes and mouse movements that enable you to form extended selection sets from non-contiguous groups of files may also be applied to groups of files in different directories.

Here's an example. Let's say that you want to copy all the files in the \WP\WPFILES directory of the current drive, plus the first ten files in the \WP\LETTERS directory to the \WP\BACKUP directory. Start by activating the directory tree window and changing to the \WP\WPFILES directory. Then activate the file list window and choose Select All from the File menu. Next, go back to the directory tree window and switch to the \WP\LETTERS directory. Then activate the file list window again, press the Ctrl key, click on the first file name in the window, move to the tenth file in the list, press Ctrl and Shift together, and click on the file name. You have now defined an extended selection set that extends across directories. Finally, select Copy from the File menu (or press F8, the shortcut key for Copy), enter \WP\BACKUP as the destination for the files in the dialog box, and click OK. The files will be copied to the new location, and the selection set will automatically be canceled.

If you use your PC daily, you'll come across plenty of opportunities to use the Shell to save time this way. As a rule, anytime you want to perform a move, copy, delete, or a similar operation on a several files at once, you can probably do it faster in the Shell than you could from the command line.

Viewing the Contents of Files

One of the little goodies buried in the Shell interface is the F9 key. This key, which has the same effect as the View File Contents menu item on the File menu, lets you view the contents of a file as if you were using a text editor or file browser. This is especially useful for peeking at the contents of text files, but it also comes in handy for browsing binary files.

To view a file, select it in the file list area of the screen and press F9. If the file is a text file, the Shell will display it in ASCII format, the way the TYPE command would display it; if it's a binary file, it will be displayed as a hex dump with file offsets shown on the left, hexadecimal numbers in the center, and the ASCII equivalents to those numbers on the right—in short, similar to the way you'd see the file if you called it up inside DEBUG. The Shell does a commendable job of guessing which are text files and which are binary. If it guesses wrong, or if you want to view the file the other way, press F9 again. F9 toggles the viewing mode between binary and ASCII.

When you're in file viewing mode, you can scroll around in the file with the Up Arrow and Down Arrow keys and the PgUp and PgDn keys. You can also go back to the beginning of the file by pressing the Home key. Unfortunately, there is no search feature that you can use to search out a particular sequence of characters or numbers in the file, but don't let that detract from the utility of this modest but important feature of the DOS 5.0 Shell. Perhaps we'll see a search command in a future version.

Adding Your Own Color Schemes

In general, when you make a configuration change to the DOS Shell through one of its many menu options, the change is written to a file called DOS-SHELL.INI located in the directory where your other DOS files are stored. DOSSHELL.INI is an ASCII text file that contains a long list of configuration directives that the Shell processes each time it is started. By browsing through the file, you can glean what most of the directives do, even though this aspect of the Shell isn't documented anywhere in your DOS manual. If you want, you can edit the file with the DOS Editor, restart the Shell, and see your configuration changes come to life.

There are some things you can do by editing DOSSHELL.INI manually that you *can't* do through the DOS Shell's menus. One of them is adding additional color schemes to the dialog box that pops up when you select the Colors option from the Options menu. By default, the Shell offers eight different predefined color schemes for you to choose from: Basic Blue, Ocean, Monochrome-2 Colors, Monochrome-4 Colors, Reverse, Hot Pink, Emerald City, and Turquoise. Trouble is, none is too exciting. All except the monochrome ones display a stark white background, and there's actually very little difference between Basic Blue, Ocean, and Turquoise. Furthermore, the Shell doesn't offer a means for adding more color schemes, so there's no obvious way to devise ones of your own. Fortunately, though, you're far from stuck. By making a few changes to DOSSHELL.INI with the DOS editor, you can design custom color schemes of your own and add them to the list of choices that the Shell presents you with.

   To start with, make a backup copy of DOSSHELL.INI and store it in a safe place, just in case something goes wrong as you make the changes. Then call up DOSSHELL.INI with the DOS Editor. About a third of the way through the file you'll see the lines

```
color =
{
```

followed by the lines

```
selection =
{
    title = Basic Blue
```

After that comes a series of commands defining the colors used for Basic Blue. The color scheme definition is terminated with a } (curly brace) character several lines further into the file, and immediately after that, the lines that define the colors for Ocean begin. Near the end of the file, a final }—the one that balances out the { following the "color =" statement—terminates the color selection options.

   All you have to do to add a new color scheme is locate the final closing curly brace (the one that begins in column 1, just above the line "associations =") and, starting on the line immediately above it, add a color scheme definition of your own. Definitions take the form

```
selection =
{
    title = title
    foreground =
    {
        base = colorcode
        highlight = colorcode
        selection = colorcode
        alert = colorcode
        menubar = colorcode
        menu = colorcode
        disabled = colorcode
        accelerator = colorcode
        dialog = colorcode
        button = colorcode
        elevator = colorcode
```

```
        titlebar = colorcode
        scrollbar = colorcode
        borders = colorcode
        drivebox = colorcode
        driveicon = colorcode
        cursor = colorcode
    }
background =
{
        base = colorcode
        highlight = colorcode
        selection = colorcode
        alert = colorcode
        menubar = colorcode
        menu = colorcode
        disabled = colorcode
        accelerator = colorcode
        dialog = colorcode
        button = colorcode
        elevator = colorcode
        titlebar = colorcode
        scrollbar = colorcode
        borders = colorcode
        drivebox = colorcode
        driveicon = colorcode
        cursor = colorcode
    }
}
```

where *title* is the title that will appear in the Color Scheme dialog box and *colorcode* is one of 16 color options: black, brightblack, blue, brightblue, green, brightgreen, cyan, brightcyan, red, brightred, magenta, brightmagenta, brown, brightbrown, white, or brightwhite. *Brightbrown* is actually an intense yellow, while *white* comes out looking more like a light gray than white. As you've probably inferred, a color code that begins with "bright" is an intensified version of the color whose name follows the prefix. For example, *red* produces a dark red that has about the same hue as a ripe red apple. *Brightred*, by contrast, is vibrant and, as the name implies, very bright.

Before you set out to create a color scheme of your own, you need to know what parts of the display the various keywords—base, highlight, selection, and so on—affect. First, for every keyword, there are two values you assign: one for the foreground color, one for the background. The foreground color goes under the foreground heading in the .INI file, while the background color goes under the background heading. Furthermore, each keyword controls a specific element of the display. For example, if you set *menu* foreground to black and *menu* background to brightwhite, the menus that you pull down from the menu bar will be displayed in—you guessed it—black letters on a white background.

Here's a short rundown on what each of the keywords does. *Base* sets the colors that the interiors of the windows are displayed in. *Highlight* controls the colors that highlighted items in active windows are displayed in (for example, file names that you highlight in the file list area and menu options highlighted in the overhead menus), while *selection* sets the colors of highlighted items in non-active windows. *Alert* controls the colors that warning messages are displayed in. *Menubar*, *menu*, and *disabled*, respectively, set the colors for the menu bar at the top of the screen, the menus that are pulled down from the menu bar, and items inside the menus that are currently disabled, while *accelerator* controls the colors that underlined letters in the menus are displayed in. *Dialog* and *button* control the colors of dialog boxes and dialog box buttons. *Elevator* sets the color of the thumb that appears inside the scroll bars, and *scrollbar* sets the color of the scroll bar itself. *Titlebar* sets the colors for the title bars of inactive windows. *Borders* controls the colors of the borders that appear at various places around the screen (for example, the borders of the pull-down menu windows). *Drivebox* and *driveicon* control the colors of the drive icons that appear near the top of the screen. Finally, *cursor* sets the color of the cursor.

The following statements, added to the color= section of DOSSHELL.INI, add a color scheme called Stars and Stripes that jazzes up the Shell with a red, white, and blue motif:

```
selection =
{
    title = Stars and Stripes
    foreground =
    {
        base = brightwhite
        highlight = brightwhite
        selection = brightwhite
        alert = brightwhite
        menubar = black
        menu = black
        disabled = white
        accelerator = cyan
        dialog = black
        button = brightwhite
        elevator = white
        titlebar = brightwhite
        scrollbar = black
        borders = black
```

```
        drivebox = brightwhite
        driveicon = brightwhite
        cursor = brightwhite
    }
    background =
    {
        base = blue
        highlight = brightred
        selection = white
        alert = cyan
        menubar = brightwhite
        menu = brightwhite
        disabled = brightwhite
        accelerator = brightwhite
        dialog = brightwhite
        button = blue
        elevator = white
        titlebar = white
        scrollbar = brightwhite
        borders = brightwhite
        drivebox = blue
        driveicon = blue
        cursor = brightblue
    }
}
```

After you've added the statements to the .INI file, restart the Shell, select Colors from the Options menu, and select Stars and Stripes at the bottom of the list. The new color scheme will be displayed.

Designing and implementing a new color scheme usually requires some trial and error because some of the color selections interact with each other in strange and sometimes not-too-obvious ways. For example, the *accelerator* colors affect the colors of hypertext links in the help screens (the lines you can double-click on to go to another part of the Help system) in addition to setting the colors of the accelerator keys in the pull-down menus. With a little work, however, you can create some pretty spiffy screens that will reward your efforts.

Searching an Entire Disk for a File or Set of Files

With DOS 5.0, you gained the ability to search an entire disk or part of a disk for files of a specified name. The command

```
DIR \BUDGET.* /S
```

lists all the files on the current drive that match the file specification BUDGET.*.
In Chapter 7, you learned how to roll this command into a macro so that typing

```
LOCATE BUDGET.*
```

does the same thing. Neither of these actions was possible in earlier versions of
DOS unless you had third-party utilities to lend a hand.

If you're running the Shell, there's an alternate way to search your hard disk
for a file or set of files without having to go out to the command prompt. Go to
the File menu and select the Search menu option. The Shell will display a dialog
box in which you can enter a file specification and indicate whether you want the
entire disk or just the current directory searched by checking or unchecking a
check box. Press OK and the Shell will display a list of all the files that meet the
criterion you specified. By default, the Shell supplies the file specification *.*
and checks the "Search entire disk" check box. So if you press OK as soon as
you enter the dialog box, the Shell will list every file on the current drive.

There's an added benefit to searching files out this way: Once the list is displayed, it's treated just like the file list that appears in the file list area. You can
move files, copy files, delete files, and do anything you can normally do with files
through the File menu, including launching application programs that appear in
the list. As an example, let's say you want to clear out all the files with the extension .BAK from your hard disk. Pull up the Search File dialog box, type ***.BAK** in
the "Search for" field, make sure the check box is checked, and press OK. When
the file list is displayed, choose Select All from the File menu (or press Ctrl-/ or
Shift-End), and then press Del. Every .BAK file on the drive will be deleted, just
as if you had manually gone through the directories and deleted them one at a
time. You just accomplished in a very short period what might have taken a long
time had your only option been to do it from the command line.

Renaming Subdirectories from Inside the Shell

Another action that you can perform from the Shell but can't from the command
line (not without a third-party utility, anyway) is renaming subdirectories. DOS's
REN command works when you're renaming files, but returns an error message
if you attempt to change the name of a subdirectory. That's why Chapter 11 contained the source code for a RENDIR (REName DIRectory) command—to
make up for this glaring omission from an otherwise rich command set.

The Shell, by contrast, makes renaming subdirectories a snap. To rename one,
highlight its name in the directory tree area, pull down the File menu from the top
of the screen, and select Rename. Then enter the new name for the subdirectory
in the ensuing dialog box. The name will be changed and the subdirectory's new
name will be reflected in the list of directories in the directory tree area. Note that
the subdirectory's position in the graphical directory tree will change if the name
change affects its position in the alphabetical list of directory names.

Interestingly, the Shell will not allow you to delete a subdirectory unless the
subdirectory is empty. To remove subdirectories that contain other files and
subdirectories, use the NUKE utility introduced in Chapter 11.

Task Switching

Even if you have a built-in aversion to running DOS shells, there's one feature of the DOS 5.0 Shell that may entice you to give the Shell a try. That feature is *task switching*, and it's only available through the Shell. Task switching is one of the most significant new features added to DOS 5.0. With it, you can have several programs active in memory at once. It's no longer necessary to terminate one application to start another. You can switch from program A to program B and leave program A behind, temporarily suspended but still active in the system. All it takes is one or two keystrokes, and you're dropped right back into the program at the same point you left off. If program A is a word processor and you left it with a document file open, that document will still be open when you get back. Contrast that to the old way of doing things—having to restart the word processor and reload the document file—and it's easy to see why task switching can help you get more from your computer.

The first thing you need to do to try out the Shell's task switcher is enable it. If you haven't already, start the Shell, pull down the Options menu, and, if the menu item named "Enable Task Swapper" isn't bulleted, select the menu item. A small bullet should appear to the left of it, indicating that the switcher (or the *swapper*, as it is called in the DOS manual) is now enabled. At the same time, a new window will appear in the lower-right quadrant of the screen that bears the title "Active Task List." This window displays a list of the programs that are active in the system at any given time. Initially, it will be empty. The next thing you need to do, then, is to add a few programs to it so you can try switching back and forth between them.

There are two ways to add a program to the active task list. The first one is to simply start the program using whatever means is most convenient (double-clicking on its name in the file list, double-clicking on the name of a data file that is *associated* with that program, starting it from the File menu with the Run command, and so on) and then, once it's running, pressing Ctrl-Esc to get back to the Shell. Notice that the name of the program you just exited appears in the active task list. The second way to add a program to the active task list is to double-click on its name while holding down either one of the Shift keys (if you're working without a mouse, highlight the program name and press Shift-Enter). When you do this, the program name appears in the active task list but the program isn't actually started until you switch to it for the first time. You can continue adding programs this way until the task list contains the names of all the programs you want loaded.

Now that you have two or more program names in the active task list, use your mouse to double-click on one of them. The Shell will drop you into that program. When you want to switch to another program, press Ctrl-Esc to return to the Shell, and double-click on the program name. Notice that when you switch back to a program you left before, it comes up in the exact state it was in when you left it. That's because DOS saves the context of the system before the switch takes place and restores it when you switch back so that the application program is unaware that the switch took place. In addition, if the number of programs active in the system at once exceeds the amount of memory available, DOS swaps some of them to disk to make room for others to run.

Pressing Ctrl-Esc and then double-clicking the name of another program in the active task list isn't the only way to switch programs. Another way makes it much faster and easier to get from one application to another. To demonstrate, double-click on one of the program names in your task list. Once you're into the program, press Alt-Tab and continue to hold the Alt key down after you've released Tab. The screen will blank out and the name of the next program in the task list will appear at the top of the screen. If that's the one you want to switch to, release the Alt key, and the Shell will switch you to that application. If it's *not* the one you want to switch to, press the Tab key again while continuing to hold down the Alt key. Each time you press Tab with Alt held down, a new program name appears at the top of the screen. Pressing Alt-Tab repeatedly cycles you through the entire list of programs in the active task list. When you find the one you want, release the Alt key, and you'll be dropped into it. You can switch back to the Shell this way, too, because the name of the Shell appears at the top of the screen, listed among the names of the programs in the active task list (although usually you can return to the Shell more quickly with Ctrl-Esc).

The Alt-Tab method of activating a program also works if you start from the Shell rather than from one of the application programs. The first press of Alt-Tab drops you into a program; each successive press displays a new program name at the top of the screen. As usual, let go of Alt when the name of the program you want to switch to is displayed, and that program will automatically be activated.

If a program is started from a program icon in the program list, and if that program item has an Application Shortcut Key defined for it in the Program Item Properties dialog box, then you can also switch to it by pressing the shortcut key. Shortcut keys appear alongside program names in the active task list. If there is no shortcut key defined for it, you can create one by selecting the program in the program list and then selecting Properties from the File menu. Move the cursor to the Application Shortcut Key field and press any letter key in combination with Shift, Ctrl, or Alt. That key combination will become the shortcut key for that program.

You can add "Command Prompt" to the active task list by pressing Shift-F9 with the task swapper enabled, or by selecting Command Prompt from the program list. The DOS command prompt then becomes just another one of the active tasks that you can switch to.

To remove a program from the active task list, switch to that program and exit it as you normally would. For example, in WordPerfect, you'd press F7; in QBasic, you'd select Exit from the File menu, or press Alt-F-X; from the command prompt, you'd type **EXIT**. When the program terminates, it is removed from the active task list. To add it back, all you have to do is start it again. With the task swapper enabled, every program you start goes on the active task list. To disable task switching altogether, go back to the Shell's Options menu and select Enable Task Swapper again. This time, the bullet will go away, indicating that the task switcher is no longer enabled. Note that you can't disable task switching until all the names have been cleared from the active task list.

Some Practical Advice on Task Switching

There's a second way to remove a program from the active task list: by highlighting its name in the list and invoking the Delete option from the Shell's file menu or pressing Del. However, you should only use this method as a last resort. It's a safety valve to be used in case a program locks up on you so you can't get out of it by conventional means. After you terminate a program this way, you should exit the DOS Shell and reboot your PC, because DOS itself may become unstable and prone to untimely crashes or unpredictable behavior.

Which brings up an interesting point: If you use the task switcher, you probably *will* experience lockups occasionally. DOS is a single-tasking operating system that was designed around the real mode of the Intel 80x86 processor family to run one program at a time. Getting it to support multiple-program contexts requires some fairly sophisticated background maneuvering on the part of the DOS Shell. In addition, certain types of programs simply don't run very well in a task-switched environment. The DOS manual warns you about 3270 and other mainframe terminal emulators and the fact that if you swap such a program out, your connection to the mainframe may be lost. The same is probably true of most communications programs. Remember that there's a difference between task switching and multitasking. In a multitasking environment, programs keep running when you switch away from them; in a task switching environment, they don't. The switcher suspends a program until the next time you switch back to it, so you cannot, for example, switch away from a communications program in the middle of downloading a file and have it continue to download data. Instead, the download will cease, and data may be lost.

Fortunately, there is relief in sight. An integral part of the programmer's reference for DOS 5.0 is a new set of calls geared toward making all programs—especially communications programs—run better in a task-switched environment. This set of calls is collectively known as the *DOS Task Switcher API* (API stands for Application Programming Interface). Among other things, the Task Switcher API allows a program to report that it is currently executing a critical section of code and prevent itself from being swapped out at the moment. This would prevent the switcher from swapping out your communications program if you interrupted it in the middle of a download, for example. Alternatively, knowing that the switcher wants to switch to another program, the communications program could elect to post a message to you informing you of the operation in progress and ask you if you really want to terminate the download. The Task Switcher API, if widely adopted, will bring other benefits to DOS users, too. For example, Microsoft has promised that the API will be implemented in future versions of real and standard mode Windows, which face some of the same sorts of problems in managing and switching between tasks that the switcher built into the DOS Shell does. The bottom line is that all programs can be made task switching aware if they choose to implement this API, and better able to run in tomorrow's environments. And it's we, as users, who will benefit. The question that remains to be answered is how enthusiastically software manufacturers will embrace this new technology, because it requires additional work on their part, the same way it takes additional programming to add to an application the ability to use extended or expanded memory. With a little luck, the Task Switcher API will become a universal standard, and we'll see fewer and fewer programs that are intolerant of switching.

Summary

In summary, let's list the things you can do with the DOS Shell that you can't do from the command line, or that you can't do from the command line without a lot of extra work. The list includes

- Loading multiple programs into memory at once so that you can switch between them without losing context

- Launching application programs by selecting data files created by those programs

- Performing operations on entire groups of files at once, with little or no more effort than is required to operate on a single file

- Renaming subdirectories

Should you run the Shell or not? The ultimate answer lies in how comfortable you feel on the command line. If you're new to DOS, you may prefer using the Shell as an intermediary to insulate you from the nuances of the command line. (If you really like the look and feel of the Shell, you might consider running Microsoft Windows on top of DOS. Windows is everything the Shell is, plus some, and it automatically takes advantage of whatever CPU it's being run on, allowing you to multitask DOS programs on a 386, for example.) If, on the other hand, you're an experienced DOS user, you may want to go to the Shell only when doing so would save you a great deal of time. Whatever your tastes, you're sure to find something to like about this latest release of the operating system—even if you don't particularly care for the command-line interface that it is famous for.

THE QBASIC INTERPRETER

MANY PROGRAMMERS CUT THEIR TEETH LEARNING TO PROGRAM IN BASIC. That's because GW-BASIC and BASICA, the first BASIC interpreters written for the IBM PC, were bundled with most versions of MS-DOS and PC-DOS, respectively. Both were simple, line-oriented programming environments, almost toys in comparison with the modern language compilers now available. But they provided the first exposure many users ever had to programming and were probably at least indirectly responsible for putting the programming bug in some of the most talented programmers working in the industry today.

DOS 5.0 features the QBasic Interpreter, a much-improved BASIC interpreter derived from Microsoft's hugely popular QuickBASIC compiler. The QBasic Interpreter is almost identical to QuickBASIC except that it does not produce stand-alone executables like QuickBASIC does; instead, you have to run QBasic programs in QBasic. (The difference between a compiler and an interpreter is that the former translates a BASIC program to machine code and saves it on disk as a stand-alone COM or EXE file, while the latter performs the translation at runtime; therefore, interpreted programs must be run under the auspices of the interpreter itself.) If you need to convert a QBasic program to .EXE format, you can port it directly to QuickBASIC, usually without changes, and compile it there. The reverse is also true: QuickBASIC programs port quickly and easily to the QBasic environment, most of them without requiring any changes whatsoever. Most GW-BASIC and BASICA programs will run in QBasic, too, complete with line numbers. Those that won't generally require only a minimal amount of patching up.

But what's most significant about the QBasic Interpreter is that it offers a structured programming environment to BASIC programmers free of charge. Its long list of features includes, among other things, support for structured decision-making constructs such as SELECT CASE, DO WHILE, and DO UNTIL, support for long integers and IEEE-format real numbers, graphics support for EGA and VGA video modes, user-defined data types, and an integrated debugger. It also features instant syntax checking, a comprehensive on-line Help system, support for recursive procedures, and an editor you're already familiar with—the DOS Editor. Plus, QBasic programs can be up to 160k long (combined length of code and data), compared with 64k for GW-BASIC and BASICA. It all adds up to a set of greatly enhanced BASIC programming tools for owners of DOS 5.0.

This chapter provides a brief but thorough overview of the QBasic Interpreter and of the QBasic programming environment in general. The first section gives you a guided tour through the Interpreter, shows you how to load and run programs and find your way through the on-line Help system, and offers some friendly advice for those endeavoring to port GW-BASIC/BASICA programs to QBasic. The second section presents a fully developed QBasic game program and analyzes it for structure and content. Finally, the third section introduces QBasic's built-in debugging features and shows you how they work.

Getting Acquainted with the QBasic Interpreter

The first step toward learning to use the QBasic Interpreter is getting acquainted with the QBasic environment—the Shell in which you load, edit, debug, and execute programs. The command for starting the QBasic Interpreter is

```
QBASIC
```

If you wish, you can also include the name of a program to load along with the interpreter, as in

```
QBASIC PASSAGES
```

Actually, the QBASIC command accepts several switches, most of which you'll never need. These switches are documented in your DOS manual and in Appendix A of this book. You can also get a list of them by typing **QBASIC /?**. As usual, it helps if you've set up your PATH statement to include the directory where QBasic is stored. In addition to the program file itself—QBASIC.EXE—DOS also needs to be able to find QBASIC.HLP, which contains the help messages that go with the interpreter, and QBASIC.INI, where your configuration changes are stored.

Two of the switches that you might find useful are /H and /RUN. Starting QBasic with a /H switch has it automatically switch into the video mode that displays the highest number of lines your adapter supports. If you're running QBasic on an EGA, you'll get 43 lines; on a VGA, you'll get 50. Having more lines displayed is very helpful when you're editing long programs. The /RUN switch has QBasic automatically run the program whose name was specified on the command line. This is a great way to run QBasic programs from batch files. Let's say you've written a QBasic program called REMBAK.BAS that sweeps through the directory structure of a hard disk deleting all the .BAK files it finds, and that you'd like to run it from your AUTOEXEC.BAT file. To do so, place the command

```
QBASIC /RUN REMBAK
```

in AUTOEXEC.BAT, and make sure there's a PATH to the directory where DOS is stored (if REMBAK.BAS isn't in the current directory, you'll need to include a path to it, too). One other thing you must make sure to do is end REMBAK.BAS with a SYSTEM statement to return control to DOS. If you don't, you'll be left inside the QBasic Interpreter when the REMBAK.BAS ends, and AUTOEXEC.BAT won't finish executing until you exit QBasic.

When QBasic is started, you'll see a screen something like the one in Figure 15.1 (if you started it without specifying the name of a BASIC program, you'll have to press Esc to bypass the Survival Guide). At the top of the screen is a menu bar containing the commands you'll use to drive the Interpreter. Below that is the window where you enter and edit programs. If there's a program loaded, its name appears at the top of the window; if there's not, then the window is labeled "Untitled." Near the bottom of the screen is another, smaller window titled "Immediate." Here, you can type QBasic commands and see them executed immediately. When you press Enter on a line that contains a QBasic command, QBasic executes the line and, if necessary, switches to the output screen so that you can see the output from the command. To see for yourself, make the Immediate window the active window by clicking inside it with the mouse (or pressing F6) and type

```
PRINT "DOS 5.0"
```

Then press Enter. The screen will immediately switch so that you can see the output from the command. Press any key and you'll be returned to the QBasic shell. We'll talk more about the Immediate window later when we discuss debugging in the QBasic environment. For now, you can remove it by clicking on the Up-Arrow symbol that appears in the upper-right corner of the screen, just under Help in the menu bar.

FIGURE 15.1

The QBasic screen

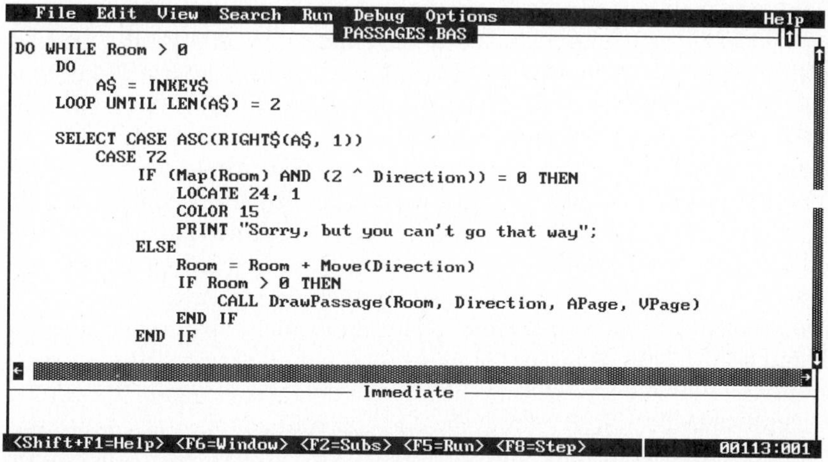

```
 File  Edit  View  Search  Run  Debug  Options                    Help
                            PASSAGES.BAS                            ↑↓
DO WHILE Room > 0
    DO
        A$ = INKEY$
    LOOP UNTIL LEN(A$) = 2

    SELECT CASE ASC(RIGHT$(A$, 1))
        CASE 72
            IF (Map(Room) AND (2 ^ Direction)) = 0 THEN
                LOCATE 24, 1
                COLOR 15
                PRINT "Sorry, but you can't go that way";
            ELSE
                Room = Room + Move(Direction)
                IF Room > 0 THEN
                    CALL DrawPassage(Room, Direction, APage, VPage)
                END IF
            END IF

─────────────────────────── Immediate ───────────────────────────
<Shift+F1=Help> <F6=Window> <F2=Subs> <F5=Run> <F8=Step>      00113:001
```

Most of the features of the QBasic Interpreter are accessed through the menus at the top of the screen. There are eight options in the menu bar: File, Edit, View, Search, Run, Debug, Options, and Help. File contains the commands you use to load, save, and print files, and to exit QBasic. Edit contains the commands you use to edit program text and create new subprograms and functions. View contains commands for selecting what program modules and windows are shown on the screen. Search contains commands for searching out text strings in the program listing and, if you wish, replacing them with other text strings. Run contains commands for starting programs and resuming them once they've stopped. Debug contains commands for program debugging, which will be discussed at length in the section entitled "Debugging Programs in the QBasic Environment." Options contains commands for customizing the display, specifying the path to the QBasic Help files, and for enabling and disabling syntax checking. Finally, the Help menu is the entry point to QBasic's extensive on-line Help system. Help is vitally important because there is no manual available for QBasic other than the books you can buy in bookstores. We'll talk more about Help and some of the hidden goodies you'll find in it later in this chapter. For reference purposes, Table 15.1 lists the contents of all eight menus and provides a brief description of each menu item.

Loading and Running Programs

Probably the best way to get a feel for the QBasic programming environment is to load a program and exercise a few of the Interpreter's features. The directory where your DOS program files are stored should contain several .BAS files (by convention, BASIC programs have the extension .BAS) that are supplied as samples. One of them is GORILLA.BAS. To load it, pull down the File menu from the menu bar at the top of the screen and select Open. Then type in the name and location of GORILLA.BAS or use the Dirs/Drives box to change to the drive and directory where GORILLA.BAS is and double-click on the file name in the File box. The listing for GORILLA.BAS will appear in the editing window. You can browse and edit the file using many of the same methods you use in the DOS Editor. In fact, you're *running* the DOS Editor, at least in a sense. When you type EDIT at the DOS command line, all EDIT.COM does is invoke QBASIC.EXE with an /EDCOM switch (for a review of the DOS Editor's text editing features, see Chapter 5).

All you have to do to run GORILLA.BAS is select Start from the Run menu, or press Shift-F5. The screen will clear and the program's output will be displayed. When you exit GORILLA.BAS, you'll be dropped back into the QBasic editor at the same point you left off. If you want to make changes to the program, all you have to do is type them in and select Start again.

As you browse through the program listing, notice that there are no subprograms or functions in the program listing itself. That's because QBasic stores subprograms and functions apart from the main body of the program. Pull down the View menu and select SUBs. From the ensuing dialog box, you can pick the name of the subprogram or function you want to edit and that subprogram or function (or *program module*) will appear in the editing window. To switch back to the main body of the program, select SUBs again and pick GORILLA.BAS,

TABLE 15.1

Summary of QBasic Menu Options

Menu Option	Shortcut Key	Description
File Menu		
New		Clears the program editing window
Open...		Loads a new program for editing
Save		Saves the current program
Save As...		Saves the current program under a new name
Print...		Prints the current program
Exit		Exits QBasic and returns to DOS
Edit Menu		
Cut	Shift-Del	Deletes the selected text from the editing window and places it in the clipboard
Copy	Ctrl-Ins	Copies the selected text from the editing window and places it in the clipboard
Paste	Shift-Ins	Pastes the contents of the clipboard into the editing window at the current cursor location
Clear	Del	Deletes the selected text without copying it to the clipboard
New SUB...		Creates a new subprogram
New FUNCTION...		Creates a new function
View Menu		
SUBs...	F2	Lets you choose the program module to display
Split		Divides the screen into two editing windows
Output Screen	F4	Displays the output screen
Search Menu		
Find...		Searches for the specified text
Repeat Last Find	F3	Searches for the next occurrence of the text specified with Find
Change...		Searches for and replaces the specified text
Run Menu		
Start	Shift-F5	Runs the current program
Restart		Clears variables and restarts the current program
Continue	F5	Continues the current program after a breakpoint is reached
Debug Menu		
Step	F8	Executes the next program statement
Procedure Step	F10	Executes the next program statement and skips procedure calls
Trace On		Enables and disables tracing
Toggle Breakpoint	F9	Sets a breakpoint at the current cursor location or removes the breakpoint if one already exists
Clear All Breakpoints		Removes all breakpoints from the program
Set Next Statement		Makes the statement at the cursor to execute the next one
Options Menu		
Display...		Lets you set screen colors and other display options
Help Path...		Lets you specify the location of Help files
Syntax Checking		Enables and disables syntax checking
Help Menu		
Index		Displays an index of Help information
Contents		Displays the table of contents for the Help system
Topic:	F1	Displays Help for the QBasic keyword that the cursor is on
Using Help	Shift-F1	Displays help on Help
About...		Displays information about the QBasic Interpreter

the first item in the list. As you browse through the list, a line at the bottom of the dialog box tells you whether the highlighted item is a subprogram, function, or, in the case of GORILLA.BAS, the "main module." This separate grouping of program modules is done for organizational purposes and does not affect the operation of QBasic in any other way. For example, when you use the Find menu option to search for a specific statement or phrase, it searches all the program modules for the specified text, not just the module that is currently displayed. Also, when you print a program listing, the subprograms and functions get printed, too. QBasic appends them to the end of the program listing, after the main body of the program.

You can also enter new programs from scratch. To do so, select New from the File menu to clear the current program from the editing window. Then start entering program lines. As you do, QBasic will automatically format the line for you, capitalizing BASIC keywords, inserting spaces after commas, adding missing quotation marks, and more. If the Syntax Checking option in the Options menu is enabled (if it's enabled, a small bullet will appear to the left of it), QBasic will check the lines you enter for syntax errors as you enter them and translate them to executable code (the ultimate goal of any compiler or interpreter) ahead of time so that the program will run faster once it's started. This is in stark contrast to most language interpreters, which wait until you press Start to start translating to machine code. To illustrate what syntax checking does for you, make sure Syntax Checking is bulleted and type

```
print "QBasic
```

As soon as you press Enter or move to another line, QBasic will amend the statement to say

```
PRINT "QBasic"
```

converting the PRINT statement to uppercase and adding the terminating quotation mark for you. As another example, try typing

```
DO WHILE Var > Ø LOOP
```

When you press Enter, QBasic will highlight the word LOOP and pop up a window with the message "Expected: end-of-statement." In other words, it's telling you that LOOP must go on the next line. Click OK in the message window, and then position the cursor in front of LOOP and press Enter to move it down a line. This time, QBasic will accept the statements because they were entered using the correct syntax. If Syntax Checking distracts you or you simply find it annoying, disable it by selecting it in the Options menu. With Syntax Checking off, QBasic will accept anything you type, and will not catch syntax errors until you run the program.

As you enter a new program from scratch, there are two ways to begin a new subprogram or function. One way is to select New SUB or New FUNCTION from the Edit menu and enter the subprogram or function name in the dialog box. The easier way is to enter the first line of the program module—the SUB or FUNCTION statement—and press Enter. QBasic will automatically supply the matching END SUB or END FUNCTION statement for you and switch you from the main program module (or whatever module you're currently working in) to the new subprogram or function module. Remember, to get back to the main program module or to any other module defined in the program, all you have to do is select SUBs from the View menu and then select the name of the module you want to edit.

When you're done, of course, you'll want to save your work to disk. You can do so using either the Save or Save As option in the File menu. QBasic saves files in plain ASCII format, so you can treat them like you would any other text file. The first time you save a file, QBasic will ask you for a name to save it under. Thereafter, it will automatically be saved under that name unless you use Save As so that you'll be prompted for a new file name.

Converting GW-BASIC and BASICA Programs for QBasic

One of the benefits of programming in QBasic is that it supports structured programming such as named procedures and functions, IF-THEN-ELSE statements, SELECT CASE constructs, DO WHILE and DO UNTIL loops, and more. It even supports recursive procedures (procedures that call themselves), something that couldn't be said about its progenitors, GW-BASIC and BASICA. In short, you can do just about anything with QBasic that you can do with any modern developmental language, and in some cases you can do it better.

In addition, QBasic features backward-compatibility with GW-BASIC and BASICA. For the most part, you can load the old programs that you ran in the earlier BASIC environments and run them with little or no modification, even if they contain line numbers—something that is not needed in a structured programming language. The one thing you must do before you transport a GW-BASIC or BASICA program to QBasic, however, is save it in ASCII format. By default, programs saved to disk in the old environments were saved in a special binary form, in which BASIC statements and functions were stored as numerical tokens rather than as plain ASCII text strings. The command for saving a file in ASCII form in both GW-BASIC and BASICA is

```
SAVE filename,A
```

where *filename* is the name of the program. Once they're saved this way, programs can be loaded directly into QBasic.

There are a few GW-BASIC/BASICA keywords that are not supported in QBasic. They are AUTO, CONT, DEF USR, DELETE, EDIT, LIST, LLIST, LOAD, MERGE, MOTOR, NEW, RENUM, SAVE, and USR. If your programs contain any of these keywords, you'll have to remove them before they'll run in QBasic. If you happen to be porting a program to QBasic from Quick-BASIC, there are a few QuickBASIC keywords that aren't supported: ALIAS, BYVAL, CDECL, COMMAND$, EVENT, $INCLUDE, INT86, INT86X, LOCAL, SADD, INTERRUPT, INTERRUPTX, SETMEM, SIGNAL, and UEVENT. With the exception of certain CALL commands, everything else should run the same in QBasic as it did in GW-BASIC, BASICA, and Quick-BASIC. CALL commands in GW-BASIC and BASICA programs must be converted to CALL ABSOLUTE to be compatible with the QBasic Interpreter.

If you have any GW-BASIC or BASICA programs that you use often and will continue to use often once they're ported to QBasic, you should consider rewriting them to take advantage of the elements of structured programming. Structured programs are generally easier to maintain, and in some cases will even run slightly faster. Unfortunately, there's no easy way to make the conversion. You have to do it yourself, and this frequently involves restructuring the program from the ground up. By definition, a fully structured program will be devoid of GOTO statements, and BASIC programs have traditionally relied on GOTO rather heavily. The first step in converting a program to structured form is removing the line numbers. To help, DOS 5.0 comes with a QBasic program called REMLINE.BAS that takes a BASIC program file as input and removes all line numbers that are not a target of a GOSUB, RETURN, GOTO, THEN, ELSE, RESUME, RESTORE, or RUN statement. It's a start, but the result is a far cry from being a structured program. If you run REMLINE, note that, by default, it'll handle a maximum of 400 program lines. If you want to use it with a program that contains more, adjust the size of the constant named MaxLines near the top of the program listing before starting it.

To illustrate the difference between the GW-BASIC/BASICA way of programming and the structured way of programming, consider the following two code fragments. Both of them print "Enter" when you press the Enter key or "spacebar" when you press the spacebar, and terminate when you press the Esc key. The first one, written for GW-BASIC and BASICA, looks like this:

```
100 A$=INKEY$:IF LEN(A$)<>1 THEN GOTO 100
110 IF A$=CHR$(13) THEN PRINT "Enter":GOTO 100
120 IF A$=CHR$(32) THEN PRINT "Spacebar":GOTO 100
130 IF A$<>CHR$(27) THEN GOTO 100
140 END
```

The same code fragment restructured for QBasic might look like this:

```
DO

    DO
        A$ = INKEY$
    LOOP UNTIL LEN(A$) = 1

    SELECT CASE ASC(A$)
        CASE 13
            PRINT "Enter"
        CASE 32
            PRINT "Spacebar"
        CASE 27
            END
```

```
        END SELECT

    LOOP WHILE LEN(A$)=1
```

The difference is striking. Even if you haven't been exposed to structured programming languages in the past, the second example is much more readable. That's why it's easier to maintain, too: When you pick up this program two years from now, it will require less effort to understand what's going on. This also illustrates why there's no easy way to translate from the old program format to the new one. The difference goes deeper than a few line numbers; it lies in the fundamental way that the program is written.

One other precaution that you should take when porting GW-BASIC/BASICA programs to QBasic relates to data files that contain strings representing real numbers that were created with the MKD$ and MKS$ functions. GW-BASIC and BASIC used the proprietary Microsoft Binary format to represent real numbers, while QBasic defaults to the more-standard IEEE floating-point format. If your QBasic program will be reading data files created by GW-BASIC or BASICA, you should use the newer CVDMBF and CVSMBF functions in place of CVD and CVS to convert the strings read from disk to IEEE format. Conversely, if you're writing real numbers to disk and want to maintain compatibility with older versions of BASIC, you should use MKDMBF$ and MKSMBF$ rather than MKD$ and MKS$. If you start QBasic with a /MBF switch, it will handle these conversions for you by substituting CVDMBF, CVSMBF, MKDMBF$, and MKSMBF$ for every occurrence of CVD, CVS, MKD$, and MKS$ when a program is run.

Navigating the QBasic Help System

Because there is precious little printed information about QBasic that comes with DOS 5.0, you'll come to rely heavily on the built-in Help system that QBasic provides. It's more than just a help system; it's a complete on-line reference to the QBasic programming environment, including documentation on every command and menu option, documentation for runtime error codes, and instructions for using the QBasic editor. It also offers helpful information on topics such as differences between GW-BASIC, BASICA, and QBasic, converting programs written for one environment to run in the other, and QBasic command-line options. In short, it's got just about everything you need except perhaps a tutorial on learning and using the language.

There are several ways to get help. If you need help on a BASIC keyword that appears in a program listing, position the cursor on the keyword and press F1 or click the right mouse button (or select Topic: from the Help menu). QBasic will open the Help window to the page that contains the documentation for that keyword. The information will include a 1- or 2-line description of the keyword, its syntax, examples of its use (examples that you can cut or copy from the Help window and paste into the editing window by using the menu options under Edit if you wish), and a list of related keywords. You can go directly to one of the related keywords by double-clicking on it. Alternatively, you can use the three buttons at the top of the Help window (Contents, Index, and Back) to display the Help system's table of contents, to display an index of BASIC keywords, or to redisplay the last Help topic you looked at. QBasic saves information on the last 20 Help topics you've reviewed and lets you cycle back through them by clicking Back repeatedly (or by pressing Alt-F1).

Sometimes you'll need information about a keyword before it's actually entered into the program listing. That's what the Index option in the Help menu is for. Index displays an alphabetical list of help topics, including BASIC language keywords. Once you find the keyword you're looking for, double-click on it (or, if you're using the keyboard, place the cursor on it and press Enter or F1). You can scroll the list using all the conventional methods, including the PgUp and PgDn keys and the scroll bar on the right. The *best* way to locate a given keyword, however, is to press the first letter of its name. The list will automatically scroll to the section that contains keywords beginning with that letter. In addition to containing BASIC keywords, the list also includes selected general topics that you can get help with. Go to the Bs, for example, and in between BLOAD and BSAVE, you'll see "Boolean Operators." Double-clicking on it produces a 2-page discourse on the use of the Boolean operators NOT, AND, OR, XOR, EQV, and IMP.

A third way to get help with QBasic is to select Contents from the Help menu. Contents displays a list of help topics grouped into the following categories:

- Orientation

- Using QBasic

- Keys

- Quick Reference

"Orientation" offers help on such topics as how to use Help and how to use dialog boxes. "Using QBasic" contains several helpful selections related to the BASIC language and BASIC programming in general, including, among other things, a list of BASIC keywords arranged by programming task (which is useful if you're not sure what statement or function you need to use but know what you want it to do), information about the limitations imposed on the QBasic environment (for example, size limits on variables and variable arrays), and advice on converting GW-BASIC/BASICA programs to work in QBasic. Through "Keys," you can get help on any of the keys and key combinations used in QBasic. Finally, "Quick Reference" contains documentation on the ASCII character set, keyboard scan codes (useful with functions such INKEY$), and runtime error codes. This is powerful stuff. How often have you had to dig through a manual for 20 minutes looking for documentation on error codes? With QBasic, it's all on-line, and just a couple of mouse clicks or keystrokes away. As usual, you can select any one topic by double-clicking on it or by positioning the cursor on it and pressing F1 or Enter.

You can even get help on Help if you wish. To do so, select Using Help from the Help menu or press Shift-F1. QBasic will present you with a concise summary of all the ways you can get help, offering helpful advice in the form of bulleted lists that get right to the heart of navigating your way through the Help system.

Keep in mind that you can print any or all of the help information the QBasic Help system contains. If you want, you can assemble a mini-manual by opening Help for all the topics you're interested in and selecting Print from the File menu. You can also get a printed copy of the ASCII character set, keyboard scan codes, and QBasic runtime error codes. To do so, select Contents from the Help menu, select the item that you want to print (for example, ASCII Character Codes), and select Print from the File menu. You may never have to hunt for an ASCII chart or a list of keyboard codes again.

Writing Programs in the QBasic Environment

Your DOS 5.0 program disks contain some wonderful sample programs to help get you up and running in the QBasic environment. Unless you've had prior experience programming in QuickBASIC, you'll have to learn how to program by example. The DOS 5.0 package does not contain any QBasic tutorials—just reference information that is supplied on-line. Fortunately, you can learn most of what you need to know about programming in QBasic by using the sample programs as a guide and, when you have questions about a particular statement or command, consulting QBasic's on-line help system for answers. It's a tough route to go, but it's better than letting a powerful tool like this go unused for lack of printed documentation.

For reference, Table 15.2 lists the QBasic statements and functions that QBasic supports, grouped by category, and provides a brief description of each. An abbreviated form of this reference is available on-line, under "Keywords by Programming Task" in the Help system's table of contents. Basically, the keywords fall into 13 different categories: Flow Control, Data Declaration and Assignment, Debugging, Device Input and Output, Event and Error Handling, File Input and Output, File System, Graphics, Math and Data Conversion, Memory Management, Procedure Call and Definition, String Management, and Time and Date. In some cases, a keyword plays a dual role as both a statement and a function; such keywords are noted with the designation "Statement" or "Function" in parentheses. Also, some keywords such as GET and PUT have different meanings depending on the context they're used in. These, too, are noted. Finally, a few keywords appear twice just because they belong under two headings.

Unfortunately, it's not possible to present a comprehensive overview of BASIC programming in this space. What the next few sections will do is analyze a living, breathing program so that you can get a feel for the dialect of BASIC supported by the QBasic Interpreter. The program is a game that runs in EGA/VGA 320 by 200 16-color graphics mode and illustrates, among other things, some of the useful graphics commands that QBasic provides. In addition to getting a working education in QBasic, you'll also gain a new game program that's fun to play. If, as you peruse the source code, you have additional questions about a particular command, function, or keyword, use the QBasic Help system to find out more about it.

TABLE 15.2

QBasic Statements and Functions by Category

Flow Control

CHAIN	Transfers control from one program to another
DO-LOOP	Repeats a block of statements while or until a condition is true
END	Ends a program, subprogram, function, or block
EXIT	Ends a subprogram or function
FOR-NEXT	Repeats a block of statements a specified number of times
IF-THEN-ELSE	Performs conditional branching
ON-GOTO/ON-GOSUB	Branches to a specified line or subroutine based on the value of an expression
SELECT CASE	Executes one of several blocks of statements based on the value of an expression
STOP	Halts the program
SYSTEM	Returns to DOS
WHILE-WEND	Repeats a block of statements while a condition is true

Data Declaration and Assignment

COMMON	Defines global variables
CONST	Declares a constant
DATA	Defines data read by READ statements
DEFDBL	Sets the default data type for double-precision variables
DEFINT	Sets the default data type for integer variables
DEFLNG	Sets the default data type for long integers
DEFSGN	Sets the default data type for single-precision variables
DEFSTR	Sets the default data type for string variables
DIM	Declares a variable and allocates storage space
ERASE	Reinitializes static arrays and deallocates dynamic arrays
LBOUND	Returns the lowest subscript for the specified dimension of an array
LET	Assigns a value to a variable
OPTION BASE	Declares the default lower bound for array subscripts
READ	Reads values stored in DATA statements into variables
REDIM	Redimensions a dynamic array
REM	Precedes remarks in a program listing
RESTORE	Specifies which DATA statement will be read next
SHARED	Shares a variable with a subprogram or function
SWAP	Exchanges the values of two variables
TYPE	Defines a new data type
UBOUND	Returns the highest subscript for the specified dimension of an array

Debugging

TRON	Enables program tracing
TROFF	Disables program tracing

Device Input and Output

BEEP	Generates a beep
CLS	Clears the screen
CSRLIN	Returns the number of the line that the cursor is on
INKEY$	Returns the key code of a key pressed on the keyboard
INP	Reads a byte from an I/O port
INPUT	Reads a string of input from the keyboard
IOCTL	Transmits a string to a device driver
IOCTL$	Reads a string from a device driver
KEY (Assignment)	Assigns a string value to a function key
LINE INPUT	Reads a line of input from the keyboard
LOCATE	Positions the cursor
LPOS	Returns the position of the print head
LPRINT	Prints data on the printer
LPRINT USING	Prints formatted data on the printer
OPEN COM	Opens a serial port for input and output
OUT	Sends a byte to an I/O port
PLAY (Function)	Returns the number of notes in the music queue
PLAY (statement)	Plays musical notes
POS	Returns the number of the column that the cursor is in
PRINT	Prints data on the screen
PRINT USING	Prints formatted data on the screen

TABLE 15.2 **(Continued)**

Device Input and Output (Continued)

SCREEN (Function)	Reads a character code or color from the screen
SCREEN (Statement)	Sets the display mode
SOUND	Generates sound through the speaker
SPC	Skips the specified number of spaces in a PRINT statement
STICK	Returns the coordinates of a joystick
STRIG	Returns the status of a joystick trigger
TAB	Moves the print position to specified column
VIEW PRINT	Defines the boundaries of a screen text viewport
WAIT	Pauses until an I/O port returns a specified value or bit pattern
WIDTH	Specifies the width of an output device

Event and Error Handling

COM	Enables or disables serial port event trapping
ERDEV	Returns an error code from the last device to generate a critical error
ERDEV$	Returns the name of the last device to generate a critical error
ERL	Returns the runtime error code for the most recent error
ERR	Returns the line number the error occurred on
ERROR	Simulates the occurrence of an error
KEY (Event Trapping)	Enables, disables, or suspends key event trapping
ON COM	Enables, disables, or suspends serial port event trapping
ON ERROR	Names an error handling routine
ON KEY	Enables, disables, or suspends key event trapping
ON PEN	Enables, disables, or suspends light pen event trapping
ON PLAY	Enables, disables, or suspends PLAY event trapping
ON STRIG	Enables, disables, or suspends joystick event trapping
ON TIMER	Enables, disables, or suspends timer event trapping
PEN	Returns light pen coordinates
PLAY (Event Trapping)	Enables, disables, or suspends PLAY event trapping
RESUME	Continues program execution after an error occurs
TIMER (Statement)	Enables, disables, or suspends timer event trapping

File Input and Output

BLOAD	Loads a file created by BSAVE into memory
BSAVE	Saves a region of memory to disk
CLOSE	Closes an open file or device
EOF	Returns true if the end of the file has been reached
FIELD	Allocates space for variables in a random access file buffer
FILEATTR	Returns information about an open file
FREEFILE	Returns the next free file number
GET (File I/O)	Reads data from disk into a buffer or variable
INPUT#	Reads data from a sequential file
INPUT$	Reads a string from a file
LINE INPUT#	Reads a line from a sequential file
LOC	Returns the current position within a file
LOCK	Locks a file or records in the file
LOF	Returns the length of a file in bytes
LSET	Moves data to a random access file buffer
OPEN	Opens a file or device for input and output
PRINT#	Writes data to a sequential file
PRINT# USING	Writes formatted data to a sequential file
PUT (File I/O)	Writes data to disk from a buffer or variable
RSET	Moves data to a random access file buffer
SEEK (Function)	Returns the current file position
SEEK (Statement)	Sets the file position for the next read or write
UNLOCK	Unlocks records locked with LOCK
WRITE	Writes data to the screen
WRITE#	Writes data to a sequential file

File System

CHDIR	Changes to the specified directory
FILES	Lists the files in a directory

TABLE 15.2

(Continued)

File System (Continued)

KILL	Deletes a file from disk
MKDIR	Creates a subdirectory
NAME	Renames a file
RMDIR	Removes a subdirectory

Graphics

CIRCLE	Draws an ellipse or circle
CLS	Clears the screen or viewport
COLOR	Sets the display colors
DRAW	Draws an object defined by a string variable
GET (Graphics)	Transfers a block of pixel data to a buffer in memory
LINE	Draws a line or box on the screen
PAINT	Fills an area with a specified color or pattern
PALETTE	Changes a color in the palette
PALETTE USING	Changes several colors in the palette
PCOPY	Copies one display page to another
PMAP	Translates between window and viewport coordinates
POINT	Returns the color of a pixel or the position of the graphics cursor
PRESET	Sets a pixel to a specified color
PSET	Sets a pixel to a specified color
PUT (Graphics)	Transfers a block of pixel data to the screen
SCREEN (Statement)	Sets the display mode
VIEW	Defines a viewport
WINDOW	Defines logical dimensions for the current viewport

Math and Data Conversion

ABS	Returns the absolute value of an expression
ASC	Returns the ASCII code for a character
ATN	Returns the arctangent value of an expression
CDBL	Converts an expression to a double-precision number
CINT	Converts an expression to an integer
CLNG	Converts an expression to a long integer
COS	Returns the cosine of an angle
CSNG	Converts an expression to a single-precision number
CVD	Converts an 8-byte string to a double-precision number
CVDMBF	Converts an 8-byte string to an IEEE-format double-precision number
CVI	Converts a 2-byte string to an integer
CVL	Converts a 4-byte string to a long integer
CVS	Converts a 4-byte string to a single-precision number
CVSMBF	Converts a 4-byte string to an IEEE-format single-precision number
EXP	Raises e to a power and returns the result
FIX	Truncates a floating-point variable to its integer portion
INT	Returns the integer portion of a variable
LOG	Returns the natural log of an expression
MKD$	Converts a double-precision number to an 8-byte string
MKDMBF$	Converts an IEEE-format double-precision number to an 8-byte string
MKI$	Converts an integer to a 2-byte string
MKL$	Converts a long integer to a 4-byte string
MKS$	Converts a single-precision number to a 4-byte string
MKSMBF$	Converts an IEEE-format single-precision number to a 4-byte string
RANDOMIZE	Initializes the random number generator
RND	Returns a random number between 0 and 1
SGN	Returns a value indicating the sign of an expression
SIN	Returns the sine of an angle
SQR	Returns the square root of a number
TAN	Returns the tangent of an angle

TABLE 15.2

(Continued)

Memory Management

CLEAR	Reinitializes variables and closes open files
DEF SEG	Sets the segment address for PEEK, POKE, BLOAD, BSAVE, and CALL ABSOLUTE statements
ENVIRON	Modifies or creates an environment string
ENVIRON$	Returns an environment string
FRE	Returns the amount of free memory (in bytes)
PEEK	Returns the value of the specified byte of memory
POKE	Sets the value of the specified byte of memory
VARPTR	Returns the offset address of a variable
VARPTR$	Returns a string representation of a variable's offset address
VARSEG	Returns the segment address of a variable

Procedure Call and Definition

CALL	Calls a subprogram
CALL ABSOLUTE	Calls a machine language procedure
DECLARE	Declares a reference to a procedure
DEF FN	Defines a function
EXIT	Exits from a subprogram or function
FUNCTION	Declares a function
GOSUB	Branches to a subroutine
RETURN	Returns from a subroutine
RUN	Runs the current program or a specified program
SHELL	Runs a program, DOS command, or batch file
STATIC	Preserves variable values between calls
SUB	Declares a subprogram

String Management

ASC	Returns the ASCII code for a character
CHR$	Returns the character whose ASCII code is specified
HEX$	Returns the hexadecimal string equivalent of a value
INSTR	Returns the position of one string within another
LCASE$	Converts the characters in a string to lowercase
LEFT$	Returns the leftmost n characters of a string
LEN	Returns the length of a string
LTRIM$	Removes leading spaces from a string
MID$ (Function)	Returns a substring of a string
MID$ (Statement)	Replaces a portion of a string with another string
OCT$	Returns a string that is the octal value of the argument
RIGHT$	Returns the rightmost n characters of a string
RTRIM$	Removes trailing spaces from a string
SPACE$	Returns a string with the specified number of spaces
STR$	Converts a numeric expression to a string variable
STRING$	Returns a string consisting of the specified character
UCASE$	Converts the characters in a string to uppercase
VAL	Converts a string to the equivalent numeric value

Time and Date

DATE$ (Function)	Returns the current date
DATE$ (Statement)	Sets the current date
SLEEP	Suspends execution for the specified number of seconds
TIMER (Function)	Returns the number of seconds elapsed since midnight
TIME$ (Function)	Returns the current time
TIME$ (Statement)	Sets the current time

Introducing *Passageways*

The name of the game is *Passageways*. The program listing is shown in Listing 15.1, and it appears on the disks in the back of the book as PASSAGES.BAS— the name we'll use for the remainder of the chapter. (For those of you who are typing in the code in Listing 15.1, note that some of the lines near the end of the listing appear as multiple lines because of space limitations; these lines are separated from the rest of the code by blank lines. Be sure to type them in as single lines, without blank lines before or after.) PASSAGES is a maze program, but one that's probably different from ones you've seen before. Rather than viewing the maze from overhead, you see 3-dimensional views of the maze looking down long rows of intersecting corridors, hence the name *Passageways*. To set the stage for the game, you're an archeological professor from a large university who has traveled to Egypt to explore the Great Pyramid of Cheops. No sooner have you entered the structure, however, than a door slams over the opening behind you. After your attempts to open the door fail, you realize that your only hope for survival lies at the end of a twisty maze of corridors whose walls haven't heard human footsteps in centuries. Your goal is to find another way out. If you find it (and it will be obvious when you do), you're rewarded with a short tune. Finding it, however, is no easy matter. The pyramid contains more than 200 different passageways, and they all look alike. Hint: If you're serious about finding your way out, take pencil and paper in hand and create maps as you go.

LISTING 15.1 PASSAGES.BAS

```
'****************************************************************************
' PASSAGES is a game program for the QBasic Interpreter in which you
' try to find your way out of a maze.  The Up-Arrow key moves you one
' step forward in the maze, while the Left-, Right-, and Down-Arrow keys
' turn you 90 degrees to the left, 90 degrees to the right, and around
' 180 degrees, respectively.  The maze has more than 200 rooms.  Your
' goal is to find the exit.  If you succeed, your efforts are rewarded
' with a short tune.  If you decide to give up, press the End key to
' terminate the program.
'
' PASSAGES runs in 320 by 200 16-color graphics mode and uses
' page-flipping for fast animation.  It requires an EGA or VGA
' video adapter.  Written June 1991.
'****************************************************************************

DEFINT A-Z
CONST LineColor = 1

DECLARE SUB DrawHeader ()
DECLARE SUB DrawPassage (Room, Direction, APage, VPage)
DECLARE SUB DrawExit ()

DIM SHARED Map(225)
DIM SHARED Move(4)
DIM SHARED RCoords(20, 5)
DIM SHARED LCoords(20, 5)
DIM SHARED FCoords(24, 5)
DIM SHARED EndCoords(8, 5)
DIM SHARED DirText$(4)

ON ERROR GOTO ScreenError
SCREEN 7, , 0, 0
ON ERROR GOTO 0
```

```
COLOR 14, 0
CLS

CALL DrawHeader
PRINT
PRINT
PRINT "Circling the globe in search of the"
PRINT "remnants of ancient civilizations and"
PRINT "cultures is not without its hazards,"
PRINT "you have found.  No sooner did you step"
PRINT "through the entrance to Egypt's Great"
PRINT "Pyramid of Cheops than a false wall"
PRINT "slammed over the opening, blocking your"
PRINT "exit.  Your attempts to open it prove"
PRINT "futile.  As you turn your back to the"
PRINT "door and peer north into the musty"
PRINT "passageways, you realize that your only"
PRINT "hope for survival lies at the end of a"
PRINT "twisty maze of corridors whose walls"
PRINT "haven't heard human footsteps in centu-"
PRINT "ries.  The lantern in your hand flickers";
PRINT "in protest as you begin your journey..."

Direction = 0
Room = 221
APage = 0
VPage = 0

FOR I = 1 TO 225
    READ Map(I)
NEXT

FOR I = 0 TO 3
    READ Move(I)
NEXT

FOR I = 0 TO 3
    READ DirText$(I)
NEXT

FOR I = 1 TO 5
    FOR J = 1 TO 20
        READ RCoords(J, I)
    NEXT
NEXT

FOR I = 1 TO 5
    FOR J = 1 TO 20
        READ LCoords(J, I)
    NEXT
NEXT

FOR I = 1 TO 4
    FOR J = 1 TO 24
        READ FCoords(J, I)
    NEXT
```

```
    NEXT

    FOR J = 17 TO 24
        READ FCoords(J, 5)
    NEXT

    FOR I = 1 TO 5
        FOR J = 1 TO 8
            READ EndCoords(J, I)
        NEXT
    NEXT

    LOCATE 23, 9
    COLOR 15
    PRINT "Press any key to begin"
    DO UNTIL INKEY$ <> ""
    LOOP

    DO WHILE INKEY$ <> ""
    LOOP

    CALL DrawPassage(Room, Direction, APage, VPage)

    DO WHILE Room > 0
        DO
            A$ = INKEY$
        LOOP UNTIL LEN(A$) = 2

        SELECT CASE ASC(RIGHT$(A$, 1))
            CASE 72
                IF (Map(Room) AND (2 ^ Direction)) = 0 THEN
                    LOCATE 24, 1
                    COLOR 15
                    PRINT "Sorry, but you can't go that way";
                ELSE
                    Room = Room + Move(Direction)
                    IF Room > 0 THEN
                        CALL DrawPassage(Room, Direction, APage, VPage)
                    END IF
                END IF

            CASE 75
                Direction = Direction + 1
                IF Direction > 3 THEN
                    Direction = Direction - 4
                END IF
                IF (Room = 4) AND (Direction = 0) THEN
                    DrawExit
                ELSE
                    CALL DrawPassage(Room, Direction, APage, VPage)
                END IF

            CASE 77
                Direction = Direction + 3
                IF Direction > 3 THEN
                    Direction = Direction - 4
```

```
                    END IF
                    IF (Room = 4) AND (Direction = 0) THEN
                        DrawExit
                    ELSE
                        CALL DrawPassage(Room, Direction, APage, VPage)
                    END IF


            CASE 79
                SCREEN 0, , 0, 0
                WIDTH 80
                END

            CASE 80
                Direction = Direction + 2
                IF Direction > 3 THEN
                    Direction = Direction - 4
                END IF
                IF (Room = 4) AND (Direction = 0) THEN
                    DrawExit
                ELSE
                    CALL DrawPassage(Room, Direction, APage, VPage)
                END IF
        END SELECT
LOOP

SCREEN 0, , 0, 0
WIDTH 80
COLOR 7, 0
LOCATE 1, 1
PRINT "Congratulations, Professor!!!"
PLAY "O3 MS L6D L6D MN L12G L12F L12D L6C P24 O1 L12G L6A L4A#"
END

ScreenError:
    CLS
    PRINT "EGA or VGA video adapter required"
    END

' Data for Map array
DATA 4,8,6,9,14,6,8,14,14,6,8,10,10,6,4
DATA 9,6,9,10,3,9,10,7,1,13,14,6,12,15,3
DATA 12,3,12,14,2,12,6,9,14,3,5,9,7,13,6
DATA 13,2,5,13,10,11,11,6,9,10,11,2,13,6,1
DATA 9,14,3,1,12,10,14,7,12,10,6,12,7,9,6
DATA 12,15,10,10,7,4,1,9,11,6,1,5,1,12,3
DATA 5,5,8,10,3,9,6,12,2,9,10,15,10,7,4
DATA 5,9,10,6,12,10,11,3,4,8,10,11,2,9,3
DATA 9,2,12,3,5,8,6,12,11,2,8,6,12,2,4
DATA 8,14,11,10,7,12,11,3,12,10,2,13,3,8,7
DATA 12,7,12,2,1,13,14,14,15,2,12,11,6,12,3
DATA 1,5,9,6,4,13,3,1,13,10,7,12,3,9,6
DATA 4,9,6,5,5,9,14,10,11,6,5,9,6,4,5
DATA 13,2,13,7,9,6,5,4,4,1,13,10,15,3,5
DATA 9,10,3,9,10,11,3,9,11,10,3,8,11,10,3
```

```
' Data for Move and DirText$ arrays
DATA -15,-1,15,1
DATA North,West,South,East

' Data for RCoords array
DATA 319,31,319,163,290,35,319,35,290,163,319,163,290,35,319,31,290,163,305,175
DATA 246,41,246,127,230,43,246,43,230,115,246,115,230,43,246,41,230,115,246,127
DATA 206,45,206,95,196,47,206,47,196,88,206,88,196,47,206,45,196,88,206,95
DATA 182,49,182,76,176,50,182,50,176,71,182,71,176,50,182,49,176,71,182,76
DATA 168,51,168,65,164,51,168,51,164,63,168,63,164,51,168,51,164,63,168,65

' Data for LCoords array
DATA 0,31,0,163,29,35,0,35,29,163,0,163,29,35,0,31,29,163,14,175
DATA 73,41,73,127,89,43,73,43,89,115,73,115,89,43,73,41,89,115,73,127
DATA 113,45,113,95,123,47,113,47,123,88,113,88,123,47,113,45,123,88,113,95
DATA 137,49,137,76,143,50,137,50,143,71,137,71,143,50,137,49,143,71,137,76
DATA 151,51,151,65,155,51,151,51,155,63,151,63,155,51,151,51,155,63,151,65

' Data for FCoords array
DATA 290,35,246,41,290,163,246,127,29,35,73,41,29,163,73,127,290,35,29,35
DATA 290,163,29,163,230,43,206,45,230,115,206,95,89,43,113,45,89,115,113,95
DATA 230,43,89,43,230,115,89,115,196,47,182,49,196,88,182,76,123,47,137,49
DATA 123,88,137,76,196,47,123,47,196,88,123,88,176,50,168,51,176,71,168,65
DATA 143,50,151,51,143,71,151,65,176,50,143,50,176,71,143,71,164,51,155,51
DATA 164,63,155,63

' Data for EndCoords array
DATA 290,35,290,163,29,35,29,163
DATA 230,43,230,115,89,43,89,115
DATA 196,47,196,88,123,47,123,88
DATA 176,50,176,71,143,50,143,71
DATA 164,51,164,63,155,51,155,63

SUB DrawExit
    CLS
    CALL DrawHeader
    LINE (0, 25)-(319, 175), LineColor, B

    LINE (319, 35)-(290, 35), LineColor
    LINE -(290, 163), LineColor
    LINE -(319, 163), LineColor

    LINE (290, 35)-(230, 43), LineColor
    LINE -(230, 115), LineColor
    LINE -(290, 163), LineColor

    LINE (230, 43)-(206, 43), LineColor
    LINE -(206, 115), LineColor
    LINE -(230, 115), LineColor

    LINE (206, 43)-(192, 45), LineColor
    LINE -(192, 103), LineColor
    LINE -(206, 115), LineColor

    LINE (192, 45)-(127, 45), LineColor
    LINE -(127, 103), LineColor
```

```
            LINE -(192, 103), LineColor

            LINE (0, 30)-(89, 43), LineColor
            LINE -(89, 115), LineColor
            LINE -(14, 175), LineColor

            LINE (89, 43)-(113, 43), LineColor
            LINE -(113, 115), LineColor
            LINE -(89, 115), LineColor

            LINE (113, 43)-(127, 45), LineColor
            LINE (113, 115)-(127, 103), LineColor
            LINE (127, 75)-(192, 75), LineColor

            LINE (144, 75)-(176, 55), LineColor
            LINE -(192, 67), LineColor
            LINE (176, 55)-(160, 75), LineColor

            PAINT (140, 55), 14, LineColor
            LOCATE 24, 1
            COLOR 15
            PRINT "Facing North... and the exit!";
    END SUB

    SUB DrawHeader
            COLOR 14
            LOCATE 2, 15
            PRINT "PASSAGEWAYS"
            LINE (25, 4)-(294, 18), LineColor, B
            LINE (0, 2)-(319, 20), LineColor, B
    END SUB

    SUB DrawPassage (Room, Direction, APage, VPage)
            APage = APage XOR 1
            SCREEN , , APage, VPage

            CLS
            CALL DrawHeader
            LINE (0, 25)-(319, 175), LineColor, B

            Level = 1
            RoomNo = Room

            DR = Direction + 3
            IF DR > 3 THEN
                DR = DR - 4
            END IF

            DL = Direction + 1
            IF DL > 3 THEN
                DL = DL - 4
            END IF

            DO
                IF (Map(RoomNo) AND (2 ^ DR)) <> 0 THEN
```

```
        LINE (RCoords(1, Level), RCoords(2, Level))-(RCoords(3, Level),
RCoords(4, Level)), LineColor

        LINE (RCoords(5, Level), RCoords(6, Level))-(RCoords(7, Level),
RCoords(8, Level)), LineColor

        LINE (RCoords(9, Level), RCoords(10, Level))-(RCoords(11, Level),
RCoords(12, Level)), LineColor

    ELSE

        LINE (RCoords(13, Level), RCoords(14, Level))-(RCoords(15, Level),
RCoords(16, Level)), LineColor

        LINE (RCoords(17, Level), RCoords(18, Level))-(RCoords(19, Level),
RCoords(20, Level)), LineColor

    END IF

    IF (Map(RoomNo) AND (2 ^ DL)) <> 0 THEN

        LINE (LCoords(1, Level), LCoords(2, Level))-(LCoords(3, Level),
LCoords(4, Level)), LineColor

        LINE (LCoords(5, Level), LCoords(6, Level))-(LCoords(7, Level),
LCoords(8, Level)), LineColor

        LINE (LCoords(9, Level), LCoords(10, Level))-(LCoords(11, Level),
LCoords(12, Level)), LineColor

    ELSE

        LINE (LCoords(13, Level), LCoords(14, Level))-(LCoords(15, Level),
LCoords(16, Level)), LineColor

        LINE (LCoords(17, Level), LCoords(18, Level))-(LCoords(19, Level),
LCoords(20, Level)), LineColor

    END IF

    IF (Map(RoomNo) AND (2 ^ Direction)) <> 0 THEN

        LINE (FCoords(1, Level), FCoords(2, Level))-(FCoords(3, Level),
FCoords(4, Level)), LineColor

        LINE (FCoords(5, Level), FCoords(6, Level))-(FCoords(7, Level),
FCoords(8, Level)), LineColor

        LINE (FCoords(9, Level), FCoords(10, Level))-(FCoords(11, Level),
FCoords(12, Level)), LineColor

        LINE (FCoords(13, Level), FCoords(14, Level))-(FCoords(15, Level),
FCoords(16, Level)), LineColor

    ELSE
```

```
                LINE (FCoords(17, Level), FCoords(18, Level))-(FCoords(19, Level),
FCoords(20, Level)), LineColor

                LINE (FCoords(21, Level), FCoords(22, Level))-(FCoords(23, Level),
FCoords(24, Level)), LineColor

        END IF

        IF (((Map(RoomNo) AND (2 ^ Direction)) <> 0) AND ((Map(RoomNo) AND
(2 ^ DR)) <> 0)) OR (((Map(RoomNo) AND (2 ^ Direction)) = 0) AND ((Map(RoomNo)
AND (2 ^ DR)) = 0)) THEN

                LINE (EndCoords(1, Level), EndCoords(2, Level))-(EndCoords
(3, Level), EndCoords(4, Level)), LineColor

        END IF

        IF (((Map(RoomNo) AND (2 ^ Direction)) <> 0) AND ((Map(RoomNo) AND
(2 ^ DL)) <> 0)) OR (((Map(RoomNo) AND (2 ^ Direction)) = 0) AND ((Map(RoomNo)
AND (2 ^ DL)) = 0)) THEN

                LINE (EndCoords(5, Level), EndCoords(6, Level))-(EndCoords
(7, Level), EndCoords(8, Level)), LineColor

        END IF

        LastRoomNo = RoomNo
        RoomNo = RoomNo + Move(Direction)
        Level = Level + 1
    LOOP UNTIL (Map(LastRoomNo) AND (2 ^ Direction)) = 0

    LOCATE 24, 1
    COLOR 15
    PRINT "Facing "; DirText$(Direction);
    VPage = APage
    SCREEN , , , VPage
END SUB
```

Figure 15.2 shows what the view looks like down a typical corridor. One corridor opens to your immediate left, and two more veer off the main corridor farther ahead, one to the left and one to the right. If you look closely, you'll also see that the corridor you're looking down eventually makes a 90-degree turn to the right. The title of the program appears at the top of the screen, and the message line at the bottom tells you what direction you're facing. Because you're walled in with no fixed points of reference, this computerized compass will prove invaluable in helping you keep your bearings straight.

You move through the maze by pressing cursor keys. The Up Arrow key moves you forward one step, while the Left and Right Arrow keys turn you 90 degrees to the left and right, respectively, without moving you. In the example shown in Figure 15.2, pressing the Left Arrow key would turn you so that you're looking down the corridor immediately to your left. You can look in all four directions from the current spot and return to the direction you're facing by pressing either Left Arrow or Right Arrow four times. The Down Arrow key turns you around 180 degrees so that you're facing in the opposite direction, again without moving you. That's the quick way to get a peek behind you. You can't move through a wall; if you try, the program will tell you "Sorry, but you can't go that way." If you finally do find the exit (you'll see a door opening to the bright sunlight outside and another pyramid off in the distance), step through it to end the game and claim your reward. Pressing the End key at any time terminates the game. Since you're running this in QBasic, you can also break out of the game by pressing Ctrl-Break.

FIGURE 15.2

The *Passageways* screen

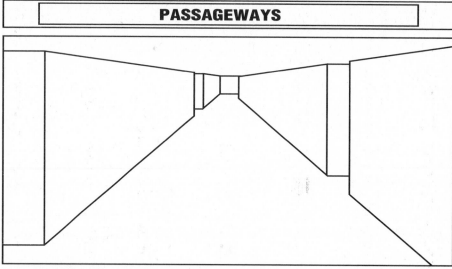

All you have to do to start the program once it's loaded is select Start from the Run menu or press Shift-F5. Before we embark on a discussion of the source code, take a few minutes to play the game and see how it works and plays. In particular, note how you do not see the screen redrawn to show the new view of the corridors when you press a key. Instead, the new screen seems to just appear all at once. That's because PASSAGES uses an animation technique called *page-flipping* to hide redraws. You'll see how it and other aspects of the program work in the sections that follow.

A Peek Inside the Source Code

PASSAGES.BAS starts off with the statement

```
DEFINT A-Z
```

which declares that, unless otherwise specified with a type-declaration character at the end of the variable name (%, &, !, #, or $), all variables that start with the letters A through Z will be integer variables. The next statement

```
CONST LineColor = 1
```

defines a constant called LineColor with the value 1. Constants appear in the program listing like variables, but their values cannot be changed like the value of a variable can. In this case, LineColor is a parameter passed to several of the graphics commands in the programs to specify the color that lines will be drawn in. By assigning it to a constant, you can change the default color (blue) to another color by changing just one line of code. Without the CONST declaration, you'd have to change several lines.

Skipping past the lines that declare subprograms (which we'll return to in a moment), the next several statements declare arrays using the SHARED keyword so that any subprogram or function in the program can access them. This is equivalent to declaring a global variable in C or Pascal. By default, variables and arrays declared in QBasic are local to the program module in which they're declared, and cannot be accessed by other program modules unless they are passed to them.

Next comes the code to switch the video adapter to graphics mode and clear the screen. The lines

```
ON ERROR GOTO ScreenError
SCREEN 7, , 0, 0
ON ERROR GOTO 0
```

set QBasic to go to the line labeled ScreenError if an error occurs when a statement is executed, change to screen mode 7 (the QBasic code for 320 by 200 16-color graphics), and then, if no error occurred, disable error trapping by setting the destination for the branch on error to 0. (The supported screen modes are documented under Screen Modes in the Help system, and Screen Modes is found in the documentation for the SCREEN statement.) It's important to use ON ERROR here because screen mode 7 is only available on systems with EGA and VGA video adapters. If the video adapter PASSAGES is running on doesn't support screen mode 7, an error occurs and execution branches to ScreenError. The code following ScreenError displays the message "EGA or VGA video adapter required." It's the most practical way to determine if the configuration you are asking for is supported by the hardware you're running on. Next, the commands

```
COLOR 14, 0
CLS
```

set the screen colors to yellow (14) on black (0) and clear the screen. CLS works no matter what screen mode you're in, and regardless of whether that mode is a text or graphics mode. In QBasic, CLS can also be used to clear just a portion of the screen.

The next several lines draw the opening screen, including the narrative that sets the scene before you're dropped into the maze. The first statement is

```
CALL DrawHeader
```

which calls the subprogram that draws "PASSAGEWAYS" enclosed by a pair of boxes at the top of the screen. The subprogram DrawHeader is defined as follows:

```
SUB DrawHeader
    COLOR 14
    LOCATE 2, 15
    PRINT "PASSAGEWAYS"
    LINE (25, 4)-(294, 18), LineColor, B
    LINE (0, 2)-(319, 20), LineColor, B
END SUB
```

DrawHeader is also declared near the top of the program with the statement

```
DECLARE SUB DrawHeader ()
```

In QBasic, subprograms (procedures that are called by name but do not return a value) are enclosed between SUB and END SUB statements. In this instance, no parameters are passed to the subprogram, but if you wish, you can write subprograms that accept parameters. You'll see an example of this later in the subprogram called DrawPassage. The subprogram terminates and returns to the statement following the one that called it when it encounters the END SUB statement. You can exit a subprogram early by inserting an EXIT SUB statement. Declaring the subprogram ahead of time isn't strictly required, but it does provide one important advantage: If the subprogram is declared, QBasic checks the arguments passed to the subprogram against the argument list you declared and warns you if there's a mismatch. If you don't declare the subprogram, QBasic has no way of knowing what the argument list should look like, so it does not perform argument checking. Note that variables or arrays defined within a subprogram are local to that subprogram unless they are explicitly declared otherwise with a SHARED statement.

While the user takes a moment to read the opening screen, PASSAGES initializes the variables and arrays that it will be using. Then it displays the message "Press any key to begin" and waits for a key press with the statements

```
DO UNTIL INKEY$ <> ""
LOOP
```

INKEY$ returns a 1- or 2-byte code identifying the key that was pressed. Unlike other BASIC input functions, it returns immediately if there is no key code waiting in the keyboard buffer and is set equal to ""—a null return. The DO UNTIL statement shown here loops repeatedly until INKEY$ is not equal to ""; therefore, execution of the program is suspended until a key is pressed.

The next two statements,

```
DO WHILE INKEY$ <> ""
LOOP
```

clear the keyboard buffer of pending keystrokes by reading them until there are no more. This way, if the user pressed any of the arrow keys while the opening screen was displayed, the keystrokes will be ignored when the view looking down the first corridor of the maze comes up. Another way to accomplish the same end is to execute the statements

```
DEF SEG = &H40
POKE &H1A, PEEK(&H1C)
```

This method takes a slightly different approach; it sets the two pointers in the BIOS Data Area that determine where the next key code in the keyboard buffer will be written to and read from equal to each other. This is slightly faster than the first method, because it removes all pending key codes from the keyboard buffer in one stroke rather than one at a time. But it's also tied a little closer to the hardware, so it's liable not to work if you port the program to a BASIC environment on another hardware platform.

After that comes the code for navigating the maze. The entire remainder of the main program module is enclosed in a loop of the form

```
DO WHILE Room > 0
    .
    .
    .
LOOP
```

which repeats until the variable named Room becomes negative. *Room* is the variable PASSAGES uses to keep track of which room in the maze you're in.

Values defining where the exits are for each room are stored in the 15 by 15 array called Map. There are 225 Map values, corresponding to the 225 rooms in the maze. Each time you press the Up Arrow key to move forward one room in the maze, the value of Room is updated. When you finally exit the maze, Room is set to some value less than zero. When that happens, the loop is terminated, and the program falls through to the statements

```
SCREEN 0, , 0, 0
WIDTH 80
COLOR 7, 0
LOCATE 1, 1
PRINT "Congratulations, Professor!!!"
PLAY "O3 MS L6D L6D MN L12G L12F L12D L6C P24 O1 L12G L6A L4A#"
END
```

which reset the video adapter to text mode, print a congratulatory message, play a tune, and end the program.

The logic PASSAGES uses to represent the characteristics of each room in the Map array is worth examining because it's a model of brevity. For each room in the maze, Map contains a value from 0 to 15. For each of the four possible exits from the room—north, west, south, and east—bit 0, 1, 2, or 3 of the corresponding Map value is set if there's an exit from the room in that direction or clear if there's not. For example, if a room has exits to the north and to the west but none to the south or east, the Map value is 3—the value you get if you set bits 0 and 1 to 1 in a 16-bit integer value, leaving all the rest 0. Similarly, if a room has an exit or entrance to the east but no others, its Map value is 8. All PASSAGES has to do to see if you've made a legal move when you press the Up Arrow key is check the Map value for that room (using Room as an index into the array) and see if the bit for the direction you're trying to move is set. If it is, then it was a legal move; if it's not, then it wasn't a legal move. PASSAGES maintains a variable called Direction that records the direction you're facing at all times. A value of 0 means north, 1 means west, 2 means south, and 3 means east. Thus, all that's required to trap illegal moves is the code sequence

```
If (Map(Room) AND (2 ^ Direction)) = 0 THEN
    LOCATE 24, 1
    COLOR 15
    PRINT "Sorry, but you can't go that way"
```

If you try to move illegally, the clause beginning with LOCATE 24, 1 is executed and the move is invalidated. Knowing how the logic works, you can design mazes of your own and plug them into the program. All you have to do is substitute new values for the first set of DATA statements in the program—the values that are read into the Map array when the variables are initialized.

To process your keystrokes, PASSAGES uses a SELECT CASE structure of the form

```
SELECT CASE ASC(RIGHT$(A$, 1))

    CASE 72
        .
        .
        .

    CASE 75
        .
        .
        .

    CASE 77
        .
        .
        .

    CASE 79
        .
        .
        .

    CASE 80
        .
        .
        .

END SELECT
```

The values 72, 75, 77, 79, and 80 are what results when you apply the expression ASC(RIGHT$(A$, 1)) to the value returned by INKEY$ for Up Arrow, Left Arrow, Right Arrow, End, and Down Arrow, respectively. A SELECT CASE structure executes the routine following the CASE statement that matches the value designated after the SELECT CASE statement at the top. In this case, it activates the routine built to handle each key code. If you press Up Arrow, the handler makes sure a move forward is legal and then modifies the value of Room accordingly. If you press one of the other arrow keys, the value of Direction is modified. And if you press End, the program is terminated with an END statement. Because of the DO UNTIL loop that the

SELECT CASE structure is contained in, SELECT CASE will continue to be executed every time a key is pressed until you find your way out of the maze or press End to terminate the program.

Any time that you press an arrow key and the value of Room or Direction is modified, PASSAGES calls the subprogram DrawPassage to draw a new view of the corridors. DrawPassage is declared with the statement

```
DECLARE SUB DrawPassage (Room, Direction, APage, VPage)
```

and defined with the statements

```
SUB DrawPassage (Room, Direction, APage, VPage)
    APage = APage XOR 1
    SCREEN , , APage, VPage
        .
        .
        .


END SUB
```

As usual, Room and Direction designate the number of the room you're in and the direction you're facing. APage and VPage designate the *active video page* and the *displayed video page*, respectively. In screen mode 7, there are two video pages in memory that you can display one at a time. The active display page is the one QBasic graphics commands such as LINE act upon; the displayed video page is the page that is shown on the screen. The two do not have to be the same. To effect smooth animation and hide the process of drawing each new screen from the user, DrawPassage switches the active video page to the one that is not displayed at the moment, draws the new screen, and then makes that page the displayed video page. All this is accomplished through the SCREEN statement, which, in addition to setting the video mode, also sets the active and displayed video pages. To toggle the active page, DrawPassage executes the statements

```
APage = APage XOR 1
SCREEN , , APage, VPage
```

XORing 0 with 1 sets it to 1; XORing 1 with 1 sets it to 0. Thus, repeatedly XORing APage with 1 toggles it back and forth between 1 and 0. A series of LINE statements are executed to draw lines depicting the new view down the corridors on the hidden video page. When drawing is completed, the statements

```
VPage = APage
SCREEN , , , VPage
```

sets the displayed video page equal to the active video page, displaying the screen that was just drawn. This animation technique, which goes by the names *page-flipping* and *double-buffering*, is similar to the process cartoon animators use to create the illusion of motion.

If you examine the source code for DrawPassage, you'll notice that it uses a temporary variable named RoomNo to stand in for Room, which is passed to it in the parameter list. It must use a local variable instead of Room because it modifies the value it's passed. When you pass a variable to a QBasic subprogram, that variable is passed by *reference*, meaning that if it's modified in the subprogram, it's modified in the program or subprogram that called it, too. Although this method can sometimes get in the way, it's a convenient way to pass arrays to subprograms. For the most part, arrays *must* be passed by reference; otherwise, they present real problems for the compiler or interpreter and slow execution down, too.

While you have PASSAGES loaded, experiment with some of the menu options available in the overhead menus to help you get accustomed to the way QBasic operates. For example, pull down the Search menu and use the Find option to search for every occurrence of DrawHeader or Direction. Or use the Split option in the View menu to split the screen and display two views of the program file at once (this is particularly useful if you're cutting and pasting between two widely separated sections of a program). The next section will take up the subject of debugging, utilizing the menu options in the Debug menu as well as other resources QBasic puts at your disposal.

PASSAGES is quite a sophisticated program for its length; it illustrates just how powerful the QBasic programming environment is—especially when you apply good, sound programming principles. If you have trouble finding your way through the maze, you'll find a map, called the Passageways Survival Guide, right after the index near the end of the book. As an alternative, you can type in the following QBasic program and have it draw a map for you:

```
DATA 4,8,6,9,14,6,8,14,14,6,8,10,10,6,4
DATA 9,6,9,10,3,9,10,7,1,13,14,6,12,15,3
DATA 12,3,12,14,2,12,6,9,14,3,5,9,7,13,6
DATA 13,2,5,13,10,11,11,6,9,10,11,2,13,6,1
DATA 9,14,3,1,12,10,14,7,12,10,6,12,7,9,6
DATA 12,15,10,10,7,4,1,9,11,6,1,5,1,12,3
DATA 5,5,8,10,3,9,6,12,2,9,10,15,10,7,4
DATA 5,9,10,6,12,10,11,3,4,8,10,11,2,9,3
DATA 9,2,12,3,5,8,6,12,11,2,8,6,12,2,4
DATA 8,14,11,10,7,12,11,3,12,10,2,13,3,8,7
DATA 12,7,12,2,1,13,14,14,15,2,12,11,6,12,3
DATA 1,5,9,6,4,13,3,1,13,10,7,12,3,9,6
DATA 4,9,6,5,5,9,14,10,11,6,5,9,6,4,5
DATA 13,2,13,7,9,6,5,4,4,1,13,10,15,3,5
```

```
DATA 9,10,3,9,10,11,3,9,11,10,3,8,11,10,3

DATA 32,189,190,188,183,186,187,185
DATA 212,200,205,202,201,204,203,206

DIM Map(1 TO 225) AS INTEGER
DIM MapChars(0 TO 15) AS INTEGER

FOR i = 1 TO 225
    READ Map(i)
NEXT

FOR i = 0 TO 15
    READ MapChars(i)
NEXT

PRINT
FOR i = 0 TO 14
    FOR j = 1 TO 15
        PRINT CHR$(MapChars(Map(i * 15 + j)));
    NEXT
    PRINT
NEXT
```

The first 15 DATA statements are identical to the ones defined for the Map array in PASSAGES.BAS. If you'd like, you can copy them directly from there. The rest of the program you can type into the QBasic editor in a matter of minutes. And no, it isn't on the disks in the back of the book. You don't want it to be *too* easy, do you?

Debugging Programs in the QBasic Environment

One of the features of the QBasic Interpreter that you'll come to appreciate if you do any significant amount of program development is its integrated debugger. A *debugger* is a program that helps you identify errors in programs so that you can fix them. Often, bugs are obvious enough that you don't need a debugger to find them. But sometimes they can be so subtle that they'll leave you pulling your hair out if you can't find help in locating them. That's what a debugger's for: weeding out the tough ones that a cursory scan through the source code will not.

The remainder of this chapter will focus on the tools that QBasic puts at your disposal for debugging programs and discuss some of the basic techniques for using them. Most of QBasic's debugging features are accessed through the Debug menu at the top of the screen. Through this menu, you have the ability to

- Step through a program one line at a time, entering or skipping over procedure calls as desired

- Perform an animated trace, highlighting each line as it is executed

- Set breakpoints in the program so that execution will stop when a certain line is reached

The Immediate window can also play a role in debugging, allowing you to examine variable values and even modify them as the program executes. This and other aspects of debugging in the QBasic environment are detailed in the sections that follow.

Single-Stepping Through a Program

QBasic gives you three options for stepping through a program a line at a time: Step, Procedure Step, and Trace. *Step* runs one statement in the program and stops before executing the next one. *Procedure Step* is identical to Step except that it steps *over* calls to subprograms and functions rather than through them. If the next statement to be executed is a call to a subprogram or function, Step will execute the call and queue up the first statement in the subprogram or function as the next to be executed. By contrast, if you select Procedure Step, the subprogram or function will be executed in its entirety and the statement following the one that called it will be the next one executed. In other words, Procedure Step saves you from stepping through procedure calls line by line. In all cases, QBasic highlights the next statement that will be executed. QBasic provides a pair of shortcut keys for Step and Procedure Step: function keys F8 and F10.

The third option, *Trace*, is just like Step except that you don't have to press F8 repeatedly. Instead, QBasic does the stepping for you. You just start the program, and then sit back and watch it go to work. You can interrupt program execution at any time by pressing Ctrl-Break.

If, as you step through a program using any of these methods, the statement that is executed produces screen output, QBasic switches to the output screen for a moment, and then switches back to the program listing. If you didn't get a good enough glimpse at the program's output, you can select Output Screen from the View menu (or press F4) to go back to the output screen at any time. When you're done, press any key to return to QBasic.

The ability to single-step through a program is a powerful capability to have because it allows you to see where the program is going, what statements it's executing, and what branches it's taking. As you single-step your way through a program, you can specify which statement should be executed next by moving the cursor to the line the statement is on and selecting Set Next Statement from the Debug menu. This enables you to jump around in the program, perhaps skipping sections of code that you know for a fact are bug-free already, and to repeat sections of code that need a second look.

Setting and Using Breakpoints

Another capability that the QBasic debugger lends you is the ability to set breakpoints in programs. A *breakpoint* is a location in a program where you want execution suspended. You set a breakpoint by moving the cursor to the statement where the breakpoint should be placed and selecting Toggle Breakpoint from the Debug menu (or pressing F9). You can create as many breakpoints as you like. To remove a breakpoint, take the cursor back to the line where the breakpoint was set (the line will be highlighted) and select Toggle Breakpoint again. Alternatively, you can remove all breakpoints in one stroke with the Clear All Breakpoints option under Debug.

An example might help to clarify how breakpoints are used. If you still have PASSAGES loaded, move the cursor to the line

```
Room = Room + Move(Direction)
```

just below the ELSE statement inside the SELECT CASE loop. This is the line that moves you from one room to another when you press the Up Arrow key. Once you're there, press F9 to set a breakpoint at that statement. QBasic will highlight the line, indicating that a breakpoint has been set. Then start the program by pressing Shift-F5. With the program running, press the Left Arrow or Right Arrow key a few times to change the direction you're facing in the maze. The program executes as it normally does, because pressing either of these keys does not cause the statement you set the breakpoint on to be executed. However, watch what happens when you press Up Arrow to move forward in the maze. Provided that move is a legal move (it is if you're not facing a wall when you press the key), the breakpoint will be reached and QBasic will drop you into the editing window at the statement where the break occurred. You can set several breakpoints like this to determine when and where a certain statement or set of statements is executed. To resume execution where you left off, press F5 (Continue). The program will continue to be interrupted every time you try to move forward until the breakpoint is cleared.

Using the Immediate Window

Single-stepping through programs and setting breakpoints are fine for seeing where the path of execution leads, but they're not much use to you beyond that. The *real* value of being able to execute a line at a time or to interrupt the program when a certain statement is reached is to be able to examine variables in the program and see what they're set to. You can examine and even change variable values in QBasic through the Immediate window, which appears at the bottom of the screen when you first start the Interpreter. The Immediate window is inextricably tied to the program that is loaded in the editing window, with the result that you can access, by name, any of the variables, arrays, subprograms, and functions contained in the program.

Let's expand on the example in the previous section by assuming that you want to see what the variable named Room is set to before and after the statement

```
Room = Room + Move(Direction)
```

is executed. First, if you removed the breakpoint set earlier, replace it by cursoring to the line that contains this statement and pressing F9. Then start the program by pressing Shift-F5 and, once you enter the maze, press Up Arrow so that the breakpoint will be reached. After QBasic has dropped you back into the editing window, activate the Immediate window by clicking on it with the mouse or pressing F6 until the window title is highlighted (F6 cycles through all the active windows). Type

```
CLS: PRINT Room
```

in the Immediate window and press Enter. QBasic will switch to its output screen, display the Room number, and prompt you to press a key to return to the QBasic screen. Next, press F8 to execute the instruction that modifies the value of Room and press F6 to switch back to the Immediate window. Cursor back up to the line where you typed "CLS: PRINT Room" and press Enter to reexecute the command. This time, the output screen will show the value for Room after the Room= statement was executed. If you wanted to verify the value of the array element that was added to Room, you could do so by typing

```
PRINT Move(Direction)
```

If you're currently facing north, QBasic will respond by displaying the number –15. By the way, you can increase or decrease the size of the Immediate window by grabbing its title bar with the mouse and dragging it up or down or by pressing Alt-Plus and Alt-Minus. The latter two key combinations increase and decrease the size of the active window a line at a time.

In addition to checking variable values, you can also *set* variable values in the Immediate window. Want to know a quick way to find the exit from the maze? Don't worry, this won't give away the route to the exit; it will just give you a glimpse of what that much-sought-for back door looks like. There are plenty of ways to go about this, but this is one. First, use Clear All Breakpoints to clear all breakpoints from the program. Then locate the lines

```
Direction = 0
Room = 221
APage = 0
VPage = 0
```

near the beginning of the program listing and set a breakpoint at Direction = 0. Next, select Start from the Run menu to start the program. Immediately after the opening screen is displayed, the breakpoint will be reached and QBasic will switch you back to the editing screen. Press F8 twice to single-step over the lines

```
Direction = 0
Room = 221
```

and press F6 to switch to the Immediate window (as an alternative, you could have cursored down to the line APage = 0 and used Set Next Statement to skip over the two lines). Inside the Immediate window, type

```
Direction = 1
Room = 6
```

and then press F5 to continue executing the program. After you press a key to dismiss the opening screen, you'll see a view that's slightly different from what you normally see when the program is started. The exit is down the hall to the right. To get there, press Up Arrow twice and Right Arrow once. You'll see the exit displayed before you in all its splendor. Press Up Arrow a final time to move through the exit, and you'll see what happens when you finally find your way through the maze.

The Immediate window is useful for other things besides debugging. In it, you can try out commands before you enter them in your programs, or use it to perform calculations using the PRINT statement. For example, the command

```
PRINT SQR(3.1415916)
```

displays the square root of 3.1415916. You can abbreviate the PRINT command with a question mark, as in

```
? SQR(3.1415916)
```

This capability is a carryover from earlier versions of BASIC, but it's a perfectly legitimate shortcut that can save you a few keystrokes.

With a few exceptions, anything you can enter into a program can be entered in the Immediate window, too. You can't do things like define subprograms there (SUB and END SUB are not accepted), but you can call subprograms that are defined in the main program. This can be a real help in isolating the effects of subprograms and functions. Suppose, for example, that the value of a variable named InitFlag is mysteriously changing when it shouldn't be and you suspect that a subprogram called DoCalc is altering it unintentionally. You could test this theory in the Immediate window by typing

```
PRINT "InitFlag="; InitFlag
CALL DoCalc
PRINT "InitFlag='"; InitFlag
```

If the two values printed out for InitFlag are not equal, then you've identified the culprit.

A final note about debugging. It's easy to become reliant on debuggers and other sophisticated tools for fine-tuning application programs. Remember that there's no substitute for good code, and good code doesn't come without effort. Here's a classic example of two ways to correct a bug in a program. Let's say you've written a program and, when you run it, you discover that if you ask it to add 2 and 2, it comes up with 3. There are two approaches to fixing the problem. The first is to find the faulty logic in the code and repair it. The second is to go to the statement that produces the output and add a statement that says if the result is 3, then the result is really 4. It should be obvious to you which is the better way. It's awfully easy to fall into the latter mode when you rely too heavily on debuggers. The moral of the story: Write good code to start with, and you'll be applying the finishing touches to your programs while others are still setting breakpoints and tracing program code.

Summary

It doesn't take long working in the QBasic environment to conclude that it's light-years beyond the BASIC interpreters that came with earlier versions of DOS. About the only way you can do better is to upgrade to full-fledged Microsoft QuickBASIC, which is very much like QBasic except that it produces stand-alone executable files that you can run from the command line.

Just so that you'll have an idea how much difference a compiler makes, the disks that came with this book include a stand-alone version of PASSAGES, compiled from the source code presented here with the Microsoft QuickBASIC compiler. You can run this version of PASSAGES from the command line. You'll notice that it runs slightly but perceptibly faster than the interpreted version. This is rather atypical of a compiled program; normally, a compiled program will run significantly faster than an interpreted program. It's not that QuickBASIC is slow, it's that QBasic is fast. The fact that the interpreted version runs almost as fast as the compiled version (and doesn't take up nearly as much disk space) is a tribute both to the power of the QBasic Interpreter and to the programmers who wrote it.

APPENDIX A

DOS COMMAND REFERENCE

Appendix A documents the DOS 5.0 commands and configuration directives. This reference is arranged in alphabetical order. The information provided for each command includes

- A short description of the command.

- The DOS version that the command first appeared in. (Some commands appeared in MS-DOS before they appeared in PC-DOS, and vice versa.)

- Just below the version number, the word *Internal*, *External*, *Batch*, or *CONFIG.SYS*, indicating whether the corresponding command is an internal DOS command, an external DOS command, a batch file command, or a CONFIG.SYS directive.

- The syntax for the command.

- A description of the command, including cross-references to chapters in the book where the command and issues related to it are discussed.

- Examples illustrating how the command is used.

- Notes containing additional information about the command.

APPEND

Set Search Path for Data Files

SYNTAX   APPEND [[*d:*]*path*;[*d:*]*path*[;...]] [/X[:ON|OFF]]
         [/PATH[:ON|OFF]] [/E]

> *path*   Directory name
> /X   Specifies whether APPEND should be extended to work with DOS's Find
>   First, Find Next, and EXEC functions
> /PATH   Specifies whether APPEND should intervene when a path name is sup-
>   plied for a data file
> /E   Stores the APPEND path as an environment variable

DESCRIPTION   APPEND sets a search path for data files the same way PATH sets a search path for executables. With APPEND installed, DOS will automatically search APPENDed directories
for data files. The /X:ON switch allows APPEND to work with a wider range of applications. The /PATH:ON switch causes APPEND to work even if the specification for a data
file includes an explicit path to the file. /E stores the APPEND path as an environment variable so that the path string can be edited using the SET command. The /X:ON and /E
switches can only be specified the first time APPEND is run; after that, /X:ON and /X:OFF
can be used to toggle extended services on and off. If a /E switch is used, APPEND ignores
path parameters on the same line. Running APPEND with nothing but a ; cancels the list
of APPENDed directories. For further discussion, see Chapter 4.

EXAMPLES   To create a search path for data files that includes the \WP\DOC and \123\BUDGET
directories of drive C, type

    APPEND C:\WP\DOC;C:\123\BUDGET

To create the same APPEND search path but have it stored as an environment variables, type

    APPEND /E
    APPEND C:\WP\DOC;C:\123\BUDGET

To create a search path that includes C:\WP\DOC and to extend APPEND's power to the
fullest, type

    APPEND C:\WP\DOC /X:ON /PATH:ON

To cancel APPEND, type

    APPEND ;

NOTES   APPEND can be a dangerous command to use because if you use it to edit a data file in
a remote directory, the file may be saved in the current directory. It also doesn't do anything for you that proper disk organization and work habits cannot.

ASSIGN

Redirect Drive Accesses

SYNTAX   `ASSIGN [x[:]=y[:] [...]] [/STATUS]`

x   Letter of the drive to redirect accesses from
y   Letter of the drive to redirect accesses to
/STATUS   Lists all redirected drives

DESCRIPTION   ASSIGN allows you to redirect disk accesses from one floppy drive to another floppy drive or a hard disk. Once accesses are redirected, all further reads and writes to drive *x* are automatically redirected to drive *y*. Running ASSIGN with no parameters cancels all drive assignments. ASSIGN is discussed in Chapter 4.

EXAMPLES   To redirect accesses from drive A to drive B, type

    `ASSIGN A=B`

To cancel all drive redirection, type

    `ASSIGN`

To list all redirected drives, type

    `ASSIGN /STATUS`

NOTES   ASSIGN is useful when you run software that doesn't allow you to choose whether it's run from drive A or drive B. If, for example, a program insists on running from drive A but you must run it from drive B because the drive is 5 1/4-inch and the disk is 3 1/2-inch (or vice versa) type **ASSIGN A=B**, then run the program from drive B. It will think it's running in A. ASSIGNed drives should not be used with the BACKUP, JOIN, LABEL, RESTORE, SUBST, DISKCOPY, and FORMAT commands.

ATTRIB

3.0
External

Change File Attributes

SYNTAX   ATTRIB [+A|-A] [+H|-H] [+R|-R] [+S|-S] [[*d:*][*path*]*filename*]
    [/S]

+A	Add archive attribute
-A	Remove archive attribute
+H	Add hidden attribute
-H	Remove hidden attribute
+R	Add read-only attribute
-R	Remove read-only attribute
+S	Add system attribute
-S	Remove system attribute
filename	Name of the file or files to process
/S	Process files in the specified directory and its descendants

DESCRIPTION ATTRIB lets you display or alter the attributes assigned to a file. Run without a + or - switch, it displays the attributes of the specified file or files. With a + or - switch, it sets or clears the specified attribute. If *filename* is omitted, ATTRIB sets or displays the attributes of all the files in the current directory. The /S switch causes ATTRIB to process files in the specified directory and its descendants. ATTRIB is discussed in Chapter 5.

EXAMPLES To display the attributes of BUDGET.DOC, type

    ATTRIB BUDGET.DOC

To remove the read-only attribute from BUDGET.DOC and make it a hidden file, type

    ATTRIB -R +H BUDGET.DOC

To set the archive bits on all files with the extension .BAK in the current directory and all its descendants, type

    ATTRIB +A *.BAK /S

NOTES The ATTRIB command is useful for setting or clearing archive attributes prior to executing a BACKUP or XCOPY command, for removing read-only, hidden, and system attributes so a file can be deleted (or for setting them so that it can't), and for hiding files in directory listings by adding a hidden attribute.

BACKUP

Back Up Files

SYNTAX

```
BACKUP source destination [/A] [/F[:size]] [/L[:log]] [/M]
    [/S] [/D:date [/T:time]]
```

source	Name and location of the file or files to back up
destination	Letter of the drive to copy files to
/A	Adds backed-up files to the destination disk without destroying backups already there
/F:*size*	Specifies the capacity the destination disk is to be formatted to. Valid values for *size* are

Disk Type	Size
160k	160, 160K, or 160KB
180k	180, 180K, or 180KB
320k	320, 320K, or 320KB
360k	360, 360K, or 360KB
720k	720, 720K, or 720KB
1.2Mb	1200, 1220K, 1200KB, 1.2, 1.2M, or 1.2 MB
1.44Mb	1440, 1440K, 1440KB, 1.44, 1.44M, or 1.44MB
2.88Mb	2880, 2880K, 2880KB, 2.88, 2.88M, or 2.88MB

/L:*log*	Write a log file named *log* summarizing the backup operation
/M	Back up only those files whose archive attributes are set
/S	Back up files in the source directory and its descendants
/D:*date*	Backup files that were modified on or after the specified date
/T:*time*	Back up files that were modified at or after the specified time

DESCRIPTION BACKUP lets you back up hard disk files to floppies. Files backed up must be restored with the RESTORE command. If you include the /L switch and omit the *log* parameter, a log file named BACKUP.LOG is created in the root directory of the source drive. If you omit the /F switch or use it but do not specify *size*, BACKUP formats unformatted destination disks to the highest capacity the drive supports. See Chapter 4 for additional information on the BACKUP command.

EXAMPLES To back up all the files on drive C to drive A, type

```
BACKUP C:\*.* A: /S
```

To back up the files in the \WP and \123 directories of drive C that have been modified since the last backup, type

```
BACKUP C:\WP\*.* A: /M
BACKUP C:\123\*.* A: /M /A
```

NOTES Files backed up with the BACKUP command can only be recovered with the RESTORE command. BACKUP will not back up the system files IO.SYS.MSDOS.SYS, and COMMAND.COM.

BREAK

Enable or Disable Break Checking

SYNTAX   BREAK [ON|OFF]

ON   Enables Break checking
OFF   Disables Break checking

DESCRIPTION   By default, DOS infrequently checks for presses of Ctrl-C and Ctrl-Break (the signal to terminate the current program). Enabling Break checking causes DOS to check for Ctrl-C and Ctrl-Break more often. If you run BREAK without an ON or OFF parameter, the current state of Break checking is displayed.

EXAMPLES   To display the current state of Break checking, type

    BREAK

To enable Break checking, type

    BREAK ON

To disable Break checking, type

    BREAK OFF

NOTES   The BREAK command can be used on the command line or inside CONFIG.SYS. The default state of Break checking is OFF.

BUFFERS

Set Disk Buffer Count

SYNTAX   BUFFERS=*n*[,*m*]

n   Number of disk buffers (range=1 to 99)

m   Number of buffers in the secondary cache (default=1, range=1 to 8)

DESCRIPTION   To speed disk accesses, DOS maintains an array of internal disk buffers where data going to and from disk is cached in case it is requested again. BUFFERS specifies the number of disk buffers and the size of the secondary cache. Normally, BUFFERS is optimized for programs that perform random reads and writes. However, increasing the size of the secondary cache benefits programs that perform sequential disk accesses. The default values for *n* depend on the amount of RAM in your system and the size of your hard disk. See the DOS manual for details.

EXAMPLES   To reserve space for 20 disk buffers, enter

```
BUFFERS=20
```

To create 20 disk buffers and set the size of the secondary cache to 4, enter

```
BUFFERS=20,4
```

NOTES   Each additional disk buffer you set up consumes about 532 bytes of RAM. However, if you load DOS in the HMA (High Memory Area), BUFFERS goes there too, provided there's room for them. Normally, you can fit up to 48 disk buffers in the HMA alongside DOS. If you use SMARTDrive or a third-party disk cache, you don't need a large number of BUFFERS.

CALL

Call Batch Program

SYNTAX   `CALL [d:][path]filename [parameters]`

filename   Name of the batch program to call
parameters   Command-line parameters passed to the batch program being called

DESCRIPTION   CALL calls a batch program from another batch file. When the CALLed batch program terminates, control returns to the program that executed the CALL. For more on batch files and the CALL command, refer to Chapter 10.

EXAMPLES   To call a batch file named BATCHSUB.BAT, enter the line

`CALL BATCHSUB`

in a batch file. To call BATCHSUB.BAT and pass the parameter BUDGET.DOC to it, enter

`CALL BATCHSUB BUDGET.DOC`

BUDGET.DOC will be substituted for the %1 parameter in BATCHSUB.BAT.

NOTES   The CALL command first appeared in DOS 3.3. Prior to that, batch files were called from within other batch files by invoking a secondary copy of the command processor with a command of the form

`COMMAND /C BATCHSUB`

If you call one batch file from another without using the CALL command, control does not return to the caller when the CALLed program terminates.

CHCP

Change Code Page

SYNTAX CHCP [*nnn*]

nnn Number of the code page to change to. Valid values are
437 United States
850 Multilingual (Latin I)
852 Slavic (Latin II)
860 Portuguese
863 Canadian-French
865 Nordic

DESCRIPTION CHCP changes the active code page. Before switching to a code page, you must execute an NLSFUNC command to install DOS's national language support functions and prepare the code page with the MODE command. If CHCP is run without a code page number, it displays the number of the active code page. For a discussion of code page switching, see Chapter 6.

EXAMPLES To display the number of the active code page, type

    CHCP

To change to code page 850, type

    CHCP 850

NOTES You can also change code pages with the MODE SELECT command. CHCP changes the code page on all devices for which code page switching is currently enabled; MODE changes the code page on one device at a time.

CHDIR (CD)

Change Directory

SYNTAX   CD [*d:*][*path*]

path   Name of the directory to change to

DESCRIPTION   CD changes the current directory. Run with no parameters, it displays the name of the current directory on the current drive. Run with a *d:* parameter but without a *path* parameter, it displays the name of the current directory on the specified drive. The CD command is discussed in Chapter 5.

EXAMPLES   To determine what directory you're in, type

```
CD
```

To change to the root directory of the current drive, type

```
CD \
```

To move up one directory level, type

```
CD ..
```

To make \123 the current directory on drive D, type

```
CD D:\123
```

NOTES   If you change directories on a remote drive, you're not automatically switched to that drive. However, when you do switch to it, the directory you named will be the current one.

CHKDSK

Check Disk

SYNTAX CHKDSK [[*d:*][*path*]*filename*] [/F] [/V]

filename   Name of the file or files to check for fragmentation
/F   Fix errors discovered on the disk
/V   Display file names as the disk is checked

DESCRIPTION CHKDSK checks a disk's file allocation table and directory entries for errors. If the /F switch is specified, CHKDSK corrects the errors it finds. If /V is included, it also displays the names of files as it encounters them. If you specify a file name, CHKDSK tells you whether the file is fragmented and, if it is, how many noncontiguous blocks it is stored in. For more information, and for examples of how to repair errors in a disk's file system after CHKDSK is done, see Chapter 4.

EXAMPLES To check the current drive for errors, type

    CHKDSK

To check drive C for errors and fix the ones that are found, type

    CHKDSK C: /F

To determine if BUDGET.DOC is stored in contiguous clusters on disk, type

    CHKDSK BUDGET.DOC

NOTES Run regularly, CHKDSK helps identify and repair disk errors before they grow to unmanageable proportions. CHKDSK checks for a variety of errors including lost clusters, cross-linked files, invalid clusters, allocation errors, and bad sectors in the FAT.

CLS

Clear Screen

SYNTAX   CLS

DESCRIPTION   CLS clears the screen. It accepts no parameters or command-line switches.

NOTES   By itself, CLS is a rather unexciting command because it offers no options for setting the screen colors. However, if you install the ANSI.SYS driver and send color commands to it, CLS will clear the screen to the colors you selected. For example, with ANSI.SYS installed, the command

```
PROMPT $e[1;37;44m
```

displays bright white text on a blue background. After issuing the command, you'll have to reset your DOS prompt with another PROMPT command.

In DOS 5.0, you can install ANSI.SYS in upper memory on 386s and 486s and not take RAM away from application programs, so it costs you nothing to be able to select the colors of your choice or to take advantage of the other enhancements ANSI.SYS has to offer. See Chapter 6 for more on the ANSI.SYS driver and selecting screen colors.

COMMAND

1.0
External

Start Command Processor

SYNTAX   `COMMAND [`*`comspec`*`] [`*`device`*`] [/C `*`command`*`] [/E:`*`size`*`] [/MSG] [/P]`

comspec	Drive and directory where COMMAND.COM resides
device	Name of the device used for command input and output (default=CON)
/C *command*	Executes *command* when COMMAND.COM is started, then terminates
/E:*size*	Specifies the size of the environment in bytes (default=160, range=160 to 32768)
/MSG	Stores error messages in memory rather than on disk
/P	Installs this copy of COMMAND.COM permanently in memory

DESCRIPTION   COMMAND.COM is the command processor DOS loads by default. If you want to install it and specify any of the parameters shown above, you must install it with a SHELL= directive in CONFIG.SYS. The *comspec* parameter tells COMMAND.COM where to find its own image on disk so that it can load itself when needed. DOS uses this parameter to create the COMSPEC environment variable. The /E switch specifies the size of the environment DOS sets up in low memory. The /P switch disables the EXIT command so that COMMAND.COM cannot be terminated.

See Chapter 2 for additional information on the SHELL= directive and COMMAND-.COM.

EXAMPLE   To install COMMAND.COM with an environment size of 512 bytes when COMMAND-.COM is located in the \DOS directory of the C drive, enter the statement

```
SHELL=C:\DOS\COMMAND.COM C:\DOS /E:512 /P
```

in your CONFIG.SYS file.

NOTES   When you install COMMAND.COM with a SHELL= statement as shown above, be sure to include the *comspec* parameter and the /P switch. Otherwise, the system may lock up after running an application program and your AUTOEXEC.BAT file will not be processed.

COMP

Compare Files

SYNTAX   COMP [[*d:*][*path*]*filename1*] [[*d:*][*path*]*filename2*] [/A] [/C]
[/D] [/L] [/N=*number*]

filename1	Name of the first file
filename2	Name of the file to compare it to
/A	Display differences as ASCII characters
/C	Disregard case in the comparison
/D	Display differences in binary form
/L	Display the line number where the difference occurred rather than the byte offset
/N=*number*	Compare the first *number* lines of the two files, even if the files are of different sizes

DESCRIPTION   COMP does a byte-by-byte comparison of two files and reports the differences. If you omit one or both of the file names, COMP will prompt you for them. The *filename1* parameters may include wildcards. For more on the COMP and FC commands, see Chapter 5.

EXAMPLES   To compare two text files named FILE1.TXT and FILE2.TXT and report the differences, type

```
COMP FILE1.TXT FILE2.TXT /A /L
```

To compare two binary files named FILE1.BIN and FILE2.BIN and report the differences, type

```
COMP FILE1.BIN FILE2.BIN /D
```

NOTES   COMP is not nearly as versatile as its cousin, FC, which offers a greater variety of command-line options and doesn't care if two files are of different sizes. After reporting ten differences, COMP quits and proceeds to the next file or asks you if you want to compare more.

COPY

1.0
Internal

Copy Files

SYNTAX   To copy a file or files:

COPY *source* [/A|/B] [*destination*] [/A|/B] [/V]

To concatenate two or more files:

COPY [*d:*][*path*]*filename1* [/A|/B] + [*d:*][*path*]*filename2* [/A|/B]
[+...] [*destination*] [/A|/B] [/V]

source   The name and location of the file or files you want to copy
destination The destination the files are copied to
/A   Treat the file as an ASCII file
/B   Treat the file as a binary file
/V   Verify that the data was copied correctly

DESCRIPTION   The COPY command has two distinct uses: copying files and concatenating files. A /A or /B switch applies to the file preceding the switch and to all subsequent files until another switch is encountered. If *destination* is omitted when files are being copied, the current drive and directory are assumed. If *destination* is omitted when files are being concatenated, COPY assigns the resultant file the name of the first file following the COPY command. You can create a duplicate with a different name by specifying a file name for *destination*. You must specify a destination file name if the file is being copied to the same directory. The COPY command is discussed in Chapter 5.

EXAMPLES   To copy all the files from the current directory to C:\BACKUP, type

COPY *.* C:\BACKUP

To copy all the files with the extension .BAK from drive A to the current directory, type

COPY A:*.BAK

To join the binary files FILE.BIN and FILE2.BIN and give the resultant file the name FILE3.BIN, type

COPY FILE1.BIN/B + FILE2.BIN FILE3.BIN

The /B switch causes DOS to treat all three files as binary files.

NOTES   When copying files, COPY assumes that all the files are binary unless otherwise specified. Thus, you rarely if ever need to use a /A or /B switch when copying files. When COPY concatenates files, it assumes that all the files are text files unless otherwise specified. Text files are only copied up to the terminating end-of-file character. Also, certain copy operations are performed more efficiently with the XCOPY command.

COUNTRY

Set Country Conventions

SYNTAX   COUNTRY=*xxx*,[*yyy*][,[*d:*][*path*]*filename*]]

xxx   3-digit country code
yyy   Default code page for the country
filename Name of the file containing country information (normally COUN-
TRY.SYS)

DESCRIPTION COUNTRY configures DOS for the language conventions used in countries outside the United States. Among other things, it affects the time and date formats used by commands such as TIME, DATE, BACKUP, and RESTORE. Valid values for *xxx* and *yyy* are shown in Table 2.2.

EXAMPLES To adapt DOS to use German language conventions when COUNTRY.SYS is located in C:\DOS, enter

    COUNTRY=Ø49,,C:\DOS\COUNTRY.SYS

To also change the default code page to 850, enter

    COUNTRY=Ø49,85Ø,C:\DOS\COUNTRY.SYS

NOTES COUNTRY is but one of many commands DOS provides for national language support. See Chapters 2 and 6 of this book and your DOS manual for additional information on adapting DOS for use in foreign countries.

CTTY

Set Console Device

SYNTAX   `CTTY` *device*

device   Name of the device to serve as the console device

DESCRIPTION By default, DOS uses the CON device driver for all its command input and output. CTTY allows you to specify an alternate device to serve in this capacity.

EXAMPLE   To use serial port COM1 for command input and output, type

`CTTY COM1`

NOTES   The most practical use for CTTY is as a means for suppressing output from DOS commands in batch files. The command CTTY NUL directs all command output to the NUL device driver until a CTTY CON command is subsequently issued. Be careful: CTTY NUL directs DOS to the NUL driver for its input as well as its output, so if something goes wrong while NUL is the console device, you'll have to reboot your PC.

DATE

Set System Date

SYNTAX   DATE [*date*]

>   *date*   Current date

DESCRIPTION DATE sets the system date. Normally, dates are entered in mm-dd-yy format. However, the format for date may change if you use the COUNTRY directive to adopt the conventions of another country. If DATE is run without a *date* parameter, it displays the current date and prompts you to enter a new one.

EXAMPLE To set the current date to September 30, 1991, type

```
DATE 9-30-91
```

or type **DATE** and enter **9-30-91** at the prompt.

NOTES In version 3.3, the DATE command gained the ability to set the CMOS calendar in a PC. In earlier versions, setting the permanent record of the date required the aid of a separate utility.

DEBUG

Start Program Debugger

SYNTAX   `DEBUG [[d:][path]filename [parameters]]`

filename   Name of the program to debug
parameters Command-line parameters passed to the program being debugged

DESCRIPTION DEBUG is DOS's built-in program debugger, which is useful for testing, creating, and modifying short COM files, entering and testing short assembly language programs, and inspecting the contents of memory. Once it's started, you can type the following commands at its command prompt:

?	Display a list of commands
A	Assemble instruction mnemonics
C	Compare two blocks of memory
D	Display the contents of a block of memory
E	Enter data into memory
F	Fill a block of memory
G	Run the current program
H	Perform hexadecimal arithmetic
I	Input a value from an I/O port
L	Load data from disk
M	Move (copy) a block of memory
N	Name the current program
O	Output a value to an I/O port
P	Execute the next program instruction, proceeding through loops and subroutines
Q	Quit
R	Display and modify register values
S	Search a block of memory
T	Execute the next program instruction
U	Unassemble machine code instructions
W	Write data to disk
XA	Allocate expanded memory
XD	Deallocate expanded memory
XM	Map expanded memory pages
XS	Display expanded memory status information

EXAMPLE To start DEBUG and load PC-DIAL.COM for inspection and debugging, type

`DEBUG PC-DIAL.COM`

NOTES DEBUG is useful to nonprogrammers for typing in short assembly language programs and patching existing programs. This book contains numerous examples in the form of DEBUG scripts.

DEL

Delete File

SYNTAX   `DEL [d:][path]filename [/P]`

filename   Name of the file or files to delete
/P   Prompt for confirmation before deleting a file

DESCRIPTION The DEL command deletes a file or set of files from disk. If you use the /P switch, DOS prompts you with the name of each file before it is deleted. *Filename* may include wildcards. DEL is discussed in Chapter 5.

EXAMPLES To delete a file named BUDGET.DOC from the current directory, type

    DEL BUDGET.DOC

To delete all the files with the extension .BAK from the current directory, type

    DEL *.BAK

To delete all files from the current directory but have DOS prompt you for confirmation before deleting each file, type

    DEL *.* /P

NOTES DEL doesn't physically remove a file from a disk. Instead, it marks it as deleted so that the space it occupies may be reused by subsequent files. Deleted files can be recovered with the UNDELETE command, assuming that the space they occupied has not already been reused.

DEVICE

Load Device Driver

SYNTAX　　DEVICE=[*d:*][*path*]*filename* [*parameters*]

filename　　Name of the device driver to load
parameters　Parameters passed to the driver being loaded

DESCRIPTION　DEVICE loads a special type of program called an *installable device driver* into memory at start-up. DOS comes with ten installable device drivers; their uses and conventions are documented in Appendix B. Other device drivers are frequently shipped with add-on peripherals such as disk drives and tape drives. If you omit *path*, DOS assumes the driver is located in the root directory of the boot drive. You can list the drivers installed and see where they were loaded with the MEM /P command. DEVICE is discused in Chapter 2.

EXAMPLE　To load SMARTDrive from C:\DOS with a cache size of 1Mb, enter

DEVICE=C:\DOS\SMARTDRV.SYS 1024

NOTES　DEVICE always loads device drivers in conventional memory. You can conserve memory in the lower 640k by loading drivers in upper memory with the DEVICEHIGH directive on 386 and 486 systems.

DEVICEHIGH

Load Device Driver High

SYNTAX   `DEVICEHIGH [SIZE=size] [d:][path]filename [parameters]`

size   Minimum amount of upper memory (in bytes) that must be available for the driver to be loaded there

filename   Name of the device driver to load

parameters Parameters passed to the driver being loaded

DESCRIPTION DEVICEHIGH works just like DEVICE except that it loads installable device drivers in upper rather than conventional memory. The *size* parameter specifies the minimum amount of upper memory required to install the driver. If you omit *path*, DEVICEHIGH assumes the driver is located in the root directory of the boot drive. Before DEVICE-HIGH may be used, both HIMEM.SYS and EMM386.EXE must be installed, and DOS must be started with the statement DOS=UMB in CONFIG.SYS. If there isn't enough room in upper memory to load the driver, or if the size of the largest remaining UMB is less than *size*, DEVICEHIGH loads the driver in conventional memory instead. DEVICEHIGH is discussed in Chapter 3.

EXAMPLES To load SMARTDrive in upper memory from C:\DOS with a cache size of 1024, enter

```
DEVICEHIGH=C:\DOS\SMARTDRV.SYS 1024
```

To load a driver named IMGDRV.SYS in upper memory and specify that it requires a minimum of 8k of RAM, enter

```
DEVICEHIGH SIZE=8192 IMGDRV.SYS
```

NOTES If a driver locks up or behaves erratically when it's loaded HIGH, the SIZE switch may help. Load the driver low and use the MEM /P command to determine how much memory it requires. Then load it high with *size* equal to that value or something slightly higher.

DIR

Display Directory Listing

SYNTAX `DIR [d:][path][filename] [/A:attr] [/B] [/L] [/O:order] [/P]`
`[/S] [/W]`

filename	File name or file specification
/A:*attr*	List files by attribute. Valid values for *attr* are

Nothing	List all files
A	List files whose archive bits are set
-A	List files whose archive bits are not set
D	List directories only
-D	List files only
H	List hidden files
-H	List files that are not hidden
R	List read-only files
-R	List files that are not read-only
S	List system files
-S	List files that are not system files

/B	List file and subdirectory names only, omitting other information such as file sizes
/L	Display file and subdirectory names in lower case
/O:*order*	Sort the listing using the specified criterion. Valid values for *order* are

Nothing	Display subdirectories first, files second, sorted by name.
D	Sort by date (oldest to newest)
-D	Sort by date (newest to oldest)
E	Sort by extension (alphabetical order)
-E	Sort by extension (reverse alphabetical order)
G	Display subdirectories first
-G	Display files first
N	Sort by name (alphabetical order)
-N	Sort by name (reverse alphabetical order)
S	Sort by size (smallest to largest)
-S	Sort by size (largest to smallest)

/P	Pause for a keystroke between screens
/S	List files in the specified directory and its descendants
/W	Display listing in wide format

DESCRIPTION The DIR command lists the contents of the current or specified directory or directories. The numerous switches, most of which were added in version 5.0, give you a great deal of flexibility in formatting the output.

EXAMPLES To list the files and subdirectories in the current directory, type

`DIR`

To list all the files with the extension .BAK on drive C, sorted by size, type

```
DIR C:\*.BAK /O:S /S
```

To list subdirectories only in the current directory, sorted by name in reverse alphabetical order, type

```
DIR /A:D /O:-N
```

NOTES The /S switch gives you a means for searching an entire disk for a misplaced file or a set of files matching a particular file specification. To list all occurrences of BUDGET.DOC on the current drive, type

```
DIR \BUDGET.DOC /S
```

or

```
DIR \BUDGET.DOC /S /B
```

You can set the default behavior for the DIR command by defining an environment variable named DIRCMD that's set equal to the switches you want appended to the command automatically. For example, type

```
SET DIRCMD=/O:N
```

and all your directory listings will appear in alphabetical order.

DISKCOMP

3.2
External

Compare Disks

SYNTAX   DISKCOMP [*d1:* [*d2:*]] [/1] [/8]

d1:	Letter of first drive
d2:	Letter of second drive
/1	Compare only the first sides of the disks
/8	Compare only eight sectors per track

DESCRIPTION   DISKCOMP compares the contents of two disks and reports discrepancies. If you omit *d2:*, DISKCOMP uses *d1:* for both disks, prompting you to insert and remove disks as needed. If you omit both drive parameters, DISKCOMP uses the current drive for both. In general, DISKCOMP cannot compare unlike disk types.

EXAMPLES   To compare the disk in drive A with the disk in drive B, type

    DISKCOMP A: B:

To compare two disks in drive A, type

    DISKCOMP A:

NOTES   You won't need the /1 and /8 switches very often. They're throwbacks to the early days of the IBM PC, when 160k, 180k, and 320k disks were common.

DISKCOPY

Copy Disk

SYNTAX   DISKCOPY [*d1:* [*d2:*]] [/1] [/V]

d1:	Letter of the drive to copy from
d2:	Letter of the drive to copy to
/1	Copy only the first side of the disk
/V	Verify that the data was copied correctly

DESCRIPTION   DISKCOPY performs a sector-by-sector disk copy, duplicating the source disk bit for bit on the destination disk. If you omit *d2:*, DISKCOPY uses *d1:* for both disks, prompting you to swap disks as needed. If you omit both drive parameters, DISKCOPY defaults to the current drive. If the destination disk is not formatted, DISKCOPY will format it to the same capacity as the source disk. DISKCOPY cannot be used on hard disks, and, in general, will not work with unlike disk types.

EXAMPLES   To make a duplicate of the disk in drive A in drive B, type

    DISKCOPY A: B:

To make a duplicate of a disk using drive A as both source and destination, type

    DISKCOPY A:

NOTES   The /V switch slows copying somewhat, but provides extra insurance that the data was copied correctly. The /V switch doesn't perform a physical comparison between the data on the source and destination disks. Instead, it has DISKCOPY read back what it wrote to the destination disk and compare it to the image of the data still in memory. If you want to perform a DISKCOPY between disks of different types, you can use the XCOPY command. See Chapter 4 for an explanation.

DOS

Configure DOS

SYNTAX   `DOS=[HIGH|LOW][,UMB|NOUMB]`

HIGH	Load DOS high (in the HMA)
LOW	Load DOS low (in conventional memory)
UMB	Establish a link to upper memory for loading TSRs and device drivers high
NOUMB	Do not establish a link to upper memory

DESCRIPTION   The DOS directive specifies where DOS should be loaded and whether it is to establish a link to upper memory. DOS=HIGH loads most of DOS itself into the 64k region of extended memory known as the High Memory Area, or HMA; DOS=LOW loads DOS the normal way, in conventional memory. The default is DOS=LOW. DOS=UMB establishes a link to upper memory so that TSRs and device drivers can be loaded high with the LOADHIGH and DEVICEHIGH commands. When DOS=UMB is specified, DOS uses HIMEM.SYS to claim all the UMBs created by EMM386.EXE for itself so that no one else may use them. The default is DOS=NOUMB. For more information on the DOS directive and other 286/386/486 memory management issues, see Chapter 3.

EXAMPLES   To load DOS into the HMA and make more room available for programs in conventional memory, enter

    `DOS=HIGH`

To establish a link to upper memory so that TSRs and device drivers can be loaded there, enter

    `DOS=UMB`

To load DOS high *and* establish a link to upper memory, enter

    `DOS=HIGH,UMB`

NOTES   Loading DOS high is the easiest and quickest way to gain more memory in your system. DOS=HIGH is only valid on 286, 386, and 486 PCs with at least 64k of extended memory. It can only be used if HIMEM.SYS is loaded, too. DOS=UMB is only valid on 386 and 486 systems with HIMEM.SYS and the EMM386.EXE driver loaded. If DOS=UMB is not specified, the LOADHIGH and DEVICEHIGH commands cannot load TSRs and device drivers into upper memory.

DOSKEY

Install Command-Line Enhancer and Macro Recorder

SYNTAX
```
DOSKEY [/REINSTALL] [/BUFSIZE=size] [/MACROS] [/HISTORY]
       [/INSERT|/OVERSTRIKE] [macro=[text]]
```

/REINSTALL	Install a new copy of DOSKEY
/BUFSIZE=*size*	Set buffer size to *size* bytes (default=512)
/MACROS	Display all currently defined macros
/HISTORY	Display command history
/INSERT	Default to insert mode when editing commands
/OVERSTRIKE	Default to overstrike mode when editing commands
macro	Macro name
text	Macro definition

DESCRIPTION DOSKEY is a memory-resident utility that adds four new features to the command line. With it installed, you can

- Edit text on the command line using the Left and Right Arrow, Ctrl-Left and Ctrl-Right, Home, End, Ctrl-Home, Ctrl-End, and Esc keys.

- Recall past commands using the Up and Down Arrow, PgUp, PgDn, F8, and F9 keys. Pressing F7 displays a numbered command history. You can execute a specific command by pressing F9 and entering the number of the command, or recall a particular command by typing the first few characters and pressing F8. Alt-F7 clears all the buffered commands.

- Enter multiple commands on a single command line by separating them with Ctrl-T, which shows up on the screen as the symbol for a paragraph marker. For example, the command

  ```
  CLS ¶ MEM
  ```

  clears the screen and executes a MEM command.

- Create command macros that act like internal DOS commands. The command

  ```
  DOSKEY WHEREIS=DIR \$1 /S
  ```

  creates a macro named WHEREIS that locates files on the current drive. The command

  ```
  WHEREIS BUDGET.DOC
  ```

  lists every occurrence of BUDGET.DOC. The command

  ```
  DOSKEY WHEREIS=
  ```

deletes the macro. You can delete all currently defined macros at once by pressing Alt-F10. DOSKEY understands the following special metacharacters in macro definitions

$B	Piping operator (|)
$G	Output redirection operator (>)
$L	Input redirection operator (<)
$T	Command separator, Ctrl-T (¶)
$$	Dollar sign
$1 through $9	Replaceable parameters 1 through 9
$*	All command-line parameters

See Chapter 7 for a detailed discussion of the DOSKEY command.

EXAMPLES To install DOSKEY with a buffer size of 2k and make insert mode the default when editing commands, type

```
DOSKEY /BUFSIZE=2048 /INSERT
```

To list all the commands currently buffered for recall, type

```
DOSKEY /HISTORY
```

To define a macro named CMEM that clears the screen and executes the MEM command, type

```
DOSKEY CMEM=CLS $T MEM
```

To delete the macro, type

```
DOSKEY CMEM=
```

To list all the macros currently defined, type

```
DOSKEY /MACROS
```

NOTES DOSKEY is a powerful command that once you try, you'll find it hard to live without. With the default buffer size of 512 bytes, DOSKEY requires about 4k of RAM. If your system is configured for loading TSRs in upper memory, load DOSKEY with LOAD-HIGH to conserve RAM. Increasing the buffer size increases the number of macros you can define and increases the number of commands that are buffered for recall.

DOSSHELL

Start the DOS Shell

SYNTAX   `DOSSHELL [/G[:res[n]]]|/T[:res[n]]] /B`

/G	Start the Shell in graphics mode
res	Screen resolution. Valid values are
	L Low
	M Medium
	H High
n	Resolution number (valid values depend on the type of video adapter being used)
/T	Start the Shell in text mode
/B	Start the Shell in black-and-white

DESCRIPTION   DOSSHELL starts the DOS Shell, a mouse-driven graphical user interface that serves as an alternative to the command line. Through the Shell, you can change drives and directories, perform file operations, launch programs, and load several programs at once and switch among them, a process known as *task-switching*. See Chapter 14 for a comprehensive discussion of the DOS Shell.

EXAMPLES   To start the DOS Shell, type

    DOSSHELL

To start the Shell in 60-line graphics mode (High Resolution 2) on a VGA video adapter, type

    DOSSHELL /G:H2

NOTES   You can determine what the valid values for *n* are by starting the Shell and selecting Display from the Options menu. The various options pertaining to screen resolution will be displayed for you. Note that there are some things you can do from the Shell that you can't do from the command line, such as renaming subdirectories.

DRIVPARM

Define Drive Parameters

SYNTAX

```
DRIVPARM=/D:drive [/F:form] [/H:heads] [/S:sectors]
    [/T:tracks] [/N] [/C] [/I]
```

/D:*drive*	Physical drive number (0=A, 1=B, and so on)
/F:*form*	Drive form factor. Valid values are

0	160k/180k/320k/360k drive
1	1.2Mb drive
2	720k drive
5	Hard disk
6	Tape drive
7	1.44Mb drive
8	Read/write optical disk
9	2.88Mb drive

/H:*heads*	Number of heads on the drive
/S:*sectors*	Number of sectors per track
/T:*tracks*	Number of tracks
/N	Drive is nonremovable
/C	Drive features change-line support
/I	Drive is unsupported by the BIOS

DESCRIPTION DRIVPARM modifies the internal drive parameter tables that DOS sets up to characterize block devices attached to your PC. You can characterize a device by the *form* factor or by the number of heads, sectors, and tracks it contains. The /N switch indicates that the drive is nonremovable (for example, a hard disk). The /C switch tells DOS that the drive features a change line, a device that enables DOS to determine when the drive door is opened. The /I switch allows DRIVPARM to support drives that are not supported by your PC's BIOS. For more on the DRIVPARM directive, see Chapter 2.

EXAMPLES To tell DOS that drive B is a 3 1/2-inch 720k drive, enter

```
DRIVPARM=/D:1 /F:2
```

To tell DOS that drive E is a tape drive with 1 head, 10 tracks, and 80 sectors per track, enter

```
DRIVPARM=/D:4 /F:6 /H:1 /T:10 /S:80
```

To configure drive A as a 1.44Mb drive when your BIOS does not support 1.44Mb drives, type

```
DRIVPARM=/D:0 /F:7 /I
```

NOTES DRIVPARM is useful for characterizing drives that DOS doesn't recognize properly. If you add a 3 1/2-inch drive to your PC and DOS treats it like a 360k or 1.2MB drive, for example, DRIVPARM with a /I switch may fix it.

ECHO

Enable or Disable Echo or Display a Message

SYNTAX   ECHO [ON|OFF] [*message*]

ON   Enable command echoing
OFF   Disable command echoing
message   Message text

DESCRIPTION The ECHO command enables or disables command echoing in batch files or outputs a message from a batch file. If ECHO is enabled, batch file commands are echoed to the screen (displayed on the screen as they are executed); if ECHO is disabled, batch file commands are not echoed to the screen. The default is ECHO ON.

EXAMPLES To disable command echo, enter the command

    ECHO OFF

To enable it again, enter

    ECHO ON

To output the message "Press any key" from a batch file, use the command

    ECHO Press any key

NOTES You can suppress the echoing of a single command in a batch file by preceding it with a @ character.

EDIT

Start DOS Editor

SYNTAX   EDIT [[*d*:][*path*]*filename*] [/B] [/G] [/H] [/NOHI]

filename	Name of the file to edit
/B	Start the Editor in black-and-white
/G	Perform fast updates on CGA monitors
/H	Display the maximum number of lines supported by the video adapter
/NOHI	Suppress the display of high-intensity colors

DESCRIPTION   The DOS Editor is a mouse-driven, full-screen text editor that serves as a functional replacement for EDLIN. Use it any time you need to edit a text file, whether it's a short AUTOEXEC.BAT file or a larger text file created by another program. The DOS Editor is covered in detail in Chapter 5.

EXAMPLES   To start the DOS Editor, type

    EDIT

To make changes to AUTOEXEC.BAT, type

    EDIT AUTOEXEC.BAT

To edit CONFIG.SYS and switch to a 50-line display on VGA video adapters, type

    EDIT CONFIG.SYS /H

NOTES   The /G switch speeds screen updates on CGA monitors, but also causes a distracting snow-like interference to appear on the screen. To start the Editor, DOS invokes QBASIC.EXE with an /EDITOR switch. QBASIC.EXE must be in the current directory, in the PATH, or in the same directory that EDIT.COM is stored in for the Editor to be started.

EDLIN

Start Line Editor

SYNTAX   EDLIN [[d:][path]filename] [/B]

filename	Name of the file to edit
/B	Ignore (Ctrl-Z) end-of-file characters

DESCRIPTION   EDLIN is the line-oriented text editor that has been part of DOS since version 1.0. Once it is started, you can type the following commands at its command prompt

?	Display a list of commands
line	Line number to edit
A	Append lines from disk
C	Copy a line or lines
D	Delete a line or lines
E	Save the file and exit
I	Insert a line or lines
L	List a line or lines
M	Move a line or lines
P	Page through the file
Q	Quit without saving the file
R	Replace text
S	Search for text
T	Transfer file (merge data from disk into the file being edited)
W	Write lines to disk (save)

EXAMPLE   To make changes to AUTOEXEC.BAT, type

    EDLIN AUTOEXEC.BAT

When the changes are complete, type **E** to save your work and exit.

NOTES   EDLIN is a throwback to line-oriented editors of yesteryear. Now that the DOS Editor is part of DOS, you won't often find a reason to use EDLIN.

EMM386

Control EMM386.EXE Driver

SYNTAX   EMM386 [ON|OFF|AUTO] [W=ON|OFF]

ON	Enable the EMM386.EXE driver
OFF	Disable the EMM386.EXE driver
AUTO	Place EMM386.EXE in AUTO mode
W=ON	Enable Weitek coprocessor support
W=OFF	Disable Weitek coprocessor support

DESCRIPTION The EMM386 command controls DOS's EMM386.EXE driver. The command is only valid if the driver is installed through CONFIG.SYS. Run without command-line parameters, EMM386 reports the current state of the driver. **EMM386 ON** enables the driver, and **EMM386 OFF** temporarily disables it. **EMM386 AUTO** places the driver in AUTO mode, which is similar to ON except that expanded memory services are provided only when a program calls for them, not before (provided EMM386.EXE was not installed with a NOEMS switch, which would prevent it from providing expanded memory services). The W=ON and W=OFF switches enable and disable support for Weitek math coprocessors.

For more information, refer to the discussion of the EMM386 command and the EMM386.EXE driver in Chapter 3.

EXAMPLES To determine the status of the EMM386.EXE driver, type

    EMM386

To temporarily disable the EMM386.EXE driver, type

    EMM386 OFF

To enable Weitek coprocessor support, type

    EMM386 W=ON

NOTES Weitek coprocessors may not work properly with EMM386.EXE installed unless you enable Weitek coprocessor support. In general, you should enable coprocessor support prior to running a program that uses the coprocessor, then disable it again after the program has terminated. Coprocessor support generally cannot be enabled if DOS is loaded in the HMA. Also, some programs will have trouble running with EMM386.EXE active because EMM386.EXE runs DOS in the Virtual-86 mode of the 386 chip. If you run across such programs, disable EMM386.EXE prior to running them with the command

    EMM386 OFF

Note that you cannot shift EMM386.EXE to OFF or AUTO mode if EMM386.EXE is currently providing expanded memory to an application program or if there are TSRs or device drivers loaded in upper memory.

ERASE

Delete File

SYNTAX   ERASE [*d:*][*path*]*filename* [/P]

filename   Name of the file or files to delete
/P   Prompt for confirmation before deleting a file

DESCRIPTION The ERASE command is identical to the DEL command. See the entry for DEL in this appendix for further information.

EXE2BIN

1.0
External

Convert EXE File to COM Format

SYNTAX   EXE2BIN [*d:*][*path*]*exefile* [[*d:*][*path*]*comfile*]

exefile   Name of the EXE file to convert
comfile   Name of the COM file to create

DESCRIPTION   EXE2BIN is used to convert binary EXE files to COM format. If you omit the *comfile* parameter, EXE2BIN defaults to a file with the same name as *exefile* and the extension BIN. An EXE file may only be converted if

- It is a valid EXE file produced by an object linker such as Microsoft's LINK utility

- The combined length of the program's code, data, and stack does not exceed 64k

- No STACK segment was declared in the source file

EXE2BIN is vital to assembly language programmers creating COM-formatted utilities, but it is of no practical use to nonprogrammers. For more information on EXE2BIN and the differences between COM and EXE files, refer to Chapter 9.

EXAMPLE   To create FINDTEXT.COM from FINDTEXT.EXE, type

    EXE2BIN FINDTEXT.EXE FINDTEXT.COM

EXIT

2.0
Internal

Terminate Command Processor

SYNTAX `EXIT`

DESCRIPTION If you're running inside a secondary command processor (for example, you've shelled to DOS from WordPerfect), EXIT is the command you type to terminate the command processor and return to the program that launched it. EXIT is ignored by the primary command processor.

EXAMPLE To return to WordPerfect after pressing Ctrl-F1 to go to DOS, type

`EXIT`

NOTES COMMAND.COM ignores the EXIT command if it was started with a /P switch. If you install COMMAND.COM with a SHELL= directive in CONFIG.SYS and forget to include the /P switch, you can crash the system by typing EXIT on the command line.

EXPAND

Expand File

SYNTAX   EXPAND [*d:*][*path*]*filename1* [...] *destination*

filename1   Name of the file or files to expand
filename2   Name of the expanded file

DESCRIPTION   EXPAND expands compressed files on the disks that came in your DOS package. Wild-cards are not accepted for *filename*, but you can specify multiple file names. *Destination* specifies where the expanded files will be placed, and may consist of a drive name, a path name, a file name, or a combination of the three. You may only include a file name in*destination* if only one file is being expanded.

EXAMPLES   To expand HIMEM.SY_, the compressed version of HIMEM.SYS, type

    EXPAND HIMEM.SY_ HIMEM.SYS

To expand HIMEM.SY_ and UNDELETE.EX_ on drive A and place the expanded versions in the \DOS directory of the C drive, type

    EXPAND A:HIMEM.SY_ A:UNDELETE.EX_ C:\DOS
    REN C:\DOS\HIMEM.SY_ HIMEM.SYS
    REN C:\DOS\UNDELETE.EX_ UNDELETE.EXE

NOTES   The files on your DOS disks are shipped in compressed form to save space and reduce the number of disks. Normally, the installation program expands them for you. However, should you ever need to expand one manually (if, for example, you delete a file from your hard disk to conserve space and then discover later that you need it), EXPAND allows you to do so without having to reinstall DOS from the ground up.

FASTOPEN

Install FASTOPEN

SYNTAX FASTOPEN d:[[=]n] [...] [/X]

    n Number of files to cache information on (default=48, range=10 to 999)

    /X   Allocate buffer space in expanded memory

DESCRIPTION FASTOPEN speeds up hard-disk operations by caching information about the physical locations of files on the disk so that once they're opened, they can be opened more quickly the second time. The n parameter specifies how many files FASTOPEN can retain information about at one time on a per-drive basis. Each file increases FASTOPEN's size in memory by about 48 bytes. You can conserve memory by using the /X switch (which allocates space for the cache in expanded memory rather than conventional memory) or by loading FASTOPEN into upper memory with the LOADHIGH command on compatible systems. FASTOPEN is discussed in Chapter 2.

EXAMPLES To install FASTOPEN and have it speed up file operations on drives C and D, type

    FASTOPEN C: D:

To install FASTOPEN on drive C only with room in the cache to retain information about 100 files, and to place the cache in expanded memory, type

    FASTOPEN C:=1ØØ /X

NOTES FASTOPEN is an easy and inexpensive way to speed up the operation of your hard disk. To speed disk operations even further, use FASTOPEN and SMARTDrive together. The two are not redundant: SMARTDrive caches data at the sector level, while FASTOPEN caches data at the file level.

FC

2.0
External

Compare Files

FC [d:][path]filename1 [d:][path]filename2 [/A] [/B] [/C]
     [/L] [/LBn] [/lines] [/N] [/T] [/W]

filename1	Name of the first file to compare
filename2	Name of the file to compare it to
/A	Abbreviate output from ASCII comparisons
/B	Perform a binary comparison
/C	Ignore case in the comparison
/L	Perform an ASCII comparison
/LBn	Set the size of the internal line buffer to *n* lines (default=100)
/lines	Number of consecutive lines required to resynchronize after a mismatch occurs (default=2)
/N	Display line numbers in ASCII comparisons
/T	Do not expand tabs to spaces
/W	Compress white space in comparisons

The FC command is COMP's more sophisticated cousin, and is a powerful tool for comparing files of any type. By default, comparisons are performed in ASCII mode unless one or more of the files being compared has the extension .EXE, .COM, .SYS, .OBJ, .LIB, or .BIN. For these, FC defaults to binary mode unless otherwise specified. See Chapter 5 for a thorough discussion of this command.

To compare two text files named FILE1.TXT and FILE2.TXT and ignore case in the comparisons, type

    FC FILE1.TXT FILE2.TXT /L /C

To perform the same comparison with regard to case while displaying line numbers and abbreviating output, type

    FC FILE1.TXT FILE2.TXT /L /N /A

To compare two binary files named FILE1.PCX and FILE2.PCX, type

    FC FILE1.PCX FILE2.PCX /B

If FC has trouble resynchronizing after a mismatch when comparing ASCII files, increase the size of the line buffer with the /LB switch. FC can't resynchronize if the mismatch exceeds the length of the line buffer.

FCBS

Set Limit on File Control Blocks

SYNTAX   FCBS=*x*

    x   Maximum number of file control blocks that can be open at one time
(default=4, range=1 to 255)

DESCRIPTION FCBS lets you specify the maximum number of file control blocks that may be open in the system concurrently. DOS limits the number of file control blocks that can be open in the system at one time, because having too many of them open can adversely affect network performance. Once the limit is reached, DOS closes old file control blocks when new ones are opened.

EXAMPLE To set the limit on file control blocks to 1, enter

    FCBS=1

NOTES If you don't run programs that use file control blocks, you can save a few bytes of memory by adding the statement FCBS=1 to your CONFIG.SYS file. If a particular program needs this setting increased, its manual should tell you what to set it to. Note that most programs do not use file control blocks for file accesses any more, opting for DOS's handle-based file functions instead.

FDISK

Configure Hard Disk

SYNTAX   FDISK

DESCRIPTION FDISK is the tool DOS provides for setting up and managing hard-disk partitions. With it, you can

- Create and remove DOS partitions, primary and extended
- Assign drive letters to and remove them from extended DOS partitions
- Specify what partition is the active partition
- Display partition data

DOS 5.0 supports partitions up to 2Gb in length. Note that when you delete a partition using FDISK, all the data stored in the partition is lost. See Chapter 4 for an in-depth discussion of FDISK.

EXAMPLE   To start FDISK so you can partition a new hard disk or change partition sizes on an old one, type

      FDISK

NOTES   A hard disk must be partitioned before it can be used (partitioning comes before formatting). Unfortunately, the only way to change the size of an existing partition is to delete it, then create a new one in its place. If you want to repartition your hard disk to take advantage of DOS 5's support for greater-than-32Mb partitions, you'll need to back up the data on it first, repartition it, then restore the data to the new partition or partitions. See Chapter 1 for a step-by-step description of this process.

FILES

Set Limit on Open Files

SYNTAX　　FILES=x

x　　　Maximum number of files that may be open in the system at once using file handles (default=8, range=8 to 255)

DESCRIPTION FILES determines how much space DOS reserves in low memory to hold information about files opened with DOS's handle-based file functions and thus sets the limit on the number of files that can be open at once. Five file handles are reserved for DOS's own internal device drivers, so the number of file handles available to application programs is actually five less than the setting of FILES.

EXAMPLE To permit up to 40 files to be open in the system at once, enter

FILES=40

NOTES At a minimum, it's advisable to set FILES to 20 in your CONFIG.SYS file, because any application that uses the disk extensively may need more file handles than are provided by default.

FIND

Find Character String

SYNTAX FIND [/C] [/I] [/N] [/V] "*string*" [[*d:*][*path*]*filename*]

/C	Display count of lines that contain the string rather than the lines them-selves
/I	Perform the search without regard to case
/N	Display line numbers
/V	Display lines that do *not* contain the specified string
string	Text string to search for
filename	Name of the file to search

DESCRIPTION FIND searches a file or a stream of characters input to it for a specified text string and either displays the lines that contain the string or, if it was started with a /V switch, displays the lines that do not contain the string. You can use the /C switch to display a count of lines that contain or do not contain the text string rather than the lines themselves. The /I switch performs searches without regard to case. If no file name is specified, FIND acts as a filter command and expects input to be provided to it via an input redirection or piping operator. By default, searches are case sensitive. The FIND command as well as redirection and piping are discussed in Chapter 8.

EXAMPLES To display all the lines in BUDGET.TXT that contain the word "Expenses," type

```
FIND "Expenses" BUDGET.TXT
```

To display line numbers, too, and to tell FIND to disregard case in the search, type

```
FIND /I /N "Expenses" BUDGET.TXT
```

To display a count of the lines in BUDGET.TXT that do not contain the string "Expenses," type

```
FIND /C /V "Expenses" BUDGET.TXT
```

To display all the files on drive C whose file names contain the letters "DOC," type

```
DIR C:\*.* /S | FIND "DOC"
```

To display a count of the files on drive C whose file names contain the letters "DOC," type

```
DIR C:\*.* /S | FIND /C "DOC"
```

NOTES FIND is one of three filter commands DOS supplies for handling text files (the other two are MORE and SORT). FIND is the only one that is capable of receiving input through a means other than redirection or piping.

FOR

Execute Command for Each Element of a Set

SYNTAX FOR %%*variable* IN (*set*) DO *command*

variable	Variable name (A through Z)
set	Set of file names or text strings to substitute for %%*variable* each iteration through the loop
command	Command to execute each time through the loop

DESCRIPTION The FOR command executes *command* once for each member of *set*. Each time through the loop, the next member of *set* is substituted for %%*variable*. If *set* includes wildcards, the wildcards are expanded as if they were file names. The %%*variable* parameter may be referenced in *command*. Chapter 10 contains more information on the FOR command.

EXAMPLES To TYPE the files FILE1.TXT, FILE2.TXT, and FILE3.TXT to the screen from a batch file, enter the command

```
FOR %%F IN (FILE1.TXT FILE2.TXT FILE3.TXT) DO TYPE %%F
```

To TYPE all files with the extension .TXT to the screen, enter

```
FOR %%F IN (*.TXT) DO TYPE %%F
```

NOTES If you run FOR from the command line, only include a single percent sign in front of *variable*.

FORMAT

Format Disk

SYNTAX   FORMAT *d:* [/1] [/4] [/8] [/B] [/F:*size*] [/N:*sectors*]
    [/T:*tracks*] [/Q] [/S] [/U] [/V:[*label*]]

d:	Letter of the drive to format
/1	Format one side of the disk only
/4	Format a 360k disk in a 1.2Mb drive
/8	Format eight sectors per track
/B	Reserve room on the disk for system files
/F:*size*	Specifies the capacity to format a floppy to
	Valid values for *size* are

Disk Type	Size
160k	160, 160k, or 160KB
180k	180, 180k, or 180KB
320k	320, 320k, or 320KB
360k	360, 360k, or 360KB
720k	720, 720k, or 720KB
1.2Mb	1200, 1200k, 1200KB, 1.2, 1.2M, or 1.2Mb
1.44Mb	1440, 1440k, 1440KB, 1.44, 1.44M, or 1.44Mb
2.88Mb	2880, 2880k, 2880KB, 2.88, 2.88M, or 2.88Mb

/N:*sectors*	Number of sectors per track
/T:*tracks*	Number of tracks on the disk
/Q	Perform a quick format
/S	Copy the system files after formatting
/U	Perform an unconditional format
/V:*label*	Add the volume label *label*

DESCRIPTION The FORMAT command is used to format hard-disk partitions and floppy disks. FOR-
MAT creates a boot sector, two copies of the file allocation table, and the root directory
on the disk or partition so that DOS can store files there. DOS 5.0 supports three types
of formats:

- The safe format (the default). Safe-formatted disks can be unformatted with the
  UNFORMAT command.

- The quick format. Quick-formatting is much faster than safe-formatting, but can
  only be performed on disks that have been formatted before. Quick-formatted
  disks, like safe-formatted disks, may be unformatted.

- The unconditional format. Unconditional formatting destroys everything on the
  disk so that the UNFORMAT command cannot recover it.

You can combine the /Q and /U switches to perform a very fast format. However, you
may not be able to unformat a disk formatted this way.

To format a floppy in drive A for the first time, type

```
FORMAT A:
```

To reformat the disk the floppy in drive A, type

```
FORMAT A: /Q
```

To format a 720k floppy in a 1.44Mb drive A and copy the system files to it, type

```
FORMAT A: /F:720 /S
```

To format the primary partition on a hard disk so that you can boot DOS from it, type

```
FORMAT C: /S
```

To format the D: drive in an extended DOS partition and add the volume label "DOS-DRIVE," type

```
FORMAT D: /V:DOS-DRIVE
```

NOTES The /1, /4, /8, /B, /N, and /T switches on the FORMAT command are now obsolete and are retained primarily for compatibility with older versions. To format a disk to a lower capacity than the maximum the drive supports, use the /F switch to specify the desired formatted capacity.

GOTO

**2.0
Batch**

Jump to Another Line

SYNTAX   GOTO *label*

label   Name of the line to jump to

DESCRIPTION The GOTO command enables batch files to jump from one line to another. The target of a GOTO command can be any line that consists of a colon followed by a label name. See Chapter 10 for details.

EXAMPLE The following batch file excerpt shows how GOTO is used to jump to the line labeled :END:

```
GOTO END
        .
        .
        .


    :END
```

NOTES You can substitute the name of an environment variable enclosed in percent signs for the *label* parameter, and GOTO will jump to the label name that the environment variable is set equal to.

GRAFTABL

Load Graphics Characters

SYNTAX   GRAFTABL [*nnn*] [/STATUS]

nnn   Code page number. Valid values are
        437   United States
        850   Multilingual (Latin I)
        852   Slavic (Latin II)
        860   Portuguese
        863   Canadian-French
        865   Nordic
/STATUS Identify the code page selected

DESCRIPTION   GRAFTABL loads a graphics character set into memory so that IBM Color Graphics Adapters can display upper-order ASCII characters. The characters can only be displayed while in graphics mode.

EXAMPLE   To load the graphics character set corresponding to code page 437, type

GRAFTABL 437

NOTES   The GRAFTABL command is not needed for most display adapters, including EGAs and VGAs. For the most part, it is one of DOS's least useful commands.

GRAPHICS

Install Graphics-Mode Screen Dump Capability

GRAPHICS [*printer*] [[*d:*][*path*]*filename*] [/B] [/R]
[/LCD][/PB:/*id*]

printer	Type of printer output will be going to. Valid values are

COLOR1	IBM Color Printer with black ribbon
COLOR4	IBM Color Printer with RGB ribbon
COLOR8	IBM Color Printer with CMY ribbon
HPDEFAULT	Any Hewlett-Packard PCL printer
DESKJET	Hewlett-Packard DeskJet printer
GRAPHICS	IBM Graphics Printer, IBM Proprinter, and most Epson printers
GRAPHICSWIDE	IBM Graphics Printer and most Epson printers with wide carriages
LASERJET	Any Hewlett-Packard LaserJet printer
LASERJETII	Hewlett-Packard LaserJet II printer
PAINTJET	Hewlett-Packard PaintJet printer
QUIETJET	Hewlett-Packard QuietJet printer
QUIETJETPLUS	Hewlett-Packard QuietJet Plus printer
RUGGEDWRITER	Hewlett-Packard RuggedWriter printer
RUGGEDWRITERWIDE	Hewlett-Packard RuggedWriter printer with wide carriage
THERMAL	IBM PC Convertible thermal printer
THINKJET	Hewlett-Packard ThinkJet printer

filename	Name of the printer profile file that contains the information GRAPHICS uses to characterize printers (normally GRAPHICS.PRO)
/B	Print the background in color on COLOR4 and COLOR8 printers
/R	Print the image as it appears on the screen rather than reversed
/LCD	Print an image from the LCD screen of the IBM PC Convertible
/PB:*id*	Specifies the aspect ratio to be used. Valid values for *id* are:

LCD	Use LCD aspect ratio (same as specifying /LCD)
STD	Use standard aspect ratio

GRAPHICS is a memory-resident program that transmits the contents of a graphics-mode screen to the printer when you press the Print Screen key. You must tell it what type of printer you have by using one of the printer codes listed above, and tell it where GRAPHICS.PRO (the file in which DOS stores information about printers) is located. If you don't supply a path to the file, GRAPHICS looks in the current directory and in the directory where GRAPHICS.COM is located.

EXAMPLES To load GRAPHICS for a LaserJet printer when GRAPHICS.PRO is located in the \DOS directory of drive C, type

```
GRAPHICS LASERJET C:\DOS\GRAPHICS.PRO
```

To load GRAPHICS for an IBM Graphics Printer or most Epson dot-matrix printers when GRAPHICS.PRO is stored in the same directory as GRAPHICS.COM, type

```
GRAPHICS GRAPHICS
```

NOTES On black-and-white printers, GRAPHICS reproduces images in up to four shades of gray. In DOS 4.0, GRAPHICS gained the ability to handle EGA and VGA screen modes. If you have a 386 or 486 configured for loading programs in upper memory, install GRAPHICS with the LOADHIGH command to conserve space in the lower 640k.

HELP

Display Help for DOS Command

SYNTAX   HELP [*command*]

command   Name of the command you want help with

DESCRIPTION   HELP invokes on-line help for a DOS command—the same help that is invoked when the command is run with a /? switch. Running HELP with no command name following it displays a list of all the DOS commands.

EXAMPLES   To get help with the FORMAT command, type

    HELP FORMAT

To list all the DOS commands, type

    HELP

NOTES   Using the /? switch is slightly faster than using the HELP command if you just want help with a single command. All DOS 5.0 commands support the /? switch. To get help with the FORMAT command, type **FORMAT /?**.

IF

Execute Command Conditionally

SYNTAX To test an exit code returned by a program:

```
IF [NOT] ERRORLEVEL exitcode command
```

To compare two strings:

```
IF [NOT] string1==string2 command
```

To see if a file exists in a specified location on disk:

```
IF [NOT] EXIST [d:][path]filename command
```

exitcode	Exit code value (0 to 255)
command	Command to execute if the test returns true
string1	Text string
string2	Text string

DESCRIPTION The IF command allows a batch file to perform a test and to act based on the results of the test. The IF ERRORLEVEL form of the command returns true if the exit code from the program most recently executed is equal to or higher than *exitcode*. The string comparison form of the command returns true if the two strings are equal. String parameters may be literal strings, replaceable batch file parameters, or environment variables with their names enclosed in percent signs. The IF EXIST form of the command returns true if the file exists in the specified location. The NOT qualifier may be used to test for the inverse of the condition. The *command* parameter can be any valid DOS command.

EXAMPLES To branch to the line labeled ERROR if RESTORE returns an exit code of 1 or higher:

```
RESTORE A: C:\*.* /S
IF ERRORLEVEL 1 GOTO ERROR
```

To branch to ERROR if the the first parameter on the line that invoked the batch file is not equal to "PARM1"

```
IF NOT "%1"=="PARM1" GOTO ERROR
```

To display the message "File does not exist" if there is no file named BUDGET.DOC in the current directory:

```
IF NOT EXIST BUDGET.DOC ECHO File does not exist
```

NOTES It's a good idea to use quotation marks when performing string comparisons with the IF command, to prevent the batch file from crashing if a comparison is performed on a null parameter. You can test for a null parameter with the following statement:

```
IF "%1"=="" GOTO END
```

INSTALL

Install Memory-Resident Program

SYNTAX   INSTALL=[*d:*][*path*]*filename* [*parameters*]

filename   Name of the program to install
parameters   Parameters passed to the program being installed

DESCRIPTION   INSTALL lets you load TSRs from CONFIG.SYS rather than from the command line. If you do not include a path to the file, INSTALL looks for it in the root directory of the drive DOS was started from. You must include the file name extension.

EXAMPLE   To install FASTOPEN from C:\DOS with space to track 40 files on drive C and 40 files on drive D, enter

    INSTALL=C:\DOS\FASTOPEN.EXE C:=40 D:=40

NOTES   Installing a TSR with INSTALL sometimes saves a few hundred bytes of RAM because INSTALL does not allocate an environment block for the TSR. It also means that some TSRs will not run correctly when they're loaded from CONFIG.SYS.

JOIN

Join Disk to Directory

SYNTAX   `JOIN [`*`d1:`* `[`*`d2:`*`]`*`path`*`] [/D]`

d1:   Drive to JOIN
d2:path   Drive and directory to JOIN the drive to
/D   UnJOINs the specified drive

DESCRIPTION   JOIN establishes a logical link between a disk and a remote directory, making it appear that an entire disk is actually a subdirectory on another drive. For example, after typing

    `JOIN A: C:\ADRIVE`

typing

    `DIR C:\ADRIVE`

will display a list of the files on the disk in drive A. You can only JOIN drives to empty directories. Running JOIN without command-line parameters lists the drives currently JOINED. Running it with a /D switch cancels JOIN for the specified drive. While a drive is JOINed, it cannot be accessed by drive letter.

EXAMPLES   To JOIN drive B to C:\BDRIVE, type

    `JOIN B: C:\BDRIVE`

To restore drive B: to its normal mode of operation, type

    `JOIN B: /D`

To list all JOINed drives, type

    `JOIN`

NOTES   JOINed drives should not be used with these commands: ASSIGN, BACKUP, CHKDSK, DISKCOMP, DISKCOPY, FDISK, FORMAT, LABEL, MIRROR, RECOVER, RESTORE, or SYS.

KEYB

Alter Keyboard Layout

SYNTAX   KEYB [*xx*[,[*yyy*][,[*d:*][*path*]*filename*]]] [/E] [/ID:*nnn*]

xx	Two-digit keyboard code
yyy	Code page number
/E	Keyboard is an enhanced keyboard
/ID:*nnn*	Specifies which keyboard layout to use when there is more than one
filename	Name of the keyboard definition file (normally KEYBOARD.SYS)

DESCRIPTION   KEYB is a TSR that remaps your keyboard to one of the alternate layouts diagrammed in your DOS manual. Valid values for all the parameters above are shown in your DOS manual. With KEYB installed, you can revert to the default configuration by pressing Ctrl-Alt-F1, and return to the new configuration by pressing Ctrl-Alt-F2. You can also enter typewriter mode by pressing Ctrl-Alt-F7.

EXAMPLE   To remap your keyboard to the Italian layout when KEYBOARD.SYS is stored in C:\DOS, type

    KEYB IT,,C:\DOS\KEYBOARD.SYS

NOTES   KEYB lets you enter accented characters using special keystroke sequences. For example, typing apostrophe-a produces the letter "a" accented with an acute diacritic in some layouts. For details, see your DOS manual.

LABEL

Set Volume Label

SYNTAX   LABEL [*d:*][*label*]

label   Volume label for the disk

DESCRIPTION   The LABEL command lets you create, modify, or delete the volume label assigned to a disk. If you run it without a *label* parameter, LABEL displays the current label (if one exists) and prompts you to enter a new one. If you press Enter without entering a new label, LABEL asks you if you want to delete the current label.

EXAMPLE   To change the volume label on drive D to DOS-DISK, type

    LABEL D:DOS-DISK

NOTES   DOS displays the volume label when you run the DIR, CHKDSK, TREE, and VOL commands. You may also specify a volume label when the disk is formatted.

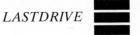

LASTDRIVE

Specify Highest Drive Letter DOS Will Support

SYNTAX   LASTDRIVE=*x*

x Letter of the highest drive DOS will support (A through Z)

DESCRIPTION   When DOS starts up, it reserves room for information about five logical drives (the current directory for the drive, the address of the device driver that services the drive, and so on) in low memory. If you plan to use a drive letter higher than E, you must use LASTDRIVE to reserve room for it.

EXAMPLE   To configure DOS to support logical drives A through Z, enter

    LASTDRIVE=Z

NOTES   Each additional drive you allocate room for consumes about 88 bytes of memory. You can conserve memory by allocating just enough memory for the drives you plan to use. If, for example, you won't be using a drive letter higher than C, then the statement LASTDRIVE=C will save 176 bytes of memory that would otherwise go unused.

LOADFIX

Load Program Above 64k Mark

SYNTAX   LOADFIX [*d:*][*path*]*filename* [*parameters*]

filename   Name of the program to run

DESCRIPTION   With DOS loaded in the HMA, there's a very good chance that programs will be loaded and run in the first 64k of memory. However, some programs do not run properly in this region. The LOADFIX command loads and runs a program above the 64k mark. LOAD-FIX searches the PATH for executable files. The *filename* parameter does not have to include the file name extension.

EXAMPLE   To run WordPerfect above the 64k mark, type

    LOADFIX WP

NOTES   Use the LOADFIX command if you receive a "Packed file corrupt" message when you try to load and run a program.

LOADHIGH (LH)

**5.0
Internal**

Load Memory-Resident Program in Upper Memory

SYNTAX   LOADHIGH [*d:*][*path*]*filename* [*parameters*]

filename   Name of the program to load high
parameters Command-line parameters passed to the program being loaded

DESCRIPTION   The LOADHIGH command loads a program into *upper memory blocks* (UMBs) established between 640k and 1Mb on 386 and 486 PCs by the EMM386.EXE driver. Before LOADHIGH may be used, both HIMEM.SYS and EMM386.EXE must be installed, and DOS must be started with the statement DOS=UMB in CONFIG.SYS. If there isn't enough room to load the specified program in upper memory, LOADHIGH loads it in conventional memory. LOADHIGH automatically searches the PATH for executables to load. The *filename* parameter need not contain an extension.

For more on the LOADHIGH command and loading TSRs and device drivers in upper memory, refer to Chapter 3.

EXAMPLE   To load a TSR named PC-DIAL into upper memory, type

    LOADHIGH PC-DIAL

NOTES   Sometimes the order in which TSRs are loaded will make a difference in how many you can fit into upper memory. If there isn't enough room for it to load a TSR into upper memory, LOADHIGH will load it in conventional memory instead. The easiest way to tell whether a TSR was loaded into upper or lower memory is to type **MEM /C**.

MEM

Profile Memory Usage

SYNTAX
```
MEM [/CLASSIFY|/DEBUG|PROGRAM]
```

/CLASSIFY   Display a list of programs loaded in upper and conventional memory
/DEBUG   Display a list of programs and internal device drivers loaded in memory
/PROGRAM   Display a list of programs loaded in memory

DESCRIPTION The MEM command profiles memory usage. Run without a command-line switch, it displays vital statistics on memory usage, such as the largest executable program size and the total amount of memory installed. The command-line switches provide information about what's loaded in memory and where; they may be abbreviated /C, /D, and /P.

EXAMPLES To determine how much memory is installed in your system and how much of it is available, type

```
MEM
```

To get a list of the programs installed in both upper and lower memory, type

```
MEM /C
```

NOTES The MEM /C command is particularly useful for determining what's loaded in upper memory and how much upper memory is still available for program loading.

MIRROR

Mirror Disk

SYNTAX To create a backup copy of a hard disk's partition tables:

```
MIRROR /PARTN
```

To create a mirror file on a disk for use by the UNFORMAT command:

```
MIRROR d: [/1]
```

To make MIRROR memory resident and have it perform delete-tracking for the UNDE-LETE command:

```
MIRROR /Tdrive[-entries] [...]
```

To remove MIRROR from memory:

```
MIRROR /U
```

/PARTN	Create a backup copy of the partition tables
/1	Retain only the latest information about a disk
/T*drive*	Specify the drive delete-tracking will be performed on
entries	Specify the number of entries in the delete-tracking file for the corresponding drive (range=1 to 999)

DESCRIPTION The MIRROR command performs three distinctly different functions. One, it creates a backup copy of a hard disk's partition tables so they can be restored if they become corrupted. Two, it creates a mirror file that the UNFORMAT command can use to restore the disk if it becomes damaged or is inadvertently formatted. Three, it performs a function known as *delete tracking*, which enables the UNDELETE command to restore some files that couldn't be restored using conventional methods. The default value for *entries* depends on the size of the disk that delete-tracking is being performed on.

EXAMPLES To make a backup copy of your hard disk's partition tables, type

```
MIRROR /PARTN
```

To create a mirror file on drive C, type

```
MIRROR C:
```

To create a delete-tracking file with the default number of entries for drive C and 200 for drive D, type

```
MIRROR /TC /TD-200
```

NOTES When you safe-format or quick-format a disk, the FORMAT command creates a mirror file on the disk just like **MIRROR d:.**

MKDIR (MD)

2.0
Internal

Make Directory

SYNTAX   `MD [d:]path`

path   Name of the subdirectory to create

DESCRIPTION The MD command creates a new subdirectory. See Chapter 5 for details.

EXAMPLES To create a subdirectory named PERSONAL as a descendant of the current directory, type

`MD PERSONAL`

To create a subdirectory named \WP that stems from the root directory, type

`MD \WP`

NOTES Subdirectories created with the MD command can be removed with the RD command.

MODE

**1.0
External**

Configure Device

SYNTAX To configure a printer attached to a parallel port:

```
MODE LPTn[:] [COLS=columns] [LINES=lines] [RETRY=r]
```

n	LPT port number (1, 2, or 3)
columns	Number of columns (80 or 132)
lines	Number of lines (6 or 8)
r	Action to take if the printer doesn't respond. Valid values are

E	Return error code if printer busy
B	Return busy code if printer busy
P	Retry indefinitely
R	Return ready code if printer busy
N	Take no action (default)

To initialize a serial port:

```
MODE COMm[:] [BAUD=baud] [PARITY=parity] [DATA=data]
[STOP=stop] [RETRY=r]
```

m	COM port number (1, 2, 3, or 4)
baud	Baud rate. Valid values are

11	110 baud
15	150 baud
30	300 baud
60	600 baud
12	1,200 baud
24	2,400 baud
48	4,800 baud
96	9,600 baud
19	19,200 baud

parity	Parity setting (N=None, E=Even, O=Odd, M=Mark, S=space)
data	Number of data bits (5, 6, 7, or 8)
stop	Number of stop bits (1, 1.5, or 2)
r	Action to take if COM port doesn't respond. Valid values are

E	Return error code if port busy
B	Return busy code if port busy
P	Retry indefinitely
R	Return ready code if port busy
N	Take no action (default)

To display the status of a device or devices:

```
MODE [device] /STATUS
```

To redirect printer output from a parallel port to a serial port:

```
MODE LPTn[:]=COMm[:]
```

n   LPT port number (1, 2, or 3)
m   COM port number (1, 2, 3, or 4)

To prepare, select, refresh, and display code pages:

```
MODE device CODEPAGE PREPARE=((yyy [...])
[d:][path]filename)
```

```
MODE device CODEPAGE SELECT=yyy
MODE device CODEPAGE REFRESH
MODE device CODEPAGE /STATUS
```

device   Name of the device being referenced
yyy   Code page number
filename   Name of the code page information file

To set the display mode:

```
MODE CON[:] [COLS=columns] [LINES=lines]
```

columns   Number of columns to display (40 or 80)
lines   Number of lines to display (25, 43, or 50)

To set the keyboard typematic rate and delay interval:

```
MODE CON[:] RATE=rate DELAY=delay
```

rate   Typematic rate (default=20, range=1 to 32)
delay   Delay interval (1=0.25 seconds, 2=0.50 seconds, 3=0.75 seconds, 4=1.0 seconds; default=2)

DESCRIPTION The MODE command is actually many commands in one. You can use it to

- Set the number of characters per inch and lines per inch for IBM-compatible printers

- Initialize a serial port to the desired baud rate, parity setting, number of data bits, and number of stop bits

- Display the status of one or more devices

- Redirect printer output from an LPT port to a COM port

- Prepare, select, refresh, and display the status of code pages

- Set the number of rows and columns of text displayed on an EGA or VGA video adapter

- Set the typematic rate and delay interval on selected keyboards

EXAMPLES To initialize serial port COM1 to 1200 baud, no parity, 8 data bits, and 1 stop bit, type

```
MODE COM1: BAUD=12 PARITY=N DATA=8 STOP=1
```

To redirect printer output from LPT1 to COM2, type

```
MODE LPT1:=COM2:
```

To switch a VGA video adapter to 50-line mode, type

```
MODE CON: LINES=50
```

To speed up keyboard operation, type

```
MODE CON: RATE=32 DELAY=1
```

NOTES You must install ANSI.SYS before using MODE to set video adapter display modes. Also, keyboard typematic and delay rates can only be set on 84-, 101-, and 102-key keyboards. MODE cannot, as is often supposed, redirect printer output from one LPT port to another LPT port, or configure your system to capture printer output to a file.

MORE

Display One Screenful of Information

SYNTAX

```
MORE < source
```

or

```
command | MORE
```

source   File or device providing the input
command Command providing the input

DESCRIPTION MORE accepts a stream of input data and outputs it one screenful at a time, pausing for a keystroke at the end of each screen. Input must be supplied to the command by an input redirection or piping operator.

EXAMPLES To display a text file named BUDGET.TXT one screenful at a time, type

```
TYPE BUDGET.TXT | MORE
```

or

```
MORE < BUDGET.TXT
```

NOTES MORE is one of three filter commands supplied with DOS; the other two are FIND and SORT.

NLSFUNC

Install National Language Support Functions

SYNTAX NLSFUNC [[*d:*][*path*]*filename*]

    filename   Name of the file that contains country-specific information (COUN-TRY.SYS)

DESCRIPTION NLSFUNC is a TSR that contains the National Language Support functions that DOS uses to support code page switching. The default value for *filename* is the name of the file specified after the COUNTRY directive in CONFIG.SYS. If there is no such directive, NLSFUNC looks for COUNTRY.SYS in the root directory of the current drive. See Chapter 6 for more examples of its use.

EXAMPLE To install NLSFUNC when COUNTRY.SYS is located in the \DOS directory of the C drive, type

    NLSFUNC C:\DOS\COUNTRY.SYS

NOTES NLSFUNC must be installed before code pages can be prepared or selected.

PATH

Set Search Path for Executable Files

SYNTAX   PATH [[*d:*]*path*[;[*d:*]*path*][;...]]

DESCRIPTION   The PATH command creates a list of directories that DOS searches for executable files whenever you type a command that is not an internal DOS command. Running PATH with no command-line parameters displays the current PATH; running it with nothing but a semicolon cancels the current PATH. PATH strings are stored as environment variables, so you can also create and modify them with the SET command. See Chapter 5 for details.

EXAMPLES   To create a PATH that contains C:\DOS, C:\SYSTEM, and C:\UTIL, type

    PATH C:\DOS;C:\SYSTEM;C:\UTIL

To display the current PATH, type

    PATH

To cancel the current PATH, type

    PATH ;

NOTES   A PATH string can't be longer than 127 characters because that's as long as DOS permits any one command to be. You can circumvent this limit for the PATH command with clever use of the SUBST command.

PAUSE

Pause Batch File Execution

SYNTAX   PAUSE

DESCRIPTION   PAUSE pauses a batch file and displays the message "Press any key to continue."

EXAMPLE   The following batch file excerpt displays the message "Insert program disk in drive A" and pauses until the user presses a key:

```
ECHO Insert program disk in drive A
PAUSE
```

NOTES   Pressing Ctrl-C or Ctrl-Break while PAUSE is waiting for a keystroke terminates a batch file. Thus, you can use PAUSE to allow a batch file to be terminated at opportune points.

PRINT

Install Print Spooler

SYNTAX

```
PRINT [/D:device] [/B:size] [/U:ticks1] [/M:ticks2] [/S:
      ticks3][/Q:qsize] [/T] [[d:][path]filename] [...] [/C] [/P]
```

/D:*device*	Name of the device to transmit print output to. The default is PRN. Valid values are PRN, LPT1, LPT2, LPT3, COM1, COM2, COM3, and COM4.
/B:*size*	Set the size of the internal buffer (in bytes) where data is stored on its way to the printer (default=512, range=512 to 16384)
/U:*ticks1*	Maximum number of clock ticks PRINT will wait for a printer to come available (default=1, range=1 to 255)
/M:*ticks2*	Maximum number of clock ticks PRINT can take to print a character (default=2, range=1 to 255)
/S:*ticks3*	Maximum number of consecutive clock ticks to be used for background printing (default=8, range=1 to 255)
/Q:*qsize*	Maximum number of files the print queue will hold (default=10, range=4 to 32)
/T	Remove all files from the print queue
filename	Name of the file to print
/C	Remove a file or files from the print queue
/P	Add a file or files to the print queue

DESCRIPTION PRINT is a TSR that allows text files to be printed in the background while you work in the foreground. The /U, /M, and /S switches allow you to fine-tune PRINT so that files print quickly, but don't steal too much time away from foreground tasks. The /B and /Q switches let you specify the sizes of the internal buffers PRINT sets up. The /C, /P, and /T switches let you control what goes into and out of the print queue. A /P or /C switch affects the file whose name precedes the switch and all subsequent files until another /P or /C switch is encountered. PRINT should be used to print text files only; printing binary files can produce strange results. To list the files currently in the print queue, run PRINT by itself on the command line. PRINT is discussed in Chapter 5.

EXAMPLES To install PRINT with a 4k buffer size and room for up to 20 files in the print queue, and to add BUDGET.TXT to the queue at the same time, type

```
PRINT /Q:2Ø /B:4Ø96 BUDGET.TXT
```

To add FILE1.TXT, FILE2.TXT, and FILE3.TXT to the print queue once PRINT is installed, type

```
PRINT FILE1.TXT FILE2.TXT FILE3.TXT
```

To remove FILE2.TXT and add FILE4.TXT, type

```
PRINT FILE2.TXT /C FILE4.TXT /P
```

To add FILE1.TXT, FILE2.TXT, and FILE3.TXT, to the print queue and remove FILE4.TXT, type

```
PRINT FILE1.TXT /P FILE2.TXT FILE3.TXT FILE4.TXT /C
```

To clear the print queue of all files, type

```
PRINT /T
```

To install PRINT if it isn't installed already, or to list the files in the print queue if it is installed, type

```
PRINT
```

NOTES If you install PRINT from your AUTOEXEC.BAT file, specify the print device with a /D switch to prevent PRINT from pausing and prompting you for a device name. Also, if you have a 386 or 486 configured for loading TSRs high, you can load PRINT in upper memory to conserve resources down low.

PROMPT

Configure Command Prompt

SYNTAX   PROMPT [*promptstring*]

promptstring   String that defines the appearance of the prompt, including metacharacters

DESCRIPTION   The PROMPT command defines the appearance of the DOS prompt. You can include the following metacharacters in a prompt string:

$b   Piping operator (|)
$d   Current date
$e   Escape character
$g   Output redirection operator (>)
$h   Backspace (delete previous character)
$l   Input redirection operator (<)
$n   Current drive
$p   Current drive and directory
$q   Equal sign (=)
$t   Current time
$v   DOS version number
$$ Dollar sign ($)
$_   Carriage return

Run without a *promptstring* parameter, PROMPT restores the default DOS prompt, which is equivalent to typing the command PROMPT ng. Chapter 6 shows some interesting command prompts for you to try out.

EXAMPLES   To configure the DOS prompt to show the current drive and directory followed by a > sign, type

    PROMPT pg

To configure the prompt to show the current time and date on separate lines, then move down a line and show the current drive and directory followed by a colon, type

    PROMPT d_t_$$p$g:

NOTES   The PROMPT command is also a convenient mechanism for passing commands to the ANSI.SYS driver, as discussed in Chapter 6.

QBASIC

Start QBasic Interpreter

SYNTAX   QBASIC [/B] [/EDITOR] [/G] [/H] [/MBF] [/NOHI]
            [[/RUN] [*d:*][*path*]*filename*]

/B	Start QBasic in black-and-white
/EDITOR	Start the DOS Editor
/G	Perform fast updates on CGA monitors
/H	Display the maximum number of lines supported by the video adapter
/MBF	Convert the built-in functions CVD, CVS, MKS$, and MKD$ to CVD-MBF, CVSMBF, MKDMBF$, and MKSMBF$, respectively
/NOHI	Suppress the display of high-intensity colors
/RUN	Run the program whose file name is specified
filename	Name of the BASIC program file to load or run

DESCRIPTION   The QBASIC command starts the QBasic Interpreter, an interpreted BASIC programming environment based on Microsoft QuickBASIC. The /MBF switch is useful for running QBasic programs that read and write data files created by GW-BASIC or BASICA.

EXAMPLES   To start QBasic, type

    QBASIC

To start QBasic in 50-line VGA mode and load PASSAGES.BAS for editing, type

    QBASIC PASSAGES /H

To start QBasic and automatically run PASSAGES.BAS, type

    QBASIC /RUN PASSAGES

NOTES   You can run BASIC programs from batch files and return control to the batch file after the program has terminated by using the /RUN switch and making the final statement in the BASIC program a SYSTEM command.

RECOVER

Recover Damaged Files

SYNTAX   To recover a file:

> RECOVER [*d:*][*path*]*filename*

To recover every file on a disk:

> RECOVER *d:*

DESCRIPTION   When a disk defect prevents a file from being read in its entirety, you can recover the part of it that lies outside the defective area with the RECOVER command. RECOVER reads the undamaged sectors and copies them to a new file. If RECOVER is applied to a single file, the recovered file is given the same name as the original; if it's applied to an entire disk, recovered files are created in the root directory with the names FILE0001.REC, FILE0002.REC, and so on. Use RECOVER when you get a data error or "Sector not found" message from DOS when trying to access a file. See Chapter 4 for more on this command.

EXAMPLES   To recover the salvageable parts of a file named BUDGET.DOC, type

> RECOVER BUDGET.DOC

To recover all the files that are salvageable on drive C, type

> RECOVER C:

NOTES   RECOVER should only be used as a last resort. Applied to a single file, it's not too dangerous a command. But applying it to an entire disk is a quick way to wipe out everything on it. You should only run RECOVER disk-wide when the system area of the disk is damaged and there is little hope of recovering files from the disk by any other method.

REM

Define Comment Line

SYNTAX   REM [*comment*]

comment   Text string

DESCRIPTION   REM can be used in batch files and in CONFIG.SYS to declare comment lines. Anything following REM is ignored.

EXAMPLE   The following lines form a typical header for a CONFIG.SYS file:

```
REM **************************************
REM
REM                 DOS 5.0
REM           Configuration File
REM
REM **************************************
```

NOTES   Although REM has been an option in batch files since DOS 2.0, it was only added to the lexicon of CONFIG.SYS in version 4.0. Another way to set off comments in batch files is to precede them with : characters, causing the batch file to interpret them as labels rather than commands.

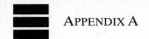

RENAME (REN)

Rename File

SYNTAX   REN [*d:*][*path*]*filename1 filename2*

filename1   Name of the file to rename
filename2   New name for the file

DESCRIPTION The REN command renames a file. You cannot specify a drive or path with *filename2* because the file cannot be "renamed" to another drive or directory. You can use wildcards to rename several files at once.

EXAMPLES To rename BUDGET.DOC to BUDGET.BAK, type

    REN BUDGET.DOC BUDGET.BAK

To change the extension of all the files in the current directory with the extension .DOC to .BAK, type

    REN *.DOC *.BAK

NOTES The REN command cannot be used to rename a subdirectory. However, the Rename function in the File menu of the DOS Shell can. For details, see Chapter 14.

REPLACE

Replace Files

SYNTAX

```
REPLACE [d:][path]filename destination [/A] [/P] [/R] [/S]
    [/U] [/W]
```

filename   Name of the file or files to copy
destination Destination to copy the files to
/A   Add new files instead of replacing existing files
/P   Prompt for confirmation before replacing a file at the destination or creating a new one
/R   Replace read-only files also
/S   Replace files in the descendants of the destination directory as well as in the directory itself (not valid if the /A switch is used)
/U   Replace only those files that are older than the files being copied (not valid if the /A switch is used also)
/W   Pause before starting

DESCRIPTION REPLACE can be used in two distinctly different ways: to replace files of a certain name at the destination, or to add files that don't already exist at the destination. It will not replace read-only files unless the /R switch is used.

EXAMPLES To transfer all the files on the disk in drive A that have counterparts in the \EXE directory of drive C, type

```
REPLACE A:\*.* C:\EXE
```

To copy files from the disk in drive A that do *not* have counterparts in the \EXE directory of drive C, type

```
REPLACE A:\*.* C:\EXE /A
```

NOTES You cannot use REPLACE to transfer system files such as IO.SYS and MSDOS.SYS, nor can you use it to copy hidden files unless you strip the attributes off with the ATTRIB command first.

RESTORE

2.0
External

Restore Backed-Up Files

SYNTAX

```
RESTORE source destination [/A:date] [/B:date] [/D]
    [/E:time] [/L:time] [/M] [/N] [/P] [/S]
```

source	Letter of the drive to restore files from
destination	Names and locations of the files to be restored
/A:*date*	Restore files that were modified on or after the specified date
/B:*date*	Restore files that were modified on or before the specified date
/D	Display a list of files without restoring any of them
/E:*time*	Restore files that were modified at or earlier than the specified time
/L:*time*	Restore files that were modified at or later than the specified time
/M	Restore files that were modified since the last backup
/N	Restore only files that do not exist on the destination disk
/P	Prompt for confirmation before restoring files whose read-only or archive attributes bits are set
/S	Restore files from the specified directory and all its descendants

DESCRIPTION RESTORE restores files backed up with the BACKUP command. You can list the name of files on the backup disks with the /D switch, which lists all files that match *filename* without actually restoring them. When RESTORE is started, it prompts you to insert the backup disks in the same order that they were inserted during the backup operation, so it's a good idea to have them labeled.

EXAMPLES To restore all the files on drive C from floppies in drive A, type

```
RESTORE A: C:\*.* /S
```

To restore all the .DOC files that were backed up from the WP\WPFILES directory of the C drive, type

```
RESTORE A: C:\WP\WPFILES\*.DOC
```

To restore all the .DOC files that were backed up from the \WP\WPFILES directory and that have been modified since the last backup, type

```
RESTORE A: C:\WP\WPFILES\*.DOC /M
```

NOTES In version 5.0, RESTORE was modified so that it could restore files backed up by any previous version of BACKUP. Before, there were version dependencies that meant you couldn't necessarily restore files backed up with an earlier version of DOS.

RMDIR (RD)

2.0
Internal

Remove Directory

SYNTAX   RD [*d:*]*path*

path   Name of the subdirectory to remove

DESCRIPTION RD removes a subdirectory. It is the counterpart to MD, which creates a subdirectory. A subdirectory cannot be removed unless it is devoid of files and other subdirectories. See Chapter 5 for more information.

EXAMPLE To remove the subdirectory named \WP\TMPFILES on the current drive, type

```
RD \WP\TMPFILES
```

NOTES If RD insists that the subdirectory is not empty, but the DIR command shows no files or subdirectories, the subdirectory may contain hidden or system files. To check, type **DIR /A** to display all files in the current directory. Then, use the ATTRIB command to strip the attributes so you can delete the files.

SET

Set Environment Variable

SYNTAX

```
SET [variable=[string]]
```

variable Name of an environment variable
string String to equate the environment variable to

DESCRIPTION SET creates, deletes, modifies, and displays environment variables. Typing SET by itself lists all the environment variables currently defined. Specifying a variable name and a text string creates that environment variable and sets it equal to the string. If you include the *variable* parameter but omit *string*, the environment variable is deleted.

EXAMPLES To create an environment variable named TEMP and set it equal to C:\SCRATCH, type

```
SET TEMP=C:\SCRATCH
```

To delete TEMP, type

```
SET TEMP=
```

To list all the environment variables currently defined, type

```
SET
```

NOTES The length of the area in low memory where environment strings are stored is fixed. Unless you declare otherwise, the default size is 160 bytes. If running the SET command produces the error message

```
Out of environment space
```

you can increase the size of the environment with a SHELL= statement such as this one, which increases the space allotted for environment strings to 512 bytes:

```
SHELL=C:\DOS\COMMAND.COM C:\DOS /E:512
```

SETVER

Set DOS Version

SYNTAX   `SETVER [`*d:path*`] [`*filename*`] [`*n.nn*`] [/DELETE] [/QUIET]`

d:path	Drive and directory where SETVER.EXE is stored
filename	File name of the application program to report a different version number to
n.nn	Version number to report (for example, 4.00)
/DELETE	Remove an entry from the version table
/QUIET	Suppress messages when /DELETE is used

DESCRIPTION   Some programs check the version of DOS that's being used and refuse to run under version 5.0. SETVER lets you set the version number that DOS will report to application programs on a program-by-program basis. To remove an entry from the table that DOS maintains internally, use the /DELETE switch. Run without switches, SETVER lists the file names in the table along with the DOS versions that are reported to them. SETVER is only effective if SETVER.EXE is loaded with a DEVICE or DEVICEHIGH directive in CONFIG.SYS. After you add or delete entries from the version table, the system must be restarted for the changes to take effect.

EXAMPLES   To make WordPerfect "think" it's running under DOS 3.30, type

```
SETVER WP.EXE 3.30
```

To delete WordPerfect from the version table, type

```
SETVER WP.EXE /DELETE
```

To list the entries currently in the version table, type

```
SETVER
```

NOTES   Some programs have good reasons for only running under certain versions of DOS. If a program is incompatible with DOS 5.0, SETVER cannot make it compatible. It will allow it to run, but it may precipitate a system crash or worse.

SHARE

Install File-Sharing Support

SYNTAX   SHARE [/F:*size*] [/L:*locks*]

/F:*size*   Allocate *size* bytes for recording file-sharing information (default=2048)
/L:*locks*   Maximum number of files that can be locked at one time (default=20)

DESCRIPTION   SHARE installs the component of DOS that supports file sharing and file locking on networks. With SHARE installed, programs written for networked environments can access files cooperatively, ensuring that one program doesn't destroy what another has done.

EXAMPLE   To install SHARE and provide 16k of buffer space for file-sharing information and room for locking up to 100 files at a time, type

    SHARE /F:16384 /L:100

NOTES   In DOS 4.0, SHARE also included the module that prevented programs that used file control blocks to access files on the hard disk from inadvertently destroying data stored in large partitions. In version 5.0, that module was moved to the DOS kernel, so SHARE is no longer required solely to support greater-than-32Mb disk partitions.

SHELL

Specify Command Processor

SYNTAX　　SHELL=[[*d:*]*path*]*filename* [*parameters*]

filename　　Name of the command processor to load
parameters　Parameters passed to the command processor being loaded

DESCRIPTION　The SHELL directive specifies what command processor is used to read and process your commands. The default command processor is COMMAND.COM. See the entry for COMMAND.COM in this appendix and in Chapter 2 for additional information.

EXAMPLE　　To load a command processor named NDOS.COM from the \SYSTEM directory of drive C, enter

　　SHELL=C:\SYSTEM\NDOS

NOTES　　SHELL is commonly used to load COMMAND.COM with a set of parameters other than the defaults. For example, the command

　　SHELL=C:\DOS\COMMAND.COM C:\DOS /E:512 /P

loads COMMAND.COM from the \DOS directory of drive C with an environment size of 512 bytes rather than the default 160.

SHIFT

Shift Replaceable Parameters

SYNTAX   `SHIFT`

DESCRIPTION The SHIFT command shifts replaceable parameters in batch files so that what was %2 is now %1, what was %3 is now %2, and so on. Batch files can use this command to access more than 10 command line parameters. See Chapter 10 for details.

EXAMPLE   To access the tenth parameter on the command as %9, type

```
SHIFT
```

NOTES   The SHIFT command is also useful for writing batch files capable of handling an unknown number of command-line parameters. For example, you can create a batch file that performs the same duty as the DEL command but accepts multiple file names with the following statements:

```
@ECHO OFF
:BEGIN
IF "%1"=="" GOTO END
DEL %1
SHIFT
GOTO BEGIN
:END
```

SORT

2.0
External

Sort Text

SYNTAX

```
SORT [/R] [/+nn] < source [> destination]
```

or

```
command | SORT [/R] [/+nn] [> destination]
```

/R   Sort in reverse order
/+nn   Sort on column number *nn*
source   File or device providing the input
destination File or device output is directed to
command   Command providing the input

DESCRIPTION SORT accepts a stream of input data and sorts it. If *destination* is not specified, SORT sends its output to the screen. Input must be supplied to the command by an input redirection or piping operator. SORT is discussed in Chapter 8.

EXAMPLES To sort a file named NAMES.TXT and display the sorted data on the screen, type

```
SORT < NAMES.TXT
```

To sort the file and store the sorted output in a file named SORTED.TXT, type

```
SORT < NAMES.TXT > SORTED.TXT
```

To list the files output by the DIR command by size, type

```
DIR | SORT /+20
```

NOTES SORT is one of three filter commands supplied with DOS; the other two are FIND and MORE. In previous versions of DOS, SORT was frequently used to sort the output from the DIR command. However, the DIR command's /O switch now makes that unnecessary.

STACKS

Configure System Stacks

SYNTAX   STACKS=*n*,*s*

n   Number of stacks to set up
s   Size of each stack (in bytes)

DESCRIPTION   To prevent your system from crashing when hardware interrupts occur too quickly in succession, DOS intercepts selected hardware interrupts and assigns them each a stack from an array of stacks it maintains internally. STACKS specifies the number of stacks created at start-up and the number of bytes allocated to each stack. On an 8088- or 8086-based PC, the default is STACKS=0,0. On all others, the default is STACKS=9,128. STACKS is discussed in Chapter 2.

EXAMPLES   To allocate no stacks at start-up, enter

    STACKS=0,0

To allocate 16 stacks of 256 bytes each, enter

    STACKS=16,256

NOTES   Increase the STACKS setting on your PC if you receive "Internal stack overflow" messages from DOS. Some PCs run fine with no internal stacks. If yours is one, and if it's a 286, 386, or 486 PC, you can conserve about 1k of memory by adding the statement STACKS=0,0 to your CONFIG.SYS file.

SUBST

Substitute Drive for Directory

SYNTAX   SUBST [*d1:* [*d2:*]*path*] [/D]

d1:   New drive letter

d2:path   Drive and directory to associate *d1:* with

/D   Delete a drive substitution

DESCRIPTION   SUBST creates a new logical drive and associates it with the specified drive and directory. DOS treats it as if it were a real drive. For example, after you type

    SUBST Z: C:\DOS5UTIL

then typing **DIR Z:** lists the contents of C:\DOS5UTIL. Running SUBST without parameters or switches displays a list of the drives currently defined with the SUBST command. SUBST is discussed in Chapter 5.

EXAMPLES   To associate drive letter E with C:\WP\DOC, type

    SUBST E: C:\WP\DOC

Thereafter, typing

    COPY FILE.TXT E:

is equivalent to typing

    COPY FILE.TXT C:\WP\DOC

To delete the drive assignment, type

    SUBST E: /D

NOTES   The SUBST command is useful when you run old application programs that do not recognize subdirectories and for creating directory aliases to circumvent the 127-character limit DOS places on PATH commands. If you plan to use a drive letter higher than E, you must make room for it by placing a LASTDRIVE directive in your CONFIG.SYS file. The following commands should not be used on drives set up by SUBST: ASSIGN, BACKUP, CHKDSK, DISKCOMP, DISKCOPY, FDISK, FORMAT, LABEL, MIRROR, RECOVER, RESTORE, and SYS.

SWITCHES

Set Configuration Switches

SYNTAX   `SWITCHES=[/K] [/W]`

/K   Treat an enhanced keyboard like a conventional keyboard
/W   Locate WINA20.386 somewhere other than the root directory

DESCRIPTION   SWITCHES is a catch-all directive that will probably be expanded in future versions of DOS. The /K switch causes DOS to ignore keys such as F11 and F12 on 101- and 102-key keyboards. The /W switch enables you to move WINA20.386, the file that SETUP placed in the root directory of your hard disk, to another drive or directory. SWITCHES is discussed in Chapter 2.

EXAMPLES   To treat an enhanced keyboard like a conventional keyboard, enter

    `SWITCHES=/K`

To tell DOS and Windows that WINA20.386 is located in the \WINDOWS directory of drive D, enter

    `SWITCHES=/W`

in CONFIG.SYS and add the statement

    `DEVICE=D:\WINDOWS\WINA20.386`

to the [386Enh] section of Windows' SYSTEM.INI file.

NOTES   The /W switch is not documented in your DOS manual, but it works, and it lets you keep your root directory clear of unnecessary files. If you use the /K switch and also use ANSI-.SYS, you should start ANSI.SYS with a /K switch also. If you don't use Windows and don't ever intend to, or if you run Windows but run it in real or standard mode, you can delete WINA20.386 and save about 10k of space on your hard disk.

SYS

1.0
External

Transfer System Files

SYNTAX
SYS [*d:*][*path*] *d:*

path   Location where the system files are stored
d: Drive to copy the system files to

DESCRIPTION For a disk to be bootable, it must contain the system files IO.SYS, MSDOS.SYS, and COMMAND.COM. SYS transfers these files to a hard disk or floppy that doesn't already contain them. If you omit the *d:* and *path* parameters, DOS looks to the root directory of the current drive for the system files. SYS is discussed in Chapter 4.

EXAMPLES To make the disk in drive A bootable, type

SYS A:

To copy the system files from drive C to drive A, type

SYS C: A:

NOTES If SYS doesn't find COMMAND.COM in the same location where IO.SYS and MSDOS.SYS are stored, it uses the COMSPEC environment variable to locate it. If SYS displays the message "Could not copy COMMAND.COM onto target disk," you can copy COMMAND.COM yourself with the COPY command or use the SET command to point COMSPEC to the drive and directory where COMMAND.COM is stored and run SYS again. Note that SYS will now work on any disk, not just one that is empty or that was formatted with a /B switch.

TIME

Set System Time

SYNTAX   TIME [*time*]

time   Current time

DESCRIPTION TIME sets the current system time. Time is entered in the format

hours[:*minutes*[:*seconds*[:*hundredths*]]][A|P]

where A or P specifies whether the time is a.m. or p.m. The default is a.m. unless *hours* is greater than 12. If you do not specify a time, TIME displays the current time and prompts you to enter a new one.

EXAMPLES   To set the current time to 10:30:00 a.m., type

    TIME 10:30

or type **TIME** and enter **10:30** at the prompt. To set the time to 2:15 p.m., type

    TIME 2:15P

or

    TIME 14:15

NOTES   In version 3.3, the TIME command gained the ability to set the CMOS clock in a PC. In earlier versions, setting the permanent record of the time required a separate utility.

TREE

2.0
External

Display Directory Tree

SYNTAX   `TREE [d:][path] [/A] [/F]`

path   Name of the subdirectory to start from
/A   Use characters from the lower half of the IBM character set to draw lines
/F   Display file names as well as subdirectory names

DESCRIPTION   TREE graphically depicts the structure of the specified drive from the specified directory down, listing all the subdirectories it encounters. If you use the /F switch, it also displays the names of the files inside those subdirectories. Use /A when you direct the output from TREE to a printer that doesn't support the upper half of the IBM character set. TREE is discussed in Chapter 5.

EXAMPLES   To display the directory structure for the current drive, type

    TREE \

To display subdirectories and file names contained in \DOS and all its descendants, type

    TREE \DOS /F

NOTES   You can use an output redirection operator to direct the output from TREE to a printer. To send it to LPT1, type

    TREE \ > LPT1

If the line-drawn characters connecting subdirectory names on the screen aren't reproduced properly on your printer, type

    TREE \ /A > LPT1

instead.

TYPE

Type Text File

SYNTAX TYPE [*d:*][*path*]*filename*

filename Name of the file to display

DESCRIPTION The TYPE command lists the contents of a file to the screen. It is designed to be used with text files, and it stops at the first occurrence of an ASCII Ctrl-Z character. TYPE does not accept wildcards in *filename*. You can pause long listings as they scroll by pressing Ctrl-S, and continue scrolling by pressing another key. TYPE is discussed in Chapter 5.

EXAMPLE To list the contents of EXPENSES.TXT to the screen, type

    TYPE EXPENSES.TXT

NOTES If the listing is more than one screen long, you can display it one page at a time by piping output from TYPE to the MORE command, as in

    TYPE EXPENSES.TXT | MORE

MORE is an external DOS command, so it must be in the current directory or in the path.

UNDELETE

Undelete File

SYNTAX   `UNDELETE [[d:][path]filename] [/LIST|/ALL] [/DOS|/DT]`

filename	Name of the file or files to undelete
/LIST	List the files that may be recovered
/ALL	Recover files without prompting for the first letter of each file name
/DOS	Ignore the delete-tracking file
/DT	Use the delete-tracking file

DESCRIPTION UNDELETE recovers files deleted with the DEL or ERASE commands. For added protection against deletions, you can use the MIRROR command to create a delete-tracking file. If UNDELETE finds a delete-tracking file when restoring files, it uses it; if there is no delete-tracking file, then it restores files using information left behind in the disk's FAT and directory entries. If you use the /ALL switch, DOS supplies a # character as the first letter in the file name. If a file of that name already exists, UNDELETE tries other characters until it finds one that works. MIRROR and UNDELETE are discussed at length in Chapter 4.

EXAMPLES To recover a file named BUDGET.DOC that was just deleted, type

```
UNDELETE BUDGET.DOC
```

To get a list of all files in the current directory that can be restored using the delete-tracking file (if it exists), type

```
UNDELETE /LIST /DT
```

To get a list of all the files in the current directory that can be restored *without* the delete-tracking file, type

```
UNDELETE /LIST /DOS
```

To recover everything than can be recovered in the current directory as quickly as possible, type

```
UNDELETE *.* /ALL
```

NOTES The sooner you restore a file after it is deleted, the greater the chance that it can be recovered. Delete tracking enables UNDELETE to recover some files that it couldn't recover otherwise, but it also adds an additional TSR to your system and slows file deletions down.

UNFORMAT

Unformat Disk

SYNTAX To restore hard-disk partition tables:

    UNFORMAT /PARTN [/L]

To unformat a hard disk or floppy:

    UNFORMAT d: [/U] [/L] [/TEST] [/P]

To verify that a disk contains a mirror file:

    UNFORMAT d: /J

/PARTN	Save a copy of a hard disk's partition tables
/L	Without the /PARTN switch: List every file and subdirectory found by UNFORMAT and ignore a mirror file if one exists. With the /PARTN switch: Display partition information for the specified drive.
/U	Unformat a disk without using the mirror file
/TEST	Perform a test unformat without actually restoring any data
/P	Send output messages to LPT1
/J	Verify that a mirror file exists and validate it

DESCRIPTION The UNFORMAT command has two distinct uses. The first is to restore a hard disk's partition tables if they become corrupted. Partition tables are saved to a floppy with the MIRROR command. The second use for UNFORMAT is to unformat a formatted disk. UNFORMAT searches the disk for a mirror file (a file created by the FORMAT or MIRROR command that contains a copy of the disk's FAT and root directory) and, if it finds it, uses it to perform the unformat. If there is no mirror file, or if UNFORMAT was started with a /U or /L switch, UNFORMAT attempts to unformat the disk using information left behind after the format. This is less reliable and much more time-consuming than an unformat performed with the aid of a mirror file. The MIRROR and UNFORMAT commands are discussed in Chapter 4.

EXAMPLES To list partition information for your hard disk, type

    UNFORMAT /PARTN /L

To restore the partition tables from a backup created earlier, type

    UNFORMAT /PARTN

To unformat a formatted disk in drive A, type

    UNFORMAT A:

NOTES When used with a disk that was just formatted with the DOS 5.0 FORMAT command, UNFORMAT will recover 100 percent of the data in its original form. If the disk was formatted with a formatting utility that does not create a mirror file, UNFORMAT will probably recover only part of the data.

VER

Display DOS Version

SYNTAX   VER

DESCRIPTION VER displays the version number of the version of DOS that is running. For DOS 5.0, it displays the message

MS-DOS Version 5.00

EXAMPLE   To determine what version of DOS is currently running, type

VER

NOTES   Some programs and utilities check the version of DOS they're running under and refuse to run under DOS 5.0. You can use the SETVER command to alter the version number that DOS reports to individual programs.

VERIFY

Enable or Disable Write Verification

SYNTAX

```
VERIFY [ON|OFF]
```

ON   Enable write verification
OFF   Disable write verification

DESCRIPTION With write verification enabled, DOS verifies that what it writes to disk is correct by reading it back and comparing it to the image of the data still in memory. This feature does *not*, as is often supposed, perform a disk-to-disk comparison when you copy a file. If you don't specify either ON or OFF, DOS displays the current status of write verification.

EXAMPLES To turn write verification on, type

```
VERIFY ON
```

To disable it, type

```
VERIFY OFF
```

To determine whether write verification is currently enabled or disabled, type

```
VERIFY
```

NOTES You can use the /V switches on the COPY, DISKCOPY, and XCOPY commands to selectively enable write-verification. These switches do not affect the global write-verification state, but they do work even if VERIFY is currently Off.

VOL

Display Volume Information

SYNTAX   VOL [*d:*]

DESCRIPTION   VOL displays the volume label and serial number of the specified drive. If you omit the drive specifier, VOL defaults to the current drive.

EXAMPLE   To determine the volume label and serial number of drive C, type

VOL C:

NOTES   Volume labels can be changed with the LABEL command and may be specified when a disk is formatted. Serial numbers are applied during the formatting process.

XCOPY

Copy File or Files

SYNTAX XCOPY *source* [*destination*] [/A] [D:*date*] [/E] [/M] [/P] [/S]
[/V] [/W]

source	Name of the file or files to copy
destination	Destination to copy the files to
/A	Copy the files whose archive bits are set and leave the archive bits intact
/D:*date*	Copy files modified on or after the specified date
/E	Copy empty subdirectories, too
/M	Copy the files whose archive bits are set and clear the archive bits
/P	Prompt for confirmation before creating a file at the destination
/S	Copy the contents of the specified directory and its descendant directories
/V	Verify that the data was copied correctly
/W	Pause for a keypress before beginning the copy operation

DESCRIPTION The XCOPY command is similar to COPY except that it uses all available memory rather than a single 64k segment, and it can copy several files at once without requiring you to swap disks when copying from floppy to floppy. It also offers a wider selection of options and, with the /S switch, will even perform a recursive copy. XCOPY will not copy hidden or system files. See Chapters 4 and 5 for details.

EXAMPLES To copy all the files from the current directory to C:\BACKUP, type

    XCOPY *.* C:\BACKUP

To copy all the files with the extension .BAK from drive A to the current directory, type

    XCOPY A:*.BAK

To copy everything from drive A to drive B, including subdirectories and their contents, type

    XCOPY A: B: /S /E

NOTES The XCOPY command is COPY's more powerful cousin. Use it if the file you are copying is longer than 64k or if you're copying two or more files. You can also use XCOPY to copy groups of files too large to fit onto a single floppy and to back up entire branches of a hard-disk directory tree.

APPENDIX B

DEVICE DRIVER REFERENCE

Appendix B documents the device drivers that come with DOS 5.0. The driver references are arranged in alphabetical order, with the name of the driver in boldface type at the top. You'll find this information for each driver:

- The syntax for the driver

- A description of the driver, including cross-references to chapters in the book where the driver and issues related to it are discussed

- Examples illustrating how the driver is used

- Notes containing additional information about the driver

ANSI.SYS

Install Extended Screen and Keyboard Control Driver

`DEVICE[HIGH]=[d:][path]ANSI.SYS [/X] [/K]`

/X   Remap extended keys separately on enhanced keyboards

/K   Ignore extended keys on enhanced keyboards (treat an enhanced keyboard like a conventional keyboard)

DESCRIPTION ANSI.SYS is DOS's extended screen and keyboard control device driver, which enables programs to control the screen and keyboard by transmitting commands to the standard output device. ANSI.SYS commands are preceded by an escape character (ASCII 27). The following table lists the escape sequences that ANSI.SYS supports. The escape character is represented by ESC. The ANSI.SYS driver is discussed in Chapter 6.

Escape Code	Description
ESC[xx;yyH	Move the cursor to row xx, column yy
ESC[xx;yyf	Move the cursor to row xx, column yy
ESC[xxA	Move the cursor up xx rows
ESC[xxB	Move the cursor down xx rows
ESC[xxC	Move the cursor right xx columns
ESC[xxD	Move the cursor left xx columns
ESC[s	Save the current cursor position
ESC[u	Restore the cursor position saved with ESC[s
ESC[2J	Clear the screen and move the cursor to row 0, column 0
ESC[K	Erase everything from the cursor to the end of the line
ESC[xx;...;xxm	Set screen attributes. Valid values for xx are:

0	All attributes off
1	Bold on
4	Underscore on (monochrome adapters only)
5	Blink on
7	Reverse video on
8	Concealed on
30	Set foreground color to black
31	Set foreground color to red
32	Set foreground color to green
33	Set foreground color to yellow
34	Set foreground color to blue
35	Set foreground color to magenta
36	Set foreground color to cyan
37	Set foreground color to white
40	Set background color to black
41	Set background color to red

42	Set background color to green
43	Set background color to yellow
44	Set background color to blue
45	Set background color to magenta
46	Set background color to cyan
47	Set background color to white

ESC[*xx*h Set display mode. Valid values for *xx* are:

0	40 by 25 monochrome (text)
1	40 by 25 color (text)
2	80 by 25 monochrome (text)
3	80 by 25 color (text)
4	320 by 200 4-color (graphics)
5	320 by 200 2-color (graphics)
6	640 by 200 2-color (graphics)
13	320 by 200 16-color (graphics)
14	640 by 200 16-color (graphics)
15	640 by 350 2-color (graphics)
16	640 by 350 16-color (graphics)
17	640 by 480 2-color (graphics)
18	640 by 480 16-color (graphics)
19	320 by 200 256-color (graphics)

ESC[7h   Enable line wrap
ESC[7l   Disable line wrap

ESC[*code*;*string*;...*string*p   Assign a string to a key. *Code* is one of the numeric values listed in Table 6.5. *String* is another value from Table 6.5, a string in quotation marks, or a combination of the two.

If ANSI.SYS is installed with a /K switch, it maps duplicate keys on 101- and 102-key keyboards separately. For example, if you redefine the Home key with an ANSI.SYS escape sequence, only the Home key on the numeric keypad will be affected. The Home key to the left of the keypad will still act as Home. Use the /K switch if ANSI.SYS doesn't respond correctly to extended keys—F11, F12, and the dedicated Arrow keys, for example. If you use the /K switch, place the statement

```
SWITCHES=/K
```

in your CONFIG.SYS file also.

EXAMPLES To load ANSI.SYS into conventional memory from C:\DOS:

```
DEVICE=C:\DOS\ANSI.SYS
```

To load ANSI.SYS in upper memory and treat duplicate keys on enhanced keyboards separately:

```
DEVICEHIGH=C:\DOS\ANSI.SYS /X
```

To transmit the escape sequence to set the screen colors to bright white on blue using the PROMPT command:

```
PROMPT $e[1;37;44m
```

To program function key F1 to clear the screen by executing a CLS command:

```
PROMPT $e[0;59;"CLS$_"p
```

See Chapter 6 for additional examples of commands transmitted to ANSI.SYS.

NOTES The two most common uses for ANSI.SYS are to set the screen colors in DOS and to assign commands to function keys. Two of the programs in this book, COLOR and FKEYS, let you perform these actions through the ANSI.SYS driver using easy-to-remember keywords rather than cryptic escape codes. COLOR and FKEYS are discussed in Chapter 12.

DISPLAY.SYS

Enable Code Page Switching (Display)

`DEVICE[HIGH]=[d:][path]DISPLAY.SYS CON[:]=(type[,[hwcp][,n]])`

type	Type of video adapter. Valid values are:
	EGA EGA or VGA video adapter
	LCD IBM PC Convertible
hwcp	Hardware code page. Valid values are:
	437 United States
	850 Multilingual (Latin I)
	852 Slavic (Latin II)
	860 Portuguese
	863 Canadian-French
	865 Nordic
n	Number of code pages the video adapter can support in addition to *hwcp*

DISPLAY.SYS provides code page switching support for EGA and VGA video adapters and for the IBM PC Convertible. DISPLAY.SYS must be loaded before you can change display code pages with the CHCP or MODE SELECT commands. For EGA and VGA adapters, the hardware code page (*hwcp*) is 437, and the number of additional code pages (*n*) may be set to any number from 0 to 6. See Chapter 6 for a detailed discussion of DIS-PLAY.SYS and of the commands that are related to it.

To load DISPLAY.SYS for an EGA video adapter and reserve room for two additional code pages to be prepared later:

```
DEVICE=C:\DOS\DISPLAY.SYS CON:=(EGA,437,2)
```

To load DISPLAY.SYS in upper memory and set it up to support a VGA video adapter with space for four additional code pages:

```
DEVICEHIGH=C:\DOS\DISPLAY.SYS CON:=(EGA,437,4)
```

The *n* parameter in the statement that loads DISPLAY.SYS determines how many code pages you can "prepare" for the video adapter with the MODE PREPARE command.

DRIVER.SYS

Create Logical Drive

SYNTAX

```
DEVICE[HIGH]=[d:][path]DRIVER.SYS /D:drive [/F:form]
    [/H:heads] [/S:sectors] [/T:tracks] [/C]
```

/D:*drive*	Drive number (0=A, 1=B, 2=Third floppy drive, and so on)
/F:*form*	Form factor for the drive. Valid values are:

        0   160k/180k/320k/360k drive
        1   1.2Mb drive
        2   720k drive
        7   1.44Mb drive
        9   2.88Mb drive

/H:*heads*	Number of heads
/S:*sectors*	Number of sectors per track
/T:*tracks*	Number of tracks
/C	Drive features change-line support

DESCRIPTION DRIVER.SYS creates a new logical drive corresponding to one of the floppy drives in the system. The /D switch tells DRIVER.SYS the physical number of the drive; the other switches are used to characterize the drive and indicate whether it features change-line support. A *change line* is a mechanism that enables DOS to determine when the drive door has been opened. Most 720k, 1.2Mb, 1.44Mb, and 2.88Mb drives have them, but 360k drives do not. The new drive assumes the next available drive letter in the system. DRIVER.SYS is discussed in Chapter 4, in the section entitled "Adding a New Floppy Drive to Your System."

EXAMPLES To load DRIVER.SYS for a 2.88Mb drive A on a system whose BIOS does not support 2.88Mb media:

```
DEVICE=C:\DOS\DRIVER.SYS /D:0 /F:9
```

To create a second drive letter for a 360k drive B and load DRIVER.SYS in upper memory:

```
DEVICEHIGH=C:\DOS\DRIVER.SYS /D:1 /F:0
```

NOTES DRIVER.SYS has two primary uses. If you add a floppy drive to your system that is not supported by the BIOS, your PC will need DRIVER.SYS or a third-party device driver to support it. You can also use DRIVER.SYS to assign a second drive letter to a drive so that files can be copied from one disk to another in the same drive.

EGA.SYS

Load EGA Task Swapper Support

SYNTAX   `DEVICE[HIGH]=[d:][path]EGA.SYS`

DESCRIPTION DOS uses EGA.SYS to save and restore the screen as you switch between active programs in the DOS Shell when task switching is enabled. EGA.SYS is not required if you have a VGA adapter.

EXAMPLES To load EGA.SYS into conventional memory:

`DEVICE=C:\DOS\EGA.SYS`

To load EGA.SYS into upper memory on properly equipped 386 and 486 systems:

`DEVICEHIGH=C:\DOS\EGA.SYS`

NOTES EGA.SYS is only required if your system has an EGA video adapter *and* you plan to run the DOS Shell with the task swapper enabled.

EMM386.EXE

Load 386 Memory Manager

DEVICE=[*d:*][*path*]EMM386.EXE [NOEMS] [RAM] [*memory*] [L=*minXMS*]
        [ON|OFF|AUTO] [I=*address-address*] [X=*address-address*]
        [W=ON|OFF] [M*x*] [FRAME=*address*] [/P*address*] [P*n*=*address*]
        [B=*address*] [A=*altregs*] [H=*handles*] [D=*nnn*] [/Y=*path*]

NOEMS   Provide upper memory services but not expanded memory services
RAM   Provide upper memory services *and* expanded memory services
memory   Number of kilobytes of memory to allocate to EMM386.EXE in addition
            to the memory used to create upper memory blocks (default=256,
            range=16 to 32768)
minXMS   Minimum amount of extended memory to be left over after
            EMM386.EXE is installed (default=0)
ON   Set EMM386.EXE to ON (default)
OFF   Set EMM386.EXE to OFF
AUTO   Set EMM386.EXE to AUTO mode
W=ON   Enable Weitek coprocessor support
W=OFF   Disable Weitek coprocessor support (default)
I=*address-address*   Include the range of upper memory between segments *address*
                        and *address*. Valid values for *address* are A000 to FFFF. Values
                        are rounded down to the nearest 100 boundary.
X=*address-address*   Exclude the range of upper memory between segments
                        address and *address*. Valid values for *address* are A000 to
                        FFFF. Values are rounded down to the nearest 100 boundary.
                        X takes precedence over I if the two ranges overlap.
M*x*   Specifies the segment address where the EMS page frame should be
            located. Valid values for *x* are:

1	C000H	8	DC00H
2	C400H	9	E000H
3	C800H	10	8000H
4	CC00H	11	8400H
5	D000H	12	8800H
6	D400H	13	8C00H
7	D800H	14	9000H

FRAME=*address*   Specifies the segment address where the EMS page frame
                    should be located. Valid values for *address* range from 8000
                    through 9000 and C000 through E000, in increments of 400.
/P*address*   Specifies the segment address where the EMS page frame should be
            located. Valid vales for *address* range from 8000 through 9000 and C000
            through E000, in increments of 400.

P*n=address*	Map EMS page *n* to the specified segment address. Valid values for *n* are 0 to 255. Valid values for *address* are 8000 through 9C00 and C000 through EC00, in increments of 400. Pages 0 through 3 must be contiguous in order to maintain compatibility with the LIM 3.2 expanded memory specification.
B=*address*	Specifies the lowest segment address where the EMS page frame may be located. The default is 4000. Valid values are 1000 through 4000.
A=*altregs*	Number of fast alternate registers to allocate space for (default=7, range=0 to 254). Each additional register set requires about 200 bytes of memory.
H=*handles*	Number of EMS handles that may be used (default=64, range=2 to 255)
D=*nnn*	Amount of memory (in kilobytes) to reserve for buffered Direct Memory Access (DMA) (default=16, range=16 to 256)
/Y=*path*	Path to where EMM386.EXE is stored (may be required if Windows is run in 386 enhanced mode)

DESCRIPTION EMM386.EXE is the memory manager that DOS uses to create upper memory blocks (UMBs) for TSRs and device drivers to be loaded into and to supply LIM 4.0 expanded memory to programs that are EMS-aware. EMM386.EXE, its uses, and its installation options are discussed in detail in Chapter 3.

EXAMPLES To load EMM386.EXE so that TSRs and device drivers can be loaded in upper memory, but without converting any extended memory to expanded memory:

```
DEVICE=C:\DOS\EMM386.EXE NOEMS
```

To load EMM386.EXE and have it supply both upper and expanded memory services and to exclude the range of memory from segment D000H to segment D200H from being used:

```
DEVICE=C:\DOS\EMM386.EXE RAM X=D000-D200
```

To load EMM.386.EXE and have it leave 1Mb of extended memory for other uses *and* to specify that EMM386.EXE is stored in the\DOS directory of drive C so that Windows can run in 386 enhanced mode:

```
DEVICE=C:\DOS\EMM386.EXE NOEMS L=1024 /Y=(:\DOS\EMM386.EXE
```

NOTES EMM386.EXE contains a dizzying array of command-line parameters that is intimidating to new users. Most of the time, you won't need any of them other than RAM and NOEMS. RAM tells EMM386.EXE to make LIM 4.0 expanded memory available to application programs and to make UMBs available to LOADHIGH and DEVICE-HIGH. NOEMS has it provide UMB support but no EMS support. If you don't specify either installation option, EMM386.EXE provides EMS support but no UMB support.

HIMEM.SYS

Load High Memory Driver

```
DEVICE=[d:][path]HIMEM.SYS [/HMAMIN=m] [/NUMHANDLES=n]
    [/INT15=memory] [/MACHINE:code] [/A20CONTROL:ON|OFF]
    [/SHADOWRAM:ON|OFF] [/CPUCLOCK:ON|OFF]
```

/HMAMIN=m
Minimum amount of memory (in kilobytes) a program must request before it can claim the HMA for itself (default=0, range=0 to 63)

/NUMHANDLES=n
Number of extended memory block (EMB) handles that HIMEM.SYS should support (default=32, range=1 to 128)

/INT15=memory
Amount of memory (in kilobytes) that HIMEM.SYS should make available using the old interrupt 15H interface for claiming extended memory (default=0, range=64 to 65535)

/MACHINE:code
Specifies which A20 handler should be used. *Code* can be a number or a text string. Valid values are:

AT	1	IBM PC/AT
PS2	2	IBM PS/2
PT1CASCADE	3	Phoenix Cascade BIOS
HPVECTRA	4	HP Vectra (A and A+)
ATT6300PLUS	5	AT&T 6300 Plus
ACER1100	6	Acer 1100
TOSHIBA	7	Toshiba 1200XE, 1600, or 5100
WYSE	8	Wyse 12.5 MHz 286
TULIP	9	Tulip SX
ZENITH	10	Zenith ZBIOS
AT1	11	IBM PC/AT
AT2	12	IBM PC/AT (alternative delay)
CSS	12	CSS Labs
AT3	13	IBM PC/AT (alternative delay)
PHILIPS	13	Philips
FASTHP	14	HP Vectra

/A20CONTROL
Specifies what action HIMEM.SYS should take if the A20 line is active when HIMEM.SYS is loaded. OFF means takes control only if A20 is initially disabled; ON means takes control whether it is enabled or disabled. The default is OFF.

/SHADOWRAM
Specifies whether HIMEM.SYS should disable shadow RAM at start-up and add that RAM to the free memory pool. The default is OFF on PCs that contain less than 2Mb of memory, ON on those that contain more. The OFF option does not work on all computers.

/CPUCLOCK
Specifies whether HIMEM.SYS has the freedom to change CPU clock speeds. The default is OFF. If your CPU's clock speed changes when HIMEM.SYS is installed, try setting CPUCLOCK to ON.

DESCRIPTION HIMEM.SYS is the driver that DOS uses to access upper and extended memory in a manner that is compatible with other XMS-aware (Extended Memory Specification) programs. HIMEM.SYS must be installed for you to load DOS in the HMA and to load programs and device drivers in upper memory. Most of the time, you won't need to use any of the switches that HIMEM.SYS supports. However, if you own one of the PCs in the list that appears under /MACHINE, you may have to use the /MACHINE switch to tell HIMEM.SYS which A20 handler (the routine HIMEM.SYS uses to toggle the A20 line on and off to gain access to the HMA) to use. Additional /MACHINE codes are listed in the README.TXT file in your DOS directory. HIMEM.SYS is discussed in Chapter 3.

EXAMPLES To load HIMEM.SYS on most PCs:

```
DEVICE=C:\DOS\HIMEM.SYS
```

To load HIMEM.SYS on an HP Vectra:

```
DEVICE=C:\DOS\HIMEM.SYS /MACHINE:FASTHP
```

or

```
DEVICE=C:\DOS\HIMEM.SYS /MACHINE:14
```

NOTES HIMEM.SYS cannot be loaded in upper memory, because nothing can be loaded there until after HIMEM.SYS and EMM386.EXE are loaded.

PRINTER.SYS

Enable Code Page Switching (Printer)

SYNTAX `DEVICE[HIGH]=[d:][path]PRINTER.SYS LPTm[:]=(type[,[hwcp][,n]])`

m LPT port number (1, 2, or 3)

type   Type of printer. Valid values are:

    4201   IBM Proprinter II and III Model 4201
            IBM Proprinter II and III XL Model 4202

    4208   IBM Proprinter X24E Model 4207
            IBM Proprinter XL24E Model 4208

    5202   IBM Quietwriter III Model 5202

hwcp   Hardware code page. Valid values are:

    437   United States
    850   Multilingual (Latin I)
    852   Slavic (Latin II)
    860   Portuguese
    863   Canadian-French
    865   Nordic

n Number of code pages the printer can support in addition to *hwcp*

DESCRIPTION PRINTER.SYS provides code page switching support for the IBM printers listed above. PRINTER.SYS must be loaded before you can change printer code pages with the CHCP or MODE SELECT commands. See Chapter 6 for further discussion of PRINTER.SYS and of the commands that are related to it.

EXAMPLES To load PRINTER.SYS for an IBM Proprinter II Model 4201 attached to LPT1, specify 850 as the hardware code page, and reserve space for two additional code pages to be prepared later on:

```
DEVICE=C:\DOS\PRINTER.SYS LPT1:=(4201,850,2)
```

NOTES PRINTER.SYS is of no use unless you own one of the IBM printers listed above. However, you can still perform switch code page on the display device with DISPLAY.SYS.

RAMDRIVE.SYS

Create RAM Disk

SYNTAX

```
DEVICE[HIGH]=[d:][path]RAMDRIVE.SYS [DiskSize] [SectorSize]
    [NumEntries] [/A|/E]
```

DiskSize	Size of the RAM Disk in kilobytes (default=64, range=16 to 4096)
SectorSize	Sector size in bytes (default=512). Valid values are 128, 256, and 512.
NumEntries	Maximum number of entries in the RAM disk's root directory (default=64, range=2 to 1024)
/A	Allocate space for the RAM disk in expanded memory
/E	Allocate space for the RAM disk in extended memory

DESCRIPTION RAMDRIVE.SYS (also known as RAMDrive) creates a RAM disk that performs just like a real drive, only much faster. You set the size of the disk with *DiskSize*. If you don't include either an /A switch or an /E switch, RAMDrive creates the disk in conventional memory. A RAM disk assumes the lowest drive letter available at the time it is created. If your hard disk has C and D partitions and RAMDRIVE.SYS is the first block device driver loaded, the RAM disk will become drive E. You can create several RAM disks by loading RAMDrive more than once. RAMDRIVE.SYS is discussed in Chapter 2.

EXAMPLES To create a 2Mb RAM disk in extended memory:

```
DEVICE=C:\DOS\RAMDRIVE.SYS 2048 /E
```

To load RAMDrive in upper memory, create a 1Mb RAM disk in expanded memory, and decrease the maximum number of files and subdirectories that can be placed in the root directory to 32:

```
DEVICEHIGH=C:\DOS\RAMDRIVE.SYS 1024 512 32 /A
```

NOTES A RAM disk is a great tool for speeding up applications that repeatedly access certain files (for example, temporary files or overlay files) on disk. If you store data files on a RAM disk, you'll need to copy them to a physical disk before turning your PC off. When the power goes away, the files stored on a RAM disk also go away.

SETVER.EXE

Load Version Table

SYNTAX   `DEVICE[HIGH]=[d:][path]SETVER.EXE`

DESCRIPTION   SETVER.EXE loads the DOS version table into memory, where DOS stores the version numbers that it reports to application programs. You can modify the version table with the SETVER command. Use SETVER when you need to use an application program that will only run under a particular version of DOS.

EXAMPLES   To load the version table into memory:

`DEVICE=C:\DOS\SETVER.EXE`

To add an entry to the version table and make WP.EXE "think" it's running under DOS 3.3, type

`SETVER WP.EXE 3.3Ø`

on the command line.

NOTES   The DOS 5.0 SETUP program places SETVER.EXE in the CONFIG.SYS file by default. If you don't run any of the applications in the list (you can list all the entries in the version table by typing **SETVER** on the command line), you can save a few hundred bytes of memory by removing the statement that loads it.

SMARTDRV.SYS

Create Disk Cache

SYNTAX　　`DEVICE[HIGH]=[d:][path]SMARTDRV.SYS [MaxSize] [MinSize] [/A]`

MaxSize　Size of the disk cache, in kilobytes (default=256, range=128 to 8192)
MinSize　Minimum size for the cache, in kilobytes (default=0)
/A　　　　Create cache in expanded memory

DESCRIPTION　SMARTDRV.SYS (also known as SMARTDrive) enhances the operation of your hard disk by setting up and maintaining a high-speed disk cache to buffer data going to and from the disk. If you do not use the /A switch, the cache goes in extended memory; if you do use the /A switch, the cache goes in expanded memory. There are no options for placing it in conventional memory. Unlike most disk caches, SMARTDrive's size isn't fixed. If it's run with Windows and Windows needs more memory, SMARTDrive will shrink itself to *MinSize* and loan the difference to Windows. If you don't specify a *MinSize*, SMARTDrive will loan all the memory it owns to Windows if needed. If you want the cache size to stay fixed, set *MinSize* equal to *MaxSize*. SMARTDRV.SYS is discussed in Chapter 2.

EXAMPLES　To establish a 1Mb disk cache in extended memory and ensure that the cache will never shrink below 512k:

```
DEVICE=C:\DOS\SMARTDRV.SYS 1024 512
```

To load SMARTDrive into upper memory and establish a 512k cache in expanded memory that is fixed in size:

```
DEVICEHIGH=C:\DOS\SMARTDRV.SYS 512 512 /A
```

NOTES　SMARTDrive can greatly enhance the performance of your hard disk. It will also prolong its life by cutting down on the number of disk accesses and reducing the physical wear and tear inflicted upon the drive. It's also one of the best ways to put extended or expanded memory to use under DOS. In general, the larger the cache size, the better SMARTDrive will perform and the faster your hard disk will operate. Don't use the /A switch to place the cache in expanded memory if that expanded memory was created with the EMM386.EXE driver; instead, locate the cache in extended memory.

APPENDIX C
SUPPLEMENTARY UTILITIES REFERENCE

Appendix C documents the utilites that come on the disks in the back of this book. The utility references are arranged in alphabetical order, with the name of the utility in boldface type in the upper-left corner. You find this information for each utility:

■ The syntax for the utility

■ A description of the utility, including cross-references to chapters in the book where the utility and issues related to it are discussed

■ Notes containing additional information about the utility

43

Display 43 Lines of Text

SYNTAX 43

DESCRIPTION 43 reprograms an EGA or VGA video adapter to display 43 lines of text in character mode. The effect is equivalent to typing

```
MODE CON: LINES=43
```

with ANSI.SYS installed. However, ANSI.SYS need not be installed for the command to work. The DEBUG script for creating 43.COM is shown in Chapter 6.

EXAMPLE To display 43 lines of text on an EGA or VGA, type

```
43
```

NOTES To get back to 25-line mode, type

```
MODE 80
```

or if ANSI.SYS is installed, type

```
MODE CON: Lines=25
```

50

Display 50 Lines of Text

SYNTAX   50

DESCRIPTION 50 reprograms a VGA video adapter to display 50 lines of text in character mode. The effect is equivalent to typing

```
MODE CON: LINES=50
```

with ANSI.SYS installed. However, ANSI.SYS need not be installed for the command to work. The DEBUG script for creating 50.COM is shown in Chapter 6.

EXAMPLE   To display 50 lines of text on a VGA, type

```
50
```

NOTES   To get back to 25-line mode, type

```
MODE 50
```

or if ANSI.SYS is installed, type

```
MODE CON: LINES=25
```

ANSIOUT

Transmit Command to ANSI.SYS

SYNTAX   ANSIOUT *text*

text   Characters to transmit to ANSI.SYS

DESCRIPTION   ANSIOUT transmits the text that follows it on the command line to the ANSI.SYS driver preceded by an escape character (ASCII 27). This provides a convenient mechanism for batch files to communicate with ANSI.SYS without having to go to extravagant lengths. The DEBUG script for ANSIOUT appears in Chapter 10.

EXAMPLE   To transmit the ANSI.SYS command to change the color that text is displayed in to intense white on a blue background, type

    ANSIOUT [1;37;44m

NOTES   ANSIOUT isn't as versatile a command for transmitting commands to ANSI.SYS as PROMPT is, but PROMPT can't be used to communicate with ANSI.SYS inside a batch file. If ANSI.SYS isn't installed when ANSIOUT is run, the output will be written to the screen instead. Batch files can use the CHKANSI utility (see Chapter 10) to determine whether ANSI.SYS is loaded prior to transmitting commands to it.

BAT2EXEC

Compile Batch File

SYNTAX   BAT2EXEC [*d:*][*path*]*filename*

filename   Name of the batch file to compile

DESCRIPTION   BAT2EXEC compiles a batch file into a stand-alone COM file. COM files produced by BAT2EXEC run several times faster than the equivalent BAT files, and the longer the batch file, the greater the difference in speed. If BAT2EXEC encounters an error while it compiles a program, it will notify you with an error message. In general, you should write and debug batch files in .BAT format, then compile them with BAT2EXEC once all the wrinkles are ironed out. The source code for BAT2EXEC is included on the disks in the back of the book.

EXAMPLE   To convert the batch file FBACKUP.BAT into a stand-alone executable called FBACK-UP.COM, type

    BAT2EXEC FBACKUP.BAT

NOTES   Programs, external commands, and other batch files referenced inside a compiled batch file must still be accessible on disk, even though the batch file itself has been compiled. For example, if the batch file calls CHKDSK, then CHKDSK.EXE must be somewhere where the compiled batch file can find it—in the current directory or in the PATH. CHKDSK.EXE does *not* become part of the COM file.

BATCHKEY

Get Keyboard Input

SYNTAX   BATCHKEY [*keylist*]

keylist   List of key codes that BATCHKEY will accept. *Keylist* values can be
entered in three forms: as literals, as ASCII codes, or as extended codes.
Examples are:

Literals	"Y"	Y key
ASCII codes	13	Enter key
Extended codes	(59)	F1 key

All three forms may be freely mixed in the key list. For a list of ASCII key codes and
extended key codes, see Tables 9.3, 9.4, and 9.5.

DESCRIPTION BATCHKEY is a utility that batch files may use to solicit keyboard input. If no key list is
supplied, BATCHKEY simply returns the ASCII code of the first key pressed. (Keys such
as F1 that produce 2-byte extended key codes return 0.) If a key list is supplied, BATCH-
KEY returns an exit code that identifies the key that was pressed by its position in the list.
For example, if the Esc key (ASCII code 27) is pressed in response to the command

```
BATCHKEY 13 27 32
```

BATCHKEY returns 2. If BATCHKEY returns 0, then the key that was pressed was not
one of the ones in the list. Note that literal values are not case-sensitive, so "Y" is the
same as "y." The source code for BATCHKEY is shown in Chapter 10.

EXAMPLES The following batch statements branch to the line labeled NO if the N key or the Esc key
is pressed, or fall through to the line labeled YES if the Y key or the Enter key is pressed:

```
:LOOP
BATCHKEY "Y" 13 "N" 27
IF ERRORLEVEL 3 GOTO NO
IF NOT ERRORLEVEL 1 GOTO LOOP
:YES
```

The following command returns 1 if A is pressed, 2 if B is pressed, 3 if C is pressed, 4 if D
is pressed, 5 if E is pressed, 6 if Enter is pressed, 7 if function key F1 is pressed, 8 if F2 is
pressed, or 9 if F3 is pressed:

```
BATCHKEY "ABCDE" 13 (59) (60) (61)
```

NOTES The only limit on the number of keys you can enter following a BATCHKEY command
is the 127-character limit DOS places on commands.

BCOPY

Background File Copy

SYNTAX   BCOPY [*source* [*destination*]] [/X] [/U]

source	Name of the file or files to copy
destination	Drive and directory to copy them to
/X	Install BCOPY's data buffer in expanded memory rather than conventional memory
/U	Uninstall the program

DESCRIPTION   BCOPY works just like DOS's COPY command, but it copies files in the background while you continue to work in the foreground. As soon as you press the Enter key, the command prompt is redisplayed, ready for you to type another command. Meanwhile, BCOPY goes to work in the background, copying the file or files you specified. If the operation is a lengthy one, BCOPY can save you a lot of time. BCOPY claims about 4k of memory for itself to use as a buffer as it copies files. If you have expanded memory, you can tell BCOPY to establish this buffer in expanded memory with the /X switch. You can also uninstall BCOPY, which goes into memory as a TSR, by running it with a /U switch. The source code for BCOPY is included on the disks in the back of the book.

EXAMPLES   To copy all the files in the current directory to drive A, type

```
BCOPY *.* A:
```

To copy all the .COM files in the \DOS directory of the current drive to the \DOS directory of a RAM disk with the drive letter E, type

```
BCOPY \DOS\*.COM E:\DOS
```

NOTES   By installing itself as a TSR and working in the background while you do other work in the foreground, BCOPY makes DOS appear to be multitasking. BCOPY is a great tool for copying files to a RAM disk in your AUTOEXEC.BAT file. Your PC will boot up much quicker, because it no longer has to wait until the files are copied to present the command prompt. You can establish BCOPY's data buffer in extended memory on a 386 or 486 by using DOS's EMM386.EXE driver to create the expanded memory, or on a 286 by using EMS40.SYS (one of the utilities included with this book) to create it.

CDX

Extended Change Directory

SYNTAX   `CDX [/B] [/+] [/F filename] [drivelist]p1 p2 ... pn`

/B	Stop at the first directory that matches the search criterion
/+	Include drives A and B in the search when * or – (minus sign) is included in the *drivelist* parameter
/F *filename*	Search for a directory that contains a file of the specified name
drivelist	List of drives to search
pn	Directory names or partial directory names

DESCRIPTION   CDX is an extended form of the CD command that does three things CD doesn't: It lets you specify partial path names, change to a directory by naming a file that's stored inside it, and change drives as well as directories. It also lets you search more than one drive for directories to switch to. When you enter the command

```
CDX W D LET
```

CDX prompts you with the name of every directory on the current drive whose path name components begin with W, D, and LET (for example, \WP\DOC\LETTERS). If you include a /B switch, CDX will change to the first directory it finds that meets these qualifications. You can include more than one drive name in the list of drives for CDX to search, or have all drives except drives A and B searched by specifying * for *drivelist*. The command

```
CDX CDE:WIN
```

searches drives C, D, and E for directories beginning with the letters WIN, while the command

```
CDX *:WIN
```

searches all drives from C on up. You can tell CDX to include drives A and B also by including the /+ switch. The command

```
CDX /+ *:WIN
```

searches every drive for the specified directory. A – (minus sign) preceding a list of drive identifiers has CDX search all drives *except* the ones named. The command

```
CDX -EF:WIN
```

searches everything but A, B, E, and F for a directory whose name begins with WIN. Finally, the command

```
CDX /F BUDGET.DOC
```

prompts you with the name of every directory on the current drive that contains a file named BUDGET.DOC. Answer yes to a prompt, and CDX will drop you into that directory. CDX is discussed in Chapter 11, and the source code (written in C) is included on the disks in the back of the book.

EXAMPLES Suppose drive C is the current drive. To change to the \WINWORD\DOC directory on drive D, type

```
CDX D:W D
```

or, if \WINWORD\DOC is the only directory that meets these criteria,

```
CDX /B D:W D
```

To list all the directories on drives C and D that contain a file with the extension .DOC, type

```
CDX /F *.DOC CD:
```

NOTES The number of *p* parameters you enter after a CDX command doesn't have to match the number of directories in the path to a subdirectory. For example, the command

```
CDX W D
```

will prompt with the directory name C:\WORDPROC\WP\DOC as well as with C:\WINWORD\DOC.

CHKANSI

Check ANSI.SYS

SYNTAX   CHKANSI

DESCRIPTION CHKANSI returns an exit code that batch files can test with the IF ERRORLEVEL command to determine whether ANSI.SYS is installed. If CHKANSI returns 0, then ANSI.SYS is loaded. If it returns 1, then ANSI.SYS is not loaded. CHKANSI only works reliably in DOS versions 4.0 and later. The DEBUG script for creating CHKANSI is shown in Chapter 10.

EXAMPLES   The following batch statements determine whether ANSI.SYS is installed and prints a message saying it is or isn't:

```
CHKANSI
IF ERRORLEVEL 1 GOTO ANSINO
ECHO ANSI.SYS is installed
GOTO END
:ANSINO
ECHO ANSI.SYS is not installed
:END
```

NOTES   In DOS 4.0 and subsequent versions, ANSI.SYS hooks into the DOS Multiplex Interrupt (interrupt 2FH) and assumes the ID code 1AH. CHKANSI checks for ANSI.SYS by calling interrupt 2FH with AH set to 1AH (the code for ANSI.SYS) and AL set to 00H. If ANSI.SYS is installed, AL returns set to FFH; if it is not installed, AL returns still set to 00H. CHKANSI adds 1 to the value returned in AL and returns the result to ERRORLEVEL.

CLEAR

Clear Screen

SYNTAX   CLEAR

DESCRIPTION   CLEAR clears the screen to a predetermined color. CLEAR behaves just like CLS except that it supports colors other than white-on-black. With DOSKEY, you can substitute CLEAR for CLS. If CLEAR is stored in the \DOS5UTIL directory of drive C, add the command

    DOSKEY CLS=C:\DOS5UTIL\CLEAR

to your AUTOEXEC.BAT file. Then, when you type CLS, DOS will run CLEAR instead. Specifying the exact location where CLEAR is stored rather than relying on the PATH lets DOS find it and execute it faster. The DEBUG script for creating CLEAR is shown in Chapter 10.

EXAMPLE   To clear the screen, type

    CLEAR

NOTES   By default, CLEAR clears the screen so that text appears in bold white on a blue background. You can change the colors selected by patching CLEAR with DEBUG. To do so, formulate a hexadecimal value that represents the color choice. Call it *xx*. Then go to the directory where CLEAR.COM is stored and type:

    DEBUG CLEAR.COM
    E 010F xx
    W
    Q

Hexadecimal color codes are formulated by pairing a hex number from 0 to 7 representing the background color with a hex number from 0 to F representing the foreground color, in that order. A list of the colors that correspond to the hex digits appears in Table 6.2.

CLRSCR

Clear Screen

SYNTAX   `CLRSCR attr [row1 col1 row2 col2]`

attr	Hexadecimal code specifying the foreground and background color
row1	Row number of the upper-left corner of the region to clear
col1	Column number of the upper-left corner of the region to clear
row2	Row number of the lower-right corner of the region to clear
col2	Column number of the lower-right corner of the region to clear

DESCRIPTION CLRSCR clears all or part of the screen to the specified color. If you omit the *row* and *col* parameters, CLRSCR clears the entire screen. If you include *row* and *col* parameters, it only clears the region bounded by those coordinates. Row and column numbers are zero-based, so the coordinates for the upper-left corner of the screen are 0,0. The source code for CLRSCR is shown in Chapter 10.

EXAMPLES To clear the entire screen to white-on-blue, type

    CLRSCR 1F

To clear a window at the center of the screen to white-on-red, type

    CLRSCR 4F 10 20 14 59

NOTES CLRSCR provides batch files a means for clearing the screen to a specified color without having to rely on ANSI.SYS. It is also useful for clearing out specific areas of the screen before using the DRAWBOX command to create borders. Hexadecimal color codes are formulated by pairing a hex number from 0 to 7 representing the background color with a hex number from 0 to F representing the foreground color, in that order. A list of the colors that correspond to the hex digits appears in Table 6.2.

COLOR

Set Screen Colors

SYNTAX   COLOR *foreground background*

foreground   Foreground color identifier
background   Background color identifier

DESCRIPTION COLOR sets the screen colors that DOS will use to display text and that the screen will be cleared to when you use the CLS command. The valid foreground and background color identifiers are BLACK, BLUE, GREEN, CYAN, RED, MAGENTA, YELLOW, and WHITE. If you wish, you may substitute BROWN or ORANGE for YELLOW. For foreground colors, you can precede the color identifier with an underscore to select the bold version of that color. The source code for COLOR is shown in Chapter 12.

EXAMPLES To change the screen colors to green on black, type

    COLOR GREEN BLACK

To change the screen colors to intense white on blue, type

    COLOR _WHITE BLUE

NOTES COLOR only runs under DOS 4.0 or higher, and it requires that the ANSI.SYS driver be installed. If ANSI.SYS is not installed, COLOR will respond with an error message when you attempt to run it.

CPI

Set Printer Characters per Inch

SYNTAX   CPI *characters*

characters   Number of characters per inch (10, 12, or 16)

DESCRIPTION DOS's MODE command can be used to configure IBM and Epson dot-matrix printers to print 10 or 16 characters per inch, but it is ineffective on LaserJet printers. CPI configures a LaserJet to print 10, 12, or 16 lines per inch. Chapter 6 contains the DEBUG script for creating CPI.

EXAMPLE   To configure a LaserJet to print 16 characters per inch, type

    CPI 16

NOTES   By default, CPI reconfigures the printer attached to LPT1. If your printer is connected to LPT2 or LPT3, you can patch CPI to work with ports other than LPT1 (see Chapter 6).

CPUTYPE

Determine Processor Type

SYNTAX   CPUTYPE

DESCRIPTION CPUTYPE runs a series of tests to determine what type of processor (8086/8088, 286, 386, or 486) is installed in your PC. In addition to outputting a message identifying the CPU type, it returns an exit code that is equal to one of the following values:

0	8086 or 8088
1	286
2	386
3	486

The source code for CPUTYPE appears in Chapter 10.

EXAMPLE   To write a batch file that aborts itself if the CPU is anything less than a 386, use the lines

```
CPUTYPE
IF NOT ERRORLEVEL 2 GOTO ABORT
```

NOTES   A companion program, NDPTYPE, described in this appendix, identifies the type of math coprocessor installed in your PC.

DRAWBOX

Draw Box

   DRAWBOX *attr width height* [*style*]

attr	Hexadecimal code specifying the foreground and background color
width	Width of the box in columns
height	Height of the box in rows
style	Box style. Valid values are:

           1   Single-line box (default)
           2   Double-line box

DESCRIPTION   DRAWBOX draws a box of the specified width and height in the specified color and in the specified style using the current cursor position for the upper-left corner of the box. The width and height specified include the box borders, so the smallest box that can be drawn has a height and width of 2. DRAWBOX provides batch files a means for drawing bordered boxes on the screen. The cursor position can be set before calling DRAWBOX with the separate SETPOS utility. The source code for DRAWBOX is shown in Chapter 10.

EXAMPLES   To draw a single-line box 40 columns wide and 10 rows high in blue-on-white, type

```
DRAWBOX 71 40 10
```

To draw a white-on-blue double-line box at the center of an 80-column by 25-line screen, paint the interior of it blue, and write "PC Magazine" at the center of it, using the batch statements

```
CLRSCR 1F 10 20 14 59
SETPOS 10 20
DRAWBOX 1F 40 5 2
SETPOS 12 34
TEXTOUT 1F "PC Magazine"
```

NOTES   Hexadecimal color codes are formulated by pairing a hex number from 0 to 7 representing the background color with a hex number from 0 to F representing the foreground color, in that order. A list of the colors that correspond to the hex digits appears in Table 6.2.

ECHOCD

Echo Current Directory

SYNTAX   ECHOCD

DESCRIPTION   ECHOCD writes the string "CD" followed by a space to the standard output device. By redirecting the output to a file with the extension .BAT and appending the output from the CD command to the file, you can create a one-line batch file that returns to the current directory. The DEBUG script for creating ECHOCD appears in Chapter 10.

EXAMPLE   To create a batch file named RETURN.BAT that contains the command to return to the current directory, type

```
ECHOCD > RETURN.BAT
CD >> RETURN.BAT
```

NOTES   ECHOCD and ECHODRV together make it easy for a batch file that changes drives and directories to return to the drive and directory it started from. The following three batch statements set up the return by creating a file called RETURN.BAT in the root directory of drive C:

```
ECHODRV > C:\RETURN.BAT
ECHOCD >> C:\RETURN.BAT
CD >> C:\RETURN.BAT
```

Then, when the batch file is ready to restore the current drive and directory, it can do so with the statement

```
CALL C:\RETURN
```

ECHODRV

Echo Current Drive

SYNTAX   ECHODRV

DESCRIPTION ECHODRV writes the letter of the current drive, a colon, and a command terminator (a carriage return character followed by a line-feed character) to the standard output device. By redirecting the output to a file with the extension .BAT, you can create a one-line batch file that returns to the current drive. The DEBUG script for creating ECHODRV appears in Chapter 10.

EXAMPLE   To create a batch file named RETURN.BAT that contains the command to return to the current drive, type

```
ECHODRV > RETURN.BAT
```

NOTES   ECHODRV and ECHOCD together make it easy for a batch file that changes drives and directories to return to the drive and directory it started from. The following three batch statements set up the return by creating a file called RETURN.BAT in the root directory of the C drive:

```
ECHODRV > C:\RETURN.BAT
ECHOCD >> C:\RETURN.BAT
CD >> C:\RETURN.BAT
```

Then, when the batch file is ready to restore the current drive and directory, it can do so with the statement

```
CALL C:\RETURN
```

EMS40.SYS

Convert Extended Memory to Expanded Memory

SYNTAX   `DEVICE=[d:][path]EMS4Ø.SYS [memory]`

memory   Number of kilobytes of extended memory to convert to expanded memory (default=384)

DESCRIPTION   EMS40.SYS does for 286s what one component of EMM386.EXE does for 386s: It takes on the role of an expanded memory manager, converting all or a part of the extended memory in your system to LIM 4.0 expanded memory, which can be used by programs that are EMS-aware. EMS40.SYS is a device driver, so it is installed in your CONFIG-.SYS file with a DEVICE directive. If you omit the *memory* parameter, it makes 384k of expanded memory available to application programs. The maximum you can specify is 15360, which corresponds to 15Mb (the maximum amount of memory the 286 will support is 16Mb, and, of that, only 15Mb of it can be extended memory), or the amount of extended memory installed in your system, whichever is smaller. Installed, EMS40.SYS consumes about 69k of RAM. All but 5k of that is devoted to the EMS page frame, the 64k region of memory that EMS pages are swapped in and out of.

EXAMPLE   To install EMS40.SYS from the \DOS5UTIL directory of drive C and provide 1Mb of LIM 4.0 expanded memory to the system at large, enter the statement

`DEVICE=C:\DOS5UTIL\EMS4Ø.SYS 1Ø24`

in your CONFIG.SYS file.

NOTES   If you own a 286 with extended memory and run programs that will use expanded memory but not extended memory, EMS40.SYS will enable you to use extended memory in place of expanded memory. If you use HIMEM.SYS, it is important that you load EMS40.SYS before you load HIMEM.SYS.

ENCRYPT

Encrypt or Unencrypt File

ENCRYPT [*d:*][*path*]*filename* "*password*"

filename   Name of the file to encrypt
password   Password to encrypt it with, enclosed in quotation marks

DESCRIPTION   ENCRYPT password-encrypts a file so that it can't be viewed by anyone who doesn't have the password. You can unencrypt an encrypted file by running it through ENCRYPT again with the same password. Passwords can be any length, up to the 127-character limit the command line imposes. In general, the longer the password, the more difficult it is to break the cipher, so the more secure the file is. For an extra measure of security, you can run a file through ENCRYPT twice to double-encrypt it. Be sure you can remember the password, though—an encrypted file can't be restored to its original form without it. The source code for ENCRYPT is shown in Chapter 11.

EXAMPLES   To encrypt a file named BUDGET.DOC with the password "PC Magazine," type

    ENCRYPT BUDGET.DOC "PC Magazine"

To unencrypt the file, type

    ENCRYPT BUDGET.DOC "PC Magazine"

again.

NOTES   To encrypt a file, ENCRYPT uses an XOR algorithm called a Vernam cipher that is simple but effective. Each character in the file is XORed with a character in the password. What is remarkable about a Vernam cipher is that XORing the file with the same characters again undoes the changes made the first time, restoring the file to its original form.

FINDTEXT

Search for Text String

SYNTAX　　FINDTEXT [*d:*][*path*][*filename*] "*text*" [/S] [/C] [/I] [/A]
　　　　　　　　[/M] [/7]

filename	Name of the file or files to search
text	Text to search for
/S	Search files in the specified directory and its descendants
/C	Make the search case sensitive
/I	Run the program in full-screen interactive mode
/M	Run the program in monochrome mode (interactive mode only)
/A	Search hidden and system files
/7	Do 7-bit comparisons, ignoring the eighth bit of the characters searched

DESCRIPTION　　FINDTEXT searches all or part of a disk for files that contain a specified text string. If *filename* is omitted, all the files in the specified directory are searched. The /S switch performs a recursive search, telling FINDTEXT to search the specified directory and all its descendants. By default, searches are not sensitive to case. You can make them case sensitive (and speed up the search somewhat) with the /C switch. In its default noninteractive mode, FINDTEXT lists the names of all files that contain the search text to the screen; in full-screen interactive mode, enabled with the /I switch, it shows the contents of the files, too. If you run FINDTEXT in interactive mode on a laptop and need maximum contrast, use the /M switch. By default, FINDTEXT ignores hidden and system files, but you can search them too with the /A switch. Finally, the /7 switch performs 7-bit comparisons, useful when you're searching Wordstar files or other files that use the eighth bit for nontext purposes. The source code for FINDTEXT is shown in Chapter 11.

EXAMPLES　　To list all the files in the current directory that contain the phrase "PC Magazine," type:

```
FINDTEXT "PC Magazine"
```

To search all files in \WP\DOC and its descendants for "PC Magazine" and ignore case and high bits in comparisons, type

```
FINDTEXT \WP\DOC "PC Magazine" /S /C /7
```

To search all the files with the extension .DOC on drive C, including hidden and system files, for "PC Magazine" and display the contents of files that are found, type

```
FINDTEXT C:\*.DOC "PC Magazine" /S /I /A
```

NOTES　　FINDTEXT is a very useful utility to have when you can't remember where you stored a certain word processing file or what you named it. If you can remember a word or phrase you put in it, you can find the file with FINDTEXT.

FKEYS

Program Function Keys

FKEYS [*shift-*]*key* ["*command*"[*]]

shift-   Identifies a shift key (Ctrl, Alt, or Shift)
key   Identifies a function key (F1 through F12)
command Command to be assigned to the function key
*   Execute the command when the function key is pressed

FKEYS programs the function keys (alone, or pressed in conjunction with Ctrl, Shift, or Alt) to execute commands. For example, the command

```
FKEYS F1 "MEM /CLASSIFY"
```

programs function key F1 to type MEM /CLASSIFY at the DOS prompt. By default, the command isn't executed until you press Enter. However, if you include an asterisk at the end of the command, as in

```
FKEYS F1 "MEM /CLASSIFY"*
```

the command will be executed as soon as you press the function key. You can program up to 48 different function keys and function key combinations this way: F1 through F12, and F1 through F12 modified with Ctrl, Shift, or Alt. The command

```
FKEYS CTRL-F1 "CLS"*
```

programs Ctrl-F1 to clear the screen. Function key assignments are only valid while you're working from the command line. When an application is running, the assignments are ignored. Function keys are deprogrammed by running FKEYS without the optional *command* parameter. For example, the command

```
FKEYS Ctrl-F1
```

erases the assignment made to Ctrl-F1 earlier.

To include a redirection operator, a piping operator, a Ctrl-T command separator, or a dollar sign in a command, use the following special metacharacters:

- ■ $B, which represents a piping symbol (|)
- ■ $G, which represents an output redirection symbol (>)
- ■ $L, which represents an input redirection symbol (<)

■ $T, which represents a Ctrl-T command separator (¶)

■ $$, which represents the dollar sign ($)

For example, the command

```
FKEYS ALT-F12 "MEM /PROGRAM $B MORE"*
```

programs Alt-F12 to execute a MEM /PROGRAM command and pipe the output to MORE so that the listing will be displayed one screenful at a time.

The source code is shown in Chapter 12.

EXAMPLES To program function key F1 to produce help for any DOS command, type

```
FKEYS F1 " /?"*
```

To program Shift-F4 to execute a CLS command followed by a MEM command (mutiple commands are only supported if DOSKEY is installed), type

```
FKEYS SHIFT-F4 "CLS $T MEM"*
```

To deprogram these function keys, type

```
FKEYS F1
FKEYS SHIFT-F4
```

NOTES FKEYS requires DOS 4.0 or later and will only work if the ANSI.SYS driver is installed.

GETHOUR

Return Current Hour

SYNTAX   GETHOUR

DESCRIPTION GETHOUR returns an exit code that is equal to the current hour (for example, the 10 in 10:00 a.m.). Hours are reported in 24-hour format, so 1:00 p.m. is 13, 2:00 p.m. is 14, and so on. Use this utility to build batch files that execute a command or set of commands at a certain time of day. The DEBUG script for creating GETHOUR appears in Chapter 10.

EXAMPLES To personalize a greeting for the time of day, enter the batch statements

```
GETHOUR
IF ERRORLEVEL 12 GOTO AFTERNOON
ECHO Good morning!
GOTO CONTINUE
:AFTERNOON
ECHO Good afternoon!
:CONTINUE
```

To pause a batch file until 9:00 p.m., then have it execute a BACKUP command, enter the statements

```
:READCLOCK
GETHOUR
IF NOT ERRORLEVEL 21 GOTO READCLOCK
BACKUP C:\*.* A: /S
```

GETKEY

Get Keyboard Input

SYNTAX   GETKEY

DESCRIPTION GETKEY pauses until a key is pressed, and then returns an exit code equal to the ASCII code for the key. A batch file can test the exit code with the IF ERRORLEVEL command. If a key that produces a 2-byte key code is pressed (for example, a function key or a cursor key), GETKEY returns 0. Thus, it cannot be used to differentiate between keys that return extended keycodes. The DEBUG script for creating GETKEY is shown in Chapter 10.

EXAMPLES The following batch statements loop until the user presses the Enter key, which produces a return code of 13:

```
ECHO Press Enter to continue...
:INPUT
GETKEY
IF ERRORLEVEL 14 GOTO INPUT
IF NOT ERRORLEVEL 13 GOTO INPUT
```

NOTES GETKEY is a quick-and-dirty way to solicit keyboard input from inside a batch file. A better way to read the keyboard from a batch file and to filter out invalid responses is to use BATCHKEY, a more sophisticated keyboard input utility developed in Chapter 10.

GETMIN

Return Current Minute

SYNTAX   GETMIN

DESCRIPTION   GETMIN returns an exit code that is equal to the number of minutes past the hour. Use it in conjunction with GETHOUR to execute a command or set of commands at a certain time of day. The DEBUG script for creating GETMIN appears in Chapter 10.

EXAMPLES   The following batch file loops until 9:30 p.m., and then executes a CHKDSK command:

```
:LOOP1
GETHOUR
IF NOT ERRORLEVEL 21 GOTO LOOP1
IF ERRORLEVEL 22 GOTO LOOP1
:LOOP2
GETMIN
IF NOT ERRORLEVEL 30 GOTO LOOP2
CHKDSK
```

INSTALL

Create Bookmark

SYNTAX `INSTALL [`*`bookmark`*`]`

bookmark   Name of the bookmark to create (maximum length is 32 characters)

DESCRIPTION INSTALL and its companion program, REMOVE, provide a means for removing TSRs from memory. Before installing a TSR, you place a bookmark in memory with INSTALL. Then, when you're ready to remove the TSR, type **REMOVE** followed by the bookmark name. When a bookmark is removed, any and all TSRs installed above it are removed from memory. If you omit the bookmark name, INSTALL assigns it the name "(No Name)". You can create as many bookmarks as you want. However, when you remove a bookmark, any bookmarks installed after it are also removed. Therefore, TSRs can be removed only in the reverse order that they were installed. For additional information concerning the use of INSTALL and REMOVE, see the entry for REMOVE in this appendix. The source code for INSTALL appears in Chapter 14.

EXAMPLES To load PC-DIAL so that it can be removed later, type

```
INSTALL PC-DIAL
PC-DIAL
```

When you're ready to remove it, type

```
REMOVE PC-DIAL
```

or, if PC-DIAL was the last bookmark installed, simply

```
REMOVE
```

NOTES INSTALL and REMOVE won't remove programs loaded with LOADHIGH. In addition, they should not be used with TSRS that claim system resources other than conventional memory and interrupts—for example, TSRs that allocate expanded memory for themselves by placing calls to an expended memory manager.

LASERLST

Print Text File

LASERLST [*d:*][*path*]*filename* [[*d:*][*path*]*outfile*] [/T*n*]

filename	Name of the text file to print
outfile	Name of a file to direct printer output to
/T*n*	Number of spaces between tab stops (default=8)

DESCRIPTION LASERLST prints text files in two-page-per-sheet format on LaserJet printers by turning the page sideways and fitting the equivalent of two 8 1/2-by-11-inch sheets onto one printed page. It not only saves trees, but also allows you to fit more information onto the page. If you want to direct the printer output to a file so that you can transport the print file to someone else's PC, use the *outfile* parameter to specify the name of the file. LASERLST is compatible with all the members of the LaserJet family and with printers that are 100-percent LaserJet-compatible. The source code for LASERLST is included on the disks in the back of the book.

EXAMPLES To print README.DOC on a LaserJet printer, type

    LASERLST README.DOC

To print README.DOC to a file named PRINTER.BIN with tab stops set four spaces apart, type

    LASERLST README.DOC PRINTER.BIN /T4

LPI

Set Printer Lines per Inch

LPI *lines*

lines   Number of lines per inch (4, 6, or 8)

DESCRIPTION DOS's MODE command can be used to configure IBM and Epson dot-matrix printers to print 6 or 8 lines per inch, but it is ineffective on LaserJet printers. LPI configures a LaserJet to print 4, 6, or 8 lines per inch. Chapter 6 contains the DEBUG script for creating LPI.

EXAMPLE To configure a LaserJet to print 8 lines per inch, type

    LPI 8

NOTES By default, LPI reconfigures the printer attached to LPT1. If your printer is connected to LPT2 or LPT3, you can patch LPI to work with ports other than LPT1 (see Chapter 6).

LPT2FILE

Capture Printer Output to a File

SYNTAX   `LPT2FILE [LPTn[:]=[d:][path]filename] [/B=size] [/C]`

n	Number of the LPT port to capture output from (1, 2, or 3)
filename	Name of the file to capture output to
/B=size	Size of LPT2FILE's internal buffer, in kilobytes (default=4, range=2 to 64)
/C	Cancel redirection

DESCRIPTION   LPT2FILE redirects output from a printer attached to a parallel port to a file. All subsequent output to the specified printer is captured in the file until another printer is redirected or until redirection is cancelled with the /C switch. You can adjust the size of the buffer set up to hold printer output on its way to the disk with the /B switch. The larger the buffer, the more memory LPT2FILE consumes, but the less frequently it pauses to access the disk. The source code for LPT2FILE is shown in Chapter 12.

EXAMPLES   To capture output from LPT1 to PRINTER.DAT, type

```
LPT2FILE LPT1:=PRINTER.DAT
```

To capture output from LPT2 to C:\TEXT\P.TXT, type

```
LPT2FILE LPT2:=C:\TEXT\P.TXT
```

To restore normal printer operation, type

```
LPT2FILE /C
```

NOTES   Certain capture operations will only work if the buffer size is set to the maximum of 64k. If you receive error messages when you attempt to print to a file, reinstall LPT2FILE with a larger buffer size and the problem may go away. LPT2FILE may be installed in upper memory with the LOADHIGH command.

LPT2LPT

Redirect LPT Port

SYNTAX   `LPT2LPT LPTm[:]=LPTn[:]`

    m   LPT port of the printer to redirect (1, 2, or 3)
    n   LPT port to direct output to (1, 2, or 3)

DESCRIPTION   DOS's MODE command can be used to redirect parallel printer output to a serial port, but it cannot be used to redirect output from one LPT port to another. LPT2LPT redirects output from parallel port to parallel port. This enables you to redirect DOS's PRN device driver (which defaults to LPT1) to LPT2 or LPT3. The DEBUG script for creating LPT2LPT appears in Chapter 6.

EXAMPLE   To redirect everything sent to LPT1 to LPT2, type

    `LPT2LPT LPT1:=LPT2:`

NOTES   To cancel printer redirection, you'll have to reboot your PC, or remove LPT2LPT from memory with the REMOVE utility, described in Chapter 14.

LZSELECT

Configure Laser Printer or Create PMF File

SYNTAX LZSELECT [/2] [/B] [/F [*d:*][*path*]*filename*]

/2   Direct output to LPT2 (default=LPT1)
/B   Run the program in black-and-white
filename Name of the PMF file to create

DESCRIPTION LZSELECT lets you create PMF files for use with the SETUP utility (Chapter 12) so that you can send control codes to LaserJet printers from SETUP's popup printer control window. You can also send control codes directly to the printer and download printer fonts through LZSELECT's menus. See Chapter 12 for a full discussion of the program and instructions for using it. The source code for LZSELECT is included on the disks in the back of the book.

EXAMPLES To start LZSELECT for the purpose of creating a PMF file called LASERJET.PMF, type

    LZSELECT LASERJET.PMF

Then, to load the menu file into SETUP, type

    SETUP LASERJET.PMF

NOTES LZSELECT is one of only three programs in this book that were written in BASIC (the other two are PCBOOK and PASSAGES).

NDPTYPE

Determine Coprocessor Type

SYNTAX   NDPTYPE

DESCRIPTION   NDPTYPE runs a series of tests to determine what type of math coprocessor (8087, 287, or 387), if any, is installed in your PC. In addition to outputting a message identifying the coprocessor type, it returns an exit code that is equal to one of the following values:

    0   No coprocessor installed
    1   8087
    2   287
    3   387

The source code for NDPTYPE appears in Chapter 10.

EXAMPLE   To write a batch file that aborts itself if there is no math coprocessor installed, use the lines

```
NDPTYPE
IF NOT ERRORLEVEL 1 GOTO ABORT
```

NOTES   A companion program, CPUTYPE, described in this appendix, identifies the type of CPU installed in your PC.

NEWPAUSE

New PAUSE Command

`NEWPAUSE`

DESCRIPTION NEWPAUSE is a humorous version of DOS's PAUSE command. When executed, it displays the message

```
Press any key to continue . . .
```

just like the PAUSE command. When you press a key, it responds with the message

```
Any key but that one . . .
```

The next keypress terminates the program. The DEBUG script for creating NEW-PAUSE appears in Chapter 10.

EXAMPLE The following batch file excerpt prompts the user to insert a disk and then press any key to continue. Little do they know...

```
ECHO Insert disk in drive A
NEWPAUSE
```

NUKE

Delete Subdirectory

SYNTAX   `NUKE [d:]path`

DESCRIPTION   NUKE deletes a subdirectory, the files in it, and all the subdirectories that stem from it. Run at the root directory level, NUKE deletes all the files and subdirectories in the root directory, but does not remove the root directory itself (the root directory cannot be removed). If the current directory is one of those deleted, NUKE changes to the parent of the highest directory that was deleted when it is done. NUKE is similar to the RD command except that it does not require that a subdirectory be empty to remove it. The source code for NUKE is shown in Chapter 11.

EXAMPLES   To remove the subdirectory \WP\WPFILES from the current drive, type

    NUKE \WP\WPFILES

To remove everything from drive A, type

    NUKE A:\

NOTES   Needless to say, you should exercise extreme caution when using NUKE. Applied to the root directory, it wipes out everything on the disk. So that you can't remove the current directory by mistake, NUKE requires that a *path* parameter be entered.

PARK

Park Hard-Disk Heads

SYNTAX　　PARK

DESCRIPTION　PARK parks the heads on hard disks whose heads do not park automatically when power is shut off. Parking the heads before you shut your PC off protects data stored on the hard disk by moving the heads to an area of the disk where no data is stored before they come in contact with the drive platters. PARK locks up your PC so that no further disk accesses may occur. If you change your mind about shutting things down after running this utility, you'll have to cycle the power off and on to get started again.

EXAMPLE　　To park your hard disk's heads, type

```
PARK
```

NOTES　　Most modern hard drives park their heads automatically when the power is shut off. If your hard disk is several years old or uses a stepper motor to actuate the heads, then the heads probably do not autopark. If this is the case, PARK can help prolong the life of your hard disk.

PASSAGES

BASIC Game Program

SYNTAX To start the stand-alone version of PASSAGES (PASSAGES.EXE):

```
PASSAGES
```

To start the QBasic version of PASSAGES (PASSAGES.BAS):

```
QBASIC /RUN PASSAGES
```

DESCRIPTION PASSAGES is a game program written in BASIC that illustrates structured BASIC programming and demonstrates the use of EGA and VGA graphics from QBasic. The object of the game is to find your way out of a maze, which you see from ground level as a series of intersecting corridors. You can move forward with the Up Arrow key, turn 90 degrees to the left or right with the Left and Right Arrow keys, or turn 180 degrees with the Down Arrow key. If you find the exit, press the Up Arrow key a final time to step through it and you'll be rewarded with a short tune. If you give up, press the End key to terminate the game. The source code for PASSAGES appears in Chapter 15.

NOTES There are two PASSAGES files on the disks in the back of this book: PASSAGES.BAS and PASSAGES.EXE. The former runs with DOS 5.0's QBasic Interpreter. The latter is a stand-alone version compiled with Microsoft QuickBASIC. Run the two one after the other to see how much (or, in this case, how little) difference a compiler makes.

PCBOOK

Print Text File in Book Form

　PCBOOK [d:][path]filename [/F] [/P] [/D] [/C] [/2] [/A] [/W]
[/S] [/R] [/I]

filename	Name of the text file to print
/F	Print file name on every page
/P	Print page numbers
/D	Print date on every page
/C	Display page count and prompt for confirmation before starting
/2	Output to LPT2 (default=LPT1)
/A	Print to a file rather than a printer
/W	Enable line wrap
/S	Turn sound on for user prompts
/R	Collate for rear paper tray
/I	Ignore printer errors

DESCRIPTION　PCBOOK prints text files in book form on LaserJet printers. Output pages can be stacked together, folded at the center, and stapled at the spine to create a book. The first pass through the printer prints everything on one side; a second pass through prints the opposite sides of the pages. Once the pages come out in the top output tray after the first pass, lay them back in the paper tray with *text facing down* to print the second side. Use the /F, /P, and /D switches to print file names, page numbers, and the current date at the top of every page if desired. If you want to know how many sheets of paper will be required, use the /C switch. PCBOOK will display a page count and ask you whether you want to proceed or quit. The /A switch lets you print to a file rather than a printer—convenient if you'll be doing the actual printing on someone else's PC. By default, lines that are more than 80 characters long are truncated. The /W switch turns line wrap on so that the lines will be printed in their entirety. The source code for PCBOOK (written in BASIC) is included on the disks in the back of the book.

EXAMPLE　To print README.DOC in booklet form and number the pages, type

```
PCBOOK README.DOC /P
```

NOTES　PCBOOK works with LaserJet II, IIP, III, and IIIP printers, and with other members of the LaserJet III line.

PCSPOOL

Install Print Spooler

SYNTAX To install PCSPOOL:

```
PCSPOOL /I [/1] [/2] [/3] [/Cnn | /D:[d:][path]]
```

/I	Install PCSPOOL and begin spooling
/1	Spool output to LPT1
/2	Spool output to LPT2
/3	Spool output to LPT3
/Cnn	Size of the print buffer in kilobytes (default=16)
/D	Locate the print buffer on disk rather than in RAM

To control the print queue:

```
PCSPOOL [/P message] [/F] [/1|/2|/3]
```

/P	Insert a pause record in the queue and, optionally, a message to be displayed
/F	Insert a form feed in the queue
/1	Direct the command to LPT1
/2	Direct the command to LPT2
/3	Direct the command to LPT3

To uninstall the program:

```
PCSPOOL /U
```

DESCRIPTION PCSPOOL spools printer output and transmits the data to the printer or printers in the background, so you can continue to work in the foreground. Using it frees up your printer much sooner after a print job begins. The command

```
PCSPOOL /I /1 /2
```

installs it and initially has it spool output going to LPT1 and LPT2. On the line that installs it, you can specify the size of the internal buffer it sets up with the /C switch, or direct PCS-POOL to create the buffer on disk instead of in memory. You can use this feature to access expanded memory indirectly by setting up a RAM disk in expanded memory and storing print data there.

Once PCSPOOL is installed, you can uninstall it by running it with a /U switch, or press Ctrl-Alt-P to open a window that displays information about the print queue and about the printers whose output is being spooled. From the window, you can issue commands to suspend or resume spooling, transmit a form feed to a printer, remove pending print jobs, skip over pending print jobs, and more. You can insert pause records in the queue from the command line with the /P switch or send form feeds with the /F switch. For example, the command

```
PCSPOOL /P /2 *** Insert Legal Tray ***
```

inserts a pause record in the queue and prompts you to insert the legal-size tray before resuming.

The source code for PCSPOOL is included on the disks in the back of the book. See Chapter 12 for additional details.

EXAMPLES To install PCSPOOL with a 32k buffer size and have it spool output to LPT1, LPT2, and LPT3, type

```
PCSPOOL /I /1 /2 /3 /C32
```

To send a form feed to LPT1 from the command line, type

```
PCSPOOL /F /1
```

To unsinstall the program, type

```
PCSPOOL /U
```

NOTES If you print long documents often, PCSPOOL will save you time by preventing your printer from being tied up for the entire time required for printing. PCSPOOL is similar to DOS's PRINT command except that it is more flexible. It is capable of handling binary files as well as text files.

PC-DIAL

Install Popup Phone Directory and Dialer

　　PC-DIAL [[*d:*][*path*]*filename*] [/B=*size*] /M]

> *filename*　　Data file to load when PC-DIAL is installed
> /B=*size*　　Set the internal buffer to *size* kilobytes (default=16, range=1 to 48)
> /M　　　　　Run in monochrome mode

DESCRIPTION　PC-DIAL is a popup phone directory and dialer that you can use to store names and phone numbers. If you have a Hayes or Hayes-compatible modem, PC-DIAL will dial the phone for you, too. The number of names and phone numbers you can store depends on the size of the buffer you allocate for PC-DIAL to store data. The default buffer size of 16k provides room for about 300 entries of 50 characters each. If you need more, increase the buffer size or divide the records up between two or more data files and shuffle them in and out as needed. Once installed, the PC-DIAL window is popped up by pressing Alt and the right Shift key and closed with the Esc key. See Chapter 13 for instructions on using PC-DIAL and for customizing it for your system, and for its source code.

EXAMPLE　To install PC-DIAL with a buffer size of 32k and load a data file named BUSINESS-.DAT, type

```
PC-DIAL BUSINESS.DAT /B=32
```

NOTES　To conserve memory below 640k, you can load PC-DIAL in upper memory with the LOADHIGH command on systems equipped for loading high. PC-DIAL is an example of a TSR that uses some rather advanced techniques for circumventing the limitations that DOS places on TSRs when it comes to performing file I/O and utilizing operating system services.

PC-LIST

List PC-DIAL Data File

SYNTAX   `PC-LIST [d:][path]filename`

filename   Name of the data file to list

DESCRIPTION PC-DIAL data files containing names, company names, and phone numbers are stored in a propietary format that lends itself to the data management scheme that PC-DIAL employs. PC-LIST reads a data file created by PC-DIAL and lists it to the screen in ASCII format. You can capture the output to a file or direct it to a printer using an output redirection operator. As a result, PC-LIST provides an indirect means for converting PC-DIAL data files to ASCII format and for printing them out. The source code for PC-LIST is contained on the disks in the back of the book.

EXAMPLES To convert a PC-DIAL file called BUSINESS.DAT to an ASCII text file name BUSI-NESS.TXT, type

    `PC-LIST BUSINESS.DAT > BUSINESS.TXT`

To print the data on LPT1, type

    `PC-LIST BUSINESS.DAT > LPT1`

NOTES Most database managers permit you to import ASCII text files and convert them into databases files. With PC-LIST serving as a translator, you can export information from PC-DIAL to database managers such as dBASE and Paradox.

PC-LOG

Maintain Log of PC Usage

SYNTAX   `PC-LOG [[d:][path]filename]`

filename   Name of the log file

DESCRIPTION PC-LOG writes a record of every program you run on your PC to a log file kept in ASCII format. If you don't specify the name and location for the log file, PC-LOG creates one called USAGE.LOG in the root directory of the current drive. For each program that you run, the log contains its name, the time it was started and ended, how long it was active, what command-line parameters it was started with, and the level at which it was run. The level refers to where the program was started relative to the primary command processor. For example, if you start a program from the command line, it runs at level 1. If you run it from the DOS Shell, it runs at level 2 or higher (the DOS Shell is level 1). If you start WordPerfect, shell out to DOS, and run a program, that program is run at level 3 (level 1=WordPerfect, level 2=COMMAND.COM). The source code for PC-LOG is shown in Chapter 14.

EXAMPLE To install PC-LOG and have it create a log file named RECORDS.TXT in C:\MISC, type

`PC-LOG C:\MISC\RECORDS.TXT`

NOTES In addition to letting you keep track of programs that are run inside other programs, PC-LOG's level-tracking feature also lets you see how application programs sometimes invoke other programs to do their work for them. For example, when you start the DOS Editor with the EDIT command, it actually launches the QBasic Interpreter to perform the text editing. As with the other TSRs in this book, you can save a few kilobytes of RAM by loading PC-LOG in upper memory.

REBOOT

Reboot the System

SYNTAX   REBOOT

DESCRIPTION REBOOT simulates a press of Ctrl-Alt-Del by stuffing the value 1234H into the word at 0040:0072 (the signal to the ROM BIOS that the next boot is supposed to be a warm boot, not a cold boot) and jumping to the instruction at address FFFF:0000 in the ROM BIOS, which is the first instruction executed when your PC is powered up. The DEBUG script for REBOOT is shown in Chapter 10.

EXAMPLE   To reboot your PC, type

    REBOOT

NOTES   REBOOT is useful when multiple CONFIG.SYS and AUTOEXEC.BAT files are a necessity. Let's say you maintain two sets of CONFIG.SYS and AUTOEXEC.BAT files: one for DOS and one for Windows. If DOS is active, the Windows versions of these files are renamed CONFIG.WIN and AUTOEXEC.WIN; if Windows is active, they're named CONFIG.DOS and AUTOEXEC.DOS. With DOS selected as the active operating environment, the following batch statements boot Windows:

```
REN \CONFIG.SYS \CONFIG.DOS
REN \CONFIG.WIN \CONFIG.SYS
REN \AUTOEXEC.BAT \AUTOEXEC.DOS
REN \AUTOEXEC.WIN \AUTOEXEC.BAT
REBOOT
```

REMOVE

Remove Bookmark

SYNTAX   `REMOVE [bookmark] [/L]`

bookmark	Name of the bookmark to remove
/L	List all bookmarks present in memory

DESCRIPTION REMOVE removes a bookmark created by INSTALL, and in the process removes TSRs installed after the bookmark. INSTALL and REMOVE provide an easy-to-use and effective means for managing the TSRs in your system. If you run REMOVE with no bookmark name, it removes the most recently installed bookmark; if you run it with the /L switch, it lists all the bookmarks it finds in memory. When it removes a bookmark, REMOVE also removes any and all bookmarks installed *after* it. Thus, bookmarks—and TSRs—can only be removed in the reverse order in which they were installed. The source code for REMOVE appears in Chapter 14.

EXAMPLES To set up your system so that SAVER, PC-DIAL, and LPT2FILE can be removed with a single command, type

```
INSTALL ALL
SAVER
PC-DIAL
LPT2FILE
```

Then, when you're ready to remove them, type

```
REMOVE ALL
```

To set them up so that they can be removed separately, type

```
INSTALL SAVER
SAVER
INSTALL PC-DIAL
PC-DIAL
INSTALL LPT2FILE
LPT2FILE
```

Then, the command

```
REMOVE LPT2FILE
```

removes LPT2FILE, the command

```
REMOVE PC-DIAL
```

removes PC-DIAL and LPT2FILE, and the command

```
REMOVE SAVER
```

removes SAVER, PC-DIAL, and LPT2FILE.

NOTES INSTALL and REMOVE won't remove programs loaded with LOADHIGH. In addition, they should not be used with TSRs that claim system resources other than conventional memory and interrupts—for example, TSRs that allocate expanded memory for themselves by placing calls to an expanded memory manager.

RENDIR

Rename Directory

SYNTAX   RENDIR [*d:*][*path*]*dirname1 dirname2*

dirname1   Name of the subdirectory to rename
dirname2   New name for the subdirectory

DESCRIPTION   RENDIR renames subdirectories just like REN renames files. RENDIR will not rename the root directory, and in DOS 5.0, it won't let you rename the current directory. However, some versions of DOS (RENDIR will run under any version from 3.0 on) *will* let you rename the current directory. If this happens, or if you rename a directory that lies in the path to the current directory, DOS may tell you that one or more subdirectories are invalid. To correct the error, CD to the root directory of the drive, then back to the current directory. The source code for RENDIR appears in Chapter 11.

EXAMPLES   To rename the subdirectory **WP** to **WPERFECT**, type

     RENDIR WP WPERFECT

To rename \WP\DOC to \WP\WPFILES, type

     RENDIR \WP\DOC WPFILES

NOTES   DOS's REN command will not rename the subdirectory, although the Rename function in the DOS Shell will. RENDIR turns the otherwise painstaking task of renaming a subdirectory into a simple six-letter command.

SAVER

Install Screen Saver

SYNTAX   SAVER [*mm*]

mm   Number of minutes of keyboard and mouse inactivity that must pass before the screen is blanked (default=5, range=0 to 60)

DESCRIPTION   SAVER protects your monitor against burn-in (a phenomenon that occurs when an image that is left on the screen too long is burned into the high-persistence phosphors used in most CRT screens) by nondestructively blanking the screen when a specified period of time goes by with no mouse or keyboard activity. When the screen goes blank, press a key, move the mouse, or click a mouse button to bring it back. You can disable screen blanking by typing **SAVER 0** and enable it again by rerunning SAVER with a nonzero *mm* value. Note that SAVER only monitors the mouse if a mouse driver is loaded when SAVER is installed. Thus, the line that loads SAVER in your AUTOEX-EC.BAT file must come after the line that loads the mouse driver. If you don't want SAVER to monitor the mouse, install it *before* you install the mouse driver. Running SAVER without an *mm* parameter tells you how many minutes it is currently set to. The source code for SAVER is shown in Chapter 12.

EXAMPLES   To install SAVER so that it will blank the screen after three minutes of inactivity, type

    SAVER 3

To temporarily disable screen blanking, type

    SAVER 0

To determine what the blanking interval is currently set to, type

    SAVER

NOTES   SAVER works with most types of video adapters used with the IBM PC, including CGAs, MDAs, EGAs, MCGAs, and VGAs. If you have a 386 or 486 configured for loading programs in upper memory, you can load SAVER high with the command **LOADHIGH SAVER**. SAVER should not be used with Microsoft Windows or with other programs that take over keyboard processing duties from the BIOS.

SETPOS

Set Cursor Position

SYNTAX   SETPOS *row col*

> *row*   Row to move the cursor to
> *col*   Column to move the cursor to

DESCRIPTION   SETPOS moves the cursor to a specified row and column. Row and column numbers are entered in decimal form and are zero-based, meaning that the coordinates of the upper-left corner of the screen are 0,0. SETPOS is used to position the cursor before executing a TEXTOUT or DRAWBOX command. The source code for SETPOS is shown in Chapter 10.

EXAMPLES   The following batch statement moves the cursor to the upper-left corner of the screen:

```
SETPOS 0 0
```

The statements below move the cursor to row 5, column 30, and display the message "Press a key to continue":

```
SETPOS 5 30
TEXTOUT 1F "Press a key to continue"
```

To move the cursor to the upper-left corner of the screen and draw a single-line box in white-on-black, enter

```
SETPOS 0 0
DRAWBOX 07 80 25
```

NOTES   You can temporarily hide the cursor by moving it to a row position higher than the number of rows displayed on the screen. For example, in a 25-line video mode, the command **SETPOS 25,0** makes the cursor disappear. It reappears when a subsequent SETPOS command moves it back into the visible viewing area.

SETUP

Install Popup Printer Utility or Transmit Control Codes

SYNTAX   SETUP [[d:][path]filename] [/C codes] [/Pn]

filename   Name of a printer menu file to load
/C *codes*   Transmit control codes defined in *codes*
/P*n*   Number of the LPT port to direct output to (1, 2, or 3; default=1)

DESCRIPTION   SETUP can be used in either of two ways. If it's run with a /C switch, it immediately outputs a code string to the printer. The code string can contain any mix of decimal, hexadecimal, and ASCII characters. ASCII characters are enclosed in quotation marks, while hexadecimal codes are preceded by the characters "0x." For example, the command

    SETUP /C 13,10,"PC Magazine",0x0D,0x0A

sends "PC Magazine" to LPT1 sandwiched between two carriage return/line-feed characters. If SETUP is run without the /C switch, it makes itself memory resident. Pressing Ctrl and the right Shift key pops up a window containing a menu of printer control options. You specify what these options are by creating a text file called a *printer menu file* (PMF) and passing SETUP the name of the file on the command line. (The format of the PMF file is documented in Chapter 12.) Once the window pops up, you can select control codes from the menus or enter codes directly. PgUp and PgDn display other menu pages, and Up and Down Arrow keys move the highlight. Enter transmits the highlighted control code, as does the function key to the left of the menu option. Press the / (slash) key to enter control codes directly. You can change where the printer output goes to by pressing the * key. The LPT port currently selected is displayed in the lower-right corner of the window. Esc closes the window. The source code for SETUP is available on the disks in the back of this book.

EXAMPLES   To reset a LaserJet printer, type

    SETUP /C 27,"E"

To set an Epson or IBM dot-matrix printer attached to LPT3 to print condensed type, type

    SETUP /C 0x0F /P3

To install SETUP as a TSR and load the menu file LASERJET.PMF, type

    SETUP LASERJET.PMF

NOTES   You can use LZSELECT, another one of the utilities included with this book, to create PMF files rather than create them with a text editor.

SLICE/SPLICE

Slice File/Splice File

SYNTAX

```
SLICE [d:][path]filename destination
```

filename   Name of the file to slice
destination   Floppy drive the file will be written to

```
SPLICE source [destination]
```

source   Drive the file will be read from
destination   Drive and directory the reassembled file will be written to

DESCRIPTION SLICE breaks a large file up into pieces and copies it to as many as 99 floppies. SPLICE reassembles the file on a hard disk at the other end. SLICE creates a copy of SPLICE on the first floppy and tailors it so that, when executed, it will reconstruct the fragmented file. The source code for SLICE is included on the disks in the back of the book.

EXAMPLES To split a file named BIGFILE.DOC and copy it to floppies in drive A, type

```
SLICE BIGFILE.DOC A:
```

To reconstruct the file in the \MISC directory of drive C at the other end, place the first disk in drive A and type

```
A:\SPLICE A: C:\MISC
```

or, if you're reading it in from drive B,

```
B:\SPLICE B: C:\MISC
```

NOTES The disks to which you copy parts of the file don't have to be empty, although using empty disks will cut down on the number of floppies required. SLICE checks the amount of free space remaining on a disk before each write and uses only that amount.

TEXTOUT

Display Text

`TEXTOUT` *attr* `"string"`

attr   Hexadecimal code specifying the foreground and background color
string   Text to display, enclosed in quotation marks

TEXTOUT provides batch files a means for displaying text on the screen in the colors of their choice without requiring that ANSI.SYS be installed. The text enclosed in quotation marks is displayed at the current cursor position, in the color specified by *attr*. A companion utility, SETPOS, can be used to set the cursor position prior to calling TEXTOUT. The source code for TEXTOUT is shown in Chapter 10.

To display "PC Magazine" in bright white on a red background, type

```
TEXTOUT 4F "PC Magazine"
```

To position the cursor at line 10, column 34, and display "Out to Lunch" in yellow on a blue background, enter the batch statements

```
SETPOS 10 33
TEXTOUT 1E "Out to Lunch"
```

Hexadecimal color codes are formulated by pairing a hex number from 0 to 7 representing the background color with a hex number from 0 to F representing the foreground color, in that order. A list of the colors that correspond to the hex digits appears in Table 6.2. You can make text output with TEXTOUT blink by adding 8 to the background color code. For example, the commands

```
SETPOS 0 76
TEXTOUT CF "WAIT"
```

display a flashing "WAIT" message in white on red in the upper right-hand corner of the screen.

TOGGLE

Toggle Keyboard States

`TOGGLE [+C|-C] [+N|-N] [+S|-S] [/L]`

+C	Turn Caps Lock on
-C	Turn Caps Lock off
+N	Turn Num Lock on
-N	Turn Num Lock off
+S	Turn Scroll Lock on
-S	Turn Scroll Lock off
/L	Toggle keyboard LEDs on systems that are not 100 percent IBM-compatible

TOGGLE gives you a means for setting Caps Lock, Num Lock, and Scroll Lock on or off from AUTOEXEC.BAT. The + operator enables a keyboard state, while - disables it. Typing

```
TOGGLE +C -N
```

turns Caps Lock on and Num Lock off. Use the /L switch if the indicator lights on your keyboard don't automatically toggle to indicate the new Lock state. On most keyboards, the lights toggle without /L. If your keyboard interface isn't 100 percent IBM-compatible, however, or if you've added a third-party keyboard that doesn't interface with the keyboard controller properly, they may not. /L will correct this on most systems. Each time it is run, TOGGLE displays the current states of Caps Lock, Num Lock, and Scroll Lock on the screen. The source code for TOGGLE appears in Chapter 12.

To turn NumLock off, type

```
TOGGLE -N
```

To turn Caps Lock on, Num Lock off, and Scroll Lock off, and to toggle the keyboard LEDs to match, type

```
TOGGLE +C -N -S /L
```

If the states of the Lock keys that TOGGLE reports don't match up with the current settings of the Caps Lock, Num Lock, and Scroll Lock LEDs, you can synchronize the lights with the actual keyboard states by typing

```
TOGGLE /L
```

WAITTIL

Pause Until a Specified Time

WAITTIL *hh*:*mm*[:*ss*]

hh   Hours
mm   Minutes
ss   Seconds

DESCRIPTION WAITTIL loops internally until the specified time arrives, then terminates and returns control to the batch program that called it. WAITTIL provides a convenient means for batch programs to execute a command or set of commands at a certain time of day or night. If you don't include the *ss* portion of the time, 0 is assumed. Hours are entered in 24-hour format. You can interrupt WAITTIL at any time by pressing Ctrl-Break or Ctrl-C. The source code for WAITTIL is shown in Chapter 10.

EXAMPLE The following two statements delay until 11:20 p.m., and then execute a BACKUP command:

```
WAITTIL 23:20
BACKUP C:\*.* A: /S
```

WHATDATE

Return Day of the Month

SYNTAX WHATDATE

DESCRIPTION WHATDATE returns an exit code that identifies the day of the month (for example, 16 for June 16th). Use it to build batch files that execute a command or set of commands based on the day of the month. The DEBUG script for creating WHATDATE appears in Chapter 10.

EXAMPLE The following batch statements execute CHKDSK on the first day of the month:

```
WHATDATE
IF ERRORLEVEL 2 GOTO CONTINUE
CHKDSK
:CONTINUE
```

WHATDAY

Return Day of the Week

SYNTAX   WHATDAY

DESCRIPTION   WHATDAY returns an exit code that identifies what day of the week it is, where 0=Sunday, 1=Monday, 2=Tuesday, and so on. Use it to create batch files that execute a command or set of commands on a certain day of the week. The DEBUG script for creating WHATDAY appears in Chapter 10.

EXAMPLE   The following batch statements execute the BACKUP command every Friday:

```
WHATDAY
IF ERRORLEVEL 6 GOTO CONTINUE
IF NOT ERRORLEVEL 5 GOTO CONTINUE
ECHO Time to back up your hard disk!
BACKUP C:\*.* A: /S
:CONTINUE
```

ZCOPY

Transfer File by Null Modem Cable

`ZCOPY source [destination] [/W] [/n] [/U] [/Ø] [/A] [/P] [/D]`

source	For the sender: name of the file or files to be transferred
	For the receiver: name of the COM port input will be read from (COM1 or COM2)
destination	For the sender: name of the COM port output will be directed to (this parameter is not optional for the sender)
	For the receiver: location the files will be copied to (the drive, directory, or both)
/W	Waive the time-out that occurs at the end of 30 seconds if a connection is not established
/n	Maximum data transfer rate. Valid values (in kilobits per second) are

	/1	115 kbps
	/2	57.6 kbps
	/3	38.4 kbps
	/4	19.2 kbps
	/5	9.6 kbps
	/6	4.8 kbps

/U	No confirmation when overwriting files at the destination if the source file is more recent
/O	Suppress all confirmation messages
/A	Abort at the first indication of a disk-full condition
/P	Pause after a connection is established
/D	Stamp received files with the current time and date

ZCOPY copies files from one PC to another via a high-speed serial data link. To initiate a transfer, connect two PCs with a null modem cable and start ZCOPY on each end. The two copies of ZCOPY attempt to establish a communications link. If 30 seconds have passed and no connection has been made, ZCOPY times out unless you started it with a /W switch on both ends. Once a link is made, ZCOPY determines the maximum data transfer rate that the two machines will support (you can limit the maximum rate it will try with the /n switch) and transfers the file or files from the sender to the receiver. Before overwriting a file on the receiving end with a file of the same name, ZCOPY will prompt you for confirmation. You can alter this default behavior with the /U (Update) and /A switches. By default, copied files retain the same date and time stamp that they had on the source machine. If you use the /D switch, files will be stamped with the current time and date at the destination. If ZCOPY detects a disk-full condition on the receiving end, it continues copying if there are smaller files yet to be transmitted that will fit on the disk. If you include an /A switch, however, it aborts at the first indication that the disk is full. The source code for ZCOPY is included on the disks in the back of the book.

EXAMPLES Suppose that you have two PCs connected with a null modem cable, and that the cable is attached to serial port COM1 on the sending PC and COM2 on the other. To copy all the files with the extension .DOC from the current directory of the sender to the \MISC directory on the receiver, type

```
ZCOPY *.DOC COM1
```

on the sending PC and

```
 ZCOPY COM2 \MISC
```

on the receiving PC.

NOTES ZCOPY is a great tool for transferring files between a desktop PC and a laptop, or between two PCs with unlike drive types. Although the exact definition of a null modem cable varies widely, ZCOPY will work with just about any of them. All it requires is that the Transmit Data and Receive Data pins (pins 2 and 3 on the RS-232 interface) be crossed over. It uses an error-free software protocol to ensure the integrity of the data that is transferred.

INDEX

A

A attribute code, 215-216, 812
"A:-C:" device driver, 78-79
About... command (QBasic), 775
About Shell command (Shell), 751
ABS_READ_INT procedure
    in LPT2FILE, 581
    in PC-DIAL, 650
ABS_WRITE_INT procedure
    in LPT2FILE, 581
    in PC-DIAL, 650-651
Absolute addresses, 23-24
Accelerator keys
    color for, 764-765
    with Editor, 240
Accented characters, 293, 865
Access codes, file, 490
"Access denied" message, 157, 229-230
Access time of RAM, 82
Accidental file erasures, preventing, 230-233
Accidental formats, recovering files from,
       178-179
Active partitions
    in master partition tables, 130-131
    setting, 135, 851
Active task list, 767-768
Active video pages, 355, 526, 800
Adapters, identifying, 555. *See also* Screen
Add-in memory boards, 88
Address lines, 87
Addresses, 22-25
Advanced program item properties, 757-758
Affine closure, 452
AH register for DOS functions, 344
AL register for DOS functions, 344
ALARM.BAT utility, 445
Alert messages, color for, 764
Alignment Check bit, 446, 449
Alignment of hard disks, 128, 182-183
"All files in directory will be deleted!" message,
       229
All Files view, 749-750
Allen, Paul, 5
Allocation chains for files
    checking, 167-168
    errors in, 172-173
"Allocation error, size adjusted" message, 172

Allocation Units, 168-173
Alt key
    with active task lists, 768
    for ASCII codes, 292, 346
    BIOS functions for, 348, 350-351
    with function key programming, 568, 946
    with hotkeys, 603
    and key codes, 263, 266
Alternate character sets, 287
    displaying, 288-290, 817
    printing, 290-292
Alternate command processors, 8, 30, 46-49, 893
Alternate register sets, 117
Alternative memory managers, 118-119
AND operations, 576
Animation, 794, 800-801
ANSI.SYS driver, 56-57, 910-912
    checking for, 407, 538, 928, 934
    for color, 253-254, 404-405, 532, 540, 820, 937
    commands for, 252-253, 404-406, 928
    for CON, 80, 247-248, 251
    DOS 2.x support for, 8
    enhancing performance with, 75
    for FKEYS, 569
    for function key assignment, 265-268
    for lines of text on screen, 258-260, 875
    remapping keyboards with, 268-269
    for screen, 403-407
    and SWITCHES directive, 58
    in upper memory, 99
"ANSI.SYS must be installed to perform
       requested function" message, 258
"ANSI.SYS not installed" message, 537
ANSIDEMO.BAT utility, 403-407
ANSIOUT utility, 404-406, 928
APPEND command, 199, 202-205, 810
    DOS 3.x support for, 10
    with SET, 33
    upper memory for, 103
Appending data
    to backup files, 158, 162
    with redirection, 317, 403
Apple Computer, 4
Application Shortcut options
    for program groups, 756
    for task switching, 768
Applications

directories for, 189
memory for, 31
Archive files and attribute, 215-216, 812
    backing up, 159, 813
    copying, 226-227, 908
    DOS function for, 363
    listing, 208-209, 831
Arrays in QBasic, 795-796, 801
ASCII codes
    Alt key for, 292, 346
    BIOS function for, 346-347
    DOS routines for, 352
    video buffers for, 89, 249-251
ASCII files. *See* Text and text files
ASCIIZ file specification, 361, 365
ASC2BIN procedure
    in BATCHKEY, 414, 416
    in CLRSCR, 428-429
    in DEMO, 438
    in DRAWBOX, 434-435
    in FKEYS, 566-567
    in LPT2FILE, 593
    in PC-DIAL, 714
    in PC-LOG, 638-639
    in SAVER, 552-553
    in SETPOS, 423-424
    in TEXTOUT, 420-421
    in WAITTIL, 444-445
Aspect ratio for printing, 284, 859
Assembly language programming, 332-344
    DEBUG for, 35-36, 827
    for directories, 364-365
    for file I/O, 361-362
    for file manipulation, 363-364
    for keyboard, 345-354
    for memory management, 365-368
    miscellaneous functions for, 370-372
    for printer, 359-361
    sample program for, 372-374
    for screen, 354-359
    for terminating programs, 369
    for time and date, 368-369
ASSIGN command, 152-153, 811
    delete tracking with, 177
    and full file names, 371
    with JOIN, 864
    with SUBST, 897
    TRUENAME with, 190
Assignment statements for QBasic, 782
Associate... command (Shell), 750
Associating programs and data files, 750,
    758-759
Associative caching, 65
ASSUME statement (assembler), 336
Asterisks (*)
    in file names, 212-214
    as macro parameter, 308-309, 837
    with Shell directories, 751-752
AT command set, 721-722

AT computers, 9-10
At signs (@) in batch files, 60, 62, 377, 840
ATTRIB command and file attributes, 140, 194,
    215-216, 812
    for AUTOEXEC.BAT file, 63
    backing up files by, 159, 813
    DOS 3.x support for, 10
    DOS function for, 363
    enhancements to, 16
    and file deletion, 229-230
    listing files by, 208-210, 831
    with Shell, 750
Attributes, screen
    address register for, 558
    ANSI.SYS for, 253, 910
    with PROMPT, 262
    TEXTOUT for, 417-421
    video buffers for, 89, 249-251, 358
A20 line, 92-96, 918
AUTO mode (EMM386.EXE), 109-110, 843, 916
AutoCAD, memory for, 73-74, 119
AUTOEXEC.BAT file, 39, 59-60
    CHKDSK in, 169
    contents of, 61-63
    executing, 30, 376
    PRINT in, 282-283
    protecting, 63-64
    in root directory, 188-189
    SETUP program for, 11
    and SHELL directive, 47, 60
    as text file, 234
    typing commands in, 270
Automatic search paths, 199-205, 810, 878
AUX device driver, 6, 78, 317
AX register, 22-23

B

$B metacharacter
    with FKEYS, 568, 570, 946
    in macros, 309-310, 837
    with PROMPT, 261, 882
B switch (EMM386.EXE), 117, 917
Back command (QBasic), 780
Background
    copying files in, 931
    printing in, 8, 280-281, 607-610, 880-881,
        963-964
Background color
    ANSI.SYS for, 253, 910-911
    batch file for, 417, 421, 976
    codes for, 255
    COLOR for, 532-540, 937
    with Editor, 244
    for printers, 284, 859
    with Shell, 763-765
    video memory for, 249-250
Backslashes (\) for root directory, 187-188, 191
Backspaces in prompt, 61-62, 261, 882
BACKUP command, 154-160, 813

with ASSIGN, 153, 811
DOS 3.x support for, 10
with JOIN, 864
with SUBST, 897
vs. XCOPY, 227
Backup files
for DOS 5.0 program disks, 38
for hard disks, 154-160, 181-182, 813
strategy for, 162-166
BACKUP.LOG file, 155-157, 813
BACKUP.001 file, 156
"Bad command or filename" message, 62
Bad sectors and clusters, 128, 140-141, 147. *See
also* Recovering files
Bank-switched memory, 83, 87-89
.BAS files, 759, 774
Basic. *See* QBasic Interpreter
BASICA programs, converting, 777-779
Batch files, 32, 375. *See also* AUTOEXEC.BAT
file
for assembly language programs, 339
calling, 10, 48, 383, 816
compiling, 456-457, 929
for coprocessor types, 449-454
creating, 376
debugging, 377, 407-408
DOS 1.x support for, 7
ECHO command in, 376-378, 840
environment variables in, 34, 63, 387-390, 862
for file backups, 162-166
FOR command in, 383-385, 854
GOTO command in, 382-383, 857
IF command in, 385-387, 862, 934
and macros, 304, 311
PAUSE command in, 379-380, 879, 958
for processor types, 445-449
for QBasic programs, 772, 883
rebooting from, 454-455, 968
redirection and piping in, 379, 395-400
REM command in, 378-379, 407
saving current drive and directory with, 400-
403, 941-942
for screen, 403-407, 417-439, 976
searching for, 200, 205
with SETUP, 600
SHIFT command in, 380-382, 894
for string comparisons, 386, 393-395, 862
subroutines in, 390-391
suppressing command output with, 399-400
as switch statements, 391-393
as text files, 234
for time and date, 439-445, 948, 950, 979-980
with user input, 408-417, 930, 949
BATCHKEY utility, 410-417, 930
Battery-operated clock, 9-10, 368-369
BAT2EXEC utility, 48, 456, 929
Baud rates for serial ports, 276, 718, 873
BCOPY command, 931
BEEP speaker program, 35-36

BEEP timer utility, 614-617
BEGIN directive (assembler), 338
Bell tone, ASCII code for, 617
Best fit memory allocation strategy, 367-368
Binary converters, 332, 338-339, 342, 845
Binary files
comparing, 217-218, 822
concatenating, 224
copying, 223, 823
displaying, 761
.EXE vs. .COM, 341-342
printing, 964
recovering, 170
vs. text, 233-234
Binary numbering system, 19-20
BIN2ASC procedure
in FKEYS, 567
in SAVER, 553
BIN2HEX procedure (PC-DIAL), 706
BIOS (Basic Input/Output System) functions,
25-29, 84, 153
for keyboard, 345-352
for printers, 360-361
with redirection, 326-327
for screen, 251, 354-357
BIOS Data Area, 85, 353-354, 575-577
BIOS_OUT procedure (FINDTEXT), 519
BIOS_OUTNUM procedure (FINDTEXT),
519-520
BIOS_OUTTEXT procedure (FINDTEXT),
519
BIOS Parameter Block, 138-139
Bits, 22
BLACK color identifier (COLOR), 532, 937
Blank lines
in batch file messages, 377
with DEBUG, 36
BLANKCELLS procedure (FINDTEXT), 520
Blanking of screen, 540-559, 972
Blinking attribute, 249-250, 253, 910
Block, 226
Block devices, 52, 78, 839
Blue bit for screen color, 249-250
BLUE color identifier (COLOR), 532, 937
Bold characters
attribute for, 249-250, 253-254, 910
with COLOR, 532, 937
with Editor, 245
Boling, Douglas, 108, 456
Book form, printing text files in, 962
Bookmarks
with Editor, 238
for TSRs, 725-744, 951, 969-970
BOOT.BAT program, 454-455
Boot indicator fields in master partition tables,
130-131
Boot sector, 138-139, 145
Bootable floppy disks, 148-149, 855, 899
Booting, DOS partitions for, 129

Bootstrap loader, 138
Borders, color for, 764
Boxes on screen, 429-436, 940
BP register, 22-23
BPB (BIOS Parameter Block), 138-139
Brackets ([]) in assembly language programs, 354
Break-checking, 523-524
BREAK directive (CONFIG.SYS), 55, 814
Breakout boxes, 278
Breakpoints with QBasic, 775, 804
BROWN color identifier (COLOR), 532, 539, 937
Buffers. *See also* Caches
    for background copying, 931
    clipboard, 239-241, 775
    for command history, 297-298, 837
    disk, 13, 40-43, 65, 68, 96-97, 362, 815
    DOS, memory for, 31
    for encryption utility, 485
    in extended memory, 81
    for file comparisons, 220, 849
    for FINDTEXT, 522
    keyboard, 263-265, 346, 351-353, 797
    for LPT2FILE, 577, 594-596, 598-599, 954
    for PC-DIAL, 644, 714-716, 965
    for print spoolers, 281-282, 607-608, 880-881, 963-964
    for string input, 353
    video, 84, 89, 248-251, 355, 358-359, 526, 720-721, 800
Burn-in, monitor, protecting against, 540-559, 972
Bus and memory, 25
Bus interface units, 21-22
Buttons, color for, 764
BX register, 22-23
Bytes, 22

C

Caches. *See also* Buffers
    with FASTOPEN disk, 64-66, 68-70, 848
    with SMARTDrive, 12, 40, 43, 57, 923
    static RAM, 82
CALIBRATE command (Norton Utilities), 185
CALL batch file command, 10, 48, 383, 816
CALL instruction (assembler), 333, 373
CALL statement (QBasic), 796
"Can't uninstall at this time" message, 608
Capacity in floppy disk formatting, 145-146, 150-151, 855
Caps Lock key
    BIOS function for, 351
    startup setting for, 570-577, 977
Carets (^) in program item help text, 758
Carriage returns
    ASCII code for, 233
    in function key assignment, 265
    in program item help text, 758

in prompts, 261, 882
Carry flag with DOS functions, 344
Case sensitivity
    of environment variables, 389, 394
    of file comparisons, 217, 822, 849
    with FIND, 321, 324, 853
    with FINDTEXT, 493, 523, 845
    of passwords, 482
    of prompt parameters, 61
    of string comparisons, 386-387, 393-395
    of text searches, 241
CASE statements (QBasic), 777, 799-800
CD command, 194, 818
CDX utility, 527-529, 932-933
Central Processing Units, 20-24, 446-450, 939
CGA (Color Graphics Adapter), 245, 247, 540
Chains
    for clusters, 139-140
    for memory, 740-743
Change Attributes command (Shell), 750
Change... command (QBasic), 775
Change lines, 53-54, 839, 914
Character bytes for video, 248-251
Character codes from scan codes, 263-264, 266
Character devices
    drivers for, 78
    for redirection, 317
Character sets, alternate, 287
    displaying, 288-290, 817
    printing, 290-292
Characters, printing, 271
CHCP command, 288-291, 817, 913
CHDIR command, 194, 818
CHECK_INSTALL procedure
    in INSTALL, 729-730
    in LPT2FILE, 591-592
    in PC-DIAL, 712-713
    in PC-LOG, 637
    in REMOVE, 735-736, 741
    in SAVER, 550, 559
CHECK_MOUSE procedure (SAVER), 545-546, 557
Child directories, 197
Child processes, 371
.CHK files, 169-170, 172
CHKANSI utility, 407, 928, 934
CHKDSK command, 819
    error checking by, 141, 154
    with JOIN, 864
    recovering files with, 167-174
    searching for files with, 214
    with SUBST, 897
Ciphers, 482-492, 944
Clear All Breakpoints command (QBasic), 775, 804
Clear command
    in Editor, 240
    in QBasic, 775
CLEAR utility, 256-257, 935

Clearing
    keyboard buffer, 353-354, 797
    screen, 6, 256-257, 424-429, 439, 796, 820,
        935-936
CLI instruction (assembler), 353
Clipboard
    with Editor, 239-241
    with QBasic, 775
CLOCK$ device driver, 78
Clocks
    battery-operated, 9-10
    DOS functions for, 368-369
    generator chips for, 24
    ticks of, 282
CLOSE_FILE procedure (PC-LOG), 628
Closing files, 362
CLRSCR utility, 424-429, 439, 936
CLS command, 6, 251, 820
    macro for, 257
    patching, 253-256
CLS statement (QBasic), 796
Clusters, 4, 139-140
    cross-linked, 170-171
    invalid, 171-172
    lost, 168-170
CMOS RAM
    for clock-calendar, 9-10
    for drive type number, 142
"Code page not prepared" message, 290
Code pages, 287-291, 817, 877
    for display, 50-51, 874, 913
    DOS 3.x support for, 10
    for graphics, 858
    for printers, 290-291, 920
Coercivity, 150-151
Cold resets, 455
Collapse Branch command (Shell), 751
Collating, international settings for, 51-52
Colons (:) for batch file labels, 382, 857, 885
Color
    ANSI.SYS for, 253-254, 404-405, 532, 540,
        820, 910-912, 928, 937
    batch file for, 417, 421, 976
    codes for, 255
    COMMAND.COM for setting, 254-256
    with Editor, 244
    functions for, 355-356
    for printers, 284, 859
    in PROMPT, 262
    with Shell, 750, 761-765
    utilities for, 256-257, 532-540, 935-937
    video buffers for, 89, 248-250
COLOR utility, 532-540, 937
COLOR4 printer type, 286, 859
COLOR8 printer type, 286, 859
Colors... command (Shell), 750
Columns
    addresses of, 358-359
    cursor positioning at, 355, 421-424, 973

setting for, 252, 258
    sorting text files by, 323, 895
.COM files, 6, 32
    from batch files, 456-457, 929
    converting .EXE to, 332, 338-339, 342, 845
    vs. .EXE, 341-342
    memory for, 367
    recovering, 170
    searching for, 200, 205
    segments for, 337
    starting location for, 336, 338
Combining files, 223-224, 823
COMMAND.COM file, 6-7, 28-29, 821
    alternatives to, 8, 30, 46-49, 893
    and AUTOEXEC.BAT, 63-64
    backing up, 157
    COMSPEC variable for, 33, 49, 74, 149
    on floppy disks, 12, 149, 899
    in HMA, 95-97
    on partitions, 141
    patching, for file protection, 231-233
    portions of, 30, 49
    on RAM disks, 74
    in root directory, 188-189
    for screen color, 254-256
    from Shell, 753
    and SHELL directive, 46-49, 388, 893
Command interpreters. *See* COMMAND.COM
        file
Command line
    and batch file commands, 378, 380-382, 894
    in PSP, 343, 416
Commands
    for ANSI.SYS, 252-253, 404-406, 928
    editing, 16, 74, 300-303, 836-837
    files for, 30-31
    function keys for, 559-570, 946-947
    help for, 15-16, 268, 861
    history for, 74, 295-301
    macros for. *See* Macros, command
    microprocessor, 333
    multiple, 304, 307, 568-569, 836-837, 947
    for program items, 756-757, 768
Commands command (Shell), 751
Commas (,) for modem pauses, 719
Comments
    in assembly language programs, 336
    in batch files, 60, 378-379, 407, 885
    in CONFIG.SYS, 55-56
    in PMF files, 601
    for print spooler commands, 609, 964
COMP command, 216-219, 822
Compaq drive tables, 142
"Compare error at OFFSET" message, 217
COMPARE_NAMES procedure (REMOVE),
        737
Comparing
    disks, 833
    files, 216-220, 822, 849

strings, 386-387, 393-395, 862
Compatibility
    and DOS 4.x, 10
    of hard drives, 142
    of QBasic, 777
Compiled programs, 436, 456
Compilers, 771
Compiling batch files, 456-457, 929
Compressed files, expanding, 847
Compressed printing mode, 272
Compressing tabs and spaces, 220, 849
COMPUTE_ADDRESS procedure (PC-
    DIAL), 664-665
COMSPEC environment variable, 33, 49, 74,
    149
COMx ports and device, 78-79
    for PC-DIAL, 716, 718-719
    for printers, 275-278, 873-874
    redirecting output to, 317
CON device driver, 6, 78-80
    ANSI.SYS for, 80, 247-248, 251
    interrupt for, 26
    for keyboard, 264
    for screen output, 345
Concatenating files, 223-224, 823
Concealed attribute, 253-254, 910
Conditional batch file commands, 385-387, 862,
    934
CONFIG.SYS file, 39-40
    BREAK directive in, 55, 814
    BUFFERS directive in, 41-43, 65, 68, 96-97,
        815
    COUNTRY directive in, 50-52, 159-160, 824
    DEVICE directive in, 8, 56-58, 70, 153, 829
    DEVICEHIGH directive in, 59, 99-103, 830
    DOS directive in, 59, 96-97, 99-101, 835
    DRIVPARM directive in, 52-55, 839
    for 8086 and 8088 systems, 121
    for 80286 systems, 121-122
    for 80386 and 80486 systems, 122-123
    FCBS directive in, 44, 850
    FILES directive in, 43-44, 852
    INSTALL directive in, 49-50, 69, 282-283,
        863
    LASTDRIVE directive in, 52, 201-202, 867
    processing of, 29
    REM directive in, 55-56, 885
    in root directory, 188-189
    SETUP program for, 11
    SETVER.EXE in, 922
    SHELL directive in, 46-49, 189, 388, 893
    STACKS directive in, 45-46, 122, 896
    SWITCHES directive in, 58-59, 252, 898
    as text file, 234
Confirmation with file operations
    copying, 226, 908
    deleting, 229, 828
    Shell, 753

Console, 8, 318, 400, 825. *See also* ANSI.SYS
    driver; CON device driver
CONST statement (QBasic), 795
Contents command (QBasic), 775, 780-781
Context-sensitive help
    with Editor, 242-244
    with Shell, 758
Continue command (QBasic), 775
Control codes
    ASCII, 233
    for printers, 271, 599-606, 956, 974
Control signals, 25
CONTROL.001 file, 156
Controllers, keyboard, 263-264
Conventional memory, 25, 83-85, 758
CONVERT_COLOR procedure (COLOR),
    536-537, 539
"Convert lost chains to files (Y/N)?" message,
    169, 173
CONVERT_MSTRING procedure (FKEYS),
    565-566, 570
Converting
    .EXE files to .COM, 332, 338-339, 342, 845
    extended memory to expanded, 106-109, 943
    GW-BASIC and BASICA programs,
        777-779
    hexadecimal numbers, 19-20
Coprocessors, 24
    batch files for type of, 449-454
    memory for, 97, 109, 118, 843, 916
    NDPTYPE for type of, 449-453, 957
Copy command
    in Editor, 239-240
    in QBasic, 775
COPY command (DOS), 152, 221-225, 228, 823
    vs. BACKUP, 160
    for printing text files, 283-284
Copy... command (Shell), 750, 755, 760
COPY CON command, 376
Copying
    files, 221-228, 750, 752-753, 760, 823, 931, 975
    floppy disks, 152, 227, 313, 834, 908
    QBasic text, 775
    ROM to RAM, 118
COPYZ procedure (PC-DIAL), 669
Corrupted files, recovering, 12, 167-174
"Could not copy COMMAND.COM onto tar-
    get disk" message, 899
Countdown timer in SAVER, 540, 553
COUNTRY directive (CONFIG.SYS), 50-52,
    159-160, 824. *See also* Code pages
COUNTRY.SYS file, 50, 58, 289
CPI utility, 273-274, 938
CP/M operating system, 3-4
CP/M-86 operating system, 5
CPUTYPE utility, 446-450, 939
CRC (Cyclical Redundancy Check) data in sec-
    tor ID headers, 127
Create Directory... command (Shell), 750, 753

Critical error flag, 596-598, 618-620, 644, 720
Cross-linked files, 170-171
CS register, 22-23, 336
Ctrl-Break and Ctrl-C keys
    with batch files, 379, 457, 879
    DOS function for, 371
    with FINDTEXT, 523-524
    with macros, 307
    setting for, 55, 814
    with TYPE, 234
Ctrl key
    BIOS functions for, 348, 350-351
    with function key programming, 568, 946
    with hotkeys, 603
    and key codes, 263, 266
Ctrl-S keys, 407
Ctrl-T keys with DOSKEY, 304, 836-837
Ctrl-Z characters in text files, 223, 376
CTS (Clear To Send) serial port pin, 277-278, 722
CTTY command, 318, 400, 825
Curly braces ({}) for Shell colors, 762
Currency symbols, international, 51
Current directory, 187, 191
    and APPEND, 204
    dot entry for, 196
    in prompt, 61, 260-261, 882
    renaming, 476, 971
    saving, 400-403, 470, 941-942
    setting, 365
Current drive, 191
    in prompt, 61, 195, 260-261, 882
    saving, 400-403, 470, 941-942
Cursor
    ANSI.SYS commands for, 261, 910
    BIOS function for, 348
    color for, 764
    with Editor, 236, 239
    hiding, 262, 424, 973
    keypad for, 262
    positioning, 355, 421-424, 973
Customizing
    Editor, 244-245
    prompts, 260-261
Cut command
    in Editor, 239-240
    in QBasic, 775
CVDMBF statement (QBasic), 779
CVSMBF statement (QBasic), 779
CX register, 22-23
CYAN color identifier (COLOR), 532, 937
Cycle time for RAM, 82
Cyclical Redundancy Check data in sector ID headers, 127
Cylinders, disk, 126, 130-131

D

$d metacharacter with PROMPT, 261, 882
D switch (EMM386.EXE), 118, 917

Data bits for serial ports, 276, 718, 873
Data bus, 20
Data Carrier Detect serial port pin, 277-278
Data-compression for backup files, 182
Data conversion statements for QBasic, 784
Data declaration statements for QBasic, 782
"Data error" message, 166
Data errors and double-density disks, 151
Data files
    associating, with programs, 750, 758-759
    directories for, 189
    paths for, 199, 202-205, 810
    QBasic, 779
Data Set Ready serial port pin, 277-278, 722
Data Terminal Ready serial port pin, 277-278
Databases
    filter commands for, 325-326
    open files needed for, 43-44
Date
    backing up files by, 159-160, 813
    batch files for, 439-445, 979-980
    copying files by, 226, 908
    DOS functions for, 368-369
    of file creation. *See* Date stamps
    international formats for, 51, 824
    with PC-LOG, 641
    in prompt, 260-261, 882
    QBasic statements for, 785
    replacing files by, 887
    restoring files by, 888
    sorting files by, 16, 211, 753, 831
DATE command, 10, 826
Date stamps, 140, 207
    DOS function for, 363
    updating, 225
    ZCOPY for, 981
Day
    in date stamps, 364
    functions for, 368-369
Day of week
    batch file for, 439-440, 980
    functions for, 368
DB directive (assembler), 337
DCD (Data Carrier Detect) serial port pin, 277-278
Dead key combinations, 865
DEBUG, 35-37, 234, 827
Debug menu (QBasic), 774-775, 802
Debugging
    batch files, 377, 407-408
    QBasic programs, 782, 802-807
Decimal numbering system, 18-20
Declaration statements for QBasic, 782
Default configuration settings, 41
Default switches for file listings, 213
Defect lists, 128
Defective sectors, 128, 140-141, 147. *See also* Recovering files
DEFINT statement (QBasic), 794-795

DEL command, 228-230, 828, 844
 modifying, 230-233, 306
 with multiple entries, 382
Delays
 batch file for, 441-445, 978
 keyboard, 269-270, 352, 874
Delete... command (Shell), 750, 755
DELETE procedure (PC-DIAL), 688-689
Delete tracking, 175-177, 871, 903
Deleted files, recovering, 11-12, 175-178, 903
Deleting
 commands from buffer, 300
 directories, 147, 192-194, 365, 459-475, 753, 766, 889, 959
 DOS partitions, 136-137, 851
 with Editor, 238-240
 environment variables, 33-34
 files, 216, 228-233, 313, 363, 382, 750, 752-753, 828, 844
 macros, 257, 310-311
 PC-DIAL records, 717
 program items, 755, 757
 programs from active task lists, 768
 QBasic text, 775
DEMO.BAT program, 436-439
Descending order, listing files in, 753
Descriptors, 86
Deselect All command (Shell), 750, 759
DESQview 386, 119
DEVICE directive (CONFIG.SYS), 8, 40, 56-58, 153, 829
 for ANSI.SYS, 252, 537
 for RAMDRIVE.SYS, 70
 for SMARTDRV.SYS, 66-67
Device drivers, 6, 27, 909
 ANSI.SYS. *See* ANSI.SYS driver
 DISPLAY.SYS, 57, 288-289, 292, 913
 DRIVER.SYS, 55-58, 153-154, 914
 EGA.SYS, 57, 915
 EMM386.EXE, 110-118, 843, 916-917
 as executable files, 32
 extended memory for, 39, 90
 HIMEM.SYS. *See* HIMEM.SYS driver
 installable, 7-8, 77-80, 829
 loading, 56, 829-830
 in MEM listings, 31, 870
 PRINTER.SYS, 57, 291-292, 920
 for printers, 270-271
 RAMDRIVE.SYS, 56-57, 70-74, 107, 921
 SETVER.EXE, 922
 SMARTDRV.SYS. *See* SMARTDRV.SYS (SMARTDrive) driver
 system file for, 28-29, 31
 upper memory for, 13, 25, 93, 97-102, 830, 869
Device independence, 6, 27
Device input and output statements for QBasic, 782-783
DEVICEHIGH directive (CONFIG.SYS), 59, 93, 97, 99-103, 830

 for alternative memory managers, 119
 for ANSI.SYS, 252, 537
 for DISPLAY.SYS, 289
 for EMM386.EXE, 115
 for HIMEM.SYS, 91
 for SMARTDRV.SYS, 66
DI register, 22-23
Diacritics, 293, 865
Diagnostic mode with CHKDSK, 168
DIAL.BAT utility, 398-399
DIAL procedure (PC-DIAL), 694-697
Dialing phones
 batch file for, 398-399
 PC-DIAL for, 644-724, 965
Dialing prefixes with PC-DIAL, 719
Dialog boxes
 color for, 764
 with Editor, 237
 with Shell, 749
Digital Research, 4-5
DIR command, 16, 28, 206-213, 831-832
DIRCMD environment variable, 16, 34, 213
Direct Memory Access
 controllers for, 24
 EMM386.EXE setting for, 118
 for file transfers, 182
 to screen, 358-359, 526, 720-721
Directories, 187-188. *See also* Current directory
 backing up, 157-158, 813
 changing, 194-197, 365, 527-529, 818, 932-933
 COMMAND.COM in, 49
 copying, 152, 222-223, 226-228, 908
 creating, 192-193, 225, 365, 750, 753, 872
 deleting, 147, 192-194, 365, 459-475, 753, 766, 889, 959
 and disk buffers, 43
 displaying structure of, 197-199, 901
 DOS functions for, 364-365
 DOS 1.x and 2.x support for, 7
 expanding and collapsing, 751-752
 file entries in, 139-140
 invalid entries in, fixing, 172-173
 joining disks to, 9, 864
 listing files in. *See* Listing files
 locating, 473-475
 managing, 188-191
 names of, 140
 NUKE for, 459-475, 959
 for program groups, 756-757
 in prompt, 61, 260-261, 882
 recovering files in, 177-178
 renaming, 14, 221, 475-481, 753, 766, 971
 restoring, 160, 888
 search paths for, 199-205, 810, 878
 with Shell, 748-749, 751-752
 substituting drives for, 9, 897
Directory attribute, listing files by, 208-209, 831
Directory tree area, 748-750

DISABLE_VIDEO procedure (SAVER), 544-545, 557-558

Disabled menus, color for, 764

Disassembling with DEBUG, 36

Disconnect command with PC-DIAL, 719

Disk drives. *See* Disks and disk drives

"Disk error reading FAT x" message, 172

DISK_INT procedure
in LPT2FILE, 581
in PC-DIAL, 650

Disk Manager program, 38, 142

Disk transfer area
DOS functions for, 370, 474
in PSP, 344
and TSRs, 619

Disk Utilities program group, 754-755

DISKCOMP command, 833
with JOIN, 864
with SUBST, 897

DISKCOPY command, 152, 834
with ASSIGN, 811
with JOIN, 864
with SUBST, 897

Disks and disk drives, 125. *See also* Floppy disks
and disk drives; Hard disks; Partitions
and partition tables
and BREAK directive, 55
buffers for, 40-43, 815
caches for, 12, 40, 42-43, 57, 64-66, 68-70, 848,
923
checking, 141, 819
defective. *See* Recovering files
directories for. *See* Directories
DOS 1.x support for, 7
interrupts for, 597
joining, to directories, 9, 864
logging, 7
parameter tables for, 53-55, 839
in prompts, 61, 195, 260-261, 882
RAM, 56-57, 70-74, 93, 107, 921
substituting, for directories, 9, 897
and TSRs, 619
verifying writes to, 906
volume labels for (*See* Volume labels)

Display... command
in QBasic, 775
in Shell, 750

DISPLAY.SYS driver, 57, 288-289, 292, 913

Displayed video pages, 800

Displaying
assembly language programs, 339-341
batch file commands, 60, 62, 252, 376-378,
407, 840
command history, 296-301
directories, 197-199, 901
file contents, 750, 761
macros, 307
volume labels, 207, 907

DMA. *See* Direct Memory Access

DO batch file statement, 383-384, 854

DO UNTIL statements (QBasic), 777, 797

DO WHILE statements (QBasic), 777

Documentation
in assembly language, 336
for QBasic, 779-781

Dollar signs ($)
with ANSI.SYS, 267-268
with FKEYS, 568-570, 946-947
for macros, 307-310, 837
for message delimiters, 337, 357
for prompts, 61-62, 195, 261, 882

DOS, locating, 85
in extended memory, 39-40, 59, 81
in High Memory Area, 59, 95-97, 835
in upper memory, 100, 835

DOS Communication Area, memory for, 85

DOS directive (CONFIG.SYS), 13, 40, 59, 96-
97, 99-101, 835

DOS Editor. *See* Editor

DOS extenders, 13, 119-120

DOS files, directory for, 189

DOS functions. *See also* Interrupt 21H
for directory manipulation, 364-365
for file I/O, 361-362
for file manipulation, 363-364
for keyboard, 352-354
for memory, 365-368
miscellaneous, 370-372
for printers, 359-360
for screen, 357
for terminating programs, 369
for time and date, 368-369

DOS Idle interrupt, 598, 618, 620

DOS_INT procedure
in LPT2FILE, 580
in PC-LOG, 621-626, 644

DOS kernel, 27-29, 31

DOS multiplex interrupt, 17, 95, 538, 556, 558-
559, 934

DOS_OUT procedure
in FINDTEXT, 514-515
in FKEYS, 567-568
in LPT2FILE, 594
in PC-LOG, 639
in REMOVE, 737

DOS_OUTNAME procedure (FINDTEXT),
513

DOS_OUTNUM procedure (FINDTEXT),
512-513

DOS partitions, 129
creating, 134-136, 851
deleting, 136-137, 851
DOS 3.x support for, 10
formatting, 141
in master partition tables, 130-133

DOS shell. *See* Shell

DOS Task Switcher API, 17-18, 769

DOS 1.x, 3-7

DOS 2.x, 7-9
DOS 3.x, 9-10
DOS 4.x, 10-11
DOS 5.0, 11-18
DOSHELP.HLP file, 16
DOSIDLE_INT procedure
    in LPT2FILE, 580-581
    in PC-DIAL, 651
DOSKEY command, 16-17, 74, 836-837
    for command history, 295-301
    editing commands with, 301-303
    installing, 297-298
    for macros, 231, 297-298, 304-313
    for multiple commands, 304, 307
    in upper memory, 99, 103
DOSSHELL.COM file, 747
DOSSHELL command, 103, 838
DOSSHELL.INI file, 761-762
Dots (.) in directory entries, 195-197
Double-buffering, 801
Double-density floppy disks, 144, 150-151
Double dots (..) in directory entries, 195-197
Double-line boxes, 429, 940
Double words, 22
DRAWBOX procedure
    in FINDTEXT, 520-522
    in PC-DIAL, 662
DRAWBOX utility, 429-436, 940
DrawExit subprogram (PASSAGES), 790-791
DrawHeader subprogram (PASSAGES), 791, 796
DRAWHORIZONTAL procedure
    in DRAWBOX, 432-433
    in FINDTEXT, 522
DrawPassage subprogram (PASSAGES), 791-793, 800-801
DRAWSTATUS procedure (FINDTEXT), 517
DRAWTITLE procedure (FINDTEXT), 516-517
DRAWVERTICAL procedure
    in DRAWBOX, 433
    in FINDTEXT, 522
    in PC-DIAL, 662-663
DRAWWINDOW procedure (FINDTEXT), 517-518
Drive icons, 748-752, 764
Drive letters
    in paths, 200, 205
    for RAM disks, 71, 921
DRIVER.SYS driver, 55-58, 153-154, 914
Drivers. *See* Device drivers
Drives. *See* Disks and disk drives
DRIVPARM directive (CONFIG.SYS), 52-55, 839
DS register, 22-23, 336
DSR (Data Set Ready) serial port pin, 277-278, 722
DTA. *See* Disk transfer area

DTR (Data Terminal Ready) serial port pin, 277-278
Dual File Lists view, 749-750
Duncan, Ray, 58
Dunford, Chris, 296
Dvorak, John, 747
DX register, 22-23
Dynamic allocation of memory, 8

E

E command (DEBUG), 255-256
$e metacharacter with PROMPT, 261, 882
EBCDIC code, 233
ECHO batch file command, 60, 62, 252, 284, 319, 376-378, 407, 840
ECHOCD utility, 402-403, 941
ECHODRV utility, 402-403, 942
ED (extra-high density) floppy disks, 12, 144, 151
EDIT command, 236, 245, 841
EDIT.HLP file, 244
Edit menu
    in Editor, 237
    in QBasic, 774-775
EDIT procedure (PC-DIAL), 691-694
EDIT_STRING procedure (PC-DIAL), 665-669
Editing
    commands, 16, 74, 300-303, 836-837
    macros, 311
    text files, 14-15, 235-245, 841-842
Editor, 14-15, 236-238, 841
    for batch files, 376
    customizing, 244-245
    cutting and pasting with, 239-241
    help for, 237, 242-244
    printing with, 242
    and QBasic, 774, 883
    searching and replacing with, 241-242
EDLIN editor, 14-15, 235-236, 842
Efficiency and cluster size, 139
EFLAGS register, 446
EGA (Enhanced Graphics Adapter), 248
    alternate character sets for, 288
    blanking screen of, 558
    DOS 4.x support for, 10
    lines of text for, 235, 245, 258-260, 926
    task switching with, 57, 915
EGA.SYS driver, 57, 915
86-DOS operating system, 4-5, 235
Electrically compatible 3 $\frac{1}{2}$-inch drives, 54-55
Elevators, color for, 764
Ellipses (...), 237, 749
EMB (Extended Memory Blocks), 95
Embedded servos, 183
EMM386 command, 109-110, 843
EMM386.EXE driver, 56-57, 70, 916-917
    for converting extended memory to expanded, 106-108

for DEVICEHIGH, 101, 869
and MEM, 90
memory used by, 77
options with, 112-118
for upper memory, 13, 17, 25, 83, 98, 110-112,
366, 368, 830
Virtual-86 mode with, 21
Empty directories, copying, 152, 227, 908
EMS. *See* Expanded memory
EMS40.SYS utility, 108-109, 943
Enable Task Swapper command (Shell), 749-
750, 767-768
ENABLE_VIDEO procedure (SAVER), 545,
557-558
ENCRYPT procedure (ENCRYPT), 489-490
ENCRYPT utility, 482-492, 944
END FUNCTION statement (QBasic), 776
END SUB statement (QBasic), 776, 796
Endless loops, 383
ENDP directive (assembler), 337
ENDS directive (assembler), 338
Enhanced keyboards, 58, 252, 262, 898, 910-911
Enhanced Small Device Interface drives, 128
EnterExecState function, 18
Environment, 33-35
appended files in, 203
and AUTOEXEC.BAT, 62
and batch files, 34, 63, 387-390, 862
capitalization of variables and strings in, 389,
394
with INSTALL, 863
and macros, 305
and PSP, 343
setting variables and strings in, 33-35, 890
size of, 9, 40, 47-48, 388, 821, 893
for TSRs, 556-557
Equal signs (=)
in batch files, 386, 393-395, 862
in prompts, 261, 882
ERASE command. *See* DEL command
Error codes for QBasic, 779
Error-handling statements for QBasic, 783
ERROR_INT procedure (PC-DIAL), 650
Error messages, suppressing, 318, 400
Error testing with DOS functions, 344-345
Error trapping with QBasic, 795
ERRORLEVEL statements
with branching, 392-393, 862
for CPU type, 446
for exit codes, 338, 385-386, 934
for keyboard values, 409-410, 416
with program termination, 369
"Errors found, F parameter not specified" mes-
sage, 168
ES register, 22-23
Escape characters
with ANSI.SYS, 251-252, 404-405, 910, 928
in prompts, 261, 882

ESDI (Enhanced Small Device Interface)
drives, 128
Event-handling statements for QBasic, 783
Exclusive-or cipher, 482-492, 944
.EXE (executable) files, 6, 31-32, 205-207
from assembly source files, 332
vs. .COM, 341-342
paths for, 9, 199-202, 878
in RAM disks, 73
recovering, 170
searching for, 200, 205
EXEC function, 18, 371, 641-643
EXEC10H procedure (FINDTEXT), 518, 526
Executable files. *See* .EXE (executable) files
Execution units, 22
EXE2BIN command, 332, 338-339, 342, 845
EXIST batch file statement, 387, 396, 862
Exit codes, 338-339, 369, 385, 862, 934
Exit command
in QBasic, 775
in Shell, 750
EXIT command (DOS), 48, 753, 846
EXIT SUB statement (QBasic), 796
Expand All command (Shell), 751
Expand Branch command (Shell), 751
EXPAND command, 847
Expand One Level command (Shell), 751
Expanded memory, 25, 81, 83. *See also*
EMM386.EXE driver
for background copying, 931
converting extended to, 106-109, 943
for disk buffers, 42-43
for disk caches, 64-68, 923
DOS 4.x support for, 10
EMS for, 87-89, 94, 107, 119
emulator for, 13
for FASTOPEN, 69, 848
page frames for, 116-117, 916
for print buffers, 282
for RAMDRIVE.SYS, 70-71, 921
for SMARTDRV.SYS, 12
for TSRs, 739-740, 743-744, 951, 970
"Expected: end-of-statement" message
(QBasic), 776
Extended character set, 232-234
Extended DOS partitions, 129
creating, 135-136, 851
DOS 3.x support for, 10
in master partition tables, 130-133
Extended error information, 345, 371, 619, 643
Extended file selections, 759-760
Extended key codes
batch file for, 416
BIOS function for, 347-350
DOS functions for, 352
Extended memory, 25, 81, 83-86
converting, to expanded, 106-109, 943
for disk caches, 64-68, 923
DOS in, 39-40, 59, 81

DOS 3.x support for, 9
for FASTOPEN, 70, 848
HIMEM.SYS for, 91-95, 918-919
for print buffers, 282
for program items, 758
for RAMDRIVE.SYS, 70-71, 921
for SMARTDRV.SYS, 12
for Windows, 119
XMS functions for, 94-95
Extended Memory Blocks, 95
Extenders, DOS, 119-120
Extensions, file, 32, 206-207
associating files by, 759
sorting files by, 211, 753
External commands, 30-31, 62, 396
Extra-high density (ED) floppy disks, 12, 144,
151

F

FAR procedures, 337
Fast alternate register sets, 117
Fastback Plus program, 181
FASTOPEN command, 68-70, 848
DOS 3.x and 4.x support for, 10
expanded memory for, 107-108
installing, 49, 69
in upper memory, 98-99, 104
FAT. *See* File allocation tables
FBACKUP.BAT utility, 162-164
FC command, 216, 218-220, 849
FCBS directive (CONFIG.SYS), 9, 44, 850
FDISK command, 16, 37, 133-137, 851
with JOIN, 864
with SUBST, 897
50 utility, 259, 927
File allocation tables, 4, 138-140
bad clusters marked in, 141
with file recovery, 166, 169-170, 172
on floppy disks, 145
and reformatting, 147-148
File control blocks, 8
directive for, 9, 44, 850
functions for, 362, 370
and PSP, 343
SHARE with, 137
"File could not be opened for writing" message,
483
File Display Options... command (Shell), 750,
753
File list area, 748-750
File menu
in Editor, 237
in QBasic, 774-775
in Shell, 748, 750
Files
access codes for, 490
allocation chains for, 167-168, 172-173
associating, 750, 758-759

attributes for. *See* ATTRIB command and
file attributes
backing up, 154-160, 162-166, 181-182, 813
batch. *See* Batch files
buffers for, 13, 40-43, 65, 68, 96-97, 362, 815
closing, 362
comparing, 216-220, 822, 849
compressed, expanding, 847
concatenating, 223-224, 823
copying, 221-228, 750, 752-753, 760, 823, 931,
975
creating, 361
cross-linked, 170-171
deleting, 216, 228-233, 313, 363, 382, 750, 752-
753, 828, 844
displaying contents of, 750, 761
DOS functions for, 361-364
DOS 1.x support for, 6-7
DOS 2.x support for, 7-8
86-DOS, 4
encrypting, 482-492, 944
.EXE vs. .COM, 341-342
executable vs. non-executable, 31-32, 205-207
existence of, 387, 396, 862
extensions for, 32, 206-207, 211, 753, 759
fragmented, 140, 182, 819
groups of, 753, 759-760
handles for. *See* Handles, file
listing. *See* Listing files
locking, 892
log. *See* Log files
for macros, 311
moving, 312, 381, 750, 752-753
names of, 140, 205, 208, 220-221, 363, 371,
750, 886
open, setting for, 43-44, 852
opening, 361-362, 619-620, 750, 754, 774-775
printing, 750, 964
printing to, 577-599, 954
program, 30-31
QBasic statements for, 783-784
on RAM disks, 71, 921
recovering. *See* Recovering files
renaming, 220-221, 363, 750, 886
replacing, 753, 887
restoring, 160-162, 165-166, 888
search paths for, 199-205, 810, 878
searching for, 214-215, 312, 364, 473-475, 750,
765-766
searching in, 493-527
selecting, 750, 759-760
sharing, 892
size of, 140, 172, 207, 362
slicing and splicing, 975
speeding access to, 68-70, 848
system. *See* System files and attributes
temporary, 34, 72, 362, 921
text. *See* Text and text files
transferring, 981-982

"Files are different sizes" message, 218
Files area
    on floppy disks, 145, 147
    on hard disks, 138
    memory used by, 77
FILES directive (CONFIG.SYS), 40, 43-44, 852
FILE0000.CHK file, 169
FILE0001.REC file, 167, 884
Filters, 315, 321-326, 853, 876, 895
FIND command, 214, 315, 320-321, 324-326,
        396, 853
Find... command (QBasic), 775
Find First function, 364, 370, 473-474, 619
Find Next function, 364, 370, 473-474, 619
FINDCHAR procedure
    in BATCHKEY, 413-414, 416
    in CLRSCR, 427
    in COLOR, 535, 539
    in DEMO, 438
    in DRAWBOX, 433
    in ENCRYPT, 488
    in FINDTEXT, 504
    in FKEYS, 564
    in INSTALL, 728-729
    in LPT2FILE, 590
    in NUKE, 464, 469-470
    in PC-DIAL, 711
    in PC-LOG, 636
    in REMOVE, 735
    in RENDIR, 476, 479
    in SAVER, 549
    in SETPOS, 423
    in TEXTOUT, 419
    in TOGGLE, 574
    in WAITTIL, 444
FINDDELIM procedure
    in COLOR, 536
    in ENCRYPT, 489
    in FINDTEXT, 504-505
    in FKEYS, 564-565
    in LPT2FILE, 591
    in NUKE, 464
    in PC-DIAL, 711-712
    in PC-LOG, 636
    in RENDIR, 479-480
FINDLAST procedure (PC-DIAL), 673-674
FINDNEXT procedure (PC-DIAL), 674
FINDREC procedure (PC-DIAL), 673
FINDTEXT utility, 493-527, 945
"First cluster number is invalid" message, 171
First fit memory allocation strategy, 367
Fixup mode with CHKDSK, 169-170
FKEYS utility, 559-570, 946-947
FLAGS register, 22-23, 448-449
Flanders, Bob, 527, 606-607
Floating-point numbers with QBasic, 779
Floppy disks and disk drives, 143-144
    adding, 153-154, 914
    ASSIGN with, 152-153, 811

comparing, 833
copying, 152, 227, 313, 834, 908
DOS 1.x support for, 7
DOS 3.x support for, 9-10
for DOS 5.0 backup, 38
extra-high density, 12, 144, 151
formatting, 145-151, 181-182, 855-856
high-density, 9-10, 126, 144, 150-151
sides on, 126
system files on, 148-149, 855, 899
unformatting, 179
Flow control statements for QBasic, 782
FLUSH procedure (LPT2FILE), 583-584
FNINIT instruction (assembler), 452
FOR batch file command, 383-385, 391-393, 854
Foreground color
    ANSI.SYS for, 253, 910
    batch file for, 417, 421, 976
    codes for, 255
    COLOR for, 532-540, 937
    with Editor, 244
    with Shell, 762-763
    video memory for, 249-250
Form factors for disk drives, 53-54, 839
Form feed character, 233, 609
FORMAT command, 12, 38, 138, 141, 145,
        855-856
    with ASSIGN, 811
    help listing for, 15
    with JOIN, 864
    with SUBST, 897
Formatting disks, 126
    DOS 3.x support for, 10
    floppy disks, 144-151, 181-182, 855-856
    hard disks, 138-142
    low-level, 127-128, 182-184
    recovering from, 11-12, 147, 154, 175, 178-
        179, 871, 904
    types of, 12
43 utility, 259-260, 926
4DOS command processor, 30
486DX, 450
Fragmented files, 140, 182, 819
FRAME parameter (EMM386.EXE), 116-117,
        916
FREEMEM procedure (REMOVE), 736-737
Full-screen text editor. *See* Editor
Fully qualified file names, 190-191, 371
Function keys, 262
    assigning commands to, 75, 265-268, 270, 559-
        570, 946-947
    batch file for, 416
    BIOS function for, 348
    with PC-DIAL, 715-716
FUNCTION statement (QBasic), 776
Functions
    DOS. *See* DOS functions; Interrupt 21H
    QBasic, 774-776
    XMS, 94-95

G

$G metacharacters
    with FKEYS, 568-570, 946
    in macros, 309-310, 837
    with PROMPT, 61, 195, 260-261, 882
Gates, Bill, 4-5
General registers, 22-23
Get Country Information function, 51
Get Extended Error Information function, 345,
    371, 619, 643
Get List of Lists function, 743
Get UMB Link Status function, 17, 366-368
GETHOUR utility, 440-441, 948
GETKEY utility, 409-410, 949
GETMIN utility, 441, 950
Global variables in QBasic, 795-796
GOTO batch file command, 382-383, 857
GOTO statement (QBasic), 778
GRAFTABL command, 858
Graphical user interface, 187
Graphics, 247-248
    code pages for, 858
    printing, 284-287, 859-860
    for QBasic, 784
    video buffers for, 89
GRAPHICS command, 284-287, 859-860
    enhancements to, 16
    as TSR, 32
    upper memory for, 103
Graphics Printer, 272
GRAPHICS.PRO file, 285-286, 859
GRAPHICSWIDE printer type, 285
Greater-than sign (>)
    in command buffer, 299
    with FKEYS, 568-569, 946
    in prompt, 61, 195, 260-261, 882
    for redirection, 309, 315-317, 400, 403
Green bit for screen color, 249-250
GREEN color identifier (COLOR), 532, 937
Ground pin for serial ports, 277
Groups of files, 753, 759-760
GUI (graphical user interface), 187
GW-BASIC programs, converting, 777-779

H

H attribute code, 215-216, 812
$h metacharacter with PROMPT, 61-62, 261,
    882
Handles, file, 7-8
    for extended memory, 93, 95, 117
    functions for, 361-362, 490, 492
Handshaking, UART, 277-278
Hard disks, 126
    backing up, 154-160, 162-166, 181-182, 813
    DOS 2.x support for, 7
    DOS 3.x support for, 9-10
    DOS 4.x support for, 10-11
    EMS data stored on, 89
    formatting, 138-142

    locating files on, 214-215
    low-level formatting of, 127-128, 182-183
    parking heads for, 179-181, 960
    partitions for. *See* Partitions and partition
        tables
    platters on, 126-127
    restoring, 160-162
    speeding operations of, 64-66, 923
    third-party maintenance tools for, 181-185
    unsupported, 142-143
Hardware, 27-28
    code pages for, 51, 288, 920
    configuration of, 58
    upper memory for, 25
Hardware interrupts, 45, 263, 896
"Has invalid cluster, file truncated" message,
    171
Hayes command set, 721-722
HDBKUP utility, 37
HDRSTORE utility, 38
Headers
    for assembly language programs, 336
    in batch files, 378-379
    for .EXE files, 341-342
    for memory, 365
    sector ID, 127
Heads, disk, 53-54, 126-127, 839
    parking, 179-181, 960
    in partition address, 130-131
HELLO1.ASM program, 334-341
HELLO1.COM program, 326
HELLO2.ASM program, 372-374
HELLO2.COM program, 327
Help, 15-16, 268, 861
    for Editor, 237, 242-244
    for program items, 757-758
    for QBasic, 772, 774-775, 779-781
    for Shell, 748, 751
HELP command, 15-16, 861
Help menu
    in Editor, 237
    in QBasic, 774-775
Help Path... command (QBasic), 775
Hercules Graphics Card, 248
Hex dumps with Shell, 761
Hexadecimal notation, 18-20
HEX2BIN procedure
    in CLRSCR, 427-428
    in DEMO, 438
    in DRAWBOX, 434
    in PC-DIAL, 705-706
    in TEXTOUT, 419-420
Hidden files and attribute, 16, 215-216, 812
    backing up, 157
    copying, 152
    deleting, 216, 230, 460, 475, 959
    and directory deletion, 194, 460, 889, 959
    DOS function for, 363
    listing, 28, 208-210, 753, 831

searching for text in, 493, 945
Hiding
    cursor, 262, 424, 973
    screen, 553, 557-558
Hierarchical file system, 7, 187-188
High-density floppy disks, 144
    DOS 3.x support for, 9-10
    formatting double-density as, 150-151
    indicator hole on 151
High first memory allocation strategy, 367
High-level formatting, 126
High Memory Area, 13, 83-84, 86-87
    for disk buffers, 42
    for DOS, 59, 95-97, 835
    with HIMEM.SYS, 92-93, 918-919
    XMS functions for, 94-95
"High Memory Area Unavailable" message, 92
High-Performance File System, 129
Highlighting
    color for, 764
    with Editor, 239-240
HIMEM.SYS driver, 13, 56-57, 918-919
    with DEVICEHIGH, 101, 869
    and EMS40.SYS, 108, 943
    for HMA, 87
    installing, 40, 91-93
    and MEM, 90-91
    memory used by, 77
    operation of, 93-95
    for SMARTDRV.SYS, 67
    for upper memory, 830
    for Windows, 119
History, command, 74, 295-301
History of DOS, 3-5
    DOS 1.x, 6-7
    DOS 2.x, 7-9
    DOS 3.x, 9-10
    DOS 4.x, 10-11
    DOS 5.0, 11-18
Hit rates with disk caches, 65
HMA. *See* High Memory Area
HMAMIN switch (HIMEM.SYS), 95
Holmes, Michael, 527, 606-607
Hotkeys, changing, 603-604
Hours
    batch file for, 440-441, 948
    functions for, 368-369
    in time stamps, 363
HPDEFAULT printer type, 284
HPFS (High-Performance File System), 129

I

IBACKUP.BAT utility, 164-165
IBM Personal Computer, 4-5
IBMBIO.COM file, 28, 56
IBMDOS.COM file, 28
IDE (Intelligent Drive Electronics) disks, 128, 143
Idle loops, 17

IEEE floating-point format, 779
IF batch file command, 63, 338, 369, 385-387, 409-410, 416, 862, 934
IF-THEN-ELSE statements (QBasic), 777
Immediate window with QBasic, 773, 803-807
IN batch file statement, 383-384, 854
Incremental backups, 159-160, 162, 164-165, 216, 227
Indentation in directory displays, 197-198
Index command
    in QBasic, 775, 780
    in Shell, 751
Indirection, 391
InDOS flag, 596-598, 618, 644, 720
Infinity control, 452
INIT procedure
    in BEEP, 615-616
    in INSTALL, 726-728
    in LPT2FILE, 585-590
    in PC-DIAL, 707-711
    in PC-LOG, 634-636
    in SAVER, 547-549
INIT_VIDEO procedure (FINDTEXT), 515-516
Initializing
    DOS, 28-29
    modems, 722
    with PC-DIAL, 719
    printer ports, 271, 276-277, 360, 873
INKEY$ statement (QBasic), 797
Input/output
    with batch files, 408-417, 930, 949
    QBasic statements for, 782-783
    redirecting. *See* Redirection
    suppressing, 317-318, 399-400, 825
Insert key, BIOS function for, 351
"Insert last backup diskette in drive A:" message, 158
Insert mode
    with DOSKEY, 298, 303
    with Editor, 238
INSERT procedure (PC-DIAL), 686-687
"INSTALL cannot be loaded high" message, 743
INSTALL directive (CONFIG.SYS), 49-50, 69, 282-283, 863
INSTALL utility, 725-730, 737-744, 951
Installable device drivers, 7-8, 77-80, 829
    as executable files, 32
    HIMEM.SYS, 40, 91-93
    loading, 56
    memory for, 31, 90, 830, 870
Installation program, 11
Installing
    DOS 5.0, 37-38
    DOSKEY, 297-298
INSTRING procedure (PC-DIAL), 670-671
Instruction decode units, 22
Instruction pointer register, 22-23

Instruction prefetch units, 22
Instruction sets, 21, 333, 335
"Insufficient room in root directory" message, 170
INT instruction (assembler), 338
Intel 80x86 microprocessor family, 4, 9, 20-24, 333
Intelligent Drive Electronics disks, 128, 143
Interactive mode in FINDTEXT, 495-496, 945
Interleave, sector, 127-128, 184-185
Interleaved memory, 82
Internal commands, 30, 62
    macros for, 304, 306
    table of, 232
Internal device drivers, 78
"Internal stack overflow" message, 46, 896
Internal stacks, 45-46, 620, 896
International support, 10. *See also* Code pages
    COUNTRY.SYS directive for, 50-52, 159-160, 824
    function for, 103, 289, 817, 877
Interpreted programs, 436, 456
Interrupt 05H, 287
Interrupt 08H, 556, 615-616
Interrupt 09H, 556
Interrupt 10H, 26, 345, 354, 526, 558, 617
    Function 0AH, 345, 356
    Function 0EH, 327, 356-357
    Function 0FH, 355-356
    Function 02H, 251, 355-356, 438
    Function 06H, 254-255, 355, 439
    Function 07H, 355
    Function 09H, 356
    Function 11H, 260, 352
Interrupt 13H, 597, 619, 720
    Function 0CH, 181
    Function 08H, 181
Interrupt 14H, 275, 722
Interrupt 15H, 93, 918
Interrupt 16H, 263-264, 345
    Function 00H, 346-349
    Function 01H, 351-352
    Function 02H, 350
    Function 03H, 352
    Function 05H, 352
    Function 10H, 348-349
    Function 11H, 351
    Function 12H, 351
Interrupt 17H, 26, 275, 345, 596, 607
    Function 00H, 271, 360, 598
    Function 01H, 271, 360, 598-599
    Function 02H, 599
Interrupt 19H, 93
Interrupt 2FH, 17, 95, 538, 556, 558-559, 934
Interrupt 20H, 342-343
Interrupt 21H, 29-30, 344
    Function 0AH, 353, 569, 618
    Function 0BH, 353, 442
    Function 0CH, 353

Function 0EH, 470
Function 0FH, 362
Function 01H, 352
Function 02H, 357, 405
Function 05H, 271, 359-360
Function 07H, 352-353
Function 08H, 352-353, 409
Function 09H, 327, 337-338, 357, 402-403, 468, 540
Function 1AH, 370, 473, 619
Function 11H, 619
Function 12H, 619
Function 19H, 402, 470
Function 2AH, 368, 440
Function 2BH, 369
Function 2CH, 368, 440, 442
Function 2DH, 369
Function 2FH, 370, 619
Function 25H, 370, 615
Function 3AH, 364-365, 470-471
Function 3BH, 364-365, 470-471
Function 3CH, 361
Function 3DH, 361, 363, 490
Function 3EH, 362, 492
Function 3FH, 362, 490-491
Function 30H, 371, 481, 538
Function 31H, 369, 555-556, 616
Function 33H, 371, 523
Function 34H, 371, 597
Function 35H, 370, 556, 615
Function 38H, 51
Function 39H, 364-365
Function 4AH, 342, 366-367
Function 4BH, 371, 641-643
Function 4CH, 338, 342, 369, 385, 555
Function 4DH, 369, 371
Function 4EH, 364, 370, 473-474, 619
Function 4FH, 364, 370, 473-474, 619
Function 40H, 362, 490, 492, 595-596, 598
Function 41H, 363, 470, 475
Function 42H, 362, 525
Function 43H, 363, 475
Function 47H, 364-365, 470
Function 48H, 366
Function 49H, 366-367, 556, 743
Function 5AH, 362
Function 5BH, 361
Function 5DH, 371, 597, 618-619, 643
Function 50H, 371, 619-620
Function 51H, 371, 620
Function 52H, 743
Function 56H, 363, 481
Function 57H, 363
Function 58H, 17, 366-368
Function 59H, 345, 371, 619, 643
Function 60H, 371
Function 62H, 371
Function 69H, 371
    non-reentrancy of, 596-598, 617-619

Interrupt 22H, 342-343
Interrupt 23H, 342-343, 524
Interrupt 24H, 342-343
Interrupt 25H, 597, 619, 720
Interrupt 26H, 597, 619, 720
Interrupt 27H, 369
Interrupt 28H, 598, 618, 620
Interrupt 33H, 555-557
Interrupts and interrupt vector table
    in assembly language programs, 338, 345
    controllers for, 24
    disabling, 353
    DOS functions for, 370
    hardware, 45, 263, 896
    for keyboard, 263-264
    memory for, 85
    software, 26, 29, 45, 338, 345
    stacks for, 45, 122, 896
    and TSRs, 554, 556, 558-559, 740, 742-743
Invalid clusters, 171-172
"Invalid drive specification" message, 52, 175, 470
"Invalid parameter" message, 278
"Invalid path, not directory, or directory not empty" message, 193
"Invalid path or file name" message, 221
"Invalid sub-directory entry" message, 173
Invisible characters, 254
I/O. *See* Input/output; Redirection
IO.SYS file, 28-31
    attributes for, 209
    backing up, 157
    in boot sector, 138
    device drivers in, 56, 78-79
    on floppy disks, 149, 899
    in HMA, 95-96
    memory for, 85
    on partitions, 141
IOCTL functions, 18
IP register, 22-23
IRET instruction (assembler), 617
ISR (interrupt service routines), 45, 85

J

JC instruction (assembler), 345
JMP instruction (assembler), 336-337
JNC instruction (assembler), 345
JOIN command, 9, 864
    with ASSIGN, 153, 811
    delete tracking with, 177
    and full file names, 371
    TRUENAME with, 190
Joining files, 223-224, 823
Jumping in batch files, 382-383, 857

K

KB_INT procedure
    in PC-DIAL, 649
    in SAVER, 542-543, 557-558

KEYB command, 103, 292-293, 865
Keyboard command (Shell), 751
KEYBOARD.SYS file, 58, 292, 865
Keyboards, 262-264
    alternate, 292-293, 865
    ANSI.SYS for, 910-912
    BIOS functions for, 345-352
    buffer for, 263-265, 346, 351-353, 797
    device drivers for, 6
    DOS 4.x support for, 10
    DOS functions for, 352-354
    with Editor, help for, 243
    enhanced, 58, 252, 262, 898, 910-911
    function key assignments on, 75, 265-268, 270, 559-570, 946-947
    remapping, 268-269, 292-293, 865
    scan codes for, 263, 266, 346, 610
    speed of, 74-75, 269-270, 352, 874
Keys
    accelerator, 240, 764-765
    command-line editing, 302
    command-recall, 299-300
    QBasic help for, 780
Keywords, QBasic, help for, 779-781
Kildall, Gary, 5

L

$L metacharacter
    with FKEYS, 568-570, 946
    in macros, 309-310, 837
    with PROMPT, 261, 882
L switch (EMM386.EXE), 114-115, 916
LABEL command, 141, 866
    with ASSIGN, 153, 811
    with JOIN, 864
    with SUBST, 897
Labels. *See also* Volume labels
    assembly language, 340
    in batch files, 382, 857, 885
Landing zones, hard disk, 142, 179, 960
Language support, 10. *See also* Code pages
    COUNTRY.SYS directive for, 50-52, 159-160, 824
    function for, 103, 289, 817, 877
Laptops with Editor, 245
Largest executable program size, 77
LaserJet printers
    for graphics, 284-286, 859-860
    pitch and line spacing for, 273-274, 938, 953
    sideways printing on, 606-607, 952
LASERLST utility, 606-607, 952
Last fit memory allocation strategy, 367-368
LASTDRIVE directive (CONFIG.SYS), 52, 201-202, 867
LC2CAP procedure (BATCHKEY), 414-415
LEDs for keyboard state, 574-575
Length
    of batch file commands, 375-376
    of page, assembler directive for, 335

of partitions, 130-131
of PATH command, 193, 200-202, 878
Less-than signs (<)
    with FKEYS, 568-569, 946
    in prompts, 261, 882
    for redirection, 309, 316
Levels with PC-LOG, 639-641, 643, 967
LH command. *See* LOADHIGH command
Lights, keyboard state, 574-575
LIM (Lotus/Intel/Microsoft) Expanded Memory Specification, 25, 87-89, 94
    and EMM386.EXE, 107
    for Windows, 119
Line buffers for file comparisons, 220, 849
Line feed character, 233
Line numbers
    for commands, 300
    for file comparisons, 217-218, 849
    with QBasic, 778
Line-oriented editors, 235
Line spacing for printers, 272-274, 938, 953
LINE statement (QBasic), 800
Line Status register, 723
Lines of text on screen
    DOS 4.x support for, 10
    with Editor, 245
    MODE settings for, 75, 874-875
    with MORE, 235
    utilities for, 257-260, 926-927
LINK command and linker, 332, 338-339
Link status of UMBs, 368
Linked lists for memory, 365, 368, 740-743
Listing files, 28, 206-207, 831-832. *See also*
    Displaying
    by attributes, 208-210, 831
    backup, 160, 888
    default switches for, 213
    deleted, 175-176
    DIRCMD environment variable for, 16, 34,
        213
    DOS 1.x support for, 7
    macros for, 312-313
    in non-current directories, 212-213
    with Shell, 750, 753
    sorting for, 210-212, 753
LOADALL instruction (assembler), 86
LOADFIX command, 16, 105-106, 868
LOADHIGH command, 59, 102-105, 869
    with alternative memory managers, 119
    for device drivers, 93
    for DOSKEY, 297
    with EMM386.EXE, 115
    for FASTOPEN, 70, 848
    for LPT2FILE, 596
    for PRINT, 283
    for TSRs, 97-99, 740, 743, 951, 970
Loading
    alternate character sets, 10, 288
    .COM files, 341

with Editor, 239
    graphics characters, 858
    installable device drivers, 56, 829-830
    QBasic programs, 774-776
Local variables in QBasic, 795-796
Lock Extended Memory Block function (XMS),
    95
Locking files, 892
Lockups with task switching, 769
LODS instruction (assembler), 416
Log files
    for backups, 155-156, 161, 813
    batch file for, 396
    for programs, 620-644, 967
Logging disks, 7
Logical drives, 12, 126, 175. *See also* Partitions
    and partition tables
    device drivers for, 79, 914
    DOS 3.x support for, 10
    in extended DOS partitions, 136
    formatting, 141
    setting for, 52, 867
    size of, 129
Logical operations, 576
Logical pages, 87
Logical volumes, 132
Look-ahead buffering, 67
LOOP statement (QBasic), 797
Lorenz cipher machines, 484
Lost clusters, 168-170
    "xx lost clusters found in y chains" message,
        168-169, 173
Lotus 1-2-3, memory for, 119
Low first memory allocation strategy, 367
Low-level formatting, 126-128, 182-184
Lowercase for file listings, 208, 831
LPI utility, 274, 953
LPT2FILE utility, 577-599, 954
LPT2LPT utility, 955
LPTx devices
    drivers for, 78-79, 270-271, 275
    redirecting output between, 278-280, 955
    redirecting output to, 317-319, 577-599, 954
LST files, 336, 339-341
LZSELECT utility, 604-606, 956

M

M-DOS operating system, 4
M switch (EMM386.EXE), 116-117, 916
Machine codes with HIMEM.SYS, 92, 95,
    918-919
"Macro storage depleted" message, 297
Macros, command, 16-17, 74, 297-298, 836-837
    vs. batch files, 304
    creating and running, 305-307
    editing and deleting, 310-311
    for file protection, 231
    for internal commands, 257
    redirection with, 309-310, 837

replaceable parameters in, 307-309
sample, 312-313
saving, 311
MAGENTA color identifier (COLOR), 532, 937
Magnetic fields and coercivity, 150-151
Main modules, QBasic, 775
Main program group, 754-755
MASM command and assembler, 332, 338-339, 342
Master partition tables, 130-133
"Match not found" message, 242
Math coprocessors, 24
  batch files for type of, 449-454
  memory for, 97, 109, 118, 843, 916
  NDPTYPE for type of, 449-453, 957
Math statements for QBasic, 784
Maze game, 785-802, 961
/MBF switch (QBasic), 779, 883
MCB (memory control blocks), 365-366, 740-743
MCGA adapters, blanking screen of, 558
MD command, 192, 872
MDA (Monochrome Display Adapter), 247, 540
MDEL.BAT utility, 382
Mefford, Michael, 262
MEM command, 75-77, 90-91, 99, 870
  DOS 4.x support for, 10
  for DOS location, 96
  enhancements to, 16
Memory, 12-13, 81-83
  addressable, 20-21
  alternative managers for, 118-119
  analyzing, 75-77, 90-91, 870
  bank-switched, 83, 87-89
  and bus, 25
  for .COM files, 342
  for command interpreter, 6-7, 30, 49
  CONFIG.SYS directives for, 59, 121-123, 830
  conventional, 25, 31, 83-85, 758
  converting, 106-109, 943
  device drivers for, 56-57, 916-917
  DEVICEHIGH directive for, 100-102
  for disk buffers, 42
  DOS configuration in, 31
  DOS directive for, 13, 40, 59, 96-97, 99-100, 835
  DOS 4.x support for, 10
  DOS functions for, 365-368
  dynamic allocation of, 8
  for environment strings, 9, 35, 40, 47-48, 388, 821, 890, 893
  expanded. *See* Expanded memory
  extended. *See* Extended memory
  for FASTOPEN, 69-70, 848
  High Memory Area. *See* High Memory Area
  HIMEM.SYS for. *See* HIMEM.SYS driver
  LOADFIX for, 105-106, 868
  LOADHIGH for. *See* LOADHIGH command
  for macros, 304-305

for NUKE, 468-469
pages in, 82-84, 87-89, 110-112, 116-117, 916-917
for program items, 758
QBasic statements for, 785
read-only, 26, 82, 118, 142
releasing, 366-367, 369, 556, 742-743
requesting, 366
resizing, 366-367
searching for free, 366-368
and task switching, 768
for TSRs, 556-557, 616, 725-744, 951, 969-970
types of, 25
upper. *See* Upper memory
with Windows, 119
with XCOPY, 226, 908
Memory control blocks, 365-366, 740-743
Memory-mapped video, 249, 358
Memory refresh, 82
Memory-resident keyboards, 293, 865
Menus and menu bars
  with ANSI.SYS, 406
  color for, 764
  with Editor, 236
  with QBasic, 773
  for SETUP, 601-602, 605-606, 974
  with Shell, 748
Messages
  in assembly language programs, 337, 357
  in batch files, 60, 62, 252, 376-378, 407, 840
Metastrings
  with FKEYS, 568-570, 946-947
  with PROMPT, 61-62, 195, 260-261, 882
Microprocessors, 4, 9, 20-24, 333
Microsoft, 4-5
Minus signs (-)
  with ATTRIB, 215-216, 812
  with file sorting, 211
  with Shell directories, 751-752
  with TOGGLE, 570-571, 977
Minutes
  batch file for, 440-441, 950
  functions for, 368-369
  in time stamps, 363
MIRROR command, 12, 154, 871
  with JOIN, 864
  for rebuilding partitions, 175-177, 903
  with SUBST, 897
  for unformatting disks, 179, 904
Misalignment, low-level formatting for, 182-183
MKDIR command, 192, 872
MKDMBF$ statement (QBasic), 779
MKSMBF$ statement (QBasic), 779
Mnemonics for assembler instructions, 333
MODE command, 873-875
  for code pages, 289-291, 817
  DOS 4.x support for, 10
  for Editor printing, 242
  for keyboard, 74-75, 269-270

for lines of text, 258
for printers, 272, 284-285
for serial ports, 275-276
as TSR, 32
upper memory for, 103
Mode select registers, 558
MODELPT utility, 278-280
Modems, dialing phone numbers with, 718-724
Modified files
backing up, 159-160, 813
copying, 226-227, 908
listing, 209, 831
restoring, 888
Monitor burn-in, protecting against, 540-559,
972
Monochrome mode
for Editor, 245
video address in, 248
Month
in date stamps, 364
functions for, 368-369
MORE command, 320-322, 396, 876
with directory displays, 199
with macros, 309
with TYPE, 235, 902
Mouse
with Editor, 236, 238, 244
with SAVER, 555, 557
with Shell, 747
MOUSE_INT procedure (SAVER), 544
MOV instruction (assembler), 333-334
Move... command (Shell), 750
MOVE.BAT utility, 381
Move Extended Memory Block function
(XMS), 95
Moving files, 312, 381, 750, 752-753
MPLEX_ID procedure
in INSTALL, 730
in LPT2FILE, 592-593
in PC-DIAL, 713
in PC-LOG, 638
in SAVER, 551, 558-559
MPLEX_INT procedure
in INSTALL, 726
in LPT2FILE, 582-583
in PC-DIAL, 651-652
in PC-LOG, 626
in SAVER, 543, 559
"MS-DOS resident in High Memory Area"
message, 96
MSDOS.SYS file, 28-30
attributes for, 209
backing up, 157
in boot sector, 138
on floppy disks, 149, 899
memory for, 85, 95-96
on partitions, 141
MSG_WINDOW procedure (PC-DIAL),
700-701

Multiline prompts, 262
Multiple commands, 304, 307, 568-569, 836-837,
947
Multiple programs, 767-770
Multiple RAM disks, 71, 921
Multitasking, 27
interrupt for, 17
vs. task switching, 769
with Windows, 119
Munro, Jay, 604

N

$n metacharacter with PROMPT, 261, 882
Names
of deleted files, 176, 903
of directories, 14, 193, 753, 766
of files, 140, 205, 208, 220-221, 363, 371, 750,
886
of macros, 306
and phone numbers, directory for, 644-724,
965
sorting files by, 16, 211, 753, 831
Nanoseconds, 82
National language support, 10. *See also* Code
pages
COUNTRY.SYS directive for, 50-52, 159-
160, 824
function for, 103, 289, 817, 877
NDPTYPE program, 449-454, 957
NEAR procedures, 337
Nested Task bit, 448
Nesting
of CALL statements, 383
of FOR statements, 384
Networks
APPEND on, 204
DOS 3.x support for, 9
and file control blocks, 44, 850
file sharing on, 892
and full file names, 371
logical drive setting for, 52
open files needed for, 43-44
TRUENAME with, 190
New command
in Editor, 239
in QBasic, 775
in Shell, 755
New FUNCTION... command (QBasic), 775-776
New SUB... command (QBasic), 775
NEWPAUSE program, 379-380, 958
NEXT procedure (PC-DIAL), 686
NEXTREC procedure (PC-DIAL), 674-675
Nishi, Kay, 5
NLSFUNC command, 103, 289, 817, 877
"No files found" message, 214
NOEMS parameter (EMM386.EXE), 106, 109,
114-115, 916-917
Non-DOS partitions, 129
deleting, 137, 851

in master partition tables, 130-131
Non-executable files, 31-32, 205-207
Non-reentrancy of TSRs, 596-598, 617-619
Non-removable disk drive parameter, 53, 839
"Non-System disk or disk error" message, 138
Normal files, 209
Norton Utilities, 178, 181-182, 185, 493
NOT batch file modifier, 385, 387, 862
NOT operations, 576
NT bit, 448
NUKE procedure (NUKE), 465-467, 471
NUKE utility, 459-475, 959
NUL device, redirecting output to, 317-318, 400, 453, 825
Null modem cable, transferring files by, 981-982
Num Lock key
    BIOS function for, 351
    startup setting for, 570-577, 977
Number signs (#)
    in deleted file names, 176, 903
    in PMF files, 601
Numbering systems, 18-20
Numeric keypad for ASCII codes, 292, 346

O

Object files, 332, 339
Oersteds, 151
Offset addresses, 23-24, 86, 354
ON ERROR statement (QBasic), 795
On-line help, 15-16, 242-244, 268, 861
Ontrack Comp. Systems, 38
Open... command (QBasic), 774-775
Open command (Shell), 750, 754-755
Open dialog box (Editor), 237-238
OPEN_FILE procedure (PC-LOG), 627-628
Open files, maximum, setting for, 43-44, 852
OPEN procedure (PC-DIAL), 690-691
OPENFILE procedure (LPT2FILE), 584
Opening
    files, 361-362, 619-620, 750, 754, 774-775
    program groups, 755
OPENWINDOW procedure (PC-DIAL), 698-699
Operating systems
    in master partition tables, 130-131
    non-disk partitions for, 129
    role of, 27-28
Optical sensors on drives, 151
Optimizing performance
    with FASTOPEN, 68-70, 848
    and interleave value, 128
    for keyboard and screen, 74-75
    memory analysis for, 75-77
    with RAMDRIVE.SYS, 70-74
    with SMARTDRV.SYS, 64-68, 923
Options menu
    in Editor, 237
    in QBasic, 774-775
    in Shell, 748-750, 752-753

OR operations, 576
ORANGE color identifier (COLOR), 532, 539, 937
ORG directive (assembler), 336
Orientation section for QBasic help, 780
OS/2 operating system, 3
OUT instruction (assembler), 723
"Out of disk space" message, 72
"Out of environment space" message, 35, 47-48, 203, 890
Output. *See* Input/output; Redirection
Output Screen command (QBasic), 775, 803
Overlays, 72-74, 641, 921
Overstrike mode
    with DOSKEY, 298, 303
    with Editor, 238

P

$p metacharacter with PROMPT, 61, 195, 260-261, 882
P switch (EMM386.EXE), 117, 916-917
"Packed file corrupt" message, 105, 868
Page description languages, 271
PAGE directive (assembler), 335-336
Page-flipping technique, 794, 800-801
Page frames, 84, 87-89, 116-117, 916-917
Page length, assembler directive for, 335
Pages
    for memory, 82-84, 87-89, 110-112, 116-117, 916-917
    for video, 355, 359, 526, 794, 800-801
Paging units, 22
Paragraphs of memory, 22, 366
Parallel ports, 360-361, 873
    device drivers for, 6, 79
    for printers, 270-271
    redirecting output between, 278-280
    redirecting output to, 955
Parameters
    in batch files, 380-382, 854, 894
    for devices, 52-55, 839
    in macros, 307-309
    with program group commands, 756-757
    with QBasic subprograms, 796
Parent directories, 196
Parity for serial ports, 276, 718, 873
PARK utility, 180-181, 960
Parking hard disk heads, 142, 179-181, 960
Parsing command lines, 416-417, 438
Partitions and partition tables, 16, 37-38, 126, 129
    creating, 134-136, 851
    deleting, 136-137, 851
    DOS 3.x support for, 9-10
    DOS 4.x support for, 10-11
    FDISK for, 133-137
    formatting, 141
    master partition tables for, 130-133
    restoring, 11-12, 154, 175, 178, 871, 904
    and SHARE, 12, 137, 892

PARTNSAV.FIL file, 175
PASSAGES.BAS program, 785-802, 961
Passageways Survival Guide, 801
Passwords
    for encryption utility, 482-492, 944
    for program groups, 756
Paste command
    in Editor, 239-240
    in QBasic, 775
PASTE procedure (PC-DIAL), 687-688
Paterson, Tim, 4-5, 235
PATH command and paths, 190, 199-205, 810,
        878
    in AUTOEXEC.BAT file, 61-62
    and batch files, 60-61, 389
    for DOS directory, 189
    DOS 2.x support for, 8
    for executable files, 9
    maximum length of, 193, 200-202, 878
PATH environment variable, 31, 33
PAUSE batch file command, 379-380, 879, 958
Pause key, 262, 351
Pause records for print spooler, 609, 964
Pausing
    batch files, 407, 949
    DOS function for, 371
    file listings, 208, 831
    with PC-DIAL, 719
    screen display, 199, 321-322, 876
    for specified time, 978
    text file viewing, 234-235
PC Backup program, 181
PC-DIAL utility, 644-724, 965
PC-LIST utility, 724, 966
PC-LOG utility, 620-644, 967
PC Tools Deluxe, 181-182
PCBOOK utility, 962
PCL (Printer Control Language), 271
PCSPOOL utility, 607-610, 963-964
Percent signs (%) for batch file parameters, 380-
        382, 388, 854, 894
Performance. *See* Optimizing performance
Periods (.) with ECHO, 377
Permanent soft fonts, 605
Perpendicular recording technology, 151
Petzold, Charles, 257
Phone numbers, dialing
    batch file for, 398-399
    PC-DIAL for, 644-724, 965
Physical memory pages, 87
Piping, 315-316, 320-321
    in batch files, 395-399
    with FKEYS, 568, 946
    with macros, 837
    in prompts, 882
    with TYPE, 235, 902
Pitch of printing, 271-274
Platters, disk, 126-127
PLAY statement (QBasic), 798

Plus signs (+)
    with ATTRIB, 215-216, 812
    with file concatenation, 223-224
    with Shell directories, 751-752
    with TOGGLE, 570-571, 977
PMF (printer menu files), 601-602, 604-606, 956,
        974
Pointers, file, 362
POP instruction (assembler), 353
Pop-up phone directory, 644-724, 965
POPUP procedure (PC-DIAL), 652-660, 721
Popup utilities, 32
Ports. *See* Parallel ports; Serial ports
POST (Power On Self-Test), 26
PostScript printer control language, 271
Precharge time for RAM, 82
"Press any key to continue..." message, 379, 879,
        958
Prevent Program Switch box, 758
Primary DOS partitions, 129
    creating, 134-135, 851
    formatting, 141
    in master partition tables, 130-131
PRINT command, 280-283, 880-881
    DOS 2.x support for, 8
    upper memory for, 103
Print... command (QBasic), 775
Print command (Shell), 750
Print Screen key, 284, 286-287, 351, 859
PRINT statement (QBasic), 806
Printable characters, 233
Printer control language, 271
PRINTER_INT procedure (LPT2FILE),
        579-580
Printer menu files, 601-602, 604-606, 956, 974
Printer status bits, 361
PRINTER.SYS driver, 57, 291-292, 920
Printers
    BIOS functions for, 360-361
    control codes for, 271, 599-606, 956, 974
    device drivers for, 6, 270-271
    DOS function for, 359-360
    interrupt for, 26
    pitch and line spacing for, 272-274, 938, 953
    redirecting output to, 278-280, 318-319
    serial ports for, 275-278, 873-874
Printing
    alternate character sets, 290-292
    background, 8, 280-281, 607-610, 880-881,
        963-964
    directories, 197, 901
    with Editor, 242
    to files, 577-599, 954
    graphics, 284-287, 859-860
    help for Editor, 244
    PC-DIAL data files, 724, 966
    QBasic documentation, 781
    QBasic programs, 775-776

text files, 242, 280-284, 319, 606-607, 750, 952, 962
PRN device driver, 6, 78, 270
  for Editor printing, 242
  redirecting output to, 317-319
"Probable non-DOS disk" message, 169
PROC directive (assembler), 337
Procedure Step command (QBasic), 775, 803
Procedures
  in assembly language programs, 337
  QBasic statements for, 785
Procedures command (Shell), 751
Processor type, determining, 446-450, 939. *See also* Coprocessors
ProComm program, 277
Program/File Lists view, 749-750
Program files, 30-32
Program groups, 754-758
Program list area, 748-750
Program List view, 749-750
Program modules, QBasic, 774
Program segment prefix, 342-344, 740
Programmable timer chips, 24
Programming. *See* Assembly language programming
Programs
  on active task list, 767
  associating data files with, 750, 758-759
  memory used by, 75-77, 84-85, 90, 740-743, 870
  multiple, 767-770
  with Shell, 754-755
Projective closure, 452
PROMPT command and prompts, 195, 882
  with ANSI.SYS, 252-253, 260-262
  assigning, to function keys, 267
  in AUTOEXEC.BAT file, 61-62
  in batch files, 60
  customizing, 260-262
  metacharacters in, 61-62, 195, 260-261, 882
PROMPT environment variable, 33
PROMPT_WINDOW procedure (PC-DIAL), 699-700
Properties command (Shell), 755
Properties for program items, 757-758, 768
Protected mode
  with EMM386.EXE, 110
  memory access in, 21, 83, 85-86
  for Windows, 119
PrtSc key, 284, 286-287, 351, 859
PSP (program segment prefix), 342-344, 740
p-System operating system, 5
PUSH instruction (assembler), 353, 448

Q

QBASIC command, 883
QBASIC.HLP file, 772
QBASIC.INI file, 245, 772
QBasic interpreter, 14, 456, 771-773
  associating files with, 759
  converting GW-BASIC and BASICA programs with, 777-779
  debugging programs with, 782, 802-807
  help system for, 779-781
  loading and running programs with, 774-777
  sample program in, 785-802
  source code files from, 234
  summary of statements for, 781-785
QEMM-386 memory manager, 12, 21, 81, 118-119
Qfiles, 280
QRAM utility, 105
QSEARCH procedure (PC-DIAL), 674
Quadwords, 22
Question marks (?)
  in file names, 212
  for help, 15-16, 268, 460, 861
  in QBasic, 806
Queues, printer, 280-282, 608, 880-881, 963-964
Quick cablers, 278
Quick formats, 12, 145, 147, 855
Quick Reference section for QBasic help, 780
QuickBASIC, 456, 771
Quotation marks (")
  for assembly language messages, 337, 357
  for function key assignment, 265, 267

R

R attribute code, 215-216, 812
RAM (Random Access Memory). *See* Memory
RAM caches, 65, 82-83
RAM disks, 9, 12, 56-57, 70-74, 93, 107, 921
RAM parameter (EMM386.EXE), 106-109, 114-115, 916-917
RAM-resident programs. *See* TSR (terminate and stay resident) programs
RAMDRIVE.SYS driver, 56-57, 70-74, 107, 921
Random disk access, caches for, 42
RD command, 192-193, 889
RD (Receive Data) serial port pin, 277
Read buffering, 67
Read Drive Parameters function, 181
Read file access, 490-491
Read-only files and attribute, 215-216, 812
  AUTOEXEC.BAT as, 63
  backup files as, 157
  deleting, 194, 216, 229-230, 460, 475, 959
  DOS function for, 363
  listing, 208-209, 831
  replacing, 887
Read/write file access, 490-491
READFILE procedure (PC-DIAL), 701-703
READKEY procedure (PC-DIAL), 660
README.TXT, 38
Real mode
  with EMM386.EXE, 111
  memory access in, 21, 83, 85-86
Real numbers with QBasic, 779

REBOOT utility, 455, 968
Rebooting
    from batch files, 454-455, 968
    for CONFIG.SYS settings, 40
.REC files, 167, 884
RECALL.BAT utility, 165-166
Receive Data serial port pin, 277
RECORD_TIME procedure (PC-LOG),
    631-632
RECOVER command, 154, 166-167, 884
    with JOIN, 864
    with SUBST, 897
Recovering files, 11-12, 166, 884, 903
    from accidental formats, 178-179
    CHKDSK for, 167-174
    deleted, 11-12, 175-178, 903
    low-level formatting for, 182-184
    partition table rebuilding for, 175
Recursion, 470-473, 777
Red bit for screen color, 249-250
RED color identifier (COLOR), 532, 937
Redirection, 315
    in batch files, 378, 395-400
    DOS 2.x support for, 8
    and DOS video functions, 357
    filters with, 321-326
    with FKEYS, 568-570, 946
    of input, 319-320
    limits of, 326-327
    with macros, 309-310, 837
    of output, 316-319
    with piping, 320-321
    of printer output, 278-280, 577-599, 954-955
    printing text files through, 283-284
    in prompts, 61, 195, 260-261, 882
Reference, passing variables by, 801
Refresh command (Shell), 750, 753
Refreshing memory, 82
Register sets, alternate, 117
Registers, 22
/REINSTALL switch (DOSKEY), 298
Relational database managers, 43
REM batch file command, 60, 378-379, 407, 885
REM directive (CONFIG.SYS), 40, 55-56, 885
Remapping keyboards, 268-269, 292-293, 865
REMLINE.BAS program, 778
REMOVE utility, 730-744, 951, 969-970
REN (RENAME) command, 220-221, 886
Rename... command (Shell), 221, 750
Renaming
    directories, 14, 221, 475-481, 753, 766, 971
    files, 220-221, 363, 750, 886
RENDIR utility, 475-481, 971
Reorder command (Shell), 755
REP MOVSW instruction (assembler), 742
Repaint Screen command (Shell), 750
Repeat Last Find command (QBasic), 775
Repeat rate for keyboards, 269-270, 352, 874
REPLACE command, 887

Replaceable parameters
    in batch files, 380-382, 854, 894
    in macros, 307-309
    with program group commands, 756-757
Replacing
    Editor text, 241-242
    files, 753, 887
    QBasic text, 775
Request To Send serial port pin, 277-278
Reserve Shortcut Keys box, 758
Reserved memory. *See* Upper memory
Resident portion of COMMAND.COM, 30, 49
Restart command (QBasic), 775
RESTORE command, 154, 156, 160-162, 888
    with ASSIGN, 153, 811
    DOS 3.x support for, 10
    enhancements to, 16
    with JOIN, 864
    with SUBST, 897
RESTORE_VIDEO procedure (FINDTEXT),
    516
Restoring files, 160-162, 165-166, 888
RESTREGION procedure (PC-DIAL), 661-
    662, 720-721
"Resynch failed" message, 219
RET instruction (assembler), 373
RET2 instruction (assembler), 643
RETURN.BAT utility, 400-401, 403
Reverse video, attribute for, 249, 253, 910
RI (Ring Indicator) serial port pin, 277
RMDIR command, 192-193, 889
ROM (Read-Only Memory), 26, 82
    copying, to RAM, 118
    for disk characteristics, 142
ROM Communication Area, 85
Root directory, 7, 140, 145, 187
    creating, 138
    defects in, 166
    files in, 188-189
    in paths, 191
    for recovered files, 884
    and reformatting, 147-148
    renaming, 476, 971
Rows, screen
    addresses of, 358-359
    cursor positioning at, 355, 421-424, 973
    setting for, 252
RS-232 breakout boxes, 278
RS-232 interface, 722-724
RTS (Request To Send) serial port pin, 277-278
Run... command (Shell), 750, 754
Run menu (QBasic), 774-775
/RUN switch (QBasic), 772, 883

S

S attribute code, 215-216, 812
S command (DEBUG), 254-255
Safe formats, 12, 145, 147, 855
Save command (QBasic), 775, 777

Save As... command (QBasic), 775, 777
SAVE procedure (PC-DIAL), 689-690
SAVEFILE procedure (PC-DIAL), 703-704
SAVER utility, 540-549, 972
SAVEREGION procedure (PC-DIAL), 660-661, 720-721
SAVESETUP procedure (PC-DIAL), 704-705
Saving
    current directory and drive, 400-403, 470, 941-942
    with Editor, 238-239
    macros, 311
    PC-DIAL records, 717
    QBasic programs, 775, 777
Scan codes, 263, 266, 346, 610
SCANHELP procedure
    in COLOR, 536
    in ENCRYPT, 489
    in FINDTEXT, 505
    in FKEYS, 565, 569-570
    in INSTALL, 729
    in LPT2FILE, 591
    in NUKE, 465, 468
    in PC-DIAL, 712
    in PC-LOG, 636-637
    in REMOVE, 735
    in RENDIR, 476, 480
    in SAVER, 549-550
    in TOGGLE, 574
Screen, 6, 247
    ANSI.SYS for, 251-254, 532, 537, 540, 875, 910-912, 937
    architecture for, 248-251
    attributes for. *See* Attributes, screen
    batch files for, 403-407, 417-439, 976
    BIOS functions for, 251, 354-357
    boxes on, 429-436, 940
    clearing, 6, 256-257, 424-429, 439, 796, 820, 935-936
    color for. *See* Color
    direct writes to, 358-359, 526, 720-721
    display mode for, 911
    DOS functions for, 357
    EGA, 915
    enhancing operations with, 75
    hiding, 553, 557-558
    lines of text on. *See* Lines of text on screen
    pages for, 355, 359, 526, 794, 800-801
    pausing, 199, 321-322, 876
    positioning cursor on, 355, 421-424, 973
    PROMPT for, 260-262
    protecting, from burn-in, 540-559, 972
    Shell commands for, 750
    splitting, with QBasic, 775, 801
    video buffers for, 89, 248-251, 355, 358-359, 526, 720-721, 800
Screen dumps, 16, 286-287, 859
Screen savers, 540-559, 972
SCREEN statement (QBasic), 795, 800

Scroll bars and scrolling
    BIOS functions for, 355, 357
    color for, 764
    with Editor, 236, 238, 244-245
Scroll Lock key
    BIOS function for, 351
    startup setting for, 570-577, 977
Search... command (Shell), 750, 766
Search menu
    in Editor, 237
    in QBasic, 774-775
Search paths, 190, 199-205, 810, 878
    in batch files, 60-61
    DOS 2.x support for, 8
    for executable files, 9
SEARCH procedure (PC-DIAL), 684-686
SEARCHDIR procedure (FINDTEXT), 505-507, 524
SEARCHFILE procedure (FINDTEXT), 507-509, 524-526
Searching
    with DEBUG, 254-255
    for directories, 473-475
    for files, 214-215, 312, 364, 473-475, 750, 765-766
    with FIND, 321, 324-326, 853
    for free memory, 366-368
    for PC-DIAL records, 717-718
    with QBasic, 774-775, 801
    for text, 241-242, 324-326, 493-527, 774-775, 853
Seattle Computer Products, 4-5
Secondary caches, 42-43
Seconds
    functions for, 368-369
    in time stamps, 363
"Sector not found" message, 166, 182
Sectors, disk, 42, 126
    bad, 128, 141, 147, 182-184
    boot, 138-139, 145
    in clusters, 139
    per cylinder, 130
    ID headers for, 127
    interleaving of, 127-128, 184-185
    low-level formatting for repairing, 182-184
    in partition address, 130-131
    for RAM disks, 70-71, 921
    per track, 53-54, 144, 839, 855
    translation of, 143
Security, encryption for, 482-492, 944
Seek function, 181
Segment address in PSP, 342-343
Segment directive (assembler), 336
Segment:offset addressing, 22-24
Segment registers, 22-23, 336
Segmentation units, 22
Segments, 22-24, 86
Select Across Directories command (Shell), 750, 760

Select All command (Shell), 750, 759
SELECT CASE statements (QBasic), 777, 799-800
Selected text with Editor, 239-240
Selections, color for, 764
Self-booting game programs, 153
Self-erasure, 151
Semicolons (;)
    for comments, 336
    with modem commands, 722
    in paths, 389
    with program group commands, 757
Sequential disk reads, caches for, 42
Serial number of disks, 207, 371
Serial ports, 78-79
    device drivers for, 6, 79
    for PC-DIAL, 716, 718-719
    for printers, 275-278, 873-874
    redirecting output to, 317
Servos in disk drives, 183
SET command, 33, 890
    in AUTOEXEC.BAT, 62-63
    in batch files, 387-390
    for path, 200
Set Country Information function, 51
Set Next Statement command (QBasic), 775, 803
Set UMB Link Status function, 17, 366-368
SETMONO procedure (FINDTEXT), 516
SETPOS utility, 421-424, 973
SETUP procedure (PC-DIAL), 675-684
SETUP program (DOS), 11, 37-38
SETUP utility, 599-606, 956, 974
SETVER command, 16, 371, 891, 905
SETVER.EXE device driver, 57, 922
SHARE command, 892
    for partitions, 12, 137
    upper memory for, 103
SHARED statement (QBasic), 795-796
Shell, 13-14, 747-754
    color with, 750, 761-765
    group operations with, 759-760
    programs with, 754-758
    renaming directories with, 766
    searching for files with, 765-766
    starting, 838
    task switching with, 767-770
    viewing file contents with, 761
Shell Basics command (Shell), 751
SHELL directive (CONFIG.SYS), 46-49, 893
    for command processor location, 30, 33, 40, 189, 821
    for environment size, 388
SHIFT batch file command, 380-382, 894
Shift keys
    BIOS functions for, 348, 350-351
    with function key programming, 568, 946
    with hotkeys, 603
    and key codes, 263, 266

Shift mask values, 603
Shift status byte, 575-577
SHORT jumps, 337
Shortcut keys
    for program groups, 756, 758
    with task switching, 768
SHOW_CHAR procedure (PC-DIAL), 664
Show Information... command (Shell), 750, 752
SHOW_STRING procedure (PC-DIAL), 663-664
SHOWFIELD procedure (PC-DIAL), 672-673
SHOWFILE procedure (FINDTEXT), 510-512, 526
SHOWLINE procedure (PC-DIAL), 672
SHOWPAGE procedure (PC-DIAL), 671-672
SHOWSTATUS procedure (LPT2FILE), 593-594
SHOWTIME procedure (SAVER), 551-552
SI register, 22-23
SideKick, 8
Sides, floppy disk, 126
Sideways printing, 606-607, 952
Single File List view, 749-750
Single-line boxes, 429, 940
Single-stepping through QBasic programs, 803
Size
    of caches, 42-43, 57, 66, 923
    of clusters, 139
    of environment, 9, 40, 47-48, 388, 821, 893
    of files, 140, 172, 207, 362
    of history buffer, 297-298, 837
    of Immediate window in QBasic, 805
    of logical drives, 129
    of LPT2FILE buffer, 577, 594-596, 954
    of memory allocated, 366-367
    of PC-DIAL buffer, 644, 714-716, 965
    of print buffers, 281-282, 607-608, 880, 963-964
    of RAM disk, 70, 921
    sorting files by, 16, 211, 323, 753, 831
    of upper memory for drivers, 101-102
SLICE utility, 975
SMARTDRV.SYS (SMARTDrive) driver, 12, 43, 56-57, 923
    expanded memory for, 107
    installing, 40, 66-68
    memory used by, 77
    speeding disk operations with, 64-66, 923
    upper memory for, 99
Snow on CGA screens, 245
Soft fonts, 605
SofTech Microsystem, 5
Software interrupts, 26, 29, 45
    in assembly language programs, 338, 345
    for keyboard, 263-264
SORT command, 315, 320-323, 895
Sorting
    file listings, 16, 210-212, 312, 753, 831
    international settings for, 51-52

text files, 315, 320-323, 895
Source code files, assemblers for, 332
SP register, 22-23
Spaces
    in environment variables, 34
    in file comparisons, 218, 220, 849
    in file names, 230
    in macro names, 306
Spacing of printing lines, 272-274
Speakers
    beeping, 35-36
    in modems, 722
SpeedStor program, 38, 142
SPICE utility, 975
SpinRite II program, 183-185
Split command (QBasic), 775, 801
Spooling of printing, 8, 280-281, 607-610, 880-881, 963-964
SQR statement (QBasic), 806
SS register, 22-23
Stacks
 command, 298-301
    internal, 45-46, 122, 620, 896
    for NUKE, 469, 472-473
    registers for, 22
    for TSRs, 620
STACKS directive (CONFIG.SYS), 45-46, 122, 896
Standard error channel, redirecting, 318, 400
Standard header for assembly language programs, 336
Standard output with ANSI.SYS, 252
Start command (QBasic), 774-775
Starting cluster numbers, 140
Startup directory for program groups, 756-757
Statements, QBasic, summary of, 781-785
Static RAM, 65, 82
Status of parallel ports, 271, 360-361
STATUS procedure (NUKE), 467
Step command (QBasic), 775, 803
STI instruction (assembler), 353, 617
Stop bits for serial ports, 276, 718, 873
Storage dimensions, 38
Stored programs, 21
STRCAT procedure (PC-DIAL), 665
Strings
    comparing, 386-387, 393-395, 862
    DOS input function for, 353
    environment, 9, 33-35, 388-389, 394, 890
    QBasic statements for, 785
    searching for, 493-527, 853
STRIPCASE procedure (FINDTEXT), 514
STRIPHIGH procedure (FINDTEXT), 514
STRLEN procedure
    in FINDTEXT, 518
    in PC-DIAL, 665
Structure of DOS, 28-31
Structured programming, 771, 777-779
SUB statement (QBasic), 776, 796

Subdirectories. *See* Directories
Subfunctions, DOS, 344
Subprograms, QBasic, 774-776, 796
Subroutines in batch files, 390-391
SUBS... command (QBasic), 775, 777
SUBST command, 9, 897
    with ASSIGN, 153, 811
    delete tracking with, 177
    and full file names, 371
    LASTDRIVE with, 52
    for paths, 201-202
    TRUENAME with, 190
Suppressing
    batch file messages, 377, 840
    command output, 317-318, 399-400, 825
Surface coercivity, 150-151
Swapping
    disk drives, 152-153, 811
    programs, 17-18, 767-770, 838
Switch statements, batch files as, 391-393
Switches, processing of, 30
SWITCHES directive (CONFIG.SYS), 58-59, 252, 898
Symbols, assembly language, 340
Syntax Checking command (QBasic), 775-776
SYS command, 12, 148-149, 899
    with JOIN, 864
    with SUBST, 897
SYSINFO.BAT utility, 397-398
SYSINIT module, 29
SysRq key, 262, 351
System area on hard disks, 138
System device drivers, 56, 78-79
System files and attributes, 16, 29-30, 32, 215-216, 812
    backing up, 157
    deleting, 216, 230, 460, 475, 959
    and directory deletion, 194, 889
    DOS function for, 363
    listing, 28, 208-209, 753, 831
    on partitions, 141
    searching for text in, 493, 945
    transferring, 12, 148-149, 152, 855, 899
System indicator byte, 130-131
SYSTEM.INI file (Windows), 59
System parameters, retrieving, 397-398
SYSTEM statement (QBasic), 773, 883

T
$T metacharacters
    with FKEYS, 568-570, 947
    in macros, 307, 310, 837
    with PROMPT, 61-62, 261, 882
Tabs
    ASCII code for, 233
    in file comparisons, 218, 220, 849
Task switching, 14, 17-18, 767-770, 838
    with EGA, 915
    memory settings for, 758

TD (Transmit Data) serial port pin, 277
TEMP environment variable, 34, 72
Temporary files, 362
    environment variables for, 34
    RAM disk for, 72, 921
Temporary fonts, 605
Terminal emulators, task switching problems
        with, 769
"Terminate batch job (Y/N)?" message, 379, 457
Terminating programs, DOS functions for, 369.
        See also TSR (terminate and stay resi-
        dent) programs
Text and text files, 233
    associating, 759
    automatic input from, 319-320
    for batch files, 7, 376
    comparing, 217-219, 822, 849
    concatenating, 224
    copying, 223, 823
    editing, 14-15, 235-245, 841-842
    for PMF, 601, 974
    printing, 242, 280-284, 319, 606-607, 750, 952,
        962
    for QBasic programs, 777
    recovering, 170
    replacing, 241-242
    searching for, 241-242, 324-326, 493-527, 774-
        775, 853
    sorting, 322-323, 895
    video buffers for, 89
    viewing, 234-235, 761, 902
TEXTOUT procedure (NUKE), 468
TEXTOUT utility, 417-421, 424, 976
Third-party utilities, 6, 181-185
386/DOSExtender, 119
386 enhanced mode, 119
386Max memory manager, 12, 21, 81, 118-119
Ticks, clock, 280-282
Time
    backing up files by, 160, 813
    batch files for, 439-445, 948, 950
    DOS functions for, 368-369
    of file creation (*See* Time stamps)
    international formats for, 51, 824
    in prompt, 61-62, 260-261, 882
    QBasic statements for, 785
    restoring files by, 888
    sorting files by, 16, 831
TIME command, 10, 900
Time-outs with printers, 360
Time stamps, 140, 207
    DOS function for, 363
    DOS 1.x support for, 7
    updating, 225
    ZCOPY for, 981
Timer chips, 24
TIMER_INT procedure
    in BEEP, 614-617
    in LPT2FILE, 578

in PC-DIAL, 648-649
    in SAVER, 541-542, 556-557
Times of program operation, logging, 620-644,
        967
Timeslices for printer spooling, 281
Timing and high-density disks, 151
Timing signals, 25
Titles and title bars
    color for, 762-764
    for program items, 756-757
    with Shell, 748, 762-763
TMP environment variable, 72
Toggle Breakpoint command (QBasic), 775, 804
TOGGLE utility, 570-577, 977
Topic: command (QBasic), 775
TPA (Transient Program Area), 31
Trace On command (QBasic), 775, 803
Tracks, disk, 53-54, 126, 839, 855
Transferring files, 981-982
Transient portion of COMMAND.COM, 30, 49
Transient Program Area, 31
Transient programs, 613
TRANSMIT_CHAR procedure (PC-DIAL),
        697-698, 722-723
Transmit Data serial port pin, 277
Transmit Holding register, 723
TRANSMIT_STRING procedure (PC-DIAL),
        697, 722
TREE command, 197-199, 901
Tree menu (Shell), 748-749, 751
Tree-structured directories, 7, 187-188
TRUENAME command, 190
Truncating files with invalid clusters, 172
TS utility (Norton Utilities), 493
TSR (terminate and stay resident) programs, 32,
        613-616
    AUTOEXEC.BAT for loading, 61
    in batch files, 929
    DOS functions for, 369, 371-372
    DOS 2.x support for, 8
    extended memory for, 39, 59, 81
    installing, 49-50, 863
    LPT2FILE, 594
    memory used by, 90
    non-reentrancy of, 596-598, 617-619
    PC-DIAL, 644-724, 965
    PC-LOG, 620-644, 967
    removing, from memory, 725-744, 951,
        969-970
    SAVER, 554-555
    SETUP, 601-602
    upper memory for, 13, 25, 93, 97-99, 102-105,
        743-744, 869, 917, 951, 970
TYPE command, 234-235, 252, 902
    batch file for, 384, 395-396
    macro for, 308
    for printing text files, 283-284
Type numbers for drives, 142-143

Typematic keyboard rates, 10, 74-75, 269-270, 352, 874

U

U command (DEBUG), 255
UART (Universal Asynchronous Receiver/ Transmitter), 24, 277, 723
UD (Unremove Directory) command (Norton Utilities), 178
UMB (upper memory blocks). *See* Upper memory
Unassembling with DEBUG, 255
Unconditional formatting, 145, 147-149, 855
UNDELETE command, 11, 154, 176, 230, 461, 828, 871, 903
Underlining, attribute for, 249, 253, 910
Underscore character (_) with COLOR, 532, 937
Undocumented DOS functions, 370-371
Undocumented interrupts, 29
UNFORMAT command, 11-12, 133, 147, 154, 175, 178-179, 871, 904
UNIX systems, 129
Unsupported hard drives, 142-143
Upgrading, 11
Upper memory, 13, 25, 59, 70, 83-84, 89, 100, 123, 830
    for applications, 17
    for device drivers, 97, 100-103, 869
    for DOS, 100, 835
    EMM386.EXE for, 110-113, 115-116
    for FASTOPEN, 108
    HIMEM.SYS for, 93-94, 97-99
    searching for free memory in, 367-368
    for TSRs, 13, 25, 93, 97-99, 102-105, 743-744, 869, 917, 951, 970
    XMS functions for, 94-95
User input, batch files for, 408-417, 930, 949
Using Help command
    in QBasic, 775
    in Shell, 751
Using QBasic help section, 780
Utilities, summary of, 925-984

V

$v metacharacter with PROMPT, 261, 882
Variables
    in batch files, 380-384, 854, 894
    environment, 9, 33-35, 388-389, 394, 890
    in QBasic, 795-796, 801, 804-806
VCPI (Virtual Control Program Interface), 13
VDISK.SYS driver, 9, 93
VER command, 905
Verification
    with disk copying, 152, 834, 906
    with file copying, 223, 226, 908
    with text replacement, 242
VERIFY command, 906
Vernam cipher, 482-492, 944

Versions
    command for setting, 16, 891
    DOS function for, 371, 481, 538
    old, 11
    in prompt, 260, 882
    retrieving, 905
    tables for, 922
Vertical bars (|) for piping, 309, 316, 320-321
    with FKEYS, 568, 946
    in prompts, 261, 882
VGA (Video Graphics Array), 248
    alternate character sets for, 288
    blanking screen of, 558
    DOS 4.x support for, 10
    lines of text on, 75, 235, 245, 258-259, 874-875, 926-927
    pausing file listings with, 208
Video. *See* Screen
Video adapters, checking for type of, 795
VIDEO_ID procedure (SAVER), 551, 555
VIDEO_INT procedure (PC-DIAL), 649-650
Video mode
    for program items, 758
    for QBasic, 772
View File Contents command (Shell), 750, 761
View menu
    in QBasic, 774-775
    in Shell, 748-750
Virtual Control Program Interface, 13
Virtual disks, 9, 12, 56-57, 70-74, 93, 107, 921
Virtual-86 mode, 21, 110-111
Virtual memory management, 110
VOL command, 907
Volume labels, 866
    attribute for, 215
    displaying, 207, 907
    DOS function for, 371
    DOS 2.x support for, 8
    with formatting, 141, 145, 319, 855
von Neumann processors, 21

W

W switch (EMM386.EXE), 109, 118, 916
Wait states, 25, 65, 83
WAITTIL utility, 441-445, 978
Warm restarts from batch files, 454-455, 968
"WARNING! Diskette is out of sequence" message, 161
"WARNING! SHARE should be loaded for large media" message, 137
Weitek math coprocessors, 97, 109, 118, 843, 916
WHATDATE utility, 439, 979
WHATDAY utility, 439-440, 980
WHEREIS macro, 297
WHITE color identifier (COLOR), 532, 937
White space in file comparisons, 218, 220, 849
Whole word matches with text searches, 241
Wide-carriage printers, 285
Width of page, assembler directive for, 335

Wildcard characters, 212-214
  with ATTRIB, 215-216
  in batch files, 384, 854
  with COPY, 222
  with DEL, 228-229
  with REN, 221, 886
WIN_SHOWDIR procedure (FINDTEXT),
    513-514
WIN_SHOWFILE procedure (FINDTEXT),
    514
WINA20.386 file, 58-59, 189, 898
Windows
  and memory, 119
  and SAVER, 554
  and SMARTdrive, 68
  and SWITCHES directive, 59
Word processing documents
  recovering, 170
  searching for text in, 493, 945
Word processors for batch files, 376
Words, 22
Wrapping with Editor, 237
WRITE_ATTR procedure (PC-DIAL), 664
WRITE_CHAR procedure (PC-DIAL), 663
WRITE_CRLF procedure (PC-LOG), 631
WRITE_DATE procedure (PC-LOG), 632-633
WRITE_DIFF procedure (PC-LOG), 629-630
WRITE_ENTRY procedure (PC-LOG), 628-
    629
Write file access, 490-491
WRITE_HEADER procedure (PC-LOG), 633
WRITE_NUM procedure (PC-LOG), 630-631
WRITE_SPACES procedure (PC-LOG), 631
WRITE_STRING procedure (PC-DIAL), 663
WRITE_TIME procedure (PC-LOG), 629
Write to File or Device function, 362, 490, 492,
    595-596, 598

X
XCOPY command, 9, 152, 160, 222, 225-228,
    908
XGA adapters, blanking screen of, 558
XMS (Extended Memory Specification), 94-95,
    112, 114-115
XT computers, support for, 7-9

Y
Y switch (EMM386.EXE), 118, 917
Year
  in date stamps, 364
  functions for, 368-369
YELLOW color identifier (COLOR), 532, 539,
    937

Z
Zbikowski, Mark, 740
ZCOPY utility, 981-982